Information Systems in Management

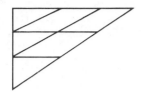

Information Systems in Management

Fourth Edition

James A. Senn
Georgia State University

Wadsworth Publishing Co.
Belmont, California
A Division of Wadsworth, Inc.

Computer Science Editor: Frank Ruggirello
Editorial Assistant: Carol Carreon
Production: Stacey C. Sawyer
Print Buyer: Martha Branch
Designer: Andrew Ogus
Copy Editor: Elizabeth Judd
Photo Researcher: Judy Mason
Technical Illustrator: Ayxa and Pat Rogondino
Compositor: Graphic Typesetting Service
Cover: Vargas/Williams/Design
Front Cover Photo: Stephen Ramsey
Back Cover Photo Research: Steuart Kenter

Printed in the United States of America
2 3 4 5 6 7 8 9 10—94 93 92 91 90

ISBN 0-534-10266-2

We appreciate the use of photographs from the following corporations: Ampex; Anderson Jacobson, Inc.; Apple Computer, Inc.; AT&T; Bell & Howell; Chrysler Corp.; Claris Corp.; Compaq Computer Group; Comshare; Cray Research; Data Products Corp.; Digital Equipment Corp.; General Electric Research and Development Center; General Motors; Hewlett-Packard; Honeywell; IBM; Intel; McDonald's; NASA; NCR Canada, Ltd.; Waterloo, Ontario; Raymond Kaiser Engineers; Sun Microsystems; Tandem; Thinking Machines Corp.; UNISYS Corp.; Wang; Xerox Corp.

Contents

Chapter 4   Views of the Organization: Human Resources, Management, and Organization Structure   94

Chapter 13   Executive Support Systems   564

Preface

To the Student

These are exciting times. Changes that were once occurring only in one's dreams seem now to be occurring daily. Economics, politics, and technology are undergoing seemingly increasing rates of profound evolution.

Throughout the United States, North America, and the world information technology is changing the way people live. Few areas of life are untouched by the rapid development of computer and communications technology. The most significant event associated with the handling of data and information—and in the communication of information—has been the introduction of the electronic computer, first as a large device and more recently as a desktop "partner" and personal assistant. Computers aren't just for big business or even just for business. They are all around us: in ATM machines dispensing cash around the clock; in cameras; in electronic components—we could develop quite a list of everyday products that use computer technology.

Ask yourself the following questions:

—Will you be affected by information systems and information systems technology more tomorrow than you are today?

—Could you be more successful or more productive by gaining a better understanding of the uses of information systems?

—Is it important for you to know about the advantages and the disadvantages associated with computer and communications technology as information systems affect *your* everyday activities—both in business and in your private life?

This book will explain why the answer to these questions is "yes"; it will show you how data and information are used in organizations and how they are managed and processed. You will also see how such systems can affect you.

Additional questions that the text will answer include:

—Why are information systems so fundamental to organizations?

—How does the use of information systems technology change the way firms compete, the services they provide, and the manner in which they treat customers?

—How can you control information systems rather than be controlled by them?

—What are the responsibilities of managers and end-users in the development and management of information systems?

These questions, none of which is trivial, concern many business activities today. To be competitive in the business community, you need the answers.

In writing this book, I assumed that you are going to be a user of information systems, not a designer. Therefore, the text includes many examples to give you a good understanding of how information systems are actually used. Many aids are included to help you learn about the field of information systems more quickly. For example, each chapter starts with key questions to guide your reading and includes a section called "Why Should You Know About . . .?", which is designed to relate the discussion that follows to one or more professions.

Minicases are used to portray the experiences and dilemmas of actual organizations: companies, municipalities, and governmental agencies. In some cases, I used real names. When fictional names have been used (to protect the innocent or the guilty), you may recognize the parties from routine monitoring of the business press. In each instance, however, the facts are correct and the situation is real. When reading the minicases, put yourself in the shoes of the manager who must decide what to do. What decision would you make if you had the problem? I believe these minicases will help clarify the concepts you read about.

The end of each chapter includes key words and review questions to help you focus your review and facilitate your learning. Many application problems are also included. By working through these real-world situations involving computer-based information systems and by developing answers or strategies as requested, you will not only be learning the terminology and concepts of information processing but you will also be making decisions about cases like those that occur constantly in organizations. You will be acting as a user of information systems—that is, learning how to use information processing tools and techniques, which is, after all, what it's all about.

Keep in mind throughout that the key to success in information processing and management is often the people—users, analysts, and managers. The underlying technology is usually reliable. People make the difference!

This fourth edition, like the previous ones, has benefited from letters, comments, and suggestions of students who have written to me. Some students relayed experiences they had after reading the book. Others sent me notes describing situations they encountered after graduation—cases that were identical to those discussed in the book, which they had remembered in surprising detail. If you would like to share similar experiences—or suggestions or ideas—please feel free to drop me a line. My address is:

James A. Senn
Computer Information Systems Department
Georgia State University
University Plaza
Atlanta, Georgia 30303

To the Instructor

Information systems and information technology are commonly discussed topics in organizations around the world. The enterprises in which they are discussed vary in size and industry type. Yet there is a common recognition that the manner in which these systems are used will not only influence the success of the organization but can change the world in which they function.

At one time, information systems were viewed as a back-office function that was the responsibility of a handful of technicians. Today, however, we find that:

——Their use can lead to distinct competitive advantages, providing they are utilized in ways that support the appropriate corporate strategy.

——Their use underlies the orderly operation of successful enterprises.

——Deployment of information systems technology can change the very basis of competition across many diverse industries.

——Responsibility for these systems is shared by senior corporate executives, operating managers, and information systems specialists.

——Knowledge of the uses of information systems is rapidly becoming a basic skill for managers, whereas in-depth understanding of business practices and principles is a fundamental requirement for computer and communications specialists.

These realizations have had a distinct influence on the fourth edition of this book. Although I have retained many of the features that helped so many adopters of previous editions, I have added other new information and insights into the information systems practice.

An information systems vision model is introduced near the beginning of the book. The vision model shows the interrelation among components of information technology and their use in an organizational setting. It also identifies the fundamental role of management theory, organization structure, and systems theory. The different types of application systems are identified in relation to these building blocks.

To assist the student in retaining a frame of reference, the vision model is used throughout the book. In each chapter, the element(s) of the model discussed are highlighted. One can quickly see where the topic(s) of the discussion fit into the larger picture.

Because information technology use is changing rapidly, keeping current is essential. This book is both current and forward looking. The following topics, discussed in depth, are new elements of this edition:

——The information systems vision (full chapter)

——Executive support systems (full chapter)

——Group decision support systems (partial chapter)

——Expert support systems (full chapter)

——Work group support systems (full chapter)

——Information systems planning and development (full chapter)

——Tools and methods for developing information systems (full chapter)

———CASE tools (partial chapter)

———Electronic data interchange (EDI) (partial chapter)

The text uses extensive examples throughout to demonstrate the principles, applications, and techniques of interest.

Personal computers are discussed throughout the book, not in a chapter by themselves. User managers, systems analysts, and virtually all organization personnel either use or are affected by personal computers. Although the unique features and opportunities associated with personal computing are emphasized as they occur, usually through application examples, they are overall fundamental tools of computing and of organizations.

There is little question that some IS areas are more developed than others. We point out weaknesses in current research and understanding—it is important for students to know where improvements must occur, and our realistic look at the state of the art in systems analysis and design methods reveals that some methods work better than others. Then, too, implementation problems are candidly discussed. Students should know that sometimes systems fail, either because of technical problems or more than likely because of ill-advised activities of end-users, managers, or systems analysts.

This text is designed to be used in a semester or a quarter course. Your students need not have prior knowledge of information systems or computers. Yet the book does not "underwhelm" students; it respects their learning capabilities and their general interest in how information technology is *used*.

A variety of learning aids are included throughout the book:

———Thought-provoking introductory anecdotes or quotations

———Key questions to focus reading and learning activities at the beginning of each chapter

———Boxed inserts to highlight important questions or issues

———Chapter summaries

———Keywords in each chapter

———Review questions

———Application problems

———Minicases detailing corporate experiences and dilemmas

———Module of extensive case studies

The telephone calls and correspondence that I have received from many instructors repeatedly emphasize the importance and usefulness of the application problems for individual student activities and the appropriate selection of case material for classroom and lecture hall discussions.

I have written this text in a modular fashion, permitting you to schedule the coverage of various aspects of information systems according to your class needs. Instructors have used the modules in three different orders:

———Introductory chapter; management information module; computer systems module; transaction processing module; information systems module; information systems management module

——Introductory chapter; computer systems module; transaction processing module; management information module; information systems module; information systems management module

——Introductory chapter; computer systems module; transaction processing module; information systems module; information systems management module; management information module

Each sequence complements the orientation of a different set of instructors and students.

Because it is important to be able to deal with information systems of all types in real settings, six classroom-tested case studies appear at the back of the book; many minicases also appear throughout the chapters. Each case, based on a real company, can be used as a term project for analysis and design or for class discussions to drive home salient points about transactions and information processing. I have found it useful to begin with one or two of the cases in the first part of the course and then return to the same cases for additional analysis and discussion later on, to refine insights into the purposes and tools of transaction and information processing systems. It has been most useful to devote a substantial amount of class time to each case. When students deal with a case, they usually think through its situations quite carefully. The cases, as all the learning tools in the book, are intended to give students a practical, applications-oriented view of information systems.

I would like to thank the following reviewers for their helpful comments:

Gary Armstrong
Shippensburg University

Gerald Braun
Xavier University

Robert Bretz
Western Kentucky University

J. Steve Davis
Clemson University

Miles Kennedy
Case Western Reserve University

Frederick Kohun
Robert Morris College

James LaSalle
University of Arizona

John Lehane
San Jose State University

John Lehman
University of Alaska

Charles Lutz
Utah State University

Ryan Nelson
University of Houston

Robert Rademacher
Colorado State

Reagan Ramsower
Baylor University

Marian Sackson
Pace University

Ken Slodden
St. John's University

Robert Stokes
University of North Carolina

Edyth Tedefalk
University of North Dakota

David Van Over
University of Georgia

The staff at Wadsworth Publishing Company has played a fundamental role in the development of this fourth edition. Frank Ruggirello has encouraged creativity in his own way, and his assistance in development of the manuscript enhanced its contents. The contributions of Mike Snell and Jon Thompson, editors on earlier editions, continue to influence the contents of the book and its usefulness to students and instructors. Andrew Ogus developed the design for the third edition. It proved to be functional and effective and so has been retained for this edition. Stacey Sawyer coordinated the production work, setting schedules and ensuring that they were met at all times.

All who participated in this project deserve credit and my thanks.

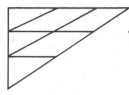

1: Introduction to Information Systems

Key Questions

What are the dominant trends in business and management? *11 Trends (7 by Tom Young)*

Why do managers need information systems? *to achieve success in a rapidly changing world.*

What role does information processing play in the management of organizations?

What are the different types of information systems? *TP   Expert Sys   MIS   Executive Sys   DSS   Work Group Sys*

How do decision support systems differ from management information systems? *unique probs vs recurring ones.*

Are transaction processing systems and information systems different? *trans processing is an IS*

What is a work group support system? *E-mail, voice mail, word processing*

What components make up a computer system? *Input (Progs, Data)   CPU   Output (Results)*

provides info to the decision maker at the right time in a media they can use.

Old Traditions and New Technology

To cherish traditions, old buildings, ancient cultures, and graceful lifestyles is a worthy thing—but in the world of technology to cling to outmoded methods of manufacture, old product lines, old markets, or old attitudes among management and workers is a prescription for suicide.

Sir Leuan Maddock
New Scientist

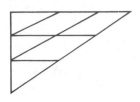

Introduction to Information Systems

The notion of successful companies brings many familiar names to mind: McDonald's, Citibank, Merrill Lynch, Sears—the list could go on. All of them depend on information systems for their day-to-day activities, and in fact information systems play a pivotal role in their success.

Information systems today touch virtually every aspect of business. And their impact is not limited to large and well-known corporations, but includes small companies as well.

The real challenge that business faces is not just to acquire computer-based information systems, nor is it to devise an information system for management. Instead the goal is the effective utilization of information systems *in* management. The effective use of information systems in management builds on a vision—an idea, often not fully articulated, of where a company can go: perhaps new services or unique products it can offer, ways of serving customers better, or ways to help employees be both more effective and more satisfied with their work. A vision also means knowing about how things are at the present time. Information describing current events, trends, and likely occurrences helps form an image of what could be—opportunities and challenges alike.

Both to inspire a vision and to make it possible to attain it, the availability of information is crucial. Information is the fundamental theme throughout this book. We will explore how information is changing organizations of all types. We also examine the underlying technology of computers (from microcomputers to mainframes) and communications and information systems that are propelling an explosion of information concerns in organizations of all types. Concepts and practices surrounding the design, development, and utilization of information systems will be examined from a management viewpoint.

These themes will be evident throughout the book:

——Having effective information systems places an organization at a distinct competitive advantage.

——Information systems do not reduce the importance of people—the human resource is more important than ever!

——The management of information systems is of concern to all members of an organization.

——Information systems affect all levels of the organization.

——Computer systems are a fundamental building block for the development of information systems.

This chapter examines these themes and introduces each of the modules that follow (which do not have to be read in the printed sequence). First we examine the enormous changes that are going on in the world of business—the world that affects every one of us. Then we define the term *information system* and show its importance to management. We also explore the different types of information systems, showing how each type has distinctive characteristics and yet uses a common focus and foundation. In the last section, we introduce some of the terminology of computers as it is applied to information systems. Throughout each section, many examples demonstrate corporate information systems use.

We will begin by looking at the dominant trends in the business world today.

Trends in Business and Management

The challenge to management of organizations today is to achieve success in a world that is changing daily. As we explore the 11 dominant trends (see Figure 1.1), note the importance of information and the way information systems are changing organizations. Increasingly, those firms that have good information and use it in the management of their organizations are much more likely to be successful. And those that do not will fall farther behind.

Blurring of Industry Boundaries

At one time, going to a local Sears store meant shopping for housewares, appliances, clothing, or hardware. Today, a trip to Sears can also involve purchasing everything from a home (through its real estate company) to insurance for home and automobile (from its insurance company) to the purchase or sale of stocks, bonds, or investment programs (from its brokerage firm). Although Sears has traditionally been one of

Figure 1.1 Trends in Business and Management

- Blurring of industry boundaries
- Deregulation of industries
- Faster pace of business
- Increasing foreign competition
- Global business community
- An information society
- Increasing complexity of management
- Interdependence of organization units
- Improvement of productivity
- Availability of computers for end-users
- Recognition of information as a resource

the largest firms in retail sales in the United States, today it is much more than a retail chain.

The banking industry has also seen enormous change. At one time, dealing with a bank mainly involved depositing or withdrawing money, and this meant going to the bank in person. Now banks handle the exchange of stocks, insurance policies, and many more nonbanking services. And money can be withdrawn from an account on street corners, in shopping malls, and at the student union, all because of the convenience of automated teller machines (ATMs). ATMs, which are only in their infancy—more sophisticated versions, with built-in intelligence, are on the horizon—have taken the requirement for brick and mortar buildings away from banking. And what about bank credit cards? We used to receive them from a bank. Now they are issued by airlines, labor unions—even football teams.

To take another example, insurance companies have become part of the financial services industry. In addition to the traditional insurance policies, these firms now offer securities and investment programs—products that compete directly with brokerage houses and investment firms. New developments have also affected brokerage houses. Merrill Lynch, Inc., traditionally considered a stockbroker, through its Cash Management Account combines information on a customer's checking, savings, credit card, and securities accounts into one monthly statement. Idle funds are swept automatically into interest-bearing money market funds. The management task is complex for Merrill Lynch, which handles $100 billion in funds, but it is probably more complex for the traditional banks, which must compete with brokerage houses and other nonbanks while at the same time addressing the competition from international lenders and the complexity of fluctuating interest rates.

Consider a final example. Home shopping, via television, is increasingly a way for busy professionals to purchase the goods they need—from food to clothing to entertainment. It is so successful that traditional catalog mail order companies find their business markedly threatened. Yet shoppers love the convenience. And they are not concerned about a line separating broadcast and retail industries. How is payment for these purchases made? Information, in the form of a bank card number, closes the sale.

In all of these instances, the money itself rarely moves. Rather, organizations move *information about money*. And their information systems are the means of managing this movement.

Deregulation of Industries

A second notable trend is the deregulation of industries. Entire industries, once regulated by government agencies to ensure the public received all possible benefits at a fair price, are now deregulated. Airlines, trucking, banking, and communications companies now conduct business in an open market where the customer determines whether price and service are acceptable. Deregulation also makes it easier for new firms to enter an industry or for an existing company to establish new lines of business as they deem appropriate. An airline, for example, can now begin service to a new city by publishing its intentions a few weeks in advance. Formal requests and approval by the Federal Aviation Association are unnecessary.

Look for the trend to continue—and not just in the United States. Deregulation is underway in many countries around the world. Elsewhere workers are demanding more free-market determination of price and service levels.

Faster Pace of Business

Third, managers find that the pace of business is increasing daily. Change is often the only constant. Most people are aware of the kinds of changes taking place: the development of new methods of production that are making assembly lines obsolete, the appearance of renewable energy sources, radical social changes, the emergence of global economic policies, and changing concentrations of money and power. Yet while these developments are occurring, managers must chart a course for their respective organizations, departments, or offices that will allow them to meet goals and objectives in an appropriate manner. As events take place, managers' information needs change. And the means of fulfilling them are under constant evolution. Throughout it all, the need for more accurate and detailed information in appropriate forms grows more critical.

(2)

Increasing Foreign Competition

The fourth trend is an increase in foreign competition. Countries around the world are developing advanced manufacturing and distribution facilities—countries that other nations did not consider global competitors. For example, automobiles enter North America from Japan, Germany, France, Sweden, Italy, and more recently from South Korea and Yugoslavia. And still other countries intend to enter the market.

Computers from South Korea, Taiwan, Hong Kong, Singapore, and Brazil compete with those manufactured by U.S. firms.

Textiles, clothing, tractors and farm machinery, insurance, and electronics products of all varieties, to cite a few other examples, compete with items manufactured in North America.

Global Business Community

A fifth change is the establishment of a global business community. At one time the notion of a global business community was of concern only to international companies, and there were a limited number of such firms. Today, the global business community exists; there is only one market—the world.

Citibank, Chase Manhattan, and many other U.S. banks do business around the world. As one bank executive recently said, "If the sun is shining in some location, you can bet we are doing business there."

The global nature of banking is typical of what is happening in other industries as well. For example, a large U.S. computer vendor does more of its business globally than in the United States. Telecommunications companies spend large amounts of time and dollars managing their international sales and service programs. The U.S. food industry serves the world (and also competes with international firms). Virtually all industries must consider what is happening around the world or risk loss of business. Even those companies that do not sell their products around the world face challenges from global competitors.

The global marketplace has another distinctive characteristic. The global economy is volatile. Currencies, markets, and political environments change continually and rapidly. Raw materials and labor sources are often contingent on factors that are beyond the control of manufacturers who depend on them. A business strategy good for today may place the firm in jeopardy tomorrow.

An Information Society

Sixth, we continue to evolve further as an information society. During the 1980s, trend watcher John Naisbitt, in his book *Megatrends: Ten Directions Transforming Our Lives,* emphasized the occurrence of an information explosion. The most dramatic of Naisbitt's trends is the recognition that we have been converted from an industrial society to an *information society.* Our economy is now built on the production, management, and use of information. Countless companies are devoted to the production of information. But perhaps more important, the companies that acquire and use information most effectively probably will be successful at the expense of those that do not.

The majority of workers today are *knowledge workers*—that is, they spend their time creating, distributing, or using information. Many experts estimate that nearly 70 percent of the American work force is employed in such knowledge worker positions as bankers, stockbrokers, computer programmers, accountants, market analysts, and insurance agents. They are participating in the transformation of a society that started as an agricultural society, became an industrial society, and is now emerging as an information society.

Managers in particular are bombarded with *data*—details and facts—continually. What they need most is *information* that is attuned to the tasks they perform or the decisions they make. (Chapters 2–4 explore information issues and their relation to management.)

Increasing Complexity of Management

A seventh trend is the increasing complexity of management. In part because of the pace of organization life and in part because of the sheer size and scope of the management task, the manager's job is increasing in complexity. Contributing factors include concerns for worker safety, product quality, public health, and competitive realities, as well as collapsed time frames (less time to do more). Greater diversity in all these categories adds a new dimension to management decision making.

Organizations themselves create new tensions as size increases or decreases and new ways of structuring the enterprise emerge for consideration. The leapfrogging pace of technology adds still other points of concern, ranging from robots and automated factory production lines to microprocessor-controlled telephones—even to the employee canteen with its microwave ovens and electronic vending machines.

The blurring of industry boundaries, increasing international competition, global business community . . . all add to the complexity of management.

And through it all, managers are expected to plan, control, and act; to turn problems into opportunities and to ensure that opportunities do not become problems; and to assist in their own fulfillment while guiding the organization toward fulfillment of its goals and objectives.

Interdependence of Organization Units

Eighth is an increase in the interdependence of organization units. Organizations are not loose confederations of workers and workstations. Because all activities are related, each individual is interconnected with colleagues. Successes and problems in one corner of the enterprise affect activities in other parts, even if they are geographically separated. Organizations are **systems**—individual components interconnected and pursuing goals and objectives. (Systems and their control are discussed in detail in Chapter 3.)

Managers use information to communicate with one another and with staff members and employees. They must convey information to others while ensuring that departments and units on which they are dependent are progressing according to anticipated goals. Information is the adhesive that holds the components of the organization system together.

Imagine the confusion—and the financial loss—that would result if sales departments did not communicate with manufacturing staff members. Or if production were scheduled without coordination with buyers and purchasing agents responsible for acquiring parts and raw materials. Unless the coordination and communication of information is planned and responsibility established, the potential for chaos is great. Information systems are thus an important element in the success of today's competitive organization.

Improvement of Productivity

The ninth trend is an accelerating demand for improved productivity. In organizations, this relates both to the improvement of processes, such as manufacturing goods or handling customer sales, and to the ability of managers to oversee a greater number of activities.

Availability of Computers for End-Users

Tenth, computer information systems are accessible to a wide variety and growing number of users. **End-users**—or just *users*—the people who utilize computers but are not systems analysts, programmers, or other information systems professionals, can have on their desktop an inexpensive personal computer (PC) that extends their capabilities to analyze, monitor, and act. (PCs are discussed in detail in Chapter 5.)

With a personal computer, the user can manipulate accounting and management information to test the effect of alternate strategies and evaluate the reason for current business results; compress large volumes of data into a single graphic display that shows trends in vivid colors; transmit and receive files of information from one end of the country to the other in seconds; prepare reports, proposals, and correspondence, making rapid revisions as needed, and automatically print the result much faster than a human typist. . . . Clearly end-user computing is an integral feature of information systems.

Recognition of Information as a Resource

The eleventh trend, the recognition of information as a resource for the organization, is a result of the others. Information has value because it influences the way the firm operates. Not having vital information can cause managers to make mistakes, miss opportunities, and encounter serious performance problems. Information systems are also a resource. They increase the capability of managers and workers, and they make it possible to achieve new levels of effectiveness and efficiency.

However, information and information systems also produce costs. For example, their development and use call for the commitment of other resources. Management information is not a by-product of processing transactions—of just buying and selling a product or a service. It involves many other activities; that is, details of events must be captured and processed to place them in a form useful to the recipient.

Because of the central importance of information, firms take steps to manage it in the same sense that any other resource must be controlled. These steps include ensuring that information is available when needed, that it is reliable and accurate, and that it is developed in a cost-effective manner, without unnecessary duplication. The management of information as a resource underlies the many information systems issues discussed throughout this book.

What Is an Information System?

As much as 80 percent of the typical executive's day is dedicated to information—receiving, communicating, and using it in a wide variety of tasks. Because information is the basis for virtually all activities performed in an organization, systems must be developed to produce and manage it. The objective of such systems is to ensure that reliable and accurate information is available when it is needed and that it is presented in a usable form.

Definition

An **information system** is a set of people, data, and procedures that work together to provide useful information. As we will see repeatedly throughout the book, the emphasis on *systems* means that the various components seek a common objective of supporting organization activities. These include day-to-day business operations, communication of information, management of activities, and decision making.

Few people in North America, and increasingly the world, are not familiar with McDonald's restaurants. The founder, Ray Kroc, created an institution out of what had been a mom-and-pop business, the operation of street corner hamburger stands. He and his staff carefully collected information to further their principle of duplication: when a strategy works, duplicate it in other locations. McDonald's assembled information on the American consumer's wishes for hamburgers and then designed the end product. It also redesigned the entire hamburger-making process and arranged a system of suppliers for each component (rolls, meat, onions, condiments, and so on). The operating system that developed around this system assured consistency and uniformity: Each hamburger, french fried potato, and pickle is identical to every other such unit. McDonald's also designed an information system, first manual and later computer-based, to monitor the performance of each restaurant; by relating customer sales and vendor purchases, labor costs, and overall profitability, management could determine when procedures were not being followed. McDonald's advanced management techniques and support systems are the basis for its continued successes in the face of aggressive competition. Its information systems are a vital tool in keeping in touch with customers, products, and restaurant performance.

You can find the same reliance on information systems in just about any area of business. Banking institutions, for instance, could not survive without information systems relating deposits, withdrawals, and loans. Many have developed specialized information systems to assist loan officers in deciding whether to lend money to an applicant (Figure 1.2): consumer information, such as applicant's credit standing, income, current and long-term liabilities, and employment status are interrelated with such loan variables as amount requested, duration of loan, and collateral offered. A database of banking and economic data is accessed to incorporate details of trends in the economy and in interest rates. Another database about banking assets is

Figure 1.2 Components of a Loan Information System

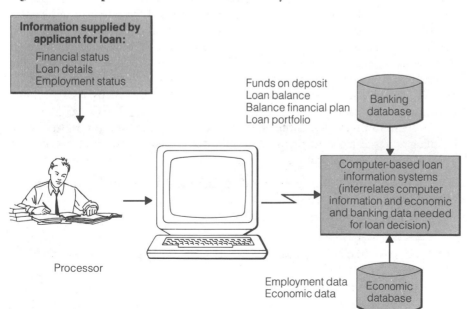

accessed to obtain information about such matters as the availability of funds and whether the loan fits the bank's financial plan and lending portfolio.

By entering and manipulating data in this information system, a loan officer can quickly prepare a prospectus for the application and can formulate a recommendation for the applicant's request. Some systems are even designed to produce a recommendation directly, which the officer can follow or ignore. Repayment terms are also suggested.

As you know, the financial world is always changing, and so banks must respond to new conditions by changing their lending policies. Through their information systems, they not only modify their loan determination procedures, but they ensure that the databases they rely on are maintained up to the minute. Few banks would be in business today without information systems support of this nature.

What Does an Information System Do?

An information system performs three general activities (Figure 1.3). First it accepts data, from sources within or external to the firm, as input. Next, it acts on data to process (produce) information; that is, it is an information-*generating* system. Procedures determine how the information is prepared. Finally, the system outputs the information for the intended user, perhaps a manager or staff member.

In the banking example above, data about the customer, bank lending policies, and interest rates are inputs to the system. System procedures determine applicant creditworthiness and assess the advisability of making a loan. System output includes a recommendation, loan conditions, and repayment terms. Of course the user, in this case the loan officer, actually makes the decision.

An airline reservation system is an information system in many ways (Figure 1.4). It assists travel agents in placing reservations for clients. Interacting through computer terminals, the travel agent, who may be located thousands of miles from the computer center, can request and receive flight information in a matter of seconds, even down to the availability of a specific seat on a certain flight. The agent can enter the reservation, enter traveler payment details, request instant credit card verification, and print the ticket and boarding pass on the spot. Furthermore, many agents all over the world can use the same system simultaneously, perhaps even booking passengers on the same flight.

We tend to think of an airline reservation system only from the viewpoint of handling tickets. But consider some of the information and the databases that support a single flight in the system:

——Passenger ticket information, including date and place of purchase and method of payment
——Passenger boarding lists
——Passenger seat assignments
——Special requirements (for example, wheelchairs, passenger escorts, nonstandard meals)
——Flight departure and arrival times
——Crew assignment

Figure 1.3 Activities Performed in an Information System

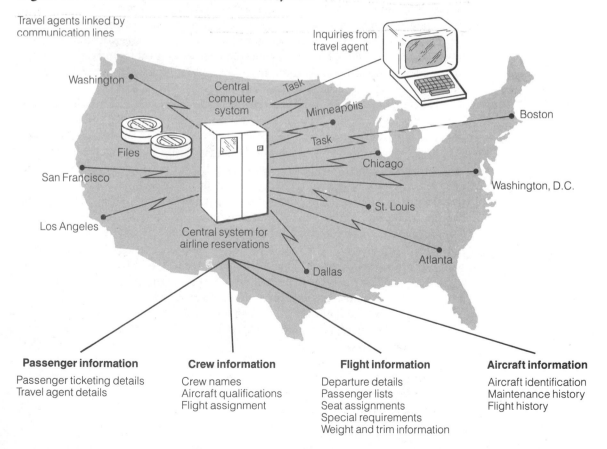

Figure 1.4 Features of an Airline Reservation System

——Aircraft assignment

——Aircraft maintenance history

——Weight of aircraft for flight (based on combined weight of aircraft, baggage, cargo, and on-board passengers and personnel)

In addition, pilots must file flight plans and keep track of weather along the route of the flight. They must know beforehand the amount of thrust needed for takeoff, taking into account the weather and temperature at that moment as well as the weight of the aircraft.

We can find similar examples of information systems throughout industry, including the hotel and restaurant fields, insurance, medicine, communications, manufacturing, and education. In each case, the nature of the activity—namely, processing data to provide the information needed by users—is the same, although the exact procedures vary.

Does an Information System Need Computers?

Information systems need not be computer-based, but often they are, as with the airline reservation system. The determining factor is whether a system can be improved by including computer processing capability. If a manual system of people and procedures can perform a task efficiently and without error, there may be little reason to use computers. Often, however, as the volume of work grows, procedures increase in complexity, or activities become more interrelated, and improvements can be gained by introducing computer assistance.

The computer complements, rather than replaces, individuals, although in instances of tasks that are particularly disliked or dangerous, computer-based systems may be designed with the intent of relieving people from exposure to such tasks. For example, clerical staff members in medical offices may dislike having to type the many insurance claim forms they must submit on behalf of patients in order to receive payment. Each form requires the entry of patient name, address, and other identification information, including many-digit policy numbers. Physician identification data must also be entered. The most important section contains the details of the diagnoses made and the medical procedures performed.. Usually the staff member must enter both the medical terminology and additional numeric codes, standardized within the medical profession. Most health-care workers feel that this job is boring and tedious. Moreover, if the office is noisy, concentration may be difficult, leading to errors. Thus doctors frequently computerize their records to improve productivity and accuracy. And the staff members are glad to be free of the clerical details.

On the other hand, computers can become valuable assistants in decision making. They can augment the capabilities of individual users by making them more productive and more effective, as we see in the next section.

Information systems that include computers are sometimes called **computer information systems.** Throughout the text, we will use the term *information system* in referring to both computer-based and noncomputer-based systems.

Table 1.1 Types of Information Systems

Transaction Processing Systems	Process data about transactions. Reasons for transaction processing include: classification, calculation, sorting, summarization, storage.
Management Information Systems (Management Reporting Systems)	Provide information for decision support where information requirements can be identified in advance (usually with respect to decisions that frequently recur).
Decision Support Systems	Assist managers with unique (nonrecurring) strategic decisions that are relatively unstructured. Part of decision process is determining what factors to consider and what information is needed.
Executive Support Systems	Assist top-level executives in acquiring and using information needed to run the organization. Enable them to be informed on day-to-day activities without becoming inundated in detail. Provide information that is used in identifying opportunities or detecting emerging problems.
Work Group Support Systems	Assist and support managers, staff, and employees in carrying out day-to-day activities. Combine computer processing, data communications, electronic message transmission, and image (fax) processing.
	Frequently draw on data stored as a result of transaction processing. Include handling of correspondence (word processing) and electronic publishing of reports and documents.
Expert Support Systems (Intelligent Support Systems)	Use computer programs to store facts and rules to mimic the decisions of a human expert. Can be used as stand-alone systems or integrated with other types of information systems.

What Types of Information Systems Exist?

Table 1.1 lists six different types of information systems: transaction processing, management information, decision support, executive support, work group support, and expert support systems. All of them are aimed at processing data for one of three reasons: to capture details of transactions, to enable people to make decisions, or to communicate information between people and locations. This section outlines the features of the various types of information systems.

Transaction Processing Systems The first type of information system is the transaction processing system. A **transaction** is an event that involves or affects a business or organization. Selling merchandise and ordering supplies from a manufacturer are common examples of transactions. As transactions occur, the data about them that are relevant or important to the organization are collected. For example, relevant data for a sales analyst might include customer's name, type, quantity, and price of merchandise sold, and whether the purchaser paid cash. Similarly, for a purchasing agent it probably is important to record the date of the order, the name of the supplier, and the quantity and type of merchandise ordered. The details of such transactions are stored for later use: comparing the number of cash versus credit sales or the number of taxable versus nontaxable transactions, determining the total sales or the amount of the average sale for a given period, referring to the record of sales to a specific customer, and so on.

Transaction processing systems process data about business activities—for instance, sales, the placing of orders, and the movement of stock and inventory. The function itself—*transaction processing*—underlies the orderly operation of any business or organization. The five reasons for transaction processing are (Figure 1.5):

—**Classification:** Grouping data according to common characteristics.

> *Example:* Classification in a university registration system. Upper division (junior and senior) undergraduates, lower division (freshmen and sophomore) undergraduates, and graduate students need different instructions to register for courses. Registration packets vary for those in each category.

—**Calculation:** Acting on the data using arithmetic procedures, such as addition or multiplication, to generate useful results.

> *Example:* Calculating the total sales tax amount to be paid for all taxable sales made throughout the three-month period.

—**Sorting:** Arranging data into a particular sequence to make processing easier and data less cumbersome.

> *Example:* Arranging invoices by postal code to speed distribution.

Figure 1.5 Data Processing Activities Generated by Transactions in Sales

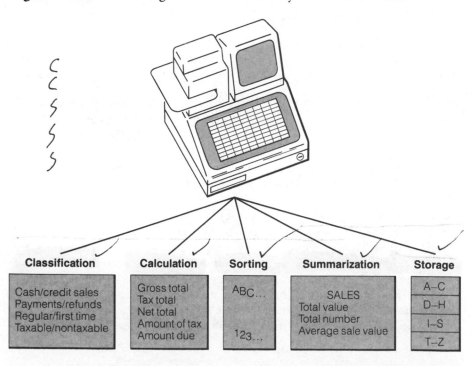

Classification	Calculation	Sorting	Summarization	Storage
Cash/credit sales Payments/refunds Regular/first time Taxable/nontaxable	Gross total Tax total Net total Amount of tax Amount due	ABC... 123...	SALES Total value Total number Average sale value	A–C D–H I–S T–Z

——**Summarization:** Reducing large amounts of transaction data to a shorter or more concise form.

> *Example:* Colleges and universities regularly compute grade-point averages on the grades students receive in each course. The average tells university officials how each student is performing and does so more effectively than a list of separate grades would.

——**Storage:** Records of events that affect the operation are retained. Some records must be retained by law.

> *Example:* The record of every check you write in your checkbook. Or, a record of each sales transaction made by a particular retailer.

Effective and accurate transaction processing underlies any orderly business organization.

Management Information Systems As stated earlier, the second reason organizations process data is to enable people to make decisions. *Information processing,* as decision-oriented data processing is commonly called, provides information to managers who have to decide what action to take in a particular situation. Managers, like the rest of us, make many decisions each day. Managers' decisions range from determining what price to set for merchandise, to determining whether more staff should be hired, to choosing the kind of advertising campaign to be used. Information processing draws on data stored through transaction processing to evaluate alternatives and select a course of action (Figure 1.6). It can also use specific data collected and processed for a particular decision.

Management information systems (MIS), also called *management reporting systems,* focus on decision support in cases of information requirements that can be identified in advance. In other words, the information needed can be determined after a thorough analysis of the decision situation. Furthermore, the decision situation is usually known to recur, perhaps frequently. Hence, reports containing the

Figure 1.6 Decisions About Sales Management Are Based on Sales Transaction Data

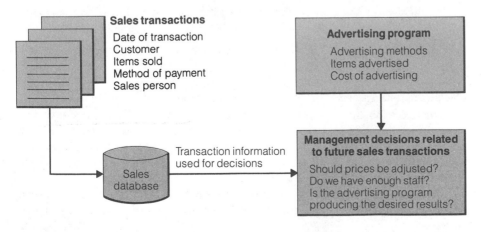

information can be produced on a recurring basis, each time incorporating new details of events since the last time the information was produced.

For example, consider a marketing manager who must decide whether to change a product's price. We can identify the following questions that will determine the information needed to make the decision:

1. What are current sales levels and what have they been historically?
2. What is the profit picture for the product? That is, how much profit is made on each item sold, and what is the total profit for all sales of the product? Has this picture changed over time?
3. When did the last price change occur?
4. Have costs of raw materials or manufacturing changed?
5. Has competition changed in a manner that affects sales or profits?
6. Are suppliers considering new pricing policies for the materials they provide to the organization?

The list could go on, but these questions give you an idea of the kind of information needed to make such a decision.

The preceding example demonstrates several important aspects of information processing:

——Most decisions are not one-time occurrences. Decision makers have a good idea of the variables to consider and the information needed.

> *Example:* Product and brand managers in companies face the decision about whether to change prices repeatedly, in some organizations as often as weekly or monthly. They know what information is needed to monitor price and product performance.

——Some of the information needed is already stored as a result of transaction processing. (Other details, such as how competition has changed or whether suppliers are considering new pricing policies, may have to be collected.)

> *Example:* Sales details and data on costs of raw materials, supplies, and services are available from within the firm.

——Data are drawn from several parts of the organization to assist the decision maker.

> *Example:* Data for pricing products will be drawn from the marketing, production, and purchasing departments.

These instances are typical of the manner in which information is gathered or prepared to assist in decision making.

Decision Support Systems   The third type of information system is the decision support system. Occasionally decisions do not recur, but involve unique situations. For example, the decision to pursue a merger with another company, to develop a large industrial park, or to seek a defense treaty with another country may come up only once. In such a situation, the risk of making an error is high, and a mistake can have serious consequences.

What information does the decision maker need in a unique situation? Some details, perhaps, can be easily identified, but a significant part of the decision problem is determining what factors to consider—that is, identifying the specific information needed. *In formulating strategic decisions, part of the problem is determining what information to gather.* (Chapters 4 and 12 discuss this topic in greater detail.)

Decision support systems (DSS) are information systems that assist managers with unique (nonrecurring) strategic decisions that are relatively unstructured. Consider the unstructured aspects of the merger and industrial park examples:

——It is not initially clear which is the best way to proceed with the decision.

——The information needed, even after it is identified, may have to be elaborated and refined through the use of discrete private sources.

——Some of the data needed may exist in part as a result of transaction systems across many different departments in the organization.

——Some of the information needed may have to be collected outside the firm.

Decision support systems exist to respond to unexpected, ad hoc needs for information. These systems are particularly important to upper-level managers who must deal with constantly changing problems and who must make decisions in situations that arise unexpectedly.

Decision support systems are discussed in Chapter 12.

Executive Support Systems The fourth type of information system is the **executive support system (ESS).** As the name suggests, ESSs are designed to assist top-level executives in acquiring and using information needed to run the organization. Because executives typically must have an overview of operations in all major business units (departments or divisions) and product lines, these systems are designed to help their users keep a pulse on the firm's activities without overloading them with unnecessary details (yet most are structured so that quick access to detail is possible when the need arises).

In addition, executive support systems may play a role in identifying opportunities that could provide the firm with a competitive edge or potential problem areas that may take an advantage away. Executives often find there are certain functions and tasks that they cannot delegate to staff members. Identification of opportunities and obstacles is often one of them.

Executives typically have not been direct users of computer information systems. However, this is changing as information systems professionals and executives gain more experience in tailoring such systems to the particular needs of top organization officials.

Work Group Support Systems **Work group support systems,** the fifth type of information system, are a special kind of information system used to support managers, staff, and employees in the day-to-day activities that must occur as they carry out their responsibilities. Work group systems often provide communications among workers through mail and message systems (often termed *electronic mail* and *voice messaging* systems because they use computers and data communications capabilities). Electronic transmission of images, in the form of *image processing* or *facsimile systems,* provides the means to communicate much more than narrative text or numeric data. Drawings, photographs, and other graphics can be transmitted in image form.

Of particular importance across all industries is *electronic data interchange (EDI)*. This type of work group support system promises to change the way firms do business. A growing number of firms are finding that they can avoid delay in completing business transactions by transmitting and receiving business documents electronically, using the power of data transmission over communication links, such as telephone lines or satellites. At the same time, they avoid having to repeatedly enter data into computers, because the data are transmitted and received in digital form through computer-to-computer transmission. Purchase orders, shipping notices, invoices, and payments are now transmitted using EDI. In some industries, such as the transportation industry, as much as 90 percent of the firms use EDI. Virtually all industries are going to depend on electronic data transmission in the future.

An additional area of work group support involves **word processing** and *electronic publishing systems*. These systems are designed to enhance the ability of both management and operating personnel to prepare correspondence, narrative reports, and special documents. Word processing systems began as stand-alone systems. But as work group activities have been influenced by computer and data communications technology, word processing and electronic publishing have gone well beyond individual devices, often involving *local area networks*, communication networks that link devices, usually at a single site, to share information and equipment. Electronic publishing systems are rapidly changing the appearance of documents prepared within a work group. Such systems allow the user to rapidly prepare documents that have a printed (typeset) appearance, including even high-quality photographs and images that previously had to be prepared by graphic artists.

Some parts of work group systems, such as word processing, are known as **office automation.** But work group systems do much more than automate the office. Often they make its location seem unimportant.

Work group systems frequently draw on data stored as a result of information processing. And they may use data communications methods for transmission of data and electronic mail. A large electrical utility, for example, established a statewide network of microcomputers, terminals, and printers to transmit information to more than 50 offices it operates. The network can be used to send an electronic message to an individual, or a communication may be broadcast to employees at all offices simultaneously. The messages range from interim company memoranda to blueprints and engineering drawings (image documents). Similarly, a user at a terminal in another part of the state can retrieve data from the company's central database at the headquarters location. This capability is not unusual; it is a fundamental feature of work group systems today. (Chapter 15 discusses the continuing evolution of work group systems.)

Expert Support Systems **Expert** systems, sometimes called *intelligent support systems*, are a special type of system in that they can be stand-alone systems or can be included within the features of the other types of systems we have discussed. Expert support systems use computer programs that store facts and rules—in what are called *knowledge bases*—to mimic the decision process of a human expert. The infusion of knowledge and decision-making characteristics with computer processing power is what sometimes leads people to refer to them as "intelligent" systems.

Expert support systems deal with situations characterized by a great deal of uncertainty and, as in decision support systems, a combination of experience and good judgment must be used to make a decision. Usually expert systems focus on a very narrow area, combining rules, assumptions, and facts to make inferences that lead to a decision. (In contrast, decision support systems rely on *factual* databases in the preparation of analyses and decision alternatives.) Expert systems are used in such areas as medical diagnosis and oil exploration. Expert systems are discussed in Chapter 14.

Computer Information Systems

As you have just seen, effective processing of data and generation of information are vital to business and organizations. At the heart of most information systems is computer power.

What Is a Computer?

In contemporary usage, "computer" has come to mean *electronic digital computer*. This device is electronic in the sense that it is composed of circuitry through which electricity flows to represent data as numbers. It operates on data to reshape them into a more useful form, at high speed and with accuracy. Because most computers are general purpose in nature, they can be instructed, through software, to perform many different functions.

Data Data can be numbers, letters, or symbols. For example, both the name of a student in a course and the account number of a bank customer are data. The computer handles **numeric data** (the digits 0–9), **alphabetic data** (the letters A–Z), and **special character data** ($, #, *, and so on). Data are generally considered to be "raw facts"—that is, facts not yet processed into information, which has significance in a decision-making situation. Data on their own are not generally useful; information is. (We'll discuss how the conversion takes place inside the computer in Chapter 5.)

Software Computers store some data and instructions internally, inside the computer cabinet, and some externally, in devices attached to the computer. Instructions are executed and data are processed automatically, after the user issues appropriate commands, usually by tapping a series of keys on the computer keyboard.

Execution instructions are spelled out in a **computer program.** Specific computer programs are purchased or written for processing applications such as processing customer orders, registering students, handling deposits and withdrawals from banks, and reporting the arrival and departure of airline flights, to name a few of many possible applications.

Computer programs are often called **software.** Software runs on computer hardware.

Hardware for Data Processing

Data processing in computer systems is performed by the equipment—the **hardware.** This section introduces the different classes of computer systems and the major hardware components: processing unit, input devices, and output devices (which together comprise a computer system *configuration*).

Classes of Computer Systems Computers are often described according to the following categories (see accompanying photos):

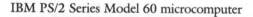

Microcomputers: **Microcomputers** are computers that are small in size, but not necessarily limited in processing power. The name originated because they are often small enough to sit on the top of a desk. The primary component is a microprocessor, the device that performs the computing. Microcomputers are then computers built from microprocessors. Microprocessors are sometimes referred to as "computers on a chip" because the main processing circuitry in each one is contained on a thin sliver or chip of silicon, smaller than a thumbnail.

IBM PS/2 Series Model 60 microcomputer

Personal computers, microcomputers of a type common in business settings, range in cost from approximately $1000 to approximately $15,000. The personal computer today has more processing capability than the large systems of a few years ago, which cost more than $1 million. Most organizations use a combination of personal and other computers to handle information processing and office system tasks.

Laptop computers are personal computers small enough to fit on a person's lap. They often are so small that they fit in a briefcase.

Home computers are a special class of microcomputers that sell for as little as $100. However, because of their limited capability, these devices seldom have a role in business environments.

Workstations are a special type of microcomputer offering extremely powerful processing capabilities and high-quality graphics. Often they are used in engineering and manufacturing environments to assist designers of buildings, automobiles, and manufactured products. Workstations are priced from approximately $7500 to $25,000. They may be used as stand-alone systems or linked together in networks.

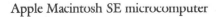

Midrange Systems: Midrange computer systems (sometimes called **minicomputers**) are designed for multiple users. They have greater speed and storage capacity than microcomputers, and they cost anywhere from approximately $15,000 to $1 million. You will find minicomputers in many different user environments, ranging from the office to the engineering department to the

Apple Macintosh SE microcomputer

Compaq Personal Computer

Sun workstation

HP 9000 Series 300 technical workstation
from Hewlett-Packard company

manufacturing floor. Because of the increasing capability of microcomputers and the decreasing cost of large computer systems, some midrange systems will be obsolete in the near future.

Mainframe computers: Medium- and large-scale systems are often referred to as **mainframe computers.** At one time they were the only means of computer power. However, the vast improvements in computer technology that brought about personal computers have changed the role of mainframe computers in many organizations. These systems are characterized by large storage capacities and extremely rapid processing speeds, measured in millions of instructions executed per second.

You will most often find mainframe computers where there are large volumes of processing (as in preparation of thousands of monthly utility bills), where large networks of users are essential (as in airline reservations systems), or where large volumes of data must be stored (as in social security or other government records).

IBM RT system; PCs used as workstations

Digital MicroVAX 3900 system, a midrange system

IBM Application System 400, another midrange system

HP 3000 system—a midrange system—with integrated workstations

IBM 3090 Model 600E mainframe system

UNISYS 2200/600 mainframe

——*Supercomputers:* **Supercomputers** are the fastest and most expensive computers available. Automobile companies employ them to design cars, aerospace companies use them to design aircraft, and the weather bureau relies on them in the forecasting of weather patterns. Some universities employ them for research.

At one time their high cost—starting at $5 million—was a deterrent to their use in business. However, with prices dropping and capabilities increasing, supercomputers will be used regularly in pharmaceutical and chemical companies, as well as in large brokerage and financial institutions.

The computer and systems development modules of the text will discuss which types of computers are suitable for meeting various information requirements.

Central Processing Unit In a computer hardware configuration, the most important element is the **central processing unit (CPU)** (see Figure 1.7). (In microprocessors, the central processing unit is on a circuitboard within the desktop unit.) All data processing involves the central processing unit, which consists of three subunits:

——*Control unit:* Examines instructions contained in computer programs and carries them out.

Cray Extended Architecture supercomputer system

Thinking Machine supercomputer

———*Arithmetic/logic unit:* Performs addition, multiplication, and so on and makes comparisons of data elements (for example, to determine whether one value is larger than another).

———*Main memory unit (also called primary storage):* Holds data processed by the arithmetic/logic unit and results of processing. Also holds some software.

Input Devices The components that feed data and instructions into the CPU are known as **input devices.** There are many different kinds, and the particular device used depends on the needs of the situation. Typewriterlike keyboards are the most common input devices, but others input data by scanning printed or written documents or even by using a microphone to accept human voice input.

Output Devices Output devices receive the processing results from the processing unit and translate them into the appropriate form for use. A printer, for example, translates electronic output signals into information that is printed (output) on paper. Other devices display output (monitor, or screen) or draw or even speak the output aloud.

Often users want to store data and instructions that they intend to use again. They must store these data in a form the CPU can understand so that they don't have to reread batches of transactions (such as sales slips) and then reenter data from terminals in what is called the *batch processing mode.* In other words, users want to store data and instructions in a computer-usable form. **Secondary storage units**

Figure 1.7 Position of the CPU in Processing Data

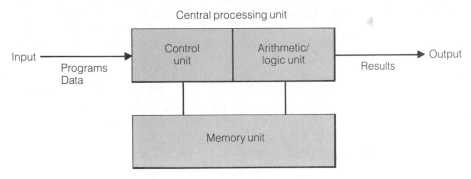

make this possible by storing data and instructions as output on magnetic devices such as magnetic disk or magnetic tape (the data are recorded in a manner similar to music recorded on magnetic tape used in home tape recorders). Data and instructions stored on these devices can be retrieved by the computer when needed and moved right into the central processing unit.

Putting Computer Technology in Perspective

Computer technology will continue to advance, and tomorrow's systems will be faster and cheaper than those available today. But in business and computer information systems, the emphasis is not on the technology; it is on the *applications*. In other words, you can assume that computer technology and information systems will be available; what you do with them is the key issue.

Why Study Information Systems?

Information systems underlie many of the business activities described in this chapter. Here are some specific reasons why you should be familiar with the characteristics of computer-based information systems:

——*Information systems are all around you.* It is virtually impossible to interact with people or organizations in most modern societies without encountering the effects of information systems, either directly or indirectly. Telephone communication, television, radio, newspapers, entertainment, transportation . . . the list could go on indefinitely.

——*You are dependent on information systems in many professions.* Information systems and computer and data communications technology are prevalent in government, medicine, law, the arts, the sciences, education, and business. In each case they have become a fundamental tool, shaping the profession and the professionals.

——*You can influence the use of information systems.* As your knowledge of information systems and their capabilities grows, you can play a role in determining when and where to consider applications of these systems and when and where not to do so. You can influence their proper use and help guard against inappropriate applications. If you don't play a role, you will have no choice but to accept the consequences of decisions others make for you.

——*You can influence the design of information systems.* It is virtually essential to know what information systems professionals do and how they go about their activities. They need your involvement in the development and deployment of information systems applications, because they recognize that the systems they develop will be used by people like you and will affect you.

——*You might choose an information systems career.* The opportunities for information systems professionals are indeed attractive. They provide exposure to many areas of endeavor and a chance to work with diverse types of people. And it's never too late for a career change. Many individuals who have established themselves in other occupations end up being drawn to the opportunities in this field. Information systems professionals must have good skills in understanding applications areas—for example, business, medicine, and so on—and in interacting with other people. The notion that information systems activities are fundamentally mathematical in nature is a fallacy; good "people skills" and the ability to tackle challenges are much more important.

In short, the demand for professionals with a background in information systems has never been higher. And few areas of society will be untouched by information systems in the years ahead.

Summary

Information systems underlie many of the activities that occur in business organizations and in society. Successful organizations have generally learned how to use information as an effective management tool, and they have developed information systems that are responsive to the needs of individuals.

Information systems are classified into six different but related types: transaction processing, management information, decision support, executive support, work group support, and expert support systems. Each type of system plays an important role in controlling and coordinating many separate and distinct organizational parts.

Computer systems and computer-based processing of data have significantly altered the capability of organizations to process transactions and make decisions. The different types of computer systems include microcomputers, minicomputers, mainframe systems, and supercomputers. Regardless of their size, the computers are controlled by sets of instructions called computer programs (that is, software). The programs tell the central processing unit how to input data, how to process data, and where to output the results. As we will be seeing throughout this book, computer systems are an integral part of information systems; however, the computer itself is secondary in importance to the information it provides to managers and other users.

Information systems are an important area for study. They are all around you and are a fundamental tool used in virtually all areas of endeavor. With a background in information systems, you can influence their design and applications. Or you may choose information systems for a career. In any event, you are increasingly likely to encounter information systems as you go about your daily activities in the future.

Key Words

Alphabetic data	Expert system	Software
Calculation	Hardware	Sorting
Central processing unit (CPU)	Information system	Special character data
	Input device	Storage
Classification	Mainframe computer	Summarization
Computer information system	Management information system (MIS)	Supercomputer
		System
Computer program	Microcomputer	Transaction
Data	Minicomputer	Transaction processing system
Decision support system (DSS)	Numeric data	
	Office automation	Word processing
End-user	Output device	Work group support system
Executive support system (ESS)	Personal computer	Workstation
	Secondary storage unit	

Review Questions

1. What trends dominate the business world today? What are their implications for the development and use of information systems?

2. What is an information system? How does it differ from a computer system?

3. What are data? How are they related to information and information systems?

4. Discuss the concept of transaction processing. What are reasons for processing transaction data? Explain each reason.

5. Businesses, governments, and organizations of other kinds are often called *systems*. What is a system in reference to organizations? What roles do information systems play in the management of systems like organizations?

6. Give a generic definition of *computer*. More specifically, what is a modern electronic digital stored-program computer?

7. What are the classes of computers? Are the members of one class more or less important than the others? Explain your answer.

8. What are computer programs? What is their purpose in data processing? In information processing?

9. Explain the following terms: central processing unit, input device, output device, batch processing mode, secondary storage unit.

10. What is the difference between decision support systems and management

information systems? What are their functions in comparison with transaction processing systems? How are they related or unrelated to work group support systems?

11. Is the term *work group support system* merely a fancy name for word processing and preparation of correspondence? Explain.

12. Why is the study of information systems important? Give as many reasons as possible.

Application Problems

1. Management is increasing in complexity, partly because of the sheer pace of activities and the magnitude of management responsibility. Yet many organizations must devote extensive time to the management of their information systems and the computers on which they are often based. Moreover, information centers and an increasing number of end-users who have personal computers generate the need for additional management and control.
   a. Do computer information systems add to or reduce the complexity of management? Explain the reason for your answer.
   b. What role should managers who are not information systems professionals take in the management of information and information systems?

2. The capability of computers to quickly process data and generate high volumes of output is well known. In this sense, they play a vital role in the information explosion. It has been said that without computers, we would not be experiencing this phenomenon.

   At the same time, managers are increasingly aware that they receive a great deal of data but very little of the information they need to make informed decisions. They point to an overload of irrelevant information and complain that much of their time is spent sifting through detail to find relevant information. Yet they often find they do not have the information they need for their most critical decisions.
   a. Are the preceding ideas contradictory?
   b. How can you avoid an overload of irrelevant information?

3. Discuss the potential effect of computer information systems on management and organization productivity:
   a. At the transaction processing level
   b. In assisting in the formulation of structured decisions
   c. In assisting managers faced with unique problems and opportunities
   d. In the communication of office information

4. The computer often is called the electronic brain. Using the ideas presented in this chapter, list the ways in which the computer and the human brain are alike and the ways they are different. Based on your findings, does the term *electronic brain* make sense? Why or why not?

5. Transaction processing is done for five reasons: classification, calculation, sorting, summarization, and storage of data. In each of the following examples, what is the most likely reason for the processing?

a. Alphabetizing the names of all credit customers of a business
b. Determining the average cost of writing a purchase order for supplies and materials
c. Keeping a carbon copy of all sales invoices in a file drawer
d. Taking notes at a board of directors meeting
e. Arranging addresses of employees by postal zip code
f. Determining the monthly payment (principal and interest) for a large business loan
g. Organizing books in a library according to topic or subject
h. Arranging the parts listed in an inventory in order from highest to lowest cost
i. Organizing the items in an inventory into two lists based on whether the parts are manufactured by your company or purchased

6. For each of the following data processing activities, state whether the data should be processed manually or whether a stored computer program would do the job better, and briefly explain why.
a. Balancing your personal checkbook
b. Calculating a table of square root values for many numbers
c. Preparing a list of parts and the quantity of each needed for every automobile being assembled today on the production line
d. Controlling the pressure and flow of chemicals through several high-pressure lines at the same time (high fluctuations in pressure are extremely dangerous)
e. Calculating the grade-point average for a specific student in the college of business
f. Calculating withholding taxes and issuing a paycheck for the net wages of all four people working for your department
g. Controlling the operation of all traffic signals in midtown Manhattan (New York City)

7. In general, what factors do you think should determine whether data should be stored or discarded after processing?

8. List at least 10 applications of computers for processing transaction data in business and government. Why would the computer, not manual methods, be used in these situations?

9. List at least 10 applications of computers for supporting decision making in business and government. Why would the computer, not manual methods, be used in these situations?

Minicase: Showtime Theatrical Services

June Russell, the president of Showtime Theatrical Services, a large firm that provides costumes, lighting equipment, and scenery to the entertainment industry, is perplexed because of her inability to obtain useful and accurate information about sales and customers. At the end of each week, the president receives a copy of all sales slips from the week. Each slip contains the customer name and details of every item rented, returned, or sold during the week. There are always several hundred slips.

Each Saturday morning, Ms. Russell scans the sales slips to determine what the level of sales has been, paying particular attention to the amounts of purchases and rentals as well as the identity of each customer. This takes several hours. At the end of the time allotted—there is seldom enough time to glance at all the slips—the president has seen many details but does not have the full sales picture.

Ms. Russell's greatest frustration is in having a great quantity of sales detail but very limited management information. For example, she cannot determine rapidly which customers made large purchases during the current or preceding weeks. Likewise, there is little control over errors. Some customers pay sales tax whereas others do not, and it is important to be sure that no mistakes are made in charging for the tax. The company must pay the tax if it is due, even if the customer was not charged for it.

Showtime Theatrical Services is growing very quickly, both in the volume of sales it makes and in the variety of items it carries. It is impossible for the sales staff to know all the customers (and their tax status). Because of competition, the company must also begin following customer purchase and rental trends to be sure they do not lose business. The sales staff will have to contact regular customers who have not purchased recently to be sure they are not being lost to a competitor.

Ms. Russell is considering the development of a sales information system to assist her in managing this portion of the business and to aid staff members in customer relations. The company is experienced in computer information systems and relies heavily on its computer-based accounting and payroll systems.

Questions

1. How might a sales information system meet Ms. Russell's concerns? Can such a system provide the information she wishes without all the detail?

2. What transaction processing functions underlie the activities described in this situation? Relate each to the handling of sales, rentals, and returns and to the preparation of pertinent management information.

Management Information Systems Module

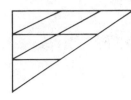

2: The Information Systems Vision

Key Questions

How is information systems thought changing organizations?

What is the information systems vision, and what is its role in the management of information systems?

How do organizations benefit from using information systems?

What are the three main benefits that organizations derive from information systems?

Why are there multiple views of information systems and organizations?

In what ways are information systems challenging for organizations?

What is the role of the corporate information manager?

Managing information technology has changed from a spectator sport to a participatory sport.

Richard L. Nolan
Chairman, Nolan, Norton, and Company

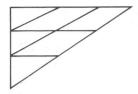

Effective information systems use is at the heart of many of the changes taking place within organizations and in the environment in which they function. Chapter 1 introduced the fundamental elements of information systems. It also outlined the transformations taking place in the global business community—changes that are expected to continue at an increasing pace.

This chapter explores a vision of information systems in organizations. It unfolds several views of the effect computer and communications technology can have on an organization, yet recognizes that there are challenges for both those who develop and those who use information systems. We begin by discussing why organizations use information technology and introduce two visions that often guide their use.

Why Use Information Systems?

Successful organizations will increasingly rely on computer information systems to meet their day-to-day needs and to manage their future. Having a vision of the role of information systems in the organization will guide development and use of information systems resources for today and tomorrow. This section explains what *vision* means in a business context and then discusses two differing information systems visions.

The Meaning of *Vision*

A **vision** is an image that grows out of a firm understanding of the area of interest, but that is produced by imagination and creativity. It is a view of what can happen by using resources to transform opportunities into reality. Successful business leaders begin with a vision. Lee Iacocca had a vision of how Chrysler Corporation could again become a successful automobile manufacturer if given the opportunity, even though the firm was bankrupt and nearly out of business when he was appointed its chief executive officer. His vision of a highly successful company with innovative products was doubted by many outside the firm. Yet Chrysler Corporation employees shared the vision, developing front-wheel drive vehicles, convertibles, and minivans by means of advanced manufacturing technology and offering warranties and guarantees unheard of in the automobile industry. Thus much of the vision became reality and has had a permanent effect on the industry. Other parts of Iacocca's vision are still unfolding—elements we will see as the firm announces new products and services and applies information technology to its operations.

Fred Smith had a different kind of vision. He foresaw the usefulness of rapid delivery of parcels, even though the firm's potential customers did not explicitly tell him they wanted an overnight express service. His sense of customer needs, coupled with a scheme for how parcels from around the country could be exchanged in a central hub location and routed to their final destination—all before 10:30 the following morning—brought about the creation of the company we know today as Federal Express. Smith continues to guide the company in finding new ways of enhancing customer service.

These are two of many examples demonstrating the importance of having a vision to guide planning and utilization of resources. Note that in each case the vision is an image, not a financial plan, a statement of market share, or a description of organization size (although these become important in trying to attain the vision). Visions generally come from within. Ideas, suggestions, and opportunities recognized by employees, staff members, customers, and suppliers form the basis of the vision. Leaders combine them with knowledge of capabilities while recognizing limitations. Visions are aimed at empowering people to see what isn't there yet, but what an organization could bring about. They suggest a direction with intentions so compelling that people are drawn to share the vision.

Two Visions of the Role of Information Systems

With respect to information systems, visions suggest the value of applying computer and communications technology to the activities of the enterprise. Members of the information systems group and the organization as a whole seek ways of utilizing information systems to achieve the vision.

Two types of visions can emerge, one more desirable than the other. As you examine each below, consider which has the most usefulness for an organization.

Information Technology Vision An **information technology vision** of an organization focuses explicitly on capabilities inherent in computer and data communications technology—such as speed of processing, storage capacity, communications capabilities, and so on—and how they can be used to gain improved efficiency. In this vision, information technology is an end in itself. Thus emphasis is placed on how well systems function with respect to processing efficiency and performance reliability, regardless of the particular uses made of their capabilities.

Strategic Business Vision In contrast, the **strategic business vision** (see Figure 2.1) focuses on the strengths and capabilities of the organization, along with the opportunities that it encounters, and assesses how information technology can be used to bring about that vision. This view considers the enabling powers of information systems technology: What does information technology allow the firm to do, such as reaching new customers or offering new products? In other words, rather than having a technology focus, the strategic business vision seeks to transform the organization by means of information systems technology.

This is the preferred vision, because it is not the computer that is important but what the computer will enable the organization to accomplish.

Figure 2.1 Information Technology and Vision of Organization

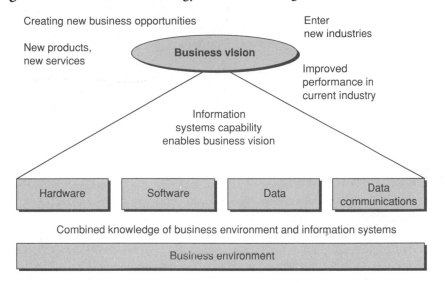

Business Vision Enabled Through Information Systems The vision of Fred Smith at Federal Express combined a knowledge of the package shipping industry, business needs, and information systems. Smith saw a market for the overnight handling of packages—a market that competitors did not envision. He recognized that the increasing pace of activities would create a need to move virtually every type of item, such as machinery parts, corporate reports, films, and so forth, from one location to another quickly. Items shipped at the end of the business day had to arrive the morning of the next business day, even if it meant the package must travel across country. That's the business part of the vision.

Smith quickly recognized the role of computers and data communications for Federal Express. He oversaw the use of information technology in such ways as:

——Electronic sorting of packages from around the country, so that when all aircraft arrived they could be unloaded and reloaded and depart for their destination within less than three hours of arrival

——Installation of terminals in Federal Express route trucks to inform drivers of customers calling for package pickup and transmission of messages

——Electronic tracking of packages from time of pickup until delivery at destination

——Use of hand-held scanners that read and store airbill numbers, eliminating the need for manual entry and thus entry errors

The business vision is intertwined with a knowledge of the capabilities provided by information systems. This is a crucial point:

There are no information systems opportunities that are not first business opportunities.

Recognizing this fact is the essential element in the information systems vision.

To understand more fully what this means, let's explore the benefits that information systems can provide to organizations.

Types of Information Systems Benefits

Information systems have the potential to provide three types of benefits to organizations: (1) gains in productivity, (2) improvements in effectiveness, and (3) competitive advantage (Figure 2.2). Whether a particular benefit will be realized depends on the vision of the firm. Each is important and sought by the management of an enterprise.

Gains in Productivity **Productivity** is the efficiency or output at a task. We say that gains in productivity occur when more work can be completed with the same or fewer resources. In organizations, this relates to business processes, such as manufacturing goods or handling customer sales, as well as to the ability of managers to oversee a greater number of activities. For example, productivity improves when an individual increases the number of sales orders that can be captured in a period of time, say an hour. Thus when an employee uses new methods to record 50 order transactions in an hour rather than 25, productivity is doubled.

Productivity Benefits of Transaction-Level Systems Many organizations first invest in information systems to obtain gains in productivity—that is, to perform current tasks, such as recording orders, in a more efficient manner. Organizations typically first become interested in computer processing because of the promise of improved operating efficiency. Common recordkeeping applications are automated: accounts receivable and payable, the general ledger, personnel records, and property management. (Chapter 10 discusses recordkeeping systems and the processing of transactions.)

Figure 2.2 Three Information Systems Benefits

Gains in productivity	Improvements in effectiveness	Gaining competitive advantage
• Increasing the efficiency of a task • More work completed with same or fewer resources	• Doing the right things • Utilization of resources to produce desirable results of high quality	• Selecting and implementing strategies that change the way a firm competes • Improved performance in comparison to competitors, using chosen criteria (e.g., market share, industry dominance, industry ranking)

Each recordkeeping application has similar features: a high volume of activities. Clearcut procedures are repeated over and over for each recordkeeping transaction. Typically a single area of the firm is involved. Each focuses on a specific file of data (for example, an accounts receivable file or a personnel file).

As firms become familiar with the potential productivity benefits of computer information systems, they expand their use of business transaction processing, still focusing on recordkeeping. Consequently, management often decides to implement computer-based order entry systems and inventory management applications.

Productivity and Computer Information Systems Computer information systems enable individual workers and staff members to become more productive because they can handle a greater number of transactions, improve quality in the processing of transactions, and achieve these results in a more timely manner.

For example, in the task of capturing order details from customers, where prices must be quoted and quantities on hand verified as the order is accepted, productivity is measured by the number of orders an individual can accurately accept in a given period of time (perhaps orders per hour). Compared to an employee using manual forms and printed inventory lists, an individual entering orders through a personal computer or terminal system that is well designed is likely to complete many more order entry tasks—two, three, even four times more in the same interval of time. The benefit from computer assistance is termed a *productivity benefit*.

Improvements in Effectiveness **Effectiveness** refers to the ability of an individual or an organization to do the things that need to be done. Individuals such as managers are judged effective when they repeatedly select actions that will have the most desirable outcome (whatever the criteria) and develop appropriate strategies to implement them. A manager who consistently foresees situations that could turn into problems, and who deals with the underlying causes before difficulties occur, is considered more effective than one who continually must solve problems that could have been prevented. An organization is effective when it utilizes its resources (financial, material, and human) in a way that ensures desirable and high-quality performance, however measured.

What is the influence of information technology on effectiveness? During **transaction processing**—that is, using information technology to facilitate productivity gains in the form of increased volume, accuracy, or consistency when processing data about business transactions—the potential exists to capture a great deal of useful data at the same time. For example, when customer orders are processed, the details of the order, the customer name, and the time at which it is placed can automatically be stored in an organized form. The details may be first written on an order form (a source document) and the document filed for reference if needed. Alternatively, the data may be entered through a computer workstation and stored in a computer database. If the details are on paper, it is difficult for more than one individual to use the data at a time. But many people can access data stored in a computer database through communications links.

Information systems that offer the potential for improvements in effectiveness are designed to draw on the rich database of details captured during transaction

Figure 2.3 Order Entry Transaction Processing and Order Fulfillment Process

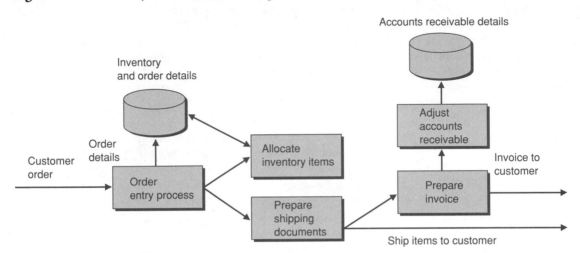

processing (Figure 2.3). In general, these systems are aimed at enhancing the effectiveness of decisions or problem-solving activities that must occur in the firm.

In the order entry example just cited, the use of information technology for improved efficiency can be extended to improve the entire order fulfillment process. Order entry is a task in the larger process of order fulfillment. The process includes the order entry task, as described earlier, but also encompasses the allocation of items in inventory, preparation of picking lists (instructions to move ordered items from the storage section to the shipping area), printing of shipping labels and related documents, preparation of the invoice, and adjusting the accounts receivable balance of the customer, if the sale is made on credit.

Efficiency in order fulfillment includes achieving an appropriate productivity level. But it also means integrating the related tasks, performing each task accurately, and capturing information needed to coordinate activities to benefit both customer and organization. In other words, it means doing order fulfillment right.

Gaining Competitive Advantage There is increasing interest in determining how information systems can make organizations more competitive. The same systems that have provided improvements in productivity and effectiveness can provide a potential for changing the way organizations compete. And they are altering the structure of entire industries. Federal Express's entry into the package transportation industry changed the nature of the industry permanently. Through its overnight delivery, it redefined the importance of time and the meaning of "fast." It also made accountability a new expectation for customers: Shippers and recipients alike want to be able to track their package from the time it is picked up until the moment it is delivered. Federal Express uses computer-based information systems to do that.

Those firms that, like Federal Express, deploy their experience and expertise in information technology for competitive advantage are likely to gain additional success in the marketplace. Those who lag behind will find themselves at a competitive disadvantage.

The interrelation between business strategy and the strategic use of computer-based information systems is becoming closer. An information systems application is *strategic* if it changes the way a firm competes. A strategy, then, is the way in which an organization tries to differentiate itself from its competitors—like Federal Express with overnight package delivery and careful tracking of shipments. Decisions about strategy should be based on corporate strengths that are utilized in such a way that allows the firm to better meet customer needs. Thus the critical question is: Can information systems be used in ways that allow an organization to be more competitive as measured by improved ability to meet customer needs, increased market share, a higher ranking in the industry, increased profits, and so on?

In the order processing example we have been using, you might envision several ways in which a firm can transform the order fulfillment process to gain an advantage over its competitors. Here are some that have been used by well-known American firms:

——*Put the customer on-line:* IBM Corporation gives customers access to product and cost information through a terminal or personal computer using ordinary communications lines. American Hospital Supply, which later became part of Baxter-Travenol, changed the pharmaceutical supply industry by allowing customers to place all orders through terminals installed on their premises. They no longer needed to contact a sales representative.

——*Capture customer preferences:* General Foods, Inc., enters into a database the questions and preferences of its customers when they telephone the consumer information center using a toll-free telephone line. The information is analyzed frequently to gain insight into new product opportunities, different ways to use existing products, and changes in product packaging.

Airline reservations systems often include passenger profiles for those passengers who fly frequently. The profiles describe individual seating preferences, meal requirements, and other information enabling the airline to better serve the customer.

——*Link suppliers into the order fulfillment process:* General Motors has requested all suppliers to be capable of receiving orders electronically, eliminating the need for paper purchase orders and compressing the time needed to communicate manufacturing and shipping information between organizations. It has extended the fulfillment process to include electronic payment to its suppliers, eliminating the need to prepare and mail thousands of bank checks each day.

——*Deliver items or services ordered electronically:* Cable television stations throughout North America deliver custom programming and pay movies, sporting events, and musical performances over the cable already wired into subscriber homes. Orders are entered through keys on the adapter box provided when cable service is installed.

Software companies are delivering programs and documentation to personal computer users. Payment is made by credit card information captured over the same data communications links used to deliver the software.

Each of these developments has brought about a permanent change in the industry represented. And each is the result of a vision based on business principles but made possible because of an understanding of and ability to use information systems.

It is not enough for an individual alone to have a vision, however. Others must share the vision.

Consider this example. Several years ago, the chief executive officer of Allegis Corporation—parent of United Airlines—formulated a vision of the airline being a "full-service" provider to the business traveler. His vision included integrated businesses in the airline, automobile rental, and hotel industries. The traveler could make reservations for each service at the same time. A range of other services were also planned. Travelers could check baggage with the airline and know their luggage would automatically be transported directly to their reserved hotel room at the destination location. The vision of simplified travel, which the executive expected would draw more travelers to Allegis, with substantial financial benefits, was to be brought about because of the firm's expertise in computer information systems.

However, the vision did not come from within. Not enough of the members of the board of directors, executives, and employees shared it, so the executive left the company and the vision was not realized. (The firm has since changed its name to UAL, Inc.)

This important lesson can be applied to information systems. A vision that is based on the technology, rather than on the organization's business, may be misguided. Perhaps even more important, the vision of information systems must emerge from within the firm. It cannot be separate from the business of the organization nor can it be dictated by information systems professionals. To do so will most likely result in failure. In the Allegis example, the vision, although achievable technically, was not shared by key corporate officials. Thus it did not become a guide to future business opportunities.

The Value of Information Systems

Computer information systems are changing the way firms compete, often at all levels of the enterprise. Therefore, they have strategic value, and they influence the vision of the firm. This section first discusses the strategic value of information systems. Then the intertwining of information systems strategies and corporate planning is considered.

Information Systems as Strategic Applications

There is often a tendency to classify information systems as strategic or nonstrategic. This is not a meaningful exercise.

Consider an operating-level application, such as the order entry system we have used as an example in this chapter. You might have a tendency to say that it is inappropriate to classify such a routine system as strategic because it encompasses a simple routine—processing orders. Yet we have already said that an application is strategic if it gives the firm a competitive advantage, or alternatively, if it changes the way a firm competes. We have discussed examples where the manner in which a firm accepts and processes orders from customers has led to an advantage.

Now, consider the opposite result. Suppose a firm cannot accept customer orders quickly or process them to deliver the right items to the customer at the proper cost (that is, it cannot process the orders accurately). You will not continue to deal with a firm that is slow or makes mistakes in handling its transactions, and neither will other businesses. The limitations of a firm's information systems, whether because of hardware, software, data, people, or anything else, becomes a competitive factor.

In summary, operating-level information systems have strategic value, and that value can be positive or negative, depending on how well the systems work.

As a matter of fact, it is difficult to think of any meaningful information systems application that does not have strategic value. If an information system has no effect on the success of an organization, then the system is useless. Having the right systems, and ensuring they function properly, is a requirement for success in business. Not having them places the firm at a distinct competitive disadvantage—one that can even lead to failure of the firm.

This means that strategic value is not something that occurs only at the executive level of a firm. It has importance throughout all levels of personnel and across all activities.

The Consideration of Information Systems in Planning for the Future

A more useful issue is how to consider the value of an organization's information systems in organization planning—that is, in decisions about products, services, facility locations, and customers. This section discusses the three alternatives for doing so (Figure 2.4).

The Development of Information Systems Without Considering Organization Strategy Information systems may be developed without explicit consideration of their effect on corporate plans or strategy. However, this does *not* mean that such systems do have strategic benefit, but rather that it is not a factor in their development.

Many productivity-oriented systems, whose aim is to improve operating costs, increase the firm's ability to accept business, or enable performance of tasks more quickly, are aimed at automating routine activities—"backoffice activities," as they are often termed. Their development may be initiated simply to solve an operating problem, such as insufficient output. Thoughts of fitting with corporate strategy and corporate goals may not have been given any significant thought.

Historically, this is how most systems have been developed.

The Development of Information Systems to Implement Corporate Strategies Gradually, manager awareness of ways in which information systems can support the mission and strategies of the organization has increased. We find growing interest in the use of these systems to support corporate strategies in dealing with customers, suppliers, and competitors, and in responding or conforming to regulatory guidelines.

Figure 2.4 The Consideration of Information Systems in Strategic Planning

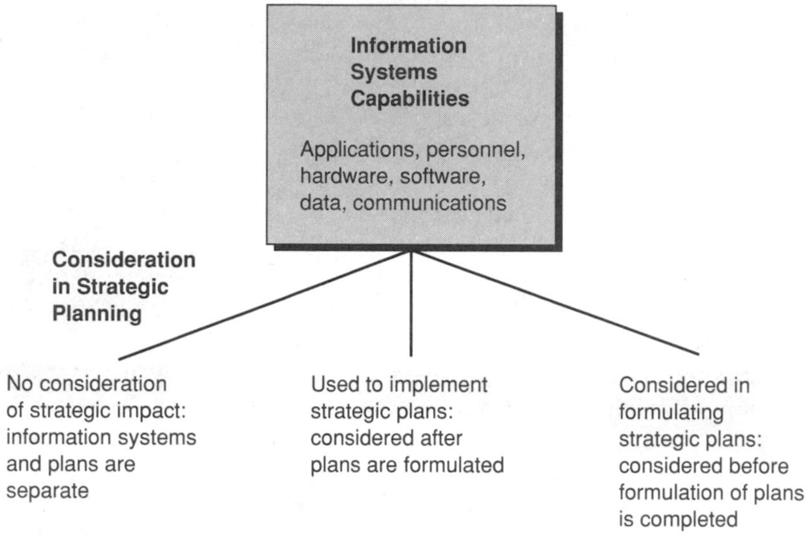

This approach typically follows these steps:

1. Corporate executives determine the strategies the firm will follow for gaining comparative advantage and competitive success.
2. The need for information systems support is identified.
3. An information systems plan is formulated to assist in implementing the organization's strategy.

As Figure 2.4 suggests, this approach requires that participants in the process know the capabilities of the organization's information systems, including current applications, personnel, and computer-related elements.

The Consideration of Information Systems in Developing Corporate Strategy Although the two preceding approaches are the most widely used, neither focuses on the manner in which an organization's information systems can influence the organization's competitive strategy. This area of opportunity can have a dramatic effect on the firm in four key areas (Table 2.1):

——**The industry in which the firm now competes:** Opportunities to use information systems technology to implement strategies for new products or services or to increase production and distribution efficiency, which in turn improve the competitive posture of the firm within its industry.

Example: Several airlines began using their computer reservations systems to provide advance seat assignments to all passengers on all flights. Doing so not only gave passengers peace of mind; it also eliminated the need to stand in check-in lines just to receive a seat number. Passengers now clearly prefer those airlines that offer this capability.

Table 2.1 Areas of Opportunity in Formulation of Corporate Strategy

Area of Opportunity	Examples
The industry in which the firm now competes	New products or services
	Improved production economies
	Improved delivery capabilities
New markets the firm can enter	Geographic expansion of market (from national to global market)
	Expansion into new market segment (begin serving retail customer, augment current wholesale market)
Industries in which the firm can begin competing	Offer services and products in industry to which firm has been supplier
	Create new industry
The elements with which the firm interacts or that influence it	Customers
	Suppliers
	Regulators
	Competitors

——**New markets the firm can enter:** Utilizing information technology to expand the reach of the firm's sales or distribution power to enter and provide support for buyers in new markets. Often involves data communications capabilities to remove the business barriers of time and geographic distance.

Example: United Parcel Service (UPS) used its effective product tracking and distribution system to expand into the North American overnight parcel delivery market, which had been developed and dominated by Federal Express. Its entry into the market and the pricing strategy it introduced changed the pricing structure of the industry, perhaps permanently. Meanwhile, both Federal Express and UPS used their communications expertise to expand into the global package delivery market.

——**Industries in which the firm can begin competing:** Gaining additional advantages from the firm's information technology to offer products and services typically associated with another industry, but in which the firm can develop and implement a competitive strategy.

Example: The brokerage firm of Merrill Lynch used its expertise in information processing to expand its services, effectively competing in the banking and financial services industry as well as its own brokerage industry. It expanded its revenue base by drawing funds previously deposited by customers in savings or commercial deposit accounts into its cash management account. Both Merrill Lynch and its customers benefited, at the expense of financial institutions.

——**The elements with which the firm interacts or that influence it:** Customers, suppliers, potential new entrants into the market, substitute products or services (discussed in greater detail later in this chapter and in Chapter 20).

Example: In the railroad industry, companies that are otherwise competitors began electronically sharing information on the location of merchandise shipped by customers. Doing so not only made it quicker and easier to track the route and location of a specific shipment, it made the railroads more competitive against the trucking industry.

The vision of information technology includes the use of computers and data communications systems as a competitive weapon. However, it requires careful assessment of the firm's expertise in information technology to determine what it does well and where improvement is needed. Similarly, management must know the firms with which it competes or wishes to compete and whether it can respond to the new information systems demands that will result if a particular strategy is further developed and implemented.

The Information Systems Environment

The information systems vision described in the preceding sections can only emerge when the information systems environment is understood and properly considered. This section describes that environment. Four components comprise the environment: (1) the business environment, (2) the organization, (3) information systems architecture, and (4) information systems applications.

The Business Environment

The foundation for all activities is the environment in which the organization operates. These components influence the products and services the enterprise offers, how it chooses to compete, and the nature of the activities it performs in carrying out its day-to-day activities. The elements that influence the organization include:

- **Customers:** Those organizations, agencies, households, or individuals who purchase the products and services of an enterprise. May be the direct consumer of the items or a distributor who in turn resells the items to the actual consumer.
- **Competitors:** Other firms, in the same or related industries, that customers may choose instead. Rivals who can capture the sales or service of a business enterprise, taking away potential revenues and market share.
- **Suppliers:** Provide the materials and services needed in an organization. Are an essential element of a firm's success since the inability of an organization to obtain needed materials and services from a supplier may limit its competitive success.
- **Regulatory agencies:** Formulate, implement, and enforce laws, regulations, and policies that determine whether a firm may compete in a specific manner. Also influence the nature of products or services and their delivery.

These elements of the business environment influence many aspects of information systems, a factor that we see throughout this book.

The Organization

It is often said that people, facilities, and financial resources are the most basic resources of any organization. Increasingly, we recognize the importance of using these resources in the most beneficial way. The organization can be looked at from these five perspectives: information, systems, human resources, management, and organization structure.

Information Have you noticed that some firms seem always to be in the right place at the right time? Or that they have the very service or product you want, available when you need it? Take airlines, for example. Some are better at scheduling their flights than others. With some, you can select a flight at just the time of day you want to depart, whether in the morning, midday, or in the evening. And if you have to connect with another flight at one of the hub cities, there is very little delay between flights (barring delays caused by weather or stacking). These airlines are experts at scheduling. They have just the information needed to know who is flying where. They also know what times of day are most beneficial to both carrier and passenger.

Of course, if you do a great deal of flying, you probably know that not all airlines provide the same service. Some seem to have their flights leave at times best suited to them, not you. And if you must change planes to connect with another flight, a two- to three-hour layover is not uncommon. What can create such a difference? In a word, information.

Managing information well means having the right type of information available when it is needed and in a form that is useful to the recipient. Chapter 3 explores the different types of information and pertinent management concerns.

Systems The term *system* refers to the manner in which the processes of an organization fit together. It recognizes that even though organizations have divisions, departments, and sections, the separate units should work together. Coordination and interaction are necessary to accomplish the objective of the organization as a whole. Information is the means of coordination.

A systems view of an organization also implies the existence of procedures to compare actual performance against expectations. Results are evaluated to determine whether adjustments are needed.

You often hear organizations described as a system. Or you may hear a manager refer to the systems in place within the organization. Both meanings fall within the systems view, discussed in detail in Chapter 3.

Human Resources The human resources in an organization are its people. There is little question that without sufficient numbers of good people, it is virtually impossible for an organization to be successful. Training and career advancement opportunities are also necessary for continued success. Continual study by researchers and practitioners alike is going on in this area.

From the perspective of information systems, the objective is to provide the type of support that will make the human resources as productive and effective as possible. Yet applications should be developed in such a way that they fit employees' interests and capabilities, thus aiding in accomplishing the personal objectives of workers as well as those of the organization.

Information systems considerations related to human resources include having the right information available in the most meaningful form for recipients to assist in assessing situations, in evaluating alternative courses of action, and in formulating decisions. They also recognize that people differ and that the information system should accommodate those differences.

Management   Management includes the functions of planning, organizing, staffing, controlling, and communicating. Although the ways in which these functions are carried out differ, there is general agreement that good managers perform them so as to produce desirable results for the organization, whether the criterion is providing good service, making a profit, or anything else.

The amount of time individuals devote to particular functions will vary according to their position in the firm and their area of responsibility—for example, marketing, manufacturing, or purchasing. Information systems support is most effective when the applications are designed to include features that accommodate the individuals' needs. (See also accompanying box on Corporate Information Managers.)

Organization Structure   Developing the right structure in an organization, including the nature of individual departments and where responsibility for decisions should rest, is an ongoing area of discussion in virtually every firm. Differing management theories have emerged through the history of organizations, each of which has many proponents who can claim successful performance as a result of following one or the other.

The structure of an organization influences the flow of information and therefore the characteristics of information systems that support the individuals within that structure. In some instances, the objective is to reduce the need for information, achieved by establishing routines and standard procedures. In other instances, organization structures are selected that allow the information to be obtained and used within a particular work group, eliminating the flow between organization units. Chapter 4 explores these concerns.

Information Systems Architecture

Information systems components include the hardware or equipment, software, data, and communications capabilities (discussed in Chapters 5–9). Although there is a tendency to focus on the equipment in a system, there is general agreement that the other components play a much greater role in obtaining value from the investment in such systems.

Architecture refers to the particular components in an organization's information systems environment and the manner in which the components fit together.

As indicated in the last chapter, all organizations undergo constant change. Some occur unexpectedly and require quick response. Others take place over time, often with people anticipating that they will occur. From an information systems perspective, the concern is whether the architecture inherent in the firm's combination of hardware, software, data, and communications resources can meet changing needs. More succinctly, if a business opportunity arises, can the firm respond or will its information technology hold it back? Information systems architecture is a

THE VISION

Corporate Information Managers

A new breed of executive has emerged in many organizations. Accorded different titles by different companies (for example, chief information officer, chief technology executive, manager of information technology), these executives have important functions and qualifications. They are not cheerleaders for new computer and communications technology, but rather experts who seek out ways to harness the power of information systems to help the organization become more productive and profitable.

Corporate information managers:

——Oversee the firm's information technology investment and plan, including information systems, data management, voice and data communications, and office systems

——Focus on information systems planning, emphasizing the coordination of corporate plans with information technology plans; they often concentrate on long-term technology

——Delegate the operation of data centers and computers to other managers who work within the information systems group headed by the corporate information manager

——Report directly to the senior executive, typically the chief executive officer or chairman of the corporation

——Have backgrounds in business that may be more extensive than their technical backgrounds

Successful corporate information managers are just as comfortable in the corporate boardroom as in the computer center.

Persons filling the role of corporate information manager in the major companies in the United States come into the position from technical positions (for example, project leaders and managers of information systems) or they may have prior experience as functional area managers (such as vice president of manufacturing or marketing). An understanding of technology is necessary, but it need not be detailed. It is much more important to corporate information managers to know *what* works than *how* it works.

Approximately 40 percent of all large firms currently have a corporate information manager and the number is growing rapidly. Many experts predict that this kind of manager will become common in all types of organizations.

CEOs typically establish the position when they recognize the strategic value of their information systems and the data they provide. This is especially true in the banking, financial service, insurance, retail, and transportation (especially airlines) industries, where information intensity is high—that is, in those industries most dependent on the availability of useful data to carry on day-to-day activities.

In firms that place high value on their information systems investments, the function of corporate information manager will increasingly be recognized as a critical one.

determining factor. Flexibility and expandability—the features that facilitate responsiveness—are accompanied by the architectural features that provide security and reliability. The data at the heart of information systems are valuable and, like any resource, should be safeguarded. Security pertains to safeguarding their existence. Reliability refers to the accuracy and integrity of the data and the information produced by the system. Architecture includes features guaranteeing both security and reliability.

Information Systems Applications

Architecture refers to structure, not content. Information systems applications draw on the structure of hardware, software, data, and communications to capture, store, and process data in a manner that meets individual and organization needs. Applications are collectively the component that users (employees, staff members, managers, executives, customers, and suppliers) see most often. It is their reason for using the information system.

Chapters 10–15 discuss the different types of information systems introduced in Chapter 1 and shown in Figure 2.5.

The Information Systems Challenge

Information systems are a challenge for organizations and their members. Yet the challenge must be met in order to achieve the vision. The nature of the challenge is sketched in the following paragraphs.

What Is the Challenge?

The challenge for information systems developers and users alike is to utilize the power of the technology to meet the ongoing needs of the organization, its members, and its customers, whether the enterprise is for profit or not and whether it offers a product or a service.

Through it all, information systems technology should be part of a solution, not a problem in and of itself. The challenge involves ensuring that the information system is transparent from the employees' standpoint and that it is a help rather than a hindrance in meeting organization goals. Everyone in an organization—not just the information systems professionals—has roles and responsibilities in developing and using information systems.

Why Are Information Systems a Challenge?

Information systems are a challenge for their developers and users. This challenge involves considerations met in other organizational areas.

Figure 2.5 Information Systems Environment

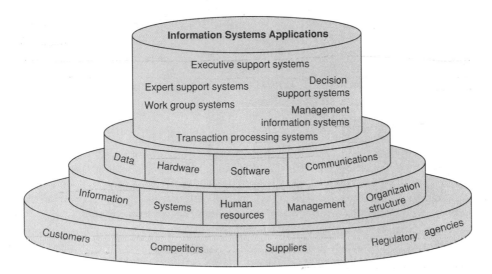

——Information and information systems requirements are constantly changing because of evolving business conditions.

——Underlying technology foundations are changing, often creating questions about whether to shift applications to new alternatives or to develop new applications.

——Software can be the most significant limitation in the deployment of information systems technology in organizations, either because it is not available or because it does not perform the necessary functions. The greatest limitation is often the inability of individuals to identify and describe applications that will have desired payoff levels for the organization, whether operationally or strategically.

——Too many information systems professionals do not have sufficient expertise in business and organizational areas to fully understand the manner in which users can most effectively utilize the capabilities of the technology.

——Information systems professionals must stop focusing on computing and start thinking about communicating.

——It is not clear how some important information needed by executives, managers, and staff members can be easily included in computer information systems.

——Information value changes, often diminishing, with the passage of time.

The information systems vision itself is both a challenge and an opportunity. It offers a direction for transforming organizations to continually more effective performance. Like a cloud, it is constantly moving, taking new shape as it moves. Not all elements of the vision are fully defined or well articulated. Thus, the vision of the moment will never be reached, but rather will always be something to be sought.

Summary

Information systems continue to play an increasingly important role in the day-to-day activities and the planning that goes on within organizations. Realizing the benefits of information systems starts with a vision that describes how such systems can be utilized in the organization's strategy for success. The vision is business oriented, not focused primarily on computer or data communications technology, and is shared by members of the enterprise.

Three benefits accrue when information systems are developed and utilized in meaningful ways. Productivity benefits provide an increase in the efficiency with which tasks are performed. Improvements in effectiveness, in contrast, result from doing the right things—that is, selecting actions and alternatives that will have the most desirable outcomes. The third benefit, gaining competitive advantage, is an outgrowth of combining a vision within the enterprise with the capabilities of information systems to meet needs of those whom the organization serves.

Information systems can be developed to meet the requirements of specific tasks, but they can also be developed to implement organization strategies or considered when strategies are formulated.

The information systems environment consists of the business environment itself and multiple views of the organization, including that of information, systems, human resources, management, and organization structure. It also includes the information systems architecture, a combination of computer hardware, software, data, and communications integrated to meet the changing needs of the enterprise. Content is an outgrowth of the applications that provide information processing, whether in the form of transaction processing, management information systems, or various support systems. The foundation on which all other elements of an information system are built is supplied by the organization environment.

The challenge for information systems developers and users alike is to apply the capabilities of information systems to meet the needs of the organization today and tomorrow. Having a vision is fundamental to meeting this challenge.

Key Words

Architecture	Productivity	Transaction processing
Effectiveness	Strategic business vision	Vision
Information technology vision		

Review Questions

1. What is a vision? What is the meaning of vision when applied to information systems?
2. How does an information technology vision differ from a strategic business vision? Which is preferred and why?

3. What types of benefits accrue from effective use of information systems? Explain the meaning of each benefit.

4. How are effectiveness and efficiency benefits different?

5. When are information systems strategic?

6. Discuss the meaning of strategic versus nonstrategic application of information systems.

7. In what ways can the value of information systems be considered when organizations plan for the future? Explain each of your answers.

8. Discuss the environment of information systems, describing each of the four components that constitute the environment.

9. What elements make up the information systems architecture? Why is the architecture important?

10. Describe the challenge of information systems. Why are information systems a challenge in organizations?

11. What is the role of the corporate information manager?

Application Problems

1. The information systems managers at two different organizations have distinctly different outlooks on their roles. The first, who has 20 years experience in the development and management of information systems applications, views the primary responsibility of the IS manager as responding to the application requirements of managers and staff members in the functional areas of the business (such as the marketing department, purchasing group, and manufacturing section). In addition, this IS manager believes that a good IS manager will be able to develop the requested applications on time, within the established budget, and with the features users indicate they want. The IS manager must accept the responsibility for ensuring that the organization's computer systems are available and functioning properly when needed around the clock.

    The second IS manager, who has 10 years broad business experience, but not extensive technical knowledge, views the responsibility of IS managers as one of pointing out business opportunities that can be taken advantage of because of the firm's expertise in information systems. As the manager often says, "IS managers who react to user requests are not doing their jobs. They should be driving the business by showing what the computer and communications technology can do. The technical issues can be handled by programmers and systems analysts, but identification of real business needs requires a management perspective."

    a. Discuss the suitability of these two differing views of IS management. Is either manager correct in his or her view?

    b. How will the view held by each IS manager affect his or her focus on planning for future information systems applications and establishment of the appropriate infrastructure?

2. It is often suggested that general managers have only a limited understanding of the computer and communications technology underlying information systems; that is, they are not information systems experts, but rather have management skills in other areas of the organization.

    a. Does the lack of detailed technical knowledge limit the ability of a manager to have a vision of the role information systems can play in the activities of an organization?

    b. In general, what level of understanding should general managers have about information systems?

3. Which type of information systems benefit (productivity, effectiveness, competitiveness) is demonstrated in each of the following examples of information systems use?

    a. Replacing manual entry of customer payments by accounting clerks with computer scanning of payments and automatic posting to accounting records. Computer scanning results in processing of each payment in one-tenth of the time normally required.

    b. Capturing data about past customer orders and maintaining the information in a form where customers can access it easily to determine the rate of usage of materials and products.

    c. Automatically sensing and calling manager's attention to areas of activity where performance, such as sales, costs, or number of returns, is higher or lower than expected.

    d. Allowing an organization to use information systems technology to provide a new service to current customers by keeping track of the rate at which they use a product and notifying them when they are likely to need a refill. Such a service is desired by customers and has attracted new customers to the organization.

    e. Scheduling the delivery route of the company's drivers so that more deliveries can be made in less time (resulting in more deliveries made per driver each day).

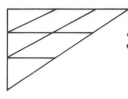

3: Information and Systems Views

Key Questions

✓ What is information?

How do accounting and management information differ?
[handwritten: exception reporting vs plan, warn, comfort, intelligence]

What are the different types of management information? *[handwritten check]*

Should information be viewed as a resource in the organization? *[handwritten: Yes]*

What is a system? *[handwritten: within enviro, I/o's, process data]*

What are the levels within any system? *[handwritten: subsystems]*

Is the modern organization a system? Why or why not?

How is an ongoing system controlled?

What is the value to organizations of using a systems approach?

Too Much!

The first thing about information systems that strikes me is that one gets too much information. The information explosion crosses and criss-crosses executive desks with a great deal of data. Much of this is only partly digested and much of it is irrelevant to what I believe to be the fundamental objective of business information, which is simplification.

Anthony J. F. O'Reilly
President, H. J. Heinz Company

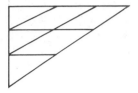

Information and Systems Views

This chapter examines the information and systems views, two components of the information systems environment introduced in Chapter 2. Managers are more interested in the usefulness of information than in the way it is produced. Information is a resource parallel in importance to people, facilities, and capital. The first portion of this chapter examines the information view, considering the types of information managers need. Next we see how data and information differ. And we look at sources and uses of information, including the communication elements associated with transmitting information from one person or location to another.

The development and use of information, and the management of organizations, must be grounded in some type of system. Systems are the underlying structure in any organization and, for that matter, in *information* systems. They are the heartbeat and the force behind an organization. The systems view describes the systems principles as they apply to organizations and to management in organizations.

Finally, we look at the implications of the information and systems views for information systems.

Managers have many different information needs, depending on their responsibilities. This section defines information and shows how it differs from data. It also points out the different types of information managers and organizations need. Then we look at the attributes of information that should concern us when using information for managerial decision making.

Information: Definition and Types

Information is data presented in a form that is meaningful to the recipient. It has real or perceived value to the user and adds to what he or she already knows about an event or an area of concern. It must tell the recipient something that was not previously known or could not be predicted. In other words, it adds to **knowledge** but must be relevant for the situation in which it will be applied (such as deciding what action to take to make the most of an opportunity or to deal with a problem).

The lack of knowledge—that is, the absence of information about a particular area of concern—is **uncertainty.**

Organization managers need two types of information, namely accounting information and management information. You should not conclude that one is more important than the other; both are essential.

Types of Accounting Information

Accounting information originates from the areas of financial and managerial accounting. The first focuses specifically on the identification and reporting of income and financial status. Income statements and balance sheets are prepared to accomplish this objective. On the other hand, managerial accounting reports business costs. Such important matters as personnel costs, operating expenses, and overhead allocation are included within the managerial accounting function. The development and administration of budgets and the analysis of organization performance, another aspect of this area of accounting, underlie management control and decision making.

Often management information is viewed as a by-product of the accounting process. On the one hand, this is because the first transaction processing systems were usually established to do accounting work. Furthermore, accounting information is so very important throughout the firm. It is in quantitative form and helps managers and supervisors answer questions about the performance of business operations and activities. For example:

——What revenue and profit levels were achieved?

——How much was sold?

——What quantity do we have on hand?

——How many meals were served?

——When did the transaction occur?

——In what sequence were the activities handled?

——What was the average cost?

As we see in this chapter, quantitative information is based on hard facts. Since we can quantify expectations (through budgets, sales quotas, and revenue levels), we are also able to compare actual performance against expectations. We call this **exception information.**

Types of Management Information

Information systems should inform managers, not overwhelm them. Managers, especially senior executives, do not routinely need or want extensive accounting detail. Summary forms of the information are typically preferred since they show the overall results and trends of interest. They also allow comparison of planned and actual performance of divisions, departments, product areas, and so on.

But, as we see in Chapter 4, many managers, especially at the upper levels, do not have the time to deliberate over large amounts of detail, *even in summary form.* Their pace is so rapid and the scope of activities in which they are involved is so broad that they must be able to pinpoint matters needing their attention. This reality dramatically influences the nature of **management information.** Often qualitative as well as soft information (estimates, opinions, and incomplete specifications) can be very useful.

Seven types of information are necessary to top-level managers (Figure 3.1).

Figure 3.1 Management Information Needs Differ by Level in the Organization

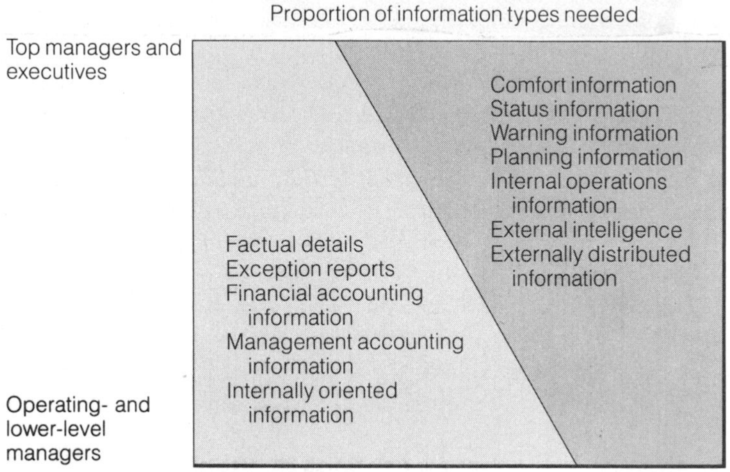

Proportion of information types needed

Top managers and executives

Operating- and lower-level managers

Factual details
Exception reports
Financial accounting
information
Management accounting
information
Internally oriented
information

Comfort information
Status information
Warning information
Planning information
Internal operations
information
External intelligence
Externally distributed
information

1. **Comfort information:** keeps managers informed about current situations or achievement levels; allows the individual to know that performance is on track and in line with general expectations in an area of interest.
   Examples:
   Yesterday's sales volumes
   This week's hotel room occupancy (management *knows* that the break-even point is 65 percent)
   Number of customers served or passengers flown
   Number of flights canceled or delayed

2. **Status information:** also called **progress information;** keeps managers abreast of current problems and crises as well as reporting advances to take advantage of opportunities that may disappear if not acted on.
   Examples:
   Progress yesterday on labor contract negotiations
   Status of construction work on new manufacturing facility
   Progress on research and development effort aimed at launching a new product to meet an emerging market
   Competitor progress on a similar product (the company introducing the item first will obtain the greatest market)

3. **Warning information:** signals that changes are occurring, either in the form of emerging opportunities or as omens of trouble ahead that will affect the success of the firm, its products or services, or its long-term viability.
   Examples:
   Significant price fluctuations in raw materials such as steel or in energy
   Increasing frequency of quality control difficulties, evidenced by higher product rejection rates at inspection stations
   Higher-than-usual position vacancies for which it is increasingly difficult

to hire qualified personnel at prevailing wage or salary rates

Test market characteristics of new product launches

4. **Planning information:** descriptions of major developments and programs due to begin in the future; includes assumptions on which plans are based or anticipated developments essential for the realization of the established plans.

   Examples:

   How the organization's market (and the overall industry) is expected to grow or shrink

   Market share the firm plans to capture over the next three years

   Entry of new competitors or product substitutes

   Breakthrough in underlying manufacturing technology

5. **Internal operations information:** key indicators of how the organization or individuals are performing; useful for reporting the overall health of an organization, subsidiary, division, or product. Areas in which actual performance does not match expectations are reported as exceptions.

   Examples:

   Accumulated return on equity

   Percent share of market held by the organization

   Sales for current month, quarter, and year-to-date plus variance from planned sales

These categories of information focus on activities internal to the organization. Senior managers also use and provide a great deal of external information, that is, information that originates outside the firm. At the same time, upper-level management is responsible for *releasing* information to individuals, agencies, and groups outside the enterprise. Thus there are two external information categories:

6. **External intelligence:** information, gossip, and opinions about activities in the environment of an organization; includes a broad range of areas such as competitor and industry changes, financial market movement, and political-economic fluctuations or expected shifts.

   Examples:

   Customer demands for new products or services

   Expert projections of behavior of the economy over the next six months

   Industry talk of impending competitor actions

   The fallout from protective or interruptive legislation in the industry or area of business

   Crop profiles for agricultural products used as raw materials

7. **Externally distributed information:** information the chief executive wishes to review before its release to stockholders or distribution to news media.

   Examples:

   Quarterly corporate earnings report

   Accumulated contributions and funds raised through the annual campaign

   Details of newly developed public service program

Table 3.1, which locates varieties of management information along the internal and external dimensions, emphasizes that both factual (numeric) and textual (narrative) information are essential. The latter form includes memos, correspondence,

Table 3.1 Types of Information by Origin and Form

	Factual	Textual
Internal	Accounting data	Office communication
	Numeric details	Planning assumptions
	Exception details	Estimates
		Opinions
External	Economic data	Industry rumors
	Purchased market data	Opinions about expected economic developments
		Legislation

expectations, general economic conditions—even rumors or personal experiences. Transaction processing systems are oriented toward processing data. In contrast, office information systems include the capability to handle text and factual information in a variety of different forms (including voice form).

The remainder of this chapter discusses the dimensions of information, focusing first on the distinction between data and information, then on the attributes we want information to have. We also see the primary and secondary sources of the different types of information we have identified.

Information Distinguished from Data

By themselves, data are meaningless; they must be changed to a usable form and placed in context to have value. **Data** become information when they are transformed to communicate meaning or knowledge (Figure 3.2), ideas or conclusions. Information, then, is knowledge based on data that have, through processing, been given meaning, purpose, and usefulness.

Relevance is a key factor in distinguishing between data and information. Not all data or facts can be relevant at a given moment. Indeed, some data may never be relevant to any event. For a marketing manager planning the sales program for the upcoming year, the accounting figure of $50 million in sales for the company's product—widgets—is relevant knowledge; that is, this information affects the decision-making activities. Likewise, the knowledge that a 10-day strike of the production personnel may occur during the first quarter is relevant information. However, the fact that the Dew Drop Inn has purchased four new pizza ovens is not relevant to the manager in developing a sales program for widgets.

Paradoxically, however, what is information for one person may not be for another. In the same sense, one person's information may be someone else's data. This analogy from a manufacturing operation will demonstrate. Company A receives daily shipments of metals and chemicals from its suppliers. These materials are used to produce copper wire. Company B purchases the wire from company A and uses it to manufacture lamps and light fixtures. The two companies operate two distinct production processes. In the first case, the raw materials include copper and the

Figure 3.2 Data Transformed into Information

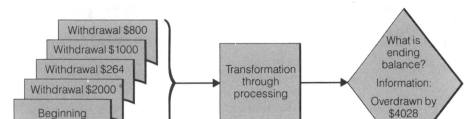

Account is posted   Information created:
                           Account is overdrawn;
                           follow-up action
                           is indicated.

product is copper wire. In the second case, the raw materials include copper wire and the finished goods are lamps. What is a finished good for company A is raw material for company B.

The same relationship exists between data and information. The copper wire produced by company A might be considered analogous to information. It has undergone a transformation to give it a specific value to the business. At the same time, copper wire is analogous to data (or raw material) for company B. The wire is transformed to be part of the finished product, lamps, which are analogous to information. In each case something more—intelligence—has been added to the data of the operation to create information.

The same transformations occur all the time in the modern organization. A cost accountant, for example, collects data on materials costs, labor costs, the hours of labor needed for a job, overhead rates, and so on, to develop standard product or production costs for given items. However, for someone developing contract bids, the standard costs are only one part of the larger cost package needed to develop information on break-even and profit points and levels.

Using the same example, the information needed to decide whether to proceed with the development of a new product will include accounting information as well as management information on the general economic outlook related to the product, insight into planned and probable competitor actions, and general sales expectations. Experienced managers will seldom formulate decisions about new products without such information.

The Attributes of Information

As we've discussed, information adds to relevant knowledge, reduces uncertainty, and supports the decision-making process in an organization. However, to be useful, information must have essential attributes, both as individual items and as a set of information (Table 3.2).

Table 3.2 The Attributes of Information

Attributes of an Item of Information		Attributes of a Set of Information	
Accuracy	Information is true or false, accurate or inaccurate. The main question is: Does the information portray the situation or status as it really is? Inaccurate information may be treated by a user as if it were accurate.	Relevance	Information is relevant if it is needed for a particular situation. Information needed once may not be relevant at all times. Likewise, information obtained "just in case it is needed" is not relevant.
Form	Distinctions of form are qualitative and quantitative, numerical and graphic, printed and displayed, summary and detail. Often a selection of one or the other alternate forms is dictated by the situation.	Completeness	Complete information provides the user with all that needs to be known about a particular situation.
Frequency	Frequency is a measure of how often information is needed, collected, or produced.	Timeliness	Timely information is available when it is needed and has not become outdated through delay.
Breadth	Breadth of information defines its scope. Some information may cover a large area of interest. Other information may be very narrow in scope. Usage determines the necessary breadth.		
Origin	Information may originate from sources inside the organization or outside it.		
Time Horizon	Information may be oriented toward the past, toward current events, or toward future activities and events.		

The **attributes of information** are the characteristics that are meaningful to the user of each individual item of information. That is, each individual item of information can be described with respect to accuracy, form, frequency, breadth, origin, and time horizon.

Information Theory

Information and its communication are the focal points of information theory, the mathematical theory of communication. We'll briefly examine the concepts of information theory in this section, since they give us some fresh insights into management and information systems.*

In the broadest sense, communication is any procedure by which one person might affect the mind of another. This includes *all* aspects of human behavior, not merely written narrative and oral speech. Following from this broad meaning, there are three levels of problems in information communication (Shannon and Weaver, 1949, p. 96):

> *Technical:* How accurately can the symbols of communication be transmitted?
> *Semantic:* How precisely do the transmitted symbols convey the desired meaning?
> *Effectiveness:* How effectively does the received meaning affect behavior in the desired way?

The *technical* problems concern the accuracy of transmission of a set of symbols from the sender to the receiver. For example, in computer processing and the generation of information to be used by a manager in decision making, information is translated from electronic signals into printed or displayed letters and characters. The next section, which deals with communication systems, discusses briefly how such technical problems are addressed. The other two levels—semantic and effectiveness problems—underlie the discussions in the management information systems and systems analysis and design modules. The *semantic* problem is concerned with how precisely the receiver understands and interprets the sender's meaning. Thus, designers of computer-based systems must ensure that output is presented in a way that can be understood and used by the recipient of the information. For example, it should be clear to the user that a sales analysis is made in terms of dollars of merchandise sold (or possibly units sold), not some other measure. In short, the user should be able to tell immediately what factor (dollar sales) is being used in the analysis. Failure in this regard indicates a semantic problem.

Effectiveness problems concern the success of the communication in producing the desired actions or conduct. Effective communication makes clear the intended meaning and results in proper action being taken. For instance, the need for any action based on a sales analysis should be clear from the information presented: If sales are lower than expected, it should be obvious to the user that sales must be improved. As we will see, the effectiveness problem as it pertains to computer-based systems means that we must be concerned with both the content of the information and the way it is presented to the recipient.

These communication problems—the technical, semantic, and effectiveness problems—are important to consider in using information systems in management. To place each of these problems in their perspective, we will look at the basic

---

*The discussion presented here is drawn from the work of Claude Shannon and Warren Weaver, *The Mathematical Theory of Communication* (Urbana: The University of Illinois Press, 1949) on the mathematical theory of communication as applied to communication systems, like the telephone and telegraph.

communications systems model for all computer-based information systems, which applies as well to communication of any type (voice, written notes, displays, and so on).

A Communications System

In its simplest form, a **communication** has four elements: a source, a communication channel, a destination, and a message. In the first stage in communication, the source selects a particular message from the available set of messages. Next, the message is transmitted through the channel to the destination. Figure 3.3 helps explain the activities involved in the basic communication process.

Source

When a message leaves the information source, it moves to a transmitter or sender, which changes it into a signal that may be sent over the channel to the receiver. This process is known as encoding—the message is reformulated into a form that can be transmitted to the recipient designated for that system. In human communication, for example, the vocal system is the encoder; it changes messages from the brain (the information source) into speech. The channel carries the encoded

Destination

message to the receiver. Then decoding occurs—the receiver converts the signal back into a message for use at the destination. Your ear is the receiving device and the brain actually decodes the words into an understandable message.

Encoding and decoding processes underlie the communication activity; that is, data are translated into machine-processable electronic signals on input, and from electronic signals to symbols and characters that can be understood by the user on output.

In theory, the communication process is very simple, but as one might expect, some complications develop. One of these is noise in the channel. During transmission, there may be certain unwanted additions to the signal. The various forms of **noise** include distortions, as of sound or shape, and errors in transmission. Noise is a problem, and defining the general characteristics of noise and its impact on a received message is important to all forms of communication, as we will see. Much work and research have gone into minimizing and eliminating the effect of noise.

The greater the amount of noise in transmission, the greater the chance that the receiver will not receive the message as it was transmitted. At worst, the message will not be received at all: for example, sometimes there is so much static on the radio that the music and announcements on a certain station are unintelligible. Similarly, in computer networks, a lot of noise on the communication lines will make

Figure 3.3 A Model of Communication

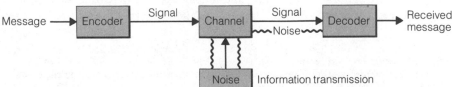

it impossible for the receiving device to get the data that have been transmitted. If transmissions are received, perhaps only a part will be correct—noise may destroy the rest.

Noise plays an important role, too, in information systems used by managers. When reports are generated, it is possible that the manager will not receive clearly the information presented in the report. For instance, suppose that the goal of a report is to signal to the receiver that sales are at a lower level than is acceptable. If there is not enough information, or if there is too much noise, the recipient may not perceive the message. With too little information, the manager will not be able to tell whether sales are at an acceptable level; for example, the report may not tell what an acceptable sales level is. If there is too much noise in the output—too many different items—the manager may not be able to pick out the important signals that sales are too low.

In these systems, it is important to provide enough information to allow the user to detect and deal with the problem easily, but not so much that its important aspects are obscured. A key element in this task is redundancy.

Redundancy

Redundancy is the repetition of part or all of a message to circumvent noise (distortion or transmission errors). Most communication is redundant to help assure complete communication. In fact, more than half of our written and spoken communication is redundant; we use more letters in words than are absolutely necessary and more words than we need. Consider this very simple example, a sentence in which half the letters are replaced by "blanks" (the small x's). Can you still read the message?

TxxS MxSxxGx xS RxDxNDxxT.

The fact that you were able to decipher "THIS MESSAGE IS REDUNDANT" indicates the effectiveness of redundancy in its coding. Of course we would not care to read an entire book in this way. Often, however, we build redundancy into a message to block out the effects of noise and to ensure that the information is received as intended.

In developing information reports for managers we also need to consider redundancy as a means of combating noise. We want managers to have enough information to be able to perceive the significance of a situation (for example, total sales as compared to expected sales), but not so much that they cannot see the forest for the trees.

If we give only the total sales figure, the communication is not very meaningful because there is no standard for comparison. If we provide both the total sales and the expected sales figures, we have improved the information presented, *but not in a satisfactory manner.* The user must further manipulate the information by determining the difference between the two figures. This step is better performed by the computer, since it will be faster and perhaps more accurate. And the user will appreciate that.

If we give the actual sales figure, the expected sales figure, *and* the percentage of variation, we have highlighted the information still further, maybe even excessively.

The recipient will get the same information about performance if only two items (actual sales and percent variation) are presented. The variation will highlight important differences without the clutter of excess details. If you ask a typical manager, you will probably find a preference for these two columns of data rather than all three. (The third one is redundant.)

Redundancy is useful if it highlights important results or issues. Too much redundancy is harmful. This concern will be discussed again later, in the design of information systems.

Information and Computer Information Systems

In Chapter 1, we introduced the fundamentals of computer information systems. We pointed out that data are collected and stored as transactions occur. We also showed that different devices can be used for preparing data, input, processing, and output by computer systems. Each configuration of computer equipment is a communication system with a source, a channel, a destination, and a message. The source may be a stored file of data that are input through a channel connecting storage devices with the central processing unit or CPU, where the data are processed. Channels also connect the CPU to the output devices (for example, printers or displays) so that the results of processing can be transmitted to the user.

Protection against noise is built into the entire processing system. For instance, checks against noise are made during processing, starting with the data preparation stage when data are keyed into a terminal or onto magnetic tape via verifying processes, and they continue to the output stage, when redundancy may be built into reports.

As indicated earlier, not all information used in management comes from transaction data. A certain amount originates from sources that are separate and distinct from business transactions. We are going to look at these sources next, but keep in mind that the same principles of information and communication apply.

Information Sources

Information, whether applied in a communication sense or in a decision-making context, obviously comes from somewhere. It is particularly important for managers to be aware of the many possible sources of information. Often managers overlook sources simply because they do not think of them when a problem arises or because they are unaware of their existence (see Table 3.3).

Awareness of information sources is only one side of this issue. Managers should also be able to identify potential problems built into the information they acquire: problems of bias, currency, fact versus opinion, and so on. As we discuss primary and secondary sources of information, you will become more aware of these difficulties.

Table 3.3 Sources of Information

Primary Source	Advantages	Disadvantages
Observation	Firsthand knowledge Avoids response bias	Observation may not be accurate Observation may affect what is being observed
Experiment	Control over variables of interest	Design of experiment May not be representative
Survey	Efficient way to reach large groups of people	Questionnaire design Size of survey
Subjective estimation	Information from experts May be only way to obtain some information	Response may be unreliable

Secondary Source	Advantages	Disadvantages
Company information	Specific to situation Already exists Relatively low cost	May not be timely May not be properly integrated or in usable form
Purchased outside sources	Not otherwise available Easily obtained	Expensive to acquire Possible bias
Publications	Low cost	May be biased
Government agencies	Impartial Large body of information	May not be in usable form

Primary and Secondary Information

Managing an organization requires both primary and secondary information. Primary information is that which must be gathered specifically for a particular problem. It is information that is being gathered for the first time for a specific party. However, what a person in one firm is collecting for the first time may have been gathered in another organization some time ago. For example, an oil-refining firm may need information on possible changes in oil costs. As a result, a study may be initiated to examine all factors that contribute to the cost of oil, including purchase price, costs of loading into tankers, and transportation costs. However, the same information may have been collected by other oil-refining companies. Does this mean that the first company does not have primary information? No, if a company collects the information itself, or if it hires a consulting firm, it is primary information even though the first company is unaware that other companies have collected it.

Secondary information, on the other hand, has already been collected and stored in an accessible location. Often a manager needs just this kind of information for a certain problem. Take the oil example. It can be expected that the Department of Energy maintains large files of information on foreign oil sources that would be useful to companies formulating long-range projections about the cost of oil and fuel. Information like this, collected by the federal government and made available to business, is typical of secondary information. Secondary information, of course, may be biased or obsolete, or it may be unusable because of the form in which it was collected. (We examine these problems shortly.)

Organizations use both kinds of information regularly for controlling internal operations and for monitoring or watching important developments outside the company. However, we cannot state conclusively that primary information is generally of higher value than secondary information—or vice versa—because organizations vary. The character of the industry or organization, coupled with the functional area (marketing, production, purchasing, and so on) in which the information is used, and the particular organizational style of management, are important in determining the usefulness of each type of information. Marketing managers, for example, may rely heavily on research information about consumer wants or needs collected firsthand (primary information). A purchasing agent may rely more on information furnished by the federal government about expected trends in prices of materials or commodities (secondary information).

Problems with Information Sources

Primary and secondary sources of information can provide management and organizations with knowledge to be used for problem-solving and decision-making activities. Because selection of a particular source depends on what information is needed and how it will be used, it is not possible to state that one source is better than another. In all cases, though, the user must be aware of possible problems with the quality of the knowledge collected. These problems are represented by the categories of impartiality, validity, reliability, consistency, and age.

Impartiality To be an effective resource, information must not reflect any bias. Such **impartiality** is instilled in the information by the person collecting or processing the data on which it is based when that person uses it the way it is intended to be used and draws only accurate inferences from the data. Impartial information does not contain intended bias or a distorted view of reality.

Validity The question of **validity** focuses on whether particular information is meaningful and relevant to the stated purpose. In other words, does the information actually answer the question being addressed? Information may be invalid if it is not used in the manner for which it was collected or formulated. Increased sales in a food store after a new manager is installed, for example, may not be a totally valid measure of the person's managerial ability. To judge whether the information is valid, we need to see whether other factors may have accounted for a change or difference in performance. In this case, new road traffic patterns, more effective corporate advertising, or especially attractive sales prices may be the true reason for the increase, which may have occurred in spite of, not because of, the new manager.

Reliability **Reliability** concerns the accuracy of the picture of what the information is trying to describe. Is the information a true indicator of a given event? If we wish to see how organizations use computers in data processing, for example, a survey of 10 companies will certainly provide information on the question. However, more reliable and complete information can be collected if 1000 companies are surveyed, and several people in each company are asked to respond to the questions.

Consistency For information to be useful, it must be based on homogeneous data; that is, the number and type of reporting units must be the same throughout. If the relevant factor shows **consistency,** we will be comparing the same factor each time. For example, if we wish to examine total sales of all corporate stores over a period of several months (a time series analysis), the number of stores examined should be constant. Information from total corporate sales would not be consistent if the number of retail stores in the chain increased or decreased from period to period. When we use any information, we should always be sure that it is consistent, that the factors on which it is based are the same for each part of the information.

Age The **age** of information is an extremely important factor in determining its worth to a user. In most instances, the greater the age, the more questionable the value for managers. The dominant factor contributing to age of information is delay.

We refer to delay as an activity (or lack of activity) that puts a time period between a user's recognition of a need for information and the receipt of it. Delays may result from the time required to collect and process data or to gain access to information. A manager may decide to collect primary data on some aspect of the company's activities. The period from that moment until the delivery of the desired information is the delay: the time necessary to develop a mechanism for collecting the data, collating them, processing them into information, and transmitting them to the user. If the period of elapsed time is too long, the knowledge may no longer be of use to the individual.

Regularly scheduled reports in organizations typically involve delay. If a weekly expense report is prepared every Monday, information on events that occurred on the preceding Monday will not be processed for a full seven days. And if it takes a day to transmit the processed report to the user, eight days will have elapsed before the manager receives knowledge of some of the events reported. Further delay will result if the manager does not use the report immediately. Computers have reduced the amount of potential delay in many situations, but too often the delay is much longer than necessary.

Secondary information, particularly from publications and industry reports, may also be characterized by delay. A consultant or researcher may perform an experiment involving a problem that is especially important and interesting to management. It may be a long time from the date of the experiment until a manager receives information on it. The experimental data must be analyzed and the findings written up, reviewed, and published. Managers have to find and read the article before the information actually reaches them, and there is still no guarantee that it will be relevant. The delay in this common situation is long, and by the time a potential user receives the information, someone else may have already gathered evidence that significantly changes it. But it may be months before this new information is distributed.

Age of information is a continual problem for organizations and users and is a central issue in the design and development of information systems. It also affects the value of information.

To establish a system, the managers of a business organization impose a scheme of order on the complex environment in which they operate. In effect, managers try to simplify their surroundings so that they can understand them and their implications. For a retail marketing manager, for example, the environment includes people, other businesses, the existing body of laws and regulations, different governments, and competitors. The environment in this context is the set of all objects that can change or be changed by the system.

In its simplest terms, a **system** is *a set of components that interact with one another for a purpose.* It is a set of objects that are related and may be described in terms of their attributes or their component parts.

Systems may be abstract or physical. An *abstract system* is conceptual, a product of the human mind. That is, it cannot be seen or pointed to as an existing entity. Social, theological, and cultural systems are abstract systems. None of these entities can be photographed, drawn, or otherwise physically pictured. However, they do exist and can be discussed, studied, and analyzed.

A *physical system,* in contrast, is a set of elements—rather than ideas or constructs—that operate in relation to one another to accomplish a common goal or purpose. Examples of physical systems include:

——*Computer systems:* collections of hardware elements that work interdependently under some means of control to process data and product output reports

——*Communication systems:* collections of components that can represent and transmit bits of information from one point to another

——*Marketing systems:* collections of people, equipment, and procedures that develop, produce, and distribute commodities, ideas, and other entities to consumers or users

The fact that a system may be classified as abstract or physical does not imply any judgment of worth or value. That is, a physical system is *not* more meaningful or more necessary than an abstract system. The distinction is for analytical purposes only.

Elements of Systems

A system is a set of components that interact with one another to accomplish a purpose or goal. Within this basic definitional framework, elements necessary for the very existence of any system may be identified. These *system elements* include the *environment, boundaries, input/output,* and *components.*

System Environment All systems operate within an **environment.*** The environment surrounds the system, both affecting it and being affected by it. What we call the

*One exception may be the universe. Since the universe is typically characterized as being "the great system," which contains all other systems, it may not be meaningful to try to delineate an environment for it.

environment depends on the system's goals, needs, and activities, as well as on whether it is physical or abstract. For example, a sociologist studying interpersonal behavior in a social group probably would consider everyone and everything not in the group as the environment. However, a psychologist studying the personality of one group member undoubtedly would consider the other group members to be part of the environment. Similarly, a computer specialist studying the processing efficiency of the central processing unit would say that the users are part of the environment, since they are not part of the CPU. However, if a computer specialist is examining the role of an organization's computer processing system in terms of reducing operating costs and decreasing errors in handling data and information, the users would definitely be a part of the system. These examples show how different environments can be defined for systems. Furthermore, the environment is a function of the individual who is observing or interacting with the system.

System Boundaries The system **boundaries** distinguish or separate the environment from the system. The system exists within the boundaries, and anything lying outside them constitutes the environment. The system's boundary line determines what is included within the system and what is not.

The particular characteristics of a boundary vary according to whether a system is physical or abstract. In a physical system, the boundary is a natural demarcation determined by the basic system structure and the system's goals and purposes. In abstract systems, on the other hand, boundaries are typically imposed by an observer. The arbitrary boundary line may therefore vary from observer to observer, unless everyone can agree on criteria for its selection. Under any circumstances, the abstract system's boundaries are determined by the observer's level of inquiry, the intent and purpose in drawing the line, and the observer's perceptions of the internal workings of the system. In a physical system, the boundaries are fixed, as in the case of the central processing unit of a computer, which contains the arithmetic/logic unit, the control unit, and the primary storage unit. However, the boundaries for an abstract system, like a production work group, may or may not include the group's supervisor, depending on the definition of the observer. One observer may feel that the supervisor is part of the work group; another, that the supervisor is outside the boundaries of the group.

Input/Output The system interacts with the environment by means of input and output. **Input** is anything entering the system from the environment; **output** is anything leaving the system, crossing the boundaries to the environment. In a computer system, data enter the system as input and leave as output in the form of information and processing results.

Information, energy, and materials can be both input and output in relation to the environment. An electrical utility takes on input from the environment in the form of raw materials (coal, oil, water power, and so on), requests for electricity from customers (shown when a consumer turns on an appliance that requires electricity), and so forth. It provides for output to the environment in the form of electricity.

Figure 3.4 The System Boundary and Input Control

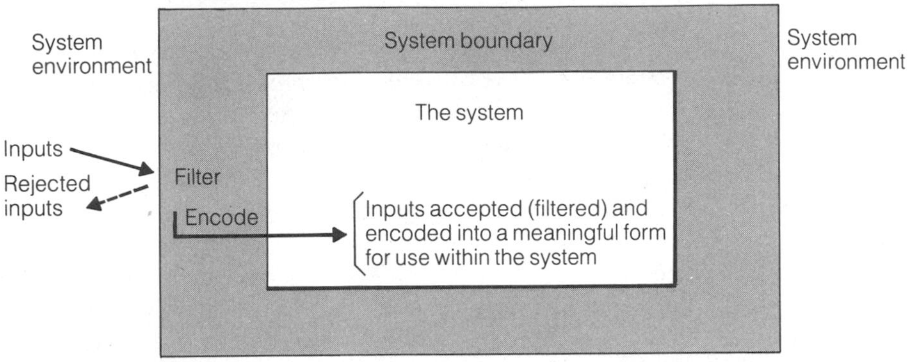

Boundaries carefully control the input and output, regulating the flow into and out of the system and protecting it from destructive or damaging agents in the environment. In essence, the boundaries are input/output filters (see Figure 3.4). For example, in an inventory control system, the regulation of "kind" determines which goods and materials should enter inventory, while the "rate" regulation focuses on how much of an item is accepted. In this way, input entering the system can be controlled.

What initially contacts the system as input often is not the same thing that actually enters. In addition to being filtered by the boundary, input is encoded there; we saw this concept earlier in this chapter. Without encoding, much input would be of little or no value after it passed the boundary.

There are two types of input: energizing input and maintenance input. Energizing input is the data or information that may be acted on by the system to produce output. A file containing transactions for accounts payable energizes the system to update files and output account statements (Figure 3.5).

Maintenance input is integrated closely with system control. When output is produced, data are frequently collected by employees of the organization to determine their appropriateness and acceptability to the environment. These data are then returned to the system, as shown in Figure 3.6, and used to regulate or improve the system's activities and processes. Large hotels and motels, for instance, ask guests to fill out cards evaluating the services (cleanliness of the rooms, quality of food in the restaurant, and so on). These data are maintenance input, used to determine whether services are being provided at a level satisfactory to the guests. If the data indicate that services should be improved, changes may be made by the managers of the business.

Output is produced from input that is operated on by the system and returned to the environment. This may be a commodity, some information, energy, or waste. In turn, the output of one system may become input to another. The waste from one organism or system may be valuable input to another (Figure 3.7). Carbon dioxide, for instance, is produced (output) when people and animals exhale and serves as input to plants.

Figure 3.5 Energizing Input for the System

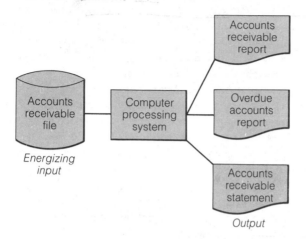

Figure 3.6 Regulation of Activities and Processes

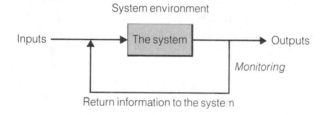

Figure 3.7 Relationship Among Systems

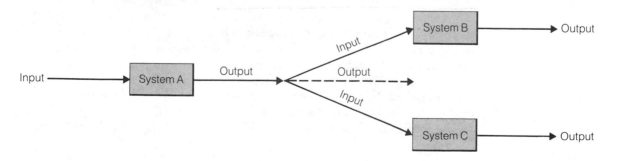

What we have been describing is an **open system**—a system that exchanges information, material, and energy with the environment. An additional feature of an open system is its ability to adapt, that is, to adjust to changes in the environment in the interest of continuing its existence. Adjustments are made on the basis of input and **feedback** (that is, input used for regulating system activities in accordance with a goal or purpose) so that the system operates in a *balanced state,* or *equilibrium.* In essence, it is a *dynamic* adjustment process because adjustments are continually being made to ensure that the system is approximately at equilibrium. If the adjustment process ceased, the system could very well run down or become disorganized. The term used for the running down or deterioration of the system is **entropy.** The process of receiving input from the environment to avoid the danger of running down is called *negative entropy.* In the motel example, if the management does not receive input from its guests, the condition of the rooms, food, and service might deteriorate (entropy) over time until one day people would stop staying at the motel. However, if the management obtains data on the services based on the feedback, the danger of going out of business would be lessened. Using feedback to maintain the services of the motel and avoid a decline in business and services is negative entropy.

In contrast, a **closed system** is self-contained and does not exchange with the environment. The tendency in a closed system is toward entropy, since there is no input from the environment to foster adaptation. In other words, without maintenance input, there is no adjustment in a closed system, and the tendency is for the system to run down or deteriorate.

Often it is necessary to study the inputs and outputs of a system in great detail. This is frequently the case when an observer does not know the processes and activities within the system. By studying and comparing inputs and outputs, insight into those particular system processes may be gained. Examining a system by studying only its inputs and outputs represents the "black box" approach. As suggested in Figure 3.8, the **black box concept** allows the investigator to neglect the internal processes and components of the system, placing them, metaphorically, in a black box. This approach is frequently used to study both abstract and physical systems, and it is very helpful to people who have the inferential and deductive abilities to get information from input and output but lack the technical background to evaluate the workings of the system.

System Components   Within the boundary lies the system itself. The system may be a single entity, or it may be made up of many components. When a system component is itself a separate system, we call it a **subsystem.** A system *component* may be defined as a unit that works with other components (or subsystems) to accomplish a specific purpose, usually to produce an output (which may be an input to another part of the system or to an entirely different system, as in Figure 3.9). The operations of each component separate, combine, or otherwise modify inputs to change their identity and produce output. Within the system, there must be connection among subsystems or components. That is, there must be a means of transferring information among the components so that each can perform its task. Information is transferred or coordinated among components or subsystems through **interfaces:** the connec-

Figure 3.8 The Black Box Concept

Figure 3.9 A System of Subsystems

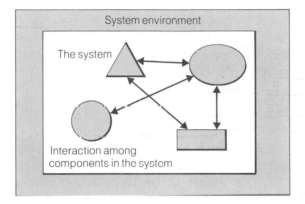

tions at system (or subsystem) boundaries that pass information across them. The interface encodes or decodes information (or energy) into a form the system can use. In a heating system, for example, a thermostat is the interface that transmits information on the temperature of the environment to the system, after converting it into an electronic signal that says to change the system (turn the heating unit on or off) or to maintain it in its current state (leave the furnace off or on). Likewise, in a computer system, a data channel serves as an interface between the central processing unit and the input devices. In elections, a voting machine or ballot box serves as an interface between the legislative system and the environment of voters and citizens. The votes are the input and the election or rejection of certain laws or candidates is the output.

Levels of Systems

Because the components within a particular system may themselves be separate systems, they must be ordered hierarchically. For example, an automobile is a multilevel system because it contains an engine system, within which is a combustion system, a carburetion system, and so on. Therefore, for meaningful study it is necessary to specify the **levels** of systems that are of interest to our investigation.

Control in Systems

Control of the system is an important concern of management in organizations. If the system is not under control, it is not serving its purpose effectively. *Control is the process that measures current performance and guides it toward a predetermined goal.* Systems can be controlled at different degrees of sophistication. Control in systems is essential for sustaining activity and existence.

Essential Control Elements

In any system or process being controlled, there are several key control elements. The particular form these elements might take varies from system to system, but they are always present. The essential elements are:

1. A *predetermined goal,* purpose, objective, or standard
2. A means of *measuring* performance
3. A means of *comparison,* to detect divergence from item 1
4. A means of *correction* and adjustment

Within any system we should know the expected performance; that is, we should know what the results of a process should be. The desired result—the goal, purpose, standard, or objective—may be a particular quantitative value, a range of values, or a certain activity. For example, the objective of a marketing system may be to produce sales of $50 million in a year; a quality control system in manufacturing might have multiple objectives: (1) keeping the defect rate for manufactured items under 2 percent and (2) removing all defective items from the final production line. There are many techniques for setting goals, objectives, and standards. The system does not evaluate the worth or the appropriateness of the goal. It merely provides the means by which activities and processes move toward that goal.

A system must have a means of measuring performance. This element frequently is the most difficult one to develop in an artificial system because a measuring tool must not affect the system it is measuring. The accuracy of measurements varies from system to system, but in all cases the measurement must be in the units stated in the predetermined goals. Thus, if we measure the percentage of defects in a certain type of production line with a specific type of equipment, the measure must be compared to a standard that involves the same kind of production process and the same equipment. It would not be appropriate to compare our operation so that of a competitor who uses different processes and equipment.

Comparison of actual performance with the predetermined goal is the third step in the control operation. Variation from a standard indicates that, to some degree, the system is not operating as well as it should. However, because variation is expected in any activity, it becomes important to determine how much variation is tolerable. For instance, if the goal of production control is to hold defective parts to 1 percent and the actual number of defects is 1.01 percent, we can probably say that an acceptable variance from the standard has been achieved. However, if the number of defects approaches 2 percent, the variance probably is not tolerable.

Finally, the system should be able to take corrective action and make adjustments to a process when significant variation is detected. The type of change depends on the system's characteristics. In the production example, changes in the equipment or in the personnel using the equipment may be necessary. However, speeding up the production process would not be sensible. Adjustments should be made only when required. Making unnecessary changes may be as serious and costly as failing to make necessary ones. Thus, our possible corrections for the production line should be made only when the defect variance is significantly different from the standard.

Introducing control elements in any system, especially one involving human interaction, can lead to potential resistance to the entire control procedure. Resistance, which is a form of dysfunctional behavior (behavior that does not contribute to organization goals), can diminish the value of the control procedure. For example, adding a new control system on the production line may irritate the employees and lead to poorer work and higher defect rates. Because of the importance of this issue, particularly in relation to computer-based information systems, it is discussed in more detail in Chapter 19.

Information is necessary to operate the control process. So is feedback. Feedback is information about system performance that is input to help adjust system activities.

Feedback and Feedback Loops

Two types of feedback are important in system activities, and both are related to system control. **Negative feedback** is corrective feedback that helps maintain the system within a critical operating range and reduces performance fluctuations around the norm or standard. Negative feedback is transmitted in **feedback control loops.** As shown in Figure 3.10, a sensor detects the effect of output on the external environment; this information is returned to the system as an input, and necessary adjustments are made according to predetermined goals. The automatic sensing mechanism in a missile system operates on the basis of negative feedback to ensure that the missile remains on the course. If the missile should change direction, a signal to the control mechanism would result in a course correction.

In contrast to negative feedback, which is *corrective,* **positive feedback** reinforces the operation of a system by causing it to continue its performance and activities

Figure 3.10 Feedback Control Loops

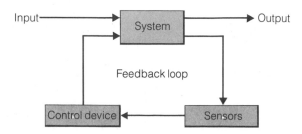

without change. A production system receiving input from management to continue production of mousetraps at the same rate as last week would be receiving positive feedback.

Systems in Management

The principles of general systems theory and systems control, which we have been examining in this chapter, have many applications in management and organizations. Because a corporate entity is continually interacting with its environment for marketing, procurement, and regulation purposes, it is an open system. Within the firm itself are identifiable subsystems (for example, the accounting system, the production system, and any computer-based information systems). However, all the subsystems must interact with other systems in the firm. A companywide information system is a network that receives input and produces output for all parts of the organization. Similarly, the accounting system provides information on operations and activities to all parts of the organization.

Typically, any system or subsystem in a firm is an open system. However, firms often develop systems that approach what we called *closed systems* earlier. Systems that have some self-regulating capabilities—that is, are partially closed systems—can be useful in business. In production and process control, for example, a control system that continually monitors production activities and makes necessary adjustments without human intervention can be very desirable. Eliminating the need for constant human interfacing can reduce personnel costs and may even lead to better control of the process. If computers are properly integrated into the control process, automatically measuring performance and making adjustments, work may take place more effectively. In other words, a control system having a *closed sequence* of steps to maintain system control can be desirable. If a monitor is placed on a liquid flow line to maintain a steady rate of flow and a constant rate of pressure, and the system is programmed to make necessary valve adjustments, the system is becoming a closed one. However, it is not totally closed. Human intervention is still necessary when the monitors detect unusual or unanticipated conditions or when a component in the system fails.

Many inventory systems are designed with a *closed loop control system* in mind. For example, if a model stock quantity or a reorder quantity is built into the inventory control mechanism, a computer program in the system generates a standard order whenever inventory reaches a specified minimum level. Since there is continual monitoring of inventory levels and adjustment of order quantities, and because the system is able to print the purchase order automatically, it is somewhat closed— some of the work can be done without human involvement. However, managers and purchasing agents must intervene, for example, when merchandise is placed on sale, when unusually large quantities of an item must be ordered, or when items are discontinued. Each of these situations, which are not uncommon in inventory control procedures, necessitates human intervention, hence would violate the integrity of a closed system.

The concept of a closed loop control system for management is receiving more and more attention. Constant advances in technology have made it possible for repetitive and well-understood tasks of the manager to be automated. This theme reappears frequently in the discussions that follow.

Multiple Uses of Information

Information is a valuable resource in any ongoing system. Information is the result of processing activities. However, it is also input to the decision processes of managers. For example, processing a file of sales data to make sales analyses results in the production of information about performance. In this sense, it is the output of a processing system. However, it is also used by a manager who must determine whether any action is needed to improve sales performance. In this sense, it is input. It is input to be acted on, a stimulus for action on some other input, and an output from system processes. Information is the central core of all resources in feedback loops and helps regulate the system's activities. The organization as a system could not survive without information.

Information Systems

Due to the tremendous needs of the organization for information on a continuing basis, it is often necessary to develop a subsystem for processing and handling the information resource alone. This *information system,* as we will refer to it, should be able to provide management with information for making the many decisions necessary in a competitive environment. Included in this system are formal channels, such as those providing reports on production, and informal channels, such as coffee break conversations, the organization's grapevine, or the *Wall Street Journal.*

Formal information channels are a recognized part of the overall organization. A description of this system includes a definition of the function it serves, as well as its technical features and output. One type of formal channel is a marketing information system, a structured system of persons, equipment, and procedures designed to maintain an orderly flow of information about marketing activities. The primary purpose of this and any information system in the firm is to show significant relationships among factors that will decrease uncertainties in the system's processes and activities. In the marketing information system, for instance, the concerns are with showing relationships among such factors as product line characteristics, price and advertising levels, distribution methods, and sales programs as they relate to the sale of specific goods or services. Each of the basic elements of a system is present in a marketing information system. Input is in the form of data about each of the factors outlined above and includes data about internal variables (such as product line policies, advertising programs, sales performances) and about the environment (for instance, competitor products and prices). Output may be the reports prepared through the system to analyze performance or to show how possible changes in price or product characteristics could change sales. Interfaces are present at the boundary; for example, accounting data on costs and profits may be incorporated into the system in a way that makes them usable for required processing. Within the overall marketing information system may be other subsystems such as the transaction processing system, the filing system, and a retrieval system to access stored data.

Many organizations have integrated computer processing into their information systems to provide better decision support to managers. This should not be confused with using the computer for conventional transaction processing, which is typically the automation of clerical activities. The discussion in the chapters that follow is centered around computer-based information systems, since this is the direction in which most organizations are moving and since this appears to be the most effective type of information system for large organizations.

Information Systems and Organizational Control

Management in any organizational system operates on the basis of the information it has about its internal and external environment. This is true whether one is concerned with top-level management, financial management, or marketing management. The information that decision makers have is the fuel for decisions about present and future activities of the organization or subsystem with which they are involved. To all managers, decisions about control of activities and processes are crucially important.

Management is the use of information to make decisions. Most managers have many information sources, but they usually use only a fraction of them. Since the information used in a particular decision can significantly affect the organization's future operation, it is vital that it be the best and most appropriate information available.

Decision makers must be concerned with three general, all-encompassing factors. They must know the state of the system, the possible changes in that state, and what effects their decisions could have on the system. Chapter 4 examines in greater detail the systems concept as it applies to management and decision making.

The Requirements of Information Systems

We have dealt quite extensively with both data and information as they apply to organizations and management. It is now evident that there is a strong relationship between data and information. Data are processed to produce information needed for decision making and problem solving. These issues have important implications for the development and use of computer information systems.

Processing Transaction Data

Organizations regularly deal with a lot of data, particularly as the result of transaction processing, the collection, sorting, classification, summarization, and storage of important data from routine events, such as ordering merchandise, controlling inventory, or giving medical treatment or diagnosis. Furthermore, data are used to produce reports that convey certain facts about an aspect of the business to managers and other users. The term we assigned to these activities is *transaction processing*.

Transaction and accounting data form the basis of many management decisions. Therefore, every effort must be made to ensure that the data are accurate and reliable. Computer information systems can be designed to monitor data entering the system for accuracy and completeness. By embedding data validation procedures in application software, the system will as a matter of procedure scrutinize incoming details to see whether they fit specified guidelines and characteristics.

Providing Data Reduction

Not all data available to a person will be needed or wanted for a specific task. For instance, a hospital administrator probably will not want or need data about the maintenance of surgical suites if the task at hand is formulating a charge policy for outpatient care in the emergency room. However, if the administrator is establishing charge policies for the use of surgery facilities, the maintenance data will be relevant and important. Managers must be given the capability, through the information system, to receive relevant information and to have the system perform the necessary summarization and presentation, even if the data originate in several different storage areas.

Information systems can provide **data reduction,** organizing many details into a format the user can work with. For example, data reduction might consist of processing a set of sales data containing the date, quantity, and dollar value of each individual sales order, into sales information, such as total dollar sales, total item sales, and sales by product type. Without data reduction managers would have a difficult time applying all the data to the problem at hand. They would be overloaded with details but short on information.

Managing Information Delay

We have already identified delay in getting the necessary information as a major problem in decision making. In both manual and computer information systems, transaction processing can be performed as soon as transactions occur, or the transactions can be grouped into batches and processed later. Batching transactions thus causes delays in processing. In some cases delay will be tolerable as, for instance, when payroll data are collected on Friday and processed during the following week. But in other instances, delay is not tolerable and, in fact, immediate processing may be needed. When information systems are designed, systems analysts decide the appropriate processing mode. They thus influence the level of transaction processing delay.

There is also delay in retrieval of information. Managers depend on the availability of the data and the capability of the information system to retrieve and process data in a timely fashion. It is generally possible to anticipate routine information requests and details needed for day-to-day operations. Thus information systems functions can be designed to furnish such information in accordance with expected needs.

Anticipating Manager Needs

Other information needs cannot be anticipated because the problems and opportunities managers will encounter are difficult to predict. For instance, it may be impossible to foresee a revolution in a foreign country that exports raw materials essential to product manufacturing. Yet such cases may have tremendous significance to the organization. Information systems that will be used in these environments must be designed with great flexibility. They will have to allow users both to develop and to retrieve information, often in varying forms. Even though the processing requirements demand more powerful software, the systems must be easy for individuals to use. They must be decision-making tools, not problem-solving obstacles.

THE VISION

Information Processing Changing the Economics of Industry

Historically economies in countries around the industrialized world have gone through periods of boom and bust. However, information systems are providing the capability to change key aspects of economic swings.

Manufacturers have often been unable to match the production of goods with demand. During the "good times" production levels increase. But when sales slow, for whatever reason, production does not halt accordingly unless manufacturers get the signal that demand is softening. More goods are produced than can be sold. Manufacturers are forced to retain excessive quantities of goods in warehouses or to decrease the price to an abnormally low level. Layoff of workers often results too, causing or deepening the severity of the economic recession.

The face of economic recessions may change through increased flow of information, resulting from effective utilization of computer and communication systems. Consequently, firms are able to assess demand as near the time of scheduled manufacturing as possible—often less than 24 hours in advance rather than days, weeks, and even months ahead. Computer systems of buyers and manufacturers are often linked electronically to share information about their plans in a way that benefits both parties.

In retailing, firms are finding ways to use their information systems to determine what is selling and what is not, adjusting orders for merchandise to avoid excessive stock. Likewise, builders and developers have either overbuilt or underbuilt, again because of an inability to match supply and demand.

In the future, then, the vision is that recessions will not be as deep because of the flow of information.

Handling Diverse Types of Information

The communication of many different types of information is a management fact of life. Both internal and external information sources are important, as are the information they provide. Managers combine key indicator information with accounting reports, estimates of performance, planning assumptions, and warnings of impending changes. Computer technology includes the capability to manage these diverse information types while not overloading end-users with irrelevant detail. Even voice information can be captured and retained. Chapter 5 examines these technologies in detail.

In the next chapter we see that information is an integral part of the processes taking place within systems like organizations. The system framework will be our vehicle for examining organizations and their networks for the gathering and transmission of information.

Summary

Information is a resource for an organization. The two types of information are accounting information, including financial and managerial forms, and management information. Often managers are provided with summaries of accounting information. However, they need many different types of management information, including comfort, status, warning, planning, and internal operations information. In addition, external intelligence and externally distributed information link the organization with its environment.

Information adds to knowledge and reduces uncertainty when provided in a meaningful form. It is characterized by the attributes of accuracy, form, frequency, breadth, origin, time horizon, relevance, completeness, and timeliness. Inappropriateness, or inadequacy, of any of these attributes diminishes the worth of the information.

Information and its communication are the focal points of information theory. In this context, information has a broader meaning; it includes not just knowledge that reduces uncertainty, but also messages for transmission, such as those in an ordinary telephone conversation. The problems in communication are:

1. How accurately are the symbols of communication transmitted?
2. How precisely do the symbols convey the desired meaning?
3. How effectively does the received meaning affect behavior in the desired way?

All information has a point of origin. In an organization it may come from internal or external sources. Identifying the various sources and being able to evaluate the reliability of each is an important task for a manager. The manner in which this is accomplished can affect the value of the information and the purpose for which it will be used.

Information systems work when essential data are carefully selected and accurately processed in a timely manner, that is, without unreasonable delay. The presentation of the information must also be acceptable to the recipients. Otherwise the potential impact of the information and the system may be lost. A system is a set of related objects. A system may be physical or abstract, but it exists to accomplish a goal or purpose. All systems are made up of a set of elements: environment, boundaries, input/output, and components. Systems that interact with the environment by means of input and output are open systems; those that do not interact with the environment are closed systems. Different types of input and output can be identified, but the main purpose of any interaction with the environment is to foster adaptation so that the system can continue to exist.

Systems are made of smaller components, some of which can be other systems or subsystems. Thus, we can have levels of systems, or systems within systems. In most systems we can identify several levels of subsystems.

In all systems, regardless of type, control is an important consideration. Control is the process of assessing current performance and making necessary adjustments to ensure that the system continues toward its predetermined goal. The essential elements of control include a goal or purpose, a means of measuring performance, a means of comparing performance against the standard, and a way of correcting or adjusting performance. Feedback and feedback loops are important factors in system performance and control.

The systems concept, as well as the control process, are important to management. Indeed, an organization is usually viewed as a system with a large number of subsystems and a common goal or purpose. These subsystems must be linked together and controlled to achieve the organization's goal. Information and a system for communicating information are important to this process. Information systems provide knowledge about the internal and the external environment and help the manager in making decisions that affect the continued existence and performance of the organization. Systems and information are central concepts in all ensuing discussions.

Key Words

Accounting information	Exception information	Open system
Accuracy	External intelligence	Output
Age	Externally distributed	Planning information
Attributes of information	information	Positive feedback
Black box concept	Feedback	Redundancy
Boundaries	Feedback control loop	Relevance
Closed system	Impartiality	Reliability
Comfort information	Information	Status (progress)
Communication	Input	information
Communications system	Interface	Subsystem
model	Internal operations	System
Completeness	information	Timeliness
Consistency	Knowledge	Uncertainty
Data	Levels	Validity
Data reduction	Management information	Warning information
Entropy	Noise	
Environment	Negative feedback	

Review Questions

1. How do accounting information and management information differ?
2. What are the different types of management information? What is the purpose of each?
3. Discuss the relationship among data, information, knowledge, and uncertainty.
4. Discuss the meaning of this statement: Information as it is commonly used is an imprecise term.
5. What are the attributes of information? Explain their meaning.
6. What are the technical, semantic, and effectiveness problems of communication? What is the relation of these concepts to computer information systems?
7. How does the meaning of *information* differ in management and in communication theory?
8. Identify and describe the components in a communications system. Are these components relevant to information and communication in management? If so, how?
9. What is noise? What is redundancy? How are these factors dealt with in communication of information?
10. Is redundancy necessary in communication? Why or why not?
11. Distinguish between primary and secondary information sources. What are some sources for each?
12. What are some of the problems with information sources?
13. Define the term *system*. What are the different types of systems?
14. Identify and discuss the different elements in a system.
15. Distinguish between *boundary* and *interface;* between *encoding* and *decoding*.
16. Define and give examples of energizing input, maintenance input, and entropy.
17. What differences exist between an open and a closed system?
18. What is the black box concept?
19. Discuss the concept of control in systems. What are the essential elements of control in a system?
20. Define and give examples of negative feedback, positive feedback, feedback loop, and information systems.

Application Problems

1. Military and government leaders all over the world rely on *briefings*—short meetings in which pertinent facts are concisely presented to keep managers and commanders informed about the status of events, recent developments and changes, potential opportunities and problems, and ideas about the significance of each. During briefings, even hearsay information is passed along if, in the opinion of the speaker, it has *potential* relevance to areas of concern. If detailed

information is needed for any of the information items included in the briefing, it can be obtained through a written report, a full briefing, or a workshop.

a. Why are briefings a useful communications tool for these busy leaders?

b. What types of information, based on the categories described in this chapter, are communicated during briefings? Give examples of each type.

c. Does the "briefing" format fit business? That is, can management briefings of the type described above become a useful tool for managers who have many diverse responsibilities? Explain.

d. What potential roles do computer information systems serve in the briefing of leaders and managers?

2. A common concern in information processing is the accuracy of the information provided to users. For some people, accuracy in information means that there can be absolutely no discrepant items in output from computer processing; everything must be very precise. For other people, the degree of accuracy in information need only be "accurate enough" for the job at hand. Thus, the first type of user requires that sales of $45,484.97 be reported as such. The other type of user feels that a report of $45,490 is sufficient.

a. Discuss the merit of these two arguments. Just what does "accuracy of information" mean?

b. What factors should determine your working definition of accuracy?

c. What role does computer processing play in accuracy of information?

3. A large product division of a company has collected and stored on various secondary storage devices all data that are potentially relevant for support of user decision making. The data are stored under a file organization that is most efficient for that type of data. When it is known specifically how the data are being or will be used, processing methods are taken into account in selecting a storage organization.

When a user needs certain types of data for problem solving, a check is made to see whether they are stored in the system. If they are, computer programs are developed that make the data accessible and process them into usable information. In some cases, data from several different files are made accessible and merged or copied into a separate file from which processing then proceeds.

a. Discuss the value of the computer in information processing for this situation.

b. What are the advantages and disadvantages of following the procedure above for data and information processing?

c. Discuss alternatives to those given.

4. Inaccurate knowledge is information if it is used as information and if the user does not realize that it is not accurate. Does this mean that information is defined by how it is used rather than in terms of accuracy and relevancy? Explain.

5. Discuss the basic model of a communications system as it applies to computer-based information systems. Identify the information system components that are comparable to the basic communication elements.

How are encoding and decoding performed in a computer information system?

What is noise in a computer information system? How is it introduced in a batch processing system and in an interactive system that uses data communications methods? How does noise in information relate to the attributes of information?

6. Redundancy is a built-in feature in modern voice transmission over telephone lines. It is also a concern in data processing.
   a. What role should redundancy play in computer information systems? What form should or could redundancy take in presentation of output to users? In hardware used in processing? In stored data?
   b. What are the dangers of too much redundancy in data or information processing? (*Hint:* Consider both economy and efficiency of the system and its user.)

7. Many organizations in all industries prepare weekly reports on such areas as orders taken from customers, merchandise withdrawn from inventory, merchandise on hand in inventory, and units manufactured on the production line. The reports frequently contain a great deal of detail (because they are the product of batch processing).
   a. Discuss the practice from the point of view of delay in processing and providing the reports to managers and users. What, if any, delay is involved? If there is delay, what factors would determine whether the delay is a problem?
   b. How does the concept of data reduction apply to this practice? Describe how the data reduction takes place.
   c. Comment on the practice from the viewpoint of the technical, semantic, and effectiveness problems associated with information.

8. What categories of primary or secondary information sources would be most useful in the situations that follow? For each, list the categories of sources that are most likely to be found in computer-processible form.
   a. Deciding on changes in sales policies
   b. Selecting a vendor from which to acquire large quantities of raw materials regularly
   c. Determining the legal ramifications of a proposed merger with another company in the same industry
   d. Predicting the rate of increase or decrease in the economy next year and determining how it will affect your company's sales
   e. Producing a mailing list of all companies that would be buyers or potential buyers for your company's products and services

9. Indicate whether the following examples of input to systems in organizations represent energizing input or maintenance input. Explain your reasoning.
   a. Marketing research data on customer opinions about product quality (for example, taste, durability, size) after use
   b. A data file containing transaction quantity data on items to be purchased from specific vendors or suppliers and used in a computer program to print purchase orders
   c. Iron ore to be used in the production of steel
   d. A file of sales and revenue data to be used in the preparation of a performance analysis report comparing actual to planned performance
   e. Data collected on frequency of use of a computer system, files and programs used, length of programs, and length of application runs
   What relation does maintenance input have to control and feedback?

10. A large medical clinic provides treatment to approximately 75,000 patients per year. The clinic is affiliated with a large hospital, but it is a separate business. Doctors are on both the clinic and the hospital staffs.

    Patients come to the clinic as a result of referrals by their private physicians or as "walk-ins." All patients are assigned a file and six-digit file number; all records about them (medical, surgical, laboratory, pharmacy, and so on) are maintained in that file.

Patients arriving at the clinic are seen first by a doctor who is on the clinic's general staff. In many cases, medication or treatments are prescribed by the general practitioner and the patient leaves. A brief notation of the date, nature of complaint or illness, and treatment prescribed is made in the patient's record.

Other patients require additional treatment in the form of x-rays, laboratory tests, surgery, or referral to a specialist. In these cases, a notation is made in the patient's record by the general practitioner and the patient is sent to the appropriate hospital department to have the tests administered; the patient then returns to the clinic for prescribed treatment.

Those requiring surgery or specialty care are sent to the appropriate hospital department. An entry is made in the patient's record and the record is then sent to the hospital department.

A central record system is maintained for use by both the hospital and the clinic. However, each facility maintains its own billing system. Thus, after treatment by both the clinic staff and the hospital, a patient receives separate statements.

   a. Identify the different systems described above. For each, what are the inputs and outputs, the boundaries and interfaces, and the specific subsystems?

   b. Briefly describe the different kinds of input and types of control mechanism identified or implied in the situation.

11. Systems that actually exist in business and government are open systems. That is, they receive input and produce output. Although we discuss the concept of a closed system, there are no truly closed systems. So, why bother to discuss closed systems? What values does the concept of a closed system have in business and in computer-based transaction processing?

12. Discuss the value of the black box concept in relation to the submission of input to computer systems for processing and the identification of output desired as a result of processing. That is, from a user's point of view, how does the black box concept relate to the central processing unit and to the software that controls the CPU?

13. The cost accounting department of a manufacturing firm has the responsibility of developing product and manufacturing costs for operation of the firm's production facilities. The department is also charged with monitoring the manufacturing operation to detect any divergence from the standard. This is accomplished by collecting data on labor, materials, maintenance, produced items, and quality control. The data are collected and encoded onto magnetic tape. The tape is processed on the firm's computer each week to generate a report on actual and standard costs. The report is sent to manufacturing management for whatever use the managers feel is most appropriate.

   a. Identify the systems that are involved in this description.

   b. Identify the control elements in the situation described above. Which ones are missing? Is this an effective control system? Explain.

14. Identify and explain the interface in the following cases:

   a. A payroll system in which employees complete time cards with work data that are later entered onto disks that are input to the computer system for processing

b. A computer-assisted instruction system in which students work at a terminal to answer questions and work problems displayed on a cathode ray tube screen

c. A banking system in which all deposit and withdrawal slips are processed manually by a bank teller

d. A telephone system

Minicase: Midwest Enterprises, Inc.

On Mondays of alternate weeks, the management team of Midwest Enterprises, Inc., a multinational company with six separate divisions, meets to review the developments of the preceding week. It examines reported sales, the status of projects, and unexpected developments, whether good or bad. There has been increased concern that a great deal of data are presented at these meetings in the form of accounting summaries and printed reports, but not enough useful information. Since new competition and economic fluctuations are of increasing concern, management is considering how to make the meetings more productive.

The chief executive officer (CEO) of the firm has indicated the need for division managers to assume greater responsibility for controlling profits and costs in their areas. At the same time, the corporate management group, consisting of the chief executive, the senior vice president, and the area vice presidents (such as finance, marketing, research and development, and manufacturing) must be kept abreast of important planning and performance activities. The CEO has suggested the following plan of action.

The management team wants to see everything condensed so that it receives essential items of information—key indicators—not complete reports. It does not want this information reported in isolation, independent of any explanation for the result, good or bad. Rather, management wants to know about actual performance this month and this year to date and in comparison to expectations.

Right next to the performance indicators, reporting managers should, if necessary, explain in one or two paragraphs why they were off-target and what they intend to do about it. If performance has exceeded expectations, they should offer reasons and indicate how they will attempt to sustain that level of performance. For example, were the results internally generated or must they be attributed to a development or activity in the firm's competitive environment?

The CEO said, "We want top management to be able to look at the key items for each area of the firm and, within an hour or so, know exactly what is good about the company and what is bad. We should be able to determine what's being done and decide whether we agree with planned actions."

This plan is under serious consideration and a decision will be made soon.

Questions

1. Discuss the usefulness of the features described in this plan. What types of management information are included in the plan? What role does accounting information play?

2. What are the implications for information systems? Will the plan change the role information systems play in management and operation of the firm's activities?

Minicase: Will the Real Information System Please Stand Up

"You asked me how effective our information systems are. And you want to know whether we are getting our money's worth from our systems investment. Well, let me tell you."

The Fortune 500 company president continued: "Our information systems are excellent for supporting day-to-day operations. We know when sales take place, who the customers are and how often they purchase, and what our profits and costs are. And we need that detail—in a reliable, accurate, and timely manner—for the company.

"However, the fact remains that we get very little management information. Most of the information I receive is summarized from our transaction processing systems. But I need *management* information. When sales targets are not reached because of competitors introducing new products, that should be reported. Perhaps you call that informal information, but our computer information systems should be capable of handling it, because it is so important to the firm.

"We also need to receive background information: *why* we took a certain action and why we avoided an alternative approach. These matters should be part of our 'corporate memory.' Rumors and incidental observations our sales staff make in their travels often provide important insights into why events occur. We also need a warning system—fluctuating costs of labor and material, possible interruption of foreign trade links, and economic predictions—that will help us keep up with developments around us. Now we do it through face-to-face conversation and over the telephone. Is there a role for information systems here? Can we benefit from computer assistance?"

Questions

1. Do you believe the comments of the president are representative of most top-level managers? Are the opinions on which these observations are based correct?

2. What is the role of computer information systems in providing the type of management information described in this example? How might these requirements be fulfilled?

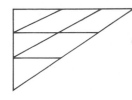

4: Views of the Organization: Human Resources, Management, and Organization Structure

Key Questions

How do similarities and differences among user managers influence information systems features?

What steps generally occur in the formulation of a decision?

What features should information systems include to overcome human limitations in the processing of information?

How do most managers divide their time between detailed problem analysis, reflection, and systematic planning?

In what ways do differing management theories affect information processing requirements?

What information processing strategies should managers consider for dealing with uncertainty? How does each impact organization design?

How do the most successful organizations use information systems to assist managers?

There's a new breed of businessmen, mostly people with MBAs, who are wary of intuitive decisions. In part, they're right. Normally, intuition is not a good enough basis for making a move. But many of these guys go to the opposite extreme. They seem to think that every business problem can be structured and reduced to a case study. That may be true in school, but in business there has to be somebody around who will say: "Okay, folks, it's time. Be ready to go in one hour."

Lee Iacocca
Chief Executive Officer
Chrysler Corporation

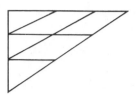

The successful management of organizations is dependent on people and information. In this chapter, we see how the two are related. First we explore the characteristics of individuals that must be taken into consideration in the development and use of information systems. Then we discuss the information systems implications for management functions and activities. Finally, we focus on how successful organizations use information systems. When you finish this chapter, you should have a good understanding of the features an information system must have to be useful in management of organizations.

Human Resources and Information Processing

As you realize, managers must be able to deal with the many diverse situations they encounter day by day. In a sense all managers have a common set of skills and limitations that influence their effectiveness in successfully running a store, department, or other type of organization. At the same time, each of us is unique in our approach to problems and in the ways in which we use information. We begin this chapter by examining how we are *alike* and how we *differ* in managing, pointing out the implications for information systems.

Ways We Are Alike in Information Processing

We know a great deal about the way individuals use information in management and decision making. The decision process itself and the way people organize the information they use is common to many situations. So are the shortcuts people take when they must make a decision. At the same time, we all have limitations that affect how well we can use information. These include limited memory capacity, the capability to do serial processing only, and the inability to estimate probability intuitively. Although as individuals we *are* different in many ways, we are also very much alike.

How We Make Decisions How are decisions made? What steps does an individual go through in formulating a decision? This section presents a model of decision making. It also examines the role of models in the overall decision-making process. Strategies

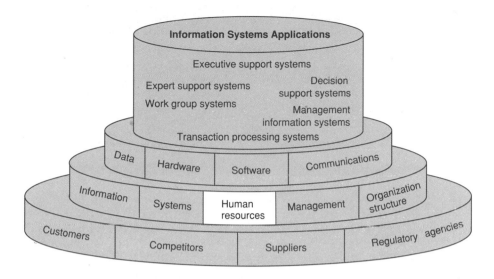

for formulating decisions in management using alternative models are examined to show you how managers can factor their level of certainty about a situation into the decision process.

Simon's Stages of Decision Making   Nobel-prize-winning economist Herbert A. Simon, one of the most often read scholars in management decision making, states that all people go through three stages in making a decision (Figure 4.1).

1. *Intelligence gathering:* searching for situations in which a decision is needed; gathering and processing data to evaluate the situation in order to understand the problem and its significance.

2. *Design of alternatives:* identifying and assessing alternative courses of action. Further understanding of the problem may arise as a result of the design process. The feasibility of possible solutions is evaluated to determine the favorable and unfavorable consequences of each approach.

3. *Selection of choice:* picking an alternative from the options generated. The decision is implemented.

As Figure 4.1 indicates, there may be interaction between the steps. For instance, suppose that you wish to plan a European travel itinerary. Working with a travel agent, you gather information about the order in which to visit the cities in which you have business. You begin by arranging the first stage—a flight from New York to London. Next a flight to Germany is planned. In the course of these arrangements you learn that a very reliable airline will begin direct flights from New York to Germany at rates 25 percent below other airlines. This new information causes you to reconsider your schedule. In other words, you reevaluate your alternatives, incorporating the new information.

Figure 4.1 Herbert A. Simon's Model of the Stages in Decision Making

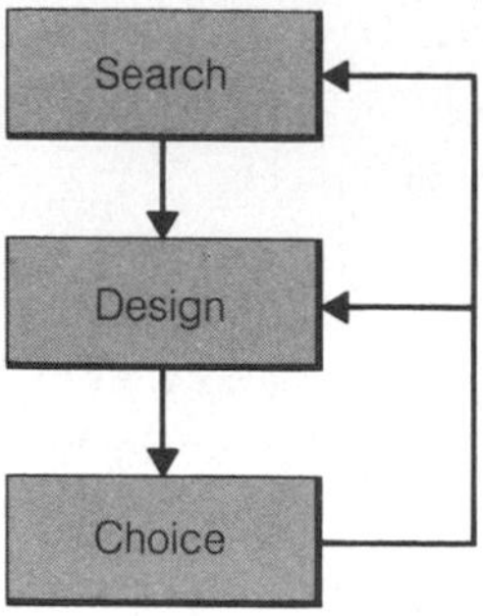

Managers alter their decision process in similar ways too. A manager considering whether to launch a new product line must balance manufacturing costs with the price for which the item can be sold. In addition, the manager may rely on the expertise of the marketing staff to advise on ways in which the product may be sold. If the marketing alternatives do not appear satisfactory, the management may go back to the product designers, seeking the right cost-and-profit combination and features that will permit formulation of an acceptable marketing program. Indeed, several iterations may be necessary before satisfactory alternatives are developed.

Models in Decision Making As we have repeatedly stressed, information for dealing with uncertainty is a key element for effective management in successful organizations. Similarly, managers confronting decision-making and problem-solving situations must often choose among alternative strategies and courses of action. This involves development and use of a model.

What Is a Model? The environment in which an organization operates is complex: Many activities are taking place, and there is a great diversity of influences on an enterprise (such as competitors, suppliers, customers, labor unions, governmental agencies, and the economy). It is impossible for people to fully grasp all the details of events and activities going on around them. Therefore, they must pay attention to the most important ones. Models assist the manager in doing this.

A **model** is an abstraction of the events surrounding a process, activity, or problem. It removes an entity from its environment so that it can be examined without the "noise" of the other influences in the environment. Simon's view of decision making is itself a model: It shows the steps in the decision without being concerned about the details of a *specific* decision or the organization in which it is being made.

A business model is also an abstraction. Unnecessary elements are discarded so the manager can focus on the particular details that affect the process, activity, or problem under study. It is an artificial representation of a real-world situation. Deciding which elements are essential depends on how the model is to be used.

Types of Decision-Making Models: Physical Models Models can lie anywhere on a continuum that ranges from those that are highly specific and applicable to a single situation (such as a working model of a particular kind of aircraft) to those that are very general and applicable to many situations (for example, a model of how to calculate net profit of any kind of business operation). One of the primary attributes of any model, however, is that only the aspects of interest in the real situation are included.

Physical models represent the entity studied in appearance and, to a certain extent, in function. Often they are scaled-down versions of the real thing—model airplanes that fly or model buildings and landscapes used by engineers, designers, and architects. These are also known as *iconic models* because they have the appearance of reality but do not behave in real ways. A different type of physical model, the *analog model,* displays the behavior of the real entity being studied but does not *appear* the same. A speedometer, for example, accurately shows the driver how fast an automobile is traveling. But the information does not appear as "speed." Analog models, therefore, are more abstract than the iconic models. Graphs and charts showing production outputs, defect rates, or penetration in the marketplace depict what is happening in the system or process but, obviously, they do not resemble them in appearance.

Types of Decision-Making Models: Symbolic Models Symbolic models attempt to duplicate systems or entities through the use of symbols to represent physical objects. The three types of symbolic model are narrative, graphic, and mathematical (see Table 4.1). A **narrative model** is a language or narrative description of the relationship among variables in a process or system. For example, the statement, "If I change my price, my competitors will match my price unless it causes them to lose money"

Table 4.1 Symbolic Models

	Explanation	Examples
Narrative Models	*Natural language* descriptions of the relationship among variables in an object or process	Narrative description of how prices are set in the marketplace under perfect competition; narrative description of how to assemble a table from precut pieces of material
Graphic Models	*Pictorial* representations of events or components that make up a complete object or process	Flowchart of the steps taken in establishing product prices; pictorial description of the parts of a table and their order of assembly
Mathematical Models	*Mathematical* representations of the system or process being studied; quantitative variables are used to represent specific components or parts	Mathematical model for product pricing; quantitative model of inventory ordering (economic order quantity)

is a typical narrative model. In this narrative describing what will happen if a selling price is changed, the model explains the relationship between price and competitor action.

Graphic models represent parts or steps in an entity or process through pictorial representation. A flowchart, used in computer application development, symbolizes events or actions and shows the sequence in which they must take place if a given action is to be completed or a specific problem solved. A different type of schematic model might show the parts used to construct an object.

Mathematical models are much more rigorous than the other types, using quantitative variables (formulas) to represent the parts of a process or system. As the name implies, they are indeed mathematical representations of the system. The model may consist of a single equation or a set of equations. Mathematical models are the most abstract and yet the simplest to use because all relationships are spelled out precisely, thus reducing the chance of misinterpretation by the model users. A good deal of insight is necessary to construct a mathematical model—perhaps more than for any other type. For example, the development of a mathematical model describing the flow of electricity in a computer system requires much more insight than the construction of a physical model of a chair. Many of us could model a chair, but only a few could mathematically model the flow of electricity. Furthermore, the model of electrical flow in a computer system is very precise. There are many different kinds of chairs, but electrical current can flow in only one way.

Example: A brief example will demonstrate the distinct features of the three types of symbolic model. A manager trying to explain the relation between sales of items (in dollars), the costs of the items sold, and the resulting profits will point out that profit is a function of quantities sold and the item costs. The interrelations can be described without discussing a specific product or an individual sale. Figure 4.2 shows how this relationship is stated in all three forms. The narrative model has no pictorial components: the relations between the variables are described through *words*. The mathematical model, on the other hand, uses symbols to represent the mathematical relations between the variables. The graphic form depicts the same relationships. Dollar values for sales are shown on the vertical axis, and items sold are shown on the horizontal scale. The lines drawn on the graph reveal how total revenue, total costs, and profits change as sales increase. The break-even point, where total costs and total revenue are identical, is readily apparent as the intersection of the two lines.

How We Search for Alternatives There are several views of the extent to which managers seek out information for the decisions they must make. Two opposing views are those of the rational manager and the administrative decision maker. You should be aware of both, but as we will see, the latter is the more common.

The Rational Manager When discussing decision making, it is easy to assume an economic, rational, and fully informed manager, who will search for the best possible alternatives. This type of manager exhibits the following characteristics:

——Searches for all alternative solutions to a problem or finds all possible courses of action to consider in selecting a decision

Figure 4.2 Alternate Models of Sales and Profit Performance

Narrative model

The total profit for sales in any period is calculated by summing the total revenue from sales and subtracting the sum of total costs of the items sold.

Mathematical model

Total profit = total sales revenue − total item costs
Total sales revenue = number × cost per item
Symbolically: TP = TR − TC where
                 TP = total profit
                 TR = total sales revenue
                 TC = total item costs

Graphic model

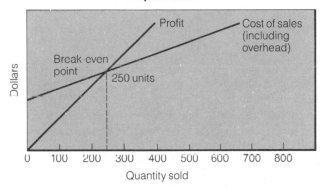

——Knows with certainty the outcome of each alternative

——Knows the benefit of each alternative

——Selects the alternative that maximizes the profit or desired benefit (utility)

As you may realize, the rational manager is an *ideal* decision maker who is working with complete information and has the ability to process and assemble the information perfectly.

The classical view of decision making represented by the rational manager is *prescriptive*. That is, it states (prescribes) how a decision *should* be made if the results are to be maximized in the most beneficial manner. Rarely if ever are decisions made like this. However, the prescription is useful as a guide.

The Administrative Decision Maker The significant flaws in the rational view include:

——Assuming the element of certainty in any aspect of the decision process

——Assuming all alternatives and their consequences to be known

The viewpoint of the administrative decision maker says that it is unlikely in business that managers will know for sure what will result if a certain, say, pricing alternative is selected. Likewise, complete knowledge of all alternatives also seldom occurs. As

Simon (1957, p. 67) states, "It is obviously impossible for the individual to know *all* his alternatives or *all* their consequences, and this impossibility is a very important departure from the model of objective rationality."

Views on Rationality The term **rationality** is used here in the sense of selecting preferred alternatives on the basis of some system of values whereby the consequences can be evaluated. But there are several kinds of rationality:

> [A] decision may be called "objectively" rational if in fact it is the correct behavior for maximizing given values in a given situation. It is "subjectively" rational if it maximizes attainment relative to the actual knowledge of the subject. It is "consciously" rational to the degree that the adjustment of means to ends is a conscious process. It is "deliberately" rational to the degree that the adjustment of means to ends has been deliberately brought about (by an individual or by the organization). A decision is "organizationally" rational if it is oriented to the organization's goals; it is "personally" rational if it is oriented to the individual's goals. (Simon, 1957, pp. 76–77)

Viewing the individual and the organization in perspective, it is virtually impossible for anyone to reach a high degree of overall rationality. Similarly, it is impossible to know all the alternatives in decision making and all their consequences, particularly in difficult and complex situations. The number of alternatives is often too high and the information requirements so vast that the rational model of a manager is unrealistic. In actuality, only a few of the possible alternatives in problem-solving activities ever come to mind.

Rationality and Satisficing Simon rejects the assumption of maximizing and substitutes the concept of **satisficing.** In place of *objective rationality,* he proposes the principle of *bounded rationality.* That is, a manager is rational *to a certain point.*

It is assumed that the manager (or administrator) will deal with the situation at hand by constructing a simplified model of it. Within this simplified model, the manager *does* behave rationally, but only according to the alternatives and consequences within the model. To predict behavior and, consequently, to support it within the organization, one must understand the model and the way it has been constructed. This is the *subjective rationality* identified by Simon.

Limits on rationality result from lack of knowledge and from the individual's capabilities. This is true for decisions made under both certainty and risk. Consequently managers do not maximize as a goal in their decisions but rather "satisfice"; that is, they find a course of action or a strategy that is *good enough.*

Satisficing means that as managers begin to look for courses of action and alternatives, they select the first alternative that meets the minimum standard of satisfaction for the values and goals being sought. This does *not* mean that an individual who is confronted with several options at the same time will not choose the best one. Rather, it implies that the factors that the person's selection process depends on are reduced in complexity. At the same time, it implies that an adjustment in the minimum acceptable satisfaction is possible. If managers easily find alternatives that meet the standard, they may continue to search longer, trying to find even more attractive strategies. Or, the next time the situation arises, they may raise their goals.

If a search for a satisfactory alternative is not successful after a period of time, they can be expected to reduce their minimum standards.

For example, a purchasing agent given the task of finding a supplier who will provide material at $10 or less a ton will try to meet this goal. If, after many telephone calls, a supplier is found who will provide the items at $10 per ton, the purchasing agent will probably stop the search. Had the search continued, a supplier who charged $9 per ton might have been found. But satisficing criteria were met when, after much searching, a supplier who would meet the stated price objective was located. If the $10-a-ton supplier had been unearthed on the first telephone call, we could predict that the purchasing agent would have continued to look for a better price. On the other hand, if no supplier had been found at the $10 level after many phone calls, we could predict that the purchasing agent would have settled for the one who came closest to the stated price objective.

It should be clear that identification of alternatives is an important part of the problem-solving process or, due to satisficing, the search process may end before the best ones are found. That is not, of course, a harsh criticism of management, but rather an acknowledgment of one of the most universal problems of organizations of all types: Managers must be able to examine alternate strategies once they have been identified. This examination has to be coupled with increased and more reliable information on performance within the organization. The basic underlying objective is to minimize risk and uncertainty in the decision process.

A number of advances and developments in management are attributed to improved modeling and information retrieval tools available to decision makers. The computer, its processing speed, and its large file capacity have been important, since they augment the capabilities of individual managers to remember and interrelate pertinent organization information.

Reliance on Both Short-Term and Long-Term Memory People use three types of memory: short-term, long-term, and external. Within the human brain are areas devoted to short- and long-term memory (Figure 4.3). All information submitted as input to an individual's thought process must first pass through **short-term memory.** The

Figure 4.3 Human Long- and Short-Term Memory

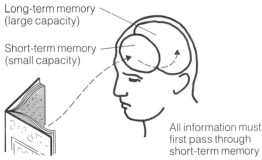

Long-term memory
(large capacity)

Short-term memory
(small capacity)

All information must
first pass through
short-term memory

short-term memory is very small. You use it, for example, when you look up a telephone number in the directory. If it is a new number, or one that has an unfamiliar exchange (the first three digits in the seven-digit number), you remember it for a brief period of time—long enough to dial the number. However, if you do not concentrate on the number and do something else between the time you look it up and the time you go to dial it, you will probably forget the sequence of digits.

Conversely, the **long-term memory** of humans is large—in fact, infinite. Although most of us cannot remember new telephone numbers for more than an instant, we can recall experiences from childhood, college days, and past business activities with vivid details. Some we remember better than others. Experiences that were particularly embarrassing, good, or unfortunate stand out the most.

Individuals use various forms of external memory to augment internal memory. Activities such as jotting a note down on paper or committing information to a magnetic file in a personal computer system are examples of external memory.

Authors recognize the distinctions between memory types when they write textbooks. One of the best ways of communicating information to readers is through the combination of both words and pictures. The reader is able to use both sides of the brain (see box, page 103). Similarly, the use of examples, inclusion of summaries, reviews, and sections of questions has proved to be an effective way of passing information into long-term memory.

Serial Processing of Information People can perform only one mental task at a time. For example, if you are focusing on the telephone number of a business associate, you cannot simultaneously think about an upcoming meeting; you must do one first, followed by the other. This is termed **serial processing.** The ability to perform multiple tasks simultaneously is **parallel processing.**

Consider another example of the serial nature of the way we operate. Can you multiply 325 by 125 in your head? Most people cannot. Even though the individual steps (multiplying 5 by 5, 2 by 5, and so on) are not difficult, people typically cannot remember each of the intermediate products that must be added up for the final result, nor can they perform the steps simultaneously. This too demonstrates the single-step, serial approach of humans to the processing of information.

However, we can switch from task to task very rapidly. For instance, people routinely stop talking on the telephone and immediately begin typing data into a computer terminal. We can switch tasks in a fraction of a second without losing our place. Indeed, if the delay is too long, we have to pause to determine where to restart. Thus when a conversation is interrupted, we may have to ask the other person a question before we can tune back into the discussion.

Computers on the other hand can process in both serial and parallel fashion. Tasks are performed one after the other or simultaneously (in parallel), depending on the type of computer system. Some of the large systems have parallel processors. But even small personal computers do some parallel processing, such as when they move groups of data at the same time or allow printing and editing simultaneously. (Because most computers currently handle only one task at a time, they are considered to be serial instruction machines.)

THE VISION

Human Information Processing

In computer information systems, heavy emphasis is placed on how the computers process data to produce information. However, the *human* information processors involved in an information system are its most important feature. As we stress throughout the text, computers are simply a tool of the people who operate the system.

Left Side, Right Side   Information processing by managers is related to basic physiological characteristics of the human brain. Researchers are studying this area intensely to learn more about the human brain and how it controls our ability to use information and to manage. We know that the brain has two sides, right and left, and we know that the human nervous system is connected to the brain in a *crossover* fashion; the left hemisphere controls the right side of the body, and the right hemisphere controls the left side (Figure A).

Evidence indicates that to a great degree the two hemispheres operate separately. Thus when a person suffers an accident or stroke to the left half of the brain, the right half of the body will be affected most seriously.

Information Processing on the Right and Left   The study of left and right brain goes far beyond the study of right- and left-handedness. Researchers are also investigating the ways in which each hemisphere processes information. Evidence indicates that the processing mode of the left hemisphere is verbal and analytic, and the mode of the right is nonverbal and global.

Figure A Crossover Pattern of Control in Human Information Processing

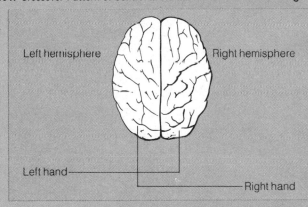

Left hemisphere   Right hemisphere

Left hand

Right hand

continued

Human Information Processing (continued)

Figure B Differences in Information Processing Between Left and Right Hemispheres

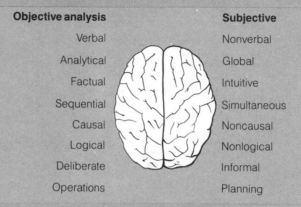

Objective analysis	Subjective
Verbal	Nonverbal
Analytical	Global
Factual	Intuitive
Sequential	Simultaneous
Causal	Noncausal
Logical	Nonlogical
Deliberate	Informal
Operations	Planning

The left side is characterized as performing objective analysis; it is good at categorizing and naming. The right side is believed to yield subjective insight into events and activities. One might use the terms factual and intuitive to describe the two hemispheres.

Figure B shows further differences between the hemispheres. Information processing on the left side will be done in a sequential fashion, while on the right more simultaneous activity occurs. Other contrasts include convergent versus divergent thinking, rational versus intuitive processing, causal versus noncausal reasoning, and logical versus nonlogical information processing. In summary, we see that the left side is characterized by more deliberate, detailed, and step-by-step processing of information. It tries to find a cause for an event. It searches for the steps needed to achieve a certain result. *On the other hand* (notice how dominant right- and left-handedness is in our language), right-side processing uses multiple pieces of data simultaneously, formulating a more global view of sets of events that relate to one another.

Two Ways of Using Information Have you ever had the experience of formulating one conclusion about a situation based on the facts and details even though your gut feeling says a different conclusion should be drawn? The right and left hemispheres provide you with two ways of using the information. The hemispheres absorb the same information but interpret and utilize it differently. Often the left hemisphere will dominate, blocking out the right

Human Information Processing (continued)

side. Thus you may encounter a situation in which you conclude that "The facts look correct, but something tells me not to trust them. I can't tell you in words exactly, but something tells me to decide against taking this step." This statement indicates that both sides of the brain are at work, processing the same information in two different ways.

Perhaps you have experienced events that led to an unexpected outcome, and you may have pored over the facts in an attempt to account for the results. Usually this will be done in a step-by-step, deliberate fashion. Even though you repeat your analysis, and know that it has been done correctly, you come up with a different result than was actually encountered. Puzzled and dejected, you decide to forget about it and move on to other work.

Later, out of nowhere, you suddenly recall the event. You may simultaneously realize: "Ah-ha! I've got it." This "ah-ha experience" indicates that your mind had not forgotten about the events even though consciously you thought you had. It indicates that the right side of the brain had been at work and, through intuition or insight, had pulled the details together in a global fashion that provided the view needed to explain the events. Such occurrences result from the simple right- and left-hemisphere ideas introduced here.

Management Implications   What do these ideas have to do with management and information systems? If you consider the operations/planning continuum in management, you should quickly realize that *operations* are more *left* hemisphere-oriented. *Planning* activities are more like *right*-hemisphere information processing. Deliberate processes, sequences, and analytical considerations are needed at the operating level. However, at the planning level strategy becomes increasingly important: The ability to assemble and integrate informal information is valuable.

Oftentimes, a successful strategist or top-level manager is one who can take a global view of an organization, or one who can process the information at hand—the same information available to many people—in new ways. A creative upper-level manager intuitively sees the possibilities for transforming ordinary data to produce new information over and above the mere facts of the situation. A manager who can do this is a valuable resource. But how does one acquire such an ability?

Due to the emphasis on routines, memorization of facts, and use of logic, our education system has been designed to develop characteristics that are more closely associated with the left hemisphere. Right-hemisphere attributes do not receive the same attention. Keep these issues in mind during investigations of information systems. When developing or using reports or information, or when following computer-oriented procedures, ask how these human information processing principles apply.

Inability to Estimate Probability Intuitively How good are you at assessing the chances that a particular event will occur or recur? Can you estimate reasonably accurately when the first autumn snow will fall in the Rocky Mountains (say in Denver)? Can you explain to a colleague the probability that the fifth sales call on a large corporate customer will land you the contract you have been seeking? Most people would not do well in any of these situations.

People are very poor intuitive statisticians. They are unable to relate the past occurrence of certain events with the likelihood of recurrence. The following situations are representative.

——People greatly overestimate the frequency of deaths caused by spectacular and dramatic causes such as accidents, homicides, cancer, and bad storms.

——Accidents are generally judged to cause as many deaths as diseases (actually disease takes approximately 15 times more lives).

——Homicides are generally estimated to occur approximately 5 times more often than suicides (actually suicides are 30 percent more frequent) (Slovic, Fischhoff, and Lichtenstein, 1980).

In general, people tend to place a higher probability on events that:

——Have occurred most recently

——Are most favorable to the individual or firm

——Are understood by the individual

——Are controlled by the individual

——Are reported most frequently in the media

In summary, our ability to correctly assess probabilities and the likelihood of certain events or outcomes is limited and will hamper our decision and management abilities, unless we receive assistance from organization information systems.

Implications of These Similarities for Information Systems The foregoing characteristics of managers and systems users have direct implications for the design of information systems. By considering them, developers can ensure a system is attractive to use and will lead to potentially productive results. If they are ignored, the information system may be ineffective.

The following guidelines suggest features that should be included in information systems to assist users:

——Embed models in the information system where appropriate. If the system is designed to support applications such as inventory management, price and profit determination, or determination of break-even points, the information system, not the user, should perform the necessary calculations and processing of data as determined by the appropriate decision model.

——Facilitate entry of inquiries and rapid retrieval of data and information so that individuals will not be tempted to rely on memory or to guess. Build essential facts or statistics into models and algorithms that guide decision making or information processing.

——Ensure that the operating characteristics of the information system do not impede the pace at which users wish to perform a specific task. Needless delays and pauses not only will frustrate individuals but may increase the likelihood of errors and mistakes from loss of concentration.

——Minimize the information people must remember to use the system or interpret its output.

——Employ meaningful and familiar codes and sequences for data.

By following these guidelines, information systems developers will assist all users, regardless of individual differences.

Ways We Differ in Information Processing

Individuals differ in information processing ability in four important areas. In this section we examine differences in dealing with an overload of information, and in cognitive styles, information-gathering styles, and problem-solving styles.

Styles of Dealing with Information Overload Managers become overloaded when they have too much information to deal with. How do they deal with this problem? Miller (1978) has identified eight common methods for managing information overload.

1. *Escape:* acting to cut off input of information
2. *Error:* incorrectly transmitting certain parts of a message
3. *Omission:* failing to transmit certain randomly distributed parts of a message
4. *Filtering:* giving priority in processing to certain messages
5. *Queuing:* delaying transmission of certain parts of a message
6. *Abstracting:* communicating a message with less than complete detail
7. *Multiple channels:* transmitting messages simultaneously over two or more channels in parallel
8. *Chunking:* transmitting meaningful information in organized chunks of symbols rather than symbol by symbol

These are very important issues for information systems developers and users. If the system design constitutes part of the problem—that is, if it produces an overload of irrelevant information—individual performance will be hindered and users will be frustrated. On the other hand, certain methods for dealing with overload, discussed in a moment, can be included as system features.

Cognitive Styles Managers are often characterized by researchers according to their individual approaches to the processing of information. One aspect of this research that has received much attention by researchers in information systems is cognitive style. The term *cognitive* refers to the way one perceives information. Thus, cognitive style is the way individuals organize and use information during decision making.

The following cognitive aspects are well documented in the research literature of information systems and psychology:

1. **Field independence/dependence:** Individuals differ in their tendency to break a set of information into discrete elements or to try to view them in context. Field-independent persons are more analytical than field-dependent persons. Field-independent persons are more attuned to pulling pieces out of the whole, while field-dependent individuals tend to emphasize the larger picture.

2. **Analytic versus heuristic:** Analytic individuals are very systematic in their evaluation of a situation. They follow a structured, well organized, and deductive approach in arriving at a decision. Heuristic people are more intuitive. They use trial and error and readily revise their plans on the basis of new information.

You should not conclude that one aspect is better than the other. By describing individuals in these different manners, however, we can point out that managers approach problems in alternative ways and want or use information in manners that are congruent with their unique characteristics.

Individuals also deal with information in different ways depending on which side of the brain is used. (See the boxed material earlier in this chapter on human information processing.)

Information-Gathering Styles Managers differ in their styles of gathering information. Two styles are recognized: global and receptive.

1. The global type of person takes an all-encompassing (perceptive) approach to a situation, marshaling perceptions about the relations among details and generalizing from them to form a "big picture."

2. The receptive type of individual focuses on details, accumulating data about specific tasks and formulating specific knowledge from the details.

These dimensions, displayed in Figure 4.4, help account for differences in the way in which the human mind organizes information. However, style of information gathering alone also interacts with the other human dimensions discussed in this section.

Problem-Solving Styles Managers fall into different categories in their assessment of problems calling for a decision or some other action. Three categories are common.

1. **Problem avoider:** tends to shun the notion that a problem exists and focuses on the positive aspects of a situation; avoids negative information; tends to use planning as a means of avoiding difficult situations or impending problems.

2. **Problem resolver:** does not seek out problems but deals with them quickly and efficiently when they arise; faces the reality of a situation and does not avoid or ignore difficulties.

3. **Problem finder:** does seek out problems, dealing with them on the one hand or turning them into advantages on the other; tends to regard problems

Figure 4.4 Dimensions for Gathering and Processing Information

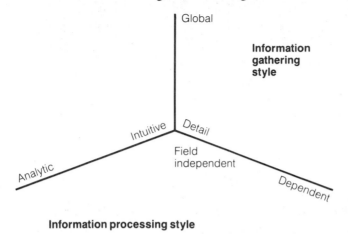

as opportunities in disguise (many successful products have been developed by this type of manager).

You can probably think of persons that fall into each of these categories. Consider whether one is more effective than the others. Now think about the way in which information systems should be designed to be used by each type of manager.

Implications of These Differences for Information Systems

Never overload users with unnecessary or confusing information. There are five ways for ensuring that this rule is followed while addressing the other individual differences discussed earlier. First, the information system itself should serve as a filter. Filtration can be accomplished by presenting averages, statistical summaries, and probability estimates. Proper use of these methods will also help avoid bias in the way information is interpreted. For example, summary information will often meet user needs, and details can be retrieved if necessary. Thus systems designers should avoid the presentation of detail information. Research has shown that when information systems are designed to provide summary information, the decision making of managers does not suffer. When speed is important, users can function more quickly and without loss of effectiveness by using summary information. Excessive detail will produce the opposite effect (Dickson, Senn, and Chervany, 1977).

Second, graphs and charts are helpful for summarizing the amount of information presented while highlighting important trends and comparisons. Research indicates that graphs and charts are most useful for:

——Detecting subtle trend changes over time (price or cost fluctuations, customer purchases, and so on)

——Searching for patterns from a vast amount of data (stock price variations in conjunction with rising and falling interest rates)

——Analyzing relationships among variables or comparing pattern changes over time (for instance, material cost and quality control rejection rates)

——Making simple impressions from large amounts of data

Graphs should not be used for presentation of specific data items or simple relationships and trends from a small amount of data. Likewise, they are not useful when it is important to read absolute or percentage changes between two numbers (Jarvenpaa and Dickson, 1986).

Graphs and charts do not make the decision or problem-solving task itself less difficult nor will they necessarily lead to more effective analysis and decision making. However, *not* using them under the foregoing conditions can impede performance.

The increasing availability of powerful software tools and application packages (discussed in Chapter 16) makes it feasible to tailor reports and information presentations to the needs and characteristics of individuals. In many cases, end-users themselves can implement this third means of avoiding information overload.

Devising ways to highlight important information constitutes a fourth approach. Often subtle differences that we tend to overlook can be important in understanding a situation or explaining a problem. Computer information systems can detect such differences more easily than many people can. Furthermore, they can emphasize them by use of color, animation, or increased intensity on a terminal display or by bold printing, color, and other graphic devices on hard copy.

Finally, presenting information in brief amounts avoids comprehension or overload difficulties while fitting differing cognitive styles. Yet it is essential for a user to be able to "browse" through the data. Conditions frequently arise that were not anticipated, and therefore were not considered in models, processing procedures, or output design. The ability to scan raw data may enable users to identify unique conditions or to uncover potential problems. Furthermore, as we discuss later in this chapter, managers may use a browsing technique to keep up to date with trends and overall business activities.

Management and Information Needs

Understanding and contributing to the interaction among internal systems and to interaction with the internal environment are key functions of management. Surely the concepts of a management hierarchy and authority are important: Whether implicit or explicit, all views of the organization are based on these concepts.

Management Functions

In general, **management** is the act or skill of transforming resources (land, labor, capital, and information) into output to accomplish a desired result or objective.

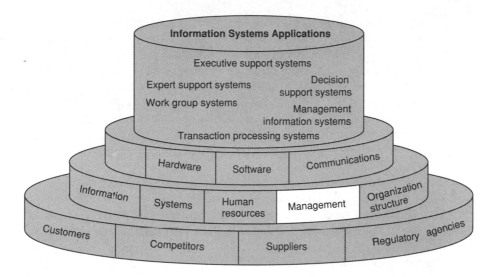

This implies that managers must be able to influence the achievement of such goals (otherwise, the activity cannot be managed).

Although management roles differ with the levels within an organization, there are some common **management functions,** including:

———**Planning:** establishing goals and developing policies, procedures, and programs to achieve them

———*Organizing:* grouping activities and establishing organizational structures and procedures to ensure that the activities are performed

———*Staffing:* obtaining and training personnel to work in the organization in order to achieve goals and objectives

———*Controlling:* measuring performance against goals and objectives and developing procedures for adjusting goals, procedures, or activities

———*Communicating:* transferring information on goals, objectives, and performance to personnel throughout the organization and the environment

All these managerial functions are vital to an organization's success. They are closely related to each other and to the concepts of hierarchy and authority at each level of management.

These universal management functions have many information systems implications. Typically goals are stated in operational and measurable terms. Thus actual performance can be monitored against planned performance, both at the strategic upper management level and at the operations level. Moreover, even though it is tedious at times for managers to plan and replan, planning remains a fact of organization life. Many planning tasks can be supported effectively through information systems capabilities. Alternative strategies may be tested by modeling the essential features of a situation and using different sets of data to estimate likely outcomes. Historical outcomes can also be reassessed to allow consideration of what the results would have been under different circumstances.

Information systems plans and corporate plans and strategies must not conflict. Rather, they should be developed together so that such predictable activities as expansion into new markets, distribution of expanded product lines, and implementation of cost containment plans do not thwart the attainment of goals and objectives or the fulfillment of plans. Many organizations now use their information systems as effective competitive weapons and are in fact changing the very nature of relationships with customers and competitors. (The deployment of information systems for competitive purposes is examined fully in Chapter 20.)

The communication of information throughout the organization is often speeded by electronic mail and computer networks linking managers and employees in widely separated locations as well as just down the hall. Many brokerage houses, for example, can instantly send messages about stock prices, buy or sell requests, or electronic funds transfers across countries and continents. This capability is changing the scope of entire industries.

Staffing may be increased or decreased because of information systems, depending on the nature of the organization. We find that the span of control, that is, number of employees reporting to managers, may increase when information systems are introduced. Computerized communication and reporting mechanisms coupled with highly effective applications software have the potential to reduce the volume of information managers must review while enlarging the scope of activity that an individual can monitor. And as indicated above, the location of staff members often does not matter, since they can "telecommute" or stay in touch electronically.

Management Hierarchies and Information Flow

To carry out organizational goals, policies, and procedures, the **management hierarchy** is organized into three levels: top, middle, and operating. The **top-management level** (Figure 4.5) performs a number of planning and strategy formulation activities. This management level is oriented toward the future of the organization and oversees the performance of a handful of key associates who are to carry out the firm's plans. Duties at this level primarily involve coordination of the overall efforts of the firm and liaison with other firms and agencies in the business community.

The **middle-management level** is concerned with overseeing performance in the organization and with controlling activities that move the organization toward the determined goals. Managers at this level are typically interested in such critical issues in performance success as employee training, personnel considerations, and equipment and material acquisition.

The **operating-management level,** the largest group of managers in the firm, is essentially supervisory; the emphasis on technical skills of employees is greater here than in either top or middle management. Operating managers ensure that employees follow procedures in work activities; they do not usually perform the

Figure 4.5 Management Hierarchy and Information Flow

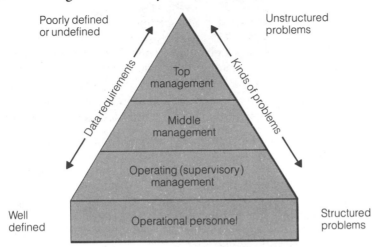

work themselves. The primary concerns of management at this level include schedules and deadlines, human relations, and cost and quality control.

An example will help to clarify the relationship among different levels of management. An important job of top management in many organizations is establishing marketing policies for the firm's products or services. Managers at this level identify the most important aspects of the marketing effort (advertising, pricing, product quality, packaging, transportation, distribution, and so forth) and establish policies to deal with each aspect. For example, top management may establish a marketing policy of advertising through mass media (newspapers, magazines, radio, television) only and avoiding door-to-door distribution of products.

At the middle-management or management control level, the policies that top management formulates are developed in greater detail. In this example, a typical management control activity is establishing advertising programs. The programs will include a statement of the message that is to encourage consumers and potential consumers to buy the product or to keep buying the product. The messages may emphasize the product characteristics most likely to sell the product, such as price, quality, and style.

After the advertising programs are outlined, operating managers determine exactly where the advertisements are to be placed. They select the newspapers and magazines that will carry the advertisements and decide when they will appear. Operating control also includes selecting the broadcast media that will carry the advertisements and arriving at daily and long-term schedules for airing them.

Similar programs will be developed by other managers to carry out management policies on transportation, packaging, and so forth. Each is a result of the attention that top management has given to formulation of marketing policies. As you can see, there is a close relationship between activities and responsibilities throughout the management hierarchy.

Management Activities

There is a tendency to view managers as well-organized, systematic thinkers who are oriented toward rational decision making. This is consistent with the view that the tasks of management are planning, organizing, controlling, and coordinating. These words dominate management literature and they do indicate the objectives of management. But we can still pose the overriding question: *What do managers do?*

To answer this question, consider the following situation from the writings of Henry Mintzberg (1975), an internationally respected researcher on management:

> A manager who is told on the telephone that one of the firm's factories has just burned down advises the caller to see whether temporary arrangements can be made to supply customers through a foreign subsidiary. Is the manager planning, organizing, coordinating, or controlling?
>
> How about a manager who presents a gold watch to a retiring employee? Or attends a conference to meet people in the trade? Or, on returning from that conference, tells one of the employees about an interesting product idea that came to mind while at the conference?

These questions point out the difficulty of describing management. But without insight into the answers, it is difficult to design planning, decision support, or information systems for managers (or for that matter, to "teach" the skills of management).

According to Mintzberg (1975), there are four myths about the manager's job. The myths, if Mintzberg is correct, have significant implications for the design and use of computer information systems. The myths are:

1. *Myth:* The manager is a reflective, systematic planner.
   Fact: Study after study has shown that managers work at an unrelenting pace, that their activities are characterized by brevity, variety, and discontinuity, and that they are strongly oriented to action and dislike reflective activities.

2. *Myth:* The effective manager has no regular duties to perform. (The good manager carefully orchestrates everything in advance, then sits back to enjoy the fruits of the labor, responding occasionally to an unforeseeable exception.)
   Fact: In addition to handling exceptions, managerial work involves performing a number of regular duties, including ritual and ceremony, negotiations, and processing of soft information that links the organization with its environment.

3. *Myth:* The senior manager needs aggregated information, which a formal management information system best provides.
   Fact: Managers strongly favor the verbal media—namely, telephone calls and meetings.

4. *Myth:* Management is, or at least is quickly becoming, a science and a profession.
   Fact: The managers' programs—to schedule time, process information, make decisions, and so on—remain locked deep inside their minds. To describe these programs, we rely on words like *judgment* and *intuition,* seldom stopping to realize that they are merely labels for our ignorance.

Figure 4.6 Typical Distribution of Time for Managers

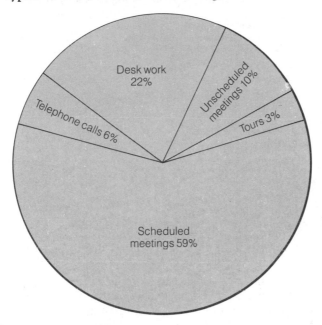

Mintzberg's breakdown of times devoted to management activities is shown in Figure 4.6.

When information systems do not fit the styles these managers use for information gathering, they will not be successful; managers will ignore them. The unstructured tasks of executives defy highly structured information systems. Therefore, decision support systems (see Chapter 14) must allow managers to quickly pose a problem and evaluate alternatives. There is no time to write software or establish databases.

The attributes of an information system that offers effective support to managers are summarized in Table 4.2 and explained as follows:

——*Offers executives quick, concise updates:* Top-level managers need to be briefed on what has changed since the last time they examined the system. If more details are needed, ready access must be assured. (See the Lockheed–Georgia Company case in the Case Study Module for an interesting system for senior executives.)

——*Permits scanning of internal and external environments:* Frequently, critical information about competitive activities, impending government legislation, or organization and product problems or opportunities does not develop from formal information reporting systems. Analysts and information system users alike must be attuned to ways in which computer-based systems can assist in scanning the environment or providing such information to managers and executives.

——*Allows users to browse:* The ability to browse through existing files and databases often provides managers with information they might not ask for or could not

---

Table 4.2 Information Systems Design Features to Aid Manager Decision Making

Offers executives quick, concise updates
Permits scanning of internal and external environments
Allows users to browse
Allows testing of strategies
Uses models
Avoids information overload
Highlights significant differences
Presents summary measures
Backs up summary information with details
Provides alternate presentation styles

---

receive in a formal report. Often they just want to "get a feel" for how the organization or department is performing. In some cases, they scan performance details hoping to discern an event or trend that went unnoticed in formal reporting systems.

Allows testing of strategies: Managers want to know the possible consequences of alternative strategies. By testing different levels and combinations of variables (perhaps labor costs, sales levels, and so on) they can see the impact of the variables on overall performance. "What if" capabilities are central to the concept of decision support systems.

Uses models: To provide a balance between rational management and satisficing, systems should be designed to take advantage of the information that models can provide. Models can be embedded in the design of an information system and the results of testing the model automatically submitted to managers.

Avoids information overload: Since people quickly become overloaded by excessive details, information systems should be designed to limit the quantity of details and number of concepts presented to management at one time. From five to nine elements are suggested. In addition, the presentation design should not require users to manipulate the details further, perhaps with a calculator, to convert them into a more appropriate form.

Highlights significant differences: The system can help ensure that managers do not overlook variations from expected performance levels by focusing attention on relevant details, not extraneous data. Graphics and highlighting techniques are essential for presenting "hard" information to managers.

Presents summary measures: Since managers are poor intuitive statisticians, the design of the system should incorporate decision aids to overcome this limitation. Carefully incorporating performance summaries such as averages and past ranges can be very helpful. Care must be taken not to include too much information, which becomes distracting or overloads the user.

Backs up summaries with detail: Summary information may provide the overall picture managers and users want. But if the information they see raises questions, they should be able to access explanatory details through the system quickly and efficiently.

——*Provides alternate presentation styles:* Since people process and use information in different ways, we can assume that some managers will prefer analytical details, whereas others will function best with graphic explanations of performance or situations. A well-designed information system should provide alternative modes for receiving information.

But information systems must also be used in concert with "soft" information—estimates, speculation, opinion, hunches, even gossip. Such information fits well with management's responsibility of *identifying opportunities,* not just solving problems. Thus the ability to store tidbits of information is no less crucial than the ability to manipulate assumptions in evaluating alternatives.

Electronic networks and voice mail systems (discussed in Chapter 14) are gaining increased recognition among executives. These innovations allow managers to keep in touch better than other alternatives.

Above all, any information system designed for the fast-paced executive must not entail long time commitments or awkward means of interaction. It also must present continuity in the face of continual interruption.

Management Theories

The practice of management and the utilization of information within an organization are guided by **management theory.** In this section we explore the role of theory in management and relate it to the fundamental principles and the use of management information.

Characteristics of a Theory

A theory provides management with a better understanding of how the complexities of business interrelate. It assists in explaining *why* a certain event or result occurs or *how* it occurs.

Since a concern of management is why things happen, a theory must have certain specific characteristics to be useful (indeed, to be considered a theory rather than a hunch or an idea):

1. A method of organizing and categorizing things (a typology) is required.
2. Future events should be predictable from the theory.
3. Past events should be explainable in terms of the theory.
4. A sense of understanding about what causes events or results should emerge from consideration of the theory.
5. The theory should bear the potential for control of events.

We will look at how this framework applies to different theories of management that are or have been in vogue in organizations.

Eras of Management Theory

The theory underlying management is changing continually (in contrast to physical laws, which are unchanging). The history of management has produced four distinct views of management and the management process. Each has been a popular approach to management, and some of the earliest ones are still widely practiced. However, each was most popular in a period, or management era, that has come to be associated with that particular theory or management school. Hence we refer to the **scientific management era,** the human relations era, the management science era, and the sociotechnical era.

Scientific Management Era Management began as an area of industrial interest during the second century of the Industrial Revolution. Frederick W. Taylor is considered to be the father of scientific management.

Taylor believed that success in business was the result of maximizing productivity. He emphasized that management had four primary responsibilities and duties:

1. To develop a science of management for each element of a job to replace the old rule-of-thumb methods, determined by the workers.
2. To select the best worker for each job and to provide training to develop the skills of all workers.
3. To develop a hearty cooperation between management and the people who carried out the work.
4. To divide work between managers and workers in almost equal shares, instead of placing most of the responsibility on the worker, as had been customary.

The key to the theory of scientific management is the belief that standards are needed to establish and communicate the level of work individuals are expected to perform. Objectives state what the organization wants to accomplish, but standards are the measures of performance that indicate how well results conform to stated objectives. Management within this viewpoint calls for information on task performance, which should assist in answering questions about work quality, the timeliness of task completion, and planned versus actual progress.

Human Relations Era Although the management pioneers associated with the scientific management era recognized the importance of the human element in organizations, most of their attention was devoted to efficiency issues. However, in the late 1920s and early 1930s, the importance of workers' social needs began to gain recognition.

Knowing how to maintain the interest and productivity of employees and managers at all levels of the organization is an important issue in modern management. This was founded on the firm belief that individuals who are not motivated in their jobs cannot be expected to produce at maximum levels of effectiveness and efficiency.

The **human relations era** increased the significance attached to managerial information about job requirements and the qualifications for effective job performance. In addition, information to match individuals with job requirements and for monitoring training needs and progress increased in importance.

Management Science Era Management science, which had its beginnings during World War II under the alternate name of *operations research,* is concerned with the application of mathematical and statistical theory to business problems. As the field grew, it also took advantage of the emerging computer technology, which enabled management scientists and operations researchers to take on problems requiring complex analysis. Before the availability of computer and modeling techniques, the problems were often so complex and time-consuming that analysts could not deal with them satisfactorily.

The techniques emerging from management science research include the following.

——*Forecasting techniques:* statistically based methods in which multiple regression and analysis of variance are to predict or explain future variables (sales, profits, market shares, error rates, defects in materials, and so forth)

——*Simulation techniques:* methods of randomly generating numbers according to assumed business characteristics that produce results to represent those that could reasonably be expected to occur if the same characteristics were found in the business environment. Different combinations of variables are used to produce simulated results describing the impact of, for example, sales price or delivery rate, on business performance.

——*Optimization techniques:* modeling and statistical methods that seek to find the best or optimum performance under certain constraints. Minimizing costs and maximizing profits or sales are commonly studied issues.

The chief tool in management science is the mathematical model—the equations or formulas that describe the variables most significant in the problem being studied. For example, models in widespread use for inventory management relate the quantity of an item on hand to the expected demand for the item. They also incorporate lead time needed to place an order and have it filled by a supplier. The model relates each of these factors to the others, allowing the user to determine when to place an order and what quantity to request.

Management science is not a redirection of management attention but rather a change in the approach to dealing with important problems and decisions. Computer and mathematical tools make it possible to deal with large problems so that many related aspects of a problem can be considered at the same time. We will see the influence of the **management science era** in many of the examples used in later discussions.

Sociotechnical Era The sociotechnical concept arose in the British coal mining industry in the 1950s, when increasing levels of technology (tools, equipment, and mining systems) were being introduced. Engineers, guided by their belief in the new technology they had developed, set up whatever organization the technology seemed to require. The "people cost" was not adequately considered. It was frequently assumed that this aspect could be taken care of by improving socioeconomic conditions, lowering unemployment, or achieving better human relations. Yet researchers were consistently finding that in spite of more progressive personnel management policies and more harmonious union-management relations, there remained significant concern over the nature of the work and the structure of jobs.

The work group in one new coal seam was particularly effective, however, outperforming all other groups. When the reason for the group's success was traced, it was found that both social (work group) and the technical systems were designed *together* in this coal seam. From this experience, the **sociotechnical era** emerged.

Sociotechnical theory is anchored in the belief that the organization consists of four interrelated components (Figure 4.7):

1. Task
2. People
3. Structure
4. Technology

There is a strong interdependence among these factors (Leavitt, 1965). If one is changed, there is a tendency of the others to adjust to damp out the effect of the change. For example, if new technology is introduced to increase productivity, the people may react in a way that counteracts the potential benefits of the new technology. This is an important concern when information systems are introduced in organizations. If the potential users of the system do not agree with the purpose or methods of the information system, they may resist it and reduce the benefits of having the system at all. (Resistance to information systems is discussed in Chapter 18.)

The sociotechnical approach to systems has emerged to implement the achievement of *both* high job satisfaction and technological efficiency.

When information systems are designed, it is just as important to consider their impact on users and managers, work groups, and organization structures as it is to

Figure 4.7 Interaction of Organization Components

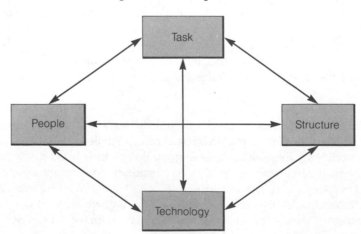

select the technical features of the system (what reports to produce, which equipment to specify, and so on). A system that is well designed technically may be ineffective— it may even fail—if its users are affected in adverse ways.

A Contingency View

The hallmark of the so-called contingency school is the fundamental belief that no single approach always works. None of the tools of the various eras discussed above are always successful in achieving certain objectives. Whether a certain approach is advisable depends on the circumstances of the moment. That is, the approach is *contingent* on the opportunity or problem at hand.

Since any of the preceding views may be useful in a specific situation, how is appropriateness determined? The contingency view suggests that the most important influences on management include: (1) the nature of the job or work the individual must perform (that is, the task), (2) the characteristics of the workers themselves (such as motivation, skill level, education, and economic class), (3) the sophistication and complexity of the tools and techniques used to perform a task, and (4) the external economic, political, and social environment of the work group and of the firm itself.

Contingency theory suggests that a large number of unskilled temporary employees in a coal mine and a small number of highly skilled research scientists striving for a breakthrough in aerospace technology should be managed differently.

According to contingency theory managers introducing information systems must constantly be aware of changes in the internal and external environment. Changes in any of the environmental components may influence selection of a different management strategy and implementation plan.

Organization Structure and Information Systems

The capabilities of computer information systems may alter the way organizations operate. As a result, managers are constantly reviewing alternatives for structuring their organizations and revising their specifications of the impact information systems should produce. This section discusses alternatives for organization design as they are influenced by information processing questions. We also explore characteristics of effective organizations, with special emphasis on the implications for information systems.

Organization Theory

Organization theory focuses on the alternate ways in which to structure an organization to best utilize its people and other resources such as equipment, material, and finances while providing for the communication of information to appropriate personnel.

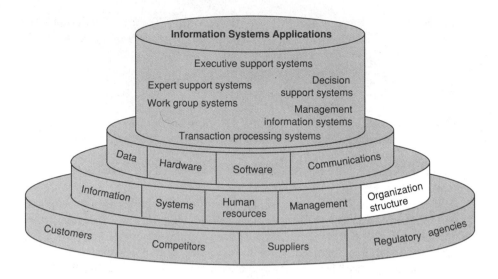

The concept of contingency theory suggests that no one approach always provides the most desirable results. Applied to the design of organizations, contingency theory suggests that there is no one best way to organize and that no single way of structuring an organization—that is, dividing work tasks and assigning responsibilities—will always produce the most effective performance results.

Concerns in Organization Design

As managers study ways of structuring their organizations, they wrestle (although not always consciously) with two design concerns:

——*Differentiation:* how to separate subtasks in an effective manner (division of labor)

——*Integration:* how to combine subtasks to complete a task successfully

A framework developed by Jay Galbraith (1973) vividly describes the alternative ways of dealing with the design problems. The framework emphasizes the belief that the best way to organize is contingent on the *uncertainty* and *diversity* of the tasks to be completed. It relates closely to the information concepts described in Chapter 3. This view of organization design is summarized below:

> If a task is well understood prior to performing it, much of the activity can be preplanned. If it is not understood, then during the actual execution of the task more knowledge is required, which leads to changes in resource allocation, schedules, and priorities. All these changes require information processing *dur-*

ing task performance. Therefore, *the greater the task uncertainty, the greater the amount of information that must be processed among decision makers during task execution in order to achieve a given level of performance*. (Galbraith, 1973, p. 4)

Uncertainty—the condition under which managers are unable to predict outcomes of activities accurately every time—limits the ability of managers to preplan and to make decisions. Therefore, various organization structures are actually variations in one of the following strategies:

——Increase the ability to *preplan*
——Increase the ability to adapt quickly to *change*
——Decrease the minimum level of acceptable performance

All organizations must do one of the foregoing when faced with uncertainty.
Increased information is needed when there is:

——A diverse number of possible results or outputs in a task or system
——A high number of different inputs
——A high level of difficulty in achieving the task or system goals and objectives

An increase in any of these produces an increase in uncertainty. Uncertainty in turn is, according to Galbraith, the difference between the information needed to perform a task and the amount of information available to the manager.

Managers must reduce uncertainty to make effective decisions and in fact to manage the enterprise. The ways to accomplish this are:

——Improve the information available
——Change the performance of the organization

The next section discusses the information processing strategies that grow out of this realization and the interrelation with organization design strategies.

Information Processing Strategies

From an information system point of view, there are two information processing strategies for dealing with uncertainty. From them, four organization design strategies are developed.

Reduce the Need for Information Processing   The first strategy is based on the assumption that some organization designs reduce the amount of information that is needed to operate and manage the organization. This strategy can be pursued by reducing the expected level of performance and by creating self-contained tasks.

Reduce Performance Level   Lowering the number of exceptions that occur in the organization's daily operation is a constant concern of some managers. Under *management by exception*, each time an anomalous event occurs, management must examine and deal with it. To understand the reason for the exception (anomaly) and to decide what to do about it or its cause, managers must collect and process information (by how much actual and expected performances differed, why the variance occurred, what the impact of the variance is, and what alternates are available to deal with the case). If too many exceptions occur, managers will be very busy and will need large amounts of information to arrive at decisions. They may even become overloaded with information and crisis situations.

On the other hand, the lower the number of exceptions occurring, the less likely that managers will become overloaded. Similarly, the need for information processing will be reduced.

Reducing performance expectations reduces the number of exceptions (provided actual performance levels do not drop or individuals do not slack off). Managers may reduce performance requirements by such actions as increasing the amount of items in inventory to guard against running out of stock, by becoming more flexible about the conditions under which overtime work is permitted, by building in extra lead time for the completion of a project or by lowering quality levels. As you can see, in each alternative above, *slack* is tolerated. That is, reducing performance levels necessitates the use of extra resources. In turn, using these additional or "slack" resources reduces the need for information processing because management has fewer exceptions to manage.

Establish Self-Contained Tasks Instead of a structure in which work groups, departments, and project teams depend on the activities and performance of other groups and departments, the self-contained approach features groups that can perform their respective tasks completely from internal resources. For example, a group may order and stock its own inventory (rather than relying on the purchasing and inventory departments), hire and train personnel (rather than using the services of the personnel department), design its own product (rather than going through the engineering department), and develop its own information systems (instead of working with a separate department).

Information processing is reduced because the group self-contained has fewer inputs from other departments (materials, designs, people, and information systems). A decreased division of labor also reduces information processing. Moreover, the group can develop its own schedules of work as long as it meets the completion requirements established for the department.

Increase Information Processing Capacity In contrast to the strategy above, whereby companies *reduce the need* for information processing, they may decide to improve their *ability to process* information. The two ways of pursuing this strategy are vertical information systems and lateral relations.

Use of Vertical Information Systems Most firms operate according to plans that offer guidance toward the achievement of goals and objectives. Under uncertainty, the ability to plan is limited by time and resources. At some point, the number of exceptions to the plan will become unacceptable and a new plan will be needed (it is better to replan than to spend substantial time modifying an old plan). How frequently replanning is needed depends on the rate at which uncertainty increases—the greater the uncertainty, the greater the frequency of replanning. But more frequent replanning calls for more resources (people, computer time, and so on).

The vertical information systems alternative improves the ability to process information by adding staff members, improving information systems, improving databases, and similar approaches. Information gathering ability is also improved by devising better methods to collect information at the points of origin and to ensure that it gets to the right person at the right time. At planning time, information processing is increased and the system is designed in such a way to have the capacity to do so.

Create a System of Lateral Relations Alternatively, it is possible to move a decision down in the organization hierarchy to the point at which the information is available rather than transmitting the information up, for a decision by higher-level managers. Lateral decision making is decentralized, but the group is not self-contained; it still depends on interaction with other functional groups.

Lateral relations occur in different forms including (in their most likely order of selection):

1. Direct contact between members of different groups
2. Liaison staffers whose responsibility is to maintain contact between groups
3. Task forces consisting of members of several groups who work together temporarily to deal with common problems or decisions
4. Teams of individuals permanently assigned to work together
5. Personnel who provide leadership of lateral processes
6. Matrix organizations for dual authority (individuals belong to project teams *and* are a member of a department in the firm)

Increasingly computer communication and lateral databases are affecting the need for lateral relations. If organizationwide databases exist and the means exist for retrieving information from them easily, the frequency of lateral relations may change, or the efficiency of the relations may improve.

Organizations need not select just one strategy. Rather several, even all, of the strategies may be used simultaneously (Figure 4.8). We would expect, however, that a greater number of methods will be applied when uncertainty is high and fewer will be needed when uncertainty is low.

Characteristics of Effective Organizations

Managers in successful organizations turn the foregoing concepts into action. They do not remain theories for discussion but are put into operation. Let's look at these characteristics of organizations and the role information systems play.

Figure 4.8 Organization Design Strategies Pertinent to Information Systems

Increase capacity to process information • Invest in *vertical* information systems 　Process information in a way that does not overload hierarchic communication channels. 　Use plans, budgets, and schedules.	Decrease need to process information • Create slack resources 　Reduce the number of exceptions that can occur by reducing expected level of performance.
• Create *lateral* relations 　Move decision down to level where information exists, avoid upward referral and overloading hierarchy; form task force of managers from various units.	• Create self-contained tasks 　Change from a functional design to one in which each group has all the resources it needs to complete the task.

The widely read best-seller *In Search of Excellence* concluded that many successful managers and companies with excellent records of performance have one thing in common: They are brilliant on the basics (Peters and Waterman, 1982). That is, in spite of the level of technology, the size of the management staff, or the nature of the product or service offered the fundamentals of management are handled exceptionally well. Wisdom prevails over intellect. Thinking is more important than the tools used to facilitate thought. Action is not impeded by overanalysis.

Peters and Waterman indicate that the following attributes distinctly characterized this elite group of firms.

1. *Bias for action:* The successful firms may approach decision making by analyzing pertinent facts and details, but they don't overdo it. They test ideas and develop information about them, but they also make a decision, monitor its effect, assess the consequences, and change course if the decision appears to have been a bad one.

2. *Close to the customer:* Successful companies listen to the comments and needs of the customers. They provide the products and services customers want, and they have the internal systems to ensure that customer information is properly managed and used in corporate decisions.

3. *Autonomy and entrepreneurship:* Innovative companies give managers and leaders the opportunity to be creative and to test ideas. They encourage risk taking and support good attempts at new ideas. A constant management commandment is: "Make sure you generate a reasonable number of mistakes."

4. *Productivity through people:* People make up the organization and they are part of a team. Respect for the individual is an underlying theme, simple in concept but effective in results. Every worker—every individual—is a source of ideas.

5. *Hands-on, value-driven:* Management involvement in day-to-day activities has more to do with achievements in an organization than the technology, resources, structure, or level of innovation in the firm.

6. *Stick to the knitting:* The companies that are most successful keep close to the business they know as they expand. They do not venture out to diverse but unfamiliar areas for the sake of commercial glamour.

7. *Simple form, lean staff:* Top management staffs are not large. The underlying organization structure is simple and unconfusing.

8. *Simultaneous loose-tight properties:* Centralized and decentralized decision authority coexist. Such activities as those associated with responsibility for product development are pushed down in the corporate hierarchy. However, organization values (such as the importance of product reliability) and operating styles are centrally encouraged from the highest management levels.

Of course, simply performing well on the basics does not guarantee success. However, it is often found that those who are successful have managed the basics well. Their information systems are equally well designed around the basics!

The management basics listed above lead to the following information processing guidelines, some of which you have already encountered (see Table 4.2).

1. Provide individuals with the information they need, free from irrelevant details and in a form that allows them to monitor performance and determine when action is needed.

2. Provide for scanning the environment in which the organization operates, paying particular attention to customer needs, activities of competition, and emerging problems, opportunities, and trends.

3. Design information systems to aid, not impede, managers. Systems that are difficult to use or do not provide useful information will be avoided.

4. Include the capability to test ideas and evaluate alternate performance strategies. "What if" testing and rapid development of information in these situations are essential.

5. Develop user-accessible information processing centers to support hands-on operation as a means of avoiding long system development times. Where appropriate, assist individuals in retrieving information from more formal information systems.

6. Match information systems plans with those of the organization. Information and information systems are resources that need management.

7. Distribute both information and information processing capability in a manner that guarantees the availability of both at the point at which decisions must be made. Provide appropriate forms of information to managers at various levels of the hierarchy.

These guidelines are basic to successful information systems in management; in the chapters that follow, we will expand their meaning and discuss the methods behind them.

Summary

Managers must continually deal with many diverse situations. We would not all handle the same situation in the same way. It follows that the way we process information will be affected by human similarities and differences.

The steps we follow in the course of making a decision include gathering intelligence, identifying options, and selecting the preferred alternative. This process may involve the repetition of steps as the need for additional alternatives or better information is realized. Sometimes managers construct physical or symbolic models to better understand the situation at hand. Models allow them to focus their attention on the most important variables and to avoid being overloaded with details. It is particularly important to ensure that decision makers are not distracted by irrelevancies because people tend not to seek optimal decisions, but rather those that meet an acceptable level of achievement. The ability to search for better alternatives usually leads to higher quality decisions.

People are alike in that they have both long- and short-term memories, they process information serially, and they cannot use their intuition to produce accurate estimates of the probability of certain events or outcomes. When designing information systems, developers use such strategies as embedding models in the system, facilitating rapid retrieval of information, minimizing the details the user must remember to interact with the system, employing meaningful codes and sequences, and ensuring that the system does not get in the way of the user.

We also *differ* in how we process information. The mechanisms we use to deal with an information load vary from making errors to grouping details into manageable chunks. Our cognitive styles influence whether we are analytic or heuristic in our evaluation of situations. Our information gathering styles lead us to seek details or to espouse global outlooks. And we fall into the categories of being problem avoiders, problem resolvers, or problem finders. Information systems can be designed to address these concerns by using techniques that will highlight important details, allow data scanning, and present information in graphic form.

Management is typically viewed as consisting of the functions of planning, organizing, staffing, controlling, and communicating. Furthermore, we distinguish top, middle, and operating level managers, each having differing performance expectations and information needs. Since managers often work at a relentless pace, they are unable to spend a great deal of time in reflection. Thus information systems characteristics must fit the varying needs of each level of manager and the activities in which each is involved.

Management theories influence the emphasis individuals place on different activities, from managing routines to giving greater emphasis to the combined influence of technology, organization structure, people, and the task to be done. Often a contingency approach is adopted: the strategy selected depends on the features of a particular situation.

The way the organization is structured will influence its overall information processing capability. There are two general information processing strategies: (1) design the organization to reduce the need for information processing and

(2) increase the capacity of the firm to process information. Both are used by successful firms.

Information processing styles vary across successful organizations. But common to all such firms is the ability to provide individuals with the information they need to deal with customers, products, and the rest of the work environment and to ensure that information systems assist, not impede, the work. They also link information systems strategies with organization plans and furnish effective access to computer information systems.

Key Words

Analytic style	Management theory	Problem avoider
Contingency theory	Mathematical model	Problem finder
Field dependence	Middle-management	Problem resolver
Field independence	level	Rationality
Graphic model	Model	Satisficing
Heuristic style	Narrative model	Scientific management
Human relations era	Operating-management	era
Long-term memroy	level	Serial processing
Management	Organization theory	Short-term memory
Management functions	Parallel processing	Sociotechnical era
Management hierarchy	Physical model	Top-management level
Management science era	Planning	Uncertainty

Review Questions

1. In what ways do individuals differ in information processing abilities? In what ways are they the same?

2. What is a model? What are the different kinds of model? Which one is the simplest to use?

3. What is satisficing? Bounded rationality?

4. Compare the classical economic manager and administrative decision maker. What is the major difference between the assumptions that each makes?

5. Describe the three steps in the decision-making process.

6. What roles does information play in uncertainty reduction in decision making? What can an increase in information accomplish for a manager?

7. What common beliefs about management may be myths? Relate the myth to reality.

8. What relation do short- and long-term memories have to human decision-making limits?

9. Discuss the various limits on rational decision making.

10. How do managers differ in information gathering style? In information processing style?

11. People are poor intuitive statisticians. Why is this the case?

12. Into what different categories do managers fall in terms of their assessment of problems calling for action or decision making?

13. Given the human limitations of managers, what attributes should information systems have to ensure that effective decision making occurs?

14. What are the functions of management? Explain each briefly.

15. Describe the responsibilities and activities of each of the three levels of management. Which group is composed of the largest number of persons? Managers have been described as either doers or watchers. Relate these notions to the three levels of management.

16. What is the role of management theory in managing organizations? How do theories affect management's viewpoints on achieving goals and objectives?

17. How do the purposes of management theory and organization theory differ?

18. Briefly describe the theories of management discussed in this chapter. What role does management information play in each?

19. According to the sociotechnical view of the organization, what is interrelationship between the components of an organization?

20. Discuss the strategies for information systems that are associated with contingency theory in the structuring of organizations.

Application Problems

1. It is well known that people differ in the ability to process and use information. Some prefer to have the detail in front of them. Others want summary information, with rapid access to details if they have a question about any item. Still others wish to receive graphic, rather than numeric, information.
   a. Taken to its logical extreme, the foregoing suggests that each user of an information system should have a personalized report that is tailored to his or her capacity to process information and to the individual's preference in display formats. Yet this is not economically feasible when there are many users. How would you address or solve this dilemma?
   b. Does the importance of information in a form that fits human information processing characteristics change between transaction processing and decision support systems? Explain.

2. Managers are described as satisficers who frequently select alternatives that meet stated goals and policies but are not the best available alternatives.
   a. Explain why this description is accurate.
   b. Can computer processing assist managers to overcome the tendency toward satisficing? Explain.

3. A new manufacturing manager is preparing to study and evaluate the efficiency with which the production line of the department operates. Among the details the manager wishes to consider are the average time to produce one item from start to finish, the average amount of material that is damaged (and becomes scrap) during the production of one item, the flow of materials and parts from

machine to machine, and the average time that each work station spends on a particular product.

After becoming familiar with the details of the manufacturing process, the manager will establish standards that can be used for comparison with the actual performance levels. If the current operation is not at a high enough standard or level of efficiency, the manager will consider new alternative procedures and evaluate them on the basis of how they could change performance levels.

   a. What kinds of model can the manager use to assist in evaluating the current process?
   b. What kinds of model can the manager use to evaluate alternative new procedures and their impact on performance?
   c. Which of these models could be programmed for use in computer processing?

4. Implementing an information system not only changes the level of technology in the area of the firm in which it is installed, it also affects the workers, the structure of the organization, and the way a certain task is performed. It is claimed that these three components interact to damp out the full effect of the new information system.
   a. Does this mean that the full potential benefit from developing and installing an information system can never be realized?
   b. What design features should be considered to obtain maximum benefit from a new system under these circumstances?
   c. What organization and user considerations should be addressed in developing and installing an information system?

5. It is often argued that a manager's information requirements differ according to the level of the management hierarchy in which the individual functions. In particular, it is stated that lower-level managers require information in very detailed form while managers at the top level use summary information. Explain why this is true. Give several examples showing how the form of information changes as it moves up the hierarchy.

6. Listed below are typical operating procedures that might be prescribed in different kinds of organizations. For each, indicate whether on-line or batch processing systems would aid the manager in following the procedures. If so, indicate what file(s) would be needed.
   a. Order inventory only when the stock level has reached the reorder point calculated for inventory control.
   b. Check all customer credit purchases against the records before the transaction is completed (because the customer's credit privileges might have been revoked).
   c. Compare all new prescriptions with the drugs the patient is already taking to ensure that the medications will not counteract each other or cause undesired side effects.
   d. Add items to the agenda of the board of directors meeting before noon of the day of the meeting.
   e. Before hiring personnel from outside the company, check the records to see whether anyone already employed by the firm has the necessary training and wishes to transfer to the open position.

7. Discuss the value of batch and on-line processing in business operations at the top-, middle-, and operating-management levels for the different kinds of environment identified in this chapter.

Minicase: Sidekick®

Many managers are adding software programs to their personal computer that allow them to perform several tasks simultaneously. For example, Sidekick (Borland International), a very popular program that costs less than $100, can be loaded into the computer along with programs for word processing, database management, decision support, and so on. It runs behind the primary program invisibly, that is, in background mode.

When users need Sidekick, they can call it into action by a single keystroke. The executing program (for example, the word processing program) stops what it is doing and turns control over to Sidekick. An additional keystroke allows the user to invoke any of Sidekick's functions, including a notepad, a calculator, a telephone directory, and a perpetual calendar that can show dates in the past and years in advance. The function initiated takes over a portion of the display screen.

Consider the following situation. A writer preparing a newspaper article about the stock market is using the word processing capability of the personal computer. In composing a paragraph on the changing market prices, it develops that the percentage increase over the past three months would offer a useful example. Not being a math whiz, the writer strikes a key and invokes Sidekick's calculator function, enters the current and previous stock prices, and tells the computer to divide and convert the result to a percentage. When the answer is displayed on the screen, the writer strikes another key and returns to the word processing function, keying the percentage into the story before the number is forgotten.

A moment later, while working on the next paragraph, an idea for another story—one that is sure to sell—comes to mind. In an instant Sidekick's notepad is invoked and the idea is keyed into the notepad (with the same commands the word processor uses). In less than 15 seconds, the writer is back in the word processor again. If the idea had not been jotted down immediately, it might have been forgotten.

Each time the background program is triggered, a portion of the screen is blocked off for the calculator, notepad, calendar, and so on. The other part of the screen continues to display the information from the foreground program. When the writer invoked the notepad, it was displayed right over a portion of the story on the screen. But the rest of the story was visible, in case the writer needed to refer to it while in Sidekick. When the writer finished entering the note, the full screen of text on the word processor reappeared.

The writer never works at the personal computer without first loading Sidekick into the background of the system.

Questions

1. What features and capabilities of Sidekick are responsible for its usefulness? What human information processing characteristics does the program accommodate?

2. Since managers are described as working at a relentless pace, jumping from task to task, is software comparable to Sidekick a good idea for corporate decision making? If so, what features and functions might be suitable for this purpose?

Minicase: No Computer Here

A very successful Fortune 500 company executive officer is fond of saying "People are always surprised when they walk into my office. They expect to see a personal computer or terminal on my desk. But I don't have one. I tell them that the biggest problem managers face is having too much information. It overwhelms them and they do not know what to do with it. The key to success is not information, but people—good people."

The executive is also quick to point out that many managers forget that whatever comes out of a computer had to be entered by someone.

Questions

1. Why is this executive most likely correct that managers don't know what to do with the information they receive? Can the problem be avoided? Why or why not?

2. Is it more important to have good people than good information? Explain your reasoning and use examples to back up your answer.

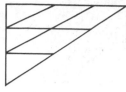

5: Computers: The Changing Frontier

Key Questions

What is the future of mainframe and personal computer systems?

How do computers process data and prepare information?

What factors distinguish personal computers from other classes of computers?

How do data enter the computer for processing?

What methods are preferred for interacting with computers?

What functions do the components of the central processing unit perform?

Are there alternatives to main memory storage?

At what speeds do computers process data?

How are optical storage and image processing changing the management of data?

The first general-purpose computer was built in the mid-1940s. It

───*Contained 18,000 vacuum tubes*
───*Weighed five tons*
───*Occupied six rooms*
───*Processed 10,000 instructions per second*
───*Required more than $5 million to build*

Today more processing power is available on a piece of silicon 5 mm square and costing less than $5 (available in an electronics store).

Few people in the United States, and even fewer organizations, are untouched by computers and information systems. They are now an integral part of everyday life, whether visibly or not. Today they are used by children in elementary schools in the learning of reading, writing, and arithmetic. Many universities are stipulating own-ership of a personal computer as a prerequisite for certain courses, and in some cases even for admission. In business, computers are a fundamental tool for the office, the warehouse, on the manufacturing floor, in the customer's office, and even in the executive suite. In many corporations, two out of every three desks will include a personal computer or management workstation.

In this chapter, we examine the components of computers. This will provide you with an understanding of what makes up a computer system and how the components work to process data. A great deal of new terminology will be introduced

Computer Systems Module

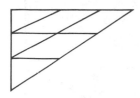

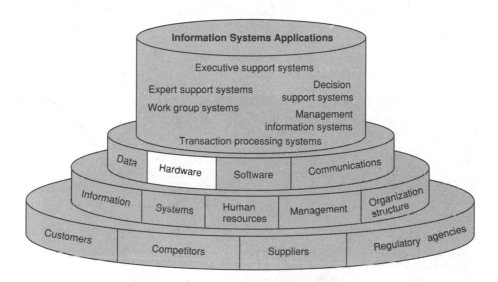

initially to familiarize you with computers and computing. The major elements of large and small computer systems will be examined from a practical viewpoint. We will see how data entry and input/output devices, the central processing unit, and secondary storage devices are used in computing and why they have contributed to so many amazing developments.

General Characteristics

Computers come in many sizes and price ranges (Table 5.1). Some you know are very small. Others—called mainframes and supercomputers—are much larger in size

Figure 5.1 Basic Computer Terms

Do you know what these terms mean?

Hardware	People	Software	Procedures
Central processing unit Configuration Mainframe Minicomputer Personal computer Workstation	Computer operator Computer programmer End-user Engineer Systems analyst Systems designer	Computer program Fourth-generation language Programming language Procedure-oriented language	Data preparation Input Output

Typical Midsize Computer Configuration

Table 5.1 Computer Cost and Performance Ranges

Class	Cost	Speed*
Microcomputer	$100 to $10,000	Up to 4 MIPS
Minicomputer	$5000 to $150,000	0.1 to 52 MIPS
Mainframe	$100,000 to $5,000,000	0.5 to 80 MIPS
Supercomputer	$2,500,000 to $25,000,000	300 megaflops to 10 gigaflops

*In millions of instructions per second (MIPS)

and capability. All have the same basic characteristics. This section introduces some terms (Figure 5.1) that are essential for gaining a better understanding of computers and data processing. The Computer Systems Module explores the related ideas in more detail.

In a general sense, computer-based data processing systems are characterized by four elements: hardware, software, procedures, and people. Each element is an integral part of the system and must be present for effective and efficient processing of transaction and decision-making data.

Hardware

The term **hardware** refers to the equipment and devices that actually process data. Used singularly, the term may refer to any single piece of equipment, while in a collective sense *hardware* may mean all the equipment in a data processing operation. We look at many of the pieces of equipment used in a computer system in this chapter.

Hardware is used to perform the functions of data entry, computation, control of computation, storage, and output (presentation or display) of results. Some of the hardware units common to a data processing system are shown in the accompanying photograph. The specific hardware used for any individual data processing installation is referred to as a **configuration.** When individual devices are coupled directly to a computer, they are said to be *on-line;* equipment that is not attached is *off-line.* Many data preparation devices, for example, are off-line. Devices such as key-to-disk systems are used to prepare data off-line. After the data have been prepared, they can be input (fed into the computer) through on-line devices.

Software

Computer users as well as computer specialists often refer to software packages when they discuss how a system will be used. *Packages* are computer programs purchased from computer stores or from vendors. For example, a manager of a small business who wants to install an accounting system on the computer will typically buy from a computer store an accounting software package that can perform the necessary accounting tasks.

Software is the general term describing programs of instructions, languages, and routines or procedures that make it possible for an individual to use the computer. In a general sense, software is any prepared set of instructions that controls the operation of the computer system for computation and processing. The term is often applied only to commercially prepared packages, as opposed to user-prepared instructions. Commercially prepared programs are developed by manufacturers or companies that specialize in software. Their primary purpose is to control all processing activities and to make sure that the resources and power of the computer are used in the most efficient manner. In Chapter 7, we examine in greater detail some of the software used to control processing.

Computer programs are sets of coded instructions that cause the computer to perform a series of operations that accomplishes a specific purpose. For example, a computer program may be developed to perform the operations of multiplication and addition in the calculation of weekly payrolls. The hours worked for each individual are multiplied by the hourly wage rate, giving the gross wage of the individual for the week. If the company wishes to compute a total wage expense, the sum of wages for all hourly personnel can be calculated. Each of these steps can be spelled out clearly in a computer program.

The programs are written in **programming languages,** specially developed languages or commands that make it possible to specify calculations and other processing in terminology that can be converted to particular operations by the computer system. The most common programming languages in use are **procedure-oriented languages** (those that allow the user to specify the procedure to be followed in processing data). These languages, such as BASIC, COBOL, FORTRAN, and PL/1, specify a set of operations or activities to be performed in sequence. The user need not be concerned with how the operations are carried out inside the computer. Because the languages allow specification of instructions at a relatively high level of notation (that is, they are close to normal English and/or use everyday arithmetic expressions), they are easy to learn and can be applied on computer systems of a number of different kinds.

Fourth-generation languages are in widespread use to supplement procedure-oriented programming languages. Such languages, discussed in detail in Chapter 7, allow users to develop sophisticated programs for retrieval of data with only a fraction of the instructions needed when programs are written in procedure-oriented languages. Because they are much easier to use than traditional programming languages, fourth-generation languages are frequently utilized by nonprogrammers (such as managers). Their use has given rise to more direct involvement of users in computing—a development often referred to as **end-user computing.**

Procedures

For a computer-based data processing system to be functional and effective, clear operating procedures are needed to define how computer resources and equipment are to be used to satisfy the needs of everyone using the system. Standard operating procedures set forth the normal day-to-day activities, and emergency procedures carefully describe steps to be taken in the event of hardware failure, fire, or other disaster.

People

One type of participant in the computer systems environment has already been identified—the end-user. End-users take the results of data processing and sometimes develop their own systems for retrieval of data from a computer. However, they are not computer specialists, nor are they part of the information systems center.

The personnel of an information systems center include systems analysts, systems designers, programmers, computer operators, and engineers. Collectively, their jobs ensure continued operation of the center under varying conditions and satisfaction of users' demands and needs. The *systems analyst/designer* is responsible for examining user requirements, designing processing systems, and specifying what activities should be performed in the computer programs to be developed. He or she frequently assumes the additional responsibility of training end-users to handle the system. The *programmer* translates program requirements into effective and efficient sets of machine-processible code, that is, computer programs. (We study the role of these people in greater depth in the Information Systems Management Module.)

Computer operators and *engineers* are directly responsible for the operation of the data processing system. The computer operator simply performs the jobs that make it possible for the system to function, including input of data and programs and removal of output from the machine. Engineers are troubleshooters who keep the system running. Their job is to replace or repair malfunctioning components and equipment and to do routine preventive maintenance. The effectiveness with which they perform this job affects the entire data processing operation.

Because of the tremendous growth in data processing, there is an overwhelming demand for trained people to work in the field (see boxed insert). There is no end in sight to the demand, and therefore it is a very good career area. The work is interesting, the opportunities exciting, and the experiences challenging.

Information Systems Careers and Occupations

Many of tomorrow's occupations will be different from those of today. This is true for information-system-related careers too. However, the work of many persons in the computer field will dramatically affect the work of persons in other fields. Thus, people in data processing will have a profound influence on business and society—they will change society as we know it today. And remember, these jobs did not even exist until the 1950s, only 40 years ago. (How long have there been physicians, accountants, and teachers?)

Systems Analysts/Designers Many business activities and scientific research projects depend on the development of ways to process data, produce information, and communicate that information to managers. This is the role of the systems analyst. Analysts begin an application by discussing the design area with managers or employees to determine the exact nature of the desired application. They break it down into its component parts so that each one can be understood. If a new inventory system is desired, for example, systems analysts must determine what data need to be collected, how they should be processed, which equipment to use, and how to present results to users. In doing this, they draw on their abilities in such areas as accounting, organizational behavior, model building, and business administration.

Information Systems Careers and Occupations (continued)

Once information needs are understood, proposals are presented to users for their approval. The proposals contain the logical "blueprint" of the system. If accepted, the logical requirements are put into specifications for programmers to follow in developing and "debugging" application software.

Some analysts work on systems improvement. They develop better procedures or adapt the application to handle additional types of data or produce different information. Others do research to develop better tools for doing systems analysis and design.

The problems analysts/designers work on vary and can span several fields. As a result, they usually specialize in either business or scientific and engineering applications. In some firms, programmer/analysts will do both problem definition and development of software.

The demand for college-trained systems analysts/designers is expanding rapidly. Organizations in business and government cannot find enough well-trained persons in these areas. It is expected that the job opportunities for systems analysts will continue to grow faster than average in the 1990s.

Figure A shows the tremendous growth in demand for trained systems analysts.

Programmers Computers can process vast quantities of data rapidly and accurately. But they can do this only when they have step-by-step instructions. Computer programmers are responsible for developing these sets of instructions, since computers cannot think for themselves. The programs list, in logical order, each step that the computer must follow to organize data, process the data to produce necessary information, and communicate the results to users.

Computer programmers usually work from problem descriptions prepared by systems analysts who have studied the task to be handled. The programmer therefore is responsible for bringing an application "to life." *Application programmers* work on business, engineering, or scientific-oriented applications, although they usually specialize in one of these areas. In contrast, *systems programmers* work on programs of instructions that control the operation of the entire computer system. The programs they develop allocate the equipment and resources among the set of applications that are to be processed during a period of time. Because of their knowledge of operating systems, systems programmers often help application programmers determine the source of problems that may occur within their programs.

The demand for good programmers in all areas is expanding, as shown in Figure A.

Computer Operating Personnel All computer centers employ people who prepare data and programs, operate the computer itself, and retrieve and distribute results. Data entry personnel punch instructions or data into cards or onto storage media. In some cases, they interact directly with the computer to do this. They may also work away from the computer (on manufacturing floors, in libraries, in medical clinics, and so on). The demand for keypunch operators has decreased dramatically due to new data entry methods. However, as Figure B shows, the demand for other computer operating personnel is increasing along with the growth of computer data processing.

Other employees run the system directly. Console operators, for example, monitor and control the computer, deciding what equipment should be set up for each job. To process the input, they make sure magnetic tapes or disks are mounted, and that printers and card readers are operable. While the system is running they watch the computer console, paying

Information Systems Careers and Occupations (continued)

special attention to signals or lights that call their attention to errors or problems. If the system "goes down" or an error is signaled, the operators either fix the problem or call an engineer who will troubleshoot the system.

General Outlook As the computer field continues to expand, the need for trained personnel will expand with it. Universities and colleges, along with business and industry, are constantly developing new tools and techniques to aid systems specialists. As a result, the field is constantly changing and so are the people in it. The past two decades have seen a great many remarkable changes in computing. The next 20 years will see at least as many more changes. Opportunities in the computing industry will grow accordingly.

Figure A Employment Demand for Systems Development Personnel (*Source:* Bureau of Labor Statistics)

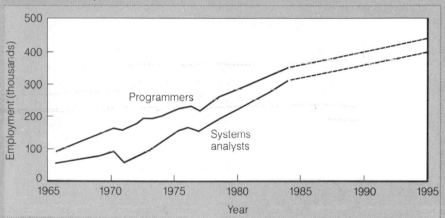

Figure B Employment Demand for Computer Equipment and Data Entry Operators (*Source:* Bureau of Labor Statistics)

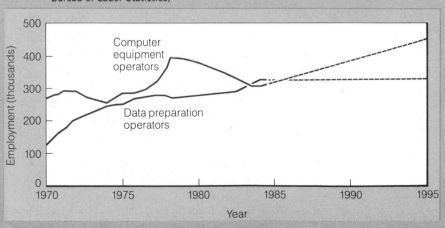

Classes of Computer Systems

The term *computer* has come to designate systems in any of several different classes. When the first computer system was introduced for business applications in the mid-1950s, however, the only alternative was a large system—often one that filled a room. And predictions were that only a handful of computers would be needed to meet business needs.

But today there are millions of computers installed around the world, and the number is growing by several million annually (see box, "Will Mainframes Disappear?"). And *computer* may now refer to a system in one of several different classes: personal computers, minicomputers, mainframe systems, and supercomputers. We explore the differences between classes of computers, emphasizing the circumstances under which each system should be considered for installation.

Personal Computers

Personal computers, or microcomputers, have become more common in business than the office copier and are predicted to soon be on two out of every three desks in many large corporations. These systems have all of the features of other classes of computers, although their storage capacities and processing speeds are generally lower. Yet today's personal computer has much greater processing power than larger systems of a few years ago, and at a fraction of the cost. (**Microprocessors,** discussed in the box, are the key to the combination of low cost and attractive processing power.)

Personal computers suitable for business use cost from $1000 to $15,000, although some home versions can be purchased for as little as $100. Additional **peripheral devices,** such as printers, add another $1000 to $5000 to the total cost. Considering the processing speed and storage capabilities that come with such a system, however, the price is remarkably attractive.

Personal computers use flexible, hard, and optical disks (explained later in this chapter). Cassette tapes are sometimes used to store backup copies of stored data as well. With these media, personal computers can store from 100,000 to more than 100 million characters of data on magnetic media. This is in contrast to typical main memory storage of from 512,000 characters up to approximately four million.

For less than $5000 you can invest in a personal computer that will do accounting, inventory control, word processing, and budgeting for business. It will also allow use of **spreadsheets**—electronic versions of an accountant's columnar worksheet, with computer processing built in. (Spreadsheets and other personal computer software are discussed in Chapter 6.)

Laptop computers are smaller than a typical attaché case. And they literally fit on your lap, even on the serving tray at a passenger's seat on an aircraft. Yet they have the same capabilities and capacities as other personal computers.

Workstations are a special type of microcomputer, known for their processing power and use of high-quality graphics. These systems, priced from approximately $7500 to $25,000, are typically used in design tasks, such as the design of buildings, manufactured products, and automobiles. Workstations are often used as stand-alone systems. However, they can be linked together through networks, facilitating the sharing of data and printers.

Midrange Computers

Midrange computers are also small and powerful and relatively inexpensive. Many cost less than a full-size automobile. Some midrange systems (also known as **mini-computers**) are the size of an ordinary office desk and a few models are small enough to sit on top of a desk (as a personal computer often does). Midrange systems generally have several hundred thousand storage locations in the main memory. As with other computers, various input/output and secondary storage devices can be attached. These computer systems range in price from less than $10,000 to $150,000.

Midrange computers are often stand-alone systems. They are also serving important roles in office environments as work group systems (see Chapter 15). However, like personal computers, they can be used to communicate with large computers, transmitting data or results.

Mainframe Computers

Mainframe computers are the large, general-purpose systems that have been traditionally associated with business. They are often classified as medium-size and large-scale systems.

Medium-size mainframes cost up to $1 million each. Prices vary due to the different equipment that can be used in the system; we discuss the various kinds of equipment in this chapter. There are from 24,000 to several million storage locations. Medium- and large-scale computer systems (in contrast to mini- and personal computers) are almost always set up in their own rooms—spaces that would be large enough to seat several hundred people.

Large-scale computers, long the pride of many manufacturers, are the most expensive of all systems, costing several million dollars to purchase and renting for up to $250,000 per month (other systems are seldom rented). Some of the biggest systems have more than 30 billion storage locations (with trillion-bit memories on the horizon).

These computers are very fast, able to execute millions of instructions in a single second. Because many secondary storage devices can be attached to extend main memory, storage is virtually limitless. The big systems are flexible, too, able to process programs written in many different languages and capable of doing processing for multiple users simultaneously.

Supercomputers

The term **supercomputer** is generally applied to the largest systems available at any time. Typically supercomputers are characterized by large memories, extremely rapid processing speeds, and multiple processors. Current models cost more than $10 million, and rental of an entire system is out of the question for private individuals.

Will Mainframes Disappear?

The computer industry has been going through a giant transformation for the past decade or more—one that has been hard for anyone to miss, whether end-user or computer professional.

Personal Computers in the Spotlight Personal computers are the focus of attention, often at the expense of mainframe systems. But will they supplant them? Asking that simple question will often instantly bring about a vigorous debate. This special insert explores both sides of the issue.

Personal computers burst onto the business scene in the late 1970s and early 1980s. At first used only by the most ardent enthusiasts, these systems received serious acceptance in 1982, when IBM introduced its personal computer. Since then, the use of personal computers in a wide variety of applications has created an industry segment where the revenues have been greater than those of mainframes since 1984. And the difference is growing.

The key to the upheaval is the microprocessor chip (see Table 5.2). Microcomputer chips (such as the Intel 8088, 80286, 80386, and 80486 used in IBM-compatible personal computers, and the Motorola 68020 and 68030, used by Apple Computer) have always been much cheaper than mainframe components, but they have also been limited in power. Hence the predominant applications for early personal computers were word processing and electronic spreadsheet analysis. Today, however, the speed and power are there, often equaling those found on mainframe systems costing several hundred thousand dollars. And the power is increasing quickly. (IBM has boasted that its Personal System/2 Model 80, selling for less than $10,000, has the raw processing speed of its 1970s-vintage 370/168 mainframe—a system that sold for $3.5 million.) Applications previously pursued on mainframes are being considered for development on personal computers: database management, manufacturing design, and so on.

Simple economics have changed the view of computer sharing. When multimillion dollar mainframes dominated the industry, the usage rule was clear: link as many terminals as possible with the mainframe, because processing power is dear. Today, the new chips and power of desktop computers and the inexpensive availability of computing power makes it attractive and feasible to do a great variety of tasks on the desktop.

Table 5.2 Computer Chips in Widespread Use

Chip	Manufacturer	Example of Use	Year Introduced
8088	Intel	IBM-compatible PCs	1981
80286	Intel	IBM-compatible PCs	1984
80386	Intel	IBM-compatible PCs	1986
80486	Intel	IBM-compatible PCs	1989
68000	Motorola	Apple Macintosh	1984
68020	Motorola	Apple Macintosh	1986
68030	Motorola	Apple Macintosh	1988

Will Mainframes Disappear? (continued)

End-users like the responsiveness of personal computers. Since these computers are not shared with other individuals, users receive almost an instant response to a command. They also like having control over the system in contrast to interacting with an invisible mainframe system located in a computer room elsewhere (perhaps not even in the same building).

Off-the-shelf software too is available to handle personal computing tasks. Rather than waiting for a member of the information systems staff to develop an application—a wait that can takes months and years because of work backlogs—users can develop many applications with commercially available software. Many also find they like working with PC programs better than mainframe programs (they appear friendlier).

Mainframes Will Not Disappear Despite the advantages and important features of personal computers, most experts do not predict the demise of mainframes. In fact, their sales continue to grow (see Figure A), although the high growth of the past will not reappear (PCs have taken over applications that would have increased growth rates).

For certain tasks, mainframes will continue to be the best tool. The storage of large volumes of information, such as databases of product inventory and manufacturing information or customer details, is best done on a mainframe. And the mainframe systems also excel at sorting through these large volumes of information.

Large systems are virtually indispensable for the management of large computer networks, which often include many personal computers attached to the network. Airline reservations systems and the banking industry's automated teller systems (ATMs) cannot be managed without mainframes. Applications like these are growing and thus are stimulating mainframe demand.

Similarly, where high volumes of transaction processing are common, you will continue to find mainframes. Nationwide order processing systems, for instance, are not candidates for personal computing.

The mainframe era is fading insofar as these computers have been the dominant force in computer information systems, though. Instead, both personal computers and mainframes will play central and important roles, even though personal computer revenues will continue to grow faster than mainframe revenues.

Figure A 10-Year View: Value of Installed Mainframes Worldwide (*Source:* International Data Corp.)

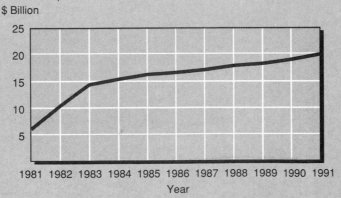

Thus in the United States, a number of universities that have been designated as centers for supercomputers receive financial support from a variety of sources in return for permitting access by researchers around the country. Supercomputers are typically used in selected corporate and U.S. government research and development centers and in such public service centers as the National Weather Service.

Processing Speeds

There is a strong correlation between the size of the computer and the speed at which it operates. The large systems operate in the realm of **picoseconds** and **nanoseconds.** A picosecond is one-trillionth of a second; a nanosecond is one-billionth of a second. To give you a better idea of just how short these fractional seconds are, compare them to a full second. A nanosecond is to 1 second what 1 second is to *30 years*. To use another example, light travels at the rate of 186,000 miles per second. During a nanosecond, light will travel less than 1 foot! You can hardly blink an eye in a few nanoseconds, which is about how long it takes the contents of a spilled cup of coffee on a desk to reach the floor; but in the same flash, a large-scale computer can add many large numbers together accurately.

The other computer systems, although very fast, often do not reach the speeds of the larger systems. Their speeds are often measured in **microseconds** (millionths of a second). Input/output operations to and from secondary storage occur as **milliseconds** (thousandths of a second).

As computer technology continues to advance, the distinctions between various computers will become blurred. For instance, many personal computers have the same processing power (measured in **MIPS**—millions of instructions per second) found in mainframe computers of a few years ago. Supercomputer processing is measured in **gigaflops**—billions of operations per second.

Size and speed are often used to compare different systems. But the system used should be selected on the basis of the work it will do in an organization or for an individual user.

Major Elements of a System

The basic physical hardware elements in a computer system can be divided into the categories of input/output devices, the central processing unit, and secondary storage devices. All these elements together make processing data and producing output possible.

Data collected for processing must first be translated into a form that can be accepted by the computer system. Then they are *input* (fed) to the computer system through some type of device. The type of **input device** depends on whether the data will be directly keyed into the system or input from a document or form.

The **central processing unit (CPU)** is the control and computational element of the computer system. (This component is what many people mean when they use the term *computer*.) All arithmetic operations take place in the three subunits of the

Figure 5.2 Major Elements in a Computer System

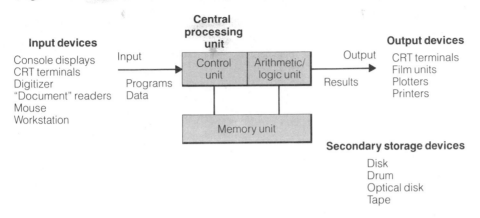

CPU: the **primary storage** or **memory unit**, the **arithmetic/logic unit**, and the **control unit** (Figure 5.2).

Not all data are held in primary storage. The amount of data may be too large to be held there, or the data may not be needed at a particular moment. Such excess data are held in **secondary storage units**, which are not part of the central processor. These cost less than primary storage and can significantly extend data storage capacity.

Output devices transfer the results of processing data (the **output**) from the computer to the user. A number of different devices have been developed and are in common use in business and organizations today. Each device is coordinated and controlled by the central processing unit.

The electronic computer can hold data and execute instructions to manipulate data with amazing speed and accuracy. Furthermore, the computer has a built-in capability to move data and instructions around so that it can complete the required operations most efficiently. And none of this movement is performed mechanically. All operations are electronic in the sense that switches, wires, and circuitry are controlled by electronic pulses or signals. All data representation and execution instructions are therefore based on the principles of electricity and magnetism. But this does not mean that you have to be an electrical engineer or a physicist to use a computer system—in fact, such training probably would not help at all.

In addition to being fast and accurate, the modern computer system can hold large quantities of data that can be accessed, or retrieved, in just a fraction of a second. The way in which the data are stored depends on the design of the computer system. However, the sequence or order in which operations occur is determined by a user-supplied computer program.

The computer does not have its own brain, as is sometimes thought. Rather, all activities and operations must be spelled out in detail, and it is the *computer program* that dictates what operations are performed and in what sequence. Without some kind of program, it would be virtually impossible to process any data.

Although when compared to a human being, the computer is faster, can store more data, and operates with a very high level of accuracy, it does not have auton-

Table 5.3 Computer and Human Capabilities

Computer Capabilities	Human Capabilities
Rapid processing	Intuition and judgment
Accuracy	Flexibility and adaptiveness
Large storage capacity	Responsiveness to unforeseen events
Effectiveness for recurring tasks	Abstract thought
Automatic	Planning and goal setting
Can run (nearly) continuously	Pattern recognition
Surveillance to detect exceptional conditions	Procedure and control establishment
Can be improved and upgraded	Capacity to read the *Wall Street Journal*
Can do only what it is told	

omous reasoning ability and cannot think intuitively (Table 5.3). Its great speed and accuracy do, however, make it a very useful tool for assisting people in business and other organizations.

Example of Using a Computer in Business

To better understand the interrelation of computers, business, and people, we will examine a common daily use of the computer in organizations: the preparation of orders for customers. The steps in order processing, as business terms this activity, are as follows (Figure 5.3):

1. Determine customer's requirement.
2. Find out the item's price and see whether the item is on hand.
3. Enter the order into the computer and have it processed.
4. Prepare an invoice.
5. Change the inventory quantity on hand to reflect the sale.
6. Store the details of the sale.

These activities will be similar whether the order processing is handled in a manual or a computerized environment. For our purposes, we assume that the business uses a desktop microcomputer for orders. And as we will see, most information processing activities combine manual and computer steps.

The sales representative must determine what item(s) the customer wishes. Only then can the computer be used to determine whether the merchandise is available. To accomplish this, details of the item are entered into the computer through the keyboard. As details are entered, they are shown on the video display terminal (Figure 5.4). Depending on how the system was designed (systems design is discussed in Chapters 16 and 17), the person using the system may "key in" a description of the product, an identifying product number, or a special code for the item. The *application*

Figure 5.3 Order Processing Activities

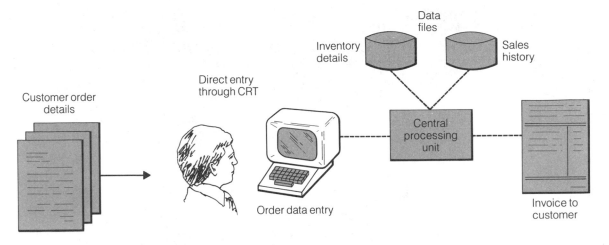

Figure 5.4 Inquiry Handling with Computer Display

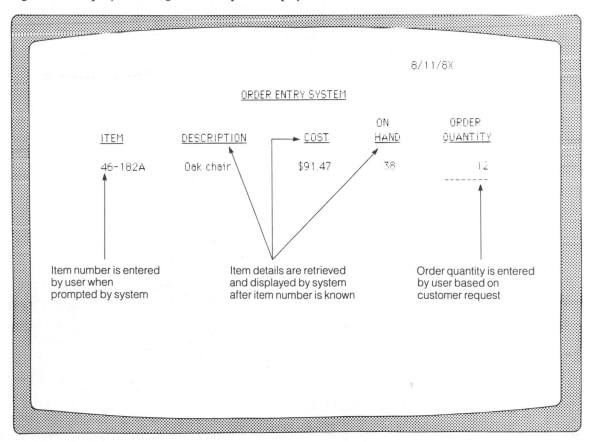

Storage of Data on Magnetic Disk

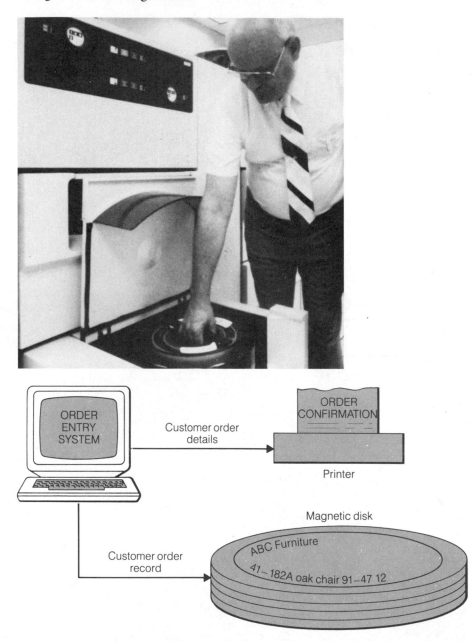

program will process the request, which is called an *inquiry,* and respond with a message on the display screen. As Figure 5.4 shows, this system has been designed and programmed to respond with a description of the item, its cost, and the quantity on hand in inventory.

Using the information on the screen, the sales agent verifies the customer's order and requests the system to process an order for a specific quantity. A copy of the transaction is prepared on a printer, one of the most common computer output devices, and given to the customer. In addition, the details of the transaction are stored on magnetic disk, an auxiliary storage device that supplements the main memory storage of the computer (accompanying photo).

The steps just described typify those associated with information systems. The participants and components are:

PEOPLE   Customer buying the items
Sales representative using the computer

HARDWARE   Input device: computer keyboard
Output devices: video display screen; printer
Auxiliary storage: flexible diskette drives
Microcomputer containing processing unit

SOFTWARE   Order entry application program
System control software (see Chapter 6)

PROCEDURES Manual: determine customer's requirements; enter item identification into system; verify order information with customer
Automated: process inquiry for item and quantity details; process order for customer; prepare printed invoice; accumulate transaction details on magnetic disk

Keep this example in mind as we examine in greater detail the various devices associated with computing and the way in which a computer operates. We will look at input and output activities next.

Input/Output of Data

As we saw earlier, data that are to be operated on by the central processing unit must be input to the system in a way that the system can understand. This process is called **data entry.** Data recorded in symbols that humans can read are converted into electronic signals that the computer accepts. After the conversion, the data are processed by the central processing unit.

There are differences in the equipment used to enter data. For convenience, we examine them in the categories of direct entry devices and document-oriented equipment.

Direct Entry Input Equipment Most organizations use the computer, regardless of size, by direct entry of data and instructions. The most common devices in this category are video display terminals (VDTs). Such input devices often are called **cathode ray tubes (CRTs).** A CRT (or simply "the terminal") looks like a television tube attached to a keyboard (much like an ordinary typewriter keyboard). The terminal may be a single unit containing the keyboard or the keyboard may be separate, connected by a short cable (see accompanying photo, p. 154).

Video Display Terminal with Detachable Keyboard

Video displays present information in a single color (often called a monochrome display) or in several colors (see Table 5.4). Color terminals capable of displaying from 4 to 16 distinct colors are most common, although with proper software the range may be expanded to several million shades.

Input is entered into the terminal through the keyboard and transmitted to the computer over cable. In small systems, such as microcomputers and personal com-

Table 5.4 Types of Graphic Boards/Monitors

Type	Acronym	Resolution Pixels (dots) per inch	Number of Colors
Monochrome	MDA	720 × 350 (no graphics)	monochrome (1 color)
Color graphics adapter	CGA	320 × 200	16
Enhanced graphics adapter	EGA	640 × 350	16
Video graphics array	VGA	640 × 480	16 (256?)

Mouse for Data Entry

puters, the terminal is attached directly to the main system unit. In larger computer environments, however, cables and telephone lines may be used to link the terminal to the more distant system. (Data communication methods are examined in Chapter 9.)

Data keyed into the system appear simultaneously on the display screen. This allows operators to see that they have entered the correct data.

Sometimes data entry is facilitated by the use of a **mouse** (accompanying photo), a lightweight device that fits in the palm of the hand and is connected to the computer or workstation by a wire. A roller or sensor on the bottom of the mouse enables the user to move it across a flat surface, causing the system to interpret the movement as an instruction to reposition the **cursor,** the spot of light on the display screen that tells the operator where the system is pointing.

Suppose you have a menu of choices for instructing the computer what action to take next in processing a customer sales order: (1) print the invoice; (2) enter an item; (3) stop processing. Using a mouse, the operator can move the cursor up and down the screen. To select option 2, "Enter an item," the operator moves the mouse until the cursor on the display screen is pointing at the menu option. When the button on top of the mouse is depressed, the system senses the signal to begin processing and it prepares to accept another item.

As this example demonstrates, the mouse provides an alternative to keying data into a computer. The mouse was pioneered by Xerox Corporation but is in wide-

Data Entry Using Light Pen

spread use on many personal computers and on workstations of larger computer systems.

Often a **light pen** (accompanying photo), looking much like an ordinary pen or pencil, is attached to a terminal for use in special applications. The light pen is connected to the terminal at one end by a wire. On the other end is a tip containing a small photosensitive element that looks like a small metal ball slightly larger than the head of a pin. The photosensitive element is the part of the light pen that actually performs the input work. When the tip touches the display screen, it creates a change in electrical currents and in this way registers the data to be input.

Light pens are often found in engineering and architectural environments, where they are used for designing automobiles, machines, and buildings. The design can be drawn on the screen using the pen and input into the system for processing (such as for structural analysis).

Light pens are also used to select answers on multiple-choice exams presented on the display, to order merchandise from warehouses, and to enter accounting data into a system. The designer may include a light pen in the design of a system for the benefit of users who are uncomfortable with typing data on a keyboard.

Have you ever wondered how computers are programmed to show symbols and graphic signs (such as corporate logos and symbols, maps, or cartoon characters)? Often **digitizers** are used to enter the data into a computer (see photo). As the digitizer scans a graphic shape, each point, dot, or line is translated into data that can be stored in the computer.

Digitizer Commonly Used for Data Entry

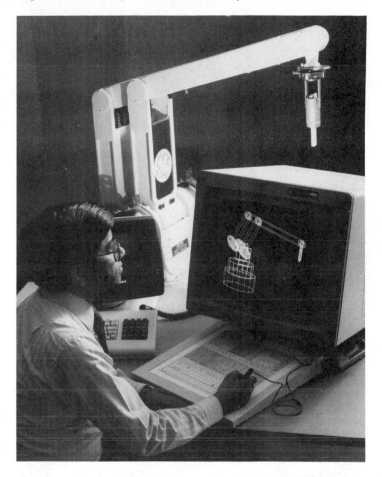

Some terminals are actually small computers in their own right. That is, they have internal processing and storage capability. The names assigned to such data entry devices vary. They may be termed **intelligent** (or "smart") **terminals,** in contrast to "dumb" terminals, which communicate but do not store or process data. Increasingly terminals of this caliber are referred to as *workstations*. Built-in memory and processing capability enable checking of data before their entry into the processing system. The microprocessors perform simple arithmetic operations and assist in finding errors in input data so that corrections can be made before the data are sent to the CPU.

Some intelligent terminals are dedicated to perform only specific tasks. One special kind of intelligent terminal is the **point-of-sale terminal,** used in the retailing industry. Computer terminals, which might have special-purpose keys like those on an ordinary cash register (for sales department, sales person's number, merchandise

Bar Code and Reader

stock number, and so on) are used to capture data about each transaction as the sale is taking place so that inventory levels can be monitored and the volume of sales transactions easily determined. These terminals are often used in conjunction with scanning devices like a light pen or wand, to speed the sales process and to minimize errors.

The grocery industry uses a bar code, the **Universal Product Code (UPC)**, for almost all products sold in the typical supermarket (see photo). Each item is identified by the familiar series of black stripes in varying patterns of wide and narrow. The bar code is printed on packages by the manufacturer. With the advent of point-of-sale transaction processing, it is possible to use a point-of-sale terminal to read the bar code and retrieve the price of the product from the memory of a small computer. Not only does this eliminate the need for stamping prices on each individual can or box, but it also makes it feasible to update inventory levels immediately so that the grocer always knows how many units of a certain item are on the shelf.

Scanners are also used to enter data into the computer (see Figure 5.5). Often used with personal computers and desktop publishing systems (see Chapter 6 for a more extensive discussion of desktop publishing), scanners enable the user to transmit an image from a paper document to the computer screen, where it can be inserted into an existing document or manipulated into a new image. For example, when a document is created for publication, a photograph can be scanned into the computer

Figure 5.5 Processing with Image Data

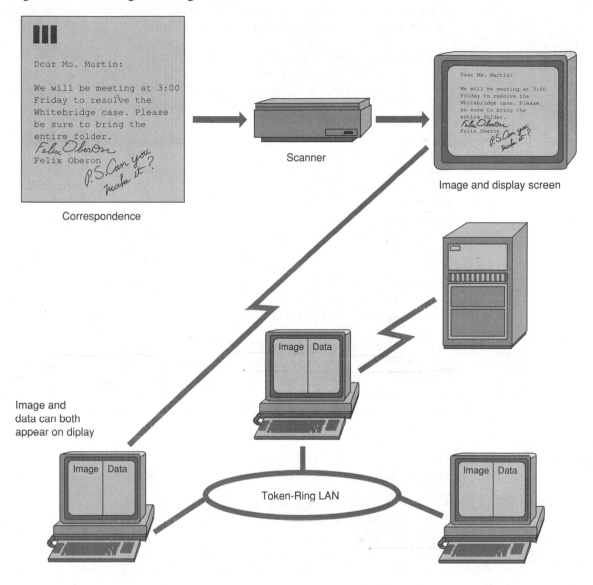

Scanner

Correspondence

Image and display screen

Image and
data can both
appear on diplay

Token-Ring LAN

and embedded within the text. Doing so eliminates the need for pasting in the photograph or manually changing its size to fit, a task that can also be done using the computer.

In addition, business and government organizations are planning increased use of scanners for capturing documents—even correspondence—in computer processable form (Figure 5.5). Once scanned into the system, they can be stored, transmitted over communication networks, or reprinted, including annotations or modifications made by users. Through this means, several individuals can share an image of the document at the same time.

Other direct input devices include typewriter terminals and *teletypes*. The user enters data or instructions by typing them on the keyboard, which contains keys for alphabetic, numeric, and special characters, and the terminal transmits the input to the processing unit. Output appears at the terminal printed on paper.

Document-Oriented Input Equipment Direct entry of data is not always desirable. For example, a bank must process many checks every day—often numbering in the millions—and it would not be cost effective to hire enough check processors to key in all the details of each check (bank number, account number, check number, date, and check amount). Instances abound of data already recorded on documents—bank checks, sales slips, and so on. It is more practical to design the system so that the computer, through document-oriented input equipment, reads the data into memory. You might consider the wand on a point-of-sale device to be document oriented: It reads printed product data from a package. The scanner discussed earlier is also document oriented: It scans images on documents into computer memory. Other common document devices are optical character readers and magnetic ink character readers. In the past, punched cards (another type of document) were in widespread use.

The **optical character reader (OCR)** (see photo) senses data that appear in predetermined locations on documents and converts the characters into electronic pulses. Optical character readers generally use an electronic light beam to sense images recorded on the documents as the beam moves back and forth. Differences in images, sensed as light is reflected from the document back to a sensing mechanism in the reader, are transformed into electronic pulses that the computer system can act on.

Many optical character readers are designed to read handwritten, printed, and typed data from documents. Consequently, there is growing use of optical character recognition for check, cash register input, sales slip, utility bill, and ticket processing. The trend toward optical character recognition is expected to continue.

Closely related to the optical character reader is the **magnetic ink character reader (MICR)**, designed to detect characters that are printed in magnetic ink. The magnetic ink images set up a magnetic field in the machine that can be transformed into an electronic signal for input to the processor. As the documents are scanned and read, they are sorted into hoppers in the machine.

The most common user of MICRs is the banking industry, which handles nearly all check processing in this way. The American Banking Association closely monitors the process to make sure the account numbering systems, the location of the numbers on the checks, and the style of type are similar so that the checks can be processed at any bank in the country.

Mark-sense documents (see Figure 5.6) constitute another method of data input. These forms contain preestablished fields or positions that are blackened by a dark pencil to represent data. You probably are familiar with mark-sense documents.

Optical Character Reader

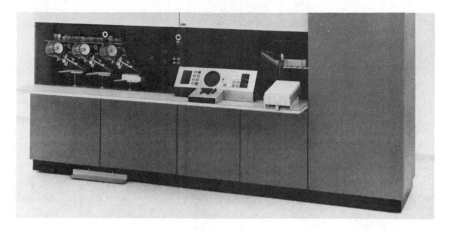

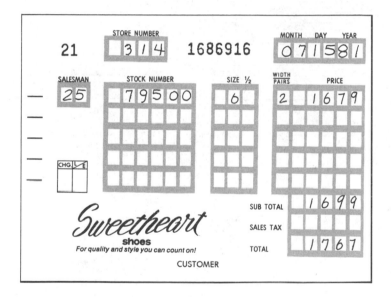

Students in large classes often take multiple-choice, computer-graded examinations in which lead pencil marks on a special sheet of paper encode each test taker's answers. The mark-sense documents thus produced can be processed by computer.

The mechanization of data processing gained a strong foothold as a result of the work of Herman Hollerith at the U.S. Census Bureau. Hollerith introduced the process of punching data into cards, which could then be processed by a machine, and for many years these cards constituted the most common input medium. The term "unit record processing" is also used because each card is a record of data—say, from a transaction. In *punched card processing* machines punch small holes in cards that can later be read by the computer. Punched card systems are now obsolete.

Figure 5.6 An Example of a Mark-Sense Document

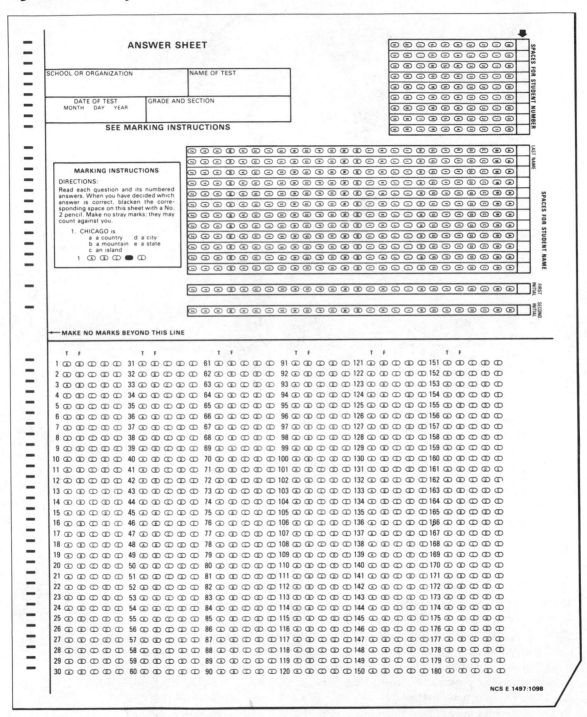

Data Entry Workgroup

Key-to-tape and **key-to-disk** devices have replaced punched card data preparation when keyed data are required. This equipment records data on a magnetic storage device, such as magnetic tape or a magnetic disk (discussed in greater detail later in this chapter), rather than on punched cards. The data are entered through keyboard-like devices, which may have special keys to set tabs, formats, and similar aids (see photo). As the data are entered, they are displayed on a small screen so that the operator can visually check for errors. Then they are stored on the magnetic tape or disk. In most cases, this operation is verified by a second person, who checks again for errors.

Data Preparation Bottleneck Data input preparation is a major **bottleneck** in most data processing operations. This buildup of a backlog of data to be prepared for input occurs because data cannot be prepared for input as fast as they can be read or accepted by the computer. In addition to data preparation delays, the time it takes to prepare and verify each input document is very costly.

To reduce the data preparation bottleneck, the following features should be incorporated into a system design:

Macintosh Computer with Multiple Windows Open

1. Provide for direct entry of small amounts of data into the system as events occur.
2. Provide for automatic examination of data for errors.
3. Utilize documents that capture data at the source of the transaction in a form for subsequent scanning or entry into the system.

Interaction with On-Line Systems

Most users, whether end-users or information systems professionals, interact with computers on-line; that is, they use the computer itself or a terminal attached to a computer. This makes the **computer interface** important.

An *interface* is the point at which the user and computer meet, that is, where they interact. Good interface designs help make the interaction comfortable for the user and prevent the making of mistakes.

When Apple Computer introduced its Macintosh computer system—see accompanying photo—it established a new standard for computer interfaces (the ideas behind the Macintosh interface were developed several years earlier by researchers at Xerox, Inc.). Previously, users interacted by entering keyword commands or selecting from menus of alternatives (Figure 5.7).

Figure 5.7 Menu Interface

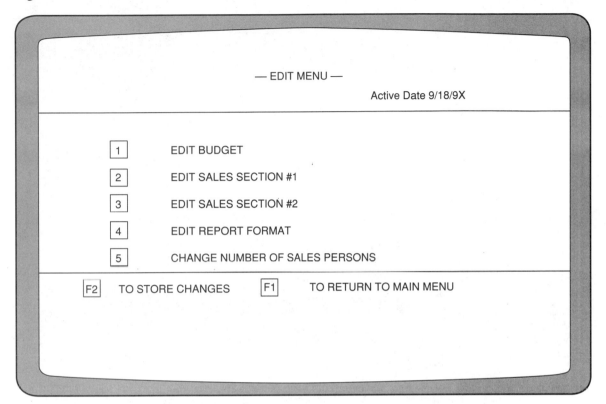

> — EDIT MENU —
>
> Active Date 9/18/9X
>
> 1   EDIT BUDGET
>
> 2   EDIT SALES SECTION #1
>
> 3   EDIT SALES SECTION #2
>
> 4   EDIT REPORT FORMAT
>
> 5   CHANGE NUMBER OF SALES PERSONS
>
> F2   TO STORE CHANGES   F1   TO RETURN TO MAIN MENU

The Macintosh design introduced windows to personal computer users. **Windows** are areas of a display screen that act independently of other areas. Each window can show information drawn from different sources. In some situations, separate applications can run in independent windows. The illustration in Figure 5.8 shows three different windows overlaid one on top of the other. Menu alternatives are shown across the top of the display screen.

Because of the popularity of windows on the Macintosh, they are now being used in a wide variety of other systems. You should expect to see window interfaces used not just on other personal computers but on mainframe and minicomputer systems as well.

The Apple Macintosh also introduced pull-down menus to personal computing. **Pull-down menus** allow the user to view operations choices by having them displayed on the screen while the information viewed by the user remains on the screen. Figure 5.9 shows a pull-down menu. Notice how it drops down from the menu bar at the top of the screen. Typically the user selects a menu alternative by pointing to it with a mouse, but other variations are possible as well, depending on the strategies selected by the vendor.

Figure 5.8 Windows Interface

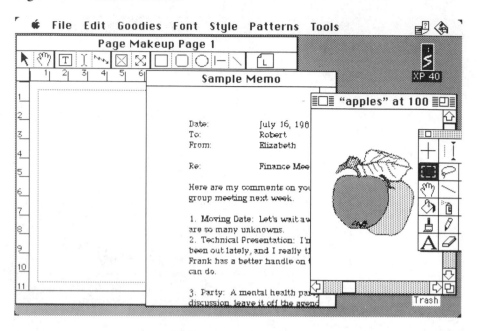

Figure 5.9 Pull-Down Menu

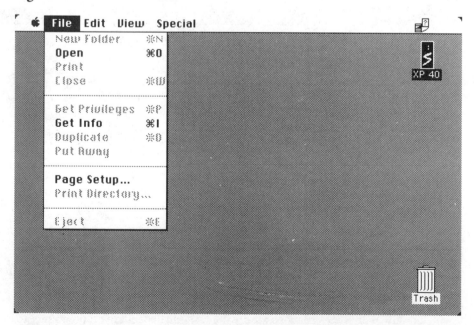

Since end-users have also shown a great liking for pull-down menus on personal computers, you should expect to see them on other systems, too.

Output Devices

Output devices transform the electronic pulses and signals from the central processing unit into results that people can use. The output may be displayed on CRT screens, printed on documents or paper, punched into cards, or displayed through photographic processes. We have already discussed several output devices. Others include printers, card punches, plotters, and audio response, as well as microfilm or microfiche units.

The most common way of doing output (for example, reports, invoices, or computer program listings) is to print it. A wide variety of printers have been developed for handling this type of output. Different ones are used for the smallest and the largest of systems. High-speed **line printers** are commonly used with large-scale systems (see photo). These units print a full line (up to 144 characters) *at one time* on continuous form paper that can be 14 inches wide. Rapid spacing of the data up, down, or across on each page and/or line must take place before the actual printing operation occurs. Table 5.5 shows the range of speeds possible on line printers.

High-Speed Computer Line Printer

Table 5.5 A Comparison of Popular Printer Technologies

Printer Technology	Price	Speed	Character Formation	Market Environment	General Characteristics
LASER (page)	$1,495 to $300,000	8 to 215 ppm	144 by 180 to 300 by 300 dpi 600 by 600 dpi	Low to High	Fast; Quiet; Graphics High Resolution
ION DEPOSITION (page)	$12,000 to $280,000	30 to 150 ppm	240 by 240 to 300 by 300 dpi	Mid to High	Fast; Quiet; Graphics High Resolution
LED ARRAY (page)	$2,995 to $200,000	8 to 92 ppm	240 by 240 to 300 by 300 dpi	Low to Mid	Fast; Quiet; Graphics High Resolution
INK JET (serial)	$400 to $14,595	20 to 240 cps	60 by 60 to 400 by 400 dpi	Low to High	Quiet; Color; Graphics High Resolution
THERMAL (serial)	$150 to $2,095	40 to 530 cps	200 by 800 to 350 by 350 dpi	Low to Mid	Quiet; Color; Graphics High Resolution
DOT MATRIX (serial/line)	$300 to $6,700 $5,780 to $30,050	40 to 1200 cps 300 lpm to 1200 lpm	1×8 to 24×127 (Draft and NLQ)	Low to High	Carbons; Graphics; Color; Inexpensive
DAISY WHEEL (serial)	$180 to $1,700	12 to 120 cps	Full Character (Draft and LQ)	Low	Best Text Quality Carbons; No graphics
BAND (line)	$4,885 to $75,000	300 to 3600 lpm	Full Character (Draft and NLQ)	High	Fast; Reliable
DRUM (column)	$4,150 to $14,000	20 cols/sec	Full Character (Draft and NLQ)	High	Fast; Reliable

dots per inch (dpi)   lines per minute (lpm)
characters per second (cps)   pages per minute (ppm)

Different types of print mechanism are used, depending on the particular manufacturer and the purpose of the device. **Impact printers** are very common in large system configurations. They usually involve either a chain or a drum that contains the character set (that is, the set of letters, numbers, symbols). In chain printers, the characters are on type slugs strung together on a horizontally moving chain (see photo). A ribbon is placed between the paper and the type chain, and as the chain moves past the paper, hammers are activated behind the paper; these force the sheet against the proper character, creating the printed image. Because the chains are interchangeable, a number of different type styles and character sets can be used.

Drum printers have the characters engraved in rows on a rotating drum, one full character set per print position. As the drum revolves, the characters are moved past the paper and ribbon. Print hammers for each position are activated and strike the paper against the type, producing the printed image.

Vertical spacing on each printed page is usually controlled by a paper or plastic tape loop inside the printer. Holes are punched in different positions in the loop,

Chain Mechanism for Printer

and when the printer control unit senses them, they control spacings on a page or cause the printer to skip to a new page. On some of the newer printers, internal programs of instructions have replaced the tape loop.

In contrast to the solid font printers, some use dot patterns to produce output. These **dot matrix printers** push wire rods against the ribbon and paper to produce the necessary characters (Figure 5.10). If you look closely at the characters produced, you can see that each is actually a collection of dots. Speed, cost, and simplicity underlie the use of the dot matrix method of printing. These printers are used with systems of many sizes.

Many mini- and microcomputers and word processing systems use **character printers,** meaning that they print one character at a time. The speeds of these printers are measured in characters per second, ranging from a very slow 10 characters to a fairly common 160 characters per second and higher. Often these printers (see photo, p. 170) look much like office typewriters. There are two types: **serial printers** transmit the code that makes up one character bit by bit, while **parallel printers** transmit all codes representing a character at once. Generally these printers are much less expensive than line printers, ranging from only a few hundred dollars to approximately $4000. Rarely does a microcomputer printer cost more than $5000.

The **daisy wheel** character printer is very popular on personal computers and word processors. The name comes from the print wheel, which resembles a flower—

Figure 5.10 Dot Matrix Printer Characters

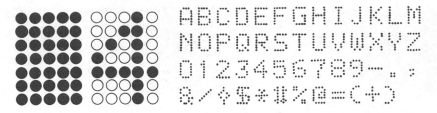

Dot Matrix Printer

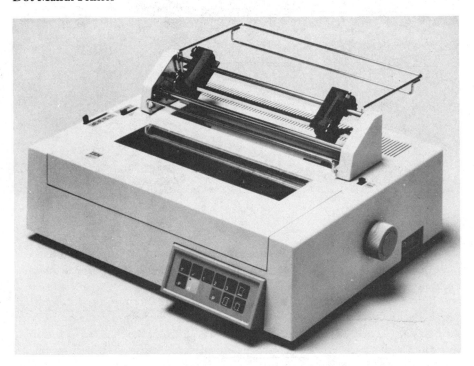

each petal contains a print character. During printing, the wheel rotates so that the appropriate character is moved into the print position.

    Nonimpact printers use photographic or chemical means for producing printed output. Some also spray ink onto paper to form the output characters. **Thermal image printers,** for example, use heat-sensitive paper and metal rods containing the print characters. When the rods are heated and pressed against the special paper, the image or letter that is on the end of the rod appears. In **photographic printing,** a light beam is focused on a rotating disk of type characters. The output from the CPU is projected onto sensitized film or paper that can be developed like photographic paper. The print image is of very high quality.

Ink jet Printer

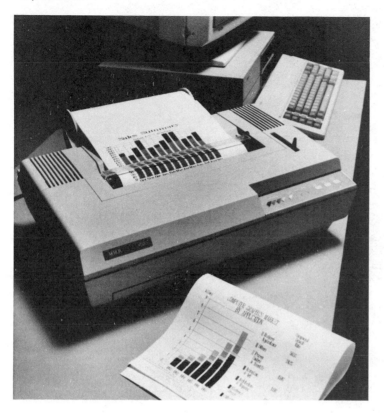

Ink jet printers (see accompanying photo) are designed so that tiny streams of ink are sprayed from holes in the print head. These streams make up a dot pattern that represents the character to be printed. Since there are no moving parts, as there are in impact printers, the printing speed is very fast. In many applications for which large volumes of output must be produced (such as in printing utility bills), ink jet printers are used to attain high output rates.

Ink jet printers, along with many dot matrix printers, will continue to increase in popularity due to their ability to print intricate graphic patterns and letters as well as their optional use of color. Graphics in business and engineering, ranging from bar and pie charts to special symbols and logos to engineering schematics, are in high demand. Computer manufacturers are responding with low-cost printers (usually less than $1000 for small units) to fulfill this need.

A great deal of attention has recently been directed to the **laser printer** (see photo, p. 172). This nonimpact printer converts data to be printed into a narrow beam of light (a laser beam) that in turn encodes a photoconductor with the data. The process forms the image of the data to be printed. A toner—a black granular dust similar to that used in many photocopiers—is used in the process. The pho-

Desktop Laser Printer

toconductor attracts toner particles and, when placed in contact with the paper, produces the printed image. Finally, the image is fused to the paper by heat and pressure.

The process is fast, and it allows printing of graphics along with text. Laser printers used with personal computers, costing less than $3000, print eight or more *pages* per minute. Larger laser printers are of course much faster and cost $40,000 or more.

Nonimpact printers will receive much more attention in the future.

Card punches or combination reader-punches convert electronic output signals into holes in punched cards in much the same way as a keypunch machine does. However, the CPU rather than a person controls the punching operation. Error checking takes place during punching. Punched output is most commonly used when the cards will be used again soon as input to the computer system—as in the case of customer bills. These materials, called **turnaround documents** because they serve both as output and input, are punched to contain such information as customer name, address, amount of bill, and date. The cards are then mailed to customers as part of the normal (monthly) statement. When customers pay their bills, they are asked to include the punched card along with their checks or money orders. The card is used as input to the central processor to post the payment to the individual's service account.

In a number of instances, graphical data are more meaningful than numerical data. **Plotters** have been developed to convert output signals from the processing

Microfiche Reader/Printer

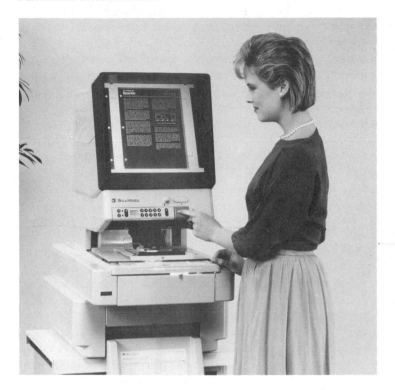

unit into lines and curves. Digital or numerical data accepted by the plotter cause a pen to move across a carriage or drum holding paper, thus creating the desired graphical output. Plotters are invaluable in the output of maps and geometrical schematics, as well as in historical trend data in the form of graphs and charts.

The **audio response unit,** a newer type of output device, is becoming increasingly common in situations in which the spoken word is more appropriate than written data or information. For example, audio response is being used on a regular basis with telephone company service operators and stock market quotation services. In these situations, prerecorded voice messages are stored in a voice unit that can be recalled on signal. The individual enters a question in the form of codes or numbers from a pushbutton telephone or similar keyboard device. The CPU then processes the question and retrieves appropriate stored voice responses for output over telephone or speaker units.

An alternative to paper output is film. **Microfilm** and **microfiche units** make this possible. Both microfilm and microfiche are used frequently in business to store large amounts of data and information inexpensively and in a small amount of space (see photo). For example, many libraries routinely record the *New York Times* or the *Wall Street Journal* on microfilm. An entire issue of the newspaper can be stored on a piece of microfilm only a few inches long, and the cost is very low. When used in computer output operations, the microfilm unit converts output signals to characters and letters, which, in turn, are "written" on a frame of microfilm. Each frame of microfilm, which is less than an inch square, can hold the same amount of data as can be printed on a regular 14-inch page of paper used in a line printer.

The microfiche unit serves the same function as the microfilm unit. However, instead of writing the output on a strip of film, the unit writes many pages of output on a film card about the size of a 3 × 5 inch index card. The film card used in some units can contain several hundred pages of output.

In general, the use of microfilm and microfiche cuts the cost of output by as much as one-third. Because of the lower cost and smaller amount of space required to store the output, we can expect to see more and more use of these media.

Central Processing Unit

As we have already discussed, the heart of the computer system is the central processing unit (CPU), where all computation actually takes place. All other devices are linked to the CPU and are under its control. Thus, the various peripheral devices examined earlier, such as card readers, printers, and terminals, are connected to the CPU and operate under its control. The CPU accepts data and instructions from input units only when the central processor signals them to feed in data; the output units print only when allowed to do so by the CPU.

All programs and data that are used for computation are stored within the CPU *memory unit*. Operations on the stored contents of the memory are performed by the *arithmetic/logic unit* under supervision of the *control unit*. Each of these three units is essential for processing data.

Storage Unit Regardless of size or type of computer, the memory unit of the CPU acts as the *primary storage unit* for the computer system. It may occupy only a single board on small computers, or a large cabinet on bigger systems. In either case, storage that takes up square centimeters today only a few years ago required several square yards. Also referred to as the main memory, the memory unit can be likened to a large set of post office boxes, each of which has a unique number assigned to it. We can visualize these boxes with numbers on them like 101, 102, . . . , 2004, and so on (Figure 5.11).

Figure 5.11 Memory Locations and Memory Addresses

101	102	103	104
105	106	107	108
109	110	111	112
113	114	115	116
117	118	119	. . .

Each location has an address

The box numbers are **addresses,** which allow us to distinguish one from another. Computer storage locations are comparable to post office boxes in that they too have assigned numbers that are their addresses.* Unlike the mail service user, however, who must know the box number in order to send anything to it, the computer system user need not know the address for a particular storage location. The control unit, which maintains the address, is responsible for inserting or removing anything from a particular location.

Each of the storage locations can hold data or instructions. In microcomputers, there are typically from 64,000 to 640,000 storage locations. The full-size computer systems used in most business applications usually have several million storage locations. Only one element of data *or* one instruction can be stored in a memory location at one time. The contents depend on the program being handled. The control unit determines what is stored in a specific storage location.

You should be aware how memory sizes are described in the computing literature. Often you see references to memories with a storage capacity of 16K, 32K, 64K, and so on. This designation refers to the number of addressable locations in the memory. The letter *K* stands for **kilobyte** and represents a value of 1024 locations in this context. Thus a reference to a memory of 16K means that it has 16,384 addressable locations.

Semiconductor Memory Memory or **storage units** can be constructed of different types of material. The materials used determine the *memory types*. **Semiconductor memories** or **integrated circuits,** as they are often called, are the dominant memory type. The familiar phrase "computer on a chip" reflects the extremely small size, and high storage capacity, of semiconductor memory components (see photo). The very thin silicon **chip** contains a number of small storage cells that can hold data. These units are not discrete, but are constructed as integrated circuits, meaning that a number of transistors are integrated or combined together on a thin silicon wafer to form a complete set of circuits.

Integrated circuits vary according to the scale of integration. Small-scale integration means that 10 or fewer transistors are tied together as a circuit. Medium- and large-scale integration involves on the order of 100 to 1,000,000 transistors. Many developments are going on currently with very large-scale integration, where several million storage units are being tied together. See the box on the language of chips, p. 176.

Semiconductor units are created by using a chemical process to etch away portions of the surface of the silicon wafers. Masks control the areas that are etched so that windows remain, forming areas where electrical currents can flow to make data representation and storage possible. This technology has made it possible to place hundreds, even thousands, of storage locations into the space that one component of earlier memory types occupied.

---

*However, each storage location in a computer system can store only one piece of data, whereas a post office box can store several letters.

Magnified Circuitry in Semiconductor Memory

Other Memory Types Semiconductor memories have replaced *ferrite core storage,* a memory type that was dominant for many years. Primary storage in the CPU is still often called "core storage," showing you how ingrained **magnetic core** memory use has been in the minds of those who use computers regularly.

Core storage consists of thousands of small donut-shaped rings of iron ferrite. Each magnetic core is about the size of a pinhead, or a little larger than the period at the end of this sentence. The iron ferrite is magnetic and can be polarized in either

The Language of Chips

bit

An acronym for binary digit. A one-digit binary number that holds one piece of data in the "zero" (off) state, or one piece of data in the "one" (on) state. A bit is the fundamental informational building block used by all computers. Eight bits comprise one byte. Eight bits were chosen to represent a character because they allow up to 256 different characters to be represented by the various combinations of ones and zeros. Some computers,

The Language of Chips (continued)

	which process one character at a time, are known as "8-bit processors." Others process two characters in parallel and are known as "16-bit processors." Some PCs and larger mainframes are "32-bit processors" and can handle four characters concurrently.
byte	Smallest addressable unit in memory. A byte is the amount of storage space needed to store one character of information—such as the letter *A*. The pattern of bits determines the meaning of a byte, just as the shape of a printed character conveys meaning. In most data processing equipment, one byte consists of eight consecutive bits.
MIPS (million instructions per second)	Represents the speed at which a central processing unit, or CPU, is capable of operating. Refers to the average number of machine language instructions the CPU performs in one second. Parameters that most affect the MIPS rate are word length and speed of the refresh cycle, measured in millions of Hertz or Megahertz (MHz). For example, the 80386 Intel chip runs at 4 MIPS, which means it is capable of performing 4 million machine language instructions per second.
DRAM (dynamic random access memory)	*(Pronounced dee-ram.)* Type of memory available through semiconductor technology. It is the storage of data (bits and bytes) in the form of charges of static electricity that are "volatile" or decay over time. The DRAM needs to be constantly refreshed or reenergized by the CPU before it decays beyond salvage. Thus, when the computer is turned off, all memory in DRAM is lost forever. Many first-time computer users lose data by turning off the computer before saving (or transferring) their work to a nonvolatile memory medium such as a floppy disk or a hard drive.
ROM (read-only memory)	Because ROM is permanently programmed at the factory, the computer retains memory even when the power is turned off. Unlike RAM, this type of memory only allows the user to read data without making changes to the copy.
CMOS (complementary metal oxide semiconductor)	*(Pronounced cee-mos.)* A process to produce integrated circuits or chips. Although chips produced through this complementary metal oxide process are generally slower than those processed with silicon, they use less power. Cooling problems result from chips that require more power, because cooling requires larger physical spaces and such power-robbing devices as fans.

of two directions (positive and negative or clockwise and counterclockwise); the direction determines whether a 0 or a 1 is stored. Wires strung through the cores carry current that changes the direction of polarity, or senses whether a 0 or a 1 value is stored.

Each core in memory is capable of representing only part of a set of numbers or letters (for example, a person's name). To represent any amount of data (or instructions), several cores must be grouped together and operated on as a single unit. For this reason, several *networks* or *planes* of cores are piled in layers and called a "stack." Often the core plane contains eight rows and eight columns; the manufacturer determines the number.

Remember the concept of an address? The address we described earlier applies to a set of cores from one matrix. The set (for example, a column from the stack) is referred to by one address. As will be explained further in the next chapter, the set is called a "byte" and can contain one character of data.

In addition, another memory type, **bubble memory** technology, is being developed primarily as an auxiliary memory to supplement main storage. However, it is finding its way into use as a primary memory component in some small systems and intelligent terminals. It is also being used in selected automatic dial telephone systems. Thus, we may see it as a prominent main memory unit medium in the future. (Discussion of bubble memories is taken up in greater detail in the following section on secondary storage devices.)

Other memory types include plated wire and thin film storage. *Plated wire storage* consists of copper wire covered by a thin metallic film. The wires are cut into lengths of about an inch each. Each "wire rod," as this short wire is called, can store data. Planes for storage are formed by inserting the rods into wire coils that charge or sense the charge in each wire. Each plane is then sealed in a plastic substance and stacks are assembled, like those in the magnetic core planes. An important advantage of these memories is that data and instructions can be moved into and out of them more rapidly than from core storage. Additionally, they can be mass produced at a much lower cost than some of the other memories. Research is continuing into the development of plated wire memories.

Thin film memory is created by depositing small, thin spots of metallic alloy on a flat film surface. Each spot can be magnetized and thus acts like a magnetic core to store data. The surface is very thin (only a few millionths of an inch) and provides for very fast access to data. Research is also continuing into the development of this memory type.

Laser memories also offer a good deal of promise for the future. Optical memories of this type use laser beams (see photo), very narrow, high-intensity beams of light, to etch data on a special light-sensitive plate. Data stored on plates in this manner create **holograms.** Data can be read from the hologram by means of a less powerful light beam.

One disadvantage of laser memories is that the photo emulsion on the plate must be developed after exposure. Therefore, it is not possible to switch different data into and out of specific storage areas. That is, the storage locations cannot be used over and over by different programs. This constraint does not exist with the

Laser Beam

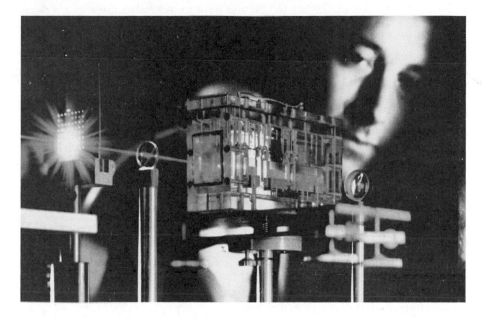

other memory types we discussed. Other methods are being studied, however, and we may soon see advances in this area.

Arithmetic/Logic Unit All calculations and computations for processing data are made in the arithmetic/logic unit, the computer's primary work unit. Such operations include addition, subtraction, multiplication, division, and exponentiation (2^2, 10^{-6}, and so on). Actually, the unit itself does all arithmetic activities through addition and subtraction. This is possible because multiplication and exponentiation are merely special cases of addition, and division is a special case of subtraction. Logical comparisons, which are performed by means of subtraction (for instance, comparing two numbers to see which one is the larger), are also performed in the arithmetic/logic unit.

Data flow into the arithmetic/logic unit on signal from the control unit, are acted on, and are returned to the primary storage unit. The number of processing activities that can be performed and the way in which they take place are determined by the design of the machine itself. A number of variations are possible, which is part of the reason for the existence of so many models and manufacturers of computer systems. The operations of the arithmetic/logic unit and the control unit are examined in greater detail in the next chapter.

The Control Unit The control unit of the CPU directs all processing and all movement of data into and out of the storage unit. This unit also directs the sequence of activities taking place within the central processing unit and maintains order in activities and operations. Therefore, the unit both moves instructions by a written program and operates in accordance with its own prewritten set of instructions established by the manufacturer. The control unit also supervises input/output activities involving peripheral and secondary storage devices.

Secondary Storage Devices

When it is neither feasible nor desirable to store all data in the main memory unit of the central processor, secondary storage devices can be linked directly to the central processor, allowing for almost unlimited storage expansion. The selection of a particular secondary storage unit depends on an organization's needs or on a specific application. The most common secondary storage devices are magnetic tape, magnetic disk, and magnetic drum.

Magnetic Tape **Magnetic tape** is a high-speed, relatively permanent storage medium for recording and retaining data. The magnetic tape has a Mylar base and is coated on one side with minute particles of iron oxide mixed with a binding agent. Data are recorded on this coating. The tape must be very carefully manufactured, since any flaw or imperfection can easily cause errors or data loss. Data are read (detected) or written (stored) on the tape as it passes through a magnetic tape unit (see Figure 5.12). The oxide side of the tape passes over read/write heads— devices in the tape drive that either read data already recorded on tape (read head) or actually write or transcribe data onto the tape (write head). The read head thus converts magnetic spots on the tape into electronic pulses the CPU can use, and the write head converts electronic pulses into spots on the magnetic tape. Each spot can store one piece of data.

Figure 5.12 Transport Mechanism for Magnetic Tape Unit

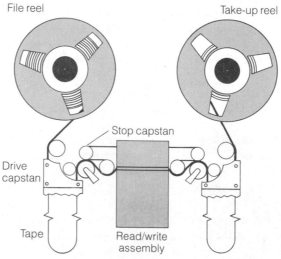

Figure 5.12 *(continued)* Magnetic Tape Unit and Tape Library

Figure 5.13 Data Representation on Seven-Track Magnetic Tape

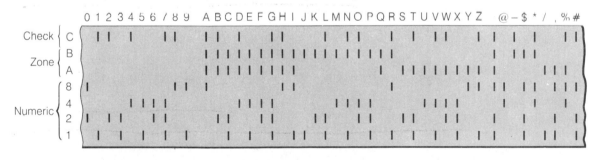

Data may be written on any of several independent tracks on the tape (Figure 5.13). A **track** is a relatively narrow area on a medium, such as magnetic tape, on which data can be recorded. If it were visible to the naked eye (normally it is not), the track would appear as a very narrow line running the length of the entire tape. The number of tracks—usually seven or nine—depends on the type of *tape drive* (the device that moves the tape forward or backward and actually performs the read or write operations). Since the recording heads are placed vertically across the tape during a read or write operation, seven or nine pieces of data may be recorded

Figure 5.14 Record Blocking on Magnetic Tape

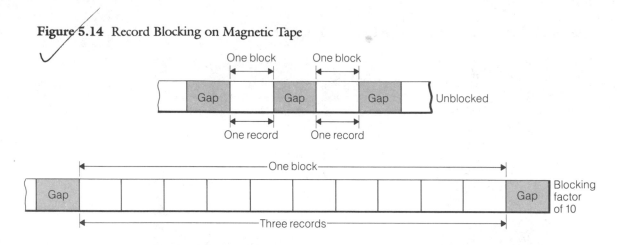

Space required to store one record = 0.5 inch
Space for interblock   = 0.3 inch

To store one record, unblocked, requires = 0.5 + 0.3 inch = 0.8 inch
To store ten records, unblocked, requires = (0.5 + 0.3) × 10 = 8 inches
If blocking factor is 10, space required = (0.5) × 10 + 0.3 = 5.3 inches
In general: (number of records in block × size of each record) × number of boxes in file

simultaneously, one bit of data on each track. In this system, magnetic particles on the tape are charged in either the positive or negative direction (that is, either magnetized or demagnetized) by an electronic signal issued from the CPU.

To understand magnetic tape properly, it is necessary to introduce some additional terminology. Data are recorded on magnetic tape in groups called "records." A **record** is a set of data pertaining to a transaction (for example, a sale of merchandise to a customer), an object (for example, the quantity of a specific item on hand in a warehouse), or a person (for instance, the name, identification number, job skill, or pay rate of an employee) of interest or importance to the person collecting or storing the data. There may be only a few characters or numbers in a record, or there may be hundreds, depending on the details of the transaction, object, or person.

Related to the concept of a record is a **block**, a physical area on the magnetic tape that contains data and is separated from other parts of the tape by blank spaces on either side. The blank areas, called **interblock gaps** (or interrecord gaps), allow the tape drive to start and stop as it reads a group of data. In other words, after a block of data has been read from magnetic tape, the tape stops moving. Data are read from magnetic tape in blocks. If there were no blank spaces on both sides of a block, data would be lost or inadvertently skipped over when the tape started to move again. Approximately 0.3–0.75 inch of tape (the length of the interblock gap) is required for the tape drive to start moving again and reach the proper speed.

Obviously the interblock gaps, which contain no data, amount to wasted space on a section of magnetic tape. One way to minimize this loss is to combine several records together and have one interblock gap for the entire group of records, as shown in Figure 5.14. If records and blocks are the same thing (that is, if one block contains one record), there is an interrecord gap on each side of every record. However, if the block contains three records, only two interrecord gaps are needed. The concept of placing more than one record in a block is referred to as **blocking.** The number of records placed in a block is called the **blocking factor.** If a block contains three records, the blocking factor is 3; if it contains seven records, the blocking factor is 7, and so on. (What is the blocking factor if a block contains only one record, that is, if the records are unblocked?)

To see the space-saving advantages of blocking, let's look at the details in Figure 5.14. The example indicates that these data require 0.5 inch of tape for each record stored (this varies for records of different length or records with different amounts of data). To this must be added the length of space needed for the interblock gap, which is a function of the tape drive being used. If we know that the interblock gap is 0.3 inch long, and that the records are stored unblocked, we can see that 1.1 inches of tape is required to store each record. (Since we are dealing with unblocked records, the length of the record and the length of the block are the same; therefore, the gap may be referred to as an *interrecord gap* rather than an interblock gap.) If we are storing 10 records on tape, unblocked, and if 0.8 inch of tape is required for each record, then 8 inches of magnetic tape is used. If 30 records are being stored, 24 inches is used.

Compare the space requirement for unblocked data with one where a blocking factor of 10 is used for the same number of records—that is, 10 records are contained in each block on the magnetic tape. Again the amount of tape required is 0.5 inch for each record stored plus 0.3 inch for the interblock gap. However, one interblock gap is needed because of the blocking factor. To store the 10 records, then, 5.3 inches of tape is used: $(10 \times 0.5) + 0.3$. If 30 records are stored, with a blocking factor of 3, a very low blocking factor, then 18 inches of magnetic tape is used. With blocking, savings in the use of magnetic tape can be significant. Furthermore, the computer user does not have to insert the interblock gap on the magnetic tape—the tape drive performs this automatically. It is common to use blocking factors of 50, 60, or more.

We have examined the interblock gap as a means of separating records and blocks of data on magnetic tape. The same principle is used to separate "files" of data. A **file** is a group of similar records. A payroll file is a group of records pertaining to payroll data; an inventory file is a set of records pertaining to items in inventory. Each file stored on a magnetic tape is separated from other files by the recording of an *end-of-file (EOF) mark* in the last record of the file. The mark is written on the tape by the tape drive on instructions from the CPU.

During manufacture, plastic strips (called *reflective spots*) are placed on the tape to enable the tape drive unit to sense the beginning and end of the usable portion of the magnetic tape. The reflective spots are placed on the base or uncoated side of the tape (that is, not the side on which data are recorded).

The back of the tape reel has a slot near the hub that accepts a plastic *file protection ring*. The purpose of this device is to prevent the loss of valuable data through accidental rewriting. Writing on a magnetic tape is possible only when the reel contains the file protection ring. However, the tape may be read with or without the ring. If someone tries to write on a protected tape—that is, if the protection ring has not been inserted into the reel—an error condition results. Presence of a ring on a reel of tape is signaled by lights on the tape drive, which turn on immediately after the tape is loaded onto the drive. The lights remain on until the ring is removed or the tape unit is unloaded. The operator must insert the ring for processing to begin, and when writing is completed, the ring should be removed from the reel to "protect" the data on the tape.

The amount of data that can be stored on a length of magnetic tape (called the "data density") is related to the recording density. **Recording density** is simply the number of characters or digits written per inch of magnetic tape. Density is determined by the physical makeup of the tape drive and, in part, by the individual who is actually writing the data on the tape. Common densities are 800, 1600, and 6250 characters per inch. The user can select one of these densities to use for recording the data; many tape drives can record (write) at all three.

The particular density used can make quite a difference in the amount of tape needed to store data. For example, if a 200-character record were recorded at a density of 1600 characters per inch, 0.125 inch of magnetic tape would be used. However, if the same record were recorded at 6250 characters per inch density, the amount of magnetic tape required would be 0.032 inch. In a large file of records, significant savings in magnetic tape can be realized by going to a higher density.

Magnetic Disk **Magnetic disks** store data in much the same way as magnetic tape. That is, electronic pulses are represented as magnetic spots, but they are stored on round, coated metal disks or plates mounted in a shaft or spindle instead of on tape. Each stack may consist of a number of plates varying in number from as few as one to more than one hundred. (Usually a single disk—that is, one not in a stack—is protected by a plastic container that surrounds it entirely. This is referred to as a *disk cartridge* and is common on older computer systems and on some of the small minicomputers.) Disks are generally from 12 to 18 inches in diameter and contain a number of concentric circles or tracks on which data can be recorded. Some disks contain more than 500 tracks per surface, depending on the size of the disk and the amount of space between each track.

The vertical alignment of one track on each surface is referred to as a **cylinder.** A **sector*** is a V- or pie-shaped section on one particular plate of the disk. The sector is comparable to a physical block of fixed length. (See Figure 5.15.)

Data are recorded on a disk by means of **read/write heads** in the disk drive unit. Some disk drives have one stationary head per track (fixed head disk); on others, read/write heads are attached to movable arms that swing back and forth across a disk surface to reach the proper track (movable head disk). Many computer systems use disk units that have removable disk packs. A **disk pack** is a stack of disks that can be lifted onto or off the disk drive. The accompanying photo shows a disk pack, the read/write heads, and a disk file. It is important to note that although the heads are very close to the disk surface, *they never actually touch the surface*. If the heads

---

*Not all disks use the sector concept. Some, like the IBM 3380 disk, use interblock gaps to separate blocks on a track.

Figure 5.15 Sectors on a Magnetic Disk

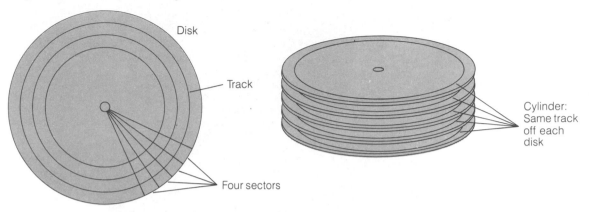

Disk

Track

Four sectors

Cylinder:
Same track
off each
disk

Disk Pack

Disk File

Read/Write Heads

were to make contact (*head crash*) with the surface, there would be a considerable amount of damage to the surface and perhaps to the heads themselves. All data recorded in those areas would be destroyed.

Disks are mounted on a magnetic disk drive unit that rotates at a rapid rate (for example, 900 revolutions per minute), thus providing rapid access to stored data (see photos).

Winchester Disk System

Winchester Disk Drives A very popular variation on disk drives is the **Winchester disk** technology. The essence of the Winchester method is that the disk read/write assembly is sealed from outside air and is nonremovable (see photo). In other words, the disks themselves, read/write heads, and actuator are contained in a sealed unit. Because the sealed environment is free from dust and dirt particles, reliability of these devices is extremely high. Maintenance is also reduced significantly, which means that operating costs are lower than for conventional disk units.

Winchester disk technology is being used on small computer systems as well as on larger business systems.

Flexible Diskettes The most widely used storage medium on personal computers is the **flexible diskette.** Also known as *floppy disks,* the most common sizes are 5¼, 3½, and 8 inches (in order of popularity). The storage capacity varies depending on the size of the disk and the computer on which it is used. However, most diskettes store between 160,000 and 2,000,000 characters of data. As electronic and storage technologies increase, it is anticipated that these storage densities will expand dramatically.

As the name implies, the diskettes are made from a soft, flexible, plasticlike material. Data are recorded around the surface on tracks (common diskettes have 40,

Portable Computer with Floppy Disk Units

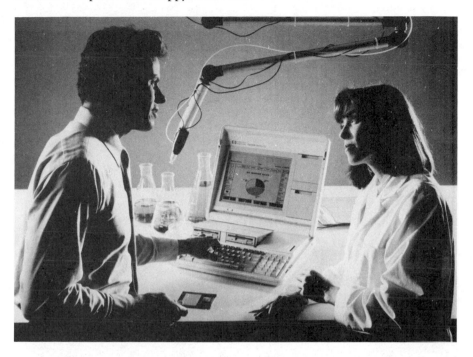

76, or 96 tracks per surface). The diskette itself is contained in a paper jacket (the most common in the 1980s) or a plastic cartridge (increasing in popularity). The disk drive rotates the diskette inside the jacket.

Computer software manufacturers usually deliver personal computer software on flexible diskettes (rather than on magnetic tape). The software is then loaded into the computer memory when it reads the contents of the diskette.

Like other types of magnetic storage, diskettes are in widespread use for the storage of data. Virtually any desktop system for word processing, accounting, or personal computing uses flexible diskettes (see photo). It is not uncommon to find a tray of 30, 40, or more diskettes beside a personal computer. Many of the diskettes will contain data (the remainder will contain a variety of software selected by the user).

You may see diskettes being used in conjunction with hard disks too. In these cases, data and programs are frequently unloaded from the **hard disks** (which cannot be removed from their housing) and written onto the diskettes. The diskettes are then stored in a desk or filing cabinet until the data or programs are needed, at which time the data can be reloaded into the computer system.

Hardcards are a special type of hard disk unit often associated with IBM standard personal computers. The name comes from the fact that they are mounted on a circuitboard that will fit inside a personal computer. The cards (see accompa-

Hardcard for Extra Disk Storage Capacity

nying photo) fit on an expansion slot rather than in the area normally used for disk drives. Thus, they have the effect of enabling the user to have more storage than normally possible. Storage capacities and performance characteristics are comparable to those of hard disks.

Many users are choosing to work with hardcards instead of internal and external disks because of the space hardcards save—they require neither desk space nor the location where a floppy diskette is normally installed. Therefore, storage capacity is increased without giving up internal or external space.

Hardcards cost from $250 to $1000 and have a storage capacity beginning at 10 megabytes and upward.

Optical Disks

Optical storage will be increasingly common over the next few years. These systems (Figure 5.16) use laser beams to store data on a special optical disk (see photo) that allows data to be written, but not erased or changed. It can be reread many times, however.

Optical disk systems allow a high storage density—15,000 bits of data per inch and higher. An optical disk for use with personal computers typically stores

Figure 5.16 Optical Disk Storage

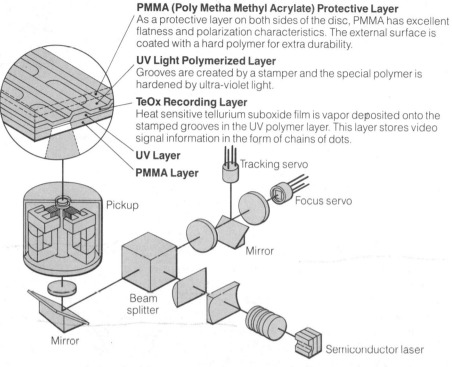

PMMA (Poly Metha Methyl Acrylate) Protective Layer
As a protective layer on both sides of the disc, PMMA has excellent flatness and polarization characteristics. The external surface is coated with a hard polymer for extra durability.

UV Light Polymerized Layer
Grooves are created by a stamper and the special polymer is hardened by ultra-violet light.

TeOx Recording Layer
Heat sensitive tellurium suboxide film is vapor deposited onto the stamped grooves in the UV polymer layer. This layer stores video signal information in the form of chains of dots.

UV Layer

PMMA Layer

Tracking servo

Focus servo

Pickup

Mirror

Beam splitter

Mirror

Semiconductor laser

Optical Disk

Table 5.6 Common Uses of Optical Storage Types

CD-ROM	WORM	Read/Write
On-line subscription services	Organizational archival storage	Graphics
Mass distribution of large documents	Medical records; bank transaction records	Artificial intelligence
	Audit trail	Desktop publishing

approximately 300 megabytes* of data (equivalent to more than 1000 flexible diskettes). The optical disks themselves range in cost from $10 to $30.

Optical disks are used in special circumstances when data are stored for archival purposes or will be referenced—not altered. When the technology for erasing and writing data on optical disks is further developed, even greater use of optical storage may follow.

Three types of optical disks are evolving (Table 5.6). **CD-ROM** (Compact Disk—Read-Only Memory) disks are similar to the compact disks now widely used with stereo music systems: They can be played but not rerecorded. CD-ROM is suitable for mass distribution of information. Examples of CD-ROM use include literary databases, stock market data, and technical documentation for such products as automobiles, aircraft, and computers. **WORM** (Write Once—Read Many) allows users to write data once to disk and read the details repeatedly. Once recorded, data cannot be modified or erased, a feature that is useful for organizations such as financial institutions which need to maintain an accurate log of business transactions over time. Widespread use of this technology is occurring slowly, largely due to the absence of standards. WORM disks are manufactured for a specific vendor's drive, and thus are not interchangeable between other drives.

Magnetic Drum **Magnetic drums** (see accompanying photo) have faster access speed than disks, but their storage capacity is often smaller. These storage units consist of metal cylinders or drums coated with magnetic material for storage of data. The tracks around the cylinder are the storage areas for vast quantities of data. As the drum rotates on the drum drive unit, data are recorded on or read from the drum tracks by fixed read/write heads.

Drums and disks allow access directly to the specific location of the needed data. This *direct access* advantage is possible because either movable or multiple read/write heads are used for each track. The tape drive, as you recall, has one head unit, which means that the tape must be passed from beginning to end, skipping over unwanted records. However, disk and drum units permit immediate access to desired records, because the tracks and records need *not* be read or passed sequentially. These direct access storage devices are more frequently used when records will not be processed sequentially and record demands are not known in advance. The organization and processing of data on these storage devices are studied further in Chapter 8.

*The term *megabyte* refers to one million bytes of storage.

Magnetic Drum

Erasable optical disks are only beginning to emerge. These disks, which will allow both writing and modification of data, may lead to innovative applications. For instance, optical memory cards may be developed to hold personal medical information, including x-ray images, sonic scans, medical notes, and other patient information. Because of the high recording density of optical storage units, the information may be stored on a card the size of ordinary credit cards.

The use of optical disks is expected to grow rapidly as the technology evolves. It is likely that many new applications will emerge.

Overlapped Processing

Speeds in the picosecond range are indeed impressive. Yet, because computer systems process such large amounts of data, both manufacturers and users want to increase the processing speed in any way possible. This is particularly true in cases of data input from outside the CPU, say from card readers or magnetic disk units, or when results are output to display or printer devices. Faster input, processing, and output of data mean that more data can be processed in a shorter amount of time.

The significance of this problem can be demonstrated through a simple example. Assume that a set of punched cards is to be processed one at a time through a

Figure 5.17 Serial and Overlapped Processing of Data

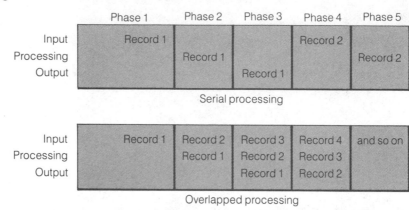

Serial processing

Overlapped processing

computer system, with the results being output to a line printer. The card reader operates at 1200 cards per minute (0.05 second per card), the line printer runs at 1500 lines per minute (0.04 second per line), and the CPU can perform the necessary processing in 0.001 second (1/1000 of a second). To input one card of data, process it, and output the results takes 0.091 second. Although this is not a long time, it is somewhat disconcerting to see that the CPU is used only 1 percent of the time and is unused for computation during the 55 percent of the time when the printer is running. Thus in an hour of data processing, using the assumptions above, the CPU is idle for all but half a minute. (Similar relations exist for input/output with other types of devices.)

When the CPU is held idle because the input and output units cannot operate at the same high speeds as the processing unit, the CPU is said to be **input/output bound** (or I/O bound). To reduce this problem somewhat, most modern computer systems have incorporated into them a procedure commonly referred to as **overlapped processing.** This simply means that instead of being performed in serial fashion, input and output operations are overlapped with processing activities, thus increasing CPU usage and decreasing the total amount of time elapsed for a program and its data to be processed (Figure 5.17).

Under nonoverlapped (or serial) processing, the first card is input, then processed; then the results are output. Each of the steps is separate and distinct—no two occur at the same time. The sequence of steps is repeated over and over for each record of data to be processed (Figure 5.18).

In overlapped processing, a number of events may occur at the same time. The first data card is input and processing begins. When processing for the *first* card of data begins (that is, at the end of the first operation), the *second* input operation begins. As the output from the first processing begins, the second data record begins processing, and the *third* record of data is input.

This sequence is repeated over and over so that at any one time there are several different activities taking place (input, processing, and output), rather than the one

Figure 5.18 Channel and Buffer Transfer of Data

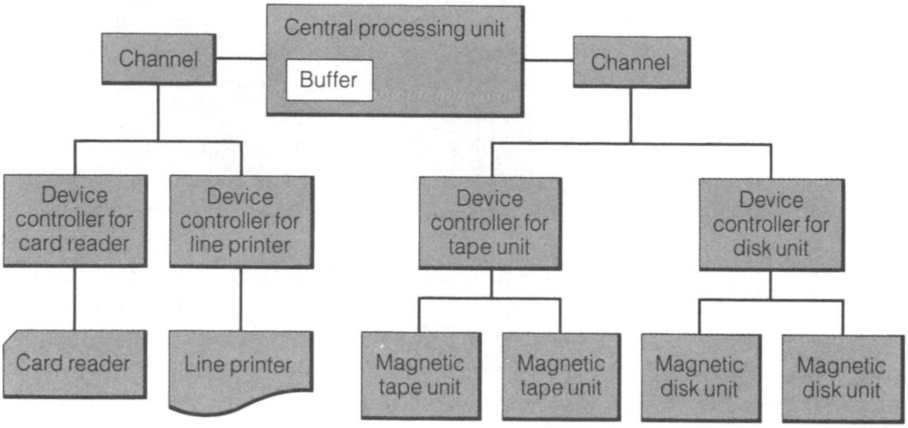

as in nonoverlapped processing. As a result of overlapping, expensive computer resources are used more efficiently and the entire processing job is completed in a much shorter time.

The example used here describes a punched card operation with printer output. However, the same principles apply for data input from magnetic devices or for output displayed on cathode ray tubes or plotters. The devices used are not the important thing in overlapping processing—rather, it is the idea of having several activities of a single computer program taking place concurrently.

Channels and Buffers

Overlapped processing is made possible through the use of special devices (called *channels* and *buffers*) that free the CPU from some of the work of data input and output. A **channel** is a hardware "pipeline" that connects an input or output unit to the memory unit of the CPU, in much the same way as a telephone in a home is connected to other telephone units by means of wires. Often, the channel is a small computer with a limited storage capacity whose main function is to connect the various devices to the CPU and make possible the transmission of data to and from each component. A channel in an ocean or large body of water connects one bay with another and allows water and ship traffic to pass back and forth. Although somewhat more sophisticated, the data channel in a computer system serves the same function.

Though the channel is a path for communication of data, instructions, and output between the CPU's components, it does not necessarily perform any of the actual computation. It operates independently of the processing unit; that is, it can be moving data to and from the CPU while the central processing unit is performing computation—thus, the channel makes overlapped processing possible.

The channel is linked to the input/output devices by a control unit. The function of the control unit (Figure 5.18), designed by the manufacturer especially for the device with which it operates, is to translate signals into a form that the device can use. Thus, a control unit or *device controller* for a magnetic disk drive would be different from one for a magnetic tape unit, even though the function is the same.

In the first computers there was typically one input device and one output device (say a card reader and a line printer). However, as technology improved and applications grew more sophisticated, this configuration was no longer sufficient. More and more peripheral devices (CRTs, printers, and so on) were added to computer system configurations, creating increased needs for data channels. Additionally, the speed of the processing unit increased so dramatically that it could outperform the input/output devices. Consequently, bottlenecks developed when input units could not keep the processor busy and output units could not dispense the output as fast as the CPU generated it. Multiple input/output systems were therefore introduced to make it possible to operate several different devices through one or more channels. In other words, under these systems several different devices could be providing input to the CPU at the same time and others could be handling the output.

Several kinds of channels are in common use today. **Selector channels** are used to feed data from fast devices (such as magnetic disk drives) directly into buffers (explained in a moment) in the CPU. They operate in **burst mode:** that is, the channels are dedicated to a single device at a particular moment and transmit data only from that one device. If a channel is handling data from a magnetic disk drive in burst mode, only the disk drive can use the channel at that time; no other devices would be able to use it then. This is possible because these devices are fast enough to use the complete capability or capacity of the channel all at once. Different units can use the channel at different times, but not at the same time.

Multiplexor channels, in contrast, are shared channels that can support several slower devices (printers, card readers, and so on) at the same time. This is accomplished by alternating the data from each device. When the data from the different devices arrive at the CPU, they are separated and the data groups from each device are reassembled into wholes for processing. With these channels, more data arrive at the CPU than would be possible if only one of the slower devices used it.

You sometimes see references to a **block multiplexor channel.** The main difference between this and the ordinary multiplexor channel is the amount of data that the former can carry to the CPU and the devices from which the data are carried. A block multiplexor channel carries longer blocks or groups of data (that is, more data at one time) from several high-speed devices. The data are interspersed on this channel, thus accommodating more than one high-speed device at a time.

As you have seen, there is usually a difference between the speeds at which different input/output units and the CPU operate. Even though the channels help improve the speed of data transmission, they are not enough to compensate for these differences in speed. **Buffers** help to adjust for differences in speeds of the CPU and peripheral devices. A buffer is a small, high-speed storage component that electronically holds data for processing or for transmission to an output device. The exact

Figure 5.19 Multiple Program Processing

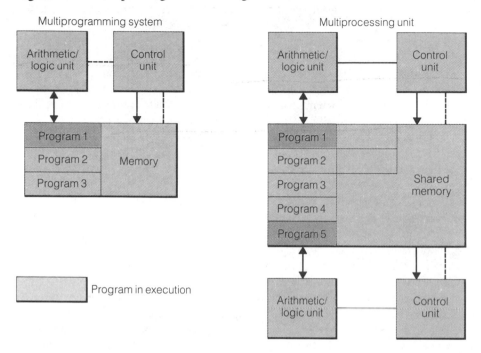

location of a buffer varies with the type of equipment in a configuration. In some cases, it is an input or output device, while in others it may be part of the CPU memory, or even in a separate storage unit between the CPU and peripheral devices.

Buffers operate under channel control (see Figure 5.18) to collect data for transmission between the CPU and input/output devices. Data from an input device are sent to the CPU and collected in the buffer. When the CPU is ready to process, data are transferred to the main storage area under the direction of the program. Processing then occurs. This sequence is reversed for output operations: The program transfers results rapidly to the buffer. The channel then moves the results to an output device so they can be printed, displayed, or whatever.

Multiprogramming **Multiprogramming** is a processing mode in which several partially completed tasks are processed *concurrently*. At any given moment, only one task or job is actually being executed, but within a larger time span of several minutes, the computer is processing several jobs or programs, alternating between actually executing, computing, and performing input/output activities. Several jobs may be in memory, but only one is executing. When one job needs to do input/output, another can begin (or resume) execution (Figure 5.19). Thus two or more independent programs are executed in the same time span by *interleaving* their execution. This is the concept that underlies overlapped processing, discussed earlier.

(overlapped processing)

The advantage of multiprogramming is that overall performance of the system can be enhanced. The great speed of the central processing unit can be used, and delays in waiting for input or output operations can be avoided.

Multiprocessing In contrast to multiprogramming, **multiprocessing** implies *simultaneous* rather than just concurrent processing. Two or more central processors of the same type are executing in parallel (that is, at the same time). Under multiprocessing, two or more different programs can be executed at the same moment because there are two or more CPUs sharing a common central memory.

(parallel processing)

Sometimes systems with *multiple different* CPUs can be configured to multiprocess. For example, a medium-size CPU and a large-scale CPU might be used in a configuration. The name given to the system of multiprocessing with different processors is *multiple-computer processing system*.

A useful processing technique that has emerged in conjunction with systems operating on more than one program at a time is **virtual memory** (also sometimes referred to as *virtual storage*). When large programs are being executed, storage available to meet the program requirements may not be sufficient, particularly when a limited *partition* or section of memory is available for each program to use. Virtual memory was developed to aid in these situations.

Virtual memory allows a system user to act as if he or she has a memory section of whatever size is needed to meet the program space requirements. In other words, one does not have to be concerned about the actual amount of space available for a program. Under this technique, the program is segmented in *pages,* which are fixed-size storage areas that contain a certain number of instructions. Most pages are kept on secondary storage devices, and only those actually needed at a particular instant are in main memory.

This means that pages are moved in and out of memory, as programs require them, by specially developed control software provided by the system manufacturers. The user need not be concerned about the memory space requirements. However, the computer system itself must do more work to move or swap the pages in and out of main memory.

Understanding the technical features of computer systems presented in this chapter will give you a good understanding of the fundamental principles underlying data processing. Now we turn to the application of these principles in data processing environments. In the next chapter, we study computer languages and software. Then we enter the next module, to explore different kinds of transaction processing systems.

Summary

Computer-based systems consist of hardware, software, procedures, and people. Each element plays an important part in transaction data processing and in decision-making activities. Hardware is the equipment that actually processes data, whereas software controls the processing within the system. Analysts, designers, programmers, operators, and engineers ensure that the system operates properly both technically and according to established procedures.

Computers vary in size, speed, and cost. Personal computers are desktop systems that cost from a few hundred dollars to approximately $15,000. Larger systems, including mainframes and supercomputers, not only cost much more but have superior processing speeds and storage capacities. These systems operate at speeds measured in nanoseconds and picoseconds. Selecting the proper system should be based on the needs of the organization and the user.

The heart of the computer system, whether large or small, is the central processing unit, which consists of the primary storage or memory unit, the arithmetic/logic unit, and the control unit. Data and instructions are held in the memory unit but may be moved about under supervision of the control unit when computation is actually being performed. The arithmetic/logic unit performs all the computations. Data are input to the CPU for processing by a wide variety of devices. Selection of a particular device depends on the medium on which data are recorded. In some cases, data are input directly to the memory unit of the CPU; in other instances, they may be written on secondary storage devices.

Results of computer processing are made accessible to users through a variety of output devices that may be part of the hardware configuration. In some cases, output may be in the form of turnaround documents that can be used later for input to the system. Selection of any output device should be based on what the results of processing are to be used for.

Data to be stored in the main memory are organized and arranged in storage locations by the control unit. However, when the data are stored on secondary storage devices, such as magnetic tape, diskette, or magnetic disk, the user has some control over how they are stored or arranged. Individual items of data are grouped into records and files. With magnetic tape, records can be grouped together through blocking. Blocking reduces the amount of space needed for interblock gaps. By increasing the blocking factor, the number of records stored between interblock gaps is increased. This makes it possible to place more records on a length of magnetic tape.

Magnetic disk and diskette storage, unlike tape, offer fixed recording density. This means that the number of characters that can be stored on a fixed section of a drum or disk is determined by the design of the devices and cannot be altered. Magnetic tape, however, can store data according to several densities, as determined by the user and the characteristics of the magnetic tape drive. Optical storage contains large quantities of data that are read through use of laser beams. Most optical disks are read-only units. All the secondary storage devices extend the storage capabilities of the computer system.

Key Words

Address	Blocking	Bubble memory
Arithmetic/logic unit	Blocking factor	Buffer
Audio response unit	Block Multiplexor Channel	Burst mode
Block	Bottleneck	Card punch

Cathode ray tube (CRT)
CD-ROM
Central processing unit (CPU)
Channel
Character printer
Chip
Computer interface
Computer program
Configuration
Control unit
Cursor
Cylinder
Daisy wheel
Data entry
Digitizer
Disk pack
Dot matrix printer
End-user computing
File
Flexible diskette
Fourth-generation language
Gigaflop
Hardcard
Hard disk
Hardware
Hologram
Impact printer
Ink jet printer
Input device
Input/output bound
Integrated circuit
Intelligent terminal
Interblock gap
Key-to-disk device

Key-to-tape device
Kilobyte
Laser printer
Light pen
Line printer
Magnetic core
Magnetic disk
Magnetic drum
Magnetic ink character reader (MICR)
Magnetic tape
Mainframe computer
Mark-sense document
Memory unit
Microcomputer
Microfiche unit
Microfilm unit
Microprocessor
Microsecond
Midrange computer
Millisecond
Minicomputer
MIPS
Mouse
Multiprocessing
Multiprogramming
Multiplexor channel
Nanosecond
Nonimpact printer
Optical character reader (OCR)
Optical storage
Output
Output device
Overlapped processing

Parallel printer
Peripheral device
Personal computer
Photographic printing
Picosecond
Plotter
Point-of-sale terminal
Primary storage unit
Procedure-oriented language
Programming language
Pull-down menu
Read/write head
Record
Recording density
Scanner
Secondary storage unit
Sector
Selector channel
Semiconductor memory
Serial printer
Software
Spreadsheet
Storage unit
Supercomputer
Thermal image printer
Track
Turnaround documents
Universal Product Code (UPC)
Virtual memory
Winchester disk
Window
Workstation
WORM

Review Questions

1. What are the main components of a computer system? What is the difference between a computer and a computer system?

2. Differentiate between hardware and software. What functions does each perform?

3. Describe the functions performed by the physical components of the central processing unit.

4. What are programming languages? What functions do they serve?

5. What are fourth-generation languages? How do they differ from traditional procedural languages such as COBOL and BASIC? What benefits do they offer to users?

6. Briefly describe the process of computing and processing transactions.

7. What are the most common data entry devices? Which do not require keying of data?

8. What are data preparation devices? Identify and describe the most important ones, indicating the medium used in each case to represent the data.

9. How are coded data represented on the different types of input media? What are the major types of codes and why do we need them?

10. If an organization does not wish to use intermediate documents to input data, what devices can be used? Since these devices exist, why are intermediate documents used?

11. How does printing occur on a line printer? How is the spacing of output on a page controlled? What different types of printers are in use today?

12. Which printers offer the greatest speeds in preparation of output? Why is this so?

13. Which printers can be used to present color or intricate graphic output? In what areas of work might this capability be needed?

14. How does laser printing differ from other printing methods?

15. What are peripheral devices?

16. What devices serve as secondary storage units? Why are they necessary? How do they differ from main memory?

17. Define the following terms: track, interblock gap, interrecord gap, file, record, end-of-file mark.

18. What is a cylinder? A sector? A head? A disk pack? A disk file?

19. What is a Winchester disk? How does it differ from a hardcard? What advantages does each offer?

20. What features characterize optical disk storage? What is the primary advantage of this storage medium? The primary disadvantage?

21. Describe the features of each type of optical disk. Which types are in most widespread use at the current time? Why?

22. What are the types of interfaces for user/system interaction? What role has the Apple Macintosh played in introducing new interfaces?

23. How are workstations and personal computers alike and how do they differ? What benefits do workstations offer for engineers and designers?

24. Discuss the future of mainframe computers, identifying the factors that will influence their utilization and the way such systems are likely to be used.

25. What purposes are served by channels and buffers? Describe the different kinds of channels and their use.

26. What are the differences between multiprocessing, multiprogramming, and multiple computer processing systems?

Application Problems

1. The president of a medium-sized department store chain has been approached by the controller about the need for acquiring a computer system to help in the routine transaction processing of the company accounting department for accounts receivable and payable and also by the purchasing department for merchandise

ordering and inventory control. However, the president has stated that she does not want a computer. She feels that it would be an added expense to her operation and would not pay for itself. She also feels that she would lose control over much of her company if she turned it over to a computer system.

What comments would you make to the president to show the benefits of computer processing? How would you deal with the expressed concern about losing control?

2. The state employment agency is preparing to purchase a computer system to process data about persons seeking jobs and companies seeking employees. A question has come up about how data should be input to the computer system for processing. Two ways are being considered:

   a. Having printed application forms, which the individual and the companies would fill out. One form would contain questions about the individual's background and the type of job being sought. A second form, to be completed by someone in the firm seeking an employee, would ask for data about the department, the job, and the type of person being sought. When the questionnaires are completed, a data entry person will key the relevant data into a workstation connected to the computer. The questionnaires are to be stored in a metal file cabinet.

   b. Having mark-sense documents on which either individuals seeking jobs or companies seeking employees would respond to questions by blackening spaces that represent the answer (for example, type of job, salary, age). The questionnaires would be input through a scanning device, which would translate the blackened spots into electronic pulses in the CPU.

   What are the advantages and disadvantages of each of these approaches? What factors should be taken into consideration in making a decision? Assume that equipment cost is not an issue.

   What other means could be used to collect and input the data for processing?

3. Intelligent terminals and microcomputers often cost more to acquire than simple terminals such as cathode ray tubes, teletypes, or on-line typewriters. What are the possible benefits of using intelligent terminals and microcomputers for input of data compared to the other devices? How does this offset the additional cost involved for microcomputers?

4. A large credit card organization uses computer processing to prepare monthly statements to mail its customers. The statement lists all purchases made during the preceding month as well as any payments made to the customer's account. The customer is supposed to tear off the top part of the statement and mail it back to the company along with a payment. Before mailing the top half, which contains the customer's name, address, and account number, the customer is requested to write the amount of the payment in a designated space on the form.

   The statement portion returned to the company is used to post the amount of the payment to the customer's account. Recently, however, the company has experienced such a large increase in customers that it can no longer keep up with the posting of the monthly payments. As a result, payments made for one month often do not appear on the next statement. This causes many customer complaints each month.

What steps could the credit card company take to improve its payment processing system? Now payments are posted to a customer account by having the account number, customer name, date, and amount of the payment punched into cards. The cards are then read into the computer and used as data for a computer program that posts the payment to the customer records stored on magnetic tape. List the alternatives the company should consider to improve this process and the benefits of each.

5. Line printers have the capacity to use continuous forms that are up to 14 inches wide. Many computer installations use only the 14-inch paper, ignoring the standard 8½-inch width. What are the advantages and disadvantages of following this strategy?

6. The Middleton Bank company prints a list of savings account interest accruals at the end of each quarter of the year. The report, printed on a line printer, contains the name, address, account number, and amount of new interest for each of the approximately 150,000 savings account holders of the bank (40 accounts per page of output). Ten copies of the report are prepared (by means of carbon paper forms, which are later burst or separated). One copy of the report is sent to each of the 10 bank offices.

The bank officers wish to reduce the cost of preparing this report. Although they realize that only about 40 percent of the entries are checked by the bank tellers during the quarter the report is used, they know that a full report must be prepared.

What options do you feel the bank officers should consider to reduce the cost associated with these paper reports? What are the benefits and possible problems with each of the alternatives you identify? (*Note:* Assume that the customers do not see the report. It is used only by the tellers.)

7. A file of 100,000 records, each of which is 32 characters long, is to be stored on magnetic disk. How many sectors, tracks, cylinders, and disk packs will be required to store the file? Assume that there are 200 cylinders on a disk pack. Each cylinder contains 20 tracks, and each track contains 20 sectors. Each sector can store 256 characters of data.

8. Bartlett Manufacturing Company is preparing to convert its employee record files from paper form to magnetic tape. There are 15,000 active records and some 115,000 inactive records (for former employees). The manager of personnel wishes to determine how many magnetic tapes to order to accommodate both the active and inactive files.

The records in the files are each 50 characters long. Between each record, when stored on tape, there will be a 0.3-inch interblock gap. The tapes that will be purchased will contain 2400 feet of usable space.

How many tapes should the personnel manager purchase to hold all the unblocked records if the recording density is 1600 characters per inch; if the recording density is 6250 characters per inch?

If the records are recorded with a blocking factor of 4, how many tapes would be required under 800, 1600, and 6250 characters-per-inch densities?

9. The Research in Marketing Company regularly conducts new-product surveys in Europe and returns the data to its New York office for processing and evaluation. Data are collected through questionnaires 10 pages long. Approximately 10,000 questionnaires are administered each time a survey is conducted.

Management is trying to determine the best means of getting the data to New York quickly while still protecting against possible loss of the valuable and sensitive data. What methods might be used to assist management with this problem? What type of computer input devices would be required for each method you identify? What are the advantages and disadvantages of each method?

10. The Brandywine Manufacturing Company is interested in finding a more accurate and efficient means of collecting data from its manufacturing line on the use of equipment and machines, production quantities, and the activities of employees. It has considered purchasing several intelligent terminals to link into the medium-size computer system it already uses for accounting, payroll, and personnel purposes. However, management is not certain whether this would be a good investment.

With the present system, each machine on the manufacturing line is numbered to make it easy to identify for routine maintenance and for assignment of employees to it. As employees begin a job they sign in on a time sheet indicating the starting time for the work, the machine to be used, and the work order number of the job. After the job is completed or at the end of the day (an individual may work on several jobs in a day or on one that lasts the entire day), the employee returns to the time sheet and adds the following data: the time of day, the amount of material used, and the amount of finished goods produced.

At the end of the day, the time sheet is sent to the processing department where the data are transferred to magnetic tape by a key-to-tape device. The tape is then read into the computer system to update the various personnel, inventory, production, and equipment maintenance files. Reports are prepared automatically at the end of the week and are distributed to manufacturing, maintenance, and payroll personnel.

Would the introduction of the data collection terminals to replace the time sheets be a good idea? What are the benefits of introducing the terminals? What problems might be expected if these terminals were used on the manufacturing line? List the major criteria you would use in making the decision.

What effect, if any, would the use of terminals have on the currency of information included in the weekly reports?

Consider error detection. What characteristics would be desirable in terminals that are to be used on the manufacturing floor?

Minicase: Optical Storage System

A large property and casualty insurance company wishes to reduce the volume of paper it circulates when processing policyholder claims. Currently, when a policy holder initiates a claim, the individual submits a letter describing the incident for which insurance coverage is requested. Often repair estimates are included (for example, to repair a damaged building or an automobile that has been in an accident) to justify the claim. In some instances, drawings and sketches are also attached.

When the claim is received, it is logged into a record book and placed in an open claim file. When processing begins, the processor removes the documents, noting on the log that the document has been removed.

When processing is completed, which consists of verification of benefits, assessment of proper coverage for the claim, preparation of payment, and correspondence with the policyholder, the documents are placed in the closed-claim file.

The firm has had difficulty in responding to inquiries from policyholders wanting to know the status of a certain claim. Location of the documentation is often time-consuming, especially if the processor is out of the office.

Management wishes to determine the feasibility of replacing the paper claim documents by the following optical storage system: When the claim is received, all documents will be scanned into computer readable form (including letters, drawings, and so forth). Handwritten annotations, signatures, and typewritten descriptions can be scanned with equal ease. After the accuracy of the scanning is verified, the paper documents will be destroyed. Only the optical version will remain.

The claims processor will work from the scanned version. Annotations and comments will be entered through a personal computer and stored with the document in the mainframe system's disk storage. Telephone inquiries can be handled by retrieving the images of the claim documents on a display screen. Even if the document is in use elsewhere, an image may be retrieved by another individual needing it.

When action on the claim is complete, the image of all documents will be moved to a closed-claim file for archival storage.

Questions

1. Is the proposed application an appropriate one for the use of scanning and optical storage? Why or why not?

2. What features must the above system have in order to be feasible?

3. What advantages and disadvantages does the proposed system provide?

Minicase: Standardize on One Computer

A common concern in many organizations, both large and small, is the issue of whether to standardize on a single vendor for all computer equipment. One company in the Northeast wrestled with this question in several meetings with management users who wished to purchase personal computers. The information systems manager, with the support of his staff, had decided several months earlier to purchase and support only personal computers produced by one large manufacturer.

To assist those wishing to use the system, the manager hired two full-time technicians who are responsible for testing, diagnosing, and repairing any malfunctioning equipment—all within a matter of hours from the time a user reports a difficulty. The technicians are also given the responsibility for monitoring new software releases and evaluating their reliability in company applications. Spare parts, ranging from memory chips to disk drives to communications devices, were ordered into stock in ample quantities.

Because of the large quantities of computers projected for use within the company under the standardization plan, the manager negotiated a special purchase agreement with the vendor. Purchase prices ranging from 25 to 35 percent below list price were agreed on, provided projected quantity levels were achieved.

It became company policy to require users to pay for computer purchases from their operating budgets (the information systems department does not *give* the computers to managers). However, when repairs are needed or parts are replaced, there is no cost to the user. The expenses are absorbed in the operating overhead of the information systems department.

The majority of users in the organization support the policy and are pleased that all departments use the same equipment. They find that the interchange of data is simplified and all users follow similar processing patterns.

Some individuals, however, are challenging this policy. Perhaps 100 of the approximately 900 users do not like the standard that has been set by the company and wish to purchase different brands of equipment. The dissenters do not agree among themselves about what other computers should be purchased: all together, about six different brands are wanted. These managers are willing to pay for the purchases from their respective budgets and will maintain the equipment as well. They argue that forcing standardization would reduce creativity, and eventually productivity. They further argue that one brand of personal computer does not meet all needs.

Questions

1. Is the development of a single standard for personal computers, considering the support facilities provided in this organization, advisable? Explain.

2. Should end-users be able to purchase whatever hardware or software they wish to use in performing their work? Should the information systems department select the equipment for users? The software?

6: Software for Information Systems

Key Questions

How does operating software differ from application software?

How do third-, fourth-, and fifth-generation programming languages differ?

When should prewritten software packages be utilized?

What are the types of fourth-generation software in widespread use?

What are the most useful personal computer software packages?

Why are developers shifting to fourth-generation software?

How do you choose a programming language?

If builders built buildings the way programmers write programs, then the first woodpecker that came along would destroy civilization.

Jerry Weinberg

Computer hardware provides the capability and the power to process data and produce the information managers, staff members, and organizations need. But the computer would not be useful without software. All of the trends in computer processing speed, higher storage densities, and decreasing costs for equivalent computing capabilities are useful only if the appropriate software is available to take advantage of the capabilities.

This chapter explores the software that underlies successful information systems. Two types of software—operating system and application software—are essential, as the first section shows. Next, we examine the five generations of languages used in application software. Third- and fourth-generation software, the types most frequently used today, are discussed in detail. The last section of this chapter covers six different types of personal computer software.

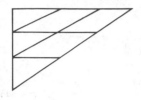

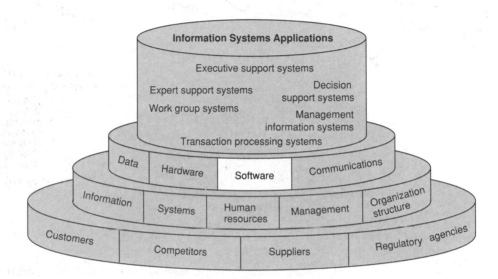

Why Should You Know About Computer Software?

Whether you use computers directly or not, it is important to understand the nature of computer software because:

—*Software controls how computers are used.* Computer systems are virtually useless without software. Alternatively, software that is not reliable—perhaps because it is not designed to perform the correct functions or to perform the functions properly—can hinder the value of any computer system, large or small.

—*You are affected by software when using computers.* You are a user of computers even when you are not aware of it, since there are many more ways of using computers than by sitting at the keyboard of a personal computer. Computers are basic to systems such as automated teller systems and scanners at the checkout counter. And all of these computers use software that affects you.

——*You can influence the selection or development of the right software.* As a member of an organization, you have many opportunities to influence the development or selection of computer software. Computers are an integral part of many business processes—the same processes in which you are involved. As you influence how the process is designed, you undoubtedly will have a role in specifying the use of computer hardware and software, whether directly or indirectly.

——*The cost of software exceeds the cost of hardware.* Computer software is expensive for several reasons. First, it is developed by a labor-intensive process, and personnel costs are increasing. Software costs are thus also increasing. Second, a great deal of software is needed for the many uses of computers. While hardware costs are plummeting, software costs are skyrocketing.

These points provide a framework for the following discussion, which begins with an overview of the different types of software used.

Types of Computer Software

Computer systems require two kinds of software: operating system software and application software.

Operating System Software

Whether the computer system is large or small, a variety of activities occur, sometimes simultaneously: data enters the system; records are written to or read from secondary storage; processing occurs; and processing results are sent to a printer or display device. And all these activities have to take place with accuracy and efficiency as well as speed. The operating system makes this possible.

The **operating system** is a group of programs that monitor and control all input/output and processing operations. As a software tool, it allocates and controls the hardware. Programs that make up the operating system are usually developed according to specifications provided by the computer manufacturers and supplied to purchasers. They are designed to make the best use of the components of each individual computer system, since an operating system that is effective for one type of system may be totally unusable on the computer of another manufacturer. In addition, even within one manufacturer's systems, different operating systems may exist.

Table 6.1 Common Operating Systems

Operating System	Computer
PC DOS	IBM personal computer
MS DOS	Microsoft Software's DOS for IBM compatible personal computers
UNIX	Large number of personal computers, midrange systems, and mainframes
AppleDos	Apple personal computers
MVS	IBM mainframe computers
VM	IBM mainframe computers
Ultrix	Digital Equipment Corporation (DEC) computer systems

Table 6.1 lists the most widely used operating systems. Personal computers often use a DOS operating system (for example, PC DOS or MS DOS). **DOS** is an acronym for disk operating system. The name indicates that the operating system modules are stored on magnetic disk. As modules are needed, they are brought into the processor.

UNIX is an increasingly popular operating system because it can be used across different manufacturers' computers. Hence when software is written to run under the UNIX operating system on one computer, it is relatively easy to adapt the same software to run on another manufacturer's computer.

Jobs

As user jobs are submitted for computer processing, they fall under operating system control. *Jobs* in this sense include control instructions that specify the system languages to be used, the necessary magnetic disk, magnetic tape, or other storage media, and other needed supervisory information such as the amount of time to be allotted and the amount of memory needed to accomplish the processing job. A job also includes the computer program, input/output requirements, and data to be used in the execution of the program. As this information enters the CPU from the input device, the operating system takes control to provide the services requested in the user's program, while at the same time making maximum use of the system resources.

Control Functions

The basic functions performed by the operating system can be divided into control functions and service functions. *Control functions* provide continuity of operation by assuring that each activity takes place correctly and in proper sequence. Most important among the various control functions are initiating input/output operations, processing interrupts (for instance, signals indicating that an input/output operation is needed or completed), recording jobs processed, and monitoring job status.

Computer systems, large and small, are interrupt driven. An **interrupt** is a signal to the operating system either that some action needs to be taken or that an action started earlier is not completed. For example, when an error occurs in processing—

perhaps the disk is full or the printer is out of paper—an interrupt is generated that tells the operating system that processing cannot continue as planned. The interrupt may lead the operating system to terminate the program and print out a message explaining the condition so that necessary action will be taken.

In short, the operating system has total responsibility for integrating all the processes and ensuring that each occurs at the proper time.

Service Functions

The operating system also performs *service functions,* the extra support activities that ensure the most advantageous use of both system and user resources. We know that the operating system is a set or collection of modules or small programs that together perform all the necessary processing in the computer programs. For the required processing to take place, each of these modules must be loaded into memory at the proper time. *Loading* is the process of moving each individual module of the operating system from the storage medium to the memory unit of the CPU. The operating system performs this service function.

Among the most important modules used in processing data are utility programs and translator programs. *Utility programs* are prewritten software modules that are frequently required in processing data. They may be as simple as a short set of instructions to take the square root or find the absolute value of a number. Or they may be quite complex, as in a sort program that arranges 15,000 names in alphabetical order. All these operations occur so often that it makes sense to have them preprogrammed and stored for rapid use as they are requested.

Translator programs are prewritten programs that convert computer programs written in a programing language into electronic pulses the computer system understands. Several different types of translator programs are in common use in modern computer systems.

Compilers are translator programs called into memory by the operating system to convert computer programs written in procedure-oriented languages (like COBOL, FORTRAN, PL/1) into executable electronic pulses or binary instructions known as *machine language.* The computer program is often called a **source program.** After it has been translated into machine language, a process called *compiling the program,* it is known as an **object program** or *object code.* All source programs must be compiled before the system can execute them.

The operating system and all the software modules that comprise it make the processing of data an easy job for the user. Without it, it would be very difficult for transaction processing to occur, and many organizations probably would not be using computer systems at all.

Application Software

Typically, when we think of computers we focus on the tasks they perform: processing customer orders, making airline reservations, scanning the product codes on food packages at the grocery checkout counter, or processing text using personal computers (that is, word processing). Each of these are *applications*—the use of computers

Figure 6.1 Relation Between Operating System and Application Program

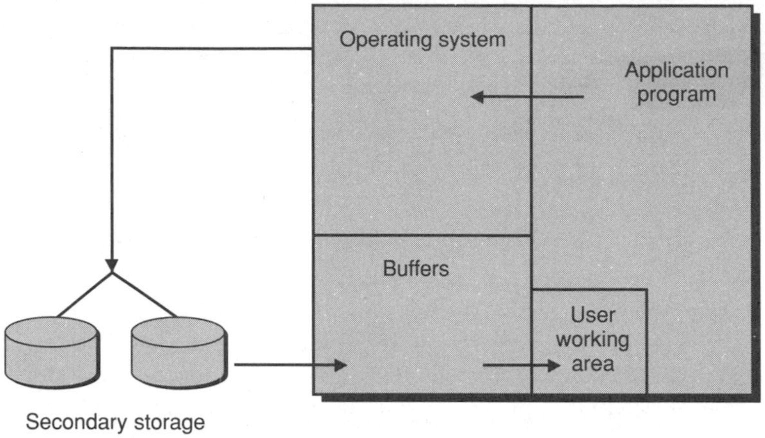

to complete a specific type of task. The software that makes these examples of processing possible is called **application software.** Hence an order processing program is an application program. So is an airline reservations system.

Application software interacts with the operating system of the computer (Figure 6.1). As you know, the operating system controls the use of computer. But the application software ensures that correct tasks are performed in the manner we wish.

The remainder of this chapter will focus on the different aspects of application software. We begin by discussing how such software is obtained.

Acquiring Application Software

In almost every case, organizations using computers purchase the operating system. One operating system is needed for a computer. But many different application programs can be run on a particular computer. When it comes to application software, there are several options for acquiring the appropriate software. This section discusses the choices for purchasing or creating application software.

Computer application software can be acquired in three ways:

— *Create the software using in-house development teams.* "In-house development" is the computer industry's term for the design and programming of software by an organization's systems analysts and computer programmers. These staff members are responsible for determining what the software must do, developing the specifications, creating the software, and testing the programs prior to implementation.

— *Develop the software using contract programming.* This involves hiring independent specialists—called contractors—in software development to create the software needed by the organization. The contractors may be responsible for the entire development process, including formulation of specifications, or for creation of the software using specifications prepared by the organization's information systems group. In some cases, contractors modify existing software to meet specifications rather than creating the entire system from scratch.

———*Purchase software packages.* In this case, a firm buys or leases prewritten software that can be quickly installed on its computer system. Typically this costs much less than actually developing the software.

All three alternatives are in widespread use in the business community.

In-House Development To determine whether the in-house development strategy is the best one for the task at hand, the following factors must be evaluated.

———Does the organization have sufficient trained staff to develop the software?

———Does the planned development schedule permit completion of the project in an acceptable time frame?

———Is the cost of developing and maintaining the system using organization personnel a good investment compared to other alternatives?

———Could the necessary software be acquired in other ways?

For many organizations, in-house development is not advisable. Often, for example, it is not cost effective for a small business organization to hire and retain a programming staff. Similarly, if a particular software requirement will lead to incurring high programming costs and a comparable package can be obtained through other means, in-house development should not be selected.

Contract Development Even if an organization hires programmers and analysts, they may not have the expertise in a particular area, nor the time to acquire it, to undertake a development task. Contractors who have expertise in a certain type of application may be able to do the task more quickly and more effectively than an in-house team.

Contracting for software is an attractive alternative under the following conditions:

———The organization does not have staff available to develop the needed software.

———No generalized prepackaged software suitable to the task is available.

———The cost of contracting for development of custom software is not prohibitive.

———Suitable arrangements can be made for maintenance of the software (that is, changes, enhancements, and corrections) after it has been delivered to the customer.

Development costs may be higher with contractors, since it is necessary to pay for their expertise. A related advantage is that they can be retained only for the duration of the project. When the job is completed, they go on to do other projects elsewhere, so that the organization no longer has them on the payroll.

The Use of Packaged Software A **software package** is a prewritten program or set of programs designed to perform specific tasks. For example, many organizations purchase payroll packages. Not only is this cheaper than writing their own, but purchasers also may benefit from changes that have been incorporated into the software package at the request of other users. In most cases, organizations using the same package form *user groups* that communicate regularly concerning the package. User groups can be instrumental in influencing the developer to enhance the software (that is, to add new features) or to provide additional services.

Note that the term *purchase* typically means "purchase a license to use" the software. The selling firm retains ownership. It may sell copies of the software to many different users, but does not give up its ownership. Licenses prevent purchasers from reselling the software, but do not restrict their use for the intended purpose. Licensing rather than sale of software generally means a firm can acquire the software at a much lower cost compared to the other alternatives we discuss.

Key questions to raise when considering software packages include:

—— Is a software package with the proper features available at a reasonable cost?

—— Is the cost of acquiring the package an acceptable alternative to custom development?

—— Is the total number of users large enough to ensure that the developer will support the package after it is purchased?

Most personal computers rely almost exclusively on purchased software. The software they need generally exists, it is reliable, and its purchase is a cost-effective investment.

In the sections that follow, we look at both programming languages used to develop application software and the package software in widespread use on computers. We begin by exploring the five generations of programming languages, first in general terms and then through a more detailed discussion of third- and fourth-generation languages.

Generations of Programming Languages

Computer software development techniques have not undergone the same extensive advances witnessed in computer hardware. The production of software remains largely a labor-intensive, manual process using little automation in the development process (Chapter 16 discusses advances occurring in automating software development). However, the increased demand for effective, efficient, and reliable computer software has caused more and more attention to be paid to this important aspect of computing.

Experts generally divide the development of computer languages into five generations.

The First Generation

The first generation began, as you would expect, with the development of computers in the 1940s and 1950s. **Machine language,** the first-generation language, consisted of strings of binary digits (the numbers 0 and 1). All instructions and commands were written by programmers using strings of these digits (Figure 6.2).

Even today the only internal language the computer understands, whether a desktop personal computer or a large supercomputer, is machine language. However,

Figure 6.2 Sample Assembly Language Program Showing Comparable Machine Instructions

Machine Code

MEMORY

LOCATION	OBJECT CODE	ADDR1	ADDR2
0000000			00000
000000	5820	F010	00010
000004	5A20	F014	00014
000008	5020	F018	0001B
00000C	07FE		
00000E	0000		
000010	00000001		
000014	00000002		
000018			

Assembly Language

STMT	SOURCE STATEMENT			
1	ADD	TEMPO		; IDENTIFIES BEGINNING/NAME OF PGM
2		USING	*,15	; IDENTIFIES R15 AS BASE REGISTER
3		l	1,A	; LOAD '7' INTO REGISTER 1
4		A	1,B	; ADD '14' TO CONTENTS OF REGISTER 1
5		ST	2,TDT	; STORE CONTENTS OF REGISTER 1 IN TDT
6		BR	14	; EXIT
7	A	DC	F'7'	; INITIALIZE TO 7
8	B	DC	F'14'	; INITIALIZE TO 14
9	SUM	DS	F	; RESERVE MEMORY LOCATION FOR SUM
10		END		

programmers no longer write in machine language. Instead, the programs are written in higher-level languages and translated into machine language.

The Second Generation

Assembly languages, which originated in the late 1950s, characterized the second generation. Programs consisted of symbolic codes that specified the actions of the computer. Common instructions in assembly language are shown in Figure 6.3. Assemblers translate assembly language programs into the machine code understood by the computer.

Some programmers still write programs in assembly language when there is a concern for peak execution efficiency or when intricate manipulations are needed. However, third- and fourth-generation languages dominate computer software today, and fifth-generation languages are emerging.

The Third Generation

Programming languages of the third generation, which began in the 1960s, are known as **higher-level** or procedural **languages.** A variety of languages were developed to meet application requirements. Hence you find scientific languages (such as FORTAN), business languages (like COBOL), and general-use languages (including BASIC).

Procedural languages must be translated into the machine code that the computer can understand. However, these languages allow the programmer to state *how to perform a task at* a much higher level than assembly languages.

The vast majority of computer applications in use today were written using **third-generation languages.** We can expect that these languages will be in use in the future. However, fourth-generation languages are now used to develop many new applications.

The Fourth Generation

A constant concern among both computer users and computer specialists is the amount of time and effort devoted to the development of computer programs. In addition, the increasing number of computers in use means that more people will be computer users. **Fourth-generation languages** were developed to meet both these concerns.

The distinguishing feature of fourth-generation languages is the emphasis on specifying *what is to be done* rather than on *how* a task should be carried out. Program specifications are developed at a higher level than with third-generation languages. What do we mean by "higher level"? The distinguishing feature of the fourth generation is a nonprocedural flavor; the programmer does not have to specify each step to complete a processing task. Processing results can be obtained with significantly fewer lines of code compared to third-generation languages (often a tenth the instructions). However, it should be noted that some fourth-generation languages include both procedural and nonprocedural elements, allowing programmers to balance ease

Figure 6.3 Common Assembly Language Commands   215

Name	Mnemonic	OP Code	For-mat	Operands
Add (c)	AR	1A	RR	R1,R2
Add (c)	A	5A	RX	R1,D2(X2,B2)
Add Decimal (c)	AP	FA	SS	D1(L1,B1),D2(L2,B2)
Add Halfword (c)	AH	4A	RX	R1,D2(X2,B2)
Add Logical (c)	ALR	1E	RR	R1,R2
Add Logical (c)	AL	5E	RX	R1,D2(X2,B2)
AND (c)	NR	14	RR	R1,R2
AND (c)	N	54	RX	R1,R2(X2,B2)
AND (c)	NI	94	SI	D1(B1),I2
AND (c)	NC	D4	SS	D1(L,B1),D2(B2)
Branch and Link	BALR	05	RR	R1,R2
Branch and Link	BAL	45	RX	R1,D2(X2,B2)
Branch and Save	BASR	0D	RR	R1,R2
Branch and Save	BAS	4D	RX	R1,D2(X2,B2)
Branch on Condition	BCR	07	RR	M1,R2
Branch on Condition	BC	47	RX	M1,D2(X2,B2)
Branch on Count	BCTR	06	RR	R1,R2
Branch on Count	BCT	46	RX	R1,D2,(X2,B2)
Branch on Index High	BXH	86	RS	R1,R3,D2(B2)
Branch on Index Low or Equal	BXLE	87	RS	R1,R3,D2(B2)
Clear Channel (c,p)	CLRCH	9F01	S	D2(B2)
Clear I/O (c,p)	CLRIO	9D01	S	D2(B2)
Compare (c)	CR	19	RR	R1,R2
Compare (c)	C	59	RX	R1,D2(X2,B2)
Compare and Swap (c)	CS	BA	RS	R1,R3,D2(B2)
Compare Decimal (c)	CP	F9	SS	D1,(L1,B1),D2(L2,B2)
Compare Double and Swap (c)	CDS	BB	RS	R1,R3,D2(B2)
Compare Halfword (c)	CH	49	RX	R1,D2(X2,B2)
Compare Logical (c)	CLR	15	RR	R1,R2
Compare Logical (c)	CL	55	RX	R1,D2(X2,B2)
Compare Logical (c)	CLI	95	SI	D1(B1),I2
Compare Logical (c)	CLC	D5	SS	D1(L,B1),D2(B2)
Compare Logical Characters under Mask (c)	CLM	BD	RS	R1,M3,D2(B2)
Compare Logical Long (c)	CLCL	0F	RR	R1,R2
Connect Channel Set (c,p)	CONCS	B200	S	D2(B2)
Convert to Binary	CVB	4F	RX	R1,D2(X2,B2)
Convert to Decimal	CVD	4E	RX	R1,D2(X2,B2)
Diagnose (p)		83		Model-dependent
Disconnect Channel Set (c,p)	DISCS	B201	S	D2(B2)

Name	Mnemonic	OP Code	For-mat	Operands
Divide	DR	1D	RR	R1,R2
Divide	D	5D	RX	R1,D2(X2,B2)
Divide Decimal	DP	FD	SS	D1(L1,B1),D2(L2,B2)
Edit (c)	ED	DE	SS	D1(L,B1),D2(B2)
Edit and Mark (c)	EDMK	DF	SS	D1(L,B1),D2(B2)
Exclusive OR (c)	XR	17	RR	R1,R2
Exclusive OR (c)	X	57	RX	R1,D2(X2,B2)
Exclusive OR (c)	XI	97	SI	D1(B1),I2
Exclusive OR (c)	XC	D7	SS	D1,(L,B1),D2(B2)
Execute	EX	44	RX	R1,D2(X2,B2)
Extract Primary ASN (s)	EPAR	B226	RRE	R1
Extract Secondary ASN (s)	ESAR	B227	RRE	R1
Halt Device (c,p)	HDV	9E01	S	D2(B2)
Halt I/O (c,p)	HIO	9E00	S	D2(B2)
Insert Address Space Control (c,s)	IAC	B224	RRE	R1
Insert Character	IC	43	RX	R1,D2(X2,B2)
Insert Characters under Mask (c)	ICM	BF	RS	R1,M3,D2(B2)
Insert PSW Key (s)	IPK	B20B	S	
Insert Storage Key (p)	ISK	09	RR	R1,R2
Insert Storage Key Extended (p)	ISKE	B229	RRE	R1,R2
Insert Virtual Storage Key (s)	IVSK	B223	RRE	R1,R2
Invalidate Page Table Entry (p)	IPTE	B221	RRE	R1,R2
Load	LR	18	RR	R1,R2
Load	L	58	RX	R1,D2(X2,B2)
Load Address	LA	41	RX	R1,D2(X2,B2)
Load Address Space Parameters (c,p)	LASP	E500	SSE	D1(B1),D2(B2)
Load and Test (c)	LTR	12	RR	R1,R2
Load Complement (c)	LCR	13	RR	R1,R2
Load Control (p)	LCTL	B7	RS	R1,R3,D2(B2)
Load Halfword	LH	48	RX	R1,D2(X2,B2)
Load Multiple	LM	98	RS	R1,R3,D2(B2)
Load Negative (c)	LNR	11	RR	R1,R2
Load Positive (c)	LPR	10	RR	R1,R2
Load PSW (n,p)	LPSW	82	S	D2(B2)
Load Real Address (c,p)	LRA	B1	RX	R1,D2(X2,B2)
Monitor Call	MC	AF	SI	D1(B1),I2
Move	MVI	92	SI	D1(B1),I2
Move	MVC	D2	SS	D1(L,B1),D2(B2)
Move Inverse	MVCIN	E8	SS	D1(L,B1),D2(B2)
Move Long (c)	MVCL	0E	RR	R1,R2
Move Numerics	MVN	D1	SS	D1(L,B1),D2(B2)

Name	Mnemonic	OP Code	Format	Operands
Move to Primary (c,s)	MVCP	DA	SS	D1(R1,B1),D2(B2),R3
Move to Secondary (c,s)	MVCS	DB	SS	D1(R1,B1),D2(B2),R3
Move with Key (c,s)	MVCK	D9	SS	D1(R1,B1),D2(B2),R3
Move with Offset	MVO	F1	SS	D1(L1,B1)D2(L2,B2)
Move Zones	MVZ	D3	SS	D1(L,B1),D2(B2)
Multiply	MR	1C	RR	R1,R2
Multiply	M	5C	RX	R1,D2(X2,B2)
Multiply Decimal	MP	FC	SS	D1(L1,B1)D2(L2,B2)
Multiply Halfword	MH	4C	RX	R1,D2(X2,B2)
OR (c)	OR	16	RR	R1,R2
OR (c)	O	56	RX	R1,D2(X2,B2)
OR (c)	OI	96	SI	D1(B1),I2
OR (c)	OC	D6	SS	D1(L,B1),D2(B2)
Pack	PACK	F2	SS	D1(L1,B1),D2(L2,B2)
Program Call (s)	PC	B218	S	D2(B2)
Program Transfer (s)	PT	B228	RRE	R1,R2
Purge TLB (p)	PTLB	B20D	S	
Read Direct (p)	RDD	85	SI	D1(B1),I2
Reset Reference Bit (c,p)	RRB	B213	S	D2(B2)
Reset Reference Bit Extended (c,p)	RRBE	B22A	RRE	R1,R2
Resume I/O (c,p)	RIO	9C02	S	D2(B2)
Set Address Space Control (s)	SAC	B219	S	D2(B2)
Set Clock (c,p)	SCK	B204	S	D2(B2)
Set Clock Comparator (p)	SCKC	B206	S	D2(B2)
Set CPU Timer (p)	SPT	B208	S	D2(B2)
Set Prefix (p)	SPX	B210	S	D2(B2)
Set Program Mask (n)	SPM	04	RR	R1
Set PSW Key from Address (s)	SPKA	B20A	S	D2(B2)
Set Secondary ASN (s)	SSAR	B225	RRE	R1
Set Storage Key (p)	SSK	08	RR	R1,R2
Set Storage Key Extended (p)	SSKE	B22B	RRE	R1,R2
Set System Mask (p)	SSM	80	S	D2(B2)
Shift and Round Decimal (c)	SRP	F0	SS	D1(L1,B1),D2(B2),I3
Shift Left Double (c)	SLDA	8F	RS	R1,D2(B2)
Shift Left Double Logical	SLDL	8D	RS	R1,D2(B2)
Shift Left Single (c)	SLA	8B	RS	R1,D2(B2)
Shift Left Single Logical	SLL	89	RS	R1,D2(B2)

c. Condition code is set
n. New condition code is loaded

p. Privileged instruction
s. Semiprivileged instruction
x. Extended-precision floating-point

Table 6.2 Comparison of Third- and Fourth-Generation Languages

Third-Generation Languages	Fourth-Generation Languages
Intended for use by professional programmers.	May be used by nonprogramming professional (that is, user) as well as professional programmer.
Requires specification of *how to perform task*.	Requires specification of *what task to perform* (system determines how to perform the task).
All alternatives must be specified.	Default alternatives are built in—user need not specify these alternatives.
Requires large number of procedural instructions.	Requires far fewer instructions (less than one-tenth in most cases).
Code may be difficult to read, understand, and maintain.	Code is easy to understand and maintain because of English-like commands.
Language developed originally for batch operation.	Language developed primarily for on-line use.
Can be difficult to learn.	Many features can be learned quickly.
Difficult to debug.	Errors easier to locate because of shorter programs, more structured code, use of defaults, and use of English-like language.
Typically file oriented.	Typically database oriented.

of programming with efficiency of operation. Table 6.2, which compares the features of third- and fourth-generation languages, shows that "higher level" means "fewer commands are needed" because each higher-level command replaces many lower-level instructions.

The Fifth Generation

As the preceding section suggests, a great deal of change has occurred in the languages and tools used to develop information systems software. Even more changes are emerging. On the horizon are **fifth-generation languages** (Figure 6.4). Although these have not yet been introduced into business usage, there has been considerable speculation on their potential. Fifth-generation languages are expected to have three major distinctions:

— *Knowledge bases as a foundation.* Knowledge bases are collections of rules and facts pertaining to an area of interest (for example, medicine or tax planning). It is anticipated that fifth-generation languages will draw on knowledge bases both to guide computer processing and to respond to user inquiries.

— *Rule-based programming.* Languages will enable programmers to describe a set of facts and rules (such as IF-THEN-ELSE statements) that comprise the knowledge base and the program. These components will be the basis for responding to inquiries or solving problems. Changing the facts or rules affecting a problem will change the processing.

Figure 6.4 Computer Usage Involving Fifth-Generation Languages

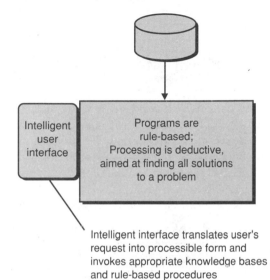

Knowledge base for
area of interest (for example, medicine)

Intelligent
user
interface

Programs are
rule-based;
Processing is deductive,
aimed at finding all solutions
to a problem

nnnnnnnnnnnnnnnnnn
nnnnnnnnnnnnnnnnnn

Users will interact with
computer using natural
language to express
inquiries or processing
needs

Intelligent interface translates user's
request into processible form and
invokes appropriate knowledge bases
and rule-based procedures

———*Artificial intelligence orientation*. Artificial intelligence (AI) refers to the teaching of computers to accomplish tasks in a manner that is considered "intelligent." Rather than following sequences of instructions, AI-based programs will have the ability to associate facts, rules, and conditions to determine an appropriate action or outcome. One area of increasing attention is the use of natural languages, like ordinary English (in contrast to traditional programming languages) to describe events or processing requirements.

PROLOG, an early form of fifth-generation language, developed in Paris, is a current rule-based language that is becoming increasingly popular. Unlike traditional programming languages, PROLOG gives the computer a description of a problem, using facts and rules, and then asks it to find all possible solutions to the problem. The computer is not told how to find the solution.

A simple example will demonstrate the power of PROLOG, as well as fifth-generation-language potential in general. Given the facts:

Terry likes Nancy.
Ted likes Mike.

and the rule:

Judy likes X if Ted likes X

PROLOG can deduce the result that:

Judy likes Mike.

In general, facts—stored in the knowledge base—and rules are processed to deduce a result. Inquiries can be posed without the need for predefined processing procedures, in contrast to the situation with current languages.

Chapter 14 discusses expert systems and knowledge-based developments in detail.

Third-Generation Languages

In this section we look at several programming languages commonly used in the United States. This discussion will not make you an expert in any of the languages, but it will give you an idea of how they are used in developing computer programs to solve business-oriented processing problems.

To help you to compare the features of the different languages, we will use a common example—a payroll processing problem—as a demonstration program. The payroll problem calls for the following procedures to be followed.

1. Input the following payroll transaction data from the workstation:
   a. Employee identification number
   b. Employee name
   c. Hours worked (40 hours per week is normal)
   d. Payroll deductions*
   e. Pay rate*
2. Test to see whether the employee worked more than 40 hours in the week.
3. If the employee worked 40 or fewer hours, calculate gross pay by multiplying the number of hours worked by the pay rate.
4. If the employee worked more than 40 hours, calculate the gross pay by multiplying the pay rate by 40 and multiplying the number of hours over 40 by 1.5 times the pay rate (overtime pay). Add the two products to compute the total gross pay.
5. Calculate the amount of tax by multiplying gross pay by the tax rate of 25 percent.
6. Determine net pay by subtracting the amount of tax and deductions from gross pay.
7. Output the following results of processing:
   a. Employee identification number
   b. Employee number
   c. Hours worked
   d. Regular pay
   e. Overtime pay
   f. Gross pay
   g. Total net pay

*In an actual business situation, these items probably would be stored in secondary storage devices and retrieved as needed. The concept of storing data in files is discussed in detail in Chapter 7.

8. Check to see whether all payroll transactions have been processed by reading the next transaction record. If the employee identification number is 99999, consider the processing to be complete.

9. If all transactions have been processed, the program is finished.

10. If all transactions have not been processed, process the transaction data just input (that is, begin again).

For each of the third-generation programming languages we study, a version of this problem statement will be coded. You will see how the instructions are used to input data, to perform calculations and tests, and to output results.

FORTRAN

The **FORTRAN** (FORmula TRANslator) programming language, designed in 1957, was originally developed for IBM computer systems. It became very widely used, however, and is available on nearly every type of computer system. Used primarily for arithmetic, algebraic, and numerical computing, FORTRAN is procedure oriented; that is, the program of instructions must clearly define the arithmetic, input/output, and other procedures that may be wanted without concern for how the operations are actually performed or carried out by the central processing unit. In working through the payroll programming problem, we will examine the kind of instructions required in FORTRAN and develop a sample program that uses them.

In FORTRAN, input/output statements and FORMAT statements are used together. READ and WRITE statements serve the input and output functions, each using a FORMAT statement that specifies the type of data, their size, and their location on the input or output medium. The sample program shown in Figure 6.5 contains the following READ and WRITE statements:

```
READ (5,100) ID, NAME, HOURS, DED, PAY
WRITE (6,110) ID, NAME, HOURS, RPAY, OPAY, GPAY, TPAY
```

The numbers 5 and 6 refer to the device or piece of computer equipment used for input and output: 5 means a card reader and 6, a line printer. The numbers 100 and 110 correspond to FORMAT statements 100 and 110 (discussed later), which specify the location of the data on the input and output media. After the right-hand parentheses come data or variable names for employee identification number, employee name, and so on, as indicated on the first page. These abbreviations are used, rather than the full word because FORTRAN places a maximum length of six letters on variable names. The variable names are assigned by the programmer, not by the computer system.

FORMAT statements are data specification statements that correspond to particular input/output instructions. Consider the following FORMAT statements:

```
100 FORMAT (I5, 2X, A4, F5.2, F5.2, F5.2)
110 FORMAT (20X, I5, 5X, A4, 5X, F7.2, 5X, F7.2, 5X, F7.2, 5X, F7.2, 5X,
    F7.2)
```

Figure 6.5 Sample FORTRAN Program

```
PROGRAM Payroll Calculation
ROUTINE Gross Pay and Net Pay

C       PROGRAM PAY
C
C       THIS PROGRAM CALCULATES PAYROLL INFORMATION USING DATA
C       INPUT FROM AN 80-COLUMN IMAGE
C
C       THE FOLLOWING DATA/VARIABLE NAMES ARE USED:
C           ITEM     MEANING
C           ====     =======
C           ID      IS  EMPLOYEE IDENTIFICATION NUMBER  (INPUT)
C           NAME    IS  EMPLOYEE NAME                   (INPUT)
C           HOURS   IS  HOURS WORKED                    (INPUT)
C           DED     IS  PAYROLL DEDUCTIONS              (INPUT)
C           PAY     IS  PAY RATE                        (INPUT)
C           RPAY    IS  REGULAR PAY
C           OPAY    IS  OVERTIME PAY
C           GPAY    IS  GROSS PAY
C           TPAY    IS  TOTAL NET TAKE-HOME PAY
C           TAX     IS  INCOME TAX
C           OHOURS  IS  TOTAL NET PAY
C
C     PRINT HEADING
      WRITE (6,50)
   50 FORMAT (20X,5HID NO.5X,NAME,5X,7HRS WKD,5X,7HREG PAY,5X,
     17HOVERTIME,4X,9HGROSS PAY,4X,7HMET PAY)
C     READ ONE CARD AND CHECK FOR END OF TRANSACTIONS
C
 1000 READ (5,100) ID,NAME, HOURS, DED, PAY
  100 FORMAT (I5,2X,A4,F5.2, F5.2,F5.2)
      IF (ID .EQ. 99999) GO TO 1300
      RPAY = 0.0
      OPAY = 0.0
C
C     CHECK FOR OVERTIME
      IF (HOURS .GT. 40.) GO TO 1100
C
C     PROCESS WITHOUT ANY OVERTIME
      GPAY = HOURS * PAY
      TAX = GPAY * .25
      TPAY = - (TAX + DED)
      GO TO 1200
C
C     PROCESS WITH OVERTIME
C
```

```
1100 RPAY = 40.0 * PAY
     OHOUR = HOURS - 40.0
     OPAY = OHOUR * (PAY * 1.5)
     GPAY = RPAY + OPAY
     TAX = GPAY * .25
     TPAY = GPAY - (TAX = DED)
C
C    OUTPUT RESULTS OF THIS TRANSACTION
C
1200 WRITE (6,110) ID, NAME, HOURS, RPAY, OPAY, GPAY, TPAY
 110 FORMAT (20X,I5,5X,A4,5X,F7.2,5X,F7.2,5X,F7.2,5X,F7.2,5X,F7.2)
     GO TO 1000
1300 STOP
     END
```

The numbers 100 and 110 correspond to the format numbers in the READ and WRITE statements. Within the parentheses are the data specifications that correspond to the variable names used in the sample READ and WRITE statements. For FORMAT 100,

I5   Integer data up to five digits long, from the first five columns of the punched data card (which is ID).

2X   A specification to skip the next two columns of the card

A4   Alphanumeric data punched into the next four columns of the card (which is NAME).

F5.2   Real/floating-point data for the next five columns—the data are five positions long, including one column for the decimal point and two digits following the decimal point. Using an F5.2 specification permits any number up to and including the value 99.99. (This specification is used for the data items HOURS, DED, and PAY.)

For FORMAT 110,

20X   Skip past the first 20 spaces (that is, columns or print positions).

I5   Integer results up to five digits long (which is ID).

5X   Skip the next five spaces (leave them blank).

A4   Alphanumeric results of four characters (which is NAME).

F7.2   Real/floating-point results for the next seven positions on the output medium (on paper). The largest value that could be printed using this specification is 9999.99. (This specification is used for the data items HOURS, RPAY, OPAY, GPAY, and TPAY.)

After the input (READ statement) in the program you see several arithmetic statements. Arithmetic statements define calculations to be performed on data. The following statements are representative of arithmetic statements:

```
RPAY = 40.0 * PAY
OHOUR = HOURS − 40.0
OPAY = OHOUR * (PAY * 1.5)
GPAY = RPAY + OPAY
TAX = GPAY * .25
TPAY = GPAY − (TAX + DED)
```

In these statements, in addition to the usual + and − for addition and subtraction, the symbol * stands for multiplication. Division, if needed, is shown by the symbol /. The symbol = means "is defined to be." In other words, RPAY (regular pay) is defined to be the product of 40.0 multiplied by PAY (hourly pay rate). Similarly, TPAY (total net pay) is defined to be GPAY (gross pay) less the sum of TAX and DED (income tax deductions).

The payroll problem requires that we use control statements to test for two conditions: whether the employee worked more than 40 hours and whether all transactions have been processed. The following statements* perform these checks:

```
IF (HOURS .GT. 40.) GO TO 1100
IF (ID .EQ. 99999) GO TO 1300
```

In the first instruction, the IF statement instructs the CPU to compare the value of the data item HOUR to the value 40. If HOUR is greater than (.GT.) 40., control for execution is transferred to the statement numbered 1100 (see Figure 6.5). The second statement performs a similar function, instructing the CPU to check ID to see if it is all 9s (99999), meaning in this case that all transactions have been processed. If there are no more data to process—if ID is 99999—the next statement to be executed is statement 1300, which stops processing, that is, ends the program.

The inclusion of notes and comments within computer programs is essential to document and explain the procedures being used. In the FORTRAN language, comment statements are inserted as desired between the executable instructions. Comment statements are designated by a "C" in the leftmost character/position of a line. The remainder of the line may contain anything the programmer wishes to say. Notice that in Figure 6.5 we have used comment statements to identify variables and to explain the processing logic (input, calculations, output, and so on).

BASIC

The **BASIC** (Beginner's All-purpose Symbolic Instruction Code) language was developed in 1964 at Dartmouth College (under a grant from the National Science Foundation). This easy-to-learn symbolic language is similar to FORTRAN. When

---

*The structured programming approach, which emerged in the early 1970s, attempts to minimize use of GOTO statements in programming.

introduced, BASIC was targeted for use on large time-sharing computers accessed by several users. It was also designed for teaching students about computers and how to program them. Thus the facilities built into BASIC are quite simple to understand and remember.

Since its introduction, BASIC has gained widespread acceptance in the fields of education, research, and industry. It is used on computers of all sizes; however, it is the dominant language on microcomputers. Many small computers include the BASIC language as part of the original purchase package, both because it is easy to learn and because of the powerful processing capability of the language itself.

In BASIC, unlike FORTRAN, it is not necessary to use FORMAT statements with INPUT and PRINT statements. The computer reads or prints the data directly as they appear, without editing or reformatting (some versions of BASIC allow use of format abilities as an option, but they are not mandatory, as in FORTRAN). Thus, if a user inputs a pay rate of $5.25, it will be accepted, as would the pay rate of $5.255578. The same INPUT statement would handle these data items equally well.

In addition to numerical data, BASIC, like many other languages, allows use of character information, called *character strings* (see Figure 6.6). These may be single letters or symbols (such as "A", "B", "1", "9", " + ", and "S"), or they may be several characters used together (such as "ABC", "PAY", and "JOHN"). Notice that the strings are enclosed in quotation marks and that the standard "series commas" necessary in English grammar are placed outside the quotation marks because the commas are not part of the character strings. This is how string data are handled in BASIC. In the payroll example, employee data would be treated as string data.

Basic arithmetic operations in BASIC are the same as in most other languages. Data items are added, subtracted, divided, or multiplied using the familiar operators of $+$, $-$, $/$, and $*$. Either variables or constants may be included in an instruction.

Control of execution is handled through IF-THEN-ELSE statements. These instructions allow the programmer to test for certain conditions and then, depending on the condition, to transfer control to an instruction elsewhere in the program. In BASIC all statements are automatically assigned identification numbers, so it is easy to refer to a specific statement.

Conditions are expressed in BASIC using the following operators:

1. Greater than: $>$
2. Less than: $<$
3. Equal: $=$
4. Greater than or equal: $>=$ or $=>$
5. Less than or equal: $<=$ or $=<$
6. Not equal: $<>$

In the payroll program, the check for 40 hours worked is IF HOURS $>$ 40 GOTO 2100. You can see how the condition is expressed very easily using the operator.

Internal documentation in computer programming helps individuals to figure out more quickly how a program operates. The REMark statement allows programmers to insert comments in their programs for this purpose. These REM statements are not executed by the computer.

Figure 6.6 Sample BASIC Program

```
10  REM    PROGRAM FOR PAYROLL CALCULATION
20  REM    THIS PROGRAM CALCULATES PAYROLL INFORMATION USING DATA
30  REM     INPUT FROM A TERMINAL KEYBOARD, I.E., USING DIRECT DATA ENTRY
40  REM
50  REM    THE FOLLOWING DATA/VARIABLE NAMES ARE USED:
60  REM            ITEM              MEANING
70  REM            ====              ========
80  REM            ID                EMPLOYEE IDENTIFICATION NUMBER   (INPUT)
90  REM            NAME              EMPLOYEE NAME                    (INPUT)
100 REM            HOURS             HOURS WORKED                     (INPUT)
110 REM            DED               PAYROLL DEDUCTIONS               (INPUT)
120 REM            PAY               PAY RATE                         (INPUT)
140 REM            OPAY              OVERTIME PAY
150 REM            GPAY              GROSS PAY
160 REM            TPAY              TOTAL NET TAKE-HOME PAY
170 REM            TAX               INCOME TAX
180 REM            OHOURS            TOTAL NET PAY
190 REM
200 REM
1000 REM                      DATA INPUT SECTION
1010 REM
1020 REM                   FIRST PROMPT USER TO INPUT NECESSARY DATA
1030 REM
1040 PRINT"ENTER: EMPLOYEE ID, NAME, HOURS WORKED, PAYROLL DEDUCTIONS, AND PAYRATE"
1060 INPUT "SEPARATE EACH ITEM BY A COMMA", ID, NAME, HOURS, DED, PAY
1095 REM  CHECK FOR LAST TRANSACTION
1100 IF  ID = 9999 THEN END ELSE NEXT SENTENCE
1200 REM         CHECK FOR OVERTIME
1210 IF HOURS > 40 GOTO 2100 ELSE NEXT SENTENCE
1220 REM
1230 REM                   PROCESS WITHOUT ANY OVERTIME
1240 GPAY = HOURS * PAY
1250 TAX = GPAY * .25
1260 TPAY = GPAY - (TAX + DED)
1270 GOTO 3190
2090 REM         PROCESS WITH OVERTIME
2095 REM
2100 RPAY = 40 * PAY
2110 OHOUR = HOURS - 40!
2120 OPAY = OHOUR * (PAY * 1.5)
2130 GPAY = RPAY + OPAY
2140 TAX = GPAY * .25
2150 TPAY = GPAY - (TAX + DED)
2160 REM
3100 REM                  PRINT RESULTS OF THIS TRANSACTION
3110 REM
3190 PRINT "  ID NO       NAME     HRS WKD    REG PAY      OVERTIME     GROSS PAY    NET PAY"
3195 PRINT " ======================================================================"
3200 PRINT TAB(3)ID; TAB (14) NAME; TAB(23) HOURS; TAB(35) RPAY; TAB(47) OPAY; TAB(59) GPAY; TAB(72)
3300 GOTO 1040
```

Because the BASIC language is easy to understand and use, many persons first learn about computing by writing programs in BASIC. Its simplicity also accounts for its popularity.

COBOL

COBOL (COmmon Business-Oriented Language) was developed by a government-sponsored committee of business and university representatives. The specifications for the language were completed in 1959 and released during 1960. Since updated and improved, it is the dominant programming language in business data processing today.

Because COBOL was explicitly designed for business use, the instructions are written in an English-like language that is similar to that used by business people. In addition, COBOL is *machine independent;* thus a program written for, say, an IBM computer can easily be transferred to other computer systems. COBOL is an easy-to-learn language that is very efficient in handling the alphabetic and alphanumerica data (for example, customer names, addresses, and merchandise descriptions) that are so often used in business organizations. These advantages will become more evident as we work through the sample program.

COBOL programs are built. The lowest-level element is a *statement*, which is comparable to an instruction in FORTRAN. Statements are grouped into *sentences* and sentences are grouped into *paragraphs*. One or more paragraphs may be used together to form a *module*. The next higher levels are *sections* and *divisions*.

COBOL programs consist of four divisions:

——*Identification division:* contains the name of the program, the programmer, date written, and other information that will help identify the program and its purpose.

——*Environment division:* names the computer system used to compile and execute the program; identifies the devices to be used for input and output or specific sets of data or results needed.

——*Data division:* carefully describes the names, type, size, and location of data and results to be input and output; shows the relationship between the sets of data.

——*Procedure division:* contain the sentences (that is, the instructions) that specify the processing and arithmetic operations and the order in which they will be performed.

The contents of the identification and environment divisions as shown on the first of the three program coding pages in Figure 6.7 are self-explanatory. However, we will look at the data division and the procedure division in greater detail. In the sample program, the data division contains a file section and a working storage section. The file section defines the set of data that is input and the results that are output (that is, the files of data). File labels are used to identify tape and disk from other tapes and disks; since, however, we are not using secondary storage devices for input/output, the file record labels are omitted. We still need to use the FD statement, which defines a set of data and gives it a name (in this case, WEEKLY-PAYROLL).

Figure 6.7 Sample COBOL Program

```
1000       IDENTIFICATION DIVISION.
1010       PROGRAM-ID.    PAYROLL.
1020       AUTHOR.
1030       DATE-WRITTEN.
1040
1050       ENVIRONMENT DIVISION.
1060       CONFIGURATION SECTION.
1070       SOURCE-COMPUTER.
1080       OBJECT-COMPUTER.
1090
1100       INPUT-OUTPUT SECTION.
1110       FILE-CONTROL.
1120          SELECT WEEKLY-PAYROLL
1130             ASSIGN TO DISC UR-S-SYSIN.
1140          SELECT PRINT-FILE
1150             ASSIGN TO DISC UR-S-SYSOUT.
1160
1170       DATA DIVISION.
1180       FILE SECTION.
1190       FD  WEEKLY-PAYROLL
1200          LABEL RECORDS ARE OMITTED
1210          DATA RECORD IS PAY-RECORD-INPUT.
1220
1230       01 PAY-RECORD-INPUT.
1240          02  ID-NUMBER           PIC  9(5).
1250          02  EMPLOYEE-NAME        PIC  X(4).
1260          02  HOURS-WORKED         PIC  99V99.
1270          02  DEDUCTIONS           PIC  99V99.
1280          02  PAY-RATE             PIC  99V99.
1290          02  FILLER               PIC  X(54).
1300
1310       FD  PRINT-FILE
1320          LABEL RECORDS ARE OMITTED
1330          DATA RECORD IS PRINT-LINE.
1340
1350       01 PRINT-LINE.
1360          02  FILLER           PIC  X(133).
1370
1380       WORKING-STORAGE SECTION.
1390
1400       01 GR-PAY               PIC  9999V99  COMP.
1410       01 REG-PAY              PIC  9999V99  COMP.
```

```
1420      01  TAXES                    PIC 9999V99   COMP.
1430      01  EOF-SWITCH           PIC  X(3).
1440          88 END-OF-FILE    VALUE 'YES'.
1450
1460      01  HEADINGS-LINE.
1470          02  FILLER  PIC X(14)   VALUE  SPACES.
1480          02  FILLER  PIC X(16)   VALUE 'EMPLOYEE ID NO.'.
1490          02  FILLER  PIC X(13)   VALUE 'EMP. NAME'.
1500          02  FILLER  PIC X(12)   VALUE 'HRS. WORKED'.
1510          02  FILLER  PIC X(13)   VALUE 'REGULAR PAY'.
1520          02  FILLER  PIC X(14)   VALUE 'OVERTIME PAY'.
1530          02  FILLER  PIC X(11)   VALUE 'GROSS PAY'.
1540          02  FILLER  PIC X(7)    VALUE 'NET PAY'.
1550          02  FILLER  PIC X(32)   VALUE  SPACES.
1560
1570      01  WEEKLY-PAYROLL-RESULTS.
1580          02  FILLER           PIC X(19)   VALUE SPACES.
1590          02  0-ID-NUMBER      PIC 9(5).
1600          02  FILLER           PIC X(0)    VALUE SPACES.
1610          02  0-EMP-NAME       PIC X(4).
1620          02  FILLER           PIC X(9)    VALUE SPACES.
1630          02  0-HRS-WORKED     PIC 99.99.
1640          02  FILLER           PIC X(6)    VALUE SPACES.
1650          02  REGULAR-PAY      PIC $$$9.99.
1660          02  FILLER           PIC X(7)    VALUE SPACES.
1670          02  OVERTIME-PAY     PIC $$$9.99.
1680          02  FILLER           PIC X(5)    VALUE SPACES.
1690          02  GROSS-PAY        PIC $$$9.99.
1700          02  FILLER           PIC X(4)    VALUE SPACES.
1710          02  NET-PAY          PIC $$$9.99.
1720          02  FILLER           PIC X(32)   VALUE SPACES.
1730
1740      PROCEDURE DIVISION.
1750
1760      00-MAIN-PROCEDURE.
1770          PERFORM 010-INITIALIZATION.
1780          PERFORM 020-PROCESS-RECORD
1790              UNTIL END-OF-FILE.
1800          PERFORM 030-CLOSING-STEPS.
1810          STOP RUN.
1820
```

```
1830        010-INITIALIZATION.
1840            OPEN INPUT WEEKLY-PAYROLL
1850                OUTPUT PRINT-FILE.
1860            MOVE HEADINGS-LINE TO PRINT-LINE.
1870            WRITE PRINT-LINE.
1880            READ WEEKLY-PAYROLL
1890                AT END MOVE 'YES' TO EOF-SWITCH.
1892            MOVE ZEROES TO OVERTIME-PAY.
1900
1910        020-PROCESS-RECORD.
1920            IF    ID-NUMBER IS EQUAL TO 99999
1930                MOVE 'YES' TO EOF-SWITCH
1940            ELSE
1950                IF HOURS-WORKED NOT GREATER THAN 40.0
1960                    MULTIPLY PAY-RATE BY HOURS-WORKED
1970                        GIVING GROSS-PAY GR-PAY REGULAR-PAY
1980                    PERFORM 025-FINISH-RECORD
1990                ELSE
2000                    MULTIPLY PAY-RATE BY 40.0 GIVING REG-PAY
2010                    COMPUTE GR-PAY = REG-PAY + 1.5 *
2020                                    (HOURS-WORKED - 40.0) * PAY-RATE
2030                    MOVE REG-PAY TO REGULAR-PAY
2040                    MOVE GR-PAY TO GROSS-PAY
2050                    SUBTRACT REG-PAY FROM GR-PAY
2060                        GIVING OVERTIME-PAY
2070                    PERFORM 025-FINISH-RECORD.
2080
2090        025-FINISH-RECORD.
2100            MULTIPLY GR-PAY BY 0.25 GIVING TAXES.
2110            SUBTRACT TAXES DEDUCTIONS FROM GR-PAY GIVING NET-PAY.
2120            MOVE ID-NUMBER TO O-ID-NUMBER.
2130            MOVE EMPLOYEE-NAME TO O-EMP-NAME
2140            MOVE HOURS-WORKED TO O-HRS-WORKED.
2150            WRITE PRINT-LINE FROM WEEKLY-PAYROLL-RESULTS
2160                AFTER ADVANCING 2 LINES
2170            MOVE ZEROES TO OVERTIME PAY.
2180            READ WEEKLY-PAYROLL
2190                AT END MOVE 'YES' TO EOF-SWITCH.
2200
2210        030-CLOSING-STEPS.
2220            CLOSE WEEKLY-PAYROLL PRINT-FILE.
```

Data are input and output in groups called records. Each item of data that is a part of the record (hours worked, pay rate, and so on) must be made known to the system, just as we did in FORTRAN through the FORMAT statement. In COBOL, this is accomplished by listing the name of the data item (notice that since the name-length restrictions are not as severe as in FORTRAN, we can use variable names that are much closer to the actual English words) and the picture or type and length specifications. The picture clause indicates how long the data item is and whether it is used in computation or is merely descriptive (like employee name, which is not added to or subtracted from). A 9 indicates numeric data and an X alphanumeric data. The V shows where a decimal point belongs. FILLER is used to indicate blank or unused spaces (columns that do not contain data).

The working storage section contains data format specifications for titles and headings, as well as for temporary data variables—that is, variables used in intermediate steps for calculating results that will be output. For example, "taxes" is an item that is neither input nor output, but is used in the intermediate step of calculating net pay from gross pay. In working storage one would find a data item for the intermediate calculation of income taxes.

In the procedure division, all the processing steps are specified. The actual computations are the same in the COBOL example as they were in FORTRAN. But notice how much easier it is to follow the logic used because of the language. The files of data are opened (that is, made ready for input and output) and the data are read by the command READ WEEKLY-PAYROLL. Then the arithmetic and comparison statements are executed to perform the payroll calculations, test for the end of processing, and so on. The statements are organized into paragraphs (PAR-1, and so on). You probably can see why COBOL has become so well ingrained in business data processing—it is a very easy language to understand and use.

Pascal

As increased attention has been paid to how application programs are designed and structured, new languages have emerged that better support structured design. One of the best known and widely used of these is **Pascal.** This language, which is used on the smallest microcomputers up to full-size mainframe systems, was introduced in 1971 by Niklaus Wirth, a Swiss researcher at the Federal Institute of Technology in Zurich. He named the language after Blaise Pascal, the famous seventeenth-century mathematician who developed the first calculating machine.

An important feature of Pascal is its requirement that the programmer plan the development. For example, all variables and constants are defined at the beginning of the program. (Other languages allow variables to be introduced into the program at any point.) Notice in Figure 6.8 that all the variables used in the payroll program are defined in lines 3 through 6 of the sample program. Pascal uses semicolons to end or separate statements (except for output statements, which end with a period). Comments and remarks are denoted by asterisks or enclosed in parentheses.

An additional built-in feature of this language is its tendency to force structuring of logic. Programs are comprised of blocks of instructions starting with BEGIN and terminating with END. The entire program is treated as one large block that can

Figure 6.8 Sample Pascal Program

```pascal
PROGRAM Payroll (Input, Output);
TYPE
    NameType = Packed Array [1..15] of char;

VAR
    ID : Integer;
    Done : Boolean;
    InputChar : Char;
    Name : NameType;
    HoursWorked, Deductions, PayRate, TakeHome,
      RegularPay, OvertimePay, GrossPay            : Real;

{******************** GetInput ********************************}
Procedure GetInput (var Done : Boolean; var ID : Integer; var Name : NameType;
                    var HoursWorked, Deductions, PayRate : Real);
Const
  BlankName =

Var
  Index : Integer;
  YesOrNo : Char;

Begin { GetInput }
    Repeat
      Writeln ( 'Do you want to continue? (Y/N)' );
      Readln (YesOrNo);
    Until YesOrNo In [ 'Y' , 'y', 'N' , 'n' ];

    If YesOrNo In [ 'N' , 'n' ]
      Then Done : = True
      Else Begin
            Writeln ( 'Please Enter ID and Name' );
            Read  (ID);
            Index  : = 1;
            Name  : = BlankName;
            While (Index <= 15) and Not EOLN (Input)
              Do Begin
                    Read (InputChar);
                    Name [Index] : = InputChar;
                    Index : = Index + 1;
                 End;
            Readln;
            Writeln ( 'Enter HoursWorked , Deductions, and PayRate." );
```

```
                    Readln (HoursWorked, Deductions, PayRate);
              End;
End; { GetInput }
{******************** ComputePay *********************************}
Procedure ComputePay (HoursWorked, Deductions, PayRate : Real;
                          var OvertimePay, RegularPay, TakeHome, GrossPay : Real);
Var
   OTHours,  IncomeTax : Real;

Begin {ComputePay}
   OTHours : = 0.0;
   If HoursWorked > 40.0
     Then Begin
            OTHours : = HoursWorked - 40.0;
            HoursWorked : = 40.0;
          End;
   OvertimePay : = OTHours * PayRate * 1.5;
   RegularPay : = HoursWorked * PayRate;
   GrossPay : = RegularPay + OvertimePay;
   IncomeTax : = GrossPay * 0.25;
   TakeHome : = GrossPay - (IncomeTax + Deductions);
End; {ComputePay}


{**************************************************************************}
BEGIN        { MAIN PROGRAM }
    Done : = False;
    While not Done
        Do Begin
            GetInput (Done, ID, Name, HoursWorked, Deductions, Payrate);
            If not Done
              Then Begin
                    ComputePay (HoursWorked, Deductions, PayRate,
                                  OvertimePay, RegularPay, TakeHome, GrossPay);
                    Writeln; Writeln;
                    Writeln ( '   ID Number' , ' Employee Name   ',
                              '   Hours ', '   Regular ',
                              '   Overtime ', ' Gross Pay ', '    Net Pay ' );
                    Writeln ( ID: 11, Name: 15,HoursWorked:10:1,RegularPay:10:2,
                                OvertimePay:10:2,GrossPay:11:2,TakeHome:11:2);
                    Writeln;
                  End;
            End; {While not Done}
END.            { MAIN PROGRAM }
```

contain other nested blocks. Figure 6.8 includes three main blocks and demonstrates the "nesting" feature of Pascal. The first, which begins at statement 7 and terminates at statement 28, controls the program, starting with the instruction to write a heading line at the top of each page. The second major block begins at statement 13 and controls pay calculation. It is executed for each data record in the input file, that is, until an end-of-file (EOF) mark is encountered in the input stream. As you know from the payroll problem that has been used throughout this chapter, some employees work overtime hours. The block that handles these calculations consists of statements 17 through 21. All results are written out by instruction 26 (WRITELN), which contains both the variable names and the output formats.

Pascal is intended to resemble the way humans approach problems more closely than other languages do. The logical stream of instructions, the distinct blocks of functions and steps, and the capability to use variables of any length demonstrate this.

Ada

The most recent language intended for universal use is **Ada,** named after the first modern computer programmer (because of her work with mathematician Charles Babbage), Ada Augusta Byron, daughter of the poet. Initiative for this language came from the U.S. Department of Defense as it attempted to acquire one programming language that could be used for business, science, math, and engineering functions. Having a single language that could be used on many different machines (thus rendering computer programs portable from one system to another) would save millions of dollars each year.

The language itself, which is only now emerging in a usable form, resembles the best features of Pascal. It also allows a variety of other custom software components to be advanced to it, should the user need them. Thus, Ada uses a concept of "plug-in" software, just as hardware people have for many years.

You will be hearing more about Ada in the coming years as the language is introduced into use in many government and business arenas, ranging from business applications to programs used for aircraft and missiles.

Choice of Third-Generation Programming Languages

Since computing centers generally have compilers and translators for several different programming languages, programmers and other systems staff members must select one to use in coding an application. (The users are generally not involved in this selection process.) We will briefly summarize the factors that should be considered in choosing a language.

The most fundamental consideration (assuming that the programmers already know the languages themselves) is the capability of each language: What kinds of processing requirement can be programmed with a particular language? After the features essential to meet a data processing or data manipulation need are known, languages should be evaluated in terms of:

——*Input/output specification:* Does the language support a variety of devices (for example, typewriter, optical scanner, terminal)? How easy is it to perform a high volume of input/output processing?

——*Data manipulation capabilities:* What types of data can be processed? What are its reformatting/editing features? What kinds of character set can be used in processing?

——*Data storage capabilities:* What kinds of file organization (discussed in the next chapter) can be used? What is its capability to store and retrieve records of variable length? How easily can stored sets of data be created or retrieved?

——*Programming aids:* How easy is it to use? What are its documentation capabilities? What are the debugging aids?

——*Efficiency:* Is the compilation process efficient? Is the code generated in compilation efficient? Is support available for modification of the features of the language?

Knowing something about the features of languages may quickly eliminate certain ones from consideration for some types of processing. FORTRAN, for example, does not have built-in features for data communication. COBOL is good for processing large amounts of data when the volume of pure calculation is low.

Ease of programming is a constant concern in selecting a language. If a language is easy to understand and use, it can reduce errors and shorten the time needed to put the program into use. The tradeoff that must be made is ease of programming versus efficiency of operation. Higher-level languages are much easier to use than assembly language, but the code is not as efficient. COBOL, for instance, is easy to learn and use because of its English-like commands and its instruction explosion features. However, because of the instruction explosion, it is much less efficient in execution than assembly language. FORTRAN is more efficient to use (to code) and it executes more quickly than COBOL, but handling alphabetic data is more complex.

Compatibility with languages being used in other application programs may also be a selection factor. If two or more applications may be combined in the near future, this possibility should be considered. Selection of the right programming language is a very important step in the programming cycle; it can make the actual coding operation much easier for you and the organization.

Fourth-Generation Languages

The preceding discussion allows us to draw some general conclusions about developing programs using third-generation languages:

1. Many instructions must be written to perform a given task.
2. Because of syntactic details such as punctuation and spacing, the process of developing a third-generation-language program tends to be error-prone— a missing comma may cause the program to fail (and it may be difficult to detect that the comma is missing).

3. Making changes in one area of a program may cause other changes through-out the entire program as well as in accompanying programs that comprise a system (for example, a change in data format may have to be made every time the data format is referenced).

4. Because of their complexity, writing programs in third-generation languages often takes longer than developers or users find acceptable.

5. Because of the labor intensity of the process coupled with the large number of instructions, the ensuing software is often too expensive.

The need for computer software is greater than ever, and the demand continues to grow as computer information systems become more widespread. When managers see the need to develop greater quantities of software, they generally must decide to pursue one or more of three strategies:

——Expand the systems development staff.

——Make the existing staff more productive.

——Let users act as their own developers.

The first alternative, hiring additional staff, raises the personnel costs of the infor-mation systems group. Many companies are unwilling to make this investment. The other two strategies are typically preferred because:

——Developers can prepare software more quickly, using fewer instructions and encountering fewer errors. Due to the nature of fourth-generation languages, both the development process and the resulting software are less complex.

——End-users can master fourth-generation languages quickly. They need not become bogged down in detailed syntax or excessively lengthy programs. Users can write short but powerful programs in fourth-generation languages. In some cases no software has to be written. Instead simple queries can be entered to retrieve the desired information.

The term *fourth-generation* applies to a broad range of languages that neverthe-less exhibit common features. This section examines the four categories of fourth-generation languages: query and retrieval languages, report generators, application generators, and decision support languages. Applications will demonstrate the fea-tures and uses of typical languages in each category.

Query and Retrieval Languages

Query and retrieval languages (or simply **query languages**) provide users with the ability to retrieve stored data without the necessity of writing lengthy procedural instructions or specifying data formats. They permit users to pose questions—that is, *queries*—in English-like or tabular formats. For example, an executive examining sales performance in an organization may wish to pose the query:

List company sales by region for the years 1986 to 1988.

The system retrieves the data needed to answer the response from the file or files associated with the program and presents an answer to the user. It must perform the following steps:

1. Sort data by year and region.
2. Prepare a total for each region.
3. Present the result in an understandable format.

However, the user need not be concerned with these steps; they are performed automatically when the query is entered. (Retrieving the same information using a third-generation language could require more than 100 instructions to produce the same result.)

Some languages in this category also allow users to enter data and update files or databases. (Query and retrieval languages sometimes parallel database management systems, a topic discussed later in this chapter and in detail in Chapter 8.)

Query-By-Example, a unique query language developed by IBM, allows users to specify queries using rows and columns of data, displayed on a screen in table form. Information is requested by placing operators in a skeleton table on the screen. The operator instructs the system to respond to the inquiry by retrieving and processing the details.

Figure 6.9 includes a brief set of data used to demonstrate the power of Query-By-Example. If it is desired to learn the names and salaries of all employees in the database, an inquiry is prepared by keying the operator P. in the name and salary columns. No data or other instructions are needed to produce the response shown in Figure 6.10. Notice in the example how the system retrieves only the data requested

Figure 6.9 Query-By-Example Database in Tabular Form

EMP	NAME	SALARY	MGR	DEPT
	JONES	8000	SMITH	HOUSEHOLD
	ANDERSON	6000	MURPHY	TOY
	MORGAN	10000	LEE	COSMETICS
	LEWIS	12000	LONG	STATIONERY
	NELSON	6000	MURPHY	TOY
	HOFFMAN	16000	MORGAN	COSMETICS
	LONG	7000	MORGAN	COSMETICS
	MURPHY	8000	SMITH	HOUSEHOLD
	SMITH	12000	HOFFMAN	STATIONERY
	HENRY	9000	SMITH	TOY

Data items

Records

Figure 6.10 Query-By-Example Print Query

Query entered:

```
EMP |       NAME      | SALARY |      MGR      |   DEPT   |
    ------------------------------------------------------------
    | P.            | P.    |              |          |
    |               |       |              |          |
```

Result displayed on screen:

```
EMP | NAME            |   SALARY |
    -------------------------------------
    | JONES          |     8000 |
    | ANDERSON       |     6000 |
    | MORGAN         |    10000 |
    | LEWIS          |    12000 |
    | NELSON         |     6000 |
    | HOFFMAN        |    16000 |
    | LONG           |     7000 |
    | MURPHY         |     8000 |
    | SMITH          |    12000 |
    | HENRY          |     9000 |
```

and ignores other items in the database. Query-By-Example works the same way regardless of the number of records and data items. And users can learn how to enter such inquiries without extensive training.

Queries can also request the arrangement of data in another sequence. Figure 6.11 shows the Query-By-Example entry to display the salesperson names in alphabetical order. The operator P. specifies the inquiry and the operator AO. indicates that the results should be in ascending order.

Users can enter conditions for the retrieval just as easily. The query in Figure 6.12 asks for the names and salaries of all employees managed by Morgan who earn at least $16,000. Conditional operators, such as greater than (>), greater than or

Figure 6.11 Query-By-Example Request to Print Results in Ascending Order

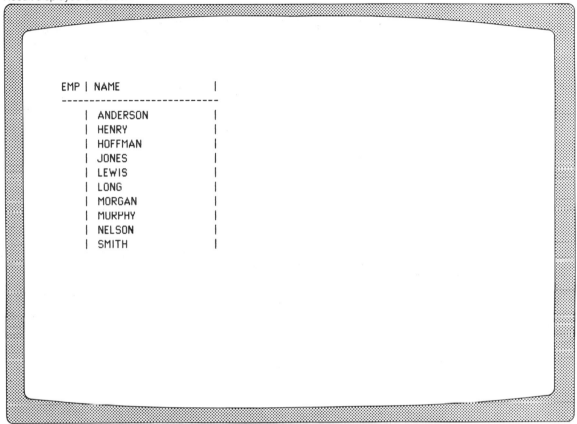

Query entered:

```
EMP |        NAME        |  SALARY  |      MGR      |    DEPT    |
    -------------------------------------------------------------
    |  P. AO.            |          |              |            |
    |                    |          |              |            |
```

Result displayed on screen:

```
EMP | NAME              |
    -------------------------
    | ANDERSON          |
    | HENRY             |
    | HOFFMAN           |
    | JONES             |
    | LEWIS             |
    | LONG              |
    | MORGAN            |
    | MURPHY            |
    | NELSON            |
    | SMITH             |
```

equal to (>=), equal (=), less than (<), and less than or equal to (<=) are expressed by including the condition in the skeleton, as illustrated.

Since the manager column includes a display request (P.) and the name Morgan, the query result displays the manager name and all details that are in answer to the query. In this example, only Hoffman meets the query requirements of earning at least $16,000 and working for Morgan.

Query-By-Example, like most query languages, makes the retrieval capability of the computer accessible to end-users without the need for extensive programming or language training. Very complex queries can be posed simply, with the burden of determining proper processing procedures falling on the software, not the user.

Figure 6.12 Query-By-Example Request Using Conditional Operator

Query entered:

```
EMP |        NAME        |  SALARY  |       MGR        |    DEPT
    -------------------------------------------------------------------
    | P.                 |P. ≥16000.|P. MORGAN         |            |
    |                    |          |                  |            |
```

Result displayed on screen:

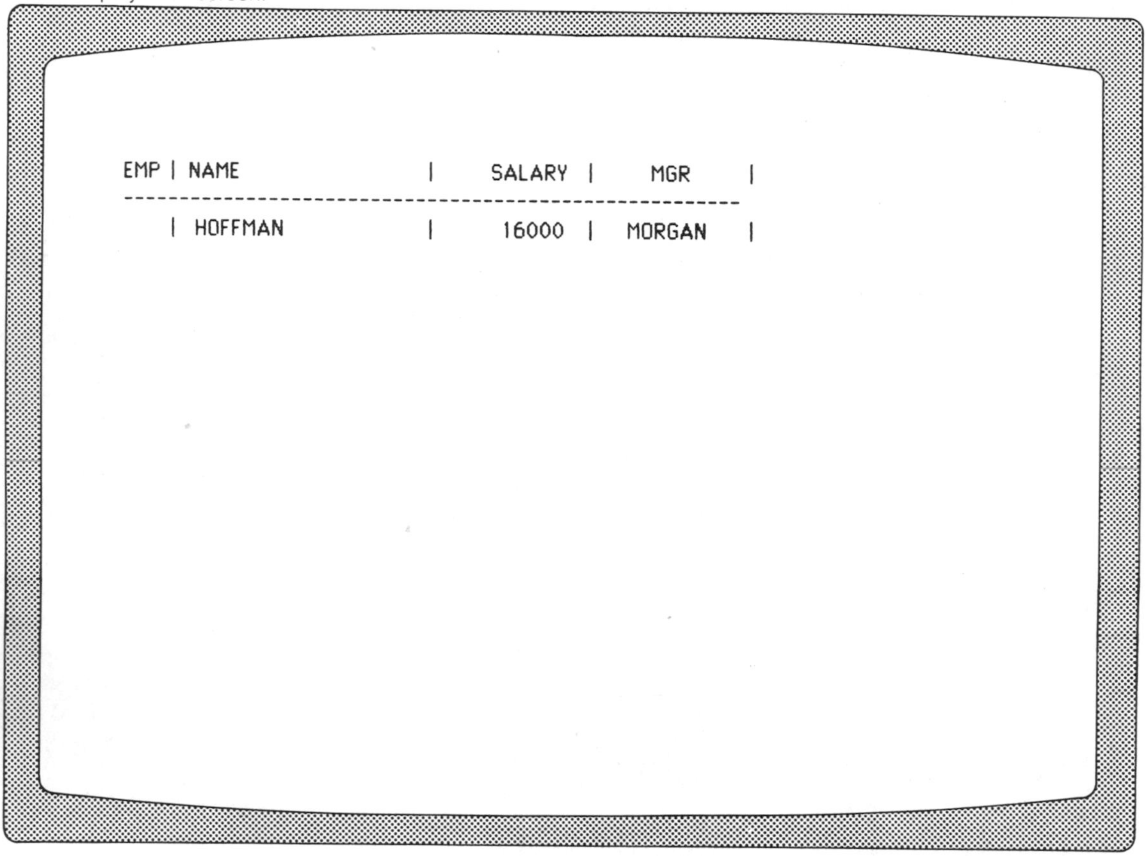

```
EMP | NAME              |   SALARY |    MGR    |
    -----------------------------------------------
    | HOFFMAN           |    16000 |   MORGAN  |
```

Report Generators

(4th
generation)

Report generators also permit users to extract (but not enter or modify) data from existing files or databases easily. Full or partial records can be extracted. In comparison with query and retrieval languages, report generators give users greater control over the appearance and content of the output, if desired. Results can be presented in a report format that is established automatically by the software, or the user can provide specifications that instruct the system to prepare customized titles for the report, page descriptions, and column headings.

Figure 6.13 contains a brief program written in the widely used report generator EASYTRIEVE PLUS. The 33 lines in this program instruct the system to retrieve

Figure 6.13 Sample EASYTRIEVE PLUS Program

```
1 FILE PRIMER FB(150 1800)
2     REGION          1    1    N
3     BRANCH          2    2    N
4     SSN             4    5    P    MASK '999-99-9999' +
                                     HEADING ('SOCIAL' 'SECURITY' 'NUMBER')
                                     HEADING ('EMPLOYEE' 'NUMBER')

5     EMP *           9    5    N
6     CODE            16   1    N
7     NAME            17   8    A
8     STREET          37   20   A
9     CITY            57   12   A
10    STATE           69   2    A
11    ZIP             71   5    N    HEADING ('ZIP' 'CODE')
12    NET             90   4    P  2 HEADING ('NET' 'PAY')
13    GROSS           94   4    P  2 HEADING ('GROSS' 'PAY')
14    DEPARTMENT      98   3    N
15    DATE-OF-BIRTH   103  6    N    MASK (Y 'Z9/99/99') +
                                     HEADING ('DATE' 'OF' 'BIRTH')
16    TELEPHONE       117  10   N    MASK '(999) 999-9999' +
                                     HEADING ('TELEPHONE' 'NUMBER')
17    SEX             127  1    A    HEADING ('SEX' 'CODE')
18                                   * 1 - FEMALE
19                                   * 2 - MALE
20    MARITAL-STAT    128  1    A    HEADING ('MARITAL' ' STATUS')
21    DEDUCTIONS      W    4    P  2
22 *
23 JOB INPUT PRIMER NAME CONTROL-2
24     DEDUCTIONS = GROSS - NET
25     PRINT CTLRPT2
26 *
27 REPORT CTLRPT2   LINESIZE 92 DTLCTL FIRST SUMCTL TAG
28     SEQUENCE REGION MARITAL-STAT BRANCH EMP* D
29     CONTROL REGION MARITAL-STAT
30     TITLE 1 'EASYTRIEVE PLUS CONTROL EXAMPLE TWO'
31     TITLE 3 'NOTICE THE CONTROL BREAK FIELDS'
32     TITLE 4 'AND CONTROL BREAK LINES'
33     LINE 1 REGION BRANCH MARITAL-STAT EMP* GROSS NET DEDUCTIONS
```

employee data and prepare a report containing the employee data (name, address, department, date of birth, and so on). The first 21 lines of the program describe the data to be included in the report and the column headings desired. Notice how little information is needed to identify the details.

The remainder of the program instructs the system to calculate deductions (GROSS − NET, in line 24) and to print the report format listed in lines 27 to 33. The instruction CONTROL REGION MARITAL-STAT, in line 29, tells the system to include a control break on the geographic region and marital status data items. The results in Figure 6.14 show subtotals for gross pay, net pay, and deductions whenever region and marital status change. A final total is also presented at the end of the report.

Typically individuals want summary information about categories of activities in the form of totals and subtotals. When using third-generation languages, programmers must specify not only what totals to produce, but how to calculate and present them. Report generators require only that users specify the field on which the subtotal should be prepared; the software works out the procedures automatically. Other arithmetic and logic operations, such as suppressing repeating data, can also be handled automatically by the software. In Figure 6.14, for example, the columns for region and marital status print data for the first occurrence of the item only and then omit the detail until the data values change again. This simple feature of the report, also established by the control break instructions in line 29, lessens clutter and makes it easier to read the report.

Application Generators

Both query and retrieval languages and report generators are output oriented; they prepare printed and display reports. In contrast, **application generators** are software programs that permit the specification of an entire application at a high level. They include the capability to develop applications that accept input, validate data, perform calculations and follow complicated processing logic, interact with files, and produce reports and output. The application generator produces source code (Figure 6.15). Some produce entire programs. Others prepare part of the program code and allow a user to link other modules into those produced by the generator.

Table 6.3 lists the most widely used application generators. We will use the product FOCUS to demonstrate the capabilities of application generators.

FOCUS is designed for use by end-users and by information systems professionals. The features for each category of user include:

———*For end-users*
　　　Report writer
　　　Graphics generator for presenting output in chart and graph form
　　　Columnar financial reporting facilities
　　　Screen editor for creating and saving processing requests
　　　Personal computer interface to transfer data to and from personal computer
　　　software

Figure 6.14 Output from EASYTRIEVE PLUS Program

EASYTRIEVE PLUS CONTROL EXAMPLE TWO   PAGE

NOTICE THE CONTROL BREAK FIELDS
AND CONTROL BREAK LINES

REGION	BRANCH	MARITAL STATUS	EMPLOYEE NUMBER	GROSS PAY	NET PAY	DEDUCTIONS
3	03	S	07781	310.40	224.36	86.04
	03		03936	324.00	242.25	81.75
	03		03890	386.40	272.53	113.87
	04		12318	282.40	195.13	87.27
	04		08262	376.00	215.95	160.05
MARITAL-STAT TOTAL				4,918.61	3,381.59	1,537.02
REGION TOTAL				7,183.61	4,915.58	2,268.03
4	01	M	05482	183.75	141.47	42.28
	02		09764	121.95	96.64	25.31
	03		11211	424.00	282.45	141.55
	04		10260	591.20	459.57	131.63
MARITAL-STAT TOTAL				1,320.90	980.13	340.77
4	01	S	10961	399.20	291.70	107.50
	01		05525	460.80	279.56	181.24
	02		06239	712.80	451.92	260.88
	03		10949	804.80	560.63	244.17
	03		04935	125.00	25.00	100.00
MARITAL-STAT TOTAL				2,502.60	1,608.81	893.79
REGION TOTAL				3,823.50	2,588.94	1,234.56
FINAL TOTAL				18,078.08	12,501.20	5,576.88

——*For information systems professionals*
   Data management facilities for creating and managing data sets
   Dialogue manager for building and maintaining processing requests, including
   condition testing and input/output activities

Figure 6.15 Activities Associated with Use of Application Generator

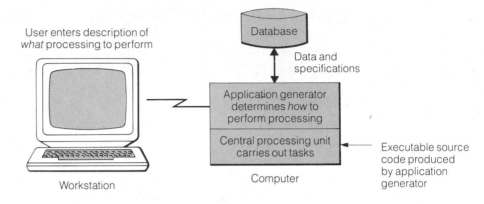

Table 6.3 Widely Used Fourth-Generation Languages

Category	Package/Language	Vendor
Query and retrieval languages	INTELLECT	Artificial Intelligence Corp.
	On-Line English	Cullinane
	Query-By-Example	IBM
	Quick Query	Caci
	SQL	IBM
Report generators	Easytrieve Plus	Panasophic
	GIS	IBM
	Mark V	Informatics
	NOMAD	NCSS
Application generators	ADS	Cullinet
	Application Factory	Cortex Corporation
	FOCUS	Information Builders
	MAPPER	Unisys (Sperry)
	MANTIS	CINCOM
	NATURAL	Software AG
	RAMIS	Mathematica, Inc.
Decision support languages	Express	Management Decision Systems
	System W	COMSHARE, Inc.
	Lotus 1-2-3	Execucom
	IFPS	

Display screen generator for creating data entry forms on workstations
Data file editor
Data security features to protect specific data items from unauthorized change

As you see, these capabilities go well beyond those of query languages and report writers. They allow the development of full processing functionality, including entry and retrieval of data, establishment and modification of data storage specifications, and data manipulation procedures. Yet, these functions are handled at a very high level; that is, the procedures to perform the tasks are not specified.

To demonstrate the power of application generators, we will examine two aspects: creating input/output display screens and creating reports.

Display Screens The creation of display screen layouts is one of the most time-consuming and error-prone areas of program development. It includes the tasks of arranging headings, instructions, and data fields on a computer display and establishing the procedures for accepting data entered through the keyboard into computer memory while at the same time showing the keyed data on the display. FOCUS, and application generators, ease this task substantially.

Figure 6.16 includes the FOCUS instructions to produce a display screen for adding new records and modifying existing records in a file. The first statement specifies that the file called EMPLOYEE will be used. CRTFORM on the next line

Figure 6.16 FOCUS Data Entry Program

```
MODIFY FILE EMPLOYEE
CRTFORM
"EMPLOYEE UPDATE"
"EMPLOYEE ID *: <EMP_ID LAST NAME: <LAST_NAME"
"DEPARTMENT: <DEPARTMENT CURRENT SALARY <CURR_SAL"
MATCH EMP_ID
    ON NOMATCH REJECT
    ON MATCH UPDATE LAST_NAME DEPARTMENT CURR_SAL
DATA VIA FI3270
END
```

Figure 6.17 FOCUS Data Entry Display Screen

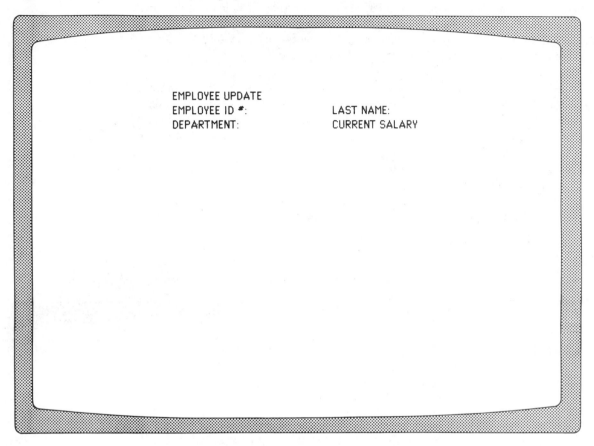

```
              EMPLOYEE UPDATE
              EMPLOYEE ID #:          LAST NAME:
              DEPARTMENT:             CURRENT SALARY
```

tells the system that a display form will be generated and thus invokes the FOCUS processing component needed to handle this activity.

Each line that will appear on the display screen begins and ends with double-quotation marks. For example, the line "EMPLOYEE UPDATE" appears on the first line of the display screen shown in Figure 6.17. The second line on the screen specifies data fields EMP ID and LAST NAME. A data entry field is indicated by the fieldname from the master file description. The text EMPLOYEE ID #: and LAST NAME: identify each field on the screen. This tells the user where to enter the data.

The instruction MATCH EMP_ID tells the system to match the entered employee identification number with one in the database in order to perform the update tasks. If there is no match—that is, if no existing record contains an employee identification corresponding to the one entered by the user—the transaction will be rejected.

Figure 6.17 shows the display screen resulting from the brief program; the colons indicate the data item field lengths, determined from the data descriptions automatically retrieved by FOCUS. All other procedural logic for clearing the display, presenting headings and user instructions, accepting and validating input, and storing modifications to the data are automatically generated by FOCUS. The short program listed in Figure 6.16 would require several hundred lines of code in third-generation languages.

Report Generation Third-generation procedural languages such as COBOL and BASIC require programs to specify how to process the data. For example, to prepare a report in COBOL, the user must state the procedures to do the following activities:

—Specify the file that will be used and its contents in detail.
—Open the file.
—Sort the file into the required order.
—Read one record at a time.
—Test to see whether there are more records to read. (If there are no more records, skip to the summary processing steps.)
—For each record to be processed, extract the data values needed for the report.
—Accumulate the totals for each data item to be reported.
—Move the fields to the output positions.
—Write the summary record to the output file.
—Go back to read another record.
—Perform the summary steps:
    Set up the report form.
    Print report and column headings.
    Write the report totals.
—Close the files.
—Stop the process.

The steps just listed would require many COBOL instructions and, typically, several attempts at compiling and running the program to remove any errors that may have been created.

With the powerful fourth-generation languages, however, only a few instructions are needed to accomplish the same processing and presentation activities. Figure 6.18 includes the entire set of FOCUS instructions to produce a selective report on sales data. Notice that the complete program is only six lines long and that the

Figure 6.18 Sample Program in Fourth-Generation Language (FOCUS)

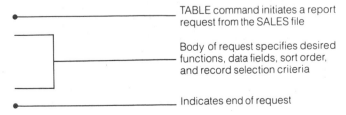

TABLE command initiates a report request from the SALES file

Body of request specifies desired functions, data fields, sort order, and record selection criteria

Indicates end of request

Figure 6.19 Sample Data for Sales Report Example

Sales File

Field Name	Meaning
REGION	Marketing region code
SITE	Store code
PONUM	Purchase order number
DATE	Order date
NAME	Customer name
AMOUNT	Total amount of order
TAX	State tax on order
FILLCODE	Indicator of shipment status
PRODUCT	Product number
UNITS	Quantity ordered

Supply File

PRODUCT	Product number
DESCRIPTION	Product description
COST	Wholesale cost
RETAIL	Retail price
VENDOR	Supplier code number
QOH	Quantity on hand in warehouse

instructions are very easy to understand. The annotations explain that the program will prepare totals by sales region for the years 1986 to 1988. The logic to read the data, test to determine whether the program has read all the data, examine the format of the data, sort and total the data, insert column headings, print the results, and so on is developed by FOCUS, rather than the programmer. FOCUS generates the application program to carry out the work. You can quickly see how the program in Figure 6.18 would facilitate the production of reports.

A more extensive example will demonstrate other features of FOCUS. Figure 6.19 lists the contents of two files we will use in an example. Figure 6.20 contains a brief program that requests a report showing all sales exceeding $1000 grouped by region and arranged in date order. The program instructs the system to insert a blank line on the report before beginning the data of each new region. The report produced by this program is shown in Figure 6.21. The headings were inserted automatically and the data proportionally spaced across the page. The name of the region prints only when it changes.

It is equally easy to build in calculations and manipulations of the data stored in the files to produce information not stored in the file. Figure 6.22 contains a

Figure 6.20 Sample Program for Sales Example

```
TABLE FILE SALES
PRINT NAME AND AMOUNT AND DATE
BY REGION BY SITE
IF AMOUNT GT 1000
ON REGION SKIP-LINE
END
```

Figure 6.21 Report Produced by Sample Program

PAGE 1

REGION	SITE	NAME	AMOUNT	DATE
------	----	-----	-------	-----
MA	NEWK	ELIZABETH GAS	$2,877.32	88 AUG
	NEWY	KOCH RECONSTRUCTION	$6,086.23	88 APR
	PHIL	ROSS INC.	$3,890.22	88 JUL
		LASSITER CONSTRUCTION	$1,120.22	88 SEP
MW	CHIC	BAKESHORE INC.	$5,678.23	88 OCT
		ROPERS BROTHERS	$2,789.20	88 AUG
	CLEV	BOVEY PARTS	$6.769.22	88 MAY
		ERIE INC.	$1,556.78	88 JAN
NE	ALBN	ROCK CITY BUILDER	$1,722.30	88 JUL
	BOST	HANCOCK RESTORERS	$8,246.20	88 FEB
		WANKEL CONTRUCTION	$2,345.25	88 JUN
		WARNER INDUSTRIES	$3,155.25	88 OCT
	STAM	ACORN INC.	$2,006.20	88 MAR
		KANGERS CONSTRUCTION	$2,790.50	88 JUN
		DART INDUSTRIES	$7,780.22	88 MAY
		ARISTA MANUFACTURING	$4,295.90	88 FEB
SE	ATL	RICH'S STORES	$1,345.17	88 AUG
	WASH	CAPITOL WHOLESALE	$3,789.00	88 JUN
		FEDERAL DEPOT	$2,195.25	88 MAR

program that totals orders, calculates percentages, and determines average order values. The program itself is both brief and easy to understand, but it involves a substantial amount of processing to produce the desired results. Figure 6.23 contains a representative report.

Figure 6.22 Order Analysis Program in Fourth-Generation Language

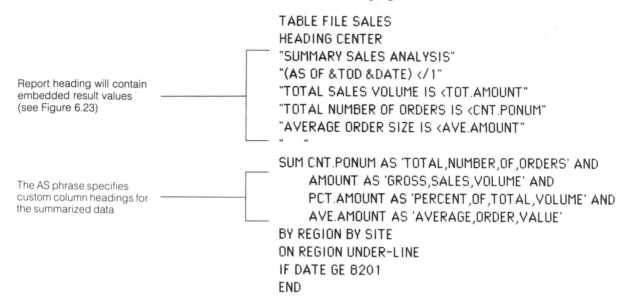

Report heading will contain embedded result values (see Figure 6.23)

```
TABLE FILE SALES
HEADING CENTER
"SUMMARY SALES ANALYSIS"
"(AS OF &TOD &DATE) </1"
"TOTAL SALES VOLUME IS <TOT.AMOUNT"
"TOTAL NUMBER OF ORDERS IS <CNT.PONUM"
"AVERAGE ORDER SIZE IS <AVE.AMOUNT"
"   "
```

The AS phrase specifies custom column headings for the summarized data

```
SUM CNT.PONUM AS 'TOTAL,NUMBER,OF,ORDERS' AND
        AMOUNT AS 'GROSS,SALES,VOLUME' AND
        PCT.AMOUNT AS 'PERCENT,OF,TOTAL,VOLUME' AND
        AVE.AMOUNT AS 'AVERAGE,ORDER,VALUE'
BY REGION BY SITE
ON REGION UNDER-LINE
IF DATE GE 8201
END
```

As these examples demonstrate, fourth-generation languages enable programmers to more quickly retrieve information needed for users. But, because the commands are relatively easy to learn and use, many nonprogramming users are developing their own programs. Furthermore, they also change and modify the programs with little difficulty to draw out the precise information they need for making a decision or managing an activity. More timely access to the appropriate information can lead to better organization performance, and that is, after all, what information systems are all about.

Decision Support Languages

Decision support languages are model oriented. They assist users and developers in analyzing data, posing "what if" questions, and describing relationships through the creation of formal models. In the past, doing this has required expertise in special languages and skill in mathematics, finance, or accounting. Decision support languages, however, provide the capability for sophisticated analysis and modeling in a form that is accessible to a much wider group of developers and users.

The simplest decision support languages are electronic spreadsheets, which are often associated with personal computers. Lotus 1-2-3 is one of the most popular spreadsheets. (Spreadsheets are discussed in the next section.) These tools allow the creation of models in two dimensions—for instance, the rows and columns of a simple table.

However, more sophisticated decision support languages are emerging that allow users to establish complex models with multiple dimensions. Each dimension

Figure 6.23 Order Analysis Report

SUMMARY OF SALES ANALYSIS
(AS OF 13.27.30 11/29/88)

TOTAL SALES VOLUME IS $2,576,655.45
TOTAL NUMBER OF ORDERS IS 3120
AVERAGE ORDER SIZE IS $825.85

REGION	SITE	TOTAL NUMBER OF ORDERS	GROSS SALES VOLUME	PERCENT OF TOTAL VOLUME	AVERAGE ORDER VALUE
MA	NEWK	256	$195,869.80	7.60	$765.12
	NEWY	398	$234,424.20	9.10	$589.01
	PHIL	144	$175,978.96	6.83	$1,222.08
	PITT	126	$109,915.62	4.27	$872.35
MW	CHIC	416	$247,770.40	9.62	$595.60
	CLEV	387	$311,936.80	12.11	$806.04
NE	ALBN	215	$115,081.30	4.47	$535.26
	BOST	306	$283,277.75	10.99	$925.74
	STAM	416	$313,448.29	12.16	$753.48
SE	ATL	156	$224,785.69	8.72	$1,440.93
	RICH	195	$146.523.74	5.69	$751.40
	WASH	215	$217,642.90	8.45	$967.30

can be viewed and analyzed independently of the others. Furthermore, analysis of the models can be performed without the creation of detailed procedural programs.

For example, the decision support language EXPRESS allows analysis of sales data on several dimensions using only a few simple statements. The program segment

LIMIT YEAR TO 1990
LIMIT CUSTOMER TO DISTRICT SOUTHEAST
DISPLAY SALES

will automatically produce a report on product sales that selects from the database according to the criteria of year, location, and the dimension of sales data. The report will be prepared with headings, totals, and so forth, whether the table includes a single entry or 1000.

Simple extraction for reporting is only the beginning. Decision support languages include powerful analytical capabilities that are just as easy to use. Among the typical capabilities associated with these languages are:

Data Analysis	Time Series Analysis	Cross-Sectional Analysis	Advanced Analysis
Mean	Moving averages	Crosstabs	Linear programming
Median	Exponential smoothing	Correlation matrices	Critical path analysis
Standard deviation	Linear extrapolation	Cluster analysis	Risk analysis
Variance	Linear growth triangles	Factor analysis	Monte Carlo simulation
Scatterplots	Multiple linear regression	Interaction detection	

Using the preceding example for sales data, it is easy to compare this year's performance with the same period last year and to have the variance reported. The EXPRESS instructions to do this are:

```
LIMIT MONTH TO CURRENT MONTH
LIMIT CUSTOMER TO DISTRICT SOUTHEAST
DISPLAY SALES LAG(SALES,12,MONTH) VARIANCE
```

The resulting report will include sales of each product in the database for the current month, the same month one year ago, and the variance from one year ago.

Decision support languages are growing in popularity on computer systems ranging from mainframes to micros.

Personal Computer Business Software

An area of special attention is the software commonly used on personal computers for business purposes. Most users of personal computers rely on purchased software packages; they do not develop their own software. This section briefly discusses the six types of computer software most often used on personal computers.

Electronic Spreadsheets

It is generally acknowledged that electronic spreadsheets are responsible for the sale of more computer systems than any other type of software. This section describes the features of spreadsheet software and the analytical powers that have led to their widespread use.

Spreadsheet software takes its name from the accountant's columnar worksheet, which it imitates. A **spreadsheet** is a worksheet consisting of a collection of cells formed by the intersection of rows and columns. Each cell can store one piece of

Figure 6.24 Window into Worksheet Produced by Spreadsheet Software

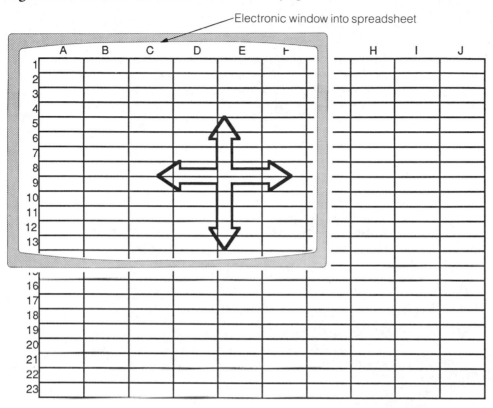

Electronic window into spreadsheet

information: a number, word or phrase, or formula. The display screen of the computer is a *window* into the worksheet. The worksheet itself can be much larger than the collection of cells that will appear on the screen at one time (Figure 6.24). Lotus 1-2-3, the most widely used spreadsheet software, provides a worksheet measuring 2048 rows by 256 columns. However typically only 6 to 10 columns and 20 rows appear on the screen. The others are in memory and appear when they are in the window (which may be moved anywhere on the spreadsheet).

Cells are uniquely identified by their row and column coordinates. Rows are numbered beginning with 1 and columns are identified by letters from A to Z followed by AA to ZZ, and so on. Thus the second cell from the left and third from the top is identified as cell B3.

The system moves between command, data entry, and other modes on instructions from the user. During command mode, the menu of information at the top of the display screen (Figure 6.25) shows the commands a user can select. In data entry mode, the detail at the top of the screen shows what the user has keyed in for the current cell. In Figure 6.25 the number 96018 appears in cell B10 and at the top of the screen. During editing, the cell data remain unmodified until the user tells the

Figure 6.25 Sales and Revenue Worksheet

B10: 96018 ◄────────── Displays contents of location B10

	A	B	C	D	E	F	G
1		GENERAL SERVICES COMPANY					
2		SALES REVENUE HISTORY					
3							
4		1986	1987	1988	1989	1990	1991
5							
6	SALES REVENUE	212456	298553	374991	425789	409554	529532
7							
8	COSTS						
9							
10	SALARIES	96018	85416	106380	106950	107490	128370
11	INTEREST	14689	19754	5890	13778	19854	24679
12	TRAVEL	42678	47345	39834	62995	48536	63886
13	MATERIALS	18343	26835	29553	27423	31995	48775
14	RENT	12000	25200	26400	29400	32100	33300
15	ADVERTISING	7900	8800	19825	24350	12000	21450
16							
17	TOTAL COSTS	191628	213350	227882	264896	251975	320460
18							
19	NET PROFIT	20828	85203	147109	160893	157579	209072
20							

@SUM(B10 . . . B15)   @SUM(C10 . . . C15)

system to change the cell contents (by depressing the "Enter" key). However, data entered for the change are displayed at the top of the screen *as they are keyed.*

Spreadsheet software packages on personal computers are widely used in business organizations because they are easy to apply and yet offer powerful calculation and data manipulation capabilities. End-users, who need not be computer experts, can instruct the software to add rows and columns, apply percentages, or use intricate accounting or financial formulas. The system automatically carries out the work and presents the results. The results and the contents of the worksheet itself can be stored on magnetic disk for later use.

Data are entered into a cell by positioning the cursor, a bar of light that shows where data will appear, and typing data on the computer keyboard. The spreadsheet software treats the data as a number or as a formula, unless the first character is an alphabetic letter. Then the software treats the data as a label (column or row heading, comment, or name). Formulas consist of numbers or cell numbers. Thus, a formula can be an instruction to add, subtract, divide, or multiply the contents of several cells (B1 + B2 − B3).

A great many functions are built into the software to assist the user in manipulating data. Typical functions include (the @ symbol tells the system to invoke the function that follows the symbol):

Financial Functions

@ PV	Computes the present value of an annuity
@ IRR	Calculates the internal rate of return of a payment series
@ PMT	Calculates the payment terms for a mortgage

Statistical Functions

@ SUM (list)	Sums the values in the list of cells indicated
@ MAX (list)	Obtains the maximum value in the list of cells indicated
@ MIN (list)	Obtains the minimum value in the list of cells indicated

Mathematical Functions

@ INT (X)	Determines the integer portion of the cell indicated
@ EXP (X)	Computes e (2.71 . . .) raised to the X power
@ LOG (X)	Computes the value of the base-10 logarithm of the number or cell indicated
@ SQRT (X)	Computes the value of the square root of the number or cell reference

Graphics functions are also included in many spreadsheet packages. They allow presentation of the data in the form of bar charts, pie charts, and line graphs. The operator need only specify the data (cells) and the graph form to be used. All manipulation of the data is performed automatically by the spreadsheet software.

The power of this software is in the development of business models. In the worksheet of data about sales revenue and associated costs (Figure 6.25), each column contains the data for one year. The last line of each column is the sum of the items identified in the rows, but the computer, not the user, has performed the arithmetic.

Figures 6.26a and 6.26b display alternate charts based on the data from the business model. All graphic data are drawn directly from the spreadsheet; users need not enter additional details.

The real power of the spreadsheet lies in the flexibility enjoyed by users: they can change single elements of data and automatically recalculate the results on the remainder of the worksheet. This feature allows managers to evaluate many alternatives in a situation without having to reenter or rekey (as on a calculator) all data for each case. For example, to see how profits for 1989 would have differed if material costs had been $5000 less, the user can key either 27423 − 5000 or 22423. Lotus 1-2-3 will automatically recalculate and display a new total cost and a different net profit result.

We can also, through a single command, tell the system to recalculate the impact of a 10 percent decrease in costs on annual and total profits. And other changes can be evaluated just as easily ("What if" the decrease is 8 percent? "What if" it increases to 13 percent?). The power of spreadsheets to perform "what if" evaluation quickly not only saves managers and users a great deal of time, but also tends to encourage people to examine more alternatives before making a decision. (Remember the

Figure 6.26a Sample Chart Showing Cost Data for 1986–1991

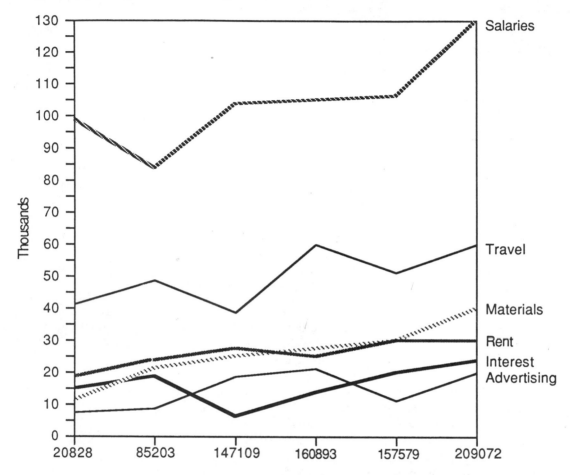

discussion of satisficing in Chapter 4. Spreadsheets are effective in reducing the frequency of satisficing.)

The most commonly used spreadsheet packages include:

——Lotus 1-2-3

——Symphony (integrated spreadsheet package)

——Framework (integrated spreadsheet package)

——Supercalc

——Visicalc

Integrated spreadsheet packages have the additional capability to perform word processing, data communications, data management, and graphics functions—all in a single package at a moderate cost. Spreadsheet software is continually being extended, and we are likely to see even more powerful systems in the future.

Figure 6.26b Sample Chart Showing Cost Data for 1991

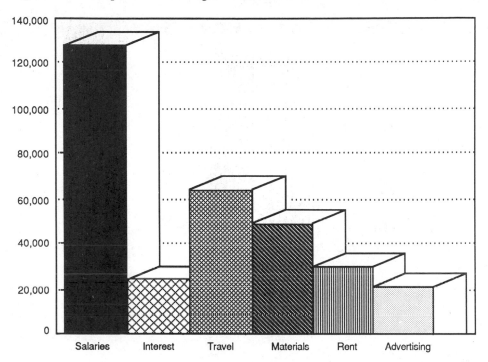

Word Processing

Word processing refers to the entry and manipulation of text, such as manuscripts, reports, and legal briefs. After spreadsheets, word processing is the most common type of software package in use on personal computers.

Word processing software allows a user to enter text data and store it on magnetic disk (Figure 6.27). It may be retrieved from storage any time and reformatted, augmented with additional text, or cut by the erasure of sentences, paragraphs, or pages. In addition, parts of several different manuscripts may be merged and reformatted to a single new document. This capability is particularly attractive when a document is repeatedly revised, each time with minor changes (for example, in legal and real estate transactions or in the preparation of sales quotations).

The most popular word processing packages for personal computers include WordPerfect, WordStar, and so on; they are listed in Table 6.4.

Many word processing packages have extended features available as options. For example, dictionaries—also called spelling checkers—can be added that will correct many typographical errors. Grammatical software checks for poor grammar and syntax, and indexing routines create tables of contents and alphabetical indexes of terms in a matter of seconds. Chapter 15 examines the topic of word processing in detail.

Figure 6.27 Main Menu Showing Word Processing Functions

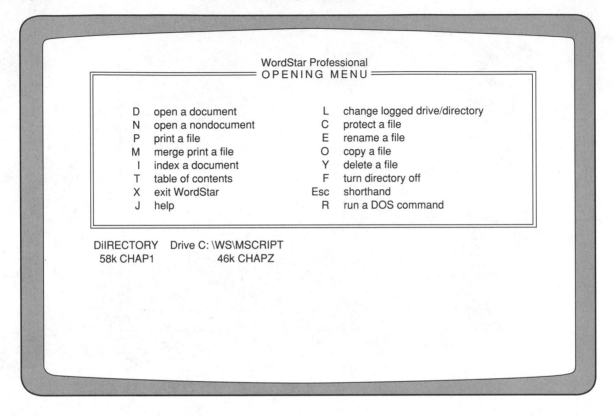

WordStar Professional
OPENING MENU

D	open a document	L	change logged drive/directory
N	open a nondocument	C	protect a file
P	print a file	E	rename a file
M	merge print a file	O	copy a file
I	index a document	Y	delete a file
T	table of contents	F	turn directory off
X	exit WordStar	Esc	shorthand
J	help	R	run a DOS command

DilRECTORY   Drive C: \WS\MSCRIPT
58k CHAP1   46k CHAPZ

Desktop Publishing

Desktop publishing involves combining text, graphics, and images—such as digitized photographs—in a single document. Emphasis is not on the entry and editing
of text, as in word processing, but on the capability to compose text in a manner
that comes close to the quality that is achieved with professional typesetting (such
as that used in this book). Table 6.5 indicates when desktop publishing is most
appropriate.

A good desktop publishing program makes it possible to develop well-designed
manuscripts. It allows users to prepare text in multiple columns, insert rules as
needed, and include graphics and illustrations in output. Proportionally spaced type
can be used and lines can be justified. Figure 6.28 illustrates a well-designed page of
information created through desktop publishing. Note the appearance of multiple
columns and the inclusion of graphics. Table 6.6 lists some widely used desktop
publishing programs. Desktop publishing is discussed in greater detail in Chapter 15.

Table 6.4 Widely Used Word Processing Programs

For IBM Personal Computer	For Apple Macintosh Computer
Multimate	Macwrite
PC Write	Word
PFS:Write	WordPerfect
Word	Word Now
WordPerfect	
WordStar	
XYWrite	

Table 6.5 Using Desktop Publishing

Use for	Not for
Newsletters	Correspondence
Catalogs	Memos
Brochures	News releases
Presentation visuals	Addressing envelopes
Published reports	Mailing lists

Data Management

The ability to store and retrieve data is fundamental to information systems. Personal computer users have many of the same requirements for managing data as users of large systems. Impressive personal computer **data management software** packages are available for well under $1000.

In many instances, personal computer data management packages include such features of fourth-generation languages as the ability to develop a data file format, a series of visual displays for entry and retrieval of data, and report layout designs without using a traditional programming language. The actual program instructions to carry out the work are developed by the data management software.

Personal computer database software allows users to:

——Create files and databases to store data

——Locate and retrieve data quickly

——Add, change, or delete records of data

——Manipulate selective data to prepare reports and summaries, or to respond to inquiries

Increasingly, data management systems include the capacity to generate entire applications without the need for users to write program instructions.

The most widely used data management packages for personal computers include:

dBASE III Plus and dBASE IV
rBASE System V (for DOS)
Paradox
PFS:File

Figure 6.28 Page Layout Created Using Desktop Publishing Software

288   *Chapter 9   Adding Graphics to Maximize Publication Effectiveness*

More about Patterns
A pattern blocks out everything behind it, as when the "Paper" shade is chosen.

Basics of Good Design
1. Organize for clarity.
2. Keep the page simple and uncluttered.
3. Establish a tone.
4. Provide visual variety.
5. Assist the reader.
6. Maintain consistency and accuracy.

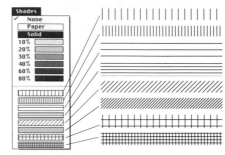

Figure 9-14
Patterns in the Shades Menu

Filling Shapes with Patterns

The bottom half of the Shades menu lets you fill PageMaker-drawn shapes with eight patterns of lines (Figure 9-14). As with the choices in the Lines menu, these patterns cannot be modified.

Patterns are especially helpful for creating borders and decorative boxes. Figure 9-15 illustrates how some of them can be paired together or with a rule to form borders.

Creating Effective Graphic Elements with PageMaker

The inclusion of drop shadows, boxed text, and other decorative elements requires design awareness as well as a knowledge of the mechanics of PageMaker's drawing tools. As you work, apply the

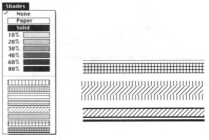

Figure 9-15
Lines and patterns can be paired to create simple borders.

(Jan Eakins, *Desktop Publishing with Pagemaker 3.0,* Watsonville, CA: Mitchell, 1990.)

Table 6.6 Widely Used Desktop Publishing Programs

For IBM Personal Computer	For Apple Macintosh Computer
Gem Publisher	Pagemaker
Interleaf	Quark Express
Pagemaker	Ready Set Go
Ventura	

Figure 6.29 dBASE IV Control Panel Showing Main Functions

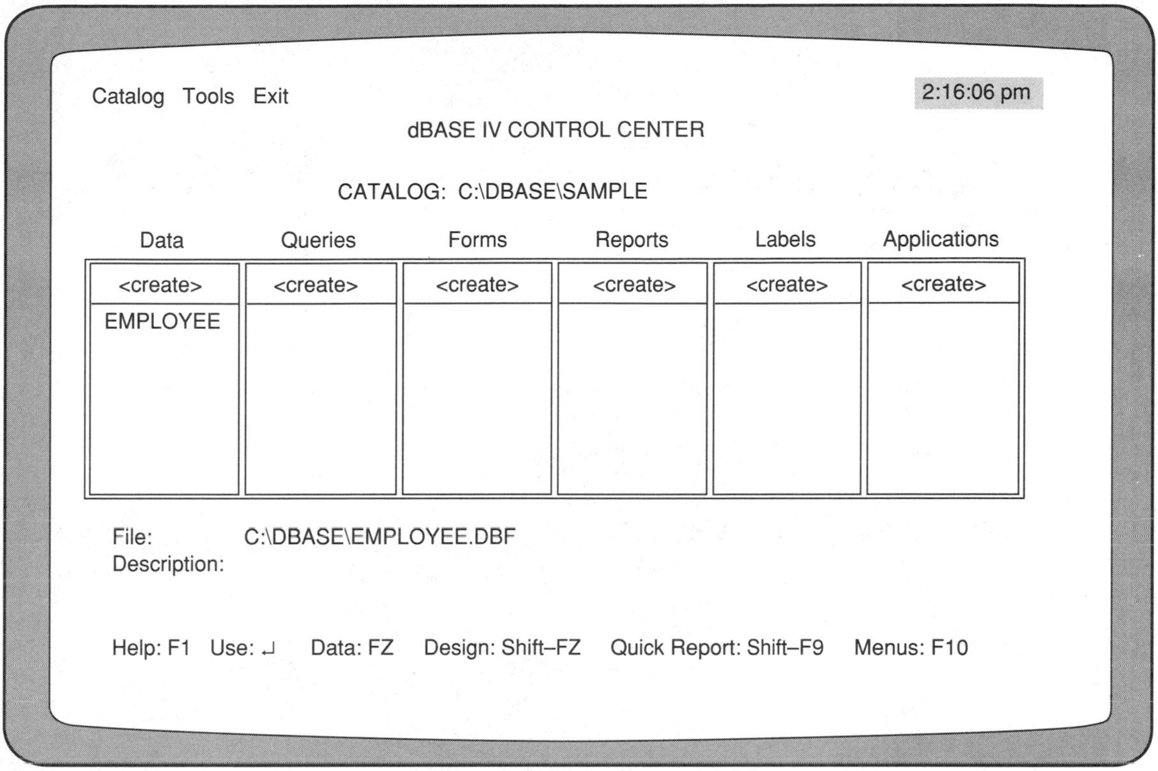

```
┌──────────────────────────────────────────────────────────────────────┐
│                                                                        │
│   Catalog  Tools  Exit                                   2:16:06 pm    │
│                         dBASE IV CONTROL CENTER                        │
│                                                                        │
│                     CATALOG:  C:\DBASE\SAMPLE                          │
│                                                                        │
│      Data      Queries     Forms      Reports     Labels    Applications │
│  ┌──────────┬──────────┬──────────┬──────────┬──────────┬──────────┐  │
│  │<create>  │<create>  │<create>  │<create>  │<create>  │<create>  │  │
│  │EMPLOYEE  │          │          │          │          │          │  │
│  │          │          │          │          │          │          │  │
│  │          │          │          │          │          │          │  │
│  │          │          │          │          │          │          │  │
│  │          │          │          │          │          │          │  │
│  └──────────┴──────────┴──────────┴──────────┴──────────┴──────────┘  │
│                                                                        │
│    File:         C:\DBASE\EMPLOYEE.DBF                                 │
│    Description:                                                        │
│                                                                        │
│                                                                        │
│   Help: F1  Use: ↵   Data: FZ   Design: Shift–FZ   Quick Report: Shift–F9   Menus: F10 │
│                                                                        │
└──────────────────────────────────────────────────────────────────────┘
```

Each of these systems can interchange data with the most popular spreadsheet packages. This feature is attractive to users because it saves time by eliminating the need to rekey or reconstruct data. It also means greater consistency, since there is less chance of introducing errors in the data during rekeying.

dBASE, the most widely used data management system on personal computers, includes many of the features of the fourth-generation languages discussed in this chapter. We will build a database using the same data as in the discussion of Query-By-Example to demonstrate the capabilities of dBASE. (*Note:* dBASE has evolved through several distinct versions, including dBASE II, dBASE III, dBASE III Plus, and dBASE IV. Each version includes significant new features. The illustrations in this chapter all use dBASE IV.)

dBASE IV stores all files in tables: Rows are records, and columns are data items. Before the data can be stored in the database, a *structure,* consisting of the names of the data items in a record, the number of characters in each, and the type of data (such as alphabetic or numeric) must be defined. dBASE IV includes an application generator that assists users in defining the structure. When the system is loaded into the computer, a menu of options appears on the display screen (Figure 6.29).

Figure 6.30 Data Descriptions Under dBASE IV

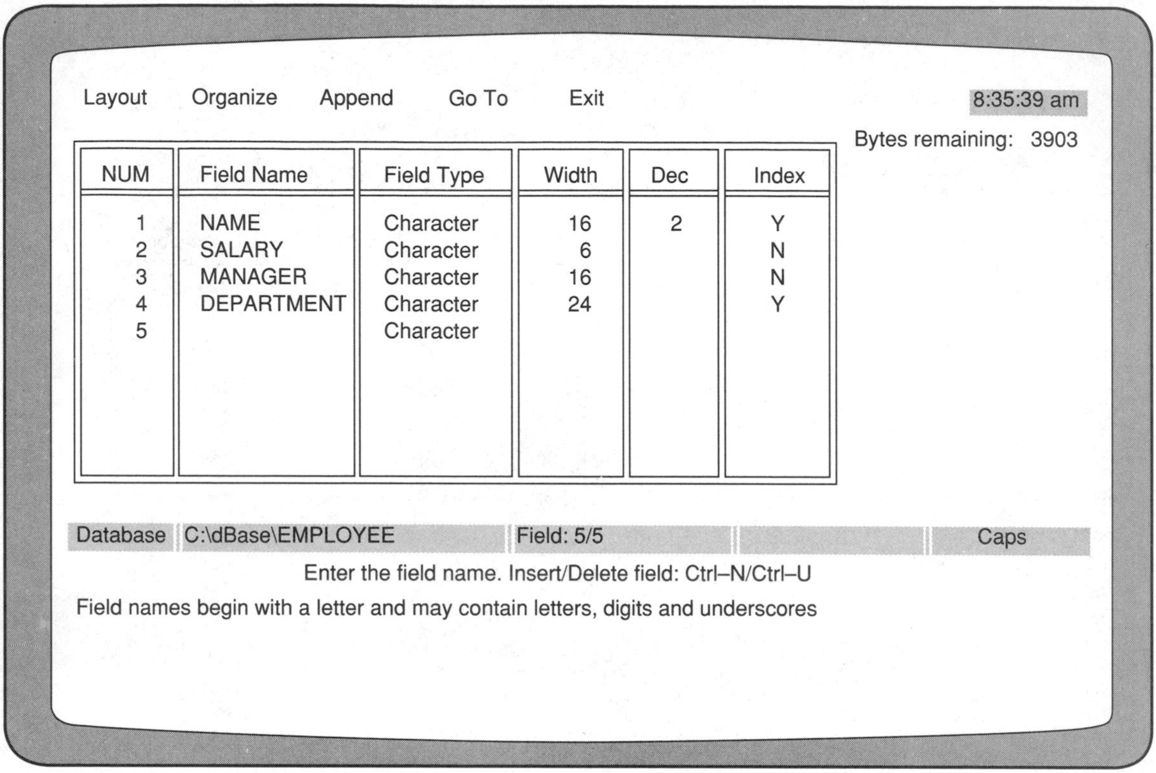

| Layout | Organize | Append | Go To | Exit | | 8:35:39 am |

Bytes remaining: 3903

NUM	Field Name	Field Type	Width	Dec	Index
1	NAME	Character	16	2	Y
2	SALARY	Character	6		N
3	MANAGER	Character	16		N
4	DEPARTMENT	Character	24		Y
5		Character			

| Database | C:\dBase\EMPLOYEE | Field: 5/5 | | Caps |

Enter the field name. Insert/Delete field: Ctrl–N/Ctrl–U

Field names begin with a letter and may contain letters, digits and underscores

The CREATE menu option allows the establishment of a file structure. To establish the structure for an employee file, we must enter the data descriptions (Figure 6.30). The application generator automatically prompts the user to supply this information; it is unnecessary to write format specifications. As each data item name, type, and length specification is entered, it is displayed on the screen. The dBASE IV software also stores the definition automatically.

dBASE IV prompts users for data, automatically accepting and storing data values as they are entered (Figure 6.31). Users need not write any program instructions to enter data.

Menus also make it possible to retrieve details and to sort data into different sequences by rearranging records or by developing indexes that permit the retrieval of data in an order different from the actual stored order. Records may be displayed on the screen (Figure 6.32) or listed on the printer. Search capabilities allow specification of conditions for retrieval or display of records (Figure 6.33). Thus, if we wish to retrieve the records for those individuals whose earnings are greater than or equal to $16,000, the query we posed using Query-By-Example, we can do so from a dBASE menu.

Figure 6.31 dBASE IV Prompt for Entry of Data

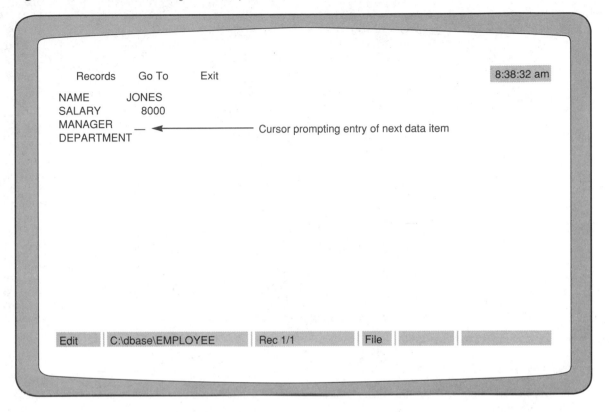

dBASE supports many reporting and retrieval options, ranging from using a built-in report writer to writing specialized report modules using procedural instructions from the dBASE command language. A "browsing" capability permits users to scan through the files of data record by record, retrieving details—even entering changes, if desired.

Because dBASE IV can join databases together in a relational manner (see Chapter 8), it is a very powerful tool for managing and retrieving data. It serves both end-users and professional programmers in many business environments, due in part to its attractive cost: The list price of dBASE IV is less than $700.

Hypertext and Data Management A special type of data management program is based around **hypertext,** such as Apple's HyperCard. The principal unit for storing information under hypertext is a **stack,** a named collection of cards. Each card is comparable to an index card and can be designed to hold whatever information its user needs.

You might think of the card as similar to an entry in a relational table. Each stack, like each database, holds data about the same entity of interest. However, cards

Figure 6.32 Retrieval of Employee Database

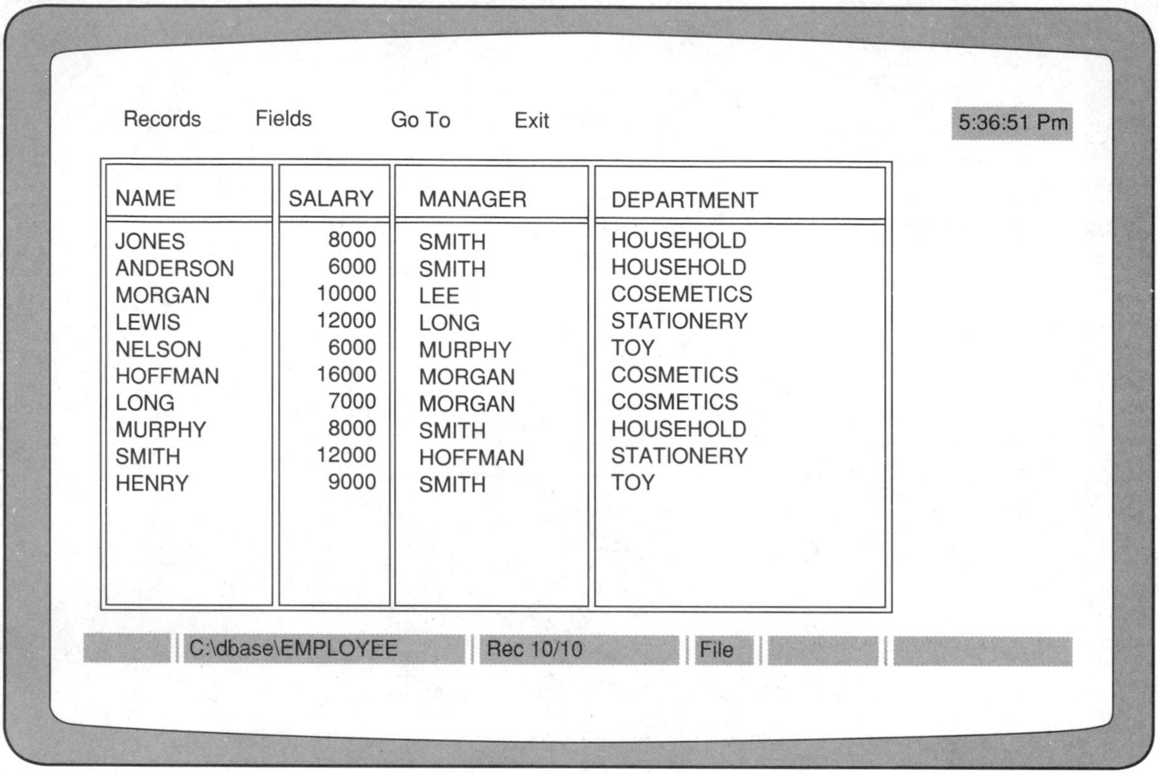

Records	Fields	Go To	Exit	5:36:51 Pm

NAME	SALARY	MANAGER	DEPARTMENT
JONES	8000	SMITH	HOUSEHOLD
ANDERSON	6000	SMITH	HOUSEHOLD
MORGAN	10000	LEE	COSEMETICS
LEWIS	12000	LONG	STATIONERY
NELSON	6000	MURPHY	TOY
HOFFMAN	16000	MORGAN	COSMETICS
LONG	7000	MORGAN	COSMETICS
MURPHY	8000	SMITH	HOUSEHOLD
SMITH	12000	HOFFMAN	STATIONERY
HENRY	9000	SMITH	TOY

C:\dbase\EMPLOYEE   Rec 10/10   File

in a HyperCard stack can also be designed to hold graphics (see Figure 6.34) that assist in entering and using information. The graphics may be a symbol or icon, or a form that shows how to enter data.

Stacks in HyperCard can be linked to other cards or stacks. Links allow the incorporation of additional details or related information of interest. For example, a stack designed to record data about customers can contain links for each customer to another stack that contains details of purchases a specific customer has made. The user can switch between order and customer stacks, depending on the needs of the situation.

Apple Computer was the first vendor to introduce hypertext into widespread use. However, because of the ease of use and powerful retrieval capabilities in HyperCard applications, other versions of hypertext are also becoming available for use.

Graphics

Graphics software used in a business environment is the functional embodiment of the phrase "A picture is worth a thousand words." In many instances, the translation of a large volume of data into a graphic form (Figure 6.35) improves communication

Figure 6.33 Conditional Retrieval of Data

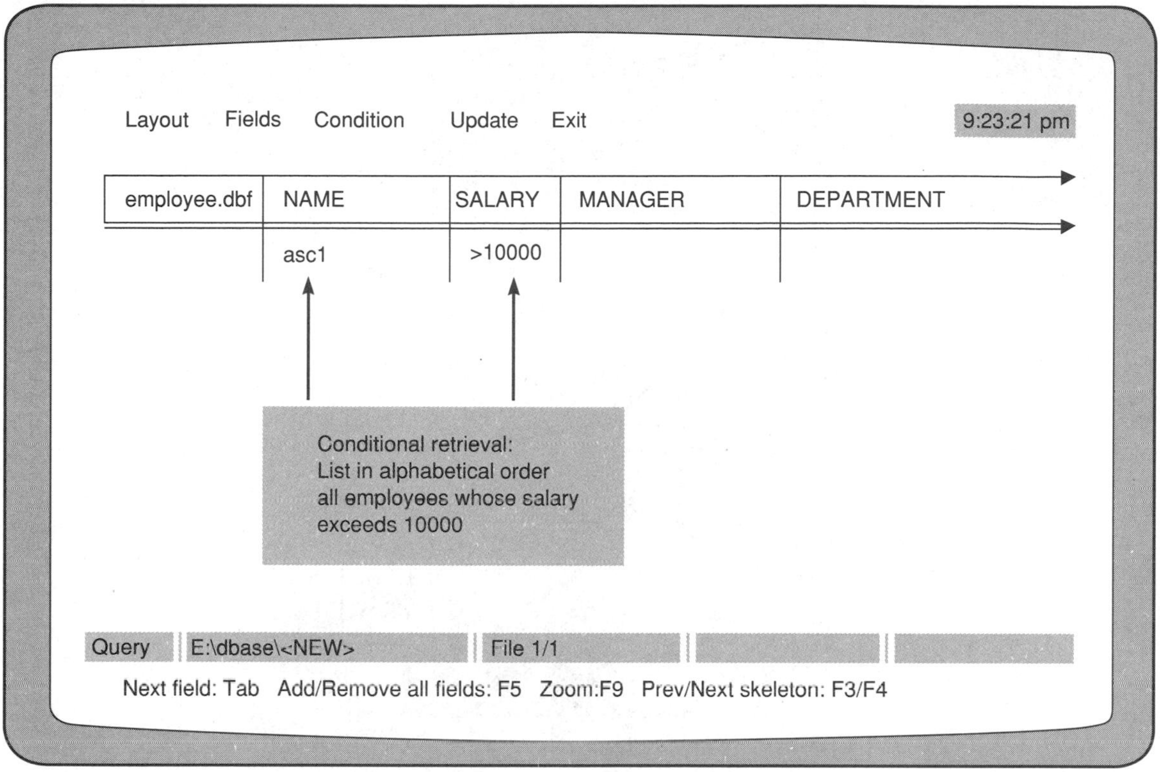

```
   Layout    Fields    Condition     Update    Exit                          9:23:21 pm

   ┌─────────────┬──────────────┬───────────┬──────────────┬─────────────────────────▶
   │ employee.dbf │ NAME        │ SALARY    │ MANAGER      │ DEPARTMENT              ▶
   └─────────────┴──────────────┴───────────┴──────────────┴─────────────────────────
                    asc1           >10000

                          ┌──────────────────────────────────┐
                          │  Conditional retrieval:           │
                          │  List in alphabetical order       │
                          │  all employees whose salary       │
                          │  exceeds 10000                    │
                          └──────────────────────────────────┘


   Query    E:\dbase\<NEW>              File 1/1
        Next field: Tab   Add/Remove all fields: F5   Zoom:F9   Prev/Next skeleton: F3/F4
```

of an idea or the meaning in the data. Charts and graphs are developed quickly using personal computer software packages. These relatively inexpensive packages process data files and display the graphics in a matter of seconds. Large volumes of data can be reduced to a single picture, usually in color. If a printed copy is needed, the graph can be sent to a printer.

You can expect that other categories of software will be added to this list in the near future. The personal computer is in widespread use in virtually all business environments. As new uses are identified, software will undoubtedly appear—at a reasonable cost—to meet the need.

Summary

Software is a vital component of information systems. The quality of the software determines the usefulness of the application and the benefits that will be gained from such systems.

The two types of software are operating systems and application software. An operating system is a group of programs that monitor and control all input/output

Figure 6.34 HyperCard Stack

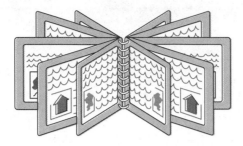

Cards ringed in a stack

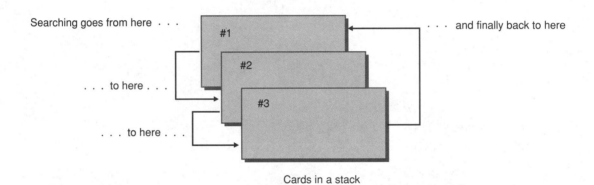

Searching goes from here . . .   . . . and finally back to here

. . . to here . . .

. . . to here . . .

Cards in a stack

and processing operations in order to ensure that the best use is made of the computer system. Application software, in contrast, is developed to carry out the procedures associated with a specific business application (such as order entry) or processing function (such as word processing).

Software may be acquired in several ways. For organizations having a programming staff, in-house development may be feasible. In many instances, however, even a firm that employs a programming staff may find it more timely and cost effective to contract for development of software packages or to purchase prewritten packages.

Computer software has developed through four generations, and a fifth generation is on the horizon. Initially all programming was done in machine language, the strings of binary digits that computers understand. Assembly language replaced machine language and then itself was replaced by procedure-oriented languages as the tool for writing computer programs. Today most programs are written in procedure-oriented languages and fourth-generation languages. The latter allow development of software by specifying what must be done rather than how to achieve the result. The four types of fourth-generation software—namely, query and retrieval languages, report generators, application generators, and decision support languages—allow users to outline complex programs without having to write detailed

Figure 6.35 Data Displayed in Graphic Format

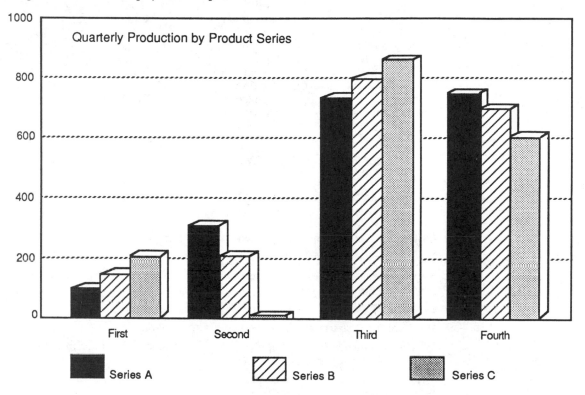

processing instructions. Programs written in these powerful languages require less than one-tenth the instructions of COBOL and BASIC programs. And they are suitable for end-users who are not professional programmers.

The spreadsheet is the most popular type of software package associated with personal computers. This package, which provides the capabilities of an accountant's columnar worksheet and the power of a computer, is the most frequently used personal computer software package. Other widely used packages perform the function of word processing, data management, and graphics. A recent method for management of data is the hypertext method.

High-quality software is an essential element in an information system. Without it, the hardware is not useful.

Key Words

Ada	Assembly language	Compiler
Application generator	BASIC	Compilation
Application software	COBOL	Data management software

Decision support
  language
Desktop publishing
DOS
Fifth-generation
  language
FORTRAN
Fourth-generation
  language
Higher-level language

Hypertext
Interrupt
Machine language
Object program
Operating system
Pascal
Query language
Query and retrieval
  language

Report generator
Software package
Source program
Spreadsheet
Stack
Syntax error
Third-generation language
Translator program
Word processing

Review Questions

1. Distinguish between operating systems and application software.

2. Discuss the different types of operating systems software.

3. Through what means can organizations acquire software? What are the advantages of each method?

4. Describe the five generations of software. Why has each new generation evolved?

5. What are the desirable attributes of a computer program?

6. Why is documentation of computer programs desirable? Distinguish between internal and external documentation.

7. Discuss the characteristics of all programming languages. What factors distinguish programming languages from each other?

8. Compare the features of the FORTRAN, BASIC, COBOL, and Pascal programming languages. How are they different?

9. What are the differences between machine and assembly language? Are programs written in these languages transferable? Why or why not?

10. Distinguish between the different types of fourth-generation languages. How do fourth- and fifth-generation languages differ?

11. If you are preparing to write a computer program, what factors should you consider in selecting a language?

12. What language is most commonly used on microcomputers? Why is this language selected over others?

13. Describe the software packages most commonly used on personal computers. Can a software package be responsible for people buying computers? Explain.

14. What characteristics distinguish desktop publishing programs? Describe the reasons to use desktop publishing software.

15. What is hypertext? What benefits does it offer for the storage and retrieval of data?

16. What is a stack? Explain how stacks store data.

Application Problems

1. James Supply Company is planning to develop a computer-based system that will perform two separate but related functions. Initially, the firm wishes to automate the order entry function. As conceived by the staff—none of whom have computer training—the system will be used to accept orders from customers, in person or over the telephone. Items wanted, quantity requested, and delivery instructions will be entered through a terminal or workstation. Using these data, the system will prepare appropriate invoices and billing notices. The order entry process used by James is typical for the industry and includes no unusual or difficult processes.

    As the system evolves, James staff wish to add computer-based inventory control processes. It is desirable to integrate inventory management with order entry so that when an order is placed, records of quantity on hand can be adjusted to reduce inventory by the amount of merchandise needed to fill the order. James's inventory procedures are currently very straightforward and there is little desire to make them more complex when an automated version is installed.

    James is about to proceed with the acquisition of the hardware and software for this system. It is considering whether to purchase software off the shelf, since there are many order entry and inventory control packages available for purchase. But, management also wants to consider asking an outside contractor to develop and install the software. Its third option is to hire a systems specialist who will design and write the application software needed. The specialist will then coordinate all installation activities and cut over to use of the new systems.

    What advantages and disadvantages do you see for each of the approaches outlined above? Which strategy do you recommend? Why?

2. What type of fourth-generation software is appropriate for each of the following situations?
    a. Formulating a printed report of selective information from an existing database; the report will group performance by categories and should include subtotals for each category.
    b. Developing source code for an application, including procedures for input of data, validation of entries, and preparation of reports summarizing input entries.
    c. Entering inquiries and displaying information from a file or database that will answer the inquiry.
    d. Entering relational inquiries to retrieve data from a database and having a formatted report prepared automatically using default headings, totals, and so on.
    e. Producing computer programs from minimal entry of processing specifications; source code may be further modified after it has been produced by the system.

3. A student planning a career as a systems analyst or programmer/analyst is faced with the task of deciding what programming languages to master, if any. The student, who wishes to work in the business community, is debating on the long-run picture for third- and fourth-generation languages. More specifically, the student is trying to decide whether to master the third-generation languages COBOL and Pascal.

The student recalls that vendors have indicated that fourth-generation languages will replace these languages and that all work will be done in one or more fourth-generation languages. At the same time, other students have suggested that fourth-generation languages are only useful in a limited number of situations, and often are used by people who cannot write "real" programs.

a. What should the student do? Will fourth-generation languages replace third-generation languages?

b. What comments can you offer about the advisability of mastering COBOL or Pascal for use in business applications?

4. Many applications running on personal computers use spreadsheet software. In fact, many business executives purchase personal computers primarily to develop spreadsheet applications. Yet only a limited number of spreadsheet packages that operate on mainframe systems are commercially available. This type of software is largely in the domain of personal computers.

Why does this situation exist? If spreadsheet software is useful, should it not also be in abundance on mainframe systems?

5. A common practice among programmers is to write sets of codes consisting of one instruction after another. Instead of grouping the instructions into modules, they use an abundance of GOTO and transfer of control statements (see the sample programs in this chapter). What problems can this kind of approach lead to in terms of documentation and program maintenance?

What would be the implications of not using GOTO statements in writing programs? That is, what would it force the programmer to do?

6. A programmer in the systems department of a business refuses to write programs in the COBOL language, preferring to use only BASIC and assembly language. The programmer says that COBOL is too wordy and awkward to use and that it requires too many instructions to process something that could be done in BASIC with just a few statements. The programs usually written in this business are oriented toward input/output of large volumes of data but require little computation and arithmetic.

What arguments could you formulate in support of and against the programmer's position?

7. You have been asked to design and develop a large, complex computer program for a new kind of operation to be installed in the company. Because of the newness of the operation, it is anticipated that a lengthy "shakedown" period will be required to develop acceptable operating procedures. This has implications for the computer program that you will be developing in that, as changes are made in operating procedures, changes will also be needed in your program. Since you are aware of this situation as you start writing the code and developing the logic, what precautions would you take to protect yourself and to ensure that future changes will be easy to make?

8. It has been said that large and complex computer programs are never completely debugged and that sooner or later unexpected errors will occur because users utilize the system in ways that the designers and programmers have not anticipated—for example, they try to input unusual data.

If this is true, how can you protect against these errors by detecting them and not processing the transactions that contain them? (*Hint:* Consider the use of test statements to deal with each of the conditions that have been thought of ahead of time.)

9. You have been assigned to design a program to process sales transactions. The following specifications have been provided:
   a. The number of transactions processed at any one time will vary.
   b. Some sales will be made to tax-exempt customers. All other customers, however, will pay a sales tax.
   c. The transaction data to be processed by the program will be keyed into the system through a workstation.
   d. Output will be printed on ledger paper by a line printer.

   Describe how you would deal with each of these specifications by identifying the general kinds of instructions in higher-level languages that you would use for each condition (for example, transfer of control statement, iteration statement). You need *not* identify them in terms of a specific programming language.

Minicase: Programmer Certification

The Data Processing Management Association, a large professional organization of the computer industry in the United States, recently queried attendees at a quality assurance symposium. This survey showed that more than 80 percent of the respondents wanted certification programs for quality assurance analysts (the persons charged with the responsibility for certifying the reliability of software).

A certification program offers a means of ensuring that individuals have demonstrated the skills and knowledge needed to perform quality assurance properly so that others can rely on their judgment when using certified software. Currently, organizations that maintain their own quality assurance staff face difficulties in determining the qualifications needed to perform as a quality assurance analyst and in verifying the capabilities of individuals considered for or occupying this important post.

There is skepticism about the usefulness of a certification program. Symposium participants questioned its feasibility because of job diversity. It was pointed out that nearly 30 different activities fall under the umbrella of "quality assurance." In addition, human factors and interpersonal skills are high on the requirements list for a certification expert, but assessing these skills is very subjective, and uniform evaluations are difficult to achieve.

An additional question is the need for recertification. Proponents point out that because of the speed with which the field is changing, it is essential for individuals to keep up. Recertification is the only way, they feel, to check on this. Opponents, in contrast, state that the purpose of certification is to determine background and qualifications to enter the certification field. It is the responsibility of the employer to ensure that a quality assurance analyst remains current in the field and able to meet the organization's requirements.

Others point to the present certification requirements for computer programmers. The certification is entirely voluntary. Neither organizations hiring programmers nor professional organizations have mandated the certification of programmers. There is no standard background of education or experience level. Yet organizations are dependent on the skill levels of the programmers.

Quality assurance certification proponents believe that it is much more important to provide standards for quality analysts than for programmers. The former are the last inspection point before software is put into actual use. Therefore it is felt that both the people and their methods must be controlled, evaluated, and reevaluated.

Questions

1. Does the certification of programmers and/or quality assurance analysts make sense from a practical viewpoint? Can certification be meaningful if it is based on the attainment of a minimum educational background and performance on a written examination? (Consider that certification in many medical fields occurs only after periods of residency working with practicing professionals and that licensing is under the control of state boards.) If certification is begun, should recertification also be required at periodic intervals, as is required for educators in many states?

2. Is it more important to monitor the qualifications and skills of computer programmers and systems analysts or of quality control specialists who scrutinize the software that programmers and analysts produce?

3. Should quality assurance practices apply to software developed by end-users? If analysis procedures are developed by end-users working with well-known spreadsheet programs on personal computers, is it necessary for certification of these procedures also?

4. If certification is eventually required for professional programmers, on the grounds that the organization relies on the quality of their programs and the information they produce, should certification requirements also apply to end-users who produce important information for the organization?

Minicase: Who Should Pay for a Software Error?

Organizations are increasingly reliant on computer software. So are individuals, whether at work, driving an automobile or flying in a commercial airliner, or even using appliances around the home. We depend on the programs of instructions that guide or operate the systems and devices.

Information systems professionals know that improvements are needed in software reliability, and well-funded efforts are continually under way to secure them. Many users of computer systems know that there are no assurances a program will not fail. And they know that as many as 40 percent of all programs are estimated to fail at one point or another.

Vigorous and costly software testing programs run for long periods of time so that errors can be detected. Yet, errors may later be revealed, perhaps originating from something as simple as the omission of a comma in a computer instruction.

The average person knows that computers will fail—everyone has encountered problems with a bank or a utility company, for example, and rightly or wrongly, the difficulties were blamed on "the computer." But most people have no idea how dependent they are on computer software in many day-to-day activities.

Suppose a programmer's mistake causes medical equipment to fail, or an on-board computer in an automobile or an aircraft causes a tragic accident. A simple typographical error can cost millions of dollars if it leads to an improper business decision. An error can also destroy volumes of data that will cost days and thousands of dollars to re-create. These are the realities of computer software.

Questions

1. Do you agree with the seriousness of software errors as presented above, or do you feel that this minicase exaggerates the problem of software reliability?

2. Should the user of a software product be informed of the risks of using the software and thus assume all liability for losses that result from its use?

3. Should the individual who writes a section of software that contains an error and ultimately causes damage be held personally liable for the damages? Should the person(s) who perform software testing be liable for damages or injury if an undetected error leads to later failure of a computer-controlled device? Is the vendor liable?

Transaction Processing Module

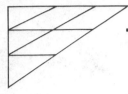

7: Files and File Processing

Key Questions

What elements are included in the hierarchy of data?

How do storage media affect data access in transaction processing?

In what ways can files be organized?

What criteria should be addressed in selecting a file organization?

Why are there so many file organization methods?

What types of files are used in transaction processing systems?

What are on-line and real-time computer systems?

What considerations must be addressed in evaluating an application for possible development as an on-line, real-time system?

Press Release Announcing UNIVAC

New York, March 25—It was announced today that a high-speed general-purpose electronic computer is being marketed by the Eckert-Mauchly Computer Corporation of Philadelphia. This instrument out-speeds and out-performs all previous electronic "brains." Speaking before a meeting of the Institute of Radio Engineers here, Dr. John W. Mauchly, the president of this company, stated that they are starting on the production of a revolutionary type of computing machine. This newest electronic brain is tiny compared with the mammoth ENIAC machine of the University of Pennsylvania and the even larger computers constructed at Harvard. In spite of its small size, however, he said, it can do many things which the earlier machines could not do but which are essential in business applications.

The Universal Automatic Computer, which was announced today, is called the UNIVAC and uses magnetic records on a metal ribbon instead of punched paper tape or cards. The ribbon of metal tape which is used in the new machine is only a few thousandths of an inch thick and about one-quarter inch wide. By a special technique over one hundred numbers can be written magnetically upon a piece of tape only an inch long. Dr. Mauchly explained that magnetic recording of numbers and letters in code on metal tapes is more permanent and durable than paper records. It can be erased or changed, he said, by special equipment built into the computing system. The ability to erase or change the information makes it possible to rearrange and alter data which have been magnetically recorded and also to completely remove data from the tapes when no longer required. In this manner, he explained, the magnetic tapes can be used repeatedly for many years.

Tapes are prepared for use in the computing system by typewriter-like recorders which can be operated by any typist. This recorder places on the magnetic surface of the tape little dots of magnetism in groups so as to represent numbers and letters in a code similar to a telegraph code. Bookkeeping data, statistics, lists of names, and similar information, when typed on the keyboard of the recorder, are stored as magnetized spots on the tape. Interspersed with such data are the instructions to the computing machine, telling what is to be done to the data. The UNIVAC then reads the tape at high speed, carrying out the instructions to rearrange the data or to perform simple arithmetic or complicated mathematical procedures with it. After the UNIVAC has completed its work, Dr. Mauchly said, the result appears upon another magnetic tape, which can then be placed in an automatic printing machine which prepares a printed page.

The new machine, Dr. Mauchly said, is an outgrowth of the remarkable work which has been done in the past few years at a number of large universities, notably the University of Pennsylvania. He said that it was here, while working with Mr. J. Presper Eckert, Jr., during the war years, that they designed the ENIAC and EDVAC electronic brains.

The ENIAC, the pioneer electronic computer, was much too large for commercial use. The EDVAC design made it possible to build better computers with much less equipment. The UNIVAC, however, is the first small electronic machine to work directly in the decimal number system and which can also handle letters and punctuation marks.

The UNIVAC is the first large electronic machine designed to classify, arrange, and sort information in a wholesale fashion. Its efficiency in this process is high because of the amazing rate (10,000 digits every second) at which it can take in and give out the data with which it deals.

Dr. Mauchly explained that in using the UNIVAC computing system there is no limitation upon the sequence of operations or the complexity of instructions. Any set of operations which can be written down can be carried out by the UNIVAC. Usually it will be possible to perform any set of operations in a number of ways, he said, and the operator is free to choose which method he should use. Those combinations of operations which occur frequently he called sub-routines, and he said they need to be recorded only once no matter how many times they are to be used.

A subroutine, he explained, is a simple series of operations which may occur frequently in the course of a given problem. An example of a subroutine would be a series of arithmetic oper-ations required to add a certain percentage of compound interest to the principal or balance of each of a number of loan accounts. The machine could at the same time perform special instructions upon each account, such as making entries of payments and transfers of funds and the formulation of new subtotals and totals. Dr. Mauchly said that the UNIVAC has special cir-cuits which make errors virtually impossible. If an error should occur, the operator is notified at once so that it will not pass unnoticed and suitable correction can be made.

The UNIVAC employs a mercury "memory" or register which can hold as many as one thousand twelve-digit numbers within the electronic machine. Data and instructions placed in this built-in memory are immediately accessible to the machine for use in computations. It is because of this high-speed built-in memory, Dr. Mauchly said, that the computer can add thou-sands of twelve-digit numbers in one second.

Part of the funds used in designing this equipment were from the U.S. Bureau of Census through a contract with the Bureau of Standards of the U.S. government. The work of the Cen-sus Bureau, as well as that of many other organizations, both governmental and commercial, has been studied, he said, in an effort to make the system as flexible and general as possible. Manufacture of the UNIVAC equipment is now being undertaken by the Eckert-Mauchly Com-puter Corporation in Philadelphia. The new computing systems, he said, are so fast and can thus handle such a large volume of data that a single machine will be able to accomplish work which now requires much larger and more expensive installations. Several large business corpo-rations, as well as statistical groups and government agencies, are preparing to install these new computing machines. A number of standard UNIVAC systems will be in use next year.

Eckert-Mauchly Computer Corporation, Release 7 P.M. March 25, 1948. (Courtesy Sperry UNIVAC)

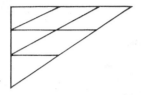

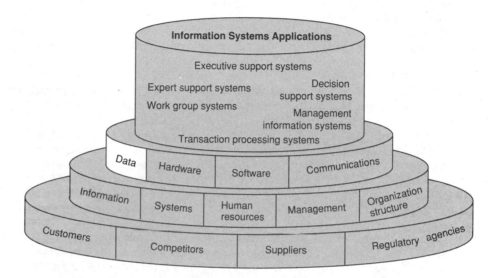

As we discussed in Chapter 1, transaction processing takes place to classify, calculate, sort, summarize, and store data. For any of these functions to occur, the data must be organized into a form that the computer can use. This means that data are not just grouped together haphazardly, but are organized into sets that make it possible to process them quickly and to use the least amount of storage space possible.

Transaction processing requires that data transaction records be grouped into **files** (collections of data) for storage and processing. These data records may be organized differently, depending on the way in which they are used.

In this chapter, we examine the hierarchical structure of files and the ways of organizing or structuring them to best meet user and processing requirements. Also, we discuss various file processing activities, including insertion and deletion of data, modification to record contents, and sorting procedures. Each of these activities is common in transaction processing systems.

Because access to the data is necessary before processing can occur, we discuss the concept of data access and describe several access methods. Each access method depends, in some sense, on the storage medium employed, and each is selected because of the way the data are expected to be used for an application or applications system.

Hierarchical Contents of Files

Files are made up of groups of data records that can be used together to provide a logical and easy way of processing data. Individual data items can be consolidated in certain ways so they can be considered as a group. For example, universities group students into classes or courses. In this way, all students who are in their third year of college can be referenced, say, for registration purposes, as juniors. Similarly, all students who are taking a course in computer-based information systems can be treated as a group for grading purposes. Thus through grouping, the entire set of data can be retrieved and used (that is, accessed) at one time, thereby eliminating the need to issue the same command or instruction with respect to each individual element.

Universities publish final examination schedules by grouping students together according to the courses they are registered in. Thus, to schedule an examination for the computer-based information systems course, the examination office can post a notice on the bulletin board stating the course name and the date and time. This is the same as posting a notice that lists the name of *each person who is registered in the course*. Listing the examination by the *name* of the course automatically refers to each of the individual persons (the elements) in the course (the group). The same principle is used in the hierarchy of data.

To fully understand the relationship of data in files, we need to focus on the lower levels in the *hierarchy of data,* including data items and records. The hierarchy calls for data items to be grouped into data records, which in turn are grouped into files (Figure 7.1). Notice that the number of items in each record and the number of records in the file are not fixed. That is, the user of the data determines which items are collected and grouped together.

Data Items and Entities

The lowest level or smallest element of data in a file, the **data item,** is a fact or statement about some *entity* (person, place, thing, or event) of interest or of potential interest for any one of a seemingly infinite number of purposes (decision making, report generation, check processing, and so on). Each fact describes the entity of interest. In a payroll situation, for example, we may wish to collect data about the entity "employee." One of the attributes that is of interest is the name of the employee. Thus we have the following:

> *Data Item*
> *of Entity*
> Name

At this point, we have established a general characteristic of interest about an entity (employee), but we have no way of distinguishing one employee from another. To do this, we need to attach a *value* to the data item for each employee.

Entity	*Data Item of Entity*	*Data Item Value*
Employee	Name	Bill Whitaker

Figure 7.1 Data Hierarchy

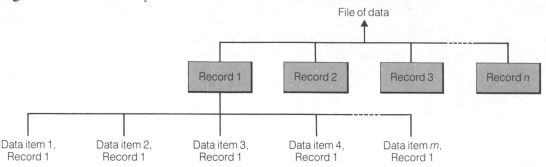

Table 7.1 Entity: Employee

Data Item Name	Size	Type	Value[a]
EMPLOYEE NAME	16	X (that is, alphanumeric—the combination of alphabetic, numeric, and special characters)	Bill Whitaker . . .
IDENTIFICATION NUMBER	6	9 (that is, numeric)	343675

[a]Blanks (. . .) count as one of the positions, so the data item EMPLOYEE NAME has a value that contains 12 letters and 4 blanks.

The specific value "Bill Whitaker" distinguishes one individual from all other individuals who fall under the entity "employee." The assignment of a value to the data item (that is, the name of Bill Whitaker) constitutes an instance of one data item (name) for the employee.

The data item itself has characteristics, including data item name, size, and type specification. The data item name enables us to distinguish one data item from all other data items. The size of the data item tells us how many characters or numbers can be used in stating its value, while the type describes whether the item is made up of alphabetic, numeric, or special characters. These characters help describe the data more fully when we are actually collecting them for storage or for use in a decision-making situation. Using the characteristics, we thus have the relationship shown in Table 7.1 between an entity and two data items describing it. Size and type more fully describe the data item. In other words, the data items have clearly identified characteristics of name, size, and type specification.

Record

Data items are the basis of records. Specifically, a **record** is a collection of data items about an entity that are usually used together in processing; these related data items are grouped together and retrievable as a single unit. In other words, a record is a

Table 7.2 Record-Employee

Data Item Name	Size	Type
EMPLOYEE NAME	16	X
IDENTIFICATION NUMBER	6	9
ADDRESS	20	X
CITY	16	X
STATE	2	X
ZIP CODE	5	9

Table 7.3 Record: EMPLOYEE (a 65-character record)

Data Item Name	Size	Type	Value
EMPLOYEE NAME	16	X	Bill Whitaker . . .
IDENTIFICATION NUMBER	6	9	343675
ADDRESS	20	X	28 Vestal Parkway . . .
CITY	16	X	Binghamton . . .
STATE	2	X	NY
ZIP CODE	5	9	13901

Table 7.4 Set of Record Instances

Record	Employee Name	ID No.	Address	City	State	Zip Code
1	Bill Whitaker	343675	28 Vestal Parkway	Binghamton	NY	13901
2	John H. Walker	18180	92 Lake Street	Vestal	NY	13902
3	Jamie Allison	47048	133 German Street	Apalachin	NY	13732
4	Barbara Rosen	107	8496 German Park	Binghamton	NY	13905

collection of data items with associated attributes to which, for reference purposes, we assign a descriptive name. Thus a record about the entity "employee," which we name EMPLOYEE, might contain the information shown in Table 7.2. Any reference to the record name EMPLOYEE will also include an implicit reference to each data item contained in it. An *instance of a record* exists when values are associated with the data items shown in Table 7.3. Of course, there can be many record instances, as shown in Table 7.4.

Sometimes some items in a record do not have values; that is, they contain only blanks. *Missing data,* as these are called, may result when, for example, a permissible value for an item is nonexistent (for example, an unknown birth date). Missing data may also result when a data item is not applicable (for instance, draft status for a woman).

The record we've been describing here is known as a **fixed-length record:** As you might expect, the number and the position of data items in such a record are of a predetermined length. Each of the records above consists of six data items or fields with fixed lengths of 16, 6, 20, 16, 2, and 5 characters, respectively.

However, not all records are fixed length. Another type, the **variable-length record,** is quite common in data processing usage. The length of records can vary due to length of data items or numbers of data items. In the first case, we may find the size of data items varying to accommodate values that differ in length. For example, one may choose to develop the EMPLOYEE NAME item as a variable-length item so that if the name is 10 characters long, the size of the field is 10; if it is 15 characters long, the size of the data item is 15 characters, and so on. Most frequently, however, the field length is fixed and any unused positions are blank. Records more often vary in length to accommodate a variable number of data items. For example, we might wish to expand the employee record to contain data pertaining to occupational skill. Since an individual may have one job skill or several, the employee record, if it is to contain these data, should be able to accommodate the listing of all pertinent skills. Therefore, an individual who has one job skill needs a record that consists of six fields, while an individual who has four different skills needs a record consisting of nine fields, four of which are fields for JOB SKILL.

Files

In the hierarchical data system, a file (also referred to as a *data set*) consists of a collection of records. Each record is a logical part of the file because it contains the same data items as all other records that are members of it. While the records in the file may be defined somewhat arbitrarily, depending on who makes up the definition, the file contents—that is, the overall collection of records—is fixed when the file is established. Thus the definition of the file, once decided, is fixed; all records must conform to the definition. A payroll file, for instance, will contain only payroll records; an employee file, only employee records, and so forth. We would not, as a general rule, find sales records in the payroll or employee files.

The collection of employee records we have been using as an example constitutes a file although it is relatively brief—only four entries. Logically, a file can contain any number of records. But each record must contain the same data items (with different instances of the data item values).

File Types

Files of several different kinds are used in transaction processing. Now we look at these types and show the role each plays in business and organizations. The main kinds—namely, master, transaction, and sort files—are summarized in Table 7.5.

Table 7.5 Forms of File Organization

Type of File	Description	Example
Master file	A relatively *permanent* collection of records that contain data about events that affect an organization. It may be historical or current-events oriented. A master file is central to the operation of the organization.	Sales history file, customer name file, parts and supplier file, inventory file, supplies and equipment file, parts explosion file
Transaction file	A relatively *temporary* collection of records that contain data about transactions that have occurred during the operation of the business or organization. This file is processed against the master file.	Account payment file, sales, order file, purchase order file, cash receipts file, changes to work-in-progress file
Sort file	A *very temporary* collection of selected records that may be from master or transaction files or may be original data. Sort files are used to arrange data records in a particular order.	Customer file (sequenced into alphabetical order) \n\n Employee file (sequenced into alphabetical order by department)

Master File

Master files are relatively permanent collections of records concerning events that affect an organization. The data may be a historical overview of events, as provided by sales history or vendor history files, or they may be current-event–oriented files, such as stock status or accounts receivable files. In either case, the files contain data that are central to the continued operation of the organization. Consequently, they must be *maintained* constantly (that is, changed to include data about any new events or to correct errors) to ensure that they are both accurate and up to date. A master file that does not contain current data—unless held strictly for archival or historical purposes—is of little or no value to an organization. Sales history or accounts receivable files may, for example, be updated daily to include new data on merchandise withdrawn from inventory or charge and credit sales that have been made during the day.

Transaction File

A **transaction file** is a relatively temporary file containing data about transactions of business activities. Transaction files may be established to capture data on sales transactions (such as number of items sold to one customer), purchase orders (such as number of items ordered or purchased from one supplier), cash receipts, and so on. These files are used mainly for posting the data to the master file much as a bookkeeper would post the data to accounts. In other words, transaction files, also called **detail files** because they contain the details of transactions, are processed against (used as data for updating) the master file.

A retail store, for example, regularly makes credit sales. The amount of these sales, as well as certain descriptive data about the transactions, must be collected and used to update the records of each customer making a purchase. Let's assume that the following data are collected on a sales slip for each transaction: (1) name of customer, (2) customer account number, (3) date of transaction, (4) description and price of each item purchased, and (5) total dollar value of the sale. At the end of each week, the store collects the data into a transaction file in the following manner. First the sales slips are collected and put into a stack or batch. Then, the data are keyed into the computer and the sales slips are put away in a steel file cabinet in case they are needed later. The computer produces a transaction file of the week's sales on magnetic tape.

This process generates a *transaction file* that contains all the relevant data from each credit sales transaction. This file is then processed against the master file of accounts receivable; that is, all new sales transactions are posted or entered into the master file. A computer program reads each individual transaction record, finds the corresponding customer's record on the master file, and the amount of the new purchase is added to the existing balance. This process, shown in flowchart form in Figure 7.2, is repeated for every transaction in the transaction file. (See the appendix, "Flowcharting Symbols and Techniques," at the end of the book.)

Transaction files may also contain data that are to be processed against the master file to change data previously recorded. Data may be changed because errors have been detected or because records must be added or deleted. In a retail store, addition or deletion entries may be the result of new accounts being opened or old accounts being closed. Transactions of this nature are just as important as the others if the master file is to be properly maintained.

We said that transaction files are temporary compared to master files. We can clarify this further. Many transaction files are, in fact, retained throughout the fiscal year because they are needed for auditing and control purposes. Frequently, it is necessary to refer to these files to verify or confirm details of particular transactions or to correct errors that were not detected earlier. Thus, while transaction files are temporary, they are often retained (off-line on magnetic storage devices) for several months before being destroyed or released.

Sort File

Like the transaction file, the **sort file** is temporary. Its sole purpose is to aid in sequencing or sorting sets of data into a particular order based on some *record key* or keys. A **key** is a field or data item in a record that is used to identify the record within a file. For example, we may wish to arrange an employee file in alphabetical order based on last names. In this case, the key is the last name, and the value for the data item is used for sorting. If, instead, we wish to sort the file into an order based on identification numbers, then the identification number would be the record key.

Sort files then are used to create new files in different sequences. They are processed against a *sort program* (a computer program that performs the sort operation) to arrange the data into a selected sequence, such as alphabetical or numerical

Figure 7.2 Transaction Processing for File Maintenance: See Appendix for Flowcharting Symbols

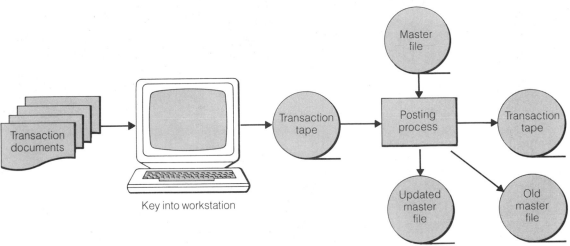

Key into workstation

order. Sorting takes place on the basis of the value in the record key that the user specifies.

Sort files may be copies of master files, collections of transactions, or the original data of either of these. In the case of transaction files, a sort file is usually created to place the transactions into the same order as the records in the master file so that updating can be performed more efficiently. Sort files may also be used in preparing reports based on either transaction or master file data. The sort file usually is not retained after the reports have been completed.

File Storage and Access Methods

The way data in files are stored on magnetic tape, magnetic disk, or magnetic drum is called a **file organization** (or storage structure). Selection of a file organization depends on the storage medium and the way the file will be used in processing. We examine each of three file organizations: serial, sequential, and random.

Types of File Organization

In **serial organization,** the most basic type of file or data set organization, records are stored in physically adjacent locations on the storage medium (for example, magnetic tape, disk, drum) *without concern for any particular order or sequencing* of records. The only concern is to store each record in the next available spot. It does not matter what the contents of a record are or what other records precede it. As Figure 7.3 indicates, to read a record stored under serial organization, the file must

Figure 7.3 Serial and Sequential Files

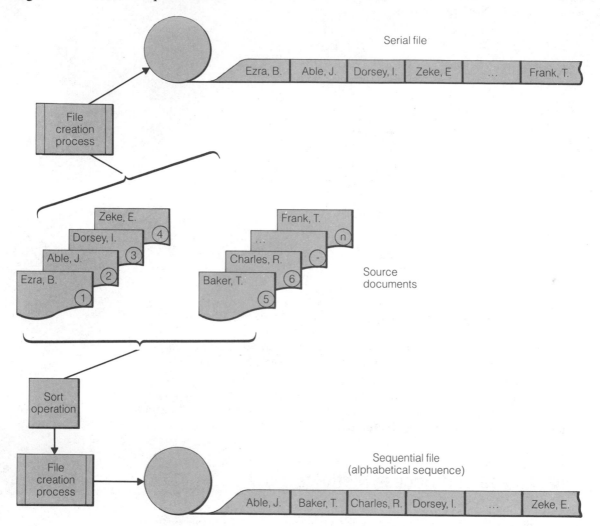

be processed from the beginning until the desired record is encountered. Because this is a haphazard way of organizing files, the serial method is seldom used for storing records in permanent files. However, it is often used for transaction data that are recorded as events occur. For instance, if sales data are entered on magnetic tape by a key-to-tape device as the transactions occur, they are being organized serially. Since the records are written one at a time, it would not matter that the records are not organized alphabetically by customer name or name of the item sold.

In **sequential organization**, records are written in the same sequence in which they are collected, but they are organized into a certain order. This means—and it is the major distinction between serial and sequential organization—that if a particular order is required, the data records must be sequenced or ordered before the file is created on the storage medium. For example, if a payroll file is to be created on magnetic tape from source documents, and alphabetical ordering on last name is wanted, the records must be alphabetized before they are put on tape. After sorting has been completed, the data are recorded and stored *in the order in which they are recorded* (Figure 7.3). In other words, the first record processed is the first record written in the second location on the tape, and so forth.

When sequentially organized files are processed, the records must be read in the same order in which they are stored, starting at the beginning of the file. The processor reads the file from the beginning, *checking each individual record* until it finds the desired one. Thus, if the particular record wanted for processing happens to be the 101st record in the file, the preceding 100 records must be read first. Sequential organization can be used on all storage media, but it is the dominant method for magnetic tape.

An alternative to sequential organization is **random organization,** sometimes called *direct address organization.* With this method, which can be used with direct access storage devices such as magnetic disk and drum, records need not be written or accessed in a sequential order but can be handled at random. Each storage spot on the storage medium has an address, and as a record is processed, it can be assigned to any storage location on the device, regardless of whether the preceding ones have been used. In other words, in creating the payroll file discussed before, the transactions can be processed from the card deck in any order and written at many locations throughout the stored file. They do not have to be written in sequential order.

To access a record stored under a random organization, prior records need not be examined first. The CPU can go directly to the desired record *without searching all the others* in the file. Obviously, then, when a single record has to be accessed, random organization is quicker than sequential organization. However, when there are a number of records to be located and read, and the transactions can be sorted into the same order as the master file, the sequential organization *may be* more efficient. These considerations are examined in more detail in the following section.

Address Systems in Random File Organization

As we have seen, random organizations offer much greater flexibility in the creation and maintenance of files than sequential organizations. We will look at two addressing systems that can be used for random organization of records. One, the direct relation method, uses the key of a record as the storage address. In the other, the key transformation method, a calculation must be performed on the key in order to derive a storage address. Either of these methods can be selected when the file is stored on direct access devices.

Direct Address Method The *direct relation* address system is the easiest and least sophisticated of all the random file systems. Because this method uses the record key or identifier as the storage address of the record in the file, there is a direct relation between the record key and the location of the record on the storage device (Figure 7.4). Under direct relation addressing, an employee identification number (the record key in this example) of 15014 would mean that the record is stored on the storage

Figure 7.4 Direct Relation Addressing

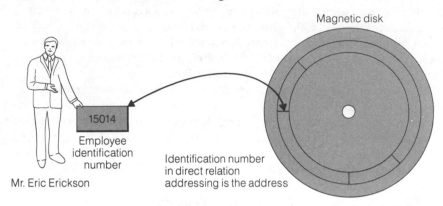

device at address 15014. (Recall that an **address** is a particular storage location on the device. It is distinguished from all other storage locations by its number.)

The **direct relation method** calls for the establishment of a set of keys that correspond to addresses on a storage device. Since the addresses are numerical, no special characters or alphabetic letters can be used in the set of established keys. Moreover, the *key set*—the set of all possible values for the key—is best established as a set of ascending, continuous (highly dense) numbers from, say, 11,000 to 11,049. Thus, 50 storage locations, each of which may eventually be used to store data for later processing, are reserved for this file. It is important to note that space is allocated for records regardless of whether they exist now, in anticipation that space will be needed as the file grows and expands.

To access a record for any purpose (to add, delete, update), one need know only the value of the record key. Because only one access is needed, this method of record location and retrieval is faster than sequential organizations or the other random addressing systems we will be examining.

However, there are potential problems and disadvantages associated with the direct address method. If a large number of locations are unused, for example, valuable storage space is wasted. Furthermore, it is a rigid method—there is one and only one way to store the data. If the record keys of a firm are not entirely numeric or if they are not in a workable numerical sequence, direct organization may prove impractical. For instance, if the key consists of alphabetic characters, such as an employee name, the direct relation method cannot be used. Likewise, if the key values cover a wide range of numbers but only a small portion of those numbers is actually used, direct organization is a poor choice.

Key Transformation Method A viable alternative to direct addressing is the **key transformation** technique. This method is used to get a random address for storage based on a record key when the key itself cannot be used directly as the address, hence must be transformed. A key transformation derives a storage address by performing

Table 7.6 Sample Randomizing Techniques

Method	Example
Division: key is divided by some selected number, the quotient is discarded and the remainder saved.	A. Divide key by total of storage locations; remainder is storage address. For example, key = 4638 range = 1000 spaces $$1000\overline{)4628}\quad 4$$ Remainder, 628, becomes the storage address 628. B. Divide key by prime number; remainder is storage address. For example, key = 4638 prime = 293 $$293\overline{)4628}\quad 15$$ Remainder, 233, becomes the storage address 233. Prime numbers can be selected from a prime number table; others include 739, 6373, and 11,069.

Folding: key is split and parts are added together to derive a storage address.	key = 148279
	split and add = 841
	                 279
	                ‾‾‾‾
	                1120
	
	Derived storage address is 1120.

Extraction: selected set of digits is extracted from key to derive a storage address.	key = 148279 Extract first, third, fifth, and sixth digits. Derived storage address is 1879.

an arithmetic or algorithmic process on the key value. In other words, the key is *not* the address, but it is used to calculate the address. For example, we could include instructions in a computer program to divide the number 111 into the key to derive a storage address. If the key of a particular record is 4567, applying the transformation technique derives a value of 41 with a remainder of 16. Either number could be used as the derived storage address, but it is the remainder, as you will see, that is usually used.

There is virtually no limit to the number of key transformation techniques. Regardless of which technique is used, however, the underlying purpose is the same: to derive a unique random address. We examine three of these techniques now: division, folding, and extraction (Table 7.6).

As we showed in the previous illustration, a common key transformation technique is to *divide* the key by some factor. For example, we can divide the key by the range of storage (that is, the total number of storage spaces available), discarding the quotient and using the remainder as the address of the record. If the range is 1000 and the record key is 4628, the result of the division is 4 with a remainder of 628. The remainder, 628, is the address of the record.

A variation on this method is to divide a record key by a prime number. A *prime number* is any number that cannot be divided evenly except by 1 or itself. The prime number is divided into the record key, and again, the remainder becomes the record address. For example, if the prime number 293 is divided into the key 4628, the remainder is 233, which is the address for storage of the record.

Folding is a second easy and efficient key transformation technique. Under this method, the value of the key is split or *partitioned* and the parts are added together to derive a storage address. The partitioning can occur in any number of ways. For example, in a six-digit key, the first, third, and fifth digits can be added to the second, fourth, and sixth. Or the first three digits can be added to the last three, and so on. If the key value is 148279, we can derive an address of 1120 by adding the third, second, and first digits to the fourth, fifth, and sixth digits respectively (see Table 7.6).

In **extraction,** one of the simplest transformation techniques, a set of digits from the key is selected for use as the address. For example, if the key is six digits long, and a four-digit address is desired, we might extract the first, third, fifth, and sixth digits as a storage address. Any number of other key transformation techniques can be developed to derive storage addresses.

Often when a large file is being handled, two keys transform into the same storage address; that is, the randomizing technique results in the same address for two different keys. When this happens, the keys are called **synonyms.** A common method of dealing with this situation uses a **distributed organization.** The distributed organization uses storage buckets for records rather than direct addresses. Records are placed into the buckets by applying the different randomizing techniques that we discussed to distribute the records as evenly as possible across the buckets.

A **bucket** is an area of storage that can contain a specific number of records. For instance, a bucket often is a track on magnetic disk. The number of buckets needed to store a file depends on the size of each record and the number of records in the file. If a file contains 10,000 records and each bucket can store 40 records, we would need 250 different buckets (and, in this case, 250 tracks). In determining the number of buckets needed, you can use a rule of thumb that each should initially be 50–75 percent full (depending on how much growth of the file is anticipated). This accommodates future expansion of records and files. If each bucket is to hold 12 records, and the file is 12,000 records long, 2000 buckets should be established to accommodate the entire file, if the buckets are initially half full (see Figure 7.5).

In adding records to a file, the address of the record (the bucket in which it is to be located) is calculated through the prescribed randomizing technique, and the record is written in the first available location in the bucket. Thus an address is calculated for the bucket, not for the individual record. Before adding the record, the bucket is searched for duplicates.

If the bucket is already full, the record is stored outside the designated bucket. The overflow can be handled in two ways. With the **consecutive spill method,** the record is written in the next available location in the next open bucket (for instance, in the next track on the disk). A more conventional method of handling overflow, however, is to use an overflow area, or bucket. A **pointer** in each bucket tells the processor where an **overflow bucket** is located (Figure 7.6). An overflow bucket is simply another bucket on the storage device.

Figure 7.5 Use of Buckets for Distributed Information

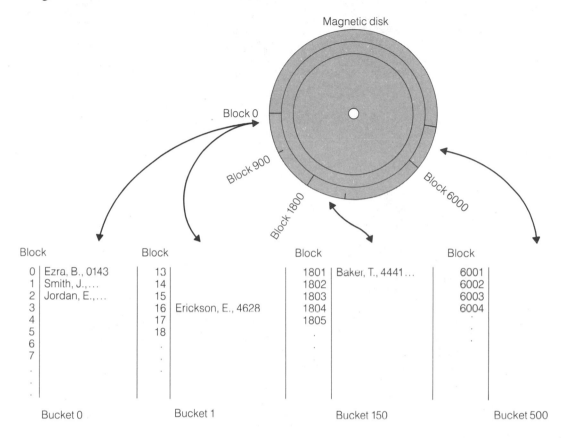

To read records, the same procedure is followed; that is, the bucket address is calculated to determine the location of the record. Then the bucket is searched to find the desired record. If it is not there and the bucket is full, a search is made in the overflow bucket.

The bucket method does not always make the most efficient use of storage space, as in the early life of a file when buckets are only half full. However, this method of assigning unused space in a small part of the file, the bucket, improves access time over, for example, sequential organizations, in which an entire file must be searched to locate a record. Hence, one must bear in mind the tradeoffs between storage space and access time when considering the distributed method of random organization.

Indexed File Organization

A common use of direct address devices for file organization involves the creation and maintenance of indexes for sequential and nonsequential storage.

An *index* in file organization techniques is comparable to the index at the back of this textbook: It is a list of record keys and addresses of associated data. In a

Figure 7.6 Overflow in Distributed Organization

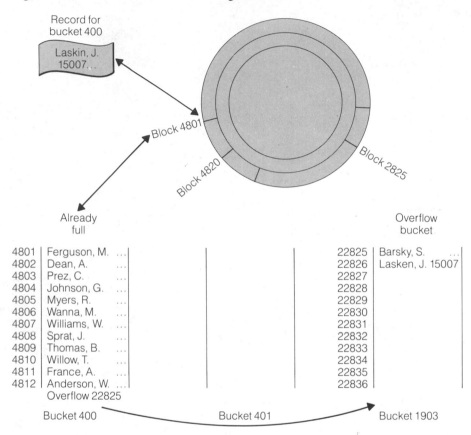

textbook, the identifier or key is a topic or a name, and the location is a page number. Indexes in files consist of a record key and a storage address. To locate a record, the index is searched until the proper record key is found. The address corresponding to the key is where the record is stored. This **indexed organization** system saves on allocated but unused space on the storage medium. Because the index keeps track of storage locations, only the storage spaces actually used need be allocated. This is in contrast to the direct and distributed methods where space is allocated in anticipation of later usage.

Indexes are used in index sequential and index nonsequential organization. The **index sequential method** combines an efficient batch capacity (that is, sequential file processing) with an inquiry operation that is efficient because records can also be accessed randomly if necessary. The file is created sequentially, with the record keys being used to place the file into an order, such as alphabetical or numerical with ascending identification numbers. Physical storage sections, called blocks, are then indexed.

Figure 7.7 Index and Stored Data in Index Sequential Organization

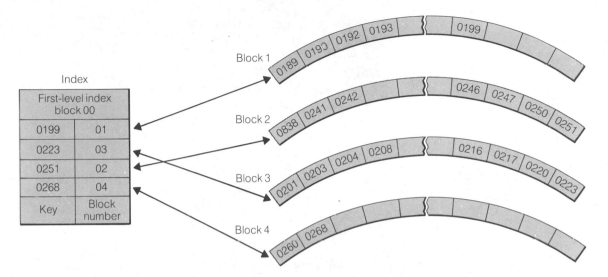

In index sequential, the index addresses a specific record in the file. However, the address in the index usually does *not* point directly to the record location (although this varies with some vendors' implementations), but rather to the block in which it is stored. The key of the last record in a block (and thus the highest key value in it) appears in the index, along with the address of the block containing it. If we wish to find a record with a key value of 0242, we would have the processor search the index to find the first entry greater than or equal to 0242. The address corresponding to that key would be the number of the block containing the record. In Figure 7.7, the key in the index that meets these criteria is 0251, which is in block 2. Block 2 would be read and then searched sequentially until the desired record was found.

In particularly large files, the index may become too long to be searched efficiently. In these cases, an index to the indexes may be created. The *master index,* as it will be termed here, contains the highest address listed in a particular subindex. Subindexes may be created for each cylinder. Subindexes, in turn, can point to still lower level indexes that pertain to a single block on a disk. If a file is stored on 10 cylinders and each cylinder contains 20 different blocks, we could have three different index levels: a master index indicating the cylinder on which a record is stored, a cylinder index indicating the group of blocks in which the record is stored, and a block index indicating the particular block in which the record is stored (Figure 7.8). To find the particular record, then, a search would first be performed on the master index; that would point to the next lower level index, and so on.

The **index nonsequential method** implies the use of an index to locate records, but here data records are not stored according to any order or sequence. (Because there is no ordering of the records, this kind of organization is also called *index random.*) Consequently, records cannot be accessed without the use of the index. To

Figure 7.8 Multiple Indices in Index Sequential Organization

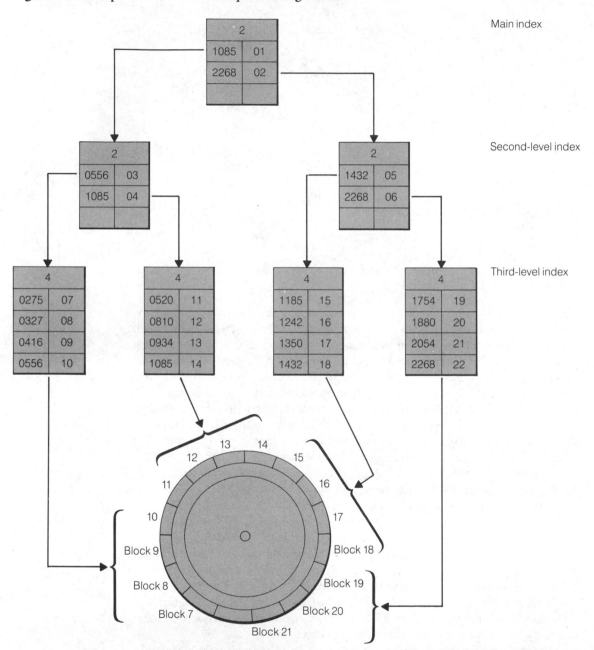

facilitate processing of files organized under the index nonsequential method, a larger index is necessary because one index entry is needed for each record in the file. Insertions are easy: A new record is simply added to the end of the file and added to the index. Deletions are also easy: An entry is removed from the index. Since there are more index entries, greater maintenance is needed to adjust the index, especially if multiple levels are used. Index nonsequential files can be processed sequentially, but this is a slow process because the index must be searched for each record.

Processing Modes

Many of the applications of transaction processing depend on the **processing mode**— the particular way in which transactions are handled. Some individual transactions are held and sorted by type into groups, while others are processed as they arrive or occur on a one-at-a-time basis. The processing mode is also related to the way users are involved in handling transactions. Sometimes users enter the transactions directly into the computer system by means of terminals or workstations. In other situations, data are recorded first on source documents, which are entered into the processing stream.

Next we examine two processing modes: batch processing and on-line processing. Both modes are in widespread use on personal computers, minicomputers, and mainframe systems.

Batch Processing

In *batch processing,* as the name indicates, all data and transactions are coded and collected into groups (batches) before processing. Data processing is therefore *periodic:* at given intervals or time periods, data that have been sorted into groups or batches are processed. The processing may be done hourly, every 2 hours, every 8 hours, and so on, depending on the organization.

When source documents (in computer-readable form) are entered into a computer together, the set is being batch processed. A batch may vary in size from a few transactions to several thousand (Figure 7.9).

Batch processing can be used, for example, for files such as accounts receivable that are stored on magnetic tape. This mode allows you to get a report with the names of all individuals who owe more than $100 simply by processing, at one time interval as a group or a batch, an accounts receivable file previously recorded on magnetic tape.

In this particular batch processing application, each record of the file must be examined to determine whether the account balance exceeds $100. Suppose we know, however, that only 50 out of, say, 5000 in the file have to be examined. If this were the case, the program would be written to examine only the 50 accounts that we specified (by providing the account numbers as keys). Such processing can be done quite easily under an index sequential organization by locating the keys (in this case,

Figure 7.9 Batch Processing Mode

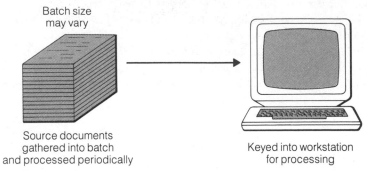

Batch size
may vary

Source documents
gathered into batch
and processed periodically

Keyed into workstation
for processing

account numbers) for the desired records in the index and accessing the proper record at the address shown. However, it still constitutes a batch processing situation.

Batch processing includes two variations: *sequential batch processing* and *random batch processing*. Assume that a master file is going to be read under the sequential batch processing mode. Before the read process, which might involve checking new credit sales amounts or cash payments to the account, the records of transactions must be sorted into the same order as records in the master file (here assumed to be on magnetic tape). The transactions are collected into a batch, sorted into the proper order for efficient access, and *then* processed against the master file. It is more efficient to have both transaction and master files in the same order because the master file can be read sequentially, record by record—otherwise, it would have to be moved back and forth for each transaction.

In random batching, the input transactions can be processed against a file (or several files) *without presorting*. This capability is useful with random organizations in which direct access to stored records is possible, as with files on magnetic disk and drum. Since neither presorting nor examination of every record is necessary, random batch processing is a comparatively faster processing mode. However, if a high percentage of the file (say 50 percent) is going to be accessed during a single processing run, it probably will save time to sort the file and then process it in sequential batches. This procedure is faster than having to calculate addresses for all the records accessed. (We look at other applications of sequential and random processing later in the chapter.)

On-Line Processing

On-line processing is virtually the opposite of batch processing. In this mode, transactions do not need to be collected into groups or batches for reading into memory. Furthermore, with on-line processing there is no need for an intermediary between the user and the computer (for example, a computer operator who runs the card reader or the line printer). The user can work directly with the processor through a terminal or workstation.

An on-line system can accept input directly from the users at their working location; that is, in an on-line system, the input data enter the system directly from the point of origin and output data are transmitted directly back to the user. The intermediate stages of writing to magnetic tape or performing off-line printing are largely avoided. On-line processing, therefore, implies direct communication between the CPU and the user for both input and output.

For example, a hospital pharmacist who wants to see whether a prescribed drug will react with other drugs a patient is taking can query the hospital's on-line patient record system and quickly retrieve a display of the individual patient's medications. In this case, the pharmacist interrogates the system directly by input of patient name or identification number and receives a response to the inquiry. There is no need to punch cards and wait for them to be processed in a batch or to wait for a report to be printed and delivered from the hospital's computer center.

On-line processing implies that activities and interaction with the processor can take place from remote locations, but typically it also implies that files are on-line. This means that files are stored on direct address storage devices so that an individual can have rapid or immediate access to the data. Such access is seldom possible with large sequential magnetic tape files.

If one uses sequential batch processing to prepare reports or obtain data from specific records, entire files must be read to locate the data. On-line processing, however, can free a user from this constraint. For example, suppose that a cashier is interested in determining whether a certain customer's credit card is valid, and the file of accounts is maintained on-line. All the cashier needs to do is enter at the terminal the account number and a symbol indicating the type of inquiry. A response or message noting the status of the account can be displayed at the terminal, often in a second or two. (*Note:* This is an on-line, real-time application. Real-time systems are discussed later in this chapter.) Inquiries of this nature are seldom possible in batch processing. Rather, the computer is used to print a complete report of "good" and "bad" accounts periodically—daily, every other day, weekly, or whatever.

On-line processing is important in file maintenance. For example, in a sales order office that uses an on-line order entry system, items ordered, quantities, prices, and customer names can be entered directly into the system file while the customer is present. In this way, the sales data update the account file, inventory levels, and so on. And often the customer can be assured that the desired merchandise is in stock before leaving the office. Under batch processing, it is necessary to collect written sales orders into batches for later data entry and processing.

Maintenance and updates can generally be performed at any time on an on-line system. Whether records are to be added to or deleted from a file, the operation can be performed through the terminal at any time if the file is continually loaded on the system. (Since extra effort is required to delete large numbers of records in a file, there is a tendency to leave in the file large chunks of obsolete or otherwise unusable data, which causes the overall file size to continually increase. The user will typically pay this cost in small amounts, due to slightly longer access times in a real-time environment.) Usually the files are stored on direct address devices that can be updated quite rapidly.

Selection of Processing Mode

On-line processing offers a number of advantages over batch processing, but it is not always the superior system. What factors should we consider in determining whether on-line processing is appropriate for an application? In general, selection criteria include response time, report detail, input volume, and file usage. All four factors affect the total cost of processing.

Response Time The amount of time needed to process an inquiry is an important factor in selecting a particular processing mode. **Response time** is the number of seconds, minutes, or hours that elapse between the time a transaction occurs or an inquiry enters the processing stream and the time the CPU issues a reply or response to it. If an immediate response is needed—one taking only a few seconds—then on-line processing is perhaps appropriate. However, if 24-hour turnaround is sufficient, there may be little need to develop an on-line system; batch processing methods probably will meet the user's needs.

For example, stockbrokers need up-to-the-minute prices from the floor of the stock exchange. Even though they may receive the latest prices a few minutes after a transaction occurs, the price may already have changed by several points. Clearly, 24-hour turnaround is not acceptable. Brokers need high-speed tickers that receive and display stock prices electronically to show the price at the last transaction. In a sense, this is an on-line system. The same type of processing could be performed through a CRT. The broker could query a direct address file through the CRT terminal and receive an immediate display of current price.

Many banks have had to develop on-line teller systems to prevent illegal withdrawals from accounts. Under the "any branch, any teller" service so popular today, it is possible to deposit money at one bank and to withdraw it at another. By using on-line processing of deposit and withdrawal transactions to update balances, banks prevent people from withdrawing the same funds several times by going to different branch offices or even different tellers in the same bank. When withdrawals are entered into account files as soon as they are made, the opportunity for these intentional overdrafts is eliminated.

Not all situations require rapid turnaround, however. For example, a payroll clerk who receives time cards on one Friday and issues pay checks for the time worked on the following Friday could manage quite well under most circumstances with a batch processing system. Similarly, a stock manager in a grocery store who orders merchandise twice a week would not need an on-line system to place an order. Rather, machine-readable cards could be filled out and read into the computer in batches.

On-line processing can also be combined with batch processing to gain sufficient response time to requests. In this case, although an on-line terminal can be used to receive responses to questions (called *queries* or *interrogations*), files need not be updated or transactions processed on-line, so the two systems can be combined. That is, queries can be made through an on-line device while actual file updating or transaction processing can be done in batches. For instance, in many large inventory control situations in manufacturing processes managers or supervisors must be able to check records to determine whether enough parts are available to complete the day's production schedule. They need to be able to query the system and receive an answer quickly. But there is no need for the files to be updated as each individual item is withdrawn from inventory. As long as the supervisor knows there are enough items to meet production demands during the day, and as long as the withdrawals are counted as they occur, it is acceptable for the files to be updated at the end of the day. Therefore, batch processing can be used to maintain the files by subtracting the withdrawal of items once daily. In this situation, *on-line query capability with batch processing maintenance* provides the best combination of response times at the lowest cost. There is nothing wrong with having both on-line query and on-line update capabilities, but there may be no reason to incur the extra expense.

Report Detail The amount of detail and number of lines in computer-prepared reports is significant in determining the processing mode. Of course line printers print at speeds much faster than most terminal devices. Furthermore, the maximum number of columns on a printed page usually is much greater for line printers than on many terminals. If a job requires the generation of long, very detailed reports, the line printer and batch processing are probably the best combination. However, if output is only a line or two for each inquiry, such as the number of units of a particular item available in inventory, the opposite may be true. Some current on-line systems make it possible for a person using a terminal to request that output be diverted to a line printer, which of course partially circumvents the problem.

Input Volume The number of items to be entered into the system for processing should also be considered when selecting a processing mode. If the number of items is large, it may be more effective to enter them directly onto a magnetic storage medium (through a key-to-storage device) than directly into main memory through a terminal. A payroll clerk, for example, typically would not enter data for 500 employees through an on-line system. Rather the data would be prepared off-line and then batch processed.

File Usage Batch processing is an effective method for processing files of, for example, 10,000 records, from beginning to end. A customer credit file in which every record is processed to prepare a monthly bill is best processed in batch. Batch processing is also often used with strictly sequential files when records can be processed from beginning to end in the order in which they are stored. However, if only a small part of a file is to be processed and the file is not sequential (that is, it is stored under one of the random organizations), it may be quicker and more efficient to access the data on-line by specifying through a terminal, one at a time, the particular records wanted.

Files that consist of simple or two-way lists may take longer to traverse or search than those established under direct organization. But, if only one record is usually accessed in a query, an on-line mode may be preferable. If groups of records are usually accessed together, batch processing is usually better.

Real-Time Systems

Some of the examples discussed in the preceding section actually dealt with real-time situations. Many times on-line and real-time systems go hand in hand. However, on-line systems need not operate in real time.

Real-Time Processing

A *real-time system* is one that can receive data, process them, and return the results to the user quickly enough to affect the user's activities, that is, quickly enough to allow the results to be used in the work being performed. This is in contrast to the built-in delay characteristic of delay batch processing systems. We will examine examples of real-time systems.

Based on this general definition, real-time processing cannot be identified in terms of seconds and minutes alone. Rather, it depends on the context in which processing is taking place. (Some claim that a system that cannot respond within milliseconds cannot be considered "real time." However, this narrow definition is not generally accepted in the computer industry or in transaction processing systems.) For example, if a stockbroker inquires about a possible market transaction and receives a price in a minute or two, this might constitute a real-time response. But a missile-tracking mechanism may need to respond in fractions of a second to be considered real-time. Thus, the important factor is not *absolute* response time, but the time elapsed relative to the needs of the user and the specific work activities.

Types of Real-Time Processing

The term *real-time* can have different meanings. We must distinguish between systems that *accept* data in real time and those that *process* it in real time. In some cases, data that must be *gathered* continuously or immediately as they become available can be processed in a slower response time frame. In other cases, **real-time processing** is necessary—for instance, in response to queries—but data need not be collected in real time. And of course in many situations both the collection and processing of data must be done in real time.

Computer collection and processing of data play an important role in modern rapid transit systems because it is always necessary to know the current location of various train cars and current track conditions. Since these data change from minute to minute, computer-operated sensors continually collect and process the data to control routing of transit cars and track utilization. Real-time software may also manage the acceleration/deceleration controller in a transit car. This both demonstrates real-time collection and processing of data and shows how data processing activities affect events as they occur. Even if data collection and processing were delayed for only a few seconds, severe problems could result. In a sense, the computer system has become part of the process and activity it is controlling. The real-time computer system is actually an *embedded computer system:* It is part of a larger system (in this example, the rapid transit system).

In an automated laboratory system in which scientists perform series of experiments, data are collected and analyzed through an on-line, real-time computer system. In this case, depending on the particular equipment, it may be necessary to collect the data continuously (real-time) since money and "nature" may prevent re-creation of a certain event or set of circumstances. Moreover, sampling of as many as 100,000 data points (single, discrete events) per second may be necessary. In this situation, it is important that the data collection take place in real-time. The actual analysis of the data usually can occur later without loss of value.

The on-line bank teller systems example is a case of both data collection and processing occurring in real time. Files are updated while the customer is at the teller's window, and the deposit or withdrawal is immediately posted to the proper account. Summary totals for all a particular teller's transactions on a given day may be made after the bank has closed; this process does not have to be in a real-time mode.

On-Line, Real-Time Processing

Generally, the data in on-line, real-time systems are maintained on-line and files are updated as transactions take place or events evolve. Furthermore, the files of data can be interrogated through remote terminals. The maintenance of data on-line implies the use of direct access storage devices. If a user needs responses to inquiries in 1 or 2 seconds, it is not possible to mount and load a magnetic disk, search it, and respond within the allowed time. Maintaining the files on direct access devices significantly reduces the time needed to respond to an inquiry. Consequently, in most on-line, real-time systems, the data files are maintained on-line while the application is in operation.

To ensure the currency of data, files are updated as soon as new data arrive. Data are not held and grouped into batches, but rather are entered into the file immediately. File updating in real time is therefore as important as real-time responses. Again, maintaining the files on-line makes this possible.

Single query and response time is so important in on-line, real-time systems that users must have rapid access to the computer and processor. When the actual processing unit is distant, users must rely on the linkage of their terminals to the CPU and the files by *remote access*. The terminals may be located in the same building or several miles—even hundreds of miles—away. In these cases the terminal is linked by a communication or telephone line over which data can be transmitted. The user operates on-line and receives responses in real time, assuming that other criteria, such as on-line files, have been met. The mere use of remote access capabilities does not guarantee real-time response. Data must be on-line and the system must be able to respond quickly without a long delay. To better understand how these processes take place, we are going to look at the functions and procedures associated with transaction processing as they apply to batch and on-line systems.

Time-Sharing Systems

In a **time-sharing computer system,** the computer's processing time is divided among two or more users. The emphasis is not on the computer's capability to handle more than one job at a time, but rather on the fact that two or more persons, each unaware of the other, can interact with the processor in the same interval of time. The term, then, pertains to the number of users on the system rather to a particular hardware configuration, although the latter also becomes important.

Interactive Computing

Many time-sharing systems are characterized by a feature called interactive computing or *conversational computing*. In this situation, a user operating from a remote terminal can submit programs (and data) to a central processor. Through commands at the terminal, the user can create the job, submit it for compilation, correct errors, and control its execution. If an error is detected, the user can correct it (by submitting new program instructions) and continue executing. The user, then, has fairly complete control over the program and data.

The interaction or conversation takes place between the terminal and the processor. Sometimes the computer responds in the form of a diagnostic or error message, which tells the user that he or she has made a mistake, but it can also just return the carriage on a typewriter to begin the next line, indicating that the user's input has been received. Other forms of interaction can be listing programs or files, asking for and receiving an explanation for an error message, or changing a line of code and having the change acknowledged.

Time-Sharing Characteristics

In the foregoing cases, users operate as if they had sole use of the entire computer system. In reality, however, a time-sharing system provides the same power and the same appearance of "ownership" to all the users, who number in the hundreds on some of the larger systems. Moreover, each user's requests are handled with relatively little delay.

Many systems allocate specific intervals of time called time slices for executing segments of programs for specific user programs being run. These time slices are measured in fractions of a second and are controlled by the hardware and software, not the users. While processing a program, a hardware clock, at regular intervals, generates electronic signals to the CPU to suspend activity on one program and begin execution of another. This constant interrupt process makes it possible for each user's program to receive attention from the processor at regular intervals. One program that requires a lot of computation time cannot tie up all the others while it runs to completion.

Since interrupts occur at the end of each user's time slice, regardless of whether a program is completed, several programs are usually partially completed at any given moment. Although extra system overhead is needed to monitor the time slice procedure, it is generally a small cost in comparison with the benefits afforded to multiple users.

Interrupts may also occur when there is a request for input/output. Thus, if a program reaches a point at which input of data from a file is required, the computer may switch control to a second program that will begin (further) execution while input operations go on for the first. In this way, although a full time slice may not have been completed, the central processor is used more effectively.

The operating system keeps track of the schedule for jobs awaiting execution. Because there is a definite order in which the programs are processed, the system is able to move to the next job in sequence after an interrupt, handling all jobs in turn for their respective time slice.

Evaluation of Time Sharing

Time-sharing operations have a number of advantages over batch systems. First, as we mentioned before, a user operating on-line through a terminal can generally receive output and results immediately. Similarly, because the terminals are relatively portable, users can move them from location to location, linking them to the central processor through telephone lines.

In a time-sharing environment, the same data files and programs are available to a number of users. This reduces storage costs and also makes it possible for several people to access the same data at the same time. Their purposes may or may not be similar, but no one is constrained by anyone else in using the files.

Time-sharing and on-line systems are not a panacea. There are drawbacks to their use. When the volume of transactions is high, the cost of system operation may force users to select batch processing, or even minicomputer preprocessing. Consequently, output flexibility and speed are reduced when compared to the possible capabilities of the central system. Furthermore, the addition of extra equipment and telephone lines creates more potential for system or mechanical problems.

Nevertheless, time sharing offers a good deal of flexibility and power to users. It must, however, be evaluated in light of the particular application in which its use is contemplated.

Transaction Processing Procedures

In all transaction processing systems, regardless of processing mode, four functions are needed, and each plays a major role in making the computer system a useful tool. We are going to examine the functions of data collection, editing, processing, and reporting. Knowing how these functions are carried out will help you to more fully understand the operation of computers for data processing. It will also show more about the interrelationships of processing modes and file organizations.

Data Collection

The most fundamental function performed in transaction processing is data collection. This necessary step in both batch and on-line systems consists of capturing, preparing, and recording data for processing. Capture of data should take place as close as possible in space and in time to the source of the transaction. Usually it is difficult, sometimes impossible, to go back and capture data after a transaction has already occurred. This is why sales documents, for example, are carefully designed to tell personnel exactly what data about the transaction are to be captured. If supervisors or managers find that the sales slips have been improperly designed or are not being correctly used, steps must be taken to improve data capture through redesign of the sales slip, procedural change, or personnel adjustment.

In addition to data capture through source documents like sales slips, we find in many systems that it is direct through terminal input. Airline reservation agents, for instance, use specially designed terminals that have keys for input of flight number, passenger name, date of flight, seat classification, and so on. Similarly, point-of-sale terminals have been introduced into the retail industry for data capture. These devices provide direct entry for such data as item number of product purchased, quantity purchased, and unit price. For credit sales, it may also be necessary to key in the buyer's account number, which can be validated immediately (see Supplement 7) by checking the credit record stored in a credit account file. If the account is not valid or has been closed, the terminal may lock, preventing a sale on credit.

Ordinary terminals (CRTs, typewriters, and so on) also can be used for direct on-line data capture if the system was designed to accommodate such input. In these cases, the users do not rely on special keys to guide their input; rather, more controls are built into the software that underlies the application. The programs tell the user what data are required and the proper order of input.

Prior to input for processing, the data must be prepared, that is, put into a form usable in the system. In on-line systems, this step may be built into the input procedure itself. But in many batch processing systems that use source documents like sales slips, separate data preparation steps may be needed. During data preparation, transaction classification and data coding occur. In many transaction processing systems we find it useful to add a data item that assigns the transaction to one of several categories. This is called *transaction classification*. For example, we may want to classify transactions on the basis of whether they are adding or deleting records or changing the contents of stored records. If we are adding a new customer to an accounts receivable file or closing (deleting) the account of another one, we want to tell the system. Thus, we can include a data item in the transaction record that tells the system the kind of transaction it is, which in turn will direct it into one processing procedure (mode) instead of another. A value of 1 may be assigned to transactions that add new records, 2 to those that delete records, and 3 to those that modify existing records. We could also use codes of A, D, and C (for add, delete, or change) or any other classification or coding scheme that might be devised by the systems people. If all transactions processed by a certain program are always the same type, we might choose to omit the classification. For example, if one program in a credit system is always used to add new accounts and never processes deletions or changes, we could omit the classification code; the program would be developed so that it always handles each transaction as an add transaction.

Data coding is the translation of data from source documents into machine-processible form. The procedure is similar to the one used for classifying transactions: the data are examined and translated into a code that is meaningful to the application program. For example, a personnel program may require data about sex, age, and department. We can use a code to present this data to the system: 0-1 or M-F for sex, 999999 for date of birth (to accommodate digits for month, day, and year), and a department number (rather than the *name* "molding department," "shipping department," or whatever).

Data must be recorded to be usable in the system. Usually when we classify transactions or code data, we do it with coding forms, similar to the ones we saw in Chapter 6 for writing programs in FORTRAN and COBOL. The forms have columns corresponding to specific data items, and we write the codes in the proper spaces on the form.

Data recording may also include punching the data from coding forms into cards or onto magnetic tape or disk. In some cases, prepunched cards are used to speed up this process. For example, *card pull files,* which consist of punched cards with prepunched data about the kind of transactions and items to be recorded, minimize or eliminate recording. If an auto supply store uses a card pull file for tires, and a separate card is "pulled" for each tire sold, we would expect to find data punched into the card to say that it is a sales transaction and to give the model, size, and stock number, and cost of the tire. In processing the transaction as a cash sale, no coding or recording would be needed, except perhaps the salesperson's number, but this could be added easily as a separate punch step. In any event, the bulk of the work would have been done ahead of time. (*Note:* If card pull files are set up so that there is one card for each unit of an item in inventory, the salespeople can quickly find out the quantity on hand in the stockroom by counting the cards.)

We are seeing more and more instances of combining the stages of data collection. For example, many retail stores are adopting source documents that can be used for direct data input. Sales slips may be like small coding forms on which the salespeople can record the pertinent items about the sales. These slips can in turn be batched and the data input by optical scanners. Such procedures can save time and eliminate the intermediate coding and recording or punching steps.

Editing

The editing function prepares the data further before application processing occurs. *Editing* is using computer programs (and possibly manual methods) to examine transactions for errors in the transaction itself and in the data. *Transaction validation* is the certification that a specific transaction can be processed by the system and is being submitted properly. For instance, if a payroll transaction were to get mixed in with purchasing transactions, we want to detect this transaction and have it removed from processing to prevent disruption of the rest of the processing stream. (A more extensive discussion of transaction and input validation is found in the supplement at the end of this chapter.)

Input validation focuses specifically on checking for errors in the data: Is the transaction complete (no data missing), and is each data item accurate and correct? Thus, in a credit system, we would have an editing program that checks each record to ensure that the customer account number is not missing and that it contains the proper number of digits or characters. We would also want to ensure that the sales data are accurate. If a transaction listed $10,428.46 as the unit price for a single passenger car tire, we would want the edit program to detect this anomaly and print an error message. (The edit program would simply be responding to the discrepancy between "$10,428.46" and the range of acceptable prices for a single tire embedded in the credit system.)

In batch processing we usually have separate computer programs that perform the editing function (Figure 7.10). They read data from storage, check the transaction and the data, and produce a list of transactions that cannot be processed (called an *exception report*). The valid transactions are written on a magnetic tape or disk file and are then ready for processing.

Applications systems vary in their handling of errors. In many applications, the valid transactions go right into the processing stream and the invalid ones are corrected and processed later. But sometimes all transactions are delayed while the erroneous ones are corrected and reedited.

Editing is also important in on-line systems, where transactions often occur on a one-at-a-time basis. Here each transaction is checked before processing. If an item is not acceptable for any reason, it is rejected and the terminal user is informed right away so that corrections can be made. Usually a log of errors is also maintained so that if the same errors are being repeated or if one particular terminal (or person) is constantly at fault, the systems staff can attempt to correct the problem identified.

Processing

The processing function encompasses the activities of sorting, file creation, and updating. We review the sorting activity first because this process often precedes either file creation or updating.

Preprocess Sorting Sorting is the arranging of records into a particular order or sequence. When we are using transaction files that are going to be processed against master files that have a sequence built into them, we want to order the transaction file into the same sequence as the master file to enhance processing efficiency. Likewise, when we are creating a master file that will be sequenced or ordered, we want to sort the transactions first. This makes processing much quicker and more efficient.

If we are batch processing credit sales transactions against a master accounts receivable file that is sorted sequentially, or is stored under an index sequential organization based on the record key of account number, we sort the transactions first. The sort operation creates a new file that is ordered by account number, say, in ascending order (Figure 7.11).

Most computer installations have one or more sort programs available. COBOL also has a sort command built into its language structure. Furthermore, *utility sort routines,* as these programs are often called, are generally very easy to use and can

Figure 7.10 Batch Editing Process

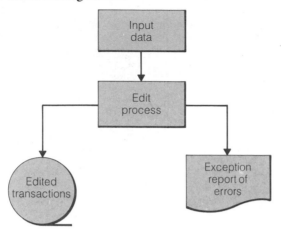

make the actual transaction processing operation much simpler and quicker. Many fourth-generation languages automatically sort output.

File Creation File creation is the process of bringing into existence a master file. Prior to the actual creation run, all the record specifications are made and a file organization selected. The specific file creation process depends on the file organization that has been selected. For sequential files on magnetic tape, magnetic disk, or magnetic drum, the completion of the sort process gives us the master file. Thus when we wish to create a sequential master file on magnetic disk from a transaction tape, we can simply have the output from the sort process written to a disk.

Creation of master files using other file organizations is slightly more complex. For these organizations (that is, random and indexed), addresses must be determined and the records written to the proper locations—for example, a block or track. With indexed organizations, the keys and addresses are also written in separate files or *indexes*. And, as we pointed out, multiple levels of indexes may be required. In most installations, utility software is used to establish the indexes so that the file creation programs need not list all the steps and instructions to create each index.

Updating In updating files, it is important to remember that *the transaction file always drives the process*. This means that before any processing with the master file occurs, a record from the transaction file is read. In the case of on-line processing, a transaction record is accepted from the user at a terminal. When the transaction record has been read, *then* the appropriate master file record is found (for deletions or changes) or the proper storage spot located (for new record additions). How these procedures are generally carried out depends on the file organization—but the transaction record is always read first. Also keep in mind the following points.

1. In updating sequential files, the transaction file should be sorted before the update process. For random processing, this is not necessary.
2. In updating sequential files, a new file is created.

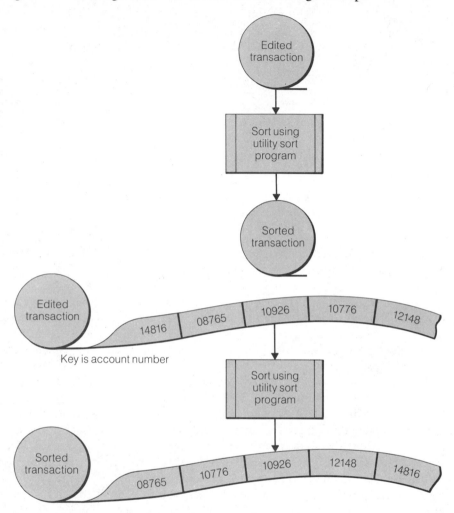

Figure 7.11 Sorting Edited Transactions Stored on Magnetic Tape

3. In updating files stored under a random organization, updating occurs in place; no new file is created.

The input to a batch update process for a sequential file (*sequential batch updating*) is a sorted transaction file and the master file. When the update process is completed, the transaction file will still exist along with the original master file (now called the *old master file*). But another file, called the *new master file*, will have been created (see Figure 7.12). This is because records are stored in sequential files by position, not by address. To change the position of the stored records, which is what happens when we add or delete records, or to change the contents of any stored record, we must recopy the file, adding the changes to another magnetic tape, magnetic disk, or other storage medium.

Since the transaction file always drives the update process, we begin the update

Figure 7.12 Sequential Batch Update Process

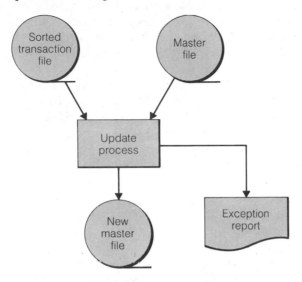

Figure 7.13 Sequential Updating of Master File

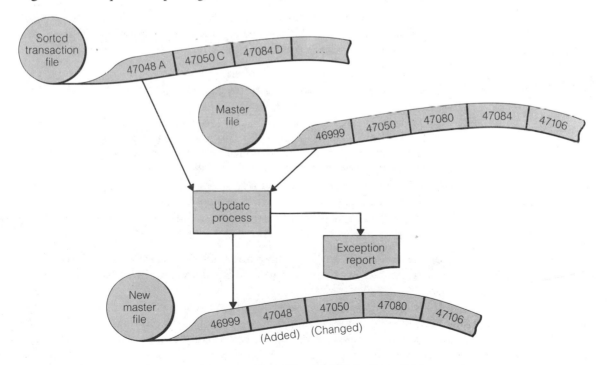

process by reading the first transaction record. In Figure 7.13 the key of this record is 47048, which contains the code A, indicating that it is an addition. Next, the first record from the master file is read. Its key is 46999, which does not correspond to the transaction record key. The master file record is written out to the new master file tape. Keeping the same transaction record in the main memory, we read the next master file record and see that it has a key of 47050, which is higher in sequence than the key of the transaction record being processed. Therefore, the program writes the transaction record on the new master file, and the CPU reads the next transaction record. Notice that the master file record in memory, with a key of 47050, remains in memory during this step.

The next transaction record contains a key of 47050 and a code of C (for "change"). To process this record, the CPU makes the change on the master file record in memory and writes it out to the new master file. After this, we read the next transaction file record, with a key of 47084, and the next master file record, with a key of 47080. Since no action is needed on the master file record, it is immediately written out to the new master file and the next record is read (with a key of 47084). Now the transaction and master record keys match so the CPU performs the action called for by the transaction code of D (for "delete"). Notice that the master file record does not exist on the new master file because it was deleted. The process continues—first a transaction record is read and then the appropriate processing is done with the records stored in the master file.

When random organized files are processed (*random batch updating*), new files are not created. Instead updating occurs *in place* on the magnetic disk or drum. A transaction record is read and the proper storage address in the master file is located (through direct address, key transformation, index search, or a search of addresses, depending on the organization used to create the file). For example, if the transaction record containing a key of 47050 is to be processed and the corresponding master file is stored by a key transformation method, we process the record in the following way:

1. The computer program calculates the storage address for the master file record containing a key of 47050.

2. The central processing unit finds the address on magnetic disk. If the record stored there contains the key of 47050, processing begins. If another record is stored there (as a result of a synonym derived from the key transformation), the overflow area is checked to find the right record.

3. When the record is found, it is read into memory, the change is made, and the record is rewritten back to the same location.

4. If the record cannot be located, a message indicating that is included in an exception report.

As you see from this example, random batch updating does not require sorting of the transaction file. Furthermore, a new file is not created, since updating can occur in place.

In *random on-line updating,* we neither batch nor sort transactions to be processed. Typically, the transactions occur on a one-at-a-time basis: For example, one savings account record is updated or one airline reservation transaction occurs. Since speed is also important, we generally find that files to be processed are stored under a random organization and are on direct access devices.

The actual processing of these transactions occurs in the same way that a *single* transaction record is processed under random batch:

1. The transaction record is read.
2. The storage address is determined.
3. The record is located in either the primary storage area or an overflow area.
4. The update is processed and the record is rewritten.
5. Any discrepancy is noted in an exception report.

Reporting

Files are created and maintained because people expect to use the data later. Therefore, transaction processing also includes the reporting function. Reports are prepared responses to direct or indirect user requests for data stored in files or the result of processing data from transactions. We have already seen one type of report, namely, the exception report that includes messages about anomalies that have occurred during processing. But others are frequently required. For example, inventory control applications typically use the computer system to generate reports on the quantity of each item on hand. Other situations call for a process of submitting inquiries and eliciting the generation of reports in response (see, for example, Figure 7.14).

Figure 7.14 Combined Sort and Update Process

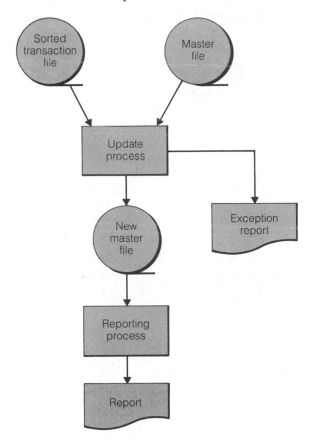

Figure 7.15 Sequential Updating Using Report File

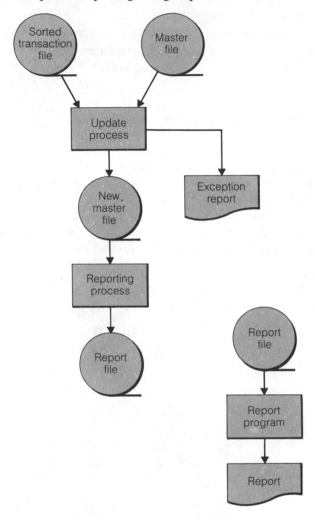

Reports may be generated as a result of batch processing or on-line inquiry, depending on the design of the applications system. Furthermore, reporting may be combined with the updating function (Figure 7.14) or remain as a separate activity. Data may be processed and reports directly output on line printers or workstations. In addition, some processing procedures lead to the creation of a *report file,* a file containing data that have been processed into report form and held on a storage device. The report is generated later by a report program (Figure 7.15).

Sorting may also be done in reporting. In the case of sequential files where records are organized in the same order that users want the report prepared in, sorting probably is not necessary. However, for files created under a random organization, sorting may be desirable to order the output into a sequence that people can easily use. In the income earned example from Chapter 6, we might find it useful to sort the processing results into alphabetical order based on employee name or by department. This may make the report easier to use.

Summary

Data need to be organized to be of value. In file processing, a hierarchy of data guides organization. The lowest unit in the hierarchy is the data item, a single factual element. Items are grouped into records and records into files to facilitate user access to data about a particular entity.

There are transaction, master, and sort files. A master file is a relatively permanent collection of records about events of the organization. Transaction files, more temporary in nature, are collections of records about activities or changes in activities that involve or affect the organization. Sort files, also temporary files, are used to sequence sets of data into a particular order based on a record key or identifier. Both sort and transaction files can be processed against the master file when ordering or updating of data is required.

Files may be stored in sequential fashion or under random or list organizations. Sequential files can be on any storage medium, while random and list organizations use random or direct access storage devices such as magnetic disk or drum. The most common random organizations are direct relation, distributed, and indexed. In some cases, transformation or randomizing techniques must be used to derive storage addresses; in other cases, the key is the address. Each form of organization has a particular advantage for applications of different types; the user should be aware of these characteristics when selecting a filing system for a specific processing purpose.

The processing mode is the way in which transactions are grouped and handled for input/output and computation. Batch processing calls for coding and collection of all data and transactions into groups before processing at periodic intervals. The on-line processing mode, in contrast, does not require batching. Rather, the user enters transactions directly into the system through a terminal or other peripheral device. On-line processing thus allows for input/output through direct communication with a user who may be at a remote location. The factors that determine which processing mode is most appropriate to a particular application include required response time, report detail and volume, input volume, and file usage.

Real-time systems control the environment in which they operate by receiving and processing data and returning results rapidly enough to affect the actions taking place. What constitutes real time is therefore relative to the activities in a given setting. In some instances, an hour or two may be considered real time, while in others real time may be just a few seconds. It is also often meaningful to distinguish between the systems that accept data in real time and those that process the data in real time.

Key Words

Address	Indexed organization	Random organization
Bucket	Index nonsequential	Real-time processing
Consecutive spill method	method	Record
Data item	Index sequential method	Response time
Detail file	Input validation	Sequential organization
Direct relation method	Key	Serial organization
Distributed organization	Key transformation	Sort file
Extraction	technique	Synonym
File	Master file	Time-sharing computer
File organization	Overflow bucket	system
Fixed-length record	Pointer	Transaction file
Folding	Processing mode	Variable-length record

Review Questions

1. Describe the hierarchy of data.

2. What is an attribute, a value, and an instance?

3. Distinguish between master, transaction, and sort files. What purposes do each serve? Give two examples of each.

4. What are the three basic methods of file organization? Describe them briefly. What limitations are there in terms of the storage devices with which each might be used?

5. Discuss randomizing and randomizing techniques. Identify and explain some of the randomizing techniques.

6. Distinguish between random and indexed file organizations.

7. How are storage addresses assigned to data that are stored under the various methods of random organization?

8. What is a pointer, an inverted file, an index, an identifier, and an overflow bucket?

9. How is a specific record located when the file is stored using an indexed sequential organization? Assume you know the record key. Describe the steps to use the index and search the file in order to retrieve the record of interest.

10. Suppose it is necessary to add *one* record to the middle of a sequential file. Is it necessary to create an entire new copy of the file if the original file contains 25,000 records? If it contains just 25 records? Explain.

11. What determines whether the processing of records in a sequential file is faster and more efficient than processing the same file stored under a randomizing structure?

12. Describe the philosophy behind time-sharing. What are some characteristics of time-sharing systems?

13. What is a time slice?

Application Problems

1. A personnel file is to be established on magnetic disk. Each record in the file will contain the following data: employee name, identification number, address, current job title, current pay rate, past job assignments and pay rates, and all employee job skills. Describe the advantages and disadvantages of creating the records in both fixed-length and variable-length form. Would the advantages and disadvantages be any different if the records were stored on magnetic tape?

2. Develop a list of file organizations that can be used for storing data in master files. For each type of organization, indicate all storage media that can use it.

3. Describe the process that would be followed for updating records stored under the file organizations listed below. The updates can consist of adding new records, deleting existing records, or changing the contents of some of the data items in a record.
   a. Index sequential organization
   b. Index nonsequential organization
   c. Sequential organization on magnetic tape
   d. Sequential organization on magnetic disk

4. Puzzled about the process of sorting transaction files used to update master files stored on magnetic tape and/or disk, a manager wishes to understand if or why sorting is necessary for files on either medium and what benefits the sort offers. List the benefits of sorting transaction files and the process followed in sorting. In a sorted file, what should order be based on?

5. Describe the process of updating master files when the unsorted transaction data and master file data are stored as follows:

Master File on	*Transaction File on*
Magnetic tape	Floppy disk
Magnetic tape	Mark-sense documents
Magnetic drum (index sequential)	Magnetic tape (unsorted)
Magnetic disk (index sequential)	Magnetic tape (unsorted)
Magnetic disk (list organization)	Magnetic tape (unsorted)
Magnetic disk (random via key transformation)	Magnetic disk (unsorted)

6. Missing data can occur in records stored under any organization. What are missing data? Are they always a problem? That is, do missing data mean that something has gone wrong? When data are missing, why not just eliminate the area of the record where the data would ordinarily be stored and save space rather than let it go unused?

7. Transaction files are used to update master files. Should a transaction file record contain *all* the same fields or data items as the record in the master file to be updated or just *a few*? Explain your answer.

8. The parts department of a large automobile and truck parts distribution center is converting its inventory file to magnetic disk pack files. Each record contains the following data items: 8-digit part number (alphanumeric), 20-character part description (alphanumeric), 5-digit "on-hand" quantity, 5-digit "on-order" quantity, and 7-digit cost figure (numeric).

The file will be relatively dynamic since quantity data changes occur quite frequently and because parts are continually being added to or discontinued from the total parts line of the center. Which random organization should the systems group select in designing the file?

9. A 2-million-character file is stored on a small system disk pack. The file contains 10,000 records, each requiring 200 characters of storage. The records contain a 16-character key. Assume that the records are blocked at one record per block. The disk pack contains 200 cylinders of 20 tracks each. There are 20 sectors per track; each sector can store 256 characters or bytes of data. How many tracks and cylinders are required to store the file of 10,000 records?

10. The Southern Tier Life and Casualty Company, which deals in life, accident and health, and automobile insurance, has approximately 3.25 million policies outstanding. Policyholder records reveal that 57 percent of the individuals hold one policy, while 36, 5, and 2 percent of the individuals have, respectively, two, three, and four policies. The present breakdown of different policies in effect is: life insurance, 757,400; accident and health, 110,700; homeowners, 1,450,150; and automobile, 942,000.

More than one policy and more than one *type* of policy may be held by an individual. Therefore the company maintains a master index that contains the name of each person, as well as the policy number of all policies he or she holds with the firm. When a transaction such as a name or address change is received by the company, the master index is first searched randomly to determine which policies must be updated. Then a mark-sense update record is prepared for each policy. The update record contains the new name or address of the individual and the number of the policy.

When the transaction records have been prepared, they are put into batches according to the type of policy being updated. At the end of the week, the batches are sorted into order based on policy number and then processed against the appropriate master file. All master files are sequential files, based on policy number, and contain standard data for insurance records (name, address, policy number, amount of coverage, and so on).

a. On what medium should the master index be sorted? On what medium should the policy master files be stored? Give the reasons for each of your answers.

b. Develop a flowchart of the computer-oriented procedures, showing all major operations performed from the time a name or address change arrives at the company through to the completion of the update. Any new files created in the update process should also be shown. (Use the symbols shown in Appendix A.)

c. What computer programs would be required to perform the general update process? That is, which activities would be performed through the computer system and which would be performed manually?

d. Suppose that instead of creating batches of mark-sense records, the changes were written onto a single unsorted transaction tape. How would updating of the master files take place?

e. What control procedures should be used to ensure accurate updating of the policy files?

11. A large poison control center located in a major metropolitan area is computerizing its files on poisons and the treatment of poisoning victims. A file will be

created to contain records on every known poison. Each record will contain the name of the substance, its characteristics when ingested into the human body, antidotes, and treatment procedures.

As telephone calls are received at the poison control center about a possible poisoning, the following information is requested: the name of the poison ingested, if known, and the symptoms of the person who has taken or been exposed to the substance. A search will then be made of the computer-based file to find out what, if any, treatment should be instituted before in-person professional assistance can be obtained. The files can be searched on the basis of the name of the poison if it is known or on the symptoms presented.

What processing mode or modes should be considered for this application? Why? Which file organizations and storage media are the most appropriate? Explain your answer.

12. A vending machine company that has approximately 5000 customers is planning to establish a computer-based file on all its clients: the number and type of machine each has, the items sold in each machine, and the average quantity of each item normally sold in a week. Creation of the file will be through batch processing.
    a. Describe the procedure that should be followed to prepare the data and create the file on magnetic disk. Several different procedures could be used; indicate the best one for this company and support your choice with reasons. What file organization is most appropriate? On what basis could the file be ordered?
    b. Describe the best procedure to follow in preparing the data and creating the file on magnetic disk. What file organization is most appropriate if the contents of the records are frequently changed and if a report is produced from the file once a week using a line printer?
    c. Is batch processing the best mode to use for creating the file? Why or why not?

13. What file organizations can be used to store data that will be processed through random batch mode? What are the criteria that determine your answer? What additional information would you have to know to select a particular one of the eligible organizations?

14. The International Olympic Games are held every four years. Although the purpose of the games and the type of games run have not changed for many years, the way the events are scored has changed significantly. For example, start and finish times for running events are captured and recorded by computers. The computer system then calculates the precise time run by each individual in each event.

    Compare the Olympic Game requirements in terms of the following system characteristics:
    a. Real-time collection of data
    b. Real-time processing of data
    c. Data communications
    d. On-line processing
    e. Time-sharing systems

15. A small manufacturer of seats, tables, stages, and sound equipment for hotel and school auditoriums has decided to computerize many of its transaction processing activities. The company has no computer staff or persons trained to use computers, and management is considering three approaches: purchasing a

small computer, renting a small computer monthly, or purchasing time from a commercial time-sharing service that has a large computer system. If the time-sharing option is selected, the firm will pay for the amount of processing time used each month plus a fee for storing data on the time-sharing company's files, as well as a fee for any programming work that the time-sharing service will have to do to make the computer usable by the new client.

Evaluate each of the three strategies on the basis of the following criteria:

a. Need for computer personnel
b. Newness of the computer for this company
c. Need for software development
d. Speed of change in computer technology
e. Control over storage of data
f. Immediacy of access to the computer

What additional information would you need to actually decide on which strategy is the *best* one for this company?

16. A time-sharing system is not necessarily a real-time system, but it provides processing results in a relatively short time frame. It is also faster than a batch processing system with respect to user turnaround time. Does this make sense? That is, is a time-sharing system faster than a batch processing system? Can a time-sharing be a real-time system? If so, under what circumstances? If not, why not?

17. A medium-sized service organization is preparing to combine its payroll and personnel files into a single file and to add an employee identification number to each employee record.

The present payroll file contains such data as name, address, pay rate, and deductions from wages. The personnel file contains name, address, job skills, and work history for each employee. All data will be combined into one file.

For payroll purposes, the file could be processed in batch mode with the employee time cards being batched to form the transaction file that will be processed against the new, single master file. However, the personnel office wishes to use the same file in an on-line fashion to be able to answer inquiries such as "Which employees have the job skills of a tool and die maker?" or "How many employees of Hispanic origin are between the ages of 21 and 40 and have at least 10 years' experience with the company?"

a. Can the same file be used in two different processing modes? Why or why not?
b. Consider batch processing of the file for payroll purposes. Should it be processed in sequential batch or random batch mode? What major criteria should decide the answer to this question?
c. What file organization should be used in establishing the combined file? Why? On what medium should the file be stored?

18. Two manufacturing companies process similar finished goods inventory files under different processing modes. Company A's file contains product identification and description, unit cost, weight, and on-hand and on-order data for each of the 1000 different items carried in stock. Items are manufactured and stored in finished goods inventory in quantities sufficient to permit the company to fill a minimum of 1 week's orders from quantities on hand. Inventory addi-

tions and deletions are posted to the file daily through a batch processing operation. Complete inventory reports are printed at the end of each business day.

Company B's file contains the same data items as listed for company A, but the second firm manufactures only about 30 different items. All orders for merchandise are made by the customer selecting the items out of the catalog and indicating how many of each one are needed. Only safety or extra stock is held in the company warehouse, to be used for emergency purposes. Unlike company A, company B has no regular "working stock." All finished goods are made to order for the customer and are immediately loaded into railroad boxcars for shipment. The inventory system for finished goods operates in an on-line processing mode and all changes to records are made as they occur. Full reports are *not* printed. All inventory data, when needed, are received by way of queries through an on-line system.

Here are two companies using almost identical files in completely different ways. Are both companies right in the way they use them or is one processing data incorrectly? What factors underlie your answer?

19. A major concern in any computer center is providing for backup of files of data. The backup is necessary in case the working file of data is destroyed or damaged in a way that results in loss of data. For example, a head crash on a disk drive could cause loss of data sorted on a disk pack mounted on the drive. In this case, data would be lost if there were no backup copy of the disk pack.

Provision for backup copies of files or for the re-creation of destroyed data is important in processing mode selection. In some cases, this provision is made by using an old master file and reprocessing all recent transactions against it to bring it up to date. In other cases, the file must be copied at intervals to ensure that a recent backup copy exists. And in still other cases, it is necessary to make copies of transactions manually so that they can be used for updating old files used as backup.

Discuss the provisions for backup in the following cases:

a. Batch processing of sequential files stored on magnetic disk—transaction data used for normal updates are on magnetic tape.

b. Batch processing of direct access files stored on magnetic disk—transaction data used for normal updates are on magnetic tape.

c. On-line processing of direct access files stored on magnetic disk—transaction data are entered into the system as transactions occur on the basis of information supplied verbally from customers.

20. Delay in receiving output from processing can cause the results to be outdated before they are received by the user. Discuss the problem of delay as it applies to batch and on-line processing systems. What causes delay under either of the processing modes? In general, does one mode result in greater delay than the other one? Explain.

Minicase: Automated Teller Machine Fraud

According to the U.S. Department of Justice, the banks in the United States lost between $70 million and $100 million during a recent year due to fraudulent use of automated teller machines (ATMs). These systems accounted for approximately $270 billion of cash transfer through 2.7 billion transactions. ATMs are specialized terminals located in shopping malls, in hotels, and at food stores, to name some of the more common sites. When customers insert their card and key in proper identification codes, they can receive cash from the machines. The use of these convenient devices is increasing rapidly.

In many cases, ATM fraud involves unauthorized transactions initiated with ATM cards that have been lost or stolen. The Department of Justice study indicates that in more than 70 percent of the cases, the individual user's identification information is either recorded on the card or is kept with it in a billfold, wallet, or purse.

A large percentage of the transactions resulted in losses to the banks. The criminals were not caught.

Since the use of ATMs is expected to increase and the emergence of new methods for electronic transfer of funds (which may involve much larger amounts of money) also is anticipated, both the banking industry and law enforcement agencies are seeking additional ways to stem the tide of fraud.

Questions

1. If the majority of fraudulent uses of ATM cards are due to human carelessness, such as writing passwords on the card itself, is fraud inevitable when cards are stolen? What protections based on information technology hardware or software solutions can you suggest? (Keep in mind that the cost must be manageable.)

2. Using current input validation methods (see Supplement 7), can you recommend guidelines to individual users or to bank officials that will eliminate the need for individuals to write down their passwords and identification codes?

Supplement 7: Input Validation Techniques

This supplement examines techniques for detecting errors in data that are being processed for use or storage in an information system. Errors may occur for a variety of reasons, ranging from mistakes made during a preparation of the data to illegal submission of transactions for processing. It is best to find these anomalies when they enter the input stream.

Input validation techniques are examined here in two broad categories. One is based on the assumption that certain types of error are best detected by checks made on the data, that is, by looking at the data items or transactions and determining whether they are acceptable. The other type helps find errors by performing operations that add extra digits to the data. Both techniques have a place in an effective input validation procedure.

Examination Techniques

The seven techniques we discuss are used to validate data or transactions by examining the input in the form in which it arrives for processing—nothing is added to the data. Each form of validation can be performed by programmed instructions or through manual procedures. While we will look at each method separately, a well-designed validation program should feature a combination of several of them, or perhaps all.

Transaction Validation

A large-scale information system processes hundreds, thousands, even millions of transactions daily, weekly, and monthly. The type of transaction processed can vary widely depending on the nature of the business and the types of activity incorporated into the system. Transactions may range from processing customer sales orders to posting payments on client accounts; from handling purchasing orders to vendors and suppliers to monitoring production and manufacturing performance; from processing payroll checks to capturing details of multimillion dollar capital expenditures. The purposes of the transactions may also vary—some are oriented toward addition of records to files and databases, others to deletion of records, and still others to changing the contents of certain data items in specific records. Moreover, some transactions originate at the site where the computer system is located, and others come from remote locations. The mode may be batch or on-line. Many different people may have the authority to submit transactions for processing, or such authority may be extremely limited.

Transaction validation ensures that actions surrounding the processing of data concerning the stored records of an enterprise are acceptable, authorized, and legitimate. This means that each aspect of a transaction must be scrutinized before the system commences processing. Once an invalid transaction has been processed, regardless of why it is invalid, the damage has been done and may be very difficult to reverse or correct. It's better to avoid the damage or problem in the first place by preventing an invalid transaction from occurring. The ways to do this are actually relatively simple.

Each transaction submitted to the information system for processing should be scrutinized to determine what type of activity it is and whether it is a valid activity. "Type of transaction" means the *business* nature of the activity—for example, sales transaction, purchasing transaction, course registration, or payroll preparation. Basic questions should be raised as the incoming transactions are screened (whether manually or by computer). For example, is the system designed to handle the transaction and if so, does it handle it only at certain times? Payroll processing, for example, may occur every second Friday. The posting of interest to personal savings accounts may occur only at the end of a fiscal quarter. If a transaction entering the system at any other time is invalid, it should be screened out. Other checks on the type of transaction should be made in cases of activities that are handled only when the purchase is from a certain set of regular suppliers and when the total value of the goods ordered does not exceed some maximum dollar value. Exceptions to these rules are invalid transactions and should not be processed by the system.

The purpose of each activity should also be checked to determine whether a transaction is valid. "Purpose" in this case means the reason for the existence of the transaction. For example, changing the dollar amount for a specific budget line in a planning file may be invalid if the change has not been authorized. Similarly, it may be invalid to delete historical records that are being kept for archival purposes. However, a transaction whose purpose is to correct a previous error may be valid and thus can be processed.

Often the location, site, or person that originates a processing activity may be a factor in determining transaction validity. A budget line change may be allowable only if an authorized person makes the change. Therefore, if a university officer submits a change for processing, it is valid. But a department chairman may not be so authorized even if his or her department is affected.

Transaction validation is a very basic way of controlling input into computer-based systems. It is relatively easy to perform, and, in fact, is so basic, obvious, and easy that many firms overlook safeguards of this nature. In the absence of well-designed transaction validation procedures, however, the risks and damages to the integrity of the data and the system can be quite substantial.

Sequence Checks

Sequence checks are a good way to validate transactions when the order of processing them is important or when it is necessary to verify that all transactions have been processed. This method simply requires that a number be assigned to each transaction or batch of transactions in sequence. As processing occurs, the number sequence is examined to verify that each transaction is handled in the proper order and that none have been missed.

This practice is quite common in industrial applications. Often, numbers are assigned to batches of accounts receivable documents when they are sent to the data entry department for keying. When actual processing takes place, the batch numbers are checked to be certain that all batches have arrived for processing and that they are in the proper order.

Sequence numbers can also be used for individual transactions. Purchasing orders, for example, are usually numbered so that controls are placed over their issuance. Again the computer can be used to check for the purchase order number of each transaction; a skip in the numbers may indicate that one or more transactions have been missed.

Batch Totals

Batch totals are used to ensure that all transactions have been processed and that, in a limited sense, the processing has taken place without error. The technique involves the addition of numbers in a specific field of a record in all transactions. A total is calculated before processing begins and another one is accumulated by the computer system as processing occurs. The two totals are compared at the end of processing. Any discrepancy between them indicates that an error has occurred that must be found and corrected.

The totals may be calculated by adding financial data in a certain field of all records, the number of transactions processed, or a *hash total*. Financial totals are easy to do. For example, in a system that processes sales transactions, a common use of batch totals is to accumulate the total sales figure for each sales translation (Table S7.1). Thus, if the transaction file contains only 10 records of sales (a relatively small set of transactions, perhaps), the dollar values from each of the 10 are added together both before processing begins and while it is taking place. Comparison of the two totals will tell the user whether all transactions were processed and whether any mistakes were made in the processing. For example, if the number 24 is recorded or processed as a 42, this will be detected because an improper total will result.

Batch totals can also be accumulated by counting the number of transaction records in the batch and then counting them again as they are processed individually. If a preprocessing count indicates that there are 10 records in the batch, the computer-prepared count, as each record is processed, should also add up to 10.

The *hash total*, also illustrated in Table S7.1, is similar to the financial total. However, instead of performing a count on fields containing financial data, the total

Table S7.1 Two Batch Total Techniques

Financial Total		Hash Total	
Quantity	Total Cost	Transaction Number	Item Number
3	$ 45.83	1	7864
14	88.96	2	1224
37	186.17	3	5815
7	44.48	4	1224
1	12.00	5	3614
1	77.07	6	4135
18	180.84	7	1789
1	7.95	8	2305
37	224.17	9	1001
4	91.12	10	9984
	958.59		38,955

is on a nonfinancial one (all records may not contain financial data), such as identification numbers or part numbers.

Format Checks

Format checks are tests of the contents of fields to ensure that the data they contain are valid according to preestablished conventions for item or field length specification, type specification, processing code, and so on. *Length checks* are used to determine whether the number of characters or numbers in the field is correct. For example, a data item that contains an eight-digit social security number is obviously wrong. Likewise, a field that is supposed to contain a six-digit employee identification number is clearly incorrect if it contains only four or five digits.

Type specification checks are made to detect any data item that contains invalid numbers or characters before the data are entered into the file or database. For example, if the social security number field is supposed to contain all numeric data, the inclusion of hyphens or letters would be incorrect.

Processing codes are often used to enable a program to first check a certain field in a transaction record to see what kind of processing is required. For example, a library researcher uses a computer program to maintain large bibliographies of literature in a certain research area. Bibliography data are still punched into cards for processing. Different cards are used for data on the author, the title, the journal title or book publisher, and volume, year, and page information. The last column of each card contains a code that tells the computer program that the card is an author card, a title card, and so on. Before processing, it is useful to have the program written to first check the processing code to determine whether it is an acceptable one. In this way invalid codes or invalid processing (such as two title cards for one book) can be detected in time to prevent errors from entering the files or database.

Reasonableness Checks

Reasonableness checks are an easy way to make an initial screening of data. This technique of checking data items to ensure that the data values fall within "reasonable" limits serves to prevent obviously unreasonable values from entering the system. Items screened this way may not necessarily be errors, but they may be questionable enough to make reverification of the item a cost-effective measure.

Both upper and lower limits may be checked by this means. For example, a computer-based university registration system may include a programmed instruction that examines the number of credits a student registers for. Thus, if students are supposed to register for 4–20 credits per term, a transaction that shows a student signing up for 22 credits should be detected. Similarly, one that lists only 2 credits should also be detected. These may not be errors, but because the number of credits on these transactions is out of the normal bounds, they should be checked.

This validation method is a quick and easy way to check data. Through it, the most obvious errors can be detected. Furthermore, it requires no work (for instance, no counting the number of transactions, totaling dollar values, and so on) before data enter the processing stream.

Audit Trail

A different type of input validation check is the *audit trail*. This approach is particularly useful for systems in which data or transactions are submitted from remote locations, although it is useful for on-site batch processing as well. The audit trail is a control technique that makes it possible to trace stored data items back to the transaction that created them or modified them to contain their current values.

To make the tracing back to original transactions possible, a list or *log* of each transaction processed is maintained, often automatically by the computer system. The log contains the contents of each transaction, the date and time of processing, and the point at which the event originated. If an error is detected, it is possible to go back to the source and reconstruct the event so that the problem can be located and the error corrected. The audit trail thus emphasizes being able to trace invalid data back to their origin and correct them.

Duplicate Processing

Sometimes it makes sense to have duplicate processing of transactions. The results can then be compared, with a difference indicating that an error has occurred. Of course, this is an expensive means of input validation since everything is done twice. However, it may be appropriate when validation is not possible through some other means or for systems that are unstable.

Check Digits

The validation techniques just examined all aid in error detection by comparing the data to a standard or parameter with which they should agree. Usually, however, these techniques offer insufficient protection against certain types of errors. An additional method, known as *check digits,* is necessary.

Principle of Check Digits

The main difference between check digits and the other validation techniques is that instead of comparing data items to standards, boundaries, or parameters, something—namely, a check digit—is added to the data.

A *check digit* is used for detection of errors in numeric data only (dollar and cents values, identification numbers, digital product codes, and so on). It is an *additional* digit or number that is appended to the original data item in a transaction to help detect errors that may occur as data are transformed from one form or medium to another. In data entry, for example, it is relatively easy to introduce errors in the form of transcriptions, transpositions, omission, or insertion of numbers. *Transcription errors* are misrecordings of numbers. For example, "3" might mistakenly be recorded as "8" or "7" as "1." *Transposition errors* consist of the reversal or juxtaposition of numbers, as when "36" is recorded as "63." These errors occur relatively frequently and are usually difficult to locate or detect.

Many such errors can be detected, however, if an additional digit (the check digit) is appended to the data item before data preparation begins. The check digit itself has no value in processing other than assuring that the data are correct, as explained below.

Development of Check Digits

Many methods of deriving check digits have been used in industry applications. Naturally some are better than others for finding errors of certain types. A full discussion of all the different methods is beyond the scope of this supplement. However, we will look at one very *basic* method here as a way of explaining the underlying principles.

One easy way to use check digits involves division by a prime number (one that can be divided evenly only by itself and 1). To develop the check digit, the data item is divided by the prime number selected. The *remainder* becomes the check digit and is added to the end of the data item.

A simple example using the prime number 7 will demonstrate how the process works. The value of the data we will use (it could be an identification number, an invoice number, or whatever) is 4713. If we divide this number by the prime number 7, we get a remainder of 2, which is the check digit. The check digit is inserted at the end of the data item so that as data preparation or processing begins, the number appears as 47132. If any error occurs that somehow changes the number, the check digit will not agree. Thus, if the value inadvertently is entered through a terminal as

41132 (notice that the 7 has been transcribed as a 1), the check digit will not match the rest of the number: Dividing 4113 by the prime number 7 yields a remainder of 4, which does not correspond with the check digit. Other numbers in the series containing 4713 also will be divided by 7, but the check digits for these numbers will vary depending on the numbers themselves. Thus 3174 and 5678 will have 3 and 1, respectively, as check digits, but 1234, like 4713, will have 2.

Comparison of check digits can be done through instructions in a computer program processing the data. Therefore, the method is easy to use in examining incoming transaction data. One disadvantage of check digits is that extra time is required to insert the digits in the data if this is done manually. Also, ironically, the data item length is increased, and this sometimes leads to additional errors. Overall, however, an input validation process can be quite effective in preventing errors from entering files or databases.

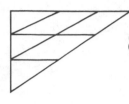

8: Database Management

Key Questions

How are databases distinguished from master files?

What are the components of database management?

How is management of the database accomplished?

Why is SQL important in database management?

Why is the separation of physical and logical views of data so important?

How do views assist in achieving the objectives of managing databases?

What is a database management system?

What data models underlie database management systems?

Why is the relational data model becoming dominant?

Through what methods of interface do users interact with database systems?

If you don't know where you are going, any road will take you there.
Lewis Carroll, *Through the Looking Glass*

Managing data is the key to successful management information support. Without proper management, vital data and essential information will not be available to support the operations of an organization. Similarly, poor management of data often results in loss of integrity and reliability in the data and the information based on it. Even if the hardware and software are well designed technically and operating properly, the value of the system will be limited if the underlying data are not reliable.

In examining the importance of database management in information systems, this chapter presents the database concept and discusses the advantages it offers in an information processing environment. Methods for managing databases are explored, along with software systems, called database management systems. Program examples from popular database management systems, including SQL, dBASE IV, and Query-By-Example, will be used to demonstrate the creation and use of databases. We will see that the different types of database management systems interact with application programs to achieve the objectives of more accessible and reliable data.

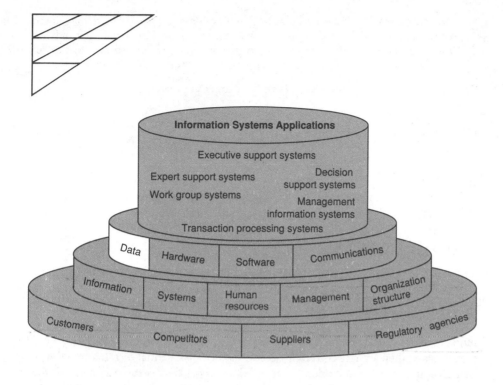

Information Systems Applications

Executive support systems

Expert support systems   Decision support systems

Work group systems

Management information systems

Transaction processing systems

Data   Hardware   Software   Communications

Information   Systems   Human resources   Management   Organization structure

Customers   Competitors   Suppliers   Regulatory agencies

Why Should You Know About Database Management?

At one time, the management of databases was largely a technical issue primarily of interest to information systems professionals. However, it is becoming increasingly important throughout all types of organizations. Among the reasons you should know about the management of databases are the following:

——*Organizations store and use large quantities of data.* Sheer volume of data alone means that proper management is essential. It is easy for any individual or organization to become inundated with data in all forms. Current and potential uses should be considered in the formulation of guidelines for the storage and use of data.

——*Data are a valuable resource that must be managed.* Value is assured by capturing, validating, and protecting the data. This is a concern throughout the organization.

——*The wrong approach to managing data adds complexity to the management of organizations.* The management of data should be part of the solution, not part of the problem, in the management of organizations. Access to reliable and accurate data should simplify—not complicate—planning and operations.

—*You have a right to influence the management of data you need.* The management of databases is not an activity that should occur in isolation. Those who rely on the data captured and stored in an organization have a need and in fact an obligation to be involved in decisions that affect their use of the data.

The discussion that follows addresses these matters in greater depth.

What Is Database Management?

Database management is the planning, organization, and control of organization databases. This section defines databases and their purpose in an information system. We also examine the objectives of managing databases.

What Is a Database?

A **database** is an integrated collection of data stored in different record types. The records are interrelated by means of relationships in the data, not their physical storage location. (The term *databank* is a synonym for database.)

Databases are distinguished from ordinary master and transaction files in four important ways. First, a file is for storage. Records comprising a file are stored together and they are retrieved by an access method (sequential or random). Recall that an important consideration in structuring master files is the way data will be processed by the application. For example, in an airline reservation system, flight records for a specific day are generally organized for direct retrieval based on the flight number. You would not want to sequentially search through a file for every flight on every day of the year until the proper one is located.

In contrast, when payroll details must be processed in the generation of employee paychecks, a sequential organization is desirable because every employee record must be examined and processed. Since all records in the payroll file are grouped together physically, searching this file, one record after the other in sequence, is a simple and efficient method.

Second, adding records to file to make it large does not turn it into a database. The existence of a database is not determined by the *number* of records stored; it is not a matter of size.

Third, records about different entities of interest may be stored within a database. In an airline database we could expect to find records of different types about aircraft, flights, crew members, and passengers—all related because these entities interact as the airline operates day after day. These four different record types will be interrelated in the same database. (In a sense, a file is a special case of a database insofar as it contains just one record type. There is no need to develop relationships between different entities or record types because there is only one type.)

Fourth, having databases does not eliminate files in an information system. Transaction files will be needed to capture details of business and organization activities. Master files may be required also, since not all data need reside in the database. And, of course, sort files are essential when data must be rearranged.

What Is the Purpose of a Database?

The purpose of storing and organizing data in a database is to represent relationships between entities of interest to the organization, a result that cannot be achieved with individual master files. Organizing data in this manner will facilitate the integration of subject areas within the enterprise. It also facilitates ad hoc inquiries, including those by nonprogrammers, as we will see—a difficult task in parameter-driven application programs.

For example, suppose airline management wants responses to the following inquiries:

——Which of our pilots are qualified on the Boeing 767 aircraft and have more than 15 years of flying experience?
——How many of our flights originate or land in Chicago on weekdays?
——Which flights average less than 50% occupancy on weekdays?

The responses to these inquiries are based on relationships built into the data (Figure 8.1):

——Pilots and their experience
——Flights and the number of passengers flying as a proportion of the seating capacity of the aircraft used on each flight
——Flights and their originations, stops en route, and destinations

Data relationships of this nature go beyond the normal physical structures of master files or the methods used to access them.

At the transaction level, the development of master files reflecting the physical relations in the data offers an efficient way of storing and retrieving data based on the intended usage.

Management applications, in contrast, focus not on storage and processing efficiency, but rather the retrieval of information needed to process inquiries. Ques-

Figure 8.1 Databases Organize Data Based on Natural Relations in the Data

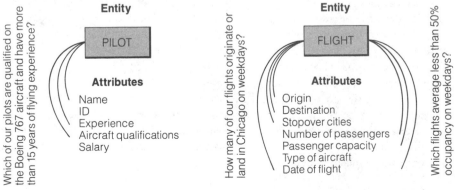

tions like those listed above are not efficiently addressed through master file storage structures because the answers depend on the relationship of data in and between records, not on the manner in which they are stored.

Consider a university environment and the data needed to manage it. The primary subject areas for management of the university are curriculum, students, personnel, finance (budget), and facilities. Databases in each of these subject areas cut across the different management levels (Figure 8.2). Within each database, many different entities, such as courses, programs, schedules, and instructors in the curriculum database are interrelated.

Because of the emphasis on a specific area of focus in an integrated database, like those in the university example, the term *subject database* is sometimes applied to emphasize that databases should not focus on individual applications, as master files do, but on integrated global areas of emphasis (like the "subject" areas of curriculum, students, personnel, finance, and facilities). Throughout this chapter, the term *database* means "subject database," that is, an *integrated* database.

We will explore the importance of managing the relationships between data in greater detail throughout the chapter.

What Are the Objectives of Managing Databases?

Many organizations have very successful information systems and have not invested in database management. However, for most firms, the only effective and efficient way to achieve the desired level of information systems support is through database management. The seven objectives of managing databases demonstrate the advantages that can be gained: avoiding unnecessary redundancy, providing access flexibility, providing relatability, maintaining data independence, ensuring evolvability, preserving data integrity, and ensuring data security.

Avoiding Unnecessary Redundancy As organizations grow to rely on information systems, more applications are implemented. Often each application is designed to use its own transaction and master files—perhaps because analysts are not aware that the same data exist in another file, or because users want control over their own files, or because the files are slightly different. The result, however, is a proliferation of data that is not in the interest of either the users or the organization (Figure 8.3).

But most important, when data are duplicated across files, it is unlikely that changes will be made simultaneously to all the files. The discrepancies that are almost certain to result make it virtually impossible to know which details are most current or which report contains the correct information.

It is expensive to store redundant data, and data maintenance is both time-consuming and costly. Recent decreases in storage costs notwithstanding, large amounts of storage are still expensive. And if different files have to be updated when events occur, there will be multiple preparation and data input steps, and more computer time must be used to process the updates.

Figure 8.2 Sample University Database

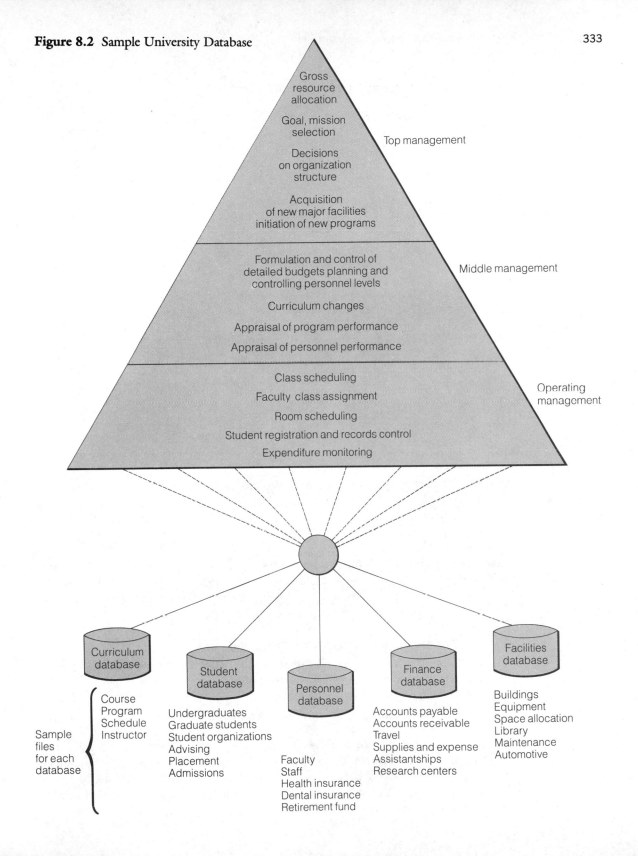

Figure 8.3 Excessive Data Redundancy in Typical University Files

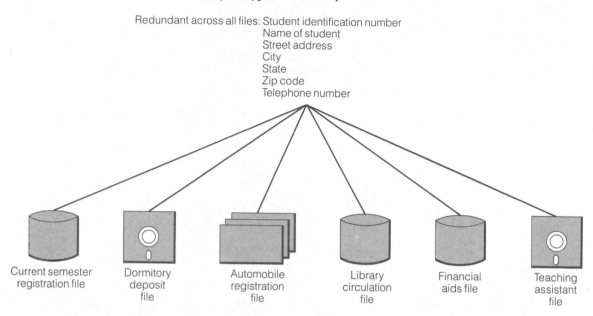

Redundant across all files: Student identification number
Name of student
Street address
City
State
Zip code
Telephone number

Current semester registration file   Dormitory deposit file   Automobile registration file   Library circulation file   Financial aids file   Teaching assistant file

Rather than permitting uncontrolled redundancy, system design should accommodate the sharing of data across applications. Common data needs can be met if the data are accessible to all applications that need it. We will see how this can be accomplished.

Providing Access Flexibility Frequently managers and other users who ask for information needed in decision making assume they can get it because they know the necessary data are stored in computer-readable form. Unfortunately, they often find that such requests cannot be met quickly because:

——The data are in several different files (Figure 8.4).

——A program must be written to pull data from the various files (then an additional report program may have to be written).

——It will take time to develop the software.

——The programmers must finish other projects first.

It is ironic that data for decisions that have the highest potential payoff frequently are not readily accessible. The nonstructured decision situations faced by upper-level managers often demand data that spans several different files. These needs call for access to any data on any key and without regard to where the data are stored or how they must be accessed.

Figure 8.4 Data Inaccessibility Due to Multiple File Locations

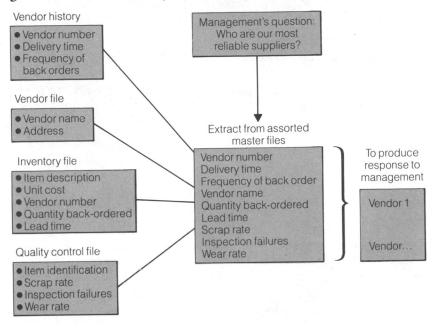

Providing Relatability *Relatability* is the capability to *define* relationships between entities or record types and to *retrieve* data based on those relationships. The importance of describing the attributes of an entity when defining records is well understood. Defining the relationship between entities is the next step.

As we will see in the discussion of relational databases later (illustrated by Figures 8.19–8.23), the management of an airline requires access to details about flights (data items such as flight number, date, origin, destination, and aircraft used) and passengers (name, origin and destination, ticket cost, and so on). To provide good management and good service, however, an airline DBMS must have the capability to *relate* these entities: What passengers are on flight 123? Who is the pilot for flight 456? How many passengers will board at the Atlanta stop on flight 789 from Miami to Chicago? These examples require the capability to connect related data items in specific ways.

Maintaining Data Independence Users should not have to constrain their view of the data because of the way the computer system stores the details. **Data independence refers to the ability to have separate logical and physical views of the data.** The terms are used as follows:

——*Logical view of data:* The user's conceptual view of the data, including the names and content of data items and the way they are organized; a certain view is selected because of the way the data will be used by an individual or in an application.

Physical view of data: The way data are organized and stored in the computer and in secondary storage, including the file structures that store the data and the access methods that retrieve details.

Complete independence is difficult to achieve. At some point, the physical and logical views must come together so that data can be processed.

Allowing the Database to Evolve *Change* is a key word in understanding the need for meeting the objective of evolvability. We can anticipate that change will occur in many areas:

——Record keys

——Physical storage structures

——Storage devices

——Programming languages

——Application programs

The list could go on.

We can seldom foresee the need for specific changes. Yet maintenance—making adjustments and enhancements in information systems—occupies a great proportion of the programmer time in many organizations. (Often more time is spent on making maintenance changes, like those specified above, than on developing new applications.)

The need for change will never be eliminated. But our objective is to ease the difficulty of making modifications when they become necessary. Some approaches to doing this are better than others.

Preserving Data Integrity *Data integrity* refers to the *reliability* of data: Is the information accurate, and can it be believed? As discussed, uncontrolled file redundancy and the need for multiple updates almost always lead to integrity problems.

Integrity problems also arise through errors in data. When files are created and maintained, checks are necessary to ensure that data are correct. Incoming data should conform to predetermined forms or ranges (a social security number should always consist of nine digits) and be stored according to precise rules (no blanks or hyphens are allowed). Data that do not conform to these definitions or rules, or contain errors, should not be allowed to enter the database.

Who is responsible for managing the data to see that errors are detected and corrected? Many times no one is responsible, and data integrity suffers to the point that managers do not have confidence in the information they receive.

Ensuring Data Security Security with respect to databases is the result of controlling the rights of access to the database and the ability of individuals to retrieve, change, add, or delete records. Security is especially important, and difficult to achieve, in large database environments where users interact with the system over communication lines. Systems operators cannot tell who is actually using the terminal or workstation at the other end of the communication link.

The objective of ensuring data security is to prevent all unauthorized access to or use of the database, whether accidental or intentional.

What Is a Database Management System?

A **database management system (DBMS)** is software. It allows the creation, use, and maintenance of databases. Yet because it is application independent, it can be used in a variety of environments and application settings. It does not depend on any application program or specific file, but can be used to make data available to *several* application programs. In other words, a DBMS is software that is not tied to a particular set of files. It eliminates the need to closely link the structure of the data in the program and the data stored on secondary storage devices. Features built into database management systems make it possible to *separate the user/program view of the data from the way the data are stored*.

As we examine the features of a DBMS and the different systems available to choose from, let's look first at how the various types have evolved.

Evolution of Database Management Systems

Like computers, database management systems have evolved through several generations. In each one, management and technical personnel realized that improvements were needed in the way computers processed data (Table 8.1).

When computers were first introduced, programmers alone were responsible for developing computer applications for the organization. The machine language

Table 8.1 Developments Leading to Database Management Systems

Development	Description
Stage 1: Machine language	All operations, including arithmetic, error test, failure protection, and read/write coding, had to be specified in detail through machine language, with a high tendency to error.
Stage 2: Input/output control system	In the generalized software to handle input of data and output of results, macroinstructions replaced complex machine language instructions to describe files, devices, formats, and storage addresses.
Stage 3: Access methods	This software made it possible to access data by location and length, rather than by contents. In some cases, a key or identifier had to be specified, but otherwise access was based on data location.
Stage 4: File management systems	These software packages allowed operations on an entire file. The format of the file and the output format had to be supplied. The software of the system could handle extraction of data, calculation, and output processes, but these capabilities were limited to single file operation.
Stage 5: Database management systems	Such software tools allow operations on multiple files, including creation, definition, update, analysis, and query. Protection features are offered for all file-related activities.

programs (see Chapter 6) specified the address of all storage locations, in binary numbers. Software was not generalized to handle a variety of data. Every read/write operation, for example, had to be recoded in detail along with error detection checks. Registers, storage addresses, numerical processing codes, and so on had to be restated each time an operation was performed—nothing was automatically determined for the users.

As computer use grew, processing capabilities also improved. Computer systems became more complex because of the growing electronic sophistication of the CPU and peripheral devices. This meant that manufacturers had to develop still more advanced software that would make using computers easier and more efficient.

General-purpose software became increasingly important. In addition to access methods, file management systems were developed to minimize the problems of dealing with a single file and individual records within it. **File management systems** require the programmer or user to supply the format of the data in the file and the desired format of the output. The system software handles the reading, extraction, and calculation or comparison operations needed to create requested output.

Database management systems arose out of the need for still more generalization of software, capable of processing data from several files simultaneously. In addition, tools to enable several programs to access the data in different forms and to allow users to arrange data into different formats was increasingly desirable. There was also a need for greater security and control of the integrity of data, and greater flexibility in output formats. Database management systems evolved as the means of meeting these objectives.

Features of Database Management Systems

A database management system is defined by its features, which include the abilities to develop data structures, define data, and interrogate and update the database after it is created, and to manage storage structure definitions.

Database Creation A database must be made known to the database management system so that it can be brought under the control of the DBMS and used for processing. To create a database, we need to define its specifications, using a data definition language that is part of the DBMS.

Creation may also include *re-creation* of a database. Some database management systems allow existing data sets, created by other programs, to be redefined to show another structure and brought under control of the DBMS.

The creation of a database, which is the responsibility of a database administrator, is based on an underlying data structure.

Data Structures The data structure feature of a DBMS permits users to utilize stored data without having to be concerned about how the data are actually stored. Database administrators can organize (structure) data according to user needs, through sub-schemas, and the database management system assembles the necessary items and records for the user. A manager who needs inventory data consisting of product number, item description, unit cost, margin, and quantity on hand can request this information with the items arranged in any desired order within or between records. It does not matter how the data are stored, which file contains the data, or whether the stored record contains more than the data items needed for a given application. It is necessary simply to specify the data desired; the database management system will locate and assemble them for use. A little later in this chapter, we see how subschemas and data structures are handled by database management systems.

Data Definition Through data independence, data are kept separate from the programs that process them. Thus, data can change without necessarily effecting changes in the programs that use them. Similarly, users can change the data requirements in programs without reorganizing the way data are stored. And as indicated earlier, data can be made available to accommodate several users with differing needs, but without changing the actual structure.

To accomplish data independence, database management systems provide for standardized **data definition.** That is, all data items must conform to standard length and type specifications, as stated in the definition.

Data are defined through one of several types of definition languages, including *free, narrative, key word, separator,* and *fixed-position forms* (Figure 8.5). The narrative is an English-like statement of data structure information, with some restriction on the particular syntax (sentence structure) used. The keyword form consists essentially of a sequence of attribute–value (description) pairs, with most of the "noise words" (that is, nonessential terms), which are present in the narrative form, eliminated. If the sequence of terms is fixed—that is, if specifications must be made using the commands in a certain order—the separator form is used. A special symbol indicates the end of each command. The attribute–values, separated by some special symbol, are required to be input. Finally, in some systems, each element of the definition appears in a fixed position for input. Often a preprinted form or questionnaire is provided to guide the user in making the specifications.

Storage Structure Definition A database administrator can choose to structure the data logically in a certain way. However, the data can actually be stored under several different **storage structures** (for example, sequential, random, or indexed), or modes of physical preservation. Database administrators select storage structures according to how the data will be used in applications.

Interrogation In interrogation, data are selected from a database and extracted or copied for processing; then the results are formatted into screen displays, printed reports, or machine-usable form for further processing. For interrogation to take place, the part of the database on which the interrogation is to be performed must be identified to the computer. After this, the computer is given a statement of the selection criteria and instructions for processing the extracted data.

Updating Updating a database means changing the values for all or selected data items in the database. It does *not* mean changing the logical data structure of a

Figure 8.5 Language Types for Data Definition (Courtesy Informatics Incorporated)

```
DISPLAY THE EFF-DATE FOR PERSONNEL SALARY
```
Free form
```
RECORD NAME IS SALARY IN DATA BASE PERSONNEL
DATA ITEM IS EFF-DATE, TYPE IS CHARACTER
LENGTH IS 6 . . .
```
Narrative form
```
RECORD: NAME = SALARY, DATA BASE = PERSONNEL
DATA-ITEM: NAME = EFF-DATE, TYPE = CHARACTER
LENGTH = 6 . . .
```
Key word form
```
DATA BASE NAME IS PERSONNEL
1. SALARY:
2. EFF-DATE (DATE IN 1), F6, CHAR: . . .
```
Separator form

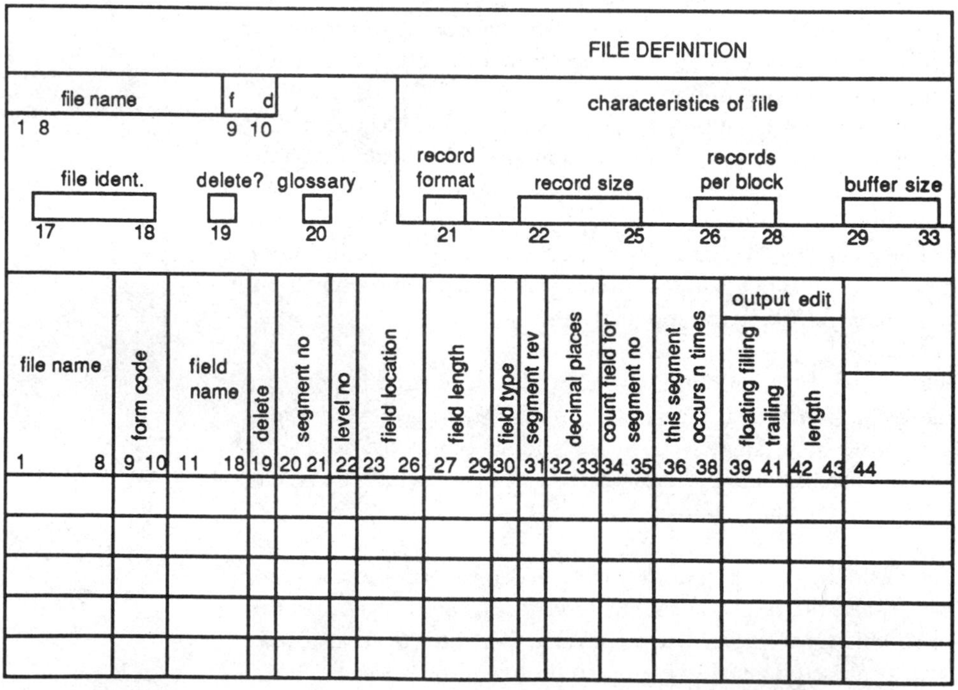

Fixed-position form

database, the validation criteria, or the security procedures. The update function requires the use of five kinds of information:

1. Description of the part of the data in the database that is to be updated
2. Data currently stored in the part of the database to be updated
3. Description of the update data to be applied to the database
4. Update data
5. Processing rules to be followed in applying the update data to the database

The update feature makes it possible to add new data to the database, change existing data items, or delete obsolete data. Updates are made by processing transaction data against the database, using the definitions that have been specified for type, length, and so on. We will look at examples of each of these features in a moment.

Types of Database Management Systems

Database management systems are generally divided into two classes: host-language and self-contained systems. But the two are not necessarily distinct. It may be beneficial to combine features of both to help achieve the objectives of database management.

Host-Language Systems Host-language systems (Figure 8.6) are extensions or enhancements of commonly used procedure-oriented languages. COBOL has been the dominant host language, although some database management systems make use of other languages. The procedure-oriented language is a "host" in the sense that it provides the basic framework for database management activities. Additions or extensions to the basic command structure of the language allow for the database management capabilities. To create the proper interface, new statements are often developed and combined with existing instructions to perform the storage and data access activities. For example, it is necessary to provide a name for the database. Therefore, a command is added to the basic language structure that allows the user to name the database (in Figure 8.6: DATABASE NAME IS PERSONNEL). By adding the data description and data manipulation language commands to the procedure language that serves as the host language, database management activities can be performed.

The user of a host-language system is considered to be an *applications programmer;* applications programmers write sets of statements or instructions that are executed sequentially as in a typical procedure-oriented language. Although users are insulated from the storage structure of the data, they exercise almost the same degree of procedural control over programs as they would working in COBOL. Thus they can direct computation and data manipulation, but need not worry about transfer of data into the user working area after it has started.

Self-Contained Systems Systems in the second DBMS category do not rely on a host procedural language for the interface but use a new language of their own. **Self-contained systems** are aimed at handling a certain set of database management

Figure 8.6 Example of a Host-Language System (Courtesy MRI Systems Corporation)

```
    PROCEDURE DIVISION
    START.
     OPEN INPUT WAGES
OPEN PERSONNEL
   MORE
     READ WAGES RECORD AT END GO TO COMPLETE
     MOVE ID TO EMP-NO
GETD EMPLOYEE WHERE EMP-NO
     IF RTN-CD NOT EQUAL TO 0 THEN GO TO ERROR
GETD SALARY LAST
     IF RTN-CD NOT EQUAL TO 0 THEN GO TO ERROR
     MULTIPLY HOURS BY BASE-RATE GIVING EMP-WAGES
     ADD EMP-WAGES TO YTD INCOME.
MODIFY SALARY YTD-INCOME
     NOTE-YTD INCOME OF THE SALARY DATA SET IS UPDATED
     IF RTN-CD NOT EQUAL TO 0 THEN GO TO ERROR
GETD WORK-AREA FIRST
     IF RTN-CD NOT EQUAL TO 0 THEN GO TO ERROR
     NOTE.
      THE ASSUMPTION IS THAT THE FIRST DEPT DATA SET IS
      THE MOST CURRENT AND THAT AT THIS POINT OUTPUT OF
      EMP-NAME, SSN, DEPT, and EMP-WAGES WOULD OCCUR.
     GO TO MORE.
    COMPLETE
     CLOSE WAGES
    CLOSE PERSONNEL
     ENTER LINKAGE
     RETURN
     ENTER COBOL
ERROR NOTE-THIS ROUTINE WOULD PROBABLY ANALYZE THE ERROR TYPE.
       PRINT COMMBLOCK CONTENTS TO THE PROGRAMMER ALONG WITH
       ERROR MESSAGE AND ABEND WITH A DUMP.
END PROCEDURE.
```

```
IDENTIFICATION DIVISION
PROGRAM-ID. 'S2KPROG'.
REMARKS. EXAMPLE OF A SYSTEM 2000 PROCEDURAL LANGUAGE PROGRAM.
DATA DIVISION.
INPUT-OUTPUT SECTION.
FD WAGES RECORD CONTAINS 80 CHARACTERS RECORDING MODE IS F
LABEL RECORDS ARE STANDARD DATA RECORD IS WAGE-IN.
01 WAGE-IN.
      02 ID          PICTURE IS 9(5).
      02 HOURS       PICTURE IS 9(3).
   WORKING-STORAGE SECTION.
COMMBLOCK OF PERSONNEL. ◄
   01 PERSONNEL.
      02 SCHEMA-NAME.
      02 RTN-CD.
      02 FILLER.
      02 LASTDS.
      02 PASSWORD.
      02 DSNO.
      02 DSPOS.
      02 LEVEL.
      02 TIME.
      02 DATE.
      02 CYCLE.
      02 SEPSYM.
      02 ENTERM.
      02 STATUS.

    01 WORK-FIELDS.
      02 EMP-WAGES        PICTURE IS 9(5)V99.

SCHEMA EMPLOYEE OF PERSONNEL.
01 EMPLOYEE.
   02 EMP-NO            PICTURE IS 9(5).
   02 EMP-NAME.         PICTURE IS X(30).
   02 SSN               PICTURE IS X(11).
SCHEMA SALARY OF PERSONNEL
01 SALARY
   02 EFF-DATE          PICTURE IS X(6).
   02 BASE-BASE         PICTURE IS 99V99.
   02 YTD-INCOME        PICTURE IS 9(5)V99.
SCHEMA WORK-AREA OF PERSONNEL.
01 WORK-AREA.
   02 DEPT              PICTURE IS X(4).
   02 MANAGER           PICTURE IS X(30).
```

To enable COBOL compiler to differentiate between the COBOL statements and System 2000 commands. System 2000 commands start in the column before the 'A' margin

Data fields EMP-NAME and MANAGER are defined for an optimum length of 18 for the database but must be redefined for the maximum in the schema

```
DATA BASE NAME IS PERSONNEL: ◀
  1 EMP-NO (INTEGER 9(5)):
  2 EMP-NAME (NAME X (18)):
  3 SSN (NAME X (11)):
  4 SEX (NON-KEY NAME X):
  5 MARITAL-STATUS (NON-KEY NAME X):
  6 SALARY (RG):
    7 EFF-DATE (DATE IN 6):
    8 BASE-RATE (NON-KEY DECIMAL 99.99 IN 6)
 10 WORK-AREA (RG):
 11 DEPT (NAME X (4) IN 10):
 12 LOCATION (NON-KEY NAME X (5) IN 10):
 13 MANAGER (NAME X (18) IN 10):
 14 EDUCATION (RG):
 15 COLLEGE (NAME X (20) IN 14):
 16 DEGREE (NAME X (3) IN 14):
 17 MAJOR (NAME X (8) IN 14):
```

Example of a COBOL program and the DBMS System 2000. The program procedure is to read a record from the WAGES file, use the ID (employee number) to access the appropriate record from the PERSONNEL database, multiply the HOURS times the BASE-RATE, write the results to an output file with EMP-NAME, SSN, and DEPT, and add the results to the YTD-INCOME field. Processing continues until all WAGES records have been read. The WAGES file contains the employee number and the number of hours each person has worked. For explanation of the schema concept, see the text accompanying Figure 8.8, below. The following database was used in this procedure.

functions so that conventional procedure (language) programming is not needed. The self-contained capabilities are tools for both the programmer and nonprogrammer.

Self-contained systems have features that make it much easier to extract data from the database, particularly for management users who are not highly trained programmers. These systems are organized around a set of general commands such as those that permit interrogation of the database or update of records. These activities, in turn, are controlled through high-level commands, so it is not possible to specify operations at the level of detail that characterizes a host-language system. By the same token, the user does not have to write highly detailed instructions about how to access and process the data.

Microcomputer database systems tend to be self-contained. Most *fourth-generation languages* that are add-ons to the database management systems are self-contained. They consist of their own command set that focuses on the functions that must be performed, not on the procedures to accomplish the task (data retrieval, report generation, or whatever).

The disadvantage of self-contained systems is the limited set of applications they can handle. However, for applications that fall within the set provided by the database management system, the self-contained systems offer significant reductions in the time needed to formulate a program.

Alternate Interface Concerns Each type of database management system must include ways for people, whether professional programmers or end-users, to interact with the system to accomplish their objectives. Programmers are concerned with developing software that functions efficiently. End-users, in contrast, want to be able to retrieve information easily without specifying a great number of technical details. Database management systems differ in the interfaces they include to meet these concerns.

The *programmer interface* is a function within self-contained or high-level systems that allows low-level programming when it is needed to achieve certain processing efficiencies or functions that are not in the self-contained language. It calls for the development of procedure-oriented programs at the computer programmer, rather than the user, level of detail. Self-contained systems are easier to use than host-language systems since the user is oriented to requesting operations on entire files rather than to the reading and writing of individual records.

The host-language systems, however, offer greater flexibility, since they are not limited to a specific set of functions or operations that can be performed on the database.

SQL, a database management system featured in examples later in this chapter, uses the same data manipulation language for host-language and self-contained applications alike. The fourth-generation language FOCUS, introduced in Chapter 6, includes both a programmer interface and an end-user interface to the underlying database.

The *user interface* permits a nonprofessional programmer or a nonprogramming user to interact with the database system. There is a distinct trend toward developing interfaces that allow individuals to control the sequence of events by initiating query and retrieval activities without the need for writing intricate procedural instructions. (Chapter 6 discusses several different examples of computer software in this category, such as Query-By-Example.)

An alternate form of user interface is system directed: The application software poses questions or presents alternatives to the user, who responds by selecting the appropriate action. Application generators often perform in this manner.

Increasing attention is being given to the development of natural language interfaces as an alternative to the artificial system interfaces described above. A *natural language interface* permits communication to the system in language as it is spoken by ordinary people. The term *English-like* is often applied to such a language (in contrast to the artificial computer languages that depend on specific vocabularies and syntax combinations).

Through a natural language interface, users will be able to pose queries and request reports in language similar to that used in conversation. The computer system in turn translates the narrative, whether verbal or keyed, into commands it understands.

There is a great deal of research under way to develop natural language interfaces. Such interfaces are not yet widely available, but this undoubtedly will change as increasing numbers of information systems and database applications emerge, coupled with greater emphasis on end-user computing.

SQL Database Management Systems

SQL (often pronounced "sequel") is a significant database language from the standpoint of all developers and users of databases, because it is influencing the characteristics of current database management systems, as indicated earlier. In some cases,

Table 8.2 Representative Database Management Systems

Database Management System	Computer System Class	Data Model
ADABAS	Mainframe	Relational (inverted file)
dBASE IV	Personal computer	Relational (SQL)
Database2 (DB2)	Mainframe	Relational (SQL)
SUPRA	Mainframe and minicomputer	Relational (SQL)
IDMS/R	Mainframe	Network/relational
IMS	Mainframe	Hierarchical
INFORMIX/SQL	Minicomputer and personal computer	Relational (SQL)
INGRES	Personal computer	Relational (SQL)
Oracle	Mainframe, minicomputer, and personal computer	Relational (SQL)
rBASE System V	Personal computer	Relational (SQL)
SQL/DS	Mainframe	Relational (SQL)
System 2000	Mainframe	Network

SQL is the language for a particular DBMS, and in others, its characteristics and commands are embedded in DBMS software.

This section introduces SQL. Later in this chapter SQL will be used to demonstrate the development and use of relational databases.

Origin of SQL SQL was designed at IBM's San Jose, California, research labs by D. Chamberlin as part of a relational database project known as System R. The project produced one of the first widely publicized relational database systems, although the system was not made available for widespread commercial use.

In the 1980s, IBM released two commercial relational database systems that were based on the original efforts: SQL/DS and Database2, also known simply as DB2. The products are similar but use different operating systems.

Today a variety of vendors provide SQL-like database systems, and the number is growing (see Table 8.2). Database management systems for mainframes, midrange systems, and personal computers are now heavily influenced by SQL features. In 1986, the American National Standards Institute (ANSI) approved SQL as the standard for relational database languages. Hence it is likely that SQL will be a component of every major DBMS that supports the relational data model (discussed later in the chapter).

Embedded SQL Depending on the particular vendor product, SQL may be a stand-alone database language or it may be embedded in a host language. When used as part of a host language like COBOL, a version known as **embedded SQL** is required.

The host-language program will contain both the normal statements of the language and SQL statements. In order for it to know that SQL statements are embedded (so they will not be treated as errors by the host language), SQL statements are set off by header and trailer statements:

```
EXEC  SQL
        SQL statements
END-EXEC.
```

Embedded SQL is often used when the system developer wants to do batch processing, accumulating transactions in files and processing them at one time to update the database. Or it may be desirable to design special display screen layouts that control the entry or display of data in a manner different from that usually provided by SQL.

How Are Databases Designed?

The preceding sections have described the rationale for database management as well as the characteristics of a DBMS. Now we focus on database designs. Database architectures *define* the database. Data structures and data models are the means of implementing a database and also provide the basis for achieving the benefits discussed previously.

Database Architectures

Architecture gives structure to the database environment. It accounts for the separation of logical and physical relationships and defines the databases through the schema and views.

Separation of Logical and Physical Relationships We know that users are going to want to view data in different ways; that is, they will want multiple views. Any one user's needs or the requirements of a specific application program will typically draw on only a portion of the database. Seldom, if ever, will all record types or every relationship be needed by an information system.

We also know that changes will be made in the system from time to time. Hardware, software, users, and of course data all change. But a change in one area should not affect the others, nor should one user's view of a set of data constrain other users.

We can satisfy each of the foregoing concerns by devising the database architecture so that the logical relationships (Figure 8.7) are separate from the physical relationships.

Specifying the physical characteristics of storing and using data means users must describe the data items in a record, including their length and type (for example, character or numeric) specifications, locations, and storage or access methods. These concerns, which represent the **physical view** and which are very important from the

348

Figure 8.7 (*a*) Different Sets of Data Relating to the Same "Entity" (*b*) Multiple Logical Views Based on the Same Set of Data

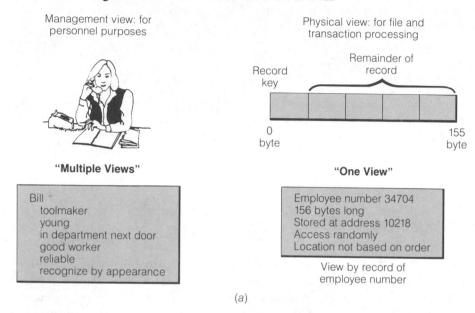

(a)

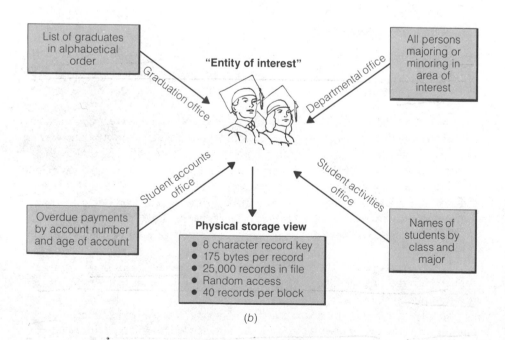

(b)

systems design aspect, should not limit the way in which users approach data and information.

The **logical view**—the user view—focuses on the data needed for a particular application, rather than on details of storage or access. For example, before staffing a new production line with people from outside the organization, a manager will want to know which current employees have experience in supervising production operations and which ones have training on the various kinds of equipment that must be run. These questions have nothing to do with the way the data are organized or stored in the system. Therefore, the user should be able to specify data needs and have them met without knowing anything about data storage.

There are three different views of stored data in a database:

1. *User's logical view of data:* the way a certain user visualizes a set of data needed for an application program; a view of part of the data in the database

2. *Data administrator's logical view of a database:* the way the entire database is viewed as it is managed by the person responsible for database design and fulfillment of the objectives of managing data

3. *Physical view of the database:* the way data are actually stored and organized on physical devices

The architecture of the database is expressed or defined through schema and views.

Schema The **schema** (sometimes called *scheme*) is a description of the *logical* view of the *entire database;* it is a list of the names and attributes of each entity and the relationships between entities about which data are stored. Notice that the data *values* are not included in the schema, which is simply a basic *framework*—a blueprint— for viewing all the entities stored without concern for how the data are actually stored. Compare this to earlier discussions of records. The contents of a data record (item names, lengths, and so on) can be described without using specific data values. The principle is the same for a schema. (Later we will see that the data model that defines the actual structure of the database is expressed as the schema. The schema will in fact look like a *schematic,* showing all the entities and the relationships between them.)

Instances of records are created when values are associated with record structures. This makes the record useful to an end-user. *Instances of a schema* are created when data values are associated with the framework—that is, when we assign specific values to each item specified in the schema (Figure 8.8).

There is one schema for a database, though one or more views may be related to the schema.

View When the data in databases are shared across different applications, it is not unusual that a specific application will require the data in another form from that used in the original definition. Similarly, there may be frequent need for using parts of several databases simultaneously. **Views** (sometimes called *subschemas*) are the means of meeting these needs. Views are logical, not physical, structures. They have

Figure 8.8 Schema Form for Entity Relationships

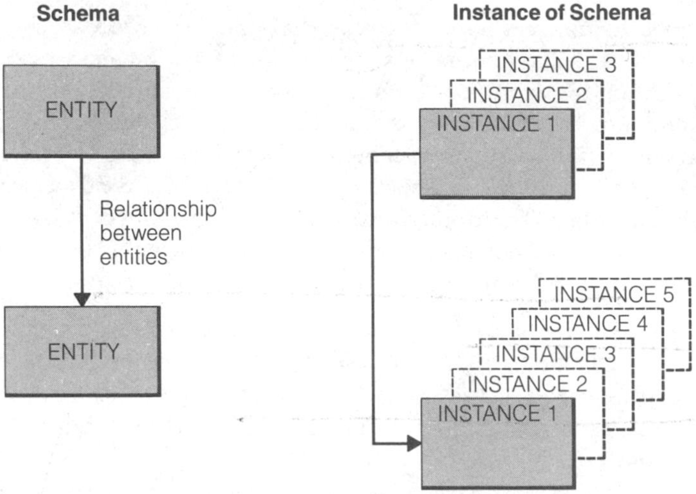

the features of a physical database, such as records and data items, but they are not permanent. Views are a subset of a database or a combination of elements from several different databases, depending on the needs of a *specific* user or group of users. Only some of the items in the schema are typically included in an individual view; the others can be ignored.

An analogy will demonstrate the relationship between schema and view. You might consider the schema to be equivalent to the road map of a large city, showing all the roads, streets, bridges, and rivers, as well as the relations among them (for example, intersections and parallel streets). However, if you want to draw a map to show the way from the university to your home, you need to represent only some of the streets that appear on the city map; that is, you draw your own map, which is a subset of the city map, giving only the streets your friend will use or pass by. Neither of you is concerned with what is on the remainder of the map (the schema). In fact, you probably do not know all the other streets on the map, and there is no reason why you should, unless you need to find your way around in those areas. A view plays a similar role in defining the architecture of a database.

(subschemas)

Benefits of Views Database developers must always balance two essential requirements: meeting the requirements of an application (and in some settings, multiple users), while avoiding unnecessary duplication of data. Views help meet these requirements by offering the following advantages:

- *Data can be seen (viewed) in different ways*. Subsets of databases can be created (with temporary copies of data) to offer the flexibility of having the data organized in just the right way. Yet the physical database remains unduplicated and in its original form.

—*Data can be manipulated without changing the original database*. Changes and adjustments can be made to a view, perhaps to test alternatives or evaluate ideas. The database remains in its original form, unaltered.

—*Database security is provided.* Only the data needed in a particular application are made available through a view. Other sensitive or protected data are not visible. Furthermore, inappropriate changes made to the data included in a view do not result in changes to the database.

—*Views shield users from changes in the physical database*. Databases evolve through use, meaning that formats and contents both change. However, when a database is shared by multiple users, there is no reason they should be concerned about changes that do not affect them. Views can remain stable while changes are made to the database.

—*Views make it unnecessary to physically extract records repeatedly*. Views can be established to extract records automatically through the creation of queries. Invoking the query will automatically initiate the steps to create the view, without the need for individual steps by the user.

Depending on the particular situation, any or all of the preceding may be reasons to create views.

The following example helps demonstrate the role of the schema and its relationship to views. An inventory database stores data about units in inventory and the vendors who supply items at particular times. It also stores data describing orders that have been placed for additional items. Hence, in a schema for an inventory database, there are records that describe the items themselves, the suppliers, the items actually on hand, and ordering data. In the schema for this hypothetical database—shown in Figure 8.9—the boxes depict entities and the connecting lines indicate relationships between the interconnected entities.

Note that the schema describes the relationships between inventory-oriented data. For instance, there is a relationship between an item and the supplier; that is, a supplier provides (supplies) an inventory item having a certain item number. In this case, the relationship might be described as "supplier of." Similarly, items ordered from a supplier by means of a purchase order are related to a specific supplier, and the relationship might be described as "ordered from." In setting up the logical structure of the database, we want to be able to establish these relationships through the schema.

In the inventory example, we can develop a view that deals with the relationship between a purchase order and vendor terms for the order (Figure 8.10). The data items of interest might include item number, item description, quantity on hand, total order value, and vendor number from one record and vendor name and sales terms from the other record. Notice that all these items are contained in the schema (Figure 8.9) that defines the database.

Through the combination of a schema and views, we can allow other users and application programs to construct different views or structures of data described in the schema. Hence a second view pertaining to the relationship between items ordered, and from whom, can be constructed. In this case, the view might show vendor number, item number, item description, and quantity ordered for one record and order number, and date of order, sales terms, and total value for the other record.

352

Figure 8.9 Sample INVENTORY Schema

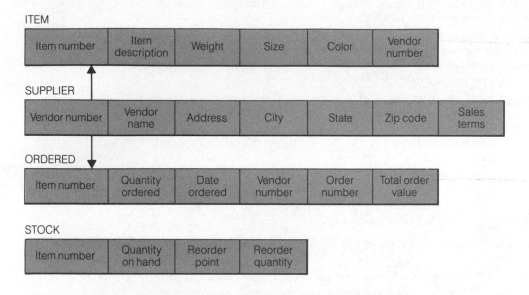

ITEM

Item number	Item description	Weight	Size	Color	Vendor number

SUPPLIER

Vendor number	Vendor name	Address	City	State	Zip code	Sales terms

ORDERED

Item number	Quantity ordered	Date ordered	Vendor number	Order number	Total order value

STOCK

Item number	Quantity on hand	Reorder point	Reorder quantity

Figure 8.10 Two Users' Views Formulated from INVENTORY Schema

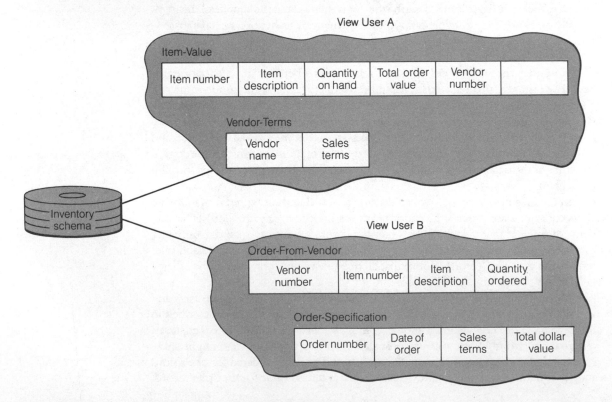

View User A

Item-Value

Item number	Item description	Quantity on hand	Total order value	Vendor number	

Vendor-Terms

Vendor name	Sales terms

Inventory schema

View User B

Order-From-Vendor

Vendor number	Item number	Item description	Quantity ordered

Order-Specification

Order number	Date of order	Sales terms	Total dollar value

We have said nothing about the storage of data or physical record keys; that is, we have not indicated that any particular storage structure or physical record key will be used to store the data on a secondary storage device. This demonstrates how the physical storage of data is independent of the way in which we logically arrange entity relationships.

Data Description Language

The details of a schema are communicated through a **data description language** (DDL) (sometimes also called a **data definition language**). Each database management system has its own data description language; there are too many to consider here, but we will use a DDL similar to COBOL in studying examples of how a schema can be formally stated. To define a schema, we must first give it a name. We will call the schema we developed for the inventory example INVENTORY. Since a schema can sometimes be quite extensive, it is often useful to divide it into subsets called *areas,* or *realms,* logical subdivisions of the total schema. Assume that the data we described in Figures 8.9 and 8.10 are actually only part of the schema and are contained in one area, which we call INVENTORY-CONTROL. Other realms could also be included, but we will confine our attention to one. After the schema name and realm have been stated through the data description language, we need to identify each record in the schema and the data items that make up each record. In our example, four records are described (ITEM, SUPPLIER, ORDERED, and STOCK). Each record is identified with a RECORD NAME IS statement and the data items are described by name, type, and length. The specification of the INVEN-TORY schema is shown in Figure 8.11. Each view must also be defined, using a data definition language that contains commands that permit specification of the view name, the name of the schema being used, and the characteristics of the data items being used in each record. Our example is a simple one that demonstrates how a schema or view is defined. In commercial database management systems other features, such as privacy and access control provisions, would also be included.

Device Media Control Language

Since the preservation of data on physical devices is separate from the logical definitions established by the data description language, another language, the **device media control language (DMCL),** is used to store the data. The device media control language (for example, JCL) is a set of commands used by systems programmers to store data. A detailed presentation of the commands is beyond the scope of our discussion. However, you should be aware that the assignment of data to physical devices is made through this language. Space is allocated and storage organizations are established, and indexing and overflow considerations can be addressed through the DMCL. Thus users can assume that all data storage is automatically taken care of by systems programmers using the device media control language. It is one more way in which independence between requirements for processing data and applications can be achieved. Applications can be modified to include additional data from a schema into a program. However, the way the data are stored need not be changed.

Figure 8.11 DDL Specification for INVENTORY Schema: INVENTORY-CONTROL Area

```
SCHEMA NAME IS INVENTORY

AREA IS INVENTORY CONTROL

RECORD NAME IS ITEM

    02    ITEM-NO               Picture 9(7).
    02    ITEM-DESCRIPTION      Picture X(20).
    02    WEIGHT                Picture 999.9.
    02    SIZE                  Picture 999.
    02    COLOR                 Picture X(5).
    02    VENDOR-NO             Picture 9(6).

RECORD NAME IS SUPPLIER

    02    VENDOR-NO             Picture 9(6).
    02    VENDOR-NAME           Picture X(25).
    02    ADDRESS               Picture X(20).
    02    CITY                  Picture X(10).
    02    STATE                 Picture X(2)
    02    ZIP-CODE              Picture 9(5).
    02    SALES-TERMS           Picture X(12).

RECORD NAME IS ORDERED

    02    ITEM-NO               Picture 9(7).
    02    QUANTITY-ORDERED      Picture 9(4).
    02    DATE-ORDERED          Picture 9(6).
    02    VENDOR-NO             Picture 9(6).
    02    ORDER-NO              Picture 9(5).
    02    TOTAL-ORDER-VALUE     Picture 999999.99.

RECORD NAME IS STOCK

    02    ITEM-NO               Picture 9(7).
    02    QUANTITY-ON-HAND      Picture 9(4).
    02    REORDER-POINT         Picture 9(2).
    02    REORDER-QUANTITY      Picture 9(4).
```

Data Manipulation Language

So far we have identified the ways in which logical and physical data definitions are formulated, but we have said nothing about the actual processing of the data in information systems application programs. To do this, we explore in greater detail the interface role of the database management system in information systems.

The ordinary application programs, which perform calculations and process data, issue commands to the database management system to retrieve data needed from secondary storage devices. This is made possible through the inclusion in the application program of **data manipulation language (DML)** commands, which specify the retrieval, modification, storage, or deletion of data stored in a database. They also establish and remove relationships between data, as we discussed during our examination of the concepts of schema and view. In other words, the data manipulation language is the language the applications programmer uses to access data stored in the database so that processing can take place in the application program. Likewise, the DML is used to transfer data from the application program to the database. This means that the DML itself does not do any processing or computation, but specifies what the data management system should do to assist the applications program.

Table 8.3 lists the data manipulation commands from several widely used mainframe and microcomputer database management systems. The functions they perform are:

1. FIND: locates a record defined and needed in processing.
2. GET: retrieves the record currently being processed and places it in the user working area

Table 8.3 Data Manipulation Commands Used by Database Management Systems

SQL	QBE	IDMS/R	IMS	System 2000	rBASE System V	dBASE IV
SELECT	P.	OBTAIN	GET*	GET1	SELECT	DISPLAY GET
INSERT	U.	STORE	ISRT	INSERT	**	APPEND STORE
UPDATE	D.	MODIFY	REPL	MODIFY	CHANGE	REPLACE
DELETE	I.	ERASE	DLET	REMOVE	DELETE	DELETE

```
* GU   GET UNIQUE
  GN   GET NEXT
  GNP  GET NEXT WITHIN PARENT
  +    also have CONNECT (into sets)
```

**Done in Load mode

3. STORE: inserts a new record in the database
4. MODIFY: changes the contents of the record currently being processed
5. ERASE: removes a record occurrence from the database

These functions are essential to make data available to the application program or to place data taken from an application program in memory in storage in the database. The next section describes how this occurs.

Interaction with Application Program

The **user working area** in the application program resides in computer memory. Each program has its own user working area, in which data are moved about by the database management system.

In processing data as specified in application programs, the database management system is an interface between the program and the stored data. Processing occurs in the following way (Figure 8.12):

1. The application program requests assistance from the database management system to retrieve data needed for processing. All requests for assistance are made through the data manipulation language commands.
2. The database management system accepts and examines the request. A comparison is made to ensure that data being requested have been properly defined in the subschema and schema.
3. The database management system requests input/output operations from the operating system of the computer.
4. The operating system in turn accesses the proper secondary storage device to transfer data to the computer system's input/output buffers.
5. The database management system takes the data from the buffer to the user working area, as requested in the initiating data manipulation commands.
6. The data in the user working area are processed in accordance with the instructions contained in the application program. This occurs just as it would in any ordinary application program.

The inventory example used earlier (Figures 8.9–8.11) will help in demonstrating this process. The instruction to read a record is originated in an application program. This results in a call to the database management system through DML commands (for example, FIND, GET); the DBMS receives from the application program the name of the record (Order-Specification) and a key (Order-No) for the particular record. From this, the DBMS locates the view associated with the application program and checks for the record type. Next, the schema (INVENTORY) is checked for the specific record type. Then the database management system determines which physical data are needed and issues a command to the operating system to read the data from secondary storage (say, magnetic disk) into a buffer in the main memory. While the data are in the buffer, the DBMS selects the items requested and performs the necessary transformations to arrange them into the form specified by the schema and view. After this, the data are transferred into the user working area (along with

Figure 8.12 Flow of Operations in Processing Data   *(primary storage)*

Main memory of the CPU

Operating system ③

Schema | Subschema

②

Database management system

① Application program

Buffers ⑤

User working area ⑥

④

Secondary storage

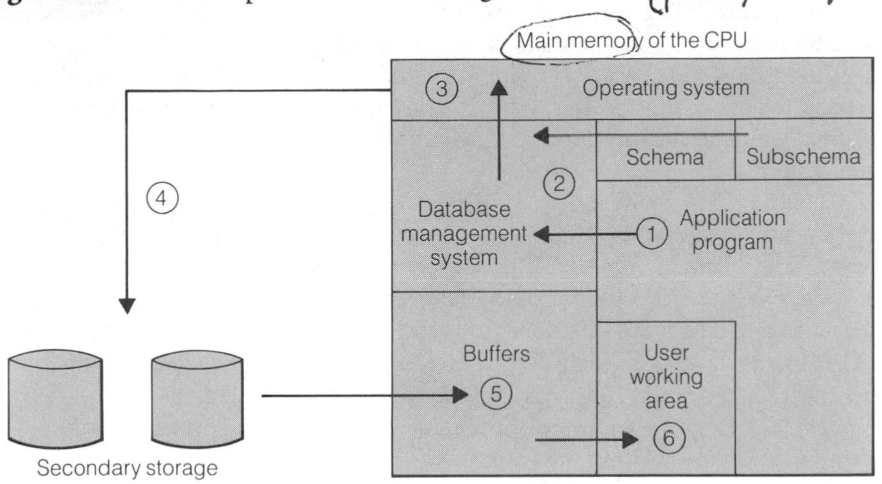

any error messages or other information), where the application program executes the programmed instructions.

This general procedure provides powerful support to users, while at the same time freeing them from concern about where the data are actually stored and how they are accessed. The schema and view, which define the data structure to the database management system, are central to the procedure and, for that matter, to the achievement of the objectives of database management.

How Do Data Models Influence Database Design?

The schema and view define the database by describing entities and relationships. However, the actual design of the database, which the schema expresses, is influenced by the data models a specific DBMS can represent. We examine the role of data models in the design of databases next. First data structures are discussed. Then the three prominent data models used in database management systems are explored in detail. Examples of how data are manipulated under each data model are included.

Data Structures

We have emphasized the separation of the logical and the physical views of data. This section examines logical data organization—that is, the data structures that are used to implement the data models (discussed later). The list structure is the basic building block. Using it, we can build more sophisticated multilist and inverted file data structures.

List Organization We alluded in Chapter 7 to the usefulness of **pointers,** that is, record addresses, in reducing the amount of search time for record processing in indexed organizations. Using the pointers in the organization of records underlies the list organization. A **list** is simply an ordered set of data. As we will see, pointers can be used in the records themselves, if the logical order of the file is not the same as the physical order, to indicate where on a storage device the records in a file or database are organized.

There are five basic types of list: simple list, two-way list, circular list, multilist, and inverted list. A *simple* list is a set of records, each containing a pointer to the next record in logical sequence. The various records may not lie next to one another in a *logical* sequential organization, and pointers are used to overcome this physical separation of data, permitting them to be processed in a logical sequence. The first record points to the (logically determined) second record, the second to the third, the third to the fourth, and so on (Figure 8.13).

For example, consider a set of personnel records concerning four employees in a single department (Figure 8.14). It has been determined that data relating to these employees should be processed sequentially in ascending order based on ID NO, which is the identifier or key. However, these four records are not stored sequentially; thus the *logical order* does not agree with the *physical order*. To resolve this dilemma, pointers are used to indicate the logical order for the records. As Figure 8.14 shows, they indicate the address of the next record in logical sequence. A pointer to the first record in the file, which tells the processor that it is in fact the initial record, is often referred to as the *external access point* or the pointer to the *head* (start) of the list (sometimes called the *database key*).

Figure 8.13 Simple List Organization

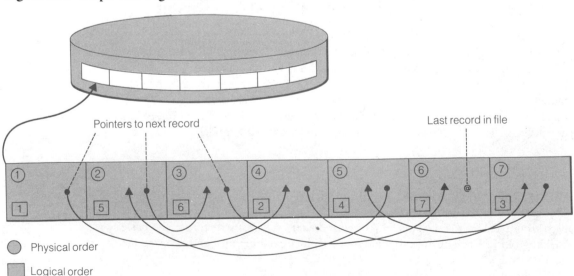

Pointers to next record

Last record in file

- ● Physical order
- ▮ Logical order

Figure 8.14 Simple List Using Pointers

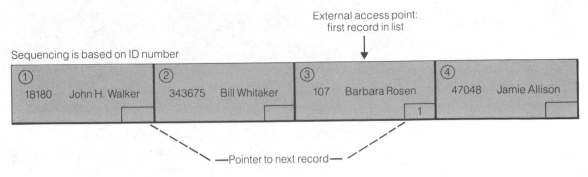

Figure 8.15 Insertion and Deletion in a Simple List

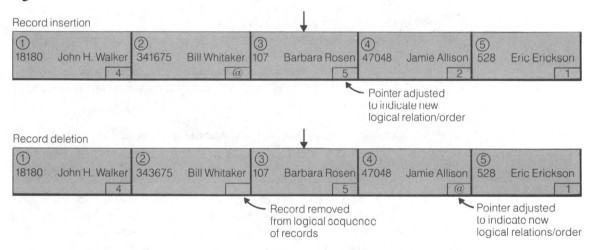

Each record in a list contains a pointer (inserted by the CPU under control of a computer program or database system) to the next record in logical sequence. How then does the processor know when it has encountered the *last* record? Often, a special symbol or a specific address, such as address 0, is inserted in the last record in the logical sequence. In our subsequent examples, the symbol @ designates the last record.

Insertion and deletion of records is relatively easy in the simple list structure. Records can be stored anywhere on the storage medium. They are linked to the list by changing the pointer in the record that the new record should follow. In Figure 8.15, the record pertaining to the new employee, Eric Erickson, should follow the record pertaining to Barbara Rosen, which previously contained a pointer to record 1 and now is modified to contain a pointer to record 5, the Eric Erickson record we just added. In this new record, a pointer is inserted to point to record 1 of the list. The process is reversed for deletion of records.

Figure 8.16 Two-Way List

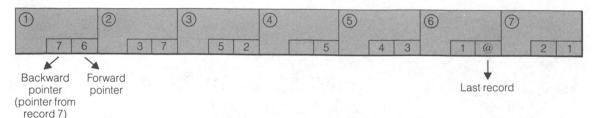

Backward pointer (pointer from record 7)

Forward pointer

Last record

Often it is desirable to have items in the list connected so that the last record in the list points back to the first. The *circular* list structure (sometimes called a *ring*) makes this possible. Contained in the last record is a pointer linking it back to the first record. Special symbols are maintained to designate the first and last records in the list, but this structure makes it impossible to enter the list and search it from *any point*.

linking

A variation on the ring structure is the *two-way list,* which contains not only forward pointers but also backward pointers (Figure 8.16). This structure makes it possible to move forward or backward, from any point in the list. Insertion and deletion are more complex, because twice as many pointers must be changed. Nevertheless, the ability to search from any point in either direction can result in more efficient search times.

Multilist A **multilist** uses the basic list structure to link together all records that have a common attribute (Figure 8.17). For example, in an airline system, all passengers on a specific flight on a certain day can be linked together in a database. The attribute is the combination of flight and date.

Each list is like a thread. Pull the end of the thread and all the records related on the attribute will be identified or reported. Each link in the chain is a record meeting the requirements of having an attribute in common. Links are created logically, through pointers. Physically the records may be stored in the database under any storage structure.

The "multi-" in multilist indicates that many lists can run through a database (for example, a list of passengers arriving in a certain city regardless of flight, a list of flights using a certain type of aircraft, or a list of flights originating or terminating in a single city). In addition, a record may belong to multiple lists (a passenger may be on city, flight, and frequent-flier lists simultaneously, even though the individual's record is stored only once in the database).

Inverted File The **inverted file** (also called *inverted list*) data structure uses an index to store information about the physical location of records having particular attributes (Figure 8.18). There are two types of inverted file. A *fully inverted file* has one index for each attribute in the records and an entry in the index for each record having a specific data value for that attribute. Each record in the index contains the storage addresses for each record in the file that meets that attribute. For instance, the record for passengers on flight 377 will contain 125 addresses if there are 125 passengers ticketed for the flight.

Figure 8.17 Multilist Structure

Storage Address	Passenger Name	Passenger Flight Number	Flight Date
1876	Linda Davant	377	2/27
1881	Glenda Gaines	428	1/24
1894	Mary Who	694	3/12
1896	Heinz Stein	694	3/12
1920	Ralph Anders	452	2/28
1928	James Thomas	428	1/24
1929	Sharon Brown	377	2/27
1931	Keith Jarvis	694	3/12
1950	David Storm	581	3/8
1986	Myron Loten	273	3/8
1991	Theresa Wilson	694	3/12
2014	Robert Sahley	694	3/12
2016	Jimmy Walker	422	1/24
2021	Tim Hoffman	377	2/27
2023	John Winkle	377	1/24

Thread for passengers on flight 428 on 1/24

Thread for passengers on flight 377 on 2/27

In a *partially inverted file,* only some of the attributes are indexed. This variation is frequently chosen because in many cases it is unlikely that certain items in the database will ever be used to retrieve data. Therefore, designers will not build an index on those items. For example, it is unlikely that a user would attempt to retrieve information about a certain flight on the basis of passenger telephone numbers. Therefore, an index would not be created to link together all persons having a common telephone number. In such a case—that is, when all attributes are not indexed—the database is partially, rather than fully, inverted.

Hierarchical and network database management systems often use either a multilist or inverted file data structure to link records together. Relational database

Figure 8.18 Inverted File Structure

Inversion on flight number:

Flight Number	Address
273	1986
377	1876, 1929, 2021, 2023 . . . . .
422	2016, 2016
428	1881, 1928
452	1920
581	1980
694	1894, 1896, 1931, 1991, 694,

Inversion on a flight date:

Flight Date	Address
1/24	1881, 1928, 2016, 2023
2/27	1876, 1929, 2021
2/28	1920
3/08	1950, 1986
3/12	1894, 1896, 1931, 1991, 2014

systems often use other structures that are beyond the scope of this discussion. The important point is that these data structures do not replace the physical storage structures used in computing. Rather, they are a technique that imparts to the retrieval of data in a database additional flexibility—flexibility that is not achievable in a physical sense.

Design Using Relational Data Model and SQL

When designing a database and establishing the schema, it is important to know the underlying data model of the database management system that will be used. The **data model** defines how relationships are shown between entities in the database. Each DBMS uses a specific data model (see Table 8.2 earlier). Three data models are in common use in database systems: the relational, hierarchical, and network models.

The **relational data model,** developed in 1970 by E. F. Codd, is the most widely used data model among those database systems currently being purchased by organizations. (Microcomputer database management systems have stimulated a substantial user interest in relational data models.) The data model itself is based on a

Figure 8.19 Components of Relation in a Relational Database

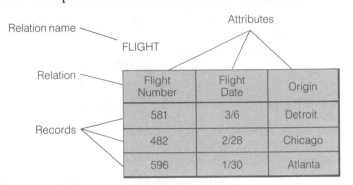

relation, which is represented as a two-dimension table. Rows in the table constitute the records, and the columns are the attributes of the entity (Figure 8.19).

There is no order or sequence in the table. Furthermore, the relation is a logical structure. When using data included in the relation, the user need not be concerned with details of storage. (Remember, ultimately, all data models will be stored in one of the file organizations a computer system can employ—a random, indexed, or sequential storage structure.)

The relational data model is currently the most popular basis for new database management systems because:

——Relational databases are conceptually simple and easy to understand.

——Since relationships need not be predefined, the database can evolve to meet changing requirements.

——Relationships are implied by the data values.

An example from the airline industry will assist in demonstrating these concepts, as well as those from the other two data models, to facilitate comparison. Figure 8.20 contains five relations: FLIGHT, PASSENGERS, AIRCRAFT, MAINTE-NANCE, and PILOT. Notice that each consists of a table with rows that represent the records of data. If we want to know the seat assignment of James Thomas on flight 428, January 24, we can scan the PASSENGERS relation looking at the data items Passenger Name and Seat Assignment.

This example probably seems very simple. That's the point of relational data-bases. The relation between entities, such as passengers and flights, should be readily understood. This model is most effective if the relationships represent the way activities really occur.

Here are four relationships of interest in airline management:

——Aircraft used on a specific flight

——Passengers on a specific flight

——Pilot of a flight

——Maintenance performed on aircraft

Figure 8.20a The FLIGHT Relation for an Airline Database

First relation for airline database:

FLIGHT

Flight Number	Flight Date	Origin	Destination	Aircraft Number	Pilot ID
581	3/6	Detroit	Memphis	18407T	334613
452	2/28	Chicago	Minneapolis	18495S	413099
596	1/30	Atlanta	Chicago	18746J	653481
428	1/24	Atlanta	San Francisco	21741L	628541
694	3/12	Boston	Chicago	21342L	131496
377	2/27	Atlanta	New York	32841L	776851
387	2/27	Minneapolis	Chicago	7465C	413099
273	3/9	Memphis	Chicago	36511A	182612
531	3/8	Detroit	Memphis	17821C	396183
273	3/12	Memphis	Chicago	18495S	413099
1536	3/1	Chicago	Milwaukee	18407T	776851

These relationships involve the entities of aircraft, flight, passenger, pilot, and maintenance. The columns in each of the relations in Figure 8.20 are the attributes that describe the entities. For instance, in Figure 8.20c, aircraft are described by the aircraft number, aircraft type, and data purchased. Similarly, Figure 8.20a describes flight entities by flight number, flight date, origin, destination, aircraft number, and pilot. For the aircraft entity, a single data item—aircraft number—is the key; it uniquely distinguishes one aircraft from all others. However, flight requires two data items: flight number and flight date. Since the airlines use the same number for a given flight every day, the date is necessary to discriminate among flights. When two data items are used to distinguish one record from another, we call the mechanism incorporating this data item pair a *concatenated key*. Concatenation is quite common in real-life applications and therefore the capability to represent this relationship is a basic feature of database management.

Figure 8.20*b* The PASSENGERS Relation for an Airline Database

Second relation for airline database:

PASSENGER

Passenger Name	Flight Number	Flight Date	Ticket Class	Seat Assignment	Telephone Number
Linda Davant	377	2/27	Y	21A	404-658-3871
Glenda Gaines	428	1/24	F	4B	404-658-3880
Mary Who	694	3/12	K	12A	607-798-2000
Heinz Stein	694	3/12	F	16C	312-644-6610
Ralph Anders	452	2/28	Q	23A	612-781-1313
James Thomas	428	1/24	Y	14C	404-394-8461
Sharon Brown	377	2/27	Y	12D	212-512-4881
Keith Jarvis	694	3/12	Y	18A	312-329-1846
David Storm	581	3/8	Y	7D	212-512-3786
Myron Loten	273	3/8	F	3C	312-486-2400
Thomas Wilson	694	3/12	K	7C	617-587-1605
Robert Sahley	694	3/12	F	2A	312-754-3000
Jimmy Walker	428	1/24	Y	28D	404-658-2121

Database Definition As noted in the earlier discussion of DBMS features, a database must be created before it can be used. In a relational database, the schema is communicated to the DBMS by creating the relations. We will use the data description language of SQL, a very popular database system, to define the four relations for our sample database. The command set of SQL (Table 8.4) is representative of other widely used relational database management systems, including those that run on microcomputers (see Chapter 6 for discussion of the popular microcomputer database management system dBASE IV).

To create the table for a relation, the data description entries must name the relation so that it can be added to the database directory. Next each data item in the

Figure 8.20c The AIRCRAFT Relation for an Airline Database

Third relation for airline database:

AIRCRAFT

Aircraft Number	Aircraft Type	Date Purchased
12476J	DC10	1/76
21342L	DC10	2/74
7465C	DC10	2/78
21667J	B747	3/74
18495S	DC9	9/81
18407T	B767	2/85
47521L	DC10	4/73
82144B	B747	5/77
16341L	B747	3/71
17821C	DC9	5/86
21741L	DC10	2/74
22321B	DC9	3/87
36511A	B767	4/85
32941L	B767	4/85
30416B	DC9	3/76

relation must be defined, including the data item name, data type, and item length. The entries for the AIRCRAFT relation are:

```
CREATE TABLE FLIGHT
(FLIGHT-NUMBER INT (4),
FLIGHT-DATE CHAR (5),
ORIGIN CHAR (16),
DESTINATION CHAR (16),
AIRCRAFT-NUMBER CHAR (6),
PILOT-ID INT (6))
```

Figure 8.20d The MAINTENANCE Relation for an Airline Database

Fourth relation for airline database:

MAINTENANCE

Aircraft Number	Date Serviced	Type of Service	Supervisor
47531L	11/18	Engine overhaul	Williams
16841L	1/26	Front gear adjustment	Roberts
30416B	3/12	Seat repair	Neal
18476J	2/28	Engine rebuild	Martin
21342L	1/4	Oxygen system replenished	Cremmins
32341L	3/1	Engine rotor replacement	Smith
18407T	11/24	Glass replacement	Neal
30416B	1/6	Microwave repair	Martin
18495S	12/18	Navigation system adjustment	Williams
21342L	1/15	Seat repair	Jackson
17821C	3/14	Engine overhaul	Ronson
21342L	12/28	Thermostat replacement	Presley

Similar entries create the other relations given in Figure 8.20.

```
CREATE TABLE PASSENGERS
(PASSENGER-NAME CHAR (24),
FLIGHT-NUMBER INT (4),
FLIGHT-DATE CHAR (5),
TICKET-CLASS CHAR (1),
SEAT-ASSIGNMENT CHAR (3),
TELEPHONE-NUMBER INT (10))

CREATE TABLE AIRCRAFT
(AIRCRAFT-NUMBER CHAR (6)
AIRCRAFT-TYPE CHAR (4)
DATE-PURCHASED CHAR (5))
```

Figure 8.20e The PILOT Relation for an Airline Database

Fifth relation for airline database:

PILOTS

Pilot Name	Pilot ID	Aircraft Qualification	Date Last Certification
Craig Neal	628541	DC10	1/28
Mike Nevert	396183	DC9	11/24
Earnest Ferell	776851	B767	12/2
Susan Baker	131496	DC10	1/18
Tom Leslie	653481	DC10	2/12
Harry Daldwell	182612	B767	3/18
Judy Lewis	334613	B747	2/1
George Tech	361219	DC10	1/24
Doug West	413099	DC9	12/14
Sherry Wilson	312643	DC10	11/28

```
CREATE TABLE MAINTENANCE
(AIRCRAFT-NUMBER CHAR (6),
SERVICE-DATE CHAR (5),
SERVICE-TYPE CHAR (24),
SUPERVISOR CHAR (24))

CREATE TABLE PILOT
(PILOT-NAME, CHAR (24),
PILOT-ID INT (6),
AIRCRAFT-QUALIFICATION CHAR (4),
DATE-LAST-CERTIFICATION CHAR (5))
```

Although these commands create the relations in Figure 8.20, they do not insert data in the database. The USE command instructs the database management system to apply the commands that follow to the specified relation. To populate a database in SQL, an INSERT command is issued. The AIRCRAFT relation in Figure 8.20c is created with the following:

```
INSERT INTO AIRCRAFT VALUES ('18476J', 'DC10', '1/76')
INSERT INTO AIRCRAFT VALUES ('21342L', 'DC10', '2/74')
INSERT INTO AIRCRAFT VALUES ('7465C', 'DC9', '2/78')
```

Table 8.4 SQL Commands

Action/Function	Command	Explanation
Database creation and description	CREATE TABLE table name	Defines table to database system
	DELETE TABLE table name	Removes table from database
	ALTER TABLE table name	Changes structure of table
Data manipulation: Retrieval	SELECT table name	Retrieves all data items of all records
	SELECT table name (data item(s))	Retrieves data item(s) of all records
	SELECT table name WHERE condition	Retrieves data items of all records
Modification	UPDATE table name SET data item = value	Changes data item to specified value
	UPDATE table name SET data item = value WHERE condition	Changes data items meeting condition to specified value
Addition	INSERT INTO table name (data items)	Adds records and data items to existing table
Deletion	DELETE FROM table name WHERE condition	Deletes data items of all records meeting a certain condition
View definition	DEFINE VIEW view name SELECT data items FROM table name	Creates temporary table by extracting data from other table(s). Can be used to restrict access to portion of database
	DROP VIEW view name	Releases view

```
INSERT INTO AIRCRAFT VALUES ('21667J', 'B747', '3/74')
INSERT INTO AIRCRAFT VALUES ('18495S', 'DC9', '9/81')
INSERT INTO AIRCRAFT VALUES ('18407T', 'B767', '2/85')
INSERT INTO AIRCRAFT VALUES ('47531L', 'DC10', '4/73')
INSERT INTO AIRCRAFT VALUES ('82144B', 'B747', '5/77')
INSERT INTO AIRCRAFT VALUES ('16841L', 'B747', '3/71')
INSERT INTO AIRCRAFT VALUES ('17821C', 'DC9', '5/86')
INSERT INTO AIRCRAFT VALUES ('21741L', 'DC10', '2/74')
INSERT INTO AIRCRAFT VALUES ('22321B', 'DC9', '3/87')
INSERT INTO AIRCRAFT VALUES ('36511A', 'B767', '4/85')
INSERT INTO AIRCRAFT VALUES ('32841L', 'B767', '4/85')
INSERT INTO AIRCRAFT VALUES ('30416B', 'DC9', '3/76')
```

The other relations are populated with data in the same manner. (In an actual environment, this type of operation would most likely be done by embedding the SQL INSERT command into a host language. A processing loop in the host language would read in data and execute the INSERT command.)

Table 8.5 Relational Operators

Relational Operator	Description of Operation
SELECT	Creates a new relation by extracting *rows* that meet the stated criteria
PROJECT	Creates a new table by extracting *columns* that meet the stated criteria
JOIN	Creates a new relation from the *rows* in two tables having attributes that meet the stated criteria

Figure 8.21 Result of Passenger Inquiry

Passenger Name	Telephone Number
Mary K Who	607-798-2000
Heinz F Stein	312-644-6610
Keith Y Jarvis	312-329-1846
Thomas K Wilson	617-537-1605
Robert F Sahley	312-754-8000

Data Manipulation The distinguishing feature of the data manipulation language in relational databases is the use of the three *relational operators:* **SELECT, JOIN,** and **PROJECT** (Table 8.5).

SELECT Relations Selection conceptually produces a new table—a new relation— that is created by the *rows* of the initial table that satisfy a condition. A projection conceptually produces a new table that is made up of *columns* from the original table that meet the processing requirements. And, the join operation conceptually creates a new table from the rows of two tables that satisfy a processing condition.

To demonstrate the power of relational databases and the three operators, we will use processing examples for querying a database and for adding, deleting, and changing records.

QUERY: WHAT ARE THE NAMES AND TELEPHONE NUMBERS OF THE PASSENGERS ON FLIGHT 694, DESTINATION CHICAGO?

The relation in Figure 8.21 includes the names of the five passengers who meet this criterion.

Using SQL, the query is posed as follows:

SELECT PASSENGER-NAME, TELEPHONE-NUMBER FROM PASSEN-GERS WHERE FLIGHT-NUMBER = '694' AND DATE = '3/12'.

This command automatically triggers the system to search the database for records that meet these criteria. The SELECT command produces an output relation that includes the data items PASSENGER-NAME and TELEPHONE-NUMBER. As this example demonstrates, the relation resulting from the query includes only the data items requested in the query.

In using dBASE IV, the same query is made by the following statement of the query:

USE PASSENGERS
SELECT PASSENGER-NAME, TELEPHONE-NUMBER
WHERE FLIGHT-NUMBER = '694' AND DATE = '3/12'

PROJECT Relations The PROJECT command creates a new table from data extracted using attributes specified in the query. In other words, PROJECT picks columns out of a relation. Consider the following example:

QUERY: WHICH PILOTS ARE TRAINED TO FLY THE DC10 AIRCRAFT?

This query requires the searching of the attribute Aircraft Qualification to find the entries that have the data value DC10. The relation in Figure 8.22 is the query result, which is obtained by expressing the query in the following DML statement:

SELECT PILOT-NAME FROM PILOT WHERE AIRCRAFT-QUALIFICA-TION = DC10

The same query is stated in QBE as follows:

PILOT-NAME   AIRCRAFT-QUALIFICATION
      P.   'DC10'

JOIN Relations The JOIN operation creates a new relation by combining two existing relations, selecting the records that meet the criteria stated in the query, and then

Figure 8.22 Result of Pilot Inquiry

```
            Pilot Name
            ----------

             Craig Neal
             Susan Baker
             Tom Leslie
             George Tech
             Sherry Wilson
```

Figure 8.23 Result of Destination Inquiry

```
       Destination
       ----------

         Chicago
       San Francisco
```

removing duplicate records. (Remember that a relational data model contains no duplicate records; this feature is part of the theory behind relational databases. However, in many implementations of the relational data model, duplicates are eliminated only when the user selects this option. We remove duplicates in the examples that follow.)

The following query demonstrates the JOIN operation:

QUERY: TO WHICH CITIES DO WE FLY THE DC10 AIRCRAFT?

Figure 8.23 shows the relation that results. The query is answered by JOINing data from the flight and aircraft relations on the common attribute Aircraft Number. Using SQL, the query is expressed as follows:

SELECT DESTINATION FROM FLIGHT, AIRCRAFT WHERE MODEL = DC10
AND AIRCRAFT.AIRCRAFT-NUMBER = FLIGHT.AIRCRAFT-NUMBER.

The powerful relational operators discussed above are the basis for all database activities. For example, the capability to add, delete, or change records depends on the operators:

ADDITION: Add the passenger James Johnson to Flight 694 on 3/12.
    A record is added to the PASSENGERS relation without affecting any other records in the table. The SQL instructions to perform the addition are:
    INSERT INTO PASSENGER VALUES ('JAMES JOHNSON', '694', '3/12')

DELETION: Pilot Mike Nevert has left the company. His name and other information must be removed from the pilot relation.
    The row of the database containing the name Mike Nevert is removed from the database. The SQL instructions are:
    DELETE FROM PILOT WHERE PILOT-NAME = 'MIKE NEVERT'

CHANGE: Change the seat assignment of passenger Sharon Brown to 7B.
    The record with the primary key of SHARON BROWN is located and the data value in the secondary attribute of seat assignment is changed according to the new data. SQL instructions for this example are:

UPDATE PASSENGER
SET SEAT-ASSIGNMENT = '7B' WHERE NAME = 'SHARON BROWN'

These examples demonstrate the power of the relational model quite vividly. Notice that in each one, the steps needed to respond to the query or to process the update requests can be visualized by examining the data. Even if a particular request is not anticipated when the database is designed, it can still be fulfilled because of the powerful operations available through the relational model. As we see in a moment, this is not necessarily the case with other data models.

The other important rational feature demonstrated by the examples above is the independence of the processing requirements from the physical storage of the data. None of the query or update steps specified file structures, access records, or physical record keys. In manipulating the database, we made no reference to physical links between relations either. Only common data items are mentioned when it is necessary to interrelate two tables (for example, pilot and aircraft type).

Design Using Hierarchical Data Model

The **hierarchical data model** follows a genealogical structure that relates entities by a superior/subordinate or parent/child relationship. A family tree (Figure 8.24), for example, shows the members of a family through four successive generations. An organization chart, another familiar hierarchical model, shows the president or chief executive officer, with layers of higher level executives, middle management people, and operating staff, in descending order.

Graphically the hierarchical data model is shown as an upside-down tree, with the highest level of the tree known somewhat paradoxically as the *root*. The *nodes* of the tree represent entities. Two types of relationship occur between nodes of the tree:

——*1 to 1* (◄——►)
An entity at one level is related to one entity at another level. For example, a pilot has one identification number. If you know the pilot, you can determine the identification number; if you know the identification number, you can determine the pilot's name.

——*1 to many* (◄——◄)
An entity at one level is related to zero, one, or more entities at the next level. For example, if you know the number of a flight on a certain day, you can determine the names of the passengers, if any (conceivably, some flights will not be booked at all).

In database design, analysts determine the entities to be included in the database and then establish each relationship between entities. The nodes represent instances of records containing the appropriate data items as determined by the systems analyst.

Figure 8.25 gives a hierarchical data model for the airline example. The entity AIRCRAFT is the root node. FLIGHT and MAINTENANCE entities are subordinate to AIRCRAFT, and the entities PASSENGERS and PILOT are related to

Figure 8.24 Basic Structure of Hierarchical Data Model

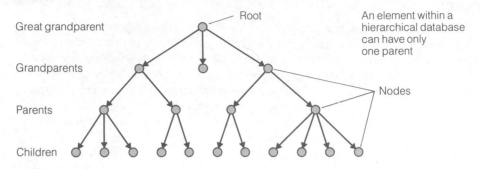

Figure 8.25 Hierarchical Structure for Airline Database

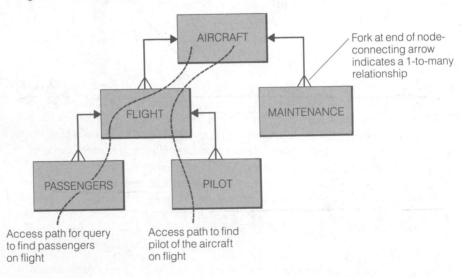

FLIGHT. The design of these relationships, which determine how data will be accessed, is very important. For example, to find information about a certain pilot, access to the record must be made through the plane and flight relationships.

In designing hierarchical databases, analysts are forced to choose between alternatives that influence accessibility of data (these tradeoffs need not be made with relational models). The data structure selected stipulates that passengers are always related to a certain *flight* and flights always to a certain *aircraft*. It is very efficient to find the flights on which a specific aircraft is used (Figure 8.26) or the *names* of the passengers on a particular flight. The database is designed to support these inquiries because they are the ones that occur most frequently.

How does this database design affect a request to list the flights on which a certain individual has been a passenger? The data model stipulates that passenger data are accessible only through an occurrence of a flight record. This relationship

Figure 8.26 Instances of Hierarchical AIRCRAFT-FLIGHT-PASSENGERS Relations

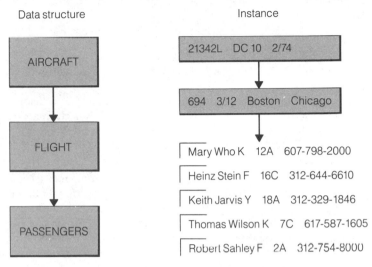

Data structure

Instance

21342L   DC 10   2/74

694   3/12   Boston   Chicago

Mary Who K   12A   607-798-2000

Heinz Stein F   16C   312-644-6610

Keith Jarvis Y   18A   312-329-1846

Thomas Wilson K   7C   617-587-1605

Robert Sahley F   2A   312-754-8000

(Notice that flight and date are *not* part of the passenger record.)

Figure 8.27 Instances of AIRCRAFT-MAINTENANCE Relationship

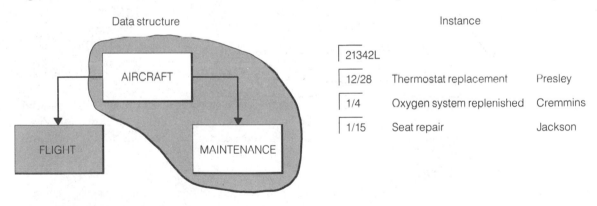

Data structure

Instance

21342L

12/28   Thermostat replacement   Presley

1/4   Oxygen system replenished   Cremmins

1/15   Seat repair   Jackson

implies that *the entire passenger list for all flights flown must be searched* to prepare the flight history for a particular passenger (airlines are interested in this information for the administration of their frequent-flier programs).

An additional example will demonstrate the importance of this matter. The relation between AIRCRAFT and MAINTENANCE shown in Figure 8.27 indicates that the set of maintenance records for a particular aircraft are linked to a record for the unit. If it is necessary to review the maintenance history of a specific aircraft, the associated maintenance records can be found very quickly. However, management may want to know how many times engines have been replaced for all DC 10s in the fleet. This seemingly simple request will require searching the entire set of maintenance records to locate a subset of DC 10 information. In a large database, such a search is difficult.

Anomalous (undesirable) side effects occur under certain database designs. Hierarchical databases involve anomalies with respect to:

——*Insertion of records:* a dependent record cannot be added to the database without a parent.

We cannot add a passenger to the database unless the individual can be linked to a specific flight. This is probably realistic. However, the same restriction implies that with the database structure in Figure 8.24 a pilot who has not been assigned a specific flight cannot be included in the database. That may not be desirable or realistic.

——*Deletion of records:* deleting a parent from the database also deletes all its descendants.

Thus if a flight is canceled, all passengers booked on that flight are deleted from the database, along with the records of their telephone numbers and other information needed to rebook them on another flight. Similarly, if a plane is sold, and the record describing it is therefore removed from the database, all flight and maintenance records pertaining to it are also deleted, useful though they might have been for purposes of comparison.

(Establishing multiple databases has been suggested to avoid this problem. However, this approach adds complexity and necessitates data redundancy and excess storage utilization.)

Design Using Network Data Model

The **network data model** is similar to the hierarchical model, except that an entity can have more than one parent. Thus, as shown in Figure 8.28, members can belong to more than one relationship (that is, have more than one owner). In the airline example, a relationship can be shown between aircraft and pilot as well as between aircraft and flight. This capability introduces the use of an additional type of relationship in the data:

——*Many to many* ($\rightarrowtail\!\!-\!\!\leftarrow$)
An entity at one level can be related to zero, one, or more than one entity at another level. For example, an individual can pilot more than one plane, and a plane can have more than one pilot. Knowing a pilot's name does not automatically tell you what plane the person flies.

The network database structure in Figure 8.29 shows the entities in the airline database we have been using. However, the relationship between entities is different.

One form of network database that has received a great deal of use is the one designed by CODASYL (the Conference on Data System Languages), an independent organization of vendors, researchers, and governmental agencies that have worked to establish guidelines and recommendations for computer software. In addition to developing the COBOL language, CODASYL established a model for

Figure 8.28 Basic Structure of Network Data Model

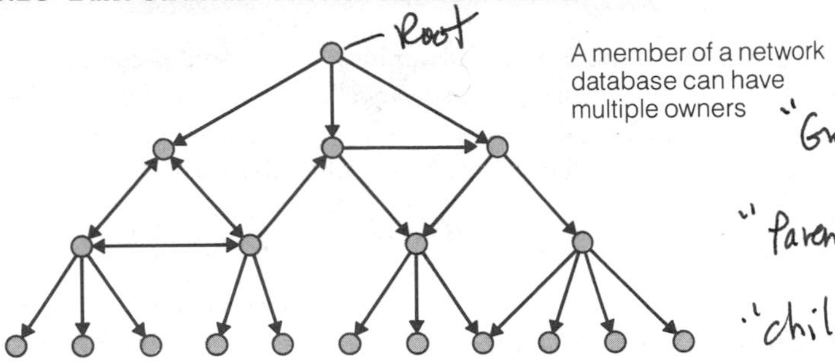

A member of a network database can have multiple owners

[handwritten annotations: "Great-Grandparents", "Grandparents", "Parents", "children"]

Figure 8.29 Network Structure for Airline Database

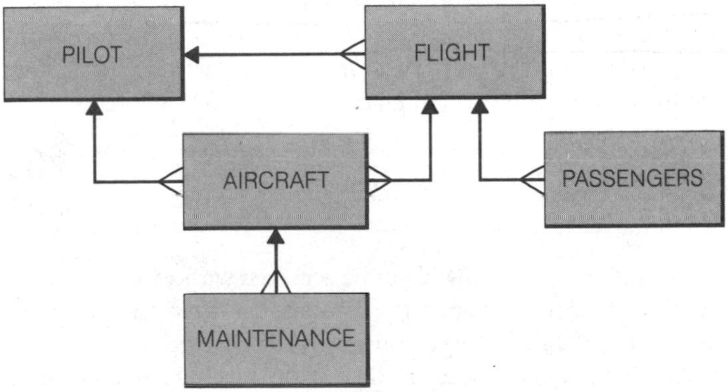

database management systems that emphasizes owner–member sets. "Owners" are analogous to parents in the hierarchical model, "members" are owned by owners, and the owner–member relation is called a *set*. Both owners and members are entities. To retrieve data from a set, the owner and the member must be specified. For example, in Figure 8.29 the database includes a set that consists of the owner PILOT and the member AIRCRAFT. Another set consists of the owner AIRCRAFT and the member MAINTENANCE. To retrieve maintenance records for an aircraft, the database system must first identify the owner record for the aircraft of interest.

In network databases, as in hierarchical databases, the relations between entities must be established at the time the data model is established and the database created (in contrast to the relational model, which does not require predefined access paths or entity relations). Similarly, the paths relating the entities must be followed when storing or retrieving data.

The network and hierarchical databases are conceptually simple and appear uncomplicated when first examined. In a large database environment, however, they can rapidly evolve into an intricate web of interrelationships that become difficult to manage as the database evolves with usage. (Consider that to find all the aircraft that have had an engine changed, it is necessary to search the entire set of maintenance records.)

Anomalies similar to those in the hierarchical data model occur. For example, if a flight is canceled, we do not want to "cancel" the aircraft, but the data model suggests that this should happen. Similarly, if a pilot is reassigned, we do not want to remove from the database the aircraft from which the reassignment occurred.

Importance of Hierarchical and Network Data Models

The preceding section points out features and drawbacks of the hierarchical and network data models in contrast to the relational model. Although systems developers are adopting relational databases because of their combined advantages of simplicity and powerful data manipulation capabilities, without the need to predefine access paths, the other data models are still important. For one thing, when access paths and relationships between entities *can be predefined,* access is usually faster and processing speed usually greater than when using relational databases. Moreover, many installed systems use network and hierarchical data models. If they are functioning well, it is unlikely that the organizations will migrate to relational models.

How Are Databases Managed?

The objectives of using databases will not be achieved without explicit action. In this sense the database must be managed as a resource for the organization—a resource that has value and usefulness. The responsibility for management, which is vested in a database administrator, must be explicitly established. In turn, the data administrator must develop guidelines and take appropriate actions, ranging from separating the logical and physical views of data to providing for data integrity and security (Table 8.6).

Database management begins with the appointment of a database administrator, as discussed in the next section. Subsequent sections cover the following aspects of database management: maintaining a data dictionary, providing for input validation, providing for backup, providing for security and privacy, and controlling concurrent operations.

Appoint a Database Administrator

The **database administrator** may be an individual or a group. In either case, the assignment is to manage and protect the database while seeking maximum benefit for all users. The underlying assumption is that in the absence of explicit designation of management responsibility and authority, the organization will not receive the benefits of developing and using the database that are desirable or possible.

The database administrator is responsible for balancing the viewpoints of all users:

——**Systems programmer:** handles storing data in database, working with the physical rather than the logical view of the data. This person organizes the data

---

Table 8.6 Actions to Manage the Database

Management Tasks

Appoint a database administrator

Separate the logical and physical views of data

Provide for input validation

Provide for backup

   Dual recording

   Dumping

   Audit trail

Provide for security and privacy

   Isolation

   Regulation

   Encryption

Control concurrent options

Maintain a data dictionary

Manage schema/subschema relationships

---

using an agreed-on storage structure in a manner that best meets all other user needs, selects storage devices, and specifies details of storage.

——**Applications programmer:** develops software, usually in third- and fourth-generation languages, to generate reports, update records, and perform other functions involving data stored in the database.

——**Specifier user (an end-user):** a manager or employee who interrogates (queries) the database to obtain data for decision making or accesses certain records to update them. This user does not need to understand conventional programming languages but must be able to enter certain key words or codes to acquire or modify records (Olle, 1970).

——**Parametric user (an end-user):** relies on predefined questions and structures (for example, "What year sales do you wish to use?") to interact with the database; may enter or extract data, but only through questions posed by the system. Typical parametric users are airline reservation agents, bank tellers, and stockroom clerks.

——**Database administrator:** also a user of the database who maintains the database in response to usage demands.

The database administrator manages the structure of the database to meet the requirements of all users. Standards must be developed and enforced. Among the most important areas of concern are:

——Development of data names, lengths, and validation criteria

——Determination of data ownership

——Designation of access and modification responsibility

The database administrator does not determine the contents of the database or the data values themselves. This is the responsibility of the systems developers and the users.

Maintain a Data Dictionary

A **data dictionary** is a collection of the definitions of data stored in the database (Figure 8.30). Definitions include specification of the characteristics of data items, such as length and type (character or numeric), descriptions, and alternate names for the data items (for example, student ID may be called by aliases such as identification number and social security number).

A data dictionary also stores cross-reference information, which is important in database management because it allows the administrator to quickly determine where a certain set of data is used.

As a management tool, a data dictionary has the following additional benefits.

—— Reduces data redundancy and inconsistency by facilitating communication between users and designers about storage and usage of data

—— Provides a central repository of design information

—— Enables designers to determine what effect a change in data requirements for an application will have on other applications and on the database itself

—— Provides reports and printed listings on the contents of the database in various formats (such as alphabetical and "where-used")

—— Provides computer-readable data specifications that in some systems can be integrated into automatic generation of application systems

The management benefits of data dictionaries are substantial. Thus even in nondatabase environments, many organizations are developing and using data dictionaries.

Provide for Input Validation

Input validation is the set of actions taken during data entry to detect errors in the data before they enter the database. Error detection at this point avoids costly updates after data have been accepted in storage and makes it easier to correct errors quickly, without having to wait for a long period of throughput and turnaround. Errors lower the quality of data and can contribute to system failure and database degradation so serious that the database is no longer an accurate, reliable resource for the organization.

In Supplement 7 we described the primary input validation techniques: transaction validation, sequence checks, batch totals, format checks, reasonableness checks, audit trail, duplicate processing, and check digits. By including instructions to perform these checks in all computer programs that input data to the database, many data errors can be detected and corrected, ensuring that invalid or erroneous data from input are not allowed to destroy the integrity of the database.

Figure 8.30 Database Dictionary   381

```
          ADD
          RECORD NAME IS EMPLOYEE VERSION 1
*+            DATE CREATED IS          11/26/85
*+            TIME LAST UPDATED IS 10304607
*+            PREPARED BY SYSMWC
*+            RECORD LENGTH IS 116
              PUBLIC ACCESS IS ALLOWED FOR ALL
              RECORD NAME SYNONYM IS EMPLOYEE VERSION 1
*+                COPIED INTO SUBSCHEMA EMPSS01 SCHEMA EMPSCHM VERSION 100
*+                COPIED INTO SCHEMA EMPSCHM VERSION 100
              RECORD NAME SYNONYM IS EMPLOYE VERSION 1
                  LANGUAGE IS ASSEMBLER
              RECORD NAME SYNONYM IS EMPLOY VERSION 1
                  LANGUAGE IS FORTRAN

              RECORD ELEMENT IS EMP-ID-0415 VERSION 1
*+            LINE IS 000100
*+            LEVEL NUMBER IS 02
              PICTURE IS 9(4)
              USAGE IS DISPLAY
              ELEMENT NAME SYNONYM IS EMPID
                  FOR RECORD SYNONYM EMPLOYE VERSION 1
              ELEMENT NAME SYNONYM IS EMPID
                  FOR RECORD SYNONYM EMPLOY VERSION 1

              RECORD ELEMENT IS EMP-NAME-0415 VERSION 1
*+            LINE IS 000200
*+            LEVEL NUMBER IS 02
              USAGE IS DISPLAY
              ELEMENT NAME SYNONYM IS EMPNAME
                  FOR RECORD SYNONYM EMPLOYE VERSION 1
              ELEMENT NAME SYNONYM IS EMPNAM
                  FOR RECORD SYNONYM EMPLOY VERSION 1

              SUBORDINATE ELEMENT IS EMP-FIRST-NAME-0415 VERSION 1
*+            LINE IS 000300
*+            LEVEL NUMBER IS 03
              PICTURE IS X(10)
              USAGE IS DISPLAY
              ELEMENT NAME SYNONYM IS EMPFNAME
                  FOR RECORD SYNONYM EMPLOYE VERSION 1
              ELEMENT NAME SYNONYM IS EMPFNM
                  FOR RECORD SYNONYM EMPLOY VERSION 1
```

SUBORDINATE ELEMENT IS EMP-LAST-NAME-0415 VERSION 1
*+   LINE IS 000400
*+   LEVEL NUMBER IS 03
      PICTURE IS X(15)
      USAGE IS DISPLAY
      ELEMENT NAME SYNONYM IS EMPLNAME
            FOR RECORD SYNONYM EMPLOYE VERSION 1
      ELEMENT NAME SYNONYM IS EMPLNM
            FOR RECORD SYNONYM EMPLOY VERSION 1

      RECORD ELEMENT IS EMP-ADDRESS-0415 VERSION 1
*+   LINE IS 000500
*+   LEVEL NUMBER IS 02
      USAGE IS DISPLAY
      ELEMENT NAME SYNONYM IS EMPADDR
            FOR RECORD SYNONYM EMPLOYE VERSION 1
      ELEMENT NAME SYNONYM IS EMPADR
            FOR RECORD SYNONYM EMPLOY VERSION 1

      SUBORDINATE ELEMENT IS EMP-STREET-0415 VERSION 1
*+   LINE IS 000600
*+   LEVEL NUMBER IS 03
      PICTURE IS X(20)
      USAGE IS DISPLAY
      ELEMENT NAME SYNONYM IS EMPSTRET
            FOR RECORD SYNONYM EMPLOYE VERSION 1
      ELEMENT NAME SYNONYM IS EMPST
            FOR RECORD SYNONYM EMPLOY VERSION 1

      SUBORDINATE ELEMENT IS EMP-CITY-0415 VERSION 1
*+   LINE IS 000700
*+   LEVEL NUMBER IS 03
      PICTURE IS X(15)
      USAGE IS DISPLAY
      ELEMENT NAME SYNONYM IS EMPCITY
            FOR RECORD SYNONYM EMPLOYE VERSION 1
      ELEMENT NAME SYNONYM IS EMPCTY
            FOR RECORD SYNONYM EMPLOY VERSION 1

      SUBORDINATE ELEMENT IS EMP-STATE-0415 VERSION 1
*+   LINE IS 000800
*+   LEVEL NUMBER IS 03
      PICTURE IS X(2)
      USAGE IS DISPLAY

```
        ELEMENT NAME SYNONYM IS EMPSTATE
            FOR RECORD SYNONYM EMPLOYE VERSION 1
        ELEMENT NAME SYNONYM IS EMPSTE
            FOR RECORD SYNONYM EMPLOY VERSION 1

        SUBORDINATE ELEMENT IS EMP-ZIP-0415 VERSION 1
*+      LINE IS 000900
*+      LEVEL NUMBER IS 03
        USAGE IS DISPLAY
        ELEMENT NAME SYNONYM IS EMPZIP
            FOR RECORD SYNONYM EMPLOYE VERSION 1
        ELEMENT NAME SYNONYM IS EMPZIP
            FOR RECORD SYNONYM EMPLOY VERSION 1

        SUBORDINATE ELEMENT IS EMP-ZIP-FIRST-FIVE-0415 VERSION 1
*+      LINE IS 001000
*+      LEVEL NUMBER IS 04
        PICTURE IS X(5)
        USAGE IS DISPLAY
        ELEMENT NAME SYNONYM IS EMPZIPF5
            FOR RECORD SYNONYM EMPLOYE VERSION 1
        ELEMENT NAME SYNONYM IS EMPZF5
            FOR RECORD SYNONYM EMPLOY VERSION 1

        SUBORDINATE ELEMENT IS EMP-ZIP-LAST-FOUR-0415 VERSION 1
*+      LINE IS 001100
*+      LEVEL NUMBER IS 04
        PICTURE IS X(4)
        USAGE IS DISPLAY
        ELEMENT NAME SYNONYM IS EMPZIPL4
            FOR RECORD SYNONYM EMPLOYE VERSION 1
        ELEMENT NAME SYNONYM IS EMPZL4
            FOR RECORD SYNONYM EMPLOY VERSION 1
```

Provide for Backup

Precautions are always necessary to ensure that data stored in a database are available when needed. For example, steps must be taken to protect the existence of the data, that is, to prevent any action that would result in the loss or destruction of data. One way to achieve protection is to maintain duplicates of files and databases called **backup copies,** which can be entered into the system if original material is lost or destroyed. There are several methods of maintaining backup, including dual record-ing of data, database dumping, and use of an audit trail with before-looks and after-looks.

Dual Recording In **dual recording,** as the name implies, the same data are recorded on two storage devices simultaneously. As transactions are processed against the database and updates or changes occur, the changes are made on both copies of the files. Therefore, if a hardware failure occurs on one device, or if an operator inad-vertently mounts the wrong device, a "clean" copy still exists and operations can be resumed. Unfortunately, in the event of a power failure, a software problem that prevents data from being written, or a natural disaster, this means of protection probably would not be sufficient.

Dumping An alternate means of protection is to copy the database periodically, for instance, daily or weekly, and store the copy. It is necessary to keep a *log,* until the next database copy is made, as a record of all interim transactions processed against the database. The log can be kept by hand on paper or electronically by the computer system itself. If data are lost, the database can easily be restored by mounting the backup copy and processing all recent transactions recorded on the log against the copy, to bring it up to date. Continual **dumping** (copying) of the database is expensive and time-consuming, however; and in addition, errors resulting in inac-curate data can occur while the files are being copied.

Audit Trail In a third means of backup protection, the **audit trail,** the contents of all input transactions are recorded as the data enter the system and maintained on a log like the one used with dumping. A list of all input transactions is kept, and a copy of each record is made before and/or after each update is recorded. These record copies are called **before-looks** and **after-looks,** respectively. If a system failure of any type occurs, this method of backup makes it possible to re-create the damaged portion of the database by using the computer to merge the transaction tapes and the copies of the updated records. Alternatively, we could work with the before-looks and the transaction tapes to bring the records forward to their current state.

The problems associated with the audit trail approach are similar to the ones mentioned for other protective measures. For example, if the system fails while the transactions are being logged, some of the changes might be lost without notice or detection. Similarly, the before-looks and after-looks could be lost in the same way if a hardware or software failure occurred while they were being recorded. In addi-tion, it is very time-consuming to record transactions and before-looks and after-looks. Hence, many installations use only one of these record-lock recordings, and if the transaction log is destroyed as a result of equipment or software failure, it is very difficult to restore the data.

Providing backup protection is an important but difficult part of managing data. There are no foolproof ways of ensuring that data loss will not occur. The problem is central to the entire area of databases and information systems, and is the subject of constant research efforts in government and industry.

Provide for Security and Privacy

Whereas backup provisions help protect against loss of data, *security provisions* are aimed at protecting the existence of data by preventing any intrusion that could lead to destruction of files and databases. *Privacy protection* consists of steps taken to guard against unauthorized distribution of data. In other words, security pertains to illegal entry to computer files (either physically or through "hacking" into an on-line system) for the purpose of destroying, modifying, or accessing data without permission. **Privacy,** on the other hand, involves the right to control distribution or dissemination of data. Thus a breach of privacy has occurred if data accessed for one purpose are distributed for another. For example, a credit report legitimately requested by a banker to assist in arriving at a loan decision should not be handed over to a life insurance company without the permission of the credit holder.

Management of databases implies protection of privacy and security. Everest (1974) identified three protection strategies: isolation, regulation, and encryption. *Isolation* is the storing of data in a physical location where they cannot readily be accessed by unauthorized persons. Maintaining the database in a concrete block room or in a steel vault is one way of achieving isolation. But the matter is more complex than this. Someone must determine who should have access to isolated data. This is *regulation*.

The three phases of regulation are identification, authorization, and monitoring. **Identification** of persons wishing to access data can be made through passwords and codes, or by badges, cards, or keys. As in the military, passwords and codes are words (names of things) used to identify "safe" people. The same principle can be used in security of computer systems and file storage areas. Some installations also use badges or cards that bear identification records on small magnetic tape strips. Sensing mechanisms read the recorded codes and screen all persons who wish to enter the data storage area.

Identification is usually matched with **authorization,** the approval to access particular files and make certain uses of the data. Someone must decide whether a particular individual is allowed to access an entire file, certain records, or just one item in each record. Decisions like these can be very difficult, but they are necessary if privacy and security are to be maintained.

A third phase of regulation is **monitoring.** Keeping records of everyone who uses the data and examining the records periodically is a relatively easy way to monitor access and possibly detect improper activities. Other problems, such as identifying people who make repeated attempts to use the database without an acceptable means of identification, can also be approached through monitoring.

Since complete isolation of data is often not feasible or sensible, other protective measures are used. Through *encryption,* unauthorized persons may find it difficult to use the data they have accessed or even to determine which records have been accessed. Encryption is the scrambling of data according to predetermined transformation rules so that they are meaningless to anyone who cannot unscramble them. For the data to be used, they must be retransformed, which can be done only on the request of an authorized person. Encryption is expensive and time-consuming, but it is a good means of protection for particularly sensitive data.

Each protective measure we have described carries a tradeoff in terms of costs and benefits. Data security is expensive because it requires extra equipment and time. Therefore, systems personnel and managers have to decide the point at which the cost of security (and privacy) exceeds the value of the data being safeguarded. Perhaps particular kinds of data—military secrets, for example—must be protected at all costs, but certainly not all data must be—or must they?

Control Concurrent Operations

Control of **concurrent operations** is important, particularly when multiple users require the same data at the same time. When two users are making changes in the database, it is possible for one of the updates to be lost. The following example illustrates how data loss can occur during concurrent operations. The initial contents of record 114 (stored on magnetic disk) were:

4629	Sonic Circles	42.18	77	144
item	description	cost	on hand	on order

——Manager 1 and manager 2 receive copies of record 114 at about the same time.

——Manager 1 changes on-hand quantity to 56 units (for example, says a transaction involving a withdrawal of 21 units has taken place) and writes the record back onto the storage device. At this point the record appears as follows:

4629	Sonic Circles	42.18	56	144

——Manager 2 changes on-hand quantity to 70 units on his or her copy of the record (that is, says that a transaction involving a withdrawal of 7 units has taken place) and writes the record back onto the storage device. This record is written *over* the existing record. Now the record appears as follows:

4629	Sonic Circles	42.18	70	144

——*Result:* the transaction consisting of the withdrawal of 21 units by manager 1 has been lost in the file. The previous balance was written over without regard for any changes that might have taken place while multiple copies of the record were with the users.

However, if one user is given exclusive use of a particular set of data while another person is waiting for it and another user has control of a set of data the first user needs, a deadlock could occur. In a **deadlock,** each user is waiting for the other to release the data he or she is using and, barring some other action, both could wait indefinitely. Since multiple-user environments facilitate the development of deadlock and problems of uncontrolled concurrent operations, it is important that these situations be anticipated and avoided.

Database Machines

As organizations increase the amount of database-oriented processing they do, or as the demand for additional database resources rises, acquisition of database machines is often considered.

Definition

A **database machine** (also called a **database computer**) is a special-purpose computer, interconnected with the main computer system, dedicated to handling database management activities. These functions include processing database inquiries and updates, storing data definitions, and storing the data dictionary.

Advantages and Disadvantages

Database machines offer the potential advantages of:

——*Reduced database processing costs:* in terms of processing resources used, database machines cost less than mainframe processing of database instructions.

——*Independence of database system and main computer system:* application developers have greater flexibility of selecting database software because they are not constrained to systems that operate on a particular mainframe (this advantage is often termed *portability*).

——*Database sharing:* the database can be shared across several different computer systems; the database computer handles concurrent processing requirements.

——*Security:* comprehensive security precautions and user validation requirements can be installed and monitored through the database machine, without utilizing mainframe resources.

The primary disadvantage of database computers lies in the added complexity that initially results, since decisions must be made about the sharing of functions. In addition, management procedures must be put in place to control the database machine.

Relation to Computer Systems

Figure 8.31 depicts the relation between database computers and mainframe systems when used together. The application programs and operating system still reside in mainframe memory. However, all DBMS inquiries are passed to the database computer, where they are interpreted. Data are retrieved from the database and transferred to the user working area of the application program. The entire procedure is transparent both to the computer system and to the end-user.

The cost and performance advances associated with database computers—similar to those occurring with computers generally—and the increasing reliance on database management systems suggests that these systems will become a common resource in organizations of all types.

Figure 8.31 Database Computer Configuration

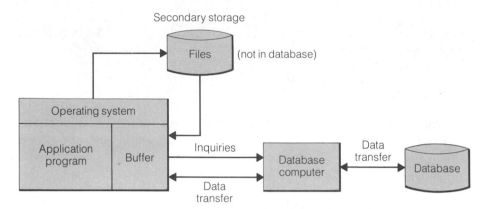

Summary

Data management underlies effective integration of stored data in automated environments. Traditional file structures are highly efficient in transaction processing, but they limit the use of the data needed in an integrated environment. Databases thus are designed to emphasize the natural relationships in the data and to facilitate ad hoc queries. At the same time, other benefits include reduced data redundancy and increased sharing and control over the data.

Components of database management include the database itself, often termed an integrated or subject database, management and administrative practices, a data dictionary, view/schema relationships, the underlying data structures, the database management system, application programs, and system interfaces. The appointment of a data administrator is essential to ensure that the needs of all users, including systems and applications programmers as well as nonprogramming users, are met. In addition, by developing and maintaining data definitions as well as logical schemas and subschemas, suitable control is achieved to facilitate effective use while protecting against change and modification from any of several sources.

A database management system is built on a data model. The hierarchical, network, and relational data models are used to define the relationships in the data to be represented in the database. The underlying data structures, based on the concept of a simple list, are the multilist and the inverted (or partially inverted) file. These logical data structures are ultimately translated into a physical storage structure, the file organization the computer understands.

Database management systems are not information systems, but the two are often used together (although it is not necessary to install a DBMS to have an information system). Whereas a database system does not give meaning to the data—that is the role of an information system—it does provide the facility for storage and recall of data and facilitates user definition of report contents. Database classes include host-language and self-contained systems.

Various interfaces, linking the user to the system, differ in their use of a traditional programming language versus a special language, even a fourth-generation language, containing database commands. There are tradeoffs between processing efficiency and ease of application development. Other interface concerns include the ability for programmers to interact at a procedural level (programmer interface), for users of different types to retrieve data (the user interface), and the inclusion of a natural language interface that resembles English narrative. In the future we will probably see continued moves toward the development of database management software that addresses these concerns as an additional way of achieving the benefits of database management. Many of the functions will likely migrate to special-purpose database machines that interconnect with mainframe systems.

Key Words

After-looks	Data manipulation language (DML)	Multilist
Applications programmer		Network data model
Audit trail	Data model	Parametric user
Authorization	Deadlock	Physical view
Backup copies	Device media control language (DMCL)	Pointer
Before-looks		Privacy
Concurrent operations	Dual recording	PROJECT
Database	Dumping	Relational data model
Database administrator	Embedded SQL	Schema
Database computer	File management system	Security
Database machine	Hierarchical data model	SELECT
Database management system (DBMS)	Host language	Self-contained system
	Identification	Specifier user
Data definition	Input validation	SQL
Data definition language	Inverted file	Storage structure
Data description language (DDL)	JOIN	Systems programmer
	List	User working area
Data dictionary	Logical view	View
Data independence	Monitoring	

Review Questions

1. What is a database? How is it related to other components of the data hierarchy?
2. "A database is a centralized resource for an organization." Explain the meaning of this statement.
3. What is the rationale for database management? Identify and explain the benefits of the database approach.
4. Identify and briefly explain the components of the database approach.
5. What is a subject database? Does it differ from the concept of an integrated database? Explain the reasoning behind your answer.

6. What measures might one take to protect data from accidental destruction?

7. Identify the different users of a database and explain the skills commonly attributed to each in interaction with the database.

8. What is the "logical view of data"? How is it different from the physical view? Does one constrain the other?

9. What is SQL? What features characterize it as a database language? How is SQL different from a specific DBMS?

10. Discuss the relationship between storage structures, accessing of data, and the logical user's view of data?

11. Explain how multiple and redundant files occur in an evolving information system. Can this be prevented? If not, why not? If yes, why is database management necessary?

12. What is deadlock? How does it occur? Does it necessarily accompany concurrent operations? Explain.

13. Discuss the benefits of a data dictionary.

14. Explain the concept of a data model. What data models are used in database management systems? Discuss the distinguishing features of each.

15. What is a list organization? What are the different types of list organization?

16. In list organizations, the physical order and the logical order are not the same. What does this mean? How is logical ordering accomplished?

17. What is a pointer? An inverted file? A partially inverted file? A multilist?

18. Identify and explain briefly the features of a database management system.

19. What is the difference between file creation, re-creation, and update? What information is required for file updating?

20. Compare the various language types used for data definition.

21. What differences exist between the host-language and self-contained database interface methods? What are the advantages and disadvantages of each from various users' points of view?

22. Explain the meaning of programmer interface, user interface, and natural language interface.

23. Describe the functioning of each of these relational database commands: JOIN, SELECT, PROJECT.

24. What are database computers? What advantages and disadvantages do they produce in the management of databases?

25. Describe the relation between databases, application programs, and database management systems when a database computer is used.

Application Problems

1. The data needs of each individual user in an information systems environment should not be affected by the data requirements of any other user. At the same time, no user should be constrained by the way data are organized and stored on secondary storage devices.

a. How does this issue relate to the objectives of database management?

b. What are the means of dealing with this issue in a database management system environment?

c. Who should be responsible for assuring that the needs of all users are met while still operating the system efficiently? Why?

2. Here is a portion of a relational database.

SUPPLIER	ITEM SUPPLIED	CITY
General Parts Company	Toy trucks	Memphis
Roberts Distributing	Crayons	Memphis
Koval Supply, Inc.	Electric trains	New York
Southern Wholesalers	Chalkboards	Atlanta
Roberts Distributing	Coloring books	Memphis
General Parts Company	Chalkboards	Memphis
Roberts Distributing	Management books	Memphis

a. State the query "Which suppliers provide our chalkboards?" in data manipulation language and name the relational operation(s) required. Show the result of the inquiry.

b. Show the query "List the name and item supplied of all Memphis suppliers" in data manipulation language. Explain how a response to the query is prepared. Show the result of the inquiry.

3. Examine the following entity relationship.

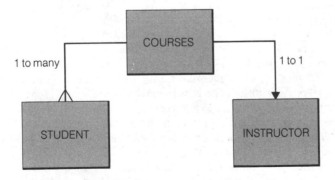

a. Based on the information provided, can you classify the model as hierarchical or network? Explain.

b. Describe how the database would have to be processed to respond to the query: "What students are registered for the course Computer Information Systems?"

c. Describe how the database would have to be processed to respond to the query: "What courses is student J. James registered for?"

d. How is an instructor record added to the database?

4. The following schema, incorporating two one-to-many relations between entities, describes data about students.

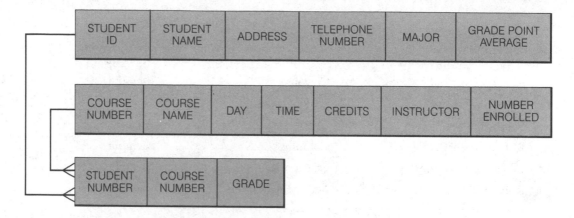

a. Show relations for each entity described above.

b. A report must be produced for each student to show name and ID as well as information about courses for which the student is registered (course number and name, credits, day, time, and instructor). Develop a subschema that will allow preparation of the report.

c. Discuss how the database would be processed to prepare a list of all students registered for CIS 400.

5. A large university uses a computer-based information system to support administrative decisions on the creation of new faculty positions, the development of new courses, and the addition of sections to existing courses. To support this decision activity, three separate master files are used.

a. *Student registration file:* includes data on student registrants (by name, identification number, and major) for each course offered by the university

b. *University teaching faculty file* (not a personnel file): includes data on what faculty members (name, identification, and department) are teaching which courses (course number), and how many students are registered for each course or section of a course

c. *University course file:* includes data on each course or section offered (course name, course number, section number, and number of credits) and the number of students registered for each

The registration and course files are maintained by the registrar's office and are based on students who register for each course at the beginning of a term. Each student must fill out a registration form that indicates the courses he or she is registering for. These documents are processed to create the file at the end of the first week of classes.

The computer center creates the university faculty file at the end of the third week of classes (after the deadline for adding or dropping classes has passed) on the basis of data received from the individual colleges, schools, and departments.

The university faculty file is used as the basis of requests from the departments to receive additional faculty lines and course offerings. University administrators make a decision on the requests based on data in the registration and course files.

a. What problems might be encountered in this system? In making faculty or course decisions based on the existing files?

b. What benefits might be realized by combining the three files into a single university course-offering database? Can the three be combined into one?

c. What problems might you encounter in combining them? How would you resolve these problems?

d. What other information would you need to deal with this data management policy?

6. An information systems manager has been resisting the introduction of database management principles by claiming that a DBMS would cause more work for the systems department and would ultimately lead to a higher level of expenses for the company. It is also argued that with the introduction of database management, in which each user can view and use the same set of data differently, the systems staff would have to try and satisfy more people individually. Yet the systems department is not satisfying management users now, with its tightly controlled files arranged so that all users are forced to view a given set of data in the same way. Now, the information systems manager says, they will have an even more difficult time because every user will want something different.

The information systems manager feels that the best way to use the data depends on the most efficient way to store them. Therefore, the systems staff should select a file organization that optimizes storage space and store the data in that format. Users can then tailor their needs to use the storage structure selected by the systems staff. Why, the manager asks, should we go to the trouble and expense of installing a database management system?

Discuss the arguments of the information systems manager. Do you agree or disagree with them? Explain.

7. The Dependable Supply Company, a wholesaler of consumer goods for local businesses, is developing an automated system to assist in its inventory control, purchasing, and order processing functions. To this end, the company has purchased a database management system.

Preliminary analysis indicates that the following data about products and vendors should be contained in the database:

—*For each product:* product number, product name, product description, and quantity on hand

—*For each supplier or vendor:* vendor number, vendor name, and vendor address

—*For each order of a product from a vendor:* quantity ordered and expected arrival date

A given vendor typically supplies more than one item. On the other hand, DSC may order the same product from any one of several suppliers.

The database will be used to support several diverse functions. Although the system may be changed in the future, it is currently expected to operate as follows.

—*Order processing:* upon receipt of a customer order, a clerk will interrogate the database for each product in the order to determine whether a sufficient quantity is on hand. If not, an inquiry will be made to see whether there has been a replenishment order, and if so, when it will arrive.

——*Purchasing:* to place a replenishment order, the purchasing agents enter the vendor number, product number, order quantity, and expected arrival date. The system will generate an order complete with the vendor's name and address.

——*Monitoring:* to maintain close control over the replenishment orders, it is desirable to monitor them so that action can be taken if it appears that an order will be late.

——*Receiving:* when a replenishment order is received from a vendor, the amount on hand is increased and the amount on order is decreased.

   a. For these four uses of the database, what record types are needed? For each, develop subschemas for the applications to indicate what data items are contained in a record and how the user might expect to access the data. Consider each use of the database independently of the other uses; that is, assume that the database can be structured so that each application will have only the data it needs and it will have the most appropriate access strategy.

   b. Consider the entire database and the four applications, and develop a schema for the database. How can the database be organized so that it will simultaneously meet the needs of all four applications? How will the schema differ if the database is organized according to a hierarchical data model? How will it vary if it is organized according to a relational model?

8. Discuss the relationship of database management systems to:
   a. Operating systems
   b. Secondary storage devices
   c. Main memory storage
   d. Procedure-oriented languages
   e. Fourth-generation languages
   f. Database computers
   g. Application programs
   h. Computer information systems

9. What value do data dictionaries have for:
   a. Modifying data structures?
   b. Modifying storage structures?
   c. Changing the storage devices on which parts of the database are stored?
   d. Determining data validation criteria?

Minicase: New York City Bus Maintenance System

If you have trouble keeping maintenance records on your personal automobile, imagine the difficulty of this task in a bus transit system for New York City. The fleet consists of nearly 5000 buses that are maintained through 22 service depots. And unlike personal automobiles, many different persons drive the city's buses over a brief period of time.

Even the simple questions so essential in managing a bus maintenance program are difficult:

——Which buses must be scheduled next week for the 9000-mile oil change and lubrication?

——How many miles have been put on each tire on each bus? (Tires are not all changed at the same time.)

——Which buses are due for safety inspection?

——Who performed each repair on each bus?

It is also difficult to determine whether there is any pattern of problems or repairs to indicate possible manufacturing defects (for example, frequent replacement of transmission seals, rapid burnout of light bulbs and ceiling lamps, high use of engine oil or refrigeration coolant).

More than 1.5 million people ride the bus every day. Thus a reliable maintenance system is essential.

Questions

1. What *features* should a maintenance system have to meet maintenance demands of the type outlined above? How would you ensure that data will be captured when work is performed? Can you guarantee the reliability of maintenance data in a system this large, or are serious problems inevitable?

2. If the buses are not always serviced at the same garage, how can the necessary maintenance data be captured and essential maintenance history details be retrieved? What physical features must the system include to make this possible?

9: Data Communications

Key Questions

What are communications networks?

How do wide-area and local-area networks differ?

In what ways are networks organized?

What roles do common carriers play in data communications?

How will ISDN change data communications?

How are computers interconnected in communications networks?

How does distributed processing benefit organizations?

What purpose do value-added carriers serve?

Connectivity

As every man goes through life he fills in a number of forms for the record, each containing a number of questions. . . . There are thus hundreds of little threads radiating from every man, millions of threads in all. If these threads were suddenly to become visible, the whole sky would look like a spider's web, and if they materialized as rubber bands, buses, trams, and even people would lose the ability to move, and the wind would be unable to carry torn-up newspapers or autumn leaves along the streets of the city. They are not visible, they are not material, but every man is constantly aware of their existence. . . . Each man, permanently aware of his own invisible threads, naturally develops a respect for the people who manipulate the threads.

A. I. Solzhenitsyn, *The Cancer Ward*. Reprinted by permission of Farrar, Straus & Giroux, Inc.

Data Communications and Networks

The communication of data between computers is nearly as important as computing itself. Scores of businesses—retailers, banks, airlines, hotels, auto rental firms—as well as government agencies and other organizations could not exist in their present form without the ability to transmit data over communication channels.

This chapter discusses the principles of data communications and addresses both the components of communications systems and their application to the management of organizations. We see how communications activities have evolved and the components that are required for data communications today. We also discuss the use of wide area and local area networks of computers. When you have completed this chapter, you will know why data communications is so vital in information systems and will have some familiarity with the alternatives available to systems developers.

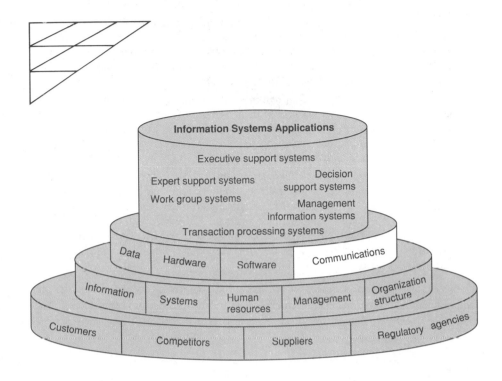

Why Should You Know About Data Communications?

Organizations of all types are paying increasing attention to the development and utilization of their data communications capabilities. Whether you are a member of a business organization or not, you will be affected by this. These are some of the reasons you should know about data communications:

——*Organizations are becoming more dependent on data communications.* At one time, telephones were used only for voice communication. However, advanced capabilities for communicating data, text, and images, as well as voice, are leading organizations to introduce new ways to improve business activities. Many firms are finding that they are unable to meet customer needs or be competitive unless they improve their communications capabilities. Data communications capabilities are evolving into a basic business requirement.

——*Data communications allows the spanning of great distances.* With data communications, whether in the form of telephone or other types of links, you can communicate with anyone in the world almost instantaneously. The trend toward globalization of business, discussed throughout this book, is in large part an outgrowth of the evolution of data communications capabilities around the world. But it goes beyond business: Television pictures of athletic competitions, political gatherings, and national celebrations around the world can be transmitted in an instant. You can be an eyewitness to events around the globe without leaving the comfort of your residence.

——*The costs and capabilities of data communications are changing.* Communications costs are dropping, both because of increased competition and because of technological advances in the telecommunications industry. At the same time, firms are spending more (often increasing from 30 to 100 percent or more per year) to improve business activities.

——*All of the preceding changes will affect everyday life.* National newspapers, printed simultaneously at many locations throughout the country, depend on data communications. So, too, do networks of automated teller machines (ATMs), providing you with access to your funds regardless of where you travel. Electronic mail allows you to remain in contact with associates and friends no matter where you are. These are only a few of the countless ways that advances in communications affect you.

In the future, more spectacular ways of using data communications technology will emerge. The combination of human creativity and technology will lead to advances that play a larger and more significant role in personal and business activities. This evolution will continue.

Evolution of Data Communications

There are many milestones in the history of data communications. Alexander Graham Bell's first words on the telephone—"Watson, come here; I want you"—are often associated with the start of **telecommunication:** the use of the telephone system as a channel for communication. Until 1983, the telephone system in the United States was dominated by the American Telephone & Telegraph Company (AT&T). That year, however, after a lengthy legal action initiated by the Justice Department, AT&T was required to divest itself of the various Bell System companies. The breakup of the telephone company created numerous Bell Operating Companies owned by seven regional Bell Operating Companies (RBOCs) (see Figure 9.1). Long-distance service is now provided by AT&T, MCI, U.S. Sprint, and other communications companies. The intent of divestiture was to provide customers with better, more economical service and new products; this goal continues to be realized. Increased competition has been another consequence of the breakup of the telephone company. In addition, a distinction is now made between service levels (Figure 9.2). *Basic service,* which is supplied by the common telephone company carriers and is regulated by the Federal Communications Commission (FCC), provides only for the transportation of messages, whether voice or data. No processing of the information occurs. *Enhanced service,* which is not regulated by the FCC, includes some processing of the information. Processing may be as simple as converting the speed or coding of transmitted information, or it may be more extensive.

Figure 9.1 Regional Bell Companies and Bell Operating Companies

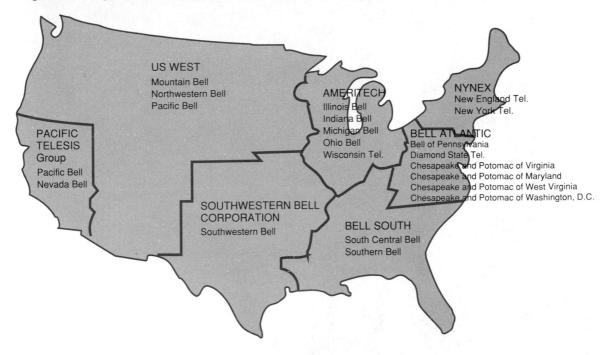

Computing continues to evolve in its use of communications for the transmission of data. The early computers required dedicated cables strung throughout buildings, with the users at the same site. Today, however, the use of ordinary voice-grade telephone lines for the transmission of data dramatically increases the number of sites that could interconnect with the computer. For all practical purposes, with the appropriate connection equipment, any location serviced by telephone lines can be put on-line as a remote user site.

Today, devices of all types—from personal computers to large mainframe systems—send and receive data involving distant locations. The public telephone network continues to play an important role in data transmission, linking locations around the world. Other means are also in widespread use.

Components of Data Communications

The components for data communications are transmission channels, communications control devices, and channel attachments. Each type is needed regardless of the size of the computer used or the nature of the data transmitted.

Transmission Channels

In data communications, a **channel** is the highway along which data travel from one location to another. It is the combination of media that interconnects the sending

Figure 9.2 Basic and Enhanced Telephone Services

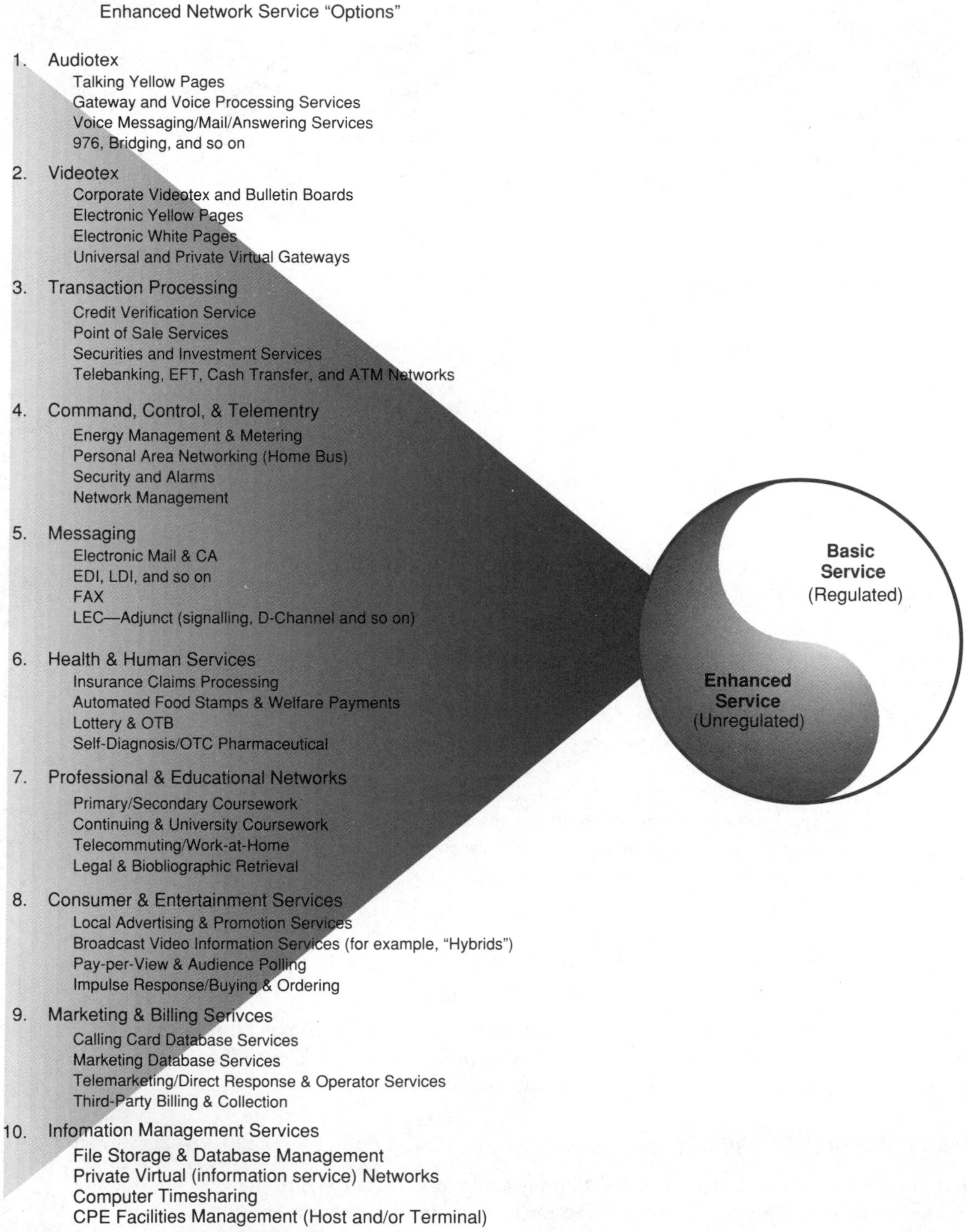

Enhanced Network Service "Options"

1. Audiotex
   Talking Yellow Pages
   Gateway and Voice Processing Services
   Voice Messaging/Mail/Answering Services
   976, Bridging, and so on

2. Videotex
   Corporate Videotex and Bulletin Boards
   Electronic Yellow Pages
   Electronic White Pages
   Universal and Private Virtual Gateways

3. Transaction Processing
   Credit Verification Service
   Point of Sale Services
   Securities and Investment Services
   Telebanking, EFT, Cash Transfer, and ATM Networks

4. Command, Control, & Telementry
   Energy Management & Metering
   Personal Area Networking (Home Bus)
   Security and Alarms
   Network Management

5. Messaging
   Electronic Mail & CA
   EDI, LDI, and so on
   FAX
   LEC—Adjunct (signalling, D-Channel and so on)

6. Health & Human Services
   Insurance Claims Processing
   Automated Food Stamps & Welfare Payments
   Lottery & OTB
   Self-Diagnosis/OTC Pharmaceutical

7. Professional & Educational Networks
   Primary/Secondary Coursework
   Continuing & University Coursework
   Telecommuting/Work-at-Home
   Legal & Biobliographic Retrieval

8. Consumer & Entertainment Services
   Local Advertising & Promotion Services
   Broadcast Video Information Services (for example, "Hybrids")
   Pay-per-View & Audience Polling
   Impulse Response/Buying & Ordering

9. Marketing & Billing Serivces
   Calling Card Database Services
   Marketing Database Services
   Telemarketing/Direct Response & Operator Services
   Third-Party Billing & Collection

10. Infomation Management Services
    File Storage & Database Management
    Private Virtual (information service) Networks
    Computer Timesharing
    CPE Facilities Management (Host and/or Terminal)

Basic Service (Regulated)

Enhanced Service (Unregulated)

Figure 9.3 Samples of Communication Cables

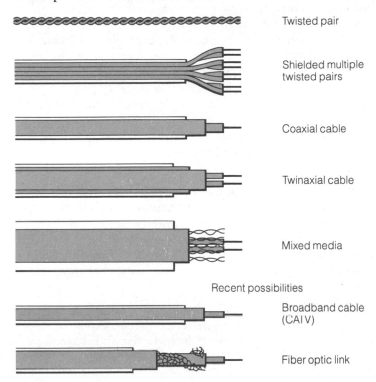

Twisted pair

Shielded multiple
twisted pairs

Coaxial cable

Twinaxial cable

Mixed media

Recent possibilities

Broadband cable
(CATV)

Fiber optic link

and receiving computers. Five media are in widespread use as data channels: tele-phone wire, coaxial cable, fiber optics, microwave transmission, and satellites.

Telephone Wire The channel most people think of for data communications is ordi-nary telephone wire, and indeed, this is the oldest type of communication channel. Telephone wire is often termed a *voice-grade* channel, since it has the properties of the communication channels used to transmit everyday spoken conversations.

The wire itself is actually a pair of wires, each wrapped in a protective coating and twisted one around the other (Figure 9.3). Therefore, information systems people often use the term **twisted pair** when referring to some voice-grade lines. The data transfer speed of voice-grade lines can be from 300 up to 100 kilobits per second. (Frequently heard references to 9600-baud lines are incorrect.*) The actual transmission depends on the modem and on the communication channel, as we will see.

*The **baud** is a variable unit of data transmission speed and the baud rate is the speed at which pulses travel. The baud rate is sometimes the same as the bit rate, but since a pulse can represent several bits at a time, at speeds greater than 1200 bits per second the bit rate generally exceeds the baud rate. Thus a 300-baud line can carry data at a rate of 300 bits per second, but the use of "9600-baud" to describe a speed of 9600 bits per second is erroneous.

The channel used to carry everyday conversations (that is, voice transmission) is limited in its transmission capacity. A voice-grade channel is subject to a variety of distortion effects, as evidenced by the slightly distorted form in which you hear the voice of the person at the other end of a telephone connection. A voice-grade channel also carries control signals such as the off-hook tone, the busy signal, and the ringing signal. All these factors both limit the capacity of the channel to carry data and affect the reliability of the transmission.

In many applications, transmission lines are leased from a common carrier* that does not have the limitations just noted. Such private leased lines have greater capacity, are not subject to control signals of the public telephone network, and provide a high-quality transmission medium.

Coaxial Cable   **Coaxial cable** consists of a single wire supported by insulating material and surrounded by a metal sheath or tube that serves as a protective coating. Because coaxial cable offers much faster data transmission than twisted pair, it is used for underground and underwater lines. It is not susceptible to noise or electrical interference (telephone wire is) and can transmit data over long distances.

There are many different types of coaxial cable, but there are two general categories:

——**Baseband:** carries a single digital signal at very high speeds (millions of bits per second). Boosters are used to overcome the weakening of the signal when transmission must occur over long distances. Signals from multiple sources can be combined on the line through *time-division multiplexing* (the multiplexing function is discussed below; p. 410). Baseband cable is relatively inexpensive and easy to maintain. Speeds range from 1 million to 50 million bits per second.

——**Broadband:** carries multiple analog signals at the same time at different frequency ranges. Suitable for transmission of voice, data, and video, broadband cable is similar to the transmission medium used for cable television. Speeds range from 20 million to 50 million bits per second.

Both types of coaxial cable are increasing in use.

Fiber Optics   The term **fiber optics** designates systems in which minute glass fibers, rather than wires, serve as the transmission media. Lasers, rather than electricity, are used to carry data. As indicated in Chapter 5, a **laser** is a coherent beam of light within a certain frequency range. The light rays are a single frequency and there is minimal distortion in transmission.

Fiber optics offers tremendous advantages in speed, enabling the transmission of data at a rate of several billion bits per second over fibers each as thin as a human hair. A pair of glass fibers can carry 1300 ordinary voice conversations simultaneously. A 1.5-pound fiber optic cable can transmit the same amount of data as 30 pounds

---

*A common carrier is a company that has filed a schedule of rates and charges (a tariff) with the Federal Communications Commission and has been approved by that agency to provide public communication service.

Communication Earth Station

of copper wire. Compared to an ordinary coaxial cable, which can carry more than 5000 voice channels, a single fiber optic cable can carry as many as 50,000 channels.

It is projected that by the mid-1990s fiber optic cables will carry approximately 30 to 50 percent of the traffic now on voice-grade lines. A lightwave system between Atlanta and Dallas makes it possible to transmit the entire contents of the *Encyclopaedia Britannica* over a single strand of glass fiber in less than 2 seconds! The expansion of such capabilities will bring about changes in data communications involving computers as yet unthought of.

Microwave Microwave transmission, which can attain speeds of 50,000 *characters* per second or even higher, involves transmission stations sending data through the air as coded signals. Relay stations or towers approximately 30 miles apart contain devices that receive and transmit data to other stations. If the stations are obstructed by geographical features that block the signals, or if the data must be transmitted over distances so long that the curvature of the earth makes a direct transmission path impossible, the signals are often relayed through orbiting satellites. Due to the increasing cost of establishing ordinary wire communication lines, microwave transmission is being used more and more in the transmission of data.

Satellite Data transmission over long distances, even between continents, often involves orbiting satellites. The data entered into a computer are sent to a microwave station, which in turn transmits them to an earth station (see accompanying photos). From the earth station, the message is beamed to an orbiting satellite (see the boxed insert), where it is relayed back to another ground station. The data are then sent through by microwave and telephone to their destination.

A transponder on the satellite receives and retransmits signals. In effect, the data are bounced off the satellite to the new location. (An intermediate satellite is used when, for example, the data must be transmitted to the other side of the earth and a direct "line-of-sight" beam is not possible.) Just three satellites can cover the entire earth.

Microwave transmission between earth and satellite offers high-speed and relatively error-free communication. An additional distinguishing feature of **satellite communications** is that the cost of transmission is independent of distance. As you know, with other methods, this may not be the case.

Orbiting Communications Satellite

Types of Transmission

Data can be transmitted in either synchronous or asynchronous fashion, depending on the type of equipment. In **asynchronous** transmission, data are transmitted one character at a time. This "start/stop" method is originated by sending a start signal over the line and halted when a stop signal is generated (Figure 9.4).

Business Satellites: A Modern Communications Dimension

At one time satellites were associated with government space programs and were used for weather predictions and defense safeguards. We have also become accustomed to radio and television programs being transmitted "live via satellite." And more than two-thirds of all overseas telephone traffic from the United States is by satellite (the rest is via undersea cable). However, the 1990s have added still another dimension to the use of satellites: Businesses have launched private satellites for commercial digital data communications and computing.

This era of satellite use for private purposes began in early 1981 with SBS-1, the first of several devices launched by Satellite Business Systems, a Virginia-based firm.

These satellites, weighing 2000 pounds apiece, are launched into orbit by powerful rockets. Approximately a half hour after liftoff, the satellite "payload" separates from its carrier. Then the communications antenna is erected as the payload moves into a permanent elliptical orbit that takes the satellite as high as 22,000 miles above the earth at speeds exceeding 20,000 mph.

The launching of these satellites (see Figure A) revolutionized voice, data, video, and document transmission. Business satellites enable users to transmit communications data at speeds of more than 3 million bits per second. And only a fraction of a second is needed to transmit the data to the opposite side of the world.

We are going to be seeing more of this new dimension in communication. Corporations that require large amounts of data transmission are investing in receiving stations to service geographically scattered facilities. Receiving station technology has developed rapidly, and a receiving "dish" about 3 feet in diameter can be located at organization facilities to send and receive data and messages. By purchasing services from satellite owners, a private, intraorganization data communications system can be operated.

The need for high-quality voice communications and face-to-face teleconferencing will undoubtedly interest more companies and federal and state agencies in sharing earth-station terminals. Business travel will probably also decrease in firms using satellite communications. As much as one-fifth of business travel will be unnecessary because of teleconferencing capabilities. Imagine an electronic mail system for major cities. Such a system would relieve many of the burden of written correspondence or difficult telephone conversation (perhaps even reducing traffic on the streets). Information could be sent across town electronically, using a communications satellite for a moderate charge. And key executives, for the cost of a receiving station—only a few thousand dollars—can even have home facilities to maintain communication on important ventures. Private communication via space is not science fiction; it is a reality that will become increasingly common.

Business Satellites (continued)

Figure A Launching Satellite Business Systems

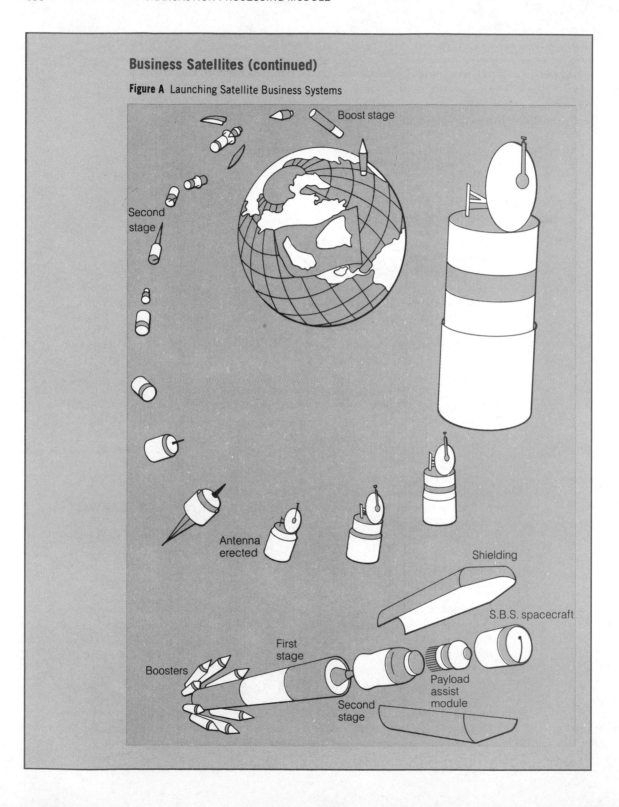

Figure 9.4 Types of Transmission

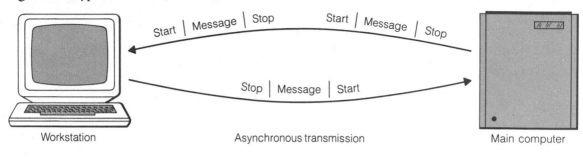

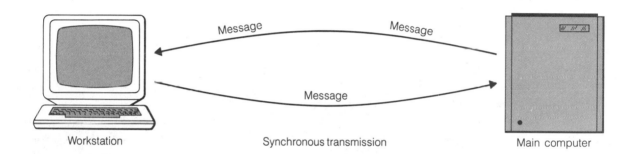

Synchronous transmission, however, is continuous. Characters follow one another over the lines without interruption. There is no need for "start" or "stop" signals, since the process is controlled by a clock mechanism in the system that regulates the transmission. Synchronous transmission is faster because extra signals do not have to be sent over the lines for each character. Large-scale or bulk transmission of data, such as magnetic tape-to-computer or computer-to-computer communication, is synchronous. (See Chapter 7 for a review of this type of communication between hardware devices.) Many keyboard devices and teleprinters, however, are designed for asynchronous transmission.

Communications Control Unit

As you can imagine, the communication of data in a computing environment must occur in a very orderly fashion to ensure that data are not lost or improperly transmitted. *Communications control devices* perform this function by performing the following tasks.

—— Detecting (and correcting where possible) errors in transmission
—— Directing a retransmission when required because of error
—— Routing messages to the proper locations
—— Temporarily storing data when destination devices are busy

Figure 9.5 Communications Equipment Configuration for Data Processing

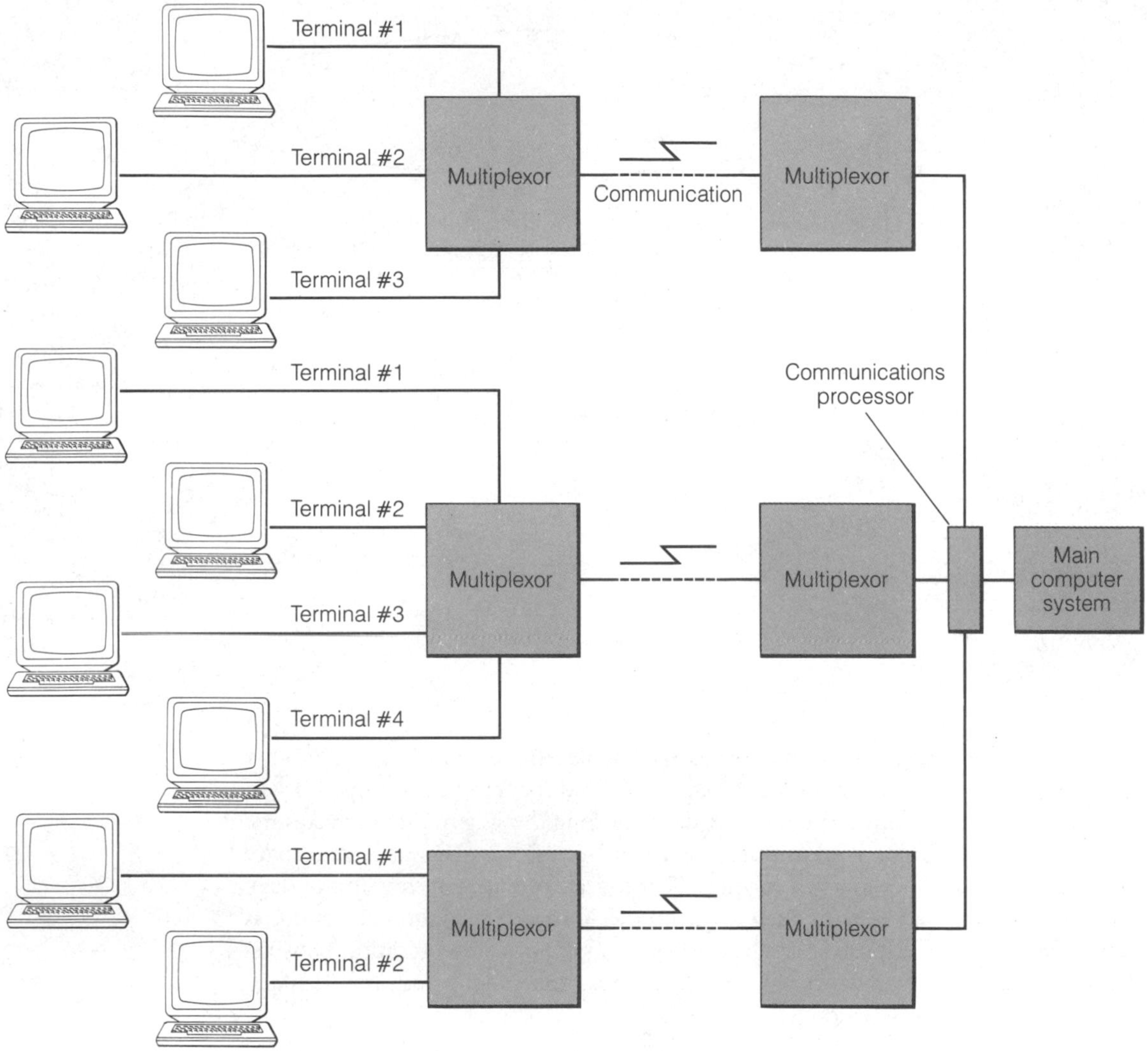

———Managing the interrelation of many communication channels into the computer

———Determining when a remote location (for example, a terminal or another computer) is ready to transmit data

Many installations today use a small computer called a **communications processor** (or a *front-end processor*) as an interface between the main computer and the associated terminals and multiplexors (Figure 9.5). (Discussion of multiplexors is deferred to the section describing channel attachments.)

The major advantage of the communications processor is that it reduces some of the communications work of the central processor. Thus, a good deal of the software that is devoted to the collection and processing of input/output data to terminals is transferred to this device, thereby freeing additional resources in the CPU.

The communications processor also serves as a character-buffering system. It can assemble groups of characters into complete messages before submission to the CPU. In the latter case, the central processor is interrupted only when a complete message has been formulated. Some communications processors can also access parts of a large filing system without going through the main system. When editing, data maintenance, and similar functions proceed in this fashion, even greater system efficiency is realized since the main system can work on more complex processing.

Protocols

For computers to communicate, rules that allow the communicating entities to understand one another must be established. Such a set of rules is called a **protocol.** Consider the conditions under which two people begin, carry on, and end a conversation. Some of the events that usually occur are:

—Gaining the attention of the person to be engaged in conversation

—Allowing each person to identify himself or herself to the other

—Affirming constantly that the speaker is being heard and understood—or advising that the speaker is *not* being heard or understood

—Taking immediate action to determine the nature of the problem if either partner ceases to acknowledge participation

—Terminating the conversation, each party having been satisfied that the other is finished

A computer protocol is a set of codes and rules to accomplish tasks such as the following:

—Getting the attention of the other device

—Identifying each device in the communication

—Verifying continuously that the messages transmitted are correctly received, or that a message cannot be correctly interpreted and must be retransmitted

—Making a recovery when errors occur

Some examples of popular communication protocols are:

—BISYNC (IBM's binary synchronous communication)

—ASCII (American Standard Code for Information Interchange)

—SDLC (IBM's synchronous data link control)

The communication software, in conjunction with hardware, is designed to use a particular protocol. Thus the protocol itself is entirely invisible to the user. For communication to occur, each device must be able to interpret the other device's protocol.

Channel Attachments

In the systems we have discussed, the workstations, terminals, and other devices must be connected to the central processor or to the communications channel. Channel attachment devices accomplish this.

Multiplexors Communications channels ordinarily transmit one message at a time. However, in many instances, better efficiency is achieved if multiple messages can be combined on a single channel. **Multiplexors** are hardware devices that achieve this purpose by collecting several low-speed signals and transmitting them together over a high-speed channel.

As indicated in Figure 9.5, a multiplexor acts as both a switching and a connecting unit when workstations and terminals are linked to the central processor. It scans all terminals and workstations connected to it in sequence, passing along to the CPU any characters or data detected on the lines. It also works in reverse, passing output signals from the CPU to the proper terminal. A multiplexor can handle a number of channels to the workstations, but only one channel is needed to link the multiplexor to the processor.

Concentrators Slower-speed, asynchronous devices are often attached to a **concentrator** to provide transmission. This store-and-forward device collects and temporarily stores the slowly collected data from several input devices in a buffer. When the buffer is full, the data are transmitted over high-speed lines to the computer. (This is in contrast to a multiplexor, which allows several devices or workstations to share a line simultaneously, transmitting data as they are received.)

Modems **Modems** connect computers to the communication channel and make it possible to transmit data over increasing distances without interference from noise and distortion on the channel. The term is a contraction of modulator–demodulator. Data can be transmitted in either analog or digital form, depending on the characteristics of the communications environment. Voice-grade channels transmit analog signals while computers send digital signals. Although many carriers are establishing digital networks specifically for the transmission of digital data, analog lines are still the most commonly used form for data communications. On the sending end, a modem converts digital signals from the computer or workstation into analog form for transmission; on the receiving end, the analog message is translated into the digital form required for processing (Figure 9.6).

In conjunction with the communications software, the modem determines the speed at which the data will be transmitted. Even though voice-grade lines can carry data at speeds up to 9600 bits per second, this cannot occur if the modem is rated at, say, 1200 or 2400 baud (rates commonly associated with personal computers). Communications environments involving midrange and mainframe systems are typically designed to transmit between 2400 and 9600 bits per second.

Direct-connect modems, which attach directly to the communications line (accompanying photos), are the most common and range in cost from approximately

Figure 9.6 Modems for Digital/Analog Signal Conversion

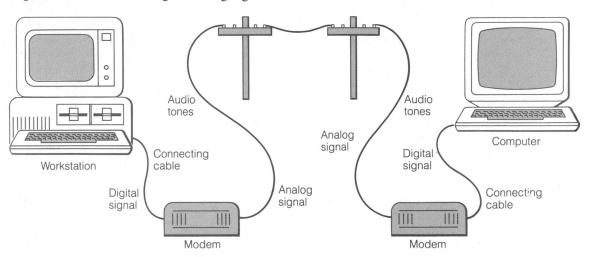

Rack-Mounted Communication Modems

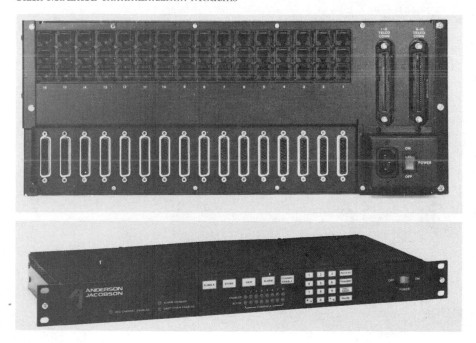

$300 to several thousand dollars. Modems capable of higher transmission speeds are more expensive.

Acoustic couplers are a less expensive form of attaching to a voice-grade line. The coupler accepts a telephone receiver into rubber cups that hold the ear and mouthpieces. Sound devices in the coupler receive and send out signals through the phone piece. The most common form of acoustic coupler transmits at 300 baud.

If the transmission facility is digital rather than analog, a device called a **data service unit** is used.

Attachment to the Modem Computers are attached to the modem through a communication channel built into the computer itself. We will use a common personal computer configuration to demonstrate. One of the most widely used communication standards in the computer industry is called the *RS-232C* interface. This recommended standard specifies the use of a **serial interface** for transmission and receipt of data (the term *port* is synonymous with interface; *serial* means data bits are transmitted one after the other, in a series, as opposed to the parallel arrangement). The type and shape of connection plug to be used are part of the standard, too. The intention is to ensure that any personal computer can be connected to a communications system without modification.

To interconnect a personal computer for data transmission, a standard cable connects the RS-232C port on the computer to a modem (Figure 9.7). The modem in turn is connected to a telephone line using an ordinary modular telephone plug.

Figure 9.7 RS-232C Interface on Personal Computer

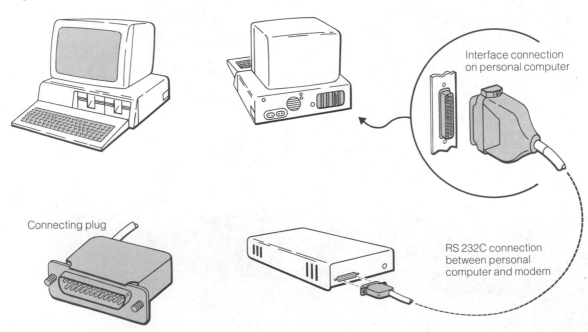

Interface connection on personal computer

Connecting plug

RS 232C connection between personal computer and modem

At the receiving end there is another modem connecting the telephone line to a communication cable, which in turn is connected to the computer system. Through this configuration, data can be quickly and easily transmitted and received. How this occurs will depend on the design of the specific communications software in use.

Data Transmission

The preceding discussion of data communications components mentioned several examples of voice and data transmission. However, additional features of communication lines must be considered, including the types of transmission line and line configurations.

Types of Line

Data transmission occurs through simplex, half-duplex, and full-duplex communication (Figure 9.8). A **simplex line** transmits data in one direction only and the direction can never be changed. To achieve two-way communication in an application, two simplex lines can be combined.

Half-duplex lines also carry data in one direction only, but the direction can be reversed. Thus this system has more flexibility than the simplex line.

A **full-duplex line** can transmit data in both directions simultaneously, as if two simplex lines were going in opposite directions.

Simplex and full- and half-duplex lines can be acquired from the telephone line supplier with different capabilities for transmission speed. Low-speed lines transmit data at rates of 50–300 bits per second and high-speed lines at 1.544 megabits per second. Hence a full-duplex line might be acquired with high or low transmission rate capacities. Full and half duplex currently are about the same in cost. Half-duplex lines are less efficient in terms of transmission because additional time is required to reverse the direction of the transmission.

Line Configurations

The term *line configuration* is used to describe the method of connecting computers, workstations, and terminals in conjunction with communication lines. There are two line configurations: point-to-point and multidrop.

Point-to-Point Lines When data communication first became important in information systems, organizations began to acquire a capacity for **point-to-point** communication of data. A data transmission line was used to connect a remote user directly with the terminal at another location (Figure 9.9). Today the user may have another computer, a workstation, or a terminal. However, the concept of a single location connected directly to a computer remains unchanged.

Point-to-point or single-drop lines are economical when the single location transmits or receives a large amount of data traffic so that there are relatively few

Figure 9.8 Types of Communication Lines

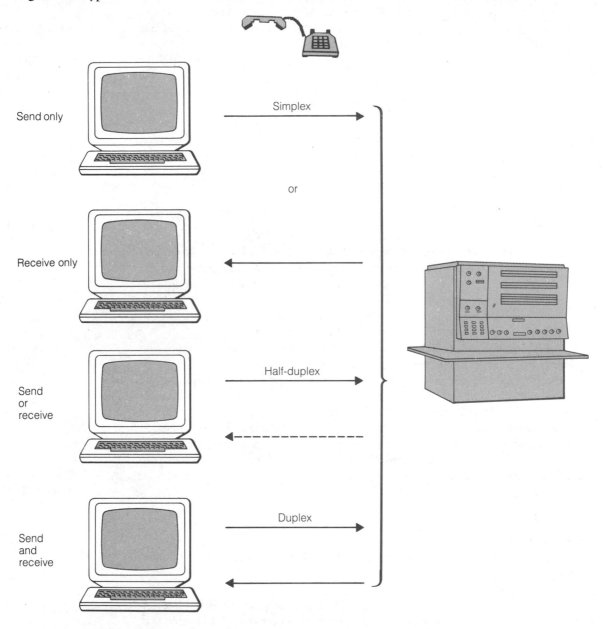

unused or idle time periods on the line. This line configuration is also used when a fast response time must be guaranteed and delays due to others sharing the line would be intolerable. Point-to-point lines are frequently used between large computers that communicate with one another continuously.

Figure 9.9 Line Configurations

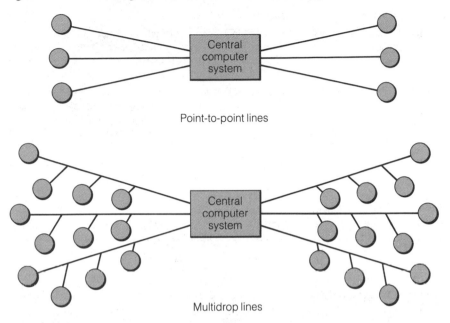

Point-to-point lines

Multidrop lines

Multidrop Lines Like telephone party lines, **multidrop lines** permit the communication channel to be shared by all users on the line. The advantage is that the total cost of the user network may be reduced, since line sharing decreases the quantity of communication lines. Furthermore, all points on the line can receive the same data at one time if necessary. This is much easier and more efficient than sending a separate communication to each workstation or computer location. However, only one site can transmit at a time. Users at other locations have to wait for access to the line. The multidrop configuration is most likely to be used when the communication lines are long and connecting sites are many miles apart.

Networks

Often the capability to communicate data or to share resources, such as occurs in time sharing, leads to the development of networks. This section examines the network concept and the most common network topologies.

The Network Concept

A **network** is a group of interconnected computers, workstations, or computer devices (such as printers and data storage systems). The devices may be near to one

Table 9.1 Well-Known Large Research and Academic Networks

Network	Sponsor	Description
ARPANET	Department of Defense	Developed in 1960s for the nationwide sharing of hardware, software, and data. Initially linked research computer centers in 20 locations on the East Coast, in the Midwest, and on the West Coast. Now includes locations in Hawaii and Europe.
BITNET	Cooperative network	Began in 1981 when City University of New York and Yale University were interconnected. Now consists of over 1300 host computers at several hundred sites, primarily universities. Also includes the constituents' networks: NETNORTH in Canada and EARN in Europe.
CSNET	Self-supporting	Developed in 1980s to facilitate development in computer science. Began with electronic mail services. Administered out of Cambridge, Mass.
NSFNET	National Science Foundation	Developed in mid-1980s to link institutions conducting research.

another or far away and may be interconnected using any of the transmission channels discussed earlier. Table 9.1 lists several well-known public networks.

There are two types of network. **Communications networks** transmit data, voice, or visual images. Computer technology is used to assist in the transmission process. In contrast, **distributed processing networks** link different components to share resources and processing capability. Both types of networks will be examined in greater detail after we have introduced the associated topologies illustrated in Figure 9.10.

Bus Topology

A **topology** is the arrangement of **nodes** (sending, receiving, or processing sites) for transmitting data. Depending on the topology, data may travel over different paths or transmission configurations. The **bus topology** is a linear channel, such as a length of cable. Taps on the cable link individual nodes to the **bus** (Figure 9.10). Thus, the configuration is that of a multidrop line.

The bus topology is often called a **broadcast topology** because every message or set of data sent on the bus goes to every node. An individual node recognizes only the messages actually addressed to it.

Star Network

In the **star topology,** many different sites are interconnected for transmission of data through a central computer system. As shown in Figure 9.10, all communication between points in the network must pass through the central computer, which in turn passes the data along to the stated location. *Network switching,* as this process is called, requires a real-time computer to analyze the transactions received to determine

Figure 9.10 Basic Network Topologies

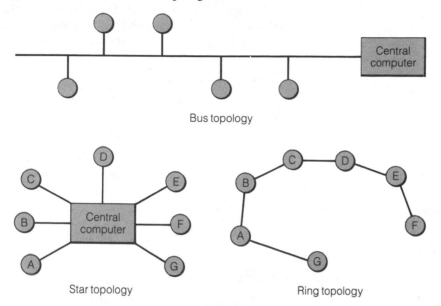

where the data are to be sent and to select the best route or line over which to transmit them. All control operations for the lines and the terminals are handled by the message switching unit (that is, the CPU) at the center of the network. Network switching centers are almost mandatory in large star networks to reduce the cost of transmitting great amounts of data.

The outlying points in a *star network* are comparable to the telephones in a single exchange. When we use the telephone to call someone, we dial a number, which is processed through a central telephone exchange. The exchange makes the proper connection so that we reach the number we have dialed. The exchange is the center of the telephone network for a small area and takes care of all the switching operations (that is, makes sure that the "data" are transmitted to the number that was dialed). Star networks do not follow a broadcast topology.

Ring Network

In the **ring topology,** data do not have to pass through a central computer system; that is, one point may communicate directly with any other point. Front-end processors (communications processors) handle communication activities at each location, storing data for brief periods before transmitting them or receiving a transmission from another location.

Ring networks use a broadcast topology. Messages pass from node to node in one direction. The computer scans the message from the preceding node for an address that it recognizes. If the message contains the proper address, it is read. Otherwise, it is sent ahead to the next node.

Selection of the proper network configuration depends on four primary criteria: the distance between points, the amount of time permissible for transmissions, the amount of data to be transmitted from one point to another, and whether each site has intelligence. Weighing each of these factors should suggest the best approach for a particular situation.

Communications Networks

The purpose of a communications network is to interconnect multiple locations that have a need to transmit or receive data. As we will see, communications networks need not provide processing capability at all. Three types of communications network are important: wide-area, local-area, and value-added networks.

Wide-Area Networks

Wide-area networks have two distinguishing characteristics:

1. They span a broad geographical distance from a few miles to thousands of miles (even between continents).
2. They use common carrier networks, such as the switched telephone network.

As the following examples indicate, the general purpose of a **wide-area network** is the transmission of data:

——A retail store accumulates sales data throughout the day and stores them on disk. At night, another computer at corporate headquarters polls the system in the retail stores. The data are transmitted over leased telephone lines back to the central site, where processing occurs and the data and the results are stored. A summary of results is returned to the retail store. This communication sequence is repeated for each of the several hundred stores owned by the corporation, which are located hundreds, even thousands, of miles apart.

——A computer vendor installs a communications modem at the customer site whenever the company puts a new computer system in place. The modem is connected to the ordinary office telephone line. Whenever a modification is made to an important software program, the vendor can transfer the software from its central computer to the customer's computer, where it replaces the earlier version. In this instance, software, not data, is transferred over the communication lines. The vendor can distribute the software over a wide area using the public dial-up telephone system.

——A researcher operates a bulletin board using a personal computer. The research-er's computer serves as a host, receiving and accepting messages from colleagues. The bulletin board is accessible on a dial-up basis, and remote users can interact by using a personal computer equipped with a simple software program and a 1200-baud modem, a dumb terminal, or a printing terminal. Individuals all over the world can tie into the bulletin board.

——A hospital leases 2400-bit-per-second communication lines to each of its four remote clinics, located 20–30 miles from the main hospital. A dumb terminal installed at each clinic allows office and medical personnel to query the hospital's patient database concerning medical history and ongoing treatments. Charges for treatments and services can be transmitted for processing on the hospital's mainframe computer. A printer in the medical office allows staff members to prepare paper copies of data retrieved from the hospital. Each clinic can access the computer system 24 hours a day, and, because of its point-to-point line, users are assured of immediate connection.

Value-Added Networks

Wide-area networks are often independently designed by organizations. Although they are controlled by common carriers in the sense that the carriers determine the transmission rates customers can acquire or the routing that will be used in interconnecting two leased lines, individual organizations often write their own network specifications. Another alternative, the **value-added network,** has emerged to improve the cost effectiveness of communications networks for some organizations. To better understand the benefits of value-added networks, which use a technique called packet switching, let's first look more closely at data movement in wide-area networks.

Data Movement Often the method of moving data in a network is the key to effectiveness. Data movement in the network configurations discussed in this chapter can be accomplished in different manners, and the following common methods are represented in Figure 9.11:

1. **Circuit switching.** In this method communication circuits are available for a transmission routing from one location to another *before* the communication process starts. While the program is running and data are being transmitted, the system has continual and exclusive use of the communication link. At the end of transmission, the link is released to other users. This approach is common in today's dial-up telephone systems. Availability of transmission links is not guaranteed, however, because it is possible to receive a "busy signal" when lines are in use. The number of paths that can be used to establish a connection between two users is limited only by the number of branch exchanges.

2. **Message switching.** Conventional message switching (sometimes called **store and forward**) is similar to circuit switching in that full messages of data are transmitted via a predetermined transmission routine. Lines are not dedicated, however. Thus in moving from node to node it is possible to encounter busy signals. When this happens, indicating that a certain link is in use, the message is temporarily stored (say on magnetic disk). When the link is available, the message is removed from storage and transmitted on toward its destination. During peak times, temporary storage of data is common.

3. **Packet switching.** Transmission routings become important in packet switching, which differs from "store and forward" mainly in that messages are stored only in primary memory; there is no temporary storage, as in

Figure 9.11 Data Movement in a Network

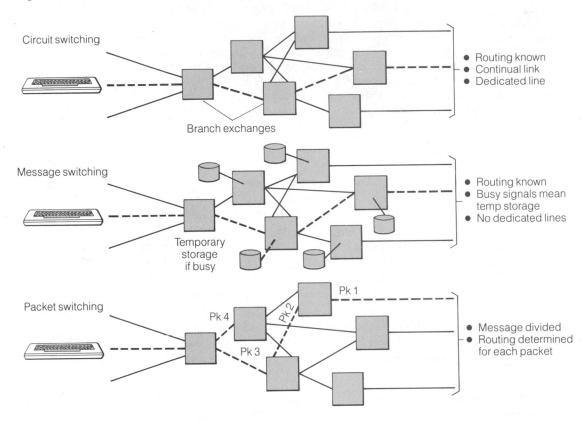

message switching. Messages are divided into blocks, or *packets,* of a standard size (often 100–250 characters each, including information to identify the packet). A complete message may therefore occupy several packets. Each packet is transmitted over a route that may be *determined at transmission time* or dynamically (that is, at each node). When two or more routes are available as options, we speak of the *alternate routing method.* There is also an *adaptive routing method,* in which routing is selected dynamically at transmission time, depending on the amount of transmission traffic and the condition of the transmission lines. Packet switching is more complex than circuit and message switching. Despite delays that are possible under heavy traffic conditions, however, this method provides more reliable transmission assurance due to the alternate routings. At the same time, it can be more economical because the network has higher utilization.

As discussed later in the chapter, packet switching is especially attractive in large distributed processing systems, since it can accommodate quite nicely changes in equipment at each location, as well as fluctuations in traffic and transmission volumes, and variety in data.

Economics of Packet Switching Value-added networks use packet switching. However, the networks are not dedicated to an individual organization. A company establishes a network and sells *subscriptions* to use it. Users pay only for the amount of data they transmit (plus perhaps a subscription fee for access privileges). Users are generally charged a rate based on the number of packets transmitted. Distance often is not a factor in determining the charge.

The "value" in value-added accrues in several ways. First the subscriber does not have to make an investment in the network equipment and software. But savings in line charges and transmission costs may also be gained. Value-added carriers lease communication channels that may consist of voice-grade lines, satellite links, and other communication channels. In turn, they provide access to their channels, sharing the costs among the users. The rate is often lower than if the users acquired their own leased lines or if they paid premium dial-up rates. But the main advantage is that growth and fluctuation are more easily accommodated.

Economic considerations play a significant role in selecting a switching method. In determining which transmission method to use, both the amount of usage over a given period and the distance the data will be transmitted are important. When a limited amount of transmission is necessary on a monthly basis and distance is short, ordinary telephone communication is probably the most economical method. When transmission distance is moderately short but monthly usage is high, leasing telephone lines is generally the most cost-effective choice. However, when transmission is over moderate to long distances and monthly usage is low to moderate, packet switching is most economical.

Local-Area Networks

A **local-area network (LAN)** is a communications network that spans a single site. "Site," however, does *not* mean "building." Rather, the term implies the interconnection of offices and buildings that are relatively close to one another and the existence of a need for regular communication (Figure 9.12). Local-area networks may link workstations, terminals, and other pieces of computer equipment that are only a few yards apart, or they may span distances of 5–10 miles. For example, a local-area network may interconnect workstations in a single office, buildings on a university campus, the baggage, ticketing, and passenger facilities at a metropolitan airport, or machines and inspection stations in a large factory.

LANs are developed for one or more of the following reasons:

———Distribution of information and messages (including electronic mail, as discussed in Chapter 15)

———Distribution of documents (such as engineering drawings and blueprints)

———Equipment sharing (including printers and disk storage file servers)

———Interconnection with a public network

LAN Carriers In contrast to wide-area networks, LANs do not use common carrier facilities but have their own networks of interconnecting devices. Coaxial cable is

Figure 9.12 Local-Area Network

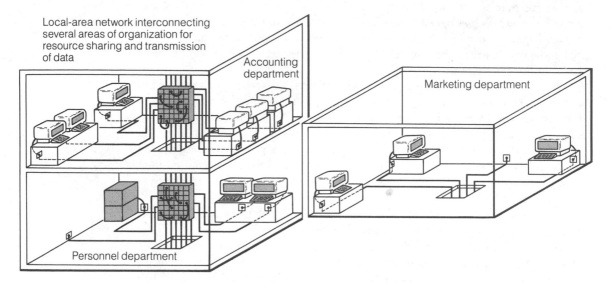

Local-area network interconnecting several areas of organization for resource sharing and transmission of data

Accounting department

Marketing department

Personnel department

the most frequent channel, although twisted-pair wire and fiber optic cable are used in some situations.

Most local area networks use a broadcast topology: Every message is sent to every node; messages are acted on at a node only if addressed to that node. Coaxial cable serves as the bus, and terminals, workstations, printers, and computers tap onto the bus (Figure 9.13).

Xerox Corporation has taken the lead in promoting the bus topology as a standard for local-area networks. Ethernet, as the standard is called, prescribes the broadcast topology and describes the appropriate coaxial cable for establishing the network. The Ethernet standard, which has been adopted by such computer manufacturers as Digital Equipment Corporation (DEC) and Apple Computer, uses the CSMA access method, described later.

The ring topology is also promoted in LAN environments. It uses twisted wire pairs but may also be designed for coaxial cable or fiber optics. This topology is often the least costly way to implement a local-area network, but allowable communication distances are shorter, and if one node fails, such that it cannot transmit or pass on data, the entire system will be unusable.

Some organizations implement local-area networks using a star topology that operates over the existing telephone switching system called the **private branch exchange (PBX)** or, if it is computer-based, the **computer branch exchange (CBX).** This strategy makes it unnecessary to rewire a building to install coaxial cable. In general, there are higher error rates on twisted-pair networks when data are transmitted at high speeds.

LAN Access Methods Two access methods are popular in the design of local area networks. The **carrier sense multiple access (CSMA) method** is used with bus

Figure 9.13 LAN Access Methods   423

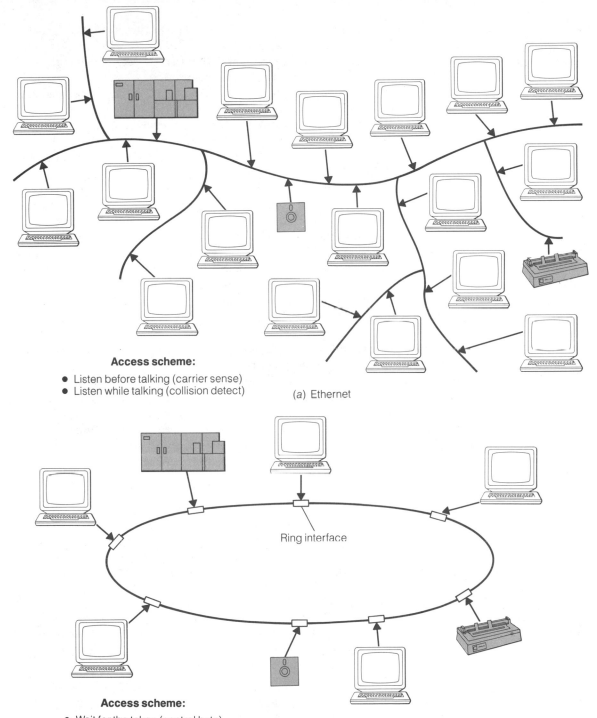

Access scheme:

- Listen before talking (carrier sense)
- Listen while talking (collision detect)

(a) Ethernet

Ring interface

Access scheme:

- Wait for the token (control byte)
- Remove the token
- Transmit your data
- Replace the token

(b) Token ring

networks and requires the workstation or other device to "listen" to the channel to determine whether it is in use; that is, it must *sense that the channel is occupied.* If the channel is not in use, a message can be sent. Otherwise, the workstation waits for a brief moment and then listens to the channel again.

Because multiple terminals may be on the line at the same time, messages sometimes "collide." This can happen if a message is about to travel past a certain point just as the line is being sensed. When the message is put on the line, it collides with the one already there. To manage the network better and to provide methods of dealing with collisions, a variation on this access method, **CSMA/CD** (where CD stands for collision detection), is often used.

The other access method we will discuss, the **token passing method,** is associated with the ring topology. A token is a string of bits sent around the network. Whenever a device wishes to transmit a message, it waits for the appearance of the token and then transmits its data on the network. After transmission, it returns the token to the network. Collisions are avoided with this method because there is only one token; hence only one node can transmit at a time. Token passing is effective in a network designed for heavy traffic, to ensure balanced access to the network. However, if traffic is intermittent, nodes will experience unnecessary delays waiting for the token when they could be transmitting.

Bridges and Gateways In some organizations, information systems requirements entail the interconnection of networks for the passing of messages, documents, or data from one network to another. If networks are of the same type—that is, are homogeneous—they are interconnected by a **bridge.** The bridge accepts transmissions from one network and directs them to appropriate locations on the other. When the networks are different, say a LAN and a wide-area network, the interconnection is made through a **gateway.** It converts message codes and formats, addresses, and data transmission rates into a form acceptable to the other network.

Connectivity

Users and computer professionals alike frequently discuss information systems in terms of connectivity. This section explains the concept of connectivity and discusses its importance in the development of computer networks.

What Is Connectivity?

Simply stated, **connectivity** is the ability of a user to interact with other elements on the system freely—that is, to connect to any other component, anytime, and anywhere. The philosophy behind connectivity is:

——Users do not care where the computing resources they use are located. Whether they are in the next room or hundreds of miles away is immaterial so long as they are accessible and meet the users' needs.

——Both computer and communications network resources should be unobtrusive from the users' standpoint. The less visible the system components are, the better, since the real reason for using the system is to retrieve and process information in support of a business activity. Users should be able to focus on this business activity, not the computer and communications components.

——Networks and information systems will increasingly be heterogeneous.

Connectivity is both a means and an objective.

Why Is Connectivity Important?

Information systems networks have evolved from their early reliance on homogeneous components to heterogeneity. *Homogeneous systems* consist of components provided by a single vendor; examples might include an all–IBM system or an all–Digital Equipment system. Often such systems have been application specific. For instance, firms developed network-based systems for linking their manufacturing plants.

Heterogeneous systems integrate multivendor components in a manner that enables all components to function together effectively and invisibly. Furthermore, heterogeneous systems are almost always application independent. Many applications share the same network simultaneously. Flexibility is thus the watchword of heterogeneous systems, and they are the basis for the connectivity in the fullest sense of the term.

Figure 9.14 illustrates the way heterogeneous networks are evolving. Local-area networks consisting of a variety of workstations and shared storage devices (file servers) are interconnected with packet networks. The same packet networks, which may be public or private—managed by the users' firms—are also shared by other dedicated applications systems.

Regional networks link other systems consisting of mainframes, workstations, and so on. And nationally based and regional networks interact to transfer information, messages, and transactions.

The entire network is flexible. It can be reconfigured to meet changing business needs. New networks can be developed and interconnected. Likewise, the components in one network can be altered without affecting other networks or the interaction between them.

Connectivity in the environment just described means that users are not aware when data is sent from one network to another. The entire system is *seamless*, since the networks interconnect and data flow across the interconnections automatically and "invisibly." As data communications capabilities increase, connectivity will expand the boundaries of distributed systems. Information systems technology will continue to evolve, making the distribution of data and information more and more effortless from the standpoint of end-users.

Distributed Processing Networks

Distributed processing networks interconnect sites not only for communication of data and messages but also for the sharing of resources. A systemwide operating system oversees the allocation of resources, but the locations of the resources used by an

Figure 9.14 Heterogeneous Network Connectivity

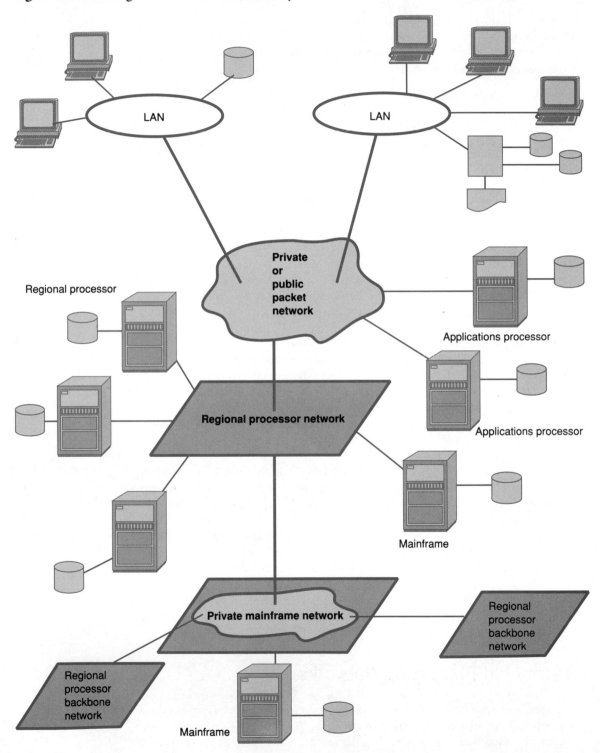

individual or an application are not necessarily known by the user. Thus distributed processing uses a communications network *plus* an additional layer of software for management and processing.

This new dimension in data processing has been made possible by such factors as the availability and affordability of mini- and microcomputers, the use of intelligent terminals, and improvements in the technology and economics of data communications. Because now small computers can do processing at locations where data are collected and events occur, data can be stored at these locations, and summary reports and information sent to other managers or to headquarters only when the need occurs (Figure 9.15). **Distributed processing,** as this is called, is the next logical step in the evolving data processing scenario. Point-of-sale systems are an example of distributed processing systems: Each terminal is a small computer that does selected data processing.

We will discuss other aspects of distributed processing in the sections that follow, but first we must establish what distributed processing is *not*. Having a front-end communications processor as part of a system to handle data communications work is not distributed processing. Neither replacing a mainframe computer with several minicomputers maintained in one center nor tying in to a computer through a typewriterlike terminal or CRT constitutes distributed processing. Remote data entry is not distributed processing either.

You may hear discussions about "distributed data entry systems," but such key-to-tape, key-to-disk, and key-to-diskette systems that allow several persons to key in data to be stored in a single system are not considered to be distributed processing as discussed in this chapter. Small, stand-alone computer systems also do not comprise distributed processing. Although these systems *could be components* in a distributed system, merely having them in an office does not constitute distributed processing. The essential communication link is missing.

To summarize, merely dividing up the work among departments and having it carried out on free-standing computer systems, as illustrated in Figure 9.16, does *not* constitute distributed processing. Rather, the features of distributed processing are: locating computing facilities at remote locations, having these systems do the majority of the data processing for that location on-site (rather than transmitting data for processing to a centralized facility), and linking these locations to a central facility or to other locations in a communications network.

Advantages of Distributed Processing

It is virtually impossible for one computer system to satisfy all processing demands that are made on it if the demand is very high or if dramatically different types of processing are required. Distributed networks allow a number of computer systems to be made available and shared by all users. The design of some computers favors business processing activities; scientific computing, on the other hand, may consist of lengthy and demanding computations performed on a relatively small amount of input. Still other computers are designed to output graphic images.

Figure 9.15 Hierarchical Distributed Processing System with Distributed Data

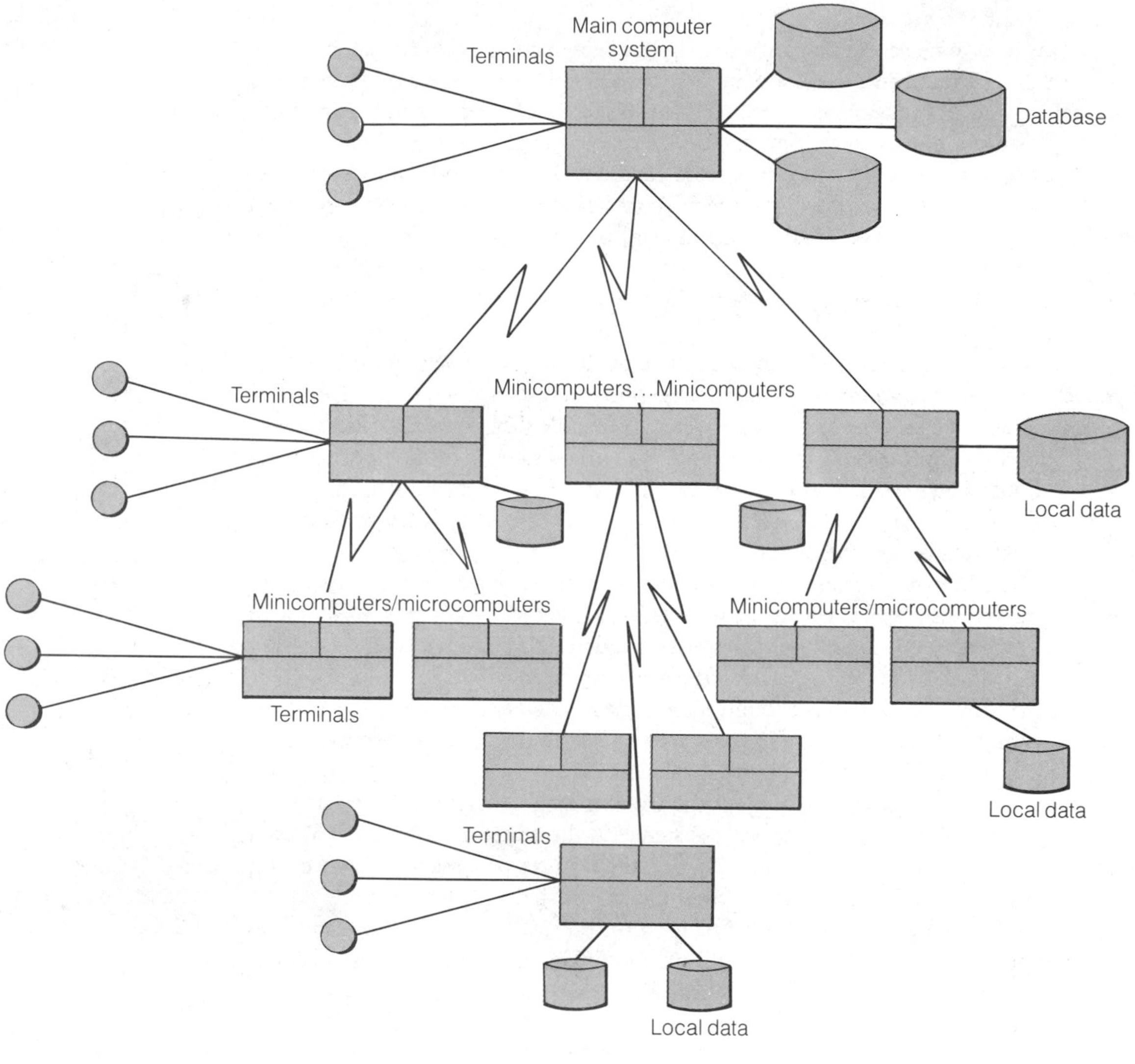

In many corporations with multiple facilities, peak computer requirements occur at different times across locations. The peak period for an East Coast facility probably will not coincide with the peak for the same company's California offices.

Distributed processing makes it possible to share systems, through communications networks, so that the proper amount of computing power is available to all users. For example, a computing job that requires more memory than is available on the user's own system can be transmitted to another system for processing. One might prefer to think of distributed processing as a set of different modules or

Figure 9.16 What Distributed Processing Is *Not*

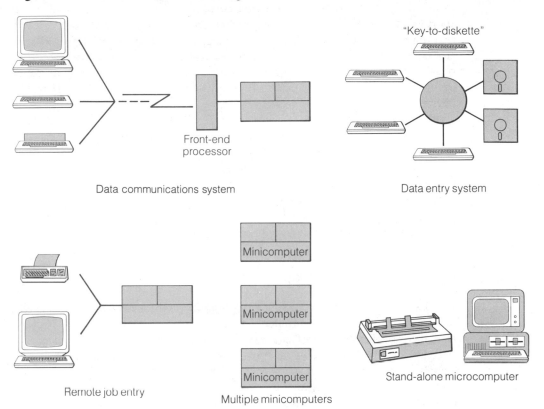

Data communications system

Data entry system

Remote job entry

Multiple minicomputers

Stand-alone microcomputer

building blocks. Each module consists of separate computer equipment programmed to do specific types of processing, depending on the needs of individuals using the equipment. Much of the processing is done within the module, thus limiting the need for communication to a larger computer.

The advantages of networks are quite significant. Individual companies are now establishing nationwide networks, and independent computing networks are being formed among a variety of organizations, both public and private. Many believe that the establishment of computer networks is a major step closer to the advent of utilities for computer power like those we now have for electric, natural gas, telephone, and other necessary services. This is particularly foreseeable for commercial networks that sell their services to anyone willing to pay the fee to utilize them. In the meantime, networking offers two advantages to present business users.

Load Sharing Distributed processing networks make available a large amount of computing power to users with small systems or just remote terminals rather than a full computer system. Since networks include connections between both computer systems and terminals at remote locations, the efficiency with which computer systems can be operated is increased. For example, a computer that is not being used for a brief period can be switched over to process work for another user. **Load sharing,** as this is called, is also helpful when one computer is overloaded or experiencing hardware problems. In these instances, the user benefits by improved turnaround and the assurance that the network will provide the necessary access to computing facilities. Access to many computers rather than just one is an attractive feature for all users who are concerned about whether their computer system will be operating when needed.

Software Sharing   An additional advantage of networks is the ability to share data and software. For example, a large file of government economic data that is used often by several sites can be stored at one site and shared by the others. This approach also serves to reduce the total cost of data storage for all users. Similarly, since fewer large systems are required, minicomputers can replace some costlier hardware. Finally, program storage can be centralized to permit the sharing of the software itself. This means that more extensive software packages can be developed at a lower cost to each installation.

Designing Distributed Systems

The design of distributed processing systems builds on the general network concepts introduced earlier. In effect, each node in the networks pictured in Figure 9.10 could be another smaller network. This means that large systems might consist of *levels* of systems. Each node undoubtedly contains some type of processor, which in turn communicates with other nodes in the system. The node unit could be a micro-, mini-, or maxicomputer. Any of the various communication methods we have discussed could be employed to link nodes together.

The systems at each node can probably be configured in various ways. As Figures 9.15 and 9.17 show, various combinations of printers, CRTs, data entry devices, and terminals may be used to accomplish the work at that location.

Distributed Data

Data too are often distributed. In fact, the very definition of distributed processing implies that sets of data will be stored at the nodes in the network, for it is at these locations that the highest use of data is most likely to be made. The data may be simple master files, or they could be formal databases. The storage of data at nodes in the distributed network was illustrated in Figure 9.15.

But merely having data stored at remote locations does not constitute distributed data. Rather, the network concept and availability of the data to other locations is important in bringing the distributed data idea to life.

Distributed Processing Applications

Many large firms in the United States manufacture and warehouse products for sales to customers. National firms tend to be regionalized to control sales and distribution of products in geographic regions. Manufacturing is often spread across more than

Figure 9.17 Distributed System for Manufacturing Enterprise

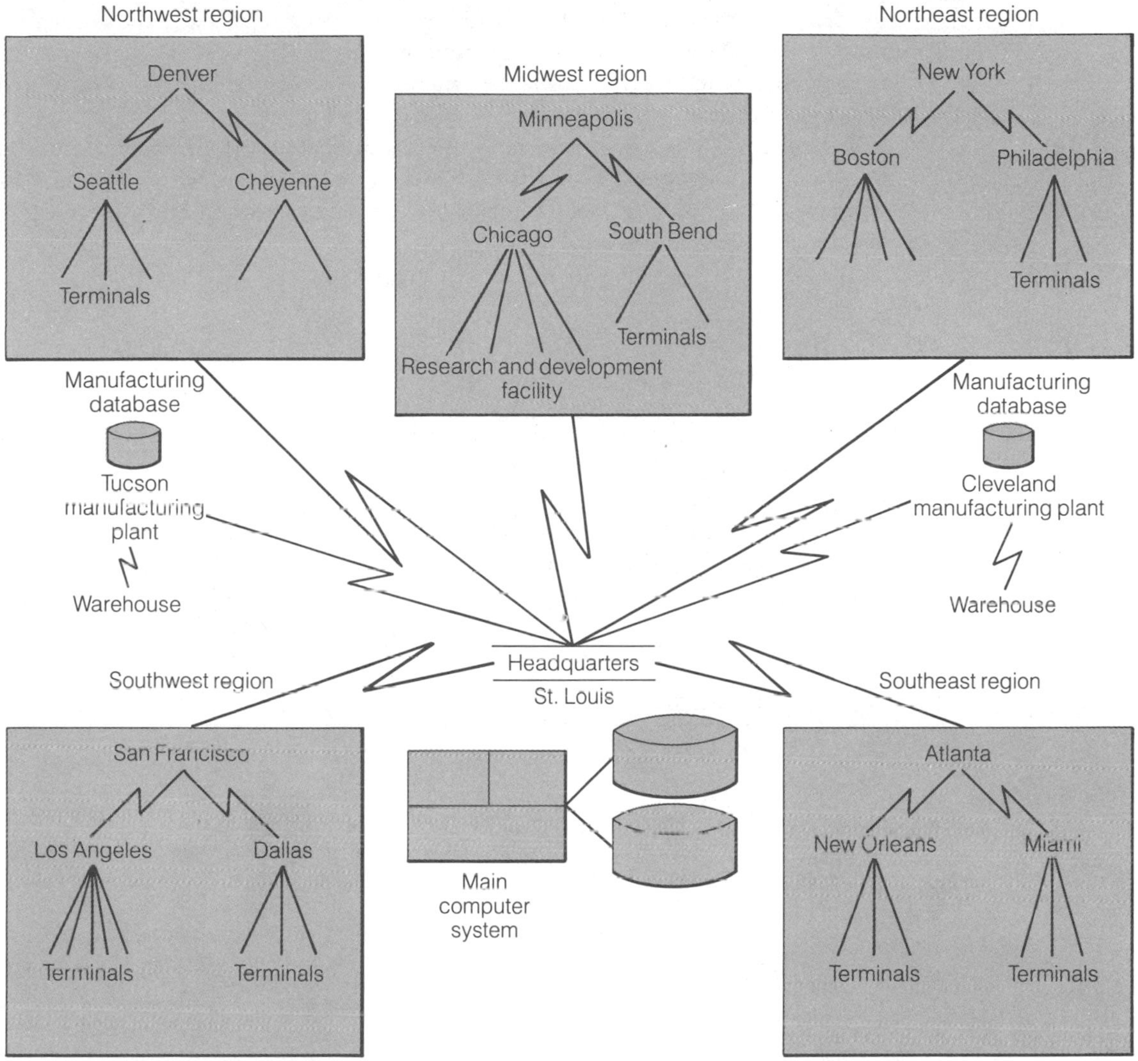

one plant, and research and development activities are performed at still another location. Each plant has its own warehouse facilities, while within the manufacturing plants there may be a need for separate computer facilities to control manufacturing operations independent of warehousing.

Corporate regions each have headquarters, along with field offices in major cities. At each regional facility, computing is done to track sales, inventory, financial information, and personnel activities. But the field offices in the major cities also use computers to do data entry, sales, and financial processing. Thus several levels of processing have been developed.

There is no need to develop distributed processing to manage and control all these facilities. However, since headquarters must have information about operations at each remote location (but not all the data needed by the field offices), a distributed network to link the facilities into the headquarters is logical. A review of Figure 9.17 will point up the linkage of the various levels in a star network. Communication between field and regional offices is also possible (in the event that transshipment of merchandise is necessary, for example) by communications through the central, headquarters node.

ISDN

The public telephone network is in transformation to an all-digital capability. This will result in new services. The most significant may be the ability to transmit all types of information (data, voice, and image) over a *single* type of network. For this reason, **Integrated Services Digital Network (ISDN)**—the name given to this network capability—is emerging as an important means of data communications (Table 9.2).

Table 9.2 ISDN Service Offerings

Residence

1. Dial tone
2. Touchtone
3. Custom calling services
   • Call forwarding
   • Call waiting
   • Three-way calling
4. Point of sale
5. Videotex
   • Home banking
   • Shopping
   • Information, reservations
   • Entertainment
6. Energy management
7. Home security
8. Meter reading
9. Class—CCS (Advanced Custom Calling Services)
   • Call block (nuisance call reject)
   • Call return
   • Repeat dialing
   • Call trace

   • Selective call forwarding
   • Selective call waiting
   • Call monitor
   • Call tracking
10. Calling party number display
11. Call completion to busy subscriber
12. Voice announcements
13. Alternate bjlling
14. Store and forward
15. Human personal service—lifeline support
16. Hi-fi voice
17. Video broadcast
18. Video billing
19. Video two-way
20. LADT (packet switching)
21. Personal computer
22. Customer direct access
23. 2B + D
24. Residence centrex

Characteristics of ISDN

ISDN is characterized by (1) all-digital communication channels that have the capability of interleaved bit streams that carry voice, text, data, and image transmissions; (2) standard interfaces for subscriber access—telephones, computers, and printers, among other devices, that will all interconnect with the network in the same manner; and (3) customer selection of a broad range of services provided by the carrier. Customers will be able to configure their communications services to meet their needs, changing from one service to another or activating additional channels, as the need arises.

ISDN is software driven. This means that new services can be added to the network at any time, and with minimal cost. Switched (dial-up), leased, and packet switched services will be available as separate services in combination with one another. All of them, including packet services (discussed later in the chapter), will be offered directly to the customer without the need for third-party involvement.

ISDN Service Levels

Two service levels—basic and primary—are available, with the service distinctions centering around line capabilities (see Figure 9.18). Basic service will include two channels that transmit data at 64 kilobits per second (KBS) and one channel that transmits at 16 KBS, all on a single fiber optic line. Enhanced service, most suitable in business rather than residence settings, includes twenty-three 64-KBS lines and data transmission and an additional 64-KBS line used for control signals (for example, call waiting).

Services and Applications

McDonald's, the well-known hamburger chain, was among the first to commit to ISDN usage, but other firms are following. Residential uses for digital transmission of voice, data, text, and image are in their infancy.

Services available through ISDN will include:

——High-speed facsimile
——Electronic mail
——Teleshopping
——Voice mail
——Automatic display of calling number
——Automated electronic filing of data

(Many of these services are described in greater detail in Chapter 15.) Since ISDN will be based on digital switches, which are for all practical purposes computers, they will be able to provide these services—ones that are not typically available through traditional telephone capabilities.

The most significant benefit could be that individuals and organizations may be able to exchange information throughout the world, at very high speeds, as easily as

Figure 9.18 ISDN Components

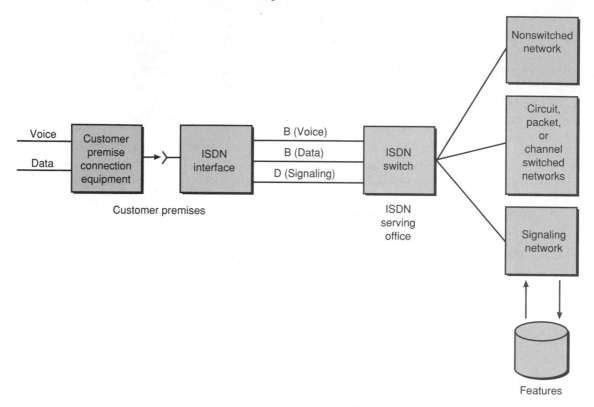

picking up a telephone. ISDN is being developed globally; for example, many European countries plan to convert large portions of their telephone system to ISDN soon.

The potential uses of ISDN is a topic of lively discussion in many organizations. Here are several examples that demonstrate the range of applications that may evolve:

——Using calling number identification to:
  - route incoming calls to the proper customer agent assigned an account
  - automatically retrieve records for better personal service
  - automatically authorize access to records or approve transactions

——Using image transmission capability to:
  - provide access to medical x-rays and images for diagnosis from any location that can be interconnected by telephone
  - deliver printed materials (books, reports, drawings, musical scores, copies of paintings, and so on, including graphics) electronically from any location to any other site

——Integrating image, voice, and data to:
  - enable conference calls featuring multiple parties at different locations, each of whom can see an image of the other on their display screens while simul-

taneously examining the same drawing or other graphic object, also appearing on their display screen

- provide on-line training, or reference video programs
- reduce the cost of communications by transmitting all three types of data over a single transmission link

Because ISDN will be available over public telephone networks, the same capabilities will be available to large and small firms alike—even to individuals.

ISDN Controversy

ISDN is not without controversy. Most of the discussion centers around whether there is a real need for ISDN. Those speaking against it point out that none of the services (for example, voice mail, electronic mail, or facsimile transmission) are new; all are available in one form or another now. Therefore, opponents suggest that ISDN may be obsolete by the time it is fully implemented sometime in the 1990s.

Proponents, on the other hand, indicate that telephone companies *around the world* are committed to ISDN as a universal system that is publicly available to all who want it. They also suggest that even though many services are available now, they are not *integrated* to the extent they will be under ISDN. And they suggest that the applications, not the technology itself, will be the key to its success. These applications will develop with experience as ISDN becomes fully implemented.

The arguments on both sides of the issue appear to have merit.

Summary

Data communications capabilities allow the interconnection of users at different locations with workstations and computers of all sizes, which also may be at different locations. The components for data communication include transmission channels, communications control devices, and channel attachments. The common transmission channels are provided by twisted wire pairs, baseband or broadband coaxial cable, fiber optics, and microwave and satellite communications. Transmission channels differ in speed of transmission, distance covered, and cost.

Communications control devices ensure that transmission occurs in an orderly fashion. A protocol specifies the rules of transmission, including the use of synchronous or asynchronous methods. It further states how communicating devices identify one another, begin and end transmission, and detect errors.

Channel attachment devices connect workstations and computers to the channel. The nature of a given device controls the speed of transmission (measured in bits per second), and also determines whether a link is dedicated or shared during a particular interval of usage.

Transmission lines are of three types: simplex, half-duplex, and duplex. Point-to-point lines connect a single location directly to the host computer, and multidrop lines allow multiple devices to share the same line.

Networks interconnect computers, workstations, and other computer devices for the transmission of data, voice, or visual images. A network that permits the sharing of resources is termed a distributed processing network. Depending on the topology used, communication may be along a linear channel (called a bus topology), through a central node (a star) or directly between points in the network (a ring configuration).

Communication networks are classified as wide-area and local-area networks. The telephone system represents the wide-area network concept; its distinguishing features are its span of a broad geographical area and the use of common carrier networks. An alternative to common carrier facilities is the value-added network. Through the technique of packet switching, a value-added carrier allows multiple users to share its communication facilities. "Value" is "added" by saving the subscriber the investment in communication facilities and managing the sharing of costs among all users. Growth and fluctuation in user transmission needs are easily accommodated.

Local-area networks, in contrast to wide-area networks, span a single site, typically interconnecting nearby buildings or offices. They do not use common carrier facilities. Most local-area networks use a broadcast topology and rely on coaxial cable to link participants in their own network of interconnecting devices. Alternate designs may use bus, ring, or star topologies. If necessary, organizations can interconnect local-area networks into wide-area networks through interface devices called gateways.

Distributed processing networks make it possible to connect different locations for the transmission of data while at the same time permitting the sharing of resources. The distributed system uses a communications network as well as a layer of software that manages the network and processing activities. The remote locations in a distributed network share data, transmit information, or even share the processing load. It is expected that distributed systems will become increasingly common as advances in hardware and communications technology continue to improve capabilities and to reduce costs.

Integrated Services Digital Network (ISDN) is the name given to the emerging network capability that will allow all users access to digital services over the public telephone network. In addition, individuals will have standard interfaces for all types of equipment and the capability to select services from a broad range of options. The two levels of service, basic and primary, will form the basis for a variety of services such as voice mail, electronic mail, high-speed facsimile, and automatic display of calling number. Many of the services already exist, but they are independent and not integrated within a single transmission source. Organizations will benefit from these services if they build them into applications that meet the needs of the enterprise.

Key Words

Acoustic coupler	Baud	Broadcast topology
Asynchronous	Bridge	Bus
Baseband	Broadband	Bus topology

Carrier sense multiple access (CSMA) method
Carrier sense multiple access/collision detection (CSMA/CD) method
Computer Branch Exchange (CBX)
Channel
Circuit switching
Coaxial cable
Communications network
Communications processor
Concentrator
Connectivity
Distributed processing

Distributed processing network
Fiber optics
Full-duplex line
Gateway
Half-duplex line
Integrated Services Digital Network (ISDN)
Laser
Load sharing
Local-area network (LAN)
Message switching
Microwave transmission
Modem
Multidrop line
Multiplexor
Network

Node
Packet switching
Point-to-point line
Private branch exchange (PBX)
Protocol
Ring topology
Satellite communications
Serial interface
Simplex line
Star topology
Store and forward
Synchronous
Telecommunication
Token passing method
Topology
Twisted pair
Value-added network
Wide-area network

Review Questions

1. What is connectivity? Why is connectivity an important concern in the integration of computers and data communications capabilities into organizations?

2. How is the advancing capability associated with data communications changing the world of business? How is it affecting individuals?

3. How are data transmitted to and from the main computer in a communications environment?

4. What are the different types of channels used in data communications? What features distinguish each?

5. How do broadband and baseband cables differ? What are the advantages and disadvantages of each?

6. In what ways will the use of fiber optics change data transmission capabilities? Why?

7. How are simplex and duplex lines different in terms of transmission capabilities?

8. What purpose is served by a protocol? Is a protocol necessary in all data communications situations? Explain.

9. What is a multiplexor, a communications processor, a concentrator?

10. Compare and contrast asynchronous and synchronous transmission.

11. Distinguish between circuit switching, message switching, and packet switching. What are the advantages and disadvantages of each?

12. What are nodes? What types of equipment can they use? What determines selection of particular equipment?

13. Why should organizations consider the user of midrange and personal computer systems in distributed systems (in contrast to having large-scale systems at each location)?

14. Discuss the costs, advantages, and disadvantages of networks.

15. What are the types of local-area networks? What features characterize each?

16. Distinguish between wide-area networks, local-area networks, and value-added networks.

17. What is the Ethernet standard? What alternatives are there to using Ethernet?

18. What is load sharing? Software sharing?

19. How is communications managed in a distributed processing system? What channel alternatives are typically used?

20. Does distributed processing automatically mean having distributed data? Explain.

21. What characteristics distinguish ISDN? Why is it important in the evolution of data communications technology?

22. "ISDN will be obsolete when it is fully implemented in the nation's public telecommunications network." Discuss both sides of this issue.

Application Problems

1. A large interior decorating firm that specializes in business offices is evaluating the value of ISDN as a way of increasing its service to customers and therefore improving day-to-day sales. The firm prides itself on good customer service. Among the many features of its service is a personal sales representative. Each customer has an assigned personal service representative who is familiar with the customer's facility, including the decorating scheme (for example, color of walls and carpet, type of draperies, and individual pieces of furniture) as well as past purchases. Customers know they can call their sales representative with a question and receive advice or suggestions that fit their particular situation.

   The sales manager wishes to devise a way to automatically have information about past sales, items currently on order, and past credit history available to the representative who accepts a call from a customer. In addition, the manager would like to assign a representative to each account and automatically have incoming calls routed to the representative, providing even more personalized service. Yet when the assigned representative is out of the office, the manager wants to have another representative accept the call, but still provide pertinent background information.

   a. How can ISDN play a role in meeting the needs of the sales manager? Explain the reason for your answer.

   b. Discuss the way features of ISDN and computer processing can be linked to provide those accepting incoming calls with the details of orders and credit.

   c. Suppose it is also desirable to have images of room interiors and layouts accessible, on-line, to the representative accepting the call. Can this be done using computer processing? Does the capability to do so depend on ISDN? Explain.

2. An information systems manager in a large organization has been asked about the feasibility of doing away with the firm's mainframe systems. Instead, they will be replaced with a distributed system that links various mid-range and personal computer systems together. It is proposed that the computers will be from different manufacturers and will each run different application software.

   What questions should be raised to determine whether the idea is feasible?

3. The Sporting Goods Company operates a chain of sporting goods stores in Florida. Each store maintains a large stock of inventory for all major sports, including golf, bowling, football, baseball, soccer, track, tennis, racquetball, and squash. In addition, the stores stock and sell exercise equipment and sports clothing. The stores are scattered throughout the state, with large concentrations around major cities, such as Jacksonville, Orlando, Tampa, and Miami. The company itself is headquartered in the northern city of Daytona. Currently the chain includes 81 stores, but an expansion program will enlarge the number to over 100 stores dispersed throughout the state.

   Because of increasing costs associated with carrying large quantities of inventory, the firm is searching for ways to reduce the stock maintained in each store. However, the firm wants to carefully balance this reduction against the consumer demand for merchandise. It does not want to be out of stock on any requested item—losing a sale or jeopardizing future sales from a customer are not acceptable alternatives.

   Each store is equipped with the latest point-of-sale terminals that accumulate data on items sold, including the stock number and quantity sold. At the end of the day, this information is printed out through the terminal, although the terminals have communication capability that would allow data to be transmitted electronically to other devices or even to different geographic locations. Each store has between 10 and 20 point-of-sale terminals.

   Management is considering the use of data communication to improve inventory management. It wants to retrieve the data from the point-of-sale terminals on a daily basis to determine what has been sold. A comparison of this information with data maintained in the company's mainframe system about merchandise sent to the store should indicate the quantity of items on hand. Inventory data can be compared with sales trends and projections to determine when additional stock should be sent.

   a. Discuss the merits of a distributed processing system versus a large network in which each terminal is connected directly to the company's central computer. For each alternative, what communication and computer equipment is needed to create an operational system? (Keep in mind that each store has multiple point-of-sale devices with communication capability.)

   b. What communication channels should management consider? Why? Explain the rationale for choosing or eliminating from consideration dial-up, leased line, microwave, and fiber optic links.

4. A nationwide insurance company wants to give its agents the ability to interconnect with a special computer system located at its headquarters. Under the plan, individual agents scattered throughout the United States will be able to dial into the system over ordinary telephone lines. Accessing the system will permit them to receive policy quotations for different types of insurance. The system will support the following functions:

   Policy premium cost quotations for different types and amounts of insurance, depending on the age, sex, occupation, and health status of the prospective policyholder

   Status reports on whether the premium is due, overdue, or paid for a particular policy; this information can be retrieved only if the agent provides the policy identification number

   A listing of all policies, including information on the type, amount of coverage, and premium amount, held by an individual; agents must provide the name and identification number of the policyholder in order to retrieve the information.

As the system is currently conceived, agents will use any of three different models of a personal computer to communicate with the main system. Option selection and data will be entered through the agents' computer keyboards. Retrieved information may be displayed or printed by the agents, depending on their needs. The delay between the agent's submission of an inquiry and the receipt of a response should typically be less than 10 seconds.

a. Is the concept of a nationwide system based around dial-up communication capabilities feasible? Why or why not? Is it cost effective for the intended usage?

b. What features must be built into the mainframe system in order to permit the system to be used as designed? What hardware and software will be needed in addition to the mainframe system itself?

c. What software must an agent have to use the system as described? What functions must the software perform? What other hardware, if any, will be required in order for the agent to use the system?

d. If the system will be designed to communicate at the rate of 2400 bits per second, can the public telephone network be used? Is transmission required to be synchronous or asynchronous due to transmission at 2400 bits per second? Is 2400 bits per second within the communication capabilities of a personal computer? Explain.

5. Which transmission channel(s) (twisted-pair, coaxial cable, fiber optics, microwave, or satellite) is/are appropriate in each of the following cases?

a. When the lowest cost voice-grade medium is specified

b. With transmission of data at rates of 75,000 characters per second over distances of 10 to 20 miles in hilly terrain

c. If transmission rates of 1 billion bits per second are needed and high communication traffic density will be common

d. If video data must be transmitted at speeds in excess of 10 billion bits per second

e. For establishment of a local-area network

f. With high-speed transmission of data combined from several different sources; transmission will occur over long distances

6. A large hospital of 1500 beds spans 6 different buildings covering a 20-acre section of land. Hospital administrators wish to improve the communication of patient data needed for diagnosis and treatment. At the same time, management of financial data must be more efficient, ensuring that charges are entered into patient records as they are incurred. The hospital operates a large computer center and has a well-trained and experienced staff.

The director of information systems has suggested to hospital management that it consider development of a local-area network to interconnect patient, treatment, and administrative areas. As proposed, physicians in laboratories will have access to the patient database to view patient medical history. Guidance on laboratory procedures can also be retrieved from a separate database.

Direct patient-care systems will be included in the planned network. Such systems will allow digital transmission of x-ray images, heart and brain scan graphs, and laboratory microscope pictures.

Patient and facility schedules (for example, surgical suites) will be maintained and updated through the local-area network. Dietary menus will be displayed over in-room televisions and patients will select the foods they wish in each meal through special terminals attached to the televisions.

The same televisions can be used by physicians to show medical data, x-rays, and medical images to patients, right in their rooms. Other televisions will be linked into the network to display images and data for training purposes elsewhere in the hospital's teaching classrooms.

General hospital and administrative procedures are also expected to benefit from a local-area network. Accounting will receive charges for medical and laboratory procedures electronically from the points of origin. Patient admission and discharge data will be received from the nursing stations. And pharmacy charges and medical supply costs will be transmitted to the accounting office from the terminals that will be located in each of the departments.

Hospital officials would also like to transmit voice data over the network.

   a. What features suggest that a local-area network is either appropriate or inappropriate for the hospital?
   b. Can the network described above also be used for voice transmissions?
   c. What transmission channels should be used to develop the network?

7. Which line configuration (point-to-point or multidrop) is most appropriate under each of the situations listed below?
   a. Financial data must be transmitted between individual locations. There is a single receiver in all cases.
   b. Catalog sales stores will submit orders to a single processing center. The center frequently wishes to transmit announcements and instructions to all stores at the same time.
   c. Individual medical clinics must communicate with an emergency center for the transmission of patient data and vital signs; delay is not permissible in emergency situations.
   d. A local-area network based on Ethernet.
   e. Sporadic data transmission will occur from various sites to a central location and economy of line costs is important.

8. A large corporation wants to increase its operating reliability by establishing two geographically separated information systems centers—one on the East Coast and another in California. The two centers will be interconnected to allow transmission of data for processing from one location to the other. If one center is experiencing computer problems but is able to transmit data, the data can be sent to the other center for processing. Similarly, the corporation wants to allow programmers at one location to work on a computer at the other location to develop and debug software.

It is expected that processing will occur at one location with the results sent to the other location for printing. Since there is a three-hour time difference between the locations, one center can take advantage of off-peak times at the other center for better resource usage.

The firm is planning to use a satellite link for transmission of data.

   a. Is this a distributed system or simply a communications network? Explain the reason for your answer.
   b. Can programmers at one location write software using a computer at a different site? If so, why? If not, why not?
   c. What advantages does a satellite link offer over leased lines between the two locations?

Minicase: The New Border Wars[1]

It is a bizarre exercise in "data transfer": computer disk packs, containing the data files of a major American bank, are loaded into a station wagon in Toronto. Then the disk packs are driven over the border to the bank's branch in Buffalo, New York, where the files are loaded onto the computer system. Why not transmit the files electronically from Toronto to Buffalo? The reason is that Canada is one of several countries with strict laws regarding transborder data flows. As a result of the Canadian Banking Act of 1980, all foreign banks in Canada must maintain and process their data within Canadian boundaries.

This is just one illustration of a new barrier that is being erected along national boundaries. It is intended to stop the passage not of political ideas or illegal aliens but of information. The combined technologies of computers and communications make it technically possible to transfer information rapidly and accurately between any two points on earth. And many of our everyday human activities depend on our doing just that, twenty-four hours a day: airline and rental car reservations, credit transactions and credit checks, stock and commodity exchanges, and so on. But many governments are not prepared to tolerate such free movement across their borders, for reasons of politics, privacy, or protectionism.

In consequence, several governments have set up legal limitations on "transborder data flow," in both directions. Brazil, Mexico, Norway, and West Germany protect their information industries by forcing foreign countries to do all their data processing within those nations. The Data Inspektionen, a privacy inspection board in Sweden, told West German computer giant Siemens A. G. in 1975 that it could not electronically transfer personnel files from its Swedish branch to Munich headquarters. Siemens wanted to use its big computers in Munich to process the branch's payroll, but the Swedes protested that the files contained private data on nationality, family, job qualifications, and education that the Germans should not have.[2]

The restrictions apply not only to bits of raw data. Information services, and the people with the skill to provide the services, must also confront the barriers. The Belgian and Canadian governments, among others, place restrictions on commercial visas, making it difficult for U.S. firms to bring American specialists into those countries to train indigenous information experts or to repair equipment. Brazil imposes controls over the import of computers and other data processing and communications hardware. U.S. airlines must overcome political barriers to obtain permission to connect up to the reservations computers in some western European countries.

Many governmental restrictions are aimed at outside companies—particularly American ones—that broadly depend on advanced systems for handling information. The Norwegian gov-

---

[1] Excerpted from John Diebold, *Making the Future Work*. New York: Simon & Schuster, 1984, pp. 308–310. Subsequent footnotes are those of the source.
[2] Bruce Nussbaum, *The World After Oil*. New York: Simon & Schuster, 1983, p. 166.

ernment, for example, has not licensed a foreign insurance firm since the 1940s. Major American law firms have been refused permission to open offices in Tokyo. Australia forbids the screening of television commercials that have been filmed overseas. West German regulations require the use of German models in all advertising produced in that country.

This type of limitation is particularly trying to the U.S. for a number of reasons. Despite recent competition from Japan and western Europe, the U.S. remains the world's dominant power in information technology. Its service industries, which largely rely on such technology, have consistently had a positive influence on the U.S. balance of trade. That influence is threatened by the restrictive information policies now being formulated and put into practice by foreign governments. Harry L. Freeman, senior vice-president of American Express, has stated the dilemma: "If we in the postindustrial West are to allow Brazilian steel and South Korean shoes to penetrate our market, our dynamic service industries must in turn be allowed to compete on world markets without unfair and burdensome restrictions."[3]

Further undermining U.S. efforts to obtain genuinely free flow of data across national borders is the fact that no international institution exists to control or encourage movement of information.

The General Agreement on Tariffs and Trade (GATT), which protects most of the trading rights of nations, is the obvious model. But no "information GATT" has yet emerged. Despite U.S. persistence, few other countries have been eager to deal with the subject through the GATT machinery. What progress has been made in controlling transborder data flows has been painstakingly hammered out in bilateral negotiations. "In the absence of international agreements that would allow nations to act together to alleviate each other's concerns, they will act alone," explained Royal Bank of Canada chairman Rowland Frazee.[4] The problem with such unilateral approaches is that they will probably produce a Balkanized international information policy—a set of rules so Byzantine that the free flow of information from one point to another around the world will become a politically unattainable goal.

We are living in an age when orbiting communications satellites can serve as Space Age traffic cops for data flows from all over the earth. They are oblivious to national boundaries. What controls are appropriate to a technology that by its very nature transcends national borders? What governing body should regulate transborder information flows? Will we ever see a global information order? What are the societal costs of not having one?

---

[3] Harry Freeman, "If America Were Allowed to Sell Its Services to the World," *Washington Post,* Jan. 25, 1983, Op Ed page.
[4] Quoted in Glenn Flanagan, "Bank Proposes Canada–U.S. Pact on Computer Services," UPI Wire, Nov. 7, 1983, 7:17 P.M. EST.

Information Systems Module

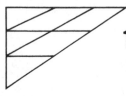

10: Transaction Processing Systems

Key Questions

What is a transaction processing system?

What sequence of activities is followed in transaction processing?

How do transaction processing system outputs differ?

What are the most common transaction processing systems in organizations?

What features are included in accounting systems?

How are accounting transaction systems organized?

How do systems for processing order transactions differ?

Automation and Change

Three phases of change related to automation:

——*First—mechanize what was done yesterday.*

——*Second—it is found that the task changes; the technology revises* what *you do, not just* how *you do it.*

——*Third, as a result of this transformation, the greatest change of all occurs in society.*

John Diebold, *Making the Future Work*

The term *information system* (or *computer-based information system*) does not refer to a single type of system, but rather to several. This module examines the features of each type of system in detail. Examples of applications in each category are also explored. Before discussing transaction processing systems, however, we review the categories of information systems introduced in Chapter 1.

Categories of Information Systems

Information systems consist of categories of systems, each system having different characteristics. Some are aimed at supporting operating-level activities, while others are oriented toward the most difficult decisions, often having an identification with top-level managers and the corporate boardroom. As outlined in Table 10.1, the categories are transaction processing systems, management information systems, and decision support systems.

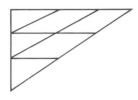

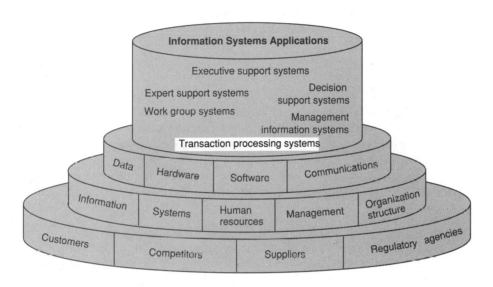

Table 10.1 Categories of Information Systems

Category of System	Characteristics
Transaction processing system	Substitutes computer-based processing for manual procedures; deals with well-structured routine processes; includes record-keeping applications
Management information system	Provides input to be used in the managerial decision process; functions to support well-structured decision situations, for which typical information requirements can be anticipated
Decision support system	Provides information to managers who must make a judgment about a particular situation; supports decision makers in situations that are not well structured

Transaction Processing Systems

The data and information processing technology available to organizations does, as we have mentioned, make it possible to process large amounts of data and information rapidly and to integrate management aids into the decision-making process. Speed of processing is particularly important when there is a high volume of transactions and operating activities. **Transaction processing systems** substitute computer processing for manual record-keeping procedures. The most important feature of these systems is their facility in dealing with well-structured and routine processes that computers can easily handle. The procedures may be repeated many times during the course of a day, week, or month. They are also well understood, to the extent that clearly specified procedures can be formulated. Because of these features, it is logical that these procedures be implemented on computers.

Typical examples of transaction processing systems include payroll preparation, account management, and savings account interest tabulations. Because these areas are well understood, clear operating procedures can be specified for each one. Organizations that invest in data processing usually start with record-keeping applications precisely because they are best understood, and because they pay for themselves quickly. However, the aim of record-keeping systems is the processing of high volumes of data, not providing support for decision making.

Management Information Systems

Some information systems applications are aimed at supporting the decisions managers make. Unlike transaction-oriented record-keeping systems, **management information systems** are aimed at assisting in decision making. They provide accurate, reliable, and valid information, whenever such information is needed.

Information systems do not make decisions or even tell managers *how* to make decisions. Rather, they provide information that is input to the decision process. Computers are not necessary to develop information systems. In fact, many effective and efficient manual information systems have been developed and are in use. However, many more are being automated. (We look at these systems in considerably more depth in Chapter 11 and throughout the remainder of the text.)

Decision Support Systems

Decision support systems provide inputs to the decision process, but they do not replace the need for human judgment. Thus they do not make decisions but provide the information managers want to make decisions. They are used more often at upper management levels, where decision making is nonroutine and highly unstructured.

In our discussion of the characteristics of decision support systems in Chapter 12, we will examine systems that must be designed for use in situations that are always changing. The individual may use various sets of data together with models to answer a series of "what if" questions on solutions to different problems. The details of decision support systems differ, but in each case the intent is to provide information processing assistance for nonroutine, and often nonrecurring, decision processes.

Why Should You Know About Transaction Processing Systems?

This chapter will explore several different kinds of transaction processing systems, including their features and their purpose. It will also point out several elements of the design of such systems with an eye on how various features affect their use. Among the reasons why it is important for you to know about transaction processing systems are the following:

⸻*Everyone uses transaction processing systems.* Even if you are not a member of a particular firm, you are often a user, whether direct or indirect, of its transaction processing systems. Placing orders for merchandise or service, making travel reservations, withdrawing money through an ATM, or making a payment to settle a bill all involve interaction with transaction processing systems. As you know, some are better designed than others.

⸻*Transaction processing is essential in business.* The collecting and processing of transactions is a daily function. Carrying out these functions properly allows the firm to conduct its business.

⸻*Reports to management depend on transaction data.* Often management's actions depend on the reliability and accuracy of the data describing business activities. If transaction data are not reliable, or if they are out of date, decisions based on the data may be inappropriate and even harmful to the longevity of the business.

⸻*Transaction processing systems involve many persons.* The day-to-day use of transaction processing applications involves customers, suppliers, staff members, and many others. They may provide data, interact with the system directly (such as by using a terminal), or use reports prepared as a result of transaction data. Information systems professionals and users alike have a responsibility to develop the right transaction processing systems.

⸻*Transaction processing is more than substituting automation for manual processes.* The capture and processing of data generates new information. Automating accounting functions, sales processes, or even the checkout process at the grocery store will simultaneously generate data useful for other purposes, such as inventory management, purchasing, marketing, or distribution systems. A single system can lead to many other changes in an organization, with benefits (or detriment) for many persons.

Depending on your background, you may wish to add other factors to this list. However, we will use the preceding reasons as a guide for the discussion that follows.

The Transaction Processing Sequence

Transaction processing follows a sequence (Table 10.2), and each activity in the sequence leads to one or more other transactions. The timing of the activities depends on the characteristics of the system. In some instances, processing must be immediate, while other systems delay processing.

Table 10.2 Activities in the Transaction Processing Sequence

Activity	Description	Form of Input or Output
Data capture	Acquisition and recording of data	Terminal
		Terminal
Transaction processing	Data validation (check for errors, missing data, reasonable values, and validity of transaction)	Exception report
	Correction of errors	
	Retrieval of data from system files to facilitate processing	
		Exception report
File maintenance	Modification of master files to reflect effect of transaction	Floppy disk
		Floppy disk
Reporting	Generation of output, including action documents, information documents, and summary reports	Printout
		Printout

Data Capture

As transactions occur, data about the events must be captured and recorded. If the system is manual, this activity may be as simple as writing down important details. For example, a manual sales system will include the handwriting of a sales slip that describes each transaction, including items sold, their cost, the amount of tax (if applicable), and the total value of the transaction.

Airline reservation transactions, in contrast, are handled on-line through terminals. Relevant details, such as passenger identification, flight number and date, and ticket price, are recorded in a file that is part of the system.

Transaction Processing

During processing, recorded data are validated and manipulated according to manual or automated procedures designed to detect and avoid errors. Common validation concerns include verifying that no data are missing, that prices or quantities are realistic, and that the transaction itself is valid. (Methods for validating data were discussed in Supplement 7.) Errors or problems detected are corrected through editing.

Some data during this step are retrieved from master files in the system. The prices of sales merchandise may be drawn from a prepared price list. Airline ticket prices are retrieved from a master ticket price file that holds all possible fares for various combinations of seating class, date of flight, advance purchase, route traveled, and destination.

File Maintenance

The occurrence of transactions leads to the maintenance of master files. When someone makes an airline reservation, seat availability records are modified to reflect the decrease in the number of seats on that flight. Passenger lists are also modified to incorporate the name of the additional person.

The sale of merchandise or the use of materials in the manufacture of finished goods should also produce file maintenance activities. In a well-run plant, for example, records are modified to show the reduction in quantities on hand whenever a shipment is made.

Transaction processing and file maintenance may occur in batch mode (that is, at some time after occurrence of the original transaction) or in on-line mode. Through on-line processing, the impact of each transaction is immediately reflected through changes to files.

Reporting

During processing, selected output may be prepared. Common categories of output, with examples, are listed below.

——*Action documents:* airline tickets, purchase orders, manufacturing orders, and merchandise withdrawal authorizations facilitate or initiate another action or transaction; turnaround documents are included in this category.

——*Information documents:* purchase order confirmations, processed orders lists, materials reject notices, and checks-paid registers confirm or inform others of a transaction or the reason for its occurrence.

——*Transaction log:* purchase order manifests, bank deposit and withdrawal listings, and sales registers offer listings of all transactions that include data to identify each transaction as well as other descriptive data.

——*Edit reports:* listings of invalid account numbers and transaction counts (see Figure 10.1) provide information on errors detected during transaction processing; information to detect missing transactions is included.

Figure 10.1 Sample Edit Report

Inventory Update Edit Report	
Record/Transaction Key	Message
777	Unable to find key on master
780	Attempt to add existing record to file
801	Unable to find key on master
815A	Nonnumeric in key field
1346	Zero data field
765	Record out of sequence
1784	Attempt to delete nonexistent record
2164	Record key out of range

Transaction Summary	
Transactions processed	1,341
Records added	186
Records deleted	34
Records updated	1,121
Errors reported	8

——*Summary monitoring reports:* balance sheets, profit and loss statements, and cash flow analyses show the impact of transactions that have occurred during a particular period or cycle of events, but without listing full details.

Multiple copies are often prepared that may, when distributed, trigger other actions (for example, investigation of material quality problems) or serve as historical reference documents (for example, check registers).

This transaction processing sequence is not unique to any particular type of application. We see it repeated in many different settings, both automated and manual.

Common Transaction Systems

Transaction processing systems make it possible for managers and employees to run the organization, providing services or products while ensuring that there is adequate control over each aspect of the business activity. This portion of the chapter describes the features of several common transaction systems: accounts receivable, accounts payable, general ledger, order entry, point of sale, and inventory control systems. As each is reviewed, notice how it fits the characteristics of record-keeping systems and also how its activities correspond to the transaction processing sequence just discussed. Many record-keeping applications have a foundation in accounting. Therefore, it is useful to first point out some important features of accounting systems.

Characteristics of Accounting Systems

Accounting systems are fundamental to business. They are the basis for determining how well or how poorly any firm is doing in its chosen enterprise. Guidelines, called *generally accepted accounting principles,* also describe the manner in which details of business activities should be recorded and managed to ensure there is a fair and objective statement of current status.

Purpose of Accounting Transactions An accounting transaction should provide details to answer four basic questions for managers, employees, auditors, stockholders, investigators from the Internal Revenue Service, and others wanting to know about the transaction.

1. What transaction occurred?
2. When did the transaction occur?
3. What was the effect of the transaction?
4. How much money was involved in the transaction?

Accounting systems are money oriented; they translate all transactions into an event that entails an increase or decrease in money (or something that can be measured in terms of money). When a transaction occurs that decreases money on the one hand, an offsetting increase in another area should result. For example, when you purchase an automobile for cash, you decrease the amount of money you have on hand. At the same time, in a business sense, you increase the value of items you own (the increase is equivalent to the amount of cash you paid for the automobile).

Double-Entry Record Keeping Another common characteristic of accounting systems is *double-entry record keeping,* in which debits to accounts must equal credits to properly balance the system. Thus in the preceding example, a decrease (credit) in the on-hand cash expended in purchasing the automobile is offset by an increase (debit) in an asset account: "automobile." Even if one part of the transaction involved several accounts (perhaps part of the cash came from a checking account and another part from a savings account), the total decreases will be offset by the amount of increase. A properly designed accounting system will preserve this aspect of financial control by always requiring that entries *balance* each other.

Auditing accounting transactions for accuracy and appropriateness is made possible by the feature known as the **audit trail,** introduced in Supplement 7, namely, a record of each transaction that is maintained in the system to show the details of the event. Auditors who use the audit trail to examine the transaction can understand what occurred and how it affects assets, liabilities, and the net worth of the organization. That is, they can answer the four important questions listed earlier. Adjustments, if necessary, can be made to correct errors or to more accurately report the effect of a transaction on the organization.

A **chart of accounts** is a document that lists all the accounting categories used in an organization. Each account named is used to report events or results of events involving that particular aspect of the firm.

The chart of accounts in Table 10.3 is typical of those used in manufacturing firms. Accounts are grouped by type (such as asset or liability) and assigned an identifying number, termed the account number, which is used to code every application of that account to a business transaction. For example, using the chart of accounts in Table 10.3, the account number 151 (Petty cash) would be applied to all transactions involving small expenditures of cash.

Basis for Reporting Transactions Accounting systems may be formulated to operate on a cash or accrual basis. **Cash accounting** transactions are reported only when cash is received or dispensed. That is, an accounting event occurs only when cash is involved.

Accrual accounting reports revenue and expense activities in the period in which they occur, regardless of whether cash changes hands. For example, if taxes that are paid quarterly are accumulated on a month-by-month basis, we say that the liability is accrued monthly. That is, the amount owed is increased each month. (In cash accounting, the expense would not be posted until the tax bill had been received and paid at the end of each quarter.) Many accountants believe that accrual accounting more accurately reports *when* a liability occurs, *who* is involved, and *what* effect the transaction has on the organization.

Distinguishing Features The following features are characteristic of accounting systems:

——*Cyclical system:* Accounting details are balanced for accuracy and summarized on a periodic basis (usually at the end of every calendar month). The "books" (accounting records) are adjusted so that all account balances reflect the transactions that occurred during the preceding month. Transactions files are prepared for the next month. The cycle in this example is a month. At the end of each monthly cycle, the same balancing and summarizing actions recur. Many business firms add quarterly cycles to be able to report performance during the preceding three months. An annual cycle for reporting accounting information is also utilized to meet legal and income tax requirements and to allow comparison of business activities from year to year.

——*Narrowness of focus:* Only transactions that directly involve the organization or its resources are reported in accounting systems. A transaction in the industry, such as the entry into the market of a new competitor who may reduce the firm's profits, does not involve the firm, hence is not reported in an accounting system.

——*Historical orientation:* An accounting system summarizes historical events, such as sales, purchases, and profit making. It reports the effects of those events by stating the current balance in accounts (such as cash on hand and debts owed

Table 10.3 Chart of Accounts Showing Account Numbers and Names

ACME CORPORATION

CHART OF ACCOUNTS

Printing Date: 05-02-XX

	Assets
100	Checking
102	Savings
150	Cash on hand
151	Petty cash
153	Certificates of deposit
156	Stock
159	Bonds
200	Accounts receivable—Sales
201	Accounts receivable—Employment
202	Accounts receivable—Other
210	Notes receivable
250	Inventory
290	Prepaid expenses
291	Accrued revenue
292	Security deposits
300	Furniture & fixtures
301	Machinery & equipment
302	Cars & trucks
303	Leasehold improvements
304	Organizational expenses
305	Patents
306	Copyrights
310	Building
330	Storage land
350	Depreciation—Furnitures & fixtures
351	Depreciation—Machinery & equipment
352	Depreciation—Cars & trucks
353	Depreciation—Leasehold improvements
354	Depreciation—Organization
355	Depreciation—Patents
356	Depreciation—Copyrights
360	Depreciation—Building
380	Goodwill
381	Trademarks

(continued)

Table 10.3 Chart of Accounts Showing Account Numbers and Names (*continued*)

Liabilities
400 Accounts Payable
405 Short-term notes payable—Lender
425 Withholding taxes payable
426 FICA taxes withheld payable
427 Sales tax payable
428 Franchise taxes payable
429 Personal property tax payable
430 Income taxes payable
431 FICA matching taxes payable
434 Real property taxes payable
445 Deferred income
446 Accrued expenses
450 Mortgage payable
452 Long-term notes payable
454 Secured long-term notes payable

Equities
500 Owner 1 — Net worth
510 Owner 1 — Contribution
520 Owner 1 — Withdrawal
530 Owner 1 — Other
540 Owner 1 — Special
550 Common stock
580 Retained earnings
585 Dividends paid
590 Fiscal year earnings

Income
600 Cash sales—Hardware
601 Cash sales—Paint
620 Credit sales—Hardware
621 Credit sales—Paint
640 Interest income
650 Cash return & allowance—Hardware
651 Cash return & allowance—Paint
670 Credit returns & allowances—Hardware
671 Credit returns & allowances—Paint
690 Earned discounts

(continued)

Table 10.3 Chart of Accounts Showing Account Numbers and Names (*continued*)

Operating Expenses

700	Cost of goods—Hardware
701	Cost of goods—Paint
750	Advertising
751	Vehicle repairs
752	Vehicle fuel
753	Salesperson expense
754	Salesperson salary
755	Store salary expense
756	Store payroll tax
757	Store insurance
758	Store rent/lease
759	Store utilities
760	Store telephone
761	Store supplies
762	Store depreciation
763	Store license/permits expenses
795	Discounts expense
800	Bank charges
801	Executive salary expense
802	Office salary/expense
803	Office payroll tax
804	Office utilities
805	Office telephone
806	Office depreciation
807	Office rent/lease expenses
808	Office supplies
809	Contributions
810	Travel
811	Legal & professional fees
812	Bad debts
813	Franchise taxes

Nonoperating Income and Expenses

900	Nonoperating income
925	Nonoperating expense
950	Federal income taxes
955	State income taxes
960	Foreign income taxes

to creditors). However, an accounting system does not predict the future. It does not, for example, report what sales will be this time next year, how much cash will be on hand, what the net value of the business will be, or what price would be received if the enterprise were offered for sale. (Managers and financial analysts might *use* accounting information, along with other types of information, to *develop* forecasts. However, those actions occur outside the accounting system.)

——*Uniformity:* Accounting systems use a routine of recording details of transactions as they occur, followed by examination of the details for accuracy. The data are posted to the appropriate accounts during or at the end of an accounting cycle. Summary reports are prepared to present an overview of accounting events and the effect of the events on the organization. This series of activities is termed *the accounting process.* It utilizes uniform rules and accepted accounting principles. An automated system for accounting must be designed to use the same rules and follow the same principles.

Accounting Software Packages Prewritten accounting software packages are available for lease or purchase from a wide variety of vendors. Different packages are available for implementation on personal computers, minicomputers, and mainframe systems. Accounting systems for use with personal computers often sell for a few hundred dollars and are designed to be used by persons with minimal computer experience and no programming capability. In contrast, accounting software for minicomputer and mainframe systems often leases for several hundred dollars monthly or can be purchased for $2500 and up.

Purchasing software packages allows an organization to implement a new system more quickly than would be possible if custom software were programmed. In addition, prewritten software has been tested in actual usage environments and is generally less expensive than specially developed programs. Other advantages of purchased software were discussed in Chapter 6.

Accounts Receivable Systems

Accounts receivable processing is a fundamental and essential transaction processing activity in any sales, service, or manufacturing organization. The term **accounts receivable** refers to revenue (cash or money) owed to a business or organization as a result of a transaction that has occurred but has not been paid for. Often sales in business are made based on purchase orders, which create sales on credit, rather than for cash. For example, when a firm orders materials needed for a manufacturing process, it does not generally send the supplier a check or cash to prepay the order. Rather it sends a purchase order requesting the materials and making a promise to pay the stated amount when the goods have arrived in satisfactory condition. In an accounting sense, the merchandise is exchanged for a promise to pay money owed. In operational terms, the balance of the supplier's accounts receivable account is increased. (If the transaction were for cash, the cash account would increase and accounts receivable would be unchanged.)

When a hospital treats a patient in the emergency room without requiring payment at the time of service, it is creating a "receivable." That is, the amount of money the patient has promised to pay is added to the balance of the accounts receivable account.

You can probably think of many examples of credit transactions in retail sales. If clothing is purchased and the cost charged on a commercial bank credit card such as Visa or MasterCard or by using private credit service extended by the store making the sale, the accounting system will require an accounts receivable transaction. Since most sales in businesses other than retail sales are made on credit, accounts receivable systems are important transaction processing systems, and the ability to handle these transactions expeditiously is an essential business activity. We will examine the purpose of accounts receivable systems in greater detail and will discuss the features of an automated accounts receivable system.

Purpose As indicated above, accounts receivable processing serves to capture and process relevant accounting data about sales made on a credit (noncash) basis. "Relevant" data include data about the sale itself as well as data about any later events that pertain to the original sale. For example, if errors are detected in the original transaction, either by the customer or by someone in the organization, they are relevant because we want to be able to correct them. Likewise, knowledge of money that is paid on the account is relevant because we need to update the account record to show the transaction.

The accounts receivable system must contain the data needed to answer the four important accounting questions as they pertain to changes in these accounting transactions: What transaction occurred? When did it occur? How much money was involved? and What was the effect of the transaction?

Types of Transactions Four types of transactions are common in accounts receivable systems.

1. *Sales transactions:* the capturing and processing of data about each credit transaction and the storage of the relevant data in a transaction record. If the sale is made to a customer who has received authorization to purchase on credit, a record already exists in the authorized customer file. If the customer is new, a record must be added to the master file.

2. *Payment transactions:* the capturing and processing of data about the payment of money on an account. The transaction data are processed and new account balances are calculated.

3. *Adjustment transactions:* the capturing and processing of data used to correct or amend data previously recorded, or to correct or amend the effect of data recorded in a previous accounting period. Adjustments may include such transactions as those to change sales amounts (because the original amount was incorrect), to change the address or name of the account holder, or to credit the amount of the adjustment.

4. *Account inquiries:* the retrieval of information from one or more accounts receivable records to answer inquiries from customers (for example, "What is the account balance?") or to print transaction details for the period.

Other types of transactions may occur, depending on the nature of the business and its particular accounting requirements.

In each of the four cases, relevant data must be captured about the transaction and put into a form the system can process. Representative data for each transaction include:

——*Sales transaction:*
   Date of transaction
   Person or organization making purchase
   Account number
   Items purchased (and quantity)
   Unit and total cost of each item
   Transaction or sales invoice number

——*Payment transaction:*
   Date of payment
   Account number (name of person or organization)
   Payment amount

——*Adjustment transaction:*
   Date of adjustment
   Type of adjustment
   Amount of adjustment
   Account number (name of person or organization)

——*Account inquiry transaction:*
   Account number (name of person or organization)

Other types of processing involve the entire file, which causes each record to be processed.

The processing of each individual transaction depends on the design of the accounts receivable system and the operating procedures that are followed. Systems in different organizations vary in the method of input, file organization, processing mode, frequency of processing, and so on.

In a typical accounts receivable system, transaction-related activities occur when a sale is made (the sale may be a transaction in an automated order entry system, or sales may be controlled manually and the details entered into this system). Transaction data are keyed into the system through a terminal and accumulated in a temporary transaction file (Figure 10.2). Throughout the day, a *batch* of transactions occurs. After each day's transactions have been entered, the accumulation of sales detail is verified to correct errors (such as invalid account numbers or wrong dollar amounts). Then the file of data is processed against the accounts receivable master file. A report listing each transaction is prepared and printed automatically (Figure 10.3).

In a system designed for *on-line* processing, of course, each transaction would be verified immediately and the detail added to the proper record to change the current month's transaction balance.

Payment transactions are handled in a manner similar to sales transactions. When a payment is received, the details are entered into the system through a terminal. Then they are processed to update the accounts receivable master file. Likewise, adjustments, taken from an account adjustment form, are entered and processed against the master file.

Figure 10.2 Overview of Transaction Processing Sequence for Accounts Receivable

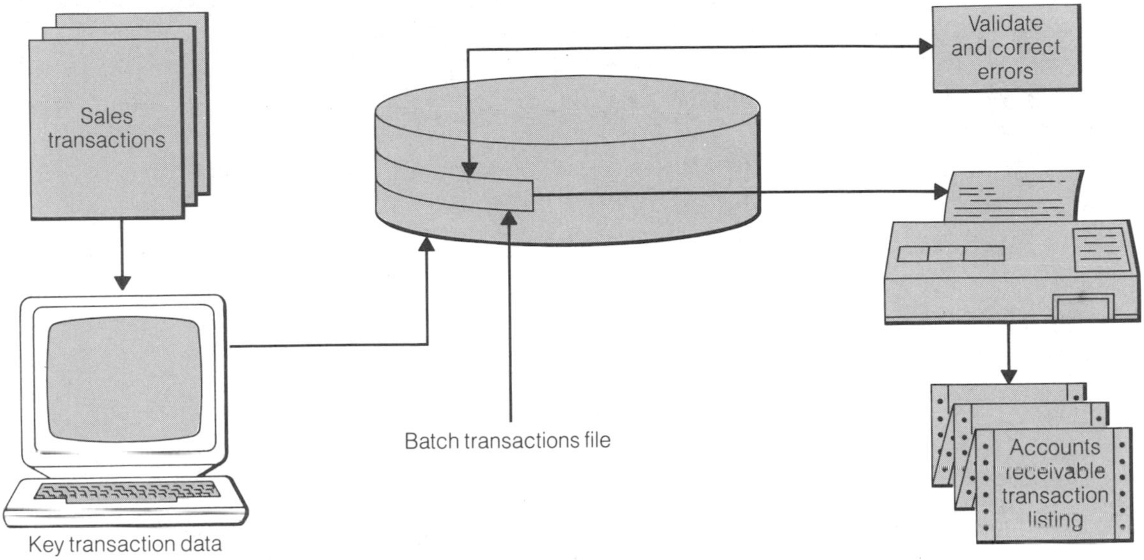

As Figure 10.4 shows, the sales, payment, and adjustment transactions can all be processed in the computer system in batch at the same time.

Output from Accounts Receivable System At the end of each month, account processing is performed to post transactions to the accounts, to perform *aging* (determine age of balance), and to change the balances to reflect activities (charges, payments, and adjustments) that occurred during the preceding month.

These reports and documents are typically generated as part of the end-of-cycle processing:

——*Statement of account:* lists the transaction details for the current period (sales and payments, and adjustments), current balance, aging details, and amount of expected payment

——*Accounts receivable register:* lists the customer names for all accounts having nonzero balances and the balance amounts

——*Accounts receivable activity summary:* summarizes accounts that had sales, payment, or adjustment activity during the period

——*High balance report:* lists the names and balance amounts of all accounts that have exceeded a prespecified floor amount

——*Aged accounts receivable register:* includes aging information for all accounts with nonzero balances

——*Monthly transaction list:* gives details of all sales, payment, and adjustment transactions entered into the system during the period (may be listed in order of entry or by type of transaction)

Figure 10.3 Accounts Receivable Transaction Listing (in order of transaction occurrence)

General Supply Company
4321 Peachtree Street
Atlanta, Georgia 30303

ACCOUNT NUMBER	AMOUNT	DATE		TYPE
3570	1677.81	830906	P	PAYMENT
83	100.40	830906	P	PAYMENT
81	9.06	830906	P	PAYMENT
3510	13.52	830908	P	PAYMENT
3540	26.91	830908	P	PAYMENT
5010	6.50	830908	P	PAYMENT
4320	36.02	830908	P	SALE
93	476.54	830908	P	PAYMENT
2970	55.64	830908	P	PAYMENT
6737	374.96	830908	P	PAYMENT
1015	60.00	830908	P	PAYMENT
5900	23.40	830908	P	PAYMENT
1100	4.42	830908	P	SALE
1850	66.05	830908	P	SALE
5280	10.73	830907	P	PAYMENT
7010	46.14	830907	P	PAYMENT
3860	29.24	830907	P	SALE
1025	3.90	830907	P	PAYMENT
6480	22.53	830907	P	PAYMENT
7610	24.56	830907	P	SALE
4960	601.55	830907	P	SALE
6400	36.75	830907	P	PAYMENT
2460	18.46	830907	P	PAYMENT
3230	9.62	830907	P	PAYMENT
5940	26.61	830907	P	PAYMENT
3300	27.54	830907	P	SALE
3990	7.80	830907	P	PAYMENT
7430	2.50	830907	P	PAYMENT
1060	10.14	830907	P	PAYMENT
7100	4.68	830907	P	SALE
2320	77.84	830907	P	SALE
83	112.25	830907	P	PAYMENT
1380	49.18	830909	P	PAYMENT
1099	3.95	830909	P	SALE
5210	16.64	830909	P	PAYMENT
3310	16.61	830909	P	PAYMENT
4600	47.90	830909	P	SALE
2730	9.75	830909	P	PAYMENT
2320	18.27	830909	P	PAYMENT
5470	18.00	830909	P	PAYMENT
4900	6.78	830909	P	PAYMENT
1830	7.80	830909	P	PAYMENT

Figure 10.4 Basic Accounts Receivable Processing

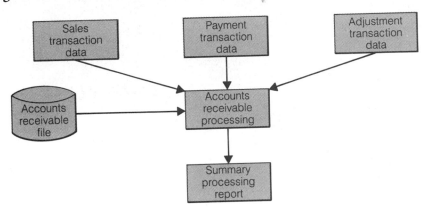

In addition, to assist in the management of accounts receivable, customer reports are also available:

——*Alphabetical customer list* (in alphabetical order by the name of the company or person responsible for the account)

——*Numeric customer list* (in numeric order based on the assigned customer account number)

These reports typify those associated with accounts receivable systems. Depending on the needs of a specific organization or the design of the particular application in use by an organization, the reports and statements may vary.

Files The two most important files in an accounts receivable system are the accounts master file and the transaction file. The master file is updated monthly, as we have discussed. The record contents for a representative master file in this system are shown in Figure 10.5.

There may be one or several transaction files. If the design of the system calls for one transaction file only, this file must be capable of holding records for each sales, payment, and adjustment transaction. In addition, the capability to add or delete customer records must be supported. The record contents for this type of transaction file are shown in Figure 10.6.

Some systems are designed to use separate transaction files for each of the foregoing maintenance functions. Usually this is to improve management control over certain transactions. For example, any person authorized to operate the system may be allowed to enter sales. Adjustments, on the other hand, may be a more sensitive area. Such transactions are often accumulated in a separate file that can be reviewed by management in batches. Payments may also be maintained in a separate file, in the interest of efficient reconciliation of payments received with those posted to the accounting system.

Figure 10.5 Contents of Accounts Receivable Master File

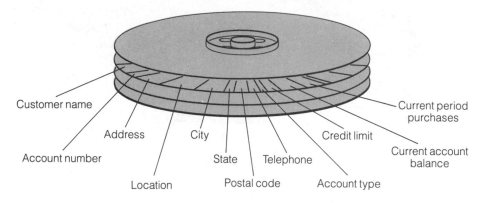

Figure 10.6 Accounts Receivable Transaction File Contents

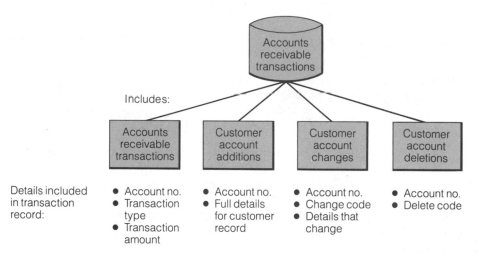

Programs An accounts receivable system, although discussed as a single application, actually consists of several different computer programs. Often the user of such a system, interacting with the computer through a terminal or workstation or using a personal computer, may not be aware of separate programs because they are activated unobtrusively when a particular function is required.

The specific programs are related to the features of the system we have been discussing (for example, file maintenance is carried out by a file maintenance program). The design of the software may also call for a program for each individual activity (one program for sales, a separate one for payments, and another for adjustments), or related activities may be included in a single program.

Programs commonly part of an accounts receivable system include those to perform these important activities:

——Customer file maintenance (add new customers or change information about existing customers)
——Transaction entry
——Validation of transaction data
——Correction of errors in transactions
——Retrieval of information to satisfy inquiries about specific accounts
——Preparation of reports from the system
——Performance of utility functions (re-sort files; delete records or reallocate storage space within files)
——Maintenance of passwords that provide for access by authorized users only

Other general-purpose programs associated with the computer operating system rather than the accounts receivable application will also be used. For example, programs to initialize disks and to monitor the size of files are essential in any transaction processing environment.

Accounts Payable Systems

The term **accounts payable** refers to money owed to a vendor or supplier for services rendered or merchandise received. The firm that is owed money is called a creditor. Rather than maintaining data about money to be received, as in accounts receivable systems, accounts payable systems store and process details about monies that must be paid out.

Purpose Accounts payable systems serve three main purposes. First they maintain records of invoices (bills) received from creditors and the total amount owed to each creditor. Every invoice is associated with a specific vendor. Typically, vendors specify a due date (such as 10, 15, or 30 days from the date of the invoice). In addition, they often offer cash discounts if payments are made quickly, say, within 10 days. These details are also maintained within the accounts payable system.

The second purpose of an accounts payable system is to maintain control over *credit levels*. Because the credit level of a firm is associated with its timely payment of bills, the accounts payable system is designed to monitor due dates and to prompt the person responsible for preparing payments. The system may also keep track of deadlines for taking cash discounts.

Bills must be paid, of course, but first there must be cash on hand to make the payment. Therefore, accounts payable systems provide periodic summaries indicating the amount of money needed to cover all invoices that are due. The accounts manager must decide which invoices to pay.

Many automated accounts payable systems can prepare company checks to pay invoices. This feature automatically supplies a record of each payment and the corresponding check number. Not only do automated systems save clerical time that otherwise would be needed to prepare and post checks, but they also provide additional security in that only certain individuals are authorized to request preparation of checks.

Managing accounts payable is much more than just paying bills. It includes accurate records management, control over cash use, maintaining good credit ratings, and protecting against unauthorized cash disbursement. Computer assistance can improve effectiveness and efficiency, provided these features are handled properly.

Types of Transaction Five types of transaction are commonly handled in computer-based accounts payable systems.

1. *Entry of invoices from vendors or suppliers:* capturing and storing data to identify each invoice or "bill" received from a creditor. If the vendor or supplier is not in the vendor master file, an entry is made to include the firm named on the invoice.

2. *Authorization for payment of invoice:* although automated systems may be designed to select automatically vendors due to receive a payment, for purposes of control, each payment should be individually authorized to prevent error or fraud.

3. *Adjustment transactions:* accepting and processing data to correct the details of an invoice previously entered into the system; includes the capability to remove from the accounts payable file an invoice already in the system, by deleting it.

4. *Invoice inquiry:* retrieving details of a particular invoice provided by a specific vendor; some systems include this feature, while others provide only for retrieval of the total amount due a specific vendor.

5. *Vendor inquiry:* retrieving details of all invoices due for a specific vendor.

The relevant data for each transaction will vary in different accounts receivable systems. However, representative data include the following:

1. *Entry of vendor invoice:*
   Date of invoice
   Date of entry into system (optional)
   Vendor number (vendor name is retrieved from vendor master file)
   Invoice number
   Purchase order number
   Invoice due date
   Discount amount
   Dollar total

2. *Authorization for payment:*
   Transaction number assigned by system when invoice was entered
   Distribution of amount between accounts in general ledger (the general ledger system is discussed in the next section of the chapter)
   Amount of payment (if not full invoice amount)

3. *Adjustment transaction:*
   Invoice number
   Type of adjustment (addition or subtraction to amount due, change of due date, hold on payment, removal of hold on payment, and so on)
   Adjustment details (format varies by type of adjustment)

4. *Invoice inquiry:* invoice number

5. *Vendor inquiry:* vendor number

In addition to these operating transactions, vendors are added to and deleted from the vendor master file, and changes in general ledger accounts and account numbers occur.

The entry of invoices into the system occurs daily in many organizations. As bills arrive, they are approved and the pertinent details are keyed into the system.

The processing of accounts payable may occur throughout the period or only near the end of the period. When there is a large volume of accounts payable or when discount dates are monitored very closely, processing may occur weekly. Some firms choose to pay bills only twice a month; still others elect to prepare checks to vendors monthly. As you can see, the management of accounts payable accommodates many variations.

In a representative system, the sequence of processing payments includes these activities (Figure 10.7):

——Print or display invoices due for payment.

——Review invoices due or suggested for payment and authorize payment.

——Enter authorization into system by:

Entering amount of payment (the default payment is the full amount of the invoice)

Entering the account numbers of the general ledger accounts that should be adjusted to show the use of the funds (for example, pay advertising, materials, or income tax expenses)

Entering the check number if the system does not automatically assign it

——Attempts to pay nonexistent invoices are disallowed.

——Each payment transaction is examined by the system to ensure that the amount of the payment is equal to the distribution of the payment across general ledger accounts.

——The checks are printed by the computer system.

——Account balances are adjusted using the payment data.

——Detail and summary reports are prepared.

These functions are equally important in on-line and batch systems. In an on-line system, authorization is typically performed by someone working interactively with the system. The payments are authorized by entering the invoice number or reference transaction number followed by the general ledger distribution. When the data are complete, a report can be requested or an instruction given to prepare the checks.

Output As with the accounts receivable system, there are a variety of reports available to oversee open accounts payable. Most systems include these reports:

——Cash requirements report

——Check register

——Checks

——General ledger summary

Figure 10.7 Accounts Payable Processing Sequence

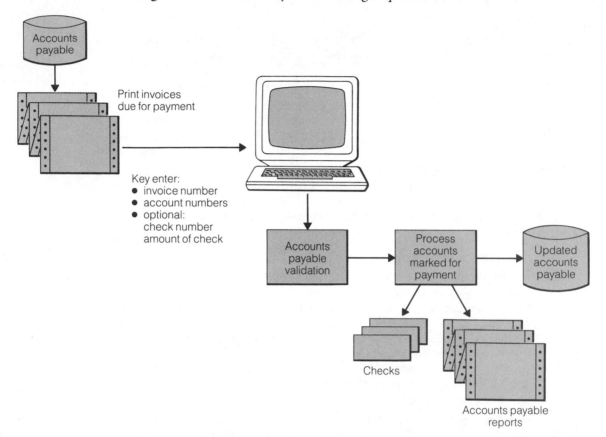

——Consolidated payables summary

——Aged payables summary

——Vendor list (alphabetical and vendor number order).

Files Three files are essential in the management of accounts payable. The *transaction file* holds details of invoices for the current accounting period. The *consolidated payables file* is the master file of details concerning outstanding invoices and money due to creditors. Depending on the design of the system, it also includes payables history, indicating the total purchases from the vendor during the current fiscal year. Aging information, typically concerning payables over 120 days by month, is retained in this file.

The *vendor master file* includes one record for every permanent supplier or vendor serving the organization. In addition to the vendor identification number, name, and address (Figure 10.8), some designs include payment terms and products or services supplied in this file.

Figure 10.8 Accounts Payable Vendor File Contracts

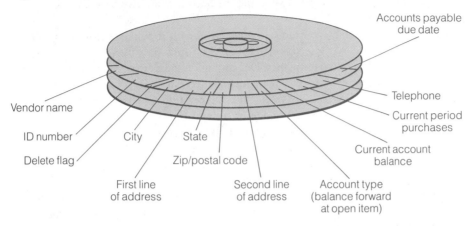

Individual programs included in this system are comparable to those discussed for accounts receivable processing. They perform data entry, input validation, file maintenance, and reporting.

General Ledger Systems

A **general ledger** system ties together all other accounting activities to show their overall effect on a business. As we discuss the purpose of this system and the underlying files and processing activities, keep in mind the activities of the accounting applications already examined.

Purpose A general ledger system serves to consolidate all financial transactions involving an organization in order to summarize and show changes in assets, liabilities, and net worth of the firm. General ledger systems are designed to assist in tracing the financial history of the company.

The chart of accounts presented in Table 10.3 was designed with the general ledger system in mind. That is, all accounts were assigned identification numbers that place them in one of the major general ledger categories: current assets, other assets, current liabilities, long-term liabilities, equity, income, and expenses. These accounts are used to classify financial activities by type, and then accounting transactions are summarized to produce financial statements.

Through the general ledger system, an organization can produce its essential financial statements:

—**Balance sheet:** comparison of assets and liabilities

—**Income statement:** profits or losses resulting from accumulation of revenues and expenses

Other reports are associated with the general ledger system, as will be discussed, but these two are of particular importance in assessing the soundness of the organization's financial status and in meeting legal reporting requirements such as those of the Internal Revenue Service and the Securities and Exchange Commission.

Input Most general ledger systems are integrated with the other accounting record-keeping systems in an organization. That is, they draw data from accounts payable, accounts receivable, and payroll files. Depending on the design, they may accept data about cash receipts, inventory, and customer orders in various ways.

Automatic posting of data from other accounting systems transfers summary totals to the appropriate general ledger accounts. In other words, the details of all the individual transactions in, say, an accounts payable system are summarized into totals for each account in the chart of accounts. The totals for cash, insurance, raw materials, taxes paid, and so on are then transferred into the general ledger system rather than the details of all individual transactions.

If there are not summary files for each activity area, special accounting journal entries are prepared and entered manually into the general ledger system. For example, if the inventory system is not integrated into the general ledger system by means of a summary file, a manual entry is prepared to post to the general ledger system the change (increase or decrease) in inventory on hand during the month. In either case, summary data must be properly posted to the general ledger system to accurately state the company's net worth as the income earned or loss incurred during the period; for example, an increase or decrease in inventory on hand changes the total value of company assets and therefore the firm's net worth.

Transactions in a general ledger system are different from those in other accounting systems. They do not include data about operation transactions. Rather, general ledger transactions are *journal* entries—the summary data pertaining to receivables, payables, and so forth. And some of the data are transferred automatically through the summary files described earlier.

Processing and Programs General ledger processing changes both current period and current year totals. One of the purposes of the general ledger is to maintain data about the performance of an organization during the current year—the financial history mentioned earlier. Therefore, in processing, year-to-date totals for each account are adjusted to reflect the effect of the current period. Thus if year-to-date cash on hand is $128,500 and the current period has generated an additional $26,400 in cash, the year-to-date total after general ledger processing will be $154,900.

The activities in general ledger processing (Figure 10.9) include the following.

——Posting summary files from other accounting systems to appropriate general ledger accounts.

——Performing manual posting of account summaries to general ledger journals.

——Preparing a trial balance to determine whether the general ledger is in balance. Assets must equal the sum of liabilities, and net worth and earnings must equal revenue less expenses. If either equation does not balance, adjustments must be made to correct errors in transaction details.

——Preparing a general ledger report of account balances and account history.

——Preparing a financial statement for the period.

Figure 10.9 General Ledger Processing

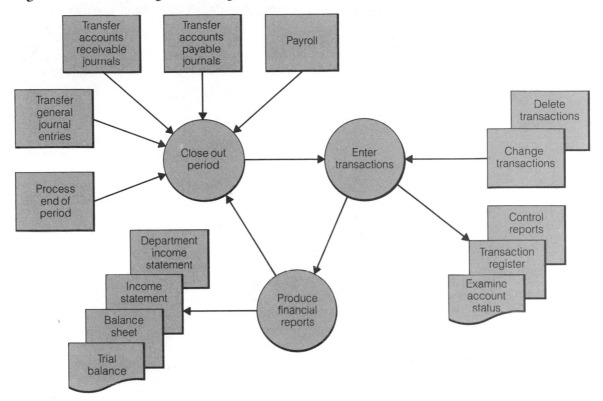

—Preparing a system for the next accounting period (closing the books for the current year if the current period is the last in the fiscal year). To close the books for the period, the current month totals for such items as income and expense are reset to zero; to close the books for the year, year-to-date totals are reset to zero.

In general, each step is easily invoked by simple entry of a keyword or by pressing of a single key on the keyboard of the workstation.

Programs The programs in a general ledger system may be organized in many different ways. Each system must have the capability to maintain the descriptive system file containing the name of the company and the individual departments (if the company is departmentalized), as well as the chart of accounts. Programs are also needed to accept journal entries and to correct them if errors occur. All transfers of summary journals from other systems must occur under program control.

Inquiries about the balances of specific accounts generally are handled by a separate program. When the user poses a query, the program is activated: It will request passwords, accounts numbers, and other necessary details to assure that the individual is authorized to retrieve the data.

At the end of a period, a special program to close out the period is run. This program, which adjusts the year-to-date totals in appropriate accounts, also clears journal entries from the current month and prepares for the receipt of new transactions during the next period.

Other utility programs may be included to check data files or to attempt recovery of lost data. These programs work together with the operating system of the computer to ensure proper use of computer resources.

Output In a typical general ledger system, you can expect to find (at a minimum) the following reports and schedules available as output.

——*Chart of accounts list:* a listing by number and name of all accounts in the chart of accounts

——*Transaction register:* a listing of all transactions entered during current period by date, account numbers used, and dollar amount involved; includes correcting transactions

——*Account status report:* a report of all or selected accounts with their beginning balances, all current activity, and new balances to date

——*Trial balance:* a list of all accounts, the total of transactions posted to each, and the beginning and ending balances; often available in summary or detail form, the trial balance is used to detect out-of-balance conditions resulting from improper posting of transactions

——*Balance sheet:* a summary of all asset, liability, and equity accounts at the close of the current accounting period

——*Income statement:* a report of income and operating expenses for the firm during the current period

——*Comparative financial statements:* totals of account balance and performance, for monitoring changes in income, expense, or assets, liabilities, and equity during previous accounting periods

——*Department income statement:* a report of income and operating expenses for a specific department during the current accounting period (for firms that maintain separate accounting records by department)

The comparative financial statements may take various forms. Some present account balances for each of the preceding months in the year while others cover only one or two months. Some present the same period one year earlier. Still others give comparative balance sheets and income statements for preceding months or years. Each system designer has a different set of organization requirements in mind when designing a general ledger system, so it is not surprising that there are many variations. Thus accounts and systems analysts must have a good idea of the information they want from the system when selecting general ledger software.

Order Entry Processing Systems

Order entry systems, whether designed for batch mode or, now more frequently, as on-line systems, underlie the very business of many organizations. Without the ability to accept and process customer orders properly, there is no reason for an organization to be in business—and it may not be for very long.

Order entry systems generally do not stand alone. As will be shown, they are often integrated with accounting systems or inventory control applications.

Purpose The general reason for operating an order entry system is of course to process customer orders. However, the features of the system determine how effectively the task can be accomplished. The objectives of order processing are to satisfy customers' needs by handling orders quickly and accurately. The application software is designed to assist in catching errors (such as incorrect prices or attempts to place orders for nonexistent items). It should also standardize the processing sequence so that each order is handled in the same manner. Consistency improves speed and reduces the chance of error.

Rapid and accurate acceptance and filling of customer orders can be an important sales asset; well-designed systems can attract customers to the organization. An on-line system that allows a firm to accept, fill, and ship an order on the same day will be attractive to customers who need to receive merchandise quickly. At the same time, the company benefits by better use of its resources. Inventory turns quickly and takes less space in the warehouse. Better inventory management is surely advantageous in business.

Order entry systems are an important source of sales and management information. Information extracted from the system permits analysis of which products are selling and to whom, and which are not. It also permits analysis of customer purchase patterns: when they buy, what quantities they select, and how they schedule shipping. Marketing, pricing, and product strategies may evolve from analysis of the information. Notice how this important management information is related to the processing of customer order transactions. (Chapter 11 examines the development and use of management information.)

Types of Transactions The most common features of order processing are associated with the following transactions:

——*Order entry:* acceptance of the details of a customer order and entry into the automated system for processing and filling

——*Order inquiry:* retrieval of information to determine the status of a previously entered order

——*Order adjustment:* editing or deleting orders already entered into the system

——*File maintenance:* adding or changing entries in the master files that comprise the order processing system, including customer master files, salesperson files, and cost or tax tables

The details needed to enter an order transaction into the system are depicted in on-line display screen format in Figure 10.10. As shown, there are two parts to the entry. The customer portion identifies the individual or organization placing the order and includes such pertinent details as shipping method, sales tax category, and salesperson. The other portion includes the details of the order: items, quantities, and costs.

Processing Orders In processing, the order is established first: an order number and date are assigned by the system and, using the customer number entered from the

Figure 10.10 Data Entry Screen for Order Entry System

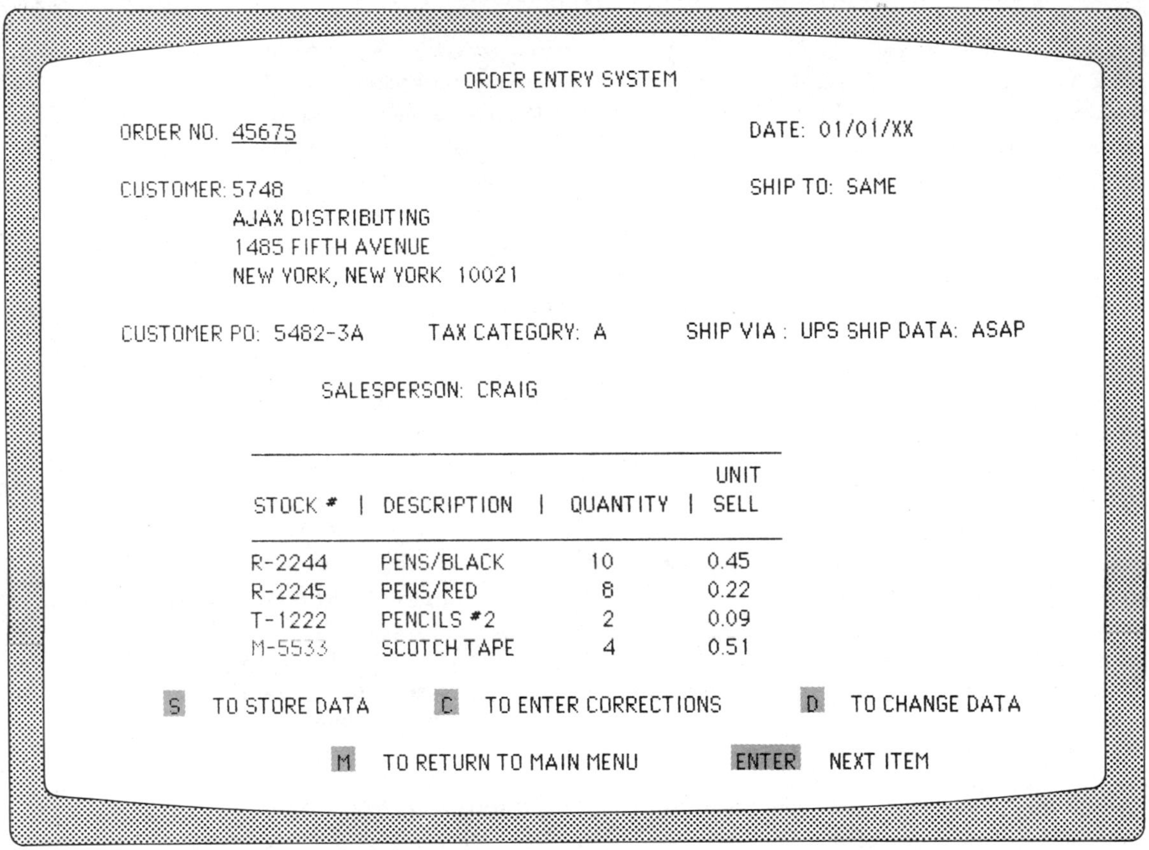

```
                        ORDER ENTRY SYSTEM

    ORDER NO. 45675                       DATE: 01/01/XX

    CUSTOMER: 5748                        SHIP TO: SAME
          AJAX DISTRIBUTING
          1485 FIFTH AVENUE
          NEW YORK, NEW YORK  10021

    CUSTOMER PO: 5482-3A     TAX CATEGORY: A     SHIP VIA: UPS SHIP DATA: ASAP

              SALESPERSON: CRAIG


                                          UNIT
        STOCK #  |  DESCRIPTION  |  QUANTITY  |  SELL

        R-2244      PENS/BLACK       10        0.45
        R-2245      PENS/RED          8        0.22
        T-1222      PENCILS #2        2        0.09
        M-5533      SCOTCH TAPE       4        0.51

     S   TO STORE DATA      C   TO ENTER CORRECTIONS      D   TO CHANGE DATA

            M   TO RETURN TO MAIN MENU      ENTER   NEXT ITEM
```

keyboard (or on the order record if the system runs in batch mode), customer information is added to the order.

Not all information needed for an order is keyed into the system. A substantial portion may be retrieved from other files: the name, address, and shipping address may be retrieved from the customer file using the customer number provided by the order taker.

If the customer requests another shipping address for this order, or wishes to provide a purchase order number for reference or to specify a method of shipment, such details are added to the record.

The body of the order contains details of the items requested. The customer requests items by name or description, but the transaction generally depends on a specific item number supplied by the salesperson or the individual preparing the order. Individual product or item descriptions and costs may be retrieved from a product or inventory file on the basis of the item number entered. When the quantity has been entered, the application software will automatically multiply quantity by cost (that is, "extend the line") to determine the cost for the entire order.

When all items on an order have been entered, a subtotal is calculated, sales tax is determined, and a total cost tallied. Depending on the design of the system, a record of the order or an invoice may be printed automatically using preprinted forms.

Different order processing systems incorporate wide variations in the specific features, partly because of the needs of individual businesses and partly because of the capabilities of the computers on which the systems will run and the cost of the software. Some optional features are the abilities to:

——Accept and track backorders for items out of stock
——Prepare *picking lists* indicating where items are stored in the warehouse or stock-room
——Calculate sales commissions
——Allow quantity discounts
——Determine the cost of the order and resulting profits
——Credit the order to a profit center within the firm
——Prepare documents for shipping the order to the customer

File structures will vary according to inclusion of any or all of these features.

Files A description of the order master file is shown in Figure 10.11. The order number permits retrieval of individual orders on request. Including the customer number in each order permits inquiries such as, How many orders are outstanding for Ace Rug Company (customer number 456679) and when were they placed?

Many order processing systems fix the number of items that may be included in a single order and in turn use **fixed-length records;** a specific number of bytes is allocated to each order, including the space for the header and for individual line

Figure 10.11 Order Master File Contents

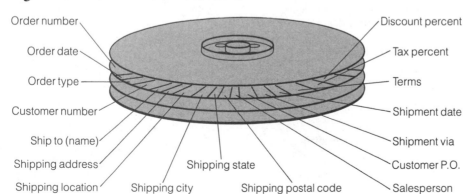

Order number
Order date
Order type
Customer number
Ship to (name)
Shipping address
Shipping location
Shipping city
Shipping state
Shipping postal code

Discount percent
Tax percent
Terms
Shipment date
Shipment via
Customer P.O.
Salesperson

Figure 10.12 Order Processing Integrated with Accounts Receivable and Inventory Management

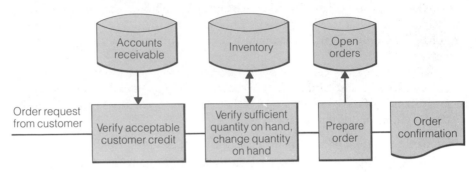

items in the order. **Variable-length records** may be used for other designs when the total number of allowable items in an order varies. Still another option uses a *linked list* (see Chapter 8). Under this format, the customer header serves as the main record and a sublist that includes individual records for each item is created.

Other important files include details of the salespeople associated with the firm and tax tables for the determination of sales taxes.

If the order entry system is integrated with inventory control and accounts receivable, it may draw data from those master files (Figure 10.12). Otherwise, the system must include such data in separate files.

Order entry systems often lead firms to consider investment in a database management system. As this discussion has shown, there is a great need to share information between accounting, inventory, and order processing systems. If these systems are not integrated, there will be unnecessary duplication of data across the applications. And as you know from previous examples, duplication between files usually leads to trouble: The data seldom are consistent.

Output The output provided in an order entry environment occurs in several different categories:

———*Documents and forms:*
     Order summary or acknowledgment
     Invoice
     Credit memo
     Backorder acknowledgment (optional)
     Shipping documents (optional)
     Item return acknowledgment (optional)
     Picking ticket
     Packing list
     Order change form
———*Order reports:*
     Open (outstanding) orders
     Items ordered
     Items backordered

Customer activity report
Salesperson activity report
Discount report
Adjustment report
Credit report
Sales tax report

——*File listings:*
Customer list
Salesperson list
Tax code list
Product list
Inventory-on-hand list

As these items should suggest, it is easy to be inundated with reports from an order entry system. Thus selective preparation of the output is suggested. When needed, the information is available. But it should not be produced routinely unless there is a clear need.

Point-of-Sale Systems

A special case of order processing is often found in retail and service settings (for example, in restaurants). **Point-of-sale (POS) systems** are small computer systems that capture order and sales data while the transaction is occurring. Unlike other order entry environments, the product or service is delivered immediately after the occurrence of the order transaction. Therefore, it is essential to capture all relevant details before the customer has left. POS systems have memory, processing ability, and data entry features much like intelligent terminals or microcomputers.

Point-of-Sale Devices POS devices may be stand-alone machines or systems of multiple terminals (see photo on next page). Each has a small memory that stores item identifications, prices, tax rates, and programs. Since a point-of-sale system has a central processing unit, there is also secondary storage that stores price and program data and accumulates sales and inventory results.

Sales data are entered through a special keyboard that has been adapted to the situation in which the POS device is being used (see section entitled "POS in Fast Foods"). Some systems use cathode ray tubes for data entry or display, while others use scanners or wands, as discussed in the section entitled "POS in the Grocery Industry." A special key, which protects against unauthorized use of the POS device, is needed to make price or programming changes.

Stand-alone terminals range in cost from approximately $2000 to $5000. POS systems cost $20,000 or more, depending on the number of terminals involved and the type of software used.

Applications of POS Systems These systems are favored in applications characterized by a heavy volume of data to be captured (because transactions occur frequently) and by a tendency toward a high error rate. Not surprisingly, the retail grocery and fast-food industries have become the biggest and most effective users of POS.

Point-of-Sale System

POS in the Grocery Industry The grocery industry is one of the leading users of scanners for point-of-sale data capture. A *scanner* is an optical reader that operates as part of the POS device to read sales and item data from each item sold. Some are hand-held wands, about the size of a pen, which the clerk moves past the price tag to read data into the system. Others are built in to the checkout counter, and data are entered into the system by sliding the item over the scanner (Figure 10.13). Most scanners read at such high speeds (about 300 inches per second) that the checker cannot move the items too fast for data entry.

In 1973 the grocery industry adopted a product identification method that advanced the use of POS devices. The *Universal Product Code (UPC)* they developed now identifies over 100,000 items, including groceries, drugs, health and beauty-

Figure 10.13 Point-of-Sale Scanning Process

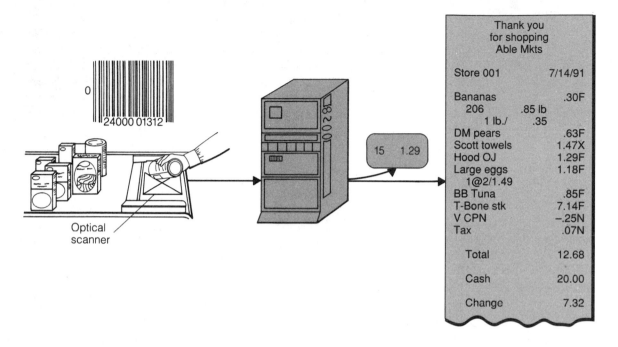

aid products, and magazines. Approximately 98 percent of all items in food stores now carry the code.

The UPC symbol is a set of narrow and wide bars representing a 10-digit number assigned to a particular product. The first five digits represent the manufacturer and the second five the product. In the grocery industry, the most common scheme also adds a check digit at the right of the symbol (check digits are explained in Supplement 7), which assists in assuring that the scanner is reading correctly.

The UPC gives only identification numbers; it does not encode the prices of items. Price data are stored in the POS system and are accessed when an identification number is entered through the scanner. As each item is scanned, the correct retail price is displayed on the checkout terminal screen where the customer can see it. The amount of the sale is automatically added to the customer order. (In addition, it is added to the daily sales volume for that checkout counter, and the quantity on hand for the item is reduced by the number of items sold.) At the end of the transaction, a detailed receipt is printed on register tape to give the customer a record of the purchase. Even coupons, the amount tendered, and change to the customer can be itemized.

The advantages of point-of-sale devices in the grocery industry are the same for both the customer and the store: faster checkout time, fewer errors, detailed transaction receipts, and lower costs.

POS in Fast Foods Fast-food outlets selling hamburgers, fried chicken, and sand-wiches have many of the same concerns about speed, accuracy, and sales data as grocery chains. However, because they offer a smaller variety of products, they frequently must serve many more people in the same interval of time. Point-of-sale devices for fast foods usually have a separate key for every menu item right on the terminal keyboard. If the menu changes during the day (for example, after breakfast), the keyboard surface often can also be changed, or different areas of the keyboard can be reserved for each type of menu. Some chains attempt to further reduce the possibility of error by using devices that show pictures of the menu items on the corresponding keys.

Fast-food orders are entered directly through the terminal keyboard. Often the operator must move on to the next customer before the first customer's order has been prepared. Many POS devices will store the first order and accept a second order, and perhaps a third. When the order is ready for the first (or second) person, the server can recall it on the terminal and complete the transaction. In each case, the POS device computes the prices and taxes, and totals the sale.

If appropriate, the terminal can accumulate sales throughout the day or the shift, and categorize them by item and by method of payment (cash, check, coupons, charge, and credit card). The terminal can even be used by management to handle time clock functions: Employees can log in and out when they begin and end work.

It is easy to see why point-of-sale devices have come into such widespread use. They offer all the features of computers, adapted to specific sales situations. And they are engineered to assist the people who are working with them, making their jobs easier and faster.

Inventory Management Systems

It should be evident that a demand for products or merchandise will go unmet if orders cannot be filled because the on-hand supply is inadequate. Inventory management is aimed at balancing supply and demand. Now we examine the features of computer-based inventory management systems.

Purpose An organization's investment in the products or merchandise it offers for sale is often sizable. Thus these items must be managed, like any other asset, to ensure the maximum possible return on the investment. Clearly **inventory management** is much more than keeping track of the quantity of items on hand in the warehouse.

Inventory control also deals with determining when orders must be placed to meet demand for an item, as well as the quantity to order. It includes the procedures for correctly accepting merchandise when it arrives and adjusting the records showing the quantity on hand in the warehouse. And it means ensuring that what the records say is on hand is actually in the warehouse. A periodic accounting for the physical quantity on hand is essential.

A large organization works with many vendors, and inventory systems must include the details of who supplies which items. Price changes from the vendors are part of business. When they occur, inventory records must be adjusted to reflect current costs. Old information is useless for determining current profit margins or estimating the value of items on hand.

Because some items are more popular than others, and because the demand for some items varies seasonally, an important feature of an inventory system is the capability to accumulate demand history throughout the month and fiscal year.

Types of Transaction The transactions associated with computer-based inventory management include the following.

—*Inventory withdrawal:* recording the removal of quantities on hand from the warehouse so that records indicate the items remaining.

—*Inventory receipt:* changing quantity-on-hand records to show the arrival of additional supplies. If the price paid for the items changes, the recorded unit cost of the item also must be adjusted to show the current purchase cost.

—*Item inquiry:* examining the record of a particular item to determine the current quantity on hand or to review other information about the item or its sales history.

—*Item maintenance:* adding or deleting items carried in inventory.

When new items are added to the list of items stocked, of course complete information must be provided to identify and describe the item, as the master file record layout shows. But when an item will be deleted, the only information that must be submitted is the identification number of the item and the instruction for the system to delete the record.

In all other cases, whether quantities, prices, or vendors require adjustment, the data to change the items must be provided, along with the identification number.

Files The primary file in an inventory system is the inventory master file. Figure 10.14 shows the data items generally included in such a file, whether used in an online or batch environment.

If the inventory application is used on a stand-alone basis, there will also be a separate vendor file. However, if the inventory function is integrated into the accounts payable system, a common master file may be used.

Output A variety of reports and listings are available from a typical inventory system. They include:

—Inventory listing
—Inventory performance report
—Vendor listing
—Suggested order list
—Receiving report
—Price change report
—Worksheets for physical inventory

Figures 10.14 and 10.15, respectively, present examples of an inventory listing and a physical inventory worksheet.

Figure 10.14 Inventory Master File List

GENERAL SUPPLY COMPANY
4321 PEACHTREE STREET
ATLANTA, GEORGIA 30303

** MASTER FILE LISTING **

STOCK #	DESCRIPTION	REFERENCE CODE	VENDOR NO.	STOCKING UNIT	ORDER UNIT	NUMBER/ UNIT	QUANTITY ON HAND	LAST COST	UNIT SELL	PERCENT MARGIN	VALUE AT LAST COST
R-2244	PENS/BLACK	A001	3	EA	BX	24	40	0.22	0.59	60.00	8.80
R-2245	PENS/RED	A002	3	EA	BX	24	50	0.22	0.59	60.00	11.00
T-1222	PENCILS #2	A010	2	EA	CS	12	100	0.09	0.14	60.00	9.00
M-5533	SCOTCH TAPE	B025	4	EA	CS	24	35	0.51	0.71	40.00	17.85
M-5525	MASKING TAPE	B028	4	EA	BX	12	40	0.40	0.80	50.00	16.00
S-4848	MARKER-BLUE	A003	2	EA	BX	24	50	0.30	0.60	50.00	15.00
S-4844	MARKER-RED	A004	2	EA	BX	24	45	0.30	0.60	50.00	13.50
S-4845	MARKER-BLACK	A005	2	EA	BX	24	38	0.30	0.60	50.00	11.40
D-1667	NOTEBOOKS 3X5	D001	6	EA	BX	12	25	0.45	0.90	50.00	11.25
D-1670	NOTEBOOKS 6X4	D002	6	EA	BX	12	35	0.52	1.05	50.00	18.20
E-1822	PADS (8X11)	D122	6	EA	BX	12	50	0.27	0.55	50.00	13.50
E-1825	PADS (8X14)	D125	6	EA	BX	12	45	0.32	0.65	50.00	14.40
Q-8971	CALENDAR	C003	12	EA	BX	6	15	0.70	0.91	30.00	10.50
C-1049	GEM CLIPS (SM)	F023	8	EA	BX	24	35	0.42	0.59	40.00	14.70
C-1050	GEM CLIPS (LG)	F025	8	EA	BX	24	45	0.50	0.70	40.00	22.50

Figure 10.15 Inventory Worksheet

Physical Inventory Worksheet
January 1, 199X

STOCK #	DESCRIPTION	VENDOR	UNIT	QUANTITY	COMMENTS
R-2244	PENS/BLACK	3	EA	_____	_____
R-2245	PENS/RED	3	EA	_____	_____
T-1222	PENCILS #2	2	EA	_____	_____
M-5533	SCOTCH TAPE	4	EA	_____	_____
M-5525	MASKING TAPE	4	EA	_____	_____
S-4848	MARKER-BLUE	2	EA	_____	_____
S-4844	MARKER-RED	2	EA	_____	_____
S-4845	MARKER-BLACK	2	EA	_____	_____
D-1667	NOTEBOOKS 3x5	6	EA	_____	_____
D-1670	NOTEBOOKS 6x4	6	EA	_____	_____
E-1822	PADS (8x11)	6	EA	_____	_____
E-1825	PADS (8x14)	6	EA	_____	_____
Q-8971	CALENDAR	12	EA	_____	_____
C-1049	GEM CLIPS (SM)	8	EA	_____	_____
C-1050	GEM CLIPS (LG)	8	EA	_____	_____

In the next chapter, which deals with management information systems, we will see how transaction systems are used to support management decision making. The data captured through applications discussed here will serve as an important element of the decision process.

Summary

Information systems can be broken into three categories: transaction processing systems, management information systems, and decision support systems. Transaction processing systems substitute computer processing for manual record-keeping procedures and are characterized by applications that deal with well-structured and routine situations. Management information systems, designed to support decision making, provide the information needed by managers who face recurring situations. Decision support systems, on the other hand, are intended to inform and assist managers who must formulate judgments in relatively unstructured situations. In the latter, part of the decision process is in determining what information is needed since the problems are typically not recurring or routine.

Transaction processing systems support the sequence of activities that includes data capture, transaction processing, file maintenance, and reporting. Output prepared includes action documents, information documents, transaction logs, edit reports, and summary monitoring reports. The particular combination of reports and output, and the manner in which they are generated, will depend on the application.

Common transaction applications include accounting systems, order entry systems, inventory management, and point-of-sale applications. Each application includes a combination of master files or databases and transaction files that store data describing the entities (for example, customers, accounts, vendors, and so on) of concern. Master files are kept current by processing transaction data against them to reflect the most recent activity. These characteristics distinguish all transaction processing systems, regardless of the application area.

Key Words

Accounts payable	Decision support system	Order entry system
Accounts receivable	Fixed-length record	Point-of-sale (POS) system
Accrual accounting	General ledger	Transaction processing
Audit trail	Income statement	system
Balance sheet	Inventory management	Variable-length record
Cash accounting	Management information	
Chart of accounts	system	

Review Questions

1. What are the categories of information systems? Which types of systems focus on routine business activities and which do not?

2. What is a transaction processing system? What characteristics distinguish this type of system from other categories of information systems?

3. How do management information systems and decision support systems differ? How are they alike?

4. In what sequence of steps does transaction processing occur? Explain each step and the activities that occur.

5. What types of output are produced from transaction systems? Identify the characteristics of each category of output.

6. Discuss the purpose of accounting systems. Why is an accounting system characterized as a transaction processing system?

7. What four questions must an accounting system be able to answer for each transaction that occurs in business?

8. How do cash and accrual methods differ? How are they alike? What is the relation of these methods to double-entry accounting?

9. Identify and discuss the distinguishing features of accounting systems.

10. What is the purpose of an accounts receivable system? Why is this system classified as a transaction processing application?

11. What types of transactions must an accounts receivable system handle? Explain the purpose of each.

12. Identify the types of output produced by a typical accounts receivable system and briefly describe the purpose of each one.

13. Discuss the types of transactions handled by accounts payable systems. To handle these transactions, what data must the master files contain?

14. How does the user control whether a specific invoice is paid through an automated accounts payable system? What other payment decisions can the user make?

15. What is the relation between the general ledger system and other accounting systems? What purpose does the general ledger system serve?

16. What is the purpose of the balance sheet and income statements produced through a general ledger system?

17. Discuss the activities included in general ledger processing.

18. What is the relation between the general ledger system and the chart of accounts?

19. Discuss the common features of automated order entry systems.

20. What is a point-of-sale system? What is its purpose?

21. What transactions must an inventory management system process? What data does the master file contain to associate transactions and inventory management details?

Application Problems

1. Major medical and health insurance carriers must process many claims for payments from physicians and policyholders each week. The amount of money paid out for the claims ranges into millions of dollars. In addition to the cost of the claims, the insurance companies must also pay staff members to enter the data from each claim into the computer system for processing. Large processing centers often employ 50 or more persons.

   One large insurance carrier, aware of the number of physicians who have purchased personal computers, wants to develop software for the physicians for handling of insurance claims. The software will allow staff members in a physician's office to enter claims data into the personal computer for storage on magnetic flexible diskette. (Staff members must now type claims data on paper forms. The forms are mailed to the carrier and are the source documents for data entry.) When diskettes are full, they will be mailed to the carrier where they will be entered directly into the processing stream—ahead of paper claim forms that must be key entered.

   a. What features should the software to be used in the physician offices have? What functions should the software perform?

   b. What additional software features will need to be added to the insurance company's processing system?

c. What advantages does the concept described above offer to the insurance company? What are the risks?

d. What advantages and disadvantages does the processing concept offer to the physician?

2. A small-business owner, with sales of approximately $5 million annually, has decided to automate the firm's accounting system. The firm's accounting requirements are somewhat unique since it deals with custom-made products. Currently all general ledger activities are performed by an outside auditor who bills the firm approximately $1000 each month for services rendered. Accounts receivable and accounts payable are handled by separate employees who are accurate and reliable. An electronic bookkeeping machine, which the firm owns, is used to post charges and payments to the paper ledger cards now used to record accounts receivable. The machine is also used to prepare checks to vendors for merchandise received or services rendered. A maintenance contract, which costs the firm approximately $125 per month, covers all parts and labor costs should repairs be needed on the machine.

When invoices are received, they are examined for accuracy and then filed by due date. Once each week the accounts payable supervisor reviews the invoices and writes the checks for those invoices to be paid (using the bookkeeping machine). A record of the payments, including the general ledger account to which they should be posted, is prepared manually. The record, along with copies of the checks, is sent to the auditor at the end of the month who reviews each transaction for accuracy and also prepares a balance sheet and profit-and-loss statements.

Customer statements are prepared and mailed once each month. Each manually prepared statement lists the name and address of the customer, the previous account balance, all charges, payments, and adjustments since the last payment, and the current balance. The accounts are not aged.

The owner wishes to purchase a personal computer to handle the accounting activities, and anticipates that all accounts receivable and accounts payable processing would be managed using the computer system. The bookkeeping machine would no longer be needed. The owner has not yet discussed the matter with the auditor who maintains the company's general ledger.

The owner is debating whether to purchase a software package for the popular brand of personal computer being considered, or contract with someone to write the software. One question that comes to mind is whether the custom product business will also mean custom software needs for accounting.

a. What factors should be considered in determining whether a personal computer is suitable for handling the firm's accounting activities?

b. What would you tell the owner about the likelihood of locating suitable accounting software to handle accounts receivable, accounts payable, and general ledger activities? What advantages or disadvantages can such software provide?

c. Suppose the personal computer costs approximately $5000 to acquire and accounting software another $3000. Is this a good investment for the company to make?

d. What role will the auditor for the company have if an accounting system is purchased that integrates accounts receivable, accounts payable, and general ledger—that is, if the system automatically posts accounting transactions to the general ledger and can provide end-of-month balance sheets and profit-

and-loss statements? Does the installation of an in-house computer system diminish the importance of the auditor to the firm?

3. An accounting system has been designed so that once a transaction is entered into the system and stored, it is not possible for the operator to change any details of the transaction (prior to telling the system to store the transaction, any data can be rekeyed or changed). All transactions must be adjusted by creating an adjusting transaction that alters the effect of the transaction in question.

For instance, if a cash payment is accidentally posted to an insurance expense account rather than to an advertising account, because the wrong account number was entered by mistake, it is not possible for the operator to retrieve the transaction and simply change the account number. Instead a new transaction must be entered that shows the adjustment of the expense from the insurance account to the advertising account.

The individuals in a company using this system are seeking to have the software changed. They indicate that the current design of the system is cumbersome and that the audit trail provisions are excessive when additional transactions are required simply to correct an error. They wish to be able to retrieve the transaction and change account numbers and dollar amounts directly, even after the transaction has been stored. They argue that the original documentation that led to the creation of the accounting transaction will still be useful in an audit to show whether a transaction was properly handled.

Are the users' criticisms of the software valid and are their assumptions regarding records for audit purposes correct? Consider the objectives for accounting and how they are met through the system described here. What recommendation would you make?

4. The university library currently uses a manual system to keep track of all books in its collection and whether they are on the shelf, in repair, or on loan to a borrower. It wishes to automate the system for better control and to provide more rapid access to information about the collection.

When books arrive, they are cataloged on 3 × 5 inch index cards: one for the name of the primary author, one by the book title, and one by subject classification. Because of the high volume of books processed, it is possible to have one copy only of each card.

After the books are recorded on catalog cards, a reference number is assigned using the Library of Congress coding system, a standard system used by many library systems to identify and catalog books. The reference number is recorded on each catalog card and on the book itself. A checkout card is placed in each book containing the title, author, and reference number of the book. A book must have this card before it can be made available for lending. After the card is inserted, the books are placed on the shelf for open borrowing.

Anyone with a library card can check out books. The authorized lending period depends on the status of the cardholder: students may check books out for two weeks; faculty members have four weeks. All other authorized cardholders have two-week borrowing privileges.

The current system requires the borrower to take the books selected to the checkout desk. A library assistant removes the checkout card from the book and enters the borrower's name and 9-digit identification number on the card (each class of borrower has a different type of identification number). A due date is determined and stamped on the card and a return card specifying this return date is inserted into the book.

As time permits, the checkout cards are filed by reference number. A cataloging assistant must then peruse all cards of checked-out books to identify those that are overdue. Form letters, with handwritten names of books and borrowers, are prepared and sent to individuals who are holding overdue books.

When a book is returned, cataloging assistants pull the checkout card from the card file and reinsert it in the book. The books are then returned to the shelf for use by other patrons.

a. What are the transactions in the library system as it currently functions? What information is captured during each transaction? What details identify a particular transaction?

b. Evaluate the efficiency of the current library transaction system. Also identify those transactions that are candidates for automation through computer processing. Indicate why you believe they should be automated.

c. What efficiency advantages can be gained through installation of a computer-based system for the library described here? For each proposed advantage indicate the processing assumptions you make. What reporting advantages are possible?

5. "Computerized inventory management systems are overrated," claims the warehouse supervisor of one company: "These systems cannot do anything that a good supervisor cannot do with accurate, up-to-date ledger cards. When items arrive, the quantity arriving is added to the quantity already on the shelf. When items leave the warehouse, the quantity removed is subtracted from the amount on hand.

"If we want to know how quickly an item is selling, we pull the card and review quantity changes. Each of the purchasing people looks at the records to determine what stock must be ordered. We seldom run out of anything. The buyers make sure we have plenty of stock.

"When you bring in a computer, you not only have inventory to manage, you must also manage the computer. When you store your records in the computer, they are inaccessible if the computer is inoperable. You become dependent on the machine. At least with manual records, you can get at them any time."

a. Is the warehouse supervisor right? How would you respond to the supervisor about the differences between manual and automated inventory management systems?

b. What transactions must be handled in an inventory management system? For each transaction, describe the data that must be processed.

c. Review the discussion of inventory systems in this chapter. What other features should an inventory system have that the supervisor does not mention?

6. Identify the type of report that each of the following transaction system output examples represents (choose between action document, information document, transaction log, edit report, or summary monitoring report).

a. A list of all library books borrowed during the day

b. Beginning and inventory item report balanced for the past week

c. Notice of insurance claims accepted for processing during the week for a specific physician

d. Overdue books report

e. Cash overage and shortage report for transactions accumulated on a specific point-of-sale terminal

f. Accounting balance sheet

g. Purchase change order

h. Hotel reservation confirmation

7. A restaurant wishes to install point-of-sale systems to increase efficiency and eliminate errors. As conceived, the system will contain prices for all individual items on the menu. When servers take a customer's order, they will go to one of the point-of-sale terminals and enter the order. The keyboard of the terminal contains a key for each item, labeled to describe the item, and each item ordered is entered separately. As the item is entered, the price is retrieved from memory and printed, along with the menu item, on the guest check inserted in the terminal's check printer.

The system also stores food inventory information, and inventory quantities are reduced each time an item is served. At the same time, a record is accumulated to show which items were served, who served them, and the time of the transaction. At the end of the day, management can print a list of transactions for the period, sales by server, and inventory quantities.

a. What transactions drive each aspect of the point-of-sale system? What data is needed for each transaction?

b. What files must be included in this system to allow it to function as described above?

c. What weaknesses do you see in this system?

d. What factors should be considered to determine whether the system described is cost effective? Acceptable to the servers? Beneficial to the organization?

Minicase: Service Merchandise Silent Sam System

Service Merchandise, Inc., is a Nashville-based chain of catalog showroom outlets. The chain includes approximately 300 stores on the East Coast. All the items carried by the store are listed in a hefty color catalog, and each bears an 8-digit identification number.

As currently structured, the system operates as follows. Customers place orders by writing the identification number, item description, and discount price on an order form, which is given to an assistant at an order desk. The assistant keys the information, along with the customer's name, into a terminal and immediately receives confirmation of the price and the availability of the item in inventory. Customers pay for the merchandise when they place the order and are given a receipt. Within approximately 5 minutes, the ordered merchandise is delivered at a counter elsewhere in the store. To pick up merchandise, a customer must show his or her receipt.

Recently, the company's information systems department has developed the concept of a Silent Sam system. Rather than going to an order desk, customers will be able to use any of several terminals scattered around the store to enter order transactions. The proposed system will allow people to enter the identification number of any item they wish to order. In turn, the system will retrieve and display information to the customer confirming that the item is on hand (in stock) and the current price. The system will automatically quote special sales prices though a customer may not be aware that an item is on sale. If an item is out of stock, a substitute will automatically be suggested by the system.

After processing each order, the system will query the customer to determine whether he or she wishes to place another order. When the last order has been confirmed, the customer will be instructed to go to the pickup desk to pay for and receive the merchandise. Using Silent Sam, customers will *not* pay for merchandise until they pick it up.

Service Merchandise feels that Silent Sam will allow the company to serve more customers, faster, without the addition of staff members.

Questions

1. Should the Silent Sam system be developed? Why or why not?

2. What features must the system have to be usable by customers who lack computer training? What procedural adjustments must be made at the pickup desk? What methods do you suggest to deal with these changes?

3. Can Service Merchandise rely on transaction information for its sales and inventory planning if customers control the entry of critical information, as specified earlier? Explain.

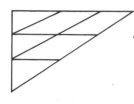

11: Management Information Systems

Key Questions

What factors underlie the complex information flows in an organization?

What distinguishes an information system from an MIS?

How are the functional elements in an MIS related to one another?

Is the total systems approach to MIS practical?

Does the federation approach to MIS provide for future flexibility?

What is the distinction between MIS and data or transaction processing?

Creating the Managerial Knowledge Base

During the last 200 years, no country has become a major economic power by following in the footsteps of earlier leaders. Each started out with what were, at the time, advanced industries and advanced production and distribution processes. And each, very fast, became a leader in management. Today, however, in part because of automation information and advanced technology, but in much larger part because of the demand for trained people in all areas of management, development requires a knowledge base that few developing countries possess or can afford. How to create an adequate managerial knowledge base fast is the critical question in economic development today. It is also one for which we have no answer so far.

Peter Drucker
"Management and the World's Work," *Harvard Business Review, 66*(5),
(September–October 1988)

Management information systems (MIS) involve more than just hardware, software, and information. They integrate different areas of the organization. This is not a new idea, nor is it synonymous with computer usage per se. The MIS has been an essential part of business management as we have known it for some time.

Why then is so much attention being given to the use of computers for supporting management decision making? The reason is that computers make the objectives more reachable. Processing data, storing and retrieving information, and improving communication throughout a firm have been fundamental concerns of managers for many years, and computer-based information systems have the potential to promote the efficient handling of these functions.

As we study the issues, a more precise meaning for the term *management information systems* will develop. The conceptual framework introduced in the preceding chapter will be extended to help the reader analyze the objectives of management information systems in this chapter and decision support systems in Chapter 12.

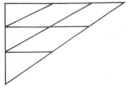

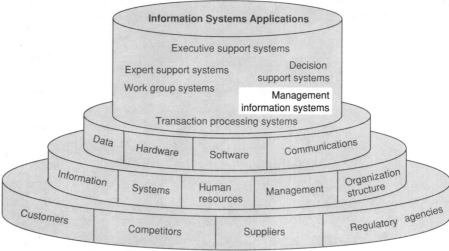

Information Systems Applications

Executive support systems

Expert support systems

Decision support systems

Work group systems

Management information systems

Transaction processing systems

Data | Hardware | Software | Communications

Information | Systems | Human resources | Management | Organization structure

Customers | Competitors | Suppliers | Regulatory agencies

We also examine examples of common management information systems. Our discussion will focus on *marketing information systems, production information systems,* and *personnel skills information systems*. Each will build on transaction processing systems discussed in Chapter 10.

Why Should You Know About Management Information Systems?

In many organizations, MIS is a commonly heard term. In others, the term is not used at all; other expressions that refer to the same type of system are used—for example, data system, computer information system, merchandise system, corporate support system, or sales system. The name is not nearly as important as the system's function, and it is the function you should know about. Here are some of the reasons why you should be familiar with management information systems:

——*Problem solving and decision making increasingly rely on MIS*. Management information systems are in widespread use throughout organizations in many industries of diverse size. They are fundamental tools. Even if you are not an information systems professional, you must be familiar with the capabilities of MIS. Otherwise, you will have a noticeable deficiency in your business and professional background.

—— *You are affected by those who use management information systems.* Even if you do not use an MIS yourself, others that you will work with probably do. The characteristics of the system and the way they use them will affect you. So will the information they draw from the system.

—— *You can influence their design and use.* Knowing what capabilities are built into an MIS gives you insight into the way such systems can be used effectively. It also enables you to recognize when expectations for a system go beyond its limits.

—— *An MIS in a firm you are familiar with may be ineffective.* Management information systems may be designed improperly. Whether you are a user or a systems developer, it is essential to be able to tell when a business problem stems from an MIS problem rather than from another source. Or stated differently, if you cannot tell when an MIS is bad, you can't tell when it is effective either.

The remainder of this chapter explores the characteristics of management information systems as well as typical examples of different types of MIS. We begin with a management framework.

A Management Framework

The term *computer-based information systems* collectively refers to both management information systems (MIS) and decision support systems (DSS). These systems operate within a management framework that ties together all parts of the organizations. The main entities of this framework have already been introduced (see Chapters 3 and 4). This section draws these elements together as they apply to the use of information systems in decision making.

Figure 11.1 represents the different components within management: multiple levels of management, activities ranging from operations to planning, and different degrees of structure in decision making and problem solving. Operating-level transactions, as you know, drive the entire organization. Important and relevant transaction data therefore are captured and stored through an organized system, as discussed in Chapter 10.

Some decisions are routine. They are called for in situations that occur often enough to warrant the development of procedures to handle them. On the other hand, some decisions are nonroutine, and the need to make them arises infrequently. Sales order processing and approving customer credit are routine: We can quickly identify the relevant factors to consider when trying to decide whether to accept an order or approve credit. Determining whether to launch a new product or to close a plant represent nonroutine, unstructured decision-making situations: Clearcut procedures seldom exist for dealing with them.

Figure 11.1 A Framework for Management and Organizations

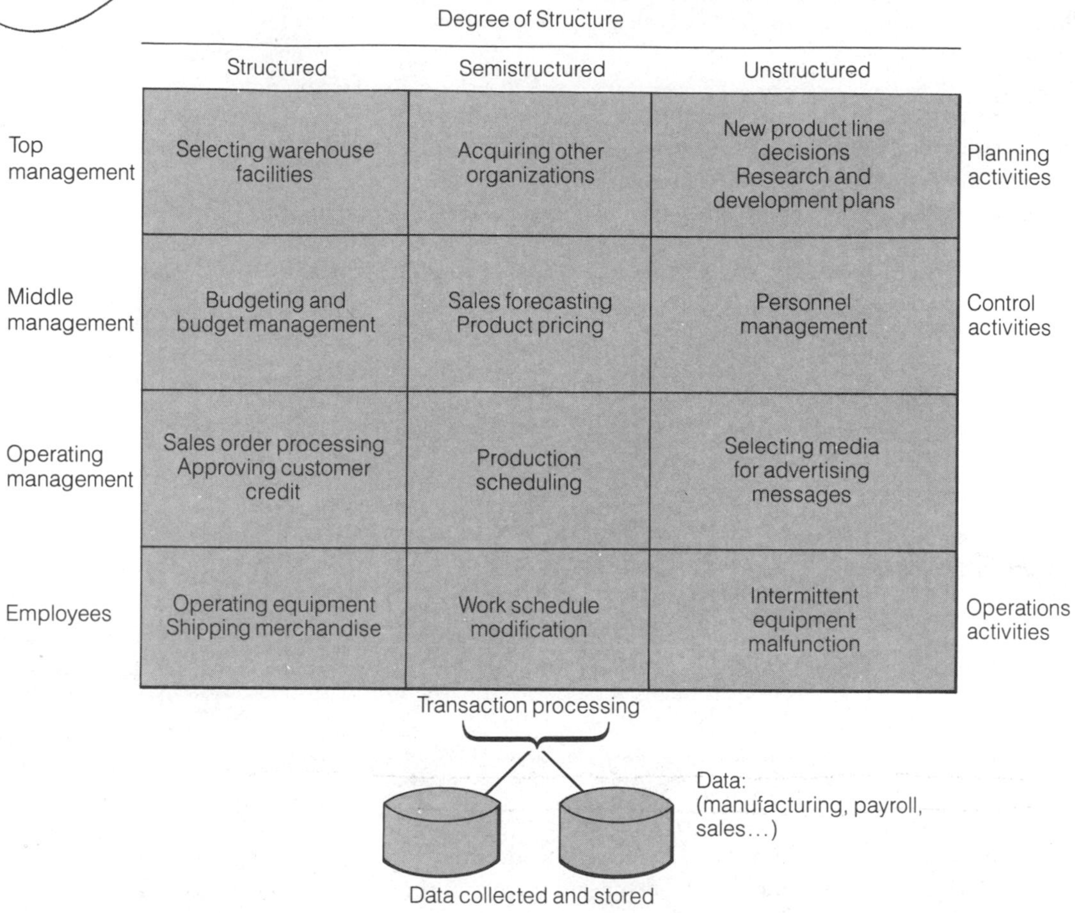

Degree of Structure

	Structured	Semistructured	Unstructured	
Top management	Selecting warehouse facilities	Acquiring other organizations	New product line decisions Research and development plans	Planning activities
Middle management	Budgeting and budget management	Sales forecasting Product pricing	Personnel management	Control activities
Operating management	Sales order processing Approving customer credit	Production scheduling	Selecting media for advertising messages	Operations activities
Employees	Operating equipment Shipping merchandise	Work schedule modification	Intermittent equipment malfunction	Operations activities

Transaction processing

Data:
(manufacturing, payroll, sales...)

Data collected and stored

Some decisions are semistructured. That is, parts of the decision can be automated, but some of the more critical aspects cannot. Instead, they need the judgment and experience of the decision makers themselves.

The same structured and unstructured relationships exist at the employee level: Many activities are structured and clearly spelled out in operating procedures, but other activities occur only infrequently and are not covered by standard routines. For instance, the procedures for operating manufacturing equipment and for shipping merchandise to customers are well defined; these activities occur regularly. However, equipment that malfunctions intermittently or merchandise that is not to be shipped until several months after it has been paid for will cause problems for a firm's employees. The experience or intuition of an individual may suggest certain actions even though no company policy clearly applies to the situation. On the other hand, a manager may have to be summoned to determine what to do.

Transaction processing is related to all levels of the organization. But, as you know, the vast majority of **transactions** occur at the operating level, and it is here that data about them are collected. Although managers further up in the hierarchy can use many of these data, they need other decision support as well. Hence, although transaction processing systems are necessary in organizations, they are not sufficient to support all managers' decision activities. This is the role of management information systems and decision support systems.

An Information Systems Perspective

Organizations are **systems** consisting of **subsystems** known as divisions, departments, functional areas, and workstations. Figure 11.2 shows some of the subsystems or areas in a manufacturing organization: Marketing, Production, Purchasing, and Inventory Control all contribute to Information Systems, and vice versa, in coordinating the aspects of the organization named inside the large box. These functional areas operate independently. Managers in the departments have the discretion to hire personnel and schedule work. But at the same time, all the subsystems must fit together so that each area performs according to expectations.

Planning and coordination of activities for all units is necessary. The subsystems must work together to accomplish common organization-wide goals. This means that each functional area must be aware both of the needs of other areas and of the demands it makes on the entire system. In short, members (managers or staff) of each subsystem need to know what is expected of them and how their input or output will be integrated with other units or functional areas. At the same time, managers who are responsible for integration must be able to keep abreast of operations. They need information about activities that tells them whether work is being

Figure 11.2 Information Concerns for Coordinating Organization Subsystems

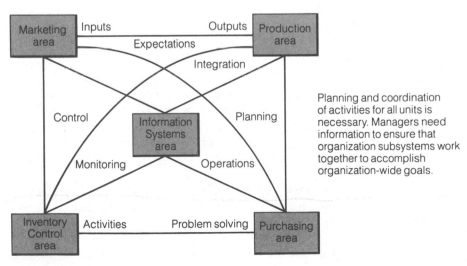

Planning and coordination of activities for all units is necessary. Managers need information to ensure that organization subsystems work together to accomplish organization-wide goals.

Figure 11.3 Information Flow to Coordinate Organizational Functions

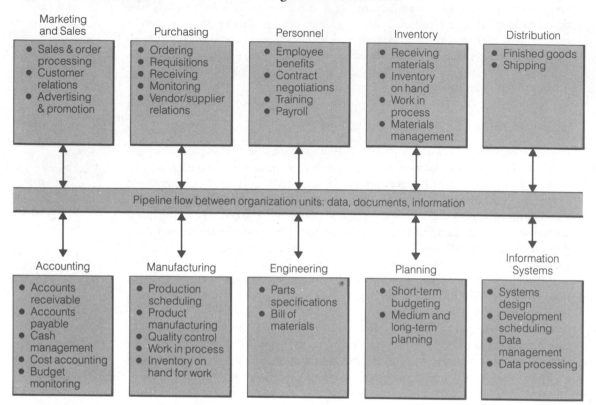

performed according to expectations. In other words, managers need information for control of operations and for problem solving.

Information Flow

Operating decisions in a complex organization call for input from the area that will generate the activity and also from areas that will be affected by the decision. Figure 11.3 identifies matters that will become the subjects of decisions by various departments. Thus marketing managers will establish sales strategies and set quotas for merchandise to be sold, and personnel managers will oversee the hiring and training of employees.

However, a decision in one area usually affects other areas of the firm as well. Salespersons can sell only what the production department manufactures. The production area is constrained by the size of the staff and the amount and kind of equipment available. Clearly, a flow of information is necessary so that activities are balanced. The decision and feedback processes for information are interconnected;

Figure 11.4 Interlocking Decisions and Information Flows

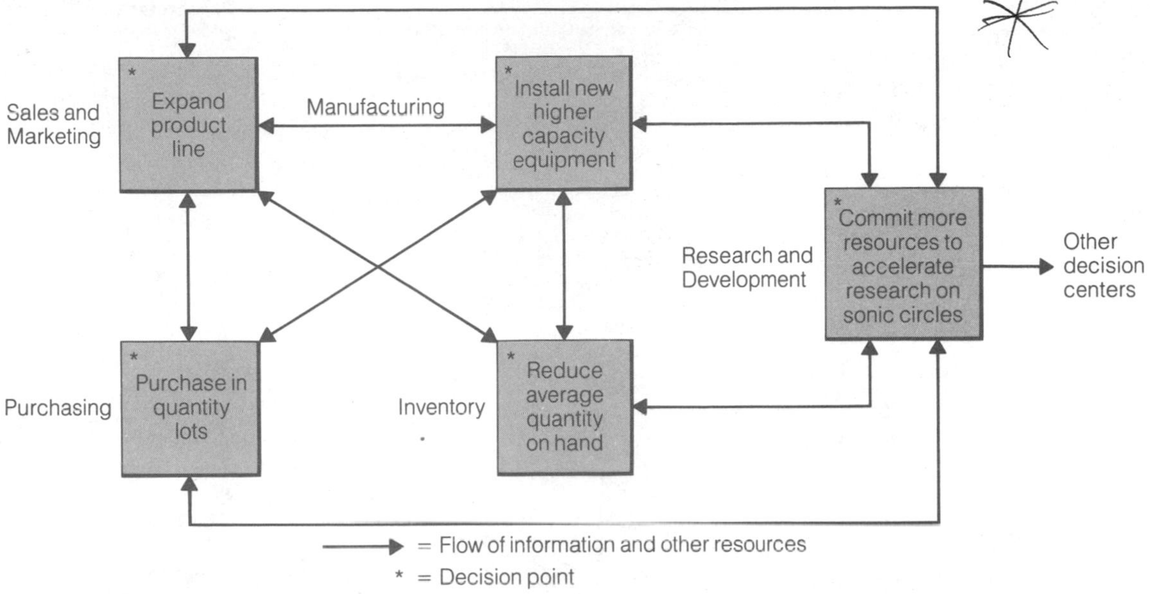

= Flow of information and other resources
* = Decision point

business centers affect each other, as suggested by the pipeline flow of informational material between departments shown in Figure 11.3.

Complex situations, however, require a set of <u>interlocking decisions</u> (Figure 11.4). The channels of information deal with everything from ordering materials to hiring employees to planning facilities expansion. Every point at which an activity or process occurs is backed up by a decision point whose information sources reach into other parts of the organization and its environment. We refer to these points as **decision centers.** As decision centers increase in importance and the decisions they make become more critical, there is a tendency to formalize the flow of information between them.

Certain data must be collected and stored for use *within* a decision center, although some of the data are processed and passed along as information to other parts of the firm (Figure 11.5). This may be done through either manual or automated means. Some information may be transmitted routinely and other items only on request. The need for the information may or may not have been anticipated.

Consider for a moment a large banking system. We can visualize a main office and a number of branch offices throughout the geographic area. Each office is operated by a bank manager and assistants. Five major activities take place at each bank office: namely, transactions involving demand deposit accounts, savings accounts, installment loans, home loans, and commercial loans. Forecasting and planning, which guide the other activities, also occur and each of these is, in turn, guided by the deposit and loan transactions.

Figure 11.5 Typical Distribution of Information Between Decision Centers

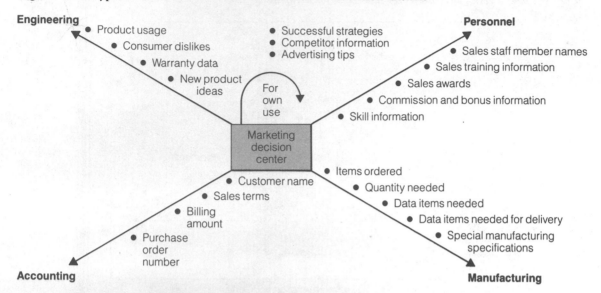

Each year individual managers lay out monthly asset, liability, income, and expense goals or projections. At the end of each month, actual balances or figures on these activities are added to those shown in the plan. Additionally, branch figures are consolidated with figures at the main office to give totals in summary form. Statements of condition and journals of transactions for all bank branches and departments are updated daily.

In this situation, many decisions and transactions take place (Figure 11.6). Incoming funds, of course, have much to do with interest rates and the availability of money for commercial loans. If total dollar deposits are increasing, more money can be allocated to loans. However, if prices are rising and unemployment is increasing in the community, families and businesses may modify their spending patterns, thus causing adjustments in the interest rates.

These changes also affect the discretion of loan officers and branch managers to accept new accounts. If credit has tightened, loan officers perhaps have fewer funds to lend out. Similarly, any loan accepted reduces the pool of money available to other branch managers for making loans. It also decreases the funds available for outside investment.

Each branch manager, along with top-level bank management, needs to be constantly abreast of the inflow and outflow of funds. Should savings or demand deposit accounts drop at one or all branches, loan policies may be adjusted. Consequently, a continual monitoring of transactions is necessary. At the same time, managers need to be able to compare their performance against planned goals and objectives, which are stated in terms of asset, liability, income, and expense projections. The success with which one manager meets the objectives and operates within constraints affects all other managers throughout the system.

Figure 11.6 Flow of Information and Control in a Bank System

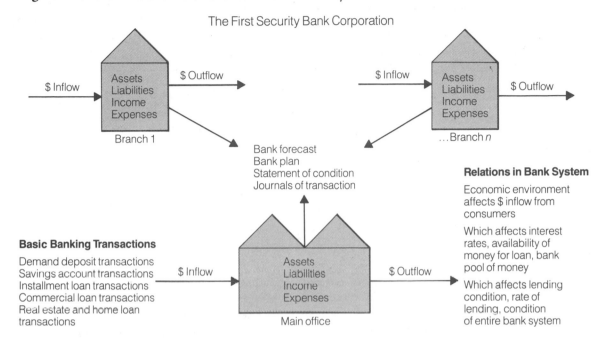

We see action–decision points in virtually all organizations. Sales force activities affect production decisions; purchasing actions directly impact what the production department can and cannot produce (and vice versa), and so on. Each point in the system needs information to keep abreast of developments in other parts of the enterprise. Should necessary information be unavailable, management actions and decisions may be less effective.

Management Information

In a certain sense, the information system of each manager in an organization is tailored to the individual's unique characteristics (attitudes and aptitudes), and any two managers are likely to have different perspectives on a given situation (Figure 11.7). For example, a decrease in the average size of payment on charge accounts may signal a potential increase in overdue or uncollectable accounts to one department store manager and a decrease in overall charges to another. How this "signal" will be interpreted depends on the information available. For example, does the first manager have aggregate data on total credit balances and related trends in charging? Prior experience in similar situations (if any) also affects one's perception of a situation. A loan or credit manager who has experienced periods of recession accompanied by slowdowns in account payments perceives the situation differently perhaps from a recent MBA.

Figure 11.7 Differing Interpretations from the Same Information: An Important Information Systems Consideration

While managers have different specific information needs, their general needs are often similar to those of their colleagues. For example, if a production schedule is being planned, managers must be aware of demands for certain products, costs associated with the production aspects of each item, the material requirements for each, and the respective inventories of materials on hand.

It is generally impossible for one person in a large firm to collect this information continually and also to have accurate and up-to-date figures. But there is no reason, for example, that production managers *should* be expected to collect all the accounting information they need. In the same sense, the accountant is not normally expected to schedule production, monitor preventive maintenance programs, or order tools and dies for manufacturing lines.

The manager needs selected information on activities throughout the organization, but it is not always easy to identify just what information is necessary. And it is not always clear how the information is to be obtained. In some cases, the information is stored knowledge on the status of projects, programs, activities, and so forth. Other information of interest to the manager may be constraints imposed on the department or division by higher-level management. Or it may be necessary to process unaggregated data to produce information not available elsewhere.

Systems for Management

Each functional area or department has its own system for gathering and using information. In a large industrial firm, there are usually systems for marketing, production, and accounting information, to name a few. In a certain sense, each system stands alone since it is used by the department in which it resides. However, since each is part of the organization, it is integrated with other systems and departments.

As we proceed to explore management information in detail, keep in mind the management framework we have been discussing.

Management Information Systems

A management information system (MIS) is an integrated system for providing information to support the planning, control, and operations of an organization. It aids operations, management, and decision making by providing past-, present-, and future-oriented information about internal operations and external intelligence (Figure 11.8). It provides uniform information in a timely fashion.

An MIS is organized to condense selected data from transaction processing and from the organization environment (competition, legislation, the economy) to develop information useful in management. It involves people, procedures, equipment, models, and data. This basic overview of MIS is expanded as we examine the following basic characteristics of MIS: relation to transaction systems, support of structured decisions, and different methods of presenting information to managers.

Relation to Transaction Processing System

In Chapter 10 we pointed out that the purpose of transaction processing is to capture and operate on data related to the business of the enterprise. The reasons for transaction processing were identified earlier as classification, sorting, calculation, summarization, and storage of data.

Transaction processing systems are not synonymous with MIS. However, an important relationship exists between them. Many of the data needed to support managerial decision-making activities originate from business transactions. For example, sales program decisions must be based partly on data pertaining to how well current sales promotions, policies, and procedures are working to meet overall marketing profit and expense objectives. Data of this nature (for example, cost of sales, number of sales made compared to calls on customers, average units sold per customer) are captured and stored in the transaction processing system. Without this system, the data would not be easily available for management use.

The mere existence of a transaction processing system, no matter how effective it may be, does not mean that the organization has an information system. Captured data must go beyond the transaction processing system. They must be selectively used and further processed (Figure 11.9) before they produce the information needed by managers. Thus, the two systems are related—transaction processing supports information systems.

Support of Structured Decisions

Whereas transaction systems are related to operating activities (sales, orders, personnel, purchasing), information systems are management tools. They support decision-making activities, particularly those that are well understood, repetitive, and structured. These decisions are most common at the operating and middle-management levels.

Since decisions supported by information systems are recurring, a substantial amount of time can be devoted to analysis of information requirements, design of

Figure 11.8 Key Elements in a Management Information System

Integrated systems	Links together functional areas that depend on each other to accomplish mission of the organization. Enables functional areas to operate and carry out activities.	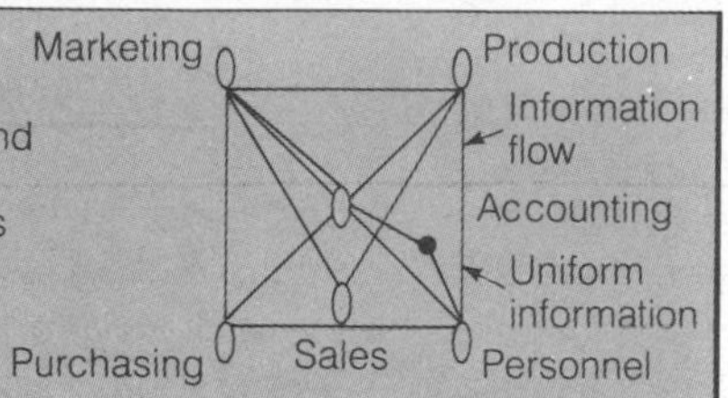 Marketing, Production, Information flow, Accounting, Uniform information, Purchasing, Sales, Personnel
Supporting planning, control, and operations	Each of these activities is required in every business area. All areas do planning and control to ensure that business occurs in a desirable (and profitable) way. Individuals must also plan and control their work, order materials in advance of need, etc.	
Management and decision making	A critical function of management is making decisions and solving problems. Some are unique; others recur frequently and regularly. In all cases, timely and accurate information is needed.	Launch new product? Accept merger offer? How to improve productivity?
Past, present, and future	Where the organization, division, or unit within the enterprise was, is now, will be, or should be tomorrow?	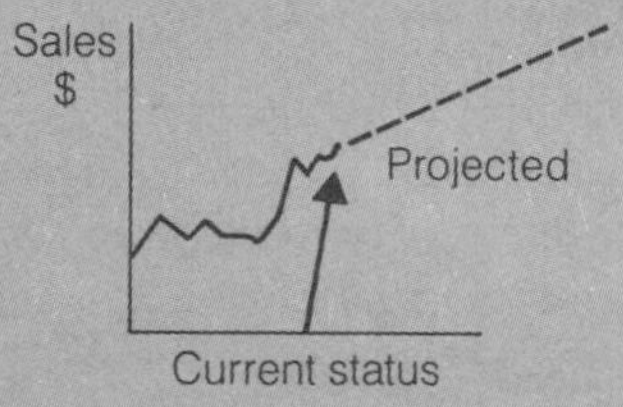 Sales $ — Projected — Current status
Internal operations	Monitoring ongoing operations, comparing them to expectations, and signaling areas in which adjustment or improvement is needed and areas that are in control.	Scrap rate? Cost of sale? Return on investment?
External intelligence	Monitoring events and opportunities outside the organization that affect or could affect the future and continued operations of the enterprise.	Regulations? Competitor pricing strategy? Overall economy? New technology?

Figure 11.9 Successive Processing of Transaction Data for Management Decisions

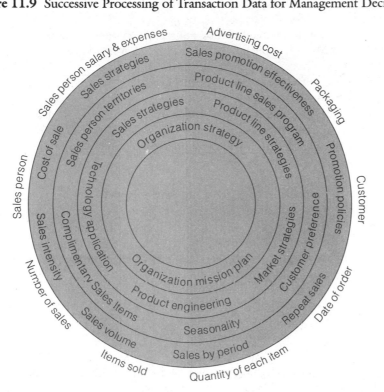

system specifications, and development of programs, procedures, and files. Components of the system will be used many times. Therefore, efficiency is important here, just as it is in transaction systems.

Presentation of Information

Report Generation To support decision making, an MIS provides reports containing relevant management information. *Report generation* involves processing data in stored files, through manual or mechanical means, to provide managers with information in convenient form. Such reports are generally summaries of events that have taken place over a period of time, although some provide a "snapshot" of the status of particular resources or processes at a specific time. Sales and inventory reports are typical examples of the latter—they show the amount of sales or number of items in stock at a given time.

The report generation function serves to get information to managers who need it for problem solving. Consequently, the focus for this function is decision-oriented reports, rather than background reports.

On-Line Retrieval The *on-line retrieval* function is a counterpart to report generation. In many situations, individuals have particular questions about work requirements that do not require the preparation of a full report. In these situations, it should be possible for the MIS to supply information on the problem or question in the proper form in a relatively short time.

For example, airline reservation systems provide agents and managers with the capability to retrieve from the system information about flight schedules, aircraft utilization, fuel availability, and other matters that will affect their decisions. Often it is not necessary to prepare a detailed printed report; only a single piece of information may be needed, and it may be wanted immediately. In these cases, the on-line retrieval capability is appreciated.

Data Sources Information systems for management draw heavily, but not exclusively, on transaction data. In addition, data about resources, budgets, and plans are used to produce the reports managers need. In most cases, the data needed to produce management information are available in one or more files. The data may be in traditional master files, or in more sophisticated databases. However, they usually exist somewhere in the organization.

A Design View of Information Systems

An MIS should not be expected to provide all the information needed for each and every decision to be made. However, a well-developed system can provide much of it. The emphasis should be on providing *integrated* information to support *integrated* decision efforts. An individual preparing a contract bid for a billion-dollar federal defense project should be able to focus on all aspects of the organization that would be involved if the firm were awarded the contract. Persons facing other decisions, such as introduction of new products, face similar problems: They need to have uniform and cohesive information, not bits and pieces.

How is this achieved? What is the structure of an MIS that will do these things? To answer these questions—that is, to show how the pieces fit together—it is necessary to view MIS from a design perspective.

Single-System View

Is there a single MIS for the firm? Would having one MIS serving the entire organization be the best way of ensuring that uniform information is distributed to managers? This is one view of MIS that has been supported in the literature and among practitioners in industry. It is often called the *total systems view of MIS.* This approach envisions a global system carefully integrated into all parts of the firm. Under this philosophy, the system is construed to be **monolithic,** with formal information networks interrelated by design prior to implementation.

The single or total systems view is based on the assumption that managers' information needs can be identified or anticipated, as can ways in which information

Figure 11.10 (*a*) Total System, Showing Ideal Integration of Information Systems Components; (*b*) Close Integration in a Total System Affects Many Applications and Makes Changes Difficult

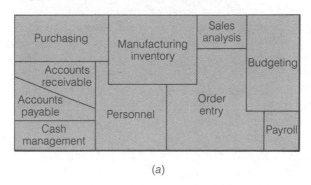

(a)

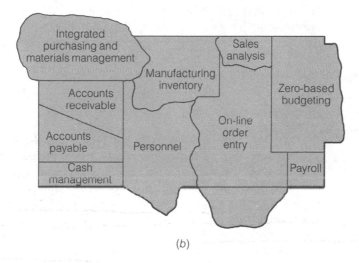

(b)

will be used. If this were completely true, we could design a system to ensure that all information was being produced and distributed to the right persons. Basically, this is the design of an ideal system (Figure 11.10*a*).

However, experience has proved that the total systems approach to MIS *does not work*. The industry no longer attempts to devise total systems. One of the most disconcerting aspects of the global systems concept is that information requirements and usage change as the MIS is used over the weeks and months of activity. Hence, what might be considered a total system when it is designed quickly becomes a deficient, partial system (Figure 11.10*b*). It is hard to imagine, for example, how a single information system could be developed to include all the accounting, manufacturing, inventory, purchasing, personnel, payroll, sales, and marketing functions. It is harder still to imagine how one information system could handle a companywide changeover to a new budgeting approach, say zero-based budgeting (where all operations must be rejustified and rebudgeted each year), without causing severe problems.

It is naive to assume that one group of persons, whether managers or systems experts, can design a single system that will meet operational requirements. And it is virtually impossible for one group of experts to have the vision and foresight to anticipate the totality of managers' needs, the various ways in which information might need to be integrated, and future changes that will be imposed by internal demands or changes in external constraints.

The total systems approach disregards the people in the system. Moreover, if all the pieces are fit carefully together, change is not possible. Compare an MIS with an automobile in which all components are built into a single frame and body; trim, lights, and even locks are part of one assembly. Now try to imagine replacing taillights without having the notion of "spare parts." It is difficult or impossible to adjust any one part. Yet this is exactly what a total system requires: a single body and frame, with all components built in.

The global MIS approach also implies that it is possible to determine which applications are economically justified and which ones are not cost effective. It is hard to believe that this is possible so far in advance of specific application projects that might be considered. We know that organizations evolve into information systems; yet a global, total systems approach does not permit this.

Multiple-System View

A more realistic view recognizes that an ideal system cannot be designed. It must be developed through experience in using the system and adding elements as they become necessary, understood, and feasible. This view also recognizes that changes are going to be needed to accommodate different managers, problems, and activities.

The multiple systems approach emphasizes the dependence of MIS on lower-level activities in the firm. It draws on and integrates information from several functional-area information systems to provide a uniform body of details and knowledge for uncertainty reduction in decision making. An MIS is therefore a collection of information systems—a cluster of related but independent business information systems that interface with one another and yet operate separately. An MIS might be considered to be a "federation" of systems or a "supersystem," in which each system is a building block in the larger organization MIS. A single system is a carefully designed and controlled component internally (perhaps analogous to the engine or transmission in an automobile), but only loosely integrated when put together with the other components (different engines or transmissions can be used in the same model automobile).

Rather than being a monolithic entity, an MIS is composed of the functional-area information systems in the organization. This structure enables specialists to collect the information they are best trained to gather. It makes sense that the accountant should be concerned with the collection of accounting information, marketing managers with marketing information, and so on. The systems are sets of computer programs and data, fed by reports generated according to system type

Figure 11.11 Federation of Information Systems with Optimal DBMS

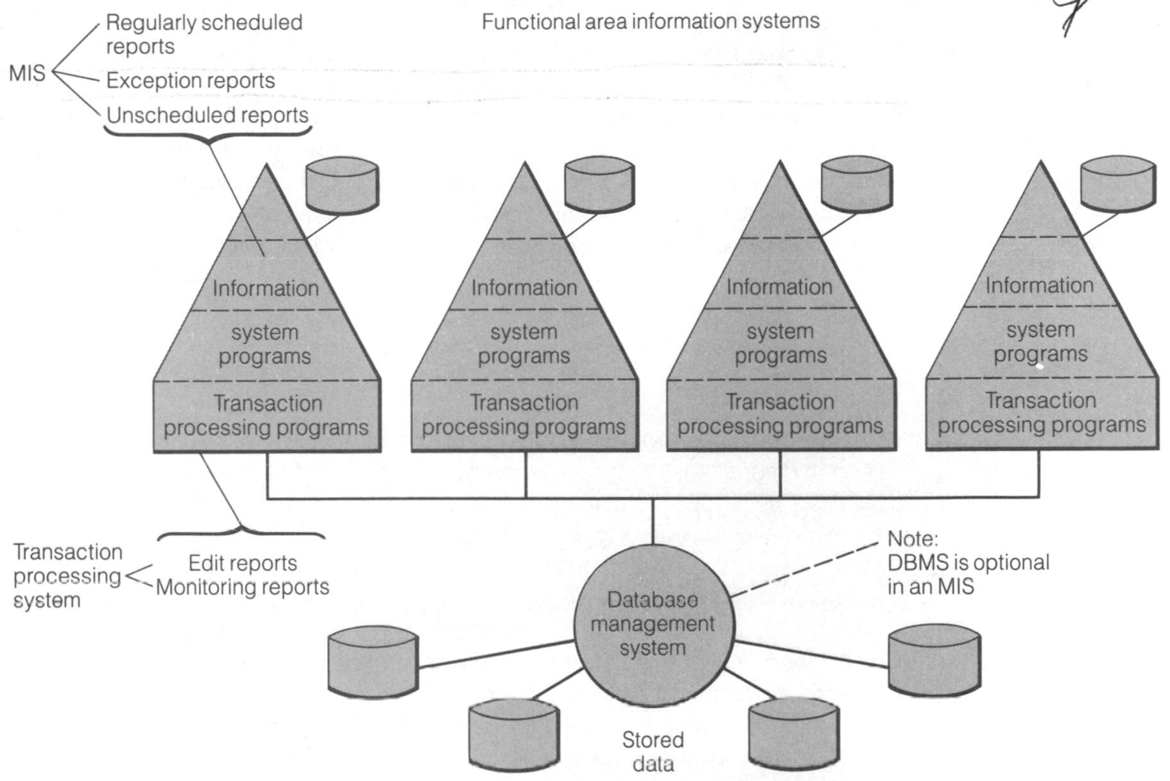

(Figure 11.11: transaction processing system reports were discussed in Chapter 10; the next section covers information systems reports).

The Role of Data

To be useful, the separate areas of an organization, as well as their information systems, must be integrated. As pointed out earlier, the continual flow of information between departments and units makes it possible to coordinate and control the activities that occur in each one. Functional-area information systems help in this traffic by providing the information necessary to integrate the activities. But the factor that integrates the separate information systems is data. In other words, a management system is constructed around a common core of data that can be used by each of the functional-area systems that comprise the MIS.

Data are stored because of their potential use in different areas of an enterprise. Because the data are a resource for the entire firm, it has become common to organize them into databases that are controlled to best meet all user requirements. Since the corporate database receives input and inquiries from throughout the firm, it serves as the center of the network of information flows. However, the way it is established, organized, maintained, and used significantly affects the success with which the MIS can function.

Not all data are stored in a centrally controlled database. Departments and functional areas may have files for their own use that do not need to be shared (but such data should not contradict the data in the database). When the same data are used in several applications and by users in different departments, however, they may be included in an organization database. These shared data files are necessary to achieve the uniformity in information that has been discussed. However, the fact that databases exist does not mean that all the data are in them.

Information Systems Reports

The information systems covered in Chapters 10–12 generate a variety of system-specific reports, which for convenience are summarized in Table 11.1. This chapter discusses only three: regularly scheduled, exception, and unscheduled reports.

Since the decisions supported through management information systems recur, many of the information requirements are known ahead of time. Consequently, the necessary supporting information can be produced regularly and according to a predetermined format. We call such documents **regularly scheduled reports.** Scheduled reports may be prepared daily, weekly, or monthly, depending on when the decision process must take place.

Regularly prepared reports are generally aimed at the operating and control levels of the organization, although a limited number may be prepared for higher-level management as well. The information supports such routine decision situations as inventory reordering and production scheduling.

Some reports are clerical and could be prepared by manual methods. However, it is often more economical and speedier to develop computer programs to generate this formatted, repetitive material.

Earlier it was pointed out that some systems support an on-line retrieval capability. In these systems, users can input keywords or commands and identification information. Prespecified routines are invoked to retrieve information and display it to the requester. Although retrieval is done on-line, the processing logic and output formats are built into the program. We compare this type of reporting with inquiry processing, to be discussed in Chapter 12.

Another kind of report generated automatically in information processing is the **exception report,** which is useful for detecting conditions that differ from those planned. For example, if the amount of scrap produced in a production and manufacturing system is supposed to be 1 percent, and during a certain week it turns out to be 5 percent, we would want to know about it. Therefore, we could program the computer system to process data about scrap rates, to ensure the production of exception reports when "out-of-bounds" cases arise.

Not all information requirements in the organization lend themselves to scheduled preparation of reports. This may be due partially to the diversity of managers'

Table 11.1 Reports Generated Through Information Systems

Type of Report	Source	Primarily Decision Oriented?	Description	Management Function(s) Supported	Discussed in
Edit	Transaction processing system	No	For detection of errors occurring during the processing of transactions and capture of data	Operations	Chapter 10
Monitoring	Transaction processing system	No	For monitoring activities and expenses that are necessary for the conduct of business but are an indirect result of the main planning and control decisions	Operations, control	Chapter 10
Regularly scheduled	Management information system	Yes	For supporting managerial decision-making efforts; generated automatically at definite intervals and in a fixed format	Operations, control	Chapter 11
Exception	Management information system	Yes	For signaling that "out-of-bounds" conditions have arisen; preformatted; automatically generated	Control	Chapter 11
Unscheduled	Management information system	Yes	For supporting managerial decision-making efforts; preformatted; prepared only when requested by managers—not automatically generated	Control, planning	Chapter 11
Special analysis	Decision support system	Yes	For supporting one-shot managerial decision-making efforts; prepared on request; based mostly on data in organization files	Planning	Chapter 12
Inquiry processing	Decision support system	Yes	For supporting managerial decision-making efforts; a special case of the special analysis report; users directly interact with the system and generate information through terminals	Planning	Chapter 12

styles of decision making or to certain "random" changes in organizational or economic climates. The need for **unscheduled reports** is most common in, but not limited to, support of top-level planning activities.

A number of information requirements are one-shot. For example, a project manager involved in contract bidding may find it necessary to ensure that a certain unique raw material will be available to the company. Consequently, it is advisable to examine records of current suppliers to see whether their delivery performance has been reliable and, if not, to develop new suppliers. It should be noted that the data necessary to produce unscheduled reports are usually in the files of the organization.

In the remainder of this chapter we will examine examples of several important functional-area information systems, discussing what each system does, to provide a general understanding of the uses of MIS in particular functional areas. Second, we will see how one system relates to other information systems. And common design features of each application will be pointed out.

Marketing Information Systems

Marketing information systems represent one type of functional-area information system in an organization. Business firms could not exist without the ability to market products or services. A company that manages the marketing function effectively may be quite successful. Poor marketing may result in the demise of the business.

A marketing information system follows the design principles outlined earlier. Such a system is actually a set of subsystems that interact in various ways to provide information needed for critical decision activities. At the same time, many of the application activities depend on data captured and stored during transaction processing.

Components of a Marketing Information System

Marketing information systems are based on the following representative objectives:

—— Management of the overall marketing process
—— Direct support of sales activities and sales personnel
—— Early identification of new product or service opportunities
—— Establishment of competitive prices without sacrificing acceptable profit levels
—— Control of costs related to marketing activities
—— Analysis of marketing effectiveness

Other objectives may apply to specific organizations.

As illustrated in Figure 11.12, our discussion presumes that a marketing information system consists of three primary subsystems, for *sales information, product management information,* and *marketing intelligence*. In a nonintegrated information system, managers would have to rely on by-products of the transaction systems alone to oversee the organization's marketing activities. However, inventory management reports and accounting ledgers—typical transaction system reports identified in Figure 11.12—give historical data only. As we examine the features of each marketing system (Figure 11.13) notice the sources of the information in each application. (Although in the ensuing discussion and the accompanying illustrations we will refer, for convenience, to "the sales information system," "the product management system," and "the marketing intelligence system," bear in mind that these are in fact *subsystems,* which in turn consist of subsystems, and so on.)

Sales Information Management of the sales function calls for the capability to close an impending sale, to understand why past sales have occurred, to know who the

Figure 11.12 Subsystems in a Marketing Information System

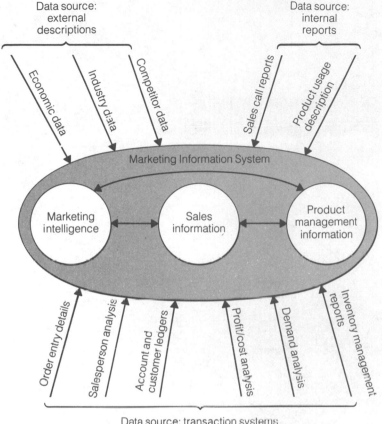

customers were, and to project future sales. Among the areas covered by the sales information system are the following:

——*Sales analysis:* monitoring locations of sales by focusing on activity by sales office or geographical region. When certain regions perform above or below expectations, it is essential to find the reasons.

——*Product analysis:* examining sales patterns for particular products by region. When new products are introduced, valuable information may be gained by following regional performance patterns and then determining why the various patterns have occurred (information may suggest that sales techniques in one region were particularly effective, that competition was weak in a given area, or that the unexpected results were attributable to temporary conditions that are not likely to recur).

——*Salesperson analysis:* determining differences in salesperson effectiveness. By monitoring performance levels, management can discover not only who the high

Figure 11.13 Features of Marketing Information Subsystems

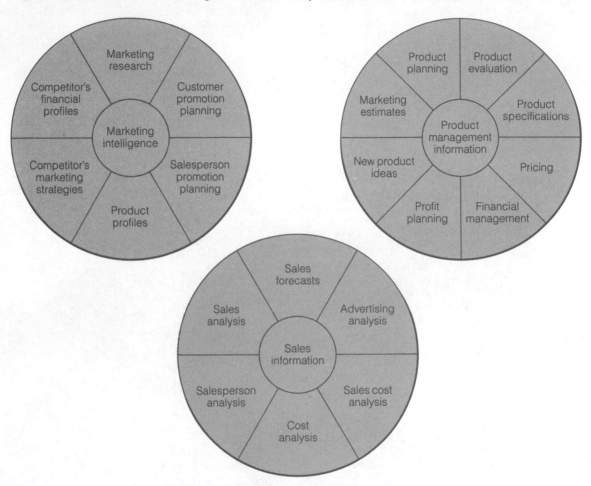

and low achievers are but may also learn why the differences occur. It may be found that some salespersons are extremely good with certain products or services and less effective with others. By correlating with historical sales in a region, management may learn that some areas are particularly sensitive to personal approaches.

——*Sales cost analysis:* determining what it costs the firm to make a sale. You would be surprised how often this question goes unanswered. Estimates are developed by combining salesperson expense data with other accounting data, such as operating overhead and management support costs. If it is the organization's marketing policy to make every effort to close a sale, costs may be found to be quite high.

——*Sales forecasts:* predicting future sales; like any prediction, forecasting the future of product sales is difficult and at best represents only an estimate.

A great deal of the data needed for the applications described above originate in the order entry and accounts receivable systems. The details captured during order processing, when analyzed, allow management to determine which customers purchase products or services regularly and which do not. This analysis may be facilitated by the simple action of cross-referencing sales with customers in the customer or accounts receivable master file. Frequently firms do not deliberately address this question. They find out about lost customers from a competitor—after the fact. Prudent monitoring of customer activity on, say, a monthly basis is a powerful means of preventing the loss of accounts. Order entry data also form the basis for salesperson analyses as well as for evaluation of regional and branch office activities.

Sales forecasting, on the other hand, uses transaction processing data in different ways. Some organizations use statistical and management science techniques to extrapolate from the data in order and accounts receivable files, evidence of evolving trends. But often useful data come from other subsystems. For example, the demand for airline travel is very sensitive to changes in the general economy of the country, and to employment levels and certain other leading economic indicators. Since the indicators appear before a change in air travel is reported, the process of developing a sales forecast must include this information. Mere reliance on historical data and extrapolation of trends in this instance would be a mistake—perhaps a costly one for the organization.

Product Management Information A product management information system depends on transaction-level systems such as those for inventory management, cost accounting, general ledger and cash management, and accounts payable. Within this system are applications for the following features (as given in Figure 11.13).

——*Pricing:* determination of the selling price of a product based on the cost to produce or acquire and market the item. This system must utilize data from the engineering or bill of materials system (discussed later in this chapter) for costs. Item costs are also received from vendors.

——*Product specifications:* features and characteristics of products; must involve the bill of materials application.

——*Profit planning:* an important aspect of new product planning that takes into account the cost of providing a product, the potential demand, and the resulting aggregate profit that can be expected. Cost analysis data originate with the cost accounting system. Market demand details are provided by other marketing system applications.

——*Financial management:* supports the organization's management of finances required to launch new products or maintain existing product lines. Intended to assist in planning for cash to ensure that adequate amounts are available to carry out tasks. Utilizes data from general ledger and cash management systems in conjunction with marketing planning information.

——*Market estimates:* indications of market size or changes anticipated for a product or product line. May be stated in quantitative form or as narrative descriptions of evolutions projected to occur.

Not all data needed in this system are stored in quantitative form as in accounting applications. Qualitative information, often in narrative form, is essential for the following applications:

——*New product ideas:* descriptions of problems identified by customers (problems may be product opportunities in disguise) or requests for new products or services.

——*Product evaluation:* comments and suggestions from current, former, or potential customers regarding the product; may include ideas for changes or modifications.

——*Product planning:* descriptions of development plans, including product features, development timetables, and marketing strategies; interrelated with new product ideas and evaluations from customers and sales staff.

Frequently the best ideas for new products or services originate with customers. Sales call reports and product usage information are often regularly solicited and entered into the marketing information system. In addition, the introduction of new technology may stimulate ideas for new products or services or ways to enhance existing product lines. Information systems technology is increasingly a factor in the formulation of corporate strategy (see Chapter 20), allowing firms to change the basis of their competition (perhaps through an improved ability to keep costs low) or to more distinctly differentiate their products.

Like many of the other marketing applications, those in the product management information system depend on information from other parts of the marketing system. Environmental data about competitors, for example, may trigger important product planning steps. The airline industry is very sensitive to competitors' changes in fares and to the introduction of new carriers into the market of a particular city. Managers must know about potential competitor changes and develop strategies for responding to them. Although transaction systems cannot supply information about competitor plans, they may provide operating details (such as current fare schedules or cost sheets) that are useful in formulating new strategies. The marketing intelligence system is also a source of important competitor information.

Marketing Intelligence *Marketing intelligence systems* focus on events occurring in the business environment of the organization. We have already emphasized the need for information about competition and concerning economic conditions. And we have pointed out how other marketing applications depend on this information.

Marketing intelligence applications produce the following information:

——*Competitors' marketing strategies:* descriptions and citations of the strategies used by others to market similar products. Describes how competitors implement such representative strategies as being the low product cost leader, providing easy accessibility to customers, promoting high-quality product features, offering a wide selection of sizes, or limiting sales to a select customer group.

——*Competitors' financial profiles:* describe the financial stability of competitors and the industry as a whole. Provide important information about the capability of other firms to compete in price-cutting wars, expensive advertising campaigns, or research and development programs. These documents stress the financial "soundness" and potential longevity of new market entrants and long-standing competitors.

——*Product profiles:* describe the strengths and weaknesses of competitors' products and services, include strategies useful to sales staff for selling or marketing against other products and suggestions for substitutes attractive to customers.

——*Marketing research:* includes details of specific product attributes (size, color, packaging, brand loyalty) gathered from purchased sources or from original data. May be general, oriented toward an entire market, or more focused, emphasizing a particular product or brand, customer segment, or geographical area. Often includes details of product substitutes (rail service rather than air travel) and complementary items (hotel and automobile requirements of arriving airline passengers).

Ideas for promotion strategies are part of the marketing intelligence system. Thus databases often include details useful in promotion:

——*Customer promotion planning:* plans for advertising and sales promotion designed to penetrate a specific market or to reach a certain type of customer. Estimates of the cost and benefit of plans may be detailed, often supplemented with quantitative data.

——*Salesperson promotion planning:* features of campaigns aimed at sales staff who market the company's product; includes anticipated cost/benefit profiles and rationale behind the promotion campaigns.

These systems are interrelated: They support the general marketing function of a business on the one hand and, on the other, they share valuable data. These characteristics are not unique to marketing. We see a similar need to integrate information in material requirements and production planning.

Material Requirements Planning Information Systems

Unless you have been a part of production management processes, it is difficult to estimate the complexity of such endeavors. However, as we will see, material requirements planning (MRP) is one of the most difficult management tasks in a manufacturing firm. At the same time, it is an area that offers many benefits with the proper use of information systems.

This section explores the features of information systems for material requirements planning, the core of the entire production management process. Although like marketing information systems, MRP depends on transaction-level data, there is also a high level of interdependence with other information systems.

Overview of Production Management

In most production environments, a finished product consists of a few or many individual components and assemblies; assemblies must be completed in time to be ready for use in finished products. Thus production managers depend on the development of a suitable production schedule (Figure 11.14) that states starting times

Figure 11.14 Production Planning Requirements

RESOURCE REPORT
FROM PLANNER 1 TO 3

DATE 7/29/9X   TIME 15.52.45   PAGE   1

MONTH	SEP	OCT	NOV	DEC	JAN	FEB	MAR	APR	MAY	JUN	JUL	AUG
UNITS	34,100	9,600	0	0	0	0	0	0	0	0	0	0
CUMULATIVE	34,100	43,700	43,700	43,700	43,700	43,700	43,700	43,700	43,700	43,700	43,700	43,700
COST	193,560	16,678	0	0	0	0	0	0	0	0	0	0
CUMULATIVE	193,560	210,238	210,238	210,238	210,238	210,238	210,238	210,238	210,238	210,238	210,238	210,238
LABOR	30,646	2,564	0	0	0	0	0	0	0	0	0	0
CUMULATIVE	30,646	33,211	33,211	33,211	33,211	33,211	33,211	33,211	33,211	33,211	33,211	33,211
MONTH	SEP	OCT	NOV	DEC	JAN	FEB	MAR	APR	MAY	JUN	JUL	AUG

PRODUCTION FORECAST

DATE 7/29/9X TIME 15.52.45 PAGE 10
START DATE 7/31/9X CURRENT DATE 9/04/9X
AVAILABLE 2,000

- ITEM -	-ENG/DRAW NO - -	DESCRIPTION	- UM LV PLANNER	VENDOR
2880	FC750035	BUCKET HANDLE 0	EA 01 00569	

NUMBER OF DAYS SUPPLY TO BE ORDERED -   AVG. SALES

- ITEM CODES -	- LOTSIZE -	LEADTIME -	UNIT	COST	ITEM CHARACTERISTICS	- - FORECAST .00
REPLAN 1 PRINT	MIN 100	TYPE M	4974		WEIGHT .000	LOCATION A124 QTY 600
TYPE 2 FORECAST 2	MAX 10,000,000	PUR 0	SETUP	7.100	SAFETY 0 SHRINK .000	NBR PER 8
					CLASS C	PER SIZ 5

PERIOD BALANCES   CURRENT BALANCES

ISSUE 0 RECEPT 0 ADJUST 0   ONHAND 2,000 ON ORDER 0 ALLOC 0 ACTIVITY 0

PLANNING DATE	ORDER DEMAND	EXPECTED INVENTORY	PLANNING DATE	EXPECTED RECEIPTS	REFERENCE
8/27	1,000.000	3,500	8/27	2,500	PLANNED
8/27	1,500.000	2,000	8/27		PLANNED
9/03	1,000.000	4,300	9/03	3,300	PLANNED
9/03	1,500.000	2,800	9/03		PLANNED
9/03	800.000	2,000	9/03		
9/04		2,000	9/04	600	PLANNED
9/07	200.000	2,000	9/07		
9/10	1,000.000	5,500	9/10	4,500	PLANNED
9/10	1,500.000	4,000	9/10		
9/10	2,000.000	2,000	9/10		
9/11		2,000	9/11	600	PLANNED
9/17	1,000.000	5,500	9/17	4,500	PLANNED
9/17	1,500.000	4,000	9/17		
9/17	2,000.000	2,000	9/17		
9/18		2,000	9/18	600	PLANNED
9/25		2,000	9/25	600	PLANNED
10/02		2,000	10/02	600	PLANNED
10/09		2,000	10/09	500	PLANNED
10/16		2,000	10/16	500	PLANNED
10/23		2,000	10/23	500	PLANNED

for each intermediate step and end dates for the finished product. Each stage depends on the timely completion of the intermediate steps. Individual steps in turn depend on many details. (You begin to see that production scheduling and management can become quite complex.)

The production scheduling process is triggered by one of two circumstances:

——*Firm customer orders have been received:* delivery of specified quantities is promised for a specific date, and production must be scheduled to meet the delivery date.

——*Products must be manufactured for anticipated sale:* sales forecasts project the demand for specific items, and manufacturing schedules must meet the forecast demand.

A system for developing a suitable schedule must draw on data from the bill of materials system and the personnel information system (discussed in detail below), the inventory management system, and the capacity database.

The *bill of materials system* provides data about the parts or components to be used in the manufacture of specified finished items. Since parts must be acquired before the item using them can be produced, it is customary to prepare a list indicating the order in which they will be needed. As shown later (Figure 11.17), such lists can take several forms. The *personnel system* provides information about the availability of employees having the job skills and training needed for the task at hand. An organization's schedule is ultimately limited by the number of people who can fulfill certain job descriptions. Wage rate information from the personnel system is used for "costing out" the job.

The *inventory management system* provides information about the quantity of materials on hand in the supply room or warehouse. This system is also the source of important data about the lead time needed to order an item and ensure that it will arrive in time for use in manufacturing process. Inventory management may also suggest order quantity lots that take advantage of cost discounts. Since many inventory systems feature decision aids, such as suggested order quantities, as well as record-keeping features, they are often quite sophisticated. And they surely are essential for proper production planning.

The *capacity planning database* contains details about machine operating rates, the speed of a particular production line, and personnel work rates. The rates usually take into account maintenance requirements, equipment setup time, and in some cases, space utilization alternatives. Capacity planning, properly done, can maximize the use of personnel and equipment, and thus contribute to meeting important completion dates.

A production schedule specifies the quantity of an item that must be manufactured, the rates at which work will be finished, the sequence in which work will be completed, and delivery date targets. Thus a production schedule is more than a timetable. Figure 11.15 shows activities that occur, including the following.

——*Material requirements planning:* developing plans to acquire and use materials in production

——*Job costing ("costing out"):* determining the sequence of costs that will be incurred in manufacturing (for example, personnel, materials, equipment, other expenses)

Figure 11.15 Production Scheduling: A Central Feature in Manufacturing Management

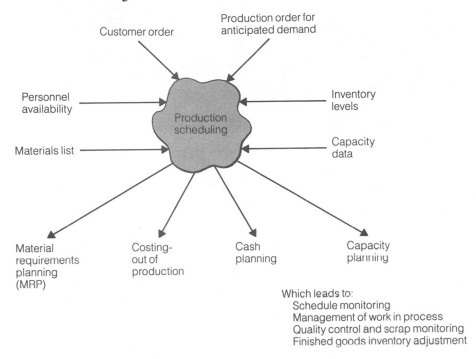

Which leads to:
Schedule monitoring
Management of work in process
Quality control and scrap monitoring
Finished goods inventory adjustment

————*Cash planning:* formulation of a plan that stipulates the amount of cash needed to manufacture scheduled products, stating the source of the cash and when it will be needed (perhaps in staged intervals)

————*Capacity planning:* workload requirements by production line, machine, and individuals

Each of these complex activities could, if not properly monitored, undermine the success or profitability of the entire project.

When manufacturing begins, other activities occur, including monitoring the schedule to see that actual work activities conform to the plan—easier said than done. The tasks of overseeing the work in process and keeping track of intermediate activities and components increase in complexity as the number of components at various manufacturing stages rises. Then there is the essential function of quality control and scrap monitoring. Information about poor quality in any raw materials or in the finished goods must be fed back to the purchasing department (which must settle the problem with the supplier or quickly find another capable of meeting the schedule) or to manufacturing supervisors and design engineers, who will adjust processes or staff assignments.

Finished goods inventory is monitored both to account for each completed item and to prepare for delivery to the customer or the warehouse.

Keep this overview in mind as we examine material requirements planning in greater detail.

Material Requirements Planning

Material requirements planning generally refers to computer software that manages the important tasks of production scheduling, determining materials requirements, planning for their acquisition, and managing the production process. The software is designed to integrate the tasks (when this job is handled manually, the tasks often are treated as independent steps). As you will see, MRP is an information system in the true sense of the term.

As Figure 11.14 showed, the system is triggered by a production schedule, of the type described earlier, that indicates what finished products must be produced and by what date. An MRP system also utilizes inventory information and bill of materials details to formulate production plans.

Bill of Materials Requirements   Bill of materials subsystems provide data about the component parts used to manufacture a certain item. You cannot, for example, manufacture typewriters without knowing that the products consist of components such as keyboards, platens, and carriage return mechanisms. Obviously, knowing what parts are needed is essential to any manufacturing process. The bill of materials subsystem addresses this data requirement.

Objectives and Purpose   There are two primary objectives in bill of materials processing:

——*Parts explosion:* identifying all items used in the manufacture of a certain finished product and the quantity of each item needed. An "item" may be an individual part, a subassembly (a set of parts used together to form a lower-level unit that is combined with other units or subassemblies), or an assembly (a set of parts and subassemblies). Material requirements planning relies heavily on the use of parts explosions from the bill of materials system in determining what items must be acquired or manufactured for the final product.

——*Where-used implosion:* identifying all products (that is, finished products, assemblies, and subassemblies) that use a certain part. A parts implosion is the opposite of the parts explosion.

The overall purpose of bill of materials processing is to provide more efficient control of production scheduling, purchasing, and inventory control activities; that is, when customers place orders for certain manufactured parts, we want to know what production work must take place, the materials needed, and whether materials are available in inventory or must be purchased.

Data in Bill of Materials Applications   The bill of materials system begins in the engineering department, where the specifications for products are developed. During design, engineers include in the product documentation a drawing of the product, as well as a list of all the parts, subassemblies, and so on that are required to manufacture it (Figure 11.16). The list typically includes a description of the part

Figure 11.16 Bill of Materials Assembly

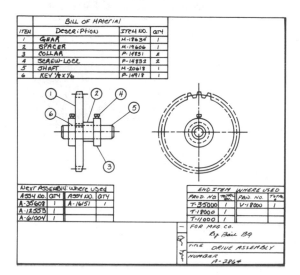

or subassembly, its inventory item number, and the quantity needed. Because items documented by the engineering department may be parts or subassemblies, many bill of materials specifications include a list of the higher-level product in which the documented item is used. In these cases, a product or assembly number, as well as the appropriate quantity, is shown on the engineering documentation.

Engineering provides inputs to the bill of materials system in the form of part numbers, product numbers, and assembly numbers. These data are used to create (or update) two sets of data:

——*Part number data:* the specifications for each individual part, including part number, part description, related engineering documentation, and selected purchasing and manufacturing specifications

——*Product structure data:* specifications for manufactured products, including parts, assemblies, and subassemblies, and the quantity of each required for the finished product

Retrieval of Bill of Materials Data Let's assume that assembly A consists of a subassembly containing items B, C, and 1, and that this subassembly is further broken down as shown in Figure 11.17*a*. The most fundamental type of retrieval of bill of materials data for assembly A is a single-level explosion (Figure 11.17*b*). From this type of retrieval, it is possible to generate other parts lists in which the items in assembly A are presented in formats that are useful in different situations. In the indented form (Figure 11.17*c*), the assembly is exploded to list each item once every time it is used. A manager can easily identify subassemblies because they are grouped vertically; that is, the indentations serve to separate the first-level assembly from the second, and so on. The summarized parts list (Figure 11.17*d*) simply gives the total

Figure 11.17 (*a*) Assembly A, Broken Down into (*b*) Single-Level Parts List, (*c*) Indented Parts List, and (*d*) Summarized, Single-Level Parts List

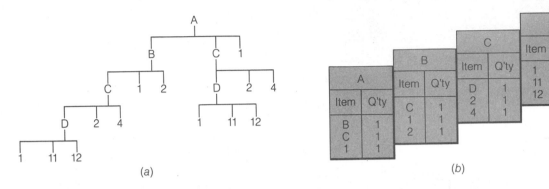

(*a*)   (*b*)

Assembly A	
Item no.	Q'ty
B	1
.C	1
..D	1
...1	1
...11	1
...12	1
..2	1
..4	1
.1	1
.2	1
C	1
.D	1
..1	1
..11	1
..12	1
.2	1
.4	1
1	1

(*c*)

Assembly A	
Item no.	Total Q'ty
B	1
C	2
D	2
1	4
2	3
4	2
11	2
12	2

(*d*)

quantity needed of each numbered item. Summarized data may also be included in a bill of materials document that gives such additional information as an item description, a code indicating the type of part (for example, a subassembly or basic part), whether the item is manufactured or purchased, units of measure (feet, meters, pounds, kilograms), and so on. The bill of materials system also can be used to produce an assembly order (Figure 11.18), which contains assembly number, order number, and quantity data, as well as the item numbers and descriptions of each entity needed for the finished product. We will return to other uses of bill of materials output in a moment.

Figure 11.18 Bill of Material and Assembly Order Documents

Bill of Materials

Assembly number:
Assembly description:
Drawing number:
Structure change: Drawing size:

Item number	Description	Type	Source	Unit of measure	Q'ty/ ass'y	Structure change	Dept ass'l'd in	Oper ass'l'd on

Assembly Order

Assembly number: 20136818
Assembly description: PUMP ASS'Y
Order quantity: 50   Order number: 337813

Item number	Description	Unit of measure	Quantity per ass'y	Expected quantity
531674	SCREW	01	6	300
531690	WASHER	01	5	250
728419	SCREW	01	5	250
1431478	SEAL	01	2	100
3519794	MOTOR	01	1	50
3572133	SPRING	01	2	100
20136130	PUMP SHAFT ASS'Y	01	1	50
20136301	SET COLLAR	01	1	50
20136315	CLAMP MOUNTING	01	1	50
20136338	SHIFTER COLLAR	01	1	50
20136345	SCREW	01	4	200

Where-used implosion reports (Figure 11.19) tell where specific parts and assemblies are used (that is, in which products). To produce these reports, the application system processes the product structure data. Internal access methods allow the software to search the data to find out where specific items are used. If necessary, cost data may also be included on reports. The ability to find out where parts and assemblies are used can be very helpful to engineers wanting to see the possible effects of parts design changes, to materials supervisors facing shortages, and to production personnel. Reports like these are also important to inventory control specialists and purchasing agents responsible for acquiring materials and supplies for the firm.

524

Figure 11.19 Where-Used Parts Implosion Documents for Assembly Shown in (*a*): (*b*) Single Level, (*c*) Indented, (*d*) Summarized, (*e*) Cost Description

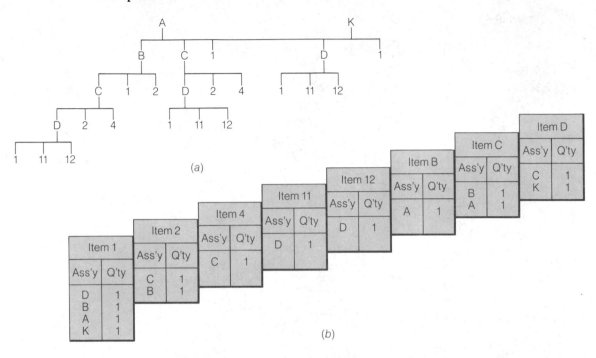

(a)

(b)

Item no. 1	
Assembly	Q'ty
D	1
.C	1
..B	1
...A	1
..A	1
.K	1
B	1
.A	1
A	1
K	1

(c)

Item no. 1	
Assembly	Total quantity
D	1
C	1
B	2
K	2
A	4

(d)

End Product Cost Change

Item number: 143652689
Item description: TAPERED ROLLER BEARING
Previous cost: 1.25
New cost: 1.45
Net change: 0.20 INCREASE

End product	Description	Cost change	Notes
1346000	SERIES 60 POWER TAKE OFF	0.80	
13462000	SERIES 62 POWER TAKE OFF	0.60	
1346800	SERIES 68 POWER TAKE OFF	1.00	
1347000	SERIES 70 POWER TAKE OFF	0.40	
1421400	SERIES 14 STD TRANSMISSION	1.80	
1451400	SERIES 14 HD TRANSMISSION	0.60	
1421600	SERIES 16 STD TRANSMISSION	1.00	
1451600	SERIES 16 HD TRANSMISSION	0.40	

(e)

Purchasing Requirements Using the exploded material requirement lists, the MRP software next identifies the materials that must be ordered and tells the user when the orders should be placed. The existing inventory management records are an important factor in this determination. Not only does the system determine the discrepancy between what is on hand and what is needed, it also is programmed to use sound purchasing policies. That is, it considers the order quantity that will provide the best discount rates while at the same time minimizing the amount of cash tied up in warehoused inventory at any time. It also takes into account lead time (that is, the time it takes a supplier to receive and fill a purchase order), from details built into the inventory management records.

MRP software will prepare purchase orders for required material and schedule them for release on dates based on the economic order quantities described above. For a long production run, many individual purchase orders will be prepared and scheduled for release.

An important variation is the inclusion of **just-in-time inventory planning** capabilities in some MRP software. Under this concept, warehousing of materials is reduced to the bare minimum, or abandoned entirely. Inventory management is based on such careful ordering of materials and timely release of purchase orders that the materials arrive "just in time" to meet production schedules. Since warehousing costs often run as high as 40 percent per year, this feature can reduce overall material costs substantially. The capacity to monitor material requirements very closely can be handled effectively through the computer-based MRP system. Of course, close coordination between manufacturer and supplier is also necessary to ensure on-time deliveries.

Manufacturing Requirements and Schedules MRP software will produce the all-important plan of production activities. Tasks and manufacturing processes are scheduled at the workstation and department level, and they include the level of detail needed by a supervisor responsible for meeting deadlines (see Figure 11.14).

Each schedule identifies individual manufacturing steps and the material needed to complete each task. A day-by-day listing of events and materials serves as a guideline for planning and for evaluating performance against the plan. Supervisors and managers have the information they need to determine whether production is on time and according to plan.

The benefits of material requirements planning are thus:

——Coordinated purchasing, inventory management, and production planning, which reduces delays and improves the capability of the firm to meet deadlines and promised delivery dates

——Better management of financial and personnel resources

——Reduction of emergency orders (supervisors term this "expediting"), which increase material costs and add to operating complexity

——Fewer "out of stock" conditions, which either halt production or require inefficient rescheduling of the production process

——The ability to commit to and meet delivery dates and thereby satisfy customer needs

The concept of material requirements planning depends on transaction data and careful interchange of information from other information systems in the organization. In the automated factory of the future, this system will increase in importance. Fully automated factories—which have the capability to manage not only materials and schedules, but also individual machine tools and production equipment—are emerging as an extension of the concepts we have discussed. Although the dependence on computer processing and information systems will increase, the heart of the system will continue to be the applications that ensure that production specifications are complete and manufacturing materials are available.

Many of the reports are automatically prepared as part of the production manufacturing process. However, others, such as the parts implosion list, will be prepared only on request. Exception reports occur for out-of-stock items or manufacturing steps that vary from the schedule.

Personnel Skills Information Systems

People—the managers, supervisors, and employees who carry out the daily activities that keep the firm going—are the most important resources in any organization. We saw the importance of having personnel skills information available when planning for production activities. As with any resource, we need to be able to capture and process data about organization personnel. Personnel information systems examples of many different kinds are discussed throughout the book. We briefly overview one type of personnel application here: the personnel skills information system.

System Features and Objectives

The basic objective of a personnel skills information system is to capture, store, and make available data about the people who work for the organization. We want to be able to identify all employees and store data about their job skills and personal attributes. A personnel skills system (Figure 11.20) should contain:

——*Identification data:* to tell who the employees are, where they are assigned, and where they are working
——*Work-related data:* to describe the jobs each employee can perform, restrictions on the work they can perform, and such background data as performance ratings and work preferences
——*Personal attributes data:* to describe employee characteristics, interests, and other personal factors that may be relevant to the organization now or in the future

Personnel Data

Data of the following kinds can be stored in the basic personnel skills information systems categories and are representative of those included in personnel databases:

——*Identification data:* employee name, employee identification number, department working number, department assigned number

Figure 11.20 Personnel Skills System

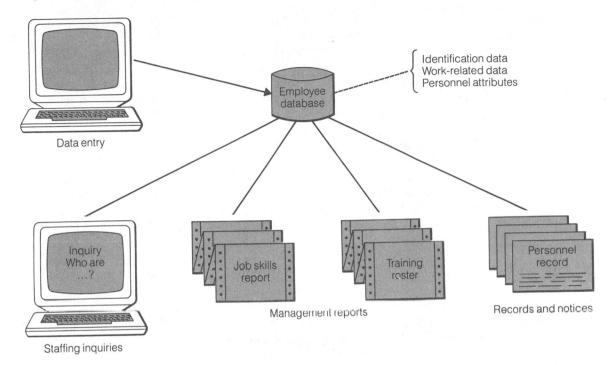

- —*Work-related data:* job code and skill level, machine operation qualifications, professional certifications, date of last job code change, current appraisal rating, work-related restrictions, previous job code experience, transfer request date and location, requirement date, emergency telephone number, awards or recognitions
- —*Personal attributes data:* hobbies, languages, proficiency ratings, education level (degree), health classification, marital status, outside activities (sports, municipal government, community work), home address

Notice the different items of personal attributes data included in the file. All are potentially relevant to the organization, although some might easily be overlooked. Languages, for example, can be very important to organizations that do business in non-English-speaking countries. Data about hobbies and outside interests can also be useful for the organization, whether for job-related purposes such as training people for new work activities, or for recruitment in connection with community service or employee recreation programs. It should be noted that this file contains no data on sex, ethnic background, or religion. Organizations often omit such items to facilitate compliance with policies relating to privacy and equal opportunity or affirmative action.

Processing and Reporting Requirements

The processing and reporting requirements for the skills file can become quite complex. For example, job code descriptions must be related to wage levels. Therefore, processing programs should, as a matter of procedure, check all these items for correspondence. If an employee's wages are too high or too low for a certain job, the discrepancy should be signaled on an exception report. Appraisal programs require that employees be scheduled for yearly updates—the need for which should be brought to management's attention during processing. Appraisals are usually tied in with wage levels for job codes; that is, skill level and appraisal rating are usually related to wages or salaries.

Updating procedures for a system as important as the personnel skills information system need to be carefully controlled and all transaction data validated. For example, personnel statistics are usually updated from personal skills and attributes forms. Employees are allowed ample time to complete these forms before processing, which makes the initial, preprocessing screening of the form easier than if the data were collected, say, on-line through a terminal. In addition to changes in personal data, update forms also usually include spaces to show appraisal changes, job code changes, rate changes, transfer requests, and awards received.

Since an organization processes many personnel action forms, each containing many data items, it makes sense to use a coding system to standardize and control responses. Therefore, we expect to find numeric or brief character codes for such factors as job skill, languages, and health. Often appraisal information and specific accomplishments on individual projects are stored as qualitative (narrative) information.

At least four representative types of report are associated with the personal skills information system. The first, information reports based on management inquiries, can be very useful for operating purposes. For instance, we can initiate selective searches of the file by job codes, personal skills, outside activities, health classifications, or work-related restrictions. If we were establishing a manufacturing facility in Paris, we might use the system to respond to an inquiry for the names and appraisal ratings for all journeymen machinists with excellent health and a knowledge of French. Similarly, if the organization has received expressions of interest in forming a photography club, the system might be used to assemble a list of all persons having photography as a hobby.

Summary reporting requires that the personnel data be processed to total counts in selected areas. These reports may be prepared for staff planning ("How many employees with a background in chemical engineering are working in other job classifications?"), plant expansion ("How many have expressed an interest in being transferred to a Sunbelt location and what are their primary job classifications?"), or any other area that may be of interest to managers.

A third kind of report uses the personnel database to generate periodic notices for appraisal scheduling, merit wage increases, and the like. If the system is programmed to review the records regularly and prepare reports like these, managers can easily receive up-to-date information.

Finally, individual employee review reports can be generated for updating and correction. If each person in the firm is supposed to be reviewed once a year on the date he or she joined the organization, much time can be saved by having the system automatically generate copies of all the records due for appraisal on the appropriate dates.

The personnel skills information system is based on processing transactions about employees. As you can see, however, it goes beyond mere transaction processing and features essential management information reporting. It is an integral system for many other information systems, such as the production information system we examined in this chapter.

Summary

Management information systems are distinguished from transaction or data processing systems by their emphasis on support of managerial decision making. Transaction processing provides some, but not all, of the data needed to produce information managers need.

An MIS deals with past, present, and projection information to support problem solving and decision making. Emphasis is on having information available in a timely fashion, with uniformity among all users regardless of the department or division in which they work. The concept of MIS is based on the realization that there is an essential requirement for communication between the various decision centers in an enterprise. Each decision maker is in some way dependent on data and information that originate in another area of the organization. The federation approach is the most feasible way of developing information support of this nature. This approach assumes that an MIS is not a monolithic entity, but consists of several functional-area information systems. Thus specialists can collect the information they are best trained to gather. In this framework, data serve to integrate the various functional areas and to assist in accomplishment of organization goals. Examples of common management information systems include marketing information systems, production management systems, and personnel skills systems.

Key Words

Decision center	Management information	Subsystem
Exception report	systems (MIS)	System
Functional-area informa-	Material requirements	Transaction
tion systems	planning (MRP)	Transaction processing
Just-in-time inventory	Monolithic	Unscheduled report
planning	Regularly scheduled report	

Review Questions

1. Define *management information system*. Explain the meaning of each component in an MIS.

2. Is on-line retrieval necessary in a management information system? Explain. How do on-line retrieval and report generation differ in meeting MIS objectives? How are they similar?

3. Why is a total system not an ideal information system?

4. What factors distinguish an edit report from a report response to an inquiry?

5. Where has the greatest success in MIS been realized? What is the apparent reason for this?

6. Compare and contrast the federation and the total systems views of MIS. What assumptions underlie each approach?

7. What role does the database play in an MIS? Is a database necessary in a functional MIS? (*Hint:* Recall the functions of an MIS.)

8. Distinguish between a management information system and a transaction processing system; between an MIS and a data processing system.

9. How can different managers use the same information to build contrasting explanations for the same situation?

10. What role does computer processing play in an information system? If computer systems play a role, is a manual information system incomplete or inadequate? Explain.

Application Problems

1. A drug wholesaler recently installed easy-to-use terminals in the offices of many of its customers. The terminals are linked to the wholesaler's computer system by ordinary telephone lines. Using the terminals, customers can place orders for merchandise, specifying the item and the quantity needed. When an order is placed, the system immediately responds with the price of the merchandise and a confirmation that the items are in stock. It also displays a date when the items will be delivered.

   Customers like the system because it allows them to order merchandise when they need it and they are not dependent on the visit of a salesperson or a telephone call to the company. The wholesaler likes the system because it provides better service to its customers as well as an efficient means of processing transactions.

   The firm has recently expanded the capabilities of the system to allow differential pricing. Customers are able to specify delivery priorities: by paying a higher price, customers can obtain very rapid delivery—faster than the normally good service the firm provides. This capability is important due to the nature of their clients' businesses, which include hospitals, emergency clinics, drug stores, and medical group facilities.

   The company has enjoyed an increased volume of business, largely attributable to the system it has evolved. It can now spot trends and customer needs simply by analyzing the data it captures as a result of processing orders. For instance, when several customers request an item the firm does not normally stock, the firm adds the item to its product line.

  a. What features make this system successful from the customer's viewpoint?

  b. Identify the system transactions needed to receive and process customer orders and ensure that merchandise is available to meet their needs. Do the transactions change when priority pricing is included as a system feature?

  c. What regularly scheduled reports should be provided to managers? What information should be available on request?

  d. Describe the relation between transaction processing and information provided to management via this system.

2. A magazine distributor wants to develop a system for monitoring the magazines and newspapers each of its customers (newsstands, book stores, drug stores, and hotel concession stands) sells. Deliveries are made to each customer twice each week, and the contents of the delivery are listed on an invoice included with the shipment. The driver of the delivery truck also picks up any unsold outdated magazines and returns them to the company. Customers receive credit for all unsold publications.

    The owner of the distributorship feels that it is important to monitor which magazines and periodicals each customer sells and which are returned in order to determine which periodicals sell well in different geographical areas and in various types of customer facilities. For example, hotels sell different items than street-corner newsstands, according to the owner.

    The current invoicing system runs on a minicomputer. It contains the name and account balance of each customer, but it does not store any product or sales information regarding the customer.

  a. Do you agree with the owner's idea of monitoring magazine sales? Why or why not?

  b. How should the transaction processing system be modified if the owner decides to go ahead? What changes must be made to gather the detailed management information the owner wants?

  c. What features should a sales information system have if the owner decides to pursue it? That is, how can the transaction system and the sales information system be related to one another? What reports do you feel the system should provide on a regular or request basis?

3. An automobile manufacturer is installing a new customer sales system throughout the country. The system will combine computer processing, videodisk storage, and graphics display capability to assist customers in ordering new automobiles and selecting accessories and options.

    As the system is designed, when the customer selects an automobile and chooses color combinations, a picture of the selection will be displayed on the color monitor. The system will also specify when a desired option can be included only if another option or feature is selected. The cost of each option and the total cost of the automobile can be displayed (and printed out) on request.

  a. What benefits accrue to the customer if this system is developed and installed in automobile showrooms? What are the benefits to the dealer?

  b. Does this system fit the definition and objectives of a management information system? Explain.

  c. What features must the system have to be useful to the customer? The dealer?

Minicase: Using Computers to Assist in Promotion Decisions

Southland Corporation, the parent of 7-Eleven convenience stores, has computerized its search for managers who have the potential of becoming executives—the so-called fast-trackers. Twice yearly, Southland managers file reports describing their subordinates' performance and assessing their promotability. The reports are consolidated into a computer database.

This approach is being used by increasing numbers of large organizations wishing to more effectively identify future managers and executives. Executive tracking systems are to personnel decision making what personal computer spreadsheets are to financial decision makers, at least in the view of firms that specialize in personnel information systems software. They allow uncovering of hidden talent, projection of future manager shortages, and analysis of individual career-development programs. Software firms are also quick to point out that the use of such systems, which often sell for less than $50,000, adds objectivity to the process (overcoming the limitations of the "old-boy" network), while assisting in meeting affirmative action and equal opportunity requirements.

When vacancies occur in management ranks, the computer-prepared profiles can be used to assess alternative staffing possibilities. It also helps point out the domino effect caused by filling one vacancy and creating another, and so on.

Some managers who are tracked this way express uneasiness over the "big brother" aspects of the program, although they do not see any real problems. Indeed, one Southland manager who uses the system and is included in it was quick to point out that people still make the promotion decisions. The computer merely catches and stores related information.

Questions

1. What features characterize the fast-track system as an information system rather than a transaction-level system? What role does computer processing play in the usefulness of the system?

2. The risks and concerns associated with relying on a computer system seem real to those whose records are included in a personnel system like that just described. What advantages does this system offer over a manual system with the same characteristics? Over a system based on "automatic succession" of individuals in the management hierarchy?

3. What are the risks in relying on a system of the type described here?

Minicase: Exception Reporting

Often users of transaction-level information systems argue that to be effective, the reporting systems they use must produce minute detail. They are convinced that unless a system places large amounts of data at their fingertips, it is of questionable value. Order processing systems are often used as examples: accountants, managers, and inventory personnel must know what has been ordered, shipped, and paid for. Without detail, they hasten to add, this knowledge cannot be had.

Information systems personnel often point out that the systems they design are reliable and that detail can be pulled from the files quickly when questions arise. They add that having too much detail can get in the way of the user and produce negative effects.

Exception reporting is presented as the most reasonable alternative. Through it, firms can focus the greatest amount of attention on cases that are out of the ordinary while still reducing the volume of data received.

Questions

1. What steps would you take to convince users and managers of the wisdom of exception reporting as an alternative to providing masses of detail?

2. Suppose that in the past, there have been severe credibility problems in the information distributed through automated systems. Although demonstrably the problems have been cleared up for several months, users and managers are reluctant to rely on the system. What general strategies can you use to convince people that the current system is reliable?

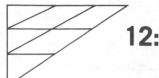

12: Decision Support Systems

Key Questions

What problems arise in supporting unstructured and semistructured situations?

How does the purpose of a decision support system differ from that of an MIS?

What different types of DSS are in use?

What capabilities are included in the design of a DSS?

How do decision support systems and group decision support systems differ?

What components make up a DSS? A GDSS?

Who uses a DSS? A GDSS?

Like management information systems, decision support systems are management tools. They support decision making and aid management, although they do not replace managers or their judgment. This chapter examines the role and structure of decision support systems. It also considers group decision support systems, a type of system designed for use by teams, committees, or other groups faced with the need to identify strategies for handling various situations that arise. By the end of the chapter, you should have a good understanding of the role of computer information systems in facilitating decisions about situations that are not well structured.

Why Should You Know About Decision Support Systems?

These reasons why you should know about **decision support systems (DSS)** hint at the nature of such systems:

——*Many decisions made in business are not well structured*. Even the best reporting systems may have limited usefulness if a situation is not structured. The question

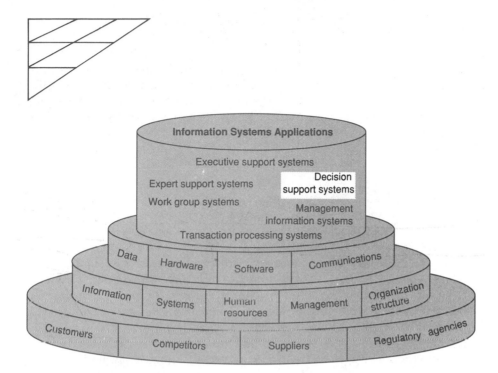

is how to use information systems to add structure to the situation. Virtually everyone faces situations like this, sometimes quite often.

——*Information systems that can support unanticipated needs are essential.* Developers of sophisticated information systems cannot possibly anticipate all the events that will occur. The unexpected situation, necessitating information that is not ordinarily available, is bound to arise at times. When it occurs, you will want computer information systems to provide support.

——*Time is becoming more and more important as an element of competitive strategy.* Rapid but effective analysis of events and possibilities, even when the need arises unexpectedly, can make the difference between capitalizing on an opportunity or missing the chance. A DSS can help to meet this need.

——*The increasing complexity of management means that more extensive analysis of alternatives is needed.* Identifying and evaluating the alternatives and options available determine success or failure in a growing number of business situations.

——*You will often be part of a group that must collectively make a decision.* Situations that are not well structured may be handled by teams and committees. Such groups have the same information needs as individuals—and perhaps even greater needs. Group decision support systems can provide additional assistance in drawing out ideas that would otherwise be overlooked.

Decision Support Systems

The characteristics of DSS distinguish these systems from automated systems of any other type. In addition, the data involved in processing originates throughout the organization. And, the scope of the system differs dramatically from transaction-level or management reporting applications. We begin by exploring each of these dimensions.

Characteristics

It has been emphasized that some decisions are routine while others are not. Decision support systems are intended to aid managers who must make decisions when only some of the pertinent details of the situations are known—that is, under unstructured or partially structured conditions.

Typically the component parts of problems managers address through MIS are known, although their interrelationships may not be fully understood. Individuals can identify the relevant factors to be studied and request the information that best sheds light on them. Then reports are formulated and programs are written to process the data needed for the report. The applications are handled on a recurring basis (daily, weekly, or monthly), and processing methods can be prespecified to provide the information needed to deal with these problems and situations. Using the terminology identified earlier, an MIS can be described as supporting structured problem solving and decision making.

In contrast, in a DSS environment, the problems under study are constantly changing, either because new sets of conditions represent one-shot, nonrecurring situations or because the problem changes as the decision makers' experience broadens.

Airline deregulation, for example, made it possible for carriers to begin serving new cities and to discontinue service to others. Now that the number of airlines serving routes from one city to another is determined by the profitability of the respective markets rather than by government regulation, there is more competition, particularly on routes between major cities. Along with route changes, deregulation has affected fares, which can be set by the carriers themselves without government approval.

An investigator studying the wisdom of deregulation would undoubtedly have some questions. Will the introduction of competition lead to overservice on certain routes? Will some cities lose air service altogether because airlines forsake smaller markets in favor of higher-volume routes? Can new airlines enter the business to service smaller cities that have lost major carrier service? Will air fares go down because of higher competition, or will they go up because of lower profit levels? All these questions arise because of the change in the carriers' regulatory status. Although the questions are important, the problem has not occurred before, so data must be developed before answers will become available.

Since deregulation of an industry is not an everyday occurrence, the problem may be unique, a one-shot item. However, the questions about deregulation will take years to answer. Analysts will be watching the ramifications of the decision unfold for 20 years or more. It is virtually impossible to design in advance a report that will remain useful over two decades or to anticipate questions that will arise. Thus, as indicated previously, the problem itself may change as more information about it is gathered. As managers begin to look at information about different parts of the original problem, the new findings may reshape the direction of analysis. Having more information about a situation may reveal aspects different from those that were originally evident. The problem being addressed then changes.

An example will demonstrate the changing nature of information requirements in partially structured situations. Ever since the energy crisis of the 1970s, worldwide attention has been focused on the amount of energy being used for transportation. To study the energy problem (Figure 12.1) as it affects and is affected by automobile transportation, one might want to know how the preference of buyers of new automobiles influence automakers' near-term planning.

When energy is in short supply and prices are rising, manufacturers might be expected to try to produce fuel-efficient automobiles. Thus one way to study this question is to assemble data about the miles per gallon (mpg) rating of new cars sold from month to month. Suppose that contrary to expectation, the data reveal that the average mpg rating of automobiles being sold goes *down,* meaning that fewer fuel-efficient cars have been purchased. An analyst might try to find out why, even though manufacturers are producing more fuel-efficient cars, consumers seem to be buying only luxury (low-mpg-rated) vehicles. This paradox might lead the analyst to broaden the scope of the investigation, speculating, for example, that because a recession is occurring, only people who can afford luxury cars are buying cars at all. Or perhaps because people expect better mpg ratings on next year's models, they are postponing purchases now. Or, again, the downtrend may have nothing to do with consumers' perceptions and preferences regarding fuel efficiency and may, instead, reflect the unusually high sales level posted last year in the industry.

Other reasons for the results could be suggested too, but the point is that as the analyst looked at the problem and received information, the formulation of the problem changed. A DSS must have built-in flexibility to respond to changing problem definitions such as this one.

Situations addressed by DSS often are not anticipated. Neither the airline deregulation nor the energy problem as it affects new car purchases were properly anticipated. Yet the need for information in both situations is evident.

The information reporting aspects of an MIS are designed carefully in advance. In a DSS, the information to be reported is often defined by the manager at the time of need—not in advance. Therefore, a DSS offers greater flexibility than an MIS. The emphasis is not so much on efficiency of processing as on getting the right information to the manager. Rapid implementation and usability of the information are the most important issues at first. (Efficient processing can be built in later if an application tends to recur in a structured manner.)

Some decisions, such as whether to pursue a merger with or acquisition of a particular firm, will not recur. Others, like preparing division budgets or financing a new sales campaign, will occur more than once but will remain semistructured,

Figure 12.1 Energy Usage Analysis Using DSS

PROBLEM: INCREASED WORLDWIDE ENERGY SHORTAGE

Focus: Effect of energy use for transportation

Question from manager: What types of automobile are consumers buying? Less fuel-efficient? More fuel-efficient?

Implicit assumption by manager: As cost of energy rises, fuel efficiency of automobiles will be increased.

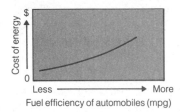

Question posed for DSS: What is the average mpg for new cars sold, month by month?

What DSS processes:

1. Mpg for each new car sold each month
2. Average mpg for all new cars sold each month
3. Plot of mpg for each month

Question posed for DSS: What is the sales volume for each type of automobile by month?

What DSS processes:

1. Class of car for each automobile sold each month
2. Average mpg for each class of car
3. Present sales by type of car by month

Results show:

1. High sale of luxury cars, which have low mpg ratings
2. Low sale of fuel-efficient cars, which have high mpg ratings

Manager interpretation: Reasons for result could be:

1. Recession.
2. Consumers are waiting for better mpg ratings expected next year.
3. High sales last year caused low sales this year.

since routines cannot be firmly stated. In both cases, data analysis and managerial input are important. A combination of management judgment, decision models, and data analysis is required. New data may be needed as more insight is gained through analysis.

Figure 12.1 *(continued)*

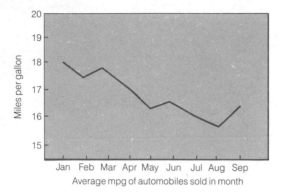

Average mpg of automobiles sold in month

Conclusion: Fewer fuel-efficient cars are being purchased by consumers.

NOT AS EXPECTED!

Change question from manager: What cars are consumers purchasing: luxury or fuel-efficient automobiles? (Assumes that manufacturers are making more fuel-efficient automobiles.)

Data Sources

Due to the uniqueness and breadth of the issues addressed through the system, the data needed to support analyses may come from many sources. Of course in DSS managers provide a greater portion of the data than in the other systems discussed, but even when relevant data are stored in master files, they are unlikely to come from a *single file*. Rather, parts of the data may be pulled from several different files and assembled into a form the DSS can use, as illustrated in Figure 12.2.

Therefore, in a DSS environment the need for powerful database management capabilities that readily permit multifile processing is evident, underscoring the importance of database management issues in MIS design and in the evolution of applications making up functional-area information systems. The objectives of managing data as a resource only increase in significance as the structure in the user's environment decreases. Later in this chapter we will see that two different types of databases are associated with decision support systems.

Scope

A DSS is *problem oriented* (in contrast to an MIS, which follows processes throughout an organization). Therefore, even though the data may originate from the enterprise as a whole, the support system itself may focus on a problem that has arisen, not an

Figure 12.2 DSS Information Sources for Inventory Control Example

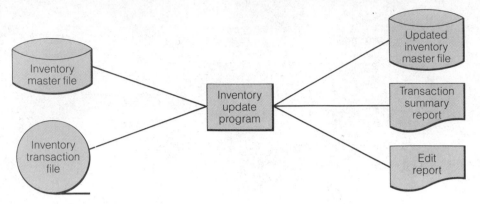

(a) Process-oriented, file-driven transaction processing

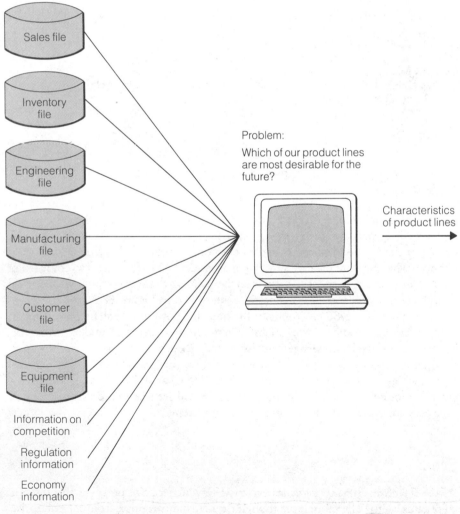

Problem:

Which of our product lines are most desirable for the future?

Characteristics of product lines →

(b) Multifile, problem-driven decision support information

Table 12.1 Representative Decision Support Systems

Decision Support System	Description	Developer
AAIMS (An Analytical Information Management System)	Supports American Airlines planning, finance, marketing, and operations functions. Also used by other airlines, engine and airframe manufacturers, airline financial analysts, consultants, and the Air Transport Association. Facilitates study of load factors, market share, seating configuration, aircraft utilization, operating statistics, traffic and capacity growth, productivity measurement, and revenue/yield.	American Airlines
BRANDAID	Models a market system so that preliminary sales forecasts and overall profitability estimates can be developed. Includes development of marketing mix budgets (price, advertising, promotion, sales force activities, and so on). Also models the market system, including competitor, retailer, consumer, and general environment variables.	J.D.C. Little
CIS (Capacity Information System)	An interactive graphics system that enables managers to assess the impact of changes in product plans on the overall manufacturing process for trucks. Includes monitoring and planning for major truck components (for example, transmissions, engines, axles) as well as capital investments and complex manufacturing schedules.	Ztrux
DAISY (Decision-Aiding Information System)	Intended to assist tactical managers in planning and carrying out missions using a set of state-of-the-art decision aids including mathematical models, large databases, and a checklist facility. Uses multimedia approach, including graphics facilities, joysticks for input, and multiple-window display screens. Excellent for maintaining mail messages, appointment schedules, and reminder lists.	The Wharton School, University of Pennsylvania
GADS (Geodata Analysis and Display System)	To assist nonprogrammers in solving unstructured problems in applications areas such as planning for urban growth, planning police beats, and redefining school district boundaries. Includes high quality graphics display capability.	IBM Research Division
MAPP (Managerial Analysis for Profit Planning)	Support financial planning and budgeting by establishing a discipline for defining products (identifying costs incurred in producing selected products, determining how resources might be shifted between product options). Aids in preparing budgets for departments and divisions producing each set of products.	Citibank

ongoing process. Table 12.1 describes some typical decision support systems designed to address specific issues.

As a rule, a DSS is developed after a firm has acquired experience in using management information systems. Thus, decision support systems are often viewed as a natural evolution of computer information systems and as a stage in the movement of information support upward in the organization hierarchy (that is, from the operating levels, into the control activities, into management planning). Even though DSS and MIS may differ in scope, they are related.

Types of Decision Support Systems

Three types of decision support system elements—institutional DSS, DSS generators, and DSS tools—are in widespread use. Each is important and is used across many different applications and organizations. You will find them on computer systems of all sizes, from microcomputers to mainframes.

Institutional DSS **Institutional DSS** are complete applications. Such systems, typically built by information systems professionals, contain many features that allow users to retrieve or generate information needed to address a general problem area, such as market analysis. These DSS are intended to be used on a continuing basis. Hence, they are designed to include features that will be useful in a variety of different situations. For example, a system designed to support market analysis will include capabilities such as:

——*Retrieval of sales and market data:* flexibility in retrieving data by region, product line, customer type, amount of sale, and so on. Aimed at reporting the results ("What happened?") for a period of time.

——*Analysis of data:* ability to interrelate business variables of interest to identify relationships between performance results and key variables. Aimed at developing explanations ("Why did it happen?").

——*Exploration of market alternatives:* ability to simulate the effect of alternative marketing strategies with business variables. Aimed at determining the impact of following various strategies ("What if?").

Marketing is not a prerogative of a single department, but a function that spans several areas of the firm. Hence, a marketing DSS will be used by more than marketing department staff members alone. This is why such a system is termed *institutional:* Its use spans many groups in the organization. (See the references for additional information on institutional DSS.)

DSS Generators In contrast to complete DSS applications, **DSS generators** are designed for use in creating or generating applications quickly. They are neither complete applications, like institutional DSS, nor are they languages. Instead, DSS generators include a *combination* of languages, user interfaces, reporting capabilities, graphics facilities, and the like that can be utilized, as needed, to create a DSS.

DSS generators can be used to assemble a DSS very quickly—one that has a limited number of features. The important thing is to be able to develop the capability (for reporting, analysis, or simulation) as fast as possible. Alternatively, a DSS generator can be used to create a DSS with many different capabilities. Such a system requires more time to develop and may be used over a more extensive period of time.

Fourth-generation languages in a sense are DSS generators when the purpose of the DSS is the retrieval and reporting of data and results (in contrast to simulating the impact of new strategies). They fit within this category because they require only a limited number of instructions to generate reports satisfying complex and sophisticated requirements.

In contrast, some packages—such as IMS—are designed to provide the user with many different capabilities, each useful with limited training or minimal operational difficulty. Such packages can be applied to many different situations, according to the needs of the user.

Applications created using DSS generators can be very powerful and efficient to use. The distinction is that the systems do not require the writing of extensive procedural instructions, say in COBOL. The generator does the work once the requirements are specified.

DSS Tools **DSS tools** are actually a special case of DSS generator. They are intended for use in the development of a DSS, but typically have a limited and special focus or strength. For example, a graphics package—designed to produce business graphics such as bar charts or data plots—can be integrated into a DSS. The graphics-generation capability is in the DSS tool, but the capability is used under control of the DSS generator. Likewise, DSS tools can be incorporated into an institutional DSS. For instance, the developers of the DSS can invoke a graphics generator when computer graphics are needed. They need not write the capabilities for computer graphics themselves.

Features of Decision Support Systems

How do decision support systems differ from information systems of other types? What do they consist of? How do they work? We look at the answers to each of these questions next.

Methods

DSS objectives are accomplished through information retrieval and information generation.

Information Retrieval In many instances, the data needed to answer a question raised by management already reside in the organization's databases. However, there has been no previous need to draw on those data in the same way as the current, unique situation requires. Therefore, no application problems exist to provide for retrieval and preparation of reports.

This important function underlies the origin of decision support systems, as we discussed earlier in this chapter. The flexibility of a database management system provides the ability to retrieve information in unexpected ways. Fourth-generation languages, with their easy-to-use command structure, also provide this capability. We will return to this question in a moment when we discuss DSS components.

Information Generation Often when new or unexpected problems arise, the information that will allow managers to address the problem does not yet exist. For example, analysts attempting to project the possible effects of airline deregulation before the new ruling had taken effect wanted to generate information about the impact on the air service to cities. Information had to be developed to determine how many cities served by a single major carrier might lose commercial air service if the lone carriers canceled their flights to those cities in order to seek higher profits on other routes. This requirement demonstrates the importance of the information generation capability of a DSS. And it emphasizes the modeling capabilities of a DSS. Using facts and data retrieved from the database or provided by users, the system can interrelate the details in a model to provide additional information (number of cities likely to be affected, probability of occurrence, alternate viewpoints, and so on). In essence, the system is creating new information, but it does so by analyzing existing and newly provided details. This is what modeling is all about.

Components

A DSS consists of three components: interface mechanism, model subsystem, and data subsystem (Figure 12.3). Component design will vary depending on the nature of the DSS.

Interface The interface provides a way for a user to interact with the system. We have discussed many types of interfaces in other sections of the book. One of the simplest interfaces is through the rows and columns of a spreadsheet. This is the vehicle for entering data and building the characteristics of a model. Single-word command alternatives may be shown across the bottom of the screen displaying the spreadsheet to remind the user of processing steps.

Other decision support systems use a rigorous command structure. In essence, the user must assemble a computer program consisting of commands and instructions that describe the model and specify the processing. Depending on the system, the commands may be stated in a procedural language or in a high-level fourth-generation language. A great deal of research is taking place in this area, resulting in the appearance of natural language interfaces (see Chapter 6).

For system output, the interface capabilities may include display or print features. Graphics capabilities, often in full color, further enhance the method of presenting information to the user.

Model Subsystem The model subsystem, an integral part of decision support, manages the storage and retrieval of the models. It also assists users in model building.

In a spreadsheet environment (Figure 12.4), models consist of one or more worksheets containing variables and parameters as well as formulas interrelating them (for example, the formula for determining profit will be stated as a sequence of adding and subtracting rows and columns). The model system allows the user to define and store the contents of the worksheet. Often the worksheet is stored in a *template* form that contains only the formulas and interrelation of variables—that is, there are no data in the cells. The templates can be distributed to other users, who add the data they wish to use in evaluating the model.

In other DSS environments, the models are described using a specially designed

Figure 12.3 Components of Decision Support System

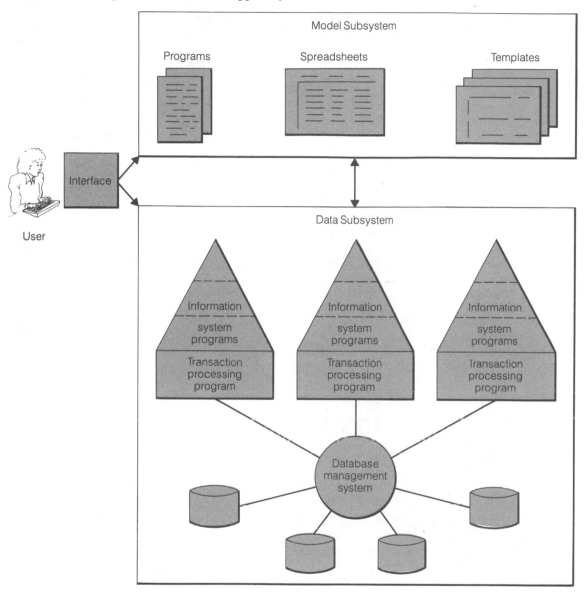

language. However, the requirements remain the same: Variables must be identified and interrelated through formulas and prescribed procedures.

The model subsystem also provides the capability to store and retrieve models. A database of models, often termed a **model bank,** stores the models, each identified with a unique name. When a user invokes a model by providing the assigned name,

Figure 12.4 Model Using Spreadsheet Format

	1985	1986	1987	1988	1989	1990
Revenues	150000.00	172500.00	198375.00	228131.25	262350.94	301703.58
Price	150.00	150.00	150.00	150.00	150.00	150.00
Units Sold	1000.00	1150.00	1322.50	1520.88	1749.01	2011.36
Materials per Unit	57.00	57.00	57.00	57.00	57.00	57.00
Materials	57000.00	65550.00	75382.50	86689.87	99693.36	114647.36
Labor per Unit	36.00	36.00	36.00	36.00	36.00	36.00
Labor	36000.00	41400.00	47610.00	54751.50	62964.22	72408.86
Cost of Goods Sold	93000.00	106950.00	122922.50	141441.38	162657.58	187056.22
Gross Margin	57000.00	65550.00	75382.50	86689.88	99693.36	114647.36
Utilities	4950.00	5197.50	5457.38	5730.24	6016.76	6317.59
Overhead	8250.00	9075.00	9982.50	10980.75	12078.83	13286.71
Depreciation	3025.00	3025.00	3025.00	3025.00	3025.00	3025.00
Selling Expenses	15000.00	17250.00	19837.50	22813.13	26235.09	30170.36
Gen and Admin	17250.00	19837.50	22813.13	26235.09	30170.36	34695.91

Revenues = Price * Units Sold
Price = 150
Units Sold = 1000, previous * 1.15
Materials per Unit = 57
Materials = Materials per Unit * Units Sold

Base Solution				VIEW MODE		Model DEMO.MOD
View	What_if	Windows	Variables	Columns		
	Set		Format	Analyze		

the model subsystem locates and retrieves it and, with the data subsystem, loads the data for processing. Processing occurs under control of the data subsystem and includes the capability to "run the model" to produce output. Models may be run periodically or to respond to needs for special analysis.

An important feature is the capability to link different models together, running them in sequence. For example, in planning a new product line, separate models must be developed for material management and operation of the production line, as well as sales and distribution. A change in one area may necessitate rerunning all the models to determine the overall impact of the change. Direct linkage between the models may allow this to occur in an integrated fashion.

Data Subsystem The data subsystem includes the means for retrieval and processing of data from formal databases and the tools to manage the data. Some of the data needed are by-products of transaction processing (for example, accounting data, inventory control details, order data). Other data originate externally, perhaps describing competitor activities, the economic outlook, or the projected future of a particular industry.

The DSS includes *two* types of databases. The organization database is a valuable data source. However, it is supplemented by a logically separate DSS database, usually a smaller unit, which contains summary information (based on that included in the organization database). Special extraction software summarizes and stores the data in the DSS database. This database may also contain data in different arrangements or it may include unique details (such as planning assumptions or goals and targets) or personal (unofficial) data.

When managers are evaluating strategies and possible problem solutions, they must be able to retrieve and use data quickly. Excessive delay in searching large databases, retrieving details, and processing them into a usable summary form cannot be tolerated. Furthermore, the arrangement of data in the organization database may be inappropriate for a DSS (and it would be illogical to reorganize the entire database, since it serves many transaction-level applications).

Processing Functions

To prepare decision-aiding information, a DSS includes sophisticated processing activities. Some are financial and are associated with accounting and money management activities. Others utilize sophisticated quantitative techniques.

Financial Functions The financial functions consist of tools for projecting the effect of interest rates, growth patterns, and economic analysis. These functions are widely understood in the management community and are used with great regularity. Thus they are a natural for inclusion in decision support systems. The following financial functions are typical of those needed:

——Present value calculation

——Internal rate of return determination

——Loan amortization

——Payment calculation

——Future value determination

Most of these functions are incorporated in spreadsheet software packages.

There are other processing functions that are not financial, which involve a greater degree of sophistication. The processing functions discussed below can be developed through such generalized DSS packages as Interactive Financial Planning System (IFPS), one of the most widely used types of DSS, or they may be included in custom-tailored decision software. Table 12.2 lists general-purpose DSS software for mainframe and microcomputer systems.

The "What If" Function The "what if" function allows the user to change the definition of one or more variables in a model. Existing values are replaced with newly selected ones and the model is rerun to determine the impact and the result. For example, managers may want to test the viability of a product in the planning phase by

Table 12.2 Representative General-Purpose DSS Packages

DSS Package	Vendor	System
Executive Information System (EIS)	Boeing Computer Services	Mainframe
Express	Tymshare	Mainframe
IFPS*	Execucom Systems	Mainframe
IFPS/Personal	Execucom Systems	Microcomputer
SAS†	SAS Institute	Mainframe
SAS/Graph	SAS Institute	Mainframe
SAS/PC	SAS Institute	Microcomputer

*Acronym for Interactive Financial Planning System

†Acronym for Statistical Analysis System

projecting sales revenues for varying degrees of market penetration: What if we achieve a 20 percent penetration? What is our estimated sales revenue if we achieve a 25 percent penetration?

Often models formulated using spreadsheets are designed with this basic function in mind. The rows and columns of the model matrix, coupled with built-in financial functions, enable the user to change the data in one or more cells in the matrix and use the "recalculate" function of the spreadsheet software to determine immediately the impact of the change.

Sensitivity Testing Sensitivity testing, a special form of "what if" analysis, is used when a manager is uncertain of assumptions made about a particular model variable. Uncertainty makes it desirable to find out whether changes from assumed values will have a major or minor impact on the result. In complex models, it is often difficult to visualize the impact without testing it through alternate data sets.

In the marketing example, analysts may use a sales model to test the sensitivity of product sales volume to advertising levels.

Goal Seeking Managers often work within the framework of goals, budgets, and quotas, which serve as a guide for formulating plans and activities. The goal-seeking function of a decision support system allows users to find out the value a particular variable must have if the desired performance level is to be achieved. Depending on the situation, users may need to specify either a single performance objective (such as a product line profit goal) or performance over the entire time horizon (say, a five-year expected life cycle).

For example, a product manager may want to know what material, labor, and sales cost levels are necessary to achieve an overall margin objective of 21 percent, when the sales forecast is prespecified. The DSS will process the data and provide output suggesting what must be done to meet the stated requirements.

The "Analyze" Function When performance in an area of interest produces unexpected or intriguing results, or when the interrelation of variables in a model is very complex, managers tend to want explanations. The "analyze" function in a DSS uses statistical methods to provide any or all of the following:

——A trend line for the variables of interest over the specified period

——The values of the variable for every period

——The values of every variable specified

The "analyze" function is generally found only in sophisticated decision support systems or modeling languages; it is not usually included in spreadsheet software.

In the marketing example, this function might be used to examine sales and cost data for other product lines for past years to permit management to determine broad trends for use in planning activities.

Simulation Most models of business performance assume average costs and expected values for important parameters, and in most cases this information provides a close enough approximation to structure a decision. However, if a decision must be made under a high degree of uncertainty or if the decision will commit a large amount of resources, managers may want to assess the risks. In other words, they will want to know how much they stand to lose if key assumptions turn out to be false.

Simulation generates the information needed to assess decision risks. Through this technique, the decision support system tests different combinations of variables to determine their impact on performance. Probability distributions are applied to the model representing typical occurrence of events.

To evaluate a new product line operation, acceptable rates of equipment failure and absenteeism, and varying levels of scrap generation may be specified. Using these data as input to the simulation model, while holding other factors constant, such as equipment operating rates and maintenance intervals, managers can estimate production delays, raw material buildups, and production bottlenecks. They can also determine the impact of these unfavorable conditions on product costs and delivery schedules. You can see how useful simulation can be in examining changes in processes or ongoing events.

Using a Decision Support System

Using a decision support system involves an iterative process. We can visualize five steps (Figure 12.5). First the problem is examined, and a formulation that permits study of the problem is developed. Next, pertinent parameters and variables are identified, to give the user an understanding of the situation. A general model may be formulated, although this is seldom done during the initial stages.

The model is built by interrelating the parameters and variables in the manner prescribed by the user. Although the user may understand clearly how the factors are related to one another, in many cases part of the original problem may be the lack of such knowledge. Therefore, the model may be only an idea that needs testing by processing.

Figure 12.5 Steps in Using a DSS

Steps

Activities

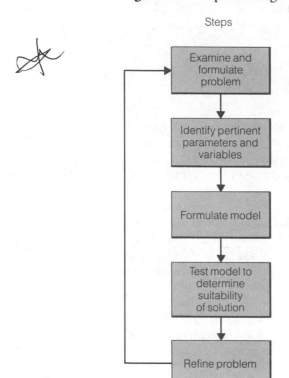

Steps	Activities
Examine and formulate problem	• Investigate problem circumstances • Determine nature and scope of problem • Assess implications of problem
Identify pertinent parameters and variables	• Discuss cause and effects with users. Determine which circumstances are fixed and which may vary • Determine possible interrelation between variables
Formulate model	• Express pertinent parameters in model form
Test model to determine suitability of solution	• Supply data needed for model • Perform processing to test model and generate results
Refine problem	• Evaluate model results • Adjust model if additional refinement is needed (will require iteration through preceding steps)

Testing the model involves supplying data for the variables and carrying out out the processing and recalculation to determine the results. Depending on the application, the test variables may be profits and losses, sales volumes, interest rates, quality levels, or almost anything else.

A model for an unstructured problem is seldom correct the first time; thus an important step in using a DSS is refinement of the problem. Users identify additional or different data for consideration. Or they rule out certain variables and add others. Remember that part of the process of addressing the problem is determining what variables are relevant.

The iterative process may be repeated a number of times until the users feel that they understand the situation as well as possible.

Decision Support System Reports

People faced with complex planning tasks need to be able to test ideas or to search through data to find explanations for situations and events. Evaluation of possible strategies that might be chosen in planning activities must be aided by the organization's information processing mechanisms. These planners must have help in examining and evaluating a number of alternatives, and subsequently, in identifying the one that is most appropriate for a particular situation.

Earlier we said that decision support systems frequently involve some type of simulation-based mechanism for evaluating "what if" questions. Representative situations calling for **special analysis reports** are: new product developments, plant expansion, change in corporate growth plans, and modifications of the corporate debt structure. Executives must have a means of addressing such questions as, "What effect will the addition of the new product line have on the funds and revenue of the company?"

Generally a fixed-format report does not support this type of process. It is often more useful for managers and their staff to construct a model containing the relevant variables. The model can be formulated and prepared as a computer program that will accept different input values for each of the variables or parameters, and so on. The computer-based model in effect *simulates* what the result of a decision would be *if* variables or parameters were at certain levels or values. After evaluating each strategy alternative, the manager should be able to arrive at a more informed decision. Of course, judgment will remain a key component in the decision process.

Inquiry processing is the generation of special analysis information by interacting directly with the computer system through terminals, rather than submitting batch programs. This special case of special analysis report generation offers users the advantage of being able to tailor and refine their information needs while actually using the computer system, rather than waiting for a batch report to be prepared, examined, data adjusted, and the report then reprocessed.

In the past, upper-level management has received only a small amount of the information it needs from automated processing systems—frequently less than 20 percent. However, as decision support systems become more widespread, the situation will change. Advances are being made in what we know about information usage in management and in ways to convey this knowledge to decision makers. In the future, it is expected that more and more attention will be given to activities for top-management planning.

Group Decision Support Systems

Group decision support systems (GDSS) are based on the principles of decision support systems discussed earlier. In addition, they offer unique features that support situations where multiple decision makers are involved, whether working face to face or not.

Rationale for a Group Decision Support System

Many uses of computing and communications technology are oriented toward individuals. Yet group decision making is a reality in business. Managers spend a great deal of their time in meetings (in Chapter 4 we saw that approximately 70 percent of a manager's time is spent in scheduled or unscheduled meetings). Typically, the individuals at a meeting have diverse experience, different points of view, and varying responsibilities. Each group member is likely to have important information that others in the group do not have. These characteristics are precisely why you want to convene a group: to draw people together in order to profit from their varying background.

The trends in business are clearly emphasizing the need to make decisions more quickly while the business situation itself is growing more complex: You must consider customers, competitors, the state of global business, government regulations—both foreign and domestic—and so on. Because the pace of change is increasingly rapid, the cost of an error is also higher than in the past, if for no other reason than that the time it takes to make a correction will give competitors an additional opportunity to take advantage of a mistake.

The exchange of information and ideas is essential. Yet lengthy meetings take away from the time available to implement decisions or carry out other managerial tasks. Group decision support systems are a type of information system whose time has come. They are receiving increased attention as organizations seek ways to deal with the increasing complexity of business.

What Is a Group Decision Support System?

A GDSS, like an individual DSS, is intended to make it easier to deal with situations that are not well structured. It is also designed to support decision makers working as a group, not just as individuals. The system is interactive. Questions may be posed, information retrieved, and information generated in response to the needs of any or all group members.

Furthermore, as we will see, the decision makers may not be hands-on users. In many cases, they do not operate the system directly.

Essential GDSS Components Like an individual DSS, a GDSS may be general in nature or specialized for use in dealing with particular topics or tasks.

The configuration of a GDSS will vary. However, several components are essential:

——Interactive computer interface

——Database

——Model base

The interactive computer interface allows users to submit inquiries, opinions, ideas, or comments, as we will see in a moment. Having such an interface is essential to provide the group support that underlies the use of these systems. Database and model base components serve the same purpose, as discussed earlier.

Computer facilities may involve personal computers, mid-range systems, or mainframes. And they may be tied together in local-area networks, in wide-area networks, or through packet switching methods. Some GDSS designs call for the use of fourth-generation languages, statistical packages, or other methods for decision analysis.

Figure 12.6 illustrates the structure of a GDSS.

Figure 12.6 Components of a GDSS

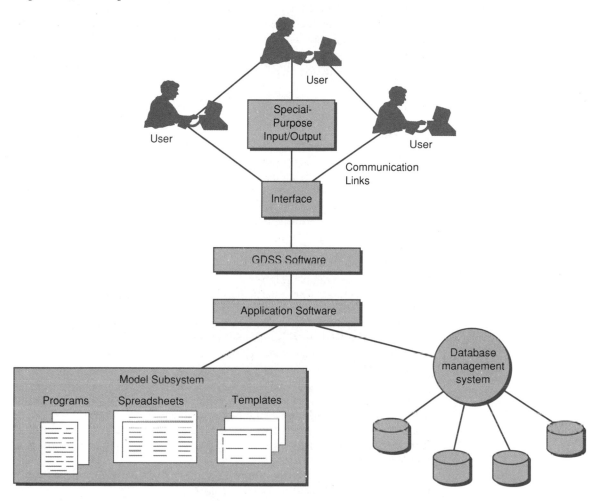

When decision makers work with a GDSS, the sessions are typically managed by a facilitator. The role of facilitators may vary. In some systems, the role is that of an intermediary between the GDSS technology and the group, while in other instances facilitators are responsible for coordinating the group's activities in an administrative sense. As group members become familiar with both procedure and system, the role of the facilitator will diminish or disappear.

On-line interaction is essential. Ideas, opinions, and suggestions that require further information usually emerge during a group session, even though the need for this information may not have been anticipated. The ability to generate or retrieve the information instantly will allow the group to continue its line of inquiry, not to mention keeping the attention of busy managers and executives.

The databases underlying the GDSS are most likely relational databases, for the same reason. Information needs cannot be anticipated nor can access paths through the database be developed in advance. When time is of the essence, flexibility in retrieval will necessitate relational databases.

In addition, multiple tools are often required. Completing a single task may require spreadsheet analysis, simulation using different probabilities, or repeated retrieval of selective historical and current events data. Both printing and display of information may be requested by participants.

Types of GDSS There are several types of GDSS (see Figure 12.7). Depending on how an organization is structured and the manner in which its managers function, one may be more appropriate than the other. The general types include:

——**Decision room:** One situation involves a boardroom or conference room equipped with special facilities that support group decision making. Seating is in a horse-shoe or U-shaped pattern, so that each individual can see the others. A large screen is often used for display of information (tables, graphs, charts, and images) and to record ideas generated by the group. The screen is visible to all group members.

Workstations may be positioned by each participant or near the group facilitator.

Example: An example might be a decision room used for quarterly price setting meetings, where participants include the corporate executives and vice presidents of each functional area, such as purchasing, personnel, marketing, manufacturing, and so on. Typically no more than 12 to 15 persons will be involved. In this example, there is continual interaction between group members as ideas are exchanged, questions are raised, and strategies are evaluated.

——**Linked decision room:** This alternative relies on videoconferencing (similar to what you see in two-way television news interviews) for linking decision rooms together for group decision making. Each decision room is outfitted in the manner described earlier. Host-based or local-area networks link each terminal or workstation into a network so that all participants see the same information simultaneously.

Videocameras in each decision room capture the discussion and transmit it to other locations, where it is viewed on projection screens.

The need for travel is reduced by this method. However, this alternative must be well managed so that the dynamics of group interchange and decision making are maintained.

Example: Some investment firms may hold weekly meetings to assess performance of securities portfolios and the need for changes in investment policies. Participants are located in regional decision rooms that are interconnected by teleconferencing.

——**Remote decision network:** This alternative brings individuals together without the use of specially outfitted decision rooms. Group members do not come face to face in a single facility, but instead are linked through networks. The GDSS design ensures that each still has access to databases and decision support software, perhaps through a central processor acting as host to the decision support system.

Emerging workstations, coupled with advanced telecommunications technology, such as ISDN, will allow all participants in the group to see and hear

Figure 12.7 Types of GDSS

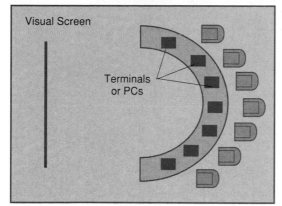

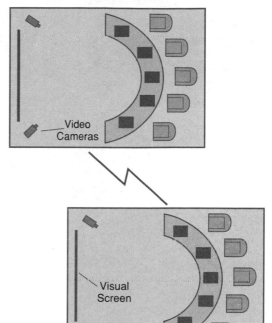

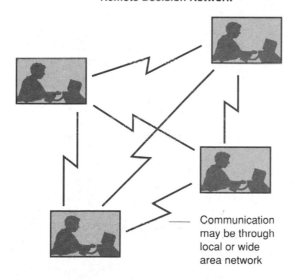

other participants on their personal display screen (Figure 12.8). In addition, identical tables, graphs, drawings, and so on can be displayed simultaneously in front of all group members.

This alternative, like the linked decision room, may rely on the use of rented technology to interconnect each site to the GDSS network. When key group members are out of town at the scheduled meeting time, they may rely on GDSS to participate in the session.

Example: Engineering teams may meet as a group electronically to explore quality control problems associated with a particular product line.

Figure 12.8 Complex Information Displayed on Screen in Advanced Communications Network

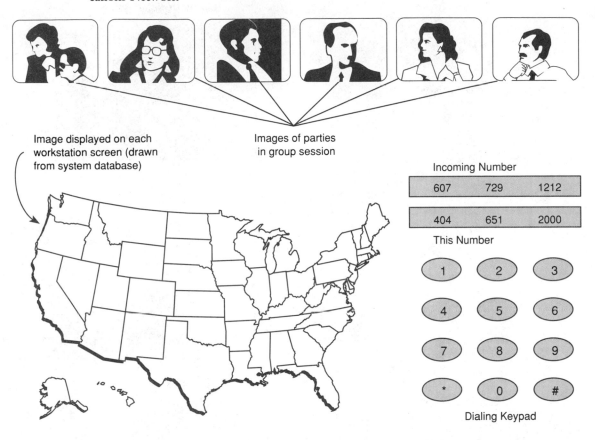

Image displayed on each workstation screen (drawn from system database)

Images of parties in group session

Incoming Number		
607	729	1212
404	651	2000

This Number

Dialing Keypad

In each of these cases, the GDSS is much more than an assembly of computer and data communications technologies (a factor that distinguishes GDSS from the office technologies discussed in Chapter 15). Keep in mind that the underlying DSS features, including real-time retrieval and generation of information, are an essential element.

Uses of GDSS   Group decision support systems offer the greatest benefit in policy-making situations or in cases where the situation at hand is not well defined. Verbal interaction is also an essential characteristic. This section discusses the types of uses where GDSS will provide the highest payoff.

Problem Clarification

Often when events do not occur as expected or when actions occur that cannot be accounted for, it is because individuals have different perceptions about the situation. Getting a group of knowledgeable individuals together with a GDSS at hand may be extremely effective in clarifying the nature and significance of a problem. When all parties have an opportunity to hear differing viewpoints and to examine underlying data, the solution frequently becomes evident.

For example, if an airline has detected a continuing drop in the number of passengers it has carried in the last six months, it will want to investigate the cause. But it must first see whether the reported drop is accurate. Among the questions that might arise in a group discussion are:

1. Was there a decline in the actual number of persons boarded or in the total dollars collected?
2. Were an excessive number of flights canceled because of bad weather? (This leads to the possibility that there was not a decline at all.)
3. Was there an industrywide decline?
4. Did certain cities have a substantial change in the number of passengers boarded?

The answers to these questions will help focus the investigation. The data to answer them will be drawn from company databases as well as from secondary sources, such as an on-line database service. Some data will be needed in tabular form, while other details will be most useful in graphic form. But the point is that the questions arise as a result of group discussion, supported by a decision support system.

Structuring a Situation

Structuring a situation means identifying the key factors influencing a situation, or surrounding an opportunity, followed by identification of strategies, procedures, or the sequence in which events must take place to meet organization needs.

In the airline example the factors of interest might include the time of the year under examination, the number of discount fares, or the number of advance purchases.

Brainstorming to Identify Alternatives

Brainstorming is an idea-generation technique developed in the 1950s to stimulate creative thought within groups. The technique calls for individuals to communicate all the ideas they have about a topic of interest (for example, what features to build into a new product or how to price airline seats) without any regard to their feasibility. Later the ideas are analyzed and evaluated from a more practical standpoint.

Some individuals, as you might suspect, are intimidated by others participating in the process. Hence they hold back their ideas, even though they may be very creative. However, brainstorming through the mechanism of GDSS allows anonymity. Participants can enter their ideas and comments into the workstation rather than voicing them aloud. Thus, electronic brainstorming encourages the free and candid flow of ideas from all participants, regardless of their managerial level or responsibilities.

Experience has shown that when a GDSS is used for electronic brainstorming, such activities as strategic planning or new product development are completed more quickly and more thoroughly than by conventional means.

Table 12.3 Advantages and Disadvantages of GDSS Use

Advantages

Act as a group memory; avoid regeneration and repeated evaluation of ideas by group members

Help identify more feasible alternatives

Make it possible to give alternatives more careful consideration

Enhance the ability of the group to communicate and utilize information

Can provide a process structure enabling the group to address the situation at hand

Serve as a means for group interaction between informed or interested parties

Disadvantages

Individuals may be uncomfortable or unwilling to operate a workstation to retrieve or enter information

May require a trained facilitator to lead sessions; otherwise benefits may not be obtained

May require all group members to be present

May require advance planning in the face of quickly developing situations

---

Evaluation of Alternatives

This task is a review of alternatives to determine which are likely to have the best outcomes and, say, an acceptable level of risk. Irrelevant ideas are also eliminated. Then a course of action can be selected.

In the airline example, possible alternatives to consider include adjusting pricing if the number of passengers or amount of revenue is falling. The increasing complexity of management, coupled with the fact that no one individual is likely to have the information needed to deal with situations that are well structured, suggests that GDSS will increase in importance.

Summary

Decision support systems aid decision makers confronted with situations that are not well structured. In these instances, part of the task of the decision maker is determining what information is required to understand the circumstances and ultimately make the decision. Because extensive reports cannot be designed in advance to address unique conditions, such material must be assembled as an understanding of the situation is gained. Iteration is common, as each new element of information raises additional questions needing investigation.

There are three types of decision support systems. Institutional DSS—the first type—are designed to be used on a continuing basis. Such systems, typically developed by information systems professionals, often span several units within an organization. DSS generators—the second type—are designed to create a DSS quickly.

They may provide only limited capabilities, or their features may be quite extensive. Often they can be employed by staff members and other users in a firm. DSS tools—the third type—are a special case of DSS generator. They have a limited focus, but can serve as components in an institutional DSS.

The components of a DSS include its method of interface, the data subsystem, and the model subsystem, which vary from system to system. Processing functions include the "analyze," "what if," and explanation functions; sensitivity testing; goal seeking; and simulation.

Group decision support systems are of growing importance in organizations as they seek ways to deal with the increasing complexity of business. These systems are designed to support decision makers who are working as a group, confronting situations that are not well structured. In addition to the model base and database associated with an individual DSS, a group DSS will also include an interactive computer interface. The need for on-line interaction is essential, since the system must have the capability of accommodating opinions, suggestions, and questions as they arise in group problem-solving sessions.

The most common ways to use GDSS are for problem clarification, structuring a situation, brainstorming to identify alternatives, or evaluation of alternatives.

Group decision support systems may include decision rooms, linked decision rooms, and remote decision networks.

Decision support systems of all types will grow in importance and frequency across all types of organizations in the future. They are an essential type of information system whose time has come.

Key Words

Decision room	DSS tool	Linked decision room
Decision support system (DSS)	Group decision support system (GDSS)	Model bank
DSS generator	Institutional DSS	Remote decision network
		Special analysis report

Review Questions

1. Distinguish between a transaction processing system and a DSS; between a DSS and an MIS.
2. What is the primary objective of a DSS? How is this objective achieved insofar as computer processing capabilities are concerned?
3. What are the different types of DSS?
4. Compare fourth-generation languages and DSS.
5. Identify and describe the components of a DSS. Give an example of each component.
6. What processing functions are included in DSS? Is it necessary to include all functions in order for a DSS to be effective? Explain.

7. What reports are produced by a DSS? Who is the intended user of each?

8. How do GDSS and individual DSS differ? How are they the same?

9. Why are GDSS a type of system whose time has come?

10. Describe how organizations use GDSS. Give examples of specific situations where a GDSS might be used. For each, indicate the role and value of a GDSS.

11. What are the essential components of a GDSS?

12. Describe the three types of GDSS, indicating the features of each. Be sure to identify the conditions under which each should be used.

Application Problems

1. City planners in urban areas are continually faced with tough decisions about road development and commercial building construction (office buildings, hotels, and retailing centers). They must consider the capacity of public facilities such as water and sewer systems and road capacity (measured in vehicles per hour) in regard to the demand that new construction will make on them.

   Decisions to approve the development of a new facility are relatively unstructured since each planning decision is unique—the project has not been built in the specific location before.

   When developers submit a plan for planning department approval, they must specify how much space the building will occupy (measured in square feet), how many floors the building will contain, and what the building will be used for— for example, office and institutional activities. The planning department then applies its standard for utility and traffic volumes to determine the impact the building will have on public resources.

   a. What features should be included in a DSS to aid city planners? Assume that standards exist for utility consumption per square foot of building and for the number of vehicles per hour a building or retail center of a specified size adds to existing traffic.

   b. If road capacity in an area is fixed and cannot be expanded, it is a constraint for all other planning. A city planning board is faced with a decision to approve one—or disapprove all—of three different proposals for use of a tract of land in an area already zoned for commercial development. The board can disapprove all three proposals if they do not fall within the constraints of public utilities. The concerns are:

      (1) Can existing roads handle traffic that would be generated by each of the projects?

      (2) Will water and sewer systems handle the demand any of the proposed projects will create?

      Which processing functions associated with DSS (financial functions, "what if," sensitivity testing, goal seeking, and analyze function) must be used to arrive at a recommendation if the recommendation will be based only on whether any of the proposals meet planning standards?

   c. What specific role do model bases and databases play in the planning decision?

   d. Is a system having the features of a DSS or those of an expert system most appropriate for the planning situation described in this problem? Explain.

2. Indicate whether the following situations are best supported by MIS, DSS, or expert systems. For each, indicate the reason for your classification.
   a. Planning the cost feasibility of a unique new product with varying material and labor costs, with market penetration, and with likely emergence of competing products during the first year. *DSS*
   b. Determining the quantity of material to order from suppliers each week. The quantity is determined by considering the amount of material currently on hand and expected demand. *MIS*
   c. Diagnosing the cause of a serious medical problem that is evidenced by multiple symptoms. Diagnosis relies on the interpretation of several different items of medical data. *expert (us*
   d. Determining whether to accept a merger of another company with your organization by considering profitability indicators, market prospects, and industry outlooks, and other factors that become apparent during the decision process. *DSS*
   e. Planning the route of mail carriers based on distance covered, amount of mail to be delivered, and overall delivery efficiency. *DSS*
   f. Determining whether to build alternative rental properties based on the construction and operating costs, tax advantages, rental demand, and alternative rental rates. *DSS*

3. A senior manager has devised a planning tool that uses an electronic spreadsheet. The rows and columns contain data about various revenue and cost categories faced by the firm. For all practical purposes, the spreadsheet is a budget. Relations are built into the system; for instance, the system will change sales levels if advertising allocations are increased or decreased. In turn, profit levels will increase or decrease.

   Similarly, the spreadsheet can be used to project the impact of different union contracts on the cost to manufacture products. The manager uses the spreadsheet to test the cost of different wage packages, determining how much a specific settlement will cost in total dollars and relating this to the level of profit for the company.

   Some of the data used in the spreadsheet is based on details captured during transaction processing; other values are estimated by the manager and entered during the actual analysis.
   a. What factors give structure to this situation? What aspects are unstructured?
   b. Is a spreadsheet model of this nature recommended for this type of analysis? Explain.
   c. Can this system be classified as a DSS? Relate the features of this system to those of a DSS or an expert system if you believe it fits this category.

4. The police department of San Jose, California, uses a computer-based system to design the patrol areas of police officers. By combining graphics display capabilities and access to police data, officers can view historical data about crime and citizen inquiries by regions of the city. The easy-to-use system allows officers to design and assess alternative patrol beats. Routes are displayed using maps that show the frequency of activity by time of day. By varying the routes, police are able to determine whether they can provide better protection and coverage when allocating themselves to larger areas or to sections needing more police saturation.
   a. What features characterize this system as a DSS?
   b. How does the system relate to the police database? To a transaction processing system?

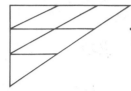

13: Executive Support Systems

Key Questions

What is an executive support system?

How do ESS differ from other information systems?

Why are ESS not universally used, in contrast to transaction processing systems?

What features are included in an ESS?

What is the relationship between executives' working habits and their use of ESS?

Are ESS developed in-house or purchased from outside vendors?

There they go;
I must hurry;
I am their leader!
Michael Hammer

Executive support systems (ESS; also known as *executive information systems*) are gaining increasing attention at the top levels of organizations of all types. This chapter examines the characteristics of these systems. It explores how executives use information, the features included in an ESS, and why executives do or do not utilize such systems. Examples of ESS will demonstrate how some firms benefit from their use.

Why You Should Know About Executive Support Systems

Even if you are not an executive, knowing about ESS is beneficial. This chapter has been prepared to help you understand

——How information systems can be made more relevant to executive-level tasks and responsibilities

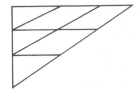

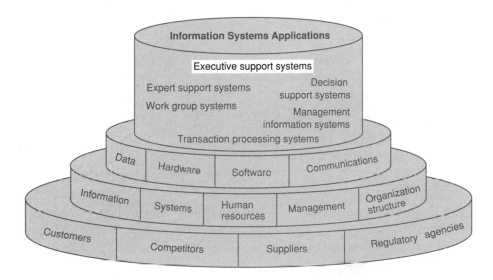

—How transaction information is both a help and a hindrance to executives

—How the role of top managers differs from that of operating managers

—How to bring problems and opportunities to the attention of senior management of an organization

We begin by examining how senior executives carry out their responsibilities.

Information Acquisition and Use by Executives

The activities of top-level executives remain a mystery to many people. This section explores the activities that are common among executives across different organizations and relates executive activities to information needs. It also introduces concerns about information needs that must be addressed in the development of computer information systems support for executives, while suggesting how to avoid the information inundation so many executives face.

Executives acquire and use information for at least seven reasons:

——To understand and assess situations quickly
——To facilitate the business of the organization
——To confront multiple problems together
——To set agendas
——To build networks
——To maintain a corporate view
——To maintain an industry perspective

Each reason will be elaborated on in the following paragraphs.

To Understand and Assess Situations Quickly

The activities of managers in general were introduced in Chapter 4. Figure 13.1 provides a breakdown of how most senior managers typically use their time. The earlier discussion explored several *myths* about the manager's job, drawing on a study by Mintzberg (1975), including the assumptions that

1. The manager is a reflective, systematic planner.
2. The effective manager has no regular duties to perform.
3. The senior manager needs aggregated information, which a formal management information structure best provides.

We also learned that effective support to managers—particularly top-level executives—requires that an information system

1. Offer quick, concise updates
2. Permit scanning of internal and external environments
3. Allow browsing through data
4. Allow testing of strategies
5. Support the use of models
6. Avoid information overload
7. Highlight significant data
8. Present summary measures
9. Back up summary information with details
10. Provide alternate presentation styles

The need to include soft information is important: Estimates, opinions, speculation, hunches, and sometimes even gossip serve the executives' purposes in identifying business opportunities.

Top-level executives—those at the level of vice president, president, and chief executive officer—maintain a fast pace, often having only a few moments to spend on a particular task. As we will emphasize throughout this chapter, they are often unable to commit long periods of time to any task, interact with computers for

Figure 13.1 How Executives Use Their Time

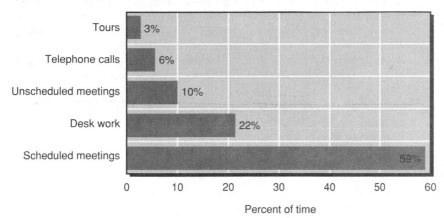

lengthy intervals, or review volumes of printed reports. They will want the capability to understand and assess a situation fast and to maintain continuity in the face of continual (but necessary) interruptions, including those from their own support staff members.

To Facilitate the Business of the Organization

The second way executives use information is to facilitate the business of the organization. Although decisions are a fact of life in corporate management, it is difficult to pinpoint if or when senior managers make decisions about major business or organization issues on their own. *Corporate-level decisions are often made by a team* involving advisors and staff members who present recommendations and alternate strategies for adoption.

Executives seldom follow a rational decision process where (1) goals are established and assessed, (2) probabilities are established for the occurrence of each alternative, and (3) the path that will provide the maximum return is chosen. (This does not mean that decisions are made without use of data or logic, of course, since they are carefully formulated in general.)

The process is often more complex than this, because senior managers frequently function more as facilitators than as decision makers (although they do make many decisions). Research tends to suggest that they focus on two kinds of problems:

1. *How to create effective organizational processes:* Major concerns include identifying the key players in a situation (a problem, opportunity, or change) as well as ways to involve them and obtain their insight and support. Other questions include how to put a process in motion and how to ensure that activities will be properly perceived and commitments obtained.

Interpersonal processes are a continual concern. Creating teamwork, where people pull together to accomplish a task, plays a central role in many accomplishments. In addition, the effective executive recognizes that individuals also have their own agenda, such as moving upward in the firm through promotion, ensuring success of their product line, improving teamwork in their division, and so on. Hence the executive will want to consider these concerns when formulating the organization processes.

2. *How to deal with one or two overriding concerns, or very general goals:* These may be very broad, such as greater overall corporate productivity, or the use of a more predictable, disciplined approach to the operations of a division. Improving stockholder benefits also fits into this category.

Often even senior managers will devote their attention to the tactics of implementation rather than formulating detailed strategies.

It appears that the general concerns of the type just mentioned are always present, and as opportunities arise that are conducive to achieving the goal, executives take advantage of them. For example, if the concern is for greater service to customers, an executive will be alert for ways to address this concern, whether chatting with potential or current customers, traveling to another city, making a purchase in a store, and so on.

Or consider the general objective of gaining greater recognition for the organization. The opportunity to sponsor a community program may arise and the executive will seize the opportunity, helping advance the community's and the firm's interests at the same time. Or the opportunity to publish a booklet on a topic of importance to the public that will be widely distributed by a service organization may be deemed an effective way to gain recognition for the firm. While neither of these is part of a calculated marketing strategy—they are not planned—they do fit in with the firm's broader strategy. Although these are not areas where information systems per se play a direct role, they can influence the activities by the way they facilitate the flow of information.

To Confront Multiple Problems Together

Third, executives assemble information to confront multiple problems together. Many problems and opportunities exist simultaneously in an organization. Each competes for the time of the senior manager.

Often the effective senior manager sees these problems as interrelated. The details of one event are reviewed with the characteristics of the others in the background. Defining the problem means getting down to the specifics to learn the cause and effect of the problem. The cause may not be the action that is noticed; the real problem may arise only after redefinition. A production shortfall, which is limiting sales levels, may in fact be the result of a conflict between manufacturing and inventory personnel over authority to determine when materials should be moved from the warehouse to the manufacturing floor. Even though one may *seem* trivial compared to the other, the fact that they are linked makes both quite important.

To Set Agendas

Fourth, information assists executives in setting agendas. Accomplishing tasks through a large and diverse group of individuals, most of whom the executive does not have direct control over, is a continual challenge. To meet this challenge, agendas have to be adopted and communicated.

Executives have agendas that are both more short-range (from today through the next 30 to 60 days) and more long-range (the next 20 to 30 years) than those of operating and middle managers. Executive-level agendas include a broad range of financial, product, market, and organizational issues. But they also include vague items as well, such as improving employee welfare.

An organization's formal plans include detailed financial objectives, but a senior manager's plans may contain less detailed financial targets while including other goals and plans that are not explicitly connected with formal plans (such as the intention to acquire a firm in another line of business, to develop an alliance with a firm in the same industry in Europe, or to sell the firm's distribution facilities in Australia). Vaguer goals may be to increase the recognition of the firm outside of its industry or to become a reference source for the media when preparing stories on the competitiveness of U.S. and Canadian firms in the industry outside of North America.

The agenda of a senior executive often will be to develop programs that will contribute to multiple objectives at once.

To Build Networks

Fifth, executives build networks. A network is an interconnection of individuals who work in cooperation with one another to achieve an objective. "People networks" are informal, differing from but compatible with the formal organization structure. For example, an executive's network may involve both superiors, such as members of the board of directors, and subordinates. It will often include others from outside the company: members of supplier, customer, and industry organizations, and so forth.

Networks facilitate the flow of information between network members, supplementing it with information from formal reports and memos. Personal observations, opinions, and early warnings of events are often communicated this way.

To Maintain a Corporate View

Sixth, executives must maintain a corporate view, and the information they use helps them do so. Division and product managers naturally focus their efforts on problems within their area of responsibility. Hence they have a narrower view than senior managers, who must take on a corporate perspective.

The line-of-business view—held by division managers—requires them to focus on sales, costs, profits, new products, and the like. In contrast, the corporate view will include assessment of whether the firm should even be in the line of business or should consider eliminating or selling the division. Or it may include discussion of mergers and acquisition of other products (even entire companies) to strengthen the line of business.

To Maintain an Industry Perspective

Seventh, in addition to looking into the firm, senior executives also take a broad **industry perspective,** keeping a close eye on the environment in which the firm operates. They pay a great deal of attention to their immediate competitors, of course, but they also study the industry as a whole and its competitors, both nationally and internationally.

Suppliers are an important influence on an industry and at the same time a key source of competitive information. Knowing the capacity of a supplier to provide a certain commodity coupled with an awareness of who it does business with will provide insight into the extent to which an industry can grow without additional sources of supplies. If supplies are short, it may be a signal to the executive to consider acquiring a supplier, to more directly control the source of materials, or to found a new company that will become a new source of supply.

Often entire industries can be influenced by an impending decision by some group outside the firm. You will often see corporate executives appear before legislative bodies to speak for or against proposed legislation or to request legislation. In recent years, senior officials of firms in some industries, including the automobile, semiconductor, and textile industries, have appeared to demand government intervention against what they perceive as unfair pricing or sales tactics by foreign competitors.

The industry perspective discussed here is also in line with the competitive role information technology may provide, as discussed in Chapters 2 and 21.

What Is an Executive Support System?

Executive support systems are computer-based systems (Table 13.1) that are compatible with the management styles and responsibilities of executives. They meet the needs discussed in the preceding section, provided certain features are included. The functions and features that characterize an ESS are discussed in this section.

The Features of an Executive Support System

Seven features are important to ensure that these systems meet the needs of executives and do not interfere with their fast pace.

Table 13.1 Commercially Available ESS

ESS	Computer System Class	Vendor
CADET EIS	PC	Cadet Executive Information Systems
Commander EIS	Mainframe/PC	Comshare, Inc. ⟵——————— 4 yrs old
FASTAR EIS	PC	Corporate Class Software, Inc.
Executive Edge	Mainframe/midrange	Execucom Systems Corp.
Express Executive Information system	PC/midrange/mainframe	Information Resources, Inc.
RESOLVE	PC	Metapraxis, Inc.
DirectLine	PC/PC-to-mainframe	MUST Software International
Pilot EIS	Mainframe-to-PC	Pilot Executive Software

Browse Capability Chapter 4 explained why information systems should make it possible to scan the environment in which organizations operate, placing particular emphasis on customer needs, activities of competition, and emerging problems, opportunities, and trends. The importance of this objective is elaborated on here.

It appears that executives are very systematic scanners when it comes to keeping up with events that affect the organization. They have a need and a knack for acquiring information about the events and activities in the competitive environment of the firm. Knowing the details of trends and emerging relationships between other relevant organizations is also important.

Such knowledge is vital in identifying opportunities as well as threats, either for new business or in new and more effective ways to compete. Such information is especially valuable in a rapidly changing environment or when the nature of the industry is becoming more complex.

Browsing and scanning also supplement data from what are otherwise considered primary sources: formatted reports, briefings, and meetings.

The greater the executives' reliance on external information, the more likely it is that the task of scanning, which encompasses many sources of information, will *not* be delegated to assistants. There are at least two reasons for this. First, executives more often than not keep strategic information in their heads, not in corporate files; therefore, they find it difficult to delegate the task, because others will have neither the same perspective nor the necessary background information. Second, much of the strategic information is from personal sources and thus available only to the executives themselves. Subordinates could not obtain the same information.

The capability to browse means that the ESS must provide a way to review a single specific file of information without the need to have formal reports prepared. Typically this means a facility for paging through records of business activities, correspondence topics, and the like. These capabilities are increasingly being incorporated in database systems. However, they are essential in an ESS.

Combining Information and Intuition

Intuition is instinctively knowing something—such as feasibility of a purchase or the likelihood of an event—without determining it through a calculated or rational process. Intuition does *not* involve guessing or trial and error. It is the result of having a thorough knowledge of facts and fundamentals—so thorough that you draw on this knowledge automatically or unconsciously. For example, you may have decided by intuition not to purchase a particular product because the price seemed too high. Later, you confirm your intuition by comparing it with the prices from other suppliers.

Research suggests that senior managers use intuition a great deal. They do so for five main purposes.

To Sense Problems Senior managers often appear to sense when a problem exists. They may review data about an area of the business, deciding that when these data are coupled with other information, something does not look right. Perhaps an event does not correspond with known trends. Or perhaps the fact that reports are late from one division signals the executive to have a more careful look. Examination reveals previously undetected difficulties that are now brought to light for a more thorough review.

To Perform Well-Learned Patterns A special way executives use intuition is to perform well-learned patterns. This involves the smooth performance of actions that have been learned through experience. For example, when a crisis occurs—perhaps a result of product tampering—the executive decides on certain actions, seemingly without delay or conscious thought: Have manufacturing identify the distributors who received the production batch in which tampering occurred; notify the distributors to recall the product from their customers; notify the news media to alert the public, providing them with all essential information; open a toll-free hot line for incoming calls about the product or problem. And almost immediately, while the impact of the problem is being contained, an investigation is getting under way to determine how it happened and how it can be avoided in the future.

Staff members may anticipate some actions, too, particularly if they have seen similar situations in the past.

To Synthesize Material In addition, intuition is an aid in synthesizing elements of data. Frequently the key to unlocking an opportunity or solving a problem is the result of *synergy*. Bits

Multiple Presentation Formats The format for presentation of data is a matter of personal preference. But too often information systems are designed to rely on a single format for the display of information.

Flexible presentation formats (Figure 13.2) are incorporated into many ESS. It is not so much that one format is better than another, but that at a given moment the user may want to see one or the other. The ability to incorporate tabular, graphic, and text data not only satisfies personal preferences but may also improve the manner in which a situation or opportunity is handled.

Combining Information and Intuition (continued)

and pieces of data, gathered from diverse sources and in different forms, can be woven into a picture that provides unexpected insight (the whole is more than the sum of the parts). Yet the manner of putting them together may be the result of relating items that one would not normally put together. That is where intuition comes in.

For example, synergy occurs when a firm's marketing executive reports that customers prefer to prepare their orders themselves rather than giving them to a salesperson. At the same time, an information systems manager recognizes that the firm's order entry system can be modified to allow customers to enter the orders on-line—a step that is in keeping with the marketing executive's realization. The combined observations aid the firm and meet customer needs.

To Doublecheck Strategies Intuition may also provide a way of doublechecking strategies, decisions, and so on. Rigorous analysis may suggest a particular strategy or tactic, which can then be evaluated intuitively. The correct action may in fact turn out to run counter to the rational one; for instance, intuition may indicate that staff members will not adopt a procedure or that it will run contrary to the culture of the organization. As an example, a firm can cut costs by laying off personnel. However, senior management may decide that doing so will have more severe consequences with investors in the face of an anticipated public stock offering in the next three-month period. Such intuitive reflection is a check on the wisdom of laying off personnel.

To Bypass In-Depth Analysis A final way to use intuition is to bypass in-depth analysis of details when there is not sufficient time to do so properly. Discussion or observation may suggest an explanation or strategy seemingly automatically. Later analysis confirms it is correct. But the action is initiated prior to the analysis. Often this results from the recognition of patterns or key details that another person might overlook or dismiss as insignificant.

These examples suggest that intuition is not a matter of guesswork. Rather it is an outgrowth of experience both in problem solving and in the analysis of details and circumstances. To the extent that experience and the lessons it brings are logical, intuition has a place in corporate management. It can serve a useful purpose in all phases of problem management, from definition to solution.

Simple Interface Executives do not want to be tied to computer keyboards or obliged to enter commands or keywords to retrieve information. Hence the most widely used ESS will rely on a simple, yet powerful, interface. Three aspects of the interface merit consideration: method of interaction, use of symbols, and levels of information presentation.

First, it is increasingly common for ESS interfaces to provide touch-screen capabilities whereby the user can have information displayed simply by touching the symbol or keyword for a display option.

Figure 13.2 Commander™ Marketshare Analysis: An ESS Presentation Format (© 1988 Comshare)

Figure 13.3 Commander™ EIS: An ESS Graphics Interface (© 1989 Comshare)

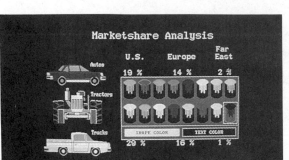

Alternatively, many ESS also support the use of a mouse to "point-and-click" when selecting an option.

A second aspect of a friendly interface uses graphics—symbols, icons, and images—to convey actions or draw attention to key information. Figure 13.3 shows the graphics interface for a widely used ESS. Notice that the screen shows six options (Status Reports, Investigate, Newswire, and so on) that can be activated simply by touching the symbol.

A third interface feature is the capability of multiple presentation levels of information, each more detailed and focused than the preceding one. Executives are constantly being interrupted, and they do not want, or have the time, to be overwhelmed with unnecessary details. However, they *do* want quick access to details when the situation warrants.

Multiple presentation levels allow executives to "drill down" to subsequent levels of detail quickly and easily. For example, learning that sales are low may lead to a review of orders. Finding that an unusually large number of orders are awaiting backordered items, the executive may want to check the manufacturing schedule. If it is found that certain items are not scheduled for manufacturing because of a shortage of materials, inventory and purchasing records may also be scanned to uncover the cause of the problem.

The executive may even be able to obtain, if desired, a reading of how the firm's stock is doing on the exchange by accessing the Dow-Jones financial database—all with a touch of the screen or a click of the mouse.

Analytical and Modeling Features As the preceding example suggests, knowing "what is" will also require the capability to determine the "why"—an explanation of how a situation has come about.

Analysis often involves the building of models that interrelate important factors.

Table 13.2 Widely Used External Databases

Database/Data Service	Vendor
Annual Reports Abstract	Western Union Telegraph
Compuserve Network	Compuserve
Dow Jones News/Retrieval	Dow Jones & Co., Inc.
Dun's Marketing Services	Dialog Information Services
Investart	Western Union Telegraph
Lexus	Mead
Nexus	Mead
Prodigy	Trintex
The Source Network	The Source
Standard and Poor's Register	Dialog Information Services
Trade and Industry ASAP	BRS Information Technologies

For example, an analysis of market share for automobiles may involve building a model that includes price, vehicle size, color, fuel utilization, and so on—factors that influence consumer purchases. Executives may have the marketing department examine the impact of advertising or pricing strategies in certain markets, or they may prefer to test assumptions themselves. You will find that a growing number of senior managers will want to find out answers to "what if" questions themselves from time to time—providing the ESS makes it easy to do so.

Tailoring and Customization Executives have preferences for the types of information and for the areas of business they wish to monitor. Over time their interests will change, usually in relation to variations in opportunities and problems and the competitive environment.

Just as executives differ, so too do their information needs. Hence the ESS must allow the tailoring of features to meet those preferences. And it must allow the design of customized reports, including specification not only of information content but also the use of symbols, colors, headings, and the like.

The Lockheed-Georgia case in the case study module at the end of the book describes how this has been accomplished very successfully in a highly regarded ESS.

Access to External Data Sources Executive support systems are effective when they incorporate external information. Many executives rely on access to commercial data services, such as those in Table 13.2. Such services not only incorporate data on industries, corporations, and so on, but they also provide news features. It is not unusual to find that executives who used to begin their day reading the *Wall Street Journal* now start by signing onto their electronic support system to see headlines of events around the world. If a particular item is of interest, a single keystroke will bring the details to the screen.

External sources include databases from which financial reports, stock prices, or foreign exchange rates are reported.

The greatest concern with using external databases is that they often provide excess detail. Some organizations synthesize and summarize the data for their executives. But in the future we can expect that commercial data services will improve their capabilities to provide multiple levels of detail and aggregation to meet diverse individual needs.

Data from Multiple Sources The earlier example of drilling down to learn more about sales fluctuations shows the need to have multiple data sources accessible through an ESS. Internal information systems are designed to draw data from a single source: When dealing with customers, the user typically accesses the order processing system. Financial questions are answered by data drawn from the general ledger system. Quantity-on-hand data originated in the inventory system. It is not surprising that, when carrying out a specific operation or managing an individual process, one uses information from a single source. However, executives do not address individual processes but broad business issues. The information they need originates in multiple data sources, both internal and external.

How Executives Use Executive Support Systems

Earlier, in Chapter 3, we discussed seven types of information needed in an organization: comfort, status (progress), warning, planning, internal operations, external intelligence, and externally distributed information. These general information types reflect the needs of senior managers, like those of others we have discussed throughout the book.

Executives use an ESS for a wide variety of reasons, ranging from keeping informed to supporting analytical requirements (Table 13.3). To illustrate the role of an ESS in meeting these needs, an example will be helpful. Large hotel chains often span many countries and even continents. But just managing the hotels in the U.S. segment of a company is challenging enough, and demands that executives keep well informed of important events at all times.

To Keep Informed Keeping informed means knowing the pulse of the organization. Although regular reports may provide averages as well as high and low levels of sales, costs, orders, and so on, they may not give executives a sense of day-to-day operations.

A hotel executive who oversees the different properties (hotels) that make up the chain wants to have a feel for the activities of the properties in various locations. The pulse of the chain can be examined by reviewing a sampling of guest records: how the guests are paying (by cash or credit card—certain credit cards suggest that a guest is a business traveler), the typical length of stay, the occupancy rates on certain days of the week, and whether there is a change in the busiest check-in day.

Sometimes simply scrolling through the actual record images will allow the

Table 13.3 How Executives Use an ESS

Reason	Explanation
To keep informed	Enables executives to stay abreast of day-to-day activities by viewing firsthand information from representative business activities and transactions without getting bogged down in details
To understand a new situation quickly	Enables rapid access to details describing business activities that provide insight into an unexpected or recently uncovered situation
To browse through data	Provides a firsthand view of activities that often cannot be achieved through the review of reports and business summaries
To maintain surveillance	Allows monitoring of a situation of special interest through specified details
To perform strategic scanning	Enables viewing of information that provides insight into a particular strategy or opportunity or brings to light the opportunity to develop a new strategy having significant potential for the organization
To analyze data	Enables examination of data or alternative scenarios through creation of spreadsheets or other forms of models; supports both "what is" and "what if" forms of analysis
To get at data directly	Enables viewing of data without waiting for staff to retrieve and extract details; also enables viewing of actual details before summarization

executive to gain a sense for changes in the firm's situation—across properties, between regions, and in categories of interest across business units.

A chief executive of a large U.S.-based international hotel chain personally reviews hundreds of guest comment cards each month. The cards are selected at random from those prepared by visitors to the different hotels managed by the firm. Keeping in touch this way allows the executive to spot trends or opportunities for new services that build the business. Delegation of this task to staff members would not provide the firsthand information that the executive views as a key to knowing the customer.

To Understand a New Situation Quickly New situations can arise on a moment's notice. Staff reports explaining the details underlying the situation may provide the data, but their usefulness depends on the staff being able to provide the details requested and their doing so in a meaningful form. And perhaps more important, obtaining these details takes time.

When alerted to the fact that profits in one region of a hotel chain are dropping, an executive may quickly assess the situation through the ESS by examining a few key variables of success:

——Is the change restricted to a few properties that are influencing the overall average, or is it occurring across the region?

——How are revenue levels changing?

——Are guest stays shorter?

——Is the number of catering functions lower than in the past?

——Are costs for food, labor, or maintenance substantially higher?

Not all information will be quantitative. For example, in the hotel business, unseasonable weather can dramatically affect business levels for better or worse. A heavy weekend snowstorm may prevent participants in large conventions and business travelers from arriving, causing business to drop for the entire week. And several successive weeks of bad weather will lead to a downturn in business indicators. Senior managers may begin asking questions before the normal end-of-the-month reports are prepared. A firsthand, on-line look at the data will help managers size up the situation.

As these examples suggest, such ESS usage is most appropriate for quickly understanding the extent of the problem and the magnitude of a change.

To Browse Through Data We have already discussed the importance of a browse feature in an ESS. Executives often use it freely. For many, there is no substitute for firsthand review of the data. Thus, **browse capability** is often an essential ESS feature. As one executive says:

> I like to take a few minutes to review details about our customers, our manufacturing, or our financial activities firsthand. Having the details flow across the screen gives me a feel for how things are going. I don't look at each record, but glance at certain elements as they scroll by. If something looks unusual, it will almost jump out at me and I can find out more about it. But if nothing is unusual, I will know that, too.

Browsing through the data can be done at any time—the first thing in the morning, before an important meeting, or even from home in the evening. When handled in this manner, it does not occupy a large segment of time (in contrast to a meeting, which can be time-consuming—it must be scheduled and a room arranged; participants must go to the meeting place; the duration is always more than five or ten minutes; often there is follow-up). Browsing is a better alternative for many executives, since it is consistent with the way they manage their time.

To Maintain Surveillance **Surveillance** means monitoring a situation. It is common for an executive to put a new program in place and monitor its impact to see if it is having the intended results (even before scheduled reports are prepared). Many executives use their ESS to do so.

In other instances, a senior manager will get an idea that food costs from a certain vendor are increasing even though no increase has been negotiated. The executive may quietly monitor the costs charged by the vendor, determining whether any other action is warranted.

In still other cases, a plan may be put in place and monitored through the ESS. The instant access to performance data through the executive's on-line workstation is more timely than periodic reports.

To Perform Strategic Scanning Since so much of the information used by senior managers originates outside the firm, it is essential that the ESS include the capability to scan so-called environmental data. Data sources for the purposes of **scanning** (multiple sources) may include commercial databanks or on-line records from industry sources. The data may be accessed from within the firm's own teleprocessing network, or a copy of the data may be purchased and loaded into the firm's databases. Industry financial data, for example, is often purchased for management's use.

Executives in a hotel chain will most likely keep an eye on such competitive data as occupancy trends and room rates. But the level of airline traffic in and out of cities where it operates hotels may be judged a useful correlate with business levels. Even more significant may be the airline fares for flights between selected cities.

Other environmental data may report the likelihood of strikes in certain related industries, overall changes in business travel across the country, and the increasing demand for electronic services (personal computers, facsimile machines, and video-conferencing) on which the hotels should capitalize.

To Support Analytical Needs Executives tend to have strong analytical skills, as we indicated in the preceding section. An ESS should include features to support this need. Spreadsheet and model-building capabilities are common. These features allow executives to combine data on "what is" with an inquisitive interest in "what if." Examples may range from changes in pricing structures, with anticipation of competitor response, to varying cost and expense levels, with an eye toward determining how revenue and income levels will change.

The sense of what is important and what is not will often depend on the larger setting in which an individual organizes his or her thoughts. Earlier in the chapter, we referred to this as the executive's agenda. *If someone else performs this function, they in essence take charge of a key portion of an executive's agenda, since they determine what is important, whether it fits a framework, and whether the manager should see it.*

Yet good ideas seem to emerge without planning. One bit of information when coupled with knowledge of a competitor's plant expansion and a piece of gossip from several days ago may reveal that a new product line will be launched by a rival company. There may not be any way that a staff member would have the same perspective, because both experiences and expectations differ. (*Note:* Senior executives do not typically rise to the top of an organization because of their analytical ability or the information they glean from reports. Rather, they combine their ability with a vision and with a network of information sources. An ESS must augment, not limit, their capability.)

To Get at Data Directly Depending on others to assemble data causes delays that can sometimes be critical. Firsthand access avoids that problem.

The ability to glance at information on certain items of interest while traveling is another reason for using ESS. A terminal and a telephone line may be all that is needed to retain access to important business details at any time of the day and from any location in the world.

Reasons Executives Do Not Use Executive Support Systems

There is not unanimous agreement on the value of ESS, however. Although the use of such systems is growing, there remains a large and substantial segment of executives who do not use ESS. This section considers five reasons for this.

Do Not Fit Individual Management Style Some executives do not want to rely on information technology as a source of information. Nor do they wish to use a keyboard or any other device in interacting with a terminal, personal computer, or workstation.

Many executives are accustomed to receiving information through management briefings and do not wish to change that. For others, their management style is one of delegation, where staff members and other managers are given assignments to obtain and present information.

Do Not Provide Type of Information Needed Others do not believe that the type of information they need can be provided through an information support system. The chance to ask questions or challenge answers when narrative and text information is transmitted verbally, whether face to face or over a telephone, is missing in on-line systems.

The hotel executive may find, for example, that annotations and comments about a particular hotel location are awkward to handle and evaluate through an ESS.

Cannot Accommodate Soft Information The handling of personal observation, opinion, and narrative commentary are considered a weakness in many ESS.

It may be difficult to incorporate these observations in an automated system: that a realtor who often represents a competing hotel chain was seen leaving the firm's headquarters; that the competitor is accumulating large quantities of cash and arranging lines of credit, and that a team of staff members recently were noticed returning on a flight from a city that is headquarters for the construction company the competitor often works with; that the president of the firm has recently made several flights to a city that has announced it wishes to build a new hotel and convention complex. Yet piecing these observations together, as you have just done by reading them, will tell you there is a good chance the competitor is planning a new hotel development.

These examples of **soft information** fit well with the environmental scanning tendencies of executives. However, the individual may not want to or be able to incorporate them into an ESS.

Involve the Risk of Improper Use Good ESS do not make good executives. Similarly, even the best intentions and the best tools do not guarantee acceptable results.

Some executives are seemingly mesmerized by automated systems and the information they produce. Such persons may accept analyses generated through spreadsheets or simulation without asking the same questions they would ask when identical information is presented by a staff member. When decisions are made without questioning results or ensuring that all pertinent factors are properly considered, the risk of error and unfortunate consequences may be substantial. Yet the manager, not the ESS, is the real culprit.

Have a Previous History of Failure Some executives do not use ESS because they have witnessed or heard of cases where systems have been discarded or have gone unused. As in any other area of life, not all attempts result in success. Executives are human, too. They may decide that if the CEO of another company whom the executive respects decided not to use an ESS, they won't either.

The reference section includes cases involving both success and failure of ESS. This is an area meriting further investigation if you are in a situation where these systems are employed.

Example of a Successful Executive Support System

This section presents an example of an effective ESS. The discussion explains how the features of the system were selected and how individuals can use it to meet their business needs.

Development Strategy

"If you had just returned from a two-week vacation, what information would you want to see on your desk?" The answer to this question tells a great deal about what information executives consider important, even critical. It also suggests the nature of information that should be available through an ESS.

Members of the MIS group at a well-known beauty products firm raised this very question to uncover the information executives needed to help run the business. Four basic groups of information, spanning a variety of information systems applications, were identified, including (1) financial, (2) human resource, (3) competitive environment, and (4) administrative support information. Key indicators were also identified in each area.

Using this information, information systems staff members developed a prototype ESS and showed it to executives. An enthusiastic endorsement by the executives led to development of the full system.

Key System Features

The ESS uses powerful personal computers attached to the firm's mainframe system. The front-end features a "point-and-click" interface where executives retrieve information using a mouse to select options. The menu-driven system was created using a well-known executive support software package. Users seldom need to use the keyboard itself to retrieve information.

Figure 13.4 Multiple Window Interface with Point-and-Click Information Expansion

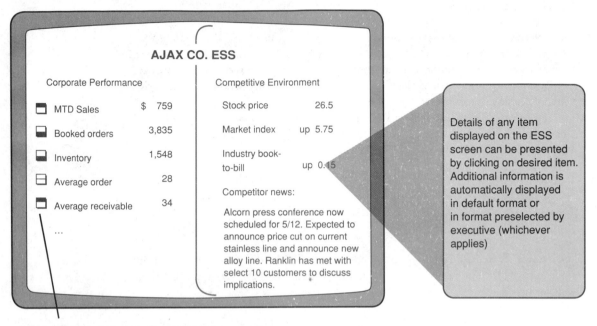

Button indicators specify performance,
using color to indicate whether results are
according to expectation

Top portion of button shows current status
compared to planned; bottom half indicates trends

When executives sign on to the system they see a display screen consisting of two windows (Figure 13.4). One window contains internal information—for example, sales levels, inventory on hand, or inventory turnover. The other displays information on the competitive environment, including pertinent news, announcements by suppliers or competitors, and consumer purchase trends. Using the mouse, the executive can point to an item, select it by clicking the mouse, and immediately see additional details on the display screen. Printed information can be requested in the same fashion.

The system incorporates both effective use of color and a graphics interface. The standard color scheme specifies that planned performance indicators (such as revenue or expense levels) are presented in red, actual performance in gold, and last year's performance in blue.

Users can define custom screens and reports that are stored in the system and retrieved on demand. Each can include comparative data on up to 15 different business units. For each, they can also define limits, say for variance from expected performance, which they want called to their attention. Doing so avoids the need to review all performance data.

Historical information is also available, including that on external events. For instance, business and financial news for the past 30 days is available on-line.

Access to external data also allows immediate comparison of sales or other performance levels of the firm with competitors. The competitive analysis feature is, as you might expect, widely used.

Hot buttons allow quick identification of dominant business trends. A *hot button* is a square, divided into two sections, that appears on the display (see Figure 13.4). The top portion is color coded to indicate performance during the current month and the bottom reflects the trend from the last two months. Hence, if the screen shows sales, the top portion of the hot button will be red if sales are behind plan and the bottom portion will be green if the trend is upward (above planned levels). Hot buttons allow quick comparison of planned versus actual performance, but quick access to the data is also possible for explanation.

Example of ESS Use An example will demonstrate how the system is used. An executive wishes to check current sales levels for a division of the company. The user first clicks the net sales indicator for the company and the information is displayed on the screen, using the color standards just described.

More details can be obtained by drilling down: Click on profit-and-loss statements to see the overall performance of the division. Click again to examine an individual line item, such as labor costs.

Using another systems feature, the executive can quickly print (also in color) a copy of the details displayed on the screen, create a custom report definition, or export the data to a spreadsheet program (Lotus 1-2-3) for additional analysis. Notes and copies of the display screens can even be sent to other people by way of an electronic mail function built into the system.

Color graphics, consisting of bar and pie charts as well as line graphs, allow executives to see trends and comparisons quickly—faster than by reviewing tables of numbers. Yet the detail is available when needed.

Several executives emphasized that if the information available through prototype had been as easily available during several recent business situations, they may have even handled the situations differently. That is the test of ESS usefulness.

Summary

Executive support systems are growing in use where they support the needs of senior executives and fit their management style. Information is a key resource for all executives, whether to facilitate the business of the organization, to build networks of individuals addressing the same business area, or to maintain corporate and industry perspectives, to mention only some of the reasons. However, the systems will be used only when they have the right features. Typically, the most desirable ESS features include the capability to access and display information easily, quickly, and in formats most suited to the wishes of the individual user. Such systems often have the capacity to retrieve data from multiple sources, both internal and external to the organization, and to provide modeling and analytical capabilities where needed.

When executives do not use ESS, the cause often can be traced to one or more of these five factors: They do not fit the executive's style of management, do not provide the information needed, cannot accommodate soft information, involve the risk of improper use, or have a previous history of failure.

Although ESS are not a panacea—they will not turn poor executive decisions into good ones—the use of these systems is growing, and effective executives often can become even more effective as a result of using them.

Key Words

Browse capability	Industry perspective	Soft information
Corporate view	Scanning	Surveillance
Executive support system (ESS)		

Review Questions

1. What are the common myths about the jobs of senior managers?
2. What characteristics should information systems have to support top-level managers effectively?
3. Describe the seven ways executives use information.
4. How do executives use information to set agendas? To build networks?
5. Distinguish between maintaining a corporate view and maintaining an industry perspective as it pertains to the use of information by executives.
6. Describe the features that distinguish an ESS.
7. What characteristics are typically attributed to a "friendly" interface for an ESS?
8. Why is the ability to tailor and customize features of an ESS important to executives?
9. How do executives use an ESS? Give examples of situations describing such use.
10. What role does an ESS play in scanning? What is scanned?
11. "Executive support systems allow individuals to get at data without staff." Explain the meaning of this statement and indicate how an ESS can provide this capability.
12. For what reasons do some executives *not* use an ESS?

Application Problems

1. An executive in a large airline company has asked the information systems department to develop a system that will support the specific needs of the chief executive officer. The development staff must decide whether to acquire a commercially available ESS package or develop its own system using staff resources.

   What questions should be addressed in determining whether to use a commercial package or design and develop a specialized ESS in-house?

2. For which of the following types of situations is assistance from an executive support system most appropriate?
   a. To monitor the progress on long-term, complex manufacturing projects
   b. To receive details of customer orders in a high-volume retailing organization
   c. To monitor actual versus planned labor costs in a labor-intensive service company
   d. To be able to retrieve customer information when telephone calls arrive from important customers located around the world
   e. To monitor bank deposits made by the firm's accounting department
   f. To retrieve stock market data from an external database service

3. The chief executive officer of a large manufacturing organization views the CEO's primary responsibility as one of creating a vision for success of the firm and then providing the leadership that will enable it to move toward achieving the vision. The CEO further emphasizes that personal contact, both inside and external to the firm, is an essential element in success of the firm.

   The same executive emphasizes that the purpose of computer information systems is to assist in facilitating the routine business of the firm (that is, processing transactions) and the generation of information in the form of timely reports. Reports, it is said, provide information about events for the most part. However, the executive also indicates that when information is needed unexpectedly, the firm's information systems should have the capability for retrieving or generating the information from existing files and databases.

   At the same time, the CEO indicates that there is no role for a specialized executive support system in the typical organization. Executive support systems cannot provide the information needed for creating a vision, and they cannot substitute for personal contacts that the CEO makes in and outside of the firm. The information on internal operations should come from the firm's existing information systems. Therefore, the executive suggests that an ESS is a useless notion and does no more than cater to the quirks of a few executives.
   a. Do you agree or disagree with the comments of this CEO? Based on the discussion in this chapter, in what ways are the views expressed accurate or inaccurate?
   b. Give several examples of situations in which an ESS can be useful to an executive who takes the view expressed in this problem.

Minicase: Executive Support Systems Put Corporate Database at Top Managers' Fingertips

The use of support systems in executive suites is on the rise throughout the United States. Today, executive support systems can, with the push of a single button, deliver information rapidly, accurately, and in graphics formats that communicate trends and patterns.

Nicknamed "graphics visual early warning systems," these new tools revitalize the relationship between top management and information systems departments. They put the resources of corporate databases at the fingertips of the people who need the data to manage the organization. They deliver the data in graphics format, usually in less than 10 seconds. And when an executive sees information that needs to be communicated to other people, he or she can, with the push of a button, automatically produce 35mm slides, overhead transparencies, or paper charts.

At General Motors Corporation headquarters in New York, executives consider their graphics executive support system so important that they will not discuss it publicly. At a GM subsidiary, Electronic Data Systems Corporation (EDS), an executive support system helps senior management monitor the performance and finances of all regional data centers.

According to one EDS executive, the graphics system made buying a mainframe unnecessary and helped to cut overhead cost growth significantly.

GM is not the only organization to discover graphics executive support systems. The U.S. Army Aviation Systems

Command pioneered an on-line system for its senior officers that includes 1400 charts, which are automatically updated each time the data change. Each chart is available at the touch of a button. The Air Force's Electronic Systems Division is prototyping a similar system.

Other organizations, both large and small, are considering extending similar capabilities to senior managers. Their goals are the same—they want to make the computer a vital tool for top management.

In commercial organizations, MIS executives recognize that today's fast-paced, competitive markets make it necessary to have the best information available immediately. That is the justification for Sears Roebuck's Easy Access System, which provides instant access to the previous day's operating results from more than 95 percent of its retail stores.

Improvements Involve Top Management

In government agencies, MIS executives recognize that productivity improvements will not happen without the involvement of top management. That involvement is made easier when management has fingertip access to the data that measures productivity.

What has surprised a number of MIS managers is how quickly demand for these systems can spread among top management.

That raises the next question. If executives are excited about these new pushbutton systems, why has it taken so long for the idea to catch on? Four barriers made these systems impractical in prior years:

——The data was not there. Either it was not on the computer or it was there and only the experts knew how to get at it. Retrieval systems required extensive training, and executives did not have the time to learn the systems.

——Equipment was expensive and communications were slow. Graphics terminals used to cost $20,000 or more. Also, communications lines were too narrow to pass pictures quickly. No one wanted to spend a lot of money, only to have to wait a minute or longer just to see the picture.

——Graphics hard-copy equipment demanded too much effort. Once a chart was created on the screen, there was no easy way to make a high-resolution 35mm slide, an overhead transparency, or a paper chart automatically. The terminal or personal computer user had to be an expert plotter operator, keep his or her own pens and paper, and even learn the switch settings. Most executives know their time is too limited for them to become machine operators.

——The personal computer arrived without connections to the data. Outfitted with Lotus Devel-

opment's 1-2-3, the personal computer provided easy executive computing, but the novelty soon wore off for senior managers.

The cost of graphics terminals has dropped below $5000. New graphics hard-copy equipment has been introduced that operates automatically and can be shared by dozens of users.

The pioneers who built their own systems spent one to two person-years creating the software and three to six months putting together the right data and the right charts to solve the business problems. All of them felt the investment was worthwhile, but they would have preferred an off-the-shelf solution.

Questions

1. Computers were introduced into business in the early 1950s, but, if the discussion above is correct, top managers are only now beginning to have direct use and benefit from the systems. This is particularly true for graphics early warning systems. What factors account for this late development? Consider whether equipment, software, or communications developments are the underlying reasons.

2. What types of information should executives monitor by use of their early warning systems? How do you suggest they use the systems and the information they can access?

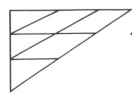

14: Expert Support Systems

Key Questions

What gives information systems intelligence?

What components comprise an expert system?

How is knowledge represented in an expert system?

Is there a relation between decision support systems and intelligent support systems?

How are expert systems used?

Who uses expert systems?

Working Smarter

Standards of living rise not because people work harder but because they work smarter. If you want to see people working hard go to almost any underdeveloped country and you will see people working like no one in America works. Economic progress is the replacement of physical exertion with brain power.

Lester C. Thurow, Dean, Sloan School of Management, MIT, 1983

You can probably recall an instance when your physician was able to diagnose a certain illness without the need for laboratory tests. You relayed a few symptoms that, when combined with your appearance and temperature, allowed the physician to diagnose your condition—perhaps in the process telling you more about how you felt than you even realized—and recommend an effective treatment. Yet you know of instances where a friend turned out to have the same ailment but whose physician had great difficulty in detecting the problem and prescribing the correct treatment. You wonder why there are different outcomes. In actuality, it is not the amount of medical training the physician has but instead his or her ability to recognize and evaluate symptoms effectively that is important.

Or take the familiar stories on the financial pages of the newspaper about individuals who have made a fortune in the stock market just by following reports about companies in the news. Others who have attempted similar investments have encountered misfortune and financial loss, even when the same companies are involved. How, you wonder, can the outcomes be so different?

While this chapter does not discuss how to become an expert like the physician or financial whiz just mentioned, it does explore the incorporation of expertise into

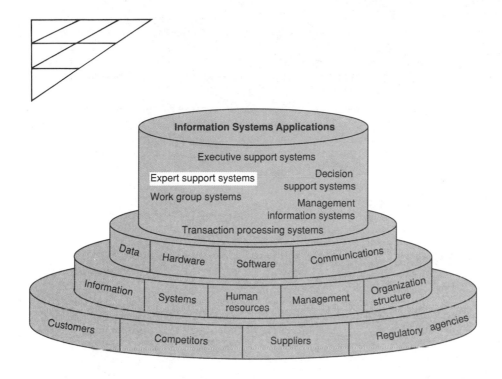

automated systems. Quite simply, there are not enough experts to go around, and so companies are looking to information systems technology for assistance in capturing the skills that make experts what they are and in making such persons even more capable.

Expert support systems is the name given to systems that meet this need. In the discussion that follows, we will consider what these systems are, what they consist of, and how they are developed. We also see how such systems differ from the other information systems we have discussed. An example will demonstrate how expert support systems can augment the capabilities of individual decision makers.

Why Should You Know About Expert Support Systems?

Even though your career focus may not be on expert support systems, there is a good chance you will encounter such systems in your chosen field in the future. Here are some of the reasons why you should be familiar with expert support systems:

——*The potential importance of being able to capture expertise in a form that can assist others is enormous.* In science, medicine, business, social science, the arts—you name it—there is an interesting way to capture the knowledge of experts so that it can be shared and its impact increased. Expert support systems are one promising approach for doing so.

——*Expert support systems can be essential components in the other information systems we have discussed.* In all fields that use information systems, whether for operating-level or executive support activities, expert support systems are increasingly under consideration or development. Both end-users and information systems professionals will be involved and affected.

——*Expert support systems will play a growing role in society.* We do not yet know the full impact expert support systems will have. However, the interest so many different professions are showing in them suggests that many people expect their impact to be wide ranging and substantial.

Expert support systems offer promise to experts and nonexperts alike. Since these systems are changing rapidly, it is important to know about the kinds of developments that are likely to take place.

What Is an Expert Support System?

An **expert support system** (often referred to simply as an **expert system**) is a computer program that uses stored facts (data) and rules to mimic a human expert. It is designed to support its user by recommending a specific decision, suggesting actions, or making predictions. This area is part of a much broader field known as **artificial intelligence,** which involves "teaching" computers to accomplish tasks in a manner that can be considered intelligent (the very concept requires a careful definition of the term *intelligence*). Many of the problems under study in the field of artificial intelligence are far from practical solutions. However, the expert support systems area of artificial intelligence is producing computer-based systems that are being put to use in the real world of business.

Expert support systems typically deal with situations characterized by a great deal of uncertainty. The strength of a *human expert* in these circumstances is the ability, usually based on a combination of experience and judgment, to determine the likelihood of a specific outcome or result when all the facts required for strictly logical decision making are not available. An expert support system is an automated system that is designed to capture the *expertise of a human expert;* it uses computer processing and software to duplicate the knowledge of an expert in a specific area. Usually expert systems are very narrowly focused. Among the most successful examples are those for configuring a specific computer system or determining whether to drill for oil at a particular location.

Uses of Expert Support Systems

Expert support systems can be used, among other things, to:

——*Provide expert advice to nonexperts:* Assist individuals encountering a situation where they are not experts but where they must take an action or make a determination. Often prompt individuals to provide information describing the situation, usually through iterative questioning. May provide possible diagnoses and actions to take.

> *Example:* To determine whether an individual has ingested poison and what precautions to take.

——*Provide assistance to experts:* Assist an expert in studying a situation, through collection of information based on observation or in evaluation of the situation. May also include recommendations for action. Often used by expert to double-check for omission of significant details.

> *Example:* Used by a physician to determine whether a patient is suffering from heart disease or cardiac malfunction.

——*Replace experts:* Utilize knowledge base and inference capabilities (discussed later) to assess situation when expert is not available.

> *Example:* Used by medical assistants in examining electrocardiogram print-outs to determine whether patient's heart is functioning properly.

——*Serve as teaching tool:* Facilitate interaction with knowledge base and inference engine to learn characteristics of certain situations and appropriate actions.

> *Example:* Interaction between physician and expert support system for the purpose of evaluating possible new cardiac diagnostic procedures.

Business organizations, government offices, defense agencies, and many other types of organizations are investigating the development and use of expert support systems. Many such systems have been developed, and countless others are under consideration (see Table 14.1).

When to Consider Expert Support Systems

Expert support systems are not a panacea; however, they can be an important tool under at least three circumstances.

To Capture Expertise Creating a base of knowledge is often reason enough to develop an expert support system. Many firms are finding that they rely on key individuals for certain tasks because those persons have a unique background or a seemingly uncanny knack for dealing with situations quickly and effectively. Such persons are, in a word, experts. As managers grasp their reliance on key persons, they often want to avoid risks to the firm if the individual becomes ill, retires, or resigns.

In these instances, specialists in expert support systems called **knowledge engineers** work with the experts to learn the way they evaluate situations, the rules of thumb (heuristics) they use, and how they decide what actions to take. The information—the knowledge—is captured in a formal fashion and stored in knowledge bases. (We will discuss knowledge bases in the next section.)

Table 14.1 Representative Expert Support Systems

DELTA	Acts as fault diagnosis system that helps maintenance personnel find malfunctions in diesel electric locomotives	General Electric
ISIS	Constructs factory job shop schedules by selecting the sequence of operations needed to complete an order and the amount of time required for each	Westinghouse Electric Corporation and Carnegie-Mellon University
MYCIN	Assists physicians in diagnosing and treating infectious blood diseases	Stanford University
REACTOR	Helps operators at nuclear facilities diagnose and respond to nuclear reactor malfunctions	EG&G Idaho
RTC	Classifies ships by interpreting radar images	Department of Defense
XCON	Ensures that components of computer systems work together and that all necessary components are included in the configuration	Digital Equipment Corporation and Carnegie-Mellon University

To Minimize Risk of Error Managers in general fear the risks and potential losses due to error, regardless of whether the price is paid financially, in loss of time, or even in loss of life. Hence, any assistance that can reduce risk deserves consideration. Because of this, you will find that expert support systems are in use or under development in such far-ranging fields as medicine, manufacturing, and aviation.

To Interrelate Large Volumes of Essential Information As indicated in Table 14.2, expert support systems can be extremely useful when large volumes of data, including qualitative details (for example, "looks feverish" or "appears tired") must be evaluated. Keeping track of details is difficult enough, but properly incorporating them into an evaluation or a decision can be even more challenging. The inferencing power of expert support systems can be a valuable aid, and therefore a reason for developing such a system.

Here are typical applications where expert support systems are appropriate:

——To diagnose the occurrence of problems in manufacturing that will lead to product failure

——To diagnose the cause of problems in a process control system

——To diagnose the location of a product failure or weakness

——To assist marketing representatives in identifying replacement products to suggest when selling against a competitor

Table 14.2 Characteristics of Expert Support Systems

Are knowledge intensive	Use large quantities of data in form of knowledge bases to produce specific output, such as a recommended action or a diagnosis
Use diverse data types	Store and process both quantitative and qualitative data rather than only numeric or character data associated with traditional data processing
Use reasoning ability	Examine details of a situation, whether facts or premises, and draw a conclusion
Use heuristics	Reason (that is, examine and solve problems) using rules of thumb provided by experts who have found them helpful in dealing with certain types of situations
Explain reasoning	Unlike decision support and management information systems, can explain the reasoning used to formulate a specific recommendation
Function even when missing data	Can work around missing details to assess the impact of certain alternatives and formulate a recommended strategy
Tolerate ambiguity	Can evaluate the likely meaning of terms or conditions that are vague or nonspecific by examining the context of use (for example, determining when *bear* refers to an animal or to an action)
Focus on limited subject domain	Designed to address a very specific type of problem or situation (the domain)

——To advise of actions to take in cleanup of chemical spills

——To advise in the trading of stocks and the management of investment portfolios

——To advise in the configuration of equipment or systems, such as computer systems

——To advise lawyers in the formulation of trial strategies

Table 14.1 includes descriptions of several expert support systems that have been developed by well-known firms.

Components of Expert Support Systems

Underlying expert support systems is the storage and representation of knowledge, which, as we will see, can be achieved in several ways. We will also see what makes knowledge-based expert support systems different from other computer programs written to solve special decision-making problems.

The features of an expert support system include a knowledge base, an inference engine, a knowledge acquisition facility, and an explanation facility (Figure 14.1).

Figure 14.1 Components of Expert Support Systems

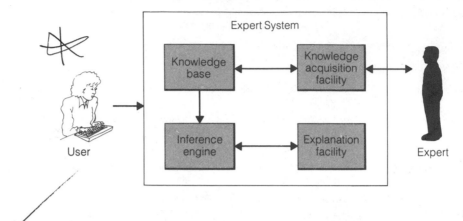

Knowledge Base

The **knowledge base** contains specific information about the area of expertise, such as facts (data) and rules that use the facts in making a decision. It is stored separately from the methods for processing the software.

Expert support systems are classified by the way they represent knowledge. There are rule-based and frame-based systems (Table 14.3).

Rule-Based Knowledge Representation Rule-based systems are the most common type of expert support system. Knowledge about a specific situation is represented as a set of conditions against which the facts or knowledge of a situation under evaluation can be checked. That is, **rules** formally state what is known about a subject area, such as tax planning. For example, one alternative to consider in selecting investment alternatives is establishment of a short-term trust. Obviously the knowledge base of a tax advisory system should contain a set of rules covering all known aspects of this subject.

Each rule in a rule-based system is in the form of an IF-THEN statement:

IF a THEN b
where a is a fact or conjunction of several facts
and b is another fact that is applied when a is true

The following rule concerning establishment of a short-term trust might be part of the knowledge base in an expert system focusing on taxes:

IF
the investor wishes to shift property income to another entity for at least 10 years
and
the investor is using some after-tax income for the benefit of some other taxpayer (for example, a child's wedding)
THEN
the investor should transfer assets to a short-term trust.

Table 14.3 Types of Knowledge Representation

Rule-Based Systems

Knowledge area (domain) is stated as set of rules

Rules are checked against facts describing current situation

When the IF portion is true, the THEN portion is performed

The matching of IF portions of rules to facts produces *inference chains*—that is, statement of how system used the rules to draw *(infer)* conclusion

Frame-Based Systems

A frame is a data structure

Each node represents an object, event, or concept

Each node in the data structure contains:
    attributes (termed *slots*)
    data values for those attributes

Slots may have procedures attached:

IF ADDED (executed when new information is inserted into slot)

IF REMOVED (executed when information is deleted from slot)

IF NEEDED (executed when information is needed from empty slot)

Program analyzes from general concepts to specific conclusions, a node at a time along a path. As each node is examined, details are analyzed and ADD/DELETE/NEEDED procedures are executed to draw an inference

---

Rules are built up consecutively by the expert support system. Thus the entire domain of knowledge about a specific situation is represented as a set of rules, against which the facts or knowledge of a situation under evaluation can be checked. When a fact is derived, it can be combined with other appropriate rules to derive additional facts. In estate planning, for example, the combination of rules will address the following interrelated questions when considering the establishment of an investment trust:

1. Does the investor wish to shift property income to another person for at least 10 years or until the death of the proposed beneficiary?

2. Does the investor desire to reclaim control of the property eventually?

3. Is the investor in a higher income tax bracket than the proposed beneficiary?

4. Is the investor willing to relinquish control of the beneficial enjoyment of the property?

5. Would the investor be able to provide for personal living needs without this income if he or she were to become disabled or unemployed?

6. Does the investor plan to have trust income pay life insurance premiums on his or her life?

7. Does the investor plan to use the trust for a leaseback of assets?

8. Is the investor supporting a person in the absence of any legal obligation to provide such support?

Depending on the nature of the expert support system, there may be anything from a few hundred rules to thousands.

Not all facts can be known, and the strength of an expert support system is a function of its ability to determine the likelihood of an outcome under the given conditions. For instance, in prospecting for oil, the best system will be the one that is most often correct in predicting which sites will be productive, based on such conditions as rock formations and the terrain in the area of exploration—regardless of any uncertainty in the situation.

The matching of the IF portions of rules produces **inference chains,** the linking of rules included in an understanding of a situation (see Figure 14.2). An inference chain, which indicates how the expert support system used the rules to infer current circumstances, can be displayed to users to show how the system has reached a given conclusion. (The importance of having an explanation will be discussed shortly.)

Frame-Based Knowledge Representation   A **frame** stores rules, processing procedures, and descriptive information about the problem, or it points to other frames in the database. Each frame is actually a network of nodes and relations organized into a hierarchy to ensure that during processing, the most important conditions are considered first. The topmost nodes represent general concepts and the lower nodes focus on more specific instances of those concepts. A particular branch of the hierarchy assumes that the preceding conditions and properties at higher levels remain true.

For example, a frame in a tax advising system may assume that preceding qualifications have determined the suitability for the investor of the trust form of financial planning. The system will then focus selection on the form of trust best suited to the situation.

Frame-based systems are most useful for handling complex subjects involving classes of objects. Frames permit the interrelation of knowledge, whereas rules isolate each assertion into a separate item and there is no interrelation of concepts expressed in rules (the processing procedures must recognize the interrelation).

Inference Engine

Inference engines are programs that consult the knowledge base to develop suggested solutions or structure a decision. That is, the inference engine includes the general problem-solving knowledge of the expert support system.

No single design is followed in the development of inference engines. Thus, to demonstrate how inferencing occurs, we will describe forward chaining and backward chaining, the two principal methods used in rule-based systems. (A third method, which we mention briefly later, consists of combining these two approaches.)

Data-Driven Forward Chaining   To use *forward chaining,* which is a data-driven method, the system works through each rule, determining all rules with statements (the a's

Figure 14.2 Inference Chains

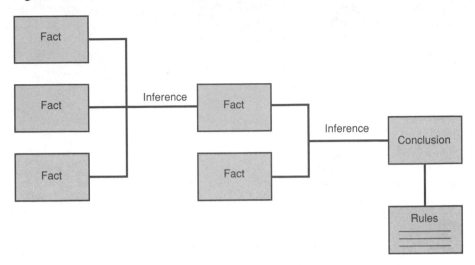

of an IF-THEN statement) that are satisfied by the contents of the database. If multiple rules apply at a single instant, the system selects one of them, evaluates it, and formulates the conclusion. This sequence is repeated until a rule causes further processing to be halted, by recommending a decision or indicating that it is impossible to formulate a decision recommendation.

Goal-Driven Backward Chaining This method starts with the desired outcome—the goal—and attempts to prove that it is achievable by *chaining backward* through the rules in the database. For example, if the goal is tax savings without risk but with the assurance of accumulated appreciation, the system looks for a rule that has this goal as its conclusion. The process is repeated until the system reaches a rule that contains an IF portion that is not true. At that point, it requests relevant facts from the user. Many researchers feel that this approach is the closest to that employed by humans: It uses information that is relevant to its goals (but it does not request that individuals provide additional information until it is stumped—a possible disadvantage).

Combination Inferencing A mixed approach is possible. Systems that allow users to submit information during processing are goal-driven in their mode of operation; but since they accept input, they are driven by data, too.

Knowledge Acquisition Subsystem

Acquiring the knowledge underlying the expert support system may be both difficult and time-consuming. Individuals must devote a large amount of time to working through the logic of their decision processing, sharing heuristics—that is, rules of thumb arrived at through experience—and communicating important facts. As a result, a great deal of research is under way to develop tools that will assist the expert and the knowledge engineer in developing or maintaining the system to create and maintain the knowledge base. In essence, these tools will provide a way of documenting the methods, rules of thumb, and inferencing procedures used by humans in their areas of expertise. You might even consider this subsystem to have the objective of "cloning" the expert.

Explanation Facility

End-users need to know what line of reasoning figures in the development of a decision. If it is determined, through the **explanation facility,** that the reasoning used by the system does not apply to current circumstances, then the solution recommended by the system may be inappropriate. Users cannot make this determination if an explanation of the inferencing process is not at hand.

Often expert support systems also use this facility to tell the user why certain information is being requested. If the importance of the question is understood, more careful thought may go into a respondent's answer.

Printing or displaying the inferencing chains discussed earlier in this chapter is one way of presenting an explanation of the system's reasoning.

Ways to Use Expert Support Systems

Previously we discussed the uses of expert support systems, indicating their value in assisting or replacing human experts or as a training tool. This section describes *how* to use the systems. The three ways discussed are as a stand-alone tool, as an information systems component, and as a controlling system.

As a Stand-Alone Tool

Expert support systems are most often thought of as stand-alone tools. That is, they are used directly, independent of any other information systems component. In these instances, the knowledge base is self-contained.

An example from the field of medicine will help to clarify this. MYCIN is a well-known expert support system used for teaching purposes. It is a stand-alone system that focuses on diagnosis and therapy in certain classes of infectious blood diseases. This system has no understanding of medical principles or science; all knowledge is derived from the rules that comprise its knowledge base. Extension of MYCIN requires the addition of new production rules.

As a Component Within an Information System

Expert support systems capabilities can be very useful as an element in an information system (Figure 14.3). According to this strategy, the system functions as a module that is invoked under control of the application problem to evaluate certain condi-

Figure 14.3 Expert Support System Embedded in Order Processing System

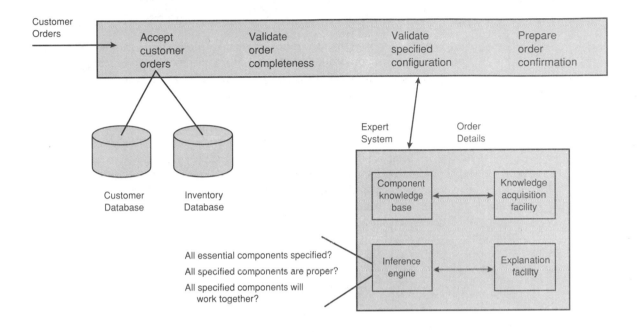

Order Processing System

tions or to suggest actions. The expert support system can be invoked automatically as part of the routine procedure or, alternatively, only on request or when certain conditions are present.

As you know, the acceptance and processing of customer orders is a fundamental activity in virtually any type of business. Routines are generally well understood and carefully worked out. Yet it is an area where mistakes can be costly. Errors can lose customers, time, or money.

Several of the leading firms in the computer industry routinely incorporate expert support systems capabilities into their order processing system. When marketing representatives enter orders for computer systems, an expert support system called a *configurator* is invoked by the order processing system to examine the details of the order (that is, the configuration).

Using the knowledge base and its inferencing capabilities, the expert support systems module examines the details to ensure that, among other things, (1) all essential components for the computer are specified in the customer order, and (2) all specified components are proper and will work together. Since there are thousands of combinations for each computer systems model, the task of evaluating the order would overwhelm an individual, not to mention the amount of time that would be needed to do the job properly.

Embedding expert support systems within information systems will most likely become increasingly common. In the future, a great many business applications will follow this strategy.

As the Controlling Program

Since expert support systems can be designed to access databases, telecommunications networks, and procedural application programs, there is no reason they cannot be the controlling program instead of a module in an information systems application. Under these circumstances, the expert support system can invoke the other components as needed.

For example, expert support systems used in quality control could be developed to access purchasing and manufacturing databases when a manufacturing defect is detected. Using data from these sources, the expert support system can prepare a report indicating the manufacturer of the parts in question, the order batch in which they are contained, and even which finished products used the part.

There really is no limit to the manner in which expert support systems can be designed. Need should be the determining factor.

Acquiring Expert Support Systems

Since expert support systems are based in software, they are acquired like any other software system (see Chapter 6): They can be built in-house or on a contract basis, or they can, in some cases, be purchased as packages.

Build In-House Using Knowledge Engineer

Many companies using expert support systems today have developed them themselves, often out of need—no expert support systems meeting their needs are available for purchase (either none exist or those that do exist were developed by firms that use them for competitive advantage and do not wish to sell their ideas).

Typically the central role in expert support systems development is, as mentioned on page 589, occupied by a *knowledge engineer*—an individual who has the responsibility and skills for eliciting the rules, heuristics, and knowledge from human experts. Using interviews, observation, and similar methods, the knowledge engineer identifies the key elements and synthesizes them into the knowledge base. Since this process must be performed carefully to ensure accuracy and completeness, it can take weeks and even years, depending on the nature and scope of the system. Even small systems consisting of, say, 50 to 100 rules may take several months. Thus you can see that a large system of several thousand rules can easily take well over a year to develop—and at a cost running into the thousands and even millions of dollars.

Knowledge engineers often use expert support systems **shells** as a development tool. A shell typically includes two key components: (1) a language for stating and managing the rules or frames that make up the knowledge base, and (2) an inference engine capable of reasoning with rule sets that the knowledge engineer builds.

Often finding a knowledge engineer is a challenge. Because the field is so new, organizations do not have individuals on staff who have the necessary training to effectively elicit rules and heuristics from the experts or for stating them in a form suitable for the knowledge base. For this reason, many firms thus contract to have expert support systems built for them.

Have a Contractor Build the System

Contracting for the development of expert support systems is similar to the contract development of application software that was discussed in Chapter 6. In this case, the contractor provides the knowledge engineers, who work with in-house experts to capture the contents of the knowledge base.

This approach has the additional advantage of allowing a firm's staff members to obtain some of the expertise in knowledge acquisition as the project progresses.

Purchase an Expert Support System

Until recently, there have been few expert support systems available in package form. Hence firms have out of necessity relied on one of the preceding alternatives.

An increasing number of firms are now developing commercial expert support systems packages. Many of these products contain a ready-made knowledge base for the area of expertise the package addresses. Others only provide a framework or structure, and the firm must enter its own rules.

The packages that have emerged to date are most often in the areas of insurance and financial planning, portfolio analysis, and project management. Table 14.4 lists several expert support systems packages.

It is expected that the number of packaged expert support systems, and the suitability of their knowledge base, will increase dramatically over the next few years.

Using an Expert Support System

An example will demonstrate the use of expert support systems in real-life decision situations. Military commanders must integrate a great deal of information about the deployment of opposing forces and equipment. Yet in nearly all instances, they have only *partial* information. They must fill in the gaps with their own expertise, using intuition and experience to estimate likely occurrences. Expert support systems are rapidly becoming an essential support tool for commanders.

The knowledge base to support commanders consists of rules that state such facts as:

——Sizes of combat units
——Distance a unit can travel in an hour, walking

Table 14.4 Representative Expert System Software

Shells

Tool Name	Host Computer	Vendor Name
ART	DEC VAX computers	Inference Corp.
KEE	Symbolics and LISP machines	Intellicorp
M.1	IBM Personal computer	Teknowledge
TIMM	IBM Personal computer DEC VAX	General Research Corp.
RuleMaster	Computers running UNIX	Radian Corp.
Guru	IBM Personal computer	MDBS, Inc.

Packages

Package Name	Intended User	Vendor Name
Lending Advisor	Financial institutions	Syntelligence
Underwriting Advisor	Insurance companies	Syntelligence
ATRANS	Banks (for money transfers)	Cognitive Systems
Streetsmart	Financial planners	Cognitive Systems

———Distance a unit can travel in an hour, by specific type of motor vehicle

———Distance a unit can travel in an hour, by specific type of water or air transport

———Distance a vehicle can move on a stated quantity of fuel at specified speeds

———Delay factors due to various weather conditions

———Deployment patterns for various types of military units

———Aggregation and organization structures of military units (for example, the relationship of squads to companies, battalions, brigades, regiments, and divisions)

———Types of military equipment typically used by various military units

———Terrain of stated geographical areas

———Location of important landmarks

———Location of roads and trains, and their condition

To these factors commanders may also add the tactics and strategies most likely to be used by friendly and opposing forces under certain conditions. These will be based on past observations, mandated policies, intelligence data, and other sources.

An expert support system containing the foregoing knowledge base can be consulted by commanders planning military strategies and evaluating alternative battle plans. The system can integrate information from intelligence reports, visual image sensors, and radar instrumentation to assist in identifying the movement of opposing forces. Similarly, commanders can pose different strategies: Which units are likely to respond if we launch a strike at a certain target? How long is it likely to take the other side to respond? What weapons and equipment is each unit outfitted with? What strategies are the opposing forces likely to use? What benefit will we gain if we plan an airdrop of troops rather than moving them by truck or ship?

Alternatives are *inferred* from the known facts in the knowledge base and entered into the system by end-users as strategies are considered. Each alternative is described in probabilistic terms; the likelihood of occurrence is stated. The inferencing process and the rationale for a certain alternative can be retrieved to assist the commander in determining the advisability of a given action.

The expert support system will not replace the military commander, nor will people automate their decisions. In the end, human judgment will be used to select desirable strategies. But the expert support system allows more complete assessment of strategies and tactics, and facilitates the incorporation of more details than might otherwise be possible under the pressures of a military conflict.

Differences Between Decision Support and Expert Support Systems

Expert support systems will continue to grow in importance in business, as well as elsewhere in society. Their usefulness is of course in being able to formulate good solutions to problems. However, expertise is not enough. It must also be possible to reach a decision quickly.

As you can see, expert support systems operate differently from decision support systems. Decision support systems contain factual data that are maintained in large files or databases. In contrast, expert support systems focus on effective manipulation of large knowledge bases containing rules of thumb (heuristics) often utilized by human experts. There is also a clear separation of knowledge, data, and processing.

The inference processing characteristics of expert support systems do not exist in decision support systems. The latter rely on use of procedural algorithms or generalized search and retrieval capabilities that draw on the database or data entered by the user.

Both systems will increase in importance in organizations of all types. Advances in computer and software technology, coupled with a better understanding of how managers and users interact with information systems generally, will determine the rate at which improvements can be realized.

Summary

Expert support systems use computer storage and processing to capture and store data and rules to mimic a human expert. They are related to decision support systems by their focus on situations that are only partially structured, but the objective of replicating the decision of human expert systems by manipulation of data and use of heuristics is a distinguishing factor of expert support systems.

These systems can be utilized in several roles, including providing expert advice to nonexperts, assisting experts, and actually replacing the expert in selected situations. They are also used as teaching tools. Frequently they are used to capture the knowledge of experts, but they also serve important roles in minimizing risk of error, particularly when there are large volumes of information that must be interrelated.

Components of an expert support system include the knowledge base containing facts and rules describing knowledge about a situation, an inferencing engine for developing suggested solutions to a problem, the knowledge acquisition subsystem, and an explanation facility. Rule-based systems are currently the most common type of expert support system. Each rule is a formal statement of a piece of knowledge about a subject area, usually stated in the IF-THEN format. Through a process called inference chaining, rules are selected and applied to a situation, eventually leading to a decision that the user can accept or reject.

Frame-based knowledge representation is an alternative to the rule-based design. Each frame stores rules, processing procedures, or descriptive information about a problem. When these entities are linked together, a network of nodes and relations, structured in hierarchical fashion, results.

Whether used as stand-alone tools or integrated into information systems applications, expert support systems will continue to grow in importance in business and management because they are effective tools for assisting managers in dealing with tough situations that call for applying their own good judgment to quantities of information.

Key Words

Artificial intelligence	Frame-based system	Rule
Expert support system	Inference chain	Rule-based system
Expert system	Inference engine	Shell
Explanation facility	Knowledge base	
Frame	Knowledge engineer	

Review Questions

1. What is the purpose of an expert support system?
2. Who are the intended users of expert support systems? Under what circumstances are expert support systems most useful?
3. In what four roles do expert support systems serve? Explain the meaning of each.
4. Define knowledge-based system. Define expert system.
5. What features characterize expert systems? How do expert systems differ from decision support and management information systems?

6. What is a knowledge base? What role do knowledge bases play in expert systems?

7. How do rule-based and frame-based systems differ? What objectives do they have in common?

8. What is a rule? A frame? A slot?

9. What is an inference? An inference engine? How do different expert systems perform inferencing?

10. Discuss the components of expert systems. Briefly describe the purpose of each component. Are these components included in decision support or management information systems? Explain.

11. Discuss the ways in which expert support systems can be used. Give an example of each.

12. How are expert support systems acquired? Which method of acquisition is most often used? Why is this the case?

Application Problems

1. Computer systems, although reliable, exhibit symptoms when they fail to function properly. Although engineers are responsible for diagnosing and repairing the systems, increased use of decision-aiding systems is changing the manner in which problems are located and fixed.

   One system, called CRIB, assists engineers in determining whether faults are hardware or software related. Engineers submit data describing their observations about symptoms and problems. These inputs are compared to symptoms in a database in order to isolate a subunit of the system that must be repaired or replaced.

   If the engineers follow the recommended action and the problem is still not corrected, the system backtracks to the last decision point and evaluates other conditions that match the criteria and symptoms provided by the engineer.

   The key feature of the system is its matching of symptoms with recommended actions.

   a. Is the system described above best classified as a decision support system or an expert system?

   b. What are the key components that lead to your classification in (a)?

2. Some investment counselors have tested a system called FOLIO with which they can advise their clients regarding performance goals. Clients, through interview, provide information about their financial status, tendency toward risk, need for tax shelters, and investment preferences.

   The system focuses on categories of investment securities (including high-risk stocks, low-risk stocks, and dividend-oriented investments). Using the information provided by the client coupled with rate of return and financial data about security classes, the system uses forward chaining to recommend the percent of the client's available fund to invest in each category.

   a. What features lead to the conclusion that the investment system can be classified as an expert system?

   b. Identify each component of an expert system in the example above.

3. If it is possible to capture the knowledge of an expert in an expert system, one can argue that there is no longer a need for an expert. Furthermore, if the data is in a database, the knowledge of the expert becomes permanent. It can be transferred to different settings and even reproduced through copying processes.

a. What factors prohibit complete duplication of an expert's knowledge?

b. Can an expert system produce more consistent, reproducible results than the human expert on which it is based? Why or why not? Is it desirable to seek this result?

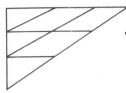

15: Work Group Support Systems

Key Questions

What are work group support systems?

How is information systems technology changing the communications in organizations?

What is electronic data interchange (EDI) and what is its significance?

What is the effect of converging information systems technologies?

How do image and voice processing have an effect on work group activities?

What features are included in personal support systems?

Why are work group systems important?

Who benefits from integrated work group support systems?

Computers and Personal Data

Today it is much easier for computer-based record keeping to affect people than for people to affect computer-based record keeping. This signal observation applies to a very broad range of automated personal data systems. When a machine tool produces shoddy products, the reaction of computers (and of the government regulatory agencies in some cases) is likely to give the factory managers prompt and strong incentives to improve their ways. This is much less likely to be the case when computerized record-keeping operations fail to meet acceptable standards.

There is some evidence that in commercial settings competition helps to prevent harmful or insensitive record-keeping practices, especially when a record-keeping organization (a bank, for instance) depends on continuous interaction with individual data subjects in order to keep its own records straight. It is also true that a number of schools and colleges have been forced to abandon automated registration and scheduling by determined student campaigns to fold, spindle, and mutilate. In governmental settings, however, the dissatisfied data subject usually has nowhere else to take his business and can even be penalized for refusing to cooperate. The result, of course, is that many organizations tend to behave like effective monopolies, which they are.

It is no wonder that people have come to distrust computer-based record-keeping operations. Even in nongovernmental settings, an individual's control over the personal information that he gives to an organization, or that an organization obtains about him, is lessening as the relationship between the giver and receiver of personal data grows more attenuated, impersonal, and diffused. There was a time when information about an individual tended to be elicited in face-to-face contacts involving personal trust and a certain symmetry, or balance, between giver and receiver. Nowadays an individual must increasingly give information about himself to large and relatively faceless institutions, for handling and use by strangers—unknown, unseen, and, all too frequently, unresponsive. Sometimes the individual does not even know that an organization maintains a record about him. Often he may not see it, much less contest its accuracy, control its dissemination, or challenge its use by others.

Records, Computers, and the Rights of Citizens, July 1973

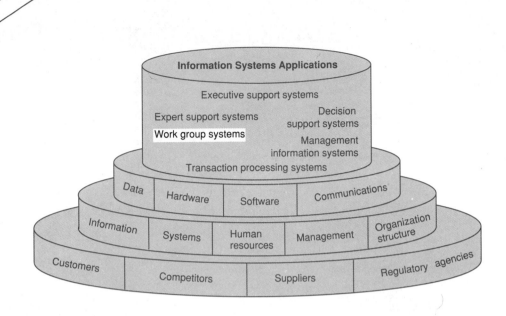

Information Systems Applications

Executive support systems

Expert support systems
Decision support systems

Work group systems

Management information systems

Transaction processing systems

Data | Hardware | Software | Communications

Information | Systems | Human resources | Management | Organization structure

Customers | Competitors | Suppliers | Regulatory agencies

Except for the introduction of the commercial typewriter three years before the death of Charles Dickens, few of the past century's changes in the operation of offices would have astonished Ebenezer Scrooge . . . until recently. Now work group support systems offer the potential to reduce the virtually total dependence of business on paper for communication of data and information, and on travel for direct and face-to-face discussion. They also have the capability to improve productivity at all levels and to form the basis for managing office activities, an area of substantial cost for most organizations.

Work group support systems have evolved from an initial emphasis on office automation—particularly the automation of the preparation of correspondence and support of secretarial functions—to what is now a wide variety of information systems applications. As this chapter will show, work group support systems go well beyond traditional office and secretarial functions. In fact, these systems represent a convergence of all of the technologies we have discussed.

The characteristics of work group support systems are considered first. Next the important application areas of word, image, and voice processing are examined in detail. Of particular importance are electronic data interchange and electronic publishing systems. The last two sections of this chapter examine video conferencing and personal support systems. When you have completed this chapter, you should have a good understanding of work group support systems and insight into how these systems will continue to evolve and grow in importance for end-users of all types.

Why Should You Know About Work Group Support Systems?

Work group support systems are closer to you than you think. Here are several ways you may be affected by such systems in your career:

——*Virtually all occupations depend on work groups.* The need to communicate and stay in touch with colleagues, whether by voice or through computer-based means, is pretty much universal. You need not work in an office, either. Construction workers, sales representatives, and law enforcement agents increasingly rely on various aspects of work group support systems to do their job. Of course, those who work on the premises of an enterprise rely on many elements of work group support.

——*Organizations and individuals want higher productivity.* Time is a resource that is always in short supply. Hence, people in all vocations are looking for ways to be more productive in the time they have available. Work group support systems offer this assistance in many ways.

——*Work group support systems can overcome distance barriers.* Through a variety of means, distances between colleagues and trading partners—even if they are on different continents—can be diminished, making rapid and efficient communication between them possible.

——*Electronic publishing has arrived.* Work group support also includes the use of computers to prepare documents ranging from résumés to newsletters to reports or even entire books. The personal computer has played a vital role in bringing this capability—which used to be something performed only by artists and printers—within reach of anyone who can operate a desktop computer.

As you read this chapter, you will find many more ways in which work group support systems are important in your career.

Characteristics of Work Group Support Systems

Whether they involve executives, middle managers, or professional persons such as attorneys, accountants, and certified financial planners, many office applications depend on the interchange of information for effective performance. Computing support for work groups is increasingly being considered to enhance the effectiveness and productivity of these individuals.

In discussing the characteristics of work group support systems, this section points out how such systems differ from computer information systems of other types and explores the integration of different information technologies.

Table 15.1 The Terminology of Work Group Support Systems

Term	Description
Electronic Data Interchange (EDI)	The use of data communications and computer processing to allow trading partners to exchange business transaction data using structured formats. The systems are interorganizational and rely on computer-to-computer exchange of data.
Electronic Publishing	The intertwining of text and image data in a single document. Incorporates formatting capabilities and the use of multiple type styles to give the document a professionally typeset appearance.
Image Processing	The processing, storage, and transmission of image data—such as drawings, blueprints, and photographs—as well as text data that has been captured as a document rather than character by character.
Video Conferencing	The use of voice or image transmission, or both, to link parties in a conversation who are at different locations. Also includes electronic publishing (that is, videotex).
Voice Processing	The transmission and receiving of voice data in digital form over various communication links. May be an integral component in large corporate systems or in personal support applications. Includes voice messaging.
Word Processing	The broad class of technology that enables manipulation, presentation, or transmission of printed, displayed, and even voice information. Usually involves narrative or text information.
Electronic Office	The result of the application of information processing and communications technology to transmit information through distributed processing and data communications methods. Aimed at speeding communication while reducing paper flow.

What Is a Work Group Support System?

Work group support systems are automated systems aimed at making knowledge workers—managers, secretaries, and administrative staff members—more productive by changing the structure and activities of the office and other work groups within an organization (Table 15.1). They utilize a portfolio of information systems technologies that facilitate information preparation, storage, retrieval, and communication.

Compared to the other systems we have discussed, the following information-handling differences distinguish work group support systems:

——*Unstructured information:* Information is often not organized into discrete components or fixed lengths. Work group information includes not only numerical details but also narrative descriptions and images, each needing managing and processing to meet user requirements.

——*Multiple functions:* These systems combine multiple technologies to support communication between people, transmission of data in various forms, and presentation of information. Voice and image processing are combined with the presentation of information or management of text information.

——*Organizationwide focus:* Work group support systems span operational systems as well as planning and control activities. They include support of clerical or administrative functions and top-level executive support. In short, they involve and affect a large segment of the organization.

Figure 15.1 Convergence of Information Technologies

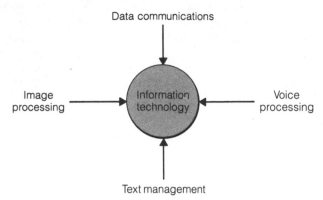

At the same time, work group support systems use the same computer and communications equipment as other information systems. The functions performed by the equipment, such as data entry, storage, processing, and retrieval, are the same. Other important information systems features included in work group support systems are:

——Data communications

——Distributed data

——Distributed users

——Distributed processing

——Database management

Integration of Technologies

Work group support systems integrate various technologies, including data, voice, text, and image systems (Figure 15.1). An organization does not have to use all these technologies to have a work group support system, however; work group systems represent varying degrees of sophistication and breadth of function.

Data-Oriented Systems The preceding chapters have introduced the concepts and processes associated with information systems, namely the processing of transactions and the support of decision situations that are well structured or *not* well structured. For each type of system, the importance of data capture, storage, processing, retrieval, and presentation was emphasized. Systems analysts and end-users alike have a variety of technologies to choose from when developing an automated system to assist in any of these activities.

The underlying feature of each category of system is data. Thus accurate and efficient data capture is a principal goal in system design. We discussed different input devices that can store and retrieve data items as well as acquiring them.

Management reporting and decision support activities focus on information. But that information can be prepared only through the processing of available data. Thus the common thread among all the systems is data.

Voice-Oriented Systems At one time, computer-based systems were characterized as stand-alone, single-site centers. Gradually, the number of users who could simultaneously submit, store, and retrieve data has increased, drawing on the voice capabilities of communications systems. Wide-area networks were augmented by PBX (private branch exchange) telephone systems for switching. The push for office productivity gave us dictation systems—voice communication of data and information to be translated into print form or retransmitted to others. Local-area networks linked units together for communication at high speeds over limited distances and involving a mixture of devices.

Voice processing allows the storage, editing, and transmission of the spoken word. And the capability is available, at a reasonable cost, to append voice messages to text and data.

A revolution in the acceptance and processing of voice is under way. Voice-input word processing systems are emerging with huge vocabularies of everyday words. Prototypes requiring mainframe systems are giving way to desktop units. (In manufacturing environments, workers will use the same technology to verbally interact with systems and applications for operation of production equipment, quality control, and materials handling. Stockbrokers will be able to retrieve market quotations "in a word.")

Text Processing Throughout the book we have shown that computers do more than transaction-oriented data processing and that telephones do not process voice alone. Now we come to the processing of *text*—manuscripts, reports, and briefs. Although many people still consider typewriters the prime tool for processing (that is, *typing*) text, the real fact is that typewriters are on the road to obsolescence. Indeed, more than 90 percent of all newly prepared text is now processed and stored in digital form.

Word processing, as we have come to know it, is not only an important office technology but another form of information processing, with the emphasis on text, not data. Yet many of the underlying methods for entry, storage, retrieval, and presentation of the text are shared with information systems.

Image Processing Pictorial information can be managed like any other type of information and can be included in office documents. To this end, **image processing** is the digitization and transmission of image information—pictures, drawings, and illustrations—between multiple locations.

But image processing offers much more. The ability to translate graphic data into digital form allows users to combine it with text, and when printed using laser capabilities, to provide publication-quality output. Graphic data can also be manipulated by removing unwanted portions or reshaped through enlargement or reduction and repositioned in a layout. Moreover, graphic data can be stored and retrieved in databases like those used for numerical data.

The development of reliable and cost-effective image processing systems will round out the integration of information technologies as we know them today.

Benefits of Work Group Support Systems

It is easy to be caught up in the computer and communications technology surrounding work group support systems. However, the real impact is on the organization of the office. The preparation of documents and the communication of messages in many different forms produce the following benefits.

——*Increased accessibility to people:* communication between individuals is facilitated both through face-to-face means and by transmission of voice and print messages.

——*Increased accessibility to information:* information can be retrieved from many locations and in diverse forms. Search time is reduced as acquisition and retrieval costs decrease.

——*Increased individual productivity:* managers and end-users can spend more time on their primary tasks and less on support activities that use up disproportionate quantities of time and effort. Reductions in meeting and travel time, coupled with the use of personal support systems, enable people to better utilize their working hours.

——*Increased continuity:* tasks can be completed with fewer transfers of control over work between different people and less effort in the transformation of information from one form to another. Frustration levels are reduced as a result.

——*Increased control over personal activities:* individuals are better able to control the pace of their activities and the frequency of interruption and disruption. People's ability to manage and interact with colleagues and staff members at different locations is greatly improved.

As this list suggests, the benefits from the development of work group support systems are wide ranging and substantial. As we examine prominent applications in the sections that follow, you will see how these benefits are realized.

Electronic Data Interchange

It is becoming more difficult to separate the office from the rest of the organization. One type of work group system that spans traditional data processing systems and the support of the work group is **electronic data interchange (EDI).** Corporations across a wide variety of industries are turning to EDI to improve the way they do business and to gain competitive advantages.

Characteristics of EDI

EDI is a form of electronic communication that allows trading partners in two or more organizations to exchange business transaction data in structured formats that can be processed by application software. EDI is an information systems concept having these features (Figure 15.2):

Figure 15.2 Business Transactions Using EDI

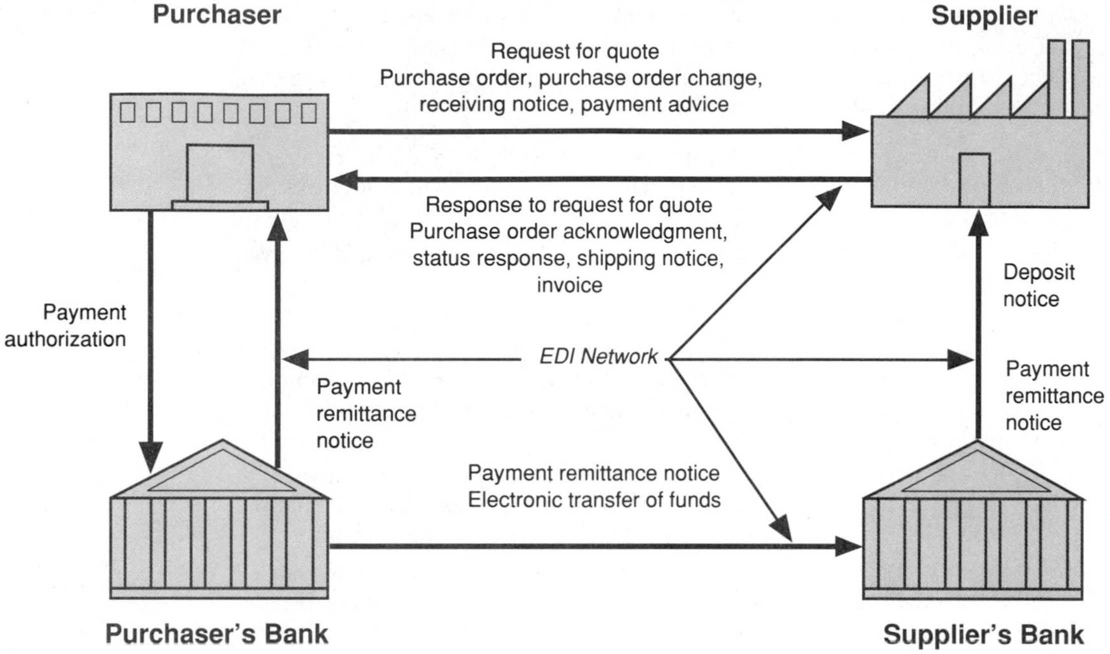

────*It is interorganizational.* EDI links trading partners (for example, organizations and their customers and suppliers) in a cooperative relationship that potentially benefits each party through improved levels of profitability, service, and productivity.

────*It involves computer-to-computer transmission.* Data are exchanged electronically, in machine-readable form and without the need for manual intervention in the data entry or manipulation process. Networks link computers within the organizations of participating firms.

────*It emphasizes the transmission of business documents.* Business documents, rather than electronic messages or narrative documents, are the substance of EDI transmissions. Typical business documents include purchase orders, quotations, invoices, bills of lading, shipping notices, and so on.

────*Formatted data are used.* In order to ensure that the data are correctly received and properly understood, carefully defined formats specify the order of data items in a transmission and the characteristics of each item.

Benefits

Three benefits stand out when organizations develop systems for EDI.

Compression of Time EDI compresses time. Business data are sent, received, and processed in a fraction of the time normally associated with business processes.

Table 15.2 EDI Industry Penetration (%)

Railroad	90
Trucking	85
Grocery	50
Automobile	35
Retail	10
Electronics	5
Banking	5

SOURCE: Gartner Group

Because data are transmitted electronically, the delay in moving information from place to place—sometimes called *information float*—is minimized. Even data moving between continents can be transferred in a matter of a few seconds.

As a result, business cycles can shrink. In some industries, the time it takes to accept orders, manufacture products, and ship them to customers has been reduced by over 25 percent as a result of EDI.

Cost Savings A study conducted by the Yankee Group, an East Coast consulting firm, revealed that 70 percent of computer output becomes input to another firm's computer system. Further, the study revealed that 25 percent of a transaction's cost is data entry and reentry. EDI eliminates the need to reenter data since data transmissions can be accepted into another firm's system in electronic form.

Entire industries have found that substantial cost savings can be achieved through EDI. The grocery industry anticipated savings in excess of $300 million per year by linking grocers and wholesalers through EDI. But they are not alone. The trucking, railroad, automobile, and retail industries rely heavily on EDI. And the apparel, pharmaceutical, and banking industries are moving rapidly into EDI to gain the business advantages outlined here (see Table 15.2).

The cost of processing purchase orders has been shown to fall from the $50 level to less than $5. And inventory only needs to be maintained at a fraction of former levels, producing significant savings in working capital.

Improved Relationships Firms increasingly need one another to be competitive and, indeed, successful. Entire industries depend on open relationships between competitive intra-industry firms. For example, competitors in the railroad industry chose to band together through open interchange of information using EDI. The trucking industry posed a massive threat to even the existence of the rail industry.

The increased dependency between competitors, suppliers, and customers is a reality of business. In many industries, failing to trade electronically may mean failure of the enterprise.

Table 15.3 Leading EDI Service Providers

Service Provider	Industry Focus
GEISCO (GE Information Services Co.)	Apparel, automotive, petrochemical, electronics, steel, international trade
McDonnell Douglas EDI Systems Co.	Grocery, transportation, chemicals, electronics
Sterling Software/Ordernet	Pharmaceutical, warehouse, medical, transportation, grocery
IBM Information Network (INN)	Insurance, retail, apparel, electronics
Kleinschmidt	Transportation, grocery, warehouse, electronics, chemicals
Control Data Corp.	Automotive, manufacturing, chemicals

Elements of EDI

The success of EDI depends on four key components: a reliable transmission network, standard data formats, product identification codes, and willing trading partners.

A Reliable Transmission Network EDI uses proven communications technology (discussed in Chapter 9). Often data are transmitted over value-added networks where service can be purchased as needed. Table 15.3 lists the leading network companies and the industries they serve. Other carriers are considering developing EDI capabilities in the near future.

Standard Data Formats Standard data formats tell trading partners what to expect in the contents, order, and form of data transmitted through EDI. The X.12 format (see Figure 15.3) is widely promoted. Among its attractions is the existence of a wide variety of transaction formats for electronic purchase orders, packing slips, invoices, payments, and so on. Each format identifies the contents of the transaction, the order in which the items will be presented, and the specifications for the data (for example, data item length and type).

Product Identification Codes Standards are also needed for identifying products. As an example, the grocery industry has had the Universal Product Code for some time. Each participant knows how products are identified and coded.

Proprietary identification systems limit the number of firms with which a corporation may interact for electronic trading. Partners may be unwilling to adopt the particular system requested unless it is industrywide. Doing so could lead them to use several different systems—one for each trading partner. This would be cumbersome indeed.

Figure 15.3 X.12 Transaction Format

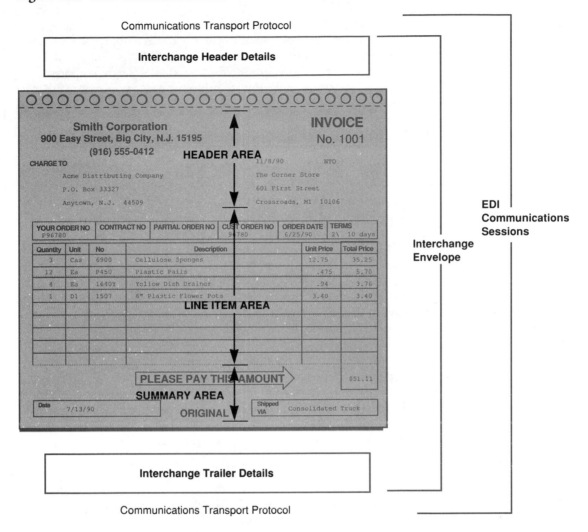

Willing Trading Partners A decision by a company to develop systems for electronic data interchange is only one step. The trading partners with which the firm interacts must also be willing to participate. If they are not, EDI will be no more than a dream.

The potential of EDI is substantial because it strengthens the relationships between trading partners while overcoming the business barriers of time and distance. EDI is rapidly becoming a standard way of doing business.

Word Processing

The manipulation of *text*—symbols, phrases, figures, and tables—is frequently referred to as **word processing.** However, this term often means different things to different people. Many people treat the "electronic office"—and increasingly, corporate publishing—as though they were equivalent to each other and synonymous with *word processing*. Some people use these terms to describe secretarial functions, while others apply them to personal computers.

Terminology

All these approaches have some validity. However, each term really describes one aspect of work group support, so that before examining word processing, it will be useful to distinguish between these ideas.

Word Processing As indicated above, *word processing* is a method of communicating text information to individuals in a manner that ensures both high quality and low costs. The preparation, formatting, and transmission of the information is achieved at high speeds. Word processing also provides a method for tailoring the presentation of information to the situation at hand. Typically, the term refers to the communication of printed information, but it is not limited to this medium.

The Electronic Office Have you ever stopped to consider the amount of information that flows within and between departments in organizations? Consider all the verbal information that passes back and forth through face-to-face conversation, over intercoms, on the telephone, and even by means of closed-circuit television. Then think about all the written information in the form of invoices, receipts, reports, memoranda, printouts, and microfilm/microfiche. The proliferation of paper in today's office has often been noted.

The electronic office is an idea whose time has come. It is intended to improve the efficiency of communication by reducing the time it takes to prepare information for communication to others and by eliminating the need to sift through a sheaf of documents to find specific pieces of information.

The electronic office also incorporates a method of handling **electronic mail.** Information that is currently prepared, stored, retrieved, and distributed *manually* can be handled *electronically*. And it does not matter whether it is stored down the hall, across the street, or across the ocean—the speed and efficiency of getting any information for any purpose will be unaffected by location.

Types of Word Processing Systems

Word processing has evolved through several types (Table 15.4). The display-based and shared-logic types are still in use. However, personal computer-based systems are the predominant choice in organizations today.

Table 15.4 Types of Word Processing Systems

Type	Description
Stand-alone system	Fully self-contained system to do input and output operations and storage of data
	Display-based: CRT used for input and visual display of data/text and operator messages. Output is produced on attached printer.
	Printer-based: data/text entry and output through typewriter-like keyboard. Special keys ease the data entry and edit operations.
Shared-logic system	Multiple users share a centrally controlled word processing system. Data entry is typically display based with output on large high-speed computer printer or through attached character printers.
Personal computer based system	A general-purpose microcomputer using word processing software handles all data/text entry, output, and storage. Usually a display-based, stand-alone system. Can do other types of business processing simply by loading different software.

As you have probably realized, personal computers are multipurpose devices. A word processing program can be loaded into the system for one job, and later accounts receivable or inventory can be handled on the same machine, simply by loading in different software packages.

Personal computers can also be integrated into local-area networks. The same flexibility is retained, but the advantage is in shared use of storage and output facilities. Software sharing is also possible because a properly licensed copy of the software can reside on a file server, available for use by anyone in the network.

Major Functions of Word Processing

The advantages of word processing become obvious as you become familiar with the functions that can be performed. You will see that corrections become trivial. Updates and extensions to stored text can easily be made. Typing can be controlled and repetitive typing reduced significantly. "Boilerplating" of much-used information is another attractive advantage of word processing.

Input The first step in word processing is to input the data, text, or information. This step is much like ordinary typing because the data are entered through a keyboard. If a visual display system is used, the text being entered appears on the videoscreen as it is typed.

As the text is entered, the word processing software controls the formatting of data on the screen (Figure 15.4). A *word wrap* feature permits entry of the text as

Figure 15.4 Data Formatting on Screen During Text Entry

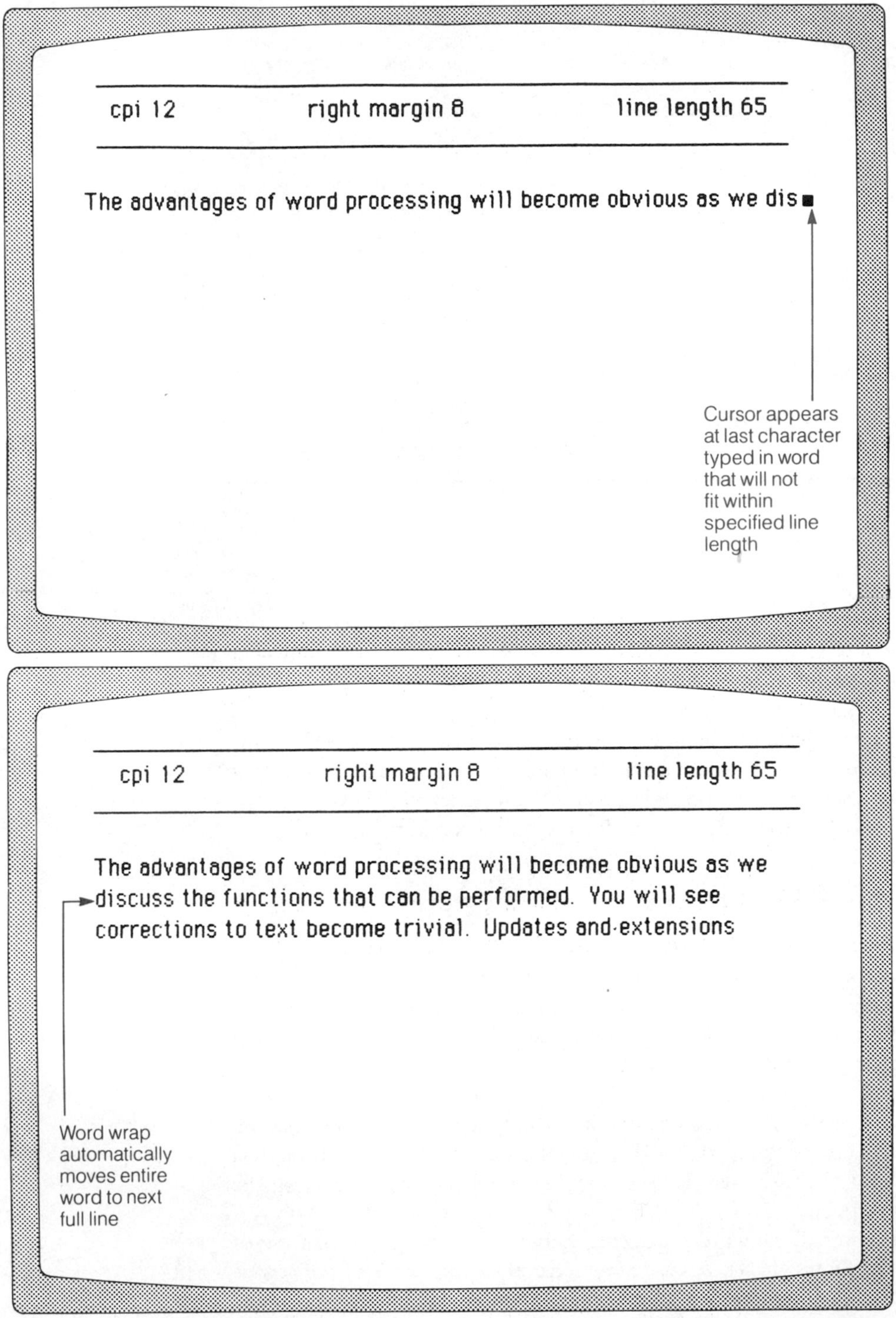

cpi 12	right margin 8	line length 65

The advantages of word processing will become obvious as we dis■

Cursor appears at last character typed in word that will not fit within specified line length

cpi 12	right margin 8	line length 65

The advantages of word processing will become obvious as we
→discuss the functions that can be performed. You will see
corrections to text become trivial. Updates and extensions

Word wrap automatically moves entire word to next full line

fast as the operator can type without concern for carriage returns. When a typed word exceeds the right margin or the right side of the screen, it is automatically moved to the next line. The line just completed is redisplayed without extraneous characters.

Revisions and corrections can be made while the text is on the screen. Typing mistakes can usually be corrected simply by typing over the letters or characters in error. If text needs to be added in the middle of a sentence or paragraph, the word processor will "open up" the line or paragraph, on command, to allow the user to make the insert. Deletions work in reverse: The word processor will remove unwanted characters and close up the remaining space so that no "holes" remain.

On-screen editing during input makes correction of errors quite easy. It also permits rearrangement of text without the need to print it first, and certainly without any retyping or cutting and pasting.

Storage Word processing systems accumulate text in memory as it is being entered. At the end of input or editing, the text can be "saved" or stored on a secondary storage medium, such as a flexible diskette. Once the operator has given the text a name (to distinguish it from all other text contained in the word processing system), it is automatically stored. The word processor determines where and how to store the data on the diskette and updates a directory that keeps track of name, location, and length for each file of text.

Some systems store the entire text as one large string of data. Others break it up into individual pages. Both methods are in widespread use.

Editing An essential feature of word processing is the edit capability. Once a file of text has been saved, it can be recalled repeatedly for editing. Each time a file is recalled, text can be added, changes and corrections can be made, and sentences, paragraphs, and pages of material can be moved around, copied, or deleted, depending on the intentions of the operator. We will see an example of editing shortly, but first we must present some important controls.

Consider that the screen on the CRT-like device is the user's "window" into the files of data that are stored within the system. From time to time, the user wants to move around in the file. As Figure 15.5 illustrates, *scrolling* makes this possible by rolling stored text up or down on the screen, letting the user move forward through the lines of text. As a new line of text comes on to the viewing screen, a line on the other side goes off. Thus, when the operator scrolls down four lines, four lines of text enter the screen at the bottom and four other lines move off the top. To make it possible to move through a long file quickly, many word processing systems permit full-screen scrolling. Rather than moving only one line at a time (that is, line scrolling), an entire screen full of data will be moved off and a new screen full of data will enter. With this method, an entire file can be examined very quickly.

Printing When a document has been edited and all changes are complete, it is ready to be printed. During printing, commands included in the file during input and editing are processed to format the output. For example, the text is broken into pages according to the operator's specifications of length. If page length is specified

Figure 15.5 Window into Electronic File of Text

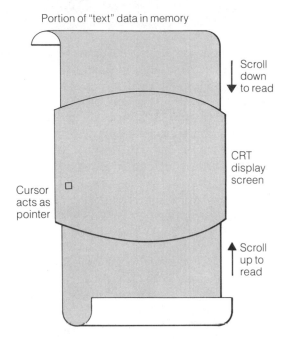

There are many possible printing enhancements. For example, key words can be underlined automatically. Subscripts and superscripts, boldface print, and paragraph indenting are also possible. Many systems will also do justified printing, producing flush margins both right and left, without ragged edges. If a typeset appearance is to be achieved by the use of variable or proportional type (that is, if the characters in the font selected occupy different amounts of space), the word processor will automatically calculate spacing and insert blanks to produce the justification.

An Example of Word Processing

The best way to see the power of word processing is to look at an example. Figure 15.6 shows a short manuscript that has been typed into a word processing system. The first four lines, starting with "\," are embedded commands. The first instructs the system that final printing should be at 12 characters per inch using a left margin of 12 and a line length (right margin) of 60 characters. As the second and third lines state, the printing should be single-spaced and justified. The embedded command "ctr" instructs the system to center the next line (in this case it is the title). The

Figure 15.6 Example of Text Marked for Word Processing Changes

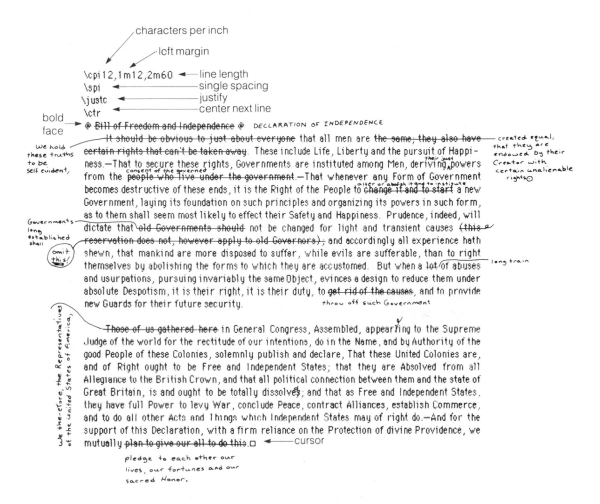

special characters (@) enclosing the fifth line indicate that the title should be printed in boldface type.

A number of changes are marked on the printed copy of the set of text shown in Figure 15.6. They can be entered into the word processing system by typing right over existing text. In some cases copy has been modified or expanded. In other cases material—for example, the phrase "(this reservation does not, however, apply to old Governors)"—has been deleted altogether. Similarly, the typographical error in the third line ("happinesss") has been corrected by deleting a letter.

All these changes can be made directly through the keyboard of a word processor, without retyping the entire text. The final version (Figure 15.7) shows what would be printed, with all the embedded commands executed and all the changes and corrections made.

Figure 15.7 Manuscript After Editing and Formatted Printing

DECLARATION OF INDEPENDENCE

We hold these truths to be self-evident, that all men are created equal, that they are endowed by their Creator with certain unalienable Rights, that among these are Life, Liberty and the pursuit of Happiness.—That to secure these rights, Governments are instituted among Men, deriving their just powers from the consent of the governed,—That whenever any Form of Government becomes destructive of these ends, it is the Right of the People to alter or to abolish it, and to institute new Government, laying its foundation on such principles and organizing its powers in such form, as to them shall seem most likely to effect their Safety and Happiness. Prudence, indeed, will dictate that Governments long established should not be changed for light and transient causes; and accordingly all experience hath shewn, that mankind are more disposed to suffer, while evils are sufferable, than to right themselves by abolishing the forms to which they are accustomed. But when a long train of abuses and usurpations, pursuing invariably the same Object, evinces a design to reduce them under absolute Despotism, it is their right, it is their duty, to throw off such Government, and to provide new Guards for their future security.

We, therefore, the Representatives of the United States of America, in General Congress, Assembled, appealing to the Supreme Judge of the world for the rectitude of our intentions, do, in the Name, and by Authority of the good People of these Colonies, solemnly publish and declare, That these United Colonies are, and of Right ought to be Free and Independent States; that they are Absolved from all Allegiance to the British Crown, and that all political connection between them and the state of Great Britain, is and ought to be totally dissolved; and that as Free and Independent States, they have full Power to levy War, conclude Peace, contract Alliances, establish Commerce, and to do all other Acts and Things which Independent States may of right do.—And for the support of this Declaration, with a firm reliance on the Protection of divine Providence, we mutually pledge to each other our Lives, our fortunes and our sacred Honor.

Word Processing and Work Group Computing

Word processing can play a special role in work groups where it is necessary to coordinate the work of two or more people in a way that will lead to results beyond what an individual could have produced alone. Since many professionals and upper-level managers depend on their ability to work in concert with others, boosting each other's skills and knowledge of a situation, you can expect work group systems to have broad appeal.

Group Use of Documents Consider the day-to-day activities of multiattorney legal firms, for example. Lawyers use standard formats or templates for planning and laying out the details of a large legal case, whether it is a civil or a criminal case. Typically a legal brief will include an outline of the complaint, a list of the parties involved on either side, and a description of the major and minor issues around which the case centers. Depending on the specific case, it may be essential to have a chronological listing of the events that transpired, a list of the witnesses involved, and a record of the facts that have been accumulated to date. A strategy for uncovering information needed to handle the case—referred to by attorneys as the *discovery plan*—and a list of pertinent facts and details to be collected are also central to the arguing of the case. Finally, an inventory of documents, records, and exhibits is sure to be included as part of the case documentation.

In many legal cases, the successful presentation of the case stems from the logic used in accumulating and organizing information coupled with the strategy for presenting the information. In this situation, the gathering of opinions, suggestions, and insight from a team of lawyers can add up to more than just the sum of the parts. It may lead to the discovery of facts and strategies that alter the entire process, even the final outcome.

Group Information Capture Word processing in work groups (sometimes you will see it called simply **work group computing**) incorporates many of the computer and communications technologies we have discussed. It is a way for individuals to screen the information they receive—which seldom can be done in electronic mail or computer conferencing—while offering comments, electronically, on the information after review. Furthermore, the comments of others are accumulated with the original document or body of information so that participants can see the comments as well and can even augment them. Often local-area networks interconnecting personal computers are used to facilitate the group communication.

Other tasks and areas where work group computing is expected to grow include sales and competitive bid proposal writing, preparation of statements of corporate policy, mission, or procedure, and research and development program statements. An increasing number of software packages are emerging to support these activities.

In each instance, word processing software is used to enter comments or revisions and to store the document containing the group annotations.

Image Processing

Managers who work not only with columns of data but with reports, blueprints, plans, budgets, facility layouts, newspaper advertising layouts, and photographs are increasingly concerned with the logistics of getting important communications and information from one place to another. Image processing is based on the realization that in some situations there is no replacement for having a document in hand.

Digitized Document Storage and Transmission

Chapter 5 introduced digitizing as an element in image processing. This section expands the discussion, with emphasis on group computing applications.

When **digitizing** occurs, the contents of a document are scanned and translated into a form that can be stored. For example, photographic images can be turned into digital form by passing a scanner over the photo. Each dot is translated into a binary digit, which is written to magnetic storage. Images are addressable; that is, they are stored at a certain location and can be retrieved when needed for modification or for output (see accompanying photo).

Architects can create building designs and store the documents digitally. Artists digitize drawings and sketches. Corporations can store a copy of their logo or letterhead on a computer-readable medium for reproduction on any document they wish to identify as "official." Universities may photograph students, storing their digitized image for later display on workstation screens for identification when the students are cashing checks, registering for courses, or checking books out of the library. Many uses like these are possible because of the reasonable cost of digitizers. Thus entire libraries or files of digitized images can be created.

Scanning Device

Once in digital form, documents and images may be modified as needed. Details can be added or taken away, color can be changed, and size can be increased or decreased.

Often images and data or text are merged for output. For example, corporate logos and advertising slogans can be combined on the cover of a brochure or report. New letterheads are quickly prepared to promote new products or announce customer services. The text–image combination can be transmitted electronically to other locations for display or for printing.

Document Facsimile Communication

A **facsimile** device (see accompanying photo) makes a copy or "fax" of an original document containing graphic or alphanumeric data and sends it electronically to another location. The receiving location reproduces a duplicate of the original copy. Typically this method uses ordinary telephone lines, although private transmission lines are becoming increasingly common. Microwave transmission is used in some cases.

Facsimile Device for Sending Documents Electronically

Almost any text, drawing, chart, or document can be sent by facsimile methods with little difficulty. No rekeying of data or redrawing of lines is needed. Basically, any two-dimensional representation that could be put in an envelope and mailed can be sent over communication lines.

Facsimile boards that fit in personal computers are also available. Using "fax boards," an individual can create a document (text, images, or a combination) on the personal computer and transmit it directly without having to first convert it to printed form.

Electronic Publishing

Image processing capabilities have created a new threshold in book and document publishing. Text is managed through word processing; and line art, like the non-photographic illustrations used in this book, can be entered through scanners or digitizers and stored. Book pages are established by arranging text and illustrations electronically. Then the pages are printed, using laser technology to produce camera-ready copy. As an alternative, laser printers will prepare many copies of a book, thus changing the normal publisher-to-printer-to-binder cycle.

Features of Publishing Systems   Computer software performs the publishing functions, taking advantage of the high-resolution display features in an appropriately equipped computer. In general, to be considered a publishing program, the software must offer the following features:

——*Allow high-quality composition of text:* Typically the results must be of typeset quality, meaning that proportional spacing and justification (alignment) of right and left margins is possible. Automatic hyphenation is also required.

——*Support page composition:* This feature allows the user to arrange text and images on the display screen in columns, as desired. The arrangement on the screen is the same as that which appears when the page is printed (termed WYSIWYG: what you see is what you get).

——*Incorporate graphics and images:* This makes it possible for the user to intersperse image and text data as desired. It typically permits images to be created outside of the program and imported for placement at the exact location desired by the user.

——*Provide editing capability:* This feature allows the user to add to, change, or remove text without leaving the program (that is, the program has word processing capability).

In addition, it is expected that the printed results will be of high quality. Typically this means the print resolution will be at least 300 dots per inch or higher (this resolution is such that the letters are solid—no dots appear when examining the makeup of the letter).

Firms of all types are taking advantage of this technology. Personnel manuals, catalogs, and important memos are prepared and stored electronically, ready to be accessed by users anywhere in the organization. They can be accessed over computer networks or by using the keyboard of the system on which they reside.

Figure 15.8 Work Surface for Desktop Publishing Program

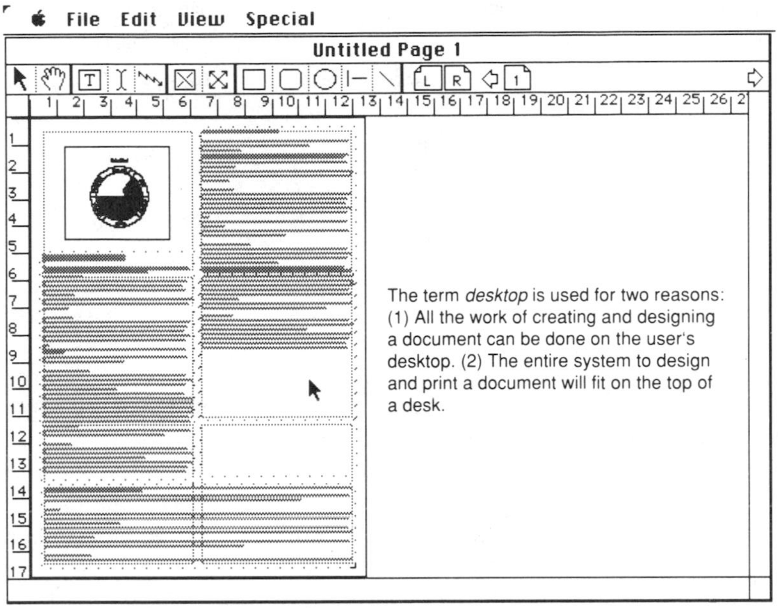

Types of Publishing Systems Image processing of this nature is not limited to large publishers. Anyone can use corporate publishing systems without a large investment of time or resources. Systems that run on personal computers are called **desktop publishing systems.** The term *desktop* is used for two reasons: (1) All the work of creating and designing a document can be done on the user's desktop—the name given to the display screen (Figure 15.8) that functions like a worktable; or (2) the entire system to design and print a document—including the printer—will fit on the top of a desk. Personal computers suitably equipped to perform desktop publishing, such as the Apple Macintosh or the IBM Personal System/2, are available for less than $10,000. Laser printers that run on a personal computer range from $2000 to $10,000.

Software packages for desktop publishing can be acquired for several hundred dollars apiece (see Table 15.5). These systems make image processing in the form of desktop publishing capabilities available in virtually any work group setting and offer the potential to combine word processing and graphics with print-quality presentation, all in an easy-to-use package.

Figure 15.9 includes a newsletter created with desktop publishing software. Notice the multiple columns, the varied type styles, and the inclusion of images. The heading is also an image.

The name **corporate publishing system** is typically applied to systems that have more capability and hence greater cost than desktop publishing systems. Such a system usually has more features in the publishing software and can produce higher

Table 15.5 Popular Desktop Publishing Programs

Publishing Program	System Type	Vendor
Gem Publisher	IBM PC	Digital Research
Interleaf Publisher	IBM PC, midrange and main-frames, DEC	Interleaf
Pagemaker	IBM PC, Apple Macintosh	Aldus Corp.
Quark	Apple Macintosh	
Ready, Set, Go	Apple Macintosh	Letraset USA
Ventura Publisher	IBM PC	Xerox Corp.

resolution in the printed result. Additional capabilities with the handling of images are built into these systems.

Often corporate publishing systems are shared by multiple users linked together in a network. Frequently they are centralized systems. Hence the computer at the heart of the system is more powerful and may be a midrange or even a mainframe system.

Voice Processing

The integration of voice capabilities into the office and into information systems in general will open up many new possibilities for the management of information. Giant leaps forward have occurred in voice input and output and in voice messaging.

Voice Output

As mentioned in Chapter 5, audio output devices are available. You hear "voice output" when you have dialed a disconnected or redirected number on the public telephone system: A speech synthesizer "speaks" data from the computer—the number you dialed and the new number. Although currently somewhat limited, the capabilities of such devices are improving rapidly.

Automobiles now include voice output devices that remind you to take your keys or to turn off your headlights. Others are embedded in the vehicle's warning system to alert the driver to low fuel, high temperature, or other such conditions.

Text-to-voice devices that scan printed text, translating the words into spoken sounds, are invaluable to the blind.

Imagine combining all the foregoing capabilities in workstations, most of which already contain a speaker. Data can be received at the terminal, including voice comments pertaining to a document or message. Better yet, take away the need to use the terminal entirely, and allow users to dial into a computer system and receive their mail *electronically and in voice form.*

Figure 15.9 Document Layout and Presentation Created Using Publishing Software

116 *Chapter 4* Communicating Through Good Design

The redesigned brochure leads the eye to important information.

Revised Version

- Even a casual viewer immediately knows that this brochure is directed at the restaurant market. (Figure 4-23)

- The streamlined product symbol, sanserif type, grid, and white space create a contemporar, look that calls for attention.

- TOM Software is clearly identified on this and the other brochures in the new series.

Wide rule identifies restaurant/food service industry by color (red)

TOM logo is emphasized by white space

Single dominant design element clearly identifies restaurant market

Figure 4-23

The redesigned brochure projects a strong message.

Reorganizing a Business Card

Project description—John Haywood, branch manager for a major risk management firm, wanted a business card that better organized information according to its importance to local clients.

Original Version

- The original business card lacks an organized visual hierarchy—the logo, description of services, and manager's name all carry approximately the same weight.

(From Jan Eakins, Desktop Publishing with Pagemaker 3.0, Watsonville, CA: Mitchell, 1990.)

Voice Input

Voice entry systems continue to be limited because of the way people speak. We say words in a continuous flow, not as discrete sounds. Along with the tremendous variation in human vocal sounds, speech production patterns pose a difficult problem for computer technicians. Even now, however, prototype systems allow the preparation of computer programs by voice entry of instructions. Because the number of commands is limited by the structure of the computer language, the task is more manageable than the case of users who wish to enter free text.

Voice-actuated typewriters have been developed, but they do not yet have the market appeal to be an integral part of office systems. The prototypes of the early 1990s have the capability to accept about 5000 words. Since the average adult vocabulary exceeds 20,000 words, however, you can see that there is a gap to close before this form of voice processing becomes commonplace in the office.

Voice Messaging

On the other hand, voice messaging is a very successful reality. It originated because of the need to dispatch communiqués without first being assured that a human being is standing by to accept the message. Voice messaging allows users to send and receive messages *using standard pushbutton telephones.* Someone wishing to leave a message for one or more persons can do so from an office, a conference room, or even a telephone booth. Messages are stored on computer media for retrieval when a recipient accesses the system.

Voice messaging allows a person to:

——Compose, edit, annotate, and review messages
——Distribute messages
——Receive messages

Such a system makes no distinction between memos, documents, notes, and letters. All are treated as messages.

To enter information into a voice messaging system typically requires a pushbutton telephone or a combination telephone/terminal. Since the telephone can be used for both input and receipt of messages, a messaging system can be used from locations throughout the world. This flexibility is extremely important when you are trying to get information to someone or receive notes left for you.

To use the system, you first enter commands to the processor through pushbuttons on the telephone; then you enter audio messages by speaking into the receiver. The messages are stored in digital form, but they can be retrieved and played out in either digital or analog form.

This capability represents a dramatic improvement over traditional dictation or recording of voice conversations. In addition to access from many locations through everyday equipment, the data are encoded to take very little space. Pauses in speaking can be compressed also. Furthermore, once stored, each message can be annotated with comments or qualifications and points of agreement or disagreement. The message itself can be sent virtually anywhere in the world, as long as there is a telephone—any telephone—to receive it. The contents of the message can be spoken to the recipient. As a matter of fact, a single message can be distributed to many different persons, and the system keeps track of who has picked up (heard) the message and who has not.

The flexibility of this type of information processing coupled with the personal touch it supplies ensures us that voice messaging will continue to increase in popularity. And undoubtedly, further enhancements will create new uses.

Video Conferencing

Image and voice come together through video conferencing. Computer conferencing and videotex are two developments that offer great promise.

Computer Conferencing

One of the most important outgrowths of the automated office is teleconferencing—the ability to link together people at remote locations *who have access to their own personal files as well as organization databases*. Teleconferencing, then, is more than a simulated face-to-face meeting. It extends the ideas proposed at conferences by permitting people to develop new information or to assemble and synthesize ideas in the midst of meetings. This is not possible during ordinary meetings, even in conversations between two people, because participants lack rapid and immediate access to information for which a need develops.

The Power of Computer Conferencing

Many large organizations today are decentralized. Senior executives are situated at remote locations—wherever division headquarters, major research facilities, or strategic production facilities may be found. Yet in doing product, investment, marketing, or other kinds of strategic planning, it is vital that the views, ideas, and information of these persons be heard and integrated into the decision process. How is this goal accomplished? One way is to ask all the executives to submit reports describing their ideas and communicating the data they have. Written reports, however, lose the nuances and emphases that can be built into voice communication. Thus, one might suggest telephone conversations and conference calls, which link several people into the same conversation simultaneously. However, telephones do not permit the dynamics of face-to-face conversation, which appear to play an important role in strategic communications.

Still another option is to have the managers and executives board an airplane and fly to a central location where a meeting can be held. This takes time and planning. It is not a productive use of managers' time, and important files and notes probably remain back at the various offices.

Computer conferencing overcomes these difficulties. It avoids the constraints of time and place. It also makes needed information available to all participants. For that matter, everyone can receive copies of information that is developed *while the conference is taking place*. Similarly, "what if" analyses or simulations can be run while all parties are linked up in conference.

Methods of Computer Conferencing

In a **computer conferencing** system, the computer structures, stores, and processes written communication among group members. As data or information are entered on one person's terminal, they can be displayed immediately on the other terminals. The same information is placed in computer storage for recall at any future time (it remains in storage until erased or purged).

A variety of devices are emerging for computer conferencing. There are even electronic blackboards: Write a set of data on your electronic blackboard and it is immediately duplicated on other connected blackboards or visual displays that are tied into the conference. Other devices are being developed as well.

Implementing computer conferencing creates a true real-time atmosphere. Information can be developed, transmitted to participants, and applied as part of the process that is being studied and controlled. This natural outgrowth of the related electronic mail, word processing, and data communications technologies undoubtedly will have increasing economic significance in the evolution of office information systems.

Videotex

The trend toward integrating digitized information with other office technologies has created **electronic publishing,** multimedia presentation of information over communication or broadcast facilities. **Videotex** is one form of electronic publishing that was originally developed for home use. Information aimed at marketing products assisting in travel planning is displayed over modified television sets. Electronic games and other forms of entertainment are also available. The recipient can control the presentation or order the services through a control device.

Videotex has been most successful in Europe, where it has emerged in a more pronounced business orientation. In the United Kingdom, nearly 90 percent of the subscribers are business users. The information generally available includes financial reports, travel schedules, and similar material clearly of business interest.

Other forms of electronic publishing include "want ads" for the sale of merchandise and electronic journalism. It is not yet clear how these forms will turn out.

Electronic publishing is important because it is an emerging information distribution structure that offers tremendous potential to business and government. The combination of data, text, voice, and image transmission capabilities appears well suited for many office system applications. The ability of developers to provide consumer and business convenience and cost advantages will determine its success.

Personal Support Systems

Personal support systems, a special type of office information system, assist executives, managers, and other end-users in their daily activities. They may reside on personal computers, as an application on an organization's communications network, or in its information center (information centers are discussed in Chapter 18).

What Functions Do Personal Support Systems Provide?

Personal support systems make it possible to reduce the dependence on mail, telephone systems, and written memos. They offer the potential to increase office efficiency by improving the organization of activities. As you will see, by providing the following services, they combine features of many of the applications we have discussed in this chapter.

——*Calendar management:* Personal calendars of events, meetings, travel plans, and important dates and times are stored in the system. Automatic reminders call the items to the user's attention. Schedules can be examined on a workstation screen or printed.

——*Meeting schedules:* Organization events are maintained on a master schedule. Some systems are programmed to be able to make reservations of special facilities or equipment. Individual schedules (for example, the teaching schedules of all department faculty members) may be maintained on a master calendar, facilitating the scheduling of meetings with students or the organizing of departmental meetings.

——*Electronic mail:* Letters, memos, and documents are sent and received. Mail can be read from the display screen of a workstation. Replies, in the form of annotations attached to the original memo, or as new documents, are entered through the workstation. Mail can be sent to individuals or broadcast to many others.

——*Document preparation:* Word processing features, such as writing and editing letters and reports, are included, as well as automatic proofing of documents for spelling errors or checking for grammatical problems such as awkward phrases or overused words.

——*Document retrieval:* Materials (both text and images) received through electronic mail or entered through the word processing feature can be found and grouped by date, origin, or topic.

——*Notes and comments:* Reminders, suggestions, and ideas that come to mind are stored. This feature functions as a scratchpad for end-users, who jot down thoughts before they are forgotten.

These services draw on the basic features of the office systems discussed throughout the chapter, as represented by the ability to manipulate data and text in conjunction with image processing, voice processing, and the use of data communications systems.

Figure 15.10 Main Menu from PROFS Office System

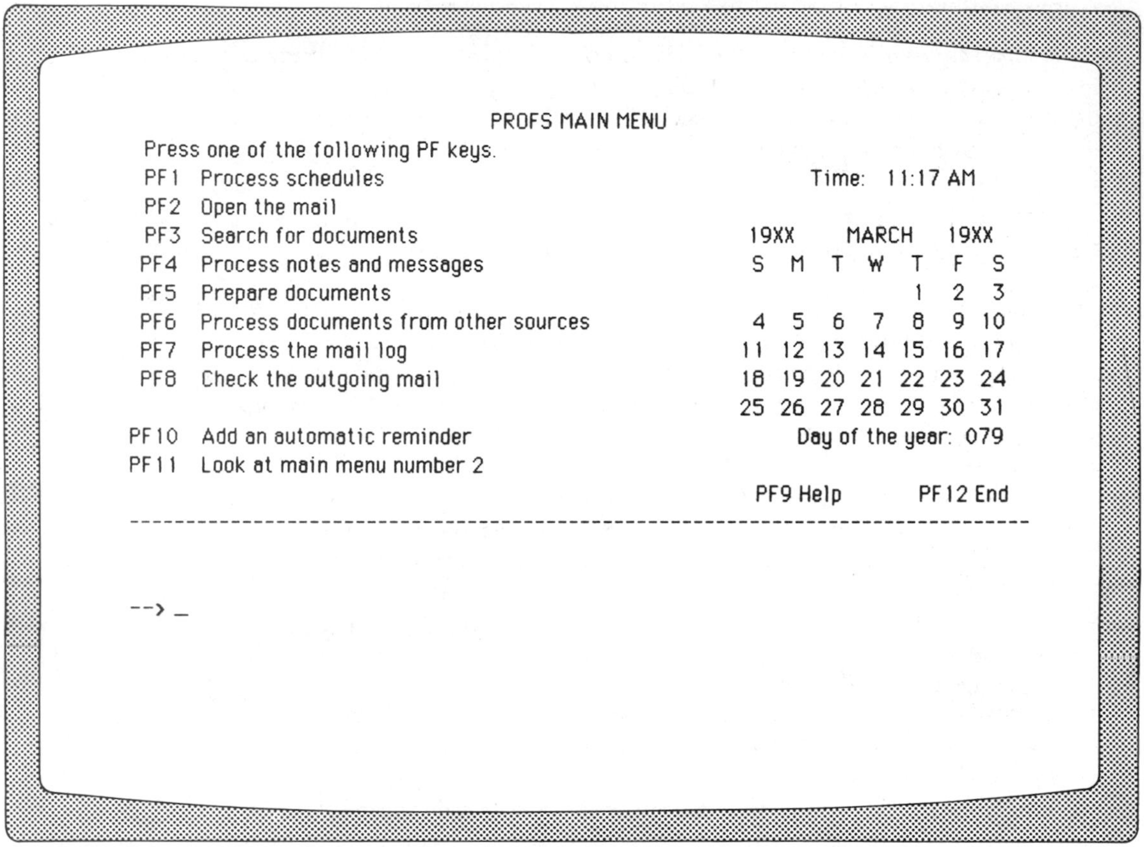

```
                        PROFS MAIN MENU
Press one of the following PF keys.
  PF1   Process schedules                              Time:   11:17 AM
  PF2   Open the mail
  PF3   Search for documents                    19XX        MARCH    19XX
  PF4   Process notes and messages              S   M   T   W   T   F   S
  PF5   Prepare documents                                       1   2   3
  PF6   Process documents from other sources    4   5   6   7   8   9  10
  PF7   Process the mail log                    11  12  13  14  15  16  17
  PF8   Check the outgoing mail                 18  19  20  21  22  23  24
                                                25  26  27  28  29  30  31
  PF10  Add an automatic reminder                    Day of the year: 079
  PF11  Look at main menu number 2
                                                PF9 Help        PF12 End
----------------------------------------------------------------------------


-->  _
```

How Are the Services Used?

Among the most widely used personal supports is IBM's PROFS, an acronym for PRofessional OFfice System (there is also a personal computer version, PROFS PC[2]). PROFS is menu driven. A list of features available to the user is presented on the display screen (Figure 15.10) along with the current month's calendar and the day and time (updated every minute). You select the option wanted from the menu. The program function key number (PF) beside each option indicates how to tell the computer to perform the function. For example, to examine an activity schedule, program function key 1 is depressed.

Figure 15.11 shows the screen display when the "schedule" function is requested. From this screen, the user can review or change a personal appointment or, if authorized, change the schedule of other users. To schedule a meeting of other users, one would enter the time and place for the meeting and the names of those who

Figure 15.11 PROFS Schedule Menu

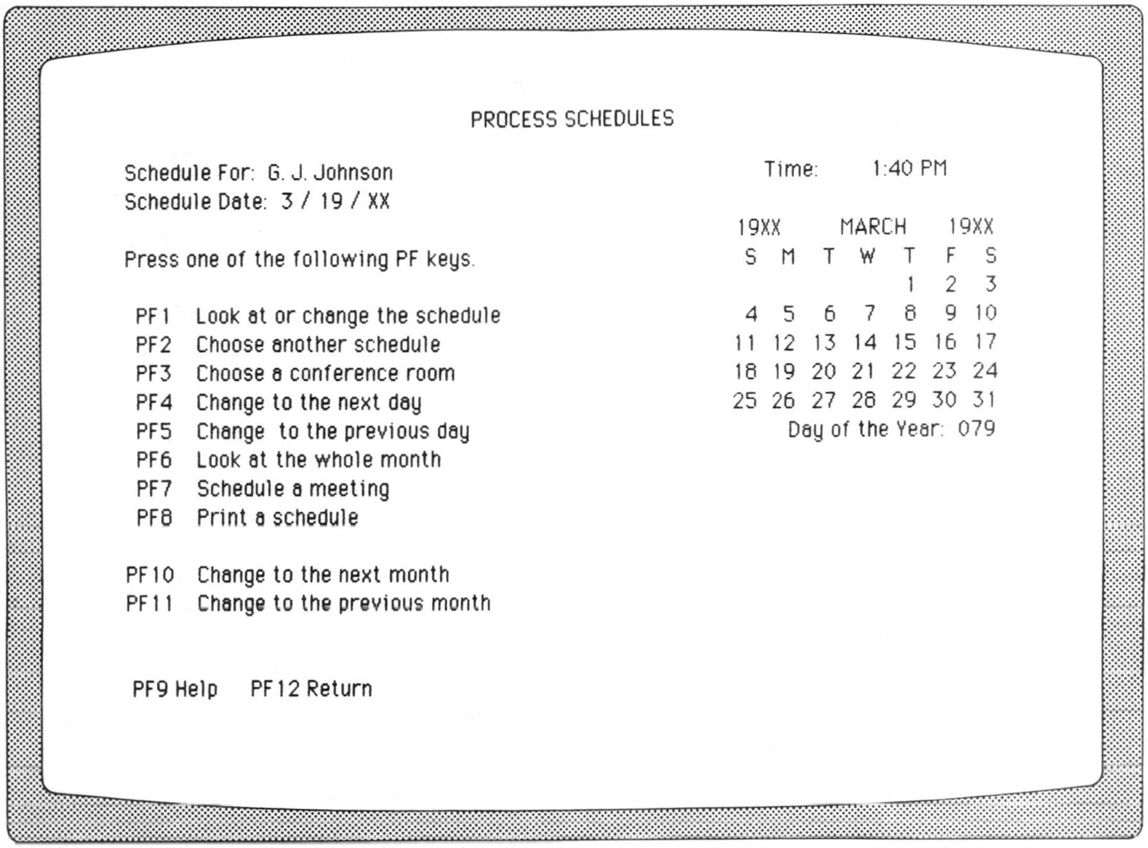

```
                              PROCESS SCHEDULES

       Schedule For:  G. J. Johnson            Time:      1:40 PM
       Schedule Date:  3 / 19 / XX
                                            19XX      MARCH     19XX
       Press one of the following PF keys.  S   M   T   W   T   F   S
                                                            1   2   3
       PF1   Look at or change the schedule   4   5   6   7   8   9  10
       PF2   Choose another schedule         11  12  13  14  15  16  17
       PF3   Choose a conference room        18  19  20  21  22  23  24
       PF4   Change to the next day          25  26  27  28  29  30  31
       PF5   Change  to the previous day          Day of the Year:  079
       PF6   Look at the whole month
       PF7   Schedule a meeting
       PF8   Print a schedule

       PF10  Change to the next month
       PF11  Change to the previous month


       PF9 Help     PF12 Return
```

should attend. PROFS will automatically review the calendars of the invitees and check the availability of the room. The system will tell the user when all the people and the room will be available at the time requested.

Arriving electronic mail may be examined by depressing function key 2. When the "open mail" function is selected from the main menu, PROFS displays a summary of each piece of mail, including the names of the sender and the original addressee (someone may have forwarded the item to you for review), the subject, the date on which any action is due, and the document number or date and time the note was sent (Figure 15.12). To view the contents of the note, simply depress the function key indicated.

These examples demonstrate the convenience of personal support systems. Other office information functions, such as document preparation and information retrieval, are also available. Image and voice processing capabilities continue to evolve.

Like the other types of applications we have discussed in this chapter, work

Figure 15.12 Message Summaries in PROFS Office System

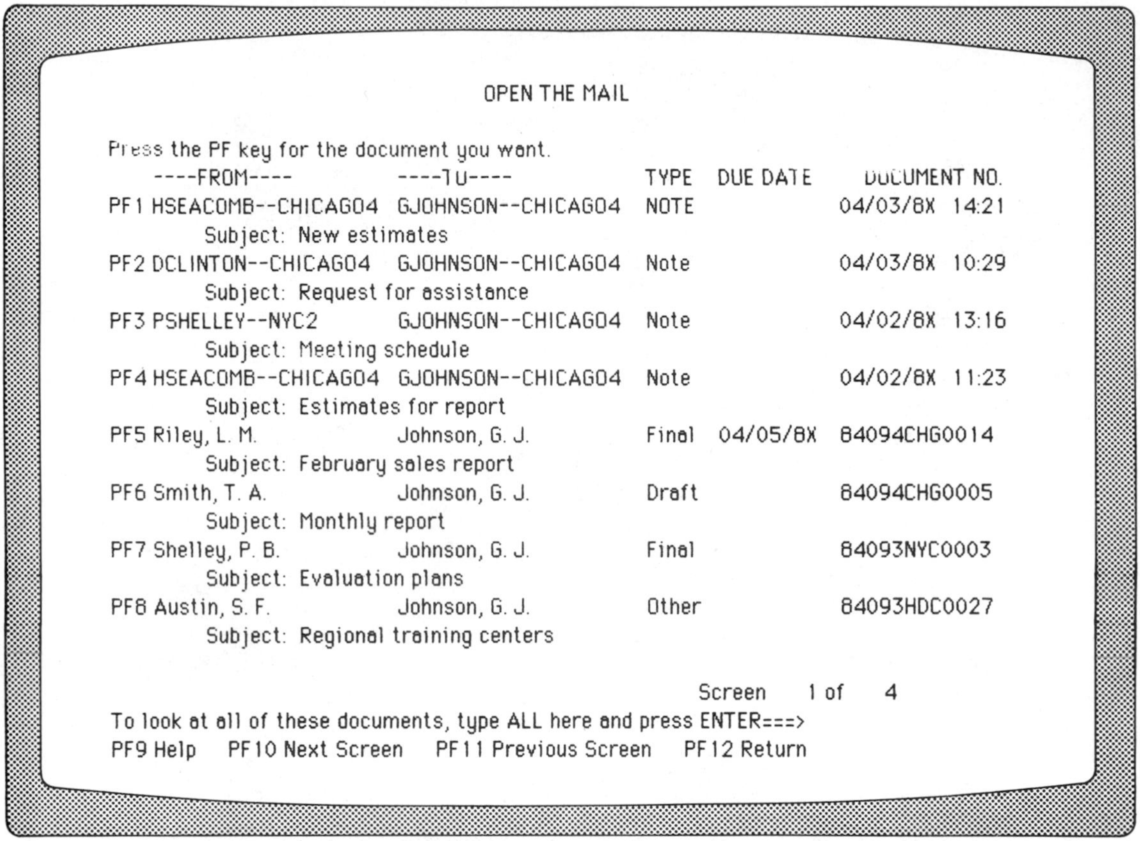

```
                          OPEN THE MAIL

Press the PF key for the document you want.
    ----FROM----          ----TO----       TYPE   DUE DATE    DOCUMENT NO.
PF1 HSEACOMB--CHICAGO4 GJOHNSON--CHICAGO4   NOTE               04/03/8X  14:21
        Subject: New estimates
PF2 DCLINTON--CHICAGO4 GJOHNSON--CHICAGO4   Note               04/03/8X  10:29
        Subject: Request for assistance
PF3 PSHELLEY--NYC2      GJOHNSON--CHICAGO4   Note               04/02/8X  13:16
        Subject: Meeting schedule
PF4 HSEACOMB--CHICAGO4 GJOHNSON--CHICAGO4   Note               04/02/8X  11:23
        Subject: Estimates for report
PF5 Riley, L. M.          Johnson, G. J.    Final  04/05/8X  84094CHG0014
        Subject: February sales report
PF6 Smith, T. A.          Johnson, G. J.    Draft             84094CHG0005
        Subject: Monthly report
PF7 Shelley, P. B.        Johnson, G. J.    Final             84093NYC0003
        Subject: Evaluation plans
PF8 Austin, S. F.         Johnson, G. J.    Other             84093HDC0027
        Subject: Regional training centers

                                        Screen    1 of    4
To look at all of these documents, type ALL here and press ENTER===>
PF9 Help   PF10 Next Screen    PF11 Previous Screen    PF12 Return
```

support systems provide users at all levels of the organization with support intended to make them more productive. They assist in formulating decisions as well as carrying out procedures and activities. The underlying computer and communications systems are the same as those used for other information systems.

Summary

As this chapter has shown, work group support systems are merging the information systems technologies for management of data, text, voice, and image processing. Each will undoubtedly play a role in the office of the future, but in many cases, the future is already here.

Electronic data interchange (EDI) spans both traditional data processing and work group support. It is characterized by computer-to-computer transfer of business data, in standard format, between organizations. Typically a public value-added network is used as the communication link spanning trading partners. Organizations are increasingly considering EDI to gain the benefits of time compression, cost savings, and improved relationships with trading partners.

Word processing involves editing, printing, and storing of text information and focuses on tailoring information to particular situations. Word processing can be done on personal computers or on systems dedicated to this function. Often, local-area networks are established to share equipment in a word processing environment or to support work group sharing of documents.

Image processing is the preparing and storing of data in graphic form, including photographs, drawings, and line art. Once digitized—that is, translated into digital form—image data can be manipulated, transmitted, or printed. Of particular importance is electronic publishing, a type of image processing that incorporates word processing capabilities. Whether performed on the desktop or through a centralized corporate publishing system, these systems have four capabilities: high-quality composition of text, makeup of pages, incorporation of graphics and images, and built-in editing capability. Publishing systems have a wide variety of uses including newsletters, catalogs, and high-quality brochures.

Electronic communications will play an increasingly important role in work group support, helping to stem the flow of paper between individuals and different locations. In some cases, images of documents are transmitted by facsimile devices. Electronic mail and computer conferencing may be used to combine voice, image, and text processing.

Work group systems will continue to evolve as advances are made in information systems technology. But the state-of-the-art systems now in place will be the basis for even more useful support systems in the future.

Key Words

Computer conferencing
Corporate publishing system
Desktop publishing system
Digitizing

Electronic data interchange (EDI)
Electronic mail
Electronic publishing
Facsimile
Image processing

Videotex
Voice processing
Word processing
Work group computing
Work group support system

Review Questions

1. What are work group support systems? How do they differ from information systems of other types?

2. What benefits do work group support systems provide to users? To organizations?

3. What is EDI? What are its characteristics?

4. Discuss the benefits of electronic data interchange to organizations.

5. What are the different types of word processing systems?

6. What are the advantages and disadvantages of using personal computers for word processing?

7. What is work group computing? What benefits does it offer to organizations?

8. What is image processing? What is the difference between document facsimile communication and image processing?

9. What is digitizing? Of what significance is digitizing to image processing?

10. What is the relationship between image processing, electronic publishing, and word processing?

11. What is desktop publishing? What does the term *desktop* refer to?

12. In what way does electronic publishing involve image processing?

13. What are the features of an electronic publishing program?

14. Distinguish between desktop publishing and corporate publishing systems.

15. Discuss the different types of voice processing. What is the impact of each on work group support systems?

16. How does the use of computer conferencing influence office and individual productivity? What features characterize computer conferencing?

17. What is videotex? Why is it important to business?

18. Discuss the functions included in personal support systems.

19. What benefits accrue to users of personal support systems? What system characteristics make these benefits possible?

Application Problems

1. The capabilities of computer conferencing systems are attracting increasing attention. Hotels, conference centers, and large corporations are establishing elaborate facilities that allow simultaneous transmission of voice and video. Although cost improvements are expected, with the result that it will be possible for more organizations to acquire facilities, the future of computer conferencing is unknown.
   a. What advantages does computer conferencing offer to busy executives who travel frequently and to organizations whose key personnel are at distant locations?
   b. What human factors may limit the success of computer conferencing?

2. Wadsworth Publishing Company is considering the development of a voice messaging system to keep in touch with its sales force around the country. The system, if developed, will allow approximately 100 field representatives to communicate with the corporate office in California from their territories around the world. Cost is not a dominant issue in the decision. Performance and improvements in communication are much more important. The vice president who will make the final decision believes that the communication improvements that can be gained through voice messaging will pay back the development costs many times over.

As an alternative, a sales representative has suggested that a new set of answering machines be acquired instead. This system is much cheaper and uses proven technology, the sales representative says. When the system answers the telephone, it plays a message prerecorded on cassette tape and allows the caller to leave a brief message. Later the messages are played back, written down on a message pad, and distributed to the proper recipients around the company. Such a system is currently in place, but the recorder, which costs approximately $250, is aging and needs replacement.

a. What are the differences between the capabilities of a voice messaging system and an answering machine?

b. Describe the advantages of the voice messaging system over the answering machine in this particular usage setting.

c. What are the disadvantages of the voice messaging system?

3. An architectural design firm is considering the implementation of a computer-based system that will allow digitizing of documents, drawings, and photographs. It currently uses a computer-assisted design (CAD) system for the preparation of mechanical, electrical, structural, spatial, and other drawings it uses in the design of buildings and landscapes of all types. The CAD system uses standard disk storage formats and coding systems. The terminals attached to the system are specially designed graphics display devices. They are necessary for the development of drawings, but not for their display. In fact, a high-quality microcomputer display can be used to show the drawings.

Frequently, architects and drafting engineers wish to digitize other drawings not in their system for combination with CAD drawings. They also want to be able to modify digitized images for use in other drawings.

Two additional important tasks are the preparation of written reports to clients and the drafting of competitive bids for contracts. The senior partners of the firm want to install an advanced word processing system for these purposes.

a. As described above, can the digitizing system be combined with a word processing system? What factors will determine the feasibility of this approach?

b. Can a personal computer be used for both purposes, assuming it has sufficient power to perform the drawing functions? Explain the reason for your answer.

4. A manager of a large department has decided to install a local-area network for word processing. As designed by the manager, the system will consist of approximately 20 workstations, a minicomputer that will function largely as a file server for storing data and information, and a laser printer. It estimated that the cost of equipping each personal computer serving as a workstation for interconnection into the LAN will be less than $1000 per station. Each workstation is expected to be actively used every day.

a. The manager is planning to interconnect the devices using the RS-232 serial port on the personal computers. Is this a good idea? What factors determine the suitability of this alternative? What other alternatives might be considered? What are the advantages of the alternatives you suggest?

b. Is a network of 20 workstations an acceptable size, considering the other equipment included in this configuration? Explain the reason for your answer.

c. What is the relation between a local-area network and an office system?

5. A major manufacturing firm that operates an extensive distributed processing network for production scheduling and inventory control has decided to invest in word processing. It has committed itself to purchase all the additional

equipment needed to handle the word processing demand for correspondence, document preparation, and information editing. Management would also like to link into existing data files from manufacturing to improve report preparation and management reporting. At least 10 areas in the firm have been identified for creation of word processing centers.

The critical question managers are addressing is whether to purchase stand-alone, dedicated word processing systems, or personal computers and printers along with suitable word processing software. The economics of hardware or software is not an issue.

    a. From the information provided, discuss the advantages and disadvantages of each alternative. Indicate any additional information you would need to reach a decision about which acquisition strategy to pursue.

    b. Are there particular reasons for the firm to insist, or not insist, on identical word processing systems in each of the 10 identified centers? Explain.

6. Which of the following tasks can be completed using word processing systems to enter, edit, and print information?

    a. Entry and storage of computer program instructions to be run on a general-purpose microcomputer

    b. Storage of names and addresses used in the production of mailing lists and individualized form letters

    c. Preparation of brief, one-time individualized memos and letters

    d. Typing of tests and examinations that are used once and discarded

    e. Entry of large-size textbook manuscripts that are updated and retyped every three years

    f. Preparation of one-page standardized letters in one of seven formats, depending on the job status of the individual receiving the letter

    g. Maintenance of personal checking account records (deposits, checks written, and adjustments)—checks are written in longhand

7. Businesses today have access to a wide variety of methods for transmitting information from one location to another. Any of these options may be attractive, depending on the nature and volume of the information to be transmitted. What factors should a manager investigate when comparing facsimile devices and document storage systems for the purpose of transmitting photographs and other documents? Explain why each factor is important and how it suggests one option or the other.

8. A manufacturing firm with a long-established and well-run set of functional-area information systems is planning to enhance its office information systems in the marketing and planning departments. Among the questions the planning team must answer is whether to integrate the office systems with the existing information systems pertinent to marketing and planning. There are no technical or economic factors to prevent such integration.

    a. Discuss the wisdom of integrating the two types of systems.

    b. What controls should be placed on the users of the office system if they are allowed to access data from the central databases and files of the marketing and planning systems?

Minicase: Voice Messaging—An In-Office Tool

"You have it all wrong," exclaimed Bo. "You think that voice mail is simply a replacement for a message recording system that captures messages left when you are out of the office. That's not it. In fact, it's the other way around. Voice messaging is for when you are *in*."

Bo works for a West Coast airline and is arguing with the freight manager about the wisdom of the new voice messaging system the airline has installed. Bo is a true aficionado of voice mail. When he comes into the office in the morning—often before any of his employees—he follows a routine: tossing his driving hat (Bo is in love with his MG) onto the hat rack, he fills a Styrofoam cup full of coffee and takes the first gulp—there's no time to mix cream or sugar. Then it's on to the telephone. After entering a code, he becomes officially "in."

Messages? Rather than barking at his assistant to bring in the messages from the night before—which he could not do anyway because no one else is in the office—Bo enters another code to retrieve messages that have been left through the voice mail system. After a brief glance he determines how to handle each one.

"Now onto the more important business," he says to himself. He presses the "*" key to send messages to the 18 managers who report to him. Speaking into the telephone he says, "We have a report that United will be adding new budget fare categories on all its West Coast flights that originate from the Midwest. Let me know what you have heard about this. If the report is true, here is our strategy. . . ." The information passed on through the phone system could easily have taken him an entire day to communicate to each manager individually. With voice mail, he has completed the task in five minutes, with full confidence that all the managers will receive the message in a timely fashion. Furthermore, they will hear it from him directly.

On to other matters. Using the telephone he cancels a golf match, schedules a haircut, gets a quotation for a new marketing brochure to send to travel agents. He leaves messages for key staff members about information he needs on American Airlines.

In every case, Bo is able to leave his message without getting put on hold and without getting tied up in distracting side conversations. He doesn't have the time today to discuss the Angels or the Forty-Niners, teams he dearly loves to watch.

He has been in the office for a half-hour now. Time for a second cup of coffee.

Bo is adamant. Voice mail is great. And it is for when you are *in*. It's for *sending* messages, not *receiving* them.

Questions

1. Is Bo right? Does the use of voice messaging appear to be more productive for sending messages than for receiving them? Are the situations described extreme ones that happen to fit Bo's style of management, or do they represent typical uses of voice mail?

2. What examples of voice messaging for managers come to mind? For administrative staff members such as administrative assistants and secretaries?

3. What future do you see for voice mail systems?

Information Systems Management Module

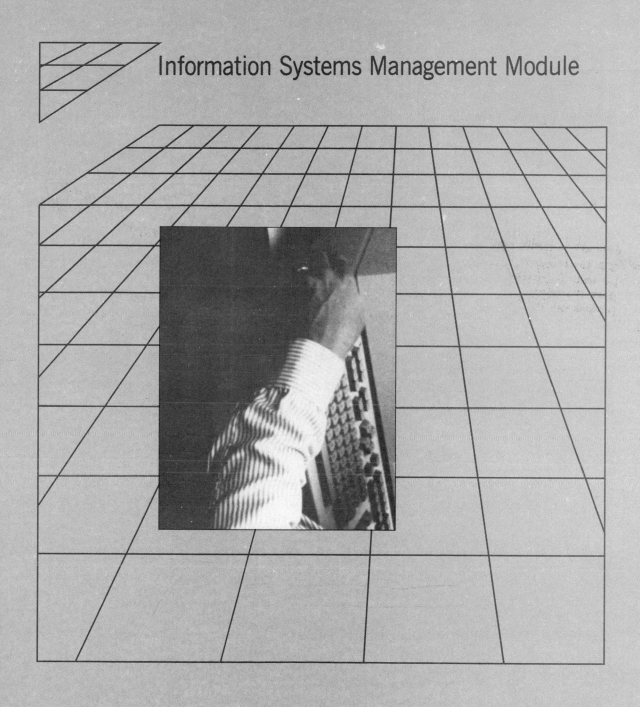

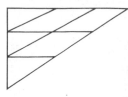

16: Information Systems Planning and Development

Key Questions

(handwritten annotations, top right:) solve a problem — capitalize on an opportunity — respond to a directive

How are information systems plans formulated?

What situations would represent good candidates for information systems development?

(handwritten annotations, left margin:) difficult to identify rqmts in advance / IS already exists, but needs modification / short time frame / integrated user input

Under what circumstances is the systems prototype methodology appropriate for developing information systems? *(handwritten:)* Table 16.4 p.671

What stages comprise the classic systems development life cycle methodology?

How should the development of information systems projects in organizations be controlled?

> *"When I use a word," Humpty Dumpty said, in a rather scornful tone, "it means just what I choose it to mean—neither more nor less."*
> *"The question is," said Alice, "whether you can make words mean so many different things."*
> *"The question is," said Humpty Dumpty, "which is to be master—that's all."*
> Lewis Carroll, *Through the Looking-Glass*

Organizations depend on successful fulfillment of two key objectives:

——Getting the right information systems

——Getting the information systems right

Unless these objectives are met, information systems will not be fully useful to the enterprise. Depending on whether the necessary information systems are planned and developed, the organization may or may not even be successful. And if the features of an information system do not suit its client population, it will not achieve its potential user objectives.

This chapter examines the planning and development of the various types of information systems discussed in preceding chapters. First we explore the characteristics of information systems planning, including its importance and the methods for formulating useful plans. Then two alternative development methods are discussed.

644

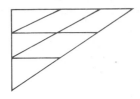

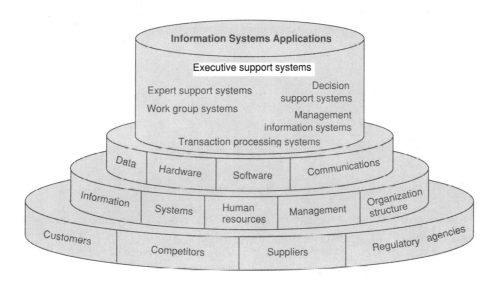

Why Should You Know About Information Systems Development?

If you are preparing for a career in the information systems field, the discussion in this chapter is fundamental to your career. But if you are going to be a user of information systems, perhaps working in marketing, manufacturing, product development, or another such function, there are other reasons why you should know about information systems planning and development. These include:

——*Users play a key role in information systems planning.* Users play a key role in the identification of information systems needs. The information systems should be developed to support the business requirements of the organization and its goals and strategies for achieving them. Articulation of these elements does not come from within the information systems group, but from throughout the organization: from executives, managers, and staff members.

——*Users need to contribute to creating systems that have the required features.* Identifying the features of each application depends on a knowledge of the business area the system will support and understanding how the application will be used once it is developed. As a user, you will interact with an information system after the analysts have finished their work and have moved on to develop other applications. Hence, you want the features to be right.

——*Users will participate in the development of information systems.* You will play an integral role in the development of some information systems, regardless of your career area. Thus, you should be familiar with the process of development.

Information systems touch virtually every profession and every career in organizations. They are a fundamental resource—a resource you will use and perhaps help develop.

Information Systems Planning

Planning for information systems (Figure 16.1) begins with the identification of needs, as we will see in this section. We will also explore the different approaches that can be used when doing planning.

Identifying Needs

Development of any type of computer-based system should be a response to need—whether at the transaction processing level or at the more complex information and support systems levels. Having the right technology and capable information systems professionals are crucial to information systems success. The third prerequisite is having the wisdom to use the information resources effectively. As mentioned earlier, managers and executives often are overloaded with irrelevant information. Yet it is not unusual to find that these same managers often receive only incidental help—or none at all—from their information systems. The fault in this case lies with both the manager and the information systems professional. Managers often cannot identify their information needs, perhaps because the situations they encounter are unique. In other instances, things are changing so quickly that it is impossible to foresee the needs that will exist by the time an appropriate system can be developed.

Information systems specialists may have difficulty understanding or correctly interpreting managers' attempts to explain their information requirements—perhaps because they are embedded in a business activity with which the analyst is not familiar.

Information systems are generally developed for one of three reasons: to solve a problem, to capitalize on an opportunity, or to respond to a directive (Table 16.1).

Solve a Problem "Problems" arise when processes or activities in an organization do not meet performance standards or expectations unless remedial action is taken. Here are four problem areas where information systems can help.

In Avoiding Errors Some situations have a high potential for error, particularly human error. Error is most common in situations where human entry of data is a driving

Figure 16.1 Information Systems Planning

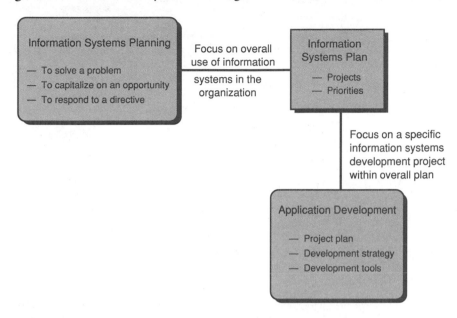

force behind the organization's operation, for example at point-of-sale locations (such as the checkout counter of a grocery store) where the number of items in a single transaction is large and many pieces of data—stock number, department number, unit price, and so on—must be collected on each.

Yet frequently these situations also involve data that are the foundation of other business functions. For instance, point-of-sale data are used for ordering merchandise, controlling price levels, and determining whether items should be discontinued. Because of the pivotal role that the capture of sales information has in cases like this, it is crucial to avoid introducing errors. This objective should guide the development of information systems applications.

In Minimizing Risk High-risk situations are those where a mistake may have significant consequences. These include situations where highly perishable or custommade products are produced, where the market is very competitive, or where a large amount of money is involved and the outcome is uncertain. For example, a decision to begin manufacturing a new line of sport automobiles means a lot of time and money will be invested before any new cars are sold: Automobile designs must be developed, equipment and materials acquired, and personnel hired.

If the success of the new line is uncertain, the risks, financial and otherwise, are very high. Therefore, it is advisable to do as much information processing as is useful before making a commitment to begin development of the new product. Failure to obtain the necessary information and to evaluate it properly could lead to disaster for the organization.

Table 16.1 Reasons for Developing Information Systems

Reasons	Description
To solve a problem	To address an area of the organization where performance does not, or will not in the future, meet expectations and where assistance can be provided by computer information systems.
	Areas of focus include:
	———where errors occur
	———where risk must be minimized
	———where there is a long time span
	———where overlapping activities must be managed
To capitalize on an opportunity	To address a business area that will benefit the organization. The development of information systems applications is an essential step in capitalizing on the opportunity.
	Reasons include:
	———taking advantage of competitive opportunities
	———increasing speed of response
	———applying new management or operations techniques
To respond to a directive	To address an order, mandate, or directive that involves information systems as an element in the response.
	Reasons include:
	———reporting on performance
	———performing required services

In Managing Over a Time Span If a particular activity spans a long time period, information systems support may help connect all the various activities that occur during the period (projects that take a long time—months and years—are often difficult to manage). In the automobile example just mentioned,

———Many months will be spent in designing all the components.
———The work will be done in different departments.
———Different locations will participate in the development process.
———Many people having diverse skills and responsibilities will be involved.

Designing, contacting suppliers for materials, acquiring equipment, hiring production people, and establishing marketing procedures with dealers will span a long period of time.

In situations like this, information systems support is useful in tracking the activities to ensure that they are actually taking place, to monitor costs, or to schedule future activities. This type of opportunity often coexists with the one that follows.

In Managing Overlapping Activities Carefully designed information systems applications can often help control activities with which several departments and functions are involved—activities that can be problematic if they do not mesh with one another as planned. When a project, or even day-to-day operations, requires the close integration of several departments, it is evident that if one falls behind or does not perform its expected function, other departments will be affected as well.

In the automobile example, if one of the design departments is not working on schedule, it may slow down all other designers, and this will surely lead to a delay in the production of the automobile. Systems support in coordinating and scheduling all efforts may help avoid problems by identifying potential difficulties far enough in advance to deal with them before any damage is done.

Capitalize on an Opportunity A second reason for planning the development of information systems is to capitalize on an opportunity. Senior executives and others are always alert to competitive opportunities. Capitalizing on such an opportunity may require speed of response or the use of new operations or management techniques, as this section discusses.

Taking Advantage of Competitive Opportunities Competitive opportunities are the chance to expand or improve business performance and competitive achievements. The chance to expand or improve business performance by offering a new service frequently arises, yet many firms cannot take advantage of the opportunity. Information systems can help in these cases.

Those airlines in the United States that have automated reservations systems have a competitive advantage over those that do not. For one thing, these airlines offer more services, such as frequent flier programs and advance seat assignments, to attract passengers. They can also provide additional services to travel agents (who are in effect a sales and marketing arm for the airlines). In some cases, airlines process reservations for the competitors, charging a fee for doing so that leads to extremely high profits.

Competitive opportunities can also arise in the form of ways to provide new products or services, change the relationship with suppliers, or even create new industries. (Chapter 20 explores the relationship between information systems and competitive strategies in detail.)

Increasing Speed The ability of computers to process data and information rapidly can benefit managers and decision makers in many ways. We have already discussed the benefits of rapid response in the management of airlines, not only to process transactions quickly but also as an aid in detecting trends and opportunities. There are similar advantages in the rapid processing and evaluation of receipts, deposits, and withdrawals from banks. In fact, in virtually any area where decisions must be made in a limited amount of time, as in stock market transactions or police activities, or where speed of response gives an essential advantage, well-developed information systems can be vital.

Operationally, if faster processing or retrieval of data saves money, increases profits, or makes performance more effective, information systems should probably play a role.

Applying New Management or Operations Techniques Business and competitive opportunities often grow out of the utilization of new management or operations techniques. In turn, the decision to pursue these methods or techniques often *creates new needs* for information systems support modules. Alternatively, if an organization has appropriate information technology in place, it may *provide the capability* to use new methods. Both forms of development are important.

New manufacturing techniques, such as just-in-time and computer-integrated manufacturing, depend on effective information systems. Just-in-time methods require close coordination between those who schedule manufacturing operations and others who provide the materials to meet the objective of having them available "just in time" to meet production needs (yet without having excessive stock on hand). Computer-integrated manufacturing means that information systems technology is an integral part of production, to the extent that some operations are turned over to computer control in their entirety.

Many other examples can be seen in business. In marketing, for instance, media selection procedures, advertising models, pricing models, market penetration techniques, and new product simulation rely on information systems technology for their implementation. In our automobile example, information processing may involve the use of techniques and models to simulate sales assuming different prices and varying marketing strategies.

In personnel management, shop floor data collection units (terminals located in different areas that employees can use to enter data about their work) are being linked to information systems to improve control processes in a way that helps the employees earn more. Control application programs can be used to monitor piecerate production and even manufacturing equipment. By having workers enter data into the collection terminal about the number of pieces of work they complete each period (hour, morning, day, or whatever) and the amount of time that a certain machine or tool is used, timelier and more accurate data about the work being done can be collected. These data can, in turn, be processed by an application program that analyzes them for management. Number of units produced, quality of production (number of defects), and level of scrap material—that is, amount of defective materials or resources damaged during production—can all be monitored. The data collected can be compared to standards to detect problems before they get out of control.

Respond to a Directive The third reason for planning the development of information systems is to respond to a directive. An order, request, or mandate originating from a legislative or management authority may require that information be provided or performance occur in a certain manner.

Reporting Performance Certain organizations in the United States, such as banks and savings institutions, must report interest earned on savings, checking, and time deposit accounts, to the U.S. Internal Revenue Service annually, using prescribed formats. Airlines must report passenger complaints as well as flight activity, delays, and so on to federal agencies. You can probably think of many other instances where directives mandate the reporting of such information.

Directives may mean that new information must be captured and reported, hence requiring the development of systems to support the activity. Or they may mean modification to existing systems, either because the directives require new reporting entirely or a change in previous reporting requirements.

Performing Services Directives can also require organizations to perform services in a way that requires computer processing. Frequently certain groups of individuals— for example, handicapped or senior citizens—are afforded special accommodations, provided they are on record as meriting such services.

Similarly, the U.S. Postal Service can direct firms to use different codes on the mail they send. Recall that it issued a directive for firms to accommodate the change from a five- to a nine-digit postal code some time ago. Firms doing business in Canada, Great Britain, and other international locations had to respond to directives requiring the use of new postal codes as well.

The planning for these developments in information systems may lead to new applications or modifications of existing ones. And they may be incorporated into advance planning processes or they may have to occur very quickly.

These guidelines identify areas where information systems are often beneficial and form the basis for planning. Table 16.2 shows the reasons firms undertake projects within the planning guidelines outlined in this section. As the table suggests, projects are generally initiated for one or more of five reasons (the Five C's):

——To increase business capability
——To improve control
——To enhance communication
——To manage cost
——To gain a competitive advantage

Planning for Systems Development

Being aware of areas for which computer-based support needs to be developed is essential to systems development, but identification is not enough. There must be a systems plan to guide all activities. Trying to develop information systems applications without a systems plan is like trying to build a house without a blueprint; at best, both would end up as helter-skelter struggles.

Planning for the development of information systems is much like strategic planning in management. Objectives, priorities, and authorization for information systems projects must be formalized. The systems development plan should identify specific projects slated for the future, priorities for each project and for resources, general procedures, and constraints for each application area. The plan must be specific enough so that anyone examining it can understand each application and

Table 16.2 Five C's: Reasons for Initiating Information Systems Projects

Reason	Explanation
Capability	
Greater Processing Speed	Using the computer's inherent ability to calculate, sort, and retrieve data and information when greater speed than that of people doing the same tasks is desired.
Increased Volume	Providing the capacity to process a greater amount of activity, perhaps to take advantage of new business opportunities. Often a result of growth that causes business to exceed the capacities and procedures underlying the achievements to date.
Faster Information Retrieval	Locating and retrieving information from storage. Conducting complex searches.
Control	
Greater Accuracy and Improved Consistency	Carrying out computing steps, including arithmetic, correctly and in the same way each time.
Better Security	Safeguarding sensitive and important data in a form that is accessible only to authorized personnel.
Communication	
Enhanced Communication	Speeding the flow of information and messages between remote locations as well as within offices. Includes the transmission of documents within offices.
Integration of Business Areas	Coordinating business activities taking place in separate areas of an organization, through capture and distribution of information.
Cost	
Cost Monitoring	Tracking the cost of labor, goods, and facilities to determine how actual costs compare with expectations.
Cost Reduction	Using computing capability to process data at a lower cost than possible with other methods, while maintaining accuracy and performance levels.
Competitive Advantage	
Lock In Customers	Changing the relationship with and services provided to customers in such a way that they will not choose to change suppliers.
Lock Out Competitors	Reducing the likelihood that competitors will be able to enter the same market because of the way the organization uses information systems.
Improve Arrangements with Suppliers	Changing the pricing, service, or delivery arrangements, or relationship between suppliers and the organization to benefit the firm.
New Product Development	Introducing new products with characteristics that use or are influenced by information technology.

Source: James A. Senn, *Analysis and Design of Information Systems* (New York: McGraw-Hill, 1989), p. 53.

know where it stands in the order of development. However, the plan should also be flexible so that priorities can be adjusted if necessary.

To avoid the creation of nonintegrated and duplicate applications, the development plan should evaluate points of contact (interface) between departments and divisions within a firm. It should focus on business functions, not business units per se, considering both present and potential applications. This requires a uniform approach to integrating individual efforts into a larger, more cohesive framework. The systems development plan should therefore be based on the objectives of:

1. Avoiding the development of systems that will duplicate others already in use in the organization
2. Providing for integration of current systems or current and proposed applications so that the resources are used wisely and efficiently
3. Ensuring that systems are developed according to an assessment of their development and operating costs and their value in achieving the specified objectives
4. Ensuring that all systems are tied to the overall master plan (unless there is a good reason for an exception)
5. Providing for continued development of the information system while ensuring that data and other resources can be shared
6. Ensuring that users want and/or need all the systems and that the systems will be used when implemented

These objectives should guide the formulation of a working **master development plan,** a formal document that describes in detail what the project is. The working master plan should clearly give:

1. The name of the project
2. The purpose of the project (project objectives)
3. A short description of the project and its users and an indication of whether it is a new application or a modification of one currently existing
4. A brief statement of the project priority
5. A short statement on the time and financial resources the project requires
6. A description of how a particular project will be developed, including use of existing equipment and personnel and any additional resources required

As work on the various projects is undertaken, these details will be expanded to include more specific data on estimated starting and completion dates, project costs, and a breakdown of major events in the systems development process.

Generic Views of Information Systems Planning

Two generic views of information systems planning are often discussed. Both are useful and will be evident in the planning methods considered in the next section. Each has its own proponents. The most common names for these approaches are "top-down" and "bottom-up" (Table 16.3).

Table 16.3 Commonly Accepted Approaches to Systems Development

Approach	Assumptions	Method
Top-down approach	There is a high degree of top-management involvement in the planning process; focus is on organization goals, objectives, and strategies.	Focus first on main goals and objectives of the organization in regard to present and future operating and planning strategies. Next, identify and examine decision areas to determine what information is needed, its form, and so on. From these examinations, design specifications can be developed.
Bottom-up approach	The basic elements in a system are the application modules and the relevant supporting data.	Identify managers' information needs and develop information systems modules to meet the needs. As the system evolves, the modules are linked together through development of a common database. Models are developed to assist with higher-level decision making. This approach is more responsive to information needs.

Top-Down Approach The **top-down approach** assumes a high degree of top-management involvement in the planning process and focuses on organization goals and strategies. The logic here is that above all, information systems need to be responsible to and supportive of an organization's basic goals. These goals should be the driving force behind the development of all information systems.

Using the top-down approach, we begin by analyzing organization objectives and goals and end by specifying application programs and modules that need to be developed to support those goals. The stages of the top-down approach outlined in the following paragraphs will illustrate how this view of planning is used.

First we must analyze the objectives and goals of the organization to determine where it is going and what management wants to accomplish. This analysis may be stated in terms of profits, growth, expansion of product lines or services, diversification, increased market share, and so on.

We also need to know what resources are available to the firm, including capital and equipment that may be acquired and raw materials that can be procured from the environment (that is, from suppliers or other manufacturers). Furthermore, information is needed on any constraints placed on the organization that affect its objectives and operation. Constraints may be due to legislative regulation, competition, public opinion, or inability to acquire resources. All of these factors shape the enterprise and, in turn, influence information systems planning.

The organization's objectives and goals influence or determine functions and activities throughout the enterprise. Therefore, we need to identify the functions (for example, marketing, production, research and development) and explain how they support the entire organization. Identifying these functions makes it possible to move to the next step in the planning process, which focuses on the major activities, decisions, and functions of managers in the various parts of the enterprise. In planning for systems, it is necessary for the systems staff to know what decisions are currently made by managers, as well as what decisions *need* to be made and when they should be made.

With activities and decisions identified, we must now identify models that guide managers and determine the information requirements for activities and decisions. The analysis should have provided insight into *what* information is needed, *when* it is needed, and *what form* is most useful. These factors provide many of the design specifications for information systems applications.

We therefore combine knowledge about decision situations and support of decisions to detail specific information processing programs (and at a lower level of detail, perhaps even modules within programs). At a still lower level of detail, databases and files for applications are identified. Some of the application programs may be executive and management oriented and others focus on transaction processing. (Remember that transaction processing systems provide many pieces of data on which organization decisions are based.)

Bottom-Up Approach   The **bottom-up approach** to systems planning begins by identifying basic transaction and information processing programs. Systems development starts from the fundamental or lifestream systems of the organization. Lifestream systems include payroll, order entry, inventory control, purchasing, and personnel processing systems that support day-to-day business activities (see Chapters 10 and 11). These systems are the easiest to identify, understand, develop, and justify (for cost savings, processing volume, and operating support reasons). As these systems are identified, the data requirements for each one can also be specified.

Once the basic transaction and information processing systems are known, planning moves to the next higher level, where integration of the applications becomes a concern. Data requirements across applications are examined and the files and records combined in order to be usable for several applications. The data management objectives of sharability and evolvability of the database (and the information system), as discussed in Chapter 8, guide this activity.

Program, systems, and data integration is followed by the formulation of models to support executive and upper-management activities. Models are used when different factors must be examined together to understand the details of a situation, to formulate alternative strategies and options, and to evaluate the advantages of each strategy.

The bottom-up approach takes us to higher and higher levels of decision making in the organization. As we approach the strategic planning level, we need to integrate more and more information systems efforts, as well as dealing with both internal and external sources of data.

Throughout the planning process, priorities are assigned to individual applications. Neither the plan nor the priorities are permanent, however. New development (for example, change in organization product strategies or perfection of new technology) may lead to a revision of the information systems plan.

Combinations The top-down approach is very useful for developing an overall plan for systems development. However, many people feel that it is not as effective in identifying specific application modules as the bottom-up approach. Consequently, we often find the two approaches combined. In these instances, the top-down method is used to generate the general perspective on how the system will evolve to support organization goals and objectives. Thus, all developments will follow in the directions established by top-level management.

A bottom-up approach is followed implementing the information systems plan. Existing lifestream systems are reassessed to determine whether they meet business needs or require enhancement. Where needed information systems do not exist, they are created.

As each step is taken, the information systems master plan is reexamined and the next stage spelled out in greater detail. In this way the information systems of an organization evolve on the basis of the experience of users, but within the overall framework and guidelines of the original master plan.

Information Systems Planning Methods

Organizations have their own ways of doing information systems planning. Some are custom-made. Others are suggested by consultants. In this section we examine four planning methods. Each has features that distinguish it from the others. As you examine them, notice the role of general managers and non–information systems personnel in the process.

The methods are the critical success factor, Business Systems Planning, and computer architecture strategic planning methods. In addition, a new method called linkage analysis will be examined.

Critical Success Factors

The **critical success factor** method focuses on the most important information needs of the organization. It does this by identifying the key factors that are essential to the survival of the organization.

Examples of Critical Success Factors Critical success factors originate from four main sources:

——*The industry in which the firm competes:* characteristics that are important throughout a particular industry and to which successful participants pay a great deal of attention

——*Competitive strategy and the historical position of the firm:* whether the firm is a dominant or minor force among competitors; the niche it occupies or the basis of its competitive strategy (such as pursuing cost containment, product pricing, or customer service advantages)

——*Environmental factors:* influences outside the firm that affect performance, such as energy cost and availability, government regulations, and changing consumer demands

———*Temporal factors:* issues of importance for a particular period which when addressed will no longer determine success or failure (for example, modernization of the physical plant or replacement of the executive management team)

Typical examples of critical success factors suggested by the MIT research team include:

Automotive Industry	Supermarket Industry	Government Hospital
Styling	Product mix	Regional integration of health care with hospitals
Quality dealer system	Inventory management	
Cost control	Sales promotion	Efficient use of scarce medical resources
Meeting energy standards	Product price	Improved cost accounting

These factors are likely to change over time and as management priorities evolve. Thus, the systems analyst must take appropriate steps to identify management's critical success factors as part of determining the requirements for an information system.

How to Identify Critical Success Factors The first step is to discuss with each manager, using interviews, the individual's goals and objectives as they relate to the organization's long- and short-term strategies:

———What role does the individual perform? What is his or her mission?

———What goals and objectives guide the manager?

———What aspects of the organization are critical concerns for the manager?

———In what areas would failure hurt the organization the most?

———What would be the most important to know about if the manager has been away or out of reach for a period of time?

The analyst will want to ensure that all critical success factors are discussed, not just those for which there are likely to be hard data. "Soft" information, such as consumer opinion about the company or relationship with competitor and regulatory agencies, may be very revealing, although such material is more difficult to collect and manage in an information system.

Next, critical success factors are prioritized. The greatest impact will result if attention is focused on three to seven factors. We want to give priority to those most closely related to organization success.

How will good or poor performance concerning a critical success factor be measured and reported? Managers and systems analysts jointly identify ways of telling how well, or how badly, things are going. This activity typically occurs during a second or third session, but rarely happens during the initial interview.

The critical success factors become the basis for developing reporting systems. They are also an invaluable tool for determining the content of corporate databases. In many instances, details that would be omitted from a formal system—such as data from customer or market surveys or assumptions built into corporate plans—will now be included in the database. The critical success factor method will often involve a mix of many different types of formal and informal data.

Another important benefit of the critical success factor method is the process

Stages of Growth

Do you wonder how some organizations have put together effective information systems, how they have determined which applications will best pay for themselves, and whether management has been responsible for all the successes of a firm in the information systems area? Organizations do not acquire sophisticated information systems applications overnight. They evolve into them, that is, they move through several different stages of learning about information systems and about the organization itself. Each stage appears to call for applications of different kinds. Similarly, increasing use of technology is in evidence at each stage.

The "stages of growth" framework has been widely discussed and applied by researchers and practitioners in information systems as well as by organization managers.* Knowing about these stages assists managers responsible for overseeing the development of their information systems to steer a course toward successful and cost-effective applications that are in the best interests of the enterprise.

Signs of Evolving Applications   The field of information systems is not old. Some organizations have several decades of experience in it, but many have only a few years. And still more firms, particularly small and middle-size organizations, have acquired computer equipment quite recently. However, it seems that all move through distinct stages—call them "growing pains" if you wish. These stages differ according to the kinds of application being developed, the control over the information systems function, and the degree of planning involved for future applications. When children are young, they stumble and fall. As they grow, they gain control of where they are headed. And as they reach maturity, we hope that each has a sound plan in mind for a career. Information systems investments often follow a similar growth curve.

Researchers have studied different organizations and their experiences when computers are first acquired, and they have studied the progression from novice to sophisticate. By looking at information systems budgets over time, the growth in applications, and growth in specialization of systems personnel, distinct stages appear evident. Several definite shifts (giving distinct stages—see Figure A) are noticed not only in expenditures, but also in management's involvement in planning and control of this organization resource. (There may be more stages, but we are not yet sure because of the field's relative newness.)

Why should firms care about stages of growth information systems? For one thing, seeing other's mistakes can show managers what to watch out for, but more importantly, the stages of growth appear to relate to organizations of many different types. Therefore, knowing what will most likely happen to *your* organization means that smooth transitions from stage to stage can be planned.

Startup   All firms go through this initiation stage. The first computer acquisition is a major step forward for an organization, but only if it is properly managed. A computer system usually is brought in on the basis of cost savings, especially for general and administrative projects and activities. At this stage, management rarely sees the long-term impact of computers for planning and control purposes.

*Richard L. Nolan, "Thoughts About the Fifth Stage," *Data Base 7*, no. 2 (1975), 4–10. C.F. Gibson and R. L. Nolan, "Managing the Four Stages of EDP Growth," *Harvard Business Review 52*, no. 1 (1974), 6–18.

Stages of Growth (continued)

Figure A Stages of Growth in Information Systems

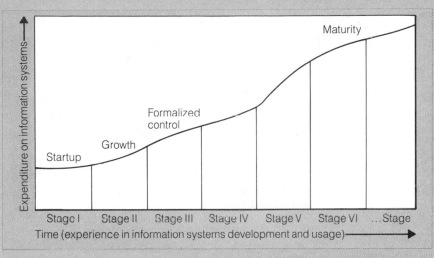

During startup an important issue to settle is the location of the computer. Usually it ends up in the accounting or controller's department, since it is often these applications that first recognize a need for computer data processing. At any rate, the computer typically is installed in the department where it is first applied. (This may not be the best location for it later.)

Initiation of computing systems brings with it many experiences, including fear. Some employees fear job loss. Others are concerned about changes in their jobs or their working habits. Managers at this stage are wise to deal with these concerns head-on. Large layoffs of people do not typically happen, although some displacement may occur. Some jobs and responsibilities will change, and management is wise not to hide this from employees. Often, however, the activities that change the most are the tasks that were the least liked when done manually.

Growth of Information Systems Initial computers frequently are larger than necessary for the jobs for which they were acquired. However, the excess capacity may be used quickly. There is unplanned growth in computing and contagious enthusiasm for the system. Control of the facility is decentralized.

Often, the economic value of new projects is overlooked. The cost justification that brought the computer through the door in the first place is not given enough attention. People become fascinated with the operation of the equipment and with the new techniques that can be applied by using it. And, it is a status symbol as well.

Considerable investment is made in new equipment when firms are in this stage. The excess capacity soon becomes a limited capacity as applications are added. But the enthusiasm at this stage becomes justification for investing in new hardware (and software). Unfortunately, there is a lack of clear management guidelines for setting project priorities or for acquiring the resources needed to support the projects.

Stages of Growth (continued)

Formalizing Control As budgets for information systems rise, the move to the third stage begins. At this stage, management sees the budget and wants to get control of it. Some firms tend to set guidelines that are too stringent—an overreaction to the limited control apparent in the preceding stage. It is hoped, however, that managers will simply recognize the growing pains for what they are and not gain control at the cost of losing innovative projects that could be of significant value to the organization in the future.

Some centralization of resources and equipment, particularly commonly used ones, occurs at this stage. In addition, we begin to see more top-management direction and user involvement in planning for information systems. Some systems analysts may move out into the user departments, providing an even closer link between person and machine.

At this stage, the focus turns from *products* to *processes* that help management and users.

Realignment and Integration of Processes Users at this stage are fairly sophisticated. Low-level information and data processing functions are no longer under the control of information systems personnel but are turned over to users. Steering committees consisting of users, top-management representatives, and systems specialists are formed to plan for application development. Both innovation in projects and stability in operations and development are now possible. The information system budget is now more in line with organization growth as well.

Particular attention is paid to underlying data driving applications. Investment may be made in database management during this stage. Sharing of information resources also begins.

Data Resource Function By now organization managers are seasoned in information systems and computing. They are experienced, learned, and educated, both in theory and practice. A

itself, since it involves senior managers directly in the information systems planning process. They provide their insight into the information important for their management activities and for the organization as a whole.

An important element in the success of this methodology is interviewer skill. One MIT team enjoys repeated success with the method, but they are experts in using it. Whether the same success can be transferred to other teams is an ongoing concern. Where it can occur, the method is very advantageous in the planning of information systems.

Business Systems Planning (BSP)

Business systems planning (BSP) has been among the most widely used methods for information systems planning. Various estimates indicate that from 20 to 30

Stages of Growth (continued)

more integrated view of information systems is evident among employees, particularly managers. They manage data as a resource, an important change from looking at computing as just another task within the enterprise. Because people understand that information systems and the databases that drive them contribute significantly to the future successes of the enterprise, systems and applications are treated in the same sense as any investment in land, capital, equipment, or personnel—as a valuable asset.

Technology may be a driving force at this stage too. Database management continues to increase in importance. Mini- and microcomputers, both for distributed networks and decision support purposes, receive increased attention. Word processing extends beyond mere secretarial functions into the information systems function. End-user computing takes on increased importance in the enterprise.

Maturity Organizations reaching more advanced stages are making effective use of their investments. However, as technological advances are made and management develops information systems even further, still other stages may emerge. But at this level computing is clearly not viewed as a necessary evil. Nor are applications developed without careful planning—above all, they are integrated into the growth and success of the enterprise. Information systems plans and corporate strategies become intertwined to gain competitive advantage.

Functional Units and Growth Stages It would be incorrect to think that the stages of growth apply only to the entire organization. They also describe the learning curves of individual departments or divisions *within* the organization. Any organization may have units at different stages while overall it is at still another level of sophistication.

Experiences within functional units can and should be shared, to enhance the success of each department individually and the organization collectively.

percent of all large organizations use or have applied BSP in formulating information systems plans. This planning method was originally developed by IBM for its internal use. However, customers quickly saw the benefits of the method. IBM thus released it as a generalized planning methodology, preparing manuals and training courses to assist firms in its proper use.

Data Emphasis The underlying theme of BSP is that data are a corporate resource. It requires the investment of time and financial resources, and a commitment of management and staff, to capture, store, and preserve the data. (Most firms have never estimated the value of their investment in data. Hence top-level executives would be astounded if they ever calculated the value, because it would range in the hundreds of millions.) Because of its value, and the limitations a corporation would face without it, the emphasis on data is easy to justify.

The <u>purpose of BSP is to identify the data necessary to run an organization</u> (whether the corporation as a whole or a large business unit or division within the firm). A top-down approach is used to identify and define the information requirements—a necessary approach for discovery of a stable architecture that will support the business processes of the firm. Data are gathered primarily through interviews and observation.

Steps Figure 16.2 depicts the 13 steps followed in conducting a BSP study. The commitment of top management is essential because of the effort that must be put forth to conduct a large-scale study. In addition, a top-level executive serves as team leader. The leader in turn selects other executives and managers to participate. (A BSP study is *not* conducted by a team of systems analysts.)

Business processes such as product development, purchasing, marketing, and manufacturing are the main activities that drive the corporation. All processes are identified independently of the organization unit responsible for carrying them out. In many cases, the processes will span organizational units. During the study, those processes critical to the success of the organization will be identified and described.

The BSP team groups all the data in the companies into data classes—that is, categories that describe entities of interest: customers, vendors, production orders, and so on. The BSP manual used in conducting the study suggests that having from 30 to 60 data classes is typical.

The architecture is the matrix of data classes and processes that are used in the organization (Figure 16.3). This tool is convenient for documenting the flow of data from the point of creation (designated in the matrix by a *C*) to its usage (designated by a *U*).

Priorities for future applications are developed using the formal descriptions as well as the information gained through the interviews. Three types of outcomes are produced:

——An information architecture that defines the systems and subsystems for information handling in the organization
——Recommendations for the management and control of data
——Priorities for the development of future information systems applications

Systems plans for each application describe costs, development times, and anticipated benefits.

Limitations Three important limitations influence BSP's value. First, the method focuses on existing details about an organization and its systems. Little guidance is given for developing improved systems. Hence, BSP describes what *is*, not what is important.

BSP can be very effective in identifying current information systems requirements. It uses the information framework as the basis for the planning of future information systems applications. However, unless those performing the study explicitly consider long-range, strategic requirements, they will not be part of the study results.

Figure 16.2 Steps in BSP Study

Control Point	Participants	Activities
①	Study team	Review study to date, documentation standards, and team understanding of results. Confirm resource allocations for the next stage.
②	Executive sponsor	Results to date. Update the study plan. Review the executive interview objectives.
③	Executive sponsor	Report on both qualitative and quantitative results of the executive interviews. Present and validate the assessment of business problems and benefits. Update the study plan.
④	Study team	Team agreement on all major issues. Review all supporting documentation to be completed. Confirm resource allocation. Update the study plan.
⑤	Executive sponsor	Review all major findings and recommendations. Demonstrate an understanding of the business and its requirements. Gain executive sponsor's agreement that the team is qualified to present the recommendations.

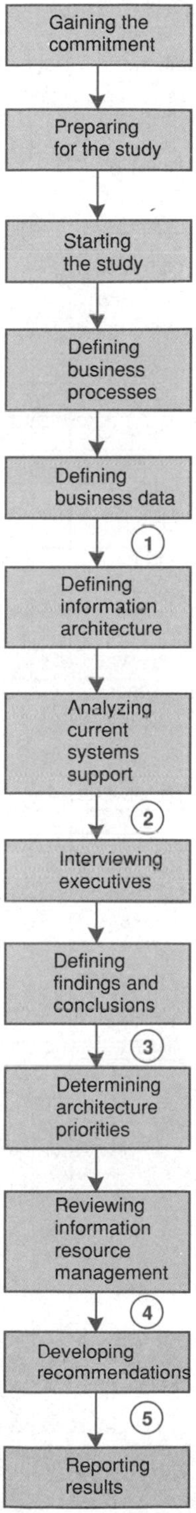

Flowchart:

Gaining the commitment → Preparing for the study → Starting the study → Defining business processes → Defining business data → ① → Defining information architecture → Analyzing current systems support → ② → Interviewing executives → Defining findings and conclusions → ③ → Determining architecture priorities → Reviewing information resource management → ④ → Developing recommendations → ⑤ → Reporting results

Figure 16.3 Process/Data Class Matrix for BSP (IBM Corporation)

Legend — Data Classes (columns): 1 Objectives · 2 Policies & Procedures · 3 Organization Unit Desc · 4 Product Forecasts · 5 Bldg & Real Estate Reqt · 6 Equipment Requirements · 7 Organization Unit Budget · 8 G/L Accounts Desc & Budget · 9 Long-Term Debt · 10 Employee Requirements · 11 Legal Requirements · 12 Competitor · 13 Marketplace · 14 Product Description · 15 Raw Material Description · 16 Vendor Description · 17 Buy Order · 18 Product Warehouse Inventory · 19 Shipment · 20 Promotion · 21 Customer Description · 22 Customer Order · 23 Seasonal Production Plan · 24 Supplier Description · 25 Purchase Order · 26 Raw Material Inventory · 27 Production Order · 28 Equipment Description · 29 Bldg & Real Estate Desc · 30 Equipment Status · 31 Accounts Receivable · 32 Product Profitability · 33 G/L Accounts Status · 34 Accounts Payable · 35 Employee Description · 36 Employee Status

(C = Create, U = Use)

Process \ Data Class	1	2	3	4	5	6	7	8	9	10	11	12	13	14	15	16	17	18	19	20	21	22	23	24	25	26	27	28	29	30	31	32	33	34	35	36
Establish Business Direction	C	C	C								U	U	U																			U	U			
Forecast Product Requirements	U			C																																
Determine Facility & Eqt Reqts	U		U		C	C																						U	U	U						
Determine & Control Fin Reqts	U		U				C	C	C																								U			U
Determine Personnel Reqts		U	U							C																									U	U
Comply with Legal Reqts										C	C			U																						
Analyze Marketplace	U											C	C	U																						
Design Product	U										U	U		C	C													U								
Buy Finished Goods														U		C	C	U																U		
Control Product Inventory				U										U			U	C	U																	
Ship Product														U				U	C			U									U					
Advertise & Promote Product													U	U						C																
Market Product (Wholesale)												U	U	U						U	C	U											U			
Enter & Cntrl Customer Order														U				U	U	U	U	C									U					
Plan Seasonal Production				U																			C													
Purchase Raw Materials															U									C	C	U								U		
Control Raw Material Inventory															U									U	U	C	U	U								
Schedule & Control Production																							U			U	C	C	C	U						
Acquire & Dispose Fac & Eqt					U	U																						C	C	C						
Maintain Equipment																												U	U	C						
Manage Facilities																					U								U	U						
Manage Cash Receipts																															C		U			
Determine Product Profitability														U				U	U						U	U	U					C	U			
Manage Accounts								U	U																						U	U	C	C		
Manage Cash Disbursements									U																								U	C		U
Hire & Terminate Personnel		U	U							U	U																								C	U
Manage Personnel		U	U																																C	C

BSP does provide an automatic method for incorporating long-range needs into the results.

The time needed to perform the study is a significant drawback. Because of the scope of the study and the methods used, a sizable number of managers must be interviewed by the analysts in order to develop a broad and comprehensive under-standing of the organization's requirements. The matrices prepared during the study help in the capture of details, but the task of analysis and synthesis of the data remains challenging.

Computer Architecture Strategic Plan

Nolan, Norton, & Co., a well-known U.S. information systems consulting firm, has developed an approach to information systems planning that links current capabilities with future needs. The computer architecture strategic plan recognizes that a port-folio of applications is built on a solid technical foundation. A model is used to link strategic visions and current resources in a manner that supports planning and development.

Application Portfolios Nolan, Norton, and Co. views information systems as consist-ing of four portfolios of applications. **Application portfolios** describe the allocation of information systems resources for the different classes of applications (Figure 16.4):

——*Institutional applications:* operating-level applications designed to facilitate the processing of applications
     Examples: payroll, accounting, personnel, and production scheduling systems
——*Professional support systems:* specialized applications such as for supporting man-agement decision making and engineering designs
     Examples: Lotus 1-2-3, electronic mail, text processing, and expert systems
——*Physical automation:* systems that replace physical activity with information technology
     Examples: robotics, CAD/CAM, and automated warehouse systems
——*Systems outside the organization:* interorganizational systems that link the firm with outside firms, such as those of customers and suppliers
     Examples: automated teller machines, home banking systems, and order entry systems installed on customer premises

Each area consists of a portfolio of applications. Depending on the structure in a particular organization, the applications may be interrelated or may be separate.

Application Foundations Firms must develop the technical foundation or **infrastruc-ture** to support the applications. Information systems are created on top of the infrastructure, as illustrated in Figure 16.4. The term *infrastructure* refers to the organization's investment in information technology that is shared by multiple portfolios.

Figure 16.4 Application Portfolios and Computer Architecture Strategic Plan
(© Copyright 1987 by Nolan, Norton & Co. All Rights Reserved.)

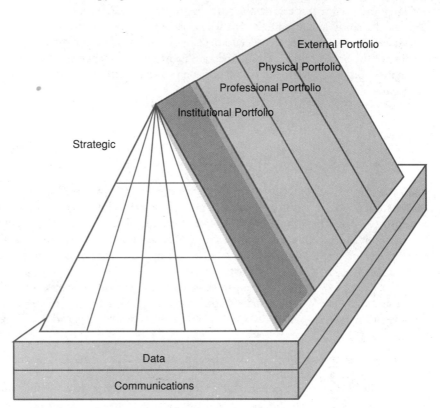

The **data architecture** describes the base of data that drives the firm. Unless this portion of the infrastructure is reliable, no applications that draw on it will be useful. Unreliable data means unreliable information systems. The architectural structure for the data will determine the accessibility of the data (data architecture is discussed in detail in Chapter 8).

The **network architecture** is the foundation of communications facilities. Data and voice transmission capabilities determine what the organization can send between locations. If the network infrastructure does not link strategic locations, it will impede the firm's competitive strategy.

Computer Architecture Information systems planning and control is architecture oriented. Nolan, Norton, & Co. call information systems architecture *computer architecture*. Figure 16.5 summarizes the elements of computer architecture as seen by this company.

Figure 16.5 Elements in Architecture (© Copyright 1987 by Nolan, Norton & Co. All Rights Reserved.)

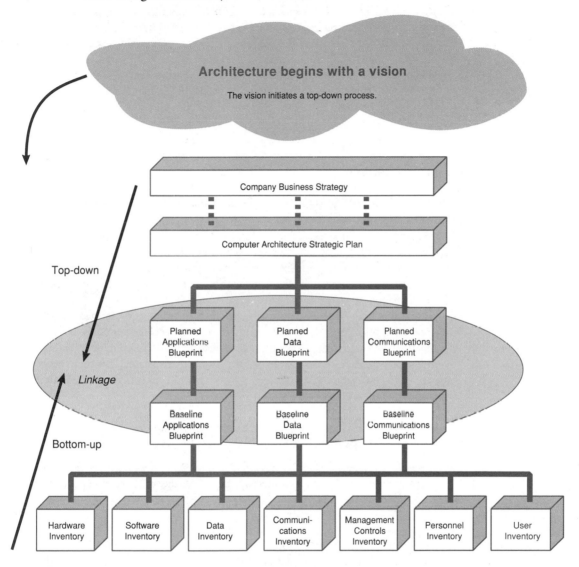

Visions and Strategies Design of new or revised architecture depends on the definition of current structures, assessment of the quality of existing information systems, and design of new information technology structures for the organization.

Information systems planning requires a *vision*—a view of the impact information systems can have on long-term corporate success, strategically and operationally.

Visions are not plans. They are not that well defined, but rather describe a direction for a firm and a conceptualization of the impact information systems have. For example, a package carrier may have a vision of becoming the largest company in the business of delivering packages and letters overnight. The vision describes where the firm wants to go, but not the means to get there. That is developed during the formulation of the company's business strategy.

Having a vision is essential, but it must be communicated. If senior managers cannot describe the vision and the strategic impact, they may be unable to mobilize the organization's personnel and the resources to build and maintain the firm's information systems plan.

The computer architecture strategic plan is an outgrowth of inventorying the current information systems resources and the formulation of information systems technology blueprints.

Blueprints A *blueprint* is an intermediate form that enables the information systems planner to link the vision, business strategy, and computer architecture strategic plan to the current system status. They aid in cutting through the complexity of many business elements, making information systems planning manageable. Building blueprints serve a similar function: They group common elements together (for example, electrical blueprints, structural blueprints, and so on) and allow the contractors and project managers to manage specialized activities.

Blueprints may be used to describe existing (baseline) or planned concerns in the areas of applications, data, and communications. *Applications blueprints* describe the information systems applications. *Data blueprints* in contrast define the data used by the applications and the extent to which data are shared between otherwise separate systems. *Communications blueprints* exist at two levels: voice and data (although companies are increasingly integrating voice and data).

Elements of Inventory As part of information systems planning, an inventory is taken to determine the current status in seven key areas:

——*Hardware inventory:* the processors, storage devices, terminals, peripherals, and communications devices installed by the organization. Each component in the inventory has an associated cost, capacity, performance characteristic (for example, speed), and maintenance requirement.

——*Software inventory:* a firm's operations systems, communications, database management systems, applications, and end-user software (spreadsheets, personal computer databases, graphics systems, and so on). Cost, age, and design characteristics have an impact on the value of the inventory.

——*Data inventory:* the data elements captured, retained, and stored. Cost considerations include the cost to maintain the data, their use, and their integrity (reliability).

——*Communications inventory:* all network links tying computers, terminals, and workstations together. Characteristics include cost, capacity, and transmission characteristics (for example, protocol and transmission speed).

——*Management controls inventory:* procedures, standards, and guidelines installed to ensure effective and efficient employment of the company's information systems architecture. Management considerations include the cost of developing and maintaining the controls and their effectiveness in achieving the objectives of control.

—*Personnel inventory:* the information systems professionals (analysts, programmers, database administrators, and so on) who are responsible for developing and maintaining the organization's information systems. Management concerns include the locations of the staff members, current and projected skill levels, and personnel costs.

—*Users' inventory:* those who use the information systems to carry out the activities of the organization, that is, the business functions. Important considerations include understanding of information systems technology, awareness of applications and their effect, and the extent of their use of applications.

Guidelines for Use The Nolan, Norton & Co. approach is built around four guidelines. First, the current status (baseline) of information systems must be assessed and documented. Second, existing computer architectures are described through three companywide blueprints: applications, data, and communications. Third, firms should strategically plan their information systems architecture five years out while specifying annual goals for application development and system evolution. Finally, responsibility must be fixed for ensuring the effort is properly focused.

Linkage Analysis Planning

Linkage analysis planning is a recent methodology developed by Kenneth Primozic and Edward Primozic, both of the IBM Corporation, with the purpose of involving an organization's senior executives explicitly in the planning for information systems. It emphasizes the competitive aspects of information technology. We introduce the method here and then explore the development of information systems for competitive advantage in greater detail in Chapter 20.

Linkage Concept The method focuses, as the name suggests, on linkages between groups of importance to the organization: customers, suppliers, competitors, industry associations, and so on.

A **linkage** is any activity that affects the cost or effectiveness of another activity. *Internal linkages* are those that exist within the organization itself. *External linkages* are those between an organization and those organizations outside the firm with which it has interaction.

Internal Linkages Planning sessions dealing with internal linkages focus on products or services, cost comparisons, and transaction-oriented customer relationships (Figure 16.6). The objective of internal linkage analysis is to identify methods to enhance a product or service by improving the support provided by information systems. The method also attempts to identify areas where productivity improvements can create substantial benefits.

External Linkages External linkage analysis addresses ways to gain competitive advantages and improved relationships with customers, leading to additional strategic

Figure 16.6 Representative Internal and External Linkages in Linkage Analysis Planning

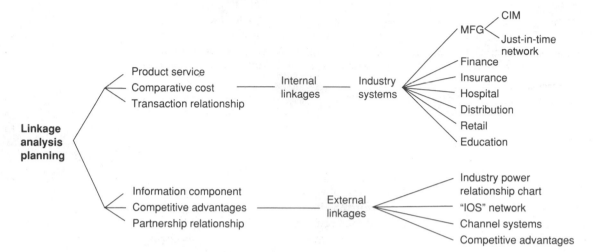

advantages. The objective is to identify methods to improve a product or service through such external relationships as interorganization systems (like electronic data interchange—see Chapter 15), the use of networks to increase the interaction between industry forces, or developing alliances and relationships between trading partners.

Analysis of Linkages This method explores answers to three key questions:

1. How each linkage affects the organization
2. How each linkage relates to other linkages and forces within the industry
3. How the linkage might change in the future

Answers to these questions are developed by examining:

——The firm's expertise as a user of information systems (what are its capabilities)

——The firm's experience in comparison to its major competitors (for example, where it is well experienced, inexperienced, and so on)

——The basis in the industry (for example, competitors, trade associations, customer groups, or suppliers)

——How the organization operates as an *extended organization* (that is, where customers, suppliers, and channels are an integral component of the organization's ability to succeed)

——Opportunities to utilize information systems technology through the creation of electronic channel support systems (for example, electronic links between trading partners) to gain advantage

In this sense, the method assists management in identifying its strengths and weaknesses in information systems in particular and in business in general.

Table 16.4 Circumstances Influencing Use of Alternate Systems Development Methods

Systems Development Life Cycle Method Is Suggested When:

Essential systems features can be identified before development begins

Design strategies are known

Operating routines with which system will be used are well understood

Data needs are clearly identified in advance

Life expectancy of application is long

Application usage will be frequent

Comprehensive system documentation is needed before application is first used

Extensive input and access controls are needed before application is first used

Tight development management and controls are required

Prototyping Method Is Suggested When:

Operational version of system must be developed quickly to provide additional development information

Changes in design specifications are anticipated

User environment is unstable

Life expectancy of application is relatively short

Application usage will be infrequent

Essential systems requirements are not known

Systems requirements are known, but alternative design strategies must be tested

Requirements are known, but user response or reaction to system is uncertain

Hardware or software requirements are unknown or unfamiliar

Broadening of application scope is anticipated after initial usage

Short-term system operating efficiency is not essential

At the completion of linkage analysis, the other methods discussed in this chapter can be used to further refine the planning effort.

Information Systems Development

Information systems planning creates the road map: where an organization is going in its use of information systems for operational and competitive purposes. Information systems development creates the road—the information systems themselves.

Information systems development utilizes two systems development strategies: (1) the systems development life cycle method and (2) the prototyping method (Table 16.4). The first has its origin in transaction processing systems, and has been a conventional approach for many years. However, the evolution of information systems development coupled with the emergence of additional development tools gave rise to the systems prototyping method. You should be familiar with both.

The Systems Development Life Cycle Method

The **systems development life cycle** method is the set of activities associated with the examination of a request for development of an information system. This approach views the process as a set of certain steps that proceed from the examination of the request to the implementation of the completed system.

Many arbitrary groupings of the activities are possible. We discuss eight stages here: (perception of) systems need, feasibility assessment, requirements analysis, logical systems design, physical systems development, testing, implementation and evaluation, and maintenance (Table 16.5). The first two stages deal with formulation of a master plan for the system. The other stages carry out the development of projects that are in the master plan.

The systems development life cycle method is most suitable for the development of information systems that will support well-understood operating routines. An order processing system (as discussed below in connection with Figure 16.8) is typical of applications that meet its criteria: The steps in performing the routine are known and easily explained; and for each step, the data needed to complete the step and the data that must be collected during processing can be identified in advance.

The life cycle method is also a convenient management tool for the development of large systems. Management of the project can focus on the completion of individual tasks at each stage (feasibility analysis, requirements analysis, design, and so on), and deadlines for their completion can be established and monitored. In addition, the assignment of activities to individual members of a project development team may appear easier if activities are staged.

In the sections that follow, we explore the eight stages of the systems development life cycle method. This overview of the analysis and design of computer-based information systems shows the series of events that must take place and the sequence in which they often occur. Remember, however, that systems personnel are likely to find themselves covering the same ground again and again, acquiring additional information about design questions as the need arises or as problems change. Can these repetitious cycles be avoided? It depends in part on how well user requirements are determined in the first place.

Systems Need In most organizations, many different applications systems are needed by users. And since transaction, management, and decision systems are all resources to the organization, they must be managed. This means that each will be developed according to its need, its value to the organization, and the availability of systems specialists to work on it. Not all development projects will be undertaken at once. But there must be a plan, similar to a corporate business plan, that tells where information systems development is going: the projects that are contemplated, the order in which they will be developed, and the resources that will be needed to do the job (Figure 16.7).

Table 16.5 Stages in the Systems Life Cycle *(2-3 yrs effort)*

Stage	Steps
Formulation of master plan	
Systems need *(prob. definition)*	Perception of need — *suggested by users*
	Clarification of purpose — *high level feasibility*
Feasibility assessment	Assessment of technical feasibility
	Assessment of economic feasibility
	Assessment of operational feasibility
Development of Projects	
Requirements analysis	Decoupling
	Determination of user information needs
	Description of user needs
	Setting detailed system requirements
Logical systems design	Specification of new system (functional)
	Specification of procedures
	Specification of input/output
	Specification of files and databases
Physical systems development	Program coding and construction
	Development of files and databases
Testing	Program testing
	Procedure testing
	File and space testing
Implementation and evaluation	Training conversion
Maintenance	Assessment of new system

Development projects are suggested by users on the basis of their perceptions of changing systems needs. Each suggestion is evaluated and determined to be either feasible or nonfeasible. All "feasible" projects are listed in the master plan.

New application needs may arise because of new demands on a manager, a department, or a division. For example, a firm doing a substantial amount of contract work for the government may need to develop a completely new cost accounting application to monitor the costs charged against a particular contract to comply with new federal regulations.

In other instances, external demands may call for modification to an existing system. Tax laws pertaining to investment credits and profit reporting change frequently. Often these changes lead to modification of applications that have been in use for some time. The change may be minor or major, affecting operating-level systems only or the whole organization.

Changes may also be needed to take advantage of new technology in the data processing field. Moving the planning activities into an on-line mode to permit the posing of a series of "what if" questions through a terminal is one type of change. Establishing a large application as a distributed processing system using mini- and microcomputers, thus shifting away from centralized processing, is another. Still

Figure 16.7 Sample Project Data for System Master Plan

Planned Project

Project number: PR6237
Project name: Order entry system
Description: Key-to-disk-based application to accept manufacturing
                   orders, edit order data, store details by customer and by
                   part(s) ordered; produce report (periodic and on request)
                   of aggregate orders for use in production scheduling

Required computer resources
New equipment   None
Estimated systems analysis hours   60
Estimated programming hours   150
Estimated debug and test hours   30
Estimated documentation hours   10

  Total personnel time   250 hours
  Estimated computer time   30 hours
  Estimated permanent computer demand   7 hours/week

Budgeting authority: Manufacturing
Estimated starting date: November
Estimated completion date: 6 months

---

other projects may arise to take advantage of new output technology, such as micro-fiche, graphics display terminals, or high-speed printers.

Furthermore, changes may come about because of the need for broad systems adjustments. Elimination of duplicate files, installation of database management systems, redesign of inefficient procedures, or consolidation of reports often call for new systems design activities.

Feasibility Assessment Before a systems request is approved and included in the master plan, its feasibility must be assessed. That is, assurance is needed that the project can be done within reasonable technical, economic, and operational constraints, as outlined in Table 16.6. *Technical* questions concern the availability of equipment, software, and know-how to develop a system that responds to a user request. For example, if the equipment needed to do the job is not available, the job

Table 16.6 Sample Questions for Feasibility Assessment

Technical Feasibility

Is the equipment needed available?

Can the equipment needed be developed?

Is software available for purchase or can it be developed?

Do our personnel have the expertise needed to develop the software?

Do our personnel have the expertise needed to develop the application?

Is there enough lead time to do the project in-house?

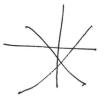

Economic Feasibility

Equipment acquisition cost?

Equipment operation and maintenance cost?

Software acquisition cost?

Software maintenance cost?

Software development cost?

Personnel training cost?

Supplies cost?

Overall operating cost?

Benefits from cost avoidance?

Operational benefits?   Rb I ?

Operational Feasibility

Will the application result in disruptive changes in current operations?

Is the equipment easy to use?

Are the procedures easy to follow?

Will the application help users and data providers?   who are the users?   will jobs be displaced?

Are the necessary data available?

Will the application cause job displacement?

Is major resistance likely?

---

is not technically feasible. If people to do the work cannot be hired or if commercially prepared software cannot be purchased, feasibility may also be limited.

Economic feasibility implies that the cost of developing the system is acceptable. As a general rule, the cost of developing and using the system should be lower than the benefits that can be enjoyed from doing so. (Economic evaluation of information systems is discussed in detail in Supplement 16.)

Operational feasibility involves the effect the system will have on the people who are going to use it and, in turn, the effect the people will have on the system. If a new application will be shunned by its intended users, there is no point in developing it.

The **feasibility study** is usually performed by a small team of systems and management personnel from different levels of the organization. Outside consultants may also be used. Rather than drafting detailed design specifications, the team examines the benefits to be gained from a new system, related costs, technical concerns, and development time. In the current business environment, technical feasibility is usually studied much more extensively than operational and economic feasibility, and this imbalance often causes problems in the implementation and maintenance stages.

Development proposals that are found to be unfeasible are discarded or returned to the originator for refinement. Those judged feasible are integrated into the master plan, where they are given a priority and scheduled. The next stage of the life cycle, requirements analysis, signals the beginning of development.

Requirements Analysis During the **requirements analysis** stage of the systems development life cycle, systems analysts assigned to the project determine and describe user information needs so that design and construction (that is, programming, file creation, and so on) can take place later. The procedures are geared to setting up more detailed requirement specifications, expanding significantly on those used to do the feasibility study, and to describing the completed system in detail.

Analysts determine how the system is operating, how information needs of various individuals are being met, and where there are problems. Often, some of the more critical pieces of information come through informal (nonprescribed) channels in an organization. The systems analyst should try to identify informal channels and learn about the information passed through them. The informal communication of information usually means that formal procedures are not adequate. For example, if a sales manager routinely uses the telephone to find out a salesperson's weekly total, the formal communication and reporting process is not adequate. This would be an area of interest for a systems analyst conducting a study for a new system.

The requirements analysis process recognizes that most systems are so complex that they cannot be studied as a single entity. The only way to make relations and interconnections perceivable is to break down (decouple) the systems and subsystems. In **decoupling,** systems are partitioned into subsystems and parts so that each part can be studied separately. Each element is analyzed independently of the others. Inputs, outputs, and their interfaces are also identified.

For example, to study a sales system, we might decouple it into the parts that accept orders, process sales order slips, record credit payments, package items for shipping, record the withdrawal of items from inventory, and analyze the results (Figure 16.8). Each activity can then be studied independently of the others. The interfaces can also be examined to see how information is transmitted between each of the system's parts.

Through decoupling we can gain a more complete understanding of the processes involved, which in turn facilitates comparisons between desired and actual performance. In the sales system, we can study how orders are processed, the volume of processing, the error rate, and how exceptional or unusual situations are handled. Necessary changes become evident, as does the need for new system specifications.

Logical Systems Design Information gathered during the requirements analysis stage is used to design the new system or to modify an existing one. During the **logical**

Figure 16.8 Decouple Subsystems for Investigation of Order Processing Systems

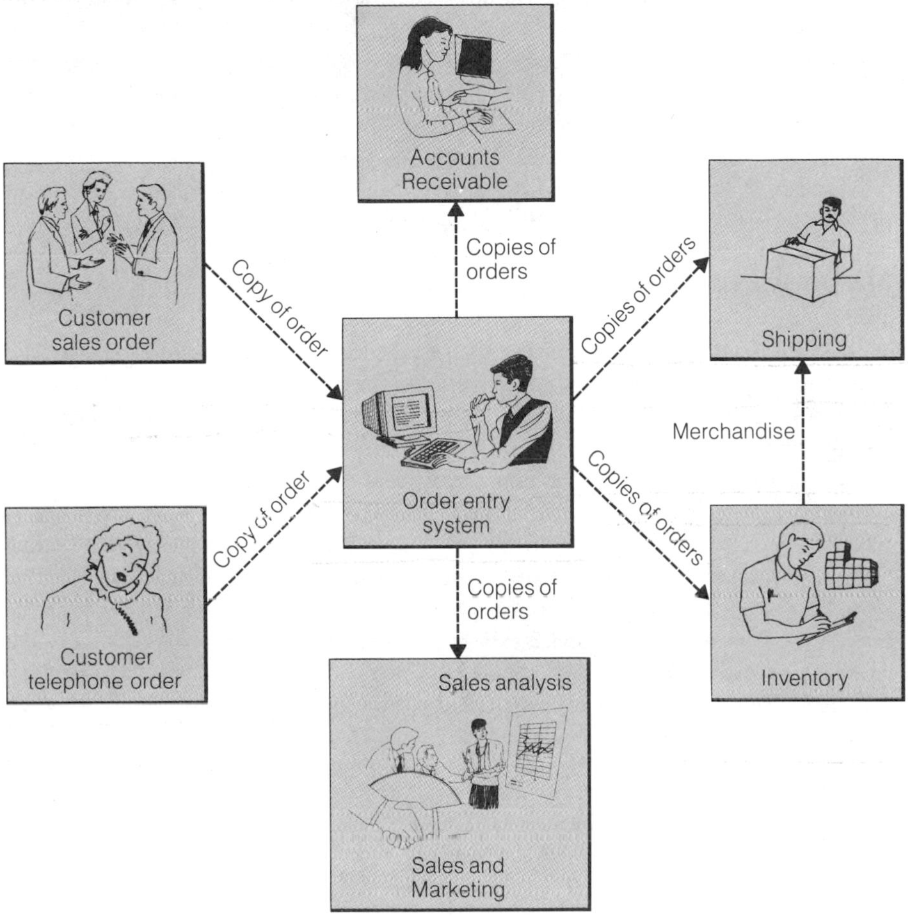

systems design stage, we are concerned with formulating *functional specifications*—statements of what the system should do, how it should do it, and in what sequence input of data, processing, output of reports, and so on should occur.

In this stage (as in all stages of the systems development life cycle), user involvement is necessary to ensure that the operating and decision procedures used in the organization are properly identified and that the new system is molded to meet them. The system must be acceptable to users; without their involvement and commitment, it may not be.

During the logical design stage, information processing procedures are detailed, such as whether the system will be an on-line or batch operation, how file updates will be made, and when reports will be prepared. In addition, input documents, output reports, control procedures, and file and database specifications are designed and described. The sizes of fields, records, and files, and the processing frequency are also specified.

Initially, several possible designs may be formulated by the designers for the future users and the programming and systems staff to discuss and criticize. Flaws in the design can be identified and corrected. Often a design's problems may be detected only during close scrutiny by the potential users. This point illustrates the importance of repeating parts of the analysis and design work to improve logical design specifications throughout the systems development life cycle. Poor designs are redone and more functional specifications are formulated on the basis of feedback from everyone who has been brought into the design process.

Physical Systems Development During the **physical systems construction** stage, the programming staff begins to build the information systems application: coding programs, developing record formats, data structures, and subschemas, and designing files and databases.

Not all software needs to be developed in-house. In many cases, organizations contract with outside firms to have software custom made to fit a specific application. In other cases, generalized ("canned") software packages are purchased from computer manufacturers or from specialists in software development (often called *software houses*). In these instances, considerable savings in programming costs can be achieved, provided the right kind of package is found. But even for off-the-shelf software packages, record formats must be defined and files established.

In addition to these file- and data-oriented activities it may be necessary to select hardware devices (for example, additional disk storage units, cathode ray tubes, data communications equipment) during construction and move them to the site where they will be used. Of course, not all applications require new hardware, so this step may be bypassed. But if new equipment is necessary, the designers should allow ample time for interviewing vendors, making selections, and receiving delivery, which may not be prompt.

Before an information systems module is brought into an organization's information and decision systems and made a part of them, steps must be taken to ensure the accuracy, correctness, and workability of the supporting software, files, and procedures. Each application series must be examined carefully to remove all difficulties. This is done through testing of the software, the information system in general, and the procedures that support and link the various processing activities.

Testing Program testing is the first phase in the overall process of application testing. A well-written program is divided into a set of integrated but logically distinct modules. Different modules, for example, should be developed to input data, perform certain processing jobs, and output reports and displays. These individual modules are tested for errors separately. Then they can be linked together and the entire program tested as a whole. By focusing first on the separate modules, coding or logic errors can be isolated and problems that might arise due to connections between modules can be avoided.

When preliminary program testing has been completed, the entire system is tested. This is one of the most critical points in the system's life cycle. Systems testing ensures that the different modules and programs in an application are compatible and that the desired operations can take place. The tests should uncover any incompatibility problems that may arise between programs or modules. For example, tests should detect a difference in data specifications (type, name, and size) output by one program and those needed for input to another. Similarly, tests should determine whether allotted file and table sizes are large enough for the application. Systems testing is the final opportunity to check out the system before implementation.

Implementation and Evaluation When all tests have been completed and the system is found to be running properly (to the best knowledge of the staff), **implementation** can begin. When the system is put in operation, the training of users in the organization can be completed. "Users" are not only the people who will deal directly with the system (for example, through cathode ray tubes or printer output) but also those who will be supplying data or forms to the system and others who will, in one way or another, be using the reports and documents it generates. All these individuals need to be aware of the importance of their roles and the way they affect or are affected by the system's activities and functions. Similarly, each person should be advised on the meaning of specific output from the system and how it affects his or her performance.

As users become familiar with the operation and use of the software, the switch to the new system can begin. Conversion includes creating the required files, establishing backup copies of master files and databases, and converting previously existing programs to operating status. Then the system itself goes into regular use in the organization.

During and after implementation, evaluations are made of the system and its operation. Users and systems staff want to be sure that the system is running correctly, that it provides the output it is supposed to, and that the users have the support it was designed to give. (A detailed discussion of systems evaluation is provided in Chapter 19.)

Maintenance All too often, systems personnel and managers feel that the systems development life cycle is completed when the system has been installed and implemented. Nothing could be further from the truth. Improvements must be made continually in almost all systems—to correct errors, to meet new needs of management, or to take advantage of new technology. In many organizations, part of the development team may be permanently assigned to the area for which the system was developed and given almost total responsibility for system **maintenance.**

The Prototyping Method

The other approach to system development is through *prototyping*. The underlying proposition for this method is that in many applications, requirements determination in advance is at best difficult. Prototyping is based on the following fundamental principle:

> Users can point to features they like or dislike in an existing system more easily than they can describe them in an imaginary or proposed system.

The **prototype** then is developed as a working system to allow users to identify the essential features in an information system. It is in essence an experimental version of a new system. However, you should be aware that prototyping in systems analysis differs significantly from the practice in, say, engineering. In the nonsystems applications, prototypes are developed over a long period of time and usually at great cost. For example, many months and millions of dollars may be required to produce a single prototype automobile that will, if approved for production, sell at a fraction of the cost of the prototype. When used in the development of information systems, however, the establishment of a prototype cannot be a long-term process, nor can the cost of the model be dramatically different from the cost of the eventual system.

Steps in Prototype Methodology There are five steps in the prototyping process:

1. Identify the user's known information requirements.
2. Develop a working model.
3. Use the model, or prototype, noting needed enhancements and changes.
4. Revise the prototype.
5. Repeat the preceding steps as needed.

During step 1, both analyst and user determine what information the system should produce and identify the data that must be processed. Emphasis is placed on the output of the system, not how it will be produced. This step takes less than a week and is usually accomplished in one or two working sessions.

Development of the working prototype is the responsibility of the systems analyst. The prototype system consists of three parts: user interface, processing routines, and output. All user dialogue must permit the individual to understand easily how to submit data or inquiries to the system and how to retrieve results. It need not, however, contain all messages and displays normally required in a completed, polished system.

The processing components of a prototype system perform processing representative of that needed in a final version, but not necessarily in an efficient manner. For example, a retrieval or response time as long as several minutes may be acceptable at this point in development. Minor processing delays generally do not impede the user in evaluating essential features.

System output also need not be complete in the prototype. Depending on the application, some nonessential output details may be dispensed with; in other instances, titles, headings, or instructional details may be unnecessary at this early stage.

Prototyping generally does not involve hand coding of programs using traditional procedural languages (like COBOL and BASIC). Rather, whenever possible, fourth-generation languages should be used. As discussed in Chapter 6, fourth-generation languages allow developers to focus on *what* should be done rather than on how to achieve desired results. This higher-level approach is particularly well-suited to prototyping.

You should remember these key points about prototyping:

— Speed of development, not efficiency of prototype performance, is the overriding concern of both systems analyst and end-user.

— The initial prototype is likely to be incomplete or unsatisfactory in one or more ways. Changes in specifications and modification of system features are *expected*.

— Users should use the system in a hands-on fashion to determine by trial and error the changes and enhancements that are desirable.

— Each iteration will result in one or more of the following changes:
Modification of the data used in processing or the manner in which data are stored in the system
Changes in existing features
Addition of new features

— A typical prototyping experience will have four to six iterations. *(-7 per Tom)*

Uses of Prototypes When user and analyst are satisfied that the process has provided the information sought, the prototype may be discarded, implemented, or redeveloped (that is, used as the basis of another prototype).

Although the first result may surprise you, in some instances it makes a lot of sense to discard a prototype and abandon the application. Perhaps the prototype has shown that the proposed system will not achieve the desired results or will be too complex to use to secure the benefits originally contemplated. Such a project should be abandoned, but because this finding was realized quickly, the prototype has been a wise investment. Consider the implications of developing a complete, working system, consuming many dollars and months of calendar time, and *then* arriving at the same conclusion. Obviously prototyping offers a better alternative. And, of course, determination that a prototype has failed can serve as impetus to begin another prototyping process, from a different angle.

On the other hand, if the level of performance efficiency, type of user interface, and output format are acceptable for the intended system usage, there is little point in investing resources in additional system development. In such cases (which represent the majority of prototyping experiences), the prototype is implemented in accordance with the design.

The third alternative—redevelopment—is used to achieve performance efficiencies. Generally the system is restarted as a new project, but the information gained through prototyping is the basis for developing a detailed design for the new system and for undertaking the programming process. In this sense, the development may use procedural or fourth-generation languages. The other option is to proceed from the prototype through subsequent steps in the traditional systems development life cycle.

The fourth alternative is to use the information gained through the prototyping process to *begin another prototyping process*. Perhaps the results provided information that indicates a system should be developed with features totally different from those originally expected; and the existing prototype is inappropriate to demonstrate those features. Rather than plunging into a full-scale development effort with the newly acquired information, creation of another prototype will add to the information at hand.

Prototyping Example   To demonstrate the use of prototyping, consider the following example. A manager assigned to the management of telecommunications expenditures after deregulation of the communications industry quickly recognized that the carrier's invoices would have to be processed to provide separate information on long distance and local calls and to identify costs by department. However, because of the rush of competition in the telephone industry, the manager was uncertain of what other information was needed or even how such information would be assembled. This manager discussed the system with a systems analyst and they decided to first construct a prototype system. The evolution of the prototype is indicated in the sequence below:

1. The initial prototype was developed after two meetings between manager and analyst. To retrieve information, the user entered a report number. Reports were printed or displayed in four different tabular formats, but in each one, departments were listed in alphabetical order.

2. After a brief period of use, it was evident that one report format was used approximately 90 percent of the time. Consequently, the prototype was modified to display that format automatically whenever the application was run. The other formats were available on request. The dialogue with the user was also modified to clear up ambiguities in words, messages, and instructions, and to allow selection of default entries simply by depressing the <ENTER> key on the workstation (initially, the user had to key each selection individually). The order of entries in the reports was also adjusted so that information was listed in descending order of usage by department rather than alphabetically. The manager found this sequence more helpful.

3. Long-distance charges were divided into in-state and out-of-state categories to permit better insight into calling expenditures. In addition, credit card call charges and those made from office telephones were listed separately, providing additional information on cost patterns. Management was surprised by the distribution of costs between these two categories—this aspect had not been examined before—and new guidelines for use of calling cards were quickly established and monitored.

4. The capability of displaying trend data from the previous 6-month period and comparative data from the same period a year earlier was added to the system. Graphics display capabilities also were added to show trends within a particular department and between departments. Other changes were made in report contents and system defaults.

The manager and the analyst agreed that the fourth iteration had resulted in a useful application and that the modifications introduced during trials with the working version would not have been identified without the prototype version. It was decided to continue to use the prototype as the working application because processing efficiency was acceptable and because changes in the source of telecommunications services were anticipated within one year. After the system had been tested thoroughly to ensure reliability, the application was used regularly.

The example application described above would have been difficult to develop using the life cycle development methodology. At best, this approach would have necessitated many changes after implementation, a point at which adjustments are both difficult and expensive.

Table 16.4 identifies factors that suggest which methodology to follow in working with a particular information systems application. In general, when system requirements are unknown and cannot be identified in advance, as in the preceding example, prototyping is the suggested strategy.

Summary

An organization's success with information systems begins with planning. Identifying needs is an essential step in planning. Information systems are generally developed for three reasons: to solve a current or anticipated problem, to capitalize on an opportunity, or to respond to a directive.

The planning process itself can be top-down, bottom-up, or a combination of the two. The planning methods discussed in this chapter included the critical success factor, BSP, and computer architecture strategic plans. In addition, an emerging method called linkage analysis was discussed. Each has particular advantages and disadvantages; however, all provide a focus for information systems planning.

Development brings a planned system into being. There are two widely used methods for the development of information systems. The classic systems development life cycle consists of the following activities: (realization of) systems need, feasibility assessment, requirements analysis, logical systems design, physical systems development, testing, implementation and evaluation, and maintenance. This methodology is most useful when systems requirements can be identified in advance—a situation common with information systems that support routine operating activities.

The prototyping methodology is used when it is difficult to identify user requirements in advance. This approach calls for the development of a working system—the prototype—that includes many of the essential features known to be needed. Through the use of the prototype, users identify additional requirements as well as necessary changes. This process is repeated several times until sufficient information has been acquired to formulate a decision about the system. At that time, the prototype may become the working system, or it may serve as the basis for designing a more efficient version that will eventually be used. In some cases, the prototype may become the basis for another prototyping sequence. And in other cases, information gained by using the prototype may lead to the decision to abandon the effort entirely.

No system will be effective if it does not meet the needs of the organization and its users. Good planning and development are essential in all organizations.

Key Words

Application portfolio	Implementation	Physical systems
Bottom-up approach	Infrastructure	construction
Business systems plan-	Logical systems design	Prototype
ning (BSP)	Linkage	Requirements analysis
Critical success factor	Linkage analysis	Systems development life
Data architecture	Maintenance	cycle
Decoupling	Master development plan	Top-down approach
Feasibility study	Network architecture	

Review Questions

1. For what three reasons are information systems generally developed? Discuss each reason, describing the types of situations most likely to occur.

2. Why are information systems projects generally initiated?

3. When planning for the development of information systems, what objectives should guide the formulation of the plan?

4. What should a development master plan contain?

5. Describe the two generic views of information systems planning. Under what circumstances can both views guide the planning effort?

6. What is the critical success factor planning method? What characteristics distinguish this method of information systems planning?

7. Describe the purpose of business systems planning (BSP). What steps comprise the method?

8. What are the limitations of the BSP method?

9. Describe the computer architecture strategic planning method. How does it differ from the critical success factor method? The BSP method?

10. What is computer architecture? What elements make up computer architecture?

11. Describe the purpose of linkage analysis planning. What does the term *linkage* mean? Why are linkages important in the planning of information systems?

12. Briefly describe the stages in the information systems life cycle. Which stages directly involve management?

13. Three sets of questions were identified as being necessary considerations in any analysis effort. What are they?

14. What is user requirements analysis?

15. Sum up the differences between logical and physical systems design and development.

16. Do managers believe transaction processing systems provide the information needed to deal with their more critical decisions? What are the apparent reasons for this attitude?

17. Describe the principle of decoupling. Why is it important or necessary in systems development?

18. What features characterize the prototyping method of information systems development? What advantages does this method offer?

19. Why is iteration important in systems development?

20. How do the classic systems development life cycle and the systems prototyping methods differ? How are they similar?

Application Problems

1. A systems analyst wants to convince a project manager of the benefits of prototyping in the development of information systems. The analyst recently used prototyping very successfully to develop a unique information system for another user, who was not able to describe information requirements in advance. After using several modified versions of the original prototype, the user acknowledged the system's effectiveness and now relies on it. This experience convinced the analyst that the only correct way to develop a system is to use prototyping.

   The project manager, in contrast, emphasizes the benefits of prototyping when used in the proper situation, such as when systems features and requirements cannot be identified in advance or through traditional methods. Prototyping should be used only when the analyst is uncertain about the new system or how it will be used. Thus it should be viewed as one tool among several in the systems analyst's repertoire of tools. The project manager agrees prototyping can be used to design a system, and also during individual steps in the systems life cycle, such as for feasibility assessment or requirements determination. However, the project manager emphasizes that prototyping is not the only development method.

   Which individual is correct? Discuss the approaches suggested by each person and determine the merits of their arguments.

2. During which stage of a system's life cycle do the following activities take place?
   a. selection of software packages to be purchased from outside vendors
   b. development of input forms
   c. construction of physical files
   d. selection of storage structures
   e. selection of data structures
   f. calculation of processing time for a typical application run on the computer system
   g. calculation of development costs
   h. calculation of costs and benefits for the new system

3. Listed below are a number of transaction and decision situations common in industrial, business, and government settings. Indicate if each is a logical or meaningful area for computer-based systems development. Explain the reason for your answer and state the nature of the systems support that would be appropriate.
   a. monitoring and control of valves that regulate high pressure in liquid-carrying lines and tubes in a chemical plant when improper pressure could result in rupture of lines and possible explosion
   b. developing individual training, rehabilitation, and guidance programs for law offenders or former prisoners

    c. designing and constructing new billion-dollar aircraft; design and building of the aircraft is a multimonth project and requires the constant interchange and monitoring of design specifications for the different component work areas (cabin sections, tail section, wing section, and so on)

    d. scheduling the arrival and departure of passenger and freight trains on specific tracks at a large railroad station

    e. selecting personnel for staffing of a new research wing of a medical center

    f. selecting stock and bond portfolios for government customers of a commercial bank

4. Managers often receive the information systems help they need only accidentally and as a result of modification in transaction processing systems. Does this mean that modification in transaction processing systems to support management decision making is not a good idea? Why or why not? What factors should be considered in a decision concerning modification of a simple transaction processing system to support managerial decision making?

5. What are the main factors of the broad area of economic evaluation of information systems? Why is each important?

6. What are the major categories in cost analysis of information systems? Which are the most difficult and least difficult to measure? Why?

7. What are the major areas of interest in benefit analysis for information systems? Give examples of each one.

8. Compare and contrast the various accounting and quantitative methods for benefit analysis. Why are they effective or ineffective methods for economic evaluation of information systems?

9. Of what value is a subjective approach to estimation of information systems benefits? How might such an approach, using the Delphi technique (see Supplement 16), be implemented?

Minicase: Prototyping—The Only Way to Build Systems?*

According to James Martin, the most widely quoted spokesman for the information systems industry, prototyping is a key productivity tool for the development of information systems. Many seminar and workshop participants have heard Martin say:

"I have never seen an example of a prototype being given to end-users without end-users changing it. So if you build a system without a prototype, you are probably going to build it wrong."

Martin speaks eloquently about the

revolutions that are occurring in the management of information systems. He foresees an ongoing increase in end-user computing, a greater use of databases in the 1990s, as well as the emergence of many tools to enhance the productivity of information systems and those who use or develop them. Many practitioners and researchers agree with Martin's vision of system development productivity.

However, there is not widespread acceptance of the vision of prototyping. Systems managers often express the following criticisms of prototyping:

1. It is difficult to manage because there are no delivery schedules, no intermediate stages (such as completion of requirements, delivery of design specifications, and design of software), and no firm date on which a system is "finished." The evolution of a prototype is ongoing and the process is unmanageable.

2. Users do not know what they want when analysts work with them. They also do not know what they want when involved in the development of a prototype, except now they have an analyst working directly with them so that many more changes can be made. In this way also, prototyping is an unmanageable process. Give users a chance to make changes, and they will *always* make changes.

3. The many applications having requirements that can be fully identified in advance are best handled through the life cycle method. Prototyping is one approach. It is not the *only* approach to design and development. If a prototype is not built first, it doesn't always mean the system will be built wrong.

Questions

1. Do you agree with Martin? If prototyping is not done, and users do not have the chance to make changes, is the system bound to be built wrong?

2. Discuss the views commonly expressed by MIS managers. Are they logical views? Does the introduction of prototyping present an unmanageable situation? Is the systems development life cycle obsolete?

× "Martin Urges MIS Managers to Automate Operations," *Computerworld,* September 23, 1985, p. 28.

Minicase: Information Systems Apprenticeship?

Information systems departments are often viewed as consisting of two kinds of people: managers and techs. Managers are generally expected to ensure that tasks are performed effectively and that employees are used in the manner that is jointly beneficial to them and to the firm. They also must receive and review reports on projects, financial statements concerning project costs, and status briefings. Information systems managers frequently interact with their counterparts in the functional areas of the firm, such as marketing, production, and accounting. In general they are expected not to solve technical problems, but to approach them from a level of sophistication that permits meaningful communication with the designated problem solvers.

The technical staff—programmers, analysts, designers—is supposed to concentrate on technical issues and not manage (except when the organization has created dual-responsibility positions). A large portion of the skills of the technician can be acquired through formal education and in-service training. However, many feel that a significant portion of the skills needed to be successful as a technician must be acquired by practice and emulation. They recommend a skilled craftsman approach whereby individuals serve a period of apprenticeship working

alongside a senior technician. During this time, the master craftsman is the manager, the technical authority, and the instructor. Emphasis is not on the working of specific systems, but on the knowledge and the techniques needed to produce successful system development.

Questions

1. The concept of apprenticeships presumes that an area is a craft or an art that cannot be learned independent of practice. Do you agree or disagree with the idea of an apprenticeship for technical staff members? What benefits might occur through apprenticeship?

2. What is the value of formal education in information systems for those who wish to pursue technical careers? How do their education and training differ from the preparation of management personnel?

3. How much technical background should a manager of information systems have? Do you agree with the portrayal of the systems manager described earlier?

Supplement 16: Cost/Benefit Analysis for Information Systems

Cost/benefit analysis is essential in the development of an information system regardless of the development methodology employed. It needs to be performed before, during, and after development of applications. Cost/benefit analysis is a critical part of the feasibility study associated with the systems life cycle. Good managers in industry do not begin to contract for new manufacturing equipment without first doing a cost/benefit analysis, and investments in information systems applications should be planned with the same foresight.

This supplement presents an in-depth look at cost/benefit analysis. We will see that cost estimates must focus on more than the capital investment for hardware and software. And it will also be evident that benefits are much more difficult to assess, whether using accounting methods or more subjective approaches. Nevertheless, to avoid investing resources blindly, managers and users must learn to determine what they will save or gain by developing and implementing an information systems application.

Cost Analysis

We can estimate the cost of systems with reasonable accuracy because the basic elements—hardware, software, personnel, and operation—can be identified readily and it is not difficult to derive a single dollar figure for each. An organization can even get hardware prices from several manufacturers without much additional effort. Rental and lease charges for both hardware and software are also easy to come by.

Personnel costs are not limited to salaries and benefits for programmers, systems analysts, systems designers, computer operators, and clerical staff. They also include costs for part of the manager's time that must be devoted to interviews, questionnaires, and related facets of the systems analysis and design investigation. Except for top management, however, it is possible to determine an hourly wage or salary figure for each individual.

Often overlooked in cost analysis are the *opportunity costs* of systems projects. Opportunity costs are benefits that would have been gained from working on another project but must be foregone because the target project was selected instead. For example, if we choose to work on project A even though we could have saved $10,000 a year in operating expenses by developing project B, we refer to the $10,000 saving that wasn't realized as an opportunity cost of project A. However, if we select project C, which will save us $50,000, we can better afford to forego the $10,000 saving. The need to compare alternative costs and benefits is the reason for doing a thorough systems analysis and drawing up a master plan for every development program. The master plan should rank the projects in terms of their overall priority and benefit to the organization, taking opportunity costs into account. The systems analysis activities should help verify that the desired benefits can be obtained and should ensure that data are collected to help get the proper system designed.

Overall, it is possible to prepare a fairly reliable cost analysis. This does not mean that we can give precise figures on what it will cost to construct a system, because we cannot. For instance, in formulating a detailed cost specification before starting to program, we need to have some idea how long it will take to code the new software. This entails a fairly accurate determination of how many instructions will be needed in a particular program and how fast the programmers will be able to think through the logic and write the instructions. Estimating these activities is not a trivial task, and often there are major discrepancies between the time allotted to construct a program and the time actually used, particularly with procedural languages such as COBOL. We also encounter difficulties in attempting to establish frameworks for program testing time and cost. We cannot accurately estimate how long it will take to identify and correct logic and syntax errors so that a program can be implemented. Since program and system testing often take 50 percent of the time devoted to a project, serious errors in this area can significantly affect the delivery date of the working application.

Nevertheless, we generally do well with cost analysis aspects of information systems. We know what factors to examine and incorporate into a cost study, and we have developed many tools to help perform the analysis. And improvements are continually being made. Benefit analysis, however, has not reached this level of sophistication.

Benefit Analysis

Benefit analysis is the study of the planning, control, and operating advantages to be gained from developing and using an information systems application. Benefits fall into three categories.

——*Cost savings benefits:* reductions in transaction processing or operational costs because the system has been introduced and used (for example, a reduced number of clerical employees, lower error rates that cut the need for time-consuming corrections, and the ability to carry a smaller inventory)

——*Operational benefits:* improvements in the way operations are carried out at different management levels (for example, faster processing, fewer forms needed, quicker access to data or information)

——*Intangible benefits:* improvements that are important to the success of the organization but do not directly affect operations, costs, or profits (for example, improved customer relations, more thorough planning, greater responsiveness to government requests for data)

Benefits of all these kinds are important. And although some may be obtained during the analysis and design or during prototyping (for example, new forms may be instituted even before the system is in use), the largest gains are found when the application is implemented. So our focus is on assessing postimplementation benefits.

There are a number of methods for assessing benefits, but these tools are not yet satisfactory—continued research and development are essential. Here we examine the tools that are available now and indicate the problems and drawbacks associated with each. Although not ideal, these tools can give us some insight into the benefits of a system.

Most benefit assessment techniques are basically accounting methods, and when they are used as tools of analysis, a time period (the *project duration period,* the amount of time the application will be used, once implemented) must be specified, along with an interest factor that indicates the growth or value of the dollars associated with the project. The interest factor in this sense might be compared with the interest an organization has to pay on money borrowed from a bank, but it is much more difficult to quantify. Traditionally, these critical factors (that is, project duration period and interest rate) have been specified by managers in the organization. Such arbitrary estimates may not be accurate enough, however, to incorporate into an evaluation.

Traditional accounting methods primarily measure *cost displacement,* that is, the cost savings realized through the application. For example, a system used in inventory control might be found to reduce the carrying cost of stock maintained in a warehouse by 20 percent a year. As another example, however, suppose that more customers are attracted to a company that has introduced an on-line sales information system because word has spread that orders are processed quickly and with few errors. It would be naive to omit such an *intangible benefit* from an overall evaluation of the project. Likewise, it would be a mistake to omit the assessment of managers' feelings about using the new system: Managers may incorporate more information into their job performance, or their work attitudes may improve. Individual details will vary, but clearly a new system will produce benefits that should be identified and assessed.

There is a tendency to evaluate systems on the basis of development costs. However, this approach is not acceptable. It is more important to determine benefits on the basis of what the system can do to help managers. This means that the value of the system should be judged according to the users' perceptions rather than according to actual cost structure. We need to examine the decisions that will be supported by the system and to learn how the application will improve the quality of the decisions. This is a more meaningful approach than merely asking what it will cost to develop and use an application. Of course, benefits have to be compared to costs before a final development decision is made. But, focusing on the decision aspects of an information system will give a better assessment of the possible benefits of the system itself and of the information it produces.

Methods of Economic Evaluation

The manager needs a method for evaluating the monetary worth of a specific information systems project or group of projects, as we showed in the preceding section. Here we examine three *economic evaluation* methods that have been developed and used in the field. The accounting methods are widely used. However, they leave much to be desired, particularly when they are applied to criteria such as cost savings, operational benefits, and intangible benefits, mentioned previously. The other methods, which are still largely experimental, are quantitative and subjective techniques of evaluation. The quantitative methods use a combination of modeling and statistics to derive project dollar benefits. The subjective approach essentially specifies project benefits in terms of what users will pay for information generated through the system.

Accounting Methods

Three methods for systems evaluation—present value, the internal rate of return, and payback period—are widely understood and used in the accounting profession. Are they, however, appropriate for use in the assessment of information systems benefits?

The Present Value Concept The purpose of the present value concept is to place a value on *future* expenses and benefits in terms of their value *today*. If we can evaluate a dollar next year, the year after, and so on, in terms of its value today, we can compare the benefits of different projects with periods of different durations based on current dollar values. We also want to evaluate costs using current money value. Organizations know the costs of many purchases or investments before they can quantify the benefits. This is certainly true for information systems, which require a heavy investment in resources long before any of the potential benefits are received. From this viewpoint, the benefit or value of the system is the *expected* dollar value we will get when the system has been implemented, less any costs or resources needed to realize those benefits (for example, the costs of programming the system or acquiring new equipment). Finding the net present value of costs and benefits makes cost and benefit comparisons more meaningful.

The *net present value method* can be applied by calculating the present value of the benefits and the present value of the costs, that is, specifying each in terms of its value today. An example will help demonstrate how this method is applied.

Let's assume we have an information system project that can be developed and completed in 18 months and will benefit the organization for 5 years. At the end of 5 years, it is expected that major revisions and modifications will be needed and large amounts of financial and human resources will have to be reinvested to maintain the benefits of the first half-decade. Thus, the project life is established at 5 years. Development costs during the 18-month cycle total $273,000: $175,000 during the first year and $98,000 during the next 6 months. We can identify benefits totaling $696,000 spread over the 5-year period of use as shown in Figure S16.1. But we also need to consider the *discount rate,* a percentage factor similar to an interest rate

Figure S16.1 Accounting Approaches to Benefit Evaluation

ASSUMPTIONS
Project development over 18 months
Expected 5-year use after development
Dollar figures assessed at beginning of year

Costs:			Benefits:	
Year 1	$175,000		Year 1	0
Year 2	98,000		Year 2	35,000
			Year 3	120,000
			Year 4	125,000
			Year 5	135,000
			Year 6	140,000
			Year 7	141,000

Total benefits $696,000

Net Present Value Method
Multiply sum of year's dollars × discount factor
(assume a 12% discount rate that reflects opportunity cost of funds):
Present value of costs: $175,000 + (98,000 × .893) = $262,514
Present value of benefits: 0 + ($35,000 × .893) + ($120,000 × .797) +
        ($125,000 × .712) + ($135,000 × .636) +
        ($140,000 × .567) + ($141,000 × .507) = $452,622

Internal Rate of Return
Compare costs and benefits, finding present value factor (PVF) that equates the two, giving the internal rate of return:
$175,000(PVF) = 98,000(PVF) = 35,000(PVF) + 120,000(PVF) + 125,000(PVF)
        + 135,000(PVF) + 140,000(PVF) + 141,000(PVF)
Using a 30 percent rate, we find a difference between the two sides of the equation of $18,625.

Using a 40 percent rate, we find a difference of −$33,000 between the two sides of the equation.

By repeating the process with different present value factors, we find that costs equal benefits at a present value of 33.15 percent.

Payback Period Method
Divide total benefits by total benefits/total costs
Total benefits = $696,000
Total costs = $273,000
Years to pay off = $696,000/$273,000 = 2.5 years

or cost of capital rate, that reflects the opportunity cost of funds. In this example, the rate has been identified as 12 percent because this is what the organization has to pay to borrow money.

To calculate the net present value of the benefits, a decimal number that represents the 12 percent rate is determined, usually by using a present value table (not shown). The number is multiplied by the value of the costs or benefits for each specific year; that is, a different decimal number is drawn from the table for each year of the project, as shown in Figure S16.1. All the yearly results are added, giving the net present value of the benefits. In the example, the net present value of the benefits is $452,622. The net present value of the system costs, assuming that the costs are figured from the beginning of each year, is $262,514. Since the benefits exceed the costs, investment in the development of the system appears to be a good idea. Of course, if the organization will not undertake a project unless benefits are expected to exceed investments by a certain percentage, the costs would have to be subtracted from the benefits and the remainder converted to a percentage for comparison to policy. On the surface, however, this seems to be a fairly good investment. Through use of the net present value concept, we see both costs and benefits expressed in terms of the dollars they represent today, rather than several years ahead, when inflation or other factors may have modified these values.

The Internal Rate of Return Concept   As an alternative to using present value, an analyst can calculate the internal rate of return of a project. The *internal rate of return* offers a means of comparing the present value of an investment with the present value of costs and benefits (cash flows) generated by the investment. To use this method we must find a present value factor (PVF) that can be multiplied by each dollar figure for costs and for benefits to produce a balanced equation. To find the present value figure that will set the two sides equal, we need to try different values, as in Figure S16.1, seeing how close we come to an equality. For example, if we evaluate the costs and benefits using 30 percent as the PVF, we find a difference of $18,625. At 40 percent, the difference is − $33,000. We want to be at zero, which means that the internal rate of return lies between 30 and 40 percent. By continuing our calculations, we find that the internal rate of return is approximately 33.15 percent. If the benefits exceed the costs and compare favorably with the firm's cost of capital, then the investment in information systems is a good one. In the example, if the firm's desired rate of return were less than 33 percent, we would expect to go ahead with the systems proposals.

The Payback Period Concept   The third accounting approach to benefit assessment is the *payback period* method. This method determines how many months or years will have to pass before the benefits exceed the costs. In other words, by using the payback method, we can find out how long it will be before the costs incurred during development have been reimbursed by the benefits from the project.

Calculation of the benefits in this manner is very simple. We divide the total benefits by total costs, yielding the number of years needed to pay off the costs. In our example, the payback period is 2.5 years ($696,000 ÷ $273,000). This figure must be compared to the organization's objectives to determine whether it is good enough.

Disadvantages of Accounting Methods   All these accounting methods are open to criticism. First, both a specific duration for the project and an interest factor or discount rate to indicate the growth or value factor of the dollar must be provided. Usually these factors are arbitrarily specified rather than estimated on the basis of completely reliable data, which leads to problems when these fundamental factors turn out to be more or less inaccurate, as often happens.

An additional problem is that these traditional accounting methods primarily measure cost displacement. As suggested previously, the intangible benefits are ignored, even though they may be the most important ones for the project. Several researchers have suggested quantitative approaches to overcome these deficiencies.

Quantitative Methods

One quantitative approach suggests applying information theory (Chapter 3) to the problem. Under this concept, the value of information is measured by the gain achieved from using it. This implies a value statement by the user of the benefits to be gained from an information systems application. The value of this approach would be increased by the provision of an operational plan for employing the concepts in an ongoing business activity.

An interesting simulation approach has also been suggested for evaluating management information systems. This method, of theoretical interest only, is aimed at making it possible to evaluate some of the intangible aspects of an information system by measuring the system's contribution to improved control of the overall organization in terms of the economic performance of the firm. In other words, the investigators want to determine whether significant performance differences can be realized as a result of changing selected aspects of the information processing system. The approach, however, suffers from overgenerality and vagueness.

The Bayesian school of statistical decision theory (see, for example, Pratt, Raiffa, and Schlaifer, 1965) has done extensive work in cost/benefit analysis. The methodology was most directly applied to management information systems evaluation by James Emery (1971). Bayesian methodology uses a procedure that combines sample information from experience with an original estimate of benefits. Suppose the initial estimate of the benefit or net gain from a project is $2600 a month with typical anticipated deviation from that amount of $130. During the first 9 months of use, let us say that the system results in benefits as follows:

First month: $2700   Sixth month: $2750
Second month: 2550   Seventh month: 2495
Third month: 2600   Eighth month: 2220
Fourth month: 2310   Ninth month: 2550
Fifth month: 2415

From this sample of monthly benefits, we calculate the average monthly benefit ($2510) and a sample deviation in monthly benefits ($173).

We want now to modify the original estimate of $2600 by combining it with the newly collected information. The formula:

$$\frac{\dfrac{9}{\$173^2} \times \$2510 + \dfrac{1}{\$130^2} \times \$2600}{\dfrac{9}{\$173^2} + \dfrac{1}{\$130^2}} = \$2525$$

is used to calculate the new benefit figure of $2525.

This method does little in the way of formalizing the original estimate, nor does it yield new sample information. There are relatively few reports in the literature of experiences with this technique, and these efforts have not been integrated into the problem of information systems evaluation.

It appears that more work is needed in all the quantitative methods, especially in means of examining costs and benefits as they are related in the organization. Furthermore, we need to evaluate these factors both before and after project development. Rather than attempting to respond to all the criticisms for the techniques discussed involving data processing cost structure, it may be preferable to determine the value of information through the eyes of the user. To this end the subjective estimation approach has been incorporated into the economic study of information systems.

Subjective Estimation

Since users are the ones who will be affected directly by a system, their inputs and evaluations should be important. Other people, such as data processing and systems staff members and higher level managers in the organization, might also have insights into the economic benefits of a particular activity and so should be consulted. One approach to this problem proposes the identification of factors besides costs and cost savings that should be considered in evaluating information systems. Its operative mechanism is a technique for gathering *subjective estimations* from people involved.

We need to incorporate into our assessments of benefits the views of people who will use or be affected by an information systems application. This means that if a systems application will affect a marketing manager in some way (for example, if the manager will provide input to the system, use reports the system produces, or be accountable for performance data about the marketing department), his or her opinion about the system should be included in the evaluation. The basis of the subjective estimation approach is the belief that by using group opinion and evaluation, we can put together a more complete evaluation of both the project and the organization. Usually when we try to assess group opinions, we form committees. However, the committee approach has its drawbacks. The member with the greatest authority may be the most influential, and any individual opinion that is unusual or significantly different from the majority view may be disregarded. The subjective estimation procedure we discuss overcomes the problems of the committee approach while still eliciting opinions from a group of people. As applied here, the subjective estimation procedure incorporates another procedure, the Delphi technique.

As part of the subjective estimation procedure, the Delphi technique involves a panel of managers, users, and systems personnel answering a sequence of questions that eventually leads to an assessment of dollar value. Inputs to the procedure include detailed specifications of the purpose of the project and sample outputs. There is no statement of costs—this avoids biasing panel members' estimates of the benefits of the project.

To obtain the dollar valuations, the following questions are posed to the panelists:

1. If you had to be 90 percent certain that the information shown on the reports would be worth more than it costs to your department, how much would you be willing to pay for it?

Figure S16.2 Outputs of Iterative Evaluation Process

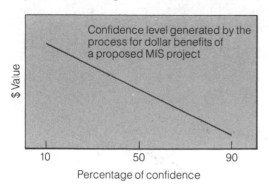

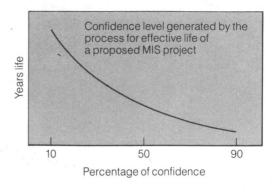

2. How much would you pay if you had to be only 50 percent sure?
3. If you had to be 10 percent certain that the project would be worth its costs to the department, how much should be paid for it?

These questions are given to the panel members several times; everyone gets feedback from the answers of others between rounds of questions. The people can then change their evaluations in light of the feedback—which contains information on why people formulated their valuations at the levels indicated. The project, then, is evaluated in terms of what the panelists would be willing to pay for the information, without reference to the vague term *information value*. The mean (average) at the three confidence levels (90 percent, 50 percent, and 10 percent) can be compared with the usefulness of the project (that is, the number of years the application can be used without major modifications—this can also be derived through questioning of the panel members) to yield a value for the application benefits (Figure S16.2).

Using subjective estimation, it is possible to take diverse opinions into account, while forcing panelists to examine their own reasoning about the system through the feedback of others. Instead of posing the question "What is the value of this information?" which relies on the ill-defined and difficult concept of the value of information, the Delphi technique asks "How much would you pay for this information?" To answer this question, panelists must face the serious task of determining how many of the organization's dollar resources should be allocated to one specific project in comparison to all other projects.

Regardless of the method employed, it is important that costs and benefits be assessed before the development of an application to determine the value of the system to the firm. It is equally important to readdress these issues after a prototype has begun operating or an application has been implemented to determine whether costs are under control and whether benefits will be realized.

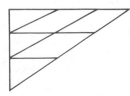

17: Tools and Methods for Developing Information Systems

Key Questions

[handwritten annotations: device that improves performance of a task. / speed development]

What are tools? What role do they play in the development of information systems?

How does the use of structured analysis change information systems development activities?

[handwritten: (Fig 17.6 p.707)] What are the steps in the design of computer-based information systems?

When is the output from an application designed? *[handwritten: first !]*

How do the features of on-line systems differ from those that run in batch? *[handwritten: smaller input file volume]*

What methods exist for structuring a design? *[handwritten: data flow diagram / flowchart]*

In what way does the use of CASE tools change the systems development process? *[handwritten: speeds ;]*

How can systems analysis and design activities be automated? *[handwritten: automates some of it.]*

Our major obligation is not to mistake slogans for solutions.
Edward R. Murrow

To an end-user, the development of an information system may seem to be a fairly straightforward and rapid process. To others, however, it may appear to be mysterious and confusing. In this chapter, we try to dispel some of this confusion by providing an overview of the development process. We begin by describing the meaning of tools in the development process. Structured analysis is one of the most widely discussed methods for developing information systems. In the chapter we will look at this method, with an eye toward the activities that occur to improve the overall development process. The last section of the chapter discusses CASE tools. CASE systems are automated tools that incorporate computer processing into the development process. CASE is growing in importance and impact.

There are two supplements at the end of the chapter. The first describes the techniques analysts use to determine application requirements, and the second describes physical construction concepts and methods.

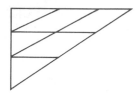

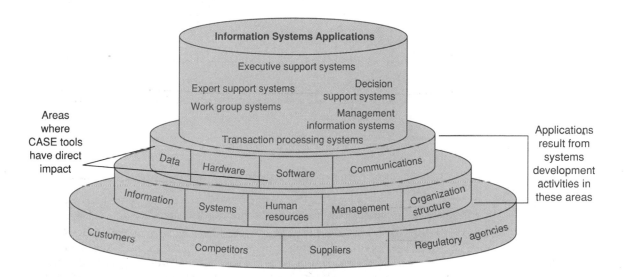

Areas where CASE tools have direct impact

Applications result from systems development activities in these areas

Information Systems Applications

Executive support systems

Expert support systems

Decision support systems

Work group systems

Management information systems

Transaction processing systems

Data | Hardware | Software | Communications

Information | Systems | Human resources | Management | Organization structure

Customers | Competitors | Suppliers | Regulatory agencies

Why Should You Know About Information Systems Development Tools and Techniques?

The process of acquiring an information system affects many people in an organization, either directly or indirectly—not just information systems professionals. The reasons why you should know about tools and methods for developing information systems include:

Knowing why the development of information systems takes time: The many development activities take time, particularly if the desired results are to be obtained. Each step provides information that determines how well the next step can be accomplished. When applications are not right, you can often retrace certain steps to find out about missing information.

——*Knowing what steps are being taken to improve systems development:* New tools, including those that use automation, are being introduced regularly. Such tools may make it possible to create applications more efficiently.

——*Knowing the role you may play in the development of information systems:* You play a key role in the development of information systems, regardless of whether you are a developer or a user of these systems. Thus, you should be familiar with the process of development.

Some organizations are questioning whether end-users can take over the development activities themselves. You might keep this question in mind as we explore the different activities and the tools that are available for assistance.

Tools for Developing Information Systems

A tool is any device that improves the performance of a task, provided the tool is used properly. A hammer, nails, and a saw—tools basic to construction work—make the building process easier and improve the results.

Types of Tools

In the development of information systems, tools fall into three categories:

——*Analysis tools:* improve the documentation of an existing system and determination of requirements for the new or modified system.

——*Design tools:* assist in formulating the features of a system that will meet the requirements outlined during systems analysis. This includes specification of features of an application, including input, output, processing, and control. It also includes layout features, such as position of data and messages on display screens, reports, and other input and output aids.

——*Development tools:* assist in translating designs into functioning applications. These include software engineering tools, code generators, and testing tools.

Purpose of Tools

Tools have two purposes: to increase developer productivity and to enhance information systems quality.

To Increase Developer Productivity The right tools should make it possible to improve developer productivity. Also, in some instances the appropriate tools will make a task possible that would otherwise be infeasible.

The productivity of analysts increases when tools reduce the amount of time needed to document, analyze, and construct information systems. The availability of structured analysis or automated tools encourages them to place greater emphasis on identification of systems requirements before initiating construction of the system. Identifying user requirements, stating them in an understandable form, and communicating them to all interested parties before construction of the system begins saves time in the long run. When used properly, therefore, tools increase the analysts' efficiency. Having and using the right tools also saves resources: people, time, and money. In the end, improved productivity is the result.

To Enhance Information Systems Quality Improving a process usually improves the resulting quality as well. Quality is the achievement of excellence in results that meet expectations, including having the right features in a system: methods of input, output, data management, and processing that will fulfill user needs. Furthermore, enhancing quality will help the system work as expected, providing the necessary information in an appropriate form.

Information systems quality results in part from having the right tools. But it also requires the knowledge to use the tools properly.

In the following section, we describe the analysis and design process in detail. Notice the manual tools that are identified in this discussion. As you read about them, consider how both tool and process could be improved.

Structured Analysis Method

Failing to determine and specify user requirements accurately and completely is a major cause of new systems failure. For example, if all needs are not identified, the system will be designed on the basis of an incomplete set of requirements. If needs have been specified inaccurately, the resulting requirements will be inconsistent and perhaps incompatible.

Thus, much of the success of the system depends on identifying the right requirements for the application and then ensuring that the development meets these requirements. This is a crucial step, because if the application that is developed does not meet the needs of the users, it may fail.

Structured Analysis

Structured analysis is aimed at avoiding potential difficulties by developing a logical, graphic model of the required system. When combined with statements of the objectives of the system (developed during system master planning) and system constraints, analysts and users alike have a meaningful requirements statement.

Structured analysis focuses on specifying *what* the system or application is required to do. It does not state how the requirements should be accomplished or how the application should be implemented. Rather, it allows individuals to see what the system should do independently of physical constraints. Later, a physical design can be developed that will be cost effective for the situation in which it is to be used.

Structured analysis uses graphic models because they show managers and non-systems personnel details of the system without introducing manual or computer processes, tape or disk files, or program and operating procedures. If the right symbols and notations are selected, virtually anyone can follow the way components in the system fit together.

Requirements Statement Using Structured Analysis

To demonstrate the use of structured analysis in assembling requirements statements, we build a **dataflow diagram** for a simple payroll application. For the logical model, the notation shown in Figure 17.1 will be used. This notation, which has become

Figure 17.1 Dataflow Diagram Symbols

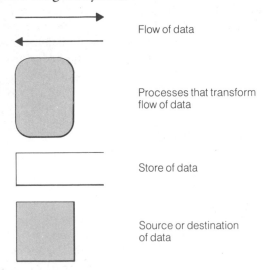

Flow of data

Processes that transform
flow of data

Store of data

Source or destination
of data

common in systems analysis, uses only four symbols: an *arrow* to show the flow of data, a *rounded box* to indicate processes that transform flow of data, an open *rectangle* to show a store of data, and a *square* to represent a source or destination of data. In addition, we can draw a line around the elements included within the system, that is, the system boundary.

For this sample analysis, the payroll system at the general level has the following description:

> The system will take time cards, ensure that each card represents an employee who is entitled to a paycheck (that is, a "valid employee"), determine pay, and produce a paycheck. Relevant payroll information will be stored.

Figure 17.2 shows a logical dataflow diagram for payroll processing. Notice that it shows the elements employees (square), employee data and payroll data (open rectangles), process time cards (rounded square), and time card and paycheck (data flow). Nothing has been said about how this system is implemented; we cannot determine whether it is a manual or an automated system. Nothing has been said about how the data are stored, either.

Earlier we pointed out the advantages of decoupling subsystems so that each can be studied separately. Then user information needs can be determined and described. The dataflow diagram aids in accomplishing this. Separate diagrams can be developed, at varying levels of detail, for each subsystem.

Levels of Analysis

The system shown in Figure 17.2 is described at a very high level, the way analysts might first approach a new application with which they were not familiar. But after seeing this very global view, they would want more information. They would prob-

Figure 17.2 Logical Dataflow Diagram for Payroll Processing

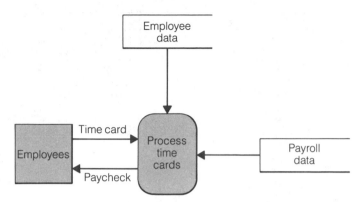

ably expand "process time cards" to develop a more specific, lower-level dataflow diagram. Figure 17.3 shows additional detail: "verify valid employee"; "determine gross pay"; "determine taxes"; "calculate net pay"; "generate paycheck." A more detailed data flow is described.

Notice that the system boundary is shown by a solid line surrounding many, but not all, of the components. "Employee" is outside the boundary of the system.

By using dataflow diagrams such as these, analysts can quickly determine where specifications are incomplete (remember that incomplete and incorrect requirements account for many new system failures). In the payroll example, nothing is said about entering new employees or about calculating deductions (union dues, donations, credit union, savings bonds) other than taxes. These could be handled in another lower-level dataflow diagram. Figure 17.4 demonstrates the hierarchies that can be built into dataflow diagrams: Deductions are explained at still a third level.

Data Dictionary of Data Stores

To define more meaningfully the data in the system, a data dictionary is developed. Asking "What do you mean by EMPLOYEE?" is a useful way of determining what data need to be stored about each component in the system. For EMPLOYEE, relevant data would include name and identification number. Other data would be necessary for such elements as taxes and pay rate. Figure 17.5a (p. 706) shows a data dictionary for the payroll example. Detailed specifications of the form of each data item are omitted here for simplicity. However, a data dictionary entry for this system might include the convention that the employee number is always seven digits and the first two indicate the year hired by the organization (68 = 1968, and so on).

Analysts should ensure that no essential data are missing and that there is no unnecessary redundancy in the data stores. Getting the data structures to a simple level should be encouraged, to make the logical dataflow clear to all users.

Once the data dictionary has been developed, analysts may indicate the data items that must be directly accessed, or they can indicate more precise logic for data

Figure 17.3 Expanded Dataflow Diagram for Payroll Processing

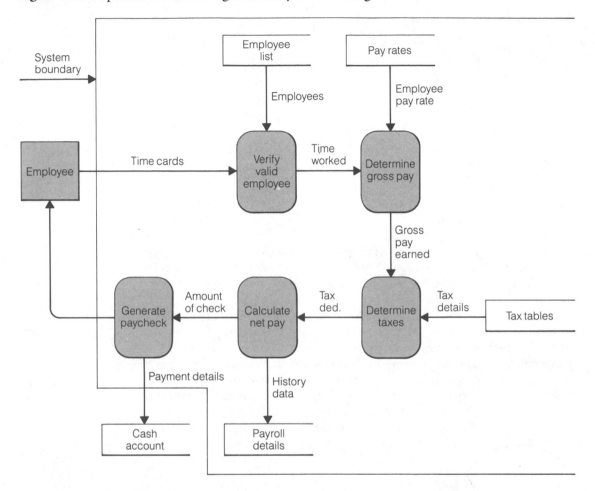

elements (for example, the overtime rate varies depending on whether the work is done on a holiday). Figure 17.5*b* shows examples of these variations.

Designing Information Systems

Requirements analysis shows what the properties of a system must be to meet users' needs but does not show how they will be developed. It is the *design* that specifies a particular solution or system. Thus a design translates a statement of the requirements into a plan or model for meeting such requirements.

This section describes the steps that are followed in the design process. Notice the tools that are utilized for each step.

Figure 17.4 Hierarchy of Definitions in Dataflow Analysis

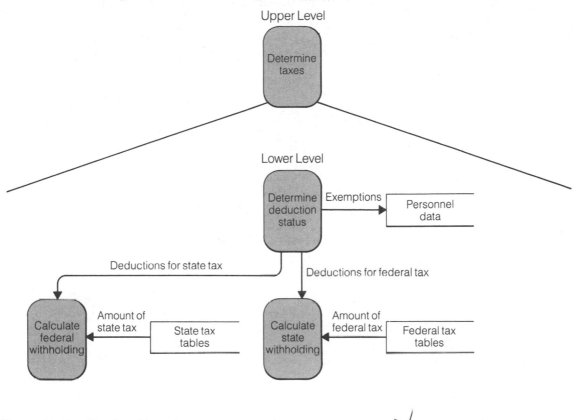

Steps in the Design Process

Systems design involves five major steps: output design, input design, processing design, data specification, and procedure specification (Figure 17.6). *Output design* focuses on selection of the content, form, and media for the reports and output the system will produce. *Input* records and methods are selected so that we know what data will be provided each time an application is run on the computer. In addition to identifying output, the *processing*—computation, data manipulation, and logic—needed to produce the output is specified. *Data specification* is also a necessary step; some data will be marked for storage in master files, and other data will be input each time an application is run. Finally, *procedures* are specified—programs and computer software as well as file and database construction are detailed.

Output Design

The first—and most important—stage in the design of a computer-based information system is to design the output the system will produce. You may be surprised to

Figure 17.5 Data Dictionary Entries for Dataflow Diagram: *(a)* Formal Definitions and *(b)* Decision Tree for Determining Overtime Status

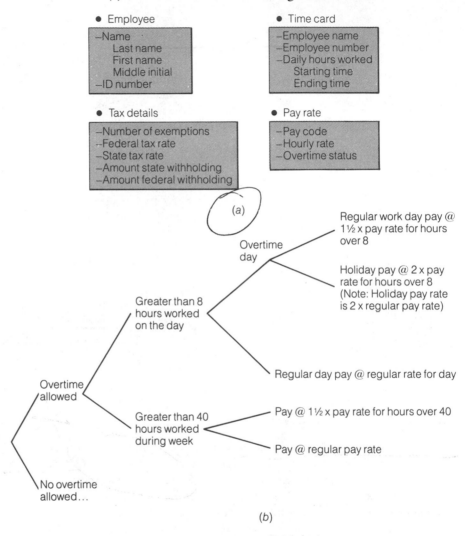

- Employee
  - –Name
    - Last name
    - First name
    - Middle initial
  - –ID number

- Time card
  - –Employee name
  - –Employee number
  - –Daily hours worked
    - Starting time
    - Ending time

- Tax details
  - –Number of exemptions
  - –Federal tax rate
  - –State tax rate
  - –Amount state withholding
  - –Amount federal withholding

- Pay rate
  - –Pay code
  - –Hourly rate
  - –Overtime status

(a)

Overtime allowed
  - Greater than 8 hours worked on the day
    - Overtime day
      - Regular work day pay @ 1½ x pay rate for hours over 8
      - Holiday pay @ 2 x pay rate for hours over 8 (Note: Holiday pay rate is 2 x regular pay rate)
    - Regular day pay @ regular rate for day
  - Greater than 40 hours worked during week
    - Pay @ 1½ x pay rate for hours over 40
    - Pay @ regular pay rate

No overtime allowed…

(b)

learn that the design of a system begins with the output and proceeds backward. After all, compared to designing files and processing, developing reports is not a complicated task.

Rationale

There are several good reasons for beginning with the output. First, a systems design is contemplated mainly, and perhaps solely, so it will produce certain output. In other words, if we don't need the output, we don't need the system! As the most important feature of the system, then, output has first priority in the design process.

Figure 17.6 Major Steps in Systems Design Process

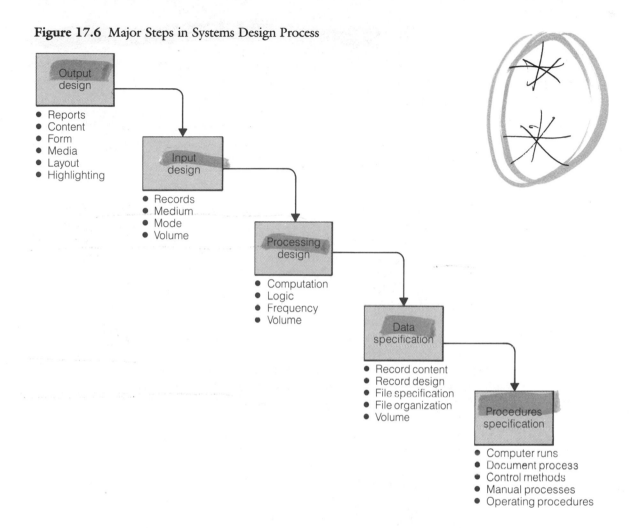

A second reason for dealing with output first comes from the strategic role it plays in the system. Although designing output is not difficult, designing good output is. To be useful and to help achieve the system's objectives, just any output will not do. It must be tailored to the individual(s) that will use it, as well as to the particular context in which it will be applied. Accomplishing this is no small task.

Still another reason for dealing with output first is that we want decisions about output to be separate from any other systems design. Within certain limits, we want to develop the best and most useful output possible without worrying about *how* we produce it. This is similar to our approach to data management, that is, the development of the logical structure of the data without concern for how the data are physically stored.

Output design should be guided by operating constraints such as hardware that is available and technology that can be applied. For example, if the computer system on which an application will be run does not include color displays and there are no plans to acquire them, output should not be developed for such displays. But other than factors like this, the design of output should be independent of the way it is produced. If we decide that a weighted moving average of items sold during the past year is needed in monthly sales reports, we should be able to incorporate this information into the report without worrying about how it is calculated. Similarly, we should not have to be concerned about how the underlying data are stored and accessed. We must, however, consider the areas of content, form, media, and layout, as discussed in the sections that follow.

Content

Content consists of the items of information that make up the output. The information that is to be conveyed to the user is the reason for the existence of the system. Selection of content for output should follow logically from the analysis of the systems purpose in terms of data to be processed (in a transaction processing system) or the decision activities to be supported. For example, in a transaction processing application such as preparation of payroll checks, the output would probably include gross pay, net pay, itemized deductions, and the name of the payee. In a more decision-oriented application such as a report of planned versus actual sales, the content could include planned sales by unit and product line and actual sales by unit and product line. In any case, the content of the reports should meet the user needs that were identified during the analysis stage.

One problem systems designers should guard against is information overload. Because computers make it possible to produce a tremendous amount of information quickly, there is a tendency to include in the output much more information than the user needs or wants. In many cases systems staffs feel they are doing the users a favor by giving them "bonus" information. In other cases, the designers do not know what to provide as output, so they provide everything. When reports contain 60,000 lines of output, of which only 60 are used, however, the design team has done users a great disservice. Output like this, which is a clear example of information overload, can easily irritate, slow down, or confuse decision makers.

Form

Another design concern is *form*, the way results are presented to users. Output may either be summarized or detailed. It may be presented numerically or graphically and in qualitative or quantitative form. A number of codes and abbreviations may be used, or all items may be spelled out. The form of output should reflect the characteristics and abilities of the users. This means that aptitudes and attitudes as well as training, experience, and other attributes of the user must be considered. If an individual is not comfortable with highly statistical output or customarily uses graphical information, systems staff should try to accommodate these preferences. All too often there is a tendency to determine output form by falling back on rules of thumb that designers have developed over time (for example, sales information should always be presented in terms of average sales, variance from planned sales, and so on). Giving greater consideration to the form of output from information systems may lead to more successful systems and more satisfied users.

Media

Media are the documents or displays used to present output and processing results. Output media such as punched cards, microfilm/microfiche, paper, and visual displays depend in part on the hardware devices used. One of the first media decisions is whether the output will be displayed or printed. If printed information is chosen, the medium on which it will be printed must be determined. The criteria for the decision include: purpose or use of output, final disposition of output, volume of output, form of information, number of copies needed, cost, and user preference.

The purpose or use of the output largely determines how much of it there should be and how the information will be communicated. Among the questions that must be answered are: Will the output have one-time or continuous use? Will it be provided regularly or only upon request or inquiry? Will it stand alone, such as a sales report? Or will it be presented with other information (for example, a report of project milestones and estimated completion dates attached to a contract proposal bid)? Answers to these questions may limit the number of media output options that can be considered. If the output is to serve as a turnaround document (for example, a utility bill), we would not consider an extensive printed report. However, a document that can later be optically scanned would be an option. Likewise, if output is going to be used repeatedly over a period of, say, a month, an easily accessible medium would be the best selection.

The volume of output also limits the design options. If the volume is high—several thousand lines, for example—visual display probably is not appropriate; paper or microfilm/microfiche might be.

Number of copies, cost of producing the copies, disposition of the output, and the form of information to be output can very quickly lead to a media decision. If the identical output is to be distributed to two or three different users at the same time and it is all quantitative, we probably would lean strongly toward using a printed report made with several carbon copies. However, if a large report is to be distributed to more than three or four people, it is better to print one copy of the output on a line printer and use other methods, such as an office copy machine or an offset printing press, to prepare the remaining copies.

Where several options are equally desirable, the final determination should be the user's preference. This is in keeping with the principle that the system should be designed to fit the user(s), rather than trying to make the user(s) fit the system.

With printed paper media, other issues such as the size of the forms or documents and the possibility of using preprinted materials must be considered. With documents such as punched cards and microfilm/microfiche, the size is fixed. However, ledger paper for use on line printers can be purchased in a number of sizes. In most offices, the standard size paper used is 8½ by 11 inches (8 by 13 inches in legal offices and 8 by 10½ inches in the armed services and the federal government). Most filing cabinets, file folders, and so on are built around these standard sizes. Yet in computer-based systems there seems to be a strong tendency to use paper 14 inches wide, which requires special filing equipment and forces the user to become accustomed to a larger, bulkier volume. Unless there is a good reason for avoiding it, however, the standard size is probably a better choice, all factors considered.

Preprinted forms are two to five times more expensive than blank paper. These useful media are more attractive for use outside the firm, however, and in some cases (for example, W-2 income tax forms), the law may require their use.

Layout

Layout specifies the location of each item of information on an output document or visual display, and any headings, titles, or page numbers that appear. Layout is an important concern in the output design stage because even if we have done a good job of defining content, form, and media, the system may be shunned if information is not well presented. If users cannot easily find the information they need in a report, they may find it too much bother to use the report at all. To be sure that poor layout of information does not decrease the value of your output, remember these simple rules:

1. List title and date prepared on each report.
2. Number all pages, and repeat title and date on each page.
3. Make the most important data or information in the report the easiest to locate.
4. Avoid overcrowding the form by including too much on a single page.
5. Use blank spots or "white areas" to enhance the appearance and readability of the output.
6. Develop the report so that the items read from left to right and from top to bottom.
7. Explain any nonstandard abbreviations used in the output. Spell out terms whenever possible.

The best way to determine whether a report of information will be legible is to use a layout form, a paper form on which sample titles, column headings, and information items can be drawn out to check for readability (Figure 17.7). Later, when computer programs are developed, instructions can be assembled to print or display output according to the format described on the layout form.

When designing systems that will display output visually on workstations, additional considerations guide the layout effort. The space available is typically 80 characters wide by 24 or 25 lines long. Thus, there is less room for data than on a printed page. Moreover, fewer pieces of data should be included on a visual display, to avoid overloading users with information. Often these restrictions result in output that spans several display screens.

When users work with printed output, they easily change the visual display by turning pages. However, when working on-line, users must be told how to move from the display currently visible to material before or after it in the system. This is

Figure 17.7 Sample Output Layout Form

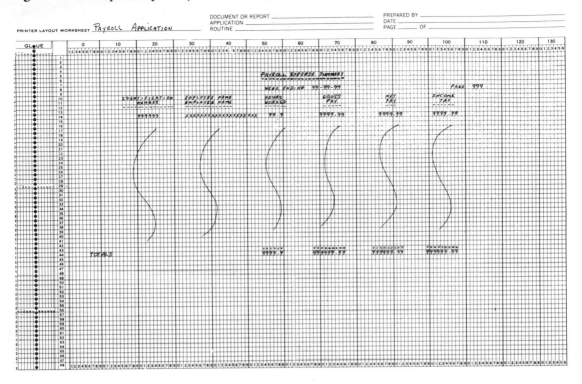

why *navigation information* telling the user how to proceed through the system is included along with the output. Such information consists of instructions on:

——How to display the next screenful of information
——How to request and retrieve information
——How to exit from the system

Figure 17.8 shows a display layout, including navigation information at the bottom of the screen. Because the layout is well designed, the user can quickly determine what key to depress to proceed by consulting the menu of options.

Highlighting Related to layout is concern for emphasizing the most important information. Although the highlighting capability is most frequently associated with visual displays, current printer technology permits highlighting on most print material as well. Output candidates for this form of emphasis include:

——Data signifying exception conditions (above or below expectations)
——Instructions to users
——Error messages

Figure 17.8 Computer Display Including Navigation Information

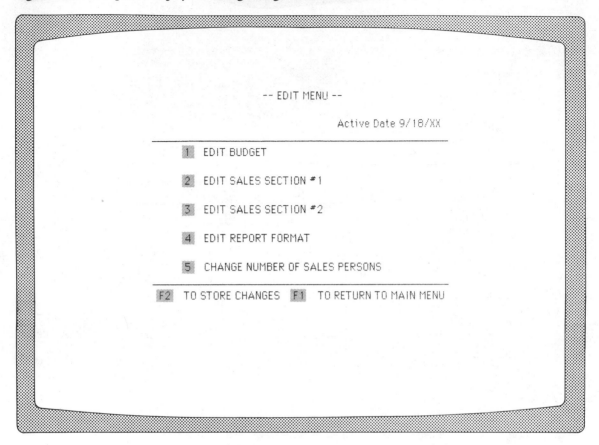

```
                        -- EDIT MENU --

                                      Active Date 9/18/XX

        ┌────────────────────────────────────────────┐

          1   EDIT BUDGET

          2   EDIT SALES SECTION #1

          3   EDIT SALES SECTION #2

          4   EDIT REPORT FORMAT

          5   CHANGE NUMBER OF SALES PERSONS
        └────────────────────────────────────────────┘
         F2   TO STORE CHANGES   F1   TO RETURN TO MAIN MENU
```

———Information about processing taking place (for example, "Sorting in process," "Processing inquiry," "Waiting for input")

Depending on the type of system, several highlighting methods may be used. Common methods for visual displays are blinking, underlining, increased/reduced light intensity, and inverse video (dark letters on a light screen). If the display uses color, red can be used for warning messages and green for normal conditions. Generally the most effective colors are red, green, blue, and yellow.

Highlighting on printed output is usually achieved by changing the spacing between letters or words, or by changing the vertical size of the letters. Italics and bold printing also are effective when properly used. Both dot matrix and laser printers include this capability as a standard feature.

Graphics The use of business graphics to enhance the presentation of information is increasing. Although the concept itself is not new, today's computer output devices are designed to perform this function especially well. The most effective use of

Inverse Video (dark letters on a light screen)

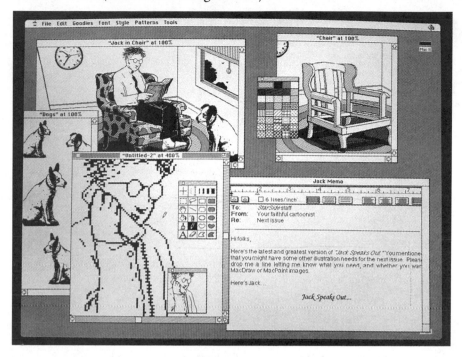

Graphics Display for Computer-Aided Design

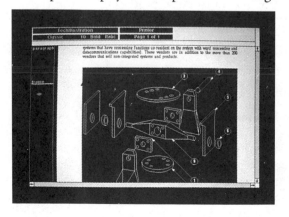

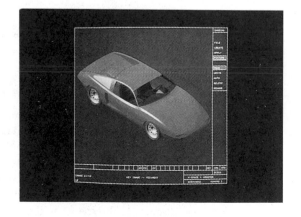

Figure 17.9 Common Types of Business Graphics

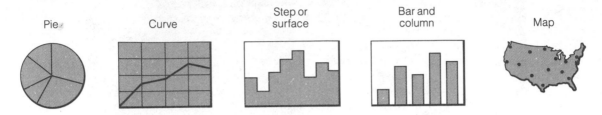

graphics as a layout tool is to display trends in data. Managers are able to see the trends much more quickly through business graphics than by examining tables of data.

Common types of business graphics (Figure 17.9) are:

——Pie charts

——Curve charts

——Bar charts

——Maps

These graphics can be displayed or printed, depending on the capabilities built into the software and the nature of the output devices in the system configuration.

Input Design

Input design involves instructing the system to guide processing or take certain actions, particularly in on-line systems. It also consists of identifying the items that will be input during an application and constructing the records in which they will be grouped for input.

Input and On-Line Systems

Most information systems are on-line, meaning that the user interacts directly with the computer: Interaction may be with a personal computer, with a personal computer attached to a communications network, or with a terminal connected to a remote computer. When planning interaction with an on-line system, the analyst must be sure to specify an easy-to-use interface. An **interface** is the common boundary between the user and the computer system, that is, the point where computer and user interact. A well-designed interface will allow the user to:

——*Tell the system what actions to take:* enter, change, or retrieve data and invoke processing actions

——*Facilitate use of the system:* allow the user to accomplish processing actions in a way that is perceived as natural and emphasizes methods that will not grow tiresome or unacceptable in frequent use

——*Avoid use errors:* prevent the user from doing things that interrupt expected actions of the computer system

And it will allow the user to do all of these easily.

The interface is often viewed as the user's window into the system, since it allows viewing of a portion of the activities that are going on within the system at a particular moment.

Actions to Specify in On-Line Systems

Three types of actions must be designed at the system interface: invoke processing, navigation, and receiving of messages.

——*Invoke processing:* Processing actions include the entry of data, editing of existing data, storage of data in memory, and retrieval of data.

——*Navigation:* **Navigation** means moving through the system, from screen to screen or page to page on a report or input form.

——*Receive messages:* Messages are the means of communication between system and user. They tell individuals when to initiate actions, the status of certain events and activities, and when an activity is completed.

Interfaces vary in form. Figure 17.8 illustrates the use of menus for taking actions and navigating. Figure 17.10 shows two alternate menu methods. The **softkey method** presents menu choices on the display screen that the user can select by *touching* the desired option. *Touch-screen* systems of this nature require special hardware features that can sense where the screen is touched. Increasingly common is the use of **pull-down menus,** discussed in Chapter 5 in conjunction with windows. This method, also shown in Figure 17.10, typically requires a mouse that functions as the pointer.

In addition to designing menus, systems designers can also design keyword dialogues to manage on-line processing. This method relies on the use of commands that the system can understand. When a particular command is entered, the system recognizes it and activates the appropriate processing activity for the command.

Moreover, advances are being made in the use of *natural language* interfaces. This approach allows users to instruct the system with less rigid commands than with the keyword method. Instead of using conventional command syntax, the users apply their own vocabulary to describe operations. The application translates the users' plain English instructions into commands it understands and takes the requested actions. Natural language interfaces are an area of vigorous research activity.

Often a **dialogue chart** is used to describe the way a particular systems design provides for navigation (see Figure 17.11). The illustration shows the functions performed by a program and the interrelationship between modules. Each box on the chart identifies the menu invoking a particular function.

Figure 17.10 Alternate Menu Forms

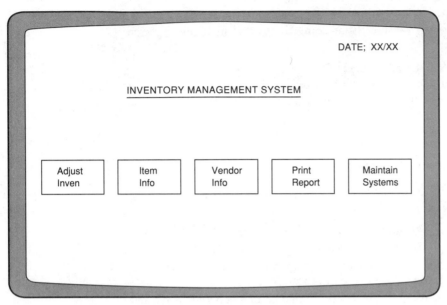

Press soft key corresponding to desired
alternative (ESCAPE to return to main menu)

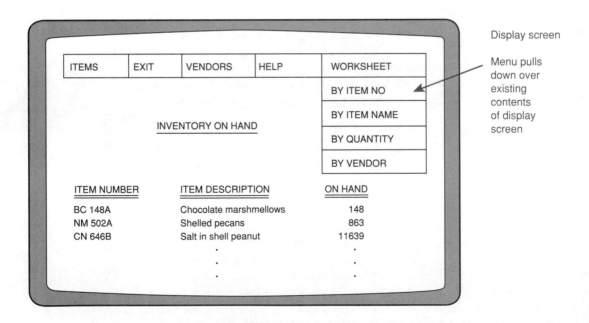

Display screen

Menu pulls
down over
existing
contents
of display
screen

Figure 17.11 Dialogue Chart for Inventory Management System

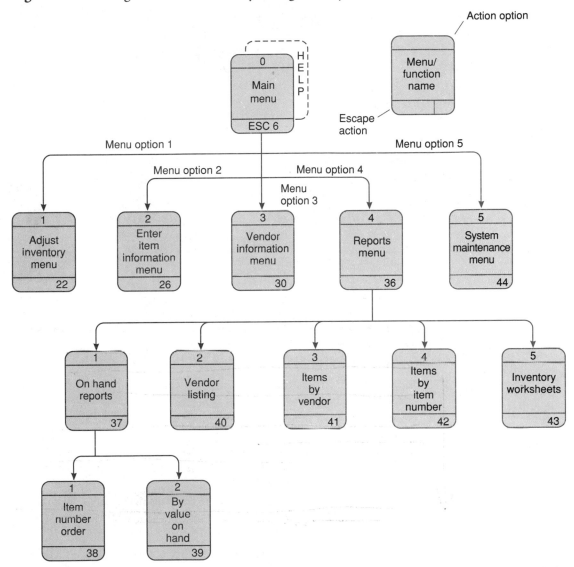

Input Record Content and Organization

Data that are needed for input to the processing stream are identified during the analysis stage and during design of output. For example, if we are processing a payroll transaction, we need to know the person being paid, perhaps an identification number, the pay period, and the number of hours worked during the period. Since those items are input to the process each time (as opposed to being stored in a

Figure 17.12 Sample Input Record

Data Item	Size	Type (9 = numeric, X = alphanumeric)	Sample Data
*Identification number	6	9*	424487
Employee name	20	X	John Livingstone
Regular hours worked	39.9	9	40.0
Overtime hours worked	39.9	9	3.8
Week ending	99999	9	101086

yte   1 2 3 4 5 6 7 8 9 10 11 12 13 14 15 16 17 18 19 20   21 22 23 24 25 26 27 28 29 30 31 32 33 34 35 36   76 77 78 79 80

master file), we want to group them together into an input record for submission for processing. It is much easier and more efficient to input these items together as a record than to submit them one at a time. The following guidelines should be followed in selecting and grouping data that will be input for processing:

1. Input only data items that will be used in processing applications; omit extraneous items.

2. Group together for input all data normally collected together as transactions or from individual documents.

3. Sequence items within a record according to the way data are collected, with the most important data (that is, the record keys that distinguish one record from another) at the front of the record.

4. In grouping data items into records, do not consider their use in the production of reports, but their use in the application. Input may be used to produce more than one report during a processing run.

After the data items have been grouped together into logical records, using a list or chart like the one shown in Figure 17.12 or a layout form, we need more information about the data item: size and type specification for each data item and items or fields that are recurring (that is, variable-length records). Figure 17.12 shows a record specification for a fixed-length record.

Input File Volume

Input volume is the size of the file based on the number of records that are to be input at one time. In batch processing systems, this can be quite substantial, while in on-line systems, it may be only one entry. In either case, the volume is determined by multiplying the size of the record (or the average size for variable-length records) by the expected number of records to be input. Since the number of records can vary dramatically, it is advisable to specify both a minimum and a maximum number, as well as an average number of records for input. (We see the mechanics of determining file volume in more detail when we look at file specification later in this chapter.)

Processing Design

After output and input have been designed, the next stages are development of computational processes, file specification, and procedure design. The order in which these three activities are handled may vary with different systems designers. In our approach we begin with the processing design, developing procedures and processes that define the ways output is produced.

Computation and Data Manipulation Requirements

When output content has been defined, we must define the data and the operations that are to be performed on the data. This is done on an item-by-item basis for every item in a report, display, or document. Not all items on a report require computation. For example, a person's name or identification number are not calculated. But since they do appear on the output, we must explain how they get there.

Definition of information that is computed from data means that the algorithm or formula that determines how the calculation is performed must be specified, either in a few brief narrative statements or according to a mathematical formula. It is essential that the data items to be used in the process be clearly indicated. Thus, if net pay is to be output on a transaction processing report, we would indicate that net pay is determined by subtracting "total deductions" from "gross pay" (Figure 17.13). This in turn requires that we define the calculations for "gross pay" and "total deductions." The same procedure is followed for all items on the output that require calculation until all have been defined at the most elementary level.

The items that are not calculated originate from one to two sources: They are retrieved directly from storage in a file or are input to the system as data.

Volume and Frequency of Output

In addition to stating or defining the items that will appear in the output, it is necessary to determine how much output there will be and how often it will be produced. For printed reports, the number of lines on a report should be determined; that is, the statement of volume should include an indication of the number of pages (minimum and maximum) that will be produced. To do this, use the number of lines printed on a single page, as determined in the layout specifications. The total length or volume can be calculated by dividing the number of lines per page into the total number of lines that will be included in the report. Thus, if we are printing a report

Figure 17.13 Sample Processing Specifications

```
NET PAY                 = GROSS PAY - TOTAL DEDUCTIONS
GROSS PAY               = REGULAR PAY + OVERTIME PAY
REGULAR PAY             = REGULAR HOURS WORKED x PAY RATE
OVERTIME PAY            = OVERTIME HOURS WORKED x OVERTIME PAY RATE
OVERTIME HOURS WORKED   = HOURS WORKED - 40
OVERTIME PAY RATE       = PAY RATE x 1.5
TOTAL DEDUCTIONS        = TOTAL INCOME TAX + TOTAL CONTRIBUTIONS
TOTAL INCOME TAX        = STATE INCOME TAX + FEDERAL INCOME TAX
```

of payroll expenses for 50,000 employees and each page of the report holds 50 lines of data, exclusive of headings and titles, the report volume would be 1000 pages.

volume

For other types of output, the number of documents prepared is a more meaningful measure. In output in the form of checks or turnaround documents, the number of separate documents that will be prepared should be calculated. When it is not possible to state the precise volume of output, it is advisable to give minimum and maximum volumes. Therefore, if a company employs many temporary workers during busy times, we would have to indicate the check-printing volume in a range showing minimum and maximum number of checks prepared year-round.

frequency →

Besides determining volume of output, it is necessary to state how often the output will be produced. In some cases, this will happen regularly (for example, daily or weekly). In other cases, output will be prepared only on request. A well-documented design states reporting frequency clearly. When the reports are not produced regularly, the design should identify the specific conditions under which the report may be requested and produced, including how often it may be done. For example, if we anticipate that a cost-variance report will be produced only when the total costs are above a certain dollar level, and we anticipate that this level will be passed every third week, we should include such a statement in our design specifications.

Data Specifications

In the process of identifying computations used to produce the system output, we saw that some of the data items were stored in databases or files maintained in the system and others were to be input each time a report was produced. The way we define and organize records has an impact on processing activities such as retrieval of the record from storage and sorting records into an order.

Record Content and Organization

The first step in developing data specification is to group all the different data items that will be used together. This helps us determine what records should be constructed and the data items that each should contain. Useful rules to guide this process are:

1. Be sure that all data items are stored data items—not those that are input each time a report is produced or output generated.
2. Be sure that all data items grouped together are used together; avoid random grouping of data items.
3. Include only data items that are actually needed and *used*; avoid gathering items just because they seem to go together.
4. In grouping items to establish logical records, do not consider file organization; treat the physical structure of files independently of the record contents, unless there is good reason for an exception.
5. Group items according to their use in the application rather than according to the specific report for which they are required.

By following these rules, we permit the development of relationships between different items. For instance, we will see that in payroll processing, wage or salary rates, income tax data, and employee deduction data will be used together. Therefore, we group them into the same record. At this point we should not be constrained by how the data will actually be stored on storage devices. This will be determined later after the logical design specifications have been established.

In discussing output, we have focused on specific reports. The design process, however, deals with information systems *applications*. This is especially important in data specification. Whereas data items are identified according to the specific report in which they are used, when records are formatted, the data should be organized as they are needed for an application, not just for a specific report. Many applications lead to the production of more than one report, as in the case of a payroll processing program that generates both paychecks and payroll expense reports. Thus certain data items may be used to produce several or even all of the reports needed in an application. In the payroll example, we need income tax data to calculate net pay printed on the checks and on the payroll expense report. But this does not mean that there should be separate records for each output or report. The same data records may be used to produce all the reports. If the payroll application produces paychecks, a report of payroll expense, and a separate report of federal and state taxes withheld for the employees, data from an individual employee's record are used to produce all three output documents. Cases like this are the reason for the recommendation to group data items according to application rather than report.

As data items are assembled, it is useful to enter them on a chart or table (see Figure 17.12) so that none are overlooked. The size or length of the data item as well as the type can also be recorded. When the list is finished, there will be a complete set of specifications for the record. Record keys (for example, employee identification number) may also be indicated on this list.

When all the items are grouped into records and key fields are specified, individual items within a record should be organized into an order (first field, second field, and so on). Working from the list of data items we have developed without concern for order, we can go back and organize the data on a record layout form such as the one shown in Figure 17.12. This method is often used in simple transaction processing systems. Another method, very common among systems that revolve around DBMS, is to establish the record organization in the form of a subschema, indicating all appropriate levels, field specifications, and so on, as we saw earlier.

File Specification

After record contents and organizations have been developed, we do **file specification;** that is, we organize the files. Master files are relatively permanent collections of records containing data about events affecting the organization. Thus, if a collection of records contains historical data or current event data that are used to monitor events or status of activities, the file should be established as a master file. If the data are temporary and are used in processing data already stored in master files, we designate these files as transaction files. Records of the number of hours employees worked during a certain week, which are used to calculate gross and net pay, are contained in transaction files. Data about regular deductions, number of dependents, and income tax calculation are stored in a master file.

In addition to specifying transaction and master files, we need to determine file volume. *File volume* is the size of the file, determined by calculating the number of characters in each record and multiplying it by the number of records in the file. However, it may not be possible to determine precisely how many records will be in the file (recall the payroll example involving records of temporary workers). In this case—and it is quite common—the best measure is the probable minimum and maximum numbers of records that will be in the file. This provides a volume figure while the system is being designed. To prevent difficulties when the system is online, we should estimate the minimum and maximum sizes of the file again after startup. Even at this early point it is important to consider the additions and deletions of records that will occur as the file is used. (Will the file grow or shrink? At what rate?)

Keep in mind that records may be fixed or variable in length, depending on the designer's specifications. For fixed-length records, there is little problem in determining the volume. For variable-length records, however, the best we can do is to estimate the average size of the records and then use the average figure in our volume calculations. This approach is not precise, but it works.

Procedure Specification

With system output, computation and data manipulation requirements, data specifications, and input requirements complete, it is possible to formulate the processing procedures, that is, the computation and data manipulation activities, that will fulfill the other specifications. At this stage of the logical systems design, the entire system begins to come together. Operating procedures and controls and processing flow-charts are developed now.

Developing Computer Processing Runs

Each system application is composed of a set of different processing activities called computer runs. A **computer run** is one routine that the computer performs. For example, there are update runs that maintain files (additions, deletions, and changes in records). Similarly, computer runs create transaction files that can be processed against master files to generate reports and output from the system.

Once the design specifications dealing with output, files, computations, and input have been completed, the runs can be identified and developed. The purpose is to formalize the processes that must be followed if the system is to operate as described in the design. This means that we have to identify all computer applications and the data or information that is input and output. The sequence of runs needs to be specified too, so that the necessary transaction data will be available when they are needed for processing. In a payroll application, for example, the transaction file containing "hours worked" data would have to be created before actual payroll processing and master file updating could occur.

As the individual processing runs are identified, processing controls should be selected and backup provisions established to ensure the integrity of the data and the continued existence of the files. Input validation techniques, such as check digits and batch totals (see Supplement 7), should be incorporated into the design of computer runs before any programming activities begin. Similarly, backup provisions such as periodic dumps of files and databases and transaction logs should be built into the systems plans at this time. When the processing activities have been identified and linked together logically, the system is ready to be flowcharted.

Flowcharting the System

A **flowchart** of the system using all the specifications guides the people who will be programming the system and constructing the files and record structures. Two types of flowchart are used: a system flowchart and a program flowchart. A *system flowchart* (also called a *macroflowchart*) shows the flow of documents and information, as well as input and output processing in the computer system. A *program flowchart* (also known as a *microflowchart*) shows the specific activities performed within sections of a single computer program, such as reading and writing operations and individual computations. We are concerned here with the system flowchart; the program flow-chart is developed when the programmers begin actual construction of the software for the new system.

The system flowchart can be developed quite easily from the new design spec-ifications, according to the following guidelines.

1. Identify the starting and ending points for the processing system.
2. Identify all data and document input and the media on which they are input using standardized symbols (shown in the appendix).

3. Identify all document and results output, medium of output, and number of copies (use standard symbols).

4. Identify all major processing requirements, such as sort routines and update modules.

5. Identify all manual and computer-based procedures in the sequence in which they are performed.

6. Identify all decisions and conditions that control the flow of processing logic.

A flowchart for a payroll processing system is shown in Figure 17.14.

Data Storage and Personal Privacy

Do you know who has access to data stored about you? Do you know who can see your personnel file or a credit file about you? If you are about to graduate from college, you will be deluged with letters and notices from companies offering their services in the form of credit cards, life insurance policies, magazine subscriptions, travel abroad, and on and on. Do you know how these companies get your name and address and how they know you are graduating? Do the implications of these questions bother you? Should it be possible for businesses to get these data about anyone?

There is little question that many data about each of us are stored in computer-based files, that the data are personal, and that we know very little about their accuracy or who has access to them. However, none of these situations exists because of the computer or information processing technology. **Invasion of privacy** is a problem, but it is not a problem *because* of computer systems. The same situations existed before computers were in use. Invasion of personal privacy is not new either; we have faced it in the past. Photography, for example, brought with it cries of invasion of privacy by those who believed that photos should not be taken without the prior consent of the subjects.

Code of Fair Information Practices A large-scale study on computers and privacy was conducted by the Department of Health, Education, and Welfare, the predecessor of the Department of Health and Human Services. The study concluded that the computer had not created any new invasion of individual privacy and that there had been no greater collection of personal or sensitive data *because* of computer systems. The study did, however, reaffirm that computer systems intensify the problems that existed with manual systems and strongly recommended that protective measures be taken to safeguard personal privacy and individual rights. A *Code of Fair Information Practices* (U.S. Department of HEW, 1973) was established that states:

1. There must be no personal-data record-keeping system whose very existence is secret.

2. There must be a way for individuals to find out what information about them is in a record and how it is used.

3. There must be a way for individuals to prevent information about themselves obtained for one purpose from being used or made available for other purposes without their consent.

We have now completed all the stages in the logical design of transaction, processing, and information systems applications. After the users, managers, and systems personnel have approved the reports and procedures, the project goes into production. During production, the programming staff begins writing computer programs, creating master and transaction files, and testing the programs. When these activities are completed, the application is implemented and goes on-line. Then the new application is evaluated to test its effectiveness and to determine its impact on the organization.

Data Storage and Personal Privacy (continued)

4. There must be a way for individuals to correct or amend a record of information about them.

5. Any organization creating, maintaining, using, or disseminating records of identifiable personal data must assure the reliability of the data for their intended use and must take reasonable precautions to prevent misuse of the data.

The Code of Fair Information Practices provides a strong set of guidelines for dealing with personal privacy. Under the code, individuals should have an opportunity to correct erroneous information about themselves that has been stored in a private or public file. But how do we find out what information *is* stored, since we may not even be aware of the existence of a particular databank? Should the organization maintaining the file bear the responsibility (and the cost) of informing people about their records? If so, how often should this be done?

Privacy Act All these questions are difficult to answer, yet somehow they have to be faced. The federal government has taken the lead with passage of landmark legislation known as the *Privacy Act of 1974*. This law is aimed at implementing the Code of Fair Information Practices. It requires that federal agencies (except as clearly specified):

1. Permit individuals to determine what information is collected about them

2. Permit individuals to prevent records obtained for one purpose from being used for another purpose

3. Permit individuals to have access to information about themselves, to have a copy made, and to correct or amend records

4. Ensure current and accurate information

5. Be subject to civil suit for damages that occur due to willful or intentional actions

The law further specifies that agencies must keep track of data and the nature and purpose of any disclosure and maintain this information for a period of five years or for the life of the record, whichever is longer. Agencies must also make this accounting of information disclosure to the individual on request and must inform any other person or agency having information from the record of any dispute about or correction of it.

726

Figure 17.14 System Flowchart for Payroll Processing

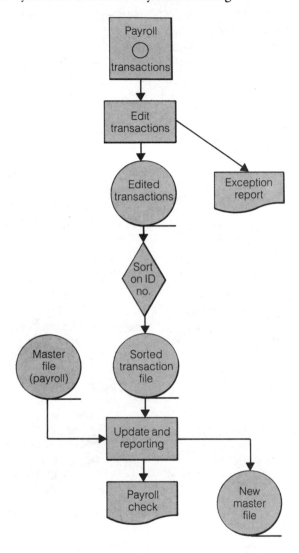

CASE Tools

As the preceding section indicates, many details must be specified in the design of an information system. In the future, automated tools—which rely on computer processing to accomplish development tasks—will replace manual tools, such as layout forms. However, only a portion of the design and development process actually tends to be automated. This section examines the benefits of CASE tools and the tasks that are being automated.

Meaning of CASE

CASE tools are receiving special attention because of their features and the promise they hold for improving analyst productivity and systems quality. The acronym **CASE** refers alternatively to *computer-aided system engineering* or *computer-aided software engineering*. Although the latter usage is more popular, the former is more accurate, since the long-term objective of CASE tools is to automate key aspects of the entire systems development process. Those who use the term *computer-aided software engineering* are quick to point out that application development begins with requirements specification, not with the actual coding of software. Thus the two expansions of CASE actually refer to the same process.

Table 17.1 includes a representative list of CASE tools.

Benefits of CASE Tools

CASE tools have the advantages of speeding the development process, automating tedious tasks, enforcing development standards, and capturing data that describe the system.

Speed the Development Process Introducing automated tools into the development of information systems can decrease the time necessary to complete the system. Tasks can often be completed more quickly either because the tool does the work or increases the speed of the work. (Imagine how much faster you can work with an electric saw compared to a manual one when constructing a wooden structure. The saw does a significant portion of the work for you.) For example, the time it takes to build a prototype is reduced compared to the time required for manual coding when a fourth-generation language is used. When a code generator (discussed in a moment) is used, the time needed will be even less.

Introducing automation is possible only when the analyst is trained in the use of tools to obtain acceptable results. Automated tools are not a cureall; knowing how to use the tools properly is a key element in their usefulness. (Imagine the damage that a novice using a high-speed electric saw can cause.)

Automate Tedious Tasks Some tasks associated with the development of information systems are just plain tedious. For instance, the creation of layout forms by inserting a position marker (an X or a 9) for each character of data is tedious but necessary.

Table 17.1 Representative CASE Tools

Tool Name	Computer System	Vendor
Analyst/Designer Toolkit	IBM PS/2; XT/AT compatible	Yourdon
CASE 2000	IBM PS/2; XT/AT compatible DEC VAX workstations	Nastec Corp.
Excelerator	IBM PS/2; XT/AT compatible Sun; Apollo	Index Technologies
Information Engineering Facility	IBM PS/2; AT compatible IBM mainframes using MVS	Texas Instruments
Information Engineering Workbench	IBM PS/2 (model 50 and higher) IBM mainframe using MVS DEC VAX	KnowledgeWare
Promod	DEC VAX, microVAX	Promod
Teamwork	Sun; Apollo, DEC VAXstation, IBM RT Workstation; HP 9000	Cadre Technologies
Visible Analyst	IBM PS/2; XT/AT compatible	Visible Systems Corp.

So is the development of dataflow diagrams when using structured analysis. Drawing charts, regardless of how useful they may be, takes time. Automated tools for creating layouts or drawing dataflow diagrams make it possible to turn the specification and drawing processes over to computer software.

Enforce Development Standards Standards specify the rules for certain development decisions. For example, an organization may have data standards that prescribe the length, type, and name to be used for particular data items. Other standards may guide the position of page numbers, dates, and the like on reports or the use of function keys for interaction with a personal computer keyboard.

When procedures are embedded in software, they are performed more consistently. Examining dataflow diagrams to ensure that they are complete and correctly drawn can be done manually. However, the task may be slow and error-prone. Automating the process will ensure that the evaluations are performed consistently each and every time.

Similarly, the generation of computer code is a task better performed by computers than by people. Generation rules can be consistently and accurately applied.

Capture Data That Describe the System Information systems development projects rely on the capture and analysis of details describing the current situation, application requirements, and design specifications. Such data may be unique to an individual application or pertinent to several systems used throughout an organization. A distinct advantage of many automated systems is the capture, storage, processing, and retrieval of system details. Once in computer-processible form, system details can be used for a variety of purposes, as we will see.

Figure 17.15 Front- and Back-End Development Activities

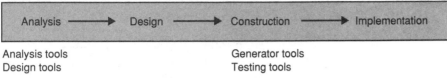

Front-end
development
activities

Back-end
development
activities

Analysis $\longrightarrow$ Design $\longrightarrow$ Construction $\longrightarrow$ Implementation

Analysis tools
Design tools

Generator tools
Testing tools

Project management tools

Activities Automated

CASE tools vary. Some automate front-end and others back-end activities. Still others are emerging that do both.

Automate Front-End of Development Process Tools that are designed to automate the early activities in the systems development process focus on requirements analysis and logical design, which are front-end activities (see Figure 17.15). Front-end tools often support the development of graphic models of systems and processes. Dataflow diagrams are representative types of front-end tools. As we have seen, dataflow diagrams depict systems processes and dataflows in graphic rather than narrative form.

Automate Back-End of Development Process Back-end tools are aimed at assisting the analyst in the formulation of program logic, processing algorithms, physical descriptions of data, and so on. These activities convert software logic designs into the actual code that brings the application into existence. Because of their use for software construction, back-end tools are sometimes referred to as *computer-aided programming tools*.

What CASE Tools Do

The features of CASE tools vary. This section describes the six activities most systems developers include in their definition of CASE.

Draw Descriptive Diagrams Many automated tools include *diagramming tools* that support systems development activities. Diagramming tools include the capacity to produce dataflow diagrams, data structure diagrams, and program structure charts (see Supplement 17B). As you know, types of diagrams are essential for support of the structured analysis methodology. And CASE tools incorporate structured analysis methods extensively.

Figure 17.16 Dataflow Drawing Screen and Command Menu (Index Technology Corp.)

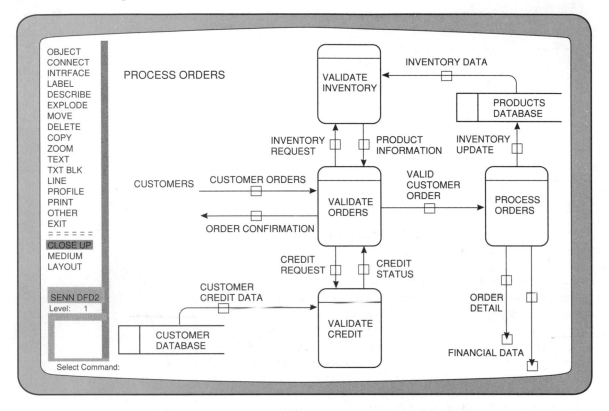

These tools support the capability to draw diagrams and charts and to store the details internally. When changes must be made, the nature of the change is described to the system, which can then redraw the entire diagram automatically. The ability to change and redraw eliminates an activity that analysts find both tedious and undesirable.

Figure 17.16 illustrates a dataflow diagram on the display screen of a personal computer.

Maintain a Descriptive Data Repository The capture, analysis, processing, and distribution of all descriptive data about information systems is aided by a data repository. The repository contains the details of systems components, such as data items, dataflows, and processes, and also includes information describing the volume and frequency of each activity (see Figure 17.17).

Repositories typically record the following types of information:

——Record and data element descriptions

Figure 17.17

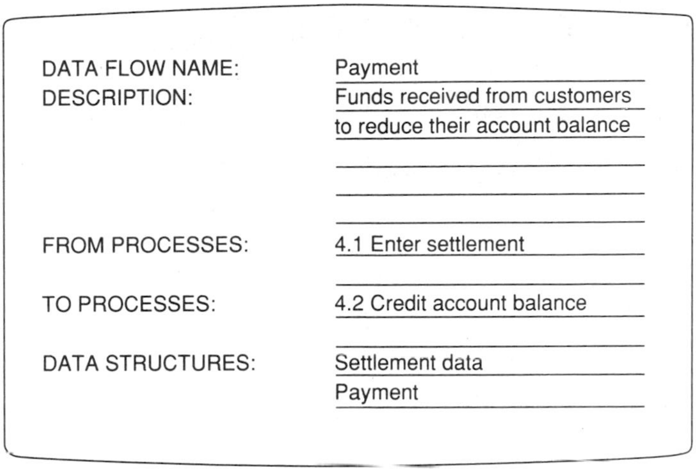

```
DATA FLOW NAME:        Payment
DESCRIPTION:           Funds received from customers
                       to reduce their account balance



FROM PROCESSES:        4.1 Enter settlement

TO PROCESSES:          4.2 Credit account balance

DATA STRUCTURES:       Settlement data
                       Payment
```

——Data details, including details of dataflows, data stores, and tables of user-defined codes (for example, the code for a cash sale, a credit sale, a cash refund, and so on)

——Systems processes, functions, and modules

——Definitions and layouts of report designs, screen designs, and data entry forms

While repositories are designed so that the information they contain is easily accessible, they also include built-in controls and safeguards that preserve the accuracy and consistency of system details. This helps make it possible to capture and maintain the descriptive data discussed earlier.

Figure 17.18 shows a repository entry for data elements using the CASE tool Excelerator.

Design Display Screens Since the data repository contains definitions of the data elements in a system and can also draw charts, it is not surprising that automated tools often have the capability to design display screens. Hence the manual process we described earlier in this chapter can be avoided if the proper tools are available.

Figure 17.19 shows a sample screen designed using Excelerator. Notice that field spaces are clearly identified. The information at the bottom of the display screen includes the specifications prepared by the analyst. Screen intensity, use of reverse letters, and inclusion of underlining, for instance, are all specified easily. Help messages are also entered at the bottom of the display screen.

Design Output Layouts Report and other layouts are created in a similar fashion to that described for display screens.

Figure 17.18 Dictionary/Repository Entry for Data Elements (Index Technology Corp.)

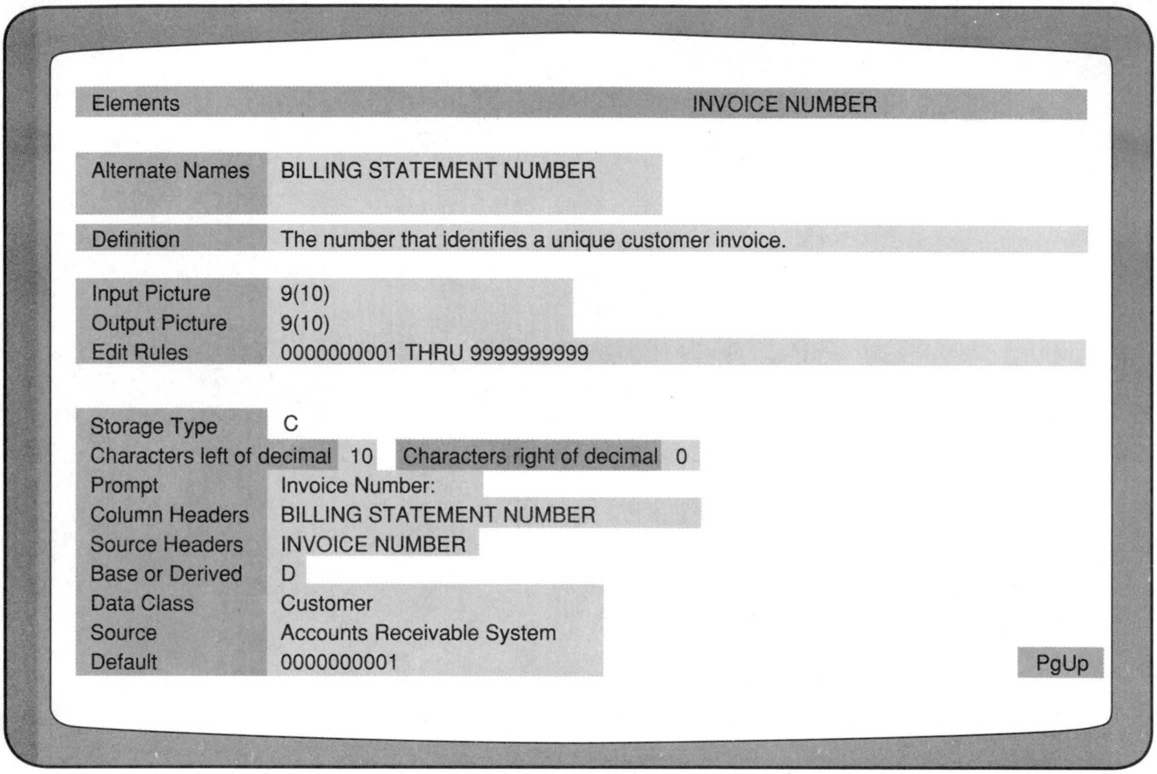

Elements	INVOICE NUMBER

Alternate Names	BILLING STATEMENT NUMBER

Definition	The number that identifies a unique customer invoice.

Input Picture	9(10)
Output Picture	9(10)
Edit Rules	0000000001 THRU 9999999999

Storage Type	C		
Characters left of decimal	10	Characters right of decimal	0
Prompt	Invoice Number:		
Column Headers	BILLING STATEMENT NUMBER		
Source Headers	INVOICE NUMBER		
Base or Derived	D		
Data Class	Customer		
Source	Accounts Receivable System		
Default	0000000001		PgUp

Some tools also store test data. In these cases, the data can be used to generate a sample report using the layout specification. The data appear in the form and position on the report chosen by the analyst. The tool does all the work, so that no computer software need be written to evaluate the report design.

The report layout in Figure 17.20 is for a parts listing. Report and column headings are entered by the user. Field-length specifications are determined automatically using the contents of the repository. The designer need only identify the items to be included; the rest is done automatically.

Generate Computer Code **Code generators** automate the preparation of computer software. They incorporate methods that allow the conversion of systems specifications into executable source code.

Code generators are most effective when they are integrated with a central repository. Such a combination achieves the objective of creating reusable computer code. When specifications change, code can be regenerated by feeding details from

Figure 17.19 Screen for Describing Data Field (Index Technology Corp.)

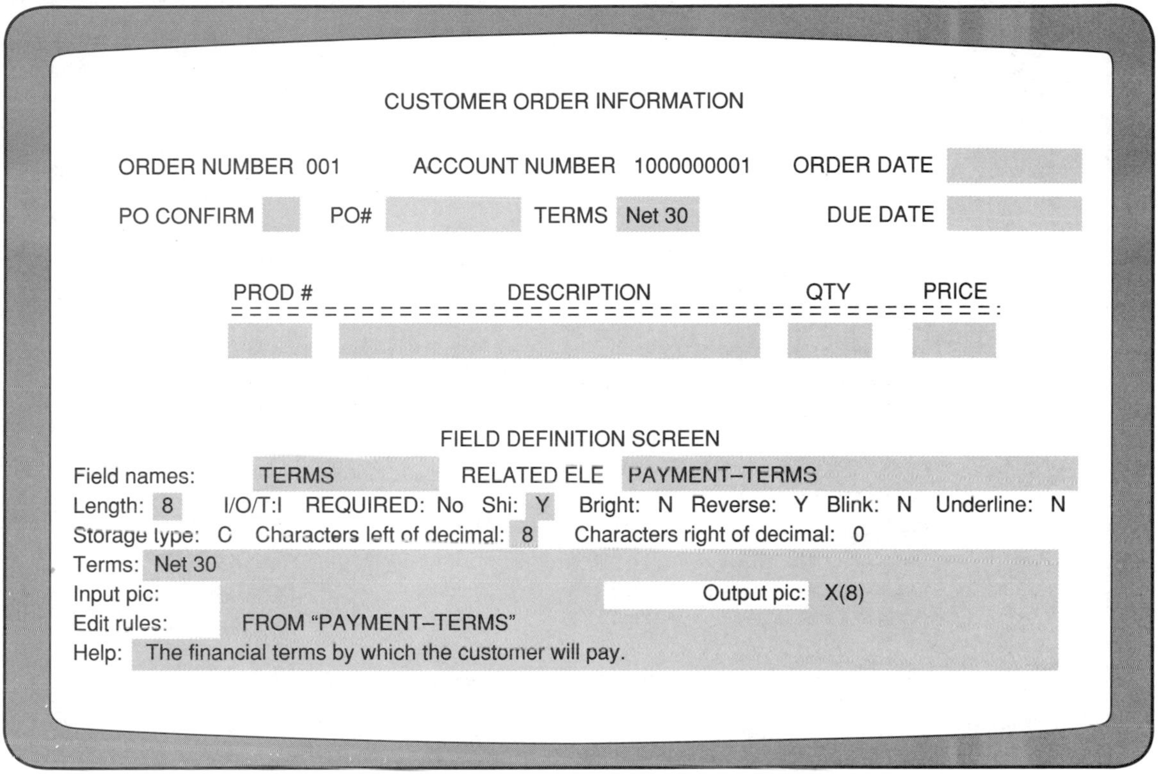

the repository through the code generator. The repository contents can be reused to prepare executable code.

Code generation is not yet perfected, however. The best code generators will produce approximately 75 percent of the source code for an application, and the rest must be written by hand. The benefits of code generators are still substantial, though.

The inclusion of code generators in CASE tools is quite common.

Assist in Managing Development CASE tools also assist project managers in maintaining project timetables. Analysis and design activities can be scheduled and resources allocated to different project activities with the help of the tool. Monitoring actual performance against planned performance is also possible. Moreover, schedules and reports can be prepared using details stored in the central repository.

CASE tools are growing in importance for the development of information systems. In the future we can expect more sophistication, especially in the area of automating the development of computer code. Everyone who uses information systems will benefit from progress in this area.

Figure 17.20 Screen for Report Design (Index Technology Corp.)

PARTS LISTING WITH SUPPLIER, CUST, AND PRICING DATA

PART#	PART NAME	UNIT PRICE	SUPPLIER	SUPPLIER NAME
Z9999	XXXXXXXXXXXXXXX	99999999	9999	XXXXXXXXXXXXXXXXXXXX
Z9999	XXXXXXXXXXXXXXX	99999999	9999	XXXXXXXXXXXXXXXXXXXX
Z9999	XXXXXXXXXXXXXXX	99999999	9999	XXXXXXXXXXXXXXXXXXXX
Z9999	XXXXXXXXXXXXXXX	99999999	9999	XXXXXXXXXXXXXXXXXXXX
Z9999	XXXXXXXXXXXXXXX	99999999	9999	XXXXXXXXXXXXXXXXXXXX
Z9999	XXXXXXXXXXXXXXX	99999999	9999	XXXXXXXXXXXXXXXXXXXX
Z9999	XXXXXXXXXXXXXXX	99999999	9999	XXXXXXXXXXXXXXXXXXXX
Z9999	XXXXXXXXXXXXXXX	99999999	9999	XXXXXXXXXXXXXXXXXXXX
Z9999	XXXXXXXXXXXXXXX	99999999	9999	XXXXXXXXXXXXXXXXXXXX
Z9999	XXXXXXXXXXXXXXX	99999999	9999	XXXXXXXXXXXXXXXXXXXX
Z9999	XXXXXXXXXXXXXXX	99999999	9999	XXXXXXXXXXXXXXXXXXXX
Z9999	XXXXXXXXXXXXXXX	99999999	9999	XXXXXXXXXXXXXXXXXXXX
Z9999	XXXXXXXXXXXXXXX	99999999	9999	XXXXXXXXXXXXXXXXXXXX
Z9999	XXXXXXXXXXXXXXX	99999999	9999	XXXXXXXXXXXXXXXXXXXX

3 EXIT 1,8 COLUMN 8 REPEAT 10 FIELD

However, we should not forget that CASE will not replace the analyst. There is no substitute for human judgment. The systems analyst remains the most important element in the development of information systems.

Summary

This chapter has examined the tools and techniques used in the design and development of information systems. Tools are devices that improve the performance of tasks, provided the tools are used properly.

Successful information systems development depends on accurately identifying the requirements the system must meet and ensuring that they are met. Effective requirements analysis is structured. Dataflows are identified and documented. The structured analysis method identifies dataflows as a way of modeling the system. Data elements are defined in data dictionaries. Different conditions and situations are explained using decision trees or similar tools.

Following a thorough requirements analysis, the logical design process begins, starting with the output and proceeding through specification of input, processing, data, and procedures. The logical design requires a knowledge of the hardware and equipment that will be available for the project as well as insight into potential users and purposes of the output. When the logical design process is completed, the project can go into production. Here programming or generation of computer code occurs and files are created and tested with the software. Finally, the new system goes into operation.

Automated tools are being used in the development process at a growing rate. Such tools are selected to increase productivity and improve system quality. CASE tools are important because they speed development, automate tedious tasks, and enforce standards and procedures. They also assist in the capture of important descriptive data. The features of CASE tools vary. However, it is evident that these tools are evolving, with more powerful versions in the offing.

Key Words

Back-end tool	File specification	Pull-down menu
CASE	Flowchart	Softkey method
Code generator	Front-end tool	Structured analysis
Computer run	Interface	Tool
Dataflow diagram	Layout	
Dialogue chart	Navigation	

Review Questions

1. What is a tool as applied to the development of information systems? What purposes do tools serve?
2. Identify the different types of tools.
3. Describe the purpose of structured analysis. What features distinguish this method?
4. What are dataflow diagrams? Why are they used? What do they consist of?
5. Compare and contrast the techniques for data gathering. At what point in the systems life cycle can each be employed? (See Supplement 17A.)
6. What objectives guide systems design?
7. Discuss the steps in the logical design of a new information systems application.
8. When is the system's output designed? Why?
9. How are input and data volume determined?
10. Describe the features of concern when designing input for on-line systems.
11. What methods of interaction can systems developers choose when designing the interface between user and system?
12. What alternatives exist for the presentation of graphic information and for highlighting of output contents?

13. What features that are unnecessary in computers that use printed output must exist in on-line systems?

14. What is meant by front-end development and back-end development?

15. What are CASE tools? Describe their purpose.

16. Identify and describe the features of CASE tools.

17. What benefits do CASE tools offer systems developers? Users of information systems?

18. What is structured programming? What are the progressions used in structured programming? What is its purpose? (See Supplement 17B.)

19. Discuss the methods of achieving a structured design. (See Supplement 17B.)

20. How are top-down design, bottom-up design, and modular programs related? Briefly describe each, pointing out the advantages they provide in software design and development. (See Supplement 17B.)

Application Problems

1. General Electronics is a distributor of electrical products of all types, ranging from home lights and lamps to industrial lighting systems. The company also stocks miscellaneous electrical items such as doorbells, electrical heating units, and a wide variety of electronic connectors.

   During the past four years, business has more than doubled, and profits have increased by 115 percent. The office staff, which processes all of the paperwork and invoices related to sales, has almost doubled during this period. At the beginning of the period, the staff consisted of a secretary and two clerks. Presently, the staff includes two secretaries and three full-time clerks, along with a part-time clerical assistant who works evenings and on Saturdays to help process customer orders.

   The customer transactions are a combination of retail cash and credit purchases, wholesale purchases to electrical contractors, and lot purchases by industrial and commercial sales organizations. Retail cash sales require that a sales slip be written up in three copies (one each for the customer, accounting, and inventory control). Credit sales are through a major national multibank credit agency. For these, the standard bank credit form is completed along with the cash sales slip. Purchases by electrical contractors and industrial and commercial customers require a purchase order form from the customer, which goes on file in the office. In turn, an invoice is typed that includes a statement of the merchandise and, of course, the customer name and address (with a shipping address if it is different from the purchaser's address). One copy goes to the customer by mail, a second copy is enclosed with the order as a shipping copy, and the other two copies are sent to inventory control and accounting.

   The part-time assistant is a graduate student at the local state university and has had courses in computer programming and introductory exposure to management information systems. The assistant has begun to think about the possibility and sensibility of introducing a computer into the operation. Might a higher level of efficiency be obtained through use of a computer? The assistant knows

---

Questions

1) What happens to credit forms?

2) bad credit processing?

3) where does ship address come from?

4) cash wholesale processing?

5) PO's reconciled with invoice?

6) Confirm order was delivered & received.

7) what if good cust. comes w/o a P.O.?

8) Are forms filed? where?

9) what do you do with cash? who receives?

10) How do you collect on credit sales?

that the company would not have to buy a computer, as the owner has access to a small machine through a friend in another company. There is little question that the owner of the company will resist the idea of computerizing the office transactions, saying that the computer cannot do anything that the clerical staff does not now do. But still the assistant wonders.

a. Develop the idea of this part-time assistant. What additional information would you need to deal with the question posed? Based on the information provided above, why would or would not the introduction of a computer into the office operation of wholesale lighting be a good idea? Take both sides of the issue.

b. Develop a flowchart that shows how orders in this company are processed. Use the standard flowcharting symbols shown in the appendix. List any information needed for a complete flowchart that is not included in the description. (*Note:* These are the kind of flaws that might be found in a poorly completed report on analysis findings.)

c. Develop a dataflow diagram for the above situation. Compare the process of doing this with the process you followed in doing the flowchart. What are the advantages and disadvantages of doing the dataflow diagram compared to the flowchart? In which can you easily develop process and data hierarchies?

2. Federal Supply Company manufactures custom-made metal and plastic parts and components. All parts and components are made to order on receipt of a firm purchase order from customers. When the required parts have been completed, they are immediately shipped to the customer. Approximately 75,000 customer-initiated purchase orders are processed by the company during a single year. A typical purchase order contains on the average a request for five different items, in quantities from 12 to 1000 each.

When customer purchase orders are received in the order processing office, an entry is made in a transaction log book, noting the customer name, date of receipt, and purchase order number (if any). The purchase orders are then sent to the accounting office for credit verification. This takes about one day. If credit is approved, the order is returned to the order processing office where the log is updated and a work order is made up. If credit is not approved, the order is returned to the customer (by the accounting office), along with a letter indicating the reason for disapproval. A pink sheet (credit action form) is sent to the order processing department indicating the credit decision. The pink sheet is used to update the transaction log book and is then discarded.

The work order is prepared in three copies. One copy is attached to the customer purchase order and is placed in the active sales file. A second copy is sent to inventory control, while the third copy is forwarded to the manufacturing office to be used in scheduling production.

The inventory control copy of the work order is used to prepare a materials requisition on the basis of information contained in the bill of materials file—a file that contains a breakdown of all parts and materials used in the manufacture of a specific item. One copy of the resulting purchase requisition, itself prepared in three copies, is sent to the purchasing department, with one copy remaining in the inventory control department (in the active purchase requisition file) and another copy being forwarded to manufacturing. When the purchasing department receives the requisition, it prepares a formal purchase order and sends it in three copies to the vendor. Fourth and fifth copies are placed in the active purchase order file and in the manufacturing office's active file.

When materials are received in the shipping room, the incoming packing list (two copies) is removed from the shipping carton(s), noted for accuracy (Did all of the billed material and parts arrive?), and copies sent to the purchasing department and manufacturing, respectively. When purchasing receives its copy of the packing list, it is compared to the original purchase order. If all ordered merchandise is received, the purchase order copy is placed in the closed purchase order file and the packing list is sent to the accounting department, where the amount is paid, by check, upon receipt of an invoice from the vendor or supplier. The purchase order remains in an accounts payable file until the vendor invoice arrives. When the bill is paid, the packing list, the invoice, and a "paid by check" form are placed in the closed accounts payable file.

When manufacturing receives its copy of the packing list, it is paired with the purchasing requisition and purchase order, and production is scheduled. After the merchandise is manufactured, it is sent to the shipping area together with the purchase requisition. The shipping office prepares a packing list (in three copies) and ships the merchandise to the customer along with two copies of the packing list.

The third copy of the packing list is sent to the accounts receivable department where an invoice is prepared and sent to the customer. A copy of the invoice is stapled to the packing list and placed in the active accounts receivable file. When payment is received from the customer, the documents are moved from the active to the closed accounts receivable file.

a. Develop a dataflow diagram for the current system. Indicate sources and destinations, data, and processes. Also develop the data dictionary entries that describe the system. Identify any areas for which you do not have sufficient data to fully describe a particular activity.

b. Assume that you have received the preceding data as a written report from which you will begin a systems investigation aimed at development of a computer-based system to replace the one described. Outline an analysis program to investigate the system and gather the facts you need to design a new system. Include a statement of where you would employ the different fact-gathering techniques and why you would use them.

3. Identify the graphic form that is most appropriate for communicating each of the following types of information:

a. The portion of each sales dollar that goes to material, labor, overhead, profit, and other usage categories.

b. The average monthly market price of a particular stock over a 2-year period.

c. A comparison of planned and actual revenues from different categories of customers.

d. Changes in automobile prices each year for the last 10 years by the three major automobile classes.

e. The percentage of income associated with each of five major product lines in a firm.

4. The design specifications for a motor vehicle licensing system calls for the following data to be entered through a computer workstation whenever a new driver registers for a license after passing the road test:

First name   (16)
Last name   (16)
Middle initial   (1)

> Street address or rural route   (24)
> Apartment number   (12)
> City or township   (24)
> County   (12)
> State   (2)
> Postal code   (9)
> Date of birth   (6)
> Height in inches   (2)
> Weight   (3)
> Restriction codes (for eyeglasses, physical handicaps, etc.)   (6)

Numbers in parentheses indicate the number of characters in the field.

Based on the guidelines discussed in the chapter, design an input screen for this system. The display screen is 80 characters wide and 24 lines long. Highlighting can be achieved through blinking characters, inverse video, and underlining. Indicate where any highlighting will be used.

Be sure the layout of the screen facilitates system use. Include appropriate headings and titles as well as navigation instructions that tell the user how to exit the screen, correct errors, or perform other tasks you anticipate.

5. The process of updating sequential files consists of the following activities (discussed in Chapter 7):

> Preparing the master file for use
> Preparing the transaction file for processing
> Reading a master file record
> Reading a transaction file

If the master and transaction file keys match, the master record is changed and written back to memory, and new master and transaction records are read into memory.

If the transaction file key is less than the master file key, a record is created and written to the master file, and the next transaction file is read.

If the transaction file key is greater than the master file record key, the master record is written to the new file, the next master record is read, and the process is repeated.

These three steps are repeated until there are no more transaction or master file records. Then the files are closed.

a. Develop a structured flowchart showing this processing procedure.

b. Develop a Warnier/Orr diagram for the procedure. (See Supplement 17B.)

6. The Morwatts Electric Company is developing a new computer-based application to improve processing of customer bills. Input to the system will consist of meter number and the most recent reading from that meter expressed as a six-digit number. When the data are input, they will be processed by a computer program that searches a file to match the input meter number with one stored in the file. This will make it possible to access the record corresponding to the customer who has been assigned the meter. In other words, the meter number is the key for the customer record. Other data contained in the record include customer name and address, last meter reading, billing code, and any unpaid balances from previous billing periods.

When the customer record is accessed, it is used to calculate the new bill and prepare a statement that can be mailed to the customer. The amount of electricity used is calculated by subtracting the previous meter reading from the new reading. The amount of electricity used is then multiplied by the appropriate unit charge, which is determined by using the customer's billing code and matching it in a file containing all unit charges. Thus, if the customer's billing code is "A," the code file is checked to determine the unit charge that corresponds to the code of "A."

Once the amount of the current bill has been calculated, a statement is output from the computer system. The statement contains the customer's name and address, the date of the statement, the amount of electricity used, the unit charge, the beginning and ending meter readings, the amount of the bill for the period, the last date to pay the bill, and the date of the next meter reading. The bill shows franchise charges and utility taxes, as applicable, along with any balance the customer owes on the preceding month's bill. Finally, the statement gives a grand total of charges and taxes.

a. Identify and describe the contents of all master files used in this system.

b. Is the file containing all unit charges a master file? Why? Do you feel it is a good idea to maintain a separate file for unit charges rather than having the charges and the codes included as instructions in the computer application program? Explain.

c. What media should be considered for input of the transaction data? Indicate the criteria you used in selecting these media over other possible input media.

d. What medium should be used for output of the statement to be mailed to the customer? Are preprinted forms a valid output option? Why or why not?

e. Develop a macroflowchart that shows all processing activities, all input and output, and all files. Assume that input data are on magnetic tape and output is produced on preprinted paper forms. Use standard flowcharting symbols.

f. A major fault in the processing system described earlier is that although a statement of electrical usage and associated charges is produced for the customer, no record of this information is maintained in the system. Develop a modified flowchart that provides for storage of this information in a system file.

7. A personnel master file pertaining to hourly employees of a business has records that contain the following data items.

> Job skill code   (4 characters)
> Job skill name   (12 characters)
> Employee last name   (12 characters)
> Employee first name   (12 characters)
> Employee middle initial   (1 character)
> Street address   (12 characters)
> City   (10 characters)
> State   (2 characters)
> Postal code   (9 characters)
> Department   (4 characters)
> Employee identification number   (8 characters)
> Hourly pay rate   (5 characters)

Since job skill and job skill name are repeating fields, these are variable-length records. There may be from one to eight job skill entries, with an average of four such entries on each record.

Employee identification number is the primary key in many applications using this file. However, name, department, and city may also be used as keys in some applications.

    a. When established, the file contained between 15,000 and 21,000 employee records. Calculate the appropriate initial file volume for the file.

    b. Develop a layout of a record for the file. Explain the reason for the order of the data items you select in developing the record layout.

8. The director of a university research center wishes to establish an information system to assist in management and control of the center's work. The research center has a staff of 41 research associates who are paid on an hourly basis and a director, an assistant director, and a research coordinator who are salaried. In addition, the research center employs 17 secretaries, technical writers, and clerical assistants who are paid a flat salary plus an hourly overtime rate for any hours in excess of 40 hours a week.

    All the center's income is through research contracts or grants obtained from sources outside the university. Research contracts are secured from private businesses and from state and local governmental units. The contracts are formal agreements between the research center and each outside organization concerning specific projects, for which the center will perform all the work. A contract includes a detailed specification of starting and completion dates for the work as well as intermediate milestone dates that indicate when critical phases of the project should be completed. A contract also specifies the sum of money the center will receive for the project, exclusive of expenses incurred. Contracts are awarded to the center for as little as $10,000 and frequently exceed $1 million. Only documented expenses are reimbursed to the center. Thus receipts for all equipment, materials and supplies, travel, and telephone expenses must be collected in a file. In addition, a statement of employee work chargeable to the contract must be maintained on hourly and daily bases, so that if, on one day, an employee works four hours on the project, a specified amount of money is charged to the contracting agency. The amount charged to the agency is independent of the compensation received by the employee.

    Research grants are obtained from government and private foundations on the basis of a clear statement of work to be performed and the starting, completion, and milestone dates for the work. However, grants, as opposed to contracts, are made for a lump sum of money that includes all expenses that are anticipated during the duration of the project. To obtain a grant, the center must submit a detailed proposal that outlines all expected expenses. When a grant is awarded to the center, the proposal of expenses becomes the project budget.

    The director wants an information system to be developed to aid in managing and monitoring work on all projects, keeping track of expenses, and comparing progress to the schedule established for each project. In addition, the director needs to develop a way of directly monitoring the work of individuals in the center, particularly the research assistants. Among the ideas that have been considered is the use of time sheets on which the assistants enter the starting and finishing times for all work performed on each project. It also has been suggested that each assistant prepare a report at the end of the week detailing the total number of hours he or she has spent on each project. Another proposal calls for the research assistants to check in with the research coordinator each time work starts and stops on an individual project. The research coordinator would then become responsible for maintaining records of individual project-chargeable hours worked.

At any one time, the center's staff may be involved with 25 to 50 projects. At the end of each month, a report must be provided to the agency funding each project about progress made to date and expenses incurred. In addition, the research center's management team wishes to have weekly information on expenses incurred, expenses billed to the contracting agency, expenses billed but not yet paid, actual versus planned progress on a project, and the activities of each staff member during the week. Management wishes to have the same information in summary form at the end of each month.

The following work and activity categories are used for reporting project-related efforts.

Typing
Printing or duplicating
Programming
Design development
Presentation preparation
Data entry
Library research
Field research
Program testing
System testing
Systems analysis
Systems analysis documentation
Staff meeting
Report writing
Report editing
Client meeting

The following expense categories are used.

Telephone
Postage and mailing
Printing and duplicating
Supplies—office
Supplies—computer
Supplies—books and manuals
Travel
Food and lodging
Entertainment
Typing
Computer charges
Equipment maintenance and repair
Facilities operating expense

a. What reports should be generated by the system for monitoring and controlling personnel activities and progress on the different projects of the center? For each report identified, provide a brief description of the nature and content of the report, the reason it is needed, and the medium on which it should be prepared. Indicate whether it is a transaction or a management decision-oriented report.

b. What other output that is not a report should be generated? Why?

c. What master files should be established as part of the center's information system? What should be the contents of each one?

d. What input should be provided for the system to produce the reports or output identified, or to maintain the system files?

Minicase: Graphics Don't Tell the Whole Story?

Lockheed-Georgia, the large aerospace company, is a sophisticated user of information systems technology for management of a broad spectrum of business activities. It is also a pioneer in the use of management information systems. The president even has a graphics terminal on his desk (see the case on MIDS in the Case Study Module that follows Chapter 21), which he uses regularly to respond to telephone calls and to keep abreast of developments in all areas of the business.

Among the features of the system used by the president is a vivid, state-of-the-art graphics display capability that can be used to show performance according to key indicators and to display trend data.

Recent conversations between the president and several key MIS advisers have centered around the appropriateness of the graphics displays. There is little question of their usefulness. However, the president is wondering whether he should develop his own graphics information. Thinking aloud, he stated that "With these graphics, somebody has already summarized the data for me. I might not agree with their summarization if I had all the information they used in generating the summary."

Some companies give end-users access to the raw data so they can develop their own graphics, but in most cases, organizations follow the same strategy as Lockheed-Georgia: They make displays of graphic data readily available. The firm's systems managers have discussed the usefulness of giving the president on-line access to raw data so that he can develop his own graphic information.

Questions

1. Does the presentation of information in graphic form mean that summarization has already taken place or that important details in the raw data may be absent?

2. What are the technical implications of giving the manager access to the raw data to develop graphic information firsthand?

3. For business firms in general, is the development of graphics displays, even if better information can be produced, a good use of a senior executive's time?

Supplement 17A: Techniques for Gathering Requirements Data

This section discusses the methods that are used to acquire the information needed to determine how an existing system is operating and to find out about user requirements. The various methods involved are described and evaluated.

Overview of Methods for Gathering Requirements Data

Through the data gathering process, we gain information to identify user and performance requirements and management needs. The synthesis of these data helps us formulate design specifications that lead to decisions about overall system data and information flows, inputs, outputs, and programs and modules for the new application. Data gathering will vary depending on whether we are developing a transaction processing application or an information systems (that is, decision-oriented) application.

Analysis of Transaction Situations In analyzing transaction processing situations, our concern is to identify and collect the documents and reports that are used or generated in handling transactions. Investigations are made to determine how the data are collected, how they are used, and whether they are needed. This may mean talking to the people who fill out sales slips when a transaction occurs and discussing the need for the data with sales managers—determining whether all the data are really needed or, alternatively, whether additional data should be collected. The systems staff must understand how transactions are processed, why they are processed, and where improvements can be made.

Analysis of Decision-Oriented Situations In a decision-oriented situation, the reason for gathering data is the same—to understand the situation. However, in this case the emphasis is on the decision and the objectives that guide its formulation. For instance, if we are studying a sales program decision (as opposed to a sales transaction), we want to learn what factors and circumstances have led to the need for such a decision. We may find that the Federal Trade Commission has outlawed certain sales techniques we have been using. Or our competitors may have introduced new incentives for consumers to purchase their products rather than ours (rebates, purchase price discounts, new buy-now/pay-later plans, and so on). Or the decision may be necessary because of changes in the size, distribution, or composition of the sales force. Whatever the reason, we have to find out what decision(s) must be made and why. In the process of learning about each decision, we must determine how it ties in to organization goals and objectives. The sales program decision, for example, may be directly tied to a company goal of increasing profits and market share through improved service to customers, higher-quality products, and more competitive prices. Knowing this goal places the sales program decision in a meaningful perspective— we can see why it is important and what its implications are.

In analyzing the decision, it is also necessary to learn about and understand any model used to guide the decision maker and to identify the data used in the model. To understand how the sales program decision is made, we must know about such inputs as number of salespersons affected and number of consumers that may be gained or lost as a result of the decision, and different incentives being considered (rebates, purchase price discounts, and so on). Understanding the model also includes having information about how sensitive it is to the data it uses. That is, how significant are data accuracy and timeliness?

Methods

There are five basic techniques for collecting needed data. Although these *data collection techniques* are often prescribed for requirements analysis, they can be used throughout the entire systems life cycle (Table S17A.1). These tools are: interview, questionnaire, observation, document examination, and measurement.

Interview Interviewing involves questioning people from various levels of the organization and making notes of their oral replies. It is an effective means of getting certain types of data, such as personal opinions about current procedures and activities, the perceived effect of competition on organization policies and procedures, impending legislation that may affect the enterprise, or new programs, products, or services being considered. Through an *interview* both qualitative and quantitative data regarding policies, procedures, and practices can be obtained, as can data about why these policies and procedures have been established. However, for reasons that become clear shortly, data gathered through interviews should be supplemented by document examination when possible.

Often the interview is the only way to find out a person's ideas or opinions. This is especially true of high-level corporate officials who are in a position to impart valuable data bearing on the information system. In addition, when serious objections to some aspects of a system are anticipated, interviewing may help detect both resistance and sources of resistance to a project, while at the same time offering an opportunity to dispel the objections. The interviewer can answer questions or clear up misconceptions and misunderstandings about the project. In some cases, this may be the only way to prevent later problems.

Although the interview is a valuable tool, it cannot be applied automatically. The success of an interview depends first on the interviewer's skills, which are

Table S17A.1 Most Likely Application of Data Gathering Tools in Systems Life Cycle

Stages	Interview	Questionnaire	Observation	Document Examination	Measurement
Perceiving need	√	√	√	√	√
Clarifying purpose	√	√	√	√	√
Determining					
Technical feasibility	√	√		√	√
Economic feasibility	√	√		√	√
Operational feasibility	√	√	√		
Decoupling	√	√	√	√	√
Determining user information needs	√	√	√	√	√
Describing user needs	√	√	√	√	√
Setting detailed system requirements	√	√	√	√	√
Specifying new system					
Procedures	√	√		√	
Input/output	√	√		√	
Files and databases	√	√			√
Coding and constructing program	√	√			
Developing files and databases	√	√		√	
Testing program	√	√		√	√
Testing procedure	√	√	√	√	√
Testing file and space			√	√	√
Implementing system	√	√	√	√	√
Maintenance	√	√	√	√	√

acquired through experience. Attitudes and motives of respondents must be discerned, along with goals and beliefs. For example, an interview might be perceived by someone who opposes a proposed system as an opportunity to sack the project by presenting comments that could lead to bad decisions. Thus the interviewer must listen carefully (see accompanying box) and probe to identify attitudes that may reflect hostility to the system.

The interviewer must be impartial and tactful both in questioning and in trying to influence others to accept advice they might prefer to ignore. The ability of the interviewers to handle themselves properly may determine the success of the interview. If an interviewer tries to sell preconceived ideas about how a system should be used without listening to the ideas, comments, and suggestions of the interviewees, valuable data and insight will be overlooked and a lesser-quality design may be established.

Interviews can be used in all phases of a system's life cycle to obtain cost and financial data and determinations of functional requirements (that is, how certain activities must be performed, perhaps because of safety laws or trade regulations), and to encourage the cooperation of users or managers. However, because of the amount of time involved in defining and phrasing questions, familiarizing interviewers with respondents' backgrounds, and analyzing the results, it is not feasible to interview large numbers of people.

Hearing Information Requirements*

What should the new application for manufacturing accomplish? What reports do we need to produce? Who really wants this project? What does the dataflow diagram show? What programming language should we use? How much time do we have?

These are typical questions in analysis and design situations. However, many novice analysts fail to address these issues properly because they do not hear what users are telling them. This has become such a widespread problem that major computer vendors are investing millions of dollars to train staff interviewers to listen.

To develop an information system that meets users' requirements an analyst must *hear* the requirements managers express. Manufacturing managers may not be computer or data processing experts, but they are experts about their business and the kinds of information needed to run it. Even though they may not express needs in a direct fashion (for example, "The information we need is . . ."), users do express their requirements. Unfortunately, analysts too often fail to assimilate what has been said and to incorporate this material into their own thinking.

Here are some suggestions for you to consider when doing requirements analysis that involves interviewing managers.

Distortion Most systems analysts consider themselves to be good listeners. But in fact, the average person *distorts* a great deal of what he or she hears and recalls only 50 percent of the original message immediately after it was delivered.

Does this description apply to you? Could it apply to anyone with whom you are or will be working? Try these tests. Do you have trouble remembering someone's name when you are introduced? Do you find yourself daydreaming, or does your mind wander from time to time when others are talking to you? When you disagree with a speaker's statement, do you become so emotionally involved that you don't even hear the remainder of the person's remarks? If these situations sound familiar, don't give up! Listening effectiveness can be improved.

Communication experts agree that the analyst shares responsibility with users or managers for ensuring that effective communication of information requirements takes place. The goal of good communication, they say, is accurately shared meaning. That is, the user must create a message that will be received by analysts in the way the user intends. And, the analyst must know how to listen to user comments. Verbal messages, however, are not like packages. They cannot be wrapped up and delivered in exactly the same manner, regardless of the destination. Numerous variables must be considered and obstacles overcome if effective communication is to occur (see Figure A).

*Courtesy Judy Brownell

Questionnaire When many people must be contacted and the questions to be posed are relatively straightforward, the *questionnaire* is effective and efficient. It is also useful when an organized, well-planned study is made across all the departments in an organization. Questionnaires should be set up to elicit brief, easily recorded, and unambiguous responses. Multiple-choice forms are often ideal. The issue here is practicality. When time is limited and the systems investigation covers several facilities or workstations in a large (decentralized) organization, the questionnaire is useful.

Hearing Information Requirements (continued)

Setting As an analyst, it is your job to make sure you can hear what is being said. Background noise, an interviewee's manner of talking, and the size of the room all influence your ability to hear. Talking with people in the middle of the production area about a particular report format is not likely to yield useful results. Instead, meet the production supervisors in a quiet office or lounge. And be sure to take the initiative: close doors, change rooms, move chairs—whatever is necessary to ensure that you can hear and concentrate on what the users or managers are telling you about their requirements.

Figure A Variables in the Listening Process

Meaning intended

Delivery
Personality
Tone of voice
Nonverbal communication
Language
Appearance

Distractions
Time of day
Distance between communicators
Physical environment
Temperature

Interests
Degree of empathy
Past experiences
Knowledge of speaker and subject
Attitude
Assumptions

Meaning assigned

Message created | Speaker variables | External variables | Listener variables | Message received

It's wise to keep the questionnaire short. People often object to the time-consuming and tedious work of answering a long series of questions. Moreover, since it is difficult to design a questionnaire that will produce the exact data required, these instruments should not be used to obtain detailed factual data about an actual operation or process (for example, the precise number of units processed through a manufacturing station on a given morning). Other data collection methods work better in such instances. Questionnaires are useful in asking a large number of people

---

Hearing Information Requirements (continued)

Analysts' listening ability may be impaired because they are in fact poorly prepared for the encounter or because the managers inaccurately assume that a system specialist will know little about business functions. Your understanding can be increased by making it a point to familiarize yourself with the jargon, background, and other relevant information about the area in which you are going to work.

Listening and communication are two-way streets. Be sure you are considering the way in which managers will hear *your* remarks as well. Ask yourself such questions as, "Is Mr. Jones likely to be familiar with the terminology I will be using?" and "Will the terms *data-flow*, *software*, and *iteration* mean the same things to us both?"

Individuals Differ! Different people hearing the same questions or responses will interpret them in very different ways, depending on their background, interests, and assumptions. Moreover, if they are tired, angry, or anxious, their attention to your discussion and questions about information requirements will be affected.

When you interpret someone's responses to your questions, it is often useful to consider the individual's position in the organization. What is this person's point of view? How will they be affected by a change resulting from the information systems application you are developing? How much do they know about the present system? *What* are they trying to tell you? *Why* are they trying to tell *you* this? These simple questions will help to interpret people's comments and answers more accurately.

Analysts are information gatherers. Often they will encounter disagreement about the need for a specific application or a certain design choice. An analyst's initial reaction may be to defend the systems point of view or to explain the designer's position more fully. But recognize the importance of thoroughly understanding the user/manager's position and why they feel the way they do.

Nonverbal Cues Don't overlook the nonverbal cues. Does the interviewee toy with a pen or pencil? Is the interviewee looking at you while speaking or fumbling through papers? Is someone waiting outside to see the manager? Increased awareness of these nonverbal cues increases your chance of interpreting responses properly and assigning appropriate weights to comments.

Effective listening in interview situations is not easy. Understanding the complexity of the entire process is helpful. Applying these basic principles will pay off later in identifying the right requirements for that new application.

if they have problems using a certain system (yes/no), how often the problems occur (once out of 10 times, once out of 100 times, and so on), and the nature of the problem (incorrect data, incomplete data, late arrival of reports). Questionnaires also can be used to present alternatives to respondents, asking that their preferences be indicated and briefly explained. Response time must be considered when using questionnaires. People always take their time to answer, if, indeed, they answer at all. Response rates often are better if each form is addressed to a specific person, rather than to a position (like manager of marketing), but the time may still be considerable.

Observation   Through _observation_ a systems investigator can see firsthand how people in the system handle certain documents and how various practices and procedures are followed under different conditions. Observation allows the investigator to detect when and where a worker goes outside the system to meet the requirements of a given situation. Having to make a telephone call to obtain information about how many sales orders were processed or paychecks written indicates a gap in the system. Likewise, it may be seen that photocopies of sales documents are made each time a sales order is processed, indicating a problem in the processing system or in the form design. Observation also helps determine where bottlenecks are occurring. Data gathered and recorded in an observation can suggest new ways to overcome such problems.

Observation, for example, is a good way to learn how employees check and process sales invoices or payroll forms. If it is found that checking is more thorough when the volume is low, but that certain items are completely ignored when there are many invoices to be processed, you have firsthand evidence of a need for control or procedure changes (perhaps nothing more than insisting on adherence to operating procedures). Similarly, if it is observed that one copy of a document is always thrown away, it probably can be concluded that the document or process needs to be redesigned.

There are two types of observation in industrial settings. In the first, the observer is someone _outside_ the actual activities: an onlooker who does not participate in the process being studied. In the second type, a _participant observer_ becomes involved in the work process, doing some of the work being studied or observed.

An outside observer is most effective when objectivity is essential. The investigator does not become involved in the emotional aspects of the situation and so can better identify the problems or processes at hand. However, and herein lies the value of participant observation, the outside observer may miss some of the dynamics of the situation. For example, subtle cues of rivalry, jealousy, or distrust between two people who depend on each other for transfer of data or information would be difficult for an outside observer to detect but would be quickly noticed by a participant.

One problem with observation is the possibility that the observer will influence the processes he or she is observing. This is known as the _Hawthorne effect_. People who know they are being observed may, for example, follow stated work rules that normally are ignored. Consequently, the observer may see only a biased picture of events, not habitual behavior.

Another problem lies in the observation process itself. The ability to view a series of activities and continually focus on the desired aspects without distortion or distraction is a special skill that cannot be easily learned; it requires special training and much practice. It is doubtful that many systems investigators have this training, which can be invaluable in ensuring an accurate analysis.

Document Examination Through _document examination,_ the analyst gets firsthand knowledge of reports, memoranda, letters, policy statements, and written procedures. This technique can involve anything from company sales literature to standard operating procedure manuals and reports of previous investigations and analyses.

Document examination should take two directions. First, the investigator should examine the documentary material provided. These data may provide insight into existing problems. However, data obtained in this manner should be verified through another data gathering technique. Often what is indicated on paper as the proper course of events is very different from what is actually taking place. For example, an organization chart is a portrait of the relationships that should exist among people in different positions in the management hierarchy. Yet, even a cursory familiarity with the firm may reveal relationships not shown on the chart. For example, although the organization chart and printed job descriptions indicate that the marketing manager decides on advertising strategies, it may be found that the sales manager actually does this. Consequently, memoranda on ad strategies sent to the marketing manager are misdirected.

The second document examination method should focus on the specific documents, forms, or records used in a process, including computer reports, ledger pages, snap-set forms, and catalogs. By examining these documents, it is possible to find out precisely what data are available (and in what form) for a specific activity in the operation. If the investigator wants to examine the content and format of all documents without having to take detailed notes, copies should be collected. The investigator must be sure to keep the documents in the order in which they are used, sorted according to department or work area being studied.

The task of collecting and examining many documents may become very tedious and time-consuming in a large-scale investigation. Also, there may be no assurance that all documents have been gathered. Informal data, such as notes that managers keep in their desks or ideas retained in their heads, probably will not be detected by this means. Moreover, even the most careful collection or examination of documents may not reveal all the critical information sources for a particular activity. In any event, the investigator may not be able to determine which data on documents are actually used or how they are used. Sales slips for cash sales of take-home merchandise often include the customer's address. But it may not be clear why the salespersons are required to collect the address data.

Document examination is useful when a limited number of documents are used, when the documents do not contain an abundance of extraneous data, and when use of the documents is well defined and routinized. Document examination should be supplemented with other factual data gathering techniques to help ensure a more complete systems investigation.

Measurement Through the technique of *measurement* (often called *sampling*), we can approximate, within reasonable and workable limits, the frequency with which certain events occur in normal work activities. Often when employees are questioned about the frequency of transactions or use of certain documents, they are unable to provide adequate answers. In such cases, it is often necessary to sample from the operation to determine how often a given type of transaction occurs, how many times a specific error occurs, or when certain other events take place. In investigating errors on source documents such as sales slips or employee time cards, for example, we could randomly select several slips or cards from a batch and examine them individually. If this is done on a large enough scale, we can project the average error rate for all documents processed.

Measurement is also used to study how long it takes to process a certain type of transaction or to complete a specific task. However, the investigator has to ensure that the chosen sample is truly representative of the usual situation.

Evaluation of Techniques

No single method can be applied across all situations, nor can one technique be used alone in an investigation. Perhaps the best strategy is to combine two or three so that data gathered through one means reinforce and confirm the data collected through another. In the case of data gathering techniques such as interviewing and observation, which require special training for the investigator, everyone involved should understand that data obtained by untrained individuals can be used only in proper perspective and should not receive too much weight in the overall evaluation. Also, as you will recall from Table S17A.1, at certain points in the systems investigation and life cycle some techniques are especially practical and others may be inadequate.

Supplement 17B: Software Engineering and Development

In this chapter and the preceding one, we examined the concepts and techniques associated with the analysis and design of computer-based data processing systems. As we discovered, both transaction processing and information processing systems are formulated and designed by following a carefully planned progression of steps ultimately leading to specifications that can be translated into software to do the processing and data manipulation needed by the organization. During the design stage, the output desired by users is the guide and objective toward which the systems staff must strive. But when the design project moves into the construction stage, fulfillment of design goals falls on the shoulders of the programming staff who develop the system software, that is, the computer programs.

This supplement examines considerations and guidelines in program and software development. We look at three major areas of concern: modularization, program design, and structured programming. Our primary goal is to identify techniques and concepts that will improve the programming *process* and *product* for organizations, users, and the systems staff.

Program Modularity

In using the English language, we have developed certain conventions that make it easier to read and write both simple and complex ideas. One such convention is to express ideas through sentences that are collected into paragraphs. Each sentence in the paragraph pertains to the same idea. Paragraphs, in turn, are grouped into minor and major sections, and sections into chapters. Chapters are grouped together to form short stories, books, or monographs. This is a convention that is widely accepted, expected, and found practical by most people who have learned to use the language. For example, we wouldn't think of writing (or reading) a 500-page novel that is written one sentence after another with no organization of ideas into paragraphs, sections, and chapters.

When we organize data for storage on auxiliary memory devices or other media, we follow similar conventions; that is, data are grouped into records and records into files and databases. This convention is pretty much universal in the data processing community. Users, systems staff members, and organizations expect it.

These same conventions should be applied to the construction of computer software: We need to formulate modules in computer software the same way we set off chapters and sections in books and novels. This section explores the module concept and the benefits of setting up modules in the construction of software.

Module Concept

You have already been introduced to one kind of modularity in information systems, namely, the idea that systems are collections of application programs. We have discussed marketing application programs (such as new product stimulation and consumer preference analysis programs), inventory application programs (such as inventory stock status and purchasing programs), and manufacturing application programs (such as production scheduling and quality control programs). Within each of these application programs, which are modules of the information system as a whole, we also identified modules for editing, file creation, file maintenance, inquiry processing, and report generation (see Chapters 7 and 10). In analysis and design, the principle of decoupling was introduced as a way of examining subsystems and interfaces between subsystems—another instance of the module concept.

Program modularity is an extension of the same principle—decomposing a larger entity into parts—applied to computer programs. In other words, we want to develop and construct the program so it is a set of modules that are each relatively small sets of coded instructions. As we will see in a moment, there are substantial benefits to using the module concept in computer programming.

Some programming managers force their staffs to write programs in modular fashion by prescribing and enforcing rules that control the length of any set of code. For example, programming managers may tell their staff that no section of code should consist of more than 50 instructions. Programmers must then code within the 50-instruction limit.* When they reach the limit, they begin another module. This is absurd.

Modular programming does not come about by dictating how many instructions should be grouped into a module. Rather, it is the result of breaking out sections of the programming based on the logic expressed or function performed by the section. Input, output, and self-contained processing routines can easily be established as modules. For example, sets of code that check for errors in incoming data, that print error messages, or that write data to secondary storage devices are logical modules because they perform specific functions that are relatively self-contained. Likewise, in an inventory control program that uses a model to determine if material needs to be ordered (for example, a reorder point model) and then prints a company purchase order, two more modules are evident. It may be helpful to think of each module as a program within a program. (Sometimes we call them *subprograms* or *routines*.) In a sense that is what they are—self-contained processing sections that interface with other modules by "communication" of data that are to be processed, results that have been produced, or information that helps control processing (for example, an error-checking module "telling" an error message module what error was detected and indicating that a specific message is to be printed or displayed).

*When this kind of rule is established, programmers often will just code instructions one after another and then go back and break them up into 50-instruction segments. Thus, they have technically followed the prescribed rule.

One module must have control over all other modules. The *main program* oversees the entire set of processing activities, calling modules into execution at the proper time.

Since modules are based on function rather than length, it makes little sense to say that the absolute number of instructions in a module is 50, 60, or any other number. However, length guidelines do apply: It is advisable to subdivide the program into small modules that can be easily managed by programmers.

Benefits of Modular Programming

Modular programming makes it possible to set up sections of code or sets of instructions that are independent of each other. As a result, it is easier to test and debug the program; one module can be worked on at a time to find and correct errors. Then several modules can be tested together for further debugging. Following this format, errors can be more quickly isolated; it is not necessary to scan thousands of individual lines of code to locate an error.

Using modular programming also provides for evolvability of the software. If a new function is to be added to a program, it can be prepared as a module and then linked/interfaced with the others according to the specifications of the programming language being used (for example, CALL statements in FORTRAN and PERFORM instructions in COBOL). Similarly, if a model included in a program has to be changed, only the module containing the instructions for the model is modified; the remainder of the program usually remains intact. These advantages are particularly important when we realize that organizations frequently spend as much as 50 percent of their information systems budget on program maintenance. Modular programming can help reduce that amount.

Program Design and Construction

Use of the modular concept also provides advantages in the design (determining how the program should process the data) and construction (writing the instructions to perform the processing) of software. Thus, we can now develop the program a module at a time, first identifying the individual modules *(design)* and then programming and testing them *(construction)*.

Top-Down Design

When modular programming is employed in software development, design is easily accomplished from the top down.* This means we start by examining the processing work that the program is supposed to accomplish. Within the overall programming

---

*Top-down design of programs should not be confused with top-down planning, discussed in Chapter 16. In top-down planning, we identify programs and applications in an information processing system by first identifying organization goals and objectives, and then moving downward a step at a time until individual programs are identified. In top-down design of programs, we formulate the design of one program called for in the systems master plan.

Figure S17B.1 Top-Down Approach to Program Design

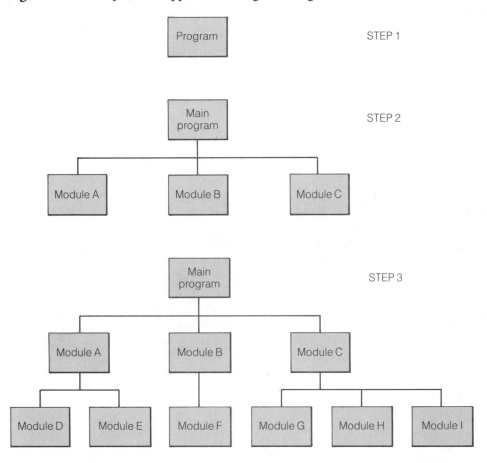

objective or purpose, individual functions and processing requirements are identified, giving a second level of design detail. Each individual processing specification can then be examined, with particularly important or independent functions being set out as separate modules at a third level, and so on, as shown in Figure S17B.1.

Suppose we are developing a program to process payroll data and print out the results. We begin with the knowledge that the program will have to accept transaction (time worked) data, calculate gross pay and net pay, and print paychecks and a payroll expense report. Analyzing this set of specifications, we find that there are several obvious modules—those to:

1. Input data from transaction file and master file (the master file will contain permanently stored data about the employee, including individual deductions for health insurance and stocks and bonds)
2. Calculate net pay (regular hours and overtime)

Figure S17B.2 Modules in Payroll Processing Program

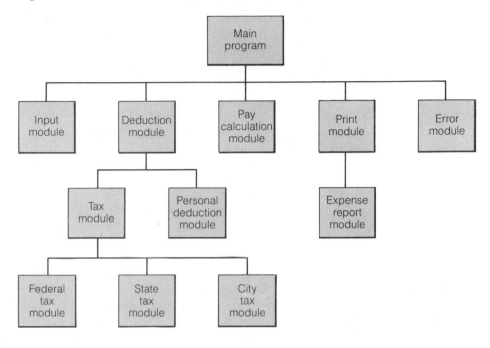

3. Calculate individual payroll deductions
4. Print results
5. Perform error checks and print exception reports

Further examination of each module indicates that another level of modularization is appropriate (see Figure S17B.2):

1. The deductions module, containing two submodules. One will compute income tax deductions and another will process individual deductions not related to income tax. Both modules are controlled by the deduction module.

2. A separate print module for payroll expense reports. This module will be controlled by the main printing routine and is needed to write expense data to a magnetic disk for every paycheck that is printed. After all paychecks are printed, the data written on the disk is read and the expense report generated.

One more level of modularization may be needed for processing income taxes. Since tax laws change frequently, it may be easier to establish separate modules to handle federal, state, and (if applicable) city income tax calculation.

By following the top-down design approach, we can easily and logically develop greater detail in the processing specifications, starting from the general statement of program purpose. Design specifications provided by the systems staff should be complete and accurate enough to do this. When the design is complete, actual construction, that is, programming, can begin.

Program Construction

Construction can take place according to a top-down or bottom-up approach. Using the top-down approach, we first establish the files and job control cards needed to process the data and generate the results. After they are tested—perhaps by writing temporary (dummy) programs—the main program is developed. Again testing occurs to eliminate any errors that have been made. With the control language and main program complete, modules on the next level can be constructed one at a time and linked to the main program. This process continues, one level at a time, until each of the modules is programmed, tested, and linked to higher-level routines.

Bottom-up construction is essentially the reverse process. The lowest-level modules are developed and debugged first, using dummy driver or calling routines that aid in testing. Sample data or files are also used. When these routines are satisfactory, the dummy calling routines are discarded and the higher-level routines are programmed and interfaced with the earlier ones. New dummy drivers may again be needed. The process continues until all of the modules and the main program are completed and the entire program has been debugged.

Modular programming can be accomplished using either the top-down or the bottom-up method. In addition, these approaches make possible *team programming*, a programming method where several different programmers work on a project at the same time, each taking responsibility for constructing different modules. Since each programmer on the team is actually working on a small program and interfacing it with other modules, fewer days, weeks, and months are needed to complete the overall programming assignment. Top-down design and modular construction are usually associated with structured programming, a technique that was developed in the mid-1960s and became widely known and accepted in the early 1970s.

Structured Programming

Structured programming is a programming philosophy aimed at making computer programs more readable and more understandable. Being able to examine instructions in a program (that is, read the program) and determine the processing logic means that errors can be detected and corrected more quickly—factors that are of interest to both programmers and users. The idea behind this philosophy is that the instructions should be written so that there is an orderly processing progression in the program. You can contrast the orderliness of a structured program with ad hoc programs containing transfer-of-control statements that branch out to different statements throughout the program. Ad hoc programs are very confusing because control is transferred to other instructions in what appears to be a haphazard way—perhaps because the individuals did not plan the logic needed ahead of time. If you tried to read or trace the logic in an ordinary program you would probably find yourself starting at the beginning, then jumping to the middle, next to someplace between the beginning and the middle, then to near the end, and so on to wherever the many branching statements sent you. Sound confusing? It is, particularly when the middle

Figure S17B.3 Structured Programming Progressions

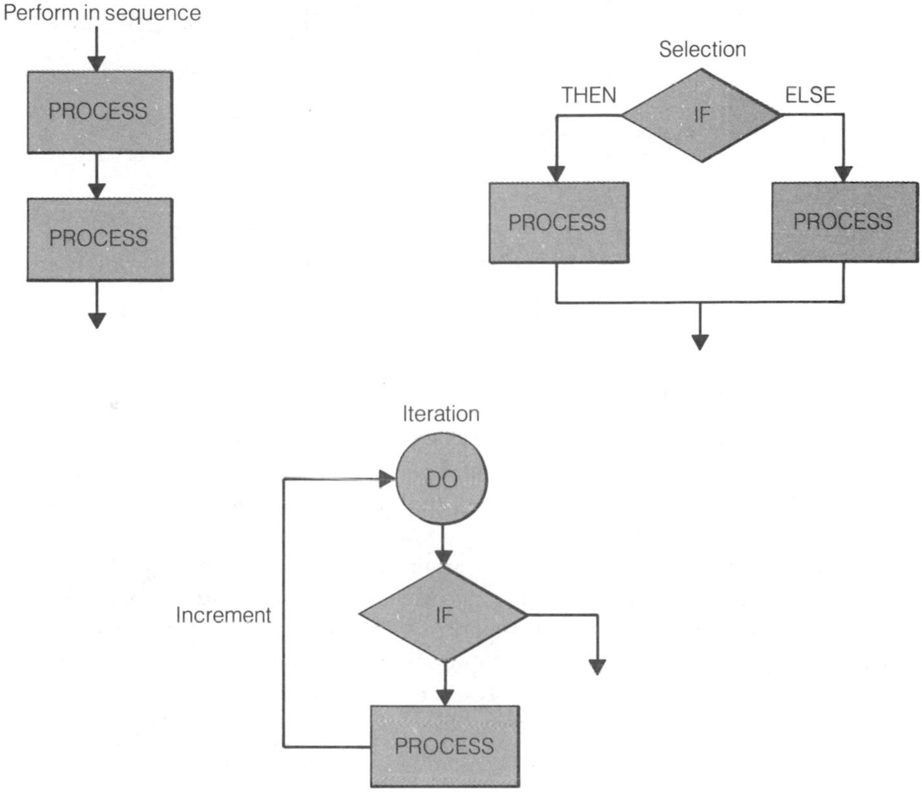

is in the midst of several thousand instructions. This is why the structured programming philosophy was devised.

The most important innovation in structured programming is to eliminate virtually all use of GOTO statements. In their place, three very simple and logically structured branching and control statements or progressions are used:

1. A series of simple *process* instructions that contain no branching or iteration
2. A *selection* process that tests for the existence of a certain condition with a choice of processing based on the results of the test
3. *Repetition* or *iteration* of processing until a condition is met

The first type of instruction is used for simple processing or calculation, like computing net pay as the difference between gross pay and total deductions. Selection statements are used in payroll processing to test for overtime, and repetition statements check whether the last transaction has been processed. These progressions are shown in Figure S17B.3. By using these progressions instead of repeated GOTO statements, it is much easier to write, read, and debug programs. This makes both construction and maintenance more efficient, freeing programmers and resources for other information systems projects. Because of the value of the structured programming philosophy, we will undoubtedly see more developments in the area.

Structured Design Methods

The principles introduced in preceding sections are in widespread use. Based on those ideas and practices, several specific methods of structuring software designs have evolved. This section provides an overview of some of them.

Warnier-Orr Method

The Warnier-Orr approach (also known as *logical construction of programs/logical construction of systems*) was developed by Jean-Dominique Warnier of Paris, France, and Kenneth Orr of the United States. It is a graphical method of identifying program structures and focusing on inputs, processes, and outputs.

The method focuses first on the output and then works backward until the processing steps, inputs, and data are identified. Thus it is consistent with the logical design approach discussed in the first part of Chapter 17. The method also uses the decoupling principle introduced in Chapter 16 where process flow was emphasized.

Warnier-Orr diagrams are basically a series of brackets used in such a way that they portray a process for development. They might even be considered hierarchical organization charts that have been tipped on their sides. The logic in these diagrams reads from left to right and top to bottom. Order and sequence are very important in these diagrams (which is an important difference from ordinary organization or hierarchy charts, where order is not significant).

In the Warnier-Orr diagrams, the name attached to a bracket describes a set of actions. The brackets to the right explain in detail how the action is accomplished. Often each piece represents a module in a program, with lower-level details being submodules or program steps.

When the structured design is complete, the problem/program is broken down into sequences of processes or steps in a hierarchical fashion. The structuring is shown through the three control progressions mentioned earlier in this supplement (sequence, alteration, and repetition). Data needed for each step can also be indicated.

In the payroll example we have been using, the design concerns of output, input, files, controls, and procedures have been emphasized. However, this example did not discuss the continuing operation of the system from day to day, week to week, and so on. Figure S17B.4 demonstrates this cycling using Warnier-Orr diagrams. Notice the left-to-right hierarchy (for example, years are made up of months). Notice also *when* various output is produced: daily summaries, weekly paychecks, and yearly tax (W-2) statements. Both scheduled and unscheduled processing is anticipated on a daily basis.

Figure S17B.4 Warnier-Orr Diagrams for Payroll Process

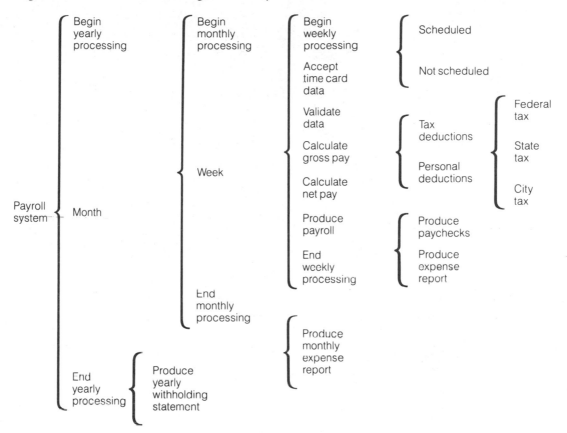

Using this method, designers can specify increased detail in the design. Programmers can also work from these specifications to develop a well-structured program or set of programs to meet processing requirements.

Structured Box Charts

This method, sometimes referred to as *Nassi-Schneiderman charts,* after the names of its developers, shows the elements of a system in a different graphic form. The diagram consists of nested boxes, each showing important logic relations. Using this notation, iterative, conditional, and sequential steps can be represented directly.

Figure S17B.5 demonstrates structured box charts for the payroll example. Notice how payroll processing steps are repeated for each employee (the outer box). File utilization and output production are shown at the bottom of the diagram.

Figure S17B.5 Structured Box Chart for Payroll Processing

Each year
Each month
Each week
Each employee
If valid
Then / Else
Compute gross pay / Print edit message
Compute net pay
Produce paycheck / Do not process record
Produce expense rpt
Produce monthly expense report
Produce yearly withholding statement

Figure S17B.6 HIPO Model for Payroll Example

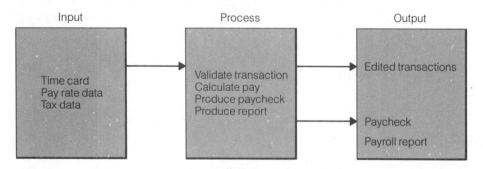

HIPO

Hierarchical, input, process, output (HIPO) charts are useful primarily for documentation purposes. They show, as the name describes, inputs to and outputs from processes.

The HIPO package has three main parts.

1. The visual table of contents shows the major modules in the application system and their hierarchical relation to one another. Figure S17B.2 typifies the visual table of contents in HIPO.

2. The HIPO overview chart shows the major input and output activities in relation to processes (Figure S17B.6).

Figure S17B.7 HIPO Chart with Embedded Structure Chart

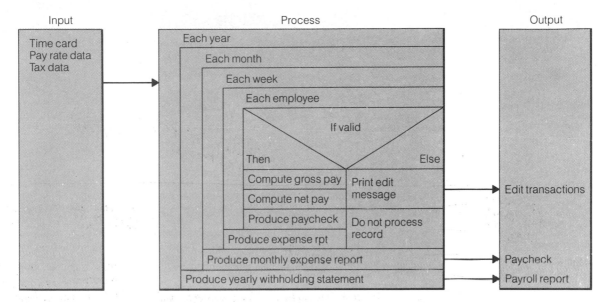

3. The detailed HIPO diagram represents module-level details, including individual inputs, processes, and files.

Although this method is not structured in the sense we have been discussing, it does aid in breaking down designs hierarchically. It also emphasizes inputs and outputs from various modules. Figure S17B.7 shows how the structure chart developed earlier could be embedded into a HIPO diagram.

Summary

Software development is still a very weak link in the systems development process. It is time consuming, costly, and error-prone. Furthermore, performing maintenance on existing systems is often difficult. The techniques and methods discussed in this supplement assist in enhancing physical development. However, continued research is needed to advance the state of the art.

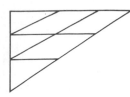

18: End-User Development of Information Systems

Key Questions

[handwritten annotations: availability of PC's — they know best what they want]

Why is end-user development of information systems of increasing importance in organizations?

[handwritten: gives them help, training hdwre/software]

How does the development of an information center facilitate end-user computing?

What types of application are most suitable for end-user development? *[handwritten: one time queries — what if / simple reports / minor changes / analyses]*

Is user development of information systems a replacement for the methods used by systems analysts? *[handwritten: No, go thru same steps]*

What are the responsibilities of the user in a user-computing environment? *[handwritten: know what you want/need — understand business prob — able to use hardware/software — do the work]*

Are there risks associated with relying on user-developed applications? *[handwritten: inaccurate specs/assumptions, bad data; incomplete info, fail to test assumptions]*

The New Generation

In the early days of the U.S. car industry, production volumes were growing fast, and a well-known sociologist was asked to predict the total number of automobiles that would ever be manufactured. After a great deal of study, the sociologist reported that no more than 2 million would be manufactured in the life cycle of the car. If the car lasted 10 years on average, the maximum annual production would never exceed 200,000. This conclusion was based on the much-researched figure that no more than 2 million people would be willing to serve as chauffeurs.

James Martin, *Fourth Generation Languages*, vol. I: *Principles*

In many organizations, end-users at all levels of the organization (managers, supervisors, engineers, and administrative staff members) are becoming directly involved in the development of information systems applications. If properly managed, this trend has the potential to increase the organizational benefits of computing.

In this chapter we examine the rationale behind end-user computing, with particular emphasis on identifying the types of applications that benefit most from direct end-user involvement. Information centers—a type of user facility particularly well suited to supporting end-user computing—are explored both from an applications perspective and operationally. We also introduce the transition to help desks, a support facility that will replace the information center as a physical location. In addition, principles and guidelines for managing end-user computing are discussed with an eye toward ways for organizations to reap its benefits while avoiding its potential risks.

764

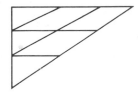

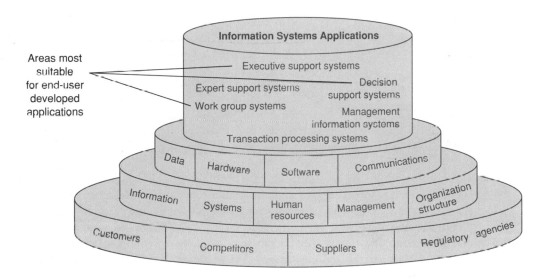

Areas most suitable for end-user developed applications

Why Should You Know About End-User Development of Information Systems?

The reasons why you should know about end-user development of information systems include the following:

——*You will be involved in end-user computing.* Computing is accessible to virtually all members of an organization who work with information. Only on rare occasions will individuals not use computers as an integral part of their job in the future. This chapter describes how end-user computing and traditional information systems are similar and how they are different, emphasizing the role that persons like you should play.

———*You can achieve substantial benefits from end-user computing.* You will realize the benefits of personal support systems, access to information through personal computers, and utilization of computer networks—characteristics of end-user computing—as you grasp the purpose of end-user systems. Benefits grow out of expectations, on the one hand, and understanding on the other.

———*You want to avoid risks of end-user computing.* Improper reliance on end-user information can lead to erroneous decisions. Knowing the risks and how to avoid them is as important as knowing the benefits of end-user computing.

Overview of End-User Computing

There is growing interest in **end-user** computing in all circles of information systems development and usage. The underlying reasons for such growth assure us that this is not a passing phenomenon but a real, and useful, development. The rationale explains the growth. However, end-user computing is not an answer to every problem. It has an appropriate place in the development of information systems applications.

Rationale

User-developed applications will proliferate because of the benefits offered through improved productivity, attention to the systems development backlog, and increased involvement of users in the systems development process.

Improvements in Productivity Shortly after the telephone was introduced and was being widely adopted, a forecaster projected the result of the rapid implementation of this communications system. The estimate concluded that in the near future, the system would fail under its own weight because there would not be enough telephone operators to meet the calling demand; everyone would have to function as a telephone operator. Of course this did not happen. The projection was wrong because it did not take into account increases in productivity due to improved telephone switching methods.

Today the demand for computer programmers is giving rise to similarly inaccurate projections. We know that the number of computer-based applications is growing rapidly; and if this growth is projected, it is possible to identify a need for *100 times* the current number of programmers. Where will we find them? Colleges and universities will not be able to meet this demand, nor will industry training programs. This estimate of programmer demand, however, is as unrealistic as the nineteenth-century prediction about the need for telephone operators. In both cases analysts overlooked productivity improvements. With respect to computer programming, the productivity improvements are related to the growth in end-user computing.

Figure 18.1 portrays the relation of computer costs to people costs. It is well known that the cost of computer equipment is dropping annually. For example, the desktop computer of today, which costs less than $10,000, only a generation ago required the investment of nearly $1 million.

At the same time, the cost of employing people to develop software is increasing rapidly—much faster than the rate at which prices for computer equipment are dropping. The trend is forcing information systems professionals to find ways to

Figure 18.1 Trends in Costs of Computers and People   767

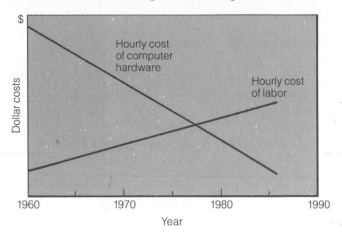

this trend not likely to reverse in near future

make the developers of computer systems applications more productive. In Chapter 16 we described the difficulty of identifying and meeting information systems requirements. Now it is clear that greater productivity and more effective information systems must be gained to offset higher costs.

Productivity benefits will result from the use of new programming languages, the *fourth-generation languages* introduced in Chapter 6. The use of *prototyping* as an alternative to the systems life cycle method of development for applications of certain types will also improve the productivity associated with systems development. Third, *involvement of users* in the systems development process is proving to be very productive. With the use of the proper tools and in the appropriate environment, managers, supervisors, and workers take responsibility for development of some systems.

Reduction of Backlog   In most organizations, there is a much greater demand for the development of new applications than the information systems staff can possibly meet. The excess demand results in a **backlog** of application requests. In some organizations, elimination of the accumulated backlog would take several years of concerted effort by systems analysts and programmers. Since they must take care of the day-to-day requirements as well, they cannot possibly catch up under current methods.

— *may be 3 years*

Managers and other end-uses, who are well aware of the size of the development backlog—equivalent to several years worth of work in some organizations—are unable to receive the application development support they need and may have several projects of their own tied up in the backlog. Indeed, sometimes they do not even request another needed application, believing that its development will not occur, or at least not within an acceptable timeframe. The collection of plans for information systems that are not even submitted as requests is often called the *hidden backlog*. Many believe that it is even larger than the apparent backlog.

— *may be 3 times the known backlog*

Reduction in Maintenance Requirements   In many information systems departments, more time and effort are devoted to maintenance of existing information systems than to the development of new ones. Several university studies carried out to learn

Table 18.1 Categories of Systems Maintenance

Type of Maintenance	Activity	Portion of Total Application Maintenance Time
Corrections	Emergency corrections of errors; routine debugging	20 percent
Adaptations	Accommodation of changes to data and files, and to hardware and system software	20 percent
Refinements to applications	User enhancement; improved documentation; recoding for computational efficiency	60 percent

more about the maintenance burden faced by systems groups identified three categories of maintenance activities (Table 18.1).

Contrary to what you might expect, most maintenance efforts are *not* devoted to the correction of errors in software. Instead, the greatest portion of the burden of maintaining information systems involves enhancements to current systems, and many of these changes would not be necessary if requirements were more accurately identified during systems development.

We refer to maintenance as a burden because of the staff time required to accomplish it. An already understaffed organization must devote a large portion of its resources to maintenance rather than to new development. In addition, maintenance priorities prevent the undertaking of important new applications and rob users of some of the benefits of the information systems support they desire and need.

The use of prototyping, discussed in Chapter 16, offers one way to reduce the maintenance burden by better identification of system requirements early in the development process. People can point to features they do not like in the prototype and at the same time determine where other features must be added. Users benefit by receiving a system better suited to their needs, and the systems department—and for that matter, the entire organization—will come out ahead, too, if it develops that maintenance demands have indeed been reduced.

Role of End-User Computing

It is possible to reduce the maintenance burden while helping to overcome the backlog and productivity problems just noted. These benefits, which are attributable to the following characteristics of end-user computing, are seen both in mainframe applications and in the area of personal computers.

——*User responsibility for systems development:* Users who develop their own applications to retrieve and manipulate information not only receive important information in a timely fashion, they eliminate a task that otherwise takes the time of systems analysts and programmers.

——*Utilization of high-level tools:* It is rare, and in fact inadvisable, for end-users to work with COBOL or other procedural programming languages. We will discuss the reasons for this later in the chapter. Instead, fourth-generation languages

---

**Table 18.2 Characteristics of Applications Appropriate for Development
by End-Users and by Information Systems Staff**

Suitable for End-User Development	Require Development by Information Systems Staff
By Application Characteristics	
One-time inquiries to prestored files and databases	High-volume transaction processing systems or applications that will be in place for long periods
Simple reports based on retrieval from organization files and using information center tools	Applications that span several departments or organization units
"What if" analysis using high-level tools	Applications that will change data values stored in organization files or databases
Applications that can be developed with pre-written software packages or with high-level tools users can understand	Applications that require use of procedural languages (does not exclude applications that use high-level languages)
By Development Process	
User must be directly involved in the development process to identify application requirements	Formal specifications are needed in advance
System is self-documenting	Extensive, formal documentation is needed
Application development time is short and suitable to user-oriented tools	Development process is long
Development by end-users can occur and standards exist to minimize the occurrence of errors or risks to the organization	

---

and special software packages provide the key to end-user application development. These tools allow them to focus on the information they want, rather than on how to produce it.

———*User development centers:* Many organizations maintain *information centers* for end-user computing, where trained staff members provide guidance on using development tools and retrieving information.

Characteristics of Suitable Applications

End-user computing is not a substitute for traditional systems development, and as you might suspect, not all information systems applications are suitable for end-user computing. The information systems department in an organization will not decrease in importance because this additional development avenue has been opened up, and it will surely not shrink in size. Rather it will grow in both respects.

Table 18.2 summarizes the applications best suited to each group. Production applications such as transaction systems, which require the processing of large volumes of data, are the responsibility of the information systems group. Management of the database, including the development and supervision of data standards and input validation requirements, are also the systems department's responsibility. Any application that spans several departments or work groups or collects or produces details used throughout the organization also must be developed by information systems specialists.

End-user computing applications, in contrast, include those that consist of:

——*One-time inquiries:* "How many of our corporate customers in the eastern region do business in excess of $100,000 annually?" "How many of our government customers have the same characteristics?"

——*Simple reports:* "List the names of all customers who have made purchases from us in the past 6 months, indicating the total amount of purchases. Prepare the report in descending order, based on amount of sales."

——*Minor changes to existing reports or inquiries:* "Modify the customer sales report to list the customers by salesperson, and rank the customers of each employee in descending order by the total amount purchased."

——*"What if" analysis:* "What would be the impact on sales if all the customers who did not purchase from us during the past 6 months had given us $1000 of business? How would our total income change if these sales produced a net profit margin of 18 percent?"

These representative (but not exhaustive) examples have in common an important feature that underlies many end-user computing applications: They draw on data that currently exist in organization files or databases. Notice also that none of the examples produced permanent changes to the organization database. As we explore information centers, we will add to the characteristics of end-user-developed applications.

The Information Center

Information centers serve a specific purpose and present important duties to members of the information systems staff. In this section, we look at the functioning of such facilities.

Purpose of the Center

An **information center** is part of the information systems department that has responsibility for the support of end-user computing. It is organized on the assumption that if end-users are provided with proper training, effective technical support, and convenient access to data and to computing facilities, they will be able to satisfy a portion of their business information requirements more or less independently (that is, without increasing the burden on the information systems department's analysts and programmers).

Relation of Center Staff to Staff of Information Systems Department

The information center staff in most organizations is one group within the IS department. It should not in any way attempt to recruit applications away from staff analysts and programmers; rather, the center staff works with applications that do not require a formal development process. Information centers do not offer a *way around* the development process, but an alternative to be used only under the circumstances mentioned previously.

Center staff members may come from user-functional areas, such as marketing, accounting, or manufacturing, or they may be systems analysts who have shifted from another area within the information systems group.

Division of Responsibility

Projects developed within the information center generally reflect an important division of responsibility. As a rule, the end-users have the best idea of what information they want and what the contents of reports should be. They are most likely to know what they need to get their jobs done. (They usually also know that they need the information quickly!) Mind you, they may *not* have complete knowledge of their needs, at least initially.

On the other hand, center staff members typically have the best insight into how results can be obtained quickly. They know the tools at hand and the data that are available.

By dividing responsibilities according to areas of greatest knowledge, it is possible for center staff and end-users to work together to get the job done. Neither group will be effective without the other. By combining their efforts, maximum productivity can be obtained. We will return to this issue later in the chapter.   *(synergism)*

Training by Center Staff

Because the success of end-user computing depends on the competence acquired by the users, the center staff maintains an ongoing training program. Activities span the gamut from providing an overview of computing facilities and processes in general (aimed at creating computer literacy) to administering exercises that teach how to use specific programs or high-level languages.

The Center as Source of Information

The center plays an important role by keeping people informed about data and information available for planning and decision making. Its staff also serves as a source of information on the retrieval and use of data. It is typical for users to want to know:

——What data are available to meet a requirement
——What program will help them to retrieve information or display results

——What equipment they can use

——What other managers or employees have needed similar information or have posed similar requests

In many organizations center staff members are the user's only constant source of answers to such questions. Too often systems analysts are unavailable because of meetings, travel, or project deadlines. The center is always there when questions arise or assistance is needed.

The Center as Management Tool

The support information centers provide to their clients is essential and of course the most obvious reason for creating the facility in the first place. But management of data, software, and equipment is an equally important function of the center.

It is best to avoid the development of applications in an uncontrolled fashion. Without explicit attention to this concern by center staff members, these representative problems are likely to arise.

——Redundant copies of data

——Incompatible data structures

——Acquisition of unreliable or inappropriate software

——Acquisition of incompatible computers and peripheral equipment

——Failure to observe house standards for data integrity

The concerns expressed during our earlier discussions of MIS and database management—for uniform information and integrity of the data—are no less important in end-user computing than in other application settings. We rely on the information center to manage and satisfy these concerns.

Hands-On Access

The center provides a broad range of computing facilities. Workstations and personal computers are available for hands-on usage. But printers, graphics display devices, and plotters are also available; and telecommunication lines and modems allow users to access remote databases or computer facilities.

Even if the users have a workstation or personal computer in their own department work area, the proper facilities for the application they have in mind may not be available. Through its facilities and resources, the information center offers users access to such equipment, and therefore to the associated software and data.

In addition, the center may maintain special application products developed by the organization's information systems department. The applications, which may run on larger mainframe or minicomputer systems, are made available for use by all managers who need the capabilities provided. Managers access the product through terminals or workstations in the center or in their respective departments, but the center provides the user support services for the product.

Two examples of business products will demonstrate this function of the center:

———A multinational manufacturing corporation developed an information system to standardize the formulation of two time-consuming and error-prone processes: manufacturing planning and cost management. All manufacturing managers— and there are hundreds in this large company—are faced constantly with the complexity of these tasks. Therefore, standard cost formulas, expense data, and production guidelines are stored as data in the system, to free managers from the chores of estimating these items and entering the data into the system. A wide variety of formats are also available.

Managers are not required to use the center product. If they do use it, the center provides full assistance for training and hands-on usage. A charge is made against the user's budget based on the amount of usage the manager has made of the product. If managers developed and used their own applications, however, the costs would be much higher.

———A large electric utility, with field offices and power generation facilities through-out several states, maintains an electronic mail system as a product of its information center. Managers can send messages and reports to one another over the mail system. They also distribute suggestions and report experiences to colleagues. Messages may be sent to all managers or addressed to specific individuals. Files may be established in the mail system to store data or information for later retrieval.

When messages are received, they may be printed or displayed. Or they may be annotated with comments and returned to the sender.

Usage is voluntary. Charges against each manager's budget are based on the amount of usage as well as file space reserved by an individual. Users agree that the charge is nominal and that the system fosters important communication that would otherwise not occur. They like the capabilities of the electronic mail system.

These examples point out two other important aspects of information centers. The center is not just an office. Rather, it represents the concept of providing user support, which goes well beyond a physical location. In fact, information centers in large organizations may well have several different locations.

Information Center Tools

We have already discussed one important tool the information center can provide, namely specially designed application products like manufacturing planning systems or electronic mail networks. And of course, the computer and communications systems themselves are also tools.

A large portion of the activity in an information center focuses on the use of different classes of software. Chapter 6 discussed one class of software that is a central component in the information center: **fourth-generation languages.** Recall that the distinguishing feature of these higher-level languages is the capability of specifying *what is to be done* rather than how a task should be accomplished. Users can focus on retrieval of data, generation of information, and creation of reports without concern for processing procedures. Thus fourth-generation languages play an important role in information centers. Commercial software is available in each of the following categories of fourth-generation software:

——**Query and retrieval languages:** allow users to pose inquiries and retrieve information from files and databases

——**Report generators:** perform extraction of stored data and preparation of formatted reports with the automatic insertion of headings and titles, totals and subtotals, and summary information

——**Application generators:** produce source code from high-level specification of input, processing, and output requirements

A great deal of tabulation and statistical analysis is often required when preparing analytical information for managers. Thus **statistical software** is an integral information center tool.

Personal computer software is widely used too. The most common types of PC software are:

——Spreadsheet packages

——Word processing programs (including spelling checkers and dictionaries)

——Data management packages

——Data communications programs

——Graphics software

As development of good software for the personal computer continues, this list will undoubtedly grow. At an information center, selected staff members have the responsibility for evaluating new packages as they are introduced into the market.

Personnel Requirements

Information center staffing requirements differ from those of the information systems department. There are five categories of center personnel. The *information center manager* oversees all activities of the center and usually reports to the senior information systems executive (Figure 18.2). Thus the manager receives information on emerging corporate strategies, policies, and operating activities.

Product managers supervise the development and use of individual applications that may be shared by multiple users. For example, the manufacturing planning and cost management system described earlier is a typical information center product. Because of the recurring need for such tools, an information systems product manager oversees general usage and coordinates support of the system as well as training of users.

Trainers work directly with the users to familiarize them with center products (such as the cost estimating system), software packages (such as spreadsheet software), or high-level languages (such as Query-By-Example or FOCUS). In addition to running individual and group classes, trainers are available for questions from users about specific features of the system or usage techniques.

Figure 18.2 Common Organization Structure for Information Systems Department

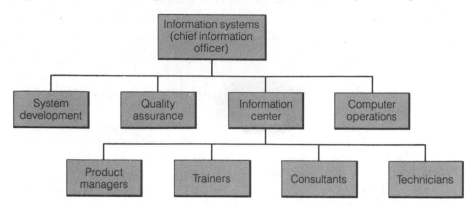

Consultants work with users who need to develop a specific application or to formulate a report of information from the database. Their responsibilities include translation of user requirements into tasks the center can address and development of strategies for meeting them. Consultants usually assist the user in choosing the right product or software to meet the identified needs. Organizations vary in their handling of the development of applications. Some allow center staff members to prepare an application, while others give initial training and require the user to do the development under the consultant's guidance. It is probably best if consultants do *some* development work to stay abreast of user questions and problems. In the long run, both they and the center will be more effective.

Technicians, who maintain the equipment in the center, are responsible for diagnosing malfunctions and making repairs. In many organizations, technicians also stay in touch with vendors and monitor new developments in software, which they evaluate for potential use in the information center.

Managing End-User Computing

End-user computing will not be successful unless it is properly managed and supported. In fact, without good management, it can be harmful to an organization. The responsibilities of all participants must be clear, and guidelines must be in place to avoid risks.

Shared Responsibilities

End-user computing means that both users and systems analysts bear responsibilities for the development and maintenance of information systems (see Table 18.3).

Table 18.3 Responsibilities in End-User Computing Environments

User Responsibilities	Information Center Responsibilities
Recognize the role of end-user development and know when applications should be handed over to the information systems department.	Recognize the benefits of end-user computing.
Understand the business problem to be addressed by the desired application.	Provide education and training programs.
Know the generic data needed to address the stated problem.	Translate generic data requirements into data specification and processing requirements.
Be able to use the necessary terminals, workstations, and related computer equipment.	Provide consulting services.
Know how to use the software.	Provide assistance in detecting and correcting errors.
Follow guidelines and adopt prescribed standards.	Watch for and evaluate new tools.
Do the work!	Assist by answering questions and solving difficult problems encountered by users.
Assess the costs and benefits.	Assess the costs and benefits.

User Responsibilities First, when doing systems development themselves, whether through an information center or on their own, end-users must have a good grip on the business problem at hand. In particular, managers should not advise center staff "I have a marketing problem" and expect to be able to sit back and await results. Consultants cannot be of assistance unless they understand the problem on a fairly detailed level.

Second, users must know what *generic data* they need to address the problem under consideration. That is, they must be able to specify details in business terms, indicating, for example, a need for data about salesperson performance, customer activity, sales by region, or market penetration by geographical region. Users are not required to consider the manner in which data will be stored in the physical organization of records, nor the format specifications. Nor do they need to think about data names.

It is, however, the responsibility of each user to know how to operate the terminals, workstations, or personal computers as well as storage devices and peripheral equipment such as printers and graphic plotters. Everyone who plans to undertake a systems development task should attend a workshop or training session to learn how to turn the equipment on and off, how to format diskettes for storage of data, how to log on to the mainframe or a shared computer system, how to retrieve output from the system, and so on. Systems staff members acting as consultants during the development of an application should not have to provide this basic training.

Similarly, end-users should acquire familiarity with the software product they will be using and generally should know about spreadsheet and data retrieval products. Sometimes, though, the analyst determines which product is most appropriate for the task at hand. When it has been decided which organization system product will be used to meet application requirements, of course learning more about that product becomes the end-user's responsibility.

Any firm's success in the management of end-user computing can be attributed in part to a policy of developing and maintaining guidelines and standards for the storage, retrieval, and use of data to avoid accidental destruction of data, loss of integrity, unauthorized access to data, and similar problems. Users are responsible for adhering to the guidelines, which often serve to protect novices from themselves!

The very phrase "end-user computing" places the responsibility of doing the work on the shoulders of the person or group that will benefit from the application. Users must develop such applications to produce the information that will meet their requirements. The initiative and commitment of time must originate with them.

Analyst Responsibilities Systems analysts also have important responsibilities in an environment of end-user computing. First, they must recognize the benefits that are attributed to user-developed applications. We have discussed them throughout this chapter. Nevertheless, systems analysts and information systems managers in some organizations still view users as a threat to their domain. They see loss of control rather than improved information systems benefits for the organization as a result of end-user computing. And they view fourth-generation languages as "taking the art out of the development of applications." Fortunately, such attitudes do not prevail in most firms today.

Systems analysts may be asked to serve as consultants to end-users, recommending appropriate software or software products to meet the needs identified. Analysts have the skills to help nonprogramming managers and employees formulate their requirements and design an approach that will produce the desired information.

Earlier we said that users must identify generic information needs. Analysts in turn translate the generic into specifics. That is, they select the available data, the format, and the method of retrieval so that the end-user can utilize the data in the application. For instance, the analysts may write the schemes or data descriptions needed to access the data.

In virtually every case, end-users will need assistance in finding and correcting errors or problems in the applications they develop. It is the responsibility of the systems analyst to address these problems and to provide debugging assistance as part of the support for an information center product or a tool designed to function in an end-user environment.

Systems professionals should continually be on the lookout for new tools—languages, packages, or computer devices—that will facilitate user-driven systems. And they are best qualified to find ways to improve the interface tools or methods. The vastly overworked term *user friendly* describes a method of interfacing with an information system that is as natural as possible, fitting the needs and characteristics of people, not computers. Good systems analysts are always alert to the development of new ideas or methods for achieving user-friendly interfaces.

Risks of End-User Computing

Throughout this chapter, we have emphasized the benefits of user-developed information systems. But you should recognize that there are risks as well. Consider the following true stories:

——One executive used a spreadsheet program to predict company sales, and the executive's colleagues used this projection to plan the hiring of additional employees and the expansion of the firm's inventory to handle the anticipated $55 million in sales.

The sales projection was wrong by more than $8 million, however. The spreadsheet user, working without assistance, had neglected to compensate for a price discount planned for a key component. Thus some of the numbers inserted into the spreadsheet's pricing formula were incorrect, and the computer, which simply processed data in accordance with programmed instructions, gave output that led to bad decisions.

——The division manager of a Fortune 500 company, working with an assistant, used a spreadsheet package to develop a profit-and-loss model for the division. The model was reviewed by several other managers in the firm, and changes were suggested. As each change was validated, it was entered into the spreadsheet model by the assistant.

After detecting an apparent error, the assistant changed one formula in the model. To avoid embarrassing the division manager, whom the assistant believed had introduced the error, the assistant did not report the change.

The model was used for several weeks and important decisions were based on information drawn from it. Then it was found that the "error" the assistant had corrected was *not* an error. This change cost the organization several hundred thousand dollars.

——A corporation was negotiating to acquire another firm. Using a personal computer, the vice president for finance constructed a model of the corporation before and after acquisition of the other company. Based on the model, the vice president arrived at a purchase offer, using stock in the parent corporation. This offer, which was based on a faulty acquisition model, overvalued the target company by 150 percent and was accepted immediately.

Unfortunately, the story doesn't end here. The owners of the target company had succeeded in obtaining unrestricted rights to sell the stock in the parent company received according to the terms of the takeover, and they sold it all. Overnight the price of the parent firm's stock dropped 40 percent.

The parent firm delayed a large planned stock offering and added to its bank borrowing but was unable to complete the financing of the integration of the other firm. Planned savings were not achieved, profits nosedived, and the bank demanded immediate payment of loans. The result was involuntary bankruptcy.

——Another company embarked on an expensive lawsuit against an end-user who was a former vice president of the firm. The executive had left to form a consulting firm, taking along computer programs and data files used in the management of company cash funds. The company sued for the return of these materials and attempted to enjoin the defendant from using them. The vice president claimed the programs and files were similar to private papers and documents traditionally removed by departing executives. The company pointed out that they had been developed on company time using company resources and claimed that they belonged to the firm.

In an out-of-court settlement, the vice president was allowed to use the system in the new consulting business. However, the vice president agreed to document the system so that it could be used by any successors. Thus the company made a tradeoff, dropping its attempt to prevent the vice president from using the files and programs in return for a promise to make the system usable by others. Without documentation, the system was worthless to all but its developer.

The number of other such examples of risks and failures is quite high.

Following is a partial list of risks that may be associated with user-developed information systems:

—Using inaccurate specifications or assumptions about organization activities
—Applying incorrect formulas or models
—Using incomplete information
—Using outdated information
—Selecting untested or inappropriate software
—Failing to follow standards or guidelines
—Failing to test assumptions or models

Avoiding the Risks

The risks pointed out above can be avoided. Properly adhered to, the guidelines in Table 18.4 will minimize the risk of relying on user-developed information systems while maximizing the benefits. The sections that follow discuss these seven rules.

Download Data **Downloading** is the term used by computer professionals to refer to the process of copying a portion of a file or database from the central computer system, often a mainframe or larger computer, to the workstation, personal computer, or departmental computer of the user. To avoid use of erroneous data, end-users should be required to download the data they use from the central system(s).

Downloading saves user time, since there is no need to key in data that already exist, but it also ensures that the same data are used in all applications and by all personnel, regardless of location or position in the firm. In addition to achieving uniformity, this practice ensures that any data used in a decision process have been properly validated, since everything in the central computer database has been processed in accordance with the standards of the information systems group.

Avoid User Data Entry Users should not enter data directly into corporate files or databases, nor should they be allowed to change data stored in them. This ensures that errors will not be introduced into valid data. All data entering the database should enter through applications developed, maintained, and managed by the information systems department.

Table 18.4 Guidelines for Effective Management of End-User Computing

Insist on downloading of system data to user system.

Avoid user entry of data into organization files and databases.

Adopt and enforce standards for data management, development of systems, and testing of applications.

Document the systems and applications using automatic documentation tools whenever possible.

Review and test user-developed software.

Provide useful end-user training.

Facilitate communication between end-users.

Standardize Standards for data, for development processes, and for testing software must be rigidly enforced. The strict adherence to careful definitions of individual items will ensure that data always have the same meaning to everyone. For example, if the meaning of "net profit" is standardized, we will be able to assume that whenever this variable appears, it includes the effect of taxes. And standardizing the meaning of "inventory value" will tell us that current purchase price data were applied to all items in the warehouse in any calculation involving this variable.

Standards should also include acceptable value ranges. This is still another aspect of providing for validation of data.

Document the Application Documentation is an aspect of systems development that causes difficulties even in the systems of computer professionals. In the user environment, the key to achieving acceptable documentation standards is to have the system automatically explain how it operates and what features characterize models and formulas.

The best spreadsheet and decision-aiding packages automatically store formulas and the relation of components in models. Although normally invisible to the user, they can be retrieved in print or display form when needed.

Many fourth-generation languages are touted as being "self-documenting" in that the programs themselves are so understandable that they serve as their own documentation. Reading through the code explains what the program does.

Unfortunately, the greatest problem in documentation is not in determining *what* was done, but *why* it was done. This aspect continues to be a source of difficulties.

Review and Test Software If all user-developed applications are reviewed by the information systems department as a matter of policy, horror stories like those recounted earlier will be avoided. Users often are reluctant to test their software; furthermore, they may not be aware of the assumptions they make about procedures and controls when designing their application—a natural tendency for us all. Systems analysts are better trained than end-users to scrutinize system requirements.

Train End-Users There is no substitute for training. Through it, mistakes can be avoided and areas for misunderstanding detected early enough to permit correction of the difficulty at the source. The discussion of information centers outlined different aspects of this activity.

Facilitate Communication A continual interchange between users will raise the level of accomplishment in end-user computing, and it will reduce risks. Common questions can be openly discussed and successful solutions publicized. Similarly, mistakes and errors can be discreetly explained with the hope of preventing their recurrence.

Common modes of communication are user groups that meet at regular intervals and newsletters, printed or shared electronically. They really work!

End-User Computing in Perspective

End-user computing is an alternative to the other development methods discussed in the preceding chapters, namely the systems development life cycle and the prototyping methodology. Each approach has distinct characteristics and provides specific advantages. There are differences, too, of course, as summarized in Table 18.5.

You should not necessarily consider any specific approach to the generation of information to be ideal. Rather, start by determining whether the information can be prepared by an end-user or whether a professional systems specialist must be engaged, and follow the method that best suits the situation at hand.

Rise of the Help Desk

Now that we have examined the importance of end-user computing, consider this proposition: End-user computing will grow in importance, and organizations will find that their need to have staffed information centers will diminish and they will close the centers. Information systems development and usage will continue to rise to new levels. (This does not eliminate the need to manage end-user computing by following the guidelines discussed in the last section; on the contrary, it makes this management more imperative.)

Let's look at this scenario more closely.

Developments Affecting Information Centers

If end-user computing will grow in importance, why will organizations not need information centers? Among the probable reasons are the following:

——*Familiarity with computing will become virtually universal.* Personal computers are now in widespread use. The number of individuals who utilize such systems in organizations reaches new highs monthly. As corporations increase their reliance on such systems, those persons who need the kind of training in their use that information centers have provided will drop.

Table 18.5 Comparison of Alternate Systems Development Methods

Characteristic	Systems Development Life Cycle Method	Prototyping Development Method	End-User Development Method
Requirements determination	Essential features are identified before development begins.	Features are identified through iteration. Requirements evolve through user response from actual usage of a working prototype.	User identifies essential features through participation in the development process directly. Adjustments to system may be ongoing.
Role of analyst	Responsible for full analysis and development process. Limited involvement of user.	Analyst involves user extensively to learn about requirements, assess system features, and react to design details or missing features.	Analyst may participate to assist or advise. User takes responsibility for defining application.
Development tools	Third- and fourth-generation languages	Fourth-generation languages	Fourth-generation languages, packaged software, and personal computer software.
Most appropriate applications	Transaction-level systems and applications where requirements are well known in advance.	Decision-oriented applications where requirements must evolve or new technology will be implemented.	Decision-oriented and personal-support applications using technology focusing on reporting and "what is" evaluations.
Data	Data entry follows validation rules built into system.	Data entry follows validation rules built into system.	User entry of data is avoided.
	Data standards maintained and enforced.	Data standards maintained and enforced.	Data standards maintained and enforced.

——*Effective training software will be generally available.* At one time software designed to train individuals in how to use computers or selected software packages was very primitive. Many packages could do little more than display text and questions to the user. But now training software can create situations, even simulations, that guide the user through personalized learning activities. Individuals thus become quite skilled in computer use.

——*The availability of software will continue to increase user needs.* An abundance of software to perform all sorts of functions is available. In the future, a growing number of information needs will be met through available software that is easy to use and includes its own training system.

——*Interfaces to all computers will become increasingly friendly.* Interfaces continue to grow more natural, through the growing use of windows, pull-down menus, and the like. Individuals are finding that they can move from application to application with little difficulty, in other words.

Collectively these developments suggest that end-user computing will proliferate, but without the need for the information center as we know it today. In its place we see the emergence of the help desk.

Reaching the Help Desk

The **help desk** will be a place where assistance is available for questions that arise. Troubleshooting and guidance, not training, will be the norm for the help desk. However, the help desk will continue to serve as a reference point for information on software, techniques, and so on, for end-user computing.

The help desk will be accessible to individuals in person and in at least two other ways:

——*By telephone:* When questions arise or difficulties are encountered using a computer component (for example, a personal computer, printer, or disk unit), help will be only a telephone call away. The help desk, staffed 24 hours per day in many firms, will be able to assist the user in identifying the source of a problem that has arisen, suggest a way to obtain needed information, or answer a simple question about an application.

——*By computer network:* With the growing reliance on network-based systems, access to the help desk through communication links will be very important. Staff assistants will be able to look inside an application to see the processing status. They will also be able to diagnose computer difficulties on-line and provide assistance. Help will be instantaneous because of the power of computer networking.

The transition to help desks will not occur to reduce costs, since it is likely that organizations may invest more in this function than in information centers. However, the investment may be more effective since it provides assistance at the time it is needed regardless of where the user is located. And it is available when the systems are in use.

Summary

End-user computing is increasing in frequency across organizations of diverse types. The underlying rationale is that through proper management of this information systems tool, users and the organization at large can benefit from improved productivity, increased involvement of users in the development process, and the potential to reduce hidden and apparent development backlogs. Similarly, application maintenance chores may be lightened.

The applications best suited to end-user computing are those that consist of one-time inquiries, simple reports, adjustments or enhancements of existing reports, and the preparation of "what if" analyses. Of particular importance is the information center, a concept embodied in a support unit designed to facilitate user-driven computing. Applications run through an information center are not confined to personal computing; they frequently involve interaction with mainframe computers and centrally managed databases. Information center staff members assume responsibility for conducting training, keeping abreast of new software and computer products, and serving as a source of information about data available to meet user needs. The tools of the center include such fourth-generation software as query and retrieval languages, report generators, and application generators, as well as statistical tabulation packages and personal computer software.

Users and systems analysts share responsibilities for application development, although the specific roles will vary across organizations. However, it is generally agreed that if end-user computing is not properly managed, significant risks can arise. As a general rule, users should not perform data entry functions or alter data stored in organization databases. Other guidelines call for adherence to data and documentation standards, and review and testing of software. There is no substitute for effective training, and the value of user-to-user communication can hardly be overstated.

As end-user computing grows in importance, help desks are likely to increasingly supplant information centers, since many of the services provided by these centers will become superfluous. However, there will still be a great need to manage end-user computing.

When kept in the proper perspective, user-driven computing is an alternative to the development of information systems through prototyping and development life cycle methods.

Key Words

Application generator	Help desk	Report generator
Backlog	Information center	Statistical software
Consultant	Personal computer software	Technician
Download	Product manager	Trainer
End-user	Query and retrieval	
Fourth-generation language	language	

Review Questions

1. What is end-user computing? What is the rationale behind this development method?
2. What is the hidden backlog? Of what significance is it to the user of computer information systems in organizations?
3. How does end-user computing affect the growing concern over the maintenance of computer software? Why is this concern important?
4. Describe the characteristics of applications suitable for end-user development.

5. Discuss the purpose of an information center. What is its relation to the information systems group? Is this relation the same across all organizations? Explain.

6. What tools are common in information centers? What benefits do they offer to users? To information systems specialists?

7. Discuss the personnel typically associated with an information center and the role each plays in supporting end-user computing.

8. In what ways are the responsibilities of end-users and systems analysts the same for end-user computing? In what ways are they different?

9. How does an organization take on risks when it supports the development of information systems by end-users? How significant are the risks? In what ways can they be avoided?

10. What types of applications are most suitable for development by end-users? What types are least suitable?

11. Why are organizations establishing help desks to support end-user computing? What functions do they perform?

Application Problems

1. Information systems managers and users alike are concerned with the large backlog of requests for the development of information systems applications. In some organizations, it is estimated that it will take years to eliminate the backlog.

   a. Suppose an information systems manager takes the position that all the talk of development backlogs is exaggerated. The manager does not deny that a backlog exists, but believes that the most important applications have been developed and are in use. The rationale behind the argument is that users asked for the most important applications first and those are the ones the systems group has developed and implemented. Applications that have been thought of later do not have the same importance as those requested first. Do you agree or disagree with this position? Explain your reason.

   the only constant is change; things that used to be important are not any more.

   b. Is the concern for a hidden backlog overstated? One might make the argument that if a user truly needs information or a new system, the request surely will be made and justified so that development can be undertaken. It is irrational to believe that a legitimate and important application will not be requested, adding to the legend of the hidden backlog. Do you agree or disagree with this argument? Why?

   some good ideas may not be brought forward

2. Which of the following types of activity are best suited for resolution through the facilities of end-user computing?

   a. Capture and entry of transaction data into a sales database

   b. Formulation of sales projections using various advertising levels, sales promotions, and product price levels

   c. Development of graphic displays of data already stored in one or more organization databases

   d. Entry of data to change or alter currently stored records about inventory usage rates

   e. Selective search through a single master file or database to retrieve data about an entity of interest

   f. Reformatting a report written in COBOL

3. Discuss the validity of the following statement: "End-user computing is vastly overrated in terms of its potential to improve organization performance. Information systems are necessarily involved with the design of files and databases, selection of file access methods, use of telecommunications facilities, incorporation of appropriate data validation methods, and the structuring of reports. Users who do not have extensive computing training cannot possibly have the expertise to make informed decisions in these areas. Therefore, end-user computing cannot be successful in the long run."

4. A salesperson in a textile firm wishes to create a database, using a personal computer and a widely marketed database management package. The total cost of the hardware and software is less than $5000. The database will contain the names and addresses of all actual and potential customers in the salesperson's region. In addition, the records will contain summaries of the purchases made by customers throughout the year, listing dollar volume by item average usage rates. The records for potential customers will tell why each firm is currently not a customer and will identify the items the firm should be purchasing. All data will be entered and maintained by the salesperson.

   The salesperson anticipates using the system to monitor current customer purchasing activities. In addition, inquiries will be made to retrieve customer information based on customer name, geographical region, and items selected. Sales calls and promotions will be targeted to individuals whose names are retrieved through one or more of the inquiries above. The salesperson will rely on the system as a primary sales tool.

   The system will fit on a standard personal computer equipped with a hard disk.

   a. Based on the preceding description, is the planned application consistent with the objectives of end-user computing? Do you think the application should be developed?

   b. Do you see any risks, inefficiencies, or inadvisable practices in the planned system?

   c. The salesperson wishes to develop the system rather than ask the information systems department to do the work. A fourth-generation database package will be used. Discuss the wisdom of having the salesperson devise this system.

5. An organization is concerned about the risks of end-user computing. It is aware of problems its competitors have encountered in user-developed systems, as a result of incomplete analysis and unreliable data. Therefore, the firm's managers insist that the information systems department oversee the development of all end-user applications, whether run on personal computers or on the firm's main-frame systems. It wants the development of all applications to be managed professionally and it insists on certification of system reliability before an application is put into daily use.

   A group of users have objected to management's position. The group claims that by installing formal management procedures for the development of applications, especially those that will run on personal computers, the benefits of end-user-developed applications will be lost. Insisting on management of the process will subject it to the same delays that, in their opinion, already hinder other systems managed by the IS department. Furthermore, they emphasize their suspicion that the IS staff can kill any application it does not wish to see developed, simply by stating that it will endanger the integrity of the firm's database.

   a. Discuss the users' position. Do you agree or disagree with their reasoning?

b. Can end-user computing be managed in the manner described above without reducing its benefits?

6. Discuss the merit of the following commonly heard comment about end-user development of information systems: "End-user computing, meaning user-developed systems, will be of limited value because the users of information systems do not know in advance what information they need from a system, and thus the basic problem of identifying information requirements remains unsolved."

Minicase: Funny Trash*

A few years ago, a city in the Netherlands had a refuse problem. A once-clean section of town had become an eyesore because people had stopped using the trash cans. Cigarette butts, beer bottles, chocolate wrappers, newspapers, and other forms of trash were littering the streets.

The municipal sanitation department sought ways to clean up the city. They tried doubling the littering fine from 25 guilders to 50 guilders for each offense, but this had little effect. They increased the number of litter agents who patrolled the area. This was another "punish the litterer" solution, and it, too, had little impact on the problem.

Then somebody asked the following question: "What if our trash cans paid people money when they deposited their litter?" The idea, to say the least, got people thinking. The what-iffer had changed a "punish the litterer" problem to a "reward the law-abider" solution. The idea had one glaring flaw, however; if the city implemented the idea, it would go bankrupt.

Fortunately, the people who were listening to this idea didn't evaluate it solely on the basis of its impracticality.

Instead, they used it as a steppingstone and asked themselves, "How else could we reward people for putting their trash in the trash cans?" This question led to the development of electronic joke-telling trash cans! When a sensing unit on the top detected the deposit of a piece of refuse, it activated a tape recorder that played a recorded joke. Some trash cans told bad puns while others told shaggy dog stories, and the jokes were changed every two weeks. As a result, people went out of their way to put their trash in the trash cans, and the town became clean once again.

Questions

1. Is there a relation between the trash problem and that of identifying user information requirements? That is, should the burden of identifying information requirements be shifted from the systems analyst to the user?

2. What creative methods, analogous to those used for handling the trash, could be applied to user development of information systems? To reducing the backlog of systems development requests?

*Based on Roger von Oech, *A Whack on the Side of the Head* (New York: Warner Books, 1983), pp. 59–60.

19: Implementing Information Systems

Key Questions

[handwritten left margin: cultural variable, work situation ", economic ", emotional ", perceptual "]

[handwritten: causes resistance]

[handwritten top right: as early as regmts analysis]

When does implementation of information systems begin?

What methods are available to convert to the use of a new system? *[handwritten: Parallel, Pilot — Phase-In — Direct Cut-Over]*

How can the impact of information systems be assessed? *[handwritten: — user attitude surveys — critical Incident logs — weighted feature evaluation — cost/benefit analysis — sys. perf. measurements — o.g. analysis]*

How does the introduction of change affect organizational structure?

How does the introduction of an information system affect an organization?

Why does resistance to computer-based information systems develop? *[handwritten: — systems oriented — people oriented — interaction of factors]*

What forms does resistance take? *[handwritten: — Aggression — Avoidance — Projection]*

How can resistance be avoided or overcome? *[handwritten: — make user friendly — involve users early — deliver system promised — provide reliable system]*

The reasonable man adapts himself to the world; the unreasonable one persists in trying to adapt the world to himself. Therefore all progress depends on the unreasonable man.

George Bernard Shaw

Implementation of information systems starts long before computer software is developed and equipment is delivered. It is not a phase of development, but rather a process in which the benefits of the system are introduced through use. Remember that the system consists not only of the computer-based portion of the application; it also entails the surrounding procedures, controls, and aids provided to users.

For systems developed through prototyping, implementation begins early, perhaps when the initial prototype is used. In some applications, the impact of the system is first noticed during requirements analysis when user and analyst begin to modify manual processes or activities in the organizational area in which the system will be used. As the prototype is refined through successive iterations, the impact of the system increases.

When end-users develop their own applications, generating reports or retrieving information in response to inquiries, the impact of the system is usually immediate. Fourth-generation languages and information center facilities encourage and make this possible. Whether one-shot or recurring, each new situation calls for modifications in which users fine-tune the application.

For applications developed using the life cycle development method, implementation takes on a different form. Early benefits of the system remain, but there is

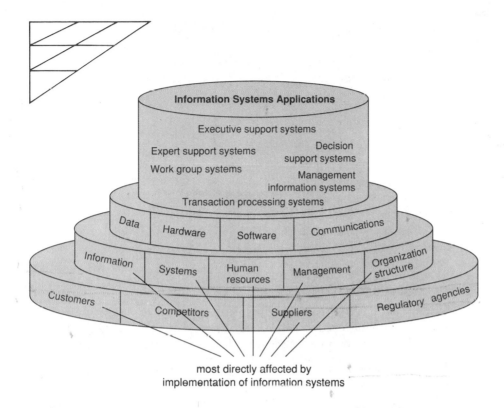

Information Systems Applications

Executive support systems

Expert support systems

Decision support systems

Work group systems

Management information systems

Transaction processing systems

Data   Hardware   Software   Communications

Information   Systems   Human resources   Management   Organization structure

Customers   Competitors   Suppliers   Regulatory agencies

most directly affected by
implementation of information systems

greater emphasis on activities that occur later in the development process. Often this is because the method tends to be chosen for applications broader in scope than those developed under other approaches. More persons are directly affected: Consider the number of bank tellers employed in a large bank that implements a new on-line deposit system. Similarly, more transactions are involved: Consider a national consumer goods firm with many regional sales offices that must process thousands of orders every day. Systems like these are not implemented without careful thought and deliberate planning.

This chapter examines the activities associated with the implementation of information systems. We look at the steps taken to prepare both the system and its users for implementation. Alternate strategies for conversion to the new system are examined. An important aspect of implementation is the evaluation of the system's impact on the enterprise and its people. Both the importance of performing the postimplementation evaluation and methods for carrying it out are discussed. We also look at various forms of resistance to the implementation of information systems, considering why they occur and learning how to avoid them. When you have completed this chapter, you should know why good planning for implementation is essential and how to plan well.

Preparing for Systems Implementation

As the development of software for the system nears completion, or the arrival date of purchased prewritten software approaches, plans are laid for ensuring that the system will perform as expected. Important preconversion activities include testing the system and conducting training.

Systems Testing

When computer software has been written, it is the responsibility of programmers and development managers to ensure that the system using it will function properly. *Program testing,* as this is termed, is performed to detect errors in the logic of the software—perhaps because of misunderstanding of the program specifications or as a result of mistakes in the code itself. To begin using a system known to contain logic errors would be unthinkable.

Another type of testing is associated with the implementation itself. **Systems testing** is performed to determine how well the system will perform and whether it meets the original specifications. The software per se is not tested; rather, the system as a whole is scrutinized. Analysts perform tests to determine whether the components of the system fit together and function properly. Typical questions that must be answered through system testing involve the following areas.

——*Data compatibility:* Are the data produced in one module in the form expected by other modules using the same data?

——*Data interrelatability:* Can data referenced by an identifying name in one module be referenced by the same name in other modules?

——*File capacity:* Are file sizes adequate to meet usage requirements?

——*Data sequencing:* Are the data stored and accessible in the proper order? Are sorting and reindexing procedures included in the system to preserve the intended order in the data?

These tests focus on the normal running of the system. Another category of testing includes special system tests. These tests (see Table 19.1) provide information on *how well* the system will run. They test documentation, procedures, performance times, and human factors concerns. Both operator and user aspects of systems usage are examined.

Systems testing is particularly important because it is often the last opportunity to find flaws that can cause the system to fail when it is converted to live use. Neither users nor computer operators care about the amount of preimplementation testing that a system went through. Their concern is whether the system will work for them. This question must be answered by systems testing. Inherent errors or problems in systems features cannot be overcome by training.

Operator Training

Training introduces both computer operators and end-users to the features of an information system (Table 19.2). And, it shows them how to take advantage of these

Table 19.1 Special Systems Tests

Type of Test	Description
✓ Peak load test	Determines whether the system can handle the volume of activities that will occur when the system is at the peak of its processing demand. *Example:* Run the system with all terminals active at the same time.
Storage testing	Determines the capacity of the system to store transaction data on a disk or in other files. *Example:* Verify documentation statements that the system will store 10,000 records of 383 bytes length on a single, flexible disk.
✓ Performance time testing	Determines the length of time used by the system to process transaction data. — 3 seconds typ *Example:* Measure response time for inquiry when system is fully loaded with operating data.
✓ Recovery testing	Determines ability of users to recover data or restart system after failure. *Example:* Load backup copy of data and try to resume processing without data or integrity loss.
✓ Procedure testing	Determines clarity of documentation on operation and use of system by having users do exactly what manuals request. *Example:* See what happens when someone tries to power down the system at the end of the week or to respond to the paper-out light on the printer.
✓ Human factors testing	Determines how users will use the system when processing data or preparing reports. *Example:* See what happens when the system does not respond immediately to an inquiry.

features. You should not consider training to be a luxury, to be attended to if time permits. Rather, it is an integral part of the development and implementation process. The quality of training in most implementations can make the difference between success and failure for the system.

Operator training involves computer staff and information center personnel who are responsible for keeping the equipment running, providing the necessary support service, or introducing the application to end-users. Their training must cover the handling of all possible operations, and the performance of routine operations (for example, starting the system, entering data, producing reports) should be second nature.

Training also involves familiarization with run procedures, including the mounting of tapes, loading of disks, copying files, or turning on communications systems. Operators must know when the various procedures are appropriate and how to accomplish them.

Table 19.2 Systems Training Activities

Type of Training	Description
Operator training	Computer staff and information center personnel who will operate the system or introduce the application to end-users acquire knowledge of routine operations, run procedures, and troubleshooting techniques.
User training	Beginners learn fundamentals, such as how to initiate processing or to format diskettes, as well as use of the system itself. Training should include hands-on experience in using the system; may be accomplished through both in-house and external facilities, including those provided by vendors or commercial sources.

Malfunctions are bound to occur. Operators and information center personnel need to know what the most likely malfunctions are, how to detect them, and what steps to follow when they arise. For example, they must know how to detect damage to data on a magnetic disk and what to do about it. They must also know the probable causes of such damage (for example, improper handling or perhaps normal wear on the disk).

In addition, operators must find out how long applications will run under normal conditions. This not only facilitates the scheduling of work activities but also enables operators to spot systems that are running longer or shorter than expected—a frequent sign of problems with a run.

User Training

When both the application itself and the equipment are new to the users, user training will address fundamental matters first. End-users need to know how to turn on a personal computer or a workstation, how to insert a diskette into a microcomputer, and how to load a program into the system. They also want to be sure when it is safe to take certain actions without risking the loss of their data (for example, when to remove a diskette or turn off the power to the computer). Usually it is not enough to ask whether a certain topic has been made clear. Some may be embarrassed to admit that they have not understood. It is much better to have the trainees demonstrate.

The bulk of user training deals with use of the system itself. Training in data handling or entry of details into the system includes both learning how to enter the data and recognizing what the data should look like (for example, an account number always has seven digits). Users must be shown how to add data, make changes (or *edit* it), formulate inquiries to retrieve specific information, and delete records of data. These functions are the most basic features of the system, and the person conducting the training session must be sure everyone understands them and can perform them comfortably.

Good documentation, although essential, does not substitute for training. Classroom activities and reading of documentation impart familiarity, but actual usage provides experience. Hands-on use of the system is the best way to ensure that people understand the system.

Weaknesses in any aspect of training, however, are likely to lead to awkward, even disastrous, situations, accompanied by high individual frustration levels.

For both operator and user training, a combination of training sources may be considered. The most often used methods include:

— In-house training, tailored to the firm's operations

— Vendor classes

— Professional industry workshops and seminars

— Purchased training films and software packages

Usually any such activities are followed up by practice time on the actual system preceding conversion to the live application.

Strategies for Conversion

Conversion is the process of cutting the new system over to use in ongoing activities. To ensure a smooth—and successful—implementation, users must be familiar with the features of the system, operators must know how to make the system function properly, and the conversion itself must go off without a hitch.

Conversion Tasks

Conversion is more than just starting to use the new system. It includes the creation of all required master and transaction files, establishing backup copies of master files and databases, and converting tested programs to operating status.

File conversion is a central part of system conversion regardless of whether the preceding system was manual or computer-based. For each file in the new system, the analyst must plan:

— The origin of the data (through data entry or by transfer from preexisting master files or databases)

— Validation of data to ensure accurate entry with no inadvertent omissions of items or records

— A schedule for performing the foregoing tasks

— The assignment of responsibility for carrying out the conversion

As you can imagine, the data conversion must be carefully planned and also cross-checked to see that it is done right. Consider the ramifications of transferring a large accounts receivable file from manual ledger cards to a computer-based system without checking for completeness and accuracy. You would not know whether all the accounts were included in the new system—and they represent real money—nor could you guarantee that the account balance for any particular customer was correct.

Any conversion plan should anticipate problems and ways to deal with them. Personnel may be absent at critical times. Data may be missing. Activities may fall behind schedule. Fallback plans must be devised to meet each such contingency.

Figure 19.1 Conversion Strategies

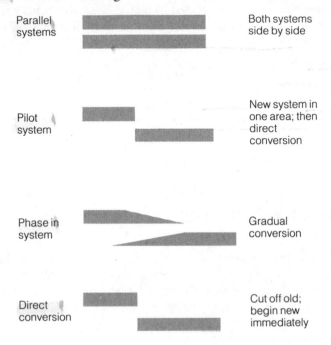

Means of Conversion

The system can go into use through one of four means (Figure 19.1).

— **Parallel systems:** The new system is operated side by side with the old one to ensure that data will not be lost if a problem arises.

— **Pilot system:** Only a small piece of the business or the function is converted to the new system. The rest of the old system remains in place for the time being. A pilot system approach involving, for example, just one part of a production line minimizes the risk to the organization as a whole if problems should develop.

— **Phase-in of system:** The old system is replaced by the new one gradually over time. This allows an organization to begin taking advantage of the newly developed support tool while retaining flexibility to cope with any deficiencies.

— **Direct cutover:** Conversion takes place all at once, rapidly (perhaps overnight). This approach has the psychological advantage of requiring everyone to try hard to make the new system work, since there is nothing else to fall back on. However, a major problem in the new system may cause the organization to suspend normal operations. This method of conversion requires much more careful and detailed planning than the other alternatives.

The specifics of a given situation may dictate the choice of one particular strategy. In general, however, long conversion periods can be frustrating for all involved and they should not be planned without very good reason.

Postimplementation Review

When the conversion to the new system is complete and operations are progressing using its features, the impact on the organization should be evaluated. Corporations and organizations that spend large amounts of money on their information systems but do not carefully assess systems impact have invested blindly. It is foolish to develop new systems without determining their costs and benefits. The postimplementation review assesses the system's impact, paying particular attention to the effects on the people in the organization and on operations, as well as differences in financial costs and benefits and overall changes in performance.

Application Impact

Impact evaluation is the determination of how the implementation and use of an information systems application affects the organization, that is, identifying the changes that are directly attributable to the system. The main areas of concern are the decision-making and operating activities, the quality of information, the structure of the organization, the attitudes of users and other employees, the number of people needed to perform the various functions, and the costs of operation and information processing. For instance, an impact study may reveal that a new customer sales order application has reduced the time required to process a single order and has boosted productivity by 30 percent a day. It may further reveal errors have been cut by 15 percent.

Even though these objectives (that is, increased productivity and fewer errors) would have been identified if not fully quantified during requirements analysis and systems design, it is important to return to them after implementation to see whether expectations have been met. The data are also useful for guiding future development projects. If optical scanning of sales slips works well in one transaction system, similar methods may be considered to process production work orders. Or, enthusiasm and improved analysis capabilities of managers using color graphics presentation of trend information may suggest uses of this feature in other management information systems.

The important areas for impact evaluation include costs and benefits, information characteristics, organizational changes, interaction between users, and individual and organizational productivity. Table 19.3 lists some representative questions to ask when assessing critical performance areas.

Often omitted from systems evaluations is consideration of the effect a new system has on the environment—elements outside the organization itself relate to the business of the firm (other businesses, government units, and so on). For example, a new system that collects and uses personal data in a manner addressed by federal privacy legislation will have an environmental impact different from a system designed for internal use in the control of inventory levels. Regardless of the application, it is important to evaluate the impact of information systems on the environment of the organization.

Table 19.3 Issues to Consider in Evaluating Information Systems*

1. Have information systems changed the cost of operation?

2. Have information systems changed the way in which operations are performed?

3. Have information systems changed the accuracy of information users receive?

4. Have information systems changed the timeliness of information and reports users receive?

5. Have information systems brought about organization changes? Are these changes for the better or for the worse?

6. Have information systems made the information available more complete?

7. Have information systems changed control or centralization? What are the effects of such changes?

8. Have information systems changed the attitudes of systems users or persons affected by the system?

9. Have information systems changed the number of users who can access the data?

10. Have information systems changed the interactions between members of the organization?

11. Have information systems changed productivity?

12. Have information systems changed the effort that must be expended to receive information for decision making?

*These evaluations should be performed both before and after installation of an information systems application.

Methods for Assessing Application Impact

There are seven basic ways of evaluating impact that should be considered in studying an information system.

Critical Incident Logs A *critical incident* is any noteworthy event involving the system. Perhaps an application feature is being applied by a user in a new way, or perhaps an exception has arisen that could not be accommodated through the system. Any event related to the information systems application should be noted.

A particularly useful method of logging incidents is to record events that are out of the ordinary or have elicited expressions of interest from systems analysts, managers, or employees, both *before* and *after* implementation. For example, recording customer complaints before and after implementation of a trust account information system will provide data on the effect of the system from the customers' point of view. The data can be recorded in a notebook, on audiotape, or in any way the organization chooses, as long as they *are* recorded.

Critical incident logging is a relatively unstructured technique, since computer hardware and software need not be involved. It is most useful when assessment takes place over a period of weeks or months, when several impacts are being measured (for example, customer complaints *and* frequency of errors of different kinds), or when quantitative measures are not possible (for instance, in listing unexpected ways in which the applications system is being used). The method is simple and can provide useful data for analysts, designers, and users. However, it is difficult to ensure that people will follow logging procedures. If they do not, of course, only part of the data will be collected (not all events will be noted) and any analysis will be only marginally useful.

User Attitude Surveys Attitude surveys gather data on individual opinions and ideas about information systems through questionnaires that are either administered in person or sent by mail. This approach makes it possible to survey many people in a relatively brief time. But attitude survey questionnaires are useful only if they are designed so that the questions can be answered quickly, and clearly enough to provide meaningful responses for the people doing the evaluation. Whether questions are open-ended, so that the user provides a written response, or multiple choice, as they often are, it is always necessary to have answers that are accurate, subject to validation, and reliable.

Questionnaires are most useful in attitude surveys if they measure something that is quantifiable: "How much faster can you perform your work by using the new order information system? 10 percent? 20 percent?" However, even if the purpose is to assess sentiments, interactions among people, or activities related to installation of a new system, the questionnaire technique, if properly applied, can also be helpful. For example, it is well established that when people are asked to indicate how others feel, they inject personal feelings into their response. Thus, if we wish to find out how people feel about using a new system, we might ask: "How do you think most of your co-workers like the new system? Like it very much? Like it some?" In this way, we can learn each individual's own feelings without having solicited them directly. Attitude surveys designed in this manner are helpful when nonquantitative responses are desired.

Weighted Feature Evaluation Weighted feature analysis is the rating of a set of characteristics or factors—the systems features—related to the impact of an information systems application. Typical concerns include ease of use, likelihood of error, suitability of the method for entering inquiries, and **user-friendliness.** Once the features have been identified, they are weighted in terms of their importance (most important to least important), and respondents evaluate how good or bad the system is with respect to these features. Features judged most important receive greater weight in subsequent analyses.

In evaluating a marketing information system, for example, we might identify the most important parameters as timeliness, accuracy, readability, and usability of information the system produces. Then we decide that accuracy is the most important factor, timeliness the next important, then usability, and finally readability. Now we ask the users how good or bad the system is in terms of these factors. To do this, we prepare a set of questions with weighted responses about each factor, using a scale of 1 (good) to 5 (bad). For example:

How timely is the information you receive from the new system?

1	2	3	4	5
Always timely	Usually timely	Sometimes timely	Seldom timely	Never timely

Answers to this question will tell us how users rate this factor.

It is often useful to compare the users' assessments with those of the systems staff—the two groups may view things quite differently. For instance, programmers and analysts may feel they have provided very timely information but the users may not agree. Evaluations like this can lead to redesigning certain features of the system.

Systems Performance Measurement This is the objective numerical evaluation—in contrast to relative subjective weighting—of the impact of the system's application. Parameters of interest are measured through observation, questionnaires, data collection by the computer system, interview, or document examination. For example, we can use measurement to assess decision-making time or use of the system to make decisions. In this case, we could determine how long a user takes to make a decision by means of observation. A questionnaire might be a good way to find out how many times a day a person looks at reports prepared by the system to make decisions. Other measurements can be taken to determine the number of reports received or the tendency to use information other than that generated through the system.

Organization Analysis The techniques used to evaluate the impact of a system are the same as those used in requirements analysis before prototyping or as an early activity in the systems development life cycle: interview, questionnaire, observation, document examination, and measurement. When used to evaluate impact, **organization analysis** focuses on the system and its uses after it has been installed. The primary concern is assessing how the system affects organization structure, procedures, and general administration policies. We are looking again at the same factors in the organization and in the newly installed system, to see how they have evolved.

The technique is useful, for example, in assessing a system's impact on the preparation of routine and special analysis reports. Outcomes in selected areas can be monitored to determine the number of decisions that have been based on the information in documents generated by the new system.

Evaluating Computer Systems Performance Performance evaluation of computer-based systems involves using monitors to collect data on how well the computer is being used and whether it is operating efficiently. Monitors are tools that collect data about use of computer system resources. **Hardware monitors** are boxlike electronic devices that can be connected to various points on computer equipment (for example, to the central processing unit or to communication channels—see Figure 19.2). During processing, the monitor records how much, how often, and in what ways the different components are used. The data are recorded on magnetic media to permit later analysis. For example, if we want to determine how often the CPU is actually processing as opposed to waiting for input/output operations to be completed, we can use a hardware monitor to collect the timing data. Analyzing these data may lead to adjustments in the computer system that will improve overlapped processing activities and eliminate bottlenecks.

A **software monitor** is a set of executable instructions embedded in the operating system to collect data about the operating system itself and about application

Figure 19.2 Monitors for Evaluating Computer Systems Performance

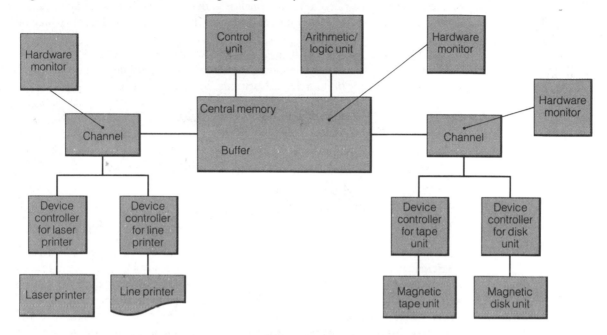

programs. That is, this monitor is itself software and collects data by being part of the operating system. Data are recorded on secondary storage for later analysis. Unlike hardware monitors, which are external to the system, software monitors require memory space and decrease processing speeds slightly. Software monitors are useful because they can keep track of what *each program* is doing.

Performance monitoring helps determine whether additional resources are needed or whether existing resources should be adjusted to improve performance. For example, if we want to add a new application to a system, we must first find out whether the computer can support it. In such a case, a hardware monitor not only could measure the amount of time the CPU is in use, it could be connected to communication channels and secondary storage devices to determine the feasibility of increasing the demands imposed on these components. In addition, during post-implementation review, performance monitoring can tell us how a new application is using computer resources.

Collection of data about the system can help an organization decide whether to add new storage units, to upgrade communications or data transfer lines, or even to purchase another central processing unit. The data can also be useful in determining whether all the present equipment is necessary or whether redesigning files would improve processing efficiency. For instance, by monitoring the use of disk drives in a configuration, we may find that only three out of the four in the system are used very often, and these three are accessed in only 65 percent of the applications. In this case, the data may lead us to the conclusion that four disk drives are unnecessary for this particular set of applications and the files may be reallocated among three or perhaps only two disk drives.

Software monitoring can help identify which languages are used most, what types of processing are most common (for example, a high volume of simple record updating versus a lot of complex calculations, or batch versus on-line processing), and how often various applications are run. Another tool for such evaluations is a record called an *accounting log*. Job accounting records maintained automatically by the operating system show what time of day a certain job is run, what systems resources or equipment are used, and how long the application runs. The data collected can be used to answer three critical evaluation questions:

——Which jobs run the most (least) often?

——Which jobs use the largest (least) amount of systems time and memory space?

——Which systems resources or components are used most (least) often?

Based on these data, adjustments can be made to improve service and increase efficiency. For example, if the data show that different operating systems are loaded and reloaded into the computer system repeatedly throughout the day, it might be best to schedule specific times for each operating system and inform users of these times—to eliminate constant reloading of that operating system. Similarly, if the data show that more computer time is spent in compiling programs than in executing them, it may be useful to acquire faster compilers.

Cost/Benefit Analysis To assess a system's impact in terms of dollars, **cost/benefit analysis** breaks down the costs of an application and, perhaps more important, the dollar benefits (for example, cost savings or increased sales through better customer service) to be gained from using the system. This is a difficult, yet very critical area that is often overlooked or neglected in systems evaluations. The cost/benefit analysis performed during the initial phase of the system provided evidence for the decision to proceed with development. After implementation, a review should be conducted to assess development costs and both accumulated and projected benefits. Has the problem addressed by the system changed? Will benefits be less or greater than expected? Will the system be even more important in the current competitive environment than originally anticipated? These important questions must not go unanswered. The answers may have implications for the whole organization.

Organizational Aspects of Information Systems Implementation

At the beginning of this chapter, it was pointed out that implementation is not an activity that is scheduled only after a system has been developed, programmed, and tested. Rather, it is an ongoing process that begins early in the development effort.

The impact of an information system on an organization and its people can be dramatic, sometimes even leading to the resistance of a new application as the conversion date approaches. Now we examine this aspect of implementation, with special attention to organization changes, possible sources of resistance, and ways to anticipate and avoid disruption or resistance.

Introduction of Change

As a general rule, *the introduction of change in corporations occurs incrementally,* rather than overnight. This is because change of any type brings uncertainty for people who perhaps previously had a good understanding and control of activities. The realization of the importance of uncertainty and how it affects the speed with which changes can be made is particularly relevant when the introduction of information systems is contemplated. Systems analysts tend to approach the development of an information system from a rational point of view, focusing on the benefits of making more information available and accessible to a greater number of people. They also tend to emphasize the value of having detail available in printed or displayed form.

What often gets overlooked is that users may not cherish the same values. Consider these thoughts:

1. Information is power to the individuals who hold it, particularly if they alone have the details.
2. The availability of better information in no way guarantees that decision making or other performance will improve or that there will be better communication between individuals or departments.
3. Components in the organization that do not customarily experience rapid technology-based change may react in ways that weaken or cancel the effects of the new technology.

Information is a political weapon and it is an element of power. While systems analysts tend to develop systems that increase its availability—through the use of database management systems or the construction of distributed systems—the individuals who will lose their political clout as a result may not support these new systems. Anyone losing an information monopoly will understandably resist the new system unless the benefits to the individual are greater than the costs. Many view the building of an information system as a declaration of war rather than a welcome avenue to improved performance.

Of course information systems are not the only focus of change in an organization. Any aspect of a firm's operation must be considered a logical target for change, the assumption being that such alterations mean improvement. Yet change may be good or bad, depending on the reason for making it and the viewpoints people have, which tend to be based on how they will be affected. For example, we would expect resistance to using a new high-speed machine if workers believed it wasn't safe and nothing was done to allay these fears. Similarly, the introduction of equipment to replace people is not likely to be enthusiastically accepted by those who will be shunted to new and perhaps unsatisfactory job situations. Others in the organization

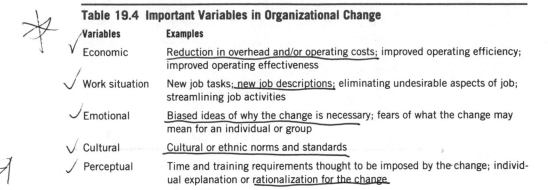

Table 19.4 Important Variables in Organizational Change

Variables	Examples
Economic	Reduction in overhead and/or operating costs; improved operating efficiency; improved operating effectiveness
Work situation	New job tasks; new job descriptions; eliminating undesirable aspects of job; streamlining job activities
Emotional	Biased ideas of why the change is necessary; fears of what the change may mean for an individual or group
Cultural	Cultural or ethnic norms and standards
Perceptual	Time and training requirements thought to be imposed by the change; individual explanation or rationalization for the change

may view the same changes favorably, however, considering the improvements in quality, productivity, cost of operations, and profitability that can be achieved.

You begin to see that information is not the only component in a decision process. Emotion, politics, and other such elements play dominant roles. Thus if an information system is designed for its information value and without serious regard for these other concerns, it may not achieve the desired level of success.

Information is not synonymous with communication. Merely giving someone more or better information may not improve either communication or the person's performance. The information may be ignored entirely. Or, it may produce an opposite result that was not wanted at all.

The way in which change affects individuals has an important bearing on the success or failure of the system that promotes it. Table 19.4 shows the strategic variables in the introduction of change, whether for computer systems or new operating procedures. People want to know *why* a change is necessary, and the reasons provided may be very important in determining the acceptance or rejection of the change.

Emotion is an important change variable. **Perception** is another factor determining the success or failure of an attempt to implement change. Redistributing information is an emotional matter that will be perceived in distinctive ways by those variously affected.

Reasons for Resistance

Better understanding of **resistance** leads to better implementation strategies and hopefully better outcomes. Researchers in the information systems field have studied the differences between systems that generate user resistance and those that do not. The differences are grouped into categories of people-oriented, systems-oriented, and people–system interaction differences (Table 19.5).

People-Oriented Reasons The extreme view that people resist all change is unlikely to be a valid one. Typically, when change is resisted there are distinct underlying reasons.

Table 19.5 Reasons for Resistance to the Introduction of Information Systems

Category	Description
People-oriented reasons	Resistance to information systems is attributed to factors inherent in people and groups within the organization. An extreme view is that people resist all change. Other perspectives focus on individual personalities, informal group relations, and formal structures involving people in the organization. Strategies for avoiding resistance include training and education of users, involvement of individuals in the development process, and creation and monitoring of organization policies related to information systems.
Systems-oriented reasons	Resistance from users stems from features of the information system such as failure to give adequate consideration to human factors in the design, awkward interaction and interface requirements, and the placing of inappropriate requirements on users. Strategies for avoiding resistance include formulating "user-friendly" designs, ensuring that the design is functional for the people who will use the system, and involving users in the design to elicit their input regarding systems features.
Interaction of factors	There is an interaction between the system and the way in which it will be used in the organization. One variation is that people and the system interact, formally and informally. The nature of the reaction determines whether resistance will occur. A political variation prescribes that resistance will occur if the features of the system dramatically disrupt the power structure of the organization. Strategies for avoiding resistance include addressing the underlying organization issues such as distribution of power and authority, facilitating open communication and good relations between users and systems designers, and ensuring that the system meets the needs and concerns of the users as well as those of higher-level management. A system cannot be designed in isolation.

For example, it is widely believed that resistance to some information systems can be traced to objections of the individual or group to changes in formal and informal organization relationships or to changes in the distribution of personal power. Alternatively, a disliked information system may simply lack features the new users had expected.

Changes in the Formal Structure Virtually all organizations can be studied in terms of the fixed boundary and departmental structures they develop for carrying out planned operations and activities. However, there are two general types of structure: formal and informal. The **formal structure** is established to create meaningful responsibility and authority relationships. Central to the formal structure in most firms is a set of departmental boundaries that define authority and responsibility and develop divisions of labor and specialization. Definitions of line and staff relationships for conducting business activities are careful and explicit. In a manufacturing firm, employees involved directly in production, including assembly line workers and their supervisors, are referred to as the **line group** of the firm.

not
covered

The other group of persons in an organization, the **staff group,** supports the line group. The purchasing department, for example, must produce raw materials, fabricated parts, and supplies for the production group. The accounting department supports the line group by monitoring expenses of and income from manufacture of goods and their sale. The operations research department provides further support by examining work methods, process flows, and machine productivity. The results of such support may be used in the design of new processes for the line aimed at improving output or increasing quality.

Changing line/staff relationships means changing the formal structure of the organization, and the magnitude of any such alteration will have a bearing on how—or indeed, whether—company personnel accept the change.

Table 19.6 summarizes the changes in formal structure that result from the introduction of a new system. Furthermore, the way any change is introduced can significantly affect the success of the new system. Automatic data collection may, for example, eliminate a sizable amount of a line supervisor's paperwork, effectively shifting the task of reporting from the line group to the staff group. Now that the reporting activity is handled "automatically" through the information system, the line supervisor is no longer responsible for it. That is, the formal structure of the organization has been changed. If no one explains to the supervisor that the change does not reflect poor performance on his or her part, however, the supervisor may try to undermine the information system.

On a larger scale, automatic data collection of the type in which one supervisor's responsibility is modified, could also change department boundaries. For example, the introduction of a computer to monitor production quantity and quality might eliminate the need for most of the clerks in a tabulating department. If the clerks who remained were reassigned to other departments, the organization chart would have to be changed accordingly.

Because a computer-based information system has vast storage and rapid retrieval capabilities, its introduction can alter formal communication channels as well. Middle management may no longer need to rely on performance reports from managers at the operating level. Rather, by using a terminal or workstation far from the production floor, middle-level managers may be able to access large files of stored data on a moment's notice and, significantly, without the immediate knowledge of the operating managers. The result is that one type of information transmission is eliminated and an entirely new communication channel is opened, through the terminal, between middle management and stored data files. And, the formal structure of the organization is altered.

Changes in the Informal Structure It would be naive to assume that all relationships in a modern organization can be or are shown on the organization chart. The **informal structure** can be just as influential as formal relationships in determining whether an information systems project is successful. The dynamics of small groups and work groups in organizational settings is well documented in the literature of social and organizational psychology. Some of those important concepts directly relate to the problems of implementing information systems, particularly to the potential problems resulting when working relations are changed, group norms are violated, and

not covered

Table 19.6 Examples of Changes in Formal Structure

Changes	Examples
Formal boundaries	Addition of an information systems department
	Reorganization of departments: some eliminated; some added; some combined with others
Formal responsibilities	Elimination of report preparation by line supervisors (automated data collection and report preparation)
	Addition of new product lines to job responsibility of marketing manager
Formal communication channels	Creation of centralized information files eliminates need for some periodic reports from managers
	Creation of new channels of communication as a result of constant monitoring of performance and activities

---

Table 19.7 Examples of Changes in Informal Structure

Area of Change	Examples
Work relations	Reorganization of job tasks and work activities results in alteration of social work groups.
	New people enter a work group.
	Some people leave the work group.
Work group norms	Information that previously might be withheld from managers is now automatically collected and reported.
	Productivity standards are altered in a way that conflicts with informal norms established within groups.
Status	New work activities become a factor in reduced or increased status of a group or individual.
	New work activities become a factor in *perceived* reduction or increase in status of a group or individual.

---

the status of people or groups is lessened by a new information systems project (see Table 19.7).

In many cases, introducing information systems in a firm, or in one department, results in changes in working relations or in work group membership. It may, for example, be necessary to do away with certain tasks in a department, reducing staffing levels, in the case of the data clerks in the earlier example whose jobs were eliminated by automation of the data collection function. This formal change in the organization of the firm was accompanied by the informal structure change of breaking up a work group.

Frequently group norms are violated when new systems are introduced. If, for example, a work group routinely refrains from giving data of certain types to management, and a new information system regularly collects such data and makes them

not covered

accessible to managers, a group norm has been rendered inoperative. It is no longer possible for group members to conceal those data.

Loss of status is another type of change in informal structure. Altering the responsibilities or tasks associated with a particular job can change the way one's co-workers view a work assignment. In many instances an individual's status is raised or lowered because of tasks that have been added or taken away. Thus management might expect a line supervisor to welcome a change that resulted in a reduced workload for the supervisor. However, if the supervisor has viewed a deskful of paperwork as a status symbol, eliminating this work may be interpreted as a reduction in status or as a sign of management's loss of confidence in the supervisor's ability to perform that portion of the job. The entire line group, in fact, may feel they are losing some control over their activities to the staff group, which now does the collecting. The change here is in the informal structure, but it stems from an adjustment in the formal lines of responsibility and authority in the firm.

Both informal and formal change can affect a firm's operating procedures and its effectiveness and efficiency. The change resulting from the introduction of computer-based information systems may foster improved operations, or it may lead to resistance and even disregard for some of the changes. The success or failure of any such change depends in large part on how it is introduced.

Systems-Oriented Reasons   Resistance may be attributed to features of the system to be implemented. Refusal to use a system that truly does not function properly—it aborts frequently or produces incorrect information—must be blamed on the system itself. Perhaps resistance is justified in these instances.

Some systems simply are too difficult to use. The method of interacting with the application for entry of data or retrieval of information may be awkward and unnatural for end-users. Perhaps an overcrowded display cannot be read without eyestrain. Maybe the system's response time is too long, or the hardware has not been located wisely—if a workstation is on the opposite side of a large room, people may resist walking over to it when they need information in response to a telephone inquiry. Any such feature is likely to raise the level of resistance among end-users.

Chapters 16 and 17 dealt with systems development issues in great detail. The guidelines presented in those discussions will help prevent systems-oriented forms of resistance. Testing strategies further assist in detecting potential problem areas in time to institute remedies before conversion.

Interaction of Factors   Neither the information system nor the population affected by it is isolated. Thus resistance may arise during implementation because of an interaction of characteristics of the new end-users and the new information system. Attempting to centralize control over data in an organization that has been operated in a very decentralized manner may provoke resistance. Here the rapid establishment of data standards and installation of a database management system would alter the balance of power in the organization. We can predict that the system will be resisted by those who lose power and accepted by those who gain it. There is a clear interaction between system and people.

Consider also an office in which clerks who process health insurance claims are evaluated on the basis of the number of correct claims they enter into an automated system during the work day. If a new system changes the manner in which data are entered, greatly increasing the number of claims that can be processed daily, we can probably expect resistance if performance expectations are altered overnight. People must be given time to get used to the new system and to learn that although they are being asked to raise their productivity, the amount of effort expected of them remains much the same.

These two examples demonstrate two kinds of interaction: political and socio-technical. Resistance for political reasons reflects changes in the distribution of power due to interaction of the users with features of the new system. The socio-technical view states that resistance arises when users perceive an unfavorable inter-action between new systems features and their work responsibilities.

Forms of Resistance

Resistance is **dysfunctional behavior;** that is, it interferes with attainment of objectives. Resistance may take many forms. For convenience, they are grouped into three categories: aggression, projection, and avoidance (Dickson and Simmons, 1970). Each of these forms of resistance causes difficult problems. Some types are more common at certain levels in the firm than at others, as shown in Table 19.8. Once resistance occurs, however, regardless of the level, it must be dealt with. This is not an easy task. It is more sensible to develop a system that does not engender resistance in the first place. If resistance never crops up, we will not have to try to correct it.

Aggression When an information systems application is introduced in a department over the members' objections, they may react with aggressive behavior. **Aggression is a form of attack on the system with the intent of making it ineffective or physically inoperative.** The most common type of physical aggression is sabotage and destruc-tion of systems components. Dumping liquids into data entry devices, demagnetizing flexible diskettes, and scratching magnetic disk plates are obvious examples of physical aggression.

A less spectacular form of aggression, called "beating the system," renders a system ineffective by defeating its purpose. Inputs of error-laden data, for example, lead to the production of faulty (inaccurate) reports, which are worse than useless; and hostile employees will be quick to try to place the blame on the system itself.

Projection Many people who dislike a particular application are not willing to risk their jobs by commiting aggressive acts that could be traced to them. **Projection** gives these dissatisfied employees a way of "energizing" their resistance. In this form of dysfunctional behavior, people wrongly blame the system for difficulties encoun-tered while using or interacting with it. Implementing an information system or systems application is a complex task, and problems often accompany its introductory phases, particularly in the training area. In such instances, the problem lies not with the application, but with the training program. Nonetheless, some people will trans-

Table 19.8 Dysfunctional Behavior at Various Levels in the Organization

Organizational Subgroup	Relation to MIS	Most Likely Dysfunctional Behavior
Operating personnel		
Clerical	Particularly affected by clerical system: job eliminated; job patterns changed	Projection
Nonclerical	Provide system inputs	Aggression
Operating management	Controlled from above by information systems	Aggression
	Job modified by information decision systems and programmed systems	Avoidance, projection
Technical staff	Systems designers and agents of systems change	None*
Top management	Generally unaffected and unconcerned with systems	Avoidance

*These employees tend to support MIS because they have had a hand in the changes. When disgruntled, however, technical staff members may exhibit creative and sophisticated forms of aggression.

fer the difficulties to the system, claiming that "the damn system" caused their mistakes.

Avoidance In the third form of resistance, which often is caused by frustration, people withdraw from or avoid interacting with the information system. For example, employees who are consistently frustrated in their attempts to input data through a shop floor data collection terminal may not use the device at all. Avoiding the terminal (and therefore the system) means avoiding frustration. **Avoidance** often takes the form of ignoring or not using reports and information generated by an information system. A materials manager who goes to the warehouse with a clipboard and records his personal count of quantities on hand because he doesn't trust an automated inventory report is avoiding the computer-based system.

Avoiding Resistance

Procedures for eliminating technical problems are fairly well established, but the methods for avoiding or eliminating resistance are less clearcut. Nevertheless, proper planning and management of development and implementation activities can be very effective. We offer several guidelines that appear to be successful in practice. The use of a change agent strategy has also been effective.

Guidelines for Avoiding Resistance As we have suggested, the acceptance/resistance factor for an information system can be anticipated long before the system is put into daily use. Therefore, steps to avoid resistance should begin early. The following guidelines are helpful:

———Involve people in the development process early, seeking out in particular those who will use the information system or be affected by it. Gain user commitment to the project.

———Ensure that the benefits of using the new system will be greater than the benefits of not using it.

———Consider the organization's record in converting smoothly to new operating systems. New systems are most readily accepted when users expect them to contribute to future success.

———Consider how previous changes were implemented. Resistance to contemplated change is least likely when past introductions have been harmonious and productive.

———Discuss the system with managers who will be affected as well as upper-level managers. Their support of the project is needed.

———Set realistic goals.

———State system and project objectives clearly.

———Design a user-friendly system.

———Deliver a system that will do what managers and end-users were promised.

———Develop a system that is *reliable.*

Throughout the entire development and implementation process, analysts must be aware of user questions and concerns. Fears of status loss and interrupted social relations are very real. So is fear of change, and uncertainties stemming from this fear have the potential to undermine a new systems application. Involving the users in the process is a powerful aid. Not only does it open important communication channels, but it gives users an opportunity to influence the development of *their* system.

The Role of the Change Agent   An information systems project creates an organization change and must be treated as an organizational phenomenon, not simply as a technical event. Unless implementation is approached from this perspective—that is, unless the systems analyst functions consciously as a change agent, not merely as a computer technician—chances of failure are higher than need be.

Researchers from the social sciences describe the role of a **change agent** in varying ways, and the person who successfully performs it will be able to implement the guidelines outlined previously. In general, there are three basic activities (Table 19.9). First, to prepare the organization or the end-user for a change, the analyst must identify and consider the barriers that constitute critical issues during requirements analysis and throughout the development process, regardless of the system development method utilized. From an organizational viewpoint, **unfreezing** prepares the firm for a change. As the name implies, attitudes need to be desolidified before a new set of operating conditions can be imposed on people who have thus far managed without them.

During the second phase, changes are introduced. New procedures are explained, additional controls are implemented, and sharing of responsibilities is begun. User training and conversion to the new system occur during this phase.

Table 19.9 Activities of Change Agents

Activity	Description
Unfreeze	Prepare the organization for the introduction of change by increasing receptivity to the change while addressing related uncertainties.
Introduce change	Implement the change, offering appropriate reasons for each new action.
Refreeze	Reinforce the new system after the change has been introduced, to return the organization to stability.

We want the change to remain in place once it has been installed, hence the **refreezing** phase in which the systems analysts reinforce the new system that has been implemented. Often they remain with the user group for several days and keep in close touch for several weeks as managers and employees acquaint themselves with the application. Questions must be answered and problems solved. It would indeed be unfortunate if a well-designed system, wanted by concerned users who had participated in its development, came unraveled because a question could not be answered or a simple mistake defied correction. And it would be equally disappointing if one dissatisfied user were to induce an entire department to resist an application. Both eventualities can be avoided through refreezing.

Throughout this discussion, we have focused on means of avoiding or overcoming resistance to the introduction of information systems in the organization. Because these methods are both time-consuming and expensive, managers often are tempted to skip some of the more difficult ones in the interest of getting the system up and operating as soon as possible. Such shortcuts are risky, however, and they may damage overall success. When there is resistance, it must be confronted. Attempts to introduce a product over objections may be fatal to the entire development process. Also, if one system is implemented without dealing with objections, the same problem may crop up when the next information systems project is introduced. The way an information systems application is introduced on one occasion will determine the level of resistance next time. It is senseless to try to "bulldoze" a major change. Patience and concern for the user are essential. And most important, effective implementation plans, including concern for the user, must be laid early in the development process.

Summary

The implementation of an information system is not an activity but rather a process that begins well before cutover to the new information system. Prior to conversion, the system must be tested to ensure that it performs according to expectations. Computer operators and users must be told what to expect and trained to handle exceptions.

Conversion to the new system can occur gradually, through initial use of pilot systems or by phasing in the new system. The parallel systems method offers the greatest security, while the highest level of risk is encountered when a new system is installed by direct cutover.

Postconversion evaluation of the system's impact is a critical step in learning how the system is operating and determining whether changes will be needed. Studying a system recently put into use can also produce information that can be used to improve future systems applications.

Although properly designed and constructed information systems surely can improve performance in an enterprise, there is more to systems development than just designing "a good one." Analysts must continually be aware of the user perspective. Information systems affect both the formal and informal structures of the organization. They may alter department boundaries as well as social and work group relations. Failure to address the importance of changes in these areas may lead to resistance in the form of aggression, projection, or avoidance of the system.

Because systems analysts act as change agents, they must focus on organizational as well as technical issues during development and implementation. Part of their responsibility is to increase the receptiveness of users to a new system. The term often applied to this activity is "unfreezing" the organization. During conversion, the new system and its associated procedures are installed and put into use. However, as a change agent, the systems analyst stays with the system after conversion, to ensure refreezing or stabilization. Questions must be answered and difficulties taken care of so they do not turn into major problems. This aspect of implementation may last several days or even weeks.

Key Words

Aggression	Hardware monitor	Projection
Attitude survey	Impact evaluation	Refreeze
Avoidance	Informal structure	Resistance
Change agent	Line group	Software monitor
Conversion	Organization analysis	Staff group
Cost/benefit analysis	Parallel system	Systems testing
Critical incident logging	Perception	Unfreeze
Direct cutover	Performance monitoring	User-friendly
Dysfunctional behavior	Phase-in of system	Weighted feature analysis
Formal structure	Pilot system	

Review Questions

1. When does systems implementation begin? Why is this activity so significant in the development of information systems?

2. Identify the activities associated with the conversion to a new system. Indicate the participants in each activity and their respective responsibilities.

3. What methods can be used to put new systems projects into operation? What are the advantages and disadvantages of each?

4. Briefly describe the means of evaluating the impact of information systems.

5. In what areas of performance evaluation are hardware monitors most helpful? Where are they least helpful?

6. What is systems testing? Is it similar to program testing? What special tests are performed?

7. What questions must be addressed by user and operator training?

8. What are the causes of resistance to change?

9. What variables are important in studying organizational change?

10. Why does the introduction of an information system often occasion much resistance among an organization's personnel? Is this resistance usually justified?

11. What effect does logic have in attempts to avoid resistance to the introduction of information systems? Explain.

12. What forms of behavior might resistance to an information system take? Give examples of each.

13. Why does the operating-level manager seem to offer the greatest resistance to the introduction of information systems?

14. What factors should be addressed in minimizing resistance?

15. What is a change agent? Why is such a person so important to the implementation of an information system?

Application Problems

1. Many computer software programs are available to train individuals in the use of particular applications. For example, people can be trained to use spreadsheet or database programs by means of commercial programs that run on personal computers. Such programs allow the trainee to interact with the software to enter data, invoke differing processing activities, or respond to questions posed by the system.

   The programs sell well largely because of their convenience and suitability for teaching the general features of packaged software. In addition, they are designed to be self-instructional; no instructor is needed to assist the trainee, at least as far as the manufacturers of the products are concerned. The programs are also reasonably priced, most likely because they sell in large volumes, like the software packages for which they provide training.

   In most cases, training programs provide instruction on the most commonly used features of a package. They often do not cover the use of advanced features or the handling of unusual situations.

   An organization is considering whether to develop a computer-based training program to train new users of an airline reservations system. The system includes many advanced features and a wide variety of options to deal with the many different circumstances that can arise when handling air travel reservations. The trainers want to allow reservations system users to learn the features of the system by working alone. At the end of the training sessions, a written test will be administered.

a. Based on the foregoing brief discussion of user training, do you believe the use of software is a good idea in this instance? Why or why not? What features must a good software training package have?

b. What disadvantages result from using prepackaged training software to train new systems users?

2. A turnkey system for the processing of accounts receivable will be installed in a retailing organization. The system will be the first computer application implemented in the organization, although sales personnel are familiar with the use of point-of-sale cash terminals.

The implementation plan that has been devised consists of the following activities:

All personnel will undergo a 3-day supervised training period. The 12 employees of the accounts receivable department will be divided into groups, and one group will receive training in the use of entry of data through terminals in each of the 3 weeks preceding the start of conversion.

During a special training session, held a day before the start of conversion, accounts receivable staff members will be allowed to test their recall of training activities by using the system to enter the types of transaction typical of those they expect to encounter daily. In addition, they will be encouraged to use the system to process the most difficult or unusual transactions they can think of. Training personnel will be on hand to answer questions and to deal with any problems that arise.

As part of the conversion, all existing accounts having balances must be keyed into the system, and all accounts receivable personnel will assist in the data entry. Each individual will be asked to enter a batch of transactions containing a given number of accounts. After each batch has been entered, a count will be made to serve as a check. The data will be entered the evening before the system is put into use. All paper ledger cards will be kept in case questions from customers arise, but the conversion itself will be direct.

After the accounts have been entered, a listing of accounts will be printed to permit verification that data entry has been complete.

a. Assess the training strategy planned for this implementation.

b. Is the conversion strategy described above a good one? If so, why? If not, how should the plan be changed or expanded?

3. People involved with or affected by computer-based information systems often try to resist the system if it is not properly developed or introduced. The forms this resistance may take are avoidance, aggression, and projection. List the type of resistance demonstrated in each of the following situations:

a. Receiving computer output and filing it away without using it

b. Ordering more inventory than necessary so that it will appear that the computer-based inventory system is responsible for extra warehouse costs

c. Telling a customer that an error on a charge account statement was caused by the computer

d. Misrouting a report from a purchasing information system to the accounting department

e. Bending, stapling, or mutilating a paper turnaround document

f. Failing to return turnaround documents for processing

4. A manager has been given a software package designed to support certain routine engineering decisions. The package was designed in-house at another firm with the constant involvement of its eventual users. It is a well-designed package that was enthusiastically accepted by the users in the other company.

   a. What kind of reaction should our manager expect in attempting to introduce the software package for the same purposes in the manager's own company? Justify your opinion. If you feel that the reaction will be a favorable one, explain why. If you feel that the reaction will be a negative one, how would you change it?

   b. Compare this situation with that encountered when an organization buys a software package from a commercial software vendor. How are they the same? How are they different?

5. The head of the grocery products division for a multinational food products company is overseeing the development of a new centralized planning system. The planning systems application will be added to the current computer-based information system that has been successful and well received by the division's members. The new application will maintain a yearly profit and performance plan for each department in the division and will provide weekly and monthly reports for comparison of planned and actual sales. A summary version of all reports will be presented to the division manager on Monday mornings. Details of reports will be mailed to the department managers each Monday.

   Since the various department managers are located all around the world, to have the on-site involvement the division head would like to see is out of the question. Thus to help maintain user involvement, a liaison team has been established in the systems and programming department. The members of the liaison team will communicate frequently both by telephone and by on-site visits with the outlying department managers so that their ideas and objectives can be incorporated into the system's design. This will give everyone a major role in the effort. The division head feels that the liaison team, by involving the department heads in the design, will cause these executives to identify with the system.

   a. Examine this situation in terms of advantages and disadvantages for preventing resistance to introduction of the system.

   b. Is the liaison team a good idea as it is employed in this case? Why or why not?

6. The employees of the check processing department in a large New York City bank are falling behind in their work. Checks that should be processed on one day often are not posted until the next morning. Even when the employees work overtime, which they do not like to do, the work often does not get completed until the following day. In addition, because of the rapid pace at which the staff must work, errors are frequent. This is embarrassing both to the bank and to the employees, who are already under a lot of pressure. The people in the department have often said there must be a better way for the work to be performed.

   A change is being contemplated in the bank's transaction processing system. If the change is implemented, the department will be restructured into a personal check processing department and another department to handle the accounts of business and governmental organizations. It will involve retraining some personnel, resulting in a complete job change for these individuals.

   Examine the situation and the proposed solution in terms of the overall effect of the change on the employees of the department. Do you feel there will be a high degree of resistance to this change? Why or why not?

7. The Acme Services Company is about to launch an investigation into the need for implementing changes and new applications into its computer-based information system. Because both management and systems staff are well aware that obstacles to such changes can develop, they wish to ensure that the analysis and design activities serve to minimize any possible resistance and at the same time to detect potential sources of trouble.

   Develop a list of guidelines that the systems staff should follow in the analysis and design work.

   Which evaluation technique(s) should be used to assess new systems impact in the following areas? Briefly explain why you recommend use of the technique(s) you select for application to the following needs.

   a. Determining areas in which resistance to use of the system is building
   b. Determining what aspects of the system are most and least important to the users
   c. Determining the average number of queries made through a new on-line system by each person, each day, in a small department
   d. Assessing a system's impact on the administration of company policies for handling customer complaints and on changing job roles and department boundaries
   e. Determining the increase in computer use due to the new system

8. A country club has installed a new computer-based billing system that processes charge slips for purchases made in the dining room, the bar, the (golf) pro shop, and the locker rooms. It features the use of mark-sense charge slips on which the number of the employee processing the purchase transaction as well as the dollar value and stock number of the item purchased are marked. The charge slips are batch processed monthly to produce bills that are sent to the members.

   The new system was developed to improve the efficiency of the billing process and to reduce errors in charges. The old manual system had been the source of numerous complaints from members and employees (waitresses, busboys, bartenders, locker room employees, and so on) alike.

   Outline an impact study to evaluate the new computer-based system.

9. A new medical information system has been designed for use in a large metropolitan hospital. The system, which is nearing completion and will be implemented soon, will provide on-line access to a large database of patient data. The patient data in the database will include a full chart on each individual being cared for. Included in the chart will be such data as notations about diagnosis, prognosis, treatment and therapy, and special care requirements. Included also are data about drug reactions, religious beliefs, and anything else that might be important in an emergency situation.

   General background data (name, age, address, next of kin, and so on) will be entered into the files when the patient is admitted to the hospital. Additional data will be added by doctors, therapists, laboratory staff, and nursing staff whenever any treatment is scheduled or administered, when drugs are prescribed or administered, and whenever any change in the patient's condition is noted. All data will be entered through specially designed terminals that can be easily operated by any medical staff member who has attended a brief training session. Terminals will be located at all nursing stations and at other key locations in the hospital.

Although computer-based systems have been used for quite some time in the administration areas of the hospital for such purposes as billing, accounts receivable maintenance, payroll, and supplies inventory control, the new medical information system will be the first entry of this type of system into mainstream medical areas. It will replace a long-standing manual system based on many paper forms and records. In addition to providing significant opportunities for improved patient care, the new system should reduce the paperwork bottleneck that continually faces medical personnel who have to keep patient records up to date and accurate.

The final testing activities for the new system are being completed, and when the time arrives to begin implementing it, it is anticipated that all errors will have been corrected.

a. List the advantages and disadvantages of each of the different implementation strategies that could be used to bring the new system into operation.

b. Which implementation strategy should be used for the medical information system? Why?

Minicase: Changeover Delays for Internal Revenue Service

As April 1 approached, the Internal Revenue Service had processed 25 percent fewer income tax returns than it had completed at the same time a year ago. As a result, millions of taxpayers were in the midst of a long wait for their refund checks.

Underlying the delay was the conversion from 1960 vintage computer systems to new multiprocessors. Part of the changeover also included the conversion of 1500 programs—3.5 million lines of code—from assembly language to COBOL (structured COBOL). The conversion plan had been established nearly four years earlier and involved IRS processing centers around the United States. The long lead time was necessary to carefully plan activities, prepare computer sites, and coordinate the arrival and installation of equipment.

The IRS was plagued with a variety of hardware and software problems from the beginning of the conversion, and Commissioner Roscoe L. Egger, Jr. publicly expressed his frustration: "With any computer [conversion] period, there are software problems and personnel adjustments. Machines break down. People push wrong buttons. . . . The results are terribly frustrating for taxpayers and us."

The problems originated in part from the following conditions.

—When equipment problems occur, IRS staff members must redo many hours of input; the system's checkpoint/restart features, which allow reprocessing from a point at which the operator knows all processing is correct, do not always work. As much as 10 to 12 hours of work may have to be redone.

——Data stored on magnetic tape from one system could not be read on the new tape drives, either because of incompatibilities or due to creases and damage to the tapes themselves.

——Programs were found to run more slowly than expected and programmers were busy trying to find and correct bugs. However, a major effort required to optimize the speed and performance of the software had not been planned when the conversion was mapped out.

The IRS was ready to begin conversion to the new system in November, knowing that the January–April tax season was just around the corner. It had to choose between going ahead with the conversion and entering the busy tax season with the old equipment. The old equipment could no longer be maintained and without question would be unable to handle the load. Performance reliability threatened to delay the processing of income tax returns. But if the IRS went ahead with the conversion, it risked the glitches and delays that occur with any changeover of this magnitude.

Questions

1. Which strategy would you recommend if you were faced with the dilemma just described for the IRS? Explain your reasoning.

2. Despite the complexity of converting hardware and software, as well as conducting training, on a nationwide basis, do you believe the changeover problems could have been avoided? Keep in mind the long lead time needed to acquire and prepare equipment for numerous processing centers.

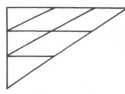

20: The Impact of Information Systems on Corporate Strategy

Key Questions

How are information systems changing the way firms compete?

How is the use of information systems altering the structure of industries?

What is a strategy?

How does one determine when information systems can be used for strategic benefit?

What strategies are generic to organizations of all types?

In what areas can information systems be applied for competitive advantage?

Do customers benefit from the incorporation of information systems technology into the strategies used by business?

How are strategies selected?

Thinking and Information

Information is no substitute for thinking and thinking is no substitute for information. The dilemma is that there is never enough time to teach all the information that could usefully be taught.

John Naisbitt and Patricia Aburdene, *Reinventing the Corporation*

Information systems are playing an increasingly important role in the success of competitive organizations and in the strategies they use to be competitive. Far from being a "back-office" function, responsible for data processing and accounting, they are taking on front-line importance.

This chapter examines the relationship between information technology and a firm's comparative advantage. We will analyze three corporate strategies for operating in a competitive environment and five competitive forces continually at work. We will also see the existence of a value chain in each organization and what it means for the organization. We will investigate the manner in which organizations use information systems to pursue these strategies with respect to customer relations, competition, new products, and suppliers. Guidelines for selecting a corporate strategy involving competitive use of information systems are included in the discussion.

Why Should You Know About Corporate Strategy?

Information systems are taking on a strategic role in organizations—a role that is changing quickly. This chapter pinpoints a major shift in management and executive

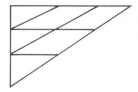

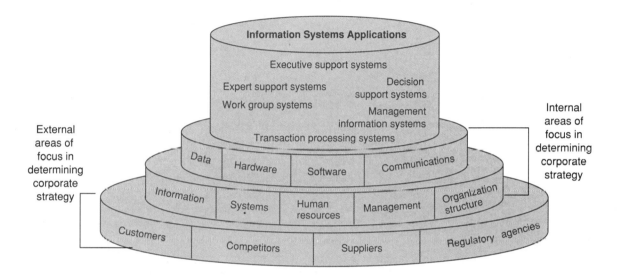

attention to information systems. Among the reasons you should know about the impact of information systems on corporate strategy are the following:

—Information systems play an increasingly important role in the formulation of competitive strategies in all industries.

—Not having the right information systems in place can lead to a distinct competitive disadvantage.

—Competitive strategy cuts across all areas of an organization and touches many types of managers and staff members.

—It may be that the concepts that you explore in this chapter will be the factors that define future competition in the marketplace.

The Challenge to Management

Chapter 2 introduced the information systems vision. We said that a vision is a concept that grows out of a firm understanding of an area, but that is produced by imagination and creativity. We also suggested that a vision is a view of what can

Figure 20.1 Three Information Systems Benefits

Gains in productivity	Improvements in effectiveness	Gaining competitive advantage
Increasing the efficiency of a task	Doing the right things	Selecting and implementing strategies that change the way a firm competes
More work completed with same or fewer resources	Utilization of resources to produce desirable results of high quality	Improved performance in comparison to competitors, using chosen criteria (e.g., market share, industry dominance, industry ranking)

happen by using resources to transform opportunities into reality. Successful opportunities begin with a vision.

Figure 20.1 restates three information systems benefits that were introduced earlier. The benefits of improvement in productivity and in effectiveness have dominated management's thinking about information systems for some time.

At one time, business regarded information systems mainly in terms of support for operating and administrative activities. Efficient transaction processing was of primary importance. Managing the paperwork explosion was also critical, because entire organizations could easily become so immersed in paper that they could not carry on normal operations.

These activities are *still* important, and if a firm is to be successful, they must be properly managed and carried out.

In many organizations, however, managers of information systems and corporate executives alike face new challenges as information systems technology advances. Information systems are changing the ways organizations compete, and they are altering the structure of entire industries. Organizations that use their good experience and expertise to effectively integrate corporate strategy, organization plans, and information systems plans will likely gain marketplace success. The others face severe constraints.

The Strategic Use of Information Systems

The task of information systems managers is expanding. Today the strategic use of information systems constitutes a major portion of their responsibilities, and they spend a large percentage of every day on such concerns. A system or application is *strategic* if it changes the way a firm competes. An example will demonstrate the significance of relating information systems technology and corporate strategy.

A large nationwide distributor of textile products looked at its method of distribution and found that even though the company was highly profitable and occupied the top position in its industry, based on market share, it was facing constraints on future expansion because:

——Its trucks could not accommodate the larger product line the firm wished to develop

——The sales personnel could not make additional sales calls (therefore more sales-persons would be needed)

——The entry of sales data occupied the time of 40 clerical staff and an additional 35 audit personnel

——The firm maintained 35 full staffed distribution centers around the United States

——A large volume of inventory was tied up in the warehouse, in distribution facilities, and on the trucks

The firm turned to information systems for assistance in developing a sales and order distribution system. The new system featured a central facility for handling of all orders that the sales staff prepared. Each night, the orders were transmitted automatically from the salesperson's personal computer over telephone lines to a central system. The order data were used in two ways: (1) Order data were used to schedule production to accommodate actual, not projected, demand; (2) orders were boxed and shipped to unstaffed drop points throughout the United States.

When the new system was installed, the firm enjoyed the following benefits:

——The product line was expanded and the existing trucks were able to accommodate the new product items with space to spare

——The sales force was able to increase the number of stores they visited by 25 percent while still handling the expanded product line

——Inventory investment dropped by the equivalent of two weeks' worth of inventory (nearly enough to pay for the entire new system)

——Field distribution expenses dropped by approximately 20 percent and all but four staffed distribution centers were closed

——All data entry clerks and audit staff positions were eliminated because of direct exchange of data

The firm's market share has increased further (by more than 10 percent) since the new system was introduced.

This example demonstrates the manner in which information systems can change the way a firm competes. Many more organizations are examining the business they are in, whether for profit or not, and assessing ways in which they can be more successful or more efficient by using their expertise in information systems to compete.

Using Strategy to Provide Competitive Advantage

Many of the applications of information technology were not possible as recently as two or three years ago. In some cases technology itself did not exist; in other cases use of the technology in the prescribed manner was economically prohibitive; and often the means of integrating different aspects of an existing, affordable technology had not emerged.

How organizations will use information systems in the next five years is sometimes difficult to predict. Experts debate where underlying computer and communications capabilities will take us. And they have differing views on the improvements that can be anticipated.

There is little disagreement, however, that information systems, properly developed, will propel a firm ahead competitively. If management ignores their potential or role in corporate strategy, information systems may become a *constraint*.

What Is a Strategy?

The application of information systems in a competitive environment calls for strategy. We define the concept in this section and discuss three generic strategies often chosen by competitive firms.

Corporate Strategy

A **strategy** is the way in which an organization endeavors to differentiate itself from its competitors, using its relative corporate strengths to better meet customer needs (Ohmae, 1982, p. 92). A strategy is successful if it ensures a better or stronger matching of corporate strengths to customer needs than is provided by competitors.

This concept is grounded in three interacting components: the *corporation* in relation to its *customers* and its *competition* (Figure 20.2). An effective management strategist is able to achieve superior performance (for example, in sales or in product quality) while making certain that the strategy chosen matches the *strengths of the firm* with the needs of the customer. In the jargon of business, "strategists leverage corporate strengths." As we will see later in this chapter, when information systems are a strength for the organization, managers should leverage information systems in formulating corporate strategy.

If a firm's approach to dealing with customers is identical to that of competition, customers may be unable to distinguish between their products or services. Situations like these lead to price wars and other unconstructive competitive methods. You can quickly see how important is to have a **competitive strategy** that builds on an organization's strengths and provides visibility to its customers.

Generic Strategies

Business organizations follow one or more of three general strategies (see Figure 20.3). Each is in widespread use and can lead to successful performance if it is the right strategy for a given corporation–customer–competition combination. The three generic strategies are: to provide low-cost products or services, to practice product differentiation, and to focus on a market niche (Porter, 1980, pp. 34–46). The skills, resources, and organizational requirements of each strategy are summarized in Table 20.1.

Figure 20.2 Elements in the Strategic Triangle

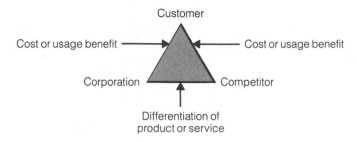

Figure 20.3 Three Generic Strategies (Adapted from Michael Porter 1985)

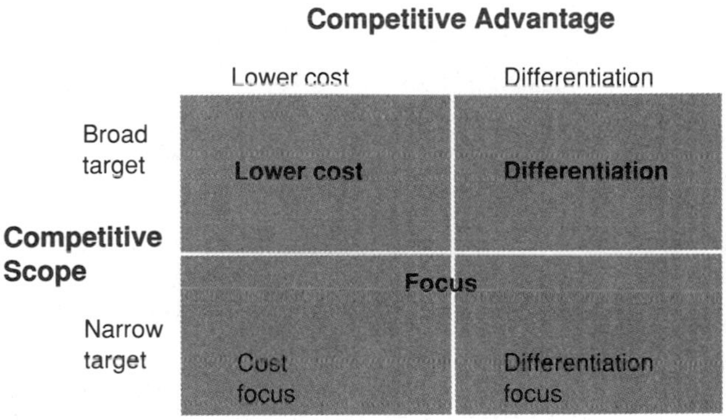

Competitive Advantage

	Lower cost	Differentiation
Broad target	**Lower cost**	**Differentiation**
Competitive Scope	**Focus**	
Narrow target	Cost focus	Differentiation focus

Low-Cost Leadership This strategy is aimed at outperforming other firms in the same industry by providing suitable quality in the firm's products or services at a lower cost than that of comparable products or services of competitors. Cost leadership is generally achieved by such techniques as careful management of overhead and production costs, selective advertising and merchandising strategies, and pinpoint marketing to customers. Lower costs generally mean that a firm can earn acceptable returns on investments even when competitors assume more aggressive pricing strategies. A low-cost leader may watch other firms compete away their profits.

   Low-cost leadership offers greater flexibility in dealing with suppliers who raise their prices to the firm, as well as buyers wishing to drive prices down and the purveyors of substitute products or services. In addition, the firm enjoying a low-cost leadership position is better able to deter potential competitors, because in addition to the other startup challenges, anyone who wished to enter the industry would have to develop strategies to deal with the low prices of the leader. Unless the wishful entrant has unique advantages, such as an edge in raw materials availability, new efficient manufacturing or distribution processes, or particularly effective

Table 20.1 Generic Competitive Strategies in Business

Strategy	Description
Low-cost leadership	Outperform other firms in the industry by providing products or services at a lower cost than competitors while sustaining or exceeding quality and service levels they provide. Provides competitive advantage when dealing with suppliers and buyers, and when offering substitute products or services.
Product differentiation	Provide a product or service that is generally recognized as distinct from competitors. Results in brand loyalty and avoids the necessity to take a low-price position; also effective in competing against substitutes.
Focus on a market niche	Indentify and compete in a market segment in which competitive advantage may be gained by concentration on a specific buyer group, product line, or geographical area. Provides advantage of better service to customers of lower costs, while producing better customer loyalty.

management practices, the chances for success in penetrating a market dominated by a low-cost leader are minimal.

Low-cost strategies may require the firm to design products for ease in manufacturing and more efficient use of raw materials. A product that requires less human intervention and more automatic control, or a manufacturing process that is as efficient in producing small quantities as it is in large production runs will visibly reduce product costs.

High market share achieved as a result of low-cost leadership can assist in sustaining a position of leadership. Better purchasing agreements, due to high volume purchases, and reinvestment of profits in new equipment and modern facilities, will further solidify the organization's cost position. For instance, a large national retail organization, able to demonstrate effective sales forecast and ordering systems, convinced its suppliers to hold inventory for the retailer and to commit to providing quick delivery as a condition of being a supplier for the firm. This agreement with the suppliers dramatically reduced the retail chain's inventory carrying costs.

Product Differentiation A product that is *differentiated* is one that is perceived throughout the industry in which it is sold as having unique features in comparison to competitive items. **Differentiation** often occurs on one or more of the dimensions shown in Table 20.2.

Differentiation can create brand loyalty among customers that will defeat low-cost pricing strategies of competitor firms. Because loyal customers must pay higher prices, the need for taking a low price position is lessened. These factors all work together to establish a barrier to competitor entry into the market.

A differentiated product is less vulnerable to substitutes—there may be no comparable alternatives—and it establishes a basis for leverage against suppliers who adjust their prices in attempts to lure customers. However, at the same time, brand loyalty and higher prices may result in lower market shares for the firm marketing

Table 20.2 Bases of Product Differentiation Using Value Chain

	Inbound Logistics	Operations	Outbound Logistics	Marketing and Sales	Service
Firm Infrastructure	Top Management Support in Selling Facilities that Enhance the Firm's Image Superior Management Information System				
Human Resource Management	Superior training of personnel	Stable workforce policies Quality of work life programs Programs to attract the best scientists and engineers		Sales incentives to retain best salespersons Recruiting better qualified sales and service personnel	Extensive training of service technicians
Technology Development	Superior material handling and sorting technology Proprietary quality assurance equipment	Unique product features Rapid model introductions Unique production process or machines Automated inspection procedures	Unique vehicle scheduling Software Special purpose vehicles or containers	Applications engineering support Superior media research Most rapid quotations for tailored models	Advanced servicing techniques
Procurement	Most reliable transportation for inbound deliveries	Highest quality raw materials Highest quality components	Best warehouse location Transportation suppliers that minimize damage	Most desirable media placements Product positioning and image	High quality replacement parts
	Handling of inputs that minimizes damage or degradation Timeliness of supply to the manufacturing process	Tight conformance to specifications Attractive product appearance Responsiveness to specification changes Low defect rates Short time to manufacture	Rapid and timely delivery Accurate and responsive order processing Handling that minimizes damage	High advertising level and quality High sales force coverage and quality Personal relationships with channels or buyers Superior technical and other sales aids Most extensive promotion Most extensive credit to buyers or channels	Rapid installation High service quality Complete field stocking of replacement parts Wide service coverage Extensive buyer training

Margin

the differentiated product or service. Even if product superiority is acknowledged, customers may not be willing to pay the premium price, thereby affecting market share.

Focus on a Market Niche   A **niche** is a focal point for a product or service; it is a *subset* of the entire industry or market. Firms that pursue the competitive strategy of concentrating on one or more market niches aim to serve a specific buyer group, segment of a product line or market, or geographical area.

This strategy is suggested when a firm believes it is better to serve a narrow target area than an entire industry. Differentiation within the segment is achieved through better meeting customers' needs or by lowering costs as a result of a narrow focus. Or, the firm may pursue both strategies within its market segment at the same time.

For example, a bank may decide to focus on industrial customers, rather than competing in the mass consumer market. Or, an airline may attempt to gain strategic advantage in its use of information systems for managing the shipment of cargo rather than passengers.

Within its chosen market segment, a firm may seek the competitive advantages offered by, for example, the strategy of low-cost leadership or product differentiation. In addition, careful selection of niches may substantially reduce vulnerability to substitution.

Evaluating the Strategic Use of Information Systems

The use of information systems for competitive purposes is a concern many managers now have. And there is growing recognition that different information systems may meet different needs.

At the same time, not all industries are the same. The strategic effect of information systems technology varies today, and it will tomorrow as well.

It is reasonable for general and information systems managers alike to ask these questions: Do we have the right information systems in place today? Is our information systems plan for the future appropriate to our competitive needs?

Assessing Information Systems Portfolios

McFarlan and others (1983) developed a framework for assessing the strategic significance of information systems technology for an organization. The framework is used to determine the characteristics of and operational dependence on an organization's existing and planned information systems technology applications—the applications portfolio—and to relate these two categories of applications on a two-dimensional matrix (see Figure 20.4). From the matrix we can identify four different types of situations, as follows:

——*Strategic:* Information technology is critical to daily operations—it is often the driving engine of key elements of the business. Future applications now under development are critical for the future competitive success of the firm.

   Example: Banks that rely on information systems to support the daily banking transactions and to provide special services to their customers, and that monitor all types of relations with customers (for example, savings, checking, trust, and investment accounts), offering new products and services that may be of interest to consumers.

——*Turnaround:* Information technology is important for ongoing operations, but the firm is not absolutely dependent on the uninterrupted cost-effective functioning of this support to achieve either short-term or long-term objectives.

   Future applications now under development are the key to revitalizing the business. They are absolutely crucial for the firm to reach its business objectives.

   Example: Rapidly growing manufacturing firm that uses information systems for inventory and accounting functions today. Must become closely integrated with both customers and suppliers in the future, relying on electronic linkages (for example, EDI) as well as sophisticated production planning and manufacturing activities or face loss of business.

——*Factory:* Information systems are essential for the smooth functioning of the firm. Disruption of service through failure of information and communications systems will severely hamper continued operation of the firm.

   Future applications under development, although important for cost-effectiveness, are not designed to change the manner in which the firm competes nor are they fundamental to the firm's ability to compete.

   Example: Airlines that operate large reservations systems that have preempted the market by contracting with a large number of travel agents to use their system and that have gained loyal customers through frequent flier programs that award bonus miles for flights (the bonus miles may be accumulated toward awards of free tickets).

——*Support:* Information systems are important to the day-to-day conduct of business, playing a supporting (back-office) role (the budget for information systems, however, may be very large because of the firm's widespread use of these systems). If the systems failed, the firm could continue to function, although perhaps in an awkward fashion.

   Future systems are not critical to the mainstream of the business, but will continue to play an important support role.

   Example: A lawn-care company that takes orders and utilizes its equipment and personnel to maintain customer premises throughout the year. Information systems are used primarily for data processing, including billing and accounts management.

Figure 20.4 Evaluating Strategic Importance of Information Systems Portfolio (Source: W. McFarlan)

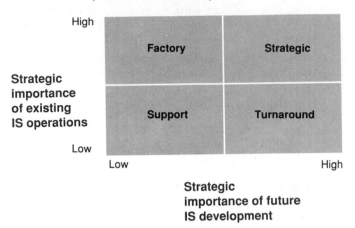

Using Portfolio Assessment

The value of examining a firm in this manner is not for purposes of classification or labeling. Rather it is to assist in identifying the role information systems are expected to play competitively, today and tomorrow.

Mere classification of an organization alone can be misinterpreted. Even if a firm is classified as a "support" or "factory" organization, information systems technology can be of strategic importance. The current and projected use of information systems technology may not be the best or even appropriate use of the resource. Moreover, factory or support firms can be *threatened* with the strategic use of information systems technology by competing firms.

The relevant issue is how to identify through the planning process those systems that would offer the greatest contribution to support the strategy of the organization (in consideration of the tradeoff between costs and benefits). Rather than classifying information systems as "support" or "strategic" after they are identified and developed, it is important that the planning process operate to identify systems with the potential to significantly enhance the competitive position of the organization. This issue is more fully addressed in the following section.

Figure 20.5 Five Competitive Forces (Adapted from Michael Porter, 1985)

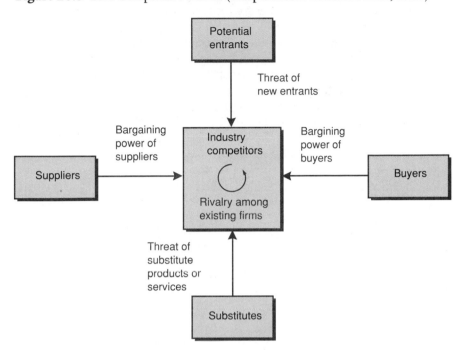

Five Competitive Forces

The competitiveness of a firm is often determined by factors that seem beyond its control; that is, they are elements outside of the firm. However, competitive advantage actually grows out of the use of strategies that enable the firm to alter competition in its favor in spite of the outside forces.

The five competitive forces shown in Figure 20.5 include the industry's own competitors, as you would expect. But also included are the bargaining power of buyers and suppliers, substitute products, and potential entrants to the industry.

The **five forces** to a great extent determine the profitability of the industry because they influence the prices, costs, and investments the firms must make. Strong buyer influence, for example, may force firms to keep prices low. So too does the threat of substitute products or services.

Some industries have few competitors, loyal buyers, and a limited threat of substitutes. The soft drink industry in the United States, for example, is certainly one that comes to mind in meeting these criteria.

On the other hand, the airline industry in the United States must continually concern itself with the impact of the competitive forces. Each force is monitored constantly by airlines.

The competitive playground of these distinctive industries is very different and so are the strategies of the firms. Soft drink firms rely heavily on advertising and the creation of image, as well as some price competition. The ingredients in their products are in relatively wide supply.

The airlines, on the other hand, must provide additional services and often extensive price competition to be successful. In addition, they must manage their internal operations carefully to control costs and ensure that their flight schedules provide the highest passenger load factor possible, while knowing who their most frequent travelers are and the special services they demand. They must also guard against frequent threats of new entrants and the power of suppliers of such essential items as aircraft (long wait from order to shipment) and fuel (prices established by supplier).

Adding value is very different between these two industries because of the role the competitive forces play.

The Value Chain

Research in competitive strategy has shown that competitive advantage cannot be understood by looking at the firm as a whole. Rather, it is a result of the many activities that go on within the enterprise and in interaction with other organizations or entities outside the firm. Thus, to understand the full meaning of the low-cost, differentiation, and focus strategies, it is useful to understand the value chain.

A **value chain** is a set of activities that are relevant to understanding the bases of cost and potential sources of differentiation in a firm. Gaining and sustaining competitive advantage depends on the ability of the firm to understand how its value chain fits in the overall value system that includes both buyers and suppliers.

Components of the Value Chain

The value chain, developed by Michael Porter (see the references), consists of the five categories divided between primary and support activities (Figure 20.6). *Primary value chain activities* are the basic business processes, fundamental in any industry. *Support value chain activities,* as the term suggests, are those activities that occur to facilitate the primary activities. The value chain categories are:

Primary Activities

——*Inbound logistics:* the activities of receiving, storing, and distributing materials and other items that serve as input to the products or services of the organization
      Examples: materials handling, inventory control, and warehousing

——*Operations:* the activities that transform input into final products or services
      Examples: manufacturing, quality control testing, packaging, and operation of the facility

Figure 20.6 The Value Chain (Source: Porter 1985)

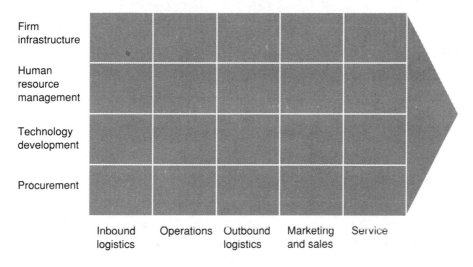

**Support
Activities**

Firm
infrastructure

Human
resource
management

Technology
development

Procurement

Inbound   Operations   Outbound   Marketing   Service
logistics   logistics   and sales

Primary Activities

—*Outbound logistics:* the activities that facilitate collecting, storing, and distributing
the finished product to buyers

    Examples: finished goods warehousing, order processing, and scheduling of
shipments

—*Marketing and sales:* the activities that facilitate or induce the purchase of the
product or service by buyers

    Examples: advertising, sales force, pricing, use of marketing channels

—*Service:* the activities associated with providing service to enhance or maintain
the value of the product or service

    Examples: installation, maintenance of repair parts, repair, and training

Support Activities

—*Procurement:* the acquisition of purchased inputs for use in the primary activities
in the value chain

    Examples: purchase of raw materials, supplies, machinery, and buildings

—*Technology development:* the broad range of activities created to improve the
product or service and the processes that make them possible (focuses on technology in general, not just information systems technology)

    Examples: machining, media research, telecommunications, metals fabrication

—*Human resource management:* the activities involved in recruiting, training, and
compensating personnel

    Examples: hiring engineers, labor negotiation, skills training

——*Firm infrastructure:* the activities that support the entire value chain, rather than individual activities

> *Examples:* general management, strategic planning, accounting, quality management, and government affairs

Each activity can be evaluated for its potential impact on competitive advantage.

Linkage and the Value Chain

Linkage between components is a key aspect of utilizing the value chain to gain competitive advantage in two ways: (1) to optimize the performance and (2) to coordinate activities.

Optimizing performance is said to occur when the firm decides to invest additional resources in the design of a product to increase quality, increase the durability of component parts, and reduce service frequency and cost. This viewpoint suggests that by optimizing performance, the firm will enjoy a competitive advantage. In the automobile industry, for example, we find that several international automobile makers, including Sweden's Volvo and West Germany's Daimler-Benz (Mercedes Benz) have chosen this strategy, recognizing that buyers are willing to pay a higher price to obtain superior quality. The generic strategy is differentiation.

Linkage through coordination recognizes the opportunity provided by closely integrating activities. Just-in-time delivery of materials and components to the manufacturing floor—meaning that inventory levels are kept very low—requires close coordination between operations, inbound and outbound logistics, and service. Many Japanese companies have been highly regarded for this type of linkage for a number of years. These firms have been able to utilize low-cost strategies resulting from perfecting this linkage very successfully. Other firms are also using the strategy successfully now and the Japanese advantage is disappearing rapidly.

Exploiting Value Chain Linkages

Exploiting the linkages requires the availability of information. The many aspects of information systems we have discussed in preceding chapters may serve as the basis for such information flows. Consider the following linkages through the flow of information using the preceding "just-in-time" example:

> Suppliers must provide materials and components needed to meet the manufacturer's production schedule. To do so, the supplier must know the production schedule, the parts needed for each item to be manufactured, and the quantity of each part to be supplied.

This linkage can produce substantial advantages to both parties, including:

——Keeping only minimal inventory on hand
——Avoiding delays in manufacturing because of materials shortages
——Reducing the order-to-manufacture-to-ship cycle
——Reducing the overall cost of manufacturing

Just-in-time manufacturing also requires linkage within the organization. Order processing, manufacturing, purchasing, inventory, and shipping must all coordinate their activities.

By examining the value chain of customers or buyers, a firm's managers may identify opportunities to gain a competitive advantage. To more fully understand the benefit of the value chain, we combine the ideas of the five forces, discussed earlier, with the capabilities of information systems to see how information systems can play a role in gaining a competitive advantage.

The Impact of Information Systems

The strategies of low-cost leadership, product differentiation, and market focus apply to all aspects of corporate strategy. But what is the role of information systems in the implementation of each strategy? In this section, we examine that role, with specific attention to relations with customers, competitors, products, and suppliers. Examples of corporate practices will be used freely to demonstrate the impact of information systems technology.

Warren McFarlan of the Harvard Business School suggests five questions to assist in evaluating the strategic impact of information systems (Table 20.3). As we examine the information systems role, notice how each strategy answers one or more of these questions.

Effects on Customer Relations

Good customer relations promote future sales, hold current customers, and gain new ones. Thus managers are in constant search of methods that will improve relations with their customers. Information systems can offer critical aid in this area by making it possible for the firm to provide better service or to sell at reduced prices. But while providing the service, which may also improve sales, a distinct competitive advantage may be gained: Customers may become unwilling to switch even if another firm becomes able to offer the same service.

Customers generally seek additional assistance in areas described by the following statements.

1. Errors are easily made.
2. Activities are labor intensive.
3. Nonperformance of activities can have serious consequences.
4. Performance of tasks is disliked.
5. Related activities must be coordinated.

Reliable performance of routine activities, surveillance of performance or resource levels, and integration of data from various records and files are among the strengths of computer-based systems that can help improve performance in the areas described

---

Table 20.3 Assessing the Competitive Potential of Information Systems Technology

Key Questions to Ask:

Where is there a potential competitive advantage from information systems technology

a. to build barriers against new entrants in the market?

b. to change the basis of competition?

c. to generate or serve as new products or services?

d. to build in switching costs to customers?

e. to strengthen a firm's power in dealing with suppliers?

---

earlier. Let's apply them to a competitive situation and develop a corporate strategy based on these advantages.

Improved Customer Service Consider a company that provides medical supplies to hospitals and large clinics. This well-established firm has relied heavily on information systems to do the "sensible things" in business, such as keeping track of orders outstanding and receiving and monitoring warehouse inventory. These fundamental information systems are essential for the orderly operation of a large enterprise. However, a firm that handles these systems effectively may still receive a poor return on its capital investments—and may even generate low profits.

This was the case for the medical supply company, and when the information systems director heard complaints from a hospital purchasing agent about long delays in the filling of orders and the trouble they were having in keeping track of outstanding orders, he looked for a more productive way to apply the firm's existing systems. After strategic consultations with top management, the information systems director installed a terminal in the hospital with a telephone link to the supply company. As a result, purchasing staff members were able to submit their orders directly to the supplier. Buyers did not have to deal with salespersons or order forms except in special cases. Hospital officials were delighted because prompt service went hand in hand with reduced paperwork. Managers of the supply firm were also pleased, not only because customer service was improved but because part of the order entry work was shifted to the customer, producing savings in staff time and payroll costs.

Soon the supply company was receiving an increasing number of orders from the hospital, which also began requesting items the company did not sell. Based on these requests, however, the supply firm began stocking additional items and gained new business as a result.

The hospital liked the system so well that it began to use it even for items that were needed in emergencies. In turn the supply firm developed a multitiered scheme wherein the customer could choose to receive guaranteed 5-hour delivery, or overnight, 3-day, or 10-day delivery. The hospital was pleased to pay a premium for more rapid delivery because it could still save money by reducing its inventory. In fact by using the vendor-provided system, inventory was reduced by more than 50 percent, saving millions of dollars.

This example demonstrates the strategic value of information systems to influence customer relations. Notice the important steps in this sequence of events:

1. The supply firm had a computerized operating system on-line.
2. In response to a customer need, the firm used existing information systems technology to improve service, benefiting customer relations.
3. New products were added to the supplier's line based on customer information. The customer, which increased its purchases from this firm, benefited by having to deal with fewer suppliers.
4. Differential pricing was installed, improving service levels and profit margins. The hospital benefited from the service by reducing its investment in inventory.

The strategic value of information systems in this example is based on improving service to the customer. Yet the supply company received valuable information about its product mix and was able to put the information to immediate use: It added products to meet demand.

The system outlined above was expanded to serve other customers as well, multiplying the competitive benefits of the strategy illustrated.

Increased Switching Costs Switching costs are the expenses that a company or individual incurs, in lost time, expenditure of resources, and hassle, when changing from one supplier or system to another. It is always good customer relations to reduce the chance that clients will switch their business to another organization. Information systems also assist in this strategic area. In the foregoing example, the hospital benefited greatly from using the supplier system: It received better service, was able to influence the supplier's product line, reduced its inventory investment, and gained automatic feedback on orders placed. Other firms (competitors) began to offer the same service to the hospital, but the purchasing agent declined. Current relations were highly satisfactory, and there was no reason to switch to another system of unproven reliability.

As you can see, information systems support can influence the ability of other firms to enter an industry or to attract customers. They can affect competition within an industry and change the balance of competition.

Effects on Competitors

Information systems can be used to change competitive environments in three ways. They can be effective tools to change intraindustry balance. At the same time, they can make it difficult or impossible for other firms to attempt to enter a market that has been dominated by a strategic user of information systems.

Altering the Intraindustry Balance Information systems can be used to change the competitive balance in an industry by altering the access of customers or suppliers to one firm over another even though multiple firms provide the same products or services. Consider the impact of telecommunications as an aid in increasing customer contact. Remote terminals linked to larger systems using telecommunications permit firms to establish a presence in many locations without opening offices in all those places.

Airline reservations operations were one of the first significant users of computer systems to improve business activities. Early systems were designed to boost operating efficiencies, by maximizing the number of persons on each flight, calculating precise weight and fuel requirements information, and so on. The remote terminals were linked into the main system through telecommunications facilities.

The first airlines to expand their view of airline reservations systems in a strategic sense shifted the balance in the industry: No longer was a reservations system an efficiency tool; it became a competitive weapon. The early reservations systems spawned travel agencies as additional arms of the airlines. People could book airline reservations at terminals installed in travel agents' offices without going near an airport. As we know, the airlines that initially developed on-line reservations systems shifted the balance of competition in their favor: Carriers that could not afford to invest in such systems did not have terminals in travel agents' offices and thus lost out on a substantial amount of potential customer contact.

In this example information systems technology permitted improved access to the customer and as a result shifted the competitive balance in an industry. Even today, many years after the first reservations systems were developed, travel agents typically have the terminals of one (at most, two) airlines in their offices. Yet they can make reservations for you on virtually any flight anywhere in the world. (Travel agents select a reservations system based in part on this capability.) This is because very soon after the first reservations systems were developed, the larger airlines made it possible for travel agents to book reservations for other carriers through their own terminals. This was done for several reasons:

1. It was good business to assist passengers whose connecting flights involved another airline.
2. The terminal access to the reservations system and to other airlines became salable as a separate product (discussed later in this chapter).
3. Legal requirements dictated that small airlines have access to computer reservations systems in the same manner as the large carriers.
4. The large carriers could charge a fee for processing reservations on the flights of other airlines.

You might suspect that the equal access requirement would diminish the intra-industry effect. However, it gave rise to still another change in competition in the industry, this one involving the positioning of information on the display screen.

Positioning refers to the location on a video display screen of information about one firm relative to all other firms. You know from the discussion of satisficing in Chapter 4 that a traveler will not have a reservations agent review all possible flight alternatives, but rather will be satisfied with the first one that meets their needs (goes to the right airport, convenient time of day, minimum number of intermediate stops, ticket class available, and so on). Based on this simple information about people, every designer of an airline reservations system positions its clients' information so that it appears first on the display screen, followed by all the other airlines' information. The information about the most competitive carrier might even be positioned last, several screens later. You can see how in a worldwide environment of air travel, positioning can affect competition and eventually balance in the industry. (Of course, if government regulators feel this creates *unfair* competitive advantage, they may publish guidelines to control it.)

The carrier can go still further by giving preferential treatment to agents who agree to use the reservations system of the carrier rather than one of the competitors. Airlines are allowed to block out certain quantities of seats on each flight so that they will not be sold over the reservations system. Imagine the competitive advantage of a carrier that offers to block out seats during peak travel times for travel agents electing to use that carrier's reservations system. Other carriers and agents cannot sell from the block even if the only unsold seats on a flight are in it. Because offers like this tend to have a high acceptance rate, the carrier benefits from having more travel agents working for the airline and multiplies the benefits enjoyed from careful flight information positioning. Moreover, monthly service charges and rental fees imposed on travel agents help the system to pay for itself.

Travel agents may have to invest, say, $75,000 to join a major carrier's reservations system, and reluctance to sacrifice such an investment can be a substantial deterrent to switching. Early identification of competitive opportunities obviously provides an important advantage.

Deterring Competitor Entry   New entrants are undesirable because they drain profits from the rest of the industry, especially if the sector is not growing fast enough to absorb the profits lost to existing firms due to competitive action. Therefore it is not surprising that information systems often assume a role in discouraging other firms from entering an industry as competitors. **Entry barriers,** as applications that achieve this purpose are called, make competition so difficult or so expensive that even when aspirants do emerge, the existing organization maintains a significant advantage.

Entry barriers are tactical. They may be evoked by the incumbent firm to make new firms reconsider the decision to enter a market. For instance, announcing a new service centered around information technology (such as advance ticketing and assignment of preferred seats on the plane) or introducing drastic price cuts while a new entrant is test marketing its product or service may emphasize the invincibility of the existing firms by reducing the effect of the competitors' marketing actions and exerting a negative influence on the test market data. Similarly, announcing that passengers can now dial into an airline's reservations system over ordinary telephone lines by using a personal computer may deter potential entrants, which may choose to postpone an engagement in such competition until they can better afford the new capability.

Creating a Barrier to Entry   Can information systems create a completely effective barrier to entry? In many instances they can. Unlike **entry deterrents,** which are tactical, entry barriers are structural in nature.

Information systems can present *structural* barriers, as illustrated by the change in the *structure* of the airline industry due to computerized reservations systems. The result was to signal any organization considering entering the airline business that an automated reservations system was a necessity. Small firms generally cannot afford to invest in such a system and therefore do not begin operation. Clearly an expensive information system constitutes a formidable defense.

The tables can also be turned. You should recognize that information systems can be used as an *offensive* resource that provides firms with a means of *entering* an industry. For example, many nonbanks, including insurance companies, realtors, and brokerage firms, were able to enter the banking industry in the 1970s and 1980s because they effectively utilized information systems and communications technologies to manage investor records. Cash management accounts offered by nonbanking firms became the most significant financial product in the banking industry in many years. Their introduction by brokerage firms changed banking permanently and at the same time immediately propelled one firm, and eventually others, into leadership positions in an industry they had been unable to enter.

Information systems are significant offensive and defensive competitive weapons. In either case, their strategic value transcends the use of systems for administrative and operational purposes, but only if the baseline systems are working properly. You would not expect a brokerage firm to be successful for long if it could not process customer transactions properly. As a matter of fact, failure to perform effectively at this level could seriously damage both the banking *and the brokerage business*.

Effects on Products

We have suggested that information systems may form the base of a new product or service. They may also offer strategic advantage by allowing a firm to differentiate its product from those offered by competitors.

An Information System as a New Product A major agricultural chemical and fertilizer firm recently started a planning service that combines its expertise in agriculture and computer processing. Customers, working with company advisers, can analyze alternative uses of their land. They evaluate strategies of planting different grains and seeds, and applying varying amounts and types of fertilizer, while estimating sensitivity to rain and other environmental conditions. Each combination can be analyzed using a model that incorporates the impact of the factors selected on land production. In turn, market price estimates can be varied to produce a range of estimates of revenues and profits generated. This "what if" strategy (What if the price is $6 per bushel? $8 per bushel? . . .) allows customers to test the sensitivity of profit to various factors from the land to the market. In a sense, the company has provided farmers with their own decision support systems (decision support systems are discussed in detail in Chapter 12).

The service is sold for a reasonable fee and is a new product for the fertilizer firm. Thus it generates revenue that would not otherwise have been realized. The company's information systems capability has been used to reap a strategic advantage from its extensive experience in agriculture. You would expect the system to generate new customers for the firm, and that is precisely what has happened.

The company also offers a spring planting program. Customers using the planning system are able to order the seeds and fertilizers they need to help ensure maximum productivity and best land use as an offshoot of the decision support system. This too has boosted profits for the firm.

Another example will demonstrate the use of an information system itself as a product. Earlier we discussed a medical supply firm that began offering an ordering service to its customers. Suppose that after the order entry system has been in use for a while, the supplier learns more about the hospital business. It finds that customers' payments for supplies depend on the receipt of revenue from patients and insurance companies. However, producing invoices and insurance claims is a large, complicated task that entail substantial cost (for personnel, equipment, supplies, space, mistakes, and so on).

Perhaps the supplier realizes that although hospitals work hard to develop expertise in delivering medical services, they are not necessarily experts in collecting money. It might start a billing service for its customers, putting to use its valuable experience in generating invoices and handling accounts receivable. The new service would bring in additional revenue without investment in new equipment, and hospitals would find that their billing was performed more efficiently and at a lower cost.

Product Differentiation Many companies sell goods or services that retail at much the same price from region to region. To achieve an identity for themselves, such firms often rely on a well-known strategy: *product differentiation,* or the emphasis on unique features that distinguish one item from another, giving certain products a real or perceived advantage over competitors. How do information systems assist in product differentiation?

Consider the cases of health studios that sell the concept of physical fitness, cosmetic firms that market beauty products, and clothing retailers that sell brand-name suits, slacks, jackets, and accessories. How does one firm distinguish itself from another in the same field? Price and quality are important, but they may not be enough. Consider the advantage that a particular firm will enjoy if it develops a "personalized" product—a computer-based personal fitness/beauty/color coordination program tailored to the individual customer or prospect.

Through an ordinary terminal the customer (alone or assisted by a sales agent) enters distinguishing personal features. The clothier needs to know about height and weight, color hair, eye color, and complexion. The cosmetic adviser and the fitness consultant will want similar information, as well as any financial constraints ("How much do you want to spend?"). The respective systems then analyze the entries to produce a personalized program of colors and fabrics of clothes, exercises and diet, or skin cremes, cosmetics, and makeup colors. Printed reports complete with headings featuring the customer's name distinguish a firm from others selling the same product or service. (Cosmetic firms may go a step further and blend the cosmetics and cremes specified by the personal profile.) The information systems feature differentiates the product from all other firms offering the same brands or services. (If it is sold for a fee, it is a new product.)

Firms follow the product differentiation strategy on the assumption that price is not always the most important consideration for the customer. In essence they use information systems to shift the emphasis from price to a feature or features not obtainable elsewhere.

Effects on Suppliers

Strategy based on information systems can in fact change a corporation's relations with suppliers.

In some industries, suppliers are strong enough to raise prices periodically without pricing themselves out of the market. The labor costs paid by manufacturing firms are a familiar example. However, the use of high technology in the form of computer-controlled robots is altering the impact of labor unions (the suppliers of laborers) on some manufacturers. Computer-controlled manufacturing plants, now in their early development phases, may turn out to have greater flexibility in the diversity and quantity of items they produce and may be able to lower their costs at the same time.

Banks are also concerned about their suppliers, although holders of savings accounts and investment certificates are seldom publicly described as such. Yet if customers decide to invest their funds with a competitor, a bank may have to increase its interest rates (a product cost) to ensure that enough funds are available to make loans. In this industry, personalized savings plans, automatic teller machines that link customers to their money regardless of where they are, and dial-up services for paying bills have been instituted in attempts to lock suppliers (depositors) into their banks.

Still other industries rely heavily on computer-aided design/computer-aided manufacturing (CAD/CAM) systems for the design and development of products. Aerospace, building, and automobile executives, for example, have found how significant information systems technology can be when dealing with suppliers. Computer graphics technology allows engineers to make in minutes and seconds design and material changes that previously took weeks and months. These firms are telling suppliers: "Do you want to be a preferred supplier? Then change to fit our system!" In large-project environments, such as in aerospace, contractors may tell potential suppliers what systems they must have or acquire to qualify as subcontractors. The change may involve CAD/CAM equipment, as in this example, order entry systems, graphics or video terminals, or communications protocols.

Table 20.4 summarizes the strategic impact that information systems may have on customers, competition, products, and suppliers. In each case the systems are built on a well-designed and effective transaction processing system. The right strategy imposed on unreliable operating systems will undermine the most well-conceived plans.

Selecting a Strategy

Because the rate of advancement in information systems and computer technology is very rapid, eventually many functions in the firms making up a specific industry will be enhanced by computer technology. For instance, nearly all airlines benefit

Table 20.4 Examples of Strategic Impact of Information Systems

Strategy	Customers (Hospitals)	Competitors— Defensive Strategy (Airline Reservations)	Competitors— Offensive Strategy (Financial Services)	Products (Agricultural Services)	Suppliers (Banking Services)
Low Cost	Reduced clerical requirements Lower inventory requirements	Reduced cost per passenger through better ticketing and load management	Shared personnel tasks reducing staff investment	Cost analysis Land productivity Reduced market risk	Free bank services instead of service charges Reduced interest rates by services provided
Product Differentiation	Differentiated pricing and delivery	On-line reservations Interairline ticketing Reserved ticket blocks Positioning	Cash management	Agricultural decision support systems	Automated teller machines Personalized savings plans

from on-line reservations systems, either because they developed their own or because they purchase access to another firm's system. However, the strategic issue is *how* the computer assistance is used. Managers must therefore select a strategy carefully, to ensure that it is the best one for their organization and that it will retain its value for an acceptable length of time.

How then does a manager select from the three strategies of low cost, product differentiation, and market niche to achieve proper leveraging of information systems?

Requirements for Following a Low-Cost Strategy

To follow the cost leadership strategy, an organization must find a way to reduce its internal costs sufficiently to permit the price of its product or service to be established below other competitors. The two means for achieving this are:

——*Reduce overall costs directly:* Manage costs by construction of efficient facilities, control of overhead expenditures, careful monitoring of customer balances, and avoidance of poor risk accounts.

——*Accumulate overall cost reductions across all functions in the organization:* Common areas for cost reduction are in the engineering (for example, CAD/CAM), design, and manufacturing functions.

Situations suitable for this strategy feature information systems that will permit major reductions in clerical or manufacturing staff or better utilization of plant and equipment. Similarly, costs may be reduced through increased organization proficiency at scheduling of personnel and equipment, improved maintenance programs, or reduced inventory levels. Finally, building billable end value into an existing system may have the effect of reducing overall costs, as shown in the hospital example.

The firm pursuing cost leadership should identify and undertake informatio systems projects that will allow it to apply this strategy successfully. The low-cost strategy may be inappropriate for a firm that is unable to develop such projects.

Requirements for Following a Product Differentiation Strategy

Bases for product differentiation include:

—Customer service

—Dealer network

—Technology

—Product features

—Product exclusivity

—Brand image

Firms most successful in following this strategy are those that can use information systems to assist in the delivery of products or services that are perceived as unique or customized. Alternatively, sharply reduced development costs may enable a firm to provide differentiated products.

Summary

Information systems are increasingly recognized for their strategic advantages in dealing with customers and competitors while forming the basis for entirely new products and services. In addition, they provide a basis for changing the relationship with "suppliers" (which can be bank depositors or labor unions, as well as vendors traditionally described by this term). Organizations that recognize the opportunity can make significant advances against competitors. Those that do not and are unable to manage information systems properly may have limited viability in the decades ahead.

Three common organization strategies are: to provide low-cost products or services, to practice product differentiation, and to focus on a market niche. Each should be evaluated when managers weigh the advantages of building barriers against competitor entry into the marketplace, changing the basis of competition in their industry, generating new products, building in switching costs, or changing the balance of power in supplier relationships. The five competitive forces affect virtually all firms, although the extent varies in each situation. In some instances, information systems offer managers a way of turning the table; that is, a firm can use the systems to enter a market that otherwise would be inaccessible.

The value chain of a firm can be examined to identify opportunities for improving the competitiveness of an organization. In addition, linkage with other firms and their value chains may offer opportunities to gain an improved relationship, add value, and therefore develop a competitive advantage.

Of course an organization must ensure that its systems perform properly. Then it should consider the role information systems should play in its own competitive strategy.

Key Words

Competitive strategy	Leverage	Support
Differentiation	Linkage	Switching cost
Entry barrier	Low-cost leadership	Turnaround
Entry deterrent	Niche	Value chain
Factory	Positioning	
Five forces	Strategy	

Review Questions

1. What new challenges must information systems managers and corporate executives generally face as a result of information technology advances? Explain.

2. What determines whether an information systems application is strategic? Give examples to support your answer.

3. Define *strategy* as it applies to the activities of an organization in a competitive environment. How does organization strategy relate to the customers and competitors that make up a competitive environment?

4. What is the value of classifying information systems portfolios into the categories based on applications in use today and those under development?

5. Discuss the meaning of *strategic, turnaround, support,* and *factory* classifications for an organization's information systems plans.

6. Identify the three generic competitive strategies organizations may choose to follow. Briefly discuss the objectives of each strategy and give examples of actions firms may take when following the strategy.

7. What are the five forces that affect firms in a competitive sense? Why are these forces significant?

8. Discuss the meaning of the value chain. What is its role in formulating competitive strategy?

9. Identify and briefly describe each of the elements in a firm's value chain. What are primary and support activities?

10. What questions should managers ask to assist them in evaluating the strategic impact of computer information systems? Explain the reason behind each question.

11. In what ways can the strategic use of information systems influence a firm's relations with its customers?

12. How can the strategic use of information systems affect an organization's competitors? Be sure to include the impact on both current and potential competitors.

13. How can information systems form the basis of new products for an organization? For an industry?

14. Discuss the ways in which information systems can change an organization's interaction with its suppliers. Why does this occur?

15. What steps and commitments are enacted when an organization decides to follow the low-cost provider strategy or decides to provide differentiated products?

16. Is the use of information systems as a competitive weapon a new phenomenon in business management? Explain the reason for your answer.

Application Problems

1. Several years ago, Avis Rent-A-Car, then the seventh largest automobile rental agency, developed the Wizzard System. Based on computer and communications technology, the Wizzard System interconnected all rental locations at airports, hotels, and so on. The system, which was the first of its kind in the industry, was attractive to customers because it allowed them to place car rental reservations from virtually any location around the country, in person or by telephone, and know instantly that an automobile would be available for them at the desired rental location. After the Wizzard System was introduced, and included in the company's advertising campaigns, Avis grew from the seventh largest national car rental firm to the second.

   The Avis system was also designed to provide management with knowledge about the location and cost of its fleet of automobiles and about the performance of various car rental locations. It helped Avis improve cost/performance ratios while forestalling the development of substitute products and services. The information captured through the Wizzard System concerning customers, vehicle demand, and performance helped Avis bargain more effectively with its suppliers.

   At the time the Wizzard System was introduced, other companies were considering entry into the automobile rental industry.
   a. Based on the above description, relate the system characteristics of the Wizzard System to its impact on:
      (1) customer relations
      (2) competitors
      (3) products
      (4) suppliers
   b. What features of the system facilitate or prohibit a sustainable competitive advantage for Avis?

2. The competitive advantages of information systems offer the potential of substantial payoffs in sales generated by the sales force. Executives are therefore concerned about leveraging the sales force through use of information systems technology, increasing the impact and productivity of the salesperson individually and collectively.

   Discuss the competitive role information systems can play in each of the following areas of sales:
   a. Allowing salespersons to increase productive selling time
   b. Providing information needed to target the sales force to specific markets or customer segments

c. Serving as a delivery vehicle for improved sales aids

d. Moving information directly to the customer

3. In many organizations, information systems are still considered an area of expense, although a necessary expense. Typically executives in such firms also view these systems as valuable for the repetitive processing of transactions data and do not consider them a potential competitive weapon.

You have been asked to lead a discussion with senior managers who are interested in considering, but skeptical about the competitive value of, information systems. What *questions* would you raise about customers, products, competitors, suppliers, or the industry, to get them thinking about this matter?

4. Many retail drug stores have developed computer-based systems that provide, as a service to their customers, a detailed accounting of all purchases of drugs and prescriptions during a particular year. A printed summary of purchases, which is useful to customers when they file income tax returns, can be prepared quickly on request.

a. What is the competitive value of such a system in dealing with customers, suppliers, and competitors?

b. A new drug store is considering installation of this type of system. Since the system will *not* be unique to the industry, would you advise the owner to cease such consideration on the grounds that not providing a unique service will diminish the competitive value of the system? Explain the reasoning behind your answer.

5. *USA Today* is a daily newspaper sold throughout the United States. This "national newspaper" uses state of the art information generation and transmission technologies to create the content of each issue at the main office. Then the copy is transmitted via satellite to 17 geographically dispersed printing plants. Each 36-page edition is created and transmitted in 8 hours, including full-color pages.

The newspaper depends on the computer and communications technology for its existence. Without it, national distribution in a timely manner would be impossible.

a. Does the above description suggest a competitive use of information technology or just creative use of basic technology? Explain the reason for your answer.

b. Do you think *USA Today* could exist without its use of data communications technology?

6. In the early 1980s, Xerox Corporation, a large manufacturer of office copiers, developed a field work support system that uses over 50 distributed minicomputers throughout North America and parts of Europe. The system provides service representatives with computerized access to information about specific customers or copiers, previous service call histories, and the workloads of service representatives in a certain geographic area.

Customers telephone the central Xerox service center when repairs are needed and a trained operator obtains a description of the problem from the customer. The customer-provided information allows the diagnosis of a substantial number of problems over the telephone, thereby reducing the total volume of service calls that must be made.

When service representatives complete a call, they contact the central service coordinator, who schedules the representative to the next customer site and provides appropriate background information about the customer, the problem the representative will encounter, and needed parts.

The distributed network permits sharing of information on parts and service problems. It also facilitates the assignment of service personnel within geographic areas, maximizing customer coverage while managing individual travel time and distance.

Xerox believes that providing rapid, but cost-effective service to customers is essential for business success.

a. What strategic advantages do you attribute to the Xerox system in improving customer support?

b. What benefits do you attribute to the system in improving the productivity of the service force by increasing the number of calls each individual can make? Are these *strategic* benefits? Why or why not?

Minicase: Delta Productivity*

Delta Airlines is one of the handful to go through deregulation with few scars on its unblemished record of strong financial performance. Delta's last strike was in 1942. The last union vote was in 1955. Francis O'Connell of the Transport Workers of America says of Delta: "[They have] a relationship with their employees that is most difficult to break into."

Delta is a people company. It advertises "the Delta Family Feeling," and lives that philosophy. The company promotes from within, pays better than most airlines, and goes to any length to avoid laying workers off in a traditionally cyclic industry. . . .

One of the more interesting notions at Delta is that of interchangeability of management parts. The chairman insists, for example, that all his senior vice presidents be trained to step into any job in the company (though not, presumably, flying the planes). Even the senior vice presidents are supposed to know one another's areas well enough to substitute for any other if need be. And, incidentally, it is a tradition for top management to pitch in and help baggage handlers at Christmastime.

Questions

1. Should the interchangeability of management parts apply also to the manager of information systems? Explain the reason for your answer.

2. Should the interchangeability of management parts pertain to the managers of information systems projects that are at the requirements analysis, design, or programming stage? Explain.

*Excerpted from Thomas J. Peters and Robert H. Waterman, Jr., *In Search of Excellence* (New York: Harper & Row, 1982), pp. 253–254.

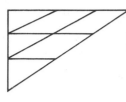

21: Information Systems in the Future

Key Questions

What are the dominant trends for information systems in the future?

How will computer costs and capabilities change?

Will mainframe systems give way to desktop systems?

What will be the dominant question about the value of information systems in organizations in the future?

What changes are most likely to occur in the way information systems are applied in organizations?

What impact will computers have on manufacturing firms?

How will management of information systems change?

What is the outlook for careers in information systems?

Quotations from Experts

1949   Popular Mechanics:
Where a calculator on the ENIAC is equipped with 18,000 vacuum tubes and weighs 30 tons, computers in the future may have only 1000 vacuum tubes and perhaps weigh only 1.5 tons.

1957   Prentice-Hall editor in deciding whether to publish a book on data processing:
I have traveled the length and breadth of this country, and have talked with the best people in business administration. I can assure you on the highest authority that data processing is a fad and won't last out the year.

1982   Kenneth Olson, President of Digital Equipment Corporation:
There is no reason for any individual to have a computer at home.

In Christopher Cerf and Victor Navasky, *The Experts Speak* (New York: Pantheon, 1984)

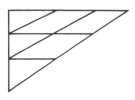

The preceding chapters focused on the way information systems are now employed. We find a solid base in computer and communications technology coupled with an intense concern for development of applications systems that meet end-user needs. These systems did not reach their current usefulness overnight but are the result of an evolution in the underlying technology and in the management philosophy that guides their use in organizations.

This chapter explores developments we should expect in the information systems of the future. Expectations are grouped in three main areas: trends in information technology, information systems applications, and information management. When you have completed this chapter, you should know what changes to watch for and how to begin preparing to take advantage of them.

Why Should You Know About the Future of Information Systems?

Everybody loves to talk about the future and speculate on what will unfold. Among the other reasons you should think about the future of information systems are the following:

—The increasing reliance on information systems is a reality for organizations of all types. The trends that are emerging suggest how organizations will be affected.

—Distinct trends suggest areas of improvement that provide new opportunities for all organization personnel.

—Developments to date are just the preliminary events. The most important developments are yet to come.

—You are part of the future.

You can undoubtedly add your own reasons to this list, whether you are planning a career in information systems, in some other area of business, or in another field.

Trends in Information Systems Technology

In the future, computers will become cheaper and more powerful because of continued technological advances. This section examines the general trends as well as computer economics and the impact of changes in this area on the use of information systems technology.

General Trends in Information Systems Technology

There are eight general trends involving pervasive expectations and developments in the use of information systems that will shape the future. This section identifies them, and we build on them in the remainder of the chapter.

Convergence Information technology will continue to evolve as a result of the convergence of what previously have been viewed as distinct technologies: data, text, voice, and image. Developers and users alike will continue to view them as inseparable and will prepare applications that presuppose their interrelationship.

Interoperability **Interoperability** is the term describing situations where users are able to exchange information, in whatever form, without difficulty or delay. Individuals need not care where other parties to communications are located or where the data and information they seek reside. This capability underlies the usefulness of information systems technology.

Achieving interoperability involves tremendous capability, and often complexity, in the components of information systems. The complexity is handled by the technology, not the user, as the next trend suggests.

Simplicity Interoperability demands that there be simplicity. There is a great deal of concern that information systems remain too complex. Requirements are not met at the rate users expect. In fact, users are reluctant to turn more and more of their day-to-day functions over to computers, even those on their own desktop, if they feel they will lose more control.

Information systems technology is definitely ahead of the users. It is time to allow the users to catch up. The additional enhancements in new software releases may be meaningless if the *last release* has more capability than necessary and performs the task users want performed. In order to move ahead, software developers and vendors alike will have to simplify the use of their systems. Simplicity begins and ends at the interface to the system.

Disintermediation Simplicity brings about **disintermediation,** the removal of unnecessary steps or persons—that is, intermediaries—who intervene on our behalf. Individuals such as technicians, and controls whose primary purpose has been that of gatekeeping, will gradually disappear. We are already seeing this in the form of end-user computing, where individuals can access data and develop their own applications without assistance from information systems professionals. In the future, disintermediation will grow in significance across all information systems application areas.

Drive Toward and Away from Single Standards Disintermediation requires standards—an area where information systems professionals will play a key role in the future, as they do today. At the personal computer level, there has been a standardization around MS-DOS, the operating system associated with IBM-compatible personal computers. The standardization has been convenient because an application written for one system could run on virtually any other DOS system.

There is a transition to multiple standards on desktop systems. MS-DOS will continue to exist and play an important role in personal computing. However, OS/2 and UNIX, both more powerful operating systems, are growing in importance across many application areas and promise to become standards in their own right. They use more memory but allow more features to be built into applications, which some users will need for such purposes as performing sophisticated analyses, creating high-resolution graphics, and doing image processing.

Applications written to run under one operating system will not function under the others. This trend is in contrast with the user demand for simplification.

On the other hand, the drive toward a single worldwide standard in the data communications area is very strong. Organizations rely on the ability to communicate electronically and need to know that they can interconnect with networks of all types and with any computer system. The open systems interconnect (OSI) standard is becoming dominant throughout the industry, and major vendors are changing their proprietary standards to accommodate its characteristics.

Creation of Group Systems Interconnecting people through computers will continue to grow in importance as the need for flow of information to coordinate activities increases. Local-area networks will proliferate. They will interconnect individuals for communication purposes and to share data and equipment. Computer systems will also continue to emerge that are designed to function as servers, directing the flow of information, sharing of data, and use of systems resources.

Increased Focus on Software Software will become an intense area of focus for vendors and users alike. Vendors will recognize the revenue potential from software and place even greater emphasis on delivering the right software and appropriate support. The largest computer vendors will look to software for as much as one-half of their revenue in the future.

Users, seeing that computers are becoming more and more alike—almost a commodity in some cases—will turn their attention to software that will meet their needs, knowing that the hardware will be available and at a reasonable cost. Purchased software will be the most attractive since it can be acquired quickly, for a known price, and with demonstrated features.

There will be increased attention to turning tasks over to software (rather than to computers). We will see companies acquiring software instead of hiring additional people.

Growing Reliance on Strategic Networking Corporations increasingly rely on the ability to transmit all types of data. Voice data and image data transmission are becoming fundamental capabilities for conducting business. In the future, a company without a reliable communications network will be at a significant disadvantage.

Figure 21.1

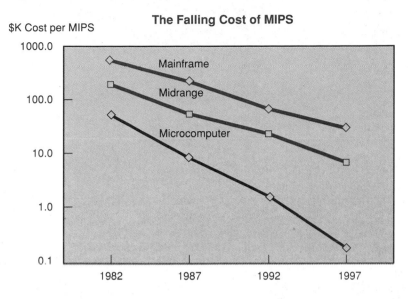

Changing Computer Economics

It is no secret that the entire economic outlook of information systems technology is changing because of shifts in the cost of computing and the resulting products available in the marketplace. Key areas of economic significance are changes in price/performance levels, product life cycles, computer chips, secondary storage, and the rise of an information utility.

Improved Price/Performance Levels There is a constant improvement in the **price/performance relationship,** since computing capability is becoming cheaper and more powerful at the same time. An equivalent amount of today's computing power will cost 20 to 30 percent less a year from today.

   Millions of Instructions Per Seconds (MIPS) continue to be the traditional—although not always the most useful—yardstick for performance comparison. Figure 21.1 shows the expected trend for the next few years, using MIPS as the guideline. As the illustration shows, the cost per MIPS will drop across all levels of systems, with microcomputers falling at the most accelerated rate. At the mainframe level, the cost per MIPS will have dropped from $1 million to less than $30,000 during the period 1965 to the early 1990s.

Product Life Cycle

Computer systems today have shorter market lives (not shorter *usable* lives) than ever. As Table 21.1 indicates for computer processors, new computer systems now

Table 21.1 Processor Performance History for IBM Processors

Year Announced	IBM Model	No. of Processors	MIPS	Cost (Millions)
1965	360/65	1	0.7	3.0
1971	370/155	1	1.8	1.6
1976	370/165	1	2.5	4.0
1978	3032	1	2.5	1.9
1978	3033	1	5.0	3.4
1982	3081K	1	13.5	4.6
1983	3084Q	4	25.7	7.9
1985	3090–200	1	28.0	5.1
1986–7	3090–400	4	55.0	9.3
1987	3090–200E	2	31.0	4.6
1988	3090–400E	4	54.0	8.4

have a life of three to four years rather than five to six years, as was common in the late 1960s.

Personal computers are replaced with newer models every three years, and there is every indication that the cycle may become even shorter. Some vendors will resist this in order to obtain maximum return from their research and development investment in a particular product line. But competitors will force their hand by the threat of bringing new products to the market in shorter time frames.

The short product life cycle is possible due partly to the change in the price/performance relationship discussed earlier. In addition, however, it is easier to build new systems with more power than to bring the selling price down accordingly (we return to this point in a moment).

Improved Chip Performance

The cost of the underlying semiconductor technology—silicon chips—continues to fall. In 1980, 64K RAM chip sets were selling for well over $100. By the mid-1980s, the same chips were down to $4, and by 1990, they were only a few cents each. However, few were being sold because new higher-density chips, holding several million characters of data each, were available for approximately $8 each.

Table 21.2 summarizes the dramatic changes in chip densities.

In spite of the amazing breakthroughs underlying semiconductor technology, it is often easier to add more capability and processing power to a new computer product than to bring down the selling price of the unmodified unit. This is because the processor and memory components are the cheapest items, thanks to the costs shifts just discussed. But costs of the most expensive parts—the packaging components—have not dropped. Keyboards and monitors cost several hundred dollars each. Cases and disk units are also priced high in relation to chips.

In general, you should expect to see a continuing stream of increasingly powerful computers entering the market. Each system will be smaller than a predecessor of

Table 21.2 Change and Predicted Change in Semiconductor Chip Density

Year	Circuit Size	Storage Capacity
1980	4 microns	64K
1985	2 microns	256K
1987	1 micron	1,024K
1990	.5 micron	4,096K
1995	.25 micron	16,384K

comparable power and speed. The price/performance relationship will continue to reflect an annual drop of 20 to 30 percent in equipment costs.

Storage

Computers of all sizes are growing in memory capacity, both because the technology allows it to occur within economic and size limits, and because applications are demanding more memory. Main memory units are growing rapidly. Where a few years ago the standard memory size of personal computers was 256K, we are now looking at systems where 2 to 4 megabytes is becoming the standard, and memories up to 16 megabytes are not uncommon. Similar growth of memories in mainframes and midrange systems is also the norm.

The capacity of secondary storage devices continues to improve at an annual rate of 40 percent. Disk drives in the 1960s had capacities of approximately 30 megabytes. Magnetic disk systems of comparable size in the 1990s store in the realm of terabytes of data each. This rate of improvement is expected to be maintained.

Optical storage will grow in popularity as well, providing even higher storage densities. Table 21.3 compares the sales volume of magnetic and optical storage. Table 21.4 shows how disk storage media was improved.

Uses of Information Technology

The advances in computer and communications technology will influence the way we use it: Mainframe functions will change, but superminicomputers will remain important. Data communications and access to databases and services will also be affected.

Mainframe Function Some people say they can hardly wait until such activities as accounting and inventory management are taken off large mainframe computers and put on desktop systems they can operate themselves. *This is unlikely to occur,* and for good reason. The attractiveness of microcomputers lies in their flexibility—they can be equipped with hardware and software appropriate for a broad range of intended uses. The capabilities of microcomputers are influencing the applications that remain on mainframe systems, but they will not replace these systems.

Table 21.3 Secondary Storage Usage by Sales Volume

Type	1985	1990
Optical	$300.0 million	$ 9.0 billion
Winchester	$ 13.0 billion	$26.2 billion
Floppy	$ 3.8 billion	$ 5.6 billion
Tape	$ 1.3 billion	$ 2.4 billion

Source: IEEE

Table 21.4 Improvements in Disk Storage Media

	1956	1978	1981	1985
Type	RAMAC	Winchester	Floppy	Optical
Space	9 × 12 ft.	8 inches	3.5 inches	1 sq. inch
Capacity	5 MB on 50 24-inch disks	11 MB	437.5K per surface	100 megabits

Mainframe systems will remain the dominant resource for the processing of transactions. Recall that transactions for a specific application are typically high in volume and all are processed in the same manner. Processing speed and storage capacity are key requirements for these applications, and they are best met by mainframe systems.

Mainframes will continue to serve as data repositories. Large volumes of data will be stored and managed by information systems professionals, such as data administrators, systems analysts, and information systems managers. Because the volume of stored data is sure to increase, the need for sound information management decisions will become even more important.

Access to data will be afforded end-users scattered among diverse locations. Thus, mainframe systems will serve a third important function, that of communications center. A large proportion of resources will handle data communications activities. The level of communications traffic will continue to grow, because of increasing demand and improved transmission capabilities. Mainframe systems will be at the center of this network, and intelligent workstations, microcomputers, and minicomputers will link the user to CPUs and databases.

Mainframe systems will function as user centers. The importance of end-user computing will continue to grow. As we discussed in Chapter 18, a significant amount will involve mainframe systems accessible through the organization's information center. Many special organization applications as well as powerful fourth-generation languages with database systems at their heart are most appropriate on mainframe systems.

Therefore, if you hear the demise of mainframe systems predicted, don't believe it. The installed base of these systems will continue to grow moderately as the function changes to meet evolving organization and user needs.

The Importance of Superminis *Superminicomputers* are high-powered systems designed for specific functions. For example, these powerful minicomputers drive automated production lines, manage communications centers, and provide the capabilities of airline flight simulators.

Some say that the expanded capabilities of low-cost desktop computers and the falling price of increased performance in mainframe systems have doomed the mini-computer. The tasks handled by small minicomputers will be given over to micro-computers, they predict, and high-end needs will be met more economically by the acquisition of small mainframe systems. This is not certain to occur, however. The combination of office information systems, oriented to departmental computing, and the growing need for data communications and distributed processing may maintain the demand for minicomputers. A related development to watch for may be a change in the definition of *minicomputer*.

These predictions notwithstanding, it is evident that superminicomputers will remain important. Improving price/performance relationships make their acquisition attractive to organizations, but their special capabilities are even more important. Often the processing capabilities of superminis exceed those of general-purpose mainframe systems. That is, more power (measured in MIPS) can be attained because the systems are designed to serve a special function and need not be all things to all users. This requirement for nonstandard capabilities is unlikely to disappear, and neither is the supermini.

The Uses of Data Communications We are still in an age of communication. Wide-area networks will continue to proliferate in the United States, in part because of dereg-ulation of the public telephone system, and also because so many communication-oriented products are available at reasonable cost. Local-area networks and private telephone systems will become more numerous and more important, as a result of the greater use of personal computers and office systems.

The *need to interconnect* will ensure the existence of a capability to link users with other users and managers with mainframe data. Data communications of all types will be widespread as entire systems are bridged to other systems and networks.

Access to Commercial Databases Managers' needs for data will not subside. But many have realized that it is impossible for an organization to collect and maintain all the details its employees and executives must work with. As a result, a growing number of firms are investing in **commercial database services.** By paying a periodic sub-scription fee, end-users are able to dial up an on-line database service containing financial, marketing, or other types of data. Special reports can be prepared or sets of data can be downloaded to the user's system. Charges are based on amount of service.

The several hundred such database services in the United States demonstrate the "commodity value" of information, and there will be more of them.

Growth of Information Utility

Information systems technology will evolve toward a utility structure. The **information utility structure** recognizes that information systems have become a corporate resource that dramatically alters not only the manner in which organizations function, but also the way in which they compete. And, as pointed out in Chapter 20, information systems technology is recognized as a critical element in the formation of corporate strategy.

Organizations will develop their information utility structures only after there is widespread investment in information systems and experience with their use by organization personnel to enhance their personal productivity, improve personal and organizational effectiveness, and influence competitive strategy. The widespread deployment of technology and dependence on its capabilities presents new opportunities, but also new demands.

The utility viewpoint will include these profound changes:

—The exercise by end-users of increased influence over individual applications and a growing discretion in the use of information technology

—The recognition of information as a resource that must be managed as an asset

—The dispersal of both users and information systems resources throughout the firm under what is termed *distributed processing*

—A growth in the importance of standards to ensure that information systems support will be available and reliable

The information utility structure is organized to provide a centralized, standard *direction,* including a means of coordination that will support the overall organizational requirements. Standards specify data organization, usage, and protection as well as guidelines for data transmission and communication (access, interface, and protocol).

The utility viewpoint depends on creation of an infrastructure that supports systems usage, not monopoly control. It is further characterized by (1) diverse (mixed-vendor and processing power) facilities installed at separate and distinct locations, (2) the distribution of data between independent locations, (3) the ability of each processing system to function separately and in concert with others in the network, and (4) a control system that links remote sites and databases into a coherent network.

Future Information Systems Applications

Information systems applications in the years ahead will be influenced by greater involvement of end-users as well as by even greater management recognition of the strategic value of such systems. Application replacement will also be a greater concern in organizations.

More Hands-on Technology

End-user computing, the term applied to applications developed or operated by managers and staff members rather than by information systems professionals, is becoming a major factor in the information/communications industry. Computing of this nature was nonexistent in 1970 and had barely emerged in 1980. But now most of the computing power in a typical organization, including a substantial proportion of mainframe resources, is used in this manner. More end-users, of course, will call for the creation of additional computing resources.

The extension of end-user applications will not occur through spreadsheets or business graphics alone but will include many other programming tools. Systems will pervade the office, the executive suite, and the information center. Office information systems and decision support systems will increase in importance, and they will provide more and better services and functions.

Widespread Image Processing

The higher storage densities, particularly those brought about by optical storage media, combined with increased processing power, are making image processing a reality (see Chapter 5). In the future, we will see image processing become widespread in many corporations.

The most visible initial applications will be those where paper documents are digitized and stored in image form. Doing so not only eliminates the flow of paper, but it also allows circulation of the document, including any handwritten annotations, to anyone linked into the system. In other words, image databases will arise and their contents will be distributable on a computer network.

In the early 1990s, image documents will be augmented by the capability of users to attach *voice messages* containing comments, narratives, and other verbal information pertaining to the document. Recall the integration of technologies earlier and you will see how this is a natural evolution of image processing. Like the image itself, voice message folders attached to the document will be accessible throughout the network and over the desktop.

Information Systems as a Strategic Tool

As Chapter 20 pointed out, managers and executives are recognizing the competitive and strategic value of information systems. The potential value of computers in relation to customers, competitors, and suppliers will lead to many uses of applications across organizations of all types. Before long the mere linking of computer information systems and corporate strategies will cease to offer a competitive advantage; *not* linking up, however, will become a competitive liability.

We will see a dramatic repositioning of information systems in organizations. The transition of these systems from supporting the business to *being the business,* when coupled with improvement in systems features such as intelligent interfaces, will facilitate more direct use of an organization's systems by outside users. The computer technology will be more invisible, but the systems themselves will be more evident than ever as customers and suppliers interact with the enterprise through terminals, workstations, and ordinary pushbutton telephones.

Applications Replacement

A growing crisis will involve the replacement of obsolete systems. The early systems were designed to support intensive transaction processing needs, and the programs of the day were coded in assembly and procedural languages. Many of these systems have been in place for 15 to 20 years. Furthermore, other applications have been built on top of them as organizations have expanded their operations and shaped their areas of emphasis. Extensive software maintenance, needed to add features or adapt applications to new facilities, has produced a series of patches and "fixes" that hamper current performance and hinder future expandability.

Many organizations find that applications replacement is their most pressing problem, but one for which there are no easy solutions. Reinvesting in replacement transaction systems will draw limited personnel and capital away from resources earmarked for new development. Yet the same new development projects, caught up in the two- to four-year backlog that characterizes the typical information systems department, have already been on the back burner too long.

One major corporation conservatively estimated the replacement cost of its applications software base at over a quarter of a billion dollars. Most companies will soon be in a similar predicament, if they are not already there.

Robotics and Computer-Integrated Manufacturing

Manufacturing companies will increase their use of information systems, not just in the transaction processing and management support areas, but in the fundamental production technologies on which the very firms are based. **Computer-integrated manufacturing (CIM)**—the name for factory automation involving computers in the many tasks associated with manufacturing—will change labor costs, productivity and product quality, and the basis of competition, to be sure. But it will continue to dramatically alter the manner in which the manufacturing process is carried out. Companies will learn that the risks of lagging behind in CIM are much greater than the short-term risks of installing these advanced systems.

General Motors, long thought to be a conservative and tradition-bound auto manufacturer, is one of the firms taking the lead in CIM. These are some of the features of GM's new systems:

——Robots will continue to take over tasks that are risky, disliked by humans, or amenable to substantial improvements in quality control. More than 15,000 such robots are anticipated to be in use within GM by 1990.

——More than 200,000 computer controlled manufacturing tools will be installed.

——Information about each *individual* automobile on order and going through the manufacturing process will be stored in a manufacturing information database. An automated vehicle identification system—based on a *computer chip affixed to each car*—will communicate with devices installed at selective manufacturing stations (for example, in the paint shop) so that data can be retrieved from the database and used to control the assembly of a particular vehicle at a particular workstation.

——Individual manufacturing stations will be integrated through a local-area network. The GM-developed system called **Manufacturing Automation Protocol (MAP)** is designed to link incompatible devices in a network by means of a single multichannel coaxial cable. Islands of automation will be interconnected for the electronic interchange of information about the product and process.

——Suppliers will use MAP to interconnect with General Motors offices. Indeed, firms that do not adopt this standard will be in jeopardy of being cut off as suppliers.

Flexible manufacturing systems will allow firms to restructure their production facilities quickly. Machines and tools will be readjusted automatically to perform a different task or to produce another product. The order of work will also be modified. All this can occur with little advance notice. The end result will be maximum operating efficiency as well as economies of scale even for short production runs.

Enterprisewide Information Systems Planning

In the future, organizations will develop strategies under which information systems are considered across the entire organization, not just for individual tasks. Many of the resources necessary to achieve this are coming into place. Database management systems, data communications methods, and enterprisewide systems planning provide the all-important foundation. The continuing emergence of data communications standards will further facilitate this trend.

One example is the just-in-time inventory concept. Instead of storing large quantities of products, parts, or materials, supplies will be delivered *to the company just before they are needed* (say, a day in advance). Inventory costs will be reduced dramatically, but this procedure will also improve quality control, since defective items can be detected when the items arrive, not after they have been in the warehouse for weeks or months.

To achieve just-in-time inventory management, organizations must coordinate marketing, product planning, manufacturing management, inventory control, and shop floor management. Information collected at all points will be communicated automatically to essential areas. This type of activity is not designed to eliminate people or jobs, but rather to make everyone more efficient.

In many instances, organizations will also form long-term partnerships with suppliers and customers. The General Motors MAP system mentioned earlier is a typical example. Suppliers will adapt to interact through GM's communications standard, since they will benefit as well as the automaker. However, the benefits will be realized over time, and because of the interdependence of systems, changes and modifications must be considered carefully, from all angles, before they are implemented. Because of the interdependence of customers and organizations, moreover, entire organizations will come to rely on one another for the communication of information and the delivery of services.

Expert Systems and Artificial Intelligence

Interest in expert systems and artificial intelligence—products now in their infancy—will mushroom. Stories of the usefulness of products are mounting, and the range of possible applications is broadening.

It appears that tools to help firms build *their own* expert systems will be an important growth area. These products will be made relatively easy to use while providing a great deal of power to those who must rely on them. They will facilitate the building of knowledge bases and inferencing procedures. This important capability will add credence to the premise that expert systems can allow individuals to shape information technology to meet their needs, rather than adjusting their requirements to fit the capabilities of the computer.

The methods for users to interface with information systems will also be influenced by artificial intelligence. Increasingly we will see methods emerging whereby computers adapt to their users, not vice versa. And as the users learn, the interface will change as well.

Many, many potential applications of artificial intelligence are in the offing. You can almost let your imagination run wild. Chances are, someone is working on products that are related to the ideas you have—computer vision, robotics, vehicle guidance systems, and so on. Ideas to exploit the power of the technology abound, but will they emerge in the form of useful products and services?

Artificial intelligence will be successful when it provides its users with improvements in productivity and effectiveness that are at least an order of magnitude higher than can be achieved without it. Productivity improvements of 20 to 30 percent may *not* be attractive enough to induce people to invest their money or their time in this facet of information systems.

These emerging technologies will influence day-to-day activities. However, they will also raise new management issues.

Information Management in the Future

The management of information systems will be a concern to organization managers for the remainder of the century. At the same time, organization management will benefit by greater participation in important decisions previously made by information systems managers.

Identifying the Business Value of Information Systems

With the increased use of information systems and the growing reliance on their capabilities for strategic purposes, executives want to know what they are getting from the investment their firms are making in information systems technology. In other words, they want to know what **business value** is accruing from the use of these systems.

Among the questions they ask are:

——How successful are we in the use of information systems? How do we gauge our success?

——What is our return on investment for information systems?

——How much does information systems contribute to the "bottom line"?

——How can we assess value from user-driven applications?

Information systems managers will be required to *demonstrate* the benefits of information systems to a skeptical corporate management—a request that is not unreasonable, but that is most assuredly a challenging one.

Identifying the business value generated from information systems will be a major topic of research and the subject of many consulting assignments as the 1990s begin. The answers that arise should prove most enlightening.

Senior Management Responsibilities

Many executives long believed that to manage information systems, they would have to become experts in the underlying computer and communications technology—something for which they had neither the time nor the interest. However, it is evident now that it is useful for managers to have significant involvement in systems development and use. Managing information systems is by no means confined to directing the area of information *technology*.

In the future, we should expect senior management to assume additional responsibility for information systems management. The following responsibilities will fall to senior managers:

——*Aligning information systems with organization objectives:* The most important objectives for the organization should also be the most important for the information systems group. Senior managers who are involved in formulation of organization plans will take greater responsibility for aligning goals for long-term benefit of the enterprise.

——*Planning for strategic information systems:* Strategic information systems, both within and between organizations, shape and support the competitive strategy of the organization and influence internal activities. Senior executives will increasingly leverage organization strategies and information systems strategies, using the information they obtain from their diverse contacts with customers, competitors, and associates.

——*Assessing information systems conformity to government regulations and corporate policy:* Senior managers, who are increasingly held accountable for violation of regulations regarding information systems, will formulate new and aggressive policies involving safeguarding personal information and the prevention of use of computer resources for unethical means or to gain unfair advantage. Senior managers will monitor conformity to the state and federal regulations that are bound to emerge, while seeing that corporate policies are in order.

——*Evaluating the benefits from the organization's investment in information systems:* Recognizing the significance of information systems as a corporate resource, and fully understanding the greater dependency on such systems than in the past, executives will face tough issues in assessing the value of their information systems investment. Their concern will lead to new procedures for assessing the economic benefit of developing and using information systems.

——*Evaluating the exposure to risk from information systems failure:* The proliferation of information systems usage, including end-user computing, many increase the gains a firm realizes. The same trend, however, increases a firm's risk if systems fail, either through excessive downtime or because of errors that go undetected. Stringent policies, guidelines, and certification procedures are likely to emerge, largely because senior management will insist on them.

Piecemeal systems development, common in the past, will gradually disappear, as organization managers for information systems enforce the same planning and control guidelines used in the traditional functions of business.

Evolving Responsibilities of Information Systems Managers

What issues are most important to information systems managers? A recent study by the Society for Information Management and the University of Minnesota's prestigious MIS Research Center identified the issues that preoccupy information systems managers (Table 21.5). As you examine the list, notice the ranking of the issues related to management and planning in contrast to those involving computer technology. The striking importance of organization issues is consistent with the emphasis we have placed on these concerns throughout the book. These issues are likely to dominate managerial efforts in the years to come.

The responsibilities of information systems managers will continue to decrease in technological orientation and to focus more heavily on management and organization skills. As summarized in Table 21.6, emphasis will shift from overseeing technology in a back-office capacity to managing key product lines; no longer computer experts pure and simple, information systems managers will develop entrepreneurial and organization skills. Future information systems managers will likely be candidates for top-management and chief executive officer posts, a rarity in the 1960s and 1970s.

Coupled with these changing responsibilities, we anticipate that some information systems managers in the future will come up through the departmental ranks. However, it is likely that a much greater proportion will assume this position after exercising other management responsibilities, perhaps as vice presidents in such other important functional areas as marketing, manufacturing, or finance.

Information Systems Career Expectations

The demand for information systems personnel continues to outstrip the supply. Educational programs at universities and colleges must keep expanding as these institutions seek to provide education and training for programmers, systems analysts, database specialists, operations personnel, and workers in other career areas related to computer information systems. The responsibilities and expectations for

Table 21.5 Most Important Issues to Information Systems and General Managers

Information Systems Manager	General Manager	
Rank	Rank	Issue
1	1	Improving information systems strategic planning
2	2	Using information systems for competitive advantage
3	3	Facilitating organizational learning and use of information systems
4	5	Increasing understanding of role and contribution of information systems
5	7	Aligning the information systems organization with that of the enterprise
6	6	Facilitating and managing end-user computing
7	8	Promoting effective use of the data resource
8	9	Developing an information architecture
9	4	Measuring information systems effectiveness and productivity
10	10	Integrating data processing, office automation, factory automation, and telecommunications
11	11	Planning, implementing, and managing telecommunications
12	13	Specifying, recruiting, and developing information systems human resources
13	12	Improving the effectiveness of software development
14	16	Enabling electronic data interchange and multivendor integration
15	NR	Managing the effect of artificial intelligence
16	15	Planning and managing the applications portfolio
17	14	Planning, implementing, and managing factory automation
18	NR	Improving information security and control
19	NR	Selecting and integrating packaged applications software
20	NR	Determining appropriate information systems funding levels

NR = not rated

Table 21.6 Evolving Role of Information Systems Manager

From	To
Overseer of technology	Diffuser of technology
Manager of technicians	Manager of key product lines and business activities
Responder to development requests	Identifier of business implications of technology
Responsible for a back-office function	Responsible for a strategic function with a path to top management
Holder of computer skills	Expert in entrepreneurial and organizational skills

all such personnel will increase because of the widespread dependence on the systems they develop.

We have already discussed the dramatic shift in involvement for senior managers. These other roles in the organization will increase in importance in the future:

——*End-users:* responsible for management of business units or for completion of operating activities; must have knowledge of business processes in which information is needed. End-users will interact with information systems to retrieve data and information stored in organization production systems and will use personal information systems to test alternative strategies and to develop information in an appropriate and useful form.

——*Information systems specialists:* responsible for determining requirements, designing systems features, selecting hardware and software, and implementing new or enhanced systems. Specialists must have in-depth knowledge of computer systems, telecommunications, and software technology, as well as an understanding of end-user business functions.

——*Functional-area analysts:* responsible for the development of requirements and implementation of new or enhanced systems. Working knowledge of information systems technology and in-depth knowledge of business functions is required; responsibility for operation of information centers may be included.

End-Users   The demand for **end-users,** and their responsibilities, have been discussed throughout the book. Computer literacy and the capability to use personal computers, spreadsheets, data management systems, and word processing packages will not be limited to information systems graduates; they will be fundamental skills mastered by graduates of business programs in general.

Information Systems Specialists   **Information systems specialists** are currently known as *systems analysts, systems designers, development specialists, information analysts,* and *programmer/analysts.* Traditionally a part of the organization's data processing or information systems group with responsibility for developing computer-based information systems for the functional areas of the organization, the information systems specialist is expected to possess technical expertise in computer hardware, software, data management, and communications functions, as well as working knowledge of selected business functions. The ability to interact with executives, managers, and staff members is essential.

Specialists in this area typically follow a career path centered around systems development activities. However, depending on industry and enterprise needs, well-qualified individuals assume substantial responsibilities for database development and management, telecommunications systems, and information resource management.

A typical educational curriculum for an information systems specialist will include programming language courses as well as coursework in the following areas:

——Computer information systems concepts

——Systems analysis and design

——Data communications

——Database management and design

——Data structures
——Software engineering
——Project management
——Management of information systems

Depending on the length of the program, advanced courses in these areas may also be provided. Graduates with this background will be employed by information systems departments.

Functional-Area Analysts With the increased use of computer information systems, and the availability of more powerful software, it appears that the functional areas of business will maintain staffs of trained systems professionals, called **functional-area analysts,** who are skilled both in information systems and in a specific business area. A broad business background, perhaps a major in a traditional area of business, will be augmented with courses in information systems. Functional-area analysts will receive training in a subset of the fields in which information systems specialists are educated (with only limited training in computer programming as we know it today). When they have completed their education, they will be hired to work in a department other than the information systems department.

The value of computer information systems as an organization resource will grow in importance in the future. But, like any resource, it is only as good as those who nurture and manage it. Therefore, there is little question that high-quality information systems personnel will be actively sought throughout the business environment.

Summary

Eight general trends are expected to affect the future of information technology, including the convergence of technologies, interoperability, simplicity, and disintermediation. We will also see a drive both toward and away from single standards, the creation of group systems, an increased focus on software, and a realization of the strategic value of computer networking.

The computer technology underlying information systems will continue to become cheaper and more powerful—trends that have been in place for several years. It is anticipated that the price of equipment will continue to drop in relation to performance at 20 to 30 percent annually. Semiconductor chips keep dropping in cost and in size. As a result, the product life for computers will be approximately three years and the equipment will be smaller but more powerful.

Secondary storage devices, although less expensive, will feature increased capacities. Optical disk storage will become a more important medium, as technology improvements increase the versatility of such devices. These improvements will be welcomed because of the constantly increasing demand for computer storage.

The functions of mainframe computers will include serving as data repositories and communications centers, as well as important resources for high volumes of transaction processing. The transaction processing function will not be moved over to microcomputers. Nor will superminis be supplanted by microcomputers; rather, they will occupy a special niche in computing—offering high-speed, specialized processing at attractive price levels.

Image processing will grow in importance in the future, made possible by advances in storage and processing capabilities. One of the most visible areas of impact will be as a replacement for the movement of documents in organizations. Instead images can be stored in the system and shared throughout the network.

End-user computing will play a much larger role in information systems in the future, both because of the accessibility of powerful computers and as a result of better, simpler software. In addition, functional-area analysts will reside in user departments to assist in the development of information systems applications. The need for information systems specialists will not, however, decrease as a result, since information systems will be even more pervasive in the organization.

A major question in the future will be how to demonstrate the business value created as a result of an organization's investment in information systems. Quantifying the value will occupy a great deal of time for both general and information systems managers.

Senior managers will take a larger and more significant role in the future as they link information systems and corporate plans to secure strategic advantage. At the same time, information systems managers will assume more important organizational roles, influencing the nature of business activities. Management of information systems has ceased to be limited to management of information technology, if indeed it ever was. In all respects, it is evident that computer information systems will be a critical resource for successful organizations of the future.

Key Words

Business value
Commercial database
  service
Computer-integrated
  manufacturing (CIM)
Disintermediation
End-user

Flexible manufacturing
  system
Functional-area analyst
Information systems
  specialist
Information utility
  structure

Interoperability
Manufacturing Automation
  Protocol (MAP)
Millions of Instructions Per
  Second (MIPS)
Price/performance
  relationship

Review Questions

1. What general trends characterize the expectations for information systems of the future?

2. What is disintermediation? Interoperability? What is the significance of each?

3. Why is software expected to play a larger role in the future of information systems?

4. How is computing power measured? How and why is its cost expected to change in the future?

5. "The usable lives of computers are decreasing." Do you agree or disagree with this statement? Explain the reason for your answer.

6. What are the most important changes in silicon chips as they pertain to computer systems and computer systems users?

7. At what rate is computer storage changing? What is the impact of this rate of change on data storage? Are data storage needs different today compared to a decade ago?

8. How will the function of mainframe computer systems change in the future? Will the number of mainframe computers installed increase, fall, or stay the same? Explain the reason for your answer.

9. What features distinguish superminicomputers from minicomputers and mainframe computers? What is the outlook for superminicomputer sales? How is this outlook explained?

10. What are the implications of linking organization strategies and information systems plans? How should this occur?

11. What problems do obsolete information systems currently pose for information systems managers? How have these problems arisen?

12. In what ways will the management of information systems change in the future?

13. What is the utility view of information systems? What assumptions underlie this view?

14. Image processing is expected to play a larger role in organizations in the future. Why is this the case? How will image processing be evident?

15. What roles will senior managers play in the management of information systems in the future? How is this change justified? Why has it not occurred before?

16. Will the responsibilities and the role of information systems managers be different in the future?

17. What is the outlook for careers in information systems?

18. How will the responsibilities of functional-area analysts differ from those of information specialists? What will functional-area analysts do that end-users will not be expected to do?

Application Problems

1. When planning new models of computer systems, vendors count on the organizations needing to increase their computing capacities. Typically, the need for both storage and processing power (MIPS) increases incrementally.

Considering the trends for end-user computing, communications and networking, personal computers, and new generations of software, is the need for increased computer storage likely to continue at current rates? Is the need for increased processing power within mainframes likely to continue to grow at current rates? Is the expectation for the power of personal computers likely to be the same as for mainframes?

2. Some senior managers are questioning whether their organizations are becoming overly dependent on computer and communications technology. They find that more computer-based intelligence is being built into products (for example, computer control systems in automobiles, production tools, and telephone systems) and that it is becoming virtually impossible to operate without such capability. Furthermore, managers increasingly have computers on their desks to perform financial analyses and evaluate alternative strategies. Even if these managers do not perform the analyses themselves, they use the computer output prepared by others.

At the same time, concern has been expressed regarding the reliability of computer-based systems. It is well known that computer software may contain errors that show up at inopportune times; worse yet, errors may go unnoticed.

Then too, the costs of maintaining computer-based systems are generally higher than those associated with manual or mechanical methods, and many more things can go wrong.
   a. Are organizations overly vulnerable to the failure of information systems due to their increased reliance on such systems? Explain.
   b. Do you agree or disagree with the notion that more can go wrong in computer-based systems than manual systems? Why or why not?

3. The number of personal computers installed in organizations is continually increasing. The cost of a personal computer is relatively low; however, some managers who must approve their firm's investment in a large number of such systems are questioning the wisdom of the overall investment. One manager calculated her firm's investment in hardware and software for personal computers and determined that the total expenditure equaled what would have been needed to purchase a mainframe system. She also pointed out that the mainframe has greater processing speed, memory, and storage capacity than the personal computer.
   a. If an organization's expected total investment in personal computers equals the cost of mainframe hardware and software, which option should be taken— a single large system or many small computers? Why?
   b. What components comprise the full cost of a single personal computer?

Minicase: Let's Wait

James Bartle, Vice President for Administration, must decide. Should the company begin installation of a local-area network to link all administrative offices, or should it wait? This is the single most important decision the VP will make all year.

Bartle is toying with the idea of linking 12 departments to share data and to facilitate electronic mail. He believes there are advantages to sharing such hardware as laser printers and color graphics devices, even though the departments have not had a great deal of experience with networking or personal computing.

Each of the departments, however, has been exposed successfully to a limited number of personal computers and to the company's large mainframe systems. The employees generally like to use the systems, which allow them to be more productive and to have information available when they need it—important benefits for any organization considering an investment in computer information systems.

The mainframe applications generally support overall corporate day-to-day operations, such as order processing, inventory management, and accounting. The dozen or so personal computers that have been installed are used for spreadsheet analysis and for some word processing. They are busy a large portion of each business day.

Given these successes, and the apparent lack of resistance by end-users to the firm's information systems, you might wonder why Bartle is pondering the networking decision. Here is what he said recently in a meeting about the decision:

> The cost of information systems is dropping rapidly—at least 25 percent annually. In addition, computers are getting smaller and faster. If we decide to proceed now, we will be making a large investment in the local-area network, buying approximately 200 personal computers, as well as printers and communications systems. The company will also have to buy a large quantity of software packages, either individually or through site licensing. Systems will have to be installed and users trained.
>
> The advances in computer technology producing the lower prices and better performance levels are expected to continue. Therefore, if we wait until next year or the year after, we will have an even better system. In fact, there is a good chance that if we install the

network system this year, it will be nearly obsolete two years from now.

> I believe an investment today would pay for itself within roughly 18 months, even though we do not have much networking experience with personal computers. But if we wait, the payback period will be even less and the hardware and software will be more powerful. This is the darndest decision I have ever had to make.

There is little question about the feasibility of the networking design and operation. All parties believe the network capabilities will function effectively and that the system will work. Moreover, the firm can well afford the purchase. Some managers, however, wonder whether the firm has enough experience with personal computers and electronic mail to warrant such an investment. That caution, coupled with the knowledge that systems will be cheaper, faster, and better next year, has been the basis for the dilemma Bartle must address.

Questions

1. Do you recommend that Bartle proceed, or wait for the anticipated price/performance improvements to occur? What reasons underlie your recommendations?

2. How significant is the company's limited experience with networking and personal computers? Should this issue alone cause the firm to wait? If so, how do you recommend the firm acquire experience without investing in a network?

3. Do the expected improvements in price/performance relationships apply equally to hardware, software, and communications technology?

Minicase

And so the discussant at the meeting went on:

"The facts are pretty clear:

——A large variety of reliable and relatively inexpensive software is available off-the-shelf for both personal computers and large systems.

——The technology of information systems is becoming much easier to use than ever before. Windows, menu-driven systems—all much simpler than previous methods of interacting with systems before.

——Standards are emerging to guarantee that computers can interconnect with networks and communicate with other systems.

——Tools are being created that allow individuals to generate their own software, eliminating the need for custom programming.

——End-user computing has proved very successful, showing that ordinary people can master computers and use them in meaningful ways.

——Senior managers now understand better than ever before that they must play a role in the development of their firm's information systems.

"I would say these are pretty exciting times to be investing in information technology. The benefits are growing and the successes of the past will pale compared to those that we will have in the future.

"Of course, if you are an information systems professional—you know, a computer person—you probably look at it differently. I don't see much need for a person like yourself in the future. Do you?"

Questions

1. If the trends in information systems (for example, simpler systems, abundant software, disintermediation, and so on) continue, will end-users be able to take over the role of developing and managing information systems?

2. What is the future role of the information systems professional? Will such persons become unnecessary, or at least necessary in fewer numbers?

Case Study Module

Sono Electronics Corporation

Sono Electronics Corporation was organized 25 years ago as a wholesale distributor of electronic products for radio and television dealers and repair shops. Over the years, it took on the retail merchandising character it now has, distributing a broad line of home entertainment products, stereo systems, televisions, radios, and repair and hobbyist parts. Approximately 7 years ago, Sono became a wholly owned subsidiary of the Midwest Commercial Holding Company, but to date its operation has remain largely unchanged. At the present time, however, Midwest is examining the entire operating procedure of Sono Electronics for purposes of trimming costs and increasing profitability (see Exhibit 1).

An Overview of Sono Electronics

Sono Electronics operates under the franchise concept. Of the current 60 stores, 54 are independently owned by individual businesspeople in major cities throughout the Midwest, West, Southwest, and Pacific Northwest. These independent owners procure almost all (approximately 90 percent) of their merchandise from the central Sono office, while the remaining store stock is purchased from rack jobbers in the owner's immediate geographical area. By purchasing the bulk of their stock from the central offices of Sono, individual franchised dealers are able to take advantage of large-quantity discounts obtained by the corporation's buying team. Also, individual owners benefit from extensive localized advertising and promotional activities of Sono.

Six of the 60 stores are wholly owned by Sono Electronics. In each case, the stores were acquired from individual owners who had run into financial difficulties for one reason or another and therefore could no longer sustain their business operations. Rather than have these six stores go out of business, Sono's central management purchased the stock and facilities and kept each one in operation at an acceptable level of profitability. It is not the intent of corporate management, however, to operate their own stores except in exceptional cases of this nature.

All individual stores are supplied from a single, centrally located warehouse. Individual stores order on a weekly basis from the warehouse, and items are subsequently shipped by truck from the warehouse to the stores some 3 days after receipt of the order at the warehouse. The ordering process will be examined in greater detail in the section on current operations.

Exhibit 1 Financial Statement for 19XX

OPERATIONS

		PER SHARE	
Net sales	$56,780,720	Earnings	.50
Gross profit	16,630,850	Dividends	.10
Income before taxes	5,942,370	Shareholders' equity	3.36
Net income	3,144,320		

FINANCIAL POSITION

RATIOS

		Gross profit/sales	29.3%
Accounts receivable	9,102,360	Income before taxes/sales	10.5%
Inventories and supplies	11,423,490	Net income/sales	5.5%
Current assets	22,690,280	Sales/average total assets	1.8x
Current liabilities	6,740,180	Sales/average shareholders' equity	2.9x
Working capital	15,950,100	Cost of goods sold/average inventory	3.5x
Fixed assets	10,972,720	Net income/average total assets	9.7%
Other assets	700,060	Net income/average shareholders' equity	16.0%
Long-term debt	6,637,520	Current assets/current liabilities	3.4x
Shareholders' equity	20,985,360	Long-term debt/capitalization	24.0%
Total assets	34,363,060	Accounts receivable/sales	16.0%

Sono Electronics plans to double the number of stores in the chain during the next 5-year period. The intent in this expansion is to continue to develop individually owned stores, concentrating on the suburban areas around major cities in the geographical regions where Sono now operates. Regional warehousing has been considered for the point in time when the number of stores doubles, but no definite plans in this direction have yet been made.

Sono Electronics considers the primary responsibilities to the franchises to include: (1) securing satisfactory store sites; (2) preparing stores for business operations; (3) providing franchisee training; (4) providing merchandise for franchise sales efforts; and (5) providing support in ensuing business operations.

Characteristics of Current Operations

Sono Electronics maintains a catalog of approximately 10,000 different items, each of which can be ordered by individual stores from the 70-page merchandise catalog/order form. All stock items are stored in the single, central warehouse facility, under the control of the warehouse foreman, Ron Stanton. Mr. Stanton is well liked by all persons under his supervision and is thought by management to be very effective in his job. Management further feels that his close and amicable relationship with his employees is a valuable asset in terms of inventory control procedures. In other words, management is confident that there is virtually no pilferage or stealing of merchandise because employees fear such actions would lose them Stanton's respect and/or friendship as well as a good job.

Maintenance of inventory stock status is through a totally manual system involving separate ledger cards for each catalog item. The ledger cards, which are coded by use of colored ink, are maintained by one person in the Accounting Department. Any changes in stock status, whether it be withdrawal of items from the warehouse, ordering of merchandise, receipt from the vendor, or placing of an item on backorder, are entered on the ledger card in an appropriate colored ink. At the end of the month all transactions are tallied and a new balance of stock determined. The new balance is entered on a new ledger card to begin the following month. A sample ledger card is shown in Exhibit 2.

Inventory control is also a problem because of the infrequent physical count of merchandise on hand. Currently, a complete item-by-item count is performed only once a year. Certain personnel may request a physical count or even go into the warehouse to check on stock levels themselves, but neither of these steps is taken very often. Consequently, Sono updates its ledger cards by write-offs, and so on, only once a year. They do not know when or why the discrepancies occur between quantities shown in the records to be in the warehouse and those quantities actually on hand.

Purchasing

In the procurement section, each of the seven purchasing agents is responsible for a specific group of stock items and support of separate product lines. Since the purchasing agent is the individual who is familiar with vendor characteristics and lead times for the specific products, he or she is the sole person who determines the quantities, order dates, and suppliers for a given purchase. No one else writes purchase orders for materials in a given area of responsibility, and likewise, each purchasing agent refrains from writing orders in anyone else's area.

When a purchasing agent reviews the inventory records or the stock ledger cards and realizes that stock of a particular item must be ordered, he or she writes a purchase order and has it formally entered on a numbered purchase order form by the typists in the secretarial pool. A copy of the order is then sent to accounting for posting of ledger cards, to receiving, and of course to the vendor. The fourth copy is returned to the buyer for his or her records. The buyer's copy is important because it makes the quantity of a particular item on order and when it is due in clear at all times. The determination of when to reorder is based almost entirely on the judgment of the responsible buyer since standard reorder points or times are not used in Sono's purchasing department.

Exhibit 2 Tab Sheet

Part number	Carried forward
9V91	*1954*

/- 8 - 3 -/2 - 36- 6 - 20 - /2 - / - 8 - 40 - 60 - 6 - 2 - 24 -
-/8 - 6 - 20 -/2 - 8 -/2 - 8 - 54 - 24 - /2 - /3 - 4 - /2 - /8 - /6 -
-/2 - 8 - /2 - 4 -/2 - 24 - 8 - 8 - /2 - 24 - 4 -/2 - 8 -/6 - 7 - / -
-/2 - /2 - 4 - 4 - /- 4 - 2 - 4 - 8 -40 - / - / - /0 - /2 - 4 - 40 -
-5 - 24 -/2 - /2 - 8 - 6 - 2 - /2 - 6 - 8 - 6 - /2 - 36 - /6 -
-5 - /2 - 3 - /2 - 8 - 80 - /2 - 30 - 4 - /5 - /2 - 24 - / -
-/2 - /2 - /2 - 6 - 8 - 8 - 20 - 7 - 36 - /2 - /2 - /0 - /2 - 8 -
-/2 - 4 - /2 - / - 2 - 4 - 24 - /2 - 6 - 4 - /2 - 4 - 4 - 24 -
-/2 - 8 - 4 - 8 - 4 - 8 - 4 - 24 - 4

Cancel 96   (554)   (302) Physical 216

SONO ELECTRONICS CORP.

The part/item number identification system causes confusion at times in both the purchasing process and the order-filling routine. Sono relies solely on product numbers assigned to individual items by the vendors or manufacturers. Because of the diversity of vendors and product number systems, errors can occur quite easily in order writing and/or filling. Management is not satisfied with its reliance on vendor product numbers but has not taken any definitive steps to correct the situation.

Order Processing

Order processing of stock requests from franchised dealers is performed manually. On an order form approximately 70 pages long (see Exhibit 3) dealers indicate, alongside the printed item number, the quantity they wish to order, if any, and any items they wish to backorder (if the items are known to be out of stock in the warehouse). When the orders arrive each week at Sono headquarters, the credit manager checks the store's credit status and approves the order. If the credit status of a store is questionable, the order form is manually extended and the credit manager makes a final approval/disapproval decision when the exact amount of the order is known.

Exhibit 3 Page from Order Form

PANASONIC (PAN)		PANASONIC (PAN)	
Tape Recorders		**Comp. receivers**	
RQ-2043	22.00	SA-40	133.17
RQ-2033	49.10	SA-6500	232.54
RQ-209A3	28.10		
		Compacts	
NEW PRODUCT 3/29 3C			
POP-UP CASSETTE RE-		SC-555A	163.40
CORDER AC/DC OPERATED		SC-666	215.99
✓ RQ-222A3	52.06		
		PE (PE)	
RQ-2263	35.21		
RS-256U3	61.42	SPECIAL PROMOTION	
RS 257S	196.39		
RS-250S	136.78	PROMOTION WILL END	
RS 801	35.08	WHEN STOCK IS DEPLETED	
RS-803US	70.23	PE-202)S	57.15
RS-820S	202.28		
		Turntables	
Tape Recorder Access.			
		PE-2035	56.17
RP-910	16.25	PE-2038	69.07
RP-932	7.03	PE-2040	86.23
RP-949	3.47		
RP-963	3.27	**Accessories**	
RP-992	3.58		
RP-8130	7.05	NEW PRODUCT 3/29 D	
		BASE FOR PE-2038	
Phonographs		✓ BV-38	6.39
SE-340	90.45	NEW PRODUCT 3/29 D	
SE-850	127.25	BASE FOR PE-2040	
SE-970	127.10	✓ BV-40	6.39
SE-990	140.27		
SE-1519	155.29	CS-1820	4.51
SS-515	49.23		
SS-674	70.30	NEW PRODUCT 3/29 B	
SS-999	139.35	CARTRIDGE SLIDE FOR	
		MODEL PE-2038	
Tape decks		✓ CS-2038	4.08
RS-736US	191.58	NEW PRODUCT 3/29 B	
RS-768US	102.02	CARTRIDGE SLIDE FOR	
RS-796US	136.05	MODEL PE-2040	
		✓ CS-2040	4.08

When credit is approved for an order, the order form is so marked and sent to the warehouse, where it is filled from inventory. Photocopies are then made of the entire order form and are enclosed in the shipping cartons as a packing slip. Nearly all 60 stores submit an order at the beginning of each week.

Accounting

After the order form has been photocopied the original copy is sent to the accounting department, where it is manually extended and totaled. Next a cover invoice is prepared. One copy is sent to the dealer and the other is used to update accounts receivable records. All receivable posting is on a Burroughs posting machine and is the responsibility of one person in the department. Payments to accounts are posted in the same manner and summary statements are prepared periodically. At the present time, the posting machine appears to be utilized to its capacity.

The source documents for accounts payable are a combination of Sono's purchase orders, the vendor packing lists, and the vendor invoices. The vendor packing list is sent to accounts payable from the warehouse after the merchandise has been received and checked in. The purchase order and packing lists are used by the accounts payable clerk to verify the accuracy of the vendor's invoice when it is received. Any discrepancy in pricing or in units received is corrected by Sono's issuance of a debit or credit memo to the vendor. The invoice is then approved for payment and filed according to due date.

Sono Electronics pays its vendors twice monthly, on the 10th and 25th of each month. Cash discounts are *always* taken, even though the discount period may have ended before payment is made. The 130 vendors who supply Sono do not have uniform terms for either cash discounts or due dates. Sono also receives late dating or special purchase terms quite frequently. On occasion, the company has *charged* a vendor for extra time spent by its personnel in correcting errors on the vendor's invoice.

Factors for Consideration in MIS Development

Both because of strong encouragement from the parent corporation and as a result of identified growth plans, Sono Electronics wishes to integrate the computer into its operation. In essence, Sono has been directed emphatically to develop a computer-based management information system for both planning and control. The design should entail more than mere automation of clerical activities. A number of areas have been pinpointed as being particularly important for incorporation into an MIS design.

Improved Inventory Control

Sono operates on the basis of, and centers its activities around, the merchandise specified in its 10,000-item catalog. Consequently, it may be surmised that a means of accurately monitoring and controlling the amount of merchandise on hand in its warehouse is one of the keys to the corporation's successful and profitable operation. With projected sales of approximately $65 million in the next fiscal year, coupled with 60 corporate or franchised stores marketing the total product mix out of a single warehouse, Sono must be able to access timely and accurate operating information. Further, it must be able to provide its buyers with the same information on a periodic basis.

Some of the primary goals in this area are maintaining satisfactory stock levels, developing a consistent and uniform method for identifying catalog items, and ensuring a more accurate accounting for merchandise quantities either on hand in inventory or withdrawn from inventory. A more accurate means of accounting for merchandise damaged or pilfered from inventory storage is also needed.

Profitability Analysis

In a field of merchandising such as the electronics industry, where a significant amount of competition exists and where the underlying technology is changing rapidly, it is important to know which items or product lines contribute the most to profits. Sono needs a means for continually identifying and monitoring fast-moving items and high-margin products in its product mix. It is also important to be able to monitor store activities continuously. When a store starts to move into a dangerous financial position, whether due to a poor product mix, slumping sales due to its physical location, or just plain poor management, Sono wants to be able to offer whatever assistance is needed to keep the dealer in business and to increase profits. Consequently, early awareness of individual store difficulties is essential for corporate management.

Planning Information

One of the potentially most valuable considerations of MIS development is how the system will support Sono's strategic planning activities. With the tremendous emphasis on growth during the next 5-year planning horizon, the need to have meaningful planning information available becomes all the more crucial. Of particular interest is the need to have information available on such wide-ranging issues as geographical areas ripe for franchised outlets, key promotional considerations for various kinds of products, and profitability (or nonprofitability) potential of specific product groups. Additionally, corporate management could benefit greatly from planning information on optimal store mixes. In other words, what assortment of merchandise is optimal for new store openings?

Operational Considerations

An MIS for Sono could assist greatly in several areas at the operational level. Stream-lining of both the ordering and billing processes could cut expenses and overhead significantly. Further, it might be possible to automate certain parts of the purchasing process. Identification of these areas and development of automation methods is an important, and not simple, task. Mechanisms might also be developed for the addition of new items and the deletion of discontinued products in the merchandise catalog. Price changes also present problems when they occur for a large number of items.

Design and Implementation of an MIS

Although management of Sono Electronics seems to be regarding development and installation of an MIS in a favorable light, no commitment has yet been made. Further, it must be remembered that the present top management developed many of the procedures that are in use currently. These procedures were instrumental in the company's success and growth, and the company is still making money by using them today. The parent company is the instigator of a large number of the possible changes discussed on the preceding pages, which may pose something of a problem when it comes time to accept a design and allocate funds for its development.

There is little question that a true management information system would be a significant asset to Sono Electronics Corporation. However, the acceptance and success of the system will depend on the particular design chosen and the way it is presented to the management and employees of the company and to key representatives of the Midwest Commercial Holding Company.

This case was prepared for class discussion rather than to illustrate either effective or ineffective handling of an administrative situation. The situation is a real one but the names of the company and its employees have been changed. Any similarity of name with existing business organizations is unintentional and by coincidence.

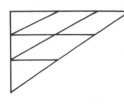

The Electron Corporation, Electrical Products Division

"You know, Denny, development and installation of any facet of an information system is an important and intricate operation in an organization as large as EPD. I think we have accomplished the task quite effectively with our shop floor data system, with a minimum disruption to personnel and procedures. Nonetheless, I'd like to evaluate our effort in some way to determine if its effectiveness is as high as we think it is."

"I agree, Tom, but you know, we have developed and installed a well-functioning system. I would hate to do something now that would disrupt the process, and an evaluation of the sort I think you are implying might do just that. As soon as you start poking around asking the people on the floor if they like the system or if there is something they would like to see improved, they start to wonder if something is wrong or if there is something they should object to but haven't realized yet. That is about the way I will state my feelings on this matter during our meeting Friday."

Tom Waterford, Manager of Information Systems at the Electrical Products Division (EPD) of the Electron Corporation, was recalling quite vividly the conversation he had had the day before with Denny Barkin, Director of Industrial Relations. He was confident that the system he had so painstakingly designed and installed was working properly in the areas of the production floor where it had been implemented. And yet, he wanted to find out if improvement were possible in the future installations. But perhaps Denny had a point. Poking around asking a lot of questions and encouraging suggestions might indeed create suspicions on the part of the workers. How could he determine if this would happen without actually sticking his neck out and beginning a study? On the other hand, how could he examine the impact of the system without doing some sort of evaluation that would involve the workers? Somehow he had to come up with a resolution for dealing with this issue. The Production Management Group would be meeting at 1:00 P.M. tomorrow and had this item at the top of the agenda.

Electron/Electrical Products Division

The Electron Corporation's Electrical Products Division, located in Ithaca, New York, is one of the largest manufacturing firms in the Tompkins, Broome, and Cortland county area of New York's southern tier. Currently it employs a work force of approximately 3500 employees. With the exception of about 200 employees at the division's two branch plants and sales personnel who staff field offices throughout the country, most of the division's employees live within a 50-mile radius of Ithaca. Electron employees live in more than 40 communities in Tompkins, Broome, and Cortland Counties—and some even come from neighboring Tioga County, a 60-minute drive away.

Dennis Barkin, Director of Industrial Relations, often comments that one of the reasons for the success of the division over its history has been its reliance on the "solid citizens" of the area. Also, Electron treats its people fairly, going out of its way to make the division a firm they can be proud of and from which they can earn a good living. In turn, the workers give "a fair day's work for a fair day's pay." It is not uncommon to find two generations of the same family employed by the EPD, a factor most attribute to the concern the division has for its employees and the fair treatment the workers continually receive from EPD.

How It All Started

The division has branch plants located in Madison, Wisconsin, and Muncie, Indiana, and a current payroll of over $30 million a year. But of course the division was not always this large.

Electron/Electrical Products Division can trace its beginning to the invention of a revolutionary type of aircraft magneto by a group of Swiss engineers during World War I. Until then, magnetos had always been built in the same old way: A coil and breaker assembly spun furiously around inside fixed magnets. Since these fragile assemblies often self-destructed, the subtle Swiss turned everything around: They let the sturdy magnets do all the spinning and kept the more fragile coils anchored in a stationary position. The new magneto made aviation history.

The Swiss electrical firm that developed the magneto opened a sales agency in New York City in 1921. The aviation industry was still just a fledgling, however, and business was far from brisk. The first upturn came when the U.S. Navy became interested in a better type of aircraft magneto. However, the interest was conditional; the Navy didn't want to be dependent on a foreign source of supply, and the Swiss were requested to establish an American manufacturing facility.

The search for a suitable site led to Ithaca. The nearby Catskill Mountains, generously sprinkled with sparkling streams and the Finger Lakes, were somewhat reminiscent of their own native Switzerland. Soon after visiting the area, management decided to set up shop in the wooden buildings of a defunct automobile company, and the business of building American-made aircraft magnetos was finally under way in 1925. The company's first Ithaca payroll numbered only 14 employees, including the officers.

The Electron Corporation, founded by Arnold Carter, began a series of acquisitions in the late 1920s and early 1930s that included the first of more than 100 companies, corporations, and partnerships that have since evolved into the highly scientific and technological corporation Electron is today. The Sparkler Magneto Company became part of the Electron organization in 1929. Originally a subsidiary, the company became a division of the corporation in 1939.

The new magneto was used by Electron until just a few years ago. The Magneto Division's name was changed at that time to Electrical Products Division, a name more descriptive of the wide diversity of products currently in production at the plant in Ithaca.

EPD and its predecessor organizations have now conducted business operations in Ithaca for more than a half century, on the site formerly occupied by the Acme Cart & Carriage Co. and later by the Juneau Automobile Company. Earlier residents of Ithaca would hardly recognize the place, however. The old, wooden Juneau Building that originally housed the division has long since been replaced by a modern, one-story structure of brick and steel. Seven acres of modern machinery and precision industrial equipment are housed in a spacious plant that covers a total floor area of more than 650,000 square feet.

The Production Line

The business of Electron in Ithaca began with an aircraft magneto, and EPD is still making aircraft magnetos. Today, however, the division makes complete ignition systems for a wide range of aircraft, industrial, and maritime applications. Electron ignition parts are now used on every type of aircraft from the smallest monoplane to the newest and largest jumbo jets such as the DC-10 airbus. For years Electron/ Electrical Products has led the entire industry in the development of new turbine ignition products and advanced concepts. Today, it is believed to be the world's leading supplier of gas turbine ignitions.

Electrical Connectors The division's biggest product line is electrical connectors. In fact, Electron is one of the world's largest manufacturers of these devices, which provide a fast, reliable means of connecting electrical circuits of all types in aircraft, automobile vehicles, space systems, ships, ground support equipment, electronic gear, and scientific instruments. Interconnections for dozens of circuits are often contained within a single plug and receptacle arrangement.

Electron has maintained a position of technical dominance in the cylindrical connector field since the early 1950s, pioneering in the introduction of miniature cylindricals. Designs developed by Electron have frequently become the accepted standard for the entire connector industry.

Diesel Fuel Injection Equipment Electron has also been a manufacturer of diesel fuel injection equipment in Ithaca since 1937. Applications for this equipment include large diesel locomotives, heavy construction machinery, farm tractors, generating stations, pipeline pumping installations, and oceangoing ships—almost anyplace where large diesel engines are used.

Micropackaging Products In today's world of microelectronics, chip-size circuitry often has thousands of electronic parts in an area no larger than a match tip. This chip-size circuitry has to have a means of getting to the outside world; micropackaging is the way it's done. The miniature circuits are enclosed in hermetically sealed flat-packs that provide protection and also enable the microelectronic circuits to be connected to a circuitboard.

Electron/EPD has recently intensified its activities in this field with the development of new micropackaging concepts and high-seal yield techniques.

New Opportunities

The trend of business activity at EPD is increasingly commercial. Divisional management is continuing an intensive effort to develop new opportunities as a means of lessening the division's dependence on government-funded programs.

An increasing number of commercial applications also require more sophisticated types of electrical connectors. The division's marketing department is focusing special attention on these opportunities. Markets for electrical connectors today are likely to include such varied applications as machine tool tape controls, hospital patient care systems, portable television cameras, medical electronic equipment, and audio systems in performing arts theaters.

Operation of the Data Collection System

The new data collection system was designed to replace a 40-year-old system that required the manual completion of time cards for all job and machine activities. Although the system served very well for most of its duration, it became obsolete with the tremendous growth in the company. For a time, consideration was given to revising the manual system to make it responsive to management's needs. However, such an overhaul did not appear to be financially feasible. The system had clearly been outgrown by the expanded activities at EPD. Instead, management indicated, a revolutionary change was needed.

Design specifications for a new system were drawn up and contract bids elicited. The contract was awarded to Data Collection, Inc., a company that specializes in shop floor data collection systems of this type.

The new system is designed to focus on labor and attendance reporting, primarily for the hourly employees. In order for the employees to interact with the system, each is provided with a new identification card. The card is essentially a badge containing information about the employee (such as name, identification number, and job title) recorded on a magnetic strip of tape on the back of the card.

Each machine in the shop is also assigned an identification number. As employees move from station to station, they insert their identification cards into the data collection station, and then enter the number of the machine they are working on, the amount of material used, the number of finished items produced, and the start and finish times.

The result is that management can automatically collect data on employee performance. This assists in determining wages, which are paid on a piece-rate basis, and in determining the flow of material through the production system. Additionally, information is collected on machine performance, so that a badly worn or poorly adjusted machine can be detected before it leads to excess material or labor costs. Finally, the data collected are useful in determining production schedules and checking adherence to the schedules. Much of this was possible under the old manual process, but because of the immense amounts of time and paperwork required, it was not practical to collect the data.

Implementation of the Shop Floor Control System

Key EPD management and systems personnel who were involved in the implementation of the data collection system believe that five major factors are responsible for an exceptionally high level of acceptance of the new system by employees and management of the division. These five factors are: (1) thorough planning, (2) organization, (3) good communication, (4) training/orientation, and (5) monitoring/feedback and follow-up.

Beginning Discussions

Discussions regarding development of the system began almost a full year prior to the first training session conducted for employees. Meetings continued from that point on, increasing in frequency 5 months before the first training sessions. Indicative of the extent of the planning involved, 27 *major* shop floor control system meetings were held between December 17 and January 30.

Planning involved both early briefing of top management and orientation of manufacturing management personnel in order to introduce and familiarize everyone concerned with the philosophy and basic principles behind the purpose and need for a shop floor control system at EPD.

Communication to Employee Units

In a project as immense as implementation of a shop floor system, communication with all parties affected is critical. Realizing this, the members of the systems and management groups responsible for the system conducted many meetings with diverse employee units.

Union officials were contacted early in the planning phase of the project, and well in advance of the first training session. The union president, business representative, and chief stewards were all given briefings early in the planning phases of the program—six weeks in advance of the first notice to employees. The operation of the system and use of the data collection terminals were explained, and a lengthy period of questions and answers followed.

A bulletin board announcement in the form of a "Notice to All Employees" was posted on March 11. Consistent with communication practices at EPD, advance copies were sent to all management personnel. Careful attention was given to the wording of the notice, which emphasized that the data collection system was being installed as a means of improving the efficiency of the complex business and would enable the division to be more competitive. (A copy of the bulletin board announcement is shown in Exhibit 1.)

The next step in the communication process involved distribution of a "Data Collection System" brochure. The brochure was written especially for employees to explain in basic terms what the system was, why it was needed, and what some of the advantages of converting to such a system were. All attempts were made to remove any technical "systems language" that might be confusing to nonsystems personnel; the brochure was not about computers.

The brochure was illustrated with contemporary-style cartoons, and the text was intentionally kept as short as possible and prepared for easy readability. The brochures were prepared and printed in plant. They were distributed with a transmittal memo to all employees through departmental supervisors.

Training Sessions

A well-conceived training and orientation program was developed, and a series of sessions started on May 9. The first of these were presentations for the general manager and staff, as well as for the superintendents, general foremen, and foremen.

Union officials and members of the Grievance Committee participated in a training session on May 13. The meetings for both management and the union representatives were held prior to the scheduling of training sessions for factory and supporting department employees.

Between May 9 and May 13, fourteen sessions were held and approximately 350 people were introduced to the shop floor control system. These training sessions are still in process, and a new series starts two months from now, as the system is implemented in additional departments.

The training sessions begin with introductory remarks by the training supervisor and include a televised, taped presentation by the general manager of EPD. Information systems management personnel handle the actual training, which includes a demonstration of the data collection terminal, as well as an opportunity for each person to operate a terminal.

Since the introduction of the system, a full-time management person has been appointed to ensure continued success with its implementation. Thirty-four departments will eventually use the system, including 1200 production workers and 1000 staff and overhead personnel. The latter are paid on an hourly basis. To date, 17 of the 34 departments have been put on to the system.

Evaluation of the System

As Tom sat in his office thinking over Denny's comments, his mind wandered back over the project and the success achieved to date. Of the departments in the plant who would be using the system, 17 had already been converted. Both workers and management wanted to move faster on the new system cutover, but they had been

Exhibit 1 The Bulletin Board Announcement of the New System

The Electron Corporation
ELECTRICAL PRODUCTS DIVISION

NOTICE TO ALL EMPLOYEES

In order to improve the efficiency of our very complex business and, as a result, be more competitive, we are preparing to install a new system of labor and attendance reporting to be used primarily by hourly employees.

This new system is known as a "Data Collection System." It takes advantage of the many advances in computer capability and will provide us with more accurate and timely information that will enable us to improve our planning, scheduling, and controls.

In the near future, you will see the installation of devices known as terminals in a few departments. A terminal is easy to operate and enables employees to report labor information and attendance directly to a computer rather than filling in job cards and ringing an attendance card. Such equipment is widely used in industry today.

The conversion to this new system will require several months and will be accomplished on a gradual basis. Before the system becomes operational in a department, all employees concerned will be scheduled to attend orientation and training sessions to become fully acquainted with the equipment and its use.

A new type of badge will be required for use with the system. Prior to the activation of the equipment in a department, new badges will be issued for all employees in that department. A new type of Hourly Lost Time Card will also become effective with the new system.

During the conversion period to the new system, your full cooperation will be very much appreciated. This is a very significant step forward in the operation of our business and is very necessary as we look to the future.

L. D. Sturgis

L. D. Sturgis
General Manager

March 11, 19XX
To: All Exempt Salaried Personnel
Copies of the above notice will be posted on all bulletin boards today.
D. Barkin

forced to wait for the remainder of the equipment. Serious delivery problems had been encountered and the rest of the equipment had just not come in from the vendor. The workers were especially eager to get going. He specifically remembered his frequent trips through the shop and the comments and questions he received from the production people: "When am I going to get on the system? . . . Are you mad at me?" or "The project that I am working on will be finished soon. What happens then? Do I get a new ID card or do I have to go back to the old system?"

Yes, the project was going along quite well. Both the men and the women on the floor appeared enthusiastic about the system. There were more women on the production equipment now than there had been any time since World War II. Further, they seemed to catch on to the new data collection system faster than the men. And it was probably their greater finger dexterity that made it easier for them to operate the keyboard on the data colletion terminals.

Prior to installation of the new system, one timekeeper had been required for every 100 people. Now there was one timekeeper for every 250 people, and yet the effectiveness with which project/machine times could be monitored had significantly improved.

The new system had drastically reduced the keypunching problem, too. Prior to introduction of the system, Tom recalled, the card volume had been in excess of 80,000 per week. Three full shifts of keypunchers had been required; now only two shifts of data entry personnel were needed.

The data collection system had replaced a 40-year-old system. Half of the benefits of the new system could have been accomplished by revising the old system, but management would not approve work on the old system. They had wanted revolution, not evolution!

Tom believed the division's adjustment to—and even dependence on—the new system had been demonstrated a few months before. One department had been using the new system for just 3 weeks. Yet when the data collection system failed, they couldn't go back to the old manual system; they had forgotten how to use it.

But the real reason the system had been so successful, he thought, might be its tie to the payroll. EDP uses both a piece rate and a group rate, along with a variety of incentives. For a while there had been a constraint on how much workers could produce—they would not be paid for anything in excess of 150 percent of the expected rate. But that had been changed 4 years ago to "no limit." An increase in production was slow in coming since workers generally avoided rate busting. But it was occurring now.

There were instances of production banking in some departments prior to the installation of the new system. However, with the data collection system this was not now possible. Had this caused dissatisfaction among the workers? Management didn't think so.

The good relationship between the workers and management of EDP was fairly evident. There had been only one strike in the history of the plant, and management and the International Machinists Union had always avoided a strike. Also, EPD was among the top in the region and nation in zero defect programs. The division had already received the Department of Defense Craftsman Award and was well on its way to receiving a Sustained Craftsman Award.

After recalling all of these details about the system, Tom turned his attention back to the evaluation problem. Less than 24 hours remained until the Production Management Group would meet. Should he push for an evaluation? Or should he continue his efforts for further implementation, assuming that everything would continue to move along smoothly?

A Proposal

After spending the rest of the day rolling back and forth on the idea of a systems evaluation effort, he decided that perhaps Denny was right. Now, this morning, right after coming into the office, he received a phone call.

"Tom, I've been thinking more about your idea to do an evaluation on the data collection system. While I haven't changed my opinion at all, it appears that others on the committee think we should at least talk about it before deciding for or against it. So, bring the proposal you worked out to the meeting this afternoon and expect to spend a considerable amount of time on it."

"But, Denny," Tom said, "I decided that perhaps you were right about not wanting to stir something up and make the workers think that something is wrong with the system. Consequently, I haven't put any proposal down on paper. I have some ideas, but nothing is written up. Do you still think the committee wants to go through a discussion on this?"

"Yes, I think they do, Tom, so put your proposal together this morning and let's at least look at it and discuss it."

"Great," Tom said to himself, "I had just convinced myself that there was no need for an evaluation, and now I am told to do a proposal on one after all—and in only a few hours."

He worked quickly and put down the evaluation ideas that had been going through his head before he had changed his mind about its merit. But they were merely ideas and had not been totally thought out; he himself was not certain about the soundness of some of them. "Well," he rationalized, "they probably won't be impressed with the idea of a systems evaluation anyhow, so it probably doesn't matter that I don't have all the details worked out."

Tom's proposal is described in the memorandum in Exhibit 2.

Tom was particularly interested in how the job activities of certain key personnel, such as foremen, had changed. In the past, foremen had felt that their primary task was expediting. However, as a result of the data collection system, they could now spend more time planning, scheduling, and analyzing (for example, determining scrap reduction via review of machine production statistics). It was also important to ascertain how the system was affecting the tasks of others in the plant, such as the various hourly groups.

The success of the system had been attributed, too, to the fact that all persons on the project team had worked in the plant at some time and could therefore relate to the current workers. Therefore it was also important to survey the members of the systems and development group to get their input about the project.

Exhibit 2 The Proposal for Systems Evaluation

MEMORANDUM

TO: Production Management Group
FROM: Tom Waterford, Manager of Information Systems
SUBJECT: A Proposal to Evaluate the Data Collection System

For years data processing people have alerted us to the problems associated with the installation of new systems. Negative attitudes toward the changes are often encountered; for hourly workers, these often take the form of actual sabotage. From all reports, however, the Electron data collection system installation is an outstanding example of a successful installation. It would be of considerable value to Electron and systems installers everywhere to know why Electron has been so successful. The proposals that follow are designed to help identify the reasons for this success.

Basic Issues to Be Addressed in the Investigation

1. Why is this system being implemented successfully when so many other companies have had insurmountable problems?

2. What parts of the training program are seen by the workers as the most valuable and essential in using the new system? How does this assessment compare with the actual costs associated with these parts of the training program?

3. How have the various jobs in the production process changed as a result of using the data collection system?

4. What problems, if any, do employees see with the data collection system?

5. What changes, if any, would floor personnel like to see made in the training program or in the way the system now operates?

Benefits to Be Gained by Electron

1. An objective evaluation of the implementation and operation of the data collection system. This would help in the planning of future systems installations.

2. Better measurement of the benefits of the data collection project.

3. An opportunity to publicize the successful efforts of Electron in using a relatively new management tool.

Exhibit 2 *(continued)*

Method

Five different groups of people will be surveyed by means of a carefully constructed questionnaire, with approximately 50 people in each group:

    a. Hourly group—departments receiving initial introduction of the system
                  —departments with recent introduction of the system
                  —departments which have not yet been introduced to the system
    b. Clerical groups—timekeepers
    c. Clerical groups—keypunchers
    d. Systems and development group
    e. Foremen/women

The purpose will be to identify dysfunctional attitudes of persons toward the system, evaluate the training program, determine the view of the employees toward the computer generally (as compared to the views of the general public), determine foreperson job changes and foreperson's perceptions of their jobs (contribution/no contribution), and attempt to determine important aspects of the job (such as communication).

The amount of time required to complete the questionnaire would be minimal (15 to 20 minutes). The questionnaires would be distributed to entire departments which (1) began using the data collection system in May, (2) began using the system only recently, and (3) have not yet begun to use the system.

This approach should provide the maximum information to EPD on the new system while minimizing the costs to the division.

        Tom had done his job and prepared a proposal on evaluation of the data collection system. But as he walked to the meeting room, questions spun around in his head: "How will the group react? Is this the right approach to take for a systems evaluation effort? Have I involved all of the right groups? Should we really even try to perform an evaluation like this, or will it merely create skepticism in the minds of the workers?"

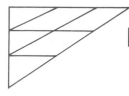

Medical Office Management Company

"Pull out the equipment! They want us to pull out the equipment! I can't understand it," said Chris. "We have installed the same system in different offices in the region and all have been well received. They work well and are in daily use. It's hard to believe that the staff in one medical office could undermine the system to such a degree that it's considered a failure."

Chris is the system supervisor for a shared medical office management system. A current problem with a new user has her and Sheila, her associate, perplexed, and she must now make recommendations about the handling of the problem. An important step is the determination of whether there is a flaw in the design of the system, an inherent problem in the particular office, weakness in training and implementation procedures, or if the current situation is a quirk that is unlikely to recur.

The Medical Office Management (MOM) Company was established one year ago to provide medical billing and management services to physicians in the region who wished to have computer service without the time and investment required to acquire an in-house system. To initiate the service, MOM purchased a midsize NCR computer system and a proven medical management software package. The package, acquired from an independent software vendor, has been installed at over 200 sites throughout North America.

The Medical Office of Dr. Jennings

Dr. Jennings is an allergist, a physician who specializes in the diagnosis and treatment of people who have sensitivities to chemicals, airborne dust, pollen, and other contaminants that affect breathing and skin conditions. In the medical profession, he is what is termed a "solo practitioner," meaning that he is the only physician associated with his practice (in contrast to a group practice, which includes multiple physicians).

The majority of Dr. Jennings' patients visit initially for a series of diagnostic procedures—skin tests, blood analyses, and so on—to allow Dr. Jennings to determine the reason for a particular allergic reaction. Common problems include allergies to airborne contaminants, as in hay fever (allergic reaction to ragweed and airborne grasses), or even to ordinary house dust. Other reactions are caused by an individual's sensitivity to certain food products, soaps, perfumes, cosmetics, or various chemicals. The tests performed to diagnose the cause of an allergy may be performed all at once, or in a sequence of visits, depending on the nature of the difficulty.

Some diagnoses may result in the presciption to avoid use of any product containing a certain food product or chemical. In these instances, the patient may never have to return to see the physician unless complications occur or a reaction recurs. For many persons, however, the diagnosis leads to the prescription of regular injections of drugs that will prevent reactions for a period of time. For instance, many hay fever patients receive weekly or biweekly shots during the summer and fall months. Each injection takes only a moment—less than thirty seconds—but may help maintain patient comfort.

Dr. Jennings is well liked by his patients, both because of the sincere concern he demonstrates for their care and because he operates his office for their convenience. His office hours include Wednesday evening hours for those patients who cannot visit during the daytime. Unless it is necessary for the patient to see him personally, they need not make advance appointments. Thus, patients who need injections for hay fever may stop by when it is convenient for them. One of the nurses will administer the needed injection. The waiting time for such drop-in patients is usually only five or ten minutes. (After the injection, they must wait in the reception room for twenty minutes to be sure there will not be a reaction to the injection. This is for the patient's own safety.)

Normal office hours are from 9:00 A.M. to 5:00 P.M. Monday, Tuesday, and Friday. On Wednesdays, the office is open until 7:00 P.M. Thursdays, hours are from 9:00 A.M. until 1:00 P.M.; the office is closed in the afternoon and the nursing staff is off.

The office staff consists of Betty and James, both trained medical office assistants. Olivia is responsible for administering allergy injections and the operation of the laboratory. She is assisted by Diane, a pre-med student at a nearby university who is employed part time, for approximately twenty hours per week. Each is paid at a salary at or above the average for the region.

Shared Medical System

Medical Office Management Company is approximately two years old. It was formed out of a recognized need to provide quality medical management support to individual medical practitioners and small group offices where the cost of an adequate computer-based system was not acceptable. Under the plan, MOM invested in the hardware and software needed for the system and hired competent operating and installation personnel. It purchased a spacious building in a pleasant suburban location. The building contains ample staff offices, a computer and communications room, and several training rooms.

Under the shared system concept, individual physicians or medical groups contract with MOM for the service. Charges are based on the number of transactions processed by the system and the number and type of forms generated for the client offices. Normal monthly summary reports are included without charge as part of the service.

Each office is linked to MOM by leased telephone lines that transmit data at 4800 baud. Modems are provided by the management company as are video display terminals. (All equipment is loaned to the physicians; they need not make any investment in computer or communications devices.) However, the medical office is responsible for the cost of the telephone lines and paper supplies. Monthly telephone line charges range from $100 to $250, depending on the distance of the office telephone exchange from MOM's location.

The rationale for the medical office management system is operating efficiency and cost reduction. The design of this system, in the eyes of MOM's management and the physicians who participated in its selection, will permit such efficiency through automation of the accounting functions inherent in accounts receivable and through automatic generation of forms and statements that would otherwise be prepared manually. The system centers around cost effective processing of accounts receivable and insurance-related transactions. It is not intended to be used for medical diagnosis.

The system has the following functions:

1. Establishment and maintenance of patient files
2. Processing of charges and payments against accounts receivable records and maintaining a payment history
3. Preparataion of monthly billing statements for mailing to patients (collection records are prepared as necessary)
4. Preparation of medical insurance information, including magnetic tape transfer of insurance information to major carriers
5. Capability to make inquiry about any patient record or transaction entered during the month (response time is two to four seconds)

In addition, reports are available on patient activities and accounting transactions. Special forms can be prepared to assist in corresponding or communicating with the patients. Reports and information available on request from the system include:

— Patient information summary
— Accounts receivable summary
— Delinquent balances report
— Credit balances report
— Missing charge slip report
— Patient telephone and account number list
— Patient mailing (label) list
— Patient card file (three-by-five cards)
— Diagnosis code file listing
— Control reports to ensure that all processing has occurred properly

Exhibit 1 gives a complete list of the reports available through MOM's system.

Accounting and transaction information can be retrieved by office, by referring physician, or by insurance company.

The software driving this system is generalized to support many different practices and medical offices. It can be expanded as necessary, providing the appropriate hardware configuration is available.

Exhibit 1 Complete MOM Report List

MOM REPORT LIST

APPOINTMENT REPORTS

Physician Day Sheet
Credit manager's report
Missing charge slip report
Missed appointment report
Reference number file listing

HOSPITAL REPORTS

Hospitalized patient report
Daily admission report
Physician report
Facility report
Daily followup report

RECALL LETTER REPORTS

INSURANCE REQUEST FILE LISTING

COLLECTION PLAN REPORTS

FILE LISTING REPORTS

Service code fil
Revenue center file
Diagnosis code file
Cause of diagnosis file
Physician file
Referring physician file
Facility file
Point-of-service file
Insurance company file
Account type file
Account letter file
Billing control file
Security file

SPECIAL REPORTS

Financial file audit report
Individual complete summary
Individual medical history
Complete summary of patient information
(alphabetical order)

All files, software, and processing hardware for the main computer system, a midsize system with ample power and storage capability for current needs and future expansion, are located at the offices of Medical Office Management Company. Only standard CRTs are at the medical practices. Data entry is handled by medical practice office personnel. All other data handling, report generation, and system maintenance is handled by personnel at MOM.

The rationale for physicians to contract with MOM is the information-handling efficiencies of an automated system whose cost is shared among many different practices. An additional feature is the degree of control and reliability that will be added to current physical office operations through use of the new system. By using this automated system, office personnel are required to follow a specific, detailed procedure for handling patient accounts and preparation of insurance statements. If properly installed, the system will *require* that patients be billed and statements submitted. Failure to do so, for any reason, will be pointed out as an exception so that action can be taken. Other control features include consistent application of rates

Exhibit 1 *(continued)*

<u>PAYMENT PLAN REPORTS</u>

Complete summary of patient information
(account number order)
Patient telephone book

<u>ACCOUNTS RECEIVABLE REPORTS</u>

Overall accounts receivable summary
Summary of accounts receivable by office
Summary of accounts receivable by referring physician
Summary of accounts receivable by account type
Summary of accounts receivable by account letter
Delinquent balances report
Credit balances report

<u>DAILY REPORTS</u>

Daily batch total report
Daily charge slip total report
Daily transaction register
Individual daily transaction register
Daily transaction analysis report generator

<u>MONTHLY REPORTS</u>

Monthly transaction register
Monthly transaction analysis report generator

<u>PATIENT MEDICAL HISTORY REPORTS</u>

Diagnosis summary report
Procedure summary report
Drug summary report
Test summary report
Patient medical database inquiry
Test flow sheets

and fees, summarization and detection of overdue accounts, maintenance of payment history, and maintenance of patient information. This level of control *is* possible in a manual sysem. However, it is seldom achieved with the same uniformity and consistency an automated system can provide.

A particularly attractive feature of the system is the additional "management" information that is automatically provided. Physicians receive details about the way in which their practice operates, the cash flow cycles, and so on. In many cases, this management information is not otherwise available to a physician in normal manual office environments.

When MOM representatives first discuss the features of the system with physicians they emphasize that the doctor should be wary of expecting reductions in the number of office personnel currently employed. Seldom in systems of this nature does the number of personnel decrease. Instead, payoffs from the investment occur in the form of (1) cost avoidance—avoiding the need for additional personnel in the future; (2) better control over personnel through enforcement of standard operating procedures; (3) reduced transaction processing costs; and (4) better operating and planning information.

Charging for System Use

The charges for use of the system depend on how much it is actually used. Physicians and medical groups pay for three types of transactions:

1. $1 for each insurance form produced by the system on behalf of a patient. (It is customary in many physician offices to type the patient's insurance claim form to ensure that the correct procedure and diagnostic information is provided—claims rejected because of improper information mean it takes that much longer for the physician to be paid.)

2. $1 for each monthly statement prepared through the system. MOM uses mailer packages that include the statement and a return envelope inside the mailer and a file copy of the statement on the outside of the mailer. The mailers include a bulk postage seal so that the office or staff members do not have to do anything except check the statements before they are mailed. (After printing, the mailers are delivered to the respective office. MOM does not automatically mail statements.) The cost of the mailers, approximately $0.20, is absorbed by MOM.

3. $0.12 for each encounter form prepared through the system. Encounter forms are statements of services performed, diagnoses rendered, and charges incurred when a patient visits an office. MOM prints these forms the night before they are needed, using patient appointment schedules on the master appointment book maintained by office staff through the computer system. Offices also keep a plentiful stock of blank encounter forms for those patients treated on an emergency or walk-in basis. There is no charge for encounter forms unless they are prepared through the computer system.

MOM provides a courier service to deliver all printed information to individual offices. Thus office staff members need not worry about operating printers, handling blank forms, or performing maintenance. This is one more way in which MOM attempts to provide a "foolproof" system of services.

System Operating Details

The medical office system is menu driven (Exhibit 2). This feature was emphasized when sales representatives from MOM introduced the system to Dr. Jennings. In presenting the system, Jonathon Edwards made the following statements:

> This system is designed so that it can be used easily by physicians, medical assistants, or clerical staff. No one need be a trained computer operator or have any knowledge of the computer portion of the system to operate it. All functions

Exhibit 2 Sample Master Menu for Selection of Processing Functions

```
                MEDICAL OFFICE MANAGEMENT COMPANY
                       DR. ROBERT JENNINGS
                          MASTER MENU

     01   Transaction file operations      12  Cycle aging

     02   Hospitalized patient control     13  Cycle billing

     03   Patient registration files       14  Periodic processing

     04   Insurance information files      15  Insurance forms request

     05   New patient financial file setup 16  Insurance forms control

     06   Financial file control           17  Collection control

     07   Maintenance of system file       18  Payment plan control

     08   Appointment control              19  Patient inquiry

     09   Demand charge slip printing      20  Reports

     10   Demand  billing

     11   Patient recall control           99  Terminate master menu


          PLEASE SELECT FUNCTION AND ENTER HERE:  *  *
```

can be selected from the menu of options, which is presented in the form of a numbered list. By pressing the number corresponding to the operation desired, that operation can be invoked.

For example, if the number 20 is entered, the Report Writing function is invoked. Entering any code other than those displayed on the display screen will *not* cause a system error; the software catches the mistake and redisplays the menu so the user can enter another request. This approach is virtually foolproof.

Once the menu code is entered, a secondary screen is displayed (Exhibit 3). The user enters the number corresponding to the type of report wanted (for example, 01 for accounts receivable reports, 02 for routine daily summary reports, 03 for monthly summary reports). As before, only valid codes will be accepted so that the operator cannot submit a transaction that will create a system fault.

The multilevel, menu-driven method of interfacing system and user is the most foolproof way of guiding personnel in repeated use of the system. It is the only way good software should be designed because it is so effective with users

Exhibit 3 Sample Report Selection Menu

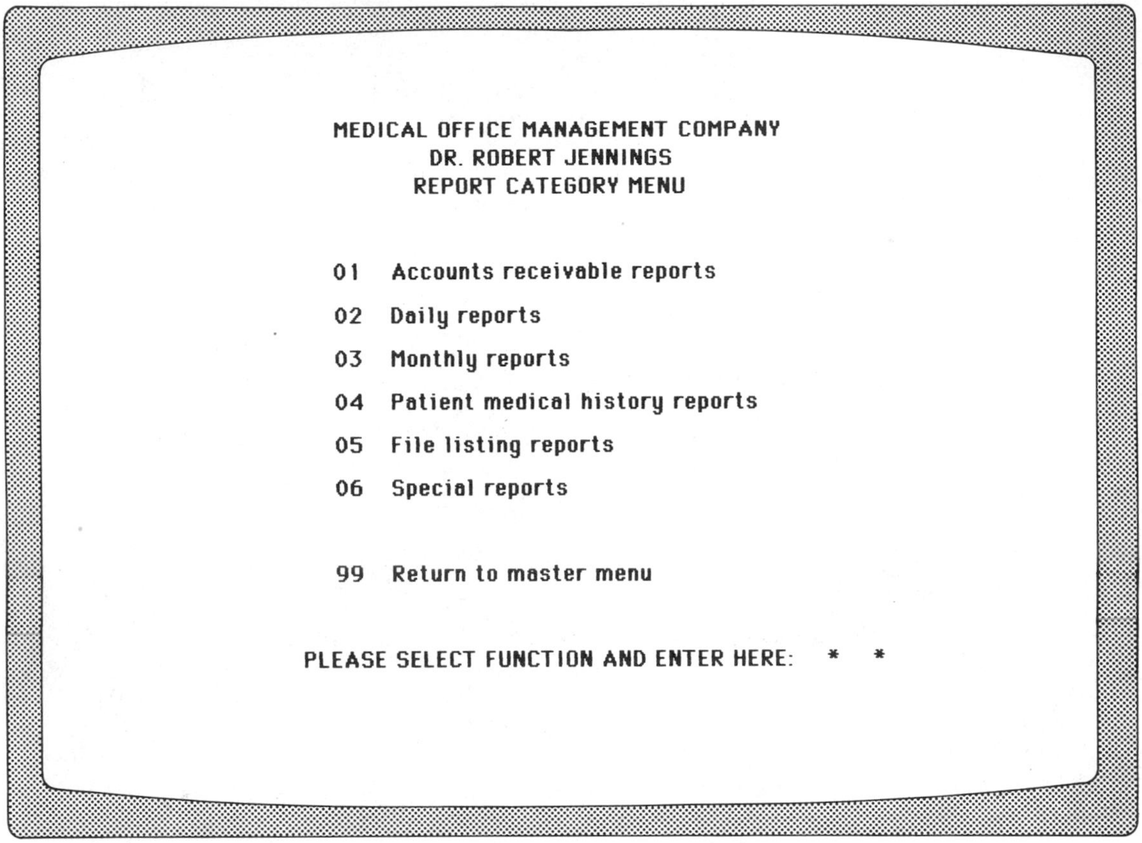

```
        MEDICAL OFFICE MANAGEMENT COMPANY
              DR. ROBERT JENNINGS
              REPORT CATEGORY MENU


    01   Accounts receivable reports

    02   Daily reports

    03   Monthly reports

    04   Patient medical history reports

    05   File listing reports

    06   Special reports


    99   Return to master menu


  PLEASE SELECT FUNCTION AND ENTER HERE:   *   *
```

who are not computer specialists. It is an attractive and functional feature of the MOM system.

When the system is initially installed for a specific practice, a separate storage section is allotted on the magnetic disk for that practice. Data and files (for example, patient data, accounts, fees, and codes) from different practices are *not* intermingled. This feature prevents accidental access to the data from another practice.

Because of the subdivision of storage, backup copies are easily and quickly made. MOM personnel do this on a regular basis. Physicians and their office personnel do not have to perform any backup or file copying work.

To prevent accidental erasure of data, a double-check has been built into the software. Before deleting records, data, or files, the operator—an end-user—must execute an additional step. This double-check feature is an important safeguard of the MOM software.

The Software System

The medical office system software was not developed by MOM. They purchased a license to use it and must pay a monthly fee for each practice in which they install it. Currently MOM pays a fee for 14 different practices.

The firm that developed and maintains the system has it installed in over 200 other medical practices, serving both individual physicians and group practices. According to the vendor's sales personnel and its technical support staff, all 200 users are very pleased with the system and would not go back to the way they handled patient records before the system was installed. During MOM's deliberation about whether to acquire this system, Jonathon Edwards contacted more than a dozen of the other practices—picking the offices at random from the full client list provided by the vendor. In each case, he discussed the system with the physician or one of the medical staff members. The enthusiasm for the system was overwhelming.

MOM's system support coordinator, Sheila Webb, also contacted the technical support personnel at other user sites. They strongly recommended the system, pointing out not only the reliability of the system, but also the willingness of the vendor to provide support when needed.

Based on their technical evaluation as well as the strong endorsement from other users, MOM acquired a license to the system and began selling its use to physicians in the region. For the first few installations, the vendor sent two staff people to assist MOM, ensuring a relatively smooth, incident-free conversion. Now MOM has 11 other practices using the system. Jonathon Edwards indicates that "Each system installed over the past 15 months is working well. There are no significant complaints or signs of problem installation."

The most frequent maintenance is due to mandated changes in claims forms by insurance and government agencies. The vendor included a forms generator in its support software when it was delivered to MOM. The generator permits replication of an insurance or claim form on the display screen so that necessary data can be keyed into the system and used in the generation of a claim. Through this tool, forms changes can, in most cases, be made right in the MOM office. Should problems arise, the vendor accepts and makes forms changes through the mail, with turnaround time of approximately two weeks.

MOM subscribers do not have to perform any maintenance on the forms layouts. That is part of the service they purchase.

Training

Medical Office Management Company set up a plush training facility where office staff come to learn to use the system. It is well lighted and furnished with comfortable chairs and furniture designed for computer terminals. Special carpeting and color schemes coupled with a quiet location encourage concentration on system activities. There is plenty of room, so participants are not crowded.

The original training program was designed to be four days with specified content.

——*Day 1:* Hardware, software concepts, and data processing procedures
——*Day 2:* Office system features, menus, and functions
——*Day 3:* Building files, charts, and patient records
——*Day 4:* Optional day for supervised practice on system

During training, the office staff members begin to build the files for their own system. They enter patient service charges, diagnostic information, and even patient information. Every effort is made to ensure the training is not only effective but useful and realistic.

After the first two installations, Chris found that the office personnel became bored by the fourth day. She restructured the training program to three days. A special training disk pack was also established so that a physician's office staff members could practice on the system from their office just before the conversion to live use of the system occurred. This practice proved useful in overcoming any lag between initial training and the conversion.

The System for Dr. Jennings

The system was installed in Dr. Jennings's office and went live on February 3. Prior to conversion, training occurred and data was entered into the system master files. Patient information for all injection patients was entered into the system. This was important because these patients visit the office most frequently and office personnel did not want to have to take the time after conversion to enter these details the first time a person came into the office for an injection.

When the system was being sold to Dr. Jennings, he and his staff were told that they would receive four days training on the system. They were assured that was more than adequate time to learn the system. It was the training period recommended by the vendor, which they followed for their own installations.

Betty—The Office Manager

Betty coordinates all activities in the office, from dealing with patients at the window when they arrive to ensuring that everyone gets time for lunch. The office is closed from 12:00 until 2:00 each day, so there had always been ample time for lunch. Often the entire office staff goes to lunch together. Dr. Jennings uses this time to visit hospital patients or to attend to other personal and medical matters away from the office.

Betty spoke freely about the system to Dr. Jennings and to others in the office—even to patients. She repeatedly emphasized: "This is a good system. But not for this office." She indicated that all persons in the office were now familiar with the system and knew how to use it properly. The conversion to the new system from the previous manual environment had occurred 6 weeks earlier.

> We got the impression when they were selling us the system last July that there would be four days of training. In actuality, I received one full day and half of another day. James received three full days.
>
> The staff did not *retain* the information they received at training. And the training stressed *how,* not *why,* something was done.
>
> We entered information into the system during the end of December. Chris put in most of the account balances at her office to help us out. Some of the patient information was put in incorrectly, especially responsible party details. Our staff had to change this information.

Betty indicated that "some patients did not receive a bill from the system when they were first sent out. We found out about this when a dunning notice was sent. Those patients who had never received first billings called us, and some were pretty mad. I assumed this was the result of something Chris had put in wrong."

Betty indicated to Dr. Jennings that the insurance speed of the system was excellent. She felt that it easily beat the old way of typing out each form. However, she wanted a way to put in transactions all at once rather than having to go from screen to screen. And she wanted to be able to retrieve patient information via the patient's name, not via their account number.

> I don't understand it. The computer seems faster in the morning than in the afternoon. Some afternoons we really get pushed. One day—an exceptional case, to be sure—we ran 105 people through the office in less than two hours. Most of them were for injections. The system was slow—we were waiting a lot. People began to back up at the window and we ran out of seats in the waiting room. We panicked! From that day on, we have had to have two people at the front window: One to do transactions with patients, another to handle the telephone, do testing, and what have you. And we have a backup of typing. Sometimes patients tell us "Forget my receipt . . . I'm going to leave." They don't like the delay.

Betty went on talking:

> Dr. Jennings wants his production statistics at the end of the day. But he just has to wait until the next morning. Oh, and the system totals and the totals for cash we have received in the mail or from the patient at the window usually do not agree. But we have no problem balancing our cash manually—you know if we ignore what the system says.

One of the features of the system is the capability to list all of the transactions occurring during the course of the day. This report is intended for audit purposes, allowing the medical staff to see that all transactions are entered properly and to assist in balancing the system against cash. Betty indicated to Chris that she thought this should be changed. She wanted transactions printed in alphabetical order, rather than in transaction number order.

She was also concerned about the bills (statements) produced by the system. Patients had called and said they did not think their insurance company would accept the statement as proof of visit and payment. And she was furious when monthly statements were run:

> That system printed 657 individual statements. That's ridiculous. We have never had more than 400 before. In some cases, four bills were sent to the same family—one for each family member. The system is supposed to consolidate them so that there is one statement for each family. That's the way we put the information in; family members were all linked to a single account number.

James—Office Assistant

Like Betty, James had received an associates degree in medical office management. Previous to using the office system, he had not had any computer experience. He went through three full days of training. "There were some confusing points. Omission of transactions was one of my concerns. Finding the cause of the problem was another. And I was not always comfortable moving from day to day on the screen."

James talked the system over with Betty, who went to training after he did. He also discussed the training activities with Dr. Jennings.

> Sheila taught me the most. She had a lot of patience and was able to stay in the training room. Chris's attention was distracted. She was running in and out for telephone calls she received. And she was not patient enough. Often it was "Do this, this, and this. *Not* why." There were some technical problems too. The keyboard on a terminal locked up and had to be replaced.
>
> The system is not a bad system. Chris must learn to critique the offices more carefully when selling the system. The main problem with the system is speed. Sometimes it seemed like it took 10 seconds to respond to our inquiries, especially in the afternoon. We also had to go in and out from menus to get from the billing portion of the system to the diagnostic section. It took us 500 percent longer to do some things.
>
> We had long lines on Wednesday afternoons anyways—that is our heaviest day. With the system the lines got up to 15 people on several occasions. It was standing room only in the office—literally. We ended up writing everything out and then doing the transactions the next morning. The stress was so intense that it took away the value of it and the fun of it. Patients noticed that we were not the same.
>
> Betty was on vacation during part of the conversion so she missed some of the problems. She did not see all of the ledger cards and beginning balances being put into the system.

As he discussed the system further, James said he was used to knowing everyone's accounts—finances, insurance, and employers. With the new system, he felt he did not know what was going on. He didn't have any facts to start from. In the office he said they increased the paper they kept, because they didn't know what was correct. Also, checks came in from patients whose records were not in the computer. This was blamed on Chris, who apparently didn't ensure that the staff had put information on all the patients in the system.

Olivia—Lab Manager

Olivia is responsible for the lab and does not operate the system very often. There was little need for her to do so, and it would in fact be difficult since she did not have a terminal installed in the lab (the lab is separate from the office area, partly because of State Department of Health requirements and also because of its unique function).

In discussing the system, Olivia stated: "It just isn't for here. People are numbers whenever you put in a computer. And my work was put aside to do computer work. But the benefits could be there if the system were programmed for this office."

"I don't run the system that much," she said, "but I did go through training. I learned more at lunch when I went through the manual. This was after we had the system here. I learned things that I did not know, even when we went live."

Chris's Dilemma

"I know this is a good system," thought Chris. "We've installed it in other offices that are busier than this one and where conditions are more difficult and they are all working well. The staff and the physicians love it—they tell us so and they tell Jonathon too. They wouldn't go back to the old way."

Dr. Jennings told Chris and Jonathon that the system would be fine if one more person were hired for his office. Chris recalled how demanding Dr. Jennings was during installation. He signed a three-year contract, a fact he made known to many of his colleagues who had not yet made the transition from manual to automated. She had spent two weeks of full-time effort working with his office—268 hours of contact time had been logged. Chris even took encounter forms home to separate and alphabetize them so that Dr. Jennings' staff would not have to do it. No other account had received that kind of service.

In discussing the system with Jonathon, Chris openly expressed her concern:

One of Dr. Jennings's staff members is very good. She saw the advantages of the system early. But she is faster than the system, and often waits for the display to present the information she wants. We are going to put in some different equipment just for this office so that will not be a concern, although I don't believe that is the source of the problem.

There were no unusual conversion problems. But Dr. Jennings is sold on his staff's credibility. He said he would be out of business the next day if any of them quit—he'd have to close the office. Even his wife told me that these people really run the office and the practice—she said he is totally dependent on them in the office.

One day he called and said separate bills were sent to all family members. When we checked this out it clearly was not true, except for a couple of isolated instances in which the patient information was not entered properly. Jennings thought MOM was trying to send extra bills to run up the charges for the month. Remember when he brought that up in our meeting with him? He really believes that because his staff told him, but he did not try to see firsthand whether it is true.

Chris went on:

Jonathon, the real problem is the system forced order and organization into an operation where there was none. The staff could no longer get off at 4:30 or 5:00 when the office door was locked. They really treasured their afternoon time off, too. Now they send 650 bills. Before 450 was the largest. The staff had complete control over who received statements. Some patients never received a statement. We checked that with some of them. Now any patient having an account balance over $5 automatically gets a statement. We put in control where there was none.

I was there one afternoon when they ran 105 patients through the office in two and one-half hours. They were busy, no question about it. They told me that is an unusual situation—it's never happened before.

I don't think the office staff is overworked. They say they are, but even their Wednesdays are not as busy as they indicate.

The staff originally perceived significant benefits. They were enthusiastic about not having to Xerox patient statements and stuff them in envelopes. And *they were glad* they would not have to fill out insurance forms. A couple of them thought it would be fun and different.

Jennings thought that the day sheets listing patient visits and charges for the day were totally messed up—they didn't balance with deposits. He was really mad about that. I finally got his accountant involved. He analyzed the situation and indicated they were correct. The deposits were wrong, not the day sheet.

As it turned out, at the end of the day, if the figures did not balance, the staff considered it a "pain" to make corrections so they just went ahead and posted it anyway. They continued practices from their old manual system, and it was bad. They were putting hospital checks in with office charges and deposits. Some payments are not even being run through the new system.

The doctor wanted posting done the same day, not the next morning. This would tie up the staff and take them away from their regular duties. That's okay, but when they are unwilling to stay a few minutes after the last patient leaves to balance the system and handle the posting, things are bound to get bogged down. The fact that Dr. Jennings will not even consider scheduling patients does not help, but I can understand him not wanting to change that part of his practice since it obviously is convenient to the patients.

The two primary office people—Betty and James—were the most positive in the beginning. Betty's husband even has an Apple Macintosh at home. She brought in signs she printed in large letters on the Macintosh to tell the patients about the system. And she was proud of the system. Olivia was against the system from the beginning. She was very negative and said she did not like computers. She thought she could not learn to use them. Rather than attacking the system outright, she convinced people the system was not right for their particular office, but that it was all right for others. Maybe that's the key to the whole mess.

Chris's dilemma now is what to do about the situation. Dr. Jennings signed a three-year contract to use the system. MOM has ordered stock preprinted with his office address and telephone number, and a year's stock was ordered to get a good price. About $1500 worth of stock is on hand. Jennings wants the contract canceled and the money he paid for the stock refunded. And he wants the equipment taken out quickly so that the staff can return to the old manual system.

This case was prepared for class discussion rather than to illustrate effective or ineffective handling of an administrative situation. The situation is a real one, but the names of the company and its employees have been changed. Any similarity of names with existing business organizations is unintentional and by coincidence.

Monroe Warner, Inc.

"Late again," Harry said. "I can't understand why we're having so much trouble with our service bureau. When they first began the contract, they were always on time. We had no difficulties, the invoices were prepared when they were needed and the weekly sales summaries were always delivered on time. Now it seems whenever the service bureau delivers something, either it is delivered late or there is a problem with it. We can't stand it anymore."

Recently, the service bureau with which Harry's dry cleaning firm—Monroe Warner, Inc.—does business has not been living up to its promises. One problem after another seems to plague the bureau. Either there are mistakes in the work when it is delivered or it is not delivered on time. Harry and those in the office who deal with customers of the laundry are very concerned about the unreliability of the bureau.

The Accounts Management System

The accoauts management system for Monroe Warner handles all sales and accounts receivable information for operation of the laundry. Monroe Warner has two types of customers: those who maintain accounts with the laundry and those who use the retail services of the laundry and pay cash for cleaning and laundry. The accounts management system includes only those customers who charge their services or arrange for them to be handled on a contract basis. Approximately 2000 customers fall into this category.

Whenever a customer receives a delivery of merchandise from Monroe Warner, a preprinted delivery slip containing the customer's name and the service performed is included with the delivery. These delivery slips are accumulated by Monroe Warner's office staff throughout the week. At the end of the week they are sent to the service bureau where the data from each delivery slip is entered into a computer system and tallied. A printed weekly service statement is produced. Copies of the delivery slip and the weekly service slip are shown in Exhibits 1 and 2, respectively.

The delivery slip details each service or item provided by Monroe Warner for a customer. For example, if mechanic uniforms are delivered, the delivery slip will indicate the item, the item number, and the quantity. All items or services performed by Monroe Warner are identified by a three-digit number. Exhibit 3 contains a representative list of items or services provided by the laundry.

For a limited number of customers, such as large industrial customers or hospitals and institutions, delivery slips are not provided. This is because these organi-

Exhibit 1 Monroe Warner Delivery Slip

MONROE WARNER, Inc.		Delivery Slip	
ACCT. NO	ROUTE	DATE	
		/ /	
QUAN.	CODE	ITEM	

ITEM NO	QTY	NOTES
1277	1	
1278	26	
401	50	
852	1	
999	43	

zations contract with Monroe Warner to pay a fixed fee. One large hospital, for example, has an ongoing contract with Monroe Warner that stipulates a monthly fee of $10,000. For this fee, the hospital receives cleaning and laundry service for all bed linens, hospital gowns, and towels and wash cloths as needed. The laundry neither counts nor weighs the items. If the hospital uses more than the expected number of pounds in any particular week, it does not change the weekly charge. Similarly if less than the average amount is used, the charge also does not vary. From time to time—typically on a quarterly basis—management will monitor the hospital's laundry and cleaning requirements and adjust the fixed fee as needed.

The weekly sales summary includes an entry for each item or service provided during the week and a total of the quantities for that item. Each line entry also includes the unit price and a total price for that line. For instance, if five uniform shirts are laundered throughout the week, the quantity entry will indicate 5, the unit cost entry will indicate $1.95, and the total cost for that line will indicate $9.75. The overall total is entered at the bottom of the summary and includes all charges for the week.

Exhibit 2 Monroe Warner Weekly Service Slip

MONROE WARNER, INC.

INCORPORATED

1200 Commonwealth Avenue, Boston, Mass 02167

This is a weekly invoice, listing total deliveries for the week. A monthly statement will be sent, to summarize the weekly invoices. Remittances may be made either weekly or monthly.

ACCOUNT NO.

Felix & Son, Inc.
2 Page Avenue
Boston, MA   02285

23650
RT   U

CLOSING DATE
3/21/XX
AMOUNT ENCLOSED

$

PLEASE RETURN THIS PORTION WITH YOUR REMITTANCE

ITEM	CODE	INVENTORY	QUANTITY	CHARGE
1277	Pant & shirt-2 Chg		1	1.90
1278	Pant & shirt-4 Chg		26	82.95
401	Shop towel		50	3.00
852	Rug 3X5		1	2.75
999	Miscellaneous		43	4.30
			121	94.90

DELIVERY SLIPS INCLUDED ON THIS INVOICE:
35

At the end of the month an account statement is sent to all customers who have nonzero balances. A copy of the monthly statement is shown in Exhibit 4. Monroe Warner's account statement is typical of those used in accounts payable operations. It identifies the customer and the month to which the statement pertains. In addition, it shows the beginning balance and aging information for the preceding 30-, 60-, 90-, and 120-day intervals. The main body of the invoice details the charges and other account activities that have occurred during the month. All charges are listed by delivery slip number. Unlike the weekly sales summary, which lists each individual item delivered during the week, the monthly statement includes only one entry for each delivery slip—the date of the delivery slip and the associated total dollar amount.

Exhibit 3 Representative List of Laundry Services

MONROE WARNER, Inc.   LINEN COUNT

/ /

	IN	OUT	
SHEET			
DRAW SHEET			
BED SPREAD			
BATH BLANKET			
PILLOW CASE			
BATH TOWEL			
HAND TOWEL			
BATH MAT			
WASH CLOTH			
PATIENT GOWN			
BED PAD			
MISC.			

Other entries in the body of the invoice include payments and adjustments to the account. When a payment is made the date of the payment and its amount are included. Credits may show as additions to or subtractions from the account, depending on the reason for the occurrence. (If customers return items that need recleaning or relaundering, a credit is made to this customer's account to remove the charge from the balance.)

Monroe Warner has a policy of charging interest for all account balances over 30 days. However, management has decided that in some instances interest is inappropriate or inadvisable, either for competitive reasons or as a courtesy to the customer. In these instances, as the system is currently designed, the statements are issued and prior to mailing, Diane, the account supervisor, makes a list of those accounts for whom interest should be subtracted. This list is sent to the service bureau and the amounts are entered into the system as credits. The credits appear on the statements the following month.

The service bureau also supplies Monroe Warner management with an accounts receivable report at the end of each month. The report lists all accounts having a

Exhibit 4 Monroe Warner Monthly Statement

MONROE WARNER, INC.
LAUNDRY & CLEANERS
1200 Commonwealth Avenue, Boston, Mass 02167

Felix & Son, Inc.   C
2 Page Avenue   4/1/XX
Boston, MA   02285

AMOUNT ENCLOSED
$

PLEASE RETURN THIS PORTION WITH YOUR REMITTANCE

DATE	REFERENCE	CHARGE	CREDIT	BALANCE
2/29/0	Previous balance			
3/03/0	Payment		322.35-	
3/07/0	Charge	102.30		
3/14/0	Charge	92.00		
3/21/0	Charge	94.00		
3/24/0	Payment		34.40-	
3/28/0	Charge	98.90		
	Column totals	388.10	656.75-	
	30-90 Day finance charge			
	1.5% of 50.70			

		AMOUNT PAST DUE			
CURRENT	30 DAYS	60 DAYS	90 DAYS		TOTAL
388.36	50.70				

nonzero balance and the amount of the balance. Aging information is also included. Those customers having a zero balance are not listed on the accounts receivable report. Report totals include current balance and totals by age category.

The Laundry and Dry Cleaning Business

Some Monroe Warner customers who use the dry cleaning and laundry *retail* services do so in large enough volume that they wish to maintain an account enabling them to charge the services and submit monthly payments. Credit is arranged prior to the initial transaction. Whenever dry cleaning or laundry service is provided, the charge for that service is automatically added to the customer's account, regardless of when they pick up the laundry or dry cleaning. The charges for these services are the same as for normal retail cash customers; the only difference is that this group of customers can charge the services against their accounts. Each of these customers is included in the overall customer file but is identified with a separate five-digit customer number. Customers in this category may be individuals, commercial establishments, medical offices, or other such businesses.

The greatest portion of Monroe Warner's business, both in revenue and in transactions generated, comes from the commercial side. Commercial customers are divided into the two categories of linen customers and uniform customers. In the laundry business, the term linen refers to bed linens, including sheets, pillowcases, blankets, and quilts, as well as bathroom linens such as hand towels, bath towels, face cloths, bath mats, and so on. Currently a specific fixed fee is charged for laundering each of these items. For example, a face cloth is charged at one price, a hand towel at another price, and so on. The amount of each charge does not vary from customer to customer nor does it change due to volume. Thus, a company using 100 pillow cases in a week pays at the same rate as another that might use 1000 in a week.

Uniform customers receive the rental and laundering of uniforms owned by Monroe Warner. Uniforms in this case include mechanic shirts and pants—the traditional type of uniform—as well as jackets, sports coats, ties, dress shirts, slacks, caps, and hats. Most of these items are laundered, although some, such as blazers and sports coats, do require dry cleaning. Each customer pays the same charge for laundering uniforms. The laundry charge also includes the rental fee for the item, but the portion due to the rental is not known to the customer.

When customers first agree to use the services of Monroe Warner, they are issued a specific number of each item. For example, when a worker needing uniforms is added to a customer's staff, he or she is given a specified supply of shirts and slacks (for example, auto mechanics receive four uniform sets). The individuals and their company are responsible for these items. Whenever an item is laundered or cleaned it is exchanged on a one-for-one basis. If one shirt and one pair of slacks are turned in for cleaning they are replaced with one shirt and one pair of slacks. As indicated above, the only charge for this service is the laundry charge. However, when a worker leaves a company or when the company decides it is no longer going to use Monroe Warner's service it is responsible for returning all rented items. Monroe Warner issues a bill for any missing items.

The only exception to the above procedure results from the limited number of institutional firms, such as hospitals and schools, that own their own linens. They do not rent from Monroe Warner and pay only the contract service price discussed earlier.

Handling Piece Goods

The laundry and dry cleaning business is characterized by high-volume activity. During the course of a single week several thousand pieces may be laundered for every customer. As items are laundered, they are pressed and folded and returned to the stockroom. As the need arises, drivers take the merchandise from the stock and deliver it to the customer.

When a driver visits a customer, he or she places all the dirty and soiled linens into one or more laundry bags containing only the items from that one customer. The bags are transported to the laundry unopened. When they arrive at the laundry they are washed as a single group. That is, all the items for one customer are washed together. At the end of the washing process the items are counted and tallied on a soil sheet. The number of shirts, pants, face cloths, hand towels, bath towels, and so on, are tallied for the group. The soil count is sent to the stockroom where the replacement items for a customer are assembled. The quantity of each item indicated on the soil sheet is pulled from the shelves and loaded onto the driver's truck. The driver in turn delivers these items to the customer. There is a one-day delay between pickup and delivery.

The soil sheet is sent to the accounting office. It contains the information needed for billing the customer for services.

Damaged items are handled by a separate process.

Developing an In-House Laundry Management System

Harry has been giving a lot of thought to terminating his contract with the service bureau. Instead, he would like to bring the laundry system in-house. He wants a computer system installed on the Monroe Warner premises that will allow his staff to maintain all accounts receivable and handle the invoicing and billing activities now performed by the serivce bureau. He is well aware of the many personal computers on the market and has often wondered whether such a system would be suitable for his operation. He has visited various computer dealers but openly admits he does not understand all of the intricacies that seem to be involved or the jargon that many computer dealers use. He is also aware that, although software is one of the most important concerns in an accounts management system, he may not be able to find a prewritten, canned software package that meets his requirements. Still, Harry finds the idea of having an in-house computer very attractive.

The accounting staff at Monroe Warner has no experience with computers of any type. In fact, Diane, the person who is most likely to be responsible for such a system if it were to be brought in-house, openly admits she fears computers and would not like to work with such a system. Harry shrugs this off and indicates that it is natural for someone to fear something they have not used before and which they do not understand. He feels that, as in many business areas, careful training is all that is required for success.

In recent years the laundry and dry cleaning business has become a stable one, largely because of the modern fabrics so widely used today. Revenue is increasing, mostly due to price changes. Harry feels Monroe Warner profits can be improved if costs can be reduced and management has information that will help them gain a larger share of the market in the area.

A primary incentive for acquiring an in-house system is to reduce the cost of outside services. Harry is aware that personal computers can be acquired for a few thousand dollars and he is quick to compare this to the $1000 monthly fee paid to the service bureau. Economically it appears to Harry that the wise investment decision is to purchase and operate a computer system. In addition to the economic reasons for in-house computing, Harry also sees an opportunity to improve the processing control he has for the account system and to enhance the information available to management. Benefits may also accrue to the customers of Monroe Warner.

Among the changes he would like to see is the development of a priced delivery slip for each customer delivery. Under this scheme customers will receive an itemized slip with each delivery that indicates what is being delivered and the cost of the delivery. The total amount of the delivery is added to their accounts receivable for the period, eliminating the need for a weekly sales summary. The new system, then, will provide a daily delivery slip and a monthly invoice; less paper will move through the laundry and yet customers will receive more timely information.

Harry is confident that the priced delivery slip system can be implemented with no additional labor cost for the laundry. The office staff can enter the appropriate delivery slip information into the system (using details provided by the laundry workers who assemble each customer's shipment) and have the slip printed immediately by the system. At the same time the cost totals for each delivery slip will be accumulated in the system and maintained throughout the month. Harry believes that the process is a very simple one—since the laundry and dry cleaning business is not complicated—and therefore the office staff should be able to adapt to a new system.

Harry is aware that a transition to a new system will not occur without some concerns and problems. It will take several months to transfer from the old system to the new one once the decision is made and software and equipment are obtained. During the transition he will want both the service bureau and the in-house system to process concurrently to compare for accuracy and to provide a backstop for the new system.

The Accounting Staff

Each member of the accounting staff has openly admitted that they do not like working with the service bureau. They acknowledge repeated problems and frequent difficulty in dealing with the service bureau, and thus would look forward to a change. However, they are reluctant to be responsible for operating a computer system, particularly when management is so attuned to having accurate accounting information. They are fearful of mistakes and the wrath of management that may result if serious mistakes occur. They are also concerned that the system have sufficient protective features to catch and correct their errors before they come to management's attention. But above all they wonder how easily they will be able to adapt to a new system.

The accounting staff is hardworking, punctual, and very reliable. Each of the seven women follows a well-established routine for monitoring accounts, handling cash and making deposits, dealing with customer problems (for example, reimbursements on clothing damaged during laundering), and reconciling receipts from each of the 15 retail stores. Since the main laundry also provides retail customer service, three of the women also monitor the customer counter, at the front of the accounting area, receiving laundry and returning cleaned items to customers. They accept the interruptions in their routines and enjoy chatting with the regular customers they have gotten to know over the years.

All of the accounting staff members are paid on an hourly basis. They will not become wealthy working for Harry, but they know they are secure in their work. Harry does not like to release employees. He gives the impression of someone who is sharp with people and abrupt in dealing with associates and employees, but he actually prefers to work around problems if they occur.

Profile of Harry

Harry is an aggressive, very successful business person. Even when he was in high school, he already owned rental property. Periodically after classes were over at the public school he attended, he visited houses or apartments to see first-hand about problems reported by his tenants, to ensure that contractors made proper repairs, or to personally collect the rent. Some tenants loved the attention he gave them.

After high school, he began classes at the Georgia Institute of Technology, aspiring to be an engineer. Although he loved the growing Atlanta metropolitan area and was proud of the education he was receiving at Georgia Tech, business opportunities in the Northeast led him to transfer to Boston and the Massachusetts Institute of Technology, where he graduated two years later with a degree in engineering.

During the two years at MIT, Harry began a series of business ventures with a friend of the same age. Between the two of them, they started six independent corporations during this two-year period. All were commercial businesses. And today, thirty years later, each continues to be highly successful and profitable.

During the three years following his education at MIT, Harry continued to pursue various business ventures, each one successful. His personal assets quickly exceeded $1 million, and the book value of his businesses was many times that amount. However, he felt that he needed to know more about business and management. A year later he entered the Harvard Business School; less than two years after that he received an MBA.

Many of Harry's classmates are now successful business developers and entrepreneurs. Some are well known in the society columns of the large-city newspapers. Others are household names in national and local government. Several have been key members of the personal staff of the President of the United States. Harry has made it a point to stay in touch with his classmates and is always present at Harvard class reunions.

While at Harvard, he developed the capability to carefully think through a problem or an opportunity to understand it from all angles. He leaves no stone unturned when evaluating a situation. He has been known to undertake an opportunity that appeared to have only minimal profit potential and turn it into a lucrative investment. He is particularly careful to find projects where he can develop either a dominant force in the market or capture the entire market.

Harry visits the laundry twice each weekday, and sometimes stops by on Saturday mornings. In the mornings, he opens the mail, sorting through the average 6-inch stack of checks, invoices, sales brochures, and correspondence in about 30 minutes. Although he passes most of it on to his office staff for handling, it is very important to him to know what is going on around the laundry. Scrutinizing the mail helps accomplish this.

Typically he is in the office for one to two hours each morning. After opening the mail, he examines performance reports—they need to be short and to the point, and their impact must be quickly evident—walks through the production areas where laundering, dry cleaning, and pressing is taking place. He knows the names of many of the over 100 employees, and will visit with some of them for a moment or two. The remainder of the time is devoted to seeing salespersons or receiving consultants, lawyers, or professionals hired to work with one of his many other business projects.

Harry will usually stop by the laundry for a few minutes late in the afternoon also. Although seldom more than a walkthrough, he finds this stop is useful to hear about any problems that have arisen during the day or to pick up telephone messages.

The remainder of the day, he is at one of his other firms. The laundry is operated for the most part by the employees. Management sets the policies, procedures, charges, and so on, and the employees carry them out. There is little argument about that.

New Design Features Desired in the Accounts Management System

The priced delivery slip is only one of the enhancements Harry would like to see implemented with the new accounts management system. He would also like to see variable pricing for the different customers. Currently, all the customers pay the same cost per item laundered or cleaned unless they are a bulk contract customer. However, since some organizations do more volume than others it may be appropriate to install a differential pricing. This could be an important benefit in a new system.

Laundry management is also very interested in linking inventory control to the accounting system. When customers first join the laundry they are issued a certain quantity of uniforms, linens, and so on and are responsible for those amounts on their account. If new items are needed they are added to their assigned inventory. Returned items are deleted from the customer's inventory. Invariably in the laundry business items are lost. Customers damage or lose track of items and have to ask for an additional supplement. In some instances rather than having the supplement added to their total, they are sent a bill equal to the value of new items. This occurs at management's discretion.

Management is also concerned with control of inventory within the laundry itself. Although a large percentage of purchased merchandise is inventoried to the customer, the laundry also maintains a stock of towels, linens, uniforms, and so on. It currently has only very loose control over the number of items purchased and maintained in-house. On an infrequent basis someone counts the items and compares the count with what has been purchased and issued to the customer. The counts never agree; there is always a discrepancy. Management would like to get a much better control over all inventory, both in-house and with the customer. Harry also feels that this may be a perfect opportunity to enhance the inventory control. With an in-house computer, changes of this nature should be considered. He would not consider them with the service bureau, however. He feels that both the cost and the problems with the service bureau make it unwise to develop any further commitment to them.

New System Proposal

Harry is interested in receiving a proposal for the new system that identifies costs, benefits, and possible risks of bringing such a system in-house. He is aware that a transition will be needed and he is also quite sure that it will be necessary to have custom software developed. However, he wants to review a full analysis of the situation and specifications for a new design. The specifications should indicate how the data will be entered, how errors will be determined and corrections made. The specifications should also show the reports and output from the system. Particular attention should be paid to controls in the system while ensuring that the design will make it possible for unskilled office workers to learn to use the system correctly and quickly. Cost, although important, should not be the primary concern in developing the new system. He believes it is better to have the right system meeting the right requirements than it is to save a few hundred dollars on the design or development.

A development plan should also be formulated. The plan should indicate the major activities that must occur, the sequencing in which they are to occur, and a time table for the systems development and implementation. The time table should also include the period needed for acquisition of the hardware configuration recommended in the design.

All software needed to run the system must be identified and cost justified. It may make sense to have a phased development, with the accounting system designed first, followed later by the inventory management system and still later by integration of the two systems. Or some other combination may be appropriate. These design alternatives should be examined and a recommendation formulated by the systems developer.

Harry has indicated that he feels an important part of a new design is understanding the current system and assessing any current weaknesses in control or operating efficiency before beginning a new venture. He must decide whether to proceed with the development of an in-house system. As he considers the importance of the special software that must be written, he also must be sure a small computer will do the necessary work.

This case was prepared for class discussion rather than to illustrate effective or ineffective handling of an administrative situation. The situation is a real one, but the names of the company and its employees have been changed. Any similarity of names with existing business organizations is unintentional and by coincidence.

Lockheed-Georgia Company

The MIDS executive support system, first conceived in 1975, continues to grow in significance. Key decision makes now have access to important information about Lockheed-Georgia Company activities. Continual evolution is a secret to the usefulness and success of MIDS.

The Lockheed-Georgia Company

The Lockheed-Georgia Company designs and builds cargo aircraft for its around-the-world market. The company, located in Marietta, Georgia, just outside of Atlanta, was started in 1951. At that time, the town was very small and depended on the railroad and farming for its existence. Lockheed-Georgia was one of the first companies to move to Marietta and played a major role in the rapid growth of the area. The company began operations in January with 150 people. By the end of the same year, 10,000 people were employed there.

Today, the Lockheed-Georgia Company's 19,000 employees come from 78 counties throughout Georgia. The annual payroll is nearly $600 million and the $1.5 billion worth of contracts that the company has awarded to other firms in the state since 1951 has greatly benefited the Georgia economy.

The Lockheed Corporation, parent of Lockheed-Georgia, consists of 17 divisions located around the United States. The Marietta company is, along with the Lockheed-California and the Lockheed Missiles and Space Company, the largest division in the corporation.

Since 1951, the company has built or modified over 7500 jet or proper aircraft. They include:

— *C-130 Hercules:* The staple of the Lockheed-Georgia Company, this aircraft is widely used by the United States military forces and by corporations and governments around the world. It has been used to carry such varying cargoes as military troops, camels, and chickens. The popularity of the plane has led to the proposal of sales not only for currency but also for in-kind trades.

— *C-5 Galaxy:* This aircraft, the largest in the West, is 247.8 feet long with a wing span of 222.8 feet. The cargo hold is 19 feet wide, 13.5 feet high, and 144.6 feet long. The plane can carry military combat units, support forces, and all types of supplies, including large vehicles and heavy weapons (for example, multiple attack helicopters). The C-5A and the newest version, the C-5B, can land on unpaved areas and provide for loading from the nose or rear of the aircraft.

——*C-141 Starlifter:* First built in 1961, and the most advanced airlift-airdrop aircraft, it is used by the U.S. Air Force for training, combat missions, and humanitarian airdrops.

In addition, the company maintains a high technology test bed—a one-of-a-kind aircraft. The test bed is the forerunner of a new-generation aircraft while also functioning as a flying laboratory for testing advanced aviation products and techniques.

Despite the impressive technologies employed in the design of aircraft today, the aircraft itself is still largely handcrafted. Employees take a great deal of pride in assembling an aircraft, watching its progress from start to finish. The manufacturing floor consists of separate production stations where, over the course of months, an aircraft is constructed rivet-by-rivet in plain view for all to see. Workers can tell when progress is moving slower than normal or at a better rate than they had anticipated.

Evolution of MIDS

Bob Ormsby, president of Lockheed-Georgia Company, was in his office surrounded by stacks of reports and paperwork. He realized that he could not possibly read and digest all of those reports and keep up with his workload—no one could. Yet, as president, he was expected to be on top of all corporate developments. He knew something had to change.

Ormsby asked the Finance and Information Services organizations for their help. He wanted them to develop a system, using computer processing, to keep him updated on all important developments within the company while eliminating the mountains of paperwork that continually accumulated in his office.

Members from these organizations started to work on a plan for the system, which they termed MIDS, an acronym for Management Information Decision Support system, in 1975. Since none of the staff members had developed a system of this nature before, they had many questions. One important issue was selection of computer hardware. The state of computer hardware was changing very quickly. Since the developers recognized that the system would require a substantial amount of development time, they did not want to select a system that would be outdated even before the working application system was installed. They decided to wait to see what new products would be introduced to the market. The information system staff continued to research new equipment as it was announced. Meanwhile, the stacks of reports and paperwork in the president's office continued to grow. In the fall of 1978 workstations with acceptable color and graphics capabilities at an appropriate price became available. Active development of MIDS began at that time.

Bob Pittman of the Finance Staff Department was selected as the development team leader. Bob had considerable experience in preparing all types of company reports and presentations, and could provide the initial information requirements. He also had an excellent rapport with executive managers. From the very start, he emphasized the need for including practical features in the system and worked closely with the information systems group to develop ways to achieve them. Useful features, not "gee-whiz" ones, were emphasized from the beginning.

In describing design requirements, Pittman stipulated that the system must:

—support Lockheed-Georgia executives and reduce the quantity of paperwork they received and had to review
—be updated continually to provide accurate and timely information
—be simple to use, without a great deal of start-up training
—contain pertinent information in comprehensible formats
—provide security to control access to information based on both access codes and user location
—interface with graphic printers to provide black-and-white as well as color print-out and color transparencies for customer and staff presentations

Planning for MIDS evolution was important, but not everything could be planned. One day, MIDS staff replaced the president's graphics terminal with a new IBM Personal Computer. The personal computer was hardwired to the system in the same way as the graphics terminal that it replaced. Furthermore, the new system provided the same quality graphics and retrieval capabilities as the terminal, and at the same time provided the capability for local storage and manipulation of MIDS data.

Within two days, the president had asked to have the old terminal back. "The PC is too noisy," he said. "My old terminal was so quiet that I didn't even know it was there. But I always know the PC is there because I hear the fan running. When it is quiet in my office, all I hear is the fan."

The PC was replaced with another to see if it was any quieter, but that did not help. He even had an IBM service engineer examine the system. According to the engineer, the fan noise is a characteristic of the PC and it could not be eliminated. The PC was removed from Ormsby's office and the original terminal was returned. A later shipment of PCs was found to include computers that were considerably quieter and the president now has a "quiet" PC.

MIDS was developed in stages. When the first MIDS system was implemented, a workstation was placed in Bob Ormsby's office. Each day he received two diskettes containing data updating the previous status indicators. To view a display, he loaded the diskettes and retrieved the specific display needed. The workstation did not actually process the data or perform calculations.

Shortly after, the first workstation was installed in Ormsby's office and seven other workstations were installed in selected management offices.

It was not long before all decided the system needed additional capabilities to support the growing number of displays that had evolved and to better meet end-user needs. For example, if someone needed to look at information from several preceding days, he or she had to send for other disks. Omsby still had to rely on paper reports to keep abreast of company activities and to communicate with Lockheed Corporation management.

The next stage of MIDS began with the purchase of a DEC 11/34 system that was used to store the displays and allowed users to interact with the system in an on-line fashion. It was later replaced by a DEC VAX 11/780 system. MIDS has now grown to over 700 displays shared by the company's top executives. The system currently has 75 users on-line and 85 connected workstations, including several in conference rooms.

In addition to the MIDS capabilities available to Lockheed-Georgia executives, subsystems have begun to emerge for various organizations, such as Manufacturing, Engineering, and Marketing. Each subsystem has its own unique display formats, tailored to the users and their information needs. The subsystems include an additional 650 display workstations.

Georgie Houdeshel, who currently directs the MIDS operations, explains the executive/subsystem interface as follows: Information requirements at various levels of management, including their integration and control, are handled in the MIDS system. Subsystems enable the heads of various organizations to develop and control their individual information requirements. Typically these subsystems contain:

——a more detailed level of data

——performance status measured against internal goals

——calendars of local organization events

——specialized data and statistics applicable to specific functional performance

——organization charts by task or group

The MIDS staff that supports the aspects of the system for executive use is responsible for meeting the management inforamtion needs for executives. These requirements necessitate flexibility to adjust the level of detail to the situation and the executive's style of management. This flexibility is accomplished by the addition of comments to explain anomalies or in some cases with follow-on displays to track a more detailed performance (these are deleted from the system when conditions warrant). For example, a schedule of major milestones to track program progress may be augmented with a more detailed schedule of a particular critical span. The detailed schedule may be provided by a subsystem.

Subsystems are controlled by the organizations that own them and access to their contents is subject to their authorization. Even company executives do not have access to subsystems without the authorization of the individual organization. There has been discussion with MIDS personnel about the fact that some data may exist in the subsystems used by middle managers that is not in the executive portion of MIDS. Some executives may feel they should have access to any information available in the organization, while middle managers want to manage their own working information, planning assumptions, and operating scenarios without having them distributed to others who do not realize the purpose and intent of the information.

The detailed data is collected and synthesized to satisfy the subsystem requirements and then summarized to provide a basis for executive information. The MIDS system is designed to take advantage of this process wherever the data system integrations permit, but individual inputs are also available to expand the total system flexibility.

Using MIDS

MIDS is easy to use, and this was an important requirement in the design of the system. One need not be an expert typist to obtain important management information.

When Lockheed-Georgia's customers spend millions of dollars for a single aircraft, they feel they have the right to call the president when they have a question. And, they expect him to have that information available. Since it is impossible for the president to remember information about the status of all orders, to be successful, MIDS had to provide the equivalent capability.

A typical instance occurred when Paul Frech, the next president of Lockheed-Georgia, received a telephone call from a defense official in Peru. The caller inquired about the pending sale of several Hercules aircraft to the Peruvian Air Force. He reasoned that since Frech was the top official at Lockheed-Georgia, he should know all the answers.

Frech was thankful to have MIDS to provide the necessary information. As the official was introducing himself, Frech called the system up and scanned information about the order—even the salesperson who had prepared the order—by executing the following steps:

———Depressing the ⟨ENTER⟩ key brought up the MIDS Major Category Menu display (see Exhibit 1)

———Selecting menu item M, by depressing the letter M on the keyboard, invoked the Marketing portion of the system. The first screen provided an index of all current Hercules prospects

———Depressing M and 5 brought up a display screen (see Exhibit 2) with all the information for the pending sale

Frech was able to provide all the information requested by the caller without delay or hesitation. This time it was a foreign official. But it could just as easily have been an Arab king, a U.S. military official, or a senior Lockheed Corporation executive. MIDS even includes a display screen containing a flight schedule for the corporate jet in case a trip must be planned as a result of a conversion.

System Features

All MIDS display subjects have the same top-down structure, selected for ease-of-use. The initial screen uses summary graphics that illustrate the status of the subject of the display. Next come the support graphics. These might include a key to the symbols used in the graphics; for instance, the notation explains that an "m" beside the image of an aircraft on the screen means that the plane is in the modification and paint stage (see Exhibit 3). The display screens are enhanced when viewed on the terminals in full color.

The last section of the display screen contains any information needed to fill in possible gaps or answer anticipated questions for the end-user. For example, the types of tests to be performed on a specific flight may be annotated.

Exhibit 1 Main Menu for MIDS System

MIDS MAJOR CATEGORY MENU

To recall this display at any time hit 'RETURN-ENTER' key.
For latest updates see S1.

A   MANAGEMENT CONTROL
     MSI'S; objectives
     organization charts;
     travel/availability/events sched.

B   C-5B ALL PROGRAM ACTIVITIES

C   HERCULES all program activities

E   ENGINEERING & ADVANCED PROGRAMS
     cost of new business; R & T;
     international developments

  EC engineering critical items

F   FINANCIAL CONTROL
     basic financial items; cost
     reduction; fixed assets; offset;
     overhead; overtime; personnel

  FC financial critical items

G   C-5A ENGINE STATUS (RESTRICTED)

H   HUMAN RESOURCES
       co-op program; employee
       statistics & participation

  HC human resources critical items

M   MARKETING
       assignments; prospects;
       sign-ups; product support

  MC marketing critical items

O   OPERATIONS
       facilities & services;
       manufacturing; material;
       product assurance & safety

  FSC facilities & serv. crit items
  MFC manufacturing critical items
  MTC material critical items
  QSC quality & safety crit. items

P   PROGRAM CONTROL
       financial & schedule
       performance

S   SPECIAL ITEMS

Exhibit 2 Typical MIDS Prospect Screen

```
    PERU/AF                        SOURCE   BUD LAWLER    5431
M5   REP: DICK SIGLER                       JIM CERTAIN   2265
```

	MON	TUE	WED	THR	FRI	SAT	SUN
REP LOCATION	---	---	---	---	---	---	---
IF AWAY				CARACAS, VENEZUELA---------			

```
FORECAST - THREE L-100-30s              PREV. HERC. BUY----8
```

```
NEXT EVENT---             |  AS OF TODAY: MEETINGS CONTINUE AMONG
  FINALIZE FINANCING      |  POTENTIAL LENDING INSTITUTIONS, INSURERS,
                          |  AND GELAC'S INTERNATIONAL MARKETING/
                          |  FINANCE/LEGAL TEAM TO DISCUSS REQUIRE-
                          |  MENTS AND CONDITIONS FOR FINANCING. GELAC
                          |  REPRESENTATIVES WILL BE IN LIMA MONDAY TO
                          |  LAY GROUNDWORK FOR FINAL NEGOTIATIONS. NO
KEY PERSON---CERTAIN      |  PROBLEMS EXPECTED.

SIGN-UP-----NEXT MONTH

PROBABILITY--GOOD

ROM VALUE----$60M

A/C DELIVERY: 4th QTR
```

This structure, used for all display screens, helps the users avoid confusion. All the information can be retrieved by using a maximum of only four keys: the ⟨ENTER⟩ key, the letter of the menu item wanted, and the ⟨PAGE FOWARD⟩ or ⟨PAGE BACKWARD⟩ keys. No jargon is used in the system displays; all narrative is stated in business terms that anyone familiar with the information displayed should be able to understand. Ease of use is the underlying design theme for MIDS. However, MIDS designers have also included the name and office telephone number for the author or source of the display contents. If additional information is needed, the user may call the person with questions.

Exhibit 3 Typical MIDS Progress Information Screen

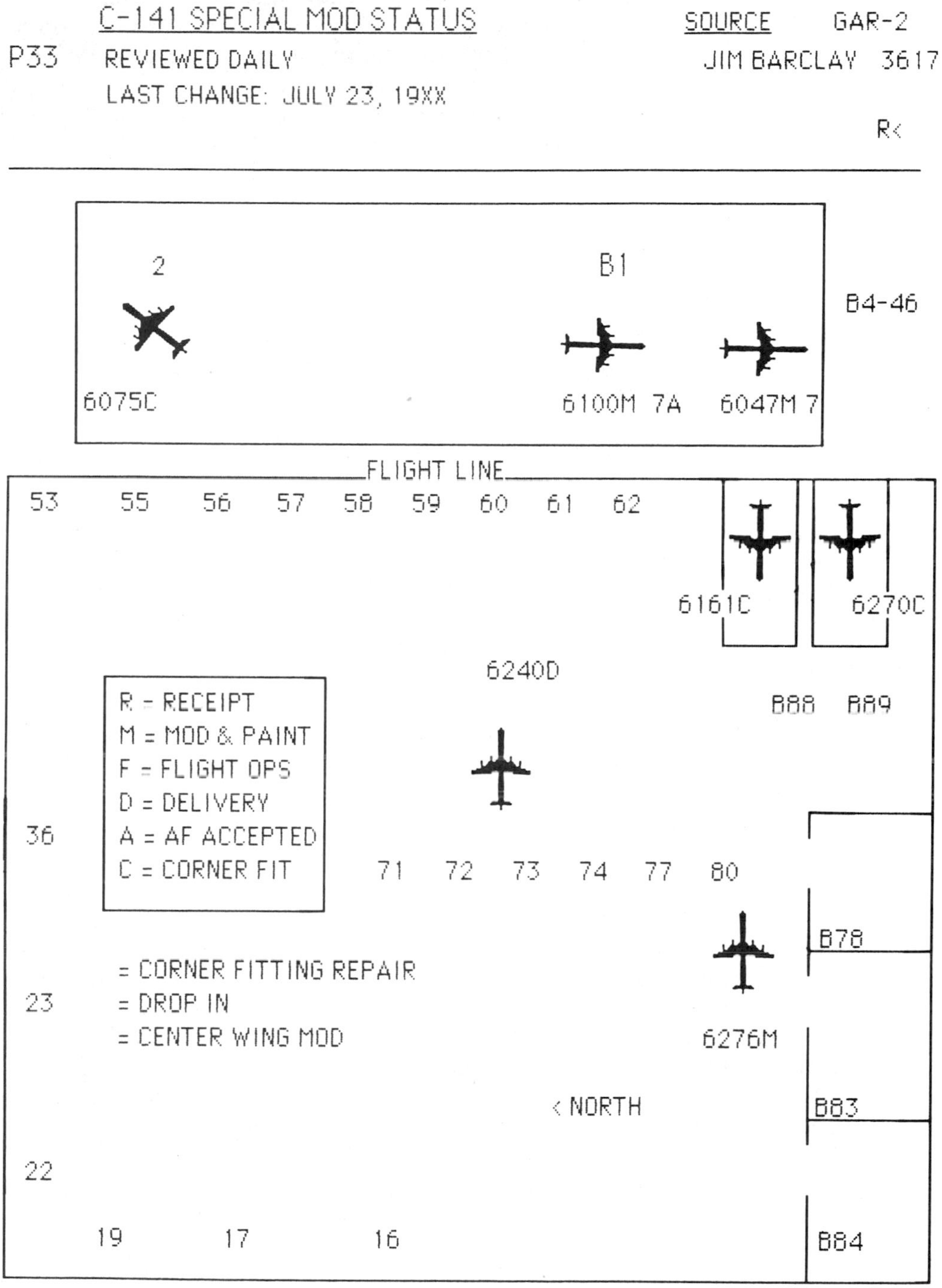

C-141 SPECIAL MOD STATUS   SOURCE   GAR-2

P33   REVIEWED DAILY   JIM BARCLAY   3617

　　　 LAST CHANGE: JULY 23, 19XX

　　　　　　　　　　　　　　　　　　　　　R<

```
2                         B1                      B4-46

6075C                 6100M 7A    6047M 7
```

FLIGHT LINE

```
53    55    56    57    58    59    60    61    62

                                            6161C        6270C

                        6240D
                                            B88   B89
R = RECEIPT
M = MOD & PAINT
F = FLIGHT OPS
D = DELIVERY
36   A = AF ACCEPTED
     C = CORNER FIT      71   72   73   74   77   80

                                                        B78
     = CORNER FITTING REPAIR
23   = DROP IN
     = CENTER WING MOD                6276M

                              < NORTH                   B83
22

     19      17      16                                 B84
```

Executives differ in the way they use MIDS. Some only browse through the displays, focusing only on those that have particular meaning at the time. At the other extreme are those who regularly and carefully examine a select set of displays, always in a certain sequence. The display of information can be tailored to one's own preferences as well. An individual is able to predefine the sequence in which a series of graphic screens is displayed. The personal profile is stored in the system and then whenever the screens are requested they will automatically be displayed in the order prescribed by the user's personal profile.

All data from MIDS may be obtained in printed form, if necessary, either on paper (black and white or color) or on transparencies. The only printer with access to MIDS is located in the office of the MIDS supervisor. The decision to use a single print location was made primarily for two reasons:

1. To control the distribution of information deemed "for limited access." Management wanted to minimize the chance of a security leak since much of the information about military aircraft or aircraft purchases by foreign governments is highly sensitive.

2. To avoid a return to the earlier "paper proliferation" days.

Each system user is assigned a password. The system provides the users access according to their passwords *and the location of the workstation they are using*. For example, if the president attempts to access the computer at a location other than his office, he will be denied access to any material designated as highly sensitive. This feature precluded exposure of information in an unauthorized area as well as to an unauthorized person.

Often users will know what information they wish to review, but may not be familiar with all the display screens that contain that information. MIDS maintains a keyword index that associates displays with key terms. By entering the first three letters of a descriptive keyword, users can quickly locate all pertinent display information.

Standardization of terminology is a continual issue in a company the size of Lockheed-Georgia. The same word or phrase may have different meanings across divisions or even departments. For instance, the marketing department might use the term *customer* to mean a person who has verbally agreed to purchase aircraft. The legal department, however, uses the term to mean the individual who has signed a contract for the purchase. Finance, on the other hand, uses *customer* to refer to the one who actually paid for the aircraft. The use of these terms was standardized early in the MIDS development and as a result there is little confusion between users.

Color usage is also standardized throughout the MIDS system. Green signals favorable performance, red means unfavorable, and yellow indicates that the data report marginal results. Goals and objectives are also color coded with cyan (light blue) indicating company goals and commitments, while magenta is used to code internal goals and objectives.

Some executives have difficulty distinguishing between colors. In these cases, special color combinations are selected to accommodate their needs.

When graphics are used, guidelines indicate which type to use. Line charts are specified for showing trends and bar charts show comparisons. Pie or stacked bar charts show percentages and parts of the whole.

All MIDS displays are designed and color coded to be effective when black and white copies are made of the screens.

Not all users have the same types of workstations, nor will this ever be the case. Therefore, the system will recognize the type of workstation at a particular location and translate display details into a form acceptable to the workstation. Likewise, it will convert input streams into an understandable form. This capability means that the company can take advantage of new equipment as it becomes available, without a system modification.

System Update Cycle

An essential set of reports supports the timely updates. Daily status reports for each screen alert operators to planned revisions, a daily "target data" report highlights events affecting the information (that is, the scheduled delivery of an aircraft), and computer-generated messages remind operators of correlating data that may be impacted by events occurring in other areas. On a typical day, approximately 15 percent of the information is updated.

The information to update MIDS records is prepared by the department responsible for a specific area. Department staff members enter data directly into the main computer system or in some cases onto floppy disks that are then submitted for processing. In both instances, the update data is double checked for accuracy before general access is granted. Only the author of the material may edit or change it. Other users may review, but cannot change, any details.

MIDS data is regarded as both timely and highly accurate.

Planned MIDS Evolution

MIDS is successful in part because it is continually evolving. All users and developers review new demands and requests and keep an eye out for computer technology that may be useful in some aspect of the system.

The system is also designed to automatically capture statistics about screen usage by individuals. Those displays that are underutilized are then examined to determine whether they are unnecessary or need to be redesigned.

Because of the increasing importance of the systems, the MIDS developers were organized into a separate department in 1985—the Management Information and Decision Support Department. They report to the Vice President—Finance.

Among the planned additions to MIDS are:

——*Three-dimensional graphics:* The display of performance information using multi-dimensional graphics will enhance the appearance of data and facilitate review of several different variables over time.

——*Audio output:* To reduce the number of words at the top of each display screen, the information support material will be spoken. Designers believe that users will better understand the message if the words are audible and only the graphics are displayed on the screen.

——*Video/computer screen interface:* The ability to capture photos, drawings, maps, or live events by means of videocamera and then digitize them for MIDS viewing. The video images will be stored on optical disks for laser reading. These disks will be linked to applicable databases and data and images can then be viewed simultaneously with a MIDS terminal.

——*"What if?" capability:* The capability for users to test the feasibility or potential impact of different business alternatives will be added to the software. For example, the effects of various fixed asset procurement plans on the company's cash flow.

——*Voice input:* A pilot program being tested by the Engineering Department will allow commands to be spoken, not entered through the keyboard, to call up MIDS displays.

MIDS continues to grow in importance. When Bob Ormsby left Lockheed-Georgia to become president of the Lockheed Aeronautical Systems Group, his successor, Paul Frech, immediately adopted MIDS as his own personal support system. His personal calendar of activities is even maintained on the system so that it is accessible to other executives.

The Lockheed-Georgia MIDS system began with a request from the president and has continued to have top-management support through several changes in executive personnel. The expansion of MIDS capabilities through subsystems, controlled by the vice-presidents of the individual organizations, is expected to increase the benefit of the system throughout the company.

This case was prepared for class discussion rather than to illustrate effective or ineffective handling of an administrative situation.

The Morgan Corporation

Bob Short, chief information officer for the Morgan Corporation, is reviewing the latest proposal from the end-user committee. This committee has been meeting for several weeks to discuss strategies, policies, and procedures for facilitating end-user computing. At the same time the committee has carefully considered the need to establish controls over end-user computing activities. This is the heart of the entire concern, as Bob sees it. The MIS Department, while generally supportive, expressed concern over the lack of control that would result as end-user computing became more predominant. The analysts raised questions about how quality control procedures would apply to user-developed systems and whether they would even be aware when user managers or their staff developed and installed applications. Bob has been placed in a position where he now must decide the future of end-user computing and strategies for managing and facilitating it within the Morgan Corporation.

History of the Morgan Corporation

The Morgan Corporation was founded in 1912 by Thomas Morgan. From the beginning it manufactured high-quality industrial tools at its northern Maryland location. Morgan purchased 150 acres in this region because it was near water and rail lines and not far from the industrial heartland of the Northeast. As manufacturing and heavy industry in the Northeast and Midwest grew, so too did the Morgan Corporation. When the nature of heavy industry in the United States changed, the Morgan Corporation adapted to stay with the changing industrial complex. The company was not affected by foreign competition or the bad economic times that the steel industry and other parts of the United States industrial complex faced.

The Morgan Corporation is still a family-owned company and currently employs 3500 employees. In 1957 Thomas Morgan, Jr. became chief executive officer and in 1967, when Thomas Morgan retired, Thomas Morgan, Jr. ascended to the position of chairman of the board. He immediately appointed Earl Dennison as president of the corporation. Dennison was succeeded in 1974 by the current president, Myron Stern.

Although the company is family owned, Thomas Morgan is careful to ensure that the best employees are always hired for the job. His own son, Gordon Morgan, has held a variety of positions within the company in order to gain the necessary experience. Currently he is vice-president of sales and oversees an annual sales volume of $74 million. Prior to this current position he was vice-president of engineering, where he learned firsthand the importance of having quality products designed and manufactured in a manner that provides the best possible value to the customer at the best return for the company.

The Morgan Corporation has been successful because it continually provides high-quality industrial tools at fair market prices. The staff continually monitors its own costs and prices very carefully. While this has always been true and is an important part of Morgan's history, it has become even more effective since the introduction of time-sharing systems in the 1960s and personal computers in the 1980s.

The Morgan Corporation is proud of the fact that it has never had an employee strike. Union stewards are involved in all manufacturing, safety, and labor management decisions. When problems arise, both management and labor always seek the most effective ways in which to resolve the dispute. All agree that Morgan is a good place to work and both management and staff want to keep it that way.

MIS Department at Morgan

The MIS Department grew as the company evolved. It uses state-of-the-art equipment and is organized to provide quality assurance for all of its applications.

Organization of the Department

The MIS Department consists of 61 people, including programmers, operations staff, quality control personnel, and information services staff members (see Exhibit 1 for the organizational breakdown). Day-to-day operations are handled by a 21-person staff that works in three shifts, six days a week. This group is responsible for running the company's IBM mainframe and maintaining the library of over 8000 magnetic tapes. The operations manager, Bill Parks, is very proud of the fact that his group is responsible for the systems' 98% "up-time" record. There is very little turnover among the operations staff. Many of the people have been there for 10-15 years and take a great deal of pride in "their system." They work diligently to ensure production schedules are met and alll jobs and reports are completed on time.

Jim O'Reilly, manager of the Systems and Programming Department, oversees 28 programmer/analysts. All are well versed in the COBOL language and some also have extensive training in assembly language. Approximately 18 months ago, Jim O'Reilly also acquired the FOCUS fourth-generation language for use in selected applications. Approximately one-third of the programming staff has become very familiar with FOCUS, and uses it when it is necessary to develop information retrieval applications quickly or when new applications are first prototyped. Jim is currently considering acquiring PC/FOCUS so that it may be installed in the company's information center and made available to end-users.

Unlike most information systems groups, O'Reilly's staff has experienced very little turnover. During the last year three programmers were added to the staff, but only one person left. Jim feels this results from the fact that Morgan is a good company to work for and the information systems group itself has much to offer.

Exhibit 1 Morgan Corporation MIS Department

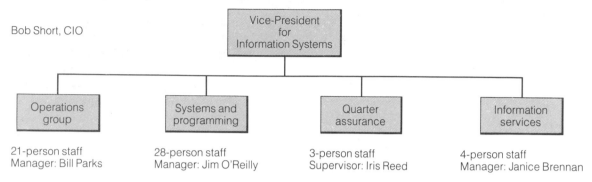

Bob Short, CIO

Vice-President for Information Systems

Operations group — 21-person staff, Manager: Bill Parks

Systems and programming — 28-person staff, Manager: Jim O'Reilly

Quarter assurance — 3-person staff, Supervisor: Iris Reed

Information services — 4-person staff, Manager: Janice Brennan

This group uses the latest computer and software technology, and it is centered around the concept of team building. When large development projects must be undertaken, Jim carefully establishes a team whose individuals complement each other. The team takes full responsibility for developing requirements specification, formulating the overall design, and then seeing the design through to its implementation.

Like most information systems staffs, the systems development group expends at least half of its effort maintaining existing systems, some of which have been placed for over 10 years. Its staff members agree that the current backlog of requests from users is at least 18 months of work.

The MIS Department operates under a charge-back policy. Whenever an application is developed, or changes are made to an existing system, the costs of doing so are billed to the department that submitted the request. Personnel costs, the largest cost component, are billed at rates from $35 to $60 per hour. Other costs, such as computer test time, or unusual equipment purchases, are also charged back. However, users do not pay for computer time or any other expenses once the application is implemented and running. The MIS operations budget covers these expenses.

Morgan's charge-back system is closely linked with the size of the systems development staff. It is expected that the budget transfers from user departments will cover 75% of the cost of the development staff salaries. (The other portion is attributed to internal needs of the department.) Thus new staff positions are justified by whether there is adequate user demand for their services.

All development activities, including statement of requirements specifications, design specifications, and testing strategies are approved by a three-person quality control group within the MIS Department. This group is responsible for ensuring that requirements for new systems or modified systems are met and for seeing that all software is appropriately tested before it is implemented. It maintains precise documentation standards and oversees the development, use, and maintenance of testing libraries. The library for each major application area contains both artificial and live data; these data are used as a database to test any new application. That is, data are read from the testing library and processed with the applications software so that the results generated can be verified for accuracy and correctness. Both the quality control group and Jim O'Reilly feel this is one of the reasons why the software development by the programming group is so reliable. (Approximately 70% of all software running at the Morgan Corporation was developed internally. Large-scale, generalized applications such as payroll and MRP were purchased from commercial vendors.)

The Information Services Group was established in 1984 to develop and operate the company's end-user oriented information center. At that time Janice Brennan, a senior analyst in the programming group, was selected to develop and launch the center. Her enthusiasm for working with staff members in the functional areas of the company (such as marketing, accounting, and personnel), coupled with her understanding of the overall development process followed at Morgan, were responsible for her selection as information services manager. The group currently consists of four other persons. The center is equipped with a number of personal computers as well as video display terminals that are connected to the mainframe system. End-users make extensive use of the information center for hands-on information processing.

Morgan Corporation Computing Complex

The heart of the computing system includes two IBM 4381 mainframe systems that were installed in 1986. Each system includes 16 megabytes of main memory and 4½ gigabytes of disk storage (IBM 3380 disk drives). Over 100 IBM 3278/3279 display terminals (or the equivalent) are attached to the system. The majority of the terminals are located in the functional areas of the company; about 40 are in the systems development group for use by programmer/analysts.

In addition to the applications software that is either purchased or developed by the systems group, Morgan also runs the PROFS personal support system and the IDMS/R database management system.

Other computer systems are installed at various locations within the company. The Production Department operates its own System 36 and uses Wang office systems for word processing and departmental computing. The Research and Development group relies heavily on a VAX system for CAD/CAM and for meeting its engineering/computing requirements. Each group is very dependent on the departmental systems. The Marketing, Finance, Accounting, and Personnel departments rely on the 4381 mainframes and are hardwired to the systems. In the past they have used only the mainframe system; however, personal computers have been popping up in these departments for use in budgeting, evaluating marketing strategies, and personnel management activities. The end-users appear very content with the personal computers and anticipate greater use of them in the future.

Bob Short, Chief Information Officer

Bob Short became the chief information officer approximately 9 months ago. Prior to that time he served for two years as vice-president for manufacturing. He has been with the company for eleven years in various management capacities and has proved to be an effective manager in each instance. Thomas Morgan has personally commented that he feels Bob will be a candidate for president of the company in the near future.

Short is not a technician and thus he views management information systems from a functional viewpoint. That is, his concern is how information systems can best be used to support the overall mission of the company; he does not get bogged down in technical details such as which programming language to use or how much memory should be purchased on a new mainframe system. Those decisions are the responsibility of his functional managers.

His extensive business background, which began after graduation from the University of Virginia with a degree in business, gives him important insight into the value of information systems from a business perspective. Two months after becoming CIO, he also enrolled in an MBA program with a concentration in MIS.

Short feels that any decision made concerning information systems is first and foremost a business decision and that the technical issues should be addressed in that light. Consequently, he is not as concerned with having the newest, latest, or fastest equipment available as he is ensuring that it will meet the needs of Morgan Corporation. Similarly, even if a project cannot be fully justified on a cost/benefit basis, if it appears that it is in line with the company's growth direction, Short is likely to endorse it and put the plan into action. As a result of these types of decisions, Bob Short has in a very short time developed a great deal of credibility with Morgan's MIS Operations Committee, the steering committee that oversees the approval of all major information systems applications for the company.

Because Short has been a member of the corporate management team for several years his office is located in the corporate suite area, rather than in the MIS Department. This location is more than symbolic in that it allows him to constantly interact with other corporate executives and to be continually aware of new planning activities and possible new developments in the company. For example, when the new Baltimore plant was under consideration, Short was an active participant in planning for the facility. His involvement ensured that MIS considerations were included in the decision process. As a result there was much closer integration between the new facility management and the information processing group than might otherwise have occurred.

Short is always careful to spend time in the MIS group even though his busy schedule of meetings at the corporate level sometimes makes this difficult. He is aware that his role is to facilitate the use of information systems in corporate activities and to link information systems plans and business activities, and he knows that the information he receives from the MIS staff is essential in achieving this objective.

MIS Operations Committee

The Morgan Corporation management team has been concerned for several years about linking information systems and corporate strategies. Therefore it was not a surprise to management when three years ago Thomas Morgan endorsed the establishment of the MIS Operations Committee. This committee reviews all project requests originated within the corporation, whether from functional-area managers or form information systems staff members.

Whenever a manager believes a new application is needed or significant changes must be made to an existing application, a project request form must be completed and submitted to the Operations Committee. This form is reviewed by the committee, which has the authority to endorse or disapprove the development of this application. All information systems applications must be approved by the Operations Committee before the systems and programming group can undertake work on them. The form, shown in Exhibit 2, indicates that managers must briefly describe the application and why it is needed. The Operations Committee then receives estimates from the Information Systems Department about the feasibility of the project and the amount of time it will take for requirements specification, systems design, programming, and testing.

The importance of and priority for the application is established by the MIS Operations Committee, not the information systems group. This committee also oversees the development backlog and establishes the priority for new requests within that backlog. Based on the information provided by the requesting manager and the committee's knowledge of existing applications, it may decide to group several applications together and improve their priority or it can consider a request as a separate application that must stand on its own merit.

Although individual managers may disagree with a particular decision about their project request, overall they feel the Operations Committee has done an effective job in maintaining applications priorities. "They have made the best of a bad situation," according to Vern Josephson, vice-president for marketing. "Managers request many more computer applications than it is physically possible for MIS to develop and maintain. Therefore, the committee has had to sort out our requests based on their individual justifications, not on political tests or technological elegance. Like any other department, we would like to do much more than we have and we would like to meet all development requests; however, that is unlikely to occur."

Since its inception three years ago, the MIS Operations Committee has focused entirely on applications for Morgan Corporation's mainframe complex. It has had little involvement with the MAPICS manufacturing planning system that runs on the Production Department's System 36 and it has not been involved in the CAD/CAM project for the R & D group. However, committee members are wondering more and more about their responsibilities for the management of end-user computing. The increasing proliferation of personal computers has raised questions for the MIS staff members and the Operations Committee participants.

The MIS Operations Committee consists of nine members; two are from the MIS department and the remainder are from other parts of the Morgan Corporation. Bob Short and Jim O'Reilly participate from the MIS Department. Other committee members include the vice-presidents of manufacturing, personnel, and R & D, as well as department managers for materials control, safety, sales, and financial accounting. June Parsons, vice-president for personnel, currently serves as chairperson of the Operations Committee. Each person on the committee serves for one calendar year. However, the committee is established so that people rotate on and off at six-month intervals. At no time does a majority of the committee's membership change. This provides continuity in all decisions and preserves the objectivity of the com-

Exhibit 2 Computer Services Project Proposal

<u>COMPUTER SERVICES PROJECT PROPOSAL</u>

Routing

1. _____
   originator

____ PROPOSAL FOR BUDGETING PURPOSES

2. _____
   comp. serv.

____ PROPOSAL FOR CURRENT IMPLEMENTATION

3. _____
   corp. dept. head

4. _____
   comp. serv.

5. _____
   committee

ORIGINATING DEPARTMENT

Requested by _____ Department _____ Location _____

Request date _____ Required date _____

Request summary

Benefits: Explain how this request will reduce expenditures, reduce manpower, or enhance company operations. Include estimated dollar savings/costs.

mittee. June is approximately halfway through her one-year term as chairperson of the committee.

All participants on the committee are at the vice-president or senior management level in the corporation. This is no accident. When the committee was established corporate management decided that the committee should be given the full authority to approve or disapprove proposals and to commit corporate and information sys-

Exhibit 2 *(continued)*

COMPUTER SERVICES DEPARTMENT
Computer Services Analysis of Request

Analysis by _____ Date _____

1. Is request for:
   a) New system or function _____ Yes _____ No
   b) Correction of an existing system

   _____
   System or Program

   c) Addition/modification of an existing system

   _____
   System or Program

   d) System or function development:
      Description of work to be done:

      _____
      _____
      _____

3. Required computer services resources:
   a) Estimated system analysis man-hours _____
   b) Estimated programming man-hours _____
   c) Estimated debug and test man-hours _____
   d) Estimated documentation man-hours _____
                  Total man-hours _____
   e) Estimated development and test computer time _____ hours
   f) Estimated production CPU time _____ per _____
   g) Special system requirements _____

4. General:
   a) Is request consistent with long-range systems objectives? _____
   b) Comments: _____
      _____
      _____
      _____

_____
_____

Approval: _____ BUDGET   _____ IMPLEMENTATION

Minor project:

_____   _____   _____   _____
Requesting Corp Dept Head   Date   Mgr – Computer Svcs   Date

Request scheduled for completion by _____

Major project:

_____   _____   _____   _____
Requesting Dept. Staff Approval   Date   Computer Priorities Comm.   Date

tems resources to projects. But management also recognized that to make decisions of this nature the participants needed to be at a level in the company where they would naturally have information about corporate plans and activities. Thus senior members of the committee were selected for membership. This decision has turned out to be wise and as a result the Operating Committee format works well.

Information Center Services

The Information Center Services Group was created by Janice Brennan and currently includes four other persons. Its mission is to facilitate end-user computing within the company, which is interpreted to mean supporting managers and staff members who have computing requirements that do not merit development within the MIS group. Often these are one-time requirements for information or applications that do not require high-volume transaction processing support. Applications developed through the information center also need not be submitted to the Operations Committee for review or approval.

The center currently includes twenty IBM personal computers, each equipped with 3278/3279 emulation boards. These boards allow the PCs to interconnect with the mainframe systems if needed or to operate on a stand-alone basis as a simple personal computer. The information center provides four IBM PC/AT 3270 computers that are connected to the 4381 systems. These computers support high-resolution graphics and allow users to run multiple sessions at the same time with up to four different windows on the display. There are also twelve 3278 terminals in the information center. Each is connected to the mainframe complex.

Several mainframe applications were developed specifically with information center users in mind. For example, a project management system runs on a mainframe and is accessible to end-users through IBM 3278 terminals or PCs with emulation boards. This system allows individuals to establish project milestones and monitor the actual and planned performance. Individuals enter the data about this project as it becomes available to them. Users are charged only for the connect time during which they are using the application. There are no development costs for these applications. Another information center application running on the mainframe assists the marketing and sales staff in preparing product quotations for customers. By interacting with the system they can examine the impact of manufacturing quantities, production costs, and profit to derive a selling price acceptable to customer and company. This application is used extensively by the sales staff.

The information services group maintains a library of personal computer software that is effective in meeting end-user needs. Among the most widely used software are such packages as dBASE III, Lotus 1-2-3, Symphony, Framework, and the Harvard Project Manager. Several word processing packages, including WordStar and Multimate, are also available through the information center. A newsletter, prepared each month by Janice Brennan, informs people in the company of new facilities in the information center, communicates user experiences, and provides tips about end-user computing. Brennan feels that the newsletter has been valuable in informing Morgan employees of the capabilities within the center as well as encouraging end-user computing in general.

End-User Computing Committee Recommendations

The end-user computing committee, established to look at necessary guidelines for encouraging the development of selective computer applications by end-users, includes representatives from each of the functional areas of the Morgan Corporation as well as the MIS Department. It is chaired by Jane Mandrell, Associate Director of the information center. The committee met several times over the past three weeks and submitted a set of recommendations, which are attached as Exhibit 3.

Among the issues of greatest importance to the Morgan Corporation are determining what controls, if any, should be placed on the development of end-user applications, and defining the MIS Department role in developing, supporting, and maintaining applications for which their department is not wholly responsible. The philosophy of the end-user computing committee is that users should be responsible for ensuring that the application is correct. That is, they feel that all risk and responsibilities should be placed on end-users, and not on the MIS Department.

Members of the MIS Department, whose opinions Bob Short greatly respects, have reviewed these recommendations and have expressed significant concerns. Bob must now deal with these concerns since ultimately he must make the recommendation to adopt or to ignore the memo from the end-user committee.

The systems development staff feels it is politically naive to assume that they will not be held responsible if there are end-user computing fiascos. Therefore, they want the quality control group to certify any application before it is put into use. This means that the group must know in advance when an application is going to be developed, what software will be used, and how it will be applied. The programmer/analysts want *each application,* and the data source for the application, registered with the MIS Department. Furthermore, they want agreement and a statement in the new guidelines that any applications not developed by the MIS Department will not be maintained by the department.

Great concern is also expressed regarding the establishment of hardware, software, and data standards. While the majority of programmer/analysts strongly support the notion of end-user computing and privately work with individuals to help them develop applications and get them into operation, they fear that standards they have worked hard to evolve in fact will be ignored. For example, they feel that a standard personal computer should be selected for predominant applications throughout the corporation. The creation of a mixed vendor environment would make it virtually impossible to standardize applications support of any form. Many end-users counter this by saying that there will be a mixed environment anyway, and that standards are impossible, so let's get on with it.

There have been instances of improper decisions due to lack of data or improper manipulation of data through end-user developed applications. Therefore the con-

Exhibit 3 Memorandum on Management of End-User Computing

Memorandum on Management of End-user Computing

MEMORANDUM: Robert Short, Vice-President for Information Systems
      FROM: Jane Mandell, Chair, End-User Computing Committee
   SUBJECT: Recommendations for Management of End-User Computing

The End-User Computing Committee has carefully examined the opportunities and concerns of providing managers and staff members with personal computers and other computing resources that are not directly within the scope of either the MIS Department or the Morgan Information Center. It is our opinion that the Morgan Corporation can receive important benefits from the judicious use of computing resources by end-users. However, we believe these activities must be managed carefully to ensure that there is no risk to the company.

This memo summarizes the recommendations formulated by the End-User Computing Committee. It outlines the basis for our recommendations and lists those types of applications that we believe are suitable for end-user development.

The issue of adequate supervision for end-user computing was discussed at length and from many angles. The committee recommends seven guidelines that will provide acceptable levels of flexibility and control.

There is not agreement by all committee members on all issues. However, each item has been recommended by at least two-thirds of the seven-person committee.

MANAGEMENT OBJECTIVES

Two objectives guided our activities and form the basis for our recommendations. They are to:

* Encourage and facilitate the use of computer resources by managers and staff members to raise personal productivity and enhance the effectiveness of decisions and departmental actions
* Improve the timeliness with which applications suitable for direct use by managers and staff members are developed

We recognize that there are many computer applications that should be developed by the MIS Department. It is explicitly noted that those computer systems suitable for end-user development are not ones normally prepared by the department's programmer/analysts, but rather new categories that current staff members are unable to support due to time constraints and workload requirements.

Exhibit 3 *(continued)*

SUITABLE APPLICATIONS

The committee believes those applications suitable for end-user development:

* Use commercially available generalized software packages (e.g., dBASE III, Lotus 1-2-3, and Microsoft Chart)
* Do not process high volumes of data or demand large storage capacities
* Do not interact with the financial control systems of the Morgan Corporation
* Produce limited quantities of printed output
* Produce information used within the originating department
* Interact with mainframe systems and databases for data retrieval only (data from end-user applications are not submitted to the mainframe systems and do not modify corporate data)
* Will be used a limited number of times and do not result in ongoing application systems

Additional characteristics may be recognized as new computer hardware and software products emerge or as experience with end-user computing provides us with new insights.

MANAGEMENT RECOMMENDATIONS

To obtain the greatest possible advantages from personal computers and end-user computing, while providing suitable management controls, the committee has determined that managers and staff members must take responsibility for the applications they develop or cause to be developed. It is unreasonable to expect that the MIS Department can be responsible for errors or inefficiencies in applications they do not prepare.

In addition, the committee believes the increased use of the Information Center demonstrates its usefulness within the company. We have placed a greater burden on the center to assist in managing end-user computing.

The following management guidelines are recommended:

1. All computer applications that are used in decision making or involve the commitment of Morgan Corporation financial and personnel resources must be approved by the Information Center.

2. Managers and staff members who develop their own computer applications, whether involving personal computers, departmental computers, or Information Center facilities, are responsible for ensuring that their application is correct and that it contains no errors.

3. The Information Center director must be notified, in writing, when managers or staff members develop and put into effect any application that was not developed by the MIS Department or Information Center personnel.

Exhibit 3 *(continued)*

4.   Any computer application developed through the Information Center will be developed without cost for assistance.

5.   Computer applications that modify the corporate databases or require high-volume transaction processing must go through normal approval and development processes. These applications should not be developed by managers or staff members.

6.   Computer applications and computer equipment that will incur a continuous cost for maintenance (such as for ongoing license or maintenance fees) or for which the total software cost is greater than $2500 must be submitted to and approved by the MIS Operations Committee.

We hope these recommendations will be openly and widely discussed by Morgan employees. Changes and additions will be welcomed. We also anticipate that the guidelines will evolve with experience. Thus, the above recommendations should not be considered final.

We also feel it is appropriate to develop an approval request form for all end-user applications.

Please contact me if any item in this statement needs clarification. I look forward to your comments and suggestions.

cerns of the MIS Department are real. They see the benefits of end-user computing and the opportunity to manage the backlog in a more effective way. But they are very uncomfortable with turning the development of any applications software over to nonprofessionals unless adequate controls are placed on them.

Bob Short is pondering his action. He wants to support end-user computing because he believes it is a valuable resource for the firm. But he knows also that the risks of errors, missing controls, and careless projects are real. "The questions are tough," he is thinking to himself. "The MIS group is already working continuously and cannot take on additional development tasks. Yet they don't want to see information systems quality get out of hand. Is there a way to achieve both objectives and not offend either group? For that matter, are there even *two sides?*"

Bob must also decide whether the end-user committee is recommending too much responsibility—and too much power—to the information center. Is the center taking on a role that may hinder the original service?

Short has been heard to ask "*Can* end-user computing be managed?" Now he must answer his own question.

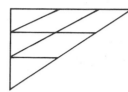

Appendix: Flowcharting Symbols and Techniques

Through symbols, flowcharts illustrate the sequence of events that takes place in processing data. The documents that are used or produced in processing and the method of data storage are included in this symbolic sequence. The symbols used in flowcharts have been standardized by the American National Standards Institute (ANSI) so that anyone who looks at a flowchart should be able to understand the sequence of events it describes.

Flowcharts and flowchart symbols are used in all phases of computer processing. They are used to describe data processing systems that are being studied and to develop the processing logic that will later translate into computer programs.

This appendix describes the standard flowchart symbols. We first introduce the symbols used to describe computer processing activities. Then we discuss flowcharting itself, pointing out which processes are generally flowcharted and why.

Flowcharting Symbols

Flowcharts pictorially describe steps and activities that take place during data processing. The symbols fall into three categories: media, processing, and descriptive symbols. Most of the symbols you see here are included in *flowchart templates,* plastic sheets used to trace the symbols onto paper. (If one uses a flowchart template, and almost everyone does, these symbols do not have to be drawn freehand and are thus standardized in shape and size.)

Media symbols show the media on which data are input or results output and also identify secondary storage devices that contain data or programs (software) stored in computer-processible form. By using these symbols, we can describe input, output, and storage operations clearly and concisely, something that is difficult to do in narrative description. Nine symbols are used to represent media (Figure A.1).

Processing symbols are used to describe calculation, input/output, and other processing activities. Some of the symbols also allow manual and noncomputer processing to be shown. There are eight processing symbols (Figure A.2).

The five **descriptive symbols** (Figure A.3) show the relationships between different individual and sets of processing activities and the sequence in which they occur. Some of the symbols in this set are also for user convenience; that is, they allow the user to follow easily the processing logic in flowcharts that are divided into segments or that extend across more than one page.

Figure A.1 Media Symbols

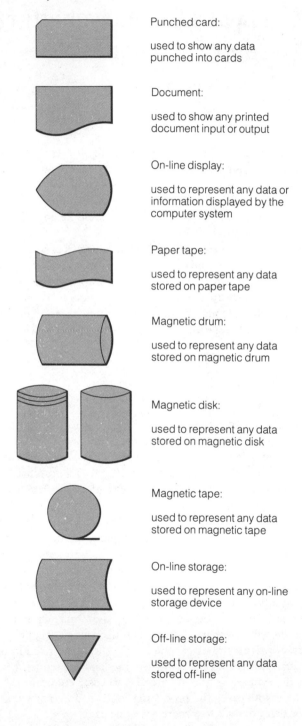

Punched card:

used to show any data punched into cards

Document:

used to show any printed document input or output

On-line display:

used to represent any data or information displayed by the computer system

Paper tape:

used to represent any data stored on paper tape

Magnetic drum:

used to represent any data stored on magnetic drum

Magnetic disk:

used to represent any data stored on magnetic disk

Magnetic tape:

used to represent any data stored on magnetic tape

On-line storage:

used to represent any on-line storage device

Off-line storage:

used to represent any data stored off-line

Figure A.2 Processing Symbols

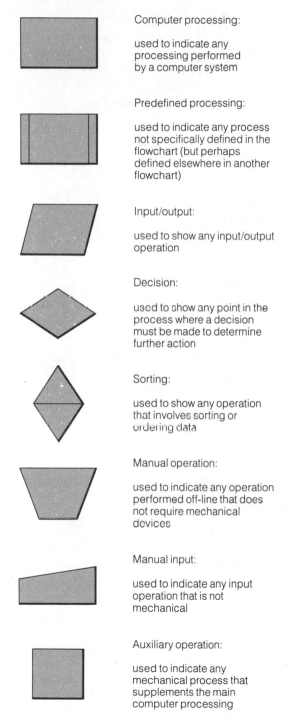

Computer processing:

used to indicate any processing performed by a computer system

Predefined processing:

used to indicate any process not specifically defined in the flowchart (but perhaps defined elsewhere in another flowchart)

Input/output:

used to show any input/output operation

Decision:

used to show any point in the process where a decision must be made to determine further action

Sorting:

used to show any operation that involves sorting or ordering data

Manual operation:

used to indicate any operation performed off-line that does not require mechanical devices

Manual input:

used to indicate any input operation that is not mechanical

Auxiliary operation:

used to indicate any mechanical process that supplements the main computer processing

Figure A.3 Descriptive Symbols

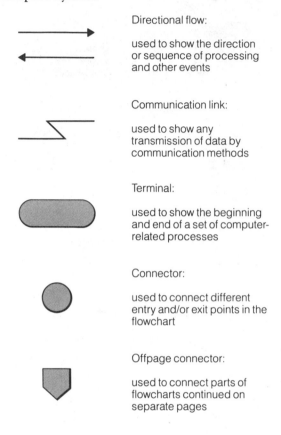

Directional flow:

used to show the direction or sequence of processing and other events

Communication link:

used to show any transmission of data by communication methods

Terminal:

used to show the beginning and end of a set of computer-related processes

Connector:

used to connect different entry and/or exit points in the flowchart

Offpage connector:

used to connect parts of flowcharts continued on separate pages

The Flowcharting Process

Flowcharting can be useful to people who actually draw the flowchart (such as programmers, systems analysts, and systems designers) and to those who read them (such as users or other systems staff members), but only if properly done. To improve their usefulness, you should be aware of why we flowchart and what should be described in the process.

Why Flowchart?

There are three primary reasons for developing flowcharts. One important reason is to identify particular processes or items processed in a computer application or processing system. In other words, we can show what processing steps take place

Figure A.4 Flowchart Segment Showing Basic Input/Output Operation

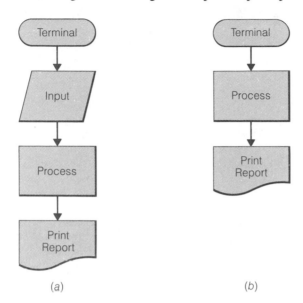

and the data acted upon during each step. For example, we can use an input/output symbol, a processing symbol, and a magnetic tape symbol to show a sequence of events for payroll calculations. Data are input from a terminal, gross pay and net pay are calculated, and a paycheck is prepared as output (Figure A.4*a*). Notice that a brief explanation is shown inside each symbol describing the document or process. Although the symbols used in flowcharting are standardized, the exact ways in which people use them can differ. In Figure A.4*b* the same payroll calculation procedure is shown, but notice that the input/output symbol has been omitted and the terminal symbol has been repeated to indicate explicitly that input is from key entry. When a document symbol is connected to a processing box, it is assumed that the document is input to that process. The reader will find both kinds of descriptions used quite frequently.

If we want to show activities for which the actual process has been predefined (for example, a utility program that is part of the computer system), we can use the predefined processing symbol. In Figure A.5 a copy routine is shown. A copy of a magnetic tape file is made, for example, as backup protection in case the original version is damaged or destroyed. Notice that the predefined process symbol is used— copy-and-sort programs are utility programs in most computer system software libraries so we do not have to program these processes ourselves.

A second reason for flowcharting is to show relationships between processes and items being processed. In large processing applications we may have to show several sets of processes; which process set is the one actually performed depends on a certain condition the program will test for. The result of the test (that is, the condition that actually exists) will determine which of the indicated processes are

Figure A.5 Flowchart Segment Showing Copy of a Magnetic Tape File

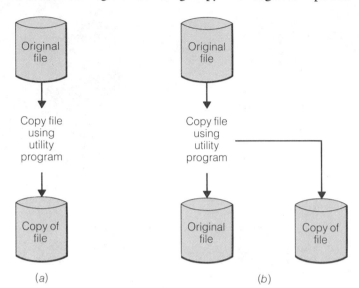

executed. In an inventory control system, for example, we will probably have the program update the balance-on-hand quantity for materials remaining in the warehouse after withdrawal transactions have been processed. Then we will check to see if the balance-on-hand is less than or equal to a preestablished reorder point (Figure A.6). If the balance is below the reorder point, a purchase order may be generated by the system.

Flowcharts also verify relationships and detect anything that has not been explained or documented. Verifying relationships means showing *all* processes and procedures needed and fitting them together so they are related to each other in a meaningful way. For example, in a production control system, we may use the computer to generate work order tickets (documents). In thinking through the design, we may have identified the need to print one copy of each ticket to be maintained in an open production order file (for work in progress). However, in actually flowcharting the system, we find that a second copy of the ticket is needed for the production employee who will begin the manufacturing work process. Having to formulate the flowchart and show the relationships between processes and documents enabled us to detect the need for the second copy. Without the flowchart process, we could easily have missed this flaw in the design. Drawing flowcharts helps tighten and integrate the system design.

What to Flowchart

Understanding the benefits of flowcharting is related to knowing what to show on the flowchart. That is, we can realize the benefits of flowcharts only if they properly

Figure A.6 Flowchart Segment of Materials Reorder Decision

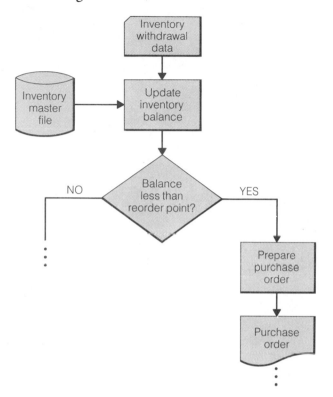

describe programs or application systems. (Program flowcharts are called *microflow-charts;* system flowcharts are *macroflowcharts.*) The flowchart should show:

1. Flow of documents through the system or program
2. Data and files used in the system or program
3. Decision and transfer of control points
4. Processes taking place
5. Sequence for processing activities

Showing the flow of documents through the system means that we must identify all documents indicating when they enter the system and how they are used. Documents produced during processing (for example, reports), and why they were produced, should be represented in the flowchart. The flowchart in Figure A.7 describes an accounts payable processing system that uses two different documents—invoices from suppliers are input to the system, used to capture data on magnetic disk, and then filed off-line; an accounts payable report is produced at the end of the update process. The processes taking place in this application system, in addition to the key-to-disk operation, are checking (editing) the data for errors and producing

Figure A.7 Systems Flowchart of Accounts Payable Processing

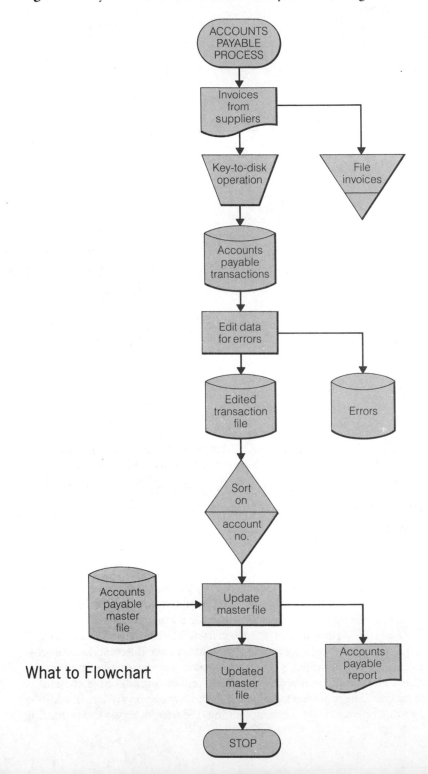

an error file on magnetic disk, sorting the transactions into order based on the account number of the supplier, and updating the accounts payable master file. Since the sequence of these activities is important to the process, it is illustrated carefully in the flowchart.

Processing takes place for the purpose of doing something with or to data. We may, for example, use data in calculation, sort data, or make copies of data. Flowcharts should clearly describe the purpose of the processing and how it is performed, including the sequence and purpose of each step. Sometimes the process actually executed depends on a certain condition, as we saw earlier in the inventory control example.

In general, flowcharts are useful for developing processing logic and sequence of activities, as well as for providing documentation so that other people can study a processing system and determine what is taking place. If properly developed, a flowchart will be an indispensable tool for all who use it.

Glossary

Access To locate data stored in the computer system or in computer-related equipment for the purpose of reading, writing, or moving data or instructions.

Accounting Information Quantitative information about income, financial status, and business costs. Contrast with *management information*.

Accounts Payable Money owed to a vendor or supplier for services rendered or merchandise received.

Accounts Receivable Money owed to a business or organization as a result of a transaction that has occurred but which the recipient has not paid.

Accrual Accounting An accounting system that reports revenue and expense activities in the period in which they occur, regardless of whether cash changes hands. Contrast with *cash accounting*.

Accumulator A special-purpose register in the central processing unit used to store the results of arithmetic operations temporarily.

Acoustic Coupler An inexpensive type of modem, in which the coupler accepts a telephone receiver into rubber cups for the ear- and mouthpieces. Usually operates at the rate of 300 baud.

Ada A programming language being developed on a variety of machines for universal use in business, science, math, and engineering.

Address The location of an area in which data or instructions can be stored in equipment such as the main memory unit of the central processing unit or on direct access devices such as magnetic disk and magnetic drum. The address is stated as a number and is maintained within the computer system. Persons working with higher-level programming languages seldom, if ever, directly use the storage address.

After-look The copy of a record made after the record is updated. Used in the *audit trail* method of backing up data.

Age How old information is greatly affects its worth to a user. Causes of delay include time needed to collect information and infrequent reports.

Aggression Aggression against a new information system is an attack on the system, such as damaging components or entering erroneous data.

Alphabetic Data Data consisting of the letters A–Z.

Alphanumeric Data The set of data that includes the letters A–Z, the numbers 0–9, and special symbols (+, −, $, #, *, etc.).

Analytic Style A systematic style of perceiving information. Analytic individuals follow a structured, well-organized, and deductive approach in arriving at a decision. Contrast with *heuristic style*.

Application The use of computer-based routines for specific purposes such as accounts receivable maintenance, inventory control, and new product selection;

software or computer programs that process data to provide output for such a purpose.

Application Generator   A program that produces application software based on information submitted by the user; software procedures produced from a description of the functions wanted by users; a type of fourth-generation language.

Application Portfolio   An organization can have four portfolios of applications: for institutional tasks such as payroll and production scheduling; professional support such as word processing and expert systems; physical automation; and systems outside the organization to link with customers and suppliers.

Application Software   See *application*.

Applications Programmer   Develops software, usually in third- and fourth-generation languages, to generate reports, update records, and perform other functions involving data stored in the database. Contrast with *systems programmer*.

Architecture   The structure under which an information system's hardware, software, data, and communications capabilities are put together. Architectures differ in flexibility, expandability, security, and reliability.

Arithmetic/Logic Unit   One of the three parts of the central processing unit of a computer system: the part in which arithmetic and logic operations are performed on data.

Artificial Intelligence   Teaching computers to accomplish tasks in a manner that is considered "intelligent," characterized by learning and making decisions. See *expert system*.

Assembly Language   A special-purpose computer program or translator that converts symbolic instructions in programs into machine-language instructions that can be executed by the computer system.

Asynchronous   Pertaining to an automatic operation (for example, computation, communication) made possible by a signal that a preceding operation has been completed and a new one can begin. Contrast with *synchronous*.

Attitude Survey   A questionnaire survey of users conducted after a new information system or application is implemented.

Attributes of Information   Characteristics of information that make the material useful to the receiver (for example, accuracy, timeliness, reliability, origin).

Audio Response Unit   A device that generates output from computer systems in the form of the spoken word. Words are stored on a magnetic medium for use in output.

Audit Trail   The technique of using system documents and other references to retrace the processing of data by following the actions taken in changing, adding, or deleting records in a file.

Authorization   Approval to access particular files in a database and make certain uses of the data.

Auxiliary Storage   Storage that supplements the main memory section of the central processing unit. Auxiliary storage may be on-line or off-line.

Avoidance   Avoidance of a new information system by the intended users is often caused by frustrating initial encounters.

Back-end Tool   Any CASE tool used in the later stages of systems development to convert software logic designs into programming code.

Backlog   In most organizations, demand for new applications requires more time than systems analysts and programmers have, resulting in a backlog.

Backup   Standby, substitute, or alternate components in a computer processing system that can be used in case of failure or damage to the primary component (for example, backup copies of data or programs; backup equipment and facilities that can be used in the event of hardware failure or other emergency).

Balance Sheet   A financial statement comparing assets and liabilities.

Baseband   A category of coaxial cable that carries a single digital signal at very high speeds and is relatively inexpensive and easy to maintain.

BASIC   Beginner's All-purpose Symbolic Instruction Code, an easy-to-learn, third-generation computer language similar to FORTRAN. Used widely, especially on microcomputers and in the fields of education, research, and industry.

Baud   The transmission speed for data, measured in bits per second.

Before-look   The copy of a record made before the record is updated. Used in the *audit trail* method of backing up data.

Binary Digit   The binary system is a two-state number system that can be used to represent the on and off states of components in computer equipment. Several binary digits, or bits, can be grouped together to represent data and instructions.

Black Box Concept   Examining a system's inputs and outputs only, as if the internal processes and components were in a "black box," allowing the investigator to analyze input and output processes without having technical knowledge about how the system works.

Block   A set of data, such as a record, that is treated as a single unit.

Blocking Factor   The number of logical records or other units of data grouped as a single unit. For example, if records are stored on magnetic tape with a blocking factor of 4, each block contains four data records.

Bottleneck   A processing slowdown that occurs because operations in certain activities or operations in the computer are lagging behind. Common bottleneck areas are data preparation, input, and output.

Bottom-up Approach   An approach to systems planning that begins by identifying basic transaction and information processing needs, then integrates those applications at each higher level in the organization to provide information for decision makers. Contrast with *top-down approach*.

Boundary   The separation between two elements, systems, or processes; a line of demarcation that separates and distinguishes two or more different entities.

Bridge   A bridge interconnects two networks of the same type, accepting transmissions from one and directing them to appropriate locations on the other.

Broadband   A category of coaxial cable that carries multiple analogue signals simultaneously at different frequency ranges, suitable for voice, data, and video transmission.

Broadcast Topology   Any computer network topology in which every transmitted message or set of data goes to every node, although each node recognizes only messages addressed to it; examples are ring and star topologies.

Browse Capability   A feature of executive support systems making it easy to page through records of business activities, correspondence topics, and other files to scan for significant information.

Buffer   A storage area or storage device that is used to assemble input and output for processing. Buffers help to compensate for speed differences between the central processing unit and various input/output devices.

Bus   A link that interconnects computer devices for data transmission.

Bus Topology   The arrangement of a computer network as a linear channel, which may be simply a cable, with taps on the cable to link the nodes.

Business Systems Planning (BSP)   A widely used method for planning information systems that uses a top-down approach to identify the data necessary to run an organization. Data are classified and put into a matrix to show their relation to the processes that create and use data. That dataflow information is used to produce an information architecture, data management recommendations, and priorities for applications development.

Business Value   To determine the business value of an information system, one may, for example, gauge how successfully the system is being used, what the system has returned on its investment, and what it contributes to the "bottom line."

Byte   The smallest storage unit in main memory or secondary storage; consists of eight bits in most computer systems.

Calculation   Using arithmetic procedures, such as addition or multiplication, on data to generate useful results.

Carrier Sense Multiple Access (CSMA) Method   A local-area network access method used with bus networks in which the transmitting device, such as a workstation, must "listen" to the channel to sense whether it is in use; if it is, the workstation waits briefly and listens again.

Carrier Sense Multiple Access/Collision Detection (CSMA/CD) Method   Same as *carrier sense multiple access* but with the addition of a detector for messages that are about to travel on a line that is being sensed, to avoid a collision.

CASE   Computer-aided system engineering, also used to mean computer-aided software engineering. CASE tools speed the system/software development process, automate tedious tasks, enforce development standards, and capture data that describe the system.

Cash Accounting   An accounting system that reports transactions only when cash is received or dispensed. Contrast with *accrual accounting*.

CBX   See *computer branch exchange*.

Central Processing Unit (CPU)   The main work unit of the computer system, the seat of all control and processing work. The unit of the computer that controls all processing of data, movement of data, and execution of instructions. Sets of circuits that together make up the control unit, the arithmetic/logic unit, and the main memory unit.

Centralization   The concept of locating decision-making authority, control, or resources at a limited number of locations in an organization. When applied to management, centralization is the location of decision-making authority at a relatively high level in the organization. Contrast with *decentralization*.

Change Agent   A social sciences term for a person introducing change to an organization, such as a systems analyst developing an information system. As change agent, the analyst must prepare users for the change (*unfreeze*), introduce the changes to them, and reinforce the new system to return the organization to stability (*refreeze*).

Channel   In data communications, the highway along which data travel from one location to another, such as telephone wire, coaxial cable, fiber optics, microwave transmission, and satellites.

Character Data   Letters and symbols (for example, $+$, $-$, $*$, $/$) that can be processed as data in a computer system.

CIM   See *computer-integrated manufacturing*.

Circuit Switching   A method of moving data in a wide-area network; communication circuits are established before communications start, and the system has continual and exclusive use of the circuit until the end of transmission. Contrast *message switching*, *packet switching*.

Classification   Grouping data according to common characteristics.

Closed System   Any system that is self-contained and does not interact with the environment.

Coaxial Cable   A single wire encased in insulating material and a protective metal casing; provides much faster data transmission than twisted pair lines, is free of noise and electrical interference, and can be used over long distances, such as in underground and underwater cables.

COBOL   COmmon Business-Oriented Language is the dominant programming language in business data processing. A third-generation, English-like language whose programs can be tranferred from one type of computer to another.

Code Generator   A CASE tool that automates some of the work of preparing computer software by converting systems specifications into executable source code.

Comfort Information   A type of information required by top-level managers to keep them informed about current situations or achievement levels; allows the manager to know that performance is in line with general expectations in an area of interest.

Commercial Database Service   Subscribers to commercial databases pay periodic fees and are able to dial up an on-line database service containing financial, marketing, or other types of data.

Communication   A communication has four essential elements: a source, a communication channel, a destination, and a message.

Communications Network   The interconnection of multiple locations via any of several channels to transmit or receive data; may be a wide-area, local-area, or value-added network.

Communications Processor   A small computer used as an interface between the main computer and associated terminals and multiplexors, freeing the central processing unit from some communications work.

Competitive Strategy   See *strategy*.

Compiler   A type of translator that converts computer programs written in higher-level programming languages into symbols and signals that are understandable and executable in the central processing unit of the computer system. Compilers are themselves computer programs that act on other computer programs written in human-understandable languages to translate them into machine-understandable signals.

Computer Branch Exchange (CBX)   A local-area network in which the existing computer-based telephone switching system is used as the center of a star topology; same as *PBX* except that the system is computer-based.

Computer Conferencing Linking together people at remote locations through their computers, where they have access to their own files as well as organization databases. The system allows one person to have information on the screen transmitted to all other members' screens, and information is stored until purged.

Computer Information System See *information system*.

Computer-Integrated Manufacturing (CIM) Factory automation using computers for manufacturing tasks.

Computer Program A set of instructions or commands that guides the processing of data in a computer system.

Computer Run One routine that the computer performs; a set of runs composes an application.

Concentrator A hardware device used to collect and temporarily store data from several input devices in a buffer. When the buffer is full, the data are transmitted to the central processing unit.

Concurrent Operations Operations on the database by two or more users at the same time. If two users make changes to the same data at the same time, one update may be lost. But controls to avoid that situation must also avoid creating deadlocks, in which each user is waiting for data reserved by the other.

Connectivity The ability of a user to interact with elements of the system freely, to connect from the station in use to any other component, regardless of location, time, or component design.

Consistency Having the relevant factor remain constant throughout units being compared; for example, information about total sales for corporate stores compared for two months can only be consistent if the number of stores is the same in both months.

Consultant In an information center within an organization, a consultant's role is to work with users who need to develop a specific application or formulate a report from the database. The consultant may do the work or may provide initial training and help as needed for users developing their own applications.

Contingency Theory A management theory calling for management strategy to be tailored to circumstances, especially the nature of the work and the workers, the sophistication and complexity of the tools and techniques, and the external environment of the work group and overall organization. As changes occur, management strategy may also need to change.

Control The concept of ensuring that operations and activities are occurring in accordance with plans and guidelines.

Control Report A non-decision-oriented report produced as a result of processing transactions in a computer system. The report points out areas in which errors have been detected in the data or in data processing.

Control Unit One of three parts of the central processing unit. This unit oversees retrieval and execution of instructions and movement and processing of data in a computer system.

Conversion The process of cutting a new information system over to use in ongoing activities; starting to use a new system.

Corporate Publishing System An electronic publishing system with greater capabilities than desktop publishing. Usually has more sophisticated publishing software and high-resolution laser printer or Linotronic output system. May also have better image handling capabilities, a network of users, and a midrange or mainframe computer.

Corporate View   The view top executives must take, assessing what lines of business the firm should be in and whether to merge with or acquire other companies or acquire product lines.

Cost/Benefit Analysis   A technique of assessing the effect of information systems in organizations by identifying the costs and benefits of the system. Analysis of costs and benefits is associated with the introduction of computer-based systems in organizations.

Critical Incident Logging   A technique for assessing effect of a new information system or application, in which users record noteworthy events during usage and may track events (for example, customer complaints) both before and after the system is in place.

Critical Success Factor   The critical success factor method of planning information systems determines information needs by identifying the factors essential to the organization's survival. Details about the organization's performance on a critical success factor will then be regularly gathered into the database and reported to the managers involved.

CSMA   See *carrier sense multiple access method.*

Cycle Clock   An electronic clock in the central processing unit that emits pulses at regular intervals to help control processing.

Cylinder   The group of tracks that can be accessed at the same time without moving the read heads on magnetic disk devices. The same track from all recording surfaces on a magnetic disk unit.

Data   Facts, ideas, or concepts that can be collected and represented electronically in digital form. Data can be captured, communicated, and processed electronically. Contrast with *information.*

Data Architecture   How data are managed to ensure reliability and access; with *network architecture* forms the infrastructure on which applications are based.

Data Definition   Specifications for the form data must take to be used in a database, as defined by a *data description language.*

Data Description Language (DDL)   The language used to describe or define all or part of a database for creation or processing. Also called *data definition language.* Contrast with *data manipulation language.*

Data Dictionary   A documentation of the data items included in a database together with their relationships with other data and programs or routines that use them.

Data Independence   The separation of data structures from storage structures. The decoupling of logical views of data and the way the data are actually stored on computer-related devices.

Data Item   The smallest unit of data stored in a computer system. The stored representation of a fact or value.

Data Management Software   Same as *database management system.*

Data Manipulation Language (DML)   The language used to transfer data between the database and computer application programs. Part of a database management system. Contrast with *data description language.*

Data Model   Defines how relationships are shown between entities in the database. *Hierarchical, network,* and *relational data models* are the most common.

Data Reduction   Obtaining or abstracting only needed data or information from a larger set of data through calculation, computation, summarization, aggregation, and so on.

Data Set   See *file.*

Data Structure   The view or conception of data held by the user; the structure or organization of data independent of its storage on physical devices. Contrast with *storage structure.*

Database   A generalized, integrated collection of data structured to model the natural relationships in the data. A collection of files. A set of data processible by several different computer programs.

Database Administrator   An individual or group whose assignment is to manage and protect the database with maximum benefit for all users.

Database Computer   Offloads the activities of a database management system to a separate computer to free up resources on the main system.

Database Machine   Same as database computer.

Database Management System (DBMS)   A software system that allows access to stored data by providing an interface between users or programs and the stored data.

Dataflow Diagram   A graphic or pictorial description of the movement of data in and out of a system and between processes and data stores; a logical view of the system and the movement and transfiguration of data in the system.

Deadlock   The situation of two or more programs waiting for data: none may continue processing because each is waiting for data controlled by the other.

Decentralization   The concept of locating decision-making authority, control, or resources at the level in an organization at which events are occurring. Contrast with *centralization.*

Decision Center   A point at which decisions are made for some part of the organization, which also affect and are affected by decisions made in other centers in the organization; information flows between centers.

Decision Room   A boardroom or conference room equipped with a group decision support system. May include a large display screen visible to all that shows tables or graphics and records ideas generated by the group, and a workstation near each participant or near the group facilitator.

Decision Support Language   Any model-oriented computer language that aids in analyzing data, posing "what if" questions, and describing relationships by creating models. Includes spreadsheets and high-level analysis software.

Decision Support System (DSS)   An information system intended to assist managers and users who must formulate decision alternatives for situations that are not well structured; a problem-oriented information system.

Decoupling   The breaking down of systems and entities into their component parts. The parts are studied independently to see how they function and how they interface with other parts of the system.

Delay   The time that elapses between the collection of data about events and receipt by the user of a report about the events. Sources of delays include time needed for data preparation, grouping data into batches, data processing, and data transmittal. See also *response time.*

Desktop Publishing   Combining text, graphics and images such as digitized photographs in a single document, using a personal computer, at a quality level close to professional typesetting.

Desktop Publishing System   An electronic publishing system that runs on a personal computer. "Desktop" refers both to the small space required for the entire system, including printer, and to the software's display screen, which is set up as a worktable.

Detail File   See *transaction file.*

Device Media Control Language (DMCL)   The language used by the systems programmer to specify the physical storage of data in a database system. Space, overflow areas, and buffering are specified.

Dialogue Chart   A chart showing the menus used to invoke each function; used to describe how a particular system design provides for navigation.

Differentiation   A descriptive term used to refer to product perceived throughout the industry as having unique features in comparison to competing items.

Digitizing   Translating text, images, or sound into a form that can be stored electronically. Once digitized, material may be modified as needed.

Direct Access   See *random access.*

Direct Cutover   A conversion to a new information system that takes place all at once, perhaps overnight.

Direct Organization   A type of random file organization that can be used when data are stored on direct address devices. The key on a record is the storage address. Hence the key in a record is its direct address on a storage device. See also *random organization.*

Disintermediation   The removal of intermediate steps or persons between the user and the information system; occurs when systems are designed to be simpler to use and end-users learn to do their own computing.

Distributed Organization   A type of file organization that can be used when data are stored on direct address devices. Addresses for storage of records are calculated by applying a randomizing algorithm to a record key. Algorithms are selected to distribute the records evenly throughout the storage space.

Distributed Processing Network   A set of hardware modules for terminals, small computers, or full-size mainframe systems, sited in different physical locations. Individual modules do stand-alone processing but can also be interconnected to share data with other locations or with a central facility.

DOS   Acronym for disk operating system, an operating system with modules stored on magnetic disk, commonly used on personal computers.

Download   To copy a portion of a file or database from the central computer system to the workstation, personal computer, or departmental computer of the user.

DSS Generator   An element of a decision support system that combines languages, user interfaces, reporting capabilities, graphics facilities and so on for use as needed in creating a decision support system. Contrast with *institutional DSS.*

DSS Tool   A limited DSS generator, specializing, for example, in generating graphics, but with the capability controlled by the DSS generator.

Dual Recording   A type of backup to protect against loss of data; the same data are recorded on two storage devices simultaneously and updates are made to both copies.

Dumping   A type of backup to protect against loss of data; the database is copied periodically, perhaps daily or weekly, and a log is kept between those periods of all transactions processed against the database.

Dysfunctional Behavior   Behavior that interferes with the attainment of objectives. Resistance to a new information system is dysfunctional behavior, often best managed by developing a system that doesn't engender resistance.

EDI   See *electronic data interchange*.

Effectiveness   The ability of an individual or organization to do the things that need to be done.

Electronic Data Interchange (EDI)   Exchanging business transaction data between organizations using electronic communications. Data are in specified formats understood by both organizations.

Electronic Mail   Electronic communications that eliminate the manual preparation, storage, retrieval, and manual distribution of information.

Electronic Publishing   Multimedia presentation of information over communication or broadcast facilities, ranging from corporate document publishing to newspapers to videotex. For printed documents, the requirements of a publishing system are that it offer typeset-quality text, page composition on the screen, incorporation of graphics and images in place, and editing capability. See also *videotex*.

Embedded SQL   SQL, the relational database language, embedded in a host language such as COBOL, the popular business transaction processing language, to provide a program containing statements from both languages. Useful for batch processing files to update the database, for example.

End-user   The individual who actually uses an information system or output; often a manager or staff member rather than an information systems professional.

Entity   An item or area of interest about which data are stored; may be a person, place, thing, or event.

Entropy   Deterioration of a system due to lack of maintenance input.

Entry Barrier   A factor in an industry that makes entering the field so difficult or expensive that existing organizations have a significant advantage. Information systems, such as computer-based airline reservation systems, can be entry barriers.

Entry Deterrent   A tactical entry barrier; may be invoked by an incumbent firm to make a new firm reconsider the decision to enter a market.

Environment   In a systems context, the environment is anything that is not a part of the system itself. Knowledge about the environment is important because of the effect it can have on the system and because interactions between the system and the environment are possible.

ESS   See *executive support system*.

Event Log   A technique for assessing the impact of information systems by maintaining a list (that is, a log) of significant events or occurrences related to the introduction and use of a system.

Evolvability   The capability of databases and/or systems to change over time to accommodate new demands placed on them by users. An objective of database management.

Exception Information   A comparison of actual performance against expectations.

Exception Report   A report produced only when certain events or circumstances are above or below prescribed standards or goals.

Execution Cycle   The phase of the operating cycle of the central processing unit during which instructions are executed; that is, the phase in which operations called for in the instructions are performed or carried out. Contrast with *instruction cycle*.

Executive Support System (ESS)   A computer-based information system designed to assist top-level executives in acquiring and using information needed to run the organization. Should provide an overview of all operations, details on request, and information to help identify opportunities and warn of potential problems.

Expert Support System   Same as *expert system*.

Expert System   A type of information system intended to replicate the decisions of a human expert; relies on manipulation of data and use of heuristics; includes knowledge base, inference engine, knowledge acquisition subsystem, and an explanation facility.

Explanation Facility   In an expert system, the explanation facility tells the user what line of reasoning was used to develop a decision, so the user can decide whether the reasoning applies to current circumstances. May also explain to the user why the system is requesting certain information.

External Intelligence   A type of information required by top-level managers; includes information, gossip, and opinions about activities in the environment of an organization, such as competitor and industry changes.

Externally Distributed Information   Information released by the organization, such as annual reports to stockholders or news of a major program in a press release; generally reviewed by the chief executive before release.

Extraction   A randomizing technique applied to record keys to derive storage addresses for records stored under random organizations. Selected digits of a key are extracted to derive the record address. For example, in the record key 578426, the first, third, fourth, and sixth digits could be extracted to derive a storage address of 5846. See also *key transformation*.

Facsimile   A copy of an original document produced by scanning the document in a facsimile device, which sends the data electronically to another location where a second facsimile device produces the copy. Also called a "fax."

Factory Situation   In assessing the significance of information systems in an organization, the factory situation is one in which current systems are essential for smooth functioning of the firm, and applications in development are not designed to change how the firm competes. Contrast *strategic, support,* and *turnaround situations*.

Feasibility Study   Examination of the workability of an information systems project proposal in terms of technical, economic, and human relations factors. If the study indicates that the project can be done (that is, is feasible), it will be incorporated into a master plan for systems development.

Feedback   Data or information collected and returned to a system or process so performance can be evaluated against expected performance and goals.

Feedback Control Loop   A loop built into an information system to sense the effect of output on the external environment and return that information to the system as an input, where adjustments can be made to meet predetermined goals.

Fiber Optics   The technology in which glass fibers are used to guide light pulses from source to destination, facilitating the transmission of data; laser beams provide the light source.

Field Dependence   A style of perceiving information in which the individual tends to emphasize the overall picture.

Field Independence   A style of perceiving information in which the individual tends to pull pieces out of the whole for analysis.

Fifth-Generation Language   A category of computer languages that are just beginning to emerge. They are expected to use knowledge bases (collections of rules and facts in areas of interest) with rules and facts fed in that describe a problem and arrive at a solution using artificial intelligence to associate rules, facts, and conditions rather than receiving a sequence of instructions.

File   A collection of related records that are stored together (also called data set). The records are organized or ordered on the basis of some common factor called a key. Records may be of fixed or varying length and can be stored on different devices and storage media. See also *file organization, record.*

File Creation   Establishing or writing records for a file on a storage medium to bring the file into existence. Making the file known to the processing system by storing the data on a medium according to a file organization and providing a way to access the stored data.

File Maintenance   Adding to, deleting from, or changing the contents of records in a file. Reorganizing the structure of a file to improve access to records or to change the storage space requirements.

File Management   Includes the functions of creation, insertion, deletion, or updating of stored files and records in files. The operations that are performed on files.

File Organization   A method for ordering data records stored as a file and providing a way to access the stored records. See *indexed organization, list organization, random organization, sequential organization.*

File Specification   In system design, organizing files into master files (relatively permanent) and transaction files (temporary data to processed) and specifying file volume, the range of number of characters the file may contain.

Five Forces   The forces that affect a firm's competitiveness: industry competitors, bargaining power of both buyers and suppliers, substitute products, and the threat of new entrants to the industry.

Fixed-Length Record   A record that always contains the same number of data items and the same number of characters in a particular data item. Contrast with *variable-length record.*

Flexible Manufacturing System   A computer-integrated manufacturing system in which a workstation can change tasks by recognizing a different computer chip affixed to the piece being worked on and asking the database what to do with the piece. Allows quick restructuring of production facilities for new products or efficiency improvements.

Flowchart   A pictorial representation of processes and procedures for operation on data. A diagram that describes documents, procedures, processes, and equipment used in processing data in a specific application.

Folding   A file randomization technique in which certain elements of a record key are used in arithmetic with other elements of a key to derive a storage address for the record. For example, if the record key 578426 is stored at address 1310, the storage address can be derived by adding the first, third, and fourth digits in the key to the other numbers.

$$
\begin{array}{r}
584 \\
+\ \underline{726} \\
1310
\end{array}
$$

See also *key transformation, random organization*.

Formal Structure   Organizational structure established to create meaningful responsibility and authority relationships; departmental boundaries and definitions of relationships between line and staff groups are usually central to the structure. Contrast *informal structure*.

FORTRAN   A third-generation programming language used widely, primarily for arithmetic, algebraic, and numerical computing, and available on most types of computer systems. FORTRAN programming must define all procedures needed by the system; the language (FORmula TRANslator) instructs the computer on how to carry them out.

Fourth-Generation Language   A group of nonprocedural languages in which the user specifies what is to be done rather than how it should be done (see also *application generator, query and retrieval language, report generator*).

Frame   In a frame-based expert support system, the frame stores rules, processing procedures, and descriptive information about the problem, or points to other frames in the database. Each frame is a hierarchy in which the most important, or general, conditions are considered before specific instances of those conditions.

Frame-Based System   An expert support system that stores knowledge in frames that permit the interrelation of knowledge and can better handle complex subjects than a rule-based system.

Front-end Tool   A CASE tool that automates the early activities in the systems development process, such as producing dataflow diagrams.

Full-Duplex Line   A communication line used in transmission of data to and from the central processing unit. A full-duplex line can carry data in both directions (to and from) simultaneously. Contrast with *half-duplex line* and *simplex line*.

Fully Connected List   A list organization in which a pointer is inserted in the last record in the list to point back to the first. All records are connected by pointers so that there appears to be no beginning or end; that is, the list appears like a ring.

Functional-Area Analyst   Has in-depth knowledge of a specific business area and working knowledge of information systems and is employed in a department other than information systems to develop requirements for and implement new or enhanced systems.

Functional-Area Information System   A system that serves one part of the organization.

Gap   See *interblock gap*.

Gateway   A gateway interconnects two different kinds of networks, such as local-area and wide-area, and converts message codes and formats, addresses, and data transmission rates into a form acceptable by the receiving network.

GDSS   See *group decision support system.*

General Ledger   A general ledger system ties together all accounting activities to summarize and show changes in assets, liabilities, and net worth, providing a financial history of an organization.

Gigabyte   One billion bytes of data.

Goals   Purposes or objectives that guide the operation of any system. Operations of systems are performed and controlled in such a way as to assist in attaining specified goals.

Graphic Model   Represents parts or steps in an entity or process pictorially; a flowchart, for example.

Group Decision Support System (GDSS)   A decision support system that also offers features to support group decision making, either in conference rooms or a computer network. See *decision room, linked decision rooms,* and *remote decision network.*

Half-Duplex Line   A communication line used in transmission of data to and from the central processing unit. A half-duplex line can carry data in either direction (to or from) but in only one direction at a time. Contrast with *full-duplex line* and *simplex line.*

Hardware   The electrical and mechanical devices that make up a computer system. The equipment that is part of a computer system. Contrast with *software.*

Hardware Monitor   A measurement device that can be attached to various parts of computer system equipment to monitor or measure their amount of use and speed in processing. Contrast with *software monitor.*

Help Desk   As end-users become more familiar with computing and systems become easier to use, information centers can be replaced by help desks, where users can get answers to questions, help in troubleshooting, and information on software and techniques.

Heuristic Style   An intuitive style of perceiving information. Heuristic individuals use trial and error and readily revise their plans on the basis of new information. Contrast with *analytic style.*

Hierarchical Data Model   Shows relationships among entities in the database in the style of a family tree. One piece of information may relate to one other piece at any level, or to many pieces at levels below it.

Higher-Level Language   See *fourth-generation language.*

Host-Language System   A class or type of database management system in which commands for data description or definition and data manipulation are embedded in a programming language. The instruction set of the programming language is expanded to include facilities for operating on databases. The language in which the database-oriented commands are embedded is called the host language. Contrast with *self-contained system.*

Human Relations Era   The era in management theory history beginning in the late 1920s and early 1930s that increased the importance attached to determining job requirements and matching them with individuals' qualifications, and monitoring training needs and progress.

Hypertext   A type of data management program that is easy to use and has powerful retrieval capabilities. User creates "stacks" of "cards" containing data on one entity of interest and related graphics such as icons or forms to help users. Stacks can be interlinked.

Identification   Part of the process of regulating access to a database, computer system, or file storage area. Persons wishing access may be required to use passwords, codes, badges, cards, or keys.

Image Processing   The digitization and transmission of image information between multiple locations. Allows graphics to be combined with text on a page, edited to change content, size or color, and stored and retrieved.

Impact Evaluation   Determining how the implementation and use of an information systems application affects the organization; identifying changes directly attributable to the system.

Impartiality   Lack of bias in the collection, processing, and use of data; not drawing inferences from data that cannot be supported by the data in the way it was collected.

Implementation   The process of putting a new system into use, including completing training of all direct and indirect users, and actual conversion and the start of regular use of the system.

Income Statement   A financial statement of profits or losses resulting from accumulation of revenues and expenses.

Indexed Organization   A file organization or storage structure in which the keys of the records are stored in a table (called an index) along with an address or pointer to the stored location of the record. Records are accessed by first searching the index to locate the proper record key and address. Access is then made to the address shown in the index. See also *inverted list, sequential organization.*

Industry Perspective   One of the perspectives top-level executives must keep, watching the environment in which the firm operates including immediate competitors, suppliers, government, and national and international competition to the industry.

Inference Chain   In using an expert system, the string of logical IF statements actually used to arrive at a solution to a problem.

Inference Engine   Programs in an expert system that interact with a knowledge base to formulate decisions or recommendations for decisions.

Informal Structure   Organizational relationships not shown on the organization chart but that are influential in functioning and that can be disrupted by a new information system.

Information   Data that have been processed into a meaningful form. Information adds to a representation and tells the recipient something that was not known before. What is information for one person may not be information for another. Information should be timely, accurate, and complete. Information reduces uncertainty. Contrast with *data.*

Information Center   An information systems facility within an organization aimed at facilitating end-user computing; trained staff members assist users with both hardware and software systems.

Information System   A (computer-based) system that processes data into a form that can be used by the recipient for decision-making purposes.

Information Systems Specialist   Has technical expertise in computer hardware, software, data management, and communications, and a working knowledge of selected business functions and ability to interact with executives, managers, and staff members. Currently known as systems analyst, systems designer, development specialist, information analyst, and programmer/analyst.

Information Technology Vision   A view of information systems in an organization focused on processing efficiency and performance reliability, rather than on uses. Contrast with *strategic business vision*.

Information Utility Structure   An infrastructure to support systems use that can develop only in an organization that has considerable investment in and experience with information technology. The structure provides a centralized, standard direction and coordination among diverse parts of the system.

Infrastructure   The *data architecture* and *network architecture* that support an organization's *application portfolios*.

Input   To submit data or instructions to the computer system for processing in the central processing unit; data or instructions that are submitted to the CPU for processing. In a general systems context, input is anything that enters the system from the environment.

Input Device   Used for submitting data or instructions to the central processing unit for processing; includes keyboards, scanners, and voice input devices.

Input/Output Bound   Describing a system in which input and output operations take place more slowly than processing in the CPU. In an input/output-bound system, the CPU's capability is degraded because it must wait for input and output operations to be complete.

Input/Output Control System   A set of software routines that control the input and output of data in the computer system. Users would have to program these processes in detail if it were not for the input/output control system.

Input Validation   Performance of tests and checks on input to ensure that the input operation is legal and the input itself is correct. A wide variety of tests can be applied to ensure the correctness of data being input to a computer system (see, for example, *audit trail*).

Institutional DSS   A decision support system provided as a complete application. Used on a continuing basis to address a general problem area, such as market analysis. Contrast with *DSS generators, DSS tools*.

Instruction Cycle   The phase in the operating cycle of the central processing unit during which instructions are moved from memory into the proper registers so that execution can take place. Contrast with *execution cycle*.

Integrated Services Digital Network (ISDN)   A single type of network in use and being advocated for universal use over public telephone lines. ISDN transmits all types of information (data, voice, and image) over an all-digital network, with standard interfaces for telephones, computers, printers, and other devices. Uses include high-speed facsimile, electronic and voice mail, and access to services offered on the network.

Integrity   The accuracy, privacy, and security of stored data.

Intelligent Terminal   A computer-oriented terminal that has built-in data checking capabilities and a small memory. Special functions may also be built into the terminal to perform certain checks on the data or to handle certain transactions (for example, bank deposit and withdrawal transactions).

Interactive Computing   Computer processing in which the user communicates directly with the system to input data and instructions and to receive output. See also *on-line*.

Interblock Gap   The area on a magnetic tape that separates blocks (physical records) from one another; the distance between the end of one block and the start of the next block. This area is used to stop and start the tape drive to avoid loss or skipping of data. Sometimes the terms *interrecord gap* and *record gap* are used as synonyms for *interblock gap*.

Interface   The point at which one system's functioning ends and another system takes over; a shared boundary between two systems.

Internal Operations Information   A type of information required by top-level managers; key indicators of how the organization or a part of it, such as a division, product, or individual, is performing.

Interoperability   The ability of users to exchange information in any form without difficulty or delay, and without concern for where another party is located or where data resides.

Interrupt   A condition, event, or signal that requires the attention of the central processing unit. An interruption of processing to attend to a specific event, condition, or signal. For example, when an input operation is completed, an interrupt is generated to tell the CPU that the operation is complete and the data are available for processing. A process that is interrupted is stopped in such a way that the processing can be resumed from the same point.

Inverted File   A storage structure in which an index is provided for all data items and the different values for the data items. In essence, every data item is a key that is indexed. A file in such a data structure. Also called *inverted list structure*. See also *indexed organization, list organization*.

ISDN   See *integrated services digital network*.

Item   See *data item*.

Job Control Language   A set of statements used to describe to the operating system a job (program) and its requirements. The language makes it possible to identify such requirements as amount of processing time, memory space, translators, and files used in execution of a job.

Job Log   A list of jobs (programs) processed through a computer system during a period, the time of processing, and other information useful in describing the job.

JOIN   One of the three relational operators in a data manipulation language. Creates a new table, or relation, from the rows, or records, of two tables that satisfy a condition. Contrast with *SELECT, PROJECT*.

Just-in-Time Inventory Planning   Inventory management based on such careful and timely ordering that materials arrive "just in time" to meet production schedules. Saves high warehousing costs; requires close coordination with suppliers. A feature of some *material requirements planning* systems.

K   See *kilobyte*.

Key   A data item within a record that identifies the record and distinguishes it from all other records. Also called *record key*.

Key Transformation   The application of an algorithm or arithmetic process on a record key to derive a storage address for the record. See also *extraction, folding, random organization.*

Keypunch Machine   A data entry device activated by depressing a key on a typewriterlike keyboard to punch holes in a card. The punched holes represent data.

Kilobyte   1024 bytes of memory or storage; in computer terminology, "K" means 1 kilobyte—thus 256K designates 256 kilobytes.

Knowledge   Collected information about an area of concern.

Knowledge Base   In an expert system, the knowledge base contains specific information about the area of expertise, such as facts (data) and rules that use the facts in making a decision.

Knowledge Engineer   Works with experts in a particular area to learn how the experts evaluate situations, the rules of thumb they use, and how they decide what actions to take. The engineer captures that knowledge in an organized way to store in a *knowledge base,* for use in an *expert support system.*

Laser   A beam of light in which light rays are a single frequency and there is minimal distortion in transmission.

Layout   Specifies the location of each item of information on an output document or visual display, and specifies any headings, titles, or page numbers that appear.

Levels   The components of an information system organized hierarchically.

Leverage   Using competitive strategies that make the most of corporate strengths; refers to how an information system that makes possible better service or cost savings can be used in a strategy to give the firm a competitive advantage.

Line Group   Employees directly involved in production in a manufacturing firm, including assembly line workers and their supervisors. Contrast *staff group.*

Linkage   Any activity that affects the cost or effectiveness of another activity. Linkages may be internal to an organization or with external entities.

Linkage Analysis   A top-down method of information systems planning that concentrates on the competitive advantages of information technology. Executives analyze where information systems support could better link related activities to enhance a product, service, or productivity.

Linked Decision Rooms   *Decision rooms* linked together by videoconferencing, using videocameras in each room to capture the discussion and transmit it to other locations. Workstations in each room are linked in a network. A type of *group decision support system.*

List   An ordered set of data; see *list organization.*

List Organization   In a list, the logical order or sequence of records is different from the physical order; a set of records stored in one order is linked together in a different logical order by the insertion of pointers in each record. See also *inverted list, sequential organization.*

Load Sharing   In a distributed processing network, several processing units sharing the workload are more efficient than one unit, taking advantage of free time on any unit and making processors available to everyone even if one unit needs repairs.

Local-Area Network (LAN)   A communication network that spans a single site covering a limited geographic distance or area; may link workstations, terminals, printers, file savers, or other computer equipment.

Logical Record A collection of data items that are used together independent of their mode of physical storage. When applied to secondary storage devices, one or more logical records are stored in a physical block. See *blocking factor*.

Logical Systems Design The stage of systems design when functional specifications are formulated, stating what the system should do, how it should do it, and in what sequence data input, processing, output of reports, and so on should occur.

Logical View The user's view of data, focusing on data needed for applications, rather than on details of storage or access. Contrast with *physical view*.

Long-Term Memory Human long-term memory has an infinite capacity for remembering experiences, though some are remembered better than others. All memories first pass through *short-term memory*.

Low-Cost Leadership The competitive strategy of offering products or services of suitable quality at a lower cost than competitors' comparable products or services.

Machine Language A language used by the central processing unit of a computer to execute instructions and process data. Machine language instructions can be executed (processed) without any translation because they are directly understandable by the CPU. Contrast with *procedure-oriented language*. See also *translator*.

Magnetic Core Storage A collection of magnetic cores that can be used to make up the memory unit of the central processing unit. Magnetic cores are tiny round pieces of iron or iron ferrite that can be magnetized to hold an electrical charge and thus store data. The magnetic cores can be strung together to form a larger memory section.

Magnetic Disk A secondary storage device, similar in appearance to a phonograph record. Data can be recorded on the magnetic surface of the disk. Several disks can be mounted together as a stack to create a disk unit or disk pack. Data are written on or read from the surface as the drum revolves at high speeds.

Magnetic Drum A secondary storage device. A circular cylinder with a magnetic surface that can store data. Data are written on or read from the surface of the drum as it revolves at high speeds.

Magnetic Ink Character Reader An input device that can recognize and accept for input data that are recorded on documents in magnetic ink.

Magnetic Tape A tape having a magnetic surface on which data can be recorded by polarization of the magnetic particles.

Mainframe The general name for a large-size computer system. Compare *microcomputer, minicomputer, supercomputer*.

Maintenance Continual improvements needed in almost all systems, to correct errors, meet new needs of management, or take advantage of new technology.

Management The act or skill of transforming resources (land, labor, capital, and information) into output to accomplish a desired result or objective.

Management Functions Planning (establishing goals and the policies, procedures and programs to achieve them); organizing; staffing; controlling (measuring performance against goals and developing procedures, to adjust goals, procedures, and activities); and communicating.

Management Hierarchy Consists of three levels; see *top-management, middle-management,* and *operating-management levels*.

Management Information Includes not only summaries of accounting information, but textual information ranging from memos to general economic conditions to rumors and personal experience, transformed into information usable to the executive. Operating level managers need less comprehensive information, including factual details, exception reports, and accounting information.

Management Information System (MIS)   An information system focused on supporting decisions in cases where information requirements can be identified in advance and the situation is known to recur, so that reports can be produced periodically. Also called *management reporting systems*. Contrast with *decision support systems*.

Management Science Era   The era in management theory that started in World War II as operations research, using mathematical and statistical tools to consider complex business problems; computers have greatly aided the process. Differs from *scientific management era*.

Management Theory   An analysis of how the complexities of business interrelate that provides a way of predicting future events, explaining past events, and understanding causes and effects.

Manufacturing Automation Protocol (MAP)   A system developed by General Motors to integrate individual manufacturing stations through a local-area network, linking even incompatible devices.

Master Development Plan   A list of projects to be designed, constructed, and implemented in a firm. Each project is identified by a name and brief description of purpose. Projects are developed by priority based on support of organization goals and objectives.

Master File   A permanent file of data pertaining to the history or current status of a factor or entity of interest to an organization. A master file is periodically updated to maintain its usefulness. Contrast with *transaction file*.

Material Requirements Planning (MRP)   Computer software that manages production scheduling, determines materials requirements and plans for their acquisition, manages the production process, and integrates the above tasks. Exchanges information with other information systems in the organization.

Mathematical Model   Mathematical representation of a process or system; the most rigorous kind of model and least subject to misinterpretation.

Megabyte   Often regarded as 1 million bytes of data, but more accurately, 1,048,576 bytes.

Message Switching   A communications method used in wide-area networks in which full messages of data are transmitted along a predetermined route, but lines are not dedicated for the transmission. If the message encounters a link in use, the message is temporarily stored, then forwarded when the line is free. Contrast with *circuit switching, packet switching*.

Microcomputer   Computers small enough to sit on a desk, but not necessarily small in processing power. A microprocessor, in which the main processing circuitry is contained on one silicon chip, performs the computing. Includes *personal computers, workstations*. Compare *minicomputer, mainframe, supercomputer*.

Microsecond   One-millionth of a second (μs; 1×10^{-6} second).

Microwave Transmission   High-speed transmission of data between stations through the air as coded signals. Satellites may also serve as transmission stations.

Middle-Management Level   Managers concerned with overseeing performance in the organization and controlling activities that move the organization toward its goals.

Typical middle-management issues are employee training, personnel considerations, and equipment and material acquisition. Contrast with *top-management level* and *operating-management level*.

Millions of Instructions Per Second (MIPS)   The measure of how fast a computer processes software.

Millisecond   One-thousandth of a second (ms; 1×10^{-3} second).

Minicomputer   Midrange computer system designed for multiple users; provides greater speed and storage than microcomputers. Market will shrink as microcomputer capabilities increase and mainframe computer prices fall. Compare *microcomputer, mainframe, supercomputer*.

MIPS   See *millions of instructions per second*.

Model   In decision making, a model is an abstraction of the events surrounding a process, activity, or problem to remove an entity from its environment for examination without the distraction of unnecessary elements. See *graphic, mathematical, narrative,* and *physical models*.

Model Bank   A database of models in a decision support system; models are identified by a unique name and stored.

Modem   A device used to connect a computer and a transmission channel that will carry data. Used to modulate and demodulate communication signals.

Monitoring   Observing for a special purpose. Monitoring who accesses certain records, checking the records for proper usage, and identifying people who repeatedly attempt to use the database without proper authorization is part of the process of regulating access to stored data. Also, monitoring hardware or software performance.

Monitoring Report   A non decision-oriented report (for example, a payroll expense report) that summarizes or describes events that have taken place.

Monolithic   A management information system (MIS) design that attempts to build a single MIS encompassing the whole organization, anticipating all needs; an unrealistic endeavor.

MRP   See *material requirements planning*.

Multidrop Line   A data line configuration that can be shared by all users on the line either for sending information from one point to another or for broadcasting to all points on the line. The line leads to a central computer, which may have other multidrop lines attached. Contrast with *point-to-point line*.

Multilist   A data structure—like list organization in which pointers connect all records with a common attribute, plus the ability to run many lists through a database in one search and to allow a single record to belong to multiple lists.

Multiplexor   A device that makes it possible to transmit two or more sets of data over the same line or channel at the same time.

Multiprocessing   The capability of executing two or more jobs simultaneously. Two or more processors that share a common memory unit are used. Contrast with *multiprogramming*.

Multiprogramming   The capability of having two or more jobs in the CPU at the same time. Execution of the programs is interleaved so that in a certain time interval each job will have been (partly) processed. Processing is not simultaneous. Contrast with *multiprocessing*.

Nanosecond   One-billionth of a second (ns; 1×10^{-9} second).

Narrative Model   A language or narrative description of the relationship among variables in a process or system, such as, "If I change my price, my competitors will match my price unless it causes them to lose money."

Navigation   Moving through the system, from screen to screen or from page to page in a report or input form.

Negative Feedback   Data or information about system performance fed back to the system through a feedback control loop to correct performance fluctuations and help maintain the system within a critical operating range.

Network   A group of interconnected computers, workstations, or computer devices such as printers and data storage systems. Networked devices may be close together or far apart and may be linked with any data transmission channels, such as coaxial cable, microwave, or fiber optics. See *local-area network, wide-area network.*

Network Architecture   Data and voice transmission capabilities in an information system; with *data architecture* the infrastructure on which applications are based.

Network Data Model   A model of relationships among entities in the database like a *hierarchical model* except that an entity can have more than one "parent," or relationship to the next higher level.

Niche   A niche is a narrow target area for a product or service within a larger market. Aiming at a market niche is a competitive strategy to win the business of a specific buyer group either by differentiating the product for that group or lowering costs as a result of the narrow focus.

Node   In a computer network, nodes are the sending, receiving, or processing sites.

Noise   Distortions in data as they are communicated to a receiver or user. The distortions may block the data or make them useless.

Nonprogrammed Decision   A decision that occurs so seldom that set routines, programs, or procedures are not devised to govern how it is made. Nonprogrammed decisions are relatively unstructured. Contrast with *programmed decision.*

Numeric Data   Data consisting of the numbers 0–9 on which arithmetic operations are performed.

Object Code   Executable instructions in machine language, created by a translation process from source code.

Office Automation   Part of the effect of work group support systems, such as word processing and other applications that automate tasks previously done manually.

Off-Line   Equipment or devices not connected to or in direct communication with the central processing unit. Contrast with *on-line.*

On-Line   Equipment or devices connected to or directly communicating with the central processing unit. Contrast with *off-line.* See also *interactive computing.*

Open System   Any system that interacts with its environment through input and output.

Operating-Management Level   Managers who are essentially supervisors; the largest group of managers in a firm. Typical concerns are schedules and deadlines, human relations, cost and quality control. Contrast with *middle-management* and *top-management levels.*

Operating System   A software system that controls the operation of a computer system by providing for input/output, allocation of memory space, translation of programs, and so on.

Order Entry System   An information system designed to accept and process customer orders; usually integrated with accounting and inventory control systems.

Organization Analysis   A technique to evaluate the impact of a recently implemented system on the organization, assessing how structure, procedures, and policies have changed and how the system is used.

Organization Theory   Focuses on alternate ways to structure an organization to best utilize people and other resources, such as equipment, material, and finances, and to provide for communication of information to appropriate personnel.

Output   Data or information that result from processing and are made available to users. In a general systems sense, output is anything that is produced by a system and movement across the boundary into the environment.

Output Device   Receives the processing results from the processing unit and translates them into the appropriate form for use. Includes printers, display screens, and voice output devices.

Overflow Area   An area of storage, particularly on secondary storage devices, in which data can be stored when the main or primary storage area is already full or in use.

Overflow Bucket   An overflow storage area.

Overlapped Processing   The occurrence of input, processing, and output operations simultaneously to improve throughput.

Packet Switching   A communication method used in wide-area networks in which messages are stored in primary memory, divided into blocks, or packets, of a standard size, and transmitted. The route may be determined when the message is sent or at each node along the way. Contrast with *circuit switching, message switching*.

Parallel Processing   The ability to perform multiple tasks simultaneously.

Parallel Systems   Conversion to a new information system while the old system continues operating for a period, to ensure that data will not be lost if a problem arises in the new system.

Parametric User   An end-user who relies on predefined questions and structures presented by the system while entering or extracting data (for example, airline reservation agents). Contrast with *specifier user*.

Pascal   A third-generation programming language used widely on various computers; introduced in 1971 as a better structured programming language. Requires the programmer to plan development by defining all variables and constants at the beginning and to structure programs logically into blocks.

PBX   See *private branch exchange*.

Perception   How an individual sees a situation, such as a new information system that changes information distribution.

Performance Monitoring   Using monitors to determine usage of components of a system to help determine whether additional resources are needed or whether existing resources should be adjusted to improve performance. See *hardware monitor, software monitor*.

Peripheral   Describing equipment attached to a computer system to augment it or to make it possible to use the central processing unit—input/output, communications, and secondary storage devices, for example.

Personal Computer   A desktop microcomputer ranging from home computers to laptops and computers used in business; has the computing functions of large systems but may be limited in speed and storage capacity. See *microcomputer*.

Personal Computer Software   Software packages designed for the personal computer; the most common are for word processing, spreadsheets, data management, data communications, and graphics.

Phase-in of System   Conversion to a new information system in which the old system is gradually replaced by the new one.

Physical File   The data contained on one storage device (for example, a magnetic tape or magnetic disk).

Physical Model   Represents the entity studied in appearance and, to some extent, in function. Iconic models, like a model airplane, appear like the entity but do not behave the same; analog models, like a speedometer, display the behavior but not the appearance.

Physical Systems Construction   The stage in systems development when the application is built: coding programs, acquiring any packaged software and new hardware needed, developing record formats, data structures, and subschemas; and designing files and databases.

Physical View   The way data are actually stored and organized on physical devices. Contrast with *logical view*.

Picosecond   One-thousandth of a nanosecond (ps; 1×10^{-12} second).

Pilot System   Conversion to a new information system in which only a small piece of the business or function is converted to the new system to see if problems develop.

Planning   Establishing goals and developing policies, procedures, and programs to achieve them.

Planning Information   A type of information required by top-level managers that describes major developments and programs being planned, including the assumptions and anticipated developments on which plans are based.

Point-of-Sale (POS) System   Small computer system to capture order and sales data while the transaction is occurring. May be a stand-alone machine or a system of multiple terminals, each with a small memory, attached to a central processing unit. Retail grocery and fast-food industries are the biggest users of POS.

Point-to-Point Line   A data line configuration that simply connects a computer, workstation, or terminal with a central computer. Contrast with *multidrop line*.

Pointer   A data item in a record that contains the storage address of another record linked or pointed to by the first record. The pointer indicates the physical location of a record in storage.

POS   See *point-of-sale system*.

Positioning   The location on a video display screen of information about one firm relative to all other firms. For example, on an airline reservation system, the airline that operates the system can position itself at the top of the display.

Positive Feedback   Data or information about the performance of a system that reinforces operation without change.

Price/Performance Relationship   The relationship between computing performance and price, usually measured in price per MIPS, or one million instructions per second executed by the computer.

Privacy   Privacy protection of records guards against unauthorized distribution of data.

Private Branch Exchange (PBX)   A local-area network in which the existing telephone switching system is used as the center of a star topology; *computer branch exchange* is a kind of PBX.

Problem Avoider   A manager who tends to shun the notion that a problem exists; avoids negative information and focuses on the positive aspects of a situation; tends to use planning to avoid difficult situations and impending problems.

Problem Finder   A manager who seeks out problems, dealing with them or turning them into advantages; regards many problems as opportunities in disguise.

Problem Resolver   A manager who does not seek out problems but deals with them quickly and efficiently when they arise; faces the reality of a situation and does not avoid or ignore difficulties.

Procedure-Oriented Language   A higher level language used to formulate computer programs by specifying the procedures or algorithms that are to be executed. Third-generation language. Contrast with *fourth-generation language, machine language.*

Processing Mode   The way transactions are handled for processing: grouped together in batches, for example, or processed as they occur. In the latter case, the user of the system is typically on-line to the central processor.

Product Manager   In an information center within an organization, a product manager supervises the development, use, and support of one or more applications to be shared by multiple users.

Productivity   The efficiency or output of a task.

Program Swapping   The movement of jobs between main memory and a secondary storage device. In some system configurations, a program may be swapped in and out of memory several times before execution is completed.

Programmed Decision   A frequently recurring decision that represents a well-understood and well-structured situation, permitting the development of routines to state how the decision should be made. Contrast with *nonprogrammed decision.*

Programming Language   Any language in which computer processing instructions (programs) are written. A language in which instructions that control the movement and processing of data are written. Most programming languages are higher level languages that must be translated into executable machine language.

PROJECT   One of the three relational operators in a data manipulation language. Creates a new table of columns, or attrributes, from the initial table that satisfy a condition. Contrast with *JOIN, SELECT.*

Projection   A form of resistance to a new information system in which people wrongly blame the system, rather than the training, for difficulties in using the system.

Protocol   The rules that allow entities to communicate with one another, including codes, identification, and acknowledgment schemes.

Prototype   A working version of an information system developed to allow users to evaluate its essential features; an experimental version of a new system.

Pull-Down Menu   Allows the user to view operations choices by having them displayed on the screen while information in use remains on the screen.

Query Language   Same as *query and retrieval language*.

Query and Retrieval Language   Provides users with the capability to retrieve stored data without writing lengthy procedural instructions or specifying data formats.

Random Access   Access to a stored record such that the next address containing the record is chosen at random (as opposed to being the next one in sequence).

Random Organization   A file organization for data stored on secondary storage devices like magnetic disk or magnetic drum (but not magnetic tape). Under random organizations, records in a file may be addressed directly without accessing any other records in the file. This is made possible by determining an address for the record and then going directly to the address. See also *direct organization, key transformation, sequential organization*.

Rationality   Selecting alternatives expected to yield the best results, evaluated on the basis of some system of values.

Real-Time Processing   The processing of a request in an on-line system in which the results are available soon enough to be useful in controlling or affecting the activity in which the user is involved.

Record   A group of data items that are stored together and/or used together in processing. A collection of related data items treated as a unit. See also *file, logical record*.

Record Key   See *key*.

Recording Density   The amount of data that can be stored in a specific section or area. For example, on magnetic tape, recording density is often expressed in terms of the number of bytes or characters of data that can be stored in an inch of tape.

Redundancy   The inclusion of extra characters or data in input, output, or storage to minimize the possibility of error or misunderstanding in the use of the data or information. Redundancy can also result when the same data are collected and stored inadvertently several times.

Reentrant Program   A program or routine that can be used by one or more computer programs at the same time and can be executed in segments with interruptions for program swapping. Reentrant programs are often used in timesharing and multiprogramming environments.

Refreeze   Reinforcing the new system after it has been introduced, to return the organization to stability. Part of the role of the systems analyst as *change agent* in introducing a new system. See also *unfreeze*.

Register   A hardware device used for temporarily storing data or instructions in the arithmetic/logic unit of the central processor.

Regularly Scheduled Report   Report needed for recurring decisions; the type of information required is known ahead of time and can be reported regularly according to a predetermined format. Reports can be daily, weekly, or monthly, depending on when the decision process must take place. Contrast with *exception report, unscheduled report*.

Relation   The underlying data structure of a relational database; a table in a relational database.

Relational Data Model   The model for a *relational database*.

Relational Database   A type of database in which the data are logically structured in relations—that is, tables of rows and columns representing records and data items.

Reliability   The accuracy of the picture provided by the information; for example, the same survey conducted randomly among 1000 people will be more reliable than one conducted among 10.

Remote Decision Network   A *group decision support system* that brings decision makers together through a network of workstations rather than in a conference room. Each member has access to databases and decision support software and can see information and graphics displayed by other members. Also, one out-of-town member of a group can join others in a conference room remotely.

Report Generator   A fourth-generation language type that allows users to extract data from files or databases and to format the output; does not require detailed statement of procedures.

Requirements Analysis   The stage in systems development in which systems analysts determine and describe user information needs so that design and construction can follow.

Resistance   Behavior that opposes a change, such as implementing a new information system. Best dealt with by preventing the rise of resistance. See *aggression, avoidance, projection*.

Response Time   The time that elapses between a request for data or processing and the receipt of the data or processing results. See also *delay*.

Ring Topology   A computer network structure in which each network point can communicate directly with any other point. Instead of a central computer directing communications, transmissions travel around the ring, and a front-end processor at each site determines whether the message is addressed to it or should be passed along.

Rule   The rules used as a knowledge base in a rule-based expert support system are represented as "IF a THEN b" statements. Facts of a situation under consideration are checked against the rules.

Rule-Based System   The most common type of expert support system. Knowledge about a specific situation is represented as a set of conditions against which the facts or knowledge of a situation under evaluation can be checked.

Satellite Communications   Microwave transmission of data from a ground station to an orbiting satellite for relay to another earth station or to other satellites and then earth; a relay using just three satellites can carry data to the furthest point on earth from the sender.

Satisficing   Finding a course of action or strategy that is "good enough," that satisfies minimum standards of a model that reduces the complexities of trying to find the ideal solution. If alternatives are difficult to find, the first acceptable one is likely to be chosen; if they are easy to find, minimum standards may be raised.

Scanning   A quick review of multiple external information sources, such as commercial databanks, using an executive support system. Also, using a scanner to digitize graphics or text for input to a computer system for storage, retrieval, and editing.

Schema   A description of a database, including a statement of the characteristics of the data and the relationship between different data elements. Contrast with *view*.

Scientific Management Era   The first era in management theory history; began in the second century of the Industrial Revolution. Aimed at maximizing productivity, scientific management required job standards to measure performance, encouraged management-worker cooperation, and increased managers' responsibilities.

Secondary Storage Unit   Device used to store data and instructions as output from a central processing unit; the stored material can be retrieved by the computer when needed. Includes magnetic hard disks and diskettes, magnetic tape and drums, and optical disks.

Sector   A pie-shaped area on the surface of a magnetic disk.

Security   Guarding against data destruction or tampering by controlling the rights of access to the database and ability to retrieve, change, add, or delete records.

SELECT   One of the three relational operators in a data manipulation language. Produces a new table of the rows, or records, of the initial table that satisfy a condition. Contrast with *JOIN, PROJECT.*

Self-Contained System   A class or type of database management system that includes its own data description and data manipulation commands. The commands are independent of any programming language. Contrast with *host-language system.*

Sequential Organization   A file organization for data stored on secondary storage devices. Under sequential organization, records are stored in a file and sequenced by key, using consecutive storage locations. During retrieval, records must be accessed sequentially. Contrast with *indexed organization, list organization, random organization.*

Serial Interface   A communication connection between two devices in which data bits are transmitted serially, one after the other, on the same wire, as opposed to a parallel interface that sends one byte (8 bits) at a time on eight wires. The standard connection from computer to modem; also called *serial port.*

Serial Processing   Processing one task at a time.

Shareability   Pertaining to the use of database resources by multiple users and programs; an objective of database management. The database is viewed as being a shared resource available to all authorized persons regardless of department.

Shell   In the field of expert support systems, shells are development tools including a language for stating and managing the rules or frames that make up the knowledge base and an inference engine capable of reasoning with rule sets.

Short-Term Memory   Human short-term memory holds very small amounts of information for a short period if attention is not interrupted. All *long-term memory* passes through short-term memory.

Simple List   A type of storage structure in which an address or pointer is included as part of the record to indicate which record in the file is next in logical sequence. By pointers, a logical sequence is distinguished from the stored physical sequence of the records. In a simple list, one pointer points to the next record in logical sequence. However, more complex lists may result if multiple pointers are included in records.

Simplex Line   A communication line that is used in transmission of data to and from the central processing unit. A simplex line can carry data in one direction only. Contrast with *half-duplex line* and *full-duplex line.*

Sociotechnical Era   The era that began in the 1950s in management theory history in which the goals are both high job satisfaction and technological efficiency, to avoid having technical advances limited by users who are affected adversely.

Soft Information   Personal observation, opinion, and narrative commentary.

Softkey Method   An interface between system and user with a touch-screen that allows the user to select menu choices by touching them on the screen.

Software   Computer programs that control the processing of data in a computer system; term includes user-written as well as commercially prepared programs like translators, utility routines, or database management systems. Contrast with *hardware*.

Software Monitor   A measurement tool for testing or monitoring the operating system. A software monitor is a set of executable instructions embedded in the operating system. Contrast with *hardware monitor*.

Software Package   Prewritten, purchased software.

Sort File   A temporary file used for sequencing or placing data into order in a transaction or master file.

Sorting   Arranging data into a particular sequence to make processing easier and data less cumbersome.

Source Code   Instructions written in a higher level programming language. Source code is translated into object code, which can be executed by the central processing unit.

Special Analysis Report   A report by a decision support system that addresses a "what if" question, such as "What effect will the product change have on revenues?"

Special Character Data   Characters other than alphabetic and numeric, such as $, #, *.

Specifier User   An end-user who queries the database for data for decision making or accesses records to update them. Needs to know key words or codes to access or modify records. Contrast with *parametric user*.

Spreadsheet   A computer program that replicates electronically the rows and columns of a worksheet; includes arithmetic capabilities and the ability to manipulate data. A type of software widely used on personal computers.

SQL   Often pronounced "sequel." A widely used relational database language.

Stack   The principal unit for storing information in hypertext, a powerful database management program. A stack is a named collection of cards holding data about one entity of interest. A stack can be linked to other cards or stacks. See *hypertext*.

Staff Group   Supports the line group, or manufacturing group, in an organization; for example, personnel in purchasing and accounting.

Star Topology   A computer network structure in which each node is connected directly to a central computer that determines where to send the data next.

Statistical Software   Any software application designed to perform statistical analysis.

Status (Progress) Information   A type of information required by top-level managers to keep them abreast of current problems and crises and aware of progress in taking advantage of opportunities.

Storage   Retaining data for later use, generally records of events affecting the organization.

Storage Structure   The physical organization of data as they are stored on a physical device. Pertaining to sequential, random, indexed, or list file organizations. Contrast with *data structure*.

Store and Forward   Same as *message switching*.

Strategic Business Vision   A view of information systems focused on the organization's strengths and capabilities and its opportunities, and what information technology will enable the firm to do. Contrast with *information technology vision*.

Strategic Situation   In assessing the significance of information systems to an organization, the strategic situation is one in which information technology is critical to daily operations, and applications in development are essential to future competitive success. Contrast with *factory, support,* and *turnaround situations*.

Strategy   The way an organization endeavors to differentiate itself from its competitors, using its relative corporate strengths to better meet customer needs.

Structured Analysis   Developing a logical, graphic model of the system required, focusing on what the system or application must do rather than how requirements will be accomplished. Uses a dataflow diagram and data dictionary.

Subschema   See *view*.

Subsystem   A part of a larger system having all the properties of a system in its own right. A system within another system.

Summarization   Reducing large amounts of transaction data to a more concise form.

Supercomputer   The fastest and most expensive computer available, used, for example, in designing cars and aircraft, weather forecasting, and research.

Support Situation   In assessing the significance of information technology to an organization, the support situation is one in which information systems play an important role in supporting (back-office) activities, although the organization could manage to function without them, and future systems will not change the situation. Contrast *factory, strategic,* and *turnaround situations*.

Surveillance   Monitoring a situation; one way in which executive support systems are used. Checking information soon after it enters the system, without waiting for a report.

Switching Costs   The expense a company or individual incurs in lost time, expenditure of resources, and hassle, when changing from one supplier or system to another. A factor in keeping customers whose needs are being satisfied.

Synchronous   Describing the control of operations by the generation of a signal from a clock when an operation is to begin. Contrast with *asynchronous*.

Synonym   Pertaining to two or more keys that derive to the same storage address under a particular key transformation algorithm.

Syntax Error   An error such as incorrect punctuation or spacing in a program that causes the program to fail; common in third-generation languages.

System   An organized entity characterized by a boundary that separates it from all other systems. A system may consist of other systems or components and may interact with its environment through input and output.

Systems Development Life Cycle   The activities in developing a computer systems project beginning with perception of a need for the project. Next a feasibility study is performed. If a project is accepted, the analysis, logical and physical design, and testing stages occur. When the system has been tested and errors corrected, it is implemented. During use, the system is evaluated, possibly leading to maintenance changes.

Systems Programmer   Handles storing data in database, working with physical rather than logical view of data. Organizes data using agreed-on storage structure to best meet other users' needs, selects storage devices, and specifies details of storage.

Systems Testing   Testing a system before implementation to determine how well it will perform and whether it meets original specifications. Separate from program testing for logic errors.

Technician   Maintains equipment, diagnosing malfunctions and making repairs. May also monitor new developments in software and evaluate them for potential use.

Telecommunication   Use of the telephone system as a channel for communication.

Third-Generation Language   The generation of programming languages beginning in the 1960s that followed machine language and assembly languages, offering programmers higher-level languages with which they can state procedures, which a compiler translates into machine language. Includes such popular programming languages as FORTRAN, BASIC, Pascal, and COBOL. See *procedure-oriented language*.

Time-Sharing   A computer system that is shared by two or more users in the same interval of time. Each user is unaffected by the others and may be unaware of anyone else's presence on the system.

Time Slice   The amount of time a particular computer program may execute in a time-sharing system. At the end of a time slice, control is transferred to another program. Control will alternate between programs, each using multiple time slices in the course of a complete program execution.

Token Passing Method   A local-area network access method used with ring networks to avoid colliding messages. A particular string of bits called the token goes around the network until a device with a message to transmit picks up the token, transmits, and returns the token to the network.

Tool   Any device that improves the performance of a task. Tools for developing information systems increase developer productivity and/or enhance system quality. Tools exist for analysis, design, and development. See also *CASE*.

Top-Down Approach   An approach to systems planning that focuses on organization goals and strategies; requires a high degree of top-management involvement. Functions such as research and development, production, and marketing are identified along with their information needs, and finally applications and databases to meet those needs are specified.

Top-Management Level   Top managers perform planning and strategy formulation; are oriented toward the future of the organization; coordinate overall efforts of the firm and act as liaisons with other agencies in the business community. Contrast with *middle-management* and *operating-management levels*.

Topology   In a computer systems network, topology is the arrangement of nodes (sending, receiving, or processing sites) for transmitting data. Some topologies are bus, star, and ring.

Track   A part of a secondary storage device that is accessed by one read/write head.

Trainer   In an information center within an organization, a trainer works directly with users to familiarize them with multiple-user applications developed by the center, with software packages, or with high-level languages such as query and retrieval.

Transaction   An event that involves or affects a business or organization. Events taking place during the course of routine business activities (for example, making sales to customers or ordering materials from a supplier).

Transaction File   A relatively temporary file for the storage of transaction data used to update a master file. Contrast with *master file*.

Transaction Processing   Using information technology to increase volume, accuracy, or consistency in processing data about business transactions.

Transaction Processing System   Processes data about business activities, such as sales and movement of inventory.

Translator   A software program that operates on or uses as data other computer programs to translate higher level instructions into machine-executable instructions. See also *machine language, object code, source code*.

Turnaround Situation   In assessing the significance of information systems to an organization, the turnaround situation is one in which current technology is important for ongoing operations, but applications being developed are essential to revitalizing the business. Contrast with *factory, strategic,* and *support situations*.

Twisted Pair   A pair of wires, each wrapped in protective coating and twisted one around the other; a voice-grade communication line such as ordinary telephone wire.

Uncertainty   The condition under which managers lack enough information to predict outcomes of activities accurately every time. Uncertainty and increased information needs occur when there are more possible results of an activity, a large number of different inputs, or difficulty in achieving goals.

Unfreeze   Preparing an organization for change by encouraging flexible attitudes. Part of the role of a systems analyst as *change agent* in introducing a new system to an organization. See also *refreeze*.

Unscheduled Report   One-time reports needed by management, usually at the top level, to make nonrecurring decisions. Contrast with *regularly scheduled report*.

User Friendly   Easy to use; a characteristic of a system or application.

User Working Area   An area in an application program in which data are brought in by the database management system, ready for use in the form required by the application; resides in the computer's main memory.

Validity   A characteristic of information; valid information is meaningful and relevant to the stated purpose. Information may be invalid if applied to a different purpose than it was collected for; for example, correlating increased sales with a new manager is invalid if other factors have contributed to the increase.

Value-Added Network   A nondedicated communication network made available on a subscription basis; users pay only for the amount of data they transmit.

Value Chain   A set of activities relevant to understanding the bases of cost and potential sources of differentiation in a firm. Consists of basic business processes such as inventory, manufacturing, order processing, marketing, and service; and support activities such as purchasing, technology development, and general management.

Variable-Length Record   A record that can contain a varying number of characters or data items. Typically in variable-length records, a certain set of data items can be repeated to handle multiple occurrences of some data (for example, a person can have several different job skills—the job skill data items might be repeated to handle each skill). Contrast with *fixed-length record*.

Videotex   A form of electronic publishing in which home or business subscribers can receive multimedia (data, text, image, and voice) presentations such as product information and video games on modified television sets. The recipient orders products or services and controls the presentation through a control device.

View A description of selected data from a database, incorporating the relationships among data as they are used in any application program. Also called *subschema*. Contrast with *schema*.

Vision A view of what can happen by using resources to transform opportunities into reality; an image that grows out of a firm understanding of the area of interest, but is produced by imagination and creativity.

Voice Processing Allows the storage, editing, and transmission of the spoken word. Still in the early stages, voice processing technology is beginning to offer voice-input word processing systems and verbal interaction with systems for information, production, quality control, and materials handling.

Warning Information A type of information required by top-level managers to signal that changes are occurring, either opportunities emerging or omens of trouble.

Weighted Feature Analysis Assessment of a new information system or application done by weighting system features, such as ease of use and likelihood of error, from least to greatest importance and having users evaluate how well the system works with respect to those features.

Wide-Area Network A communication network spanning a broad geographical distance and utilizing common carrier networks.

Word A fixed-length set of bits that are operated on as a single unit to hold data or instructions.

Word Processing A system of equipment that assists in preparation and communication of written, displayed, or voice information. Often used to refer to input, editing, and printing or display of written information, including reports, documents, and manuscripts.

Work Group Computing Using word processing in work groups to screen information and offering comments on it electronically. May be used in preparing documents such as sales proposals, policy statements, and research reports, allowing several users to enter revisions or add comments to the document file.

Work Group Support System A type of information system used to support managers, staff, and employees in day-to-day activities. May provide electronic and voice mail, image processing or a facsimile system, electronic data interchange, word processing, and electronic publishing.

Workstation A microcomputer offering extremely powerful processing capabilities and high-quality graphics, often used in engineering design. See *microcomputer*.

References

Chapter 1: Introduction to Information Systems

Kanter, Rosabeth Moss. *The Change Masters* (New York: Simon and Schuster), 1984.

Naisbitt, John. *Megatrends* (New York: Warner Books), 1982.

Peters, Thomas J., and Robert H. Waterman, Jr. *In Search of Excellence* (New York: Harper & Row), 1982.

Peters, Tom. *Thriving on Chaos* (New York: Knopf), 1987.

Toffler, Alvin. *Future Shock* (New York: Bantam Books), 1970.

Toffler, Alvin. *The Third Wave* (New York: William Morrow), 1980.

Chapter 2: The Information Systems Vision

Cash, James I., Jr., F. Warren McFarlan, and James L. McKenney. *Corporate Information Systems Management: The Issues Facing Senior Executives* (2nd ed.) (Homewood, IL: Irwin), 1988.

Elam, Joyce, et al. *Transforming the IS Organization* (Washington, D.C.: ICIT Press), 1988.

King, William R. "Strategic Planning for Management Information Systems," *MIS Quarterly* (2)1 (March 1978), pp. 27–37.

Senn, James A. "Linking Corporate Strategy and Information Technology: Three Views On Planning," *INTEC Report* (Atlanta: INTEC: Information Technology Management Center), 1989.

Senn, James A., and Ronald E. Wilkes. "Corporate Strategy and the Information Resource: Confronting The Issues," *Proceedings of Joint International Symposium On Information Systems* (Sydney, Australia: Australian Computer Society), 1988, pp. 165–187.

Zubuff, Shoshana. *In the Age of the Smart Machine* (New York: Basic Books), 1988.

Chapter 3: Systems Concepts

Anthony, Robert N. *Planning and Control Systems: A Framework for Analysis* (Boston: Division of Research, Graduate School of Business Administration, Harvard University), 1965.

Bertalanffy, L. V. "General Systems Theory: A Critical Review," *General Systems 7* (1962), pp. 1–20.

Boulding, K. E. "General Systems Theory—The Skeleton of Science," *Management Science 5* (April 1956), pp. 197–208.

Shannon, Claude, and Warren Weaver. *The Mathematical Theory of Communication* (Urbana: The University of Illinois Press), 1949.

Chapter 4: Information Systems in the Organization

Ackoff, Russell L. *A Concept of Corporate Planning* (New York: Wiley-Interscience), 1970.

Anthony, Robert N. *Planning and Control Systems: A Framework for Analysis* (Boston: Division of Research, Graduate School of Business Administration, Harvard University), 1965.

Dickson, Gary W., James A. Senn, and Norman L. Chervany. "Research in Management Information Systems: The Minnesota Experiments," *Management Science 23* (May 1977), pp. 913–923.

Galbraith, Jay. *Organizational Design: An Information Processing View* (Reading, MA: Addison-Wesley), 1973.

Hubert, Georgia P. "Cognitive Style as a Basis for MIS and DSS Design: Much Ado About Nothing?" *Management Science 29* (May 1983), pp. 567–597.

Iacocca, Lee. *Iacocca: An Autobiography* (New York: Bantam Books), 1984.

Ives, Blake, and M. H. Olson. "Manager or Technician? The Nature of the Information System's Manager's Job," *MIS Quarterly 5,* no. 4 (December 1981), pp. 49–62.

Jarvenpaa, Sirkka L., and Gary W. Dickson. "Myths vs. Facts about Graphics in Decision Making," *Spectrum 3,* no. 1 (February 1986).

Leavitt, H. J. "Applying Organizational Change in Industry: Structural, Technological and Humanistic Approaches." In *Handbook of Organizations,* J. G. March (Ed.) (Chicago: Rand McNally), 1965.

Miller, J. G. *Living Systems* (New York: McGraw-Hill), 1978.

Mintzberg, H. "The Manager's Job: Folklore and Fact," *Harvard Business Review 53,* no. 4 (July–August 1975), pp. 49–61.

Peters, Thomas J., and Robert H. Waterman, Jr. *In Search of Excellence* (New York: Harper and Row), 1982.

Pounds, W. F. "The Process of Problem Finding," *Sloan Management Review 1,* no. 2 (Fall 1969), pp. 1–19.

Simon, Herbert A. *Administrative Behavior* (2nd ed.) (Englewood Cliffs, NJ: The Free Press), 1957.

Simon, Herbert A. *The New Science of Management Decision* (New York: Harper & Row), 1960.

Slovic, Paul, Baruch Fischhoff, and Sarah Lichtenstein. "Risky Assumptions," *Psychology Today* (June 1980), pp. 44–48.

Chapter 8: Database Management

Atre, S. *Data Base: Structured Techniques for Design, Performance, and Management* (New York: Wiley-Interscience), 1980.

Canning, Richard G. "The Debate on Data Base Management," *EDP Analyzer 10* (March 1972).

CODASYL Systems Committee. *Data Base Task Group Report* (New York: Association for Computing Machinery), April 1971.

CODASYL Systems Committee. *Feature Analysis of Generalized Data Base Management Systems* (New York: Association for Computing Machinery), May 1971.

CODASYL Systems Committee. *Selection and Acquisition of Data Base Management Systems* (New York: Association for Computing Machinery), March 1976.

CODASYL Systems Committee. *A Survey of Generalized Data Base Management Systems* (New York: Association for Computing Machinery), May 1969.

Date, C. J. *An Introduction to Database Systems* (3rd ed.) (Reading, MA: Addison-Wesley), 1980.

Everest, Gordon C. "Objectives of Database Management," *Information Systems,* Proceedings of the Fourth International Symposium on Computer and Information Sciences (COINS-72), December 14–16, 1972. (New York: Plenum Press), 1974.

Everest, Gordon C., *Database Management: Objectives, System Functions, and Administration* (New York: McGraw-Hill), 1986.

McFadden, Fred R., and Jeffrey A. Hoffer. *Data Base Management* (Menlo Park, CA: Benjamin/Cummings), 1985.

Martin, James. *Computer Data-Base Organization* (2nd ed.) (Englewood Cliffs, NJ: Prentice-Hall), 1977.

Olle, T. William. "MIS: Data Bases," *Datamation 16,* no. 15 (November 15, 1970), pp. 47–50.

Teorey, Toby J., and James P. Fry. "The Logical Record Access Approach to Database Design," *Computing Surveys 12,* no. 2 (June 1980), pp. 179–212.

Chapter 11: Management Information Systems

Brancheau, James, and James C. Wetherbe. "Key Information System Issues," *MIS Quarterly, 11* (March 1987), pp. 23–46.

Davis, Gordon B., and Margethe Olson. *Management Information Systems: Conceptual Foundations, Structure, and Development* (2nd ed.) (New York: McGraw-Hill), 1985.

Dickson, Gary W. "Management Information Systems: Evolution and Status." In *Advances in Computers,* Marshal Youts (Ed.) (New York: Academic Press), 1981.

Gorry, G. A., and Michael S. Scott Morton. "A Framework for Management Information Systems," *Sloan Management Review 13,* no. 1 (Fall 1971), pp. 55–69.

Ives, Blake, Scott Hamilton, and Gordon B. Davis. "A Framework for Research in Computer-Based Management Information Systems," *Management Science 26* (September 1980), pp. 910–934.

Ives, B., and M. H. Olson. "Manager or Technician? The Nature of the Information System's Manager's Job," MIS Quarterly 5, no. 4 (December 1981), pp. 49–62.

Keen, Peter G. W., and Michael S. Scott Morton. *Decision Support Systems: An Organizational Perspective* (Reading, MA: Addison-Wesley), 1978.

King, William R. "Strategic Planning for Management Information Systems," *MIS Quarterly 2,* no. 1 (March 1978), pp. 27–37.

McFarlan, F. Warren, and James F. McKenney. "The Information Archipelago—Maps and Bridges," *Harvard Business Review 61,* no. 5 (September–October 1982), pp. 109–119. *See also other articles in the series:* "The Information Archipelago—Plotting A Course" (January–February 1983), with Philip Pyburn; and "The Information Archipelago—Governing the New World" (July–August 1983).

Martin, James. *An Information Systems Manifesto* (Englewood Cliffs, NJ: Prentice-Hall), 1984.

Rockart, John F. "Chief Executives Define Their Own Data Needs," *Harvard Business Review 58,* no. 2 (March–April 1979), pp. 81–93.

Chapter 12: Decision Support Systems

Alter, Steven. *Decision Support Systems: Current Practice and Continuing Challenges* (Reading, MA: Addison-Wesley), 1980.

Alter, Steven. "A Taxonomy of Decision Support Systems," *Sloan Management Review 19,* no. 1 (Fall 1977), pp. 39–56.

DeSanctus, Gerardine, and Brent Gallupe. "Group Decision Support Systems: A New Frontier," *Data Base,* no. 16 (Winter 1985) pp. 3–10.

Ginzberg, Michael J., W. Reitman, and Edward A. Stohr (Eds.). *Decision Support Systems* (New York: Elsevier), 1982.

Jarvenpa, Sirkka L., V. Srinivasan Rao, and George P. Huber. "Computer Support for Meetings of Groups Working on Unstructured Problems: A Field Experiment," *MIS Quarterly,* no. 12 (December 1988) pp. 645–665.

McLean, Ephraim R. "Decision Support Systems and Managerial Decision Making," *Spectrum 1,* no. 2 (July–August 1984).

Nunamaker, Jay F., Jr., L. M. Applegate, and Benn R. Konsynski. "Facilitating Group Creativity with GOSS," *MIS Quarterly,* no. 3 (Spring 1987) pp. 5–19.

Sprague, Ralph J., Jr. "A Framework for the Development of Decision Support Systems," *MIS Quarterly 4,* no. 4 (December 1980), pp. 1–26.

Sprague, Ralph J., Jr., and Eric D. Carlson. *Building Effective Decision Support Systems* (Englewood Cliffs, NJ: Prentice-Hall), 1982.

Chapter 13: Executive Support Systems

Crescenzi, Adam D., and John F. Rockart. "Engaging Top Management in Information Technology." In *The Rise of Managerial Computing,* (John F. Rockart and Christine V. Bullen (Eds.) (Homewood, IL: Irwin), 1986.

Houdeshel, George, and Hugh J. Watson. "The Management Information and Decision Support (MIDS) System at Lockheed-Georgia," *MIS Quarterly,* no. 10 (March 1987).

Huber, George P. "The Nature and Design of Post-Industrial Organizations," *Management Science,* no. 30 (August 1984), pp. 928–951.

Isenberg, Daniel J. "How Senior Managers Think," *Harvard Business Review,* no. 62 (November–December 1984), pp. 81–90.

Kotter, John P. "What Effective General Managers Really Do," *Harvard Business Review,* no. 60 (November–December 1982), pp. 156–167.

Mintzberg, H. "The Manager's Job: Folklore and Fact," *Harvard Business Review 53,* no. 4 (July–August 1975), pp. 49–61.

Rockart, John F., and David W. DeLong. *Executive Support Systems* (Homewood, IL: Irwin), 1988.

Rockart and Treacy. "The CEO Goes On-Line," *Harvard Business Review,* no. 60 (January–February 1982), pp. 82–88.

Sprague, Ralph J., Jr., and Erick D. Carlson. *Building Effective Decision Support Systems* (Englewood Cliffs, NJ: Prentice-Hall), 1982.

Chapter 14: Expert Support Systems

Bobrow, D. G., S. Mittal, and M. J. Stefik. "Expert Systems: Perils and Promises," *Communications of the ACM,* no. 29 (September 1986), pp. 880–994.

Feigenbaum, Edward, Pamela McCorduck, and H. Penny Nii. *The Rise of the Expert Company* (New York: Times Books), 1988.

Harmon, P., and D. King. *Expert Systems: Artificial Intelligence in Business* (New York: Wiley), 1985.

Hayes-Roth, F. "Rule-Based Systems," *Communications of the ACM,* no. 28 (September 1985), pp. 921-932.

Weitzel, R., Jr., and K. R. Andrews. "A Company/University Joint Venture to Build a Knowledge-Based System," *MIS Quarterly,* no. 12 (March 1988), pp. 23–36.

Chapter 15: Office Information Systems

Allen, Robert J. "Office Technology: Putting the Pieces Together," *Management Technology* (January 1984).

Guilliano, Vincent E. "The Mechanization of Office Work," *Scientific American* (September 1982), pp. 148–165.

Olson, Margarethe H. "Remote Office Work: Changing Patterns in Space and Time," *Communications of the ACM 26* (March 1983), pp. 182–187.

Olson, Margarethe H., and Henry C. Lucas. "The Impact of Office Automation on the Organization: Some Implications for Research and Practice," *Communications of the ACM 25* (November 1982), pp. 838–847.

Pava, Calvin, *Managing New Office Technology: An Organizational Strategy* (New York: Free Press), 1983.

Poppel, Harvey L. "Who Needs the Office of the Future?" *Harvard Business Review 61,* no. 6 (November–December 1982), pp. 146–167.

Tapscott, Don. *Office Automation: A User-Driven Method* (New York: Plenum Press), 1982.

Yankee Group. *Electronic Data Interchange,* April 1988.

Zisman, Michael D. "Office Automation: Revolution or Evolution?" *Sloan Management Review 19,* no. 3 (Spring 1978), pp. 1–16.

Chapter 16: Information System Planning and Development

Bedford, Morton M., and Mohamed Onsi. "Measuring the Value of Information—An Information Theory Approach," *Management Services 3* (January–February 1966), pp. 15–22.

Blumenthal, Sherman C. *Management Information Systems: A Framework for Planning and Development* (Englewood Cliffs, NJ: Prentice-Hall), 1969.

Boyd, D. F., and H. S. Krasnow. "Economic Evaluation of Management Information Systems," *IBM Systems Journal 3* (March 1963), pp. 2–23.

Chervany, Norman L., and Gary W. Dickson. "Economic Evaluation of Management Information Systems: An Analytical Framework," *Decision Sciences 1,* no. 3 (1970), pp. 296–308.

Constantine, Larry, and Edward Yourdon. *Structured Design* (New York: Yourdon), 1975.

Cougar, Daniel J., and Robert W. Knapp (Eds.) *Systems Analysis Techniques* (New York: Wiley), 1974.

Davis, Gordon B. "Strategies for Information Requirements Determination," *IBM Systems Journal 21,* no. 1 (1982), pp. 4–30.

Davis, Gordon B., and Margrethe H. Olson. *Management Information Systems: Conceptual Foundations, Structure, and Development.* (2nd ed.) (New York: McGraw-Hill), 1985.

DeMarco, Tom. *Structured Analysis and System Specification* (New York: Yourdon), 1978.

Dickson, Gary W., Robert L. Leitheiser, James C. Wetherbe, and Mal Nechis. "Key Information Systems Management Issues," *Spectrum 1,* no. 3 (September–October 1984).

Dooley, Richard E. "Linking Business and Information System Planning," *Spectrum,* no. 3 (June 1986), pp. 1–6.

Emery, James C. *Cost/Benefit Analysis of Information Systems: SMIS Workshop Report No. 1* (Chicago: Society for Management Information Systems), 1971.

Gane, Chris, and Trish Sarsons. *Structured Systems Analysis* (Englewood Cliffs, NJ: Prentice-Hall), 1979.

Gibson, Cyrus F., and Richard L. Nolan. "Managing the Four States of EDP Growth," *Harvard Business Review 52,* no. 1 (January–February 1974), pp. 76–88.

IBM Corporation. *Business System Planning—Information Systems Planning Guide,* 1985.

Ives, Blake, Scott Hamilton, and Gordon B. Davis. "A Framework for Research in

Computer-Based Management Information Systems," *Management Science 26* (September 1980), pp. 910–934.

Jenkins, A. Milton. "Prototyping: A Methodology for the Design and Development of Application Systems," *Spectrum 2,* no. 2 (April 1985). *See also* Part II, Volume 2, no. 3 (June 1985).

King, John Leske, and Edward L. Schrems. "Cost Benefit Analysis in Information Systems Development and Operation," *Computing Surveys 10,* no. 1 (March 1978), pp. 19–34.

King, William R. "Strategic Planning For Management Information Systems," *MIS Quarterly,* no. 2 (March 1978), pp. 27–37.

Laning, Laurence. "Corporate Data Architecture: The Key to Supporting Management," *Data Base,* no. 14 (Summer 1983), pp. 14–15.

McKeen, James D. "Successful Development Strategies for Business Application Systems." *MIS Quarterly 7,* no. 3 (September 1983), pp. 47–65.

Martin, James, and Joe Leben. *Strategic Information Planning Methodologies.* Englewood Cliffs: Prentice-Hall, Inc., 1989.

Munro, Malcolm C., and Gordon B. Davis. "Determining Management Information Needs: A Comparison of Methods," *MIS Quarterly 1,* no. 2 (June 1977), pp. 55–67.

Nunamann, J. David, and A. Milton Jenkins. "Prototyping: The New Paradigm for Systems Development," *MIS Quarterly 6,* no. 3 (September 1982), pp. 29–44.

Nolan, Richard L. "Managing the Crises in Data Processing," *Harvard Business Review 57,* no. 2 (March–April 1979), pp. 115–126.

Nolan, Richard L., and Alex J. Pollock. "Organization and Architecture or Architecture and Organization," *Stage By Stage,* no. 6 (October 1966), pp. 1–10.

Nolan, Richard L., and James C. Wetherbe. "Toward a Comprehensive Framework for MIS Research," *MIS Quarterly 4,* no. 2 (June 1980), pp. 1–20.

North, Harper Q., and Donald L. Pyke. "Probes of the Technological Future," *Harvard Business Review 47,* no. 3 (May–June 1969), pp. 68–82.

Powers, Richard F., and Gary W. Dickson. "MIS Project Management: Myths, Opinions, and Reality," *California Management Review 15,* no. 3 (Spring 1973), pp. 147–156.

Pratt, J. W. H. Raiffa, and R. Schlaifer. *Introduction to Statistical Decision Theory* (New York: McGraw-Hill), 1965.

Ross, Douglas T. "Structured Analysis for Requirements Definition," *Proceedings of the Second International Conference on Software Engineering* (San Francisco, New York: Association for Computing Machinery), 1976.

Senn, James A. "A Management View of Systems Analysts: Failures and Shortcomings," *MIS Quarterly 2,* no. 3 (September 1978), pp. 25–32.

Senn, James A. *Analysis and Design of Information Systems* (New York: McGraw-Hill), 1984.

Vitalari, Nicholas P., and Gary W. Dickson. "Problem Solving for Effective Systems Analysis," *Communications of the ACM 26* (November 1983), pp. 948–956.

Wetherbe, James C., and Gordon B. Davis. "Developing a Long-Range Information Architecture," *Proceedings of the National Computer Conference* (Anaheim, CA: AFITS Press), *52* (May 1983), pp. 261–269.

Wetherbe, James C., and Gary W. Dickson. *MIS Management* (New York: McGraw-Hill), 1984.

Willoughby, Theodore C., and James A. Senn. *Business Systems* (Cleveland: Association for Systems Management), 1975.

Chapter 17: Tools And Methods for Developing Information Systems

Brooks, Fred P. "The Silver Bullet: Essence and Accidents of Software Engineering," *Computer 20* (April 1987), pp. 10–19.

Constantine, Larry, and Edward Yourdon. *Structured Design* (New York: Yourdon), 1975.

Cougar, Daniel J., and Robert W. Knapp (Eds.). *Systems Analysis Techniques* (New York: Wiley), 1974.

Dahl, O., Edward Dijkstra, and Charles Hoare. *Structured Programming* (New York: Academic Press), 1972.

Davis, Gordon B. *Management Information Systems: Conceptual Foundations, Structure, and Development* (New York: McGraw-Hill), 1974.

DeMarco, Tom. *Structured Analysis and System Specification.* (New York: Yourdon), 1978.

Gane, Chris, and Trish Sarsons. *Structured Systems Analysis* (Englewood Cliffs, NJ: Prentice-Hall), 1979.

Higgins, David A. *Program Design and Construction* (Englewood Cliffs, NJ: Prentice-Hall), 1979.

Jackson, Michael A. *Principles of Program Design* (New York: Academic Press), 1979.

McClure, Carma. *CASE Is Software Automation* (Englewood Cliffs, NJ: Prentice-Hall), 1989.

Munro, Malcolm C., and Gordon B. Davis. "Determining Management Information Needs: A Comparison of Methods," *MIS Quarterly 1,* no. 2 (June 1977), pp. 55–68.

Myers, Glenford J. *Software Reliability: Principles and Practices* (New York: Wiley), 1976.

Orr, Kenneth T. *Structured Systems Development* (New York: Yourdon), 1977.

Senn, James A. *Analysis and Design of Information Systems* (2nd ed.) (New York: McGraw-Hill), 1989.

Willoughby, Theodore C., and James A. Senn. *Business Systems* (Cleveland: Association for Systems Management), 1975.

Yourdon, Edward N. (Ed.). *Classics in Software Engineering* (New York: Yourdon), 1979.

Yourdon, Edward. *Modern Structured Analysis* (New York: Yourdon Press), 1989.

Chapter 18: End-User Development of Information Systems

Alloway, R. M., and J. A. Quillard. "User Manager's Systems Needs," *MIS Quarterly 7* (June 1983), pp. 27–41.

Hammond, L. W. "Management Considerations for an Information Center," *IBM Systems Journal 21,* no. 2 (1982), pp. 131–161.

McLean, Ephraim R. "End-Users as Application Developers," *MIS Quarterly 3,* no. 4 (December 1979), pp. 37–46.

Martin, James. *Application Development without Programmers* (Englewood Cliffs, NJ: Prentice-Hall), 1982.

Martin, James. *An Information Systems Manifesto* (Englewood Cliffs, NJ: Prentice-Hall), 1984.

Rockart, John F., and L. Flannery. "The Management of End-User Computing," *Communications of the ACM 26* (October 1983), pp. 776–784.

Chapter 19: Implementing Information Systems

Argyris, Chris. "Resistance to Rational Management Systems," *Innovation* (1969), pp. 28–42.

Argyris, Chris. "Management Information Systems: The Challenge to Reality and Emotionality," *Management Science 17,* no. 6 (February 1971), pp. B275–B292.

Argyris, Chris. "Organizational Learning and Management Information Systems," *Data Base 13,* no. 2–3 (Winter–Spring 1982), pp. 3–11.

Carlson, Eric D. "Evaluating the Impact of Information Systems," *Management Informatics 3,* no. 2 (April 1974), pp. 57–67.

Cougar, J. Daniel, and Robert A. Zawacki. *Motivating and Managing Computer Personnel.* (New York: Wiley), 1980.

DeSanctus, Gerardine, and James F. Courtney. "Toward Friendly User MIS Implementation," *Communications of the ACM 26* (October 1983), pp. 732–738.

Dickson, Gary W., and John K. Simmons. "The Behavioral Side of MIS," *Business Horizons 13* (August 1970), pp. 59–71.

Fried, Louis. "Hostility in Organization Change," *Journal of Systems Management 23* (June 1972), pp. 14–21.

Ginzberg, Michael J. "Key Recurrent Issues in MIS Implementation Process," *MIS Quarterly 5,* no. 2 (June 1981), pp. 47–60.

Keen, Peter G. W. "Information Systems and Organizational Change," *Communications of the ACM 24* (January 1981), pp. 24–33.

Kolb, D. A., and L. A. Frohman. "An Organization Development Approach to Consulting," *Sloan Management Review 12* (1970), pp. 51–65.

Lucas, Henry C., Jr. *Toward Creative Systems Design* (New York: Columbia University Press), 1974.

McKeen, James D. "Successful Development Strategies for Business Application Systems," *MIS Quarterly 7,* no. 3 (September 1983), pp. 47–65.

Markus, M. Lynne. "Power, Politics, and MIS Implementation," *Communications of the ACM 26* (June 1983), pp. 430–444.

Markus, M. Lynne. *Systems in Organizations* (Boston: Pitman), 1984.

Powers, Richard F., and Gary W. Dickson. "MIS Project Management: Myths, Opinions, and Reality." *California Management Review 15* (Spring 1973), pp. 147–156.

Williams, L. L. "The Human Side of Systems Change," *Systems and Procedures Journal 15,* no. 4 (July 1964), pp. 40–43.

Wolk, S. "Resistance to EDP: An Employee-Management Dilemma," *Data Management 6* (September 1968), pp. 44ff.

Zmud, Robert W., and James F. Cox. "The Implementation Process: A Change Approach," *MIS Quarterly 3,* no. 2 (June 1979), pp. 35–43.

Chapter 20: The Impact of Information Systems on Corporate Strategy

Applegate, Lynda M., James I. Cash, and D. Quinn Mills. "Information Technology And Tomorrow's Manager," *Harvard Business Review,* no. 66 (November–December 1988), pp. 128–136.

Benjamin, Robert I., John F. Rockart, Michael S. Scott Morton, and John Wayman. "Information Technology: A Strategic Opportunity," *Sloan Management Review 25,* no. 3 (Spring 1984), pp. 3–10.

Cash, James I., Jr., F. Warren McFarlan, and James L. McKenney. *Corporate Information Systems Management: The Issues Facing Senior Executives* (2nd ed.) (Homewood, IL: Irwin), 1988.

Ives, Blake, and Gerald P. Learmonth. "The Information System as a Competitive Weapon," *Communications of the ACM 27* (December 1984), pp. 1193–1201.

McFarlan, F. Warren, and James L. McKenney. *Corporate Information Systems Management* (Homewood, IL: Irwin), 1983.

McFarlan, F. Warren, James L. McKenney, and Phillip Pyburn. "The Information Archipelago—Plotting the Course," *Harvard Business Review 61,* no. 1 (January–February 1983), pp. 145–156.

Naisbitt, John, and Patricia Aburdene. *Reinventing the Corporation* (New York: Warner Books), 1985.

Ohmae, Kenneth. *The Mind of the Strategist* (New York: McGraw-Hill), 1982.

Peters, Thomas J., and Robert H. Waterman, Jr. *In Search of Excellence* (New York: Harper & Row), 1982.

Porter, Michael E. *Competitive Strategy* (New York: Free Press), 1980.

Porter, Michael E. *Competitive Advantage* (New York: Free Press), 1985.

Chapter 21: Information Systems in the Future

Benjamin, Robert I. "Information Technology in the 1990s: A Long-Range Planning Scenario," *MIS Quarterly 6,* no. 2 (June 1982), pp. 11–32.

Brancheau, James, and James C. Wetherbe. "Key Information System Issues," *MIS Quarterly 11* (March 1987), pp. 23–46.

Davenport, Thomas H., Michael Hammer, and Metsisto Tauno. "How Executives Can Shape Their Company's Information Systems," *Harvard Business Review,* no. 67 (March–April 1989), pp. 130–134.

Dickson, Gary W., Robert L. Leitheiser, James C. Wetherbe, and Mal Nechis. "Key Information Systems Management Issues," *Spectrum 1,* no. 3 (September/October 1984).

Naisbitt, John. *Megatrends* (New York: Warner Books), 1982.

Naisbitt, John, and Patricia Aburdene. *Reinventing the Corporation* (New York: Warner Books), 1985.

Robinson, David G. "Dilemma of Obsolete Systems: Alternatives to Replacement," *Indications 1,* no. 4 (Summer 1984).

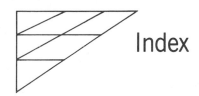

Index